Houghton Mifflin Company Boston

New York Atlanta Geneva, Illinois Dallas Palo Alto

Comedy:

A Critical Anthology

Edited and with an introduction by

Robert W. Corrigan
California Institute of the Arts

Headnotes by

Glenn M. Loney
Brooklyn College

Printed in the U.S.A.

Library of Congress Catalog Card Number: 78–150137

ISBN: 0–395–04325–5

Maurice Valency. Reprinted from The Modern Library volume, *Four Contemporary French Plays*, by permission of Random House, Inc.

Puntila and His Hired Man by Bertolt Brecht. Copyright 1957 by Suhrkamp Verlag, Berlin. Acting version translated by Gerhard Nellhaus, reprinted by permission of the translator, Suhrkamp Verlag Frankfurt am Main, and Methuen & Co. Ltd.

The Last Analysis by Saul Bellow. Copyright © 1965 by Saul Bellow. All rights reserved. Reprinted by permission of The Viking Press, Inc. *Caution Notice*: This play in its printed form is designed for the reading public only. All dramatic rights in it are fully protected by copyright, and no public or private performance — professional or amateur — may be given without the written permission of the author and the payment of royalty. As the courts have also ruled that the public reading of a play constitutes a public performance, no such reading may be given except under the conditions stated above. Communication should be addressed to the author's representative, Russell and Volkening, 551 Fifth Avenue, Room 1517, New York, New York 10017.

Contents

ROBERT W. CORRIGAN

Comedy and the Comic Spirit

A few years ago in a seminar on comedy I asked the students in the class to give a definition of comedy in one hundred words or less. After what seemed an interminable silence — we all knew that I had asked the impossible, and that the question really reflected my own frustration in attempting to deal with comedy's many baffling problems — a young man reached into his pocket and pulled out a crumpled newspaper clipping and passed it over to me, mumbling something to the effect that "this is it!" Though it was not a definition, it certainly did indicate in a grotesque manner several of the elements related to this complex subject which Dr. Johnson so correctly observed "has been particularly unpropitious to definers." The article read as follows:

MAN'S CORK LEG CHEATS DEATH

Keeps Him Afloat After Leap Into River

A carpenter's cork leg kept him afloat and prevented him from taking his life by jumping into the Mississippi River from a Canal St. ferry, Fourth District police reported Monday.

Taken to Charity hospital after his rescue was Jacob Lewis, Negro, 52, 2517 Annette. Suffering from possible skull fracture and internal injuries, he was placed in a psychiatric ward for examination.

Police said that after his release from the hospital he would be booked for disturbing the peace by attempting to commit suicide.

The incident occurred about 11:25 P.M. Sunday while the ferry M.P. *Crescent* was tied up on the Algiers side of the river.

Police quoted a ferry passenger as saying he saw the man leap from a rest-room window into the water. When the call was sounded, two employees, James McCaleb, 43, 709 Wilks Lane, and Edward Johnson, 54, 2113 Whitney, Algiers, both Negroes, lowered a boat and rescued Lewis.

He was brought into the boat about 100 yards from the ferry after he refused to grab life preservers the men threw him.

Ferry employees said he told them he had no desire to live. His attempt on his life might have succeeded if his cork leg had not kept him afloat, police said.

(New Orleans *Times Picayune*)

We cannot help laughing at this report of a thwarted suicide. The situation is ludicrous, if not downright absurd; death and utter despair are cheated in such a preposterous fashion that they are not taken seriously. Even the physical injury is all but ignored, and we are more conscious of the insult — being booked for disturbing the peace — than we are of the pain. And, finally, in its own grim way the story underscores the commonplace that comedy and laughter are serious business. In short, it is an analog to several of the plays in this volume.

However, as we enter the realm of comedy we must proceed with caution. There are countless pitfalls to be avoided, the most important of them being the tendency to get so caught up in related but peripheral issues — the psychology or physiology of laughter, the politics of humor, conventions of comic acting, etc. — that we forget the main subject altogether. Nor should we forget the lesson to be learned from the first recorded attempt to take comedy seriously. Recall the prophecy of Plato's *Symposium*: It is early morning and Socrates is still rambling on. He finally begins talking about comedy and proposes his theory that tragedy and comedy spring from the same roots. "To this they were constrained to assent, being drowsy, and not quite following the argument. And first of all Aristophanes dropped off to sleep." "Such was the charm," as Henry Myers has pointed out, "of the first theory of comedy! We leave the *Symposium* with an unforgettable picture of an eminent philosopher putting an eminent comic poet to sleep with a lecture on the comic spirit."

A second warning: In our investigation of the general nature of comedy we must resist falling victim to what I have called the "formalistic fallacy" in the study of dramatic genres. This is the kind of thinking about drama which assumes that comedy of all ages has certain formal and structural characteristics in common. But where in the history of drama will one find such formal consistency? Certainly not in classical Greek or Roman drama; nor in English stage comedy of the Elizabethan, Restoration, or eighteenth-century periods; nor, for that matter, in the so-called "black" comedy of our own age. Though it is true that some characteristics of comedy seem to be "universal" — the presence of lovers, the defeat of an imposter figure and his subsequent assimilation into the restored social fabric, an inverted Oedipal pattern in which the son triumphs over the father, and the presence of violence without its consequences — these finally have thematic rather than structural significance. The structure of each play is unique, and even within the work of a given playwright there is an evolution of form which makes it impossible to consider his work in terms of consistent structural patterns.

The constant in comedy is the comic view of life or the comic spirit: the sense that no matter how many times man is knocked down he somehow manages to pull himself up and keep on going. Tragedy, on the other hand, has always dealt with that rebellious spirit in man which resists the limitations of being human, including the limits imposed on him by society. It focuses on man's heroic capacity to suffer in his rebellion, and celebrates the essential nobility of the rebellious spirit. Thus, while tragedy celebrates the hero's capacity to suffer, and thereby earn a new and deeper knowledge of himself and his universe, comedy tends to be more concerned with the fact that despite all our individual defeats, life does nonetheless continue on its merry way. Comedy, then, celebrates man's capacity to endure; such capacity is ultimately conserving in spirit and quality. Eric Bentley describes this relationship in his *The Life of the Drama* as follows: "In tragedy, but by no means comedy, the self-preservation instinct is overruled. . . . The comic sense tries to cope with the daily, hourly, inescapable difficulty of being. For if everyday life has an undercurrent or cross-current of the tragic, the main current is material for comedy."

However, while identifying the continuing spirit of comedy is essential, it is not enough. Because it does not help us very much when it comes to explaining why particular plays which we are accustomed to calling comedies are comic. For, though it is true that it is almost impossible to say what comedy is, we do nonetheless know that it exists and is readily identifiable. We laugh at Volpone even when his situation is desperate, and we are moved to tears by Charlie Chaplin at the end of *City Lights* in spite of the ludicrousness of some of the early scenes. Even in those plays where the laughable and the painful are inextricably combined — for example, the Falstaff plays or any of Chekhov's plays — audiences have no difficulty following the right threads in the design. In short, the problems of comedy are seldom artistic; playwrights know how to write plays which their audiences will recognize as comic. The big question is: How do we know?

One important clue in our search for an answer to "How do we know?" is the fact that, invariably, every discussion of comedy begins with (or eventually reaches) at least a passing reference to tragedy. The reverse is seldom true: in most essays on tragedy, comedy is never mentioned. In this regard, an apparent exception to the rule is illuminating. In the beginning of the fifth chapter of *The Poetics*, Aristotle defines comedy as follows:

> Comedy is an artistic imitation of men of an inferior moral bent; faulty, however, not in so far as their shortcomings are ludicrous; for the Ludicrous is a species or part, not all, of the Ugly. It may be described as that kind of shortcoming and deformity which does not strike us as painful, and causes no harm to others; a ready example is afforded by the comic mask, which is ludicrous, being ugly and distorted, without any suggestion of pain.

The two key ideas in this definition are *the Ludicrous* and *the absence of pain;* and although it is clear from what follows that Aristotle is more concerned with their tragic contrasts — *the serious* and *the painful* — he does establish two fundamental boundaries of the comic. Let us examine them briefly.

In making this distinction between the ludicrous and the serious Aristotle was not denying the potential seriousness of comedy; rather, much like Plato, he was postulating the idea that comedy — as well as tragedy — derives from positive attitudes toward value. For something to be serious we must assign it serious value, and this can occur only when there exists a larger system of values which we accept as valid and of which the specific value is a part. Thus, while Aristotle describes the ludicrous as a species of the ugly which has no painful effects, it is impossible to set the limits of the ludicrous until the serious has first been defined and accepted. A thing cannot be ugly or immoral until we have first agreed on what is beautiful and moral. This explains why it is we can discuss tragedy (which deals directly with the serious) without reference to comedy, but when talking about comedy must always refer to the standards of seriousness which give it its essential definition.

Thus, for all of its positive characteristics, comedy is negative in its definition. An audience will refuse to react positively (in this case, laugh) to any presentation in a ludicrous manner of what it believes to be the true, the good, or the beautiful. We laugh, for example, at the absent-minded professor not because of his learning but because his absent-mindedness is not consistent with his erudition. When Trofimov falls down the stairs in the Third Act of *The Cherry Orchard* it is a comic event. Not because falling down stairs is funny — it obviously is not — but because it undercuts his pompous posturings about love which preceded his fall. Similarly, we can never be induced to laugh at the beautiful *as* beautiful. A beautiful woman is not funny; a beautiful woman who speaks in a high, squeaking voice is very funny because she fails to measure up to the standard which her appearance had previously established. Such a standard may not always be a logically defensible one — more often than not it is not — but it holds in the theatre so long as the audience takes it to be so. Such is also the case with the beautiful but dumb blonde. The dumbness is an analog to the squeaking voice, though there is no logical, necessary relationship between beauty and intelligence. It is merely that we somehow expect it.

However, our laughter in these instances cannot be explained in the simple terms of incongruity. For incongruity, no matter how it is conceived — expectation and consequence, tension and elasticity, reality and illusion — does not, as many theorists have maintained, necessarily evoke a comic response, nor is it unique to the comic form. Incongruity has been effectively used in all dramatic forms — serious and comic. It can produce dire emotions as well as side-splitting laughter. The coming of Birnam Wood to Dunsinane in *Macbeth* is unquestionably incongruous, but no one in the play or the audience thinks it is funny. The same is true of Richard III's seduction of Lady Anne. Indeed, as Aristotle pointed out in Chapter XIV of *The Poetics*, to show a terrible act committed by a character from whom we expect love (hence, an incongruous act) is the most effective way of producing a tragic effect. In fact, I believe a good case could be made for the idea that incongruity is the cause of horror in the theatre as well as laughter. What is operative in the ludicrous is not a question of mere incongruity, but a perceptible falling short of an already agreed-upon standard of seriousness which we have set for the object, or which is set by the object for itself.

One boundary of the comic's realm, then, is that line where the ludicrous and the serious meet. We turn now to its other boundary. In *The Life of the Drama,* Bentley characterizes farce as that form in which violence can operate without fear of consequence. He goes on to show how the violence of farce becomes the basic ore of comedy. This observation is significant, but it needs enlarging. One essential difference between comedy and farce is that in the action of the former there are definite consequences (one reason why we say comedy *is* of greater consequence than farce). But these consequences have had all of the elements of pain and permanent defeat removed. Thus it is that the pratfall is the symbol of the comic. This symbol can be carried to its outermost limits by saying that in comedy death is never taken seriously or even considered as a serious threat. Aristotle perceived, correctly, that while the ludicrous (whether it take the form of the grotesque, of exaggeration or of physical deformity) was the proper subject matter for comedy, manifestations of the ludicrous must be made painless before they can become comic. The writhings of the cartoon character who has just received a blow on the head, the violent events in some of Molière's plays, or the mayhem committed on and by slapstick clowns remains funny only so long as it is quite clear that no real pain is involved. One reason why the violence of slapstick is so effective in films (one thinks of the pies and boppings of the Three Stooges or the Ritz Brothers) is that it is virtually impossible to fear for the characters since the actors have no physical reality. On the stage, if a fight — even one intended to be funny — appears to be an actual fight, the audience may well begin to fear for the actors, that is, take seriously the possibility of pain. Thus it is that whenever a serious deed or event is allowed to enter the field of comedy (as frequently happens) the serious effect must, in some way, be cut off. Such is the case in Jonson's *Volpone,* in which the possibility of the rape is never seriously considered because of the circumstances in which the scene occurs. Similarly, in *The Playboy of the Western World* we never take Christy's threat to murder old Mahon seriously because all of the prior fantasizing about Oedipal murder assures us that the dreadful threat will never be carried out. Conversely, one of the reasons *The Cherry Orchard* is so difficult to interpret is that the line between the characters' self-dramatizing about suffering and actual pain is such a tenuous one. If we miss all the subtle clues Chekhov gives us to indicate that Madame Ranevsky does not really care about the orchard and is actually enjoying being at the center of a teapot drama, then it is impossible for us to think of it as the comedy ("at times even a farce") which Chekhov intended. The same kind of ambiguity exists in *Twelfth Night* with Malvolio. Shakespeare pushes the cruelty almost too far, and if we begin to feel sorry for Malvolio the comic effect of the rest of the play is jeopardized.

From these examples we may draw our second conclusion: comedy operates in that middle zone between the serious and the absurd which Aristotle called the Ludicrous. It is an area which excludes nobility of character, painful consequences, and the consummation of any events which are likely to offend our moral sensibilities.

Another false but widely held assumption about comedy is that there are themes, situations, or character types which are the special province of comedy, or are at least thought to be especially compatible to the comic muse. But if we examine the history of drama, we discover that we must reject the assumption. *Oedipus Rex*, for example, is the story of "the lost one found." As such, it is, like *The Importance of Being Earnest*, a "success" story, a story type which traditionally has been particularly well-suited to comedy. There is no doubt that *Oedipus Rex* is a success story, but no one would ever call it a comedy. The reverse is equally true: *The Playboy of the Western World* is, as I have already noted, a story of Oedipal murder, but no one has ever thought of it as a tragedy.

All of the materials available to the dramatist, whether they be from his own experience, from history, or from the accrued traditions of the drama itself are, in fact, neutral. It is only by the playwright's shaping of them that they take on meaning — a meaning which may be tragic, comic, melodramatic, farcical, or what have you. Not to understand this fact is to blur the crucial distinctions which exist between art and life. In life, the meaning we assign to any situation will be the product of personal determinants. But our response to an event which occurs in a play will be the product of the causes built into that play by the playwright. In both cases it is the view and the value assigned to it which will determine whether we consider a situation serious or comic, or remain completely indifferent to it. For example, the "battle of the sexes" is usually mentioned as a typical comic plot. And while it is true that the struggle for power in the home has provided a comic impetus for many plays, beginning with *Lysistrata* right up to *The Last Analysis*, this same struggle is also at the heart of such eminently serious works as *Macbeth* and Strindberg's *The Father*. Or again, a girl surrounded by a host of suitors has been used as the basic predicament of countless comic plots, but surely this is the situation of Homer's Penelope, O'Neill's Nina Leeds, and even (in a perverted way) of Ibsen's Hedda Gabler as well. Nor will it do for us to claim that comedy generates action out of ignorance or wrong reason, since *Oedipus Rex*, *King Lear*, and *Othello* come to mind as readily as *Twelfth Night*, *Tartuffe*, and *The School for Scandal*. Even plays universally accepted as tragic or comic can be transformed. Tom Stoppard turned *Hamlet* into an absurdist comedy with *Rosencrantz and Guildenstern Are Dead*, and one of the fascinating aspects of Nicol Williamson's interpretation of the Dane was the way he created numerous comic effects simply by making unexpected changes in phrasing. In short, for every comic use made of a given situation, one can find examples of a serious use of the same situation. And the reverse of this is equally true. In each case the deciding factor is the way the artist has used his materials so they will assume a comic or a serious shape. In so doing he will also shape the audience's response to his creation.

One other broad area of misunderstanding needs to be clarified before the reader enters the world of comedy. Living, as we do, in a time when our next tomorrow must always be in question, comedy's tenacious greed for life, its instinct for self-preservation, and its attempts to mediate the pressures of our daily life seem to qualify it as the most appropriate mode for the drama of the second half of the twentieth century. However, one of the most striking characteristics of the modern drama is the way the age-old distinctions between the tragic and the comic (the serious and the ludicrous, the painful and the painless) have been obliterated. This has not been a process of commingling as so many critics have, I believe, erroneously asserted. The combining of the tragic and the comic in a single play is nearly as old as the drama itself — I can trace it back to Sophocles. But what is happening today is something quite different. So much so, that it has become increasingly difficult to use the terms comedy and tragedy with any precision. There are a number of reasons for this.

As I indicated earlier, both tragedy and comedy depend upon generally accepted standards of values. Such norms make it possible to establish those hierarchies of seriousness upon which the drama has been traditionally based. It is this public truth which in earlier periods of history provided the artist with his means of communication. It enabled him to communicate emotion and attitude by simply describing incidents; it provided him with a storehouse of symbols with guaranteed responses; it enabled him to construct a plot by selecting and patterning events which, by means of this public criterion, were significant. But once public truth is shattered into innumerable separate and mutually incommunicable private truths, all experience tends to become equally serious or equally ludicrous. Or, as Eugène Ionesco, one of the founding fathers of the Theatre of the Absurd, put it: "It all comes to the same thing anyway; comic and tragic are merely two aspects of the same situation, and I have now reached the stage when I find it hard to distinguish one from the other."

Any examination of the theatre of the past century makes it abundantly clear that the drama's general pattern of development during this time can best be described as a gradual but steady shift away from universal philosphical and social concerns toward the crises and conflicts of man's inner and private life. One of the dominant ideas of the modern *Weltanschauung* is the belief that it is impossible to know what the world is really like. Beginning with Luther's refusal to accept that there was any intelligible relationship between faith and works, the sacramental view of experience gradually disappeared. In rejecting the phenomenal world as an outward and visible manifestation of man's spiritual condition, Luther began a revolution in thought which, because of the achievements of science and technology in the past two hundred years, now makes it impossible for man to attach any objective value to the observations of his senses. This insistence on such a clear-cut division between the physical and the spiritual aspects of reality had a profound effect on the modern dramatist. Inevitably, it made him increasingly distrustful of his sensory responses to the "outside" world, and at the same time it tended to negate whatever belief he might have had in the objective validity of his subjective feelings and sensations. The modern artist no longer holds a mirror up to nature, at least not with any confidence; he can only stare at his own image. He becomes a voyeur to his own existence.

Probably no force in the nineteenth century did more to destroy man's belief in an established norm of human nature, and hence begin this process of internalization in the theatre, than the advent of psychology as a systematized field of study. By convincingly demonstrating that normal people are not as rational as they seem, and that abnormal people do not act in a random and unintelligible way, psychology has made it difficult, if not impossible, for the dramatist to present his characters in a direct way. In earlier times when it was believed that there was a sharp distinction between the sane and the insane, the irrational "aberrations" of human behavior were dramatically significant because they could be defined in terms of a commonly accepted standard of sane conduct. However, once a playwright believes that the meaning of every human action is relative and intelligible only in terms of a unique and subsurface combination of forces, the dramatic events of the plot cease to have meaning in themselves, and they take on significance only as the secret motivations of the characters who participate in them are revealed. (The technique of earlier drama is just the reverse: the motivations of the characters are revealed by the events of the plot.)

Nowhere are the profound effects of these changes of attitude more evident than in those modern plays we call comedies. The plays in the last half of this volume attest to this fact. Historically, comedy has as often as not been exceedingly complex — the typical comic plot is a labyrinth of complexity — but it has seldom been ambiguous. And ours is an age of ambiguity. One of the reasons we tend to dismiss the frothy Broadway comedy as irrelevant or escapist is that it is so clear-cut; it lacks the dimension of ambiguity. Thus, while the playwright may approach experience with a comic sense, *i.e.*, man's need and capacity to endure, he is acutely aware that not only is the serious inseparable from the ludicrous, but also that it is impossible for him to remove the pain of experience from his representation of life if that representation is to have the ring of truth.

We see this clearly in the plays of Chekhov where the ludicrous and the painful are so inextricably linked that they make us laugh with a lump in our throats. O'Neill sensed something similar when in 1939 he remarked:

> "It's struck me as time goes on, how something funny, even farcical, can suddenly, without apparent reason, break up into something gloomy and tragic . . . A sort of unfair *nonsequitur*, as though events, through life, were manipulated just to confuse us. I think I'm aware of comedy more than I ever was before — a big kind of comedy that doesn't stay funny very long."

The most striking thing about Gogo and Didi as they wait for Godot is that they are two irreducible specimens of humanity whose only capacity is to remain comically, tragically, ambiguously alive with the courage of their hallucinations. (Anouilh appropriately described *Waiting for Godot* as Pascal's *Pensées* "acted out by circus clowns.") Finally, Saul Bellow is a great comic artist not because he pokes fun at humanity's shortcomings, but because he sees the comic as the most appropriate weapon in man's struggle for survival in an absurd world. Life as revealed in *The Last Analysis* is a Grand Guignol but with less sense.

With increasing frequency the contemporary theatre reveals (and sometimes celebrates) that to live is to make the comic gesture, or what Pirandello called the comic grimace. Today, the comic view of life is comic in the sense that the lines of the comic mask are indistinguishable from those of the tragic. In them we find that the relationship of means to ends is a paradox. In the plays in the first half of this volume we have a sense that a destiny is being fulfilled: as the comic action is completed, all the complexities and disruptions of the plot have been resolved and the social fabric has been restored. We have no sense of such natural or inevitable resolution in the plays of the second section. Whenever the boundaries between the serious and the ludicrous tend to dissolve, clear-cut resolution gives way to ambiguity, fantasy, or philosophic sleight of hand.

And yet this should not be cause for despair, for from its very beginnings comedy — no matter what form it has taken — has always been one of the human spirit's most effective strategies for drawing life into a stalemate in our cold war with existence. Perhaps Aristophanes was right to fall asleep after all. In his infinite wisdom he knew that the lines between comedy and tragedy were at best tenuous, and often artificial. Certainly that latter-day Aristophanes, James Joyce, did. And as we enter comedy's realm we should do so in the litanal spirit which brings *Finnegan's Wake* to a close:

> "Loud, heap miseries upon us yet entwine our arts with laughters low. In the name of the former and of the latter and of their holocaust, All men."

PART ONE

THE PLAYS

Aristophanes · *Lysistrata*

Shakespeare · *Twelfth Night*

Jonson · *Volpone*

Molière · *Tartuffe*

Sheridan · *The School for Scandal*

Wilde · *The Importance of Being Earnest*

Chekhov · *The Cherry Orchard*

Synge · *The Playboy of the Western World*

Shaw · *Misalliance*

Giraudoux · *The Madwoman of Chaillot*

Brecht · *Puntila and His Hired Man*

Bellow · *The Last Analysis*

Aristophanes (c. 446–385 B.C.) frequently creates a central figure who is thoroughly and delightfully ridiculous. His comic misadventures proceed helter-skelter with a crazy kind of illogical logic. Often, however, to achieve the satire he desires, his central character, though fond of fun and full of clever puns and tricks, really represents common sense, as does Dicaeopolis in *The Acharnians* or Strepsiades in *The Clouds*. He is the norm against which the patent ridiculousness of the other characters can be measured. If the comedy had no sane men in it at all, it could easily be dismissed as merely a wild fantasy with no point of valid contact with — or just criticism of — the society.

In *Lysistrata* (411 B.C.), the central or title role belongs to a woman who is anything but comic or ridiculous. She is, in fact, a strong, clever, attractive heroine whom George Bernard Shaw might have been proud to create: the first feminist, but *not* unfeminine. Although she demands that all the women cease having sexual relations with their men, as a means of stopping the disastrous war that was actually to lay Greece open to barbarian conquests, she is as much a proponent and bearer of the Life Force which obsessed Shaw as are Major Barbara, Candida, or Dona Ana.

Although all Greek comedies had their share of bawdiness, the very nature of Lysistrata's "happy idea" — as the central comic device is called — is such that graphic representation on stage of sexual frustration and excitation not only cannot be avoided but is deliberately encouraged. The Greeks were living, of course, in an agrarian society. Their lives were bound up with human, animal, and vegetable fertility. Dionysus was a cult god of fertility, but Demeter and others were also invoked for growth of crops, richness of harvest, and other kinds of increase and fulfillment. The human form, draped or undraped, was a thing of unashamed beauty to the Greeks. The genital organs, sometimes carved in marble as cult symbols, were not at all objects of fear or shame. In the garb of Dionysus's attendants, the Corybants, or in the outfits of the chorus in the Satyr plays, or, frequently, in the comic costume, the male phallus — on occasion grotesquely enlarged — was a customary appendage. This explains some of the indicated and implied stage action in *Lysistrata* and why the Greeks were amused rather than embarrassed by it.

Of the surviving Aristophanic comedies, *Lysistrata* is the one most often successful in modern performance. There are several good reasons. Although *The Birds, The Frogs,* and *The Clouds* have been justly admired by scholars, the men and the affectations they mock need some explanation before an average reader or audience can appreciate the points of satire. A knowledge of the Peloponnesian War, on the other hand, is not essential to enjoying the action or the humorous irony of *Lysistrata*. True, some of the specific references to persons and historical details or customs are puzzling today, but they are not fundamental to appreciation. Not only does *Lysistrata* enjoy the advantage of a remarkably simple plot, capable of many amusing variations on the basic theme, but its theme is so *very* basic that it commands a universality of interest and understanding that almost no other Aristophanic comedies can.

Man's sex drives, after all, are certainly central to his existence, as is his fear of death. What more novel form of blackmailing males into giving up war than denying them the gratification they seek from their wives and sweethearts! There is an added subtlety in the fact that this threat is able to win the desired goal when the threats of death, drought, and destruction, caused by battle, have failed to move the warriors on either side.

The bawdier elements in this comedy push it in the direction of farce, but the skillful revelation of the various frailties of the men and women of Athens and Sparta pull it in the opposite direction, toward social comedy or comedy of manners. Such terms would have meant little to Aristophanes, for Classic comedy had a formula, a structure within whose limits he worked with great variety and flexibility. Revealing their foibles, though, he showed his fellow Greeks how ridiculous they could be.

Aristophanes' use of the comic chorus is most engaging. Traditionally, the chorus served at least two functions: the twenty-four members could split into two sides of twelve each and debate the merits of the "happy idea," and they gave the playwright an ingenious means of reflecting audience attitudes — without encouraging verbal interruptions — which he could then bend to agree with his thesis. In *Lysistrata,* Aristophanes goes even farther by turning his debate teams into old men and old women, whose sharp wrangling offers a Senior Citizens' subplot version of the battle of the sexes which is raging stage center most of the time. These contrasts are both richly comic and devastatingly incisive.

When one looks at the work of the Greek tragic playwrights, it is apparent that the real horrors of war — the psychic and spiritual ones — were only too well understood. Despite that fact, Aristophanes may have believed that he had more chance to sway the minds of his audiences by making them laugh at lust and stupidity and false valor than by arousing them to guilt and tears, as either *The Trojan Woman* or *The Phoenician Women* might. This raises a question for those who are interested not only in Greek plays but in modern theatre as well: Which has greater power to reach an audience, to change its mind — tragedy or comedy? Another question a modern reader might well ask himself as he enjoys *Lysistrata* is how much like us these comic characters really are. Do they have any counterpart in our time, in our own country, in our community, even?

G. L.

ARISTOPHANES

Lysistrata

TRANSLATED BY DONALD SUTHERLAND

Characters

LYSISTRATA, KALONIKE, MYRRHINA — *Athenian women*
LAMPITO, *a Spartan woman*
CHORUS OF OLD MEN
CHORUS OF WOMEN
ATHENIAN COMMISSIONER
OLD MARKET-WOMEN
CINESIAS, *an Athenian, husband of Myrrhina*
SPARTAN HERALD
SPARTAN AMBASSADORS
ATHENIAN AMBASSADORS

(*A street in Athens before daylight.*)

LYSISTRATA. If anyone had asked them to a festival
of Aphrodite or of Bacchus or of Pan,
you couldn't get through Athens for the tambourines,
but now there's not one solitary woman here.
Except my next-door neighbor. Here she's coming out.
Hello, Kalonike.

KALONIKE. Hello, Lysistrata.
What are you so upset about? Don't scowl so, dear.
You're less attractive when you knit your brows and glare.

LYSISTRATA. I know, Kalonike, but I am smoldering
with indignation at the way we women act.
Men think we are so gifted for all sorts of crime
that we will stop at nothing —

KALONIKE. Well, we are, by Zeus!

LYSISTRATA. — but when it comes to an appointment here with me
to plot and plan for something really serious
they lie in bed and do not come.

KALONIKE. They'll come, my dear.
You know what trouble women have in going out:
one of us will be wrapped up in her husband still,

another waking up the maid, or with a child
to put to sleep, or give its bath, or feed its pap.

LYSISTRATA. But they had other more important things to do than those.

KALONIKE. What ever is it, dear Lysistrata?
What have you called us women all together for?
How much of a thing is it?

LYSISTRATA. Very big.

KALONIKE. And thick?

LYSISTRATA. Oh very thick indeed.

KALONIKE. Then *how* can we be late?

LYSISTRATA. That's not the way it is. Or we would all be here.
But it is something I have figured out myself
and turned and tossed upon for many a sleepless night.

KALONIKE. It must be something slick you've turned and tossed upon!

LYSISTRATA. So slick that the survival of all Greece depends
upon the women.

KALONIKE. On the women? In that case
poor Greece has next to nothing to depend upon.

LYSISTRATA. Since now it's we who must decide affairs of state.
either there is to be no Spartan left alive —

KALONIKE. A very good thing too, if none were left, by Zeus!

LYSISTRATA. — and every living soul in Thebes to be destroyed —

KALONIKE. Except the eels! Spare the delicious eels of Thebes!

LYSISTRATA. — and as for Athens — I can't bring myself to say
the like of that for us. But just think what I mean!
Yet if the women meet here as I told them to
from Sparta, Thebes, and all of their allies,
and we of Athens, all together we'll save Greece.

KALONIKE. What reasonable thing could women ever do,
or glorious, we who sit around all prettied up
in flowers and scandalous saffron-yellow gowns,
groomed and draped to the ground in oriental stuffs
and fancy pumps?

LYSISTRATA. And those are just the very things
I count upon to save us — wicked saffron gowns,
perfumes and pumps and rouge and sheer transparent frocks.

KALONIKE. But what use can they be?

LYSISTRATA. So no man in our time
will raise a spear against another man again —

KALONIKE. I'll get a dress dyed saffron-yellow, come what may!

LYSISTRATA. — nor touch a shield —

KALONIKE. I'll slip into the sheerest gown!

LYSISTRATA. — nor so much as a dagger —

KALONIKE. I'll buy a pair of pumps!

LYSISTRATA. So don't you think the women should be here by now?

KALONIKE. I don't. They should have *flown* and got here long ago.

LYSISTRATA. You'll see, my dear. They will, like good Athenians,
do everything too late. But from the coastal towns
no woman is here either, nor from Salamis.

KALONIKE. I'm certain those from Salamis have crossed the strait:
they're always straddling *something* at this time of night.

LYSISTRATA. Not even those I was expecting would be first
to get here, from Acharnae, from so close to town,
not even they are here.

KALONIKE. But one of them, I know,
is under way, and three sheets to the wind, by now.
But look — some women are approaching over there.

LYSISTRATA. And over here are some, coming this way —

KALONIKE. Phew! Phew!
Where are they from?

LYSISTRATA. Down by the marshes.

KALONIKE. Yes, by Zeus!
It smells as if the bottoms had been all churned up!

(*Enter* MYRRHINA, *and others.*)

MYRRHINA. Hello Lysistrata. Are we a little late?
What's that? Why don't you speak?

LYSISTRATA. I don't think much of you,
Myrrhina, coming to this business only now.

MYRRHINA. Well, I could hardly find my girdle in the dark.
If it's so urgent, tell us what it is. We're here.

KALONIKE. Oh no. Let's wait for just a little while until
the delegates from Sparta and from Thebes arrive.

LYSISTRATA. You show much better judgment.

(*Enter* LAMPITO, *and others.*)

Here comes Lampito!

LYSISTRATA. Well, darling Lampito! My dearest Spartan friend!
How very sweet, how beautiful you look! That fresh
complexion! How magnificent your figure is!
Enough to crush a bull!

LAMPITO. Ah shorely think Ah could.
Ah take mah exacise. Ah jump and thump mah butt.

KALONIKE. And really, what a handsome set of tits you have!

LAMPITO. You feel me ovah lahk a cow fo sacrafahce!

LYSISTRATA. And this other young thing — where ever is *she* from?

LAMPITO. She's prominent, Ah sweah, in Thebes — a delegate
ample enough.

LYSISTRATA. By Zeus, she represents Thebes well,
having so trim a ploughland.

KALONIKE. Yes, by Zeus, she does!
There's not a weed of all her field she hasn't plucked.

LYSISTRATA. And who's the other girl?

LAMPITO. Theah's nothing small, Ah sweah, or tahght about her folks in Corinth.

KALONIKE. No, by Zeus! — to judge by this side of her, nothing small or tight.

LAMPITO. But who has called togethah such a regiment of all us women?

LYSISTRATA. Here I am. I did.

LAMPITO. Speak up, just tell us what you want.

KALONIKE. Oh yes, by Zeus, my dear, do let us know what the important business is!

LYSISTRATA. Let me explain it, then. And yet . . . before I do . . . I have one little question.

KALONIKE. Anything you like.

LYSISTRATA. Don't you all miss the fathers of your little ones,
your husbands who have gone away to war? I'm sure
you all have husbands in the armies far from home.

KALONIKE. Mine's been away five months in Thrace — a general's guard,
posted to see his general does not desert.

MYRRHINA. And mine has been away in Pylos seven whole months.

LAMPITO. And mahn, though he does get back home on leave sometahms,
no soonah has he come than he is gone again.

LYSISTRATA. No lovers either. Not a sign of one is left.
For since our eastern allies have deserted us
they haven't sent a single six-inch substitute
to serve as leatherware replacement for our men.
Would you be willing, then, if I thought out a scheme,
to join with me to end the war?

KALONIKE. Indeed I would,
even if I had to pawn this very wrap-around
and drink up all the money in one day, I would!

MYRRHINA. And so would I, even if I had to see myself
split like a flounder, and give half of me away!

LAMPITO. And so would Ah! Ah'd climb up Mount Taygetos
if Ah just had a chance of seeing peace from theah!

LYSISTRATA. Then I will tell you. I may now divulge my plan.
Women of Greece! — if we intend to force the men
to make a peace, we must abstain . . .

KALONIKE. From what? Speak out!

LYSISTRATA. But will you do it?

KALONIKE. We will, though death should be the price!

LYSISTRATA. Well then, we must abstain utterly from the prick.
Why do you turn your backs? Where are you off to now?
And you — why pout and make such faces, shake your heads?

Why has your color changed? Why do you shed those tears?
Will you do it or will you not? Why hesitate?
KALONIKE. I will not do it. Never. Let the war go on!
MYRRHINA. Neither will I. By Zeus, no! Let the war go on!
LYSISTRATA. How can you say so, Madam Flounder, when just now
you were declaiming you would split yourself in half?
KALONIKE. Anything else you like, anything! If I must
I'll gladly walk through fire. That, rather than the prick!
Because there's nothing like it, dear Lysistrata.
LYSISTRATA. How about you?
MYRRHINA. I too would gladly walk through fire.
LYSISTRATA. Oh the complete depravity of our whole sex!
It is no wonder tragedies are made of us,
we have such unrelenting unity of mind!
But you, my friend from Sparta, dear, if you alone
stand by me, only you, we still might save the cause.
Vote on my side!
LAMPITO. They'ah hahd conditions, mahty hahd,
to sleep without so much as the fo'skin of one . . .
but all the same . . . well . . . yes. We need peace just as bad.
LYSISTRATA. Oh dearest friend! — the one real woman of them all!
KALONIKE. And if we really should abstain from what you say —
which Heaven forbid! — do you suppose on that account
that peace might come to be?
LYSISTRATA. I'm absolutely sure.
If we should sit around, rouged and with skins well creamed,
with nothing on but a transparent negligé,
and come up to them with our deltas plucked quite smooth,
and, once our men get stiff and want to come to grips,
we do not yield to them at all but just hold off,
they'll make a truce in no time. There's no doubt of that.
LAMPITO. We say in Spahta that when Menelaos saw
Helen's ba'e apples he just tossed away his swo'd.
KALONIKE. And what, please, if our husbands just toss *us* away?
LYSISTRATA. Well, you have heard the good old saying: Know Thyself.
KALONIKE. It isn't worth the candle. I hate cheap substitutes.
But what if they should seize and drag us by brute force
into the bedroom?
LYSISTRATA. Hang onto the doors!
KALONIKE. And if —
they beat us?
LYSISTRATA. Then you must give in, but nastily,
and do it badly. There's no fun in it by force.
And then, just keep them straining. They will give it up
in no time — don't you worry. For never will a man
enjoy himself unless the woman coincides.
KALONIKE. If both of you are for this plan, then so are we.

LAMPITO. And we of Spahta shall persuade ouah men to keep
the peace sinceahly and with honah in all ways,
but how could anyone pe'suade the vulgah mob
of Athens not to deviate from discipline?

LYSISTRATA. Don't worry, we'll persuade our men. They'll keep the peace.

LAMPITO. They won't, so long as they have battleships afloat
and endless money sto'ed up in the Pahthenon.

LYSISTRATA. But that too has been carefully provided for:
we shall take over the Acropolis today.
The oldest women have their orders to do that:
while *we* meet here, *they* go as if to sacrifice
up there, but really seizing the Acropolis.

LAMPITO. All should go well. What you say theah is very smaht.

LYSISTRATA. In that case, Lampito, what are we waiting for?
Let's take an oath, to bind us indissolubly.

LAMPITO. Well, just you show us what the oath is. Then we'll sweah.

LYSISTRATA. You're right. Where is that lady cop? (*To the armed* LADY COP *looking around for a* LADY COP.) What do you think
you're looking for? Put down your shield in front of us,
there, on its back, and someone get some scraps of gut.

KALONIKE. Lysistrata, what in the world do you intend
to make us take an oath on?

LYSISTRATA. What? Why, on a shield,
just as they tell me some insurgents in a play
by Aeschylus once did, with a sheep's blood and guts.

KALONIKE. Oh *don't*, Lysistrata, don't swear upon a *shield*,
not if the oath has anything to do with peace!

LYSISTRATA. Well then, what *will* we swear on? Maybe we should get
a white horse somewhere, like the Amazons, and cut
some bits of gut from it.

KALONIKE. *Where* would we get a horse?

LYSISTRATA. But what kind of an oath *is* suitable for us?

KALONIKE. By Zeus, I'll tell you if you like. First we put down
a big black drinking-cup, face up, and then we let
the neck of a good jug of wine bleed into it,
and take a solemn oath to — add no water in.

LAMPITO. Bah Zeus, Ah jest can't tell you how Ah lahk that oath!

LYSISTRATA. Someone go get a cup and winejug from inside.

(KALONIKE *goes and is back in a flash.*)

KALONIKE. My dears, my dearest dears — how's *this* for pottery?
You feel good right away, just laying hold of it.

LYSISTRATA. Well, set it down, and lay your right hand on this pig.
O goddess of Persuasion, and O Loving-cup,
accept this victim's blood! Be gracious unto us.

KALONIKE. It's not anaemic, and flows clear. Those are good signs.
LAMPITO. What an aroma, too! Bah Castah it *is* sweet!
KALONIKE. My dears, if you don't mind — I'll be the first to swear.
LYSISTRATA. By Aphrodite, no! If you had drawn first place
by lot — but now let all lay hands upon the cup.
Yes, Lampito — and now, let one of you repeat
for all of you what I shall say. You will be sworn
by every word she says, and bound to keep this oath:
No lover and no husband and no man on earth —
KALONIKE. No lover and no husband and no man on earth —
LYSISTRATA. *shall e'er approach me with his penis up.* Repeat.
KALONIKE. shall e'er approach me with his penis up. Oh dear,
my knees are buckling under me, Lysistrata!
LYSISTRATA. *and I shall lead an unlaid life alone at home,*
KALONIKE. and I shall lead an unlaid life alone at home,
LYSISTRATA. *wearing a saffron gown and groomed and beautified*
KALONIKE. wearing a saffron gown and groomed and beautified
LYSISTRATA. *so that my husband will be all on fire for me*
KALONIKE. so that my husband will be all on fire for me
LYSISTRATA. *but I will never willingly give in to him*
KALONIKE. but I will never willingly give in to him
LYSISTRATA. *and if he tries to force me to against my will*
KALONIKE. and if he tries to force me to against my will
LYSISTRATA. *I'll do it badly and not wiggle in response*
KALONIKE. I'll do it badly and not wiggle in response
LYSISTRATA. *nor toward the ceiling will I lift my Persian pumps*
KALONIKE. nor toward the ceiling will I lift my Persian pumps
LYSISTRATA. *nor crouch down as the lions on cheese-graters do*
KALONIKE. nor crouch down as the lions on cheese-graters do
LYSISTRATA. *and if I keep my promise, may I drink of this —*
KALONIKE. and if I keep my promise, may I drink of this —
LYSISTRATA. *but if I break it, then may water fill the cup!*
KALONIKE. but if I break it, then may water fill the cup!
LYSISTRATA. Do you all swear to this with her?
ALL. We do, by Zeus!
LYSISTRATA. I'll consecrate our oath now.
KALONIKE. Share alike, my dear,
so we'll be friendly to each other from the start.
LAMPITO. What was that screaming?
LYSISTRATA. That's what I was telling you:
the women have already seized the Parthenon
and the Acropolis. But now, dear Lampito,
return to Sparta and set things in order there —
but leave these friends of yours as hostages with us —
And let us join the others in the citadel
and help them bar the gates.
KALONIKE. But don't you think the men

will rally to the rescue of the citadel,
attacking us at once?

LYSISTRATA. They don't worry me much:
they'll never bring against us threats or fire enough
to force open the gates, except upon our terms.

KALONIKE. Never by Aphrodite! Or we'd lose our name
for being battle-axes and unbearable!

(*Exeunt. The scene changes to the Propylaea of the Acropolis. A* CHORUS *of very old men struggles slowly in, carrying logs and firepots.*)

ONE OLD MAN. Lead on! O Drakës, step by step, although your
shoulder's aching
and under this green olive log's great weight
your back be breaking!

ANOTHER. Eh, life is long but always has
more surprises for us!
Now who'd have thought we'd live to hear
this, O Strymodorus? —

The wives we fed and looked upon
as helpless liabilities
now dare to occupy the Parthenon,
our whole Acropolis, for once they seize
the Propylaea, straightway
they lock and bar the gateway.

CHORUS. Let's rush to the Acropolis with due precipitation
and lay these logs down circlewise, till presently we turn them
into one mighty pyre to make a general cremation
of all the women up there — eh! with our own hands we'll burn them,
the leaders and the followers, without discrimination!

AN OLD MAN. They'll never have the laugh on me!
Though I may not look it,
I rescued the Acropolis
when the Spartans took it
about a hundred years ago.
We laid a siege that kept their king
six years unwashed, so when I made him throw
his armor off, for all his blustering,
in nothing but his shirt he
looked very very dirty.

CHORUS. How strictly I besieged the man! These gates were all invested
with seventeen ranks of armored men all equally ferocious!
Shall women — by Euripides and all the gods detested —

not be restrained — with me on hand — from something so atrocious?
They shall! — or may our trophies won at Marathon be bested!

But we must go a long way yet
up that steep and winding road
before we reach the fortress where we want to get.
How shall we ever drag this load,
lacking pack-mules, way up there?
I can tell you that my shoulder has caved in beyond repair!
Yet we must trudge ever higher,
ever blowing on the fire,
so its coals will still be glowing when we get where we are going
Fooh! Fooh!
Whoo! I choke!
What a smoke!

Lord Herakles! How fierce it flies
out against me from the pot!
and like a rabid bitch it bites me in the eyes!
It's female fire, or it would not
scratch my poor old eyes like this.
Yet undaunted we must onward, up the high Acropolis
where Athena's temple stands
fallen into hostile hands.
O my comrades! shall we ever have a greater need to save her?
Fooh! Fooh!
Whoo! I choke!
What a smoke!

FIRST OLD MAN. Well, thank the gods, I see the fire is yet alive and waking!

SECOND OLD MAN. Why don't we set our lumber down right here in handy batches,
then stick a branch of grape-vine in the pot until it catches

THIRD OLD MAN. and hurl ourselves against the gate with battering and shaking?

FIRST OLD MAN. and if the women won't unbar at such an ultimatum
we'll set the gate on fire and then the smoke will suffocate 'em.

SECOND OLD MAN. Well, let's put down our load. Fooh fooh, what smoke! But blow as needed!

THIRD OLD MAN. Your ablest generals *these* days would not carry wood like *we* did.

SECOND OLD MAN. At last the lumber ceases grinding my poor back to pieces!

THIRD OLD MAN. These are your orders, Colonel Pot: wake up the coals and bid them
report here and present to me a torch lit up and flaring.

FIRST OLD MAN. O Victory, be with us! If you quell the women's daring
we'll raise a splendid trophy of how you and we undid them!

(*A* CHORUS *of middle-aged women appears in the offing.*)

A WOMAN. I think that I perceive a smoke in which appears a flurry
of sparks as of a lighted fire. Women, we'll have to hurry!

CHORUS OF WOMEN.

Oh fleetly fly, oh swiftly flit,
my dears, e'er Kalykë be lit
and with Kritylla swallowed up alive
in flames which the gales dreadfully drive
and deadly old men fiercely inflate!
Yet one thing I'm afraid of: will I not arrive too late?
for filling up my water-jug has been no easy matter
what with the crowd at the spring in the dusk and the clamor and pottery clatter.
Pushed as I was, jostled by slave-
women and sluts marked with a brand
yet with my jug firmly in hand
here I have come, hoping to save
my burning friends and brave,

for certain windy, witless, old,
and wheezy fools, so I was told,
with wood some tons in weight crept up this path,
not having in mind heating a bath
but uttering threats, vowing they will
consume those nasty women into cinders on grill!
But O Athena! never may I see my friends igniting!
Nay! — let them save all the cities of Greece and their people from folly and fighting!
Goddess whose crest flashes with gold,
they were so bold taking your shine
only for this — Goddess who hold
Athens — for *this* noble design,
braving the flames, calling on you
to carry water too!

(*One of the old men urinates noisily.*)

CHORUS OF WOMEN. Be still! What was that noise? Aha! Oh, wicked and degraded!
Would any good religious men have ever done what *they* did?

CHORUS OF MEN. Just look! It's a surprise-attack! Oh, dear, we're being raided
by swarms of them below us when we've got a swarm above us!

CHORUS OF WOMEN. Why panic at the sight of us? This is not many of us.
We number tens of thousands but you've hardly seen a fraction.

CHORUS OF MEN. O Phaidrias, shall they talk so big and we not take some action?
Oh, should we not be bashing them and splintering our lumber? (*The* OLD MEN *begin to strip for combat.*)

CHORUS OF WOMEN. Let us, too, set our pitchers down, so they will not encumber
our movements if these gentlemen should care to offer battle.

CHORUS OF MEN. Oh someone should have clipped their jaws — twice, thrice, until they rattle —
(as once the poet put it) — then we wouldn't hear their prating.

CHORUS OF WOMEN. Well, here's your chance. Won't someone hit me? Here I stand, just waiting!
No other bitch will ever grab your balls, the way I'll treat you!

CHORUS OF MEN. Shut up — or I will drub you so old age will never reach you!

CHORUS OF WOMEN. Won't anyone step and lay one finger on Stratyllis?

CHORUS OF MEN. And if we pulverize her with our knuckles, will you kill us?

CHORUS OF WOMEN. No, only chew your lungs out and your innards and your eyes, sir.

CHORUS OF MEN. How clever is Euripides! There is no poet wiser: he says indeed that women are the worst of living creatures.

CHORUS OF WOMEN. Now is the time, Rhodippe: let us raise our brimming pitchers.

CHORUS OF MEN. Why come up here with water, you, the gods' abomination?

CHORUS OF WOMEN. And why come here with fire, you tomb? To give yourself cremation?

CHORUS OF MEN. To set your friends alight upon a pyre erected for them.

CHORUS OF WOMEN. And so we brought our water-jugs. Upon your pyre we'll pour them.

CHORUS OF MEN. *You'll* put my fire out?

CHORUS OF WOMEN. Any time! You'll see there's nothing to it.

CHORUS OF MEN. I think I'll grill you right away, with just this torch to do it!

CHORUS OF WOMEN. Have you some dusting-powder? Here's your wedding-bath all ready.

CHORUS OF MEN. *You'll* bathe me, garbage that you are?

CHORUS OF WOMEN. Yes, bridegroom, just hold steady!

CHORUS OF MEN. Friends, you have heard her insolence —
CHORUS OF WOMEN. I'm free-born, not your slave, sir.
CHORUS OF MEN. I'll have this noise of yours restrained —
CHORUS OF WOMEN. Court's out — so be less grave, sir.
CHORUS OF MEN. Why don't you set her hair on fire?
CHORUS OF WOMEN. Oh, Water, be of service!
CHORUS OF MEN. Oh woe is me!
CHORUS OF WOMEN. Was it too hot?
CHORUS OF MEN. Oh, stop! What *is* this? Hot? Oh no!
CHORUS OF WOMEN. I'm watering you to make you grow.
CHORUS OF MEN. I'm withered from this chill I got!
CHORUS OF WOMEN. You've got a fire, so warm yourself. You're trembling: are you nervous?

(*Enter a* COMMISSIONER, *escorted by* FOUR SCYTHIAN POLICEMEN *with bows and quivers slung on their backs.*)

COMMISSIONER. Has the extravagance of women broken out
into full fury, with their banging tambourines
and constant wailings for their oriental gods,
and on the roof-tops their Adonis festival,
which I could hear myself from the Assembly once?
For while Demostratos — that numbskull — had the floor,
urging an expedition against Sicily,
his wife was dancing and we heard her crying out
"Weep for Adonis!" — so the expedition failed
with such an omen. When the same Demostratos
was urging that we levy troops from our allies
his wife was on the roof again, a little drunk:
"Weep for Adonis! Beat your breast!" says she. At that,
he gets more bellicose, that god-Damn-ox-tratos.
To this has the incontinence of women come!

CHORUS OF MEN. You haven't *yet* heard how outrageous they can be!
With other acts of violence, these women here
have showered us from their jugs, so now we are reduced
to shaking out our shirts as if we'd pissed in them.

COMMISSIONER. Well, by the God of Waters, what do you expect?
When we ourselves conspire with them in waywardness
and give them good examples of perversity
such wicked notions naturally sprout in them.
We go into a shop and say something like this:
"Goldsmith, about that necklace you repaired: last night
my wife was dancing, when the peg that bolts the catch
fell from its hole. I have to sail for Salamis,
but if you have the time, by all means try to come
towards evening, and put in the peg she needs."
Another man says to a cobbler who is young

and has no child's-play of a prick, "Cobbler," he says,
"her sandal-strap is pinching my wife's little toe,
which is quite delicate. So please come by at noon
and stretch it for her so it has a wider play."
Such things as that result of course in things like this:
when I, as a Commissioner, have made a deal
to fit the fleet with oars and need the money now,
I'm locked out by these women from the very gates.
But it's no use just standing here. Bring on the bars,
so I can keep these women in their proper place.
What are *you* gaping at, you poor unfortunate?
Where are *you* looking? Only seeing if a bar
is open yet downtown? Come, drive these crowbars in
under the gates on that side, pry away, and I
will pry away on this.

(LYSISTRATA *comes out.*)

LYSISTRATA. No need to pry at all.
I'm coming out, of my own will. What use are bars?
It isn't bolts and bars we need so much as brains.

COMMISSIONER. Really, you dirty slut? Where is that officer?
Arrest her, and tie both her hands behind her back.

LYSISTRATA. By Artemis, just let him lift a hand at me
and, public officer or not, you'll hear him howl.

COMMISSIONER. You let her scare you? Grab her round the middle, you.
Then *you* go help him and between you get her tied.

(KALONIKE *comes out.*)

KALONIKE. By Artemis, if you just lay one hand on her
I have a mind to trample the shit out of you.

COMMISSIONER. It's out already! Look! Now where's the other one?
Tie up *that* woman first. She babbles, with it all.

(MYRRHINA *comes out.*)

MYRRHINA. By Hecatë, if you just lay a hand on her
you'll soon ask for a cup — to get your swellings down!

(*The* POLICEMAN *dashes behind the* COMMISSIONER *and clings to him for protection.*)

COMMISSIONER. What happened? Where's that bowman, now? Hold onto *her!* (*He moves quickly away downhill.*)
I'll see that none of you can get away through here!

LYSISTRATA. By Artemis, you come near her and I'll bereave
your head of every hair! You'll weep for each one, too.

COMMISSIONER. What a calamity! This one has failed me too.
But never must we let ourselves be overcome
by women. All together now, O Scythians! —
let's march against them in formation!

LYSISTRATA. You'll find out
that inside there we have four companies
of fighting women perfectly equipped for war.

COMMISSIONER. Charge! Turn their flanks, O Scythians! and tie their hands!

LYSISTRATA. O allies — comrades — women! Sally forth and fight!
O vegetable vendors, O green-grocery-
grain-garlic-bread-bean-dealers and inn-keepers all!

(*A group of fierce* OLD MARKET-WOMEN, *carrying baskets of vegetables, spindles, etc., emerges. There is a volley of vegetables. The* SCYTHIANS *are soon routed.*)

Come pull them, push them, smite them, smash them into bits!
Rail and abuse them in the strongest words you know!
Halt, Halt! Retire in order! We'll forego the spoils!

COMMISSIONER (*tragically, like say Xerxes*). Oh what reverses have my bowmen undergone!

LYSISTRATA. But what did you imagine? Did you think you came
against a pack of slaves? Perhaps you didn't know
that women can be resolute?

COMMISSIONER. I know they can —
above all when they spot a bar across the way.

CHORUS OF MEN. Commissioner of Athens, you are spending words unduly,
to argue with these animals, who only roar the louder,
or don't you know they showered us so coldly and so cruelly,
and in our undershirts at that, and furnished us no powder?

CHORUS OF WOMEN. But beating up your neighbor is inevitably bringing
a beating on yourself, sir, with your own eyes black and bloody.
I'd rather sit securely like a little girl demurely
not stirring up a single straw nor harming anybody,
So long as no one robs my hive and rouses me to stinging.

CHORUS OF MEN. How shall we ever tame these brutes? We cannot tolerate
the situation further, so we must investigate
this occurrence and find
with what purpose in mind
they profane the Acropolis, seize it, and lock

the approach to this huge and prohibited rock,
to our holiest ground!
Cross-examine them! Never believe one word
they tell you — refute them, confound them!
We must get to the bottom of things like this
and the circumstances around them.

COMMISSIONER. Yes indeed! and I want to know first one thing:
just *why* you committed this treason,
barricading the fortress with locks and bars —
I insist on knowing the reason.

LYSISTRATA. To protect all the money up there from you —
you'll have nothing to fight for without it.

COMMISSIONER. You think it is *money* we're fighting for?

LYSISTRATA. All the troubles we have are about it.
It was so Peisander and those in power
of his kind could embezzle the treasure
that they cooked up emergencies all the time.
Well, let them, if such is their pleasure,
but they'll never get into this money again,
though you men should elect them to spend it.

COMMISSIONER. And just what will *you* do with it?

LYSISTRATA. Can you ask?
Of course we shall superintend it.

COMMISSIONER. You will superintend the treasury, *you?!*

LYSISTRATA. And why should it strike you so funny?
when we manage our houses in everything
and it's we who look after your money.

COMMISSIONER. But it's not the same thing!

LYSISTRATA. Why not?

COMMISSIONER. It's war,
and *this* money must pay the expenses.

LYSISTRATA. To begin with, you needn't be waging war.

COMMISSIONER. To survive, we don't need our defenses?

LYSISTRATA. You'll survive: we shall save you.

COMMISSIONER. Who? You?

LYSISTRATA. Yes, we.

COMMISSIONER. You absolutely disgust me.

LYSISTRATA. You may like it or not, but you *shall* be saved.

COMMISSIONER. I protest!

LYSISTRATA. If you care to, but, trust me,
this has got to be done all the same.

COMMISSIONER. It has?
It's illegal, unjust, and outrageous!

LYSISTRATA. We must save you, sir.

COMMISSIONER. Yes? And if I refuse?

LYSISTRATA. You will much the more grimly engage us.

COMMISSIONER. And whence does it happen that war and peace
are fit matters for women to mention?

LYSISTRATA. I will gladly explain —

COMMISSIONER. And be quick, or else
you'll be howling!

LYSISTRATA. Now, just pay attention
and keep your hands to yourself, if you can!

COMMISSIONER. But I can't. You can't think how I suffer
from holding them back in my anger!

AN OLD WOMAN. Sir —
if you don't you will have it much rougher.

COMMISSIONER. You may croak that remark to yourself, you hag!
Will *you* do the explaining?

LYSISTRATA. I'll do it.

Heretofore we women in time of war
have endured very patiently through it,
putting up with whatever you men might do,
for never a peep would you let us
deliver on your unstatesmanly acts
no matter how much they upset us,
but we knew very well, while we sat at home,
when you'd handled a big issue poorly,
and we'd ask you then, with a pretty smile
though our heart would be grieving us sorely,
"And what were the terms for a truce, my dear,
you drew up in assembly this morning?"
"And what's it to you?" says our husband, "Shut up!"
— so, as ever, at this gentle warning
I of course would discreetly shut up.

KALONIKE. Not me!
You can bet I would never be quiet!

COMMISSIONER. I'll bet, if you weren't, you were beaten up.

LYSISTRATA. *I'd* shut up, and I do not deny it,
but when plan after plan was decided on,
so bad we could scarcely believe it,
I would say "This last is so mindless, dear,
I cannot think how you achieve it!"
And then he would say, with a dirty look,
"Just you think what your spindle is for dear,
or your head will be spinning for days on end —
let the *men* attend to the war, dear."

COMMISSIONER. By Zeus, *he* had the right idea!

LYSISTRATA. You fool!
Right ideas were quite out of the question,
when your reckless policies failed, and yet
we never could make a suggestion.

And lately we heard you say so yourselves:
in the streets there'd be someone lamenting:
"There's not one man in the country now!"
— and we heard many others assenting.
After that, we conferred through our deputies
and agreed, having briefly debated,
to act in common to save all Greece
at once — for why should we have waited?
So now, when we women are talking sense,
if you'll only agree to be quiet
and to listen to us as we did to you,
you'll be very much edified by it.

COMMISSIONER. *You* will edify *us!* I protest!

LYSISTRATA. Shut up!

COMMISSIONER. *I'm* to shut up and listen, you scum, you?!
Sooner death! And a veil on your head at that!

LYSISTRATA. We'll fix that. It may really become you:
do accept this veil as a present from me.
Drape it modestly — so — round your head, do you see?
And now — *not* a word more, sir.

KALONIKE. Do accept this dear little wool-basket, too!
Hitch your girdle and card! Here are beans you may chew
the way all of the nicest Athenians do —
and the *women* will see to the war, sir!

CHORUS OF WOMEN. Oh women, set your jugs aside and keep a closer distance:
our friends may need from us as well some resolute assistance.

Since never shall I weary of the stepping of the dance
nor will my knees of treading, for these ladies I'll advance
anywhere they may lead,
and they're daring indeed,
they have wit, a fine figure, and boldness of heart,
they are prudent and charming, efficient and smart,
patriotic and brave!

But, O manliest grandmothers, onward now!
And you matronly nettles, don't waver!
but continue to bristle and rage, my dears,
for you've still got the wind in your favor!

(*The* CHORUS OF WOMEN *and the* OLD MARKET-WOMEN *join.*)

LYSISTRATA. But if only the spirit of tender Love
and the power of sweet Aphrodite
were to breathe down over our breasts and thighs
an attraction both melting and mighty,

and infuse a pleasanter rigor in men,
raising only their cudgels of passion,
then I think we'd be known throughout all of Greece
as makers of peace and good fashion.

COMMISSIONER. Having done just what?

LYSISTRATA. Well, first of all
we shall certainly make it unlawful
to go madly to market in armor.

AN OLD MARKET-WOMAN. Yes!
By dear Aphrodite, it's awful!

LYSISTRATA. For now, in the midst of the pottery-stalls
and the greens and the beans and the garlic,
men go charging all over the market-place
in full armor and beetling and warlike.

COMMISSIONER. They must do as their valor impels them to!

LYSISTRATA. But it makes a man only look funny
to be wearing a shield with a Gorgon's head
and be wanting sardines for less money.

OLD MARKET-WOMAN. Well, I saw a huge cavalry-captain once
on a stallion that scarcely could hold him,
pouring into his helmet of bronze a pint
of pea-soup an old woman had sold him,
and a Thracian who, brandishing shield and spear
like some savage Euripides staged once,
when he'd frightened a vendor of figs to death,
gobbled up all her ripest and aged ones.

COMMISSIONER. And how, on the international scale,
can you straighten out the enormous
confusion among all the states of Greece?

LYSISTRATA. Very easily.

COMMISSIONER. How? Do inform us.

LYSISTRATA. When our skein's in a tangle we take it thus
on our spindles, or haven't you seen us? —
one on this side and one on the other side,
and we work out the tangles between us.
And that is the way we'll undo this war,
by exchanging ambassadors, whether
you like it or not, one from either side,
and we'll work out the tangles together.

COMMISSIONER. Do you really think that with wools and skeins
and just being able to spin you
can end these momentous affairs, you fools?

LYSISTRATA. With any intelligence in you
you statesmen would govern as we work wool,
and in everything Athens would profit.

COMMISSIONER. How so? Do tell.

LYSISTRATA. First, you take raw fleece
and you wash the beshittedness off it:
just so, you should first lay the city out
on a washboard and beat out the rotters
and pluck out the sharpers like burrs, and when
you find tight knots of schemers and plotters
who are out for key offices, card them loose,
but best tear off their heads in addition.
Then into one basket together card
all those of a good disposition
be they citizens, resident aliens, friends,
an ally or an absolute stranger,
even people in debt to the commonwealth,
you can mix them all in with no danger.
And the cities which Athens has colonized —
by Zeus, you should try to conceive them
as so many shreddings and tufts of wool
that are scattered about and not leave them
to lie around loose, but from all of them
draw the threads in here, and collect them
into one big ball and then weave a coat
for the people, to warm and protect them.

COMMISSIONER. Now, isn't this awful? They treat the state
like wool to be beaten and carded,
who have nothing at all to do with war!

LYSISTRATA. Yes we do, you damnable hard-head!
We have none of your honors but we have more
than double your sufferings by it.
First of all, we bear sons whom you send to war.

COMMISSIONER. Don't bring up our old sorrows! Be quiet!

LYSISTRATA. And now, when we ought to enjoy ourselves,
making much of our prime and our beauty,
we are sleeping alone because all the men
are away on their soldierly duty.
But never mind *us* — when young girls grow old
in their bedrooms with no men to share them.

COMMISSIONER. You seem to forget that men, too, grow old.

LYSISTRATA. By Zeus, but you cannot compare them!
When a man gets back, though he be quite gray,
he can wed a young girl in a minute,
but the season of woman is very short:
she must take what she can while she's in it.
And you know she must, for when it's past,
although you're not awfully astute, you're
aware that no man will marry her then
and she sits staring into the future.

COMMISSIONER. But he who can raise an erection still —

LYSISTRATA. Is there some good reason you don't drop dead?
We'll sell you a coffin if you but will.
Here's a string of onions to crown your head
and I'll make a honey-cake large and round
you can feed to Cerberus underground!

FIRST OLD MARKET-WOMAN. Accept these few fillets of leek from me!

SECOND OLD MARKET-WOMAN. Let me offer you these for your garland, sir!

LYSISTRATA. What now? Do you want something else you see?
Listen! Charon's calling his passenger —
will you catch the ferry or still delay
when his other dead want to sail away?

COMMISSIONER. Is it not downright monstrous to treat *me* like this?
By Zeus, I'll go right now to the Commissioners
and show myself in evidence, just as I am! (*He begins to withdraw with dignity and his* FOUR SCYTHIAN POLICEMEN.)

LYSISTRATA. Will you accuse us of not giving you a wake?
But your departed spirit will receive from us
burnt offerings in due form, two days from now at dawn!

(LYSISTRATA *with the other women goes into the Acropolis. The* COMMISSIONER, *etc., have left. The* MALE CHORUS *and the mixed* FEMALE CHORUS *are alone.*)

CHORUS OF MEN. No man now dare fall to drowsing, if he wishes to stay free!
Men, let's strip and gird ourselves for this eventuality!

To me this all begins to have a smell
of bigger things and larger things as well:
most of all I sniff a tyranny afoot. I'm much afraid
certain secret agents of the Spartans may have come,
meeting under cover here, in Cleisthenes's home,
instigating those damned women by deceit to make a raid
upon our treasury and that great sum
the city paid my pension from.

Sinister events already! — think of lecturing the state,
women as they are, and prattling on of things like shields of bronze,
even trying hard to get us reconciled to those we hate —
those of Sparta, to be trusted like a lean wolf when it yawns!
All of this is just a pretext, men, for a dictatorship —
but to me they shall not dictate! Watch and ward! A sword I'll hide
underneath a branch of myrtle; through the agora I'll slip,
following Aristogeiton, backing the tyrannicide!

(*The* OLD MEN *pair off to imitate the gestures of the famous group statue of the tyrannicides Harmodius and Aristogeiton.*)

Thus I'll take my stand beside him! Now my rage is goaded raw
I'm as like as not to clip this damned old woman on the jaw!

CHORUS OF WOMEN. Your own mother will not know you when you come home, if you do!
Let us first, though, lay our things down, O my dear old friends and true.

For now, O fellow-citizens, we would
consider what will do our city good.
Well I may, because it bred me up in wealth and elegance:
letting me at seven help with the embroidering
of Athena's mantle, and at ten with offering
cakes and flowers. When I was grown and beautiful I had my chance
to bear her baskets, at my neck a string
of figs, and proud as anything.

Must I not, then, give my city any good advice I can?
Need you hold the fact against me that I was not born a man,
when I offer better methods than the present ones, and when
I've a share in this economy, for I contribute men?
But, you sad old codgers, *yours* is forfeited on many scores:
you have drawn upon our treasure dating from the Persian wars,
what they call grampatrimony, and you've paid no taxes back.
Worse, you've run it nearly bankrupt, and the prospect's pretty black.
Have you anything to answer? Say you were within the law
and I'll take this rawhide boot and clip you one across the jaw!

CHORUS OF MEN. Greater insolence than ever! —
that's the method that she calls
"better" — if you would believe her.

But this threat must be prevented! Every man with both his balls
must make ready — take our shirts off, for a man must reek of male
outright — not wrapped up in leafage like an omelet for sale!

Forward and barefoot: we'll do it again
to the death, just as when we resisted
tyranny out at Leipsydrion, when
we really existed!

Now or never we must grow
young again and, sprouting wings
over all our bodies, throw
off this heaviness age brings!

For if any of us give them even just a little hold
nothing will be safe from their tenacious grasp. They are so bold

they will soon build ships of war and, with exorbitant intent,
send such navies out against us as Queen Artemisia sent.
But if they attack with horse, our knights we might as well delete:
nothing rides so well as woman, with so marvelous a seat,
never slipping at the gallop. Just look at those Amazons
in that picture in the Stoa, from their horses bringing bronze
axes down on men. We'd better grab *these* members of the sex
one and all, arrest them, get some wooden collars on their necks!

CHORUS OF WOMEN. By the gods, if you chagrin me
or annoy me, if you dare,
I'll turn loose the sow that's in me

till you rouse the town to help you with the way I've done your hair!
Let us too make ready, women, and our garments quickly doff
so we'll smell like women angered fit to bite our fingers off!

Now I am ready: let one of the men
come against me, and *he'll* never hanker
after a black bean or garlic again:
no woman smells ranker!

Say a single unkind word,
I'll pursue you till you drop,
as the beetle did the bird.
My revenge will never stop!

Yet you will not worry me so long as Lampito's alive
and my noble friends in Thebes and other cities still survive.
You'll not overpower us, even passing seven decrees or eight,
you, poor brutes, whom everyone and everybody's neighbors hate.
Only yesterday I gave a party, honoring Hecatë,
but when I invited in the neighbor's child to come and play,
such a pretty thing from Thebes, as nice and quiet as you please,
just an eel, they said she couldn't, on account of your decrees.
You'll go on forever passing such decrees without a check
till somebody takes you firmly by the leg and breaks your neck!

(LYSISTRATA *comes out. The* CHORUS OF WOMEN *addresses her in the manner of tragedy.*)

Oh Queen of this our enterprise and all our hopes,
wherefore in baleful brooding hast thou issued forth?

LYSISTRATA. The deeds of wicked women and the female mind
discourage me and set me pacing up and down.

CHORUS OF WOMEN. What's that? What's that you say?

LYSISTRATA. The truth, alas, the truth!

CHORUS OF WOMEN. What is it that's so dreadful? Tell it to your friends.

LYSISTRATA. A shameful thing to tell and heavy not to tell.

CHORUS OF WOMEN. Oh, never hide from me misfortune that is ours!

LYSISTRATA. To put it briefly as I can, we are in heat.

CHORUS OF WOMEN. Oh Zeus!

LYSISTRATA. Why call on Zeus? This is the way things are.
At least it seems I am no longer capable
of keeping them from men. They are deserting me.
This morning I caught one of them digging away
to make a tunnel to Pan's grotto down the slope,
another letting herself down the parapet
with rope and pulley, and another climbing down
its sheerest face, and yesterday was one I found
sitting upon a sparrow with a mind to fly
down to some well-equipped whoremaster's place in town.
Just as she swooped I pulled her backward by the hair.
They think of every far-fetched excuse they can
for going home. And here comes one deserter now.
You there, where are you running?

FIRST WOMAN. I want to go home,
because I left some fine Milesian wools at home
that must be riddled now with moths.

LYSISTRATA. Oh, damn your moths!
Go back inside.

FIRST WOMAN. But I shall come back right away,
just time enough to stretch them out upon my bed.

LYSISTRATA. Stretch nothing out, and don't you go away at all.

FIRST WOMAN. But shall I let my wools be ruined?

LYSISTRATA. If you must.

SECOND WOMAN. Oh miserable me! I sorrow for the flax
I left at home unbeaten and unstripped!

LYSISTRATA. One more —
wanting to leave for stalks of flax she hasn't stripped.
Come back here!

SECOND WOMAN. But, by Artemis, I only want
to strip my flax. Then I'll come right back here again.

LYSISTRATA. Strip me no strippings! If you start this kind of thing
some other woman soon will want to do the same.

THIRD WOMAN. O lady Artemis, hold back this birth until
I can get safe to some unconsecrated place!

LYSISTRATA. What is this raving?

THIRD WOMAN. I'm about to have a child.

LYSISTRATA. But you weren't pregnant yesterday.

THIRD WOMAN. I am today.
Oh, send me home this instant, dear Lysistrata,
so I can find a midwife.

LYSISTRATA. What strange tale is this?
What is this hard thing you have here?

THIRD WOMAN. The child is male.

LYSISTRATA. By Aphrodite, no! You obviously have some hollow thing of bronze. I'll find out what it is. You silly thing! — you have Athena's helmet here — and claiming to be pregnant!

THIRD WOMAN. So I am, by Zeus!

LYSISTRATA. In that case, what's the helmet for?

THIRD WOMAN. So if the pains came on me while I'm still up here, I might give birth inside the helmet, as I've seen the pigeons do.

LYSISTRATA. What an excuse! The case is obvious. Wait here. I want to show this bouncing baby helmet off. (*She passes the huge helmet around the* CHORUS OF WOMEN.)

SECOND WOMAN. But I can't even sleep in the Acropolis, not for an instant since I saw the sacred snake!

FOURTH WOMAN. The owls are what are killing *me*. How can I sleep with their eternal whit-to-whoo-to-whit-to-whoo?

LYSISTRATA. You're crazy! Will you stop this hocus-pocus now? No doubt you miss your husbands: don't you think that they are missing us as much? I'm sure the nights they pass are just as hard. But, gallant comrades, do bear up, and face these gruelling hardships yet a little while. There is an oracle that says we'll win, if we only will stick together. Here's the oracle.

CHORUS OF WOMEN. Oh, read us what it says!

LYSISTRATA. Keep silence, then and hear:
"*Now when to one high place are gathered the fluttering swallows,*
Fleeing the Hawk and the Cock however hotly it follows,
Then will their miseries end, and that which is over be under:
Thundering Zeus will decide.

A WOMAN. Will we lie on top now, I wonder?

LYSISTRATA. *But if the Swallows go fighting each other and springing and winging*
Out of the holy and high sanctuary, then people will never
Say there was any more dissolute bitch of a bird whatsoever."

A WOMAN. The oracle is clear, by Zeus!

LYSISTRATA. By *all* the gods! So let us not renounce the hardships we endure. But let us go back in. Indeed, my dearest friends, it would be shameful to betray the oracle.

(*Exeunt into the Acropolis.*)

CHORUS OF MEN. Let me tell you a story I heard one day when I was a child:

There was once a young fellow Melanion by name
who refused to get married and ran away
to the wild.

To the mountains he came
and inhabited there
in a grove
and hunted the hare
both early and late
with nets that he wove
and also a hound
and he never came home again, such was his hate,
all women he found
so nasty, and we
quite wisely agree.

Let us kiss you, dear old dears!

CHORUS OF WOMEN. With no onions, you'll shed tears!

CHORUS OF MEN. I mean, lift my leg and *kick*.

CHORUS OF WOMEN. My, you wear your thicket thick!

CHORUS OF MEN. Great Myronides was rough
at the front and black enough
in the ass to scare his foes.
Just ask anyone who knows:
it's with hair that wars are won —
take for instance Phormion.

CHORUS OF WOMEN. Let me tell you a story in answer to Melanion's case.

There is now a man, Timon, who wanders around
in the wilderness, hiding his face from view
in a place
where the brambles abound
so he looks like a chip
off a Fur-
y, curling his lip.
Now Timon retired
in hatred and pure
contempt of all men
and he cursed them in words that were truly inspired
again and again
but women he found
delightful and sound.

Would you like your jaw repaired?

CHORUS OF MEN. Thank you, no. You've got me scared.

CHORUS OF WOMEN. Let me jump and kick it though.

CHORUS OF MEN. You will let your man-sack show.

CHORUS OF WOMEN. All the same you wouldn't see,
old and gray as I may be,
any superfluity

of unbarbered hair on me;
it is plucked and more, you scamp,
since I singe it with a lamp!

(*Enter* LYSISTRATA *on the wall.*)

LYSISTRATA. Women, O women, come here quickly, here to me!
WOMEN. Whatever is it? Tell me! What's the shouting for?
LYSISTRATA. I see a man approaching, shaken and possessed,
seized and inspired by Aphrodite's power.
O thou, of Cyprus, Paphos, and Cythera, queen!
continue straight along this way you have begun!
A WOMAN. Whoever he is, where is he?
LYSISTRATA. Near Demeter's shrine.
A WOMAN. Why yes, by Zeus, he is. Who ever can he be?
LYSISTRATA. Well, look at him. Do any of you know him?
MYRRHINA. Yes.
I do. He's my own husband, too, Cinesias.
LYSISTRATA. Then it's your duty now to turn him on a spit,
cajole him and make love to him and not make love,
to offer everything, short of those things of which
the wine-cup knows.
MYRRHINA. I'll do it, don't you fear.
LYSISTRATA. And I
will help you tantalize him. I will stay up here
and help you roast him slowly. But now, disappear!

(*Enter* CINESIAS.)

CINESIAS. Oh how unfortunate I am, gripped by what spasms,
stretched tight like being tortured on a wheel!
LYSISTRATA. Who's there? Who has got this far past the sentries?
CINESIAS. I.
LYSISTRATA. A man?
CINESIAS. A man, for sure.
LYSISTRATA. Then clear away from here.
CINESIAS. Who're you, to throw me out?
LYSISTRATA. The look-out for the day.
CINESIAS. Then, for the gods' sake, call Myrrhina out for me.
LYSISTRATA. You don't say! Call Myrrhina out! And who are you?
CINESIAS. Her husband. I'm Cinesias Paionides.
LYSISTRATA. Well, my dear man, hello! Your name is not unknown
among us here and not without a certain fame,
because your wife has it forever on her lips.
She can't pick up an egg or quince but she must say:
Cinesias would enjoy it so!
CINESIAS. How wonderful!

LYSISTRATA. By Aphrodite, yes. And if we chance to talk
of husbands, your wife interrupts and says the rest
are nothing much compared to her Cinesias.

CINESIAS. Go call her.

LYSISTRATA. Will you give me something if I do?

CINESIAS. Indeed I will, by Zeus, if it is what you want.
I can but offer what I have, and I have this.

LYSISTRATA. Wait there. I will go down and call her.

CINESIAS. Hurry up!
because I find no charm whatever left in life
since she departed from the house. I get depressed
whenever I go into it, and everything
seems lonely to me now, and when I eat my food
I find no taste in it at all — because I'm stiff.

MYRRHINA (*offstage*). I love him, how I love him! But he doesn't want
my love! (*On wall.*) So what's the use of calling me to him?

CINESIAS. My sweet little Myrrhina, why do you act like that?
Come down here.

MYRRHINA. There? By Zeus, I certainly will not.

CINESIAS. Won't you come down, Myrrhina, when I'm calling you?

MYRRHINA. Not when you call me without needing anything.

CINESIAS. Not needing anything? I'm desperate with need.

MYRRHINA. I'm going now.

CINESIAS. Oh no! No, don't go yet! At least
you'll listen to the baby. Call your mammy, you.

BABY. Mammy mammy mammy!

CINESIAS. What's wrong with you? Have you no pity on your child
when it is six days now since he was washed or nursed?

MYRRHINA. Oh, *I* have pity. But his father takes no care
of him.

CINESIAS. Come down, you flighty creature, for the child.

MYRRHINA. Oh, what it is to be a mother! I'll come down,
for what else can I do? (*Exits to reenter below.*)

CINESIAS. It seems to me she's grown
much younger, and her eyes have a more tender look.
Even her being angry with me and her scorn
are just the things that pain me with the more desire.

MYRRHINA. Come let me kiss you, dear sweet little baby mine,
with such a horrid father. Mammy loves you, though.

CINESIAS. But why are you so mean? Why do you listen to
those other women, giving me such pain? — And you,
you're suffering yourself.

MYRRHINA. Take your hands off of me!

CINESIAS. But everything we have at home, my things and yours,
you're letting go to pieces.

MYRRHINA. Little do I care!

CINESIAS. Little you care even if your weaving's pecked apart
and carried off by chickens?

MYRRHINA (*bravely*). Little I care, by Zeus!

CINESIAS. You have neglected Aphrodite's rituals
for such a long time now. Won't you come back again?

MYRRHINA. Not I, unless you men negotiate a truce
and make an end of war.

CINESIAS. Well, if it's so decreed,
we will do even that.

MYRRHINA. Well, if it's so decreed,
I will come home again. Not now. I've sworn I won't.

CINESIAS. All right, all right. But now lie down with me once more.

MYRRHINA. No! No! — yet I don't say I'm not in love with you.

CINESIAS. You love me? Then why not lie down, Myrrhina dear?

MYRRHINA. Don't be ridiculous! Not right before the child!

CINESIAS. By Zeus, of course not. Manes, carry him back home.
There now. You see the baby isn't in your way.
Won't you lie down?

MYRRHINA. But *where*, you rogue, just where
is one to do it?

CINESIAS. Where? Pan's grotto's a fine place.

MYRRHINA. But how could I come back to the Acropolis
in proper purity?

CINESIAS. Well, there's a spring below
the grotto — you can very nicely bathe in that.

(*Ekkyklema or inset-scene with grotto.*)

MYRRHINA. And then I'm under oath. What if I break my vows?

CINESIAS. Let me bear all the blame. Don't worry about your oath.

MYRRHINA. Wait here, and I'll go get a cot for us.

CINESIAS. No, no,
the ground will do.

MYRRHINA. No, by Apollo! Though you are
so horrid, I can't have you lying on the ground. (*Leaves.*)

CINESIAS. You know, the woman loves me — *that's* as plain as day.

MYRRHINA. There. Get yourself in bed and I'll take off my clothes.
Oh, what a nuisance! I must go and get a mat.

CINESIAS. What for? I don't need one.

MYRRHINA. Oh yes, by Artemis!
On the bare cords? How ghastly!

CINESIAS. Let me kiss you now.

MYRRHINA. Oh, very well.

CINESIAS. Wow! Hurry, hurry and come back.

(MYRRHINA *leaves. A long wait.*)

MYRRHINA. Here is the mat. Lie down now, while I get undressed. Oh, what a nuisance! You don't have a pillow, dear.

CINESIAS. But I don't need one, not one bit!

MYRRHINA. By Zeus, *I* do! (*Leaves.*)

CINESIAS. Poor prick, the service around here is terrible!

MYRRHINA. Sit up, my dear, jump up! Now I've got everything.

CINESIAS. Indeed you have. And now, my golden girl, come here.

MYRRHINA. I'm just untying my brassiere. Now don't forget: about that treaty — you won't disappoint me, dear?

CINESIAS. By Zeus, no! On my life!

MYRRHINA. You have no blanket, dear.

CINESIAS. By Zeus, I do not need one. I just want to screw.

MYRRHINA. Don't worry, dear, you will. I'll be back right away. (*Leaves.*)

CINESIAS. This number, with her bedding, means to murder me.

MYRRHINA. Now raise yourself upright.

CINESIAS. But *this* is upright now!

MYRRHINA. Wouldn't you like some perfume?

CINESIAS. By Apollo, no!

MYRRHINA. By Aphrodite, yes! You must — like it or not. (*Leaves.*)

CINESIAS. Lord Zeus! Just let the perfume spill! That's all I ask!

MYRRHINA. Hold out your hand. Take some of this and rub it on.

CINESIAS. This perfume, by Apollo, isn't sweet at all. It smells a bit of stalling — not of wedding nights!

MYRRHINA. I brought the *Rhodian* perfume! How absurd of me!

CINESIAS. It's fine! Let's keep it.

MYRRHINA. You *will* have your little joke. (*Leaves.*)

CINESIAS. Just let me at the man who first distilled perfumes!

MYRRHINA. Try this, in the long vial.

CINESIAS. I've got one like it, dear. But don't be tedious. Lie down. And please don't bring anything more.

MYRRHINA (*going*). That's what I'll do, by Artemis! I'm taking off my shoes. But dearest, don't forget you're going to vote for peace.

CINESIAS. I will consider it. She has destroyed me, murdered me, that woman has! On top of which she's got me skinned and gone away!

What shall I do? Oh, whom shall I screw,
cheated of dear Myrrhina, the first
beauty of all, a creature divine?
How shall I tend this infant of mine?
Find me a pimp: it has to be nursed!

CHORUS OF MEN (*in tragic style, as if to Prometheus or Andromeda bound*). In what dire woe, how heavy-hearted

I see thee languishing, outsmarted!
  I pity thee, alas I do.
What kidney could endure such pain,
what spirit could, what balls, what back,
what loins, what sacroiliac,
If they came under such a strain
and never had a morning screw?

CINESIAS. O Zeus! the twinges! Oh, the twitches!

CHORUS OF MEN. And this is what she did to you,
that vilest, hatefullest of bitches!

CINESIAS. Oh nay, by Zeus, she's dear and sweet!

CHORUS OF MEN. How can she be? She's vile, O Zeus, she's vile!
Oh treat her, Zeus, like so much wheat —
O God of Weather, hear my prayer —
and raise a whirlwind's mighty blast
to roll her up into a pile
and carry her into the sky
far up and up and then at last
drop her and land her suddenly
astride that pointed penis there!

(*The ekkyklema turns, closing the inset-scene. Enter, from opposite sides, a* SPARTAN *and an* ATHENIAN OFFICIAL.)

SPARTAN. Wheah is the Senate-house of the Athenians?
Ah wish to see the chaihman. Ah have news fo him.

ATHENIAN. And who are you? Are you a Satyr or a man?

SPARTAN. Ah am a herald, mah young friend, yes, by the gods,
and Ah have come from Sparta to negotiate.

ATHENIAN. And yet you come here with a spear under your arm?

SPARTAN. Not Ah, bah Zeus, not Ah!

ATHENIAN. Why do you turn around?
Why throw your cloak out so in front? Has the long trip
given you a swelling?

SPARTAN. Ah do think the man is queah!

ATHENIAN. But you have an erection, oh you reprobate!

SPARTAN. Bah Zeus, Ah've no sech thing! And don't you fool around!

ATHENIAN. And what have you got there?

SPARTAN. A Spahtan scroll-stick, suh.

ATHENIAN. Well, if it is, *this* is a Spartan scroll-stick, too.
But look, I know what's up: you can tell *me* the truth.
Just how are things with you in Sparta: tell me that.

SPARTAN. Theah is uprising in all Spahta. Ouah allies
are all erect as well. We need ouah milkin'-pails.

ATHENIAN. From where has this great scourge of frenzy fallen on you?
From Pan?

SPARTAN. No, Ah think Lampito began it all,
and then, the othah women throughout Spahta joined
togethah, just lahk at a signal fo a race,
and fought theah husbands off and drove them from theah cunts.

ATHENIAN. So, how're you getting on?

SPARTAN. We suffah. Through the town
we walk bent ovah as if we were carrying
lamps in the wind. The women will not let us touch
even theah berries, till we all with one acco'd
have made a peace among the cities of all Greece.

ATHENIAN. This is an international conspiracy
launched by the women! Now I comprehend it all!
Return at once to Sparta. Tell them they must send
ambassadors fully empowered to make peace.
And our Assembly will elect ambassadors
from our side, when I say so, showing them this prick.

SPARTAN. Ah'll run! Ah'll flah! Fo all you say is excellent!

CHORUS OF MEN. No wild beast is more impossible than woman is to fight,
nor is fire, nor has the panther such unbridled appetite!

CHORUS OF WOMEN. Well you know it, yet you go on warring with me without end,
when you might, you cross-grained creature, have me as a trusty friend.

CHORUS OF MEN. Listen: I will never cease from hating women till I die!

CHORUS OF WOMEN. Any time you like. But meanwhile is there any reason why
I should let you stand there naked, looking so ridiculous?
I am only coming near you, now, to slip your coat on, thus.

CHORUS OF MEN. That was very civil of you, very kind to treat me so,
when in such uncivil rage I took it off a while ago.

CHORUS OF WOMEN. Now you're looking like a man again, and not ridiculous.
If you hadn't hurt my feelings, I would not have made a fuss,
I would even have removed that little beast that's in your eye.

CHORUS OF MEN. *That* is what was hurting me! Well, won't you take my ring to pry
back my eyelid? Rake the beast out. When you have it, let me see,
for some time now it's been at my eye and irritating me.

CHORUS OF WOMEN. Very well, I will — though you were *born* an irritable man.
What a monster of a gnat, by Zeus! Look at it if you can.
Don't you see it? It's a native of great marshes, can't you tell?

CHORUS OF MEN. Much obliged, by Zeus! The brute's been digging at me like a well!
So that now you have removed it, streams of tears come welling out.

CHORUS OF WOMEN. I will dry them. You're the meanest man alive, beyond a doubt,
yet I will, and kiss you, too.

CHORUS OF MEN. Don't kiss me!

CHORUS OF WOMEN. If you will or not!

CHORUS OF MEN. Damn you! Oh, what wheedling flatterers you all are, born and bred!
That old proverb is quite right and not inelegantly said:
"There's no living *with* the bitches and, without them, even *less*" —
so I might as well make peace with you, and from now on, I guess,
I'll do nothing mean to you and, from you, suffer nothing wrong.
So let's draw our ranks together now and start a little song:

For a change, we're not preparing
any mean remark or daring
aimed at any man in town,
but the very opposite: we plan to do and say
only good to everyone,
when the ills we have already are sufficient anyway.
Any man or woman who
wants a little money, oh
say three minas, maybe two,
kindly let us know.
What we have is right in here.
(Notice we have purses, too!)
And if ever peace appear,
he who takes our loan today
never need repay.

We are having guests for supper,
allies asked in by our upper
classes to improve the town.
There's pea-soup, and I had killed a sucking-pig of mine:
I shall see it is well done,
so you will be tasting something very succulent and fine.
Come to see us, then, tonight
early, just as soon as you
have a bath and dress up right:
bring your children, too.
Enter boldly, never mind
asking anyone in sight.
Go straight in and you will find
you are quite at home there, but
all the doors are shut.

And here come the Spartan ambassadors,
dragging beards that are really the biggest I

have ever beheld, and around their thighs
they are wearing some sort of a pig-sty.

Oh men of Sparta, let me bid you welcome first,
and then you tell us how you are and why you come.

SPARTAN. What need is theah to speak to you in many words?
Fo you may see youahself in what a fix we come.

CHORUS OF MEN. Too bad! Your situation has become
terribly hard and seems to be at fever-pitch.

SPARTAN. Unutterably so! And what is theah to say?
Let someone bring us peace on any tuhms he will!

CHORUS OF MEN. And here I see some natives of Athenian soil,
holding their cloaks far off their bellies, like the best
wrestlers, who sicken at the touch of cloth. It seems
that overtraining may bring on this strange disease.

ATHENIAN. Will someone tell us where to find Lysistrata?
We're men, and here we are, in this capacity.

CHORUS OF MEN. This symptom and that other one sound much alike.
Toward morning I expect convulsions do occur?

ATHENIAN. By Zeus, we are exhausted with just doing that,
so, if somebody doesn't reconcile us quick,
there's nothing for it: we'll be screwing Cleisthenes.

CHORUS OF MEN. Be careful — put your cloaks on, or you might be seen
by some young blade who knocks the phalluses off herms.

ATHENIAN. By Zeus, an excellent idea!

SPARTAN (*having overheard*). Yes, bah the gods!
It altogethah is. Quick, let's put on our cloaks.

(*Both groups cover quickly and then recognize each other with full diplomatic pomp.*)

ATHENIAN. Greetings, O men of Sparta! (*To his group.*) We have been disgraced!

SPARTAN (*to one of his group*). Mah dearest fellah, what a dreadful thing fo us,
if these Athenians had seen ouah wo'st defeat!

ATHENIAN. Come now, O Spartans: one must specify each point.
Why have you come here?

SPARTAN. To negotiate a peace.
We ah ambassadahs.

ATHENIAN. Well put. And so are we.
Therefore, why do we not call in Lysistrata,
she who alone might get us to agree on terms?

SPARTAN. Call her or any man, even a Lysistratus!

CHORUS OF MEN. But you will have no need, it seems, to call her now, for here she is. She heard you and is coming out.

CHORUS OF MEN *and* CHORUS OF WOMEN. All hail, O manliest woman of all!

It is time for you now to be turning
into something still better, more dreadful, mean,
unapproachable, charming, discerning,
for here are the foremost nations of Greece,
bewitched by your spells like a lover,
who have come to you, bringing you all their claims,
and to you turning everything over.

LYSISTRATA. The work's not difficult, if one can catch them now
while they're excited and not making passes at
each other. I will soon find out. Where's Harmony?

(*A naked maid, perhaps wearing a large ribbon reading* HARMONY, *appears from inside.*)

Go take the Spartans first, and lead them over here,
not with a rough hand nor an overbearing one,
nor, as our husbands used to do this, clumsily,
but like a woman, in our most familiar style:
If he won't give his hand, then lead him by the prick.
And now, go bring me those Athenians as well,
leading them by whatever they will offer you.
O men of Sparta, stand right here, close by my side,
and *you* stand over there, and listen to my words.
I am a woman, yes, but there is mind in me.
In native judgment I am not so badly off,
and, having heard my father and my elders talk
often enough, I have some cultivation, too.
And so, I want to take and scold you, on both sides,
as you deserve, for though you use a lustral urn
in common at the altars, like blood-relatives,
when at Olympia, Delphi, or Thermopylae —
how many others I might name if I took time! —
yet, with barbarian hordes of enemies at hand,
it is Greek men, it is Greek cities, you destroy.
That is one argument so far, and it is done.

ATHENIAN. My prick is skinned alive — that's what's destroying *me*.

LYSISTRATA. Now, men of Sparta — for I shall address you first —
do you not know that once one of your kings came here
and as a suppliant of the Athenians
sat by our altars, death-pale in his purple robe,
and begged us for an army? For Messenë then
oppressed you, and an earthquake from the gods as well.

Then Cimon went, taking four thousand infantry,
and saved the whole of Lacedaemon for your state.
That is the way Athenians once treated you;
you ravage their land now, which once received you well.

ATHENIAN. By Zeus, these men are in the wrong, Lysistrata!

SPARTAN (*with his eyes on* HARMONY). We'ah wrong . . . What an unutterably lovely ass!

LYSISTRATA. Do you suppose I'm letting you Athenians off?
Do you not know that once the Spartans in their turn,
when you were wearing the hide-skirts of slavery,
came with their spears and slew many Thessalians,
many companions and allies of Hippias?
They were the only ones who fought for you that day,
freed you from tyranny and, for the skirt of hide,
gave back your people the wool mantle of free men.

SPARTAN. Ah nevah saw a woman broadah — in her views.

ATHENIAN. And I have never seen a lovelier little nook.

LYSISTRATA. So why, when you have done each other so much good,
go on fighting with no end of malevolence?
Why don't you make a peace? Tell me, what's in your way?

SPARTAN. Whah, we ah willin', if *they* will give up to us
that very temptin' cuhve (*of* HARMONY, *as hereafter*).

LYSISTRATA. What curve, my friend?

SPARTAN. The bay
of Pylos, which we've wanted and felt out so long.

ATHENIAN. No, by Poseidon, you will not get into that!

LYSISTRATA. Good friend, do let them have it.

ATHENIAN. No! What other town
can we manipulate so well?

LYSISTRATA. Ask them for one.

ATHENIAN. Damn, let me think! Now first suppose you cede to us
that bristling tip of land, Echinos, behind which
the gulf of Malia recedes, and those long walls,
the legs on which Megara reaches to the sea.

SPARTAN. No, mah deah man, not *everything*, bah Castah, no!

LYSISTRATA. Oh, give them up. Why quarrel for a pair of legs?

ATHENIAN. I'd like to strip and get to plowing right away.

SPARTAN. And *Ah* would lahk to push manuah, still earliah.

LYSISTRATA. When you have made a peace, then you will do all that.
But if you want to do it, first deliberate,
go and inform your allies and consult with them.

ATHENIAN. Oh, damn our allies, my good woman! We are stiff.
Will all of our allies not stand resolved with us —
namely, to screw?

SPARTAN. And so will ouahs, Ah'll guarantee.

ATHENIAN. Our mercenaries, even, will agree with us.

LYSISTRATA. Excellent. Now to get you washed and purified

so you may enter the Acropolis, where we
women will entertain you out of our supplies.
You will exchange your pledges there and vows for peace.
And after that each one of you will take his wife,
departing then for home.

ATHENIAN. Let's go in right away.

SPARTAN. Lead on, ma'am, anywheah you lahk.

ATHENIAN. Yes, and be quick.

(*Exeunt into Acropolis.*)

CHORUS OF MEN *and* CHORUS OF WOMEN.

All the rich embroideries, the
scarves, the gold accessories, the
trailing gowns, the robes I own
I begrudge to no man: let him take what things he will
for his children or a grown
daughter who must dress for the procession up Athena's hill.
Freely of my present stocks
I invite you all to take.
There are here no seals nor locks
very hard to break.
Search through every bag and box,
look — you will find nothing there
if your eyesight isn't fine —
sharper far than mine.

Are there any of you needing
food for all the slaves you're feeding,
all your little children, too?
I have wheat in tiny grains for you, the finest sort,
and I also offer you
plenty of the handsome strapping grains that slaves get by the quart.
So let any of the poor
visit me with bag or sack
which my slave will fill with more
wheat than they can pack,
giving each his ample share.
Might I add that at my door
I have watch-dogs? — so beware.
Come too close by day or night,
you will find they bite.

(*Voice of drunken* ATHENIANS *from inside.*)

FIRST ATHENIAN. Open the door! (*Shoves the porter aside.*) And will you get out of my way?

(*A second drunken* ATHENIAN *follows. The first sees the* CHORUS.)

What are you sitting *there* for? Shall I, with this torch,
burn you alive? (*Drops character.*) How vulgar! Oh, how commonplace!
I can not do it!

(*Starts back in. The second* ATHENIAN *stops him and remonstrates with him in a whisper. The first turns and addresses the audience.*)

Well, if it really must be done
to please you, we shall face it and go through with it.

CHORUS OF MEN *and* CHORUS OF WOMEN. And we shall face it and go through with it with you.

FIRST ATHENIAN (*in character again, extravagantly*). Clear out of here!
Or you'll be wailing for your hair!

(CHORUS OF WOMEN *scours away in mock terror.*)

Clear out of here! so that the Spartans can come out
and have no trouble leaving, after they have dined.

(CHORUS OF MEN *scours away in mock terror.*)

SECOND ATHENIAN. I never saw a drinking-party like this one:
even the Spartans were quite charming, and of course
we make the cleverest company, when in our cups.

FIRST ATHENIAN. You're right, because when sober we are not quite sane.
If I can only talk the Athenians into it,
we'll always go on any embassy quite drunk,
for now, going to Sparta sober, we're so quick
to look around and see what trouble we can make
that we don't listen to a single word they say —
instead we think we hear them say what they do not —
and none of our reports on anything agree.
But just now everything was pleasant. If a man
got singing words belonging to another song,
we all applauded and swore falsely it was fine!
But here are those same people coming back again
to the same spot! Go and be damned, the pack of you!

(*The* CHORUS, *having thrown off their masks, put on other cloaks, and rushed back on stage, stays put.*)

SECOND ATHENIAN. Yes, damn them, Zeus! Just when the party's coming out!

(*The party comes rolling out.*)

A SPARTAN (*to another*). Mah very chahmin friend, will you take up youah flutes?
Ah'll dance the dipody and sing a lovely song
of us and the Athenians, of both at once!

FIRST ATHENIAN (*as pleasantly as he can*). Oh yes, take up your little reeds, by all the gods:
I very much enjoy seeing you people dance.

SPARTAN. Memory, come,
come inspiah thah young
votaries to song.
come inspiah theah dance!

(*Other* SPARTANS *join*).

Bring thah daughtah, bring the sweet
Muse, fo well she knows
us and the Athenians,
how at Ahtemisium
they in godlike onslaught rose
hahd against the Puhsian fleet,
drove it to defeat!
Well she knows the Spartan waws,
how Leonidas
in the deadly pass
led us on lahk baws
whettin' shahp theah tusks, how sweat
on ouah cheeks in thick foam flowahed,
off ouah legs how thick it showahed,
fo the Puhsian men were mo'
than the sands along the sho'.
Goddess, huntress, Ahtemis,
slayeh of the beasts, descend:
vuhgin goddess, come to this
feast of truce to bind us fast
so ouah peace may nevah end.
Now let friendship, love, and wealth
come with ouah acco'd at last.
May we stop ouah villainous
wahly foxy stealth!
Come, O huntress, heah to us,
heah, O vuhgin, neah to us!

LYSISTRATA. Come, now that all the rest has been so well arranged,
you Spartans take these women home; these others, you.

Let husband stand beside his wife, and let each wife
stand by her husband: then, when we have danced a dance
to thank the gods for our good fortune, let's take care
hereafter not to make the same mistakes again.

ATHENIAN. Bring on the chorus! Invite the three Graces to follow,
and then call on Artemis, call her twin brother,
the leader of choruses, healer Apollo!

CHORUS (*joins*). Pray for their friendliest favor, the one and the other.

Call Dionysus, his tender eyes casting
flame in the midst of his Maenads ecstatic with dancing.
  Call upon Zeus, the resplendent in fire,
  call on his wife, rich in honor and ire,
call on the powers who possess everlasting
memory, call them to aid,
call them to witness the kindly, entrancing
peace Aphrodite has made!
    Alalai!
    Bound, and leap high! Alalai!
    Cry, as for victory, cry
    Alalai!

LYSISTRATA. Sing us a new song, Spartans, capping our new song.

SPARTANS. Leave thah favohed mountain's height,
Spahtan Muse, come celebrate
Amyclae's lord with us and great
Athena housed in bronze;
praise Tyndareus' paih of sons,
gods who pass the days in spoht
wheah the cold Eurotas runs.

(*General dancing.*)

Now to tread the dance,
now to tread it light,
praising Spahta, wheah you find
  love of singing quickened bah the pounding beat
    of dancing feet,
when ouah guhls lahk foals cavoht
wheah the cold Eurotas runs,
when they fleetly bound and prance
  till theah haih unfilleted shakes in the wind,
as of Maenads brandishin'
ahvied wands and revelin',
  Leda's daughtah, puah and faiah,
  leads the holy dances theah.

FULL CHORUS (*as everyone leaves dancing*).
So come bind up youah haih with youah hand,
    with youah feet make a bound
lahk a deeah; fo the chorus clap out
    an encouragin' sound,
singin' praise of the temple of bronze
    housin' her we adaw:
sing the praise of Athena: the goddess unvanquished in waw!

Curtain

Plagiarism, as Shakespeare's career amply demonstrates, is no vice if used with style and wit to improve on the play plots of others. One such instance was *Twelfth Night* (1600), which takes its main plot from an Italian tale translated into English. The tale was itself based on an Italian play, *Gli Ingannati* (1531). Indeed, in Italy the play was so popular that it had gone through eight editions by 1585.

Curiously, in England it was not only Englished but Latinized. A Latin version, *Laelia,* was twice performed at Queens College, Cambridge, once with Queen Elizabeth's favorite, the Earl of Essex, in attendance. It must also have been known at court, and the Queen's own fondness for Latin and for dramas may have prompted Shakespeare to adapt it for an Epiphany entertainment.

The title alone, alluding to the twelfth day after Christmas, customarily a time for dramatic festivities at the court, suggests that, at least. And critic Leslie Hotson argues that the character of Malvolio is based on Sir William Knollys, the puritanical comptroller of Queen Elizabeth's household. He was a well-known figure of ridicule among the courtiers. Hotson also believes that the play was specifically intended as the high point of the state visit of Don Virginio Orsino, a Tuscan duke, to the English court. Whatever the truth of these suggestions, they do add a dimension of historical interest to the drama. The reader who knows something of the Elizabethan passion for allegory and concealed meaning may enjoy studying this play with special attention to the possible parallels between the dramatic fiction and the royal reality.

The main plot, a staple of the Italian *commedia,* is set in motion by the mistaken identities of identical twins — or, since they are sister and brother, *almost* identical twins. This significant difference, however, is not apparent, thanks to another common device of the *commedia* — that of the pert young girl disguised as a page. These twin plot tricks served Shakespeare extremely well on several counts. First and most obvious: since women were not yet permitted to appear on the English stage, female roles had to be played by boys. This probably galled Shakespeare, who once referred to "squeaking Cleopatras." If Lady Macbeth taxed both the boy-player's powers and the audience's belief, a role like Viola/Cesario capitalized on the youthful attractiveness of the actor and the audience's acceptance of the convention.

Second, the device of the disguised and mistaken identities permits Shakespeare to explore the nature of true love, as opposed to mere infatuation. Both the Duke and Olivia are at first in love with externals, with appearances. And appearances, as the old saying so wisely has it, are not what they seem. Viola's awkward situation, caught between Olivia's hopeless love for her and her own hopeless love for the Duke, is the occasion of gentle comedy. Even better than the pleasant, sad humor, however, is the richness of the lyrics Shakespeare has given her.

Feste, the clown, also has some delightful songs. If, to modern readers, his chop-logic humor seems labored and heavy — as the patter of Shakespeare's fools so often does now, thanks partly to the shifts in the meanings of words or their obsolescence — it must be remembered that it was funny to the age of Elizabeth I. Feste may very well be looked upon as the unifying, if not the central, character in this comedy.

When the play is produced with that in mind, it can have an integrity and a harmony it too often lacks when the romantic plot is allowed to exist almost in isolation from the satiric subplot. Because the idiocies and impostures of Sir Toby Belch and Sir Andrew Aguecheek are so exaggerated, they tend to draw attention to themselves rather than to their dramatic function, which is a distorted image of the Count's courting of Olivia. Sir Andrew's suit to Olivia is promoted virtually *in absentia*, as is the Count's. The comic difference is that, while Olivia is so cold to Orsino that he has to use his page as an intermediary, Sir Andrew is constantly in evidence in Olivia's household — mostly in the kitchen — but cannot gain a hearing. He relies instead on Sir Toby, who, if a bit fat and foolish, is not nearly so much a fool as Sir Andrew. Thus, Sir Toby makes both profit and sport of a courtship which can have no success, though he keeps giving Sir Andrew encouragement.

This farcical underweaving of the main romantic theme is effective as counterpoint, but Shakespeare has woven an even richer, thicker comic texture with the deliberate deception of Malvolio, who is tricked into believing that Olivia favors him. His self-importance, arrogance, and pretension give him no occasion for doubt, and to some degree they justify his humiliation. Feste and Maria provide a restraint, a control on the excesses of Sir Toby and Sir Andrew, as well as upon the punishment of Malvolio.

Modern readers and audiences, living in times of Mental Health Dinner Dances and compassion for the insane, may find Malvolio's "cure" a bit extreme, rather too cruel. In Shakespeare's day, and indeed well into the nineteenth century, visiting madhouses to laugh at the deranged was a popular entertainment. Even though Malvolio's character and manner may justify his shaming, it is still a dark moment in this romantic froth. If at the end of the play the rest of the lovers and would-be lovers know more about themselves, each other, and love, Malvolio's new knowledge is no pleasure to him, and he is *not* placated.

G. L.

WILLIAM SHAKESPEARE

Twelfth Night

or

What You Will[1]

Characters

[ORSINO, *Duke of Illyria*
SEBASTIAN, *brother to Viola*
ANTONIO, *a sea captain, friend to Sebastian*
A SEA CAPTAIN, *friend to Viola*
VALENTINE, CURIO, } *gentlemen attending on the Duke*
SIR TOBY BELCH, *uncle to Olivia*
SIR ANDREW AGUECHEEK
MALVOLIO, *steward to Olivia*
FABIAN, FESTE, *a clown,* } *servants to Olivia*
OLIVIA, *a rich countess*
VIOLA
MARIA, *Olivia's woman*
Lords, Priests, Sailors, Officers, Musicians, and other Attendants

SCENE: *A city in Illyria, and the sea-coast near it.*]

ACT ONE

SCENE 1. [*A room in the* DUKE'S *palace.*][2]

Enter ORSINO, DUKE OF ILLYRIA, CURIO, *and other Lords* [Musicians attending].

DUKE. If music be the food of love, play on!
Give me excess of it, that, surfeiting,

[1] "The printing of *Twelfth Night* in the Folio of 1623 was the first, and upon this the present text is based." (Neilson and Hill, p. 279.) Bracketed passages have been supplied from other sources with the suppliers recorded in the notes in parentheses: (Pope), (Hanmer), etc. A capital F in the notes stands for "Folio." Lines have been renumbered for this volume.

[2] "Stage directions, if modern, are enclosed in [brackets]; when they are sub-

The appetite may sicken, and so die.
That strain again! It had a dying fall.
O, it came o'er my ear like the sweet sound
That breathes upon a bank of violets,
Stealing and giving odour. Enough! no more!
'Tis not so sweet now as it was before.
O spirit of love, how quick and fresh art thou,
That, notwithstanding thy capacity
Receiveth as the sea, nought enters there,
Of what validity and pitch soe'er,
But falls into abatement and low price
Even in a minute! So full of shapes is fancy
That it alone is high fantastical.

CURIO. Will you go hunt, my lord?

DUKE. What, Curio?

CURIO. The hart.

DUKE. Why, so I do, the noblest that I have.
O, when mine eyes did see Olivia first,
Methought she purg'd the air of pestilence!
That instant was I turn'd into a hart;
And my desires, like fell and cruel hounds,
E'er since pursue me.

Enter VALENTINE.

How now! what news from her?

VALENTINE. So please my lord, I might not be admitted,
But from her handmaid do return this answer:
The element itself, till seven years' heat,
Shall not behold her face at ample view;
But, like a cloistress, she will veiled walk,
And water once a day her chamber round
With eye-offending brine: all this to season
A brother's dead love, which she would keep fresh
And lasting in her sad remembrance.

DUKE. O, she that hath a heart of that fine frame
To pay this debt of love but to a brother,
How will she love when the rich golden shaft
Hath kill'd the flock of all affections else

stantially those of editions not later than 1623, they are unbracketed, or are set aside by a single bracket only, or, when occurring within a line, are enclosed in (parentheses)." (Neilson and Hill, p. v.)

Act I, Scene i, line 5. **sound** Ff. Pope's emendation, *south,* has been followed by many editors. 12. **validity:** value. **pitch:** height. 14. **fancy:** love. 15. **fantastical:** imaginative. 21–23. **That . . . pursue me.** Allusion to Actæon, who, seeing Diana naked, was changed into a hart and killed by his own dogs. 26. **element:** sky. **years' heat:** summers. 35. **shaft:** *i.e.,* Cupid's.

That live in her; when liver, brain, and heart,
These sovereign thrones, are all suppli'd, and fill'd
Her sweet perfections with one self king!
Away before me to sweet beds of flowers;
Love-thoughts lie rich when canopi'd with bowers.

[*Exeunt.*

SCENE 2. [*The sea-coast.*]

Enter VIOLA, *a* CAPTAIN, *and Sailors.*

VIOLA. What country, friends, is this?
CAPTAIN. This is Illyria, lady.
VIOLA. And what should I do in Illyria?
My brother he is in Elysium.
Perchance he is not drown'd. What think you, sailors?
CAPTAIN. It is perchance that you yourself were saved.
VIOLA. O my poor brother! and so perchance may he be.
CAPTAIN. True, madam; and, to comfort you with chance,
Assure yourself, after our ship did split,
When you and those poor number sav'd with you
Hung on our driving boat, I saw your brother,
Most provident in peril, bind himself,
Courage and hope both teaching him the practice,
To a strong mast that liv'd upon the sea;
Where, like [Arion] on the dolphin's back,
I saw him hold acquaintance with the waves
So long as I could see.
VIOLA. For saying so, there's gold.
Mine own escape unfoldeth to my hope,
Whereto thy speech serves for authority,
The like of him. Know'st thou this country?
CAPTAIN. Ay, madam, well; for I was bred and born
Not three hours' travel from this very place.
VIOLA. Who governs here?
CAPTAIN. A noble duke, in nature as in name.
VIOLA. What is his name?
CAPTAIN. Orsino.
VIOLA. Orsino! I have heard my father name him.
He was a bachelor then.
CAPTAIN. And so is now, or was so very late;
For but a month ago I went from hence,

37. **liver . . . heart.** The supposed seats of the passions. 39. **self:** sole.
Scene ii, 15. [Arion] (Pope). *Orion* F. Arion was a Greek poet, saved from drowning by dolphins who were so ravished by his lyre that they carried him to land.

And then 'twas fresh in murmur — as, you know,
What great ones do the less will prattle of —
That he did seek the love of fair Olivia.

VIOLA. What's she?

CAPTAIN. A virtuous maid, the daughter of a count
That died some twelvemonth since, then leaving her
In the protection of his son, her brother,
Who shortly also died; for whose dear love,
They say, she hath abjur'd the [company
And sight] of men.

VIOLA. O that I serv'd that lady,
And might not be delivered to the world,
Till I had made mine own occasion mellow,
What my estate is!

CAPTAIN. That were hard to compass,
Because she will admit no kind of suit,
No, not the Duke's.

VIOLA. There is a fair behaviour in thee, captain;
And though that nature with a beauteous wall
Doth oft close in pollution, yet of thee
I will believe thou hast a mind that suits
With this thy fair and outward character.
I prithee, and I'll pay thee bounteously,
Conceal me what I am, and be my aid
For such disguise as haply shall become
The form of my intent. I'll serve this duke.
Thou shalt present me as an eunuch to him.
It may be worth thy pains, for I can sing
And speak to him in many sorts of music
That will allow me very worth his service.
What else may hap, to time I will commit,
Only shape thou thy silence to my wit.

CAPTAIN. Be you his eunuch, and your mute I'll be.
When my tongue blabs, then let mine eyes not see.

VIOLA. I thank thee. Lead me on.

[*Exeunt.*

SCENE 3. [*A room in* OLIVIA'S *house.*]

Enter SIR TOBY BELCH *and* MARIA.

SIR TOBY. What a plague means my niece, to take the death of her brother thus? I am sure care's an enemy to life.

40–41. [**company And sight**] (Hanmer). *sight And company* F. 42–44. **And . . . estate is.** *I.e.*, And might not have my true condition known until a suitable time. 59. **allow**: show, prove. 61. **wit**: design.

MARIA. By my troth, Sir Toby, you must come in earlier o' nights. Your cousin, my lady, takes great exceptions to your ill hours.

SIR TOBY. Why, let her except before excepted.

MARIA. Ay, but you must confine yourself within the modest limits of order.

SIR TOBY. Confine! I'll confine myself no finer than I am. These clothes are good enough to drink in, and so be these boots too; an they be not, let them hang themselves in their own straps.

MARIA. That quaffing and drinking will undo you. I heard my lady talk of it yesterday, and of a foolish knight that you brought in one night here to be her wooer.

SIR TOBY. Who? Sir Andrew Aguecheek?

MARIA. Ay, he.

SIR TOBY. He's as tall a man as any's in Illyria.

MARIA. What's that to th' purpose?

SIR TOBY. Why, he has three thousand ducats a year.

MARIA. Ay, but he'll have but a year in all these ducats. He's a very fool and a prodigal.

SIR TOBY. Fie, that you'll say so! He plays o' the viol-de-gamboys, and speaks three or four languages word for word without book, and hath all the good gifts of nature.

MARIA. He hath indeed, almost natural; for besides that he's a fool, he's a great quarreller; and but that he hath the gift of a coward to allay the gust he hath in quarrelling, 'tis thought among the prudent he would quickly have the gift of a grave.

SIR TOBY. By this hand, they are scoundrels and substractors that say so of him. Who are they?

MARIA. They that add, moreover, he's drunk nightly in your company.

SIR TOBY. With drinking healths to my niece. I'll drink to her as long as there is a passage in my throat and drink in Illyria. He's a coward and a coystrill that will not drink to my niece till his brains turn o' th' toe like a parish-top. What, wench! *Castiliano vulgo!* for here comes Sir Andrew Agueface.

Enter SIR ANDREW AGUECHEEK.

SIR ANDREW. Sir Toby Belch! How now, Sir Toby Belch!

SIR TOBY. Sweet Sir Andrew!

SIR ANDREW. Bless you, fair shrew.

MARIA. And you too, sir.

SIR TOBY. Accost, Sir Andrew, accost.

SIR ANDREW. What's that?

SIR TOBY. My niece's chambermaid.

Scene iii, 5. except before excepted. Quibble upon the legal phrase, *exceptis excipiendis*, "with the exceptions before named." 16. **tall:** fine. 21. **viol-de-gamboys:** bass viol. 24. **natural:** (1) naturally, (2) like an idiot. 26. **gust:** gusto, zest. 33. **coystrill:** knave. 34. ***Castiliano vulgo.*** Probably nonsense.

SIR ANDREW. Good Mistress Accost, I desire better acquaintance.

MARIA. My name is Mary, sir.

SIR ANDREW. Good Mistress Mary Accost, —

SIR TOBY. You mistake, knight. "Accost" is front her, board her, woo her, assail her.

SIR ANDREW. By my troth, I would not undertake her in this company. Is that the meaning of "accost"?

MARIA. Fare you well, gentlemen.

SIR TOBY. An thou let part so, Sir Andrew, would thou mightst never draw sword again.

SIR ANDREW. An you part so, mistress, I would I might never draw sword again. Fair lady, do you think you have fools in hand?

MARIA. Sir, I have not you by th' hand.

SIR ANDREW. Marry, but you shall have; and here's my hand.

MARIA. Now, sir, "thought is free." I pray you, bring your hand to th' butt'ry-bar and let it drink.

SIR ANDREW. Wherefore, sweetheart? What's your metaphor?

MARIA. It's dry, sir.

SIR ANDREW. Why, I think so. I am not such an ass but I can keep my hand dry. But what's your jest?

MARIA. A dry jest, sir.

SIR ANDREW. Are you full of them?

MARIA. Ay, sir, I have them at my fingers' ends. Marry, now I let go your hand, I am barren. [*Exit.*

SIR TOBY. O knight, thou lack'st a cup of canary. When did I see thee so put down?

SIR ANDREW. Never in your life, I think, unless you see canary put me down. Methinks sometimes I have no more wit than a Christian or an ordinary man has; but I am a great eater of beef and I believe that does harm to my wit.

SIR TOBY. No question.

SIR ANDREW. An I thought that, I'd forswear it. I'll ride home to-morrow, Sir Toby.

SIR TOBY. *Pourquoi*, my dear knight?

SIR ANDREW. What is "*pourquoi*"? Do or not do? I would I had bestowed that time in the tongues that I have in fencing, dancing, and bear-baiting. O, had I but followed the arts!

SIR TOBY. Then hadst thou had an excellent head of hair.

SIR ANDREW. Why, would that have mended my hair?

SIR TOBY. Past question; for thou seest it will not [curl by] nature.

SIR ANDREW. But it becomes me well enough, does't not?

SIR TOBY. Excellent; it hangs like flax on a distaff, and I hope to see a housewife take thee between her legs, and spin it off.

58. **butt'ry-bar.** Where drinks were served. 60. **It's dry.** Signifying lack of amorousness. 63. **dry jest:** dull jest. 67. **canary:** a sweet wine (from the Canary Islands). 80. **head of hair.** Sir Toby puns on *tongues* (l. 78) and (curling) *tongs*. 82. [**curl by**] (Theobald). *coole my* F.

SIR ANDREW. Faith, I'll home to-morrow, Sir Toby. Your niece will not be seen, or if she be, it's four to one she'll none of me. The Count himself here hard by wooes her.

SIR TOBY. She'll none o' th' Count. She'll not match above her degree, neither in estate, years, nor wit; I have heard her swear't. Tut, there's life in't, man.

SIR ANDREW. I'll stay a month longer. I am a fellow o' the strangest mind i' th' world; I delight in masques and revels sometimes altogether.

SIR TOBY. Art thou good at these kickshawses, knight?

SIR ANDREW. As any man in Illyria, whatsoever he be, under the degree of my betters; and yet I will not compare with an old man.

SIR TOBY. What is thy excellence in a galliard, knight?

SIR ANDREW. Faith, I can cut a caper.

SIR TOBY. And I can cut the mutton to't.

SIR ANDREW. And I think I have the back-trick simply as strong as any man in Illyria.

SIR TOBY. Wherefore are these things hid? Wherefore have these gifts a curtain before 'em? Are they like to take dust, like Mistress Mall's picture? Why dost thou not go to church in a galliard and come home in a coranto? My very walk should be a jig. I would not so much as make water but in a sink-a-pace. What dost thou mean? Is it a world to hide virtues in? I did think, by the excellent constitution of thy leg, it was form'd under the star of a galliard.

SIR ANDREW. Ay, 'tis strong, and it does indifferent well in a damn'd colour'd stock. Shall we [set] about some revels?

SIR TOBY. What shall we do else? Were we not born under Taurus?

SIR ANDREW. Taurus! That's sides and heart.

SIR TOBY. No, sir, it is legs and thighs. Let me see thee caper. Ha! Higher! Ha, ha! Excellent!

[*Exeunt.*

SCENE 4. [*A room in the* DUKE'*s palace.*]

Enter VALENTINE, *and* VIOLA *in man's attire.*

VALENTINE. If the Duke continue these favours towards you, Cesario, you are like to be much advanc'd. He hath known you but three days, and already you are no stranger.

91. **there's life in't:** there's still hope. 94. **kickshawses:** trifles. 96. **old:** (possibly) experienced. 97. **galliard:** a lively dance. 99. Sir Toby puns: mutton is often served with *caper* sauce. 100. **back-trick:** *i.e.*, the reverse step (in the galliard). 105. **coranto:** a fast dance. 106. **sink-a-pace:** (cinque pace) a five-step dance. 109–110. **damn'd colour'd.** Many editors amend to *flame-coloured.* 110. **stock:** stocking. [**set**] (Rowe). *sit* F. 112. **Taurus.** In the old medical astrology the constellation Taurus was held to control the neck and throat; so both Sir Andrew and Sir Toby are wrong.

VIOLA. You either fear his humour or my negligence, that you call in question the continuance of his love. Is he inconstant, sir, in his favours?

VALENTINE. No, believe me.

Enter DUKE, CURIO, *and Attendants.*

VIOLA. I thank you. Here comes the Count.

DUKE. Who saw Cesario, ho?

VIOLA. On your attendance, my lord; here.

DUKE. Stand you a while aloof. Cesario,
Thou know'st no less but all. I have unclasp'd
To thee the book even of my secret soul;
Therefore, good youth, address thy gait unto her.
Be not deni'd access, stand at her doors,
And tell them, there thy fixed foot shall grow
Till thou have audience.

VIOLA. Sure, my noble lord,
If she be so abandon'd to her sorrow
As it is spoke, she never will admit me.

DUKE. Be clamorous and leap all civil bounds
Rather than make unprofited return.

VIOLA. Say I do speak with her, my lord, what then?

DUKE. O, then unfold the passion of my love,
Surprise her with discourse of my dear faith.
It shall become thee well to act my woes.
She will attend it better in thy youth
Than in a nuncio's of more grave aspect.

VIOLA. I think not so, my lord.

DUKE. Dear lad, believe it;
For they shall yet belie thy happy years,
That say thou art a man. Diana's lip
Is not more smooth and rubious; thy small pipe
Is as the maiden's organ, shrill and sound;
And all is semblative a woman's part.
I know thy constellation is right apt
For this affair. Some four or five attend him, —
All, if you will; for I myself am best
When least in company. Prosper well in this,
And thou shalt live as freely as thy lord,
To call his fortunes thine.

VIOLA. I'll do my best
To woo your lady, — [*aside*] yet, a barful strife!
Whoe'er I woo, myself would be his wife.

[*Exeunt.*

Scene iv, 30. **rubious:** ruby-colored. 31. **sound:** clear. 32. **semblative:** like. 33. **constellation:** nature (which the stars determined). 39. **barful strife:** task full of obstacles.

SCENE 5. [*A room in* OLIVIA'S *house.*]

Enter MARIA *and* CLOWN.

MARIA. Nay, either tell me where thou hast been, or I will not open my lips so wide as a bristle may enter, in way of thy excuse. My lady will hang thee for thy absence.

CLOWN. Let her hang me! He that is well hang'd in this world needs to fear no colours.

MARIA. Make that good.

CLOWN. He shall see none to fear.

MARIA. A good lenten answer. I can tell thee where that saying was born, of "I fear no colours."

CLOWN. Where, good Mistress Mary?

MARIA. In the wars; and that may you be bold to say in your foolery.

CLOWN. Well, God give them wisdom that have it; and those that are fools, let them use their talents.

MARIA. Yet you will be hang'd for being so long absent; or, to be turn'd away, is not that as good as a hanging to you?

CLOWN. Many a good hanging prevents a bad marriage; and, for turning away, let summer bear it out.

MARIA. You are resolute, then?

CLOWN. Not so, neither; but I am resolv'd on two points.

MARIA. That if one break, the other will hold; or, if both break, your gaskins fall.

CLOWN. Apt, in good faith; very apt. Well, go thy way. If Sir Toby would leave drinking, thou wert as witty a piece of Eve's flesh as any in Illyria.

MARIA. Peace, you rogue, no more o' that. Here comes my lady. Make your excuse wisely, you were best. [*Exit.*]

Enter LADY OLIVIA [*and retinue*] *with* MALVOLIO.

CLOWN. Wit, an't be thy will, put me into good fooling! Those wits, that think they have thee, do very oft prove fools; and I, that am sure I lack thee, may pass for a wise man; for what says Quinapalus? "Better a witty fool than a foolish wit." — God bless thee, lady!

OLIVIA. Take the fool away.

CLOWN. Do you not hear, fellows? Take away the lady.

OLIVIA. Go to, you're a dry fool, I'll no more of you; besides, you grow dishonest.

CLOWN. Two faults, madonna, that drink and good counsel will amend; for give the dry fool drink, then is the fool not dry: bid the dishonest man mend himself; if he mend, he is no longer dishonest; if he

Scene v, 5. **colours:** flags (*i.e.,* foes), with a pun on *collars* (the hangman's noose). 8. **lenten:** scanty. 19. **points:** (1) counts, (2) laces to hold up the *gaskins* or breeches. 29. **Quinapalus.** Feste's invention. 33. **dry:** dull.

cannot, let the botcher mend him. Any thing that's mended is but patch'd; virtue that transgresses is but patch'd with sin, and sin that amends is but patch'd with virtue. If that this simple syllogism will serve, so; if it will not, what remedy? As there is no true cuckold but calamity, so beauty's a flower. The lady bade take away the fool; therefore, I say again, take her away.

OLIVIA. Sir, I bade them take away you.

CLOWN. Misprision in the highest degree! Lady, "*cucullus non facit monachum*"; that's as much to say as I wear not motley in my brain. Good madonna, give me leave to prove you a fool.

OLIVIA. Can you do it?

CLOWN. Dexteriously, good madonna.

OLIVIA. Make your proof.

CLOWN. I must catechise you for it, madonna. Good my mouse of virtue, answer me.

OLIVIA. Well, sir, for want of other idleness, I'll bide your proof.

CLOWN. Good madonna, why mournest thou?

OLIVIA. Good fool, for my brother's death.

CLOWN. I think his soul is in hell, madonna.

OLIVIA. I know his soul is in heaven, fool.

CLOWN. The more fool, madonna, to mourn for your brother's soul being in heaven. Take away the fool, gentlemen.

OLIVIA. What think you of this fool, Malvolio? Doth he not mend?

MALVOLIO. Yes, and shall do till the pangs of death shake him. Infirmity, that decays the wise, doth ever make the better fool.

CLOWN. God send you, sir, a speedy infirmity, for the better increasing your folly! Sir Toby will be sworn that I am no fox, but he will not pass his word for twopence that you are no fool.

OLIVIA. How say you to that, Malvolio?

MALVOLIO. I marvel your ladyship takes delight in such a barren rascal. I saw him put down the other day with an ordinary fool that has no more brain than a stone. Look you now, he's out of his guard already. Unless you laugh and minister occasion to him, he is gagg'd. I protest, I take these wise men that crow so at these set kind of fools no better than the fools' zanies.

OLIVIA. O, you are sick of self-love, Malvolio, and taste with a distemper'd appetite. To be generous, guiltless, and of free disposition, is to take those things for bird-bolts that you deem cannon-bullets. There is no slander in an allow'd fool, though he do nothing but rail; nor no railing in a known discreet man, though he do nothing but reprove.

CLOWN. Now Mercury endue thee with leasing, for thou speak'st well of fools!

38. **botcher:** mender of old clothes. 45. **Misprision:** mistake, with a possible reference to the literal sense, taking the wrong person. 45–46. ***cucullus . . . monachum:*** the cowl does not make the monk. 46. **motley:** the parti-colored costume of jesters. 51. **mouse:** term of affection. 51–52. **of virtue:** virtuous. 72. **zanies:** imitators. 75. **bird-bolts:** blunt arrows. 76. **allow'd:** licensed. 78. **leasing:** (gift of) lying. Mercury was the god of thieves and liars.

Re-enter MARIA.

MARIA. Madam, there is at the gate a young gentleman much desires to speak with you.

OLIVIA. From the Count Orsino, is it?

MARIA. I know not, madam. 'Tis a fair young man, and well attended.

OLIVIA. Who of my people hold him in delay?

MARIA. Sir Toby, madam, your kinsman.

OLIVIA. Fetch him off, I pray you. He speaks nothing but madman; fie on him!

[*Exit* MARIA.]

Go you, Malvolio; if it be a suit from the Count, I am sick, or not at home, — what you will, to dismiss it.

(*Exit* MALVOLIO.)

Now you see, sir, how your fooling grows old, and people dislike it.

CLOWN. Thou hast spoke for us, madonna, as if thy eldest son should be a fool; whose skull Jove cram with brains! for — here he comes —

Enter SIR TOBY.

one of thy kin has a most weak *pia mater*.

OLIVIA. By mine honour, half drunk. What is he at the gate, cousin?

SIR TOBY. A gentleman.

OLIVIA. A gentleman! What gentleman?

SIR TOBY. 'Tis a gentleman here — a plague o' these pickle-herring! How now, sot!

CLOWN. Good Sir Toby!

OLIVIA. Cousin, cousin, how have you come so early by this lethargy?

SIR TOBY. Lechery! I defy lechery. There's one at the gate.

OLIVIA. Ay, marry, what is he?

SIR TOBY. Let him be the devil, an he will, I care not; give me faith, say I. Well, it's all one. [*Exit*.

OLIVIA. What's a drunken man like, fool?

CLOWN. Like a drown'd man, a fool, and a madman. One draught above heat makes him a fool, the second mads him, and a third drowns him.

OLIVIA. Go thou and seek the crowner and let him sit o' my coz, for he's in the third degree of drink, he's drown'd. Go, look after him.

CLOWN. He is but mad yet, madonna; and the fool shall look to the madman. [*Exit*.

Re-enter MALVOLIO.

93. *pia mater*: brain. 109. crowner: coroner.

MALVOLIO. Madam, yond young fellow swears he will speak with you. I told him you were sick. He takes on him to understand so much, and therefore comes to speak with you. I told him you were asleep. He seems to have a foreknowledge of that too, and therefore comes to speak with you. What is to be said to him, lady? He's fortified against any denial.

OLIVIA. Tell him he shall not speak with me.

MALVOLIO. Has been told so; and he says, he'll stand at your door like a sheriff's post, and be the supporter to a bench, but he'll speak with you.

OLIVIA. What kind o' man is he?

MALVOLIO. Why, of mankind.

OLIVIA. What manner of man?

MALVOLIO. Of very ill manner. He'll speak with you, will you or no.

OLIVIA. Of what personage and years is he?

MALVOLIO. Not yet old enough for a man, nor young enough for a boy; as a squash is before 'tis a peascod, or a codling when 'tis almost an apple. 'Tis with him in standing water, between boy and man. He is very well-favour'd and he speaks very shrewishly. One would think his mother's milk were scarce out of him.

OLIVIA. Let him approach. Call in my gentlewoman.

MALVOLIO. Gentlewoman, my lady calls. [*Exit.*

Re-enter MARIA.

OLIVIA. Give me my veil. Come, throw it o'er my face.
We'll once more hear Orsino's embassy.

Enter [VIOLA *and Attendants*].

VIOLA. The honourable lady of the house, which is she?

OLIVIA. Speak to me; I shall answer for her. Your will?

VIOLA. Most radiant, exquisite, and unmatchable beauty, — I pray you, tell me if this be the lady of the house, for I never saw her. I would be loath to cast away my speech, for besides that it is excellently well penn'd, I have taken great pains to con it. Good beauties, let me sustain no scorn. I am very comptible, even to the least sinister usage.

OLIVIA. Whence came you, sir?

VIOLA. I can say little more than I have studied, and that question's out of my part. Good gentle one, give me modest assurance if you be the lady of the house, that I may proceed in my speech.

OLIVIA. Are you a comedian?

VIOLA. No, my profound heart; and yet, by the very fangs of malice I swear, I am not that I play. Are you the lady of the house?

OLIVIA. If I do not usurp myself, I am.

120. **sheriff's post:** post before a sheriff's house for notices. 127. **squash:** unripe pea pod. **codling:** unripe apple. 128. **standing water:** at turn of the tide. 129. **shrewishly:** crossly. 135. S.D. VIOLA. *Violenta* F. 140. **con:** memorize. 141. **comptible:** sensitive.

VIOLA. Most certain, if you are she, you do usurp yourself; for what is yours to bestow is not yours to reserve. But this is from my commission. I will on with my speech in your praise, and then show you the heart of my message.

OLIVIA. Come to what is important in't. I forgive you the praise.

VIOLA. Alas, I took great pains to study it, and 'tis poetical.

OLIVIA. It is the more like to be feigned. I pray you, keep it in. I heard you were saucy at my gates, and allow'd your approach rather to wonder at you than to hear you. If you be not mad, be gone. If you have reason, be brief. 'Tis not that time of moon with me to make one in so skipping a dialogue.

MARIA. Will you hoist sail, sir? Here lies your way.

VIOLA. No, good swabber, I am to hull here a little longer. Some mollification for your giant, sweet lady. Tell me your mind. I am a messenger.

OLIVIA. Sure, you have some hideous matter to deliver, when the courtesy of it is so fearful. Speak your office.

VIOLA. It alone concerns your ear. I bring no overture of war, no taxation of homage. I hold the olive in my hand. My words are as full of peace as matter.

OLIVIA. Yet you began rudely. What are you? What would you?

VIOLA. The rudeness that hath appear'd in me have I learn'd from my entertainment. What I am, and what I would, are as secret as maidenhead; to your ears, divinity, to any other's, profanation.

OLIVIA. Give us the place alone; we will hear this divinity.

[*Exeunt* MARIA *and Attendants.*]

Now, sir, what is your text?

VIOLA. Most sweet lady, —

OLIVIA. A comfortable doctrine, and much may be said of it. Where lies your text?

VIOLA. In Orsino's bosom.

OLIVIA. In his bosom! In what chapter of his bosom?

VIOLA. To answer by the method, in the first of his heart.

OLIVIA. O, I have read it; it is heresy. Have you no more to say?

VIOLA. Good madam, let me see your face.

OLIVIA. Have you any commission from your lord to negotiate with my face? You are now out of your text, but we will draw the curtain and show you the picture. Look you, sir, such a one I was — this present. Is't not well done? [*Unveiling.*]

VIOLA. Excellently done, if God did all.

151. **from:** out of. 160. **skipping:** flighty. 162. **swabber:** washer of decks — keeping up the nautical metaphor in "hoist sail." **hull:** float, drift. 163. **giant.** Ironical reference to Maria's small stature. 167–168. **taxation:** demand. 171–172. **my entertainment:** the way I have been received here. 186. **this present:** just now.

OLIVIA. 'Tis in grain, sir; 'twill endure wind and weather.

VIOLA. 'Tis beauty truly blent, whose red and white
Nature's own sweet and cunning hand laid on.
Lady, you are the cruell'st she alive
If you will lead these graces to the grave
And leave the world no copy.

OLIVIA. O, sir, I will not be so hard-hearted; I will give out divers schedules of my beauty. It shall be inventoried, and every particle and utensil labell'd to my will: as, item, two lips, indifferent red; item, two grey eyes, with lids to them; item, one neck, one chin, and so forth. Were you sent hither to praise me?

VIOLA. I see you what you are, you are too proud;
But, if you were the devil, you are fair.
My lord and master loves you. O, such love
Could be but recompens'd, though you were crown'd
The nonpareil of beauty!

OLIVIA. How does he love me?

VIOLA. With adorations, [with] fertile tears,
With groans that thunder love, with sighs of fire.

OLIVIA. Your lord does know my mind; I cannot love him.
Yet I suppose him virtuous, know him noble;
Of great estate, of fresh and stainless youth,
In voices well divulg'd, free, learn'd, and valiant,
And in dimension and the shape of nature
A gracious person. But yet I cannot love him.
He might have took his answer long ago.

VIOLA. If I did love you in my master's flame,
With such a suff'ring, such a deadly life,
In your denial I would find no sense.
I would not understand it.

OLIVIA. Why, what would you?

VIOLA. Make me a willow cabin at your gate,
And call upon my soul within the house;
Write loyal cantons of contemned love
And sing them loud even in the dead of night;
Halloo your name to the reverberate hills
And make the babbling gossip of the air
Cry out "Olivia!" O, you should not rest
Between the elements of air and earth,
But you should pity me!

OLIVIA. You might do much.
What is your parentage?

VIOLA. Above my fortunes, yet my state is well.
I am a gentleman.

189. **in grain:** indelible, not painted. 197. **labell'd:** attached (as a codicil). 199. **praise:** appraise. 205. **[with]** (Pope). Omitted in F. 210. **In . . . divulg'd:** of good repute. 214. **flame:** passion. 215. **deadly:** doomed to die. 220. **cantons:** cantos, songs.

OLIVIA. Get you to your lord.
I cannot love him. Let him send no more, —
Unless, perchance, you come to me again
To tell me how he takes it. Fare you well!
I thank you for your pains. Spend this for me.
VIOLA. I am no fee'd post, lady. Keep your purse.
My master, not myself, lacks recompense.
Love make his heart of flint that you shall love;
And let your fervour, like my master's, be
Plac'd in contempt! Farewell, fair cruelty. [*Exit.*
OLIVIA. "What is your parentage?"
"Above my fortunes, yet my state is well.
I am a gentleman." I'll be sworn thou art.
Thy tongue, thy face, thy limbs, actions, and spirit
Do give thee five-fold blazon. Not too fast! Soft, soft!
Unless the master were the man. How now!
Even so quickly may one catch the plague?
Methinks I feel this youth's perfections
With an invisible and subtle stealth
To creep in at mine eyes. Well, let it be.
What ho, Malvolio!

Re-enter MALVOLIO.

MALVOLIO. Here, madam, at your service.
OLIVIA. Run after that same peevish messenger,
The County's man. He left this ring behind him,
Would I or not. Tell him I'll none of it.
Desire him not to flatter with his lord,
Nor hold him up with hopes. I'm not for him.
If that the youth will come this way to-morrow,
I'll give him reasons for't. Hie thee, Malvolio.
MALVOLIO. Madam, I will. [*Exit.*
OLIVIA. I do I know not what, and fear to find
Mine eye too great a flatterer for my mind.
Fate, show thy force; ourselves we do not owe;
What is decreed must be, and be this so. [*Exit.*]

ACT TWO

SCENE 1. [*The sea-coast.*]

Enter ANTONIO *and* SEBASTIAN.

ANTONIO. Will you stay no longer? Nor will you not that I go with you?

234. **post:** messenger. 243. **blazon:** proof of nobility. 260. **owe:** own.

SEBASTIAN. By your patience, no. My stars shine darkly over me. The malignancy of my fate might perhaps distemper yours, therefore I shall crave of you your leave that I may bear my evils alone. It were a bad recompense for your love, to lay any of them on you.

ANTONIO. Let me yet know of you whither you are bound.

SEBASTIAN. No, sooth, sir. My determinate voyage is mere extravagancy. But I perceive in you so excellent a touch of modesty, that you will not extort from me what I am willing to keep in; therefore it charges me in manners the rather to express myself. You must know of me then, Antonio, my name is Sebastian, which I call'd Roderigo. My father was that Sebastian of Messaline, whom I know you have heard of. He left behind him myself and a sister, both born in an hour. If the heavens had been pleas'd, would we had so ended! But you, sir, alter'd that; for some hour before you took me from the breach of the sea was my sister drown'd.

ANTONIO. Alas the day!

SEBASTIAN. A lady, sir, though it was said she much resembled me, was yet of many accounted beautiful; but, though I could not with such estimable wonder overfar believe that, yet thus far I will boldly publish her: she bore a mind that envy could not but call fair. She is drown'd already, sir, with salt water, though I seem to drown her remembrance again with more.

ANTONIO. Pardon me, sir, your bad entertainment.

SEBASTIAN. O good Antonio, forgive me your trouble.

ANTONIO. If you will not murder me for my love, let me be your servant.

SEBASTIAN. If you will not undo what you have done, that is, kill him whom you have recover'd, desire it not. Fare ye well at once. My bosom is full of kindness, and I am yet so near the manners of my mother, that upon the least occasion more mine eyes will tell tales of me. I am bound to the Count Orsino's court. Farewell. [*Exit.*

ANTONIO. The gentleness of all the gods go with thee!
I have many enemies in Orsino's court,
Else would I very shortly see thee there.
But, come what may, I do adore thee so
That danger shall seem sport, and I will go. [*Exit.*

SCENE 2. [*A street.*]

Enter VIOLA *and* MALVOLIO, *at several doors.*

MALVOLIO. Were you not even now with the Countess Olivia?

VIOLA. Even now, sir. On a moderate pace I have since arriv'd but hither.

Act II, Scene i, 4. distemper: disorder. 8–9. **My . . . extravagancy:** my destination is mere wandering. 11. **express:** reveal. 16. **breach:** breakers, surf. 21. **estimable wonder:** admiring esteem.

MALVOLIO. She returns this ring to you, sir. You might have saved me my pains, to have taken it away yourself. She adds, moreover, that you should put your lord into a desperate assurance she will none of him; and — one thing more — that you be never so hardy to come again in his affairs, unless it be to report your lord's taking of this. Receive it so.

VIOLA. She took the ring of me. I'll none of it.

MALVOLIO. Come, sir, you peevishly threw it to her; and her will is, it should be so return'd. If it be worth stooping for, there it lies in your eye; if not, be it his that finds it. [*Exit.*

VIOLA. I left no ring with her. What means this lady?
Fortune forbid my outside have not charm'd her!
She made good view of me; indeed, so much
That [sure] methought her eyes had lost her tongue,
For she did speak in starts distractedly.
She loves me, sure. The cunning of her passion
Invites me in this churlish messenger.
None of my lord's ring! Why, he sent her none.
I am the man! If it be so, as 'tis,
Poor lady, she were better love a dream.
Disguise, I see thou art a wickedness
Wherein the pregnant enemy does much.
How easy is it for the proper-false
In women's waxen hearts to set their forms!
Alas, [our] frailty is the cause, not we!
For such as we are made [of], such we be.
How will this fadge? My master loves her dearly;
And I, poor monster, fond as much on him;
And she, mistaken, seems to dote on me.
What will become of this? As I am man,
My state is desperate for my master's love;
As I am woman, — now alas the day! —
What thriftless sighs shall poor Olivia breathe!
O time! thou must untangle this, not I.
It is too hard a knot for me t' untie! [*Exit.*]

SCENE 3. [*A room in* OLIVIA'*s house.*]

Enter SIR TOBY *and* SIR ANDREW.

SIR TOBY. Approach, Sir Andrew. Not to be a-bed after midnight is to be up betimes; and "*deliculo surgere,*" thou know'st, —

Scene ii, 6. **desperate:** hopeless. 16. [**sure**] F_2. Om. F_1. **lost:** *i.e.,* put at a loss. 24. **pregnant:** resourceful. 25. **proper-false:** handsome deceivers. 27. [**our**] F_2. O F_1. 28. **made** [**of**] (Tyrwhitt). *made, if* F_1. 29. **fadge:** turn out.

Scene iii, 2. ***deliculo surgere*** (*saluberrimum est*): to rise early is most healthful. An extract from Lilly's *Latin Grammar.*

SIR ANDREW. Nay, by my troth, I know not; but I know, to be up late is to be up late.

SIR TOBY. A false conclusion. I hate it as an unfill'd can. To be up after midnight and to go to bed then, is early; so that to go to bed after midnight is to go to bed betimes. Does not our lives consist of the four elements?

SIR ANDREW. Faith, so they say; but I think it rather consists of eating and drinking.

SIR TOBY. Thou'rt a scholar; let us therefore eat and drink. Marian, I say! a stoup of wine!

Enter CLOWN.

SIR ANDREW. Here comes the fool, i' faith.

CLOWN. How now, my hearts! Did you never see the picture of "we three"?

SIR TOBY. Welcome, ass. Now let's have a catch.

SIR ANDREW. By my troth, the fool has an excellent breast. I had rather than forty shillings I had such a leg, and so sweet a breath to sing, as the fool has. In sooth, thou wast in very gracious fooling last night, when thou spok'st of Pigrogromitus, of the Vapians passing the equinoctial of Queubus. 'Twas very good, i' faith. I sent thee sixpence for thy leman. Hadst it?

CLOWN. I did impeticos thy gratillity; for Malvolio's nose is no whipstock. My lady has a white hand, and the Mermidons are no bottle-ale houses.

SIR ANDREW. Excellent! Why, this is the best fooling, when all is done. Now, a song.

SIR TOBY. Come on; there is sixpence for you. Let's have a song.

SIR ANDREW. There's a testril of me too. If one knight give a —

CLOWN. Would you have a love-song, or a song of good life?

SIR TOBY. A love-song, a love-song.

SIR ANDREW. Ay, ay. I care not for good life.

CLOWN (*sings*). O mistress mine, where are you roaming?
O, stay and hear, your true love's coming,
That can sing both high and low.
Trip no further, pretty sweeting;
Journeys end in lovers meeting,
Every wise man's son doth know.

SIR ANDREW. Excellent good, i' faith.

12. **stoup:** cup. 14–15. A picture of two asses or fools entitled "we three," the spectator making the third. 16. **catch:** round. 17. **breast:** voice. 20–21. **Pigrogromitus . . . Queubus.** Mock learning. 22. **leman:** sweetheart. 23. **impeticos thy gratillity.** Nonsensical mode of saying "pocket thy gratuity." 23–24. **whipstock:** whip handle (*i.e.*, Malvolio's nose is keen). 24. **Mermidons:** followers of Achilles. 29. **testril:** sixpence.

SIR TOBY. Good, good.

CLOWN [*sings*]. What is love? 'Tis not hereafter.
Present mirth hath present laughter;
  What's to come is still unsure.
In delay there lies no plenty;
Then come kiss me, sweet and twenty,
  Youth's a stuff will not endure.

SIR ANDREW. A mellifluous voice, as I am true knight.

SIR TOBY. A contagious breath.

SIR ANDREW. Very sweet and contagious, i' faith.

SIR TOBY. To hear by the nose, it is dulcet in contagion. But shall we make the welkin dance indeed? Shall we rouse the night-owl in a catch that will draw three souls out of one weaver? Shall we do that?

SIR ANDREW. An you love me, let's do't. I am dog at a catch.

CLOWN. By'r lady, sir, and some dogs will catch well.

SIR ANDREW. Most certain. Let our catch be, "Thou knave."

CLOWN. "Hold thy peace, thou knave," knight? I shall be constrain'd in't to call thee knave, knight.

SIR ANDREW. 'Tis not the first time I have constrained one to call me knave. Begin, fool. It begins, "Hold thy peace."

CLOWN. I shall never begin if I hold my peace.

SIR ANDREW. Good, i' faith. Come, begin.

[*Catch sung. Enter* MARIA.

MARIA. What a caterwauling do you keep here! If my lady have not call'd up her steward Malvolio and bid him turn you out of doors, never trust me.

SIR TOBY. My lady's a Cataian, we are politicians, Malvolio's a Peg-a-Ramsey, and "Three merry men be we." Am not I consanguineous? Am I not of her blood? Tilly-vally. Lady! [*Sings.*] "There dwelt a man in Babylon, lady, lady!"

CLOWN. Beshrew me, the knight's in admirable fooling.

SIR ANDREW. Ay, he does well enough if he be dispos'd, and so do I too. He does it with a better grace, but I do it more natural.

SIR TOBY [*sings*]. "O, the twelfth day of December," —

MARIA. For the love o' God, peace!

Enter MALVOLIO.

MALVOLIO. My masters, are you mad, or what are you? Have you no wit, manners, nor honesty, but to gabble like tinkers at this time of night? Do ye make an alehouse of my lady's house, that ye squeak out your

48. **contagious breath:** catchy song. 51. **welkin:** sky. 65. **Cataian:** Chinese, rascal. 65–66. **Peg-a-Ramsey:** a character in a ballad. 66. **Three merry men** (etc.). This and subsequent quotations are from popular songs.

coziers' catches without any mitigation or remorse of voice? Is there no respect of place, persons, nor time in you?

SIR TOBY. We did keep time, sir, in our catches. Sneck up!

MALVOLIO. Sir Toby, I must be round with you. My lady bade me tell you that, though she harbours you as her kinsman, she's nothing alli'd to your disorders. If you can separate yourself and your misdemeanours, you are welcome to the house; if not, an it would please you to take leave of her, she is very willing to bid you farewell.

SIR TOBY. "Farewell, dear heart, since I must needs be gone."

MARIA. Nay, good Sir Toby.

CLOWN. "His eyes do show his days are almost done."

MALVOLIO. Is't even so?

SIR TOBY. "But I will never die."

CLOWN. Sir Toby, there you lie.

MALVOLIO. This is much credit to you.

SIR TOBY. "Shall I bid him go?"

CLOWN. "What an if you do?"

SIR TOBY. "Shall I bid him go, and spare not?"

CLOWN. "O no, no, no, no, you dare not."

SIR TOBY. Out o' tune, sir! Ye lie. Art any more than a steward? Dost thou think, because thou art virtuous, there shall be no more cakes and ale?

CLOWN. Yes, by Saint Anne, and ginger shall be hot i' th' mouth too.

SIR TOBY. Thou'rt i' th' right. Go, sir, rub your chain with crumbs. A stoup of wine, Maria!

MALVOLIO. Mistress Mary, if you priz'd my lady's favour at anything more than contempt, you would not give means for this uncivil rule. She shall know of it, by this hand. [*Exit.*

MARIA. Go shake your ears.

SIR ANDREW. 'Twere as good a deed as to drink when a man's a-hungry, to challenge him the field, and then to break promise with him and make a fool of him.

SIR TOBY. Do't, knight. I'll write thee a challenge, or I'll deliver thy indignation to him by word of mouth.

MARIA. Sweet Sir Toby, be patient for to-night. Since the youth of the Count's was to-day with my lady, she is much out of quiet. For Monsieur Malvolio, let me alone with him. If I do not gull him into a nayword, and make him a common recreation, do not think I have wit enough to lie straight in my bed. I know I can do it.

SIR TOBY. Possess us, possess us. Tell us something of him.

MARIA. Marry, sir, sometimes he is a kind of puritan.

SIR ANDREW. O, if I thought that, I'd beat him like a dog!

SIR TOBY. What, for being a puritan? Thy exquisite reason, dear knight?

77. **coziers'**: cobblers'. 79. **Sneck up**: go hang. 100. **chain**: *i.e.*, steward's badge. 114. **nayword**: byword. 116. **Possess**: inform.

SIR ANDREW. I have no exquisite reason for't, but I have reason good enough.

MARIA. The devil a puritan that he is, or anything constantly, but a time-pleaser; an affection'd ass, that cons state without book and utters it by great swarths; the best persuaded of himself, so cramm'd, as he thinks, with excellencies, that it is his grounds of faith that all that look on him love him; and on that vice in him will my revenge find notable cause to work.

SIR TOBY. What wilt thou do?

MARIA. I will drop in his way some obscure epistles of love; wherein, by the colour of his beard, the shape of his leg, the manner of his gait, the expressure of his eye, forehead, and complexion, he shall find himself most feelingly personated. I can write very like my lady your niece. On a forgotten matter we can hardly make distinction of our hands.

SIR TOBY. Excellent! I smell a device.

SIR ANDREW. I have't in my nose too.

SIR TOBY. He shall think, by the letters that thou wilt drop, that they come from my niece, and that she's in love with him.

MARIA. My purpose is, indeed, a horse of that colour.

SIR ANDREW. And your horse now would make him an ass.

MARIA. Ass, I doubt not.

SIR ANDREW. O, 'twill be admirable!

MARIA. Sport royal, I warrant you. I know my physic will work with him. I will plant you two, and let the fool make a third, where he shall find the letter. Observe his construction of it. For this night, to bed, and dream on the event. Farewell. [*Exit.*

SIR TOBY. Good night, Penthesilea.

SIR ANDREW. Before me, she's a good wench.

SIR TOBY. She's a beagle, true-bred, and one that adores me. What o' that?

SIR ANDREW. I was ador'd once too.

SIR TOBY. Let's to bed, knight. Thou hadst need send for more money.

SIR ANDREW. If I cannot recover your niece, I am a foul way out.

SIR TOBY. Send for money, knight. If thou hast her not i' the end, call me cut.

SIR ANDREW. If I do not, never trust me, take it how you will.

SIR TOBY. Come, come, I'll go burn some sack; tis too late to go to bed now. Come, knight; come, knight.

[*Exeunt.*

124. **affection'd:** affected. **cons . . . book:** memorizes courtly speeches. 125. **swarths:** swaths. 147. **Penthesilea:** Queen of the Amazons. 154. **recover:** win. **out:** *i.e.*, of money. 156. **cut:** horse with docked tail. 158. **burn:** heat and spice. **sack:** a Spanish wine.

SCENE 4. [*A room in the* DUKE'S *palace*.]

Enter DUKE, VIOLA, CURIO, *and others*.

DUKE. Give me some music. Now, — good morrow, friends, —
Now, good Cesario, but that piece of song,
That old and antique song we heard last night.
Methought it did relieve my passion much,
More than light airs and recollected terms
Of these most brisk and giddy-paced times.
Come, but one verse.

CURIO. He is not here, so please your lordship, that should sing it.

DUKE. Who was it?

CURIO. Feste, the jester, my lord; a fool that the lady Olivia's father took much delight in. He is about the house.

DUKE. Seek him out, and play the tune the while.

[*Exit* CURIO.] *Music plays*.

Come hither, boy. If ever thou shalt love,
In the sweet pangs of it remember me;
For such as I am all true lovers are,
Unstaid and skittish in all motions else,
Save in the constant image of the creature
That is belov'd. How dost thou like this tune?

VIOLA. It gives a very echo to the seat
Where Love is thron'd.

DUKE. Thou dost speak masterly.
My life upon't, young though thou art, thine eye
Hath stay'd upon some favour that it loves.
Hath it not, boy?

VIOLA. A little, by your favour.

DUKE. What kind of woman is't?

VIOLA. Of your complexion.

DUKE. She is not worth thee, then. What years, i' faith?

VIOLA. About your years, my lord.

DUKE. Too old, by heaven. Let still the woman take
An elder than herself; so wears she to him,
So sways she level in her husband's heart.
For, boy, however we do praise ourselves,
Our fancies are more giddy and unfirm,
More longing, wavering, sooner lost and worn,
Than women's are.

VIOLA. I think it well, my lord.

DUKE. Then let thy love be younger than thyself,

Scene iv, 5. recollected terms: studied phrases. 16. **motions:** emotions. 22. **favour:** face.

Or thy affection cannot hold the bent.
For women are as roses, whose fair flower
Being once display'd, doth fall that very hour.

VIOLA. And so they are; alas, that they are so!
To die, even when they to perfection grow!

Re-enter CURIO *and* CLOWN.

DUKE. O, fellow, come, the song we had last night.
Mark it, Cesario, it is old and plain.
The spinsters and the knitters in the sun
And the free maids that weave their thread with bones
Do use to chant it. It is silly sooth,
And dallies with the innocence of love,
Like the old age.

CLOWN. Are you ready, sir?

DUKE. Ay; prithee, sing.

[*Music.*

SONG.

[CLOWN.] Come away, come away, death,
And in sad cypress let me be laid.
Fly away, fly away, breath;
I am slain by a fair cruel maid.
My shroud of white, stuck all with yew,
O, prepare it!
My part of death, no one so true
Did share it.

Not a flower, not a flower sweet,
On my black coffin let there be strown.
Not a friend, not a friend greet
My poor corpse, where my bones shall be thrown.
A thousand thousand sighs to save,
Lay me, O, where
Sad true lover never find my grave,
To weep there!

DUKE. There's for thy pains.

CLOWN. No pains, sir; I take pleasure in singing, sir.

DUKE. I'll pay thy pleasure then.

CLOWN. Truly, sir, and pleasure will be paid, one time or another.

DUKE. Give me now leave to leave thee.

35. **the bent:** its intensity. 43. **free:** carefree. **bones:** bobbins (of bone). 44. **silly sooth:** simple truth. 46. **old age:** golden age. 50. **cypress:** coffin of cypress wood. 55–56. **My . . . share it:** *i.e.,* No truer lover ever died than I.

CLOWN. Now, the melancholy god protect thee, and the tailor make thy doublet of changeable taffeta, for thy mind is a very opal. I would have men of such constancy put to sea, that their business might be everything and their intent everywhere; for that's it that always makes a good voyage of nothing. Farewell. [*Exit.*

DUKE. Let all the rest give place.

[CURIO *and Attendants retire.*]

Once more, Cesario,
Get thee to yond same sovereign cruelty.
Tell her, my love, more noble than the world,
Prizes not quantity of dirty lands.
The parts that fortune hath bestow'd upon her,
Tell her, I hold as giddily as fortune;
But 'tis that miracle and queen of gems
That nature pranks her in attracts my soul.

VIOLA. But if she cannot love you, sir?

DUKE. [I] cannot be so answer'd.

VIOLA. Sooth, but you must.
Say that some lady, as perhaps there is,
Hath for your love as great a pang of heart
As you have for Olivia. You cannot love her.
You tell her so. Must she not then be answer'd?

DUKE. There is no woman's sides
Can bide the beating of so strong a passion
As love doth give my heart; no woman's heart
So big, to hold so much. They lack retention.
Alas, their love may be call'd appetite,
No motion of the liver, but the palate,
That suffer surfeit, cloyment, and revolt;
But mine is all as hungry as the sea,
And can digest as much. Make no compare
Between that love a woman can bear me
And that I owe Olivia.

VIOLA. Ay, but I know —

DUKE. What dost thou know?

VIOLA. Too well what love women to men may owe.
In faith, they are as true of heart as we.
My father had a daughter lov'd a man,
As it might be, perhaps, were I a woman,
I should your lordship.

DUKE. And what's her history?

VIOLA. A blank, my lord. She never told her love,

71. **changeable taffeta**: shot silk. 80. **giddily**: carelessly. 82. **pranks**: adorns. 84. [I] (Hanmer). *It* F. 92. **retention**: stability. 95. **cloyment**: satiety. **revolt**: revulsion.

But let concealment, like a worm i' the bud,
Feed on her damask cheek. She pin'd in thought,
And with a green and yellow melancholy
She sat, like Patience on a monument,
Smiling at grief. Was not this love indeed?
We men may say more, swear more; but indeed
Our shows are more than will, for still we prove
Much in our vows, but little in our love.

DUKE. But died thy sister of her love, my boy?

VIOLA. I am all the daughters of my father's house,
And all the brothers too; — and yet I know not.
Sir, shall I to this lady?

DUKE. Ay, that's the theme.
To her in haste. Give her this jewel. Say
My love can give no place, bide no denay.

[*Exeunt.*

SCENE 5. [OLIVIA'S *garden.*]

Enter SIR TOBY, SIR ANDREW, *and* FABIAN.

SIR TOBY. Come thy ways, Signior Fabian.

FABIAN. Nay, I'll come. If I lose a scruple of this sport, let me be boil'd to death with melancholy.

SIR TOBY. Wouldst thou not be glad to have the niggardly rascally sheep-biter come by some notable shame?

FABIAN. I would exult, man. You know, he brought me out o' favour with my lady about a bear-baiting here.

SIR TOBY. To anger him we'll have the bear again, and we will fool him black and blue. Shall we not, Sir Andrew?

SIR ANDREW. An we do not, it is pity of our lives.

Enter MARIA.

SIR TOBY. Here comes the little villain. How now, my metal of India!

MARIA. Get ye all three into the box-tree; Malvolio's coming down this walk. He has been yonder i' the sun practising behaviour to his own shadow this half hour. Observe him, for the love of mockery, for I know this letter will make a contemplative idiot of him. Close, in the name of jesting! Lie thou there [*throws down a letter*], for here comes the trout that must be caught with tickling. [*Exit.*

Enter MALVOLIO.

108 **thought:** brooding. 109. **green and yellow,** signifying hope and jealousy. 110. **monument:** tomb.

Scene v, 5. **sheep-biter:** a vicious dog. 11. **metal of India:** gold. 15. **contemplative:** staring or self-regarding; cf. "Contemplation" (l. 24). 17. **tickling.** Trout can be caught by being stroked.

MALVOLIO. 'Tis but fortune. All is fortune. Maria once told me she did affect me; and I have heard herself come thus near, that, should she fancy, it should be one of my complexion. Besides, she uses me with a more exalted respect than any one else that follows her. What should I think on't?

SIR TOBY. Here's an overweening rogue!

FABIAN. O, peace! Contemplation makes a rare turkey-cock of him. How he jets under his advanc'd plumes!

SIR ANDREW. 'S light, I could so beat the rogue!

SIR TOBY. Peace, I say.

MALVOLIO. To be Count Malvolio!

SIR TOBY. Ah, rogue!

SIR ANDREW. Pistol him, pistol him.

SIR TOBY. Peace, peace!

MALVOLIO. There is example for't. The lady of the Strachy married the yeoman of the wardrobe.

SIR ANDREW. Fie on him, Jezebel!

FABIAN. O, peace! now he's deeply in. Look how imagination blows him.

MALVOLIO. Having been three months married to her, sitting in my state, —

SIR TOBY. O, for a stone-bow, to hit him in the eye!

MALVOLIO. Calling my officers about me, in my branch'd velvet gown, having come from a day-bed, where I have left Olivia sleeping, —

SIR TOBY. Fire and brimstone!

FABIAN. O, peace, peace!

MALVOLIO. And then to have the humour of state; and after a demure travel of regard, telling them I know my place as I would they should do theirs, to ask for my kinsman Toby, —

SIR TOBY. Bolts and shackles!

FABIAN. O peace, peace, peace! Now, now.

MALVOLIO. Seven of my people, with an obedient start, make out for him. I frown the while, and perchance wind up my watch, or play with my — some rich jewel. Toby approaches, curtsies there to me, —

SIR TOBY. Shall this fellow live?

FABIAN. Though our silence be drawn from us with cars, yet peace.

MALVOLIO. I extend my hand to him thus, quencing my familiar smile with an austere regard of control, —

SIR TOBY. And does not Toby take you a blow o' the lips then?

MALVOLIO. Saying, "Cousin Toby, my fortunes, having cast me on your niece, give me this prerogative of speech," —

SIR TOBY. What, what?

MALVOLIO. "You must amend your drunkenness."

25. **jets:** struts. 32. **Strachy.** This lady, unidentified, obviously married below her station. 38. **state:** chair of state. 40. **branch'd:** flowered. 44. **humour of state:** mood of authority. 44–45. **demure . . . regard:** grave look about (me). 55. **control:** authority.

SIR TOBY. Out, scab!

FABIAN. Nay, patience, or we break the sinews of our plot.

MALVOLIO. "Besides, you waste the treasure of your time with a foolish knight," —

SIR ANDREW. That's me, I warrant you.

MALVOLIO. "One Sir Andrew," —

SIR ANDREW. I knew 'twas I; for many do call me fool.

MALVOLIO. What employment have we here? [*Taking up the letter.*]

FABIAN. Now is the woodcock near the gin.

SIR TOBY. O, peace, and the spirit of humours intimate reading aloud to him!

MALVOLIO. By my life, this is my lady's hand. These be her very C's, her U's, and her T's; and thus makes she her great P's. It is, in contempt of question, her hand.

SIR ANDREW. Her C's, her U's, and her T's: why that?

MALVOLIO [*reads*]. "To the unknown belov'd, this, and my good wishes": — her very phrases! By your leave, wax. Soft! And the impressure her Lucrece, with which she uses to seal. 'Tis my lady. To whom should this be?

FABIAN. This wins him, liver and all.

MALVOLIO [*reads*].
"Jove knows I love;
But who?
Lips, do not move;
No man must know."

"No man must know." What follows? The numbers alter'd! "No man must know!" If this should be thee, Malvolio?

SIR TOBY. Marry, hang thee, brock!

MALVOLIO [*reads*].
"I may command where I adore;
But silence, like a Lucrece knife,
With bloodless stroke my heart doth gore.
M, O, A, I, doth sway my life."

FABIAN. A fustian riddle!

SIR TOBY. Excellent wench, say I.

MALVOLIO. "M, O, A, I, doth sway my life." Nay, but first, let me see, let me see, let me see.

FABIAN. What dish o' poison has she dress'd him!

SIR TOBY. And with what wing the [staniel] checks at it!

MALVOLIO. "I may command where I adore." Why, she may command me. I serve her. She is my lady. Why, this is evident to any formal

69. **woodcock:** a bird noted for its stupidity. **gin:** snare. 73–74. **in contempt of:** beyond. 77. **By . . . wax.** Spoken as he breaks the seal. 85. **numbers:** metre. 87. **brock:** badger. 92. **fustian:** ridiculous. 97. **[staniel]** (Hanmer): untrained falcon. *stallion* F. **checks at it:** turns aside (as to inferior prey). Cf. III.i.53. 99. **formal:** normal.

capacity, there is no obstruction in this. And the end, — what should that alphabetical position portend? If I could make that resemble something in me! — Softly; M, O, A, I, —

SIR TOBY. O, ay, make up that. He is now at a cold scent.

FABIAN. Sowter will cry upon't for all this, though it be as rank as a fox.

MALVOLIO. M, — Malvolio; M, — why, that begins my name.

FABIAN. Did not I say he would work it out? The cur is excellent at faults.

MALVOLIO. M, — but then there is no consonancy in the sequel. That suffers under probation. A should follow, but O does.

FABIAN. And O shall end, I hope.

SIR TOBY. Ay, or I'll cudgel him, and make him cry O!

MALVOLIO. And then I comes behind.

FABIAN. Ay, an you had any eye behind you, you might see more detraction at your heels than fortunes before you.

MALVOLIO. M, O, A, I; this simulation is not as the former. And yet, to crush this a little, it would bow to me, for every one of these letters are in my name. Soft! here follows prose. [*Reads.*]

"If this fall into thy hand, revolve. In my stars I am above thee, but be not afraid of greatness. Some are [born] great, some achieve greatness, and some have greatness thrust upon 'em. Thy Fates open their hands, let thy blood and spirit embrace them; and, to inure thyself to what thou art like to be, cast thy humble slough and appear fresh. Be opposite with a kinsman, surly with servants; let thy tongue tang arguments of state; put thyself into the trick of singularity: she thus advises thee that sighs for thee. Remember who commended thy yellow stockings, and wish'd to see thee ever cross-garter'd. I say, remember. Go to, thou art made if thou desir'st to be so; if not, let me see thee a steward still, the fellow of servants, and not worthy to touch Fortune's fingers. Farewell. She that would alter services with thee,

THE FORTUNATE UNHAPPY."

Daylight and champaign discovers not more. This is open. I will be proud, I will read politic authors, I will baffle Sir Toby, I will wash off gross acquaintance, I will be point-device the very man. I do not now fool myself, to let imagination jade me; for every reason excites to this, that my lady loves me. She did commend my yellow stockings of late, she did praise my leg being cross-garter'd; and in this she manifests herself to my love, and with a kind of injunction drives me to these habits of

104–105. **Sowter . . . fox.** *I.e.*, Even Sowter (a stupid hound) will catch this scent though, in fact, it is as strong as a fox's. 108. **faults:** failure of the scent. 109. **consonancy:** agreement. 110. **probation:** testing. 116. **stimulation:** suggestion. 117. **crush:** force (the meaning). 119. **revolve:** consider. 120. **[born]** (Rowe). *become* F. Cf. III.iv.37 and V.i.347. 123. **slough:** skin (of a snake). **opposite:** contradictory. 132. **champaign:** open country. 133. **politic:** *i.e.*, who treat state affairs. 134. **point-device:** precisely. 135. **jade:** trick.

her liking. I thank my stars I am happy. I will be strange, stout, in yellow stockings, and cross-garter'd, even with the swiftness of putting on. Jove and my stars be praised! Here is yet a postscript. [*Reads.*]

"Thou canst not choose but know who I am. If thou entertain'st my love, let it appear in thy smiling. Thy smiles become thee well; therefore in my presence still smile, dear my sweet, I prithee."

Jove, I thank thee. I will smile; I will do everything that thou wilt have me. [*Exit.*

FABIAN. I will not give my part of this sport for a pension of thousands to be paid from the Sophy.

SIR TOBY. I could marry this wench for this device —

SIR ANDREW. So could I too.

SIR TOBY. And ask no other dowry with her but such another jest.

Re-enter MARIA.

SIR ANDREW. Nor I neither.

FABIAN. Here comes my noble gull-catcher.

SIR TOBY. Wilt thou set thy foot o' my neck?

SIR ANDREW. Or o' mine either?

SIR TOBY. Shall I play my freedom at tray-trip, and become thy bond-slave?

SIR ANDREW. I' faith, or I either?

SIR TOBY. Why, thou hast put him in such a dream, that when the image of it leaves him he must run mad.

MARIA. Nay, but say true. Does it work upon him?

SIR TOBY. Like aqua-vitae with a midwife.

MARIA. If you will then see the fruits of the sport, mark his first approach before my lady. He will come to her in yellow stockings, and 'tis a colour she abhors, and cross-garter'd, a fashion she detests; and he will smile upon her, which will now be so unsuitable to her disposition, being addicted to a melancholy as she is, that it cannot but turn him into a notable contempt. If you will see it, follow me.

SIR TOBY. To the gates of Tartar, thou most excellent devil of wit!

SIR ANDREW. I'll make one too.

[*Exeunt.*

139. **stout:** haughty. 148. **Sophy:** Shah of Persia. 156. **tray-trip:** a game with dice. 169. **Tartar:** Tartarus (Hell).

ACT THREE

SCENE 1. [OLIVIA's *garden*.]

Enter VIOLA *and* CLOWN [*with a tabor*].

VIOLA. Save thee, friend, and thy music! Dost thou live by thy tabor?

CLOWN. No, sir, I live by the church.

VIOLA. Art thou a churchman?

CLOWN. No such matter, sir. I do live by the church; for I do live at my house, and my house doth stand by the church.

VIOLA. So thou mayst say, the king lies by a beggar, if a beggar dwells near him; or, the church stands by thy tabor, if thy tabor stand by the church.

CLOWN. You have said, sir. To see this age! A sentence is but a chev'ril glove to a good wit. How quickly the wrong side may be turn'd outward!

VIOLA. Nay, that's certain. They that dally nicely with words may quickly make them wanton.

CLOWN. I would, therefore, my sister had had no name, sir.

VIOLA. Why, man?

CLOWN. Why, sir, her name's a word, and to dally with that word might make my sister wanton. But, indeed, words are very rascals since bonds disgrac'd them.

VIOLA. Thy reason, man?

CLOWN. Troth, sir, I can yield you none without words; and words are grown so false, I am loath to prove reason with them.

VIOLA. I warrant thou art a merry fellow and car'st for nothing.

CLOWN. Not so, sir, I do care for something; but in my conscience, sir, I do not care for you. If that be to care for nothing, sir, I would it would make you invisible.

VIOLA. Art not thou the Lady Olivia's fool?

CLOWN. No, indeed, sir; the Lady Olivia has no folly. She will keep no fool, sir, till she be married; and fools are as like husbands as pilchards are to herrings, the husband's the bigger. I am indeed not her fool, but her corrupter of words.

VIOLA. I saw thee late at the Count Orsino's.

CLOWN. Foolery, sir, does walk about the orb like the sun, it shines everywhere. I would be sorry, sir, but the fool should be as oft with your master as with my mistress. I think I saw your wisdom there.

VIOLA. Nay, an thou pass upon me, I'll no more with thee. Hold, there's expenses for thee.

Act III, Scene i, 1. **tabor:** small drum. 10. **chev'ril:** kid. 13. **wanton:** equivocal (*unchaste,* l. 17). 18. **disgrac'd them:** *i.e.,* became necessary to bind them. 28. **pilchards:** fish like herring. 35. **pass upon:** jest at.

CLOWN. Now Jove, in his next commodity of hair, send thee a beard!

VIOLA. By my troth, I'll tell thee, I am almost sick for one, — [*aside*] though I would not have it grow on my chin. Is thy lady within?

CLOWN. Would not a pair of these have bred, sir?

VIOLA. Yes, being kept together and put to use.

CLOWN. I would play Lord Pandarus of Phrygia, sir, to bring a Cressida to this Troilus.

VIOLA. I understand you, sir. 'Tis well begg'd.

CLOWN. The matter, I hope, is not great, sir, begging but a beggar. Cressida was a beggar. My lady is within, sir. I will construe to them whence you come. Who you are and what you would are out of my welkin — I might say "element," but the word is overworn. [*Exit.*

VIOLA. This fellow is wise enough to play the fool,
And to do that well craves a kind of wit.
He must observe their mood on whom he jests,
The quality of persons, and the time,
And, like the haggard, check at every feather
That comes before his eye. This is a practice
As full of labour as a wise man's art;
For folly that he wisely shows is fit,
But wise men, folly-fall'n, quite taint their wit.

Enter SIR TOBY *and* SIR ANDREW.

SIR TOBY. Save you, gentleman.

VIOLA. And you, sir.

SIR ANDREW. *Dieu vous garde, monsieur.*

VIOLA. *Et vous aussi; votre serviteur.*

SIR ANDREW. I hope, sir, you are; and I am yours.

SIR TOBY. Will you encounter the house? My niece is desirous you should enter, if your trade be to her.

VIOLA. I am bound to your niece, sir; I mean, she is the list of my voyage.

SIR TOBY. Taste your legs, sir; put them to motion.

VIOLA. My legs do better understand me, sir, than I understand what you mean by bidding me taste my legs.

SIR TOBY. I mean, to go, sir, to enter.

VIOLA. I will answer you with [gait] and entrance. But we are prevented.

Enter OLIVIA *and Gentlewoman.*

37. **commodity**: consignment. 40. **these**: *i.e.*, coins (see l. 36). 41. **use**: interest. 42. **Pandarus**: uncle to Cressida, who brought her and Troilus together. 46. **Cressida . . . beggar.** In Henryson's *Testament of Cresseid*, Cressida became a leper and begged by the roadside. 53. **haggard**: untrained hawk. 57. **folly-fall'n**: acting like fools. 60–61. ***Dieu . . . serviteur:*** God keep you, sir. And you, too; I am your servant. 65. **list**: goal. 71. **[gait]** (Johnson). *gate* F. A pun on the two words. 71–72. **prevented**: anticipated.

Most excellent accomplish'd lady, the heavens rain odours on you!

SIR ANDREW. That youth's a rare courtier. "Rain odours;" well.

VIOLA. My matter hath no voice, lady, but to your own most pregnant and vouchsafed ear.

SIR ANDREW. "Odours," "pregnant," and "vouchsafed"; I'll get 'em all three all ready.

OLIVIA. Let the garden door be shut, and leave me to hearing.

[*Exeunt all but* OLIVIA *and* VIOLA.]

Give me your hand, sir.
VIOLA. My duty, madam, and most humble service.
OLIVIA. What is your name?
VIOLA. Cesario is your servant's name, fair princess.
OLIVIA. My servant, sir! 'Twas never merry world
Since lowly feigning was call'd compliment.
You're servant to the Count Orsino, youth.
VIOLA. And he is yours, and his must needs be yours.
Your servant's servant is your servant, madam.
OLIVIA. For him, I think not on him. For his thoughts,
Would they were blanks, rather than fill'd with me!
VIOLA. Madam, I come to whet your gentle thoughts
On his behalf.
OLIVIA. O, by your leave, I pray you,
I bade you never speak again of him;
But, would you undertake another suit,
I had rather hear you to solicit that
Than music from the spheres.
VIOLA. Dear lady, —
OLIVIA. Give me leave, beseech you. I did send,
After the last enchantment you did here,
A ring in chase of you; so did I abuse
Myself, my servant, and, I fear me, you.
Under your hard construction must I sit,
To force that on you, in a shameful cunning,
Which you knew none of yours. What might you think?
Have you not set mine honour at the stake
And baited it with all th' unmuzzled thoughts
That tyrannous heart can think? To one of your receiving
Enough is shown. A cypress, not a bosom,
Hides my heart. So, let me hear you speak.
VIOLA. I pity you.
OLIVIA. That's a degree to love.

75. **pregnant:** ready. 102. **to force:** for forcing. 104–105. **Have . . . thoughts.** The figure of speech comes from bear-baiting. 106. **receiving:** intelligence. 107. **cypress:** thin crepe. 109. **degree:** step.

VIOLA. No, not a grize; for 'tis a vulgar proof,
That very oft we pity enemies.
OLIVIA. Why, then, methinks 'tis time to smile again.
O world, how apt the poor are to be proud!
If one should be a prey, how much the better
To fall before the lion than the wolf!

[*Clock strikes.*

The clock upbraids me with the waste of time.
Be not afraid, good youth, I will not have you;
And yet, when wit and youth is come to harvest,
Your wife is like to reap a proper man.
There lies your way, due west.
VIOLA. Then westward-ho! Grace and good disposition
Attend your ladyship!
You'll nothing, madam, to my lord by me?
OLIVIA. Stay!
I prithee, tell me what thou think'st of me.
VIOLA. That you do think you are not what you are.
OLIVIA. If I think so, I think the same of you.
VIOLA. Then think you right. I am not what I am.
OLIVIA. I would you were as I would have you be!
VIOLA. Would it be better, madam, than I am?
I wish it might, for now I am your fool.
OLIVIA. O, what a deal of scorn looks beautiful
In the contempt and anger of his lip!
A murd'rous guilt shows not itself more soon
Than love that would seem hid. Love's night is noon.
Cesario, by the roses of the spring,
By maidhood, honour, truth, and everything,
I love thee so, that, maugre all thy pride,
Nor wit nor reason can my passion hide.
Do not extort thy reasons from this clause,
For that I woo, thou therefore hast no cause;
But rather reason thus with reason fetter,
Love sought is good, but given unsought is better.
VIOLA. By innocence I swear, and by my youth,
I have one heart, one bosom, and one truth,
And that no woman has; nor never none
Shall mistress be of it, save I alone.
And so adieu, good madam; nevermore
Will I my master's tears to you deplore.

110. **grize:** step. **vulgar proof:** common experience. 138. **maugre:** in spite of. 141. **no cause:** *i.e.*, to woo.

OLIVIA. Yet come again; for thou perhaps mayst move
That heart, which now abhors, to like his love.

[*Exeunt.*

SCENE 2. [*A room in* OLIVIA'S *house.*]

Enter SIR TOBY, SIR ANDREW, *and* FABIAN.

SIR ANDREW. No, faith, I'll not stay a jot longer.

SIR TOBY. Thy reason, dear venom, give thy reason.

FABIAN. You must needs yield your reason, Sir Andrew.

SIR ANDREW. Marry, I saw your niece do more favours to the Count's serving-man than ever she bestow'd upon me. I saw't i' th' orchard.

SIR TOBY. Did she see thee the while, old boy? Tell me that.

SIR ANDREW. As plain as I see you now.

FABIAN. This was a great argument of love in her toward you.

SIR ANDREW. 'Slight, will you make an ass o' me?

FABIAN. I will prove it legitimate, sir, upon the oaths of judgement and reason.

SIR TOBY. And they have been grand-jurymen since before Noah was a sailor.

FABIAN. She did show favour to the youth in your sight only to exasperate you, to awake your dormouse valour, to put fire in your heart, and brimstone in your liver. You should then have accosted her; and with some excellent jests, fire-new from the mint, you should have bang'd the youth into dumbness. This was look'd for at your hand, and this was balk'd. The double gilt of this opportunity you let time wash off, and you are now sailed into the north of my lady's opinion, where you will hang like an icicle on a Dutchman's beard, unless you do redeem it by some laudable attempt either of valour or policy.

SIR ANDREW. An't be any way, it must be with valour; for policy I hate. I had as lief be a Brownist as a politician.

SIR TOBY. Why, then, build me thy fortunes upon the basis of valour. Challenge me the Count's youth to fight with him; hurt him in eleven places; my niece shall take note of it; and assure thyself, there is no love-broker in the world can more prevail in man's commendation with woman than report of valour.

FABIAN. There is no way but this, Sir Andrew.

SIR ANDREW. Will either of you bear me a challenge to him?

SIR TOBY. Go, write it in a martial hand. Be curst and brief. It is no matter how witty, so it be eloquent and full of invention. Taunt him with the license of ink. If thou thou'st him some thrice, it shall not be amiss; and as many lies as will lie in thy sheet of paper, although the sheet were

Scene ii, 9. **'Slight:** by God's light. 23. **policy:** tact (Sir Andrew interprets as *intrigue*). 24. **Brownist:** member of the sect of Independents, founded by Robert Brown. 32. **curst:** surly. 34. **thou'st:** use "thou" as to an inferior.

big enough for the bed of Ware in England, set 'em down. Go about it. Let there be gall enough in thy ink. Though thou write with a goose-pen, no matter. About it.

SIR ANDREW. Where shall I find you?

SIR TOBY. We'll call thee at the cubiculo. Go.

[*Exit* SIR ANDREW.

FABIAN. This is a dear manikin to you, Sir Toby.

SIR TOBY. I have been dear to him, lad, some two thousand strong, or so.

FABIAN. We shall have a rare letter from him. But you'll not deliver't?

SIR TOBY. Never trust me, then; and by all means stir on the youth to an answer. I think oxen and wainropes cannot hale them together. For Andrew, if he were open'd and you find so much blood in his liver as will clog the foot of a flea, I'll eat the rest of the anatomy.

FABIAN. And his opposite, the youth, bears in his visage no great presage of cruelty.

Enter MARIA.

SIR TOBY. Look, where the youngest wren of mine comes.

MARIA. If you desire the spleen, and will laugh yourselves into stitches, follow me. Yond gull Malvolio is turned heathen, a very renegado; for there is no Christian that means to be saved by believing rightly can ever believe such impossible passages of grossness. He's in yellow stockings.

SIR TOBY. And cross-garter'd?

MARIA. Most villanously; like a pedant that keeps a school i' th' church. I have dogg'd him like his murderer. He does obey every point of the letter that I dropp'd to betray him. He does smile his face into more lines than is in the new map with the augmentation of the Indies. You have not seen such a thing as 'tis. I can hardly forbear hurling things at him. I know my lady will strike him. If she do, he'll smile and take't for a great favour.

SIR TOBY. Come, bring us, bring us where he is.

[*Exeunt.*

36. **bed of Ware:** a famous bed (nearly twelve feet square) in an inn at Ware in Hertfordshire. 40. **cubiculo:** *i.e.,* Sir Andrew's apartment. 46. **wainropes:** cart-ropes. 49. **opposite:** opponent. 51. **mine** Ff. *nine* (Theobald). 52. **spleen:** fit of laughter. 55. **impossible . . . grossness:** incredible acts of stupidity. 60. **new . . . Indies.** Probably a map published about 1599 by Emerie Molyneux, giving more of the East Indies than any earlier one.

Scene 3. [*A street.*]

Enter SEBASTIAN *and* ANTONIO.

SEBASTIAN. I would not by my will have troubled you;
But, since you make your pleasure of your pains,
I will no further chide you.
ANTONIO. I could not stay behind you. My desire,
More sharp than filed steel, did spur me forth,
And not all love to see you, though so much
As might have drawn one to a longer voyage,
But jealousy what might befall your travel,
Being skilless in these parts; which to a stranger,
Unguided and unfriended, often prove
Rough and unhospitable. My willing love,
The rather by these arguments of fear,
Set forth in your pursuit.
SEBASTIAN. My kind Antonio,
I can no other answer make but thanks,
And thanks, and ever [thanks. Too] oft good turns
Are shuffl'd off with such uncurrent pay;
But, were my worth as is my conscience firm,
You should find better dealing. What's to do?
Shall we go see the reliques of this town?
ANTONIO. To-morrow, sir. Best first go see your lodging.
SEBASTIAN. I am not weary, and 'tis long to night.
I pray you, let us satisfy our eyes
With the memorials and the things of fame
That do renown this city.
ANTONIO. Would you'd pardon me.
I do not without danger walk these streets.
Once, in a sea-fight, 'gainst the Count his galleys
I did some service; of such note indeed,
That were I ta'en here it would scarce be answer'd.
SEBASTIAN. Belike you slew great number of his people?
ANTONIO. Th' offence is not of such a bloody nature,
Albeit the quality of the time and quarrel
Might well have given us bloody argument.
It might have since been answer'd in repaying
What we took from them, which, for traffic's sake,
Most of our city did; only myself stood out,
For which, if I be lapsed in this place,
I shall pay dear.

Scene iii, 8. **jealousy:** suspicion. 9. **skilless:** unacquainted. 15. **And thanks . . . oft** (Seymour). *And thankes; and ever oft* F. 16. **uncurrent:** worthless. 17. **worth:** wealth. 28. **answer'd:** atoned for. 31. **quality:** nature. 36. **lapsed:** caught.

SEBASTIAN. Do not then walk too open.
ANTONIO. It doth not fit me. Hold, sir, here's my purse.
In the south suburbs, at the Elephant
Is best to lodge. I will bespeak our diet,
Whiles you beguile the time and feed your knowledge
With viewing of the town. There shall you have me.
SEBASTIAN. Why I your purse?
ANTONIO. Haply your eye shall light upon some toy
You have desire to purchase; and your store,
I think, is not for idle markets, sir.
SEBASTIAN. I'll be your purse-bearer and leave you
For an hour.
ANTONIO. To th' Elephant.
SEBASTIAN. I do remember.

[*Exeunt.*

SCENE 4. [OLIVIA'S *garden.*]

Enter OLIVIA *and* MARIA.

OLIVIA [*aside*]. I have sent after him; he says he'll come.
How shall I feast him? What bestow of him?
For youth is bought more oft than begg'd or borrow'd.
I speak too loud. —
Where is Malvolio? He is sad and civil,
And suits well for a servant with my fortunes.
Where is Malvolio?

MARIA. He's coming, madam, but in very strange manner. He is, sure, possess'd, madam.

OLIVIA. Why, what's the matter? Does he rave?

MARIA. No, madam, he does nothing but smile. Your ladyship were best to have some guard about you, if he come; for, sure, the man is tainted in's wits.

OLIVIA. Go call him hither.

Enter MALVOLIO.

I am as mad as he,
If sad and merry madness equal be.
How now, Malvolio!
MALVOLIO. Sweet lady, ho, ho.
OLIVIA. Smil'st thou?
I sent for thee upon a sad occasion.

MALVOLIO. Sad, lady? I could be sad. This does make some obstruc-

46. **idle markets:** frivolous purchases.
Scene iv, 5. sad: grave.

tion in the blood, this cross-gartering; but what of that? If it please the eye of one, it is with me as the very true sonnet is, "Please one, and please all."

[OLIVIA]. Why, how dost thou, man? What is the matter with thee?

MALVOLIO. Not black in my mind, though yellow in my legs. It did come to his hands, and commands shall be executed. I think we do know the sweet Roman hand.

OLIVIA. Wilt thou go to bed, Malvolio?

MALVOLIO. To bed! Ay, sweet heart, and I'll come to thee.

OLIVIA. God comfort thee! Why dost thou smile so and kiss thy hand so oft?

MARIA. How do you, Malvolio?

MALVOLIO. At your request! Yes. Nightingales answer daws.

MARIA. Why appear you with this ridiculous boldness before my lady?

MALVOLIO. "Be not afraid of greatness:" 'twas well writ.

OLIVIA. What mean'st thou by that, Malvolio?

MALVOLIO. "Some are born great," —

OLIVIA. Ha!

MALVOLIO. "Some achieve greatness," —

OLIVIA. What say'st thou?

MALVOLIO. "And some have greatness thrust upon them."

OLIVIA. Heaven restore thee!

MALVOLIO. "Remember who commended thy yellow stockings," —

OLIVIA. Thy yellow stockings!

MALVOLIO. "And wish'd to see thee cross-garter'd."

OLIVIA. Cross-garter'd!

MALVOLIO. "Go to, thou art made, if thou desir'st to be so;" —

OLIVIA. Am I made?

MALVOLIO. "If not, let me see thee a servant still."

OLIVIA. Why, this is very midsummer madness.

Enter SERVANT.

SERVANT. Madam, the young gentleman of the Count Orsino's is return'd. I could hardly entreat him back. He attends your ladyship's pleasure.

OLIVIA. I'll come to him.

[*Exit* SERVANT.]

Good Maria, let this fellow be look'd to. Where's my cousin Toby? Let some of my people have a special care of him. I would not have him miscarry for the half of my dowry.

[*Exeunt* [OLIVIA *and* MARIA].

22. **sonnet:** ballad, of which the quotation is the refrain. 24. [OLIVIA] F_2. *Malvolio* F_1. 56–57. **miscarry:** suffer harm.

MALVOLIO. O, ho! do you come near me now? No worse man than Sir Toby to look to me! This concurs directly with the letter. She sends him on purpose, that I may appear stubborn to him, for she incites me to that in the letter. "Cast thy humble slough," says she; "be opposite with a kinsman, surly with servants; let thy tongue tang with arguments of state; put thyself into the trick of singularity;" and consequently sets down the manner how; as, a sad face, a reverend carriage, a slow tongue, in the habit of some sir of note, and so forth. I have lim'd her; but it is Jove's doing, and Jove make me thankful! And when she went away now, "Let this fellow be looked to"; "fellow!" not Malvolio, nor after my degree, but "fellow." Why, everything adheres together, that no dram of a scruple, no scruple of a scruple, no obstacle, no incredulous or unsafe circumstance — What can be said? Nothing that can be can come between me and the full prospect of my hopes. Well, Jove, not I, is the doer of this, and he is to be thanked.

Re-enter MARIA, *with* SIR TOBY *and* FABIAN.

SIR TOBY. Which way is he, in the name of sanctity? If all the devils of hell be drawn in little, and Legion himself possess'd him, yet I'll speak to him.

FABIAN. Here he is, here he is. How is't with you, sir? How is't with you, man?

MALVOLIO. Go off; I discard you. Let me enjoy my private. Go off.

MARIA. Lo, how hollow the fiend speaks within him! Did not I tell you? Sir Toby, my lady prays you to have a care of him.

MALVOLIO. Ah, ha! Does she so?

SIR TOBY. Go to, go to; peace, peace. We must deal gently with him. Let me alone. How do you, Malvolio? How is't with you? What, man, defy the devil! Consider, he's an enemy to mankind.

MALVOLIO. Do you know what you say?

MARIA. La you, an you speak ill of the devil, how he takes it at heart! Pray God he be not bewitch'd!

FABIAN. Carry his water to the wise woman.

MARIA. Marry, and it shall be done to-morrow morning if I live. My lady would not lose him for more than I'll say.

MALVOLIO. How now, mistress!

MARIA. O Lord!

SIR TOBY. Prithee, hold thy peace; this is not the way. Do you not see you move him? Let me alone with him.

FABIAN. No way but gentleness; gently, gently. The fiend is rough, and will not be roughly us'd.

SIR TOBY. Why, how now, my bawcock! How dost thou, chuck?

58. **come near:** begin to understand. 63. **consequently:** thereupon. 65. **lim'd:** caught. 67. **fellow:** originally *companion*, and so taken by Malvolio. 69. **incredulous:** incredible. 74. **little:** miniature. **Legion.** See *Mark* v.9. 95. **rough:** violent. 97. **bawcock:** fine fellow.

MALVOLIO. Sir!

SIR TOBY Ay, "Biddy, come with me." What, man, 'tis not for gravity to play at cherry-pit with Satan. Hang him, foul collier!

MARIA. Get him to say his prayers, good Sir Toby, get him to pray.

MALVOLIO. My prayers, minx!

MARIA. No, I warrant you, he will not hear of godliness.

MALVOLIO. Go, hang yourselves all! You are idle shallow things; I am not of your element. You shall know more hereafter. [*Exit.*

SIR TOBY. Is't possible?

FABIAN. If this were played upon a stage now, I could condemn it as an improbable fiction.

SIR TOBY. His very genius hath taken the infection of the device, man.

MARIA. Nay, pursue him now, lest the device take air and taint.

FABIAN. Why, we shall make him mad indeed.

MARIA. The house will be the quieter.

SIR TOBY. Come, we'll have him in a dark room and bound. My niece is already in the belief that he's mad. We may carry it thus, for our pleasure and his penance, till our very pastime, tired out of breath, prompt us to have mercy on him; at which time we will bring the device to the bar and crown thee for a finder of madmen. But see, but see.

Enter SIR ANDREW.

FABIAN. More matter for a May morning.

SIR ANDREW. Here's the challenge, read it. I warrant there's vinegar and pepper in't.

FABIAN. Is't so saucy?

SIR ANDREW. Ay, is't, I warrant him. Do but read.

SIR TOBY. Give me. [*Reads.*] "Youth, whatsoever thou art, thou art but a scurvy fellow."

FABIAN. Good, and valiant.

SIR TOBY [*reads*]. "Wonder not, nor admire not in thy mind, why I do call thee so, for I will show thee no reason for't."

FABIAN. A good note. That keeps you from the blow of the law.

SIR TOBY [*reads*]. "Thou com'st to the lady Olivia, and in my sight she uses thee kindly. But thou liest in thy throat; that is not the matter I challenge thee for."

FABIAN. Very brief, and to exceeding good sense — less.

SIR TOBY [*reads*]. "I will waylay thee going home; where if it be thy chance to kill me," —

FABIAN. Good.

SIR TOBY [*reads*]. "Thou kill'st me like a rogue and a villain."

FABIAN. Still you keep o' th' windy side of the law; good.

100. **cherry-pit:** child's game of throwing cherry stones into a hole. 105. **element:** sphere. 110. **take . . . taint:** become known and spoiled. 126. **admire:** be amazed. 128. **note:** point. 137. **windy:** safe.

SIR TOBY [*reads*]. "Fare thee well, and God have mercy upon one of our souls! He may have mercy upon mine; but my hope is better, and so look to thyself. Thy friend, as thou usest him, and thy sworn enemy,

ANDREW AGUECHEEK."

If this letter move him not, his legs cannot. I'll give't him.

MARIA. You may have very fit occasion for't. He is now in some commerce with my lady, and will by and by depart.

SIR TOBY. Go, Sir Andrew, scout me for him at the corner of the orchard like a bum-baily. So soon as ever thou seest him, draw; and, as thou draw'st, swear horrible; for it comes to pass oft that a terrible oath, with a swaggering accent sharply twang'd off, gives manhood more approbation than ever proof itself would have earn'd him. Away!

SIR ANDREW. Nay, let me alone for swearing. [*Exit.*

SIR TOBY. Now will not I deliver his letter; for the behaviour of the young gentleman gives him out to be of good capacity and breeding; his employment between his lord and my niece confirms no less; therefore this letter, being so excellently ignorant, will breed no terror in the youth; he will find it comes from a clodpole. But, sir, I will deliver his challenge by word of mouth, set upon Aguecheek a notable report of valour, and drive the gentleman, as I know his youth will aptly receive it, into a most hideous opinion of his rage, skill, fury, and impetuosity. This will so fright them both that they will kill one another by the look, like cockatrices.

Re-enter OLIVIA *with* VIOLA.

FABIAN. Here he comes with your niece. Give them way till he take leave, and presently after him.

SIR TOBY. I will meditate the while upon some horrid message for a challenge.

[*Exeunt* SIR TOBY, FABIAN, *and* MARIA.]

OLIVIA. I have said too much unto a heart of stone,
And laid mine honour too unchary on't.
There's something in me that reproves my fault;
But such a headstrong potent fault it is
That it but mocks reproof.

VIOLA. With the same 'haviour that your passion bears
Goes on my master's grief.

OLIVIA. Here, wear this jewel for me; 'tis my picture.
Refuse it not; it hath no tongue to vex you;
And I beseech you come again to-morrow.

146. **bum-baily:** petty sheriff's officer (who arrested debtors). 148–149. **approbation:** credit. 149. **proof:** trial. 159–160. **cockatrices:** basilisks, fabulous creatures suppose to kill by a mere look. 162. **presently:** immediately. 166. **on't** Ff. *out* (Theobald).

What shall you ask of me that I'll deny,
That honour sav'd may upon asking give?

VIOLA. Nothing but this, — your true love for my master.

OLIVIA. How with mine honour may I give him that
Which I have given to you?

VIOLA. I will acquit you.

OLIVIA. Well, come again to-morrow. Fare thee well!
A fiend like thee might bear my soul to hell. [*Exit.*]

Re-enter SIR TOBY *and* FABIAN.

SIR TOBY. Gentleman, God save thee!

VIOLA. And you, sir.

SIR TOBY. That defence thou hast, betake thee to't. Of what nature the wrongs are thou hast done him, I know not; but thy intercepter, full of despite, bloody as the hunter, attends thee at the orchard-end. Dismount thy tuck, be yare in thy preparation, for thy assailant is quick, skilful, and deadly.

VIOLA. You mistake, sir, I am sure. No man hath any quarrel to me. My remembrance is very free and clear from any image of offence done to any man.

SIR TOBY. You'll find it otherwise, I assure you; therefore, if you hold your life at any price, betake you to your guard; for your opposite hath in him what youth, strength, skill, and wrath can furnish man withal.

VIOLA. I pray you, sir, what is he?

SIR TOBY. He is knight, dubb'd with unhatch'd rapier and on carpet consideration; but he is a devil in private brawl. Souls and bodies hath he divorc'd three; and his incensement at this moment is so implacable, that satisfaction can be none but by pangs of death and sepulchre. Hob, nob, is his word; give't or take't.

VIOLA. I will return again into the house and desire some conduct of the lady. I am no fighter. I have heard of some kind of men that put quarrels purposely on others, to taste their valour. Belike this is a man of that quirk.

SIR TOBY. Sir, no; his indignation derives itself out of a very competent injury; therefore, get you on and give him his desire. Back you shall not to the house, unless you undertake that with me which with as much safety you might answer him; therefore, on, or strip your sword stark naked; for meddle you must, that's certain, or forswear to wear iron about you.

VIOLA. This is as uncivil as strange. I beseech you, do me this courteous office, as to know of the knight what my offence to him is. It is something of my negligence, nothing of my purpose.

186–187. **Dismount thy tuck:** draw thy sword. 187. **yare:** quick. 196. **unhatch'd:** unhacked. 196–197. **carpet consideration.** A "carpet knight" was one who had been dubbed not on the battlefield for valor, but on a carpet for money paid to the king. 201. **conduct:** escort. 204. **quirk:** humor. 209. **meddle:** fight.

SIR TOBY. I will do so. Signor Fabian, stay you by this gentleman till my return. [*Exit.*

VIOLA. Pray you, sir, do you know of this matter?

FABIAN. I know the knight is incens'd against you, even to a mortal arbitrement, but nothing of the circumstance more.

VIOLA. I beseech you, what manner of man is he?

FABIAN. Nothing of that wonderful promise, to read him by his form, as you are like to find him in the proof of his valour. He is, indeed, sir, the most skilful, bloody, and fatal opposite that you could possibly have found in any part of Illyria. Will you walk towards him? I will make your peace with him if I can.

VIOLA. I shall be much bound to you for't. I am one that had rather go with sir priest than sir knight. I care not who knows so much of my mettle.

[*Exeunt. Re-enter* SIR TOBY, *with* SIR ANDREW.

SIR TOBY. Why, man, he's a very devil; I have not seen such a firago. I had a pass with him, rapier, scabbard, and all, and he gives me the stuck in with such a mortal motion, that it is inevitable; and on the answer, he pays you as surely as your feet hits the ground they step on. They say he has been fencer to the Sophy.

SIR ANDREW. Pox on't, I'll not meddle with him.

SIR TOBY. Ay, but he will not now be pacified. Fabian can scarce hold him yonder.

SIR ANDREW. Plague on't, an I thought he had been valiant and so cunning in fence, I'd have seen him damn'd ere I'd have challeng'd him. Let him let the matter slip, and I'll give him my horse, grey Capilet.

SIR TOBY. I'll make the motion. Stand here; make a good show on't. This shall end without the perdition of souls. [*Aside.*] Marry, I'll ride your horse as well as I ride you.

Re-enter FABIAN *and* VIOLA.

[*To* FABIAN.] I have his horse to take up the quarrel. I have persuaded him the youth's a devil.

FABIAN. He is as horribly conceited of him; and pants and looks pale, as if a bear were at his heels.

SIR TOBY [*to* VIOLA]. There's no remedy, sir; he will fight with you for's oath sake. Marry, he hath better bethought him of his quarrel, and he finds that now scarce to be worth talking of; therefore draw, for the supportance of his vow. He protests he will not hurt you.

VIOLA [*aside*]. Pray God defend me! A little thing would make me tell them how much I lack of a man.

FABIAN. Give ground, if you see him furious.

218. **arbitrement:** trial. 228. **firago:** virago. 229–230. **stuck in:** thrust. 230. **on the answer:** on the return. 231. **pays you:** does for you. 242. **take up:** settle. 244. **is . . . conceited:** has as horrible a conception.

SIR TOBY. Come, Sir Andrew, there's no remedy; the gentleman will, for his honour's sake, have one bout with you. He cannot by the duello avoid it; but he has promised me, as he is a gentleman and a soldier, he will not hurt you. Come on; to't.

SIR ANDREW. Pray God, he keep his oath!

Enter ANTONIO.

VIOLA. I do assure you, 'tis against my will.

[*They draw.*

ANTONIO. Put up your sword. If this young gentleman
Have done offence, I take the fault on me;
If you offend him, I for him defy you.

SIR TOBY. You, sir! Why, what are you?

ANTONIO. One, sir, that for his love dares yet do more
Than you have heard him brag to you he will.

SIR TOBY. Nay, if you be an undertaker, I am for you.

[*They draw. Enter Officers.*

FABIAN. O good Sir Toby, hold! Here come the officers.

SIR TOBY. I'll be with you anon.

VIOLA. Pray, sir, put your sword up, if you please.

SIR ANDREW. Marry, will I, sir; and, for that I promis'd you, I'll be as good as my word. He will bear you easily and reins well.

FIRST OFFICER. This is the man; do thy office.

SECOND OFFICER. Antonio, I arrest thee at the suit of Count Orsino.

ANTONIO. You do mistake me, sir.

FIRST OFFICER. No, sir, no jot. I know your favour well,
Though now you have no sea-cap on your head.
Take him away; he knows I know him well.

ANTONIO. I must obey. [*To* VIOLA.] This comes with seeking you.
But there's no remedy; I shall answer it.
What will you do, now my necessity
Makes me to ask you for my purse? It grieves me
Much more for what I cannot do for you
Than what befalls myself. You stand amaz'd,
But be of comfort.

SECOND OFFICER. Come, sir, away.

ANTONIO. I must entreat of you some of that money.

VIOLA. What money, sir?
For the fair kindness you have show'd me here,
And, part, being prompted by your present trouble,
Out of my lean and low ability

254. **duello**: code of duelling. 265. **undertaker**: meddler.

I'll lend you something. My having is not much.
I'll make division of my present with you.
Hold, there's half my coffer.

ANTONIO. Will you deny me now?
Is't possible that my deserts to you
Can lack persuasion? Do not tempt my misery,
Lest that it make me so unsound a man
As to upbraid you with those kindnesses
That I have done for you.

VIOLA. I know of none,
Nor know I you by voice or any feature.
I hate ingratitude more in a man
Than lying, vainness, babbling, drunkenness,
Or any taint of vice whose strong corruption
Inhabits our frail blood.

ANTONIO. O heavens themselves!

SECOND OFFICER. Come, sir, I pray you, go.

ANTONIO. Let me speak a little. This youth that you see here
I snatch'd one half out of the jaws of death,
Reliev'd him with such sanctity of love,
And to his image, which methought did promise
Most venerable worth, did I devotion.

FIRST OFFICER. What's that to us? The time goes by; away!

ANTONIO. But, O, how vile an idol proves this god!
Thou hast, Sebastian, done good feature shame.
In nature there's no blemish but the mind;
None can be call'd deform'd but the unkind.
Virtue is beauty, but the beauteous evil
Are empty trunks o'erflourish'd by the devil.

FIRST OFFICER. The man grows mad; away with him!
Come, come, sir.

ANTONIO. Lead me on. [*Exit* [*with Officers*].

VIOLA. Methinks his words do from such passion fly
That he believes himself; so do not I.
Prove true, imagination, O, prove true,
That I, dear brother, be now ta'en for you!

SIR TOBY. Come hither, knight; come hither, Fabian; we'll whisper o'er a couplet or two of most sage saws.

VIOLA. He nam'd Sebastian. I my brother know
Yet living in my glass; even such and so
In favour was my brother, and he went
Still in this fashion, colour, ornament,
For him I imitate. O, if it prove,
Tempests are kind and salt waves fresh in love. [*Exit.*]

291. **present:** present means. 313. **unkind:** unnatural. 315. **o'erflourish'd:** ornamented. 325–326. **I . . . glass:** I know I look like my brother. 329. **prove:** *i.e.*, prove true.

SIR TOBY. A very dishonest paltry boy, and more a coward than a hare. His dishonesty appears in leaving his friend here in necessity and denying him; and, for his cowardship, ask Fabian.

FABIAN. A coward, a most devout coward, religious in it.

SIR ANDREW. 'Slid, I'll after him again and beat him.

SIR TOBY. Do; cuff him soundly, but never draw thy sword.

SIR ANDREW. An I do not, —

FABIAN. Come, let's see the event.

SIR TOBY. I dare lay any money 'twill be nothing yet.

[*Exeunt.*

ACT FOUR

Scene 1. [*Before* OLIVIA'*s house.*]

Enter SEBASTIAN *and* CLOWN.

CLOWN. Will you make me believe that I am not sent for you?

SEBASTIAN. Go to, go to, thou art a foolish fellow; let me be clear of thee.

CLOWN. Well held out, i' faith! No, I do not know you; nor I am not sent to you by my lady, to bid you come speak with her; nor your name is not Master Cesario; nor this is not my nose neither. Nothing that is so is so.

SEBASTIAN. I prithee, vent thy folly somewhere else. Thou know'st not me.

CLOWN. Vent my folly! He has heard that word of some great man and now applies it to a fool. Vent my folly! I am afraid this great lubber, the world, will prove a cockney. I prithee now, ungird thy strangeness and tell me what I shall vent to my lady. Shall I vent to her that thou art coming?

SEBASTIAN. I prithee, foolish Greek, depart from me. There's money for thee. If you tarry longer, I shall give worse payment.

CLOWN. By my troth, thou hast an open hand. These wise men that give fools money get themselves a good report — after fourteen years' purchase.

Enter SIR ANDREW, SIR TOBY, *and* FABIAN.

SIR ANDREW. Now, sir, have I met you again? There's for you.

335. **'Slid:** by God's eyelid.

Act IV, Scene i, 12. cockney: fop. 15. **Greek:** jester. 18–19. **after . . . purchase:** *i.e.*, at a high price. The value of land was figured in terms of its annual rental.

SEBASTIAN. Why, there's for thee, and there, and there. Are all the people mad?

SIR TOBY. Hold, sir, or I'll throw your dagger o'er the house.

CLOWN. This will I tell my lady straight. I would not be in some of your coats for two pence. [*Exit.*]

SIR TOBY. Come on, sir. Hold!

SIR ANDREW. Nay, let him alone. I'll go another way to work with him. I'll have an action of battery against him, if there be any law in Illyria. Though I struck him first, yet it's no matter for that.

SEBASTIAN. Let go thy hand.

SIR TOBY. Come, sir, I will not let you go. Come, my young soldier, put up your iron; you are well flesh'd. Come on.

SEBASTIAN. I will be free from thee. What wouldst thou now?
If thou dar'st tempt me further, draw thy sword.

SIR TOBY. What, what? Nay, then I must have an ounce or two of this malapert blood from you.

Enter OLIVIA.

OLIVIA. Hold, Toby! On thy life I charge thee, hold!

SIR TOBY. Madam —

OLIVIA. Will it be ever thus? Ungracious wretch,
Fit for the mountains and the barbarous caves,
Where manners ne'er were preach'd! Out of my sight!
Be not offended, dear Cesario.
Rudesby, be gone!

[*Exeunt* SIR TOBY, SIR ANDREW, *and* FABIAN.]

I prithee, gentle friend,
Let thy fair wisdom, not thy passion, sway
In this uncivil and unjust extent
Against thy peace. Go with me to my house,
And hear thou there how many fruitless pranks
This ruffian hath botch'd up, that thou thereby
Mayst smile at this. Thou shalt not choose but go.
Do not deny. Beshrew his soul for me,
He started one poor heart of mine in thee.

SEBASTIAN. What relish is in this? How runs the stream?
Or I am mad, or else this is a dream.
Let fancy still my sense in Lethe steep.
If it be thus to dream, still let me sleep!

OLIVIA. Nay, come, I prithee. Would thou'dst be rul'd by me!

32. **flesh'd:** initiated in bloodshed. 36. **malapert:** saucy. 43. **Rudesby:** ruffian. 45. **extent:** attack. 48. **botch'd up:** crudely contrived. 51. **started:** roused. **heart:** with pun on *hart*. 52. **relish:** meaning. 54. **Lethe:** river of forgetfulness.

SEBASTIAN. Madam, I will.

OLIVIA. O, say so, and so be!

[*Exeunt.*

SCENE 2. [OLIVIA'S *house.*]

Enter MARIA *and* CLOWN.

MARIA. Nay, I prithee, put on this gown and this beard. Make him believe thou art Sir Topas the curate. Do it quickly; I'll call Sir Toby the whilst. [*Exit.*]

CLOWN. Well, I'll put it on, and I will dissemble myself in't; and I would I were the first that ever dissembled in such a gown. I am not tall enough to become the function well, nor lean enough to be thought a good student; but to be said an honest man and a good housekeeper goes as fairly as to say a careful man and a great scholar. The competitors enter.

Enter SIR TOBY [*and* MARIA].

SIR TOBY. Jove bless thee, master Parson.

CLOWN. *Bonos dies*, Sir Toby: for, as the old hermit of Prague, that never saw pen and ink, very wittily said to a niece of King Gorboduc, "That that is is"; so I, being master Parson, am master Parson; for, what is "that" but "that," and "is" but "is"?

SIR TOBY. To him, Sir Topas.

CLOWN. What, ho, I say! Peace in this prison!

SIR TOBY. The knave counterfeits well; a good knave.

MALVOLIO (*within*). Who calls there?

CLOWN. Sir Topas the curate, who comes to visit Malvolio the lunatic.

MALVOLIO. Sir Topas, Sir Topas, good Sir Topas, go to my lady.

CLOWN. Out, hyperbolical fiend! How vexest thou this man! Talkest thou nothing but of ladies?

SIR TOBY. Well said, master Parson.

MALVOLIO. Sir Topas, never was man thus wronged. Good Sir Topas, do not think I am mad. They have laid me here in hideous darkness.

CLOWN. Fie, thou dishonest Satan! I call thee by the most modest terms, for I am one of those gentle ones that will use the devil himself with courtesy. Say'st thou that house is dark?

MALVOLIO. As hell, Sir Topas.

CLOWN. Why, it hath bay windows transparent as barricadoes, and the clerestories toward the south north are as lustrous as ebony; and yet complainest thou of obstruction?

MALVOLIO. I am not mad, Sir Topas. I say to you, this house is dark.

Scene ii, 7. housekeeper: host. 8. **competitors:** confederates. 10. **hermit of Prague.** Invented by Feste. 11. **Gorboduc:** mythical British king. 20. **hyperbolical:** extravagant. 30. **clerestories:** windows high up in the wall.

CLOWN. Madman, thou errest. I say, there is no darkness but ignorance, in which thou art more puzzl'd than the Egyptians in their fog.

MALVOLIO. I say, this house is dark as ignorance, though ignorance were as dark as hell; and I say, there was never man thus abus'd. I am no more mad than you are. Make the trial of it in any constant question.

CLOWN. What is the opinion of Pythagoras concerning wild fowl?

MALVOLIO. That the soul of our grandam might haply inhabit a bird.

CLOWN. What think'st thou of his opinion?

MALVOLIO. I think nobly of the soul, and no way approve his opinion.

CLOWN. Fare thee well. Remain thou still in darkness. Thou shalt hold th' opinion of Pythagoras ere I will allow of thy wits, and fear to kill a woodcock lest thou dispossess the soul of thy grandam. Fare thee well.

MALVOLIO. Sir Topas, Sir Topas!

SIR TOBY. My most exquisite Sir Topas!

CLOWN. Nay, I am for all waters.

MARIA. Thou mightst have done this without thy beard and gown. He sees thee not.

SIR TOBY. To him in thine own voice, and bring me word how thou find'st him. I would we were well rid of this knavery. If he may be conveniently deliver'd, I would he were, for I am now so far in offence with my niece that I cannot pursue with any safety this sport to the upshot. Come by and by to my chamber. [*Exit* [*with* MARIA].

CLOWN [*singing*]. "Hey, Robin, jolly Robin,
Tell me how thy lady does."

MALVOLIO. Fool!

CLOWN. "My lady is unkind, perdy."

MALVOLIO. Fool!

CLOWN. "Alas, why is she so?"

MALVOLIO. Fool, I say!

CLOWN. "She loves another" — Who calls, ha?

MALVOLIO. Good fool, as ever thou wilt deserve well at my hand, help me to a candle, and pen, ink, and paper. As I am a gentleman, I will live to be thankful to thee for't.

CLOWN. Master Malvolio?

MALVOLIO. Ay, good fool.

CLOWN. Alas, sir, how fell you besides your five wits?

MALVOLIO. Fool, there was never man so notoriously abus'd. I am as well in my wits, fool, as thou art.

CLOWN. But as well? Then you are mad indeed, if you be no better in your wits than a fool.

MALVOLIO. They have here propertied me, keep me in darkness, send ministers to me, asses, and do all they can to face me out of my wits.

34. **Egyptians . . . fog.** See *Exodus* x.21. 37. **constant:** logical, rational. 47. **I . . . waters:** I can assume any rôle. 68. **wits.** Five by analogy with the five senses; they were common wit, imagination, fantasy, estimation, and memory. 73. **propertied:** treated as a tool.

CLOWN. Advise you what you say; the minister is here. Malvolio, Malvolio, thy wits the heavens restore! Endeavour thyself to sleep, and leave thy vain bibble babble.

MALVOLIO. Sir Topas!

CLOWN. Maintain no words with him, good fellow. Who, I, sir? Not I, sir. God buy you, good Sir Topas. Marry, amen. I will, sir, I will.

MALVOLIO. Fool, fool, fool, I say!

CLOWN. Alas, sir, be patient. What say you, sir? I am shent for speaking to you.

MALVOLIO. Good fool, help me to some light and some paper. I tell thee, I am as well in my wits as any man in Illyria.

CLOWN. Well-a-day that you were, sir!

MALVOLIO. By this hand, I am. Good fool, some ink, paper, and light; and convey what I will set down to my lady. It shall advantage thee more than ever the bearing of letter did.

CLOWN. I will help you to't. But tell me true, are you not mad indeed, or do you but counterfeit?

MALVOLIO. Believe me, I am not. I tell thee true.

CLOWN. Nay, I'll ne'er believe a madman till I see his brains. I will fetch you light and paper and ink.

MALVOLIO. Fool, I'll requite it in the highest degree. I prithee, be gone.

CLOWN [*singing*].
I am gone, sir,
And anon, sir,
I'll be with you again,
In a trice,
Like to the old Vice,
Your need to sustain;

Who, with dagger of lath,
In his rage and his wrath,
Cries, ah, ha! to the devil,
Like a mad lad.
Pare thy nails, dad.
Adieu, goodman devil. [*Exit.*

SCENE 3. [OLIVIA'S *garden.*]

Enter SEBASTIAN.

SEBASTIAN. This is the air, that is the glorious sun,
This pearl she gave me, I do feel't and see't;
And though 'tis wonder that enwraps me thus,

75. **Advise you:** take care. From this point through l. 80 Feste alternates speaking as Sir Topas and in his own voice. 80. **buy:** be with. 82. **shent:** reproved. 101. **the old Vice,** the Fool of the Moralities and Interludes, carried a wooden dagger with which he would attempt to pare the Devil's nails.

Yet 'tis not madness. Where's Antonio, then?
I could not find him at the Elephant;
Yet there he was, and there I found this credit,
That he did range the town to seek me out.
His counsel now might do me golden service;
For though my soul disputes well with my sense,
That this may be some error, but no madness,
Yet doth this accident and flood of fortune
So far exceed all instance, all discourse,
That I am ready to distrust mine eyes
And wrangle with my reason that persuades me
To any other trust but that I am mad
Or else the lady's mad; yet, if 'twere so,
She could not sway her house, command her followers,
Take and give back affairs and their dispatch
With such a smooth, discreet, and stable bearing
As I perceive she does. There's something in't
That is deceivable. But here the lady comes.

Enter OLIVIA *and* PRIEST.

OLIVIA. Blame not this haste of mine. If you mean well,
Now go with me and with this holy man
Into the chantry by; there, before him,
And underneath that consecrated roof,
Plight me the full assurance of your faith,
That my most jealous and too doubtful soul
May live at peace. He shall conceal it
Whiles you are willing it shall come to note,
What time we will our celebration keep
According to my birth. What do you say?
SEBASTIAN. I'll follow this good man, and go with you;
And, having sworn truth, ever will be true.
OLIVIA. Then lead the way, good father; and heavens so shine
That they may fairly note this act of mine!

[*Exeunt.*

Scene iii, 6. **was:** had been. **credit:** belief. 12. **instance:** example, precedent. **discourse:** reason. 15. **trust:** belief. 18. **Take . . . dispatch:** undertake and discharge affairs. 21. **deceivable:** deceptive. 24. **chantry:** private chapel. 29. **Whiles:** until. 30. **What:** at which.

ACT FIVE

SCENE 1. [*Before* OLIVIA'S *house.*]

Enter CLOWN *and* FABIAN.

FABIAN. Now, as thou lov'st me, let me see his letter.

CLOWN. Good Master Fabian, grant me another request.

FABIAN. Anything.

CLOWN. Do not desire to see this letter.

FABIAN. This is to give a dog and in recompense desire my dog again.

Enter DUKE, VIOLA, CURIO, *and Lords.*

DUKE. Belong you to the Lady Olivia, friends?

CLOWN. Ay, sir! we are some of her trappings.

DUKE. I know thee well; how dost thou, my good fellow?

CLOWN. Truly, sir, the better for my foes and the worse for my friends.

DUKE. Just the contrary; the better for thy friends.

CLOWN. No, sir, the worse.

DUKE. How can that be?

CLOWN. Marry, sir, they praise me and make an ass of me. Now my foes tell me plainly I am an ass; so that by my foes, sir, I profit in the knowledge of myself, and by my friends I am abused; so that, conclusions to be as kisses, if your four negatives make your two affirmatives, why then, the worse for my friends and the better for my foes.

DUKE. Why, this is excellent.

CLOWN. By my troth, sir, no; though it please you to be one of my friends.

DUKE. Thou shalt not be the worse for me. There's gold.

CLOWN. But that it would be double-dealing, sir, I would you could make it another.

DUKE. O, you give me ill counsel.

CLOWN. Put your grace in your pocket, sir, for this once, and let your flesh and blood obey it.

DUKE. Well, I will be so much a sinner, to be a double-dealer. There's another.

CLOWN. Primo, secundo, tertio, is a good play; and the old saying is, the third pays for all. The triplex, sir, is a good tripping measure; or the bells of Saint Bennet, sir, may put you in mind; one, two, three.

DUKE. You can fool no more money out of me at this throw. If you will let your lady know I am here to speak with her, and bring her along with you, it may awake my bounty further.

Act V, Scene i, 1. **his:** Malvolio's. 15. **abused:** deceived. 29. **Primo . . . tertio:** possibly alluding to throws at dice. 30. **triplex:** triple time in music. 31. **Saint Bennet:** the church of St. Benedict in London.

CLOWN. Marry, sir, lullaby to your bounty till I come again. I go, sir, but I would not have you to think that my desire of having is the sin of covetousness; but, as you say, sir, let your bounty take a nap, I will awake it anon. [*Exit.*

Enter ANTONIO *and Officers.*

VIOLA. Here comes the man, sir, that did rescue me.
DUKE. That face of his I do remember well,
Yet, when I saw it last, it was besmear'd
As black as Vulcan in the smoke of war.
A bawbling vessel was he captain of,
For shallow draught and bulk unprizable,
With which such scatheful grapple did he make
With the most noble bottom of our fleet,
That very envy and the tongue of loss
Cri'd fame and honour on him. What's the matter?
FIRST OFFICER. Orsino, this is that Antonio
That took the *Phoenix* and her fraught from Candy,
And this is he that did the *Tiger* board,
When your young nephew Titus lost his leg.
Here in the streets, desperate of shame and state,
In private brabble did we apprehend him.
VIOLA. He did me kindness, sir, drew on my side,
But in conclusion put strange speech upon me.
I know not what 'twas but distraction.
DUKE. Notable pirate! Thou salt-water thief!
What foolish boldness brought thee to their mercies
Whom thou, in terms so bloody and so dear,
Hast made thine enemies?
ANTONIO. Orsino, noble sir,
Be pleas'd that I shake off these names you give me.
Antonio never yet was thief or pirate,
Though I confess, on base and ground enough,
Orsino's enemy. A witchcraft drew me hither.
That most ingrateful boy there by your side,
From the rude sea's enrag'd and foamy mouth
Did I redeem. A wreck past hope he was.
His life I gave him, and did thereto add
My love, without retention or restraint,
All his in dedication. For his sake
Did I expose myself, pure for his love,
Into the danger of this adverse town;
Drew to defend him when he was beset;

43. **bawbling:** trifling. 44. **unprizable:** worthless. 45. **scatheful:** damaging. 50. **Candy:** Candia, Crete. 54. **brabble:** brawl. 57. **distraction:** madness. 60. **dear:** dangerous.

Where being apprehended, his false cunning,
Not meaning to partake with me in danger,
Taught him to face me out of his acquaintance,
And grew a twenty years removed thing
While one would wink; deni'd me mine own purse,
Which I had recommended to his use
Not half an hour before.

VIOLA. How can this be?

DUKE. When came he to this town?

ANTONIO. To-day, my lord; and for three months before,
No int'rim, not a minute's vacancy,
Both day and night did we keep company.

Enter OLIVIA *and Attendants.*

DUKE. Here comes the countess; now heaven walks on earth.
But for thee, fellow; fellow, thy words are madness.
Three months this youth hath tended upon me;
But more of that anon. Take him aside.

OLIVIA. What would my lord, but that he may not have,
Wherein Olivia may seem serviceable?
Cesario, you do not keep promise with me.

VIOLA. Madam!

DUKE. Gracious Olivia, —

OLIVIA. What do you say, Cesario? Good my lord, —

VIOLA. My lord would speak; my duty hushes me.

OLIVIA. If it be aught to the old tune, my lord,
It is as fat and fulsome to mine ear
As howling after music.

DUKE. Still so cruel!

OLIVIA. Still so constant, lord.

DUKE. What, to perverseness? You uncivil lady,
To whose ingrate and unauspicious altars
My soul the faithfull'st off'rings have breath'd out
That e'er devotion tender'd! What shall I do?

OLIVIA. Even what it please my lord, that shall become him.

DUKE. Why should I not, had I the heart to do it,
Like to th' Egyptian thief at point of death,
Kill what I love? — a savage jealousy
That sometime savours nobly. But hear me this:
Since you to non-regardance cast my faith,
And that I partly know the instrument
That screws me from my true place in your favour,
Live you the marble-breasted tyrant still;

98. **fat and fulsome:** *i.e.*, repulsive. 107. **Egyptian thief.** The *Ethiopica* of Heliodorus tells how a robber tried to kill his mistress rather than let her fall into the hands of his enemies.

But this your minion, whom I know you love,
And whom, by heaven I swear, I tender dearly,
Him will I tear out of that cruel eye,
Where he sits crowned in his master's spite.
Come, boy, with me; my thoughts are ripe in mischief.
I'll sacrifice the lamb that I do love,
To spite a raven's heart within a dove.

VIOLA. And I, most jocund, apt, and willingly,
To do you rest, a thousand deaths would die.

OLIVIA. Where goes Cesario?

VIOLA. After him I love
More than I love these eyes, more than my life,
More, by all mores, than e'er I shall love wife.
If I do feign, you witnesses above
Punish my life for tainting of my love!

OLIVIA. Ay me, detested! How am I beguil'd!

VIOLA. Who does beguile you? Who does do you wrong?

OLIVIA. Hast thou forgot thyself? Is it so long?
Call forth the holy father.

DUKE. Come, away!

OLIVIA. Whither, my lord? Cesario, husband, stay.

DUKE. Husband!

OLIVIA. Ay, husband! Can he that deny?

DUKE. Her husband, sirrah!

VIOLA. No, my lord, not I.

OLIVIA. Alas, it is the baseness of thy fear
That makes thee strangle thy propriety.
Fear not, Cesario; take thy fortunes up.
Be that thou know'st thou art, and then thou art
As great as that thou fear'st.

Enter PRIEST.

O, welcome, father!
Father, I charge thee by thy reverence
Here to unfold, though lately we intended
To keep in darkness what occasion now
Reveals before 'tis ripe, what thou dost know
Hath newly pass'd between this youth and me.

PRIEST. A contract of eternal bond of love,
Confirm'd by mutual joinder of your hands,
Attested by the holy close of lips,
Strength'ned by interchangement of your rings;
And all the ceremony of this compact
Seal'd in my function, by my testimony;

114. **minion:** favorite. 136. **strangle thy propriety:** deny thysef. 150. **function:** official capacity.

Since when, my watch hath told me, toward my grave
I have travell'd but two hours.

DUKE. O thou dissembling cub! What wilt thou be
When time hath sow'd a grizzle on thy case?
Or will not else thy craft so quickly grow,
That thine own trip shall be thine overthrow?
Farewell, and take her; but direct thy feet
Where thou and I henceforth may never meet.

VIOLA. My lord, I do protest —

OLIVIA. O, do not swear!
Hold little faith, though thou hast too much fear.

Enter SIR ANDREW.

SIR ANDREW. For the love of God, a surgeon! Send one presently to Sir Toby.

OLIVIA. What's the matter?

SIR ANDREW. Has broke my head across and has given Sir Toby a bloody coxcomb too. For the love of God, your help! I had rather than forty pounds I were at home.

OLIVIA. Who has done this, Sir Andrew?

SIR ANDREW. The Count's gentleman, one Cesario. We took him for a coward, but he's the very devil incardinate.

DUKE. My gentleman, Cesario?

SIR ANDREW. 'Od's lifelings, here he is! You broke my head for nothing; and that that I did, I was set on to do't by Sir Toby.

VIOLA. Why do you speak to me? I never hurt you.
You drew your sword upon me without cause;
But I bespake you fair, and hurt you not.

Enter SIR TOBY *and* CLOWN.

SIR ANDREW. If a bloody coxcomb be a hurt, you have hurt me. I think you set nothing by a bloody coxcomb. Here comes Sir Toby halting. You shall hear more; but if he had not been in drink, he would have tickl'd you othergates than he did.

DUKE. How now, gentleman! How is't with you?

SIR TOBY. That's all one. Has hurt me, and there's th' end on't. Sot, didst see Dick surgeon, sot?

CLOWN. O, he's drunk, Sir Toby, an hour agone. His eyes were set at eight i' th' morning.

SIR TOBY. Then he's a rogue, and a passy measures [pavin]. I hate a drunken rogue.

154. **grizzle:** gray hair. **case:** skin. 156. **trip:** *i.e.*, as in wrestling. 165. **coxcomb:** head. 169. **incardinate:** incarnate. 179. **othergates:** otherwise. 185. [**pavin**] (Malone). *panyn* F. "Passy measures pavin" is an English form of the Italian "Passamezzo pavana," a measured dance with strains of eight bars each. Toby's outburst is inspired by "set at eight" (ll. 183–184).

OLIVIA. Away with him! Who hath made this havoc with them?

SIR ANDREW. I'll help you, Sir Toby, because we'll be dress'd together.

SIR TOBY. Will you help? — an ass-head and a coxcomb and a knave, a thin-fac'd knave, a gull!

OLIVIA. Get him to bed, and let his hurt be look'd to.

[*Exeunt* CLOWN, FABIAN, SIR TOBY, *and* SIR ANDREW.] *Enter* SEBASTIAN.

SEBASTIAN. I am sorry, madam, I have hurt your kinsman;
But, had it been the brother of my blood,
I must have done no less with wit and safety.
You throw a strange regard upon me, and by that
I do perceive it hath offended you.
Pardon me, sweet one, even for the vows
We made each other but so late ago.

DUKE. One face, one voice, one habit, and two persons,
A natural perspective, that is and is not!

SEBASTIAN. Antonio, O my dear Antonio!
How have the hours rack'd and tortur'd me,
Since I have lost thee!

ANTONIO. Sebastian are you?

SEBASTIAN. Fear'st thou that, Antonio?

ANTONIO. How have you made division of yourself?
An apple, cleft in two, is not more twin
Than these two creatures. Which is Sebastian?

OLIVIA. Most wonderful!

SEBASTIAN. Do I stand there? I never had a brother,
Nor can there be that deity in my nature,
Of here and everywhere. I had a sister,
Whom the blind waves and surges have devour'd.
Of charity, what kin are you to me?
What countryman? What name? What parentage?

VIOLA. Of Messaline; Sebastian was my father;
Such a Sebastian was my brother too;
So went he suited to his watery tomb.
If spirits can assume both form and suit
You come to fright us.

SEBASTIAN. A spirit I am indeed;
But am in that dimension grossly clad
Which from the womb I did participate.
Were you a woman, as the rest goes even,
I should my tears let fall upon your cheek,
And say, "Thrice welcome, drowned Viola!"

199. **habit:** dress. 200. **natural perspective:** an optical illusion produced by nature. 204. **Fear'st:** doubtest. 210–211. **Nor . . . everywhere:** nor can I, God-like, be everywhere. 217. **suited:** clothed. 220. **in . . . clad:** clothed in that material form. 221. **Which . . . participate:** which I have possessed since birth. 222. **goes even:** agrees.

VIOLA. My father had a mole upon his brow.
SEBASTIAN. And so had mine.
VIOLA. And died that day when Viola from her birth
Had numb'red thirteen years.
SEBASTIAN. O, that record is lively in my soul!
He finished indeed his mortal act
That day that made my sister thirteen years.
VIOLA. If nothing lets to make us happy both
But this my masculine usurp'd attire,
Do not embrace me till each circumstance
Of place, time, fortune, do cohere and jump
That I am Viola; which to confirm,
I'll bring you to a captain in this town,
Where lie my maiden weeds; by whose gentle help
I was preserv'd to serve this noble count.
All the occurrence of my fortune since
Hath been between this lady and this lord.
SEBASTIAN [*to* OLIVIA]. So comes it, lady, you have been mistook;
But nature to her bias drew in that.
You would have been contracted to a maid;
Nor are you therein, by my life, deceiv'd,
You are betroth'd both to a maid and man.
DUKE. Be not amaz'd, right noble is his blood.
If this be so, as yet the glass seems true,
I shall have share in this most happy wreck.
[*To* VIOLA.] Boy, thou hast said to me a thousand times
Thou never shouldst love woman like to me.
VIOLA. And all those sayings will I over-swear;
And all those swearings keep as true in soul
As doth that orbed continent the fire
That severs day from night.
DUKE. Give me thy hand,
And let me see thee in thy woman's weeds.
VIOLA. The captain that did bring me first on shore
Hath my maid's garments. He upon some action
Is now in durance, at Malvolio's suit,
A gentleman, and follower of my lady's.
OLIVIA. He shall enlarge him; fetch Malvolio hither.
And yet, alas, now I remember me,
They say, poor gentleman, he's much distract.

Re-enter CLOWN *with a letter, and* FABIAN.

232. **lets:** prevents. 235. **jump:** agree. 240. **occurrence:** course. 243. **nature . . . drew** *i.e.,* nature followed her own inclination. 248. **glass.** Probably an allusion to the "perspective" of l. 200. 254. **orbed continent:** the sphere of the sun (according to the Ptolemaic cosmology). 259. **in durance:** under arrest.

A most extracting frenzy of mine own
From my remembrance clearly banish'd his.
How does he, sirrah?

CLOWN. Truly, madam, he holds Belzebub at the stave's end as well as a man in his case may do. Has here writ a letter to you. I should have given 't you to-day morning, but as a madman's epistles are no gospels, so it skills not much when they are deliver'd.

OLIVIA. Open 't and read it.

CLOWN. Look then to be well edified when the fool delivers the madman. [*Shouts.*] "By the Lord, madam," —

OLIVIA. How now, art thou mad?

CLOWN. No, madam, I do but read madness. An your ladyship will have it as it ought to be, you must allow Vox.

OLIVIA. Prithee, read i' thy right wits.

CLOWN. So I do, madonna; but to read his right wits is to read thus; therefore perpend, my princess, and give ear.

OLIVIA. Read it you, sirrah. [*To* FABIAN.]

FABIAN (*reads*). "By the Lord, madam, you wrong me, and the world shall know it. Though you have put me into darkness and given your drunken cousin rule over me, yet have I the benefit of my senses as well as your ladyship. I have your own letter that induced me to the semblance I put on; with the which I doubt not but to do myself much right, or you much shame. Think of me as you please. I leave my duty a little unthought of and speak out of my injury.

THE MADLY-US'D MALVOLIO."

OLIVIA. Did he write this?

CLOWN. Ay, madam.

DUKE. This savours not much of distraction.

OLIVIA. See him deliver'd, Fabian; bring him hither.

[*Exit* FABIAN.]

My lord, so please you, these things further thought on,
To think me as well a sister as a wife,
One day shall crown th' alliance on't, so please you,
Here at my house and at my proper cost.

DUKE. Madam, I am most apt t' embrace your offer.
[*To* VIOLA.] Your master quits you; and for your service done him,
So much against the mettle of your sex,
So far beneath your soft and tender breeding,
And since you call'd me master for so long,
Here is my hand. You shall from this time be
Your master's mistress.

264. **extracting:** distracting. 267. **at . . . end:** at staff's length. 270. **skills:** matters. 276. **Vox:** *i.e.*, the appropriate (loud) voice. 279. **perpend:** consider. 296. **proper:** own. 297. **apt:** ready. 298. **quits:** releases. 299. **mettle:** character.

OLIVIA. A sister! You are she.

Enter MALVOLIO [*and* FABIAN].

DUKE. Is this the madman?
OLIVIA. Ay, my lord, this same.
How now, Malvolio!
MALVOLIO. Madam, you have done me wrong,
Notorious wrong.
OLIVIA. Have I, Malvolio? No.
MALVOLIO. Lady, you have. Pray you, peruse that letter;
You must not now deny it is your hand.
Write from it, if you can, in hand or phrase;
Or say 'tis not your seal, not your invention.
You can say none of this. Well, grant it then
And tell me, in the modesty of honour,
Why you have given me such clear lights of favour,
Bade me come smiling and cross-garter'd to you,
To put on yellow stockings and to frown
Upon Sir Toby and the lighter people;
And, acting this in an obedient hope,
Why have you suffer'd me to be imprison'd,
Kept in a dark house, visited by the priest,
And made the most notorious geck and gull
That e'er invention play'd on? Tell me why.
OLIVIA. Alas, Malvolio, this is not my writing,
Though, I confess, much like the character;
But out of question 'tis Maria's hand.
And now I do bethink me, it was she
First told me thou wast mad. Then cam'st in smiling,
And in such forms which here were presuppos'd
Upon thee in the letter. Prithee, be content.
This practice hath most shrewdly pass'd upon thee;
But when we know the grounds and authors of it,
Thou shalt be both the plaintiff and the judge
Of thine own cause.
FABIAN. Good madam, hear me speak,
And let no quarrel nor no brawl to come
Taint the condition of this present hour,
Which I have wond'red at. In hope it shall not
Most freely I confess, myself and Toby
Set this device against Malvolio here,
Upon some stubborn and uncourteous parts
We had conceiv'd against him. Maria writ

309. **from:** *i.e.,* differently from. 316. **lighter:** lesser. 320. **geck and gull:** fool and dupe. 327. **presuppos'd:** suggested. 329. **practice:** trick. **pass'd:** imposed. 338. **parts:** qualities.

The letter at Sir Toby's great importance,
In recompense whereof he hath married her.
How with a sportful malice it was follow'd
May rather pluck on laughter than revenge,
If that the injuries be justly weigh'd
That have on both sides pass'd.

OLIVIA. Alas, poor fool, how have they baffl'd thee!

CLOWN. Why, "some are born great, some achieve greatness, and some have greatness thrown upon them." I was one, sir, in this interlude; one Sir Topas, sir; but that's all one. "By the Lord, fool, I am not mad." But do you remember? "Madam, why laugh you at such a barren rascal? An you smile not, he's gagg'd." And thus the whirligig of time brings in his revenges.

MALVOLIO. I'll be reveng'd on the whole pack of you. [*Exit.*]

OLIVIA. He hath been most notoriously abus'd.

DUKE. Pursue him, and entreat him to a peace;
He hath not told us of the captain yet.
When that is known and golden time convents,
A solemn combination shall be made
Of our dear souls. Meantime, sweet sister,
We will not part from hence. Cesario, come;
For so you shall be, while you are a man;
But when in other habits you are seen,
Orsino's mistress and his fancy's queen.

[*Exeunt* [*all, except* CLOWN].

CLOWN (*sings*). When that I was and a little tiny boy,
With hey, ho, the wind and the rain,
A foolish thing was but a toy,
For the rain it raineth every day.

But when I came to man's estate,
With hey, ho, &c.
'Gainst knaves and thieves men shut their gate,
For the rain, &c.

But when I came, alas! to wive,
With hey, ho, &c.
By swaggering could I never thrive,
For the rain, &c.

But when I came unto my beds,
With hey, ho, &c.

340. **importance:** importunity. 343. **pluck on:** excite. 357. **convents:** suits. 366. **toy:** trifle.

With toss-pots still had drunken heads,
  For the rain, &c.

A great while ago the world begun,
  With hey, ho, &c.
But that's all one, our play is done,
And we'll strive to please you every day. [*Exit.*]

Curtain

378. toss-pots: drunkards.

Greed is not an admirable character trait, but it has often proved a powerful element in satiric comedy. *Volpone* (1605–1606), if for no other reason than that it has so many grasping, avaricious birds roosting on the same perch, deserves a place of honor in comedy's Pantheon.

But it is not for the *number* of greedy comic types alone that Ben Jonson (1572–1637) can claim laurels as the portraitist of avarice. Each of his eager acquisitors is a cameo of rare carving; a type, true, but nonetheless a marvellously accurate abstract of recognizable human specifics. Jonson reinforced his slashing satire by giving the various scoundrels the names of the animals they most resemble in their frantic clawing for wealth. Not only does this allow in makeup and costume for a *commedia dell'arte* touch — even to the point of using animal masks — thoroughly appropriate to the time and place, but it also underlines the real loss in humanity that occurs when evil or unworthy passions drive men to forget their better selves. And because the major figures — the Fox, the Fly, the Vulture, the Raven, and the Crow — have allowed themselves to become more animal than man, readers and audiences can laugh easily at them and enjoy their comeuppance.

Jonson could, as Shakespeare so often did, borrow plots and ideas from earlier plays, histories, and prose works. Several of his most distinctive comedies, however, are originals. *Volpone* is perhaps the best of them.

Jonson's peculiar talent in *Volpone* lies in the combination of types he has assembled and in the intricate manner in which he has interwoven their separate connections with Volpone and his parasite, Mosca. What could have developed as an episodic morality drama — in fact, this play does have both episodes and a stinging moral message — has been cleverly structured to offer instead a complex plot which rises in tension to a mirth-ridden climax, followed by an astonishing reversal. This, in turn, has its reversal, until all is brought to rest with fiercely severe sentences for the miscreants.

With his theory of Comedy and Humors, Jonson sought to poke fun at human folly by dealing with characters in terms of one special comic flaw. In *Every Man Out of His Humor*, he set forth his ideas:

> As when some one peculiar quality
> Doth so possess a man, that it doth draw
> All his affects, his spirits, and his powers,
> In their confluctions all to run one way,
> This may be said to be a humor.

Sir Politick Would-Be, with his idiotic notions of meddling in state affairs, is a good example of this comic oversimplification for purposes of emphasis. The Raven, the Crow, and the Vulture, however, are more or less alike in their humor, which is greed. But to keep that from becoming dramatically and visually boring, the various animal qualities have been cleverly introduced. Each one is willing to sacrifice different things — things which should be precious to them or to their sense of honor — in order to be made Volpone's heir. None sees, so blinded by avarice is he, that Volpone has no real reason to cherish any one, despite his degrading sacrifices and gifts. The will of man to believe in his potential good fortune, especially when he has earned none, is an amazingly potent force, as Jonson eloquently demonstrates.

Complementing the humor generated by the outlines of animal nature in the major characters is the entertaining irony of imposture. As Mosca deludes the panting would-be heirs, urging them on to greater excesses of humiliation and generosity to win Volpone's favor, the audience can enjoy, with the Fox and the Fly, the tremendous joke being played on them. It would be cruel, were they not so eager to have what they do not deserve. As a result, they get exactly what they deserve — twice — but not what they bargained for. The first time around, they find they are not only not inheritors, but that they have lost all they gave to Volpone. In the second instance, they are punished by the Venetian State according to the quality of their crimes.

Jonson may have had fun deluding the petitioners for Volpone's fortune, but he is a stern moralist at the last. Not even Volpone escapes. Or Mosca. All are corrupt, so all are punished.

Celia, the wife who is forced by her husband to submit to Volpone's lust, is rewarded for her virtue. Although Jonson manages to subject her to Volpone's eager importunities — rising lecherously as he does from his supposed sick-bed — he does effect her rescue before she can be ravished. Her lines, as she pleads for her honor, can be very comic indeed, considering her situation.

All Volpone's viciousness and imposture, all his evil practices — Celia's plight excluded — fall only on those who deserve them by trying to work on him schemes which are just as sordid but not half so clever. This being so, it is not difficult to savor the success of his disguise and deception, to empathize with his delight as it progresses. This empathy, which can be greatly reinforced by an actor who gives Volpone's role a human zest for a game wittily played and a sense of a man who knows how to enjoy life, can make Volpone's final punishment seem unduly harsh. If the actor makes Volpone meanly vicious and as cunning as his adversaries, of course, no such problem arises. In that case, however, the play can be merely unpleasant, rather than wildly funny.

G. L.

BEN JONSON

Volpone

Characters

VOLPONE, *a Magnifico*
MOSCA, *his Parasite*
VOLTORE, *an Advocate*
CORBACCIO, *an old Gentleman*
CORVINO, *a Merchant*
BONARIO, *son to Corbaccio*
SIR POLITICK WOULD-BE, *a Knight*
PEREGRINE, *a Gentleman Traveller*
NANO, *a Dwarf*
CASTRONE, *a Eunuch*
ANDROGYNO, *a Hermaphrodite*
LADY WOULD-BE, *Sir Politick's Wife*
CELIA, *Corvino's Wife*
COMMANDADORI, *Officers of Justice*
MERCATORI, *three Merchants*
AVOCATORI, *four Magistrates*
NOTARIO, *the Register*
SERVITORI, *Servants*
TWO WAITING-WOMEN
GREGE (or Mob)

(SCENE: *Venice.*)

THE ARGUMENT

V olpone, childless, rich, feigns sick, despairs,
O ffers his state to hopes of several heirs,
L ies languishing: his parasite receives
P resents of all, assures, deludes; then weaves
O ther cross plots, which ope themselves, are told.
N ew tricks for safety are sought; they thrive; when bold,
E ach tempts the other again, and all are sold.

PROLOGUE

Now, luck yet send us, and a little wit
    Will serve to make our play hit;
(According to the palates of the season)
    Here is rhime, not empty of reason.
This we were bid to credit from our poet,
    Whose true scope, if you would know it,
In all his poems still hath been this measure,
    To mix profit with your pleasure;
And not as some, whose throats their envy failing,
    Cry hoarsely, All he writes is railing:
And when his plays come forth, think they can flout them,
    With saying, he was a year about them.
To this there needs no lie, but this his creature,
    Which was two months since no feature;
And though he dares give them five lives to mend it,
    'Tis known, five weeks fully penn'd it,
From his own hand, without a co-adjutor,
    Novice, journey-man, or tutor.
Yet thus much I can give you as a token
    Of his play's worth, no eggs are broken,
Nor quaking custards with fierce teeth affrighted,
    Wherewith your rout are so delighted;
Nor hales he in a gull old ends reciting,
    To stop gaps in his loose writing;
With such a deal of monstrous and forced action,
    As might make Bethlem a faction:[1]
Nor made he his play for jests stolen from each table,
    But makes jests to fit his fable;
And so presents quick comedy refined,
    As best critics have designed;
The laws of time, place, persons he observeth,
    From no needful rule he swerveth.
All gall and copperas[2] from his ink he draineth,
    Only a little salt remaineth,
Wherewith he'll rub your cheeks, till red, with laughter,
    They shall look fresh a week after.

[1] **Bethlem a faction**: disrupt Bedlam (the famous madhouse at Bethlehem Green).

[2] **Copperas**: green vitriol, used in making ink.

ACT ONE

Scene 1

(*A room in* VOLPONE's *house. Enter* VOLPONE *and* MOSCA.)

VOLPONE. Good morning to the day; and next, my gold!
Open the shrine, that I may see my saint.

(MOSCA *draws the curtain, and discovers piles of gold, plate, jewels, etc.*)

Hail the world's soul, and mine! More glad than is
The teeming earth to see the longed-for sun
Peep through the horns of the celestial Ram,
Am I, to view thy splendor darkening his;
That lying here, amongst my other hoards,
Show'st like a flame by night, or like the day
Struck out of chaos, when all darkness fled
Unto the center. O thou son of Sol,
But brighter than thy father, let me kiss,
With adoration, thee, and every relic
Of sacred treasure in this blessed room.
Well did wise poets, by thy glorious name,
Title that age which they would have the best;
Thou being the best of things, and far transcending
All style of joy in children, parents, friends,
Or any other waking dream on earth.
Thy looks when they to Venus did ascribe,
They should have given her twenty thousand Cupids;
Such are thy beauties and our loves! Dear saint,
Riches, the dumb god, that giv'st all men tongues,
That can'st do nought, and yet mak'st men do all things;
The price of souls; even hell, with thee to boot,
Is made worth heaven. Thou art virtue, fame,
Honor, and all things else. Who can get thee,
He shall be noble, valiant, honest, wise —
MOSCA. And what he will, sir. Riches are in fortune
A greater good than wisdom is in nature.
VOLPONE. True, my beloved Mosca. Yet I glory
More in the cunning purchase of my wealth,
Than in the glad possession, since I gain
No common way; I use no trade, no venture;
I wound no earth with plowshares, fat no beasts,
To feed the shambles; have no mills for iron,
Oil, corn, or men to grind them into powder:
I blow no subtle glass, expose no ships

To threat'nings of the furrow-faced sea;
I turn no moneys in the public bank,
Nor usure private.
MOSCA. No, sir, nor devour
Soft prodigals. You shall have some will swallow
A melting heir as glibly as your Dutch
Will pills of butter, and ne'er purge for it;
Tear forth the fathers of poor families
Out of their beds, and coffin them alive
In some kind clasping prison, where their bones
May be forthcoming, when the flesh is rotten:
But your sweet nature doth abhor these courses;
You loathe the widow's or the orphan's tears
Should wash your pavements, or their piteous cries
Ring in your roofs, and beat the air for vengeance.
VOLPONE. Right, Mosca; I do loathe it.
MOSCA. And besides, sir,
You are not like the thresher that doth stand
With a huge flail, watching a heap of corn,
And, hungry, dares not taste the smallest grain,
But feeds on mallows, and such bitter herbs;
Nor like the merchant, who hath filled his vaults
With Romagnia, and rich Canadian wines,
Yet drinks the lees of Lombard's vinegar.
You will lie not in straw, whilst moths and worms
Feed on your sumptuous hangings and soft beds;
You know the use of riches, and dare give now
From that bright heap, to me, your poor observer,
Or to your dwarf, or your hermaphrodite,
Your eunuch, or what other household trifle
Your pleasure allows maintenance —
VOLPONE. Hold thee, Mosca (*gives him money*);
Take of my hand! thou strik'st on truth in all,
And they are envious term thee parasite.
Call forth my dwarf, my eunuch, and my fool,
And let them make me sport.

(*Exit* MOSCA.)

What should I do,
But cocker up[3] my genius, and live free
To all delights my fortune calls me to?
I have no wife, no parent, child, ally
To give my substance to; but whom I make

[3] **Cocker up**: indulge.

Must be my heir: and this makes men observe me:
This draws new clients daily to my house,
Women and men of every sex and age,
That bring me presents, send me plate, coin, jewels,
With hope that when I die (which they expect
Each greedy minute) it shall then return
Tenfold upon them; whilst some, covetous
Above the rest, seek to engross me whole,
And counterwork the one unto the other,
Contend in gifts, as they would seem in love:
All which I suffer, playing with their hopes,
And am content to coin them into profit,
And look upon their kindness, and take more,
And look on that; still bearing them in hand,
Letting the cherry knock against their lips,
And draw it by their mouths, and back again.—
How now!

(*Enter* MOSCA *with* NANO, ANDROGYNO, *and* CASTRONE.)

NANO. Now, room for fresh gamesters, who do will you to know,
They do bring you neither play nor university show:
And therefore do entreat you, that whatsoever they rehearse,
May not fare a whit the worse, for the false pace of the verse.
If you wonder at this, you will wonder more ere we pass,
For know, here is enclosed the soul of Pythagoras,
That juggler divine, as hereafter shall follow.
Which soul, fast and loose, sir, came first from Apollo,
And was breathed into Aethalides, Mercurius his son,
Where it had the gift to remember all that ever was done.
From thence it fled forth, and made quick transmigration
To goldilocked Euphorbus, who was killed in good fashion
At the siege of old Troy, by the cuckold of Sparta.
Hermotimus was next (I find it in my charta)
To whom it did pass, where no sooner it was missing
But with one Pyrrhus of Delos it learned to go a-fishing;
And thence did it enter the sophist of Greece.
From Pythagore, she went into a beautiful piece
Hight Aspasia, the meretrix; and the next toss of her
Was again of a whore, she became a philosopher,
Crates the cynic, as it self doth relate it:
Since kings, knights, and beggars, knaves, lords, and fools gat it,
Besides ox and ass, camel, mule, goat, and brock,
In all which it hath spoke, as in the cobler's cock.
But I come not here to discourse of that matter,
Or his one, two, or three, or his great oath, *By quater!*

His musics, his trigon, his golden thigh,
Or his telling how elements shift; but I
Would ask how of late thou hast suffered translation,
And shifted thy coat in these days of reformation.
ANDROGYNO. Like one of the reformed, a fool, as you see,
Counting all old doctrine heresy.
NANO. But not on thine own forbid meats hast thou ventured?
ANDROGYNO. On fish, when first a Carthusian I entered.
NANO. Why, then thy dogmatical silence hath left thee?
ANDROGYNO. Of that an obstreperous lawyer bereft me.
NANO. O wonderful change, when sir lawyer forsook thee!
For Pythagore's sake, what body then took thee?
ANDROGYNO. A good dull mule.
NANO. And how! by that means
Thou wert brought to allow the eating of beans?
ANDROGYNO. Yes.
NANO. But from the mule into whom didst thou pass?
ANDROGYNO. Into a very strange beast, by some writers called an ass;
By others, a precise, pure illuminate brother,[4]
Of those devour flesh, and sometimes one another;
And will drop you forth a libel or a sanctified lie,
Betwixt every spoonful of a nativity-pie.
NANO. Now quit thee, for heaven, of that profane nation,
And gently report thy next transmigration.
ANDROGYNO. To the same that I am.
NANO. A creature of delight,
And, what is more than a fool, an hermaphrodite!
Now, prithee, sweet soul, in all thy variation,
Which body would'st thou choose to keep up thy station?
ANDROGYNO. Troth, this I am in: even here would I tarry.
NANO. 'Cause here the delight of each sex thou canst vary?
ANDROGYNO. Alas, those pleasures be stale and forsaken;
No, 'tis your fool wherewith I am so taken,
The only one creature that I can call blessed;
For all other forms I have proved most distressed.
NANO. Spoke true, as thou wert in Pythagoras still.
This learned opinion we celebrate will,
Fellow eunuch, as behoves us, with all our wit and art,
To dignify that whereof ourselves are so great and special a part.
VOLPONE. Now, very, very pretty! Mosca, this
Was thy invention?
MOSCA. If it please my patron,
Not else.
VOLPONE. It doth, good Mosca.
MOSCA. Then it was, sir.

[4] **A precise, pure illuminate brother**: a Puritan.

NANO *and* CASTRONE (*sing*).

Fools, they are the only nation
Worth men's envy or admiration;
Free from care or sorrow-taking,
Selves and others merry making:
All they speak or do is sterling.
Your fool he is your great man's darling,
And your ladies' sport and pleasure;
Tongue and bauble are his treasure.
E'en his face begetteth laughter,
And he speaks truth free from slaughter;
He's the grace of every feast,
And sometimes the chiefest guest;
Hath his trencher and his stool,
When wit waits upon the fool.
O, who would not be
He, he, he?

(*Knocking without.*)

VOLPONE. Who's that? Away!

(*Exeunt* NANO *and* CASTRONE.)

Look, Mosca. Fool, begone!

(*Exit* ANDROGYNO.)

MOSCA. 'Tis Signior Voltore, the advocate;
I know him by his knock.

VOLPONE. Fetch me my gown.
My furs and nightcaps; say, my couch is changing,
And let him entertain himself awhile
Without i' the gallery.

(*Exit* MOSCA.)

Now, now, my clients
Begin their visitation! Vulture, kite,
Raven, and gorcrow, all my birds of prey,
That think me turning carcase, now they come;
I am not for them yet.

(*Enter* MOSCA, *with the gown, etc.*)

How now! the news?

MOSCA. A piece of plate, sir.

VOLPONE. Of what bigness?
MOSCA. Huge,
Massy, and antique, with your name inscribed,
And arms engraven.
VOLPONE. Good! and not a fox
Stretched on the earth, with fine delusive sleights,
Mocking a gaping crow? ha, Mosca!
MOSCA. Sharp, sir.
VOLPONE. Give me my furs. (*Puts on his sick dress.*)
Why dost thou laugh so, man?
MOSCA. I cannot choose, sir, when I apprehend
What thoughts he has without now, as he walks:
That this might be the last gift he should give;
That this would fetch you; if you died today,
And gave him all, what he should be tomorrow;
What large return would come of all his ventures;
How he should worshipped be, and reverenced;
Ride with his furs, and foot-cloths; waited on
By herds of fools and clients; have clear way
Made for his mule, as lettered as himself;
Be called the great and learned advocate:
And then concludes, there's nought impossible.
VOLPONE. Yes, to be learned, Mosca.
MOSCA. O, no: rich
Implies it. Hood an ass with reverend purple,
So you can hide his two ambitious ears,
And he shall pass for a cathedral doctor.
VOLPONE. My caps, my caps, good Mosca. Fetch him in.
MOSCA. Stay, sir; your ointment for your eyes.
VOLPONE. That's true;
Dispatch, dispatch: I long to have possession
Of my new present.
MOSCA. That, and thousands more,
I hope to see you lord of.
VOLPONE. Thanks, kind Mosca.
MOSCA. And that, when I am lost in blended dust,
And hundred such as I am, in succession —
VOLPONE. Nay, that were too much, Mosca.
MOSCA. You shall live
Still to delude these harpies.
VOLPONE. Loving Mosca!
'Tis well: my pillow now, and let him enter.

(*Exit* MOSCA.)

Now, my feigned cough, my phthisic, and my gout,
My apoplexy, palsy, and catarrhs,

Help, with your forced functions, this my posture,
Wherein, this three year, I have milked their hopes.
He comes; I hear him — Uh! (*coughing*) uh! uh! uh! O —

(*Enter* MOSCA, *introducing* VOLTORE, *with a piece of plate.*)

MOSCA. You still are what you were, sir. Only you,
Of all the rest, are he commands his love,
And you do wisely to preserve it thus,
With early visitation and kind notes
Of your good meaning to him, which I know
Cannot but come most grateful! Patron! sir!
Here's Signior Voltore is come —
VOLPONE (*faintly*). What say you?
MOSCA. Sir, Signior Voltore is come this morning
To visit you.
VOLPONE. I thank him.
MOSCA. And hath brought
A piece of antique plate, bought of St. Mark,[5]
With which he here presents you.
VOLPONE. He is welcome.
Pray him to come more often.
MOSCA. Yes.
VOLTORE. What says he?
MOSCA. He thanks you, and desires you see him often.
VOLPONE. Mosca.
MOSCA. My patron!
VOLPONE. Bring him near, where is he?
I long to feel his hand.
MOSCA. The plate is here, sir.
VOLTORE. How fare you, sir?
VOLPONE. I thank you, Signior Voltore;
Where is the plate? mine eyes are bad.
VOLTORE (*putting it into his hands*). I'm sorry
To see you still thus weak.
MOSCA (*aside*). That he's not weaker.
VOLPONE. You are too munificent.
VOLTORE. No, sir; would to heaven,
I could as well give health to you, as that plate!
VOLPONE. You give, sir, what you can: I thank you. Your love
Hath taste in this, and shall not be unanswered:
I pray you see me often.
VOLTORE. Yes, I shall, sir.
VOLPONE. Be not far from me.
MOSCA. Do you observe that, sir?

[5] **St. Mark:** in St. Mark's place.

VOLPONE. Hearken unto me still; it will concern you.
MOSCA. You are a happy man, sir; know your good.
VOLPONE. I cannot now last long —
MOSCA. You are his heir, sir.
VOLTORE. Am I?
VOLPONE. I feel me going; Uh! uh! uh! uh!
I'm sailing to my port, Uh! uh! uh! uh!
And I am glad I am so near my haven.
MOSCA. Alas, kind gentleman! Well, we must all go —
VOLTORE. But, Mosca —
MOSCA. Age will conquer.
VOLTORE. Pray thee, hear me;
Am I inscribed his heir for certain?
MOSCA. Are you!
I do beseech you, sir, you will vouchsafe
To write me in your family. All my hopes
Depend upon your worship: I am lost,
Except the rising sun do shine on me.
VOLTORE. It shall both shine and warm thee, Mosca.
MOSCA. Sir,
I am a man that hath not done your love
All the worst offices: here I wear your keys,
See all your coffers and your caskets locked,
Keep the poor inventory of your jewels,
Your plate and moneys; am your steward, sir,
Husband your goods here.
VOLTORE. But am I sole heir?
MOSCA. Without a partner, sir; confirmed this morning:
The wax is warm yet, and the ink scarce dry
Upon the parchment.
VOLTORE. Happy, happy me!
By what good chance, sweet Mosca?
MOSCA. Your desert, sir;
I know no second cause.
VOLTORE. Thy modesty
Is loath to know it; well, we shall require it.
MOSCA. He ever liked your course, sir; that first took him.
I oft have heard him say how he admired
Men of your large profession, that could speak
To every cause, and things mere contraries,
Till they were hoarse again, yet all be law;
That with most quick agility, could turn,
And return; make knots, and undo them;
Give forked counsel; take provoking gold
On either hand, and put it up: these men,
He knew, would thrive with their humility.
And, for his part, he thought he should be blest

To have his heir of such a suffering spirit,
So wise, so grave, of so perplexed a tongue,
And loud withal, that would not wag, nor scarce
Lie still, without a fee; when every word
Your worship but lets fall, is a chequin![6] —

(*Knocking without.*)

Who's that? one knocks; I would not have you seen, sir.
And yet — pretend you came, and went in haste:
I'll fashion an excuse — and, gentle sir,
When you do come to swim in golden lard,
Up to the arms in honey, that your chin
Is borne up stiff, with fatness of the flood,
Think on your vassal; but remember me:
I have not been your worst of clients.
VOLTORE. Mosca! —
MOSCA. When will you have your inventory brought, sir?
Or see a copy of the will? — Anon! —
I'll bring them to you, sir. Away, be gone,
Put business in your face.

(*Exit* VOLTORE.)

VOLPONE (*springing up*). Excellent Mosca!
Come hither, let me kiss thee.
MOSCA. Keep you still, sir.
Here is Corbaccio.
VOLPONE. Set the plate away:
The vulture's gone, and the old raven's come.
MOSCA. Betake you to your silence, and your sleep.
Stand there and multiply. (*Putting the plate onto the rest.*)
Now shall we see
A wretch who is indeed more impotent
Than this can feign to be; yet hopes to hop
Over his grave —

(*Enter* CORBACCIO.)

Signior Corbaccio!
You're very welcome, sir.
CORBACCIO. How does your patron?
MOSCA. Troth, as he did, sir; no amends.
CORBACCIO. What! mends he?
MOSCA. No, sir: he's rather worse.

[6] **Chequin**: a gold coin, or sequin.

CORBACCIO. That's well. Where is he?
MOSCA. Upon his couch, sir, newly fallen asleep.
CORBACCIO. Does he sleep well?
MOSCA. No wink, sir, all this night
Nor yesterday; but slumbers.
CORBACCIO. Good! he should take
Some counsel of physicians. I have brought him
An opiate here, from mine own doctor.
MOSCA. He will not hear of drugs.
CORBACCIO. Why? I myself
Stood by while it was made, saw all the ingredients;
And know it cannot but most gently work:
My life for his, 'tis but to make him sleep.
VOLPONE (*aside*). Ay, his last sleep, if he would take it.
MOSCA. Sir.
He has no faith in physic.
CORBACCIO. Say you, say you?
MOSCA. He has no faith in physic: he does think
Most of your doctors are the greater danger,
And worse disease, to escape. I often have
Heard him protest that your physician
Should never be his heir.
CORBACCIO. Not I his heir?
MOSCA. Not your physician, sir.
CORBACCIO. O, no, no, no,
I do not mean it.
MOSCA. No, sir, nor their fees
He cannot brook: he says they flay a man
Before they kill him.
CORBACCIO. Right, I do conceive you.
MOSCA. And then they do it by experiment;
For which the law not only doth absolve them,
But gives them great reward: and he is loath
To hire his death, so.
CORBACCIO. It is true, they kill
With as much license as a judge.
MOSCA. Nay, more;
For he but kills, sir, where the law condemns,
And these can kill him too.
CORBACCIO. Ay, or me;
Or any man. How does his apoplex?
Is that strong on him still?
MOSCA. Most violent.
His speech is broken, and his eyes are set,
His face drawn longer than 'twas wont —
CORBACCIO. How! how!
Stronger than he was wont?

MOSCA. No, sir: his face
Drawn longer than 'twas wont.
CORBACCIO. O, good!
MOSCA. His mouth
Is ever gaping, and his eyelids hang
CORBACCIO. Good.
MOSCA. A freezing numbness stiffens all his joints,
And makes the color of his flesh like lead.
CORBACCIO. 'Tis good.
MOSCA. His pulse beats slow, and dull.
CORBACCIO. Good symptoms still.
MOSCA. And from his brain —
CORBACCIO. I conceive you; good.
MOSCA. Flows a cold sweat, with a continual rheum,
Forth the resolved corners of his eyes.
CORBACCIO. Is't possible? Yet I am better, ha!
How does he, with the swimming of his head?
MOSCA. O, sir, 'tis past the scotomy,[7] he now
Hath lost his feeling, and hath left to snort:
You hardly can perceive him, that he breathes.
CORBACCIO. Excellent, excellent! sure I shall outlast him:
This makes me young again, a score of years.
MOSCA. I was a coming for you, sir.
CORBACCIO. Has he made his will?
What has he given me?
MOSCA. No, sir.
CORBACCIO. Nothing! ha?
MOSCA. He has not made his will, sir.
CORBACCIO. O, O, O!
What then did Voltore, the lawyer, here?
MOSCA. He smelt a carcase, sir, when he but heard
My master was about his testament;
As I did urge him to it for your good —
CORBACCIO. He came unto him, did he? I thought so.
MOSCA. Yes, and presented him this piece of plate.
CORBACCIO. To be his heir?
MOSCA. I do not know, sir.
CORBACCIO. True:
I know it too.
MOSCA (*aside*). By your own scale, sir.
CORBACCIO. Well,
I shall prevent him yet. See, Mosca, look!
Here I have brought a bag of bright chequines,
Will quite weigh down his plate.
MOSCA (*taking the bag*). Yea, marry, sir.

[7] **Scotomy:** dimness of sight accompanied by dizziness.

This is true physic, this your sacred medicine;
No talk of opiates, to this great elixir!
CORBACCIO. 'Tis *aurum palpabile*, if not *potabile*.[8]
MOSCA. It shall be ministered to him in his bowl.
CORBACCIO. Ay, do, do, do.
MOSCA. Most blessed cordial!
This will recover him.
CORBACCIO. Yes, do, do, do.
MOSCA. I think it were not best, sir.
CORBACCIO. What?
MOSCA. To recover him.
CORBACCIO. O, no, no, no, by no means.
MOSCA. Why, sir, this
Will work some strange effect, if he but feel it.
CORBACCIO. 'Tis true, therefore forbear; I'll take my venture:
Give me it again.
MOSCA. At no hand; pardon me:
You shall not do yourself that wrong, sir. I
Will so advise you, you shall have it all.
CORBACCIO. How?
MOSCA. All, sir; 'tis your right, your own: no man
Can claim a part: 'tis yours, without a rival,
Decreed by destiny.
CORBACCIO. How, how, good Mosca?
MOSCA. I'll tell you, sir. This fit he shall recover.
CORBACCIO. I do conceive you.
MOSCA. And, on first advantage
Of his gained sense, will I re-importune him
Unto the making of his testament:
And show him this. (*Pointing to the money.*)
CORBACCIO. Good, good.
MOSCA. 'Tis better yet,
If you will hear, sir.
CORBACCIO. Yes, with all my heart.
MOSCA. Now would I counsel you, make home with speed;
There, frame a will, whereto you shall inscribe
My master your sole heir.
CORBACCIO. And disinherit
My son?
MOSCA. O, sir, the better: for that color
Shall make it much more taking.
CORBACCIO. O, but color?[9]
MOSCA. This will, sir, you shall send it unto me.
Now, when I come to enforce, as I will do,

[8] ***Aurum palpabile*, if not *potabile*:** palpable gold, if not potable (medicinal) gold.
[9] **O, but color?** only a pretense?

Your cares, your watchings, and your many prayers,
Your more than many gifts, your this day's present,
And last, produce your will; where, without thought,
Or least regard, unto your proper issue,
A son so brave, and highly meriting,
The stream of your diverted love hath thrown you
Upon my master, and made him your heir;
He cannot be so stupid, or stone-dead,
But out of conscience and mere gratitude —

CORBACCIO. He must pronounce me his?

MOSCA. 'Tis true.

CORBACCIO. This plot
Did I think on before.

MOSCA. I do believe it.

CORBACCIO. Do you not believe it?

MOSCA. Yes, sir.

CORBACCIO. Mine own project.

MOSCA. Which, when he hath done, sir —

CORBACCIO. Published me his heir?

MOSCA. And you so certain to survive him —

CORBACCIO. Ay.

MOSCA. Being so lusty a man —

CORBACCIO. 'Tis true.

MOSCA. Yes, sir —

CORBACCIO. I thought on that too. See, how he should be
The very organ to express my thoughts!

MOSCA. You have not only done yourself a good —

CORBACCIO. But multiplied it on my son.

MOSCA. 'Tis right, sir.

CORBACCIO. Still, my invention.

MOSCA. 'Las, sir! heaven knows.
It hath been all my study, all my care,
(I e'en grow gray withal) how to work things —

CORBACCIO. I do conceive, sweet Mosca.

MOSCA. You are he,
For whom I labor here.

CORBACCIO. Ay, do, do, do:
I'll straight about it. (*Going.*)

MOSCA (*aside*). Rook go with you,[10] raven!

CORBACCIO. I know thee honest.

MOSCA (*aside*). You do lie, sir!

CORBACCIO. And —

MOSCA (*aside*). Your knowledge is no better than your ears, sir.

CORBACCIO. I do not doubt, to be a father to thee.

MOSCA (*aside*). Nor I to gull my brother of his blessing.

[10] **Rook go with you:** I hope you get rooked (cheated).

CORBACCIO. I may have my youth restored to me, why not?
MOSCA (*aside*). Your worship is a precious ass!
CORBACCIO. What say'st thou?
MOSCA. I do desire your worship to make haste, sir.
CORBACCIO. 'Tis done, 'tis done; I go. (*Exit.*)
VOLPONE (*leaping from his couch*). O, I shall burst!
Let out my sides, let out my sides —
MOSCA. Contain
Your flux of laughter, sir: you know this hope
Is such a bait, it covers any hook.
VOLPONE. O, but thy working, and thy placing it!
I cannot hold; good rascal, let me kiss thee:
I never knew thee in so rare a humor.
MOSCA. Alas, sir, I but do as I am taught;
Follow your grave instructions; give them words;
Pour oil into their ears, and send them hence.
VOLPONE. 'Tis true, 'tis true. What a rare punishment
Is avarice to itself!
MOSCA. Ay, with our help, sir.
VOLPONE. So many cares, so many maladies,
So many fears attending on old age,
Yea, death so often called on, as no wish
Can be more frequent with them, their limbs faint,
Their senses dull, their seeing, hearing, going,
All dead before them; yea, their very teeth,
Their instruments of eating, failing them:
Yet this is reckoned life! nay, here was one,
Is now gone home, that wishes to live longer!
Feels not his gout, nor palsy; feigns himself
Younger by scores of years, flatters his age
With confident belying it, hopes he may
With charms, like Æson, have his youth restored:
And with these thoughts so battens, as if fate
Would be as easily cheated on as he,
And all turns air!

(*Knocking within.*)

Who's that there, now? a third!
MOSCA. Close, to your couch again; I hear his voice:
It is Corvino, our spruce merchant.
VOLPONE (*lies down as before*). Dead.
MOSCA. Another bout, sir, with your eyes (*anointing them*). — Who's there?

(*Enter* CORVINO.)

Signior Corvino! come most wished for! O,
How happy were you, if you knew it, now!
CORVINO. Why? what? wherein?
MOSCA. The tardy hour is come, sir.
CORVINO. He is not dead?
MOSCA. Not dead, sir, but as good;
He knows no man.
CORVINO. How shall I do then?
MOSCA. Why, sir?
CORVINO. I have brought him here a pearl.
MOSCA. Perhaps he has
So much remembrance left, as to know you, sir:
He still calls on you; nothing but your name
Is in his mouth. Is your pearl orient, sir?
CORVINO. Venice was never owner of the like.
VOLPONE (*faintly*). Signior Corvino!
MOSCA. Hark.
VOLPONE. Signior Corvino!
MOSCA. He calls you; step and give it to him. — He's here, sir,
And he has brought you a rich pearl.
CORVINO. And how do you, sir?
Tell him, it doubles the twelfth carat.
MOSCA. Sir,
He cannot understand, his hearing's gone;
And yet it comforts him to see you —
CORVINO. Say,
I have a diamond for him, too.
MOSCA. Best show it, sir;
Put it into his hand; 'tis only there
He apprehends: he has his feeling yet.
See how he grasps it!
CORVINO. 'Las, good gentleman!
How pitiful the sight is!
MOSCA. Tut! forget, sir.
The weeping of an heir should still be laughter
Under a visor.
CORVINO. Why, am I his heir?
MOSCA. Sir, I am sworn, I may not show the will
Till he be dead; but here has been Corbaccio,
Here has been Voltore, here were others too,
I cannot number 'em, they were so many;
All gaping here for legacies: but I,
Taking the vantage of his naming you,
Signior Corvino, Signior Corvino, took
Paper and pen and ink and there I asked him,
Whom he would have his heir? *Corvino*. Who
Should be executor? *Corvino*. And,

To any question he was silent to,
I still interpreted the nods he made,
Through weakness, for consent: and sent home th' others
Nothing bequeathed them, but to cry and curse.

CORVINO. O, my dear Mosca!

(*They embrace.*)

Does he not perceive us?

MOSCA. No more than a blind harper. He knows no man,
No face of friend, nor name of any servant,
Who 'twas that fed him last, or gave him drink:
Not those he hath begotten, or brought up,
Can he remember.

CORVINO. Has he children?

MOSCA. Bastards,
Some dozen or more, that he begot on beggars,
Gypsies and Jews and blackamoors, when he was drunk.
Knew you not that, sir? 'tis the common fable.
The dwarf, the fool, the eunuch, are all his;
He's the true father of his family.
In all save me: — but he has given 'em nothing.

CORVINO. That's well, that's well! Art sure he does not hear us?

MOSCA. Sure, sir! why, look you, credit your own sense. (*Shouts in* VOLPONE'*s ear.*)
The pox approach, and add to your diseases,
If it would send you hence the sooner, sir,
For your incontinence, it hath deserved it
Thoroughly, and thoroughly, and the plague to boot! —
You may come near, sir. — Would you would once close
Those filthy eyes of yours, that flow with slime,
Like two frog-pits; and those same hanging cheeks,
Covered with hide instead of skin — Nay, help, sir —
That look like frozen dish-clouts set on end!

CORVINO (*aloud*). Or like an old smoked wall, on which the rain
Ran down in streaks!

MOSCA. Excellent, sir! speak out:
You may be louder yet; a culverin
Discharged in his ear would hardly bore it.

CORVINO. His nose is like a common sewer, still running.

MOSCA. 'Tis good! And what his mouth?

CORVINO. A very draught.

MOSCA. O, stop it up —

CORVINO. By no means.

MOSCA. 'Pray you, let me:
Faith I could stifle him rarely with a pillow,
As well as any woman that should keep him.

CORVINO. Do as you will; but I'll begone.
MOSCA. Be so:
It is your presence makes him last so long.
CORVINO. I pray you, use no violence.
MOSCA. No, sir! why?
Why should you be thus scrupulous, pray you, sir?
CORVINO. Nay, at your discretion.
MOSCA. Well, good sir, begone.
CORVINO. I will not trouble him now, to take my pearl.
MOSCA. Puh! nor your diamond. What a needless care.
Is this afflicts you? Is not all here yours?
Am not I here, whom you have made your creature?
That owe my being to you?
CORVINO. Grateful Mosca!
Thou art my friend, my fellow, my companion,
My partner, and shalt share in all my fortunes.
MOSCA. Excepting one.
CORVINO. What's that?
MOSCA. Your gallant wife, sir.

(*Exit* CORVINO.)

Now is he gone: we had no other means
To shoot him hence, but this.
VOLPONE. My divine Mosca!
Thou hast today outgone thyself.

(*Knocking within.*)

Who's there?
I will be troubled with no more. Prepare
Me music, dances, banquets, all delights;
The Turk is not more sensual in his pleasures,
Than will Volpone.

(*Exit* MOSCA.)

Let me see; a pearl!
A diamond! plate! chequines! Good morning's purchase.
Why, this is better than rob churches, yet;
Or fat, by eating, once a month, a man —

(*Enter* MOSCA.)

Who is't?
MOSCA. The beauteous lady Would-be, sir,
Wife to the English knight, Sir Politick Would-be
(This is the style, sir, is directed me),

Hath sent to know how you have slept tonight,
And if you would be visited?

VOLPONE. Not now:
Some three hours hence —

MOSCA. I told the squire[11] so much.

VOLPONE. When I am high with mirth and wine; then, then:
'Fore heaven, I wonder at the desperate valor
Of the bold English, that they dare let loose
Their wives to all encounters!

MOSCA. Sir, this knight
Had not his name for nothing, he is *politic*,
And knows, howe'er his wife affect strange airs,
She hath not yet the face to be dishonest:
But had she Signior Corvino's wife's face —

VOLPONE. Has she so rare a face?

MOSCA. O, sir, the wonder,
The blazing star of Italy! a wench
Of the first year! a beauty ripe as harvest!
Whose skin is whiter than a swan all over,
Than silver, snow, or lilies! a soft lip,
Would tempt you to eternity of kissing!
And flesh that melteth in the touch to blood!
Bright as your gold, and lovely as your gold!

VOLPONE. Why had not I known this before?

MOSCA. Alas, sir,
Myself but yesterday discovered it.

VOLPONE. How might I see her?

MOSCA. O, not possible;
She's kept as warily as is your gold;
Never does come abroad, never takes air,
But at a window. All her looks are sweet,
As the first grapes or cherries, and are watched
As near as they are.

VOLPONE. I must see her.

MOSCA. Sir,
There is a guard of spies ten thick upon her,
All his whole household; each of which is set
Upon his fellow, and have all their charge,
When he goes out, when he comes in, examined.

VOLPONE. I will go see her, though but at her window.

MOSCA. In some disguise then.

VOLPONE. That is true; I must
Maintain mine own shape still the same: we'll think.

(*Exeunt.*)

[11] **The squire**: the messenger.

ACT TWO

Scene 1

(St. Mark's Place; a retired corner before CORVINO's *house. Enter* SIR POLITICK WOULD-BE, *and* PEREGRINE.)

SIR POLITICK. Sir, to a wise man, all the world's his soil:
It is not Italy, nor France, nor Europe,
That must bound me, if my fates call me forth.
Yet, I protest, it is no salt desire
Of seeing countries, shifting a religion,
Nor any disaffection to the state
Where I was bred, and unto which I owe
My dearest plots, hath brought me out; much less,
That idle, antique, stale, gray-headed project
Of knowing men's minds and manners, with Ulysses!
But a peculiar humor of my wife's
Laid for this height of Venice, to observe,
To quote, to learn the language, and so forth —
I hope you travel, sir, with license?
PEREGRINE. Yes.
SIR POLITICK. I dare the safelier converse — How long, sir,
Since you left England?
PEREGRINE. Seven weeks.
SIR POLITICK. So lately!
You have not been with my lord ambassador?
PEREGRINE. Not yet, sir.
SIR POLITICK. Pray you, what news, sir, vents our climate?
I heard last night a most strange thing reported
By some of my lord's followers, and I long
To hear how 'twill be seconded.
PEREGRINE. What was't, sir?
SIR POLITICK. Marry, sir, of a raven that should build
In a ship royal of the king's.
PEREGRINE (*aside.*) This fellow,
Does he gull me, trow? or is gulled? Your name, sir?
SIR POLITICK. My name is Politick Would-be.
PEREGRINE (*aside*). O, that speaks him. —
A knight, sir?
SIR POLITICK. A poor knight, sir.
PEREGRINE. Your lady
Lies here in Venice, for intelligence
Of tires and fashions and behavior
Among the courtesans? the fine Lady Would-be?

SIR POLITICK. Yes, sir; the spider and the bee, ofttimes,
Suck from one flower.
PEREGRINE. Good Sir Politick,
I cry you mercy; I have heard much of you:
'Tis true, sir, of your raven.
SIR POLITICK. On your knowledge?
PEREGRINE. Yes, and your lion's whelping in the Tower.
SIR POLITICK. Another whelp!
PEREGRINE. Another, sir.
SIR POLITICK. Now heaven!
What prodigies be these? The fires at Berwick!
And the new star! these things concurring, strange,
And full of omen! Saw you those meteors?
PEREGRINE. I did, sir.
SIR POLITICK. Fearful! Pray you, sir, confirm me,
Were there three porpoises seen above the bridge,
As they give out?
PEREGRINE. Six, and a sturgeon, sir.
SIR POLITICK. I am astonished.
PEREGRINE. Nay, sir, be not so;
I'll tell you a greater prodigy than these.
SIR POLITICK. What should these things portend?
PEREGRINE. The very day
(Let me be sure) that I put forth from London,
There was a whale discovered in the river,
As high as Woolwich, that had waited there,
Few know how many months, for the subversion
Of the Stode fleet.
SIR POLITICK. Is't possible? believe it,
'Twas either sent from Spain, or the archdukes:
Spinola's[12] whale, upon my life, my credit!
Will they not leave these projects? Worthy sir,
Some other news.
PEREGRINE. Faith, Stone the fool is dead,
And they do lack a tavern fool extremely.
SIR POLITICK. Is Mass Stone dead?
PEREGRINE. He's dead, sir; why, I hope
You thought him not immortal? — (*Aside.*) O, this knight,
Were he well known, would be a precious thing
To fit our English stage: he that should write
But such a fellow, should be thought to feign
Extremely, if not maliciously.
SIR POLITICK. Stone dead!
PEREGRINE. Dead. — Lord! how deeply, sir, you apprehend it!
He was no kinsman to you?

[12] **Spinola**: a Spanish general (1569–1630).

SIR POLITICK. That I know of.
Well! that same fellow was an unknown fool.
PEREGRINE. And yet you knew him, it seems?
SIR POLITICK. I did so. Sir,
I knew him one of the most dangerous heads
Living within the state, and so I held him.
PEREGRINE. Indeed, sir?
SIR POLITICK. While he lived, in action,
He has received weekly intelligence,
Upon my knowledge, out of the Low Countries,
For all parts of the world, in cabbages;
And those dispensed again to ambassadors,
In oranges, musk-melons, apricots,
Lemons, pome-citrons, and such-like; sometimes
In Colchester oysters, and your Selsey cockles.
PEREGRINE. You make me wonder.
SIR POLITICK. Sir, upon my knowledge.
Nay, I've observed him, at your public ordinary,
Take his advertisement[13] from a traveller,
A concealed statesman, in a trencher of meat;
And instantly, before the meal was done,
Convey an answer in a tooth-pick.
PEREGRINE. Strange!
How could this be, sir?
SIR POLITICK. Why, the meat was cut
So like his character, and so laid, as he
Must easily read the cipher.
PEREGRINE. I have heard,
He could not read, sir.
SIR POLITICK. So 'twas given out,
In policy, by those that did employ him:
But he could read, and had your languages,
And to't, as sound a noddle —
PEREGRINE. I have heard, sir,
That your baboons were spies, and that they were
A kind of subtle nation near to China.
SIR POLITICK. Ay, ay, your Mamaluchi. Faith, they had
Their hand in a French plot or two; but they
Were so extremely given to women, as
They made discovery of all: yet I
Had my advices here, on Wednesday last.
From one of their own coat, they were returned,
Made their relations, as the fashion is,
And now stand fair for fresh employment.
PEREGRINE (*aside*). Heart!

[13] **Advertisement:** information.

This Sir Pol will be ignorant of nothing.
It seems, sir, you know all.
SIR POLITICK. Not all, sir, but
I have some general notions. I do love
To note and to observe: though I live out,
Free from the active torrent, yet I'd mark
The currents and the passages of things,
For mine own private use; and know the ebbs
And flows of state.
PEREGRINE. Believe it, sir, I hold
Myself in no small tie unto my fortunes,
For casting me thus luckily upon you,
Whose knowledge, if your bounty equal it,
May do me great assistance, in instruction
For my behavior and my bearing, which
Is yet so rude and raw.
SIR POLITICK. Why, came you forth
Empty of rules for travel?
PEREGRINE. Faith, I had
Some common ones, from out that vulgar grammar,
Which he that cried Italian to me, taught me.
SIR POLITICK. Why, this it is that spoils all our brave bloods,
Trusting our hopeful gentry unto pedants,
Fellows of outside, and mere bark. You seem
To be a gentleman, of ingenuous race: —
I not profess it, but my fate hath been
To be, where I have been consulted with,
In this high kind, touching some great men's sons,
Persons of blood and honor. —

(*Enter* MOSCA *and* NANO *disguised, followed by persons with materials for erecting a stage.*)

PEREGRINE Who be these, sir?
MOSCA. Under that window, there 't must be. The same.
SIR POLITICK. Fellows, to mount a bank. Did your instructor
In the dear tongues, never discourse to you
Of the Italian mountebanks?
PEREGRINE. Yes, sir.
SIR POLITICK. Why,
Here you shall see one.
PEREGRINE. They are quacksalvers;
Fellows, that live by venting[14] oils and rugs.
SIR POLITICK. Was that the character he gave you of them?
PEREGRINE. As I remember.

[14] **Venting**: selling.

SIR POLITICK. Pity his ignorance.
They are the only knowing men of Europe!
Great general scholars, excellent physicians,
Most admired statesmen, professed favorites,
And cabinet counselors to the greatest princes;
The only languaged men of all the world!

PEREGRINE. And, I have heard, they are most lewd[15] imposters;
Made all of terms and shreds; no less beliers
Of great men's favors, than their own vile med'cines;
Which they will utter upon monstrous oaths:
Selling that drug for two-pence, ere they part,
Which they have valued at twelve crowns before.

SIR POLITICK. Sir, calumnies are answered best with silence.
Yourself shall judge. — Who is it mounts, my friends?

MOSCA. Scoto of Mantua,[16] sir.

SIR POLITICK. Is't he? Nay, then
I'll proudly promise, sir, you shall behold
Another man than has been phant'sied to you.
I wonder yet, that he should mount his bank,
Here in this nook, that has been wont t'appear
In face of the Piazza! — Here he comes.

(*Enter* VOLPONE, *disguised as a mountebank Doctor, and followed by a crowd of people.*)

VOLPONE (*to* NANO). Mount, zany.

MOB. Follow, follow, follow, follow!

SIR POLITICK. See how the people follow him! he's a man
May write ten thousand crowns in bank here. Note,

(VOLPONE *mounts the stage.*)

Mark but his gesture: — I do use to observe
The state he keeps in getting up.

PEREGRINE. 'Tis worth it, sir.

VOLPONE. Most noble gentlemen, and my worthy patrons! It may seem strange, that I, your Scoto Mantuano, who was ever wont to fix my bank in face of the public Piazza, near the shelter of the Portico to the Procuratia, should now, after eight months' absence from this illustrious city of Venice, humbly retire myself into an obscure nook of the Piazza.

SIR POLITICK. Did not I now object to same?

PEREGRINE. Peace, sir.

VOLPONE. Let me tell you: I am not, as your Lombard proverb saith, cold on my feet; or content to part with my commodities at a cheaper rate, than I accustomed: look not for it. Nor that the calumnious reports

[15] **Lewd**: ignorant.
[16] **Scoto of Mantua**: an Italian juggler.

of that impudent detractor, and shame to our profession (Alessandro Buttone, I mean), who gave out, in public, I was condemned *a sforzato*[17] to the galleys, for poisoning the Cardinal Bembo's —— cook, hath at all attached, much less dejected me. No, no, worthy gentlemen; to tell you true, I cannot endure to see the rabble of these ground *ciarlitani*,[18] that spread their cloaks on the pavement, as if they meant to do feats of activity, and then come in lamely, with their mouldy tales out of Boccacio, like stale Tabarine, the fabulist:[19] some of them discoursing their travels, and of their tedious captivity in the Turks' galleys, when, indeed, were the truth known, they were the Christians' galleys, where very temperately they ate bread, and drunk water, as a wholesome penance, enjoined them by their confessors, for base pilferies.

SIR POLITICK. Note but his bearing, and contempt of these.

VOLPONE. These turdy-facy-nasty-paty-lousy-fartical rogues, with one poor groat's-worth of unprepared antimony, finely wrapt up in several *scartoccios*,[20] are able, very well, to kill their twenty a week, and play; yet these meagre, starved spirits, who have half stopped the organs of their minds with earthy oppilations,[21] want not their favorers among your shrivelled salad-eating artisans, who are overjoyed that they may have their half-pe'rth of physic; though it purge them into another world, it makes no matter.

SIR POLITICK. Excellent! have you heard better language, sir?

VOLPONE. Well, let them go. And, gentlemen, honorable gentlemen, know, that for this time, our bank, being thus removed from the clamors of the *canaglia*,[22] shall be the scene of pleasure and delight; for I have nothing to sell, little or nothing to sell.

SIR POLITICK. I told you, sir, his end.

PEREGRINE. You did so, sir.

VOLPONE. I protest, I, and my six servants, are not able to make of this precious liquor, so fast as it is fetched away from my lodging by gentlemen of your city; strangers of the Terrafirma; worshipful merchants: ay, and senators too: who, ever since my arrival, have detained me to their uses, by their splendidous liberalities. And worthily; for, what avails your rich man to have his magazines stuffed with *moscadelli*,[23] or of the purest grape, when his physicians prescribe him, on pain of death, to drink nothing but water cocted with aniseeds? O health! health! the blessing of the rich! the riches of the poor! who can buy thee at too dear a rate, since there is no enjoying this world without thee? Be not then so sparing of your purses, honorable gentlemen, as to abridge the natural course of life —

17 **A *sforzato*:** with hard labor.
18 ***Ciarlitani*:** charlatans.
19 **Tabarine, the fabulis:** a popular French story teller.
20 ***Scartoccios*:** wrapping paper.
21 **Oppilations:** obstructions
22 ***Canaglia*:** riff-raff.
23 ***Moscadelli*:** muscatel.

PEREGRINE. You see his end.

SIR POLITICK. Ay, is't not good?

VOLPONE. For, when a humid flux, of catarrh, by the mutability of air, falls from your head into an arm or shoulder, or any other part; take you a ducat, or your chequin of gold, and apply to the place affected: see what good effect it can work. No, no, 'tis this blessed *unguento,*[24] this rare extraction, that hath only power to disperse all malignant humors, that proceed either of hot, cold, moist, or windy causes —

PEREGRINE. I would he had put in dry too.

SIR POLITICK. 'Pray you, observe.

VOLPONE. To fortify the most indigest and crude stomach, ay, were it of one that, through extreme weakness, vomited blood, applying only a warm napkin to the place, after the unction and fricace;[25] — for the *vertigine*[26] in the head, putting but a drop into your nostrils, likewise behind the ears; a most sovereign and approved remedy: the *mal caduco,*[27] cramps, convulsions, paralyses, epilepsies, *tremorcordia,*[28] retired nerves, ill vapors of the spleen, stopping of the liver, the stone, the *strangury, hernia ventosa, iliaca passio,*[29] stops a *dysenteria* immediately; easeth the torsion of the small guts; and cures *melanchoia hypondriaca,* being taken and applied according to my printed receipt. (*Pointing to his bill and his vial.*) For this is the physician, this the medicine; this counsels, this cures; this gives the direction, this works the effect; and, in sum, both together may be termed an abstract of the theoric and practic in the Æsculapian art. 'Twill cost you eight crowns. And, — Zan Fritada, prithee sing a verse extempore in honor of it.

SIR POLITICK. How do you like him, sir?

PEREGRINE. Most strangely, I!

SIR POLITICK. Is not his language rare?

PEREGRINE. But alchemy, I never heard the like; or Broughton's[30] books.

NANO (*sings*). Had old Hippocrates, or Galen,
That to their books put med'cines all in,
But known this secret, they had never
(Of which they will be guilty ever)
Been murderers of so much paper,
Or wasted many a hurtless taper;
No Indian drug had e'er been famed,
Tobacco, sassafras not named;
Ne yet, of guacum[31] one small stick, sir,

[24] ***Unguento:*** ointment.
[25] **Fricace:** salve.
[26] ***Vertigine:*** dizziness.
[27] ***Mal caduco:*** epilepsy.
[28] ***Tremorcordia:*** palpitations of the heart.
[29] ***Hernia ventosa, iliaca passio:*** types of colic.
[30] **Broughton:** an English theologian and dabbler in the occult.
[31] **Guacum:** a medicinal resin.

Nor Raymund Lully's[32] great elixir.
Ne had been known the Danish Gonswart,[33]
Or Paracelsus,[34] with his long sword.

VOLPONE. No more. — Gentlemen, if I had but time to discourse to you the miraculous effects of this my oil, surnamed Oglio del Scoto; with the countless catalogue of those I have cured of the aforesaid, and many more diseases; the patents and privileges of all the princes and commonwealths of Christendom; or but the depositions of those that appeared on my part, before the Signiory of the Sanita and most learned College of Physicians; where I was authorised, upon notice taken of the admirable virtues of my medicaments, and mine own excellency in matter of rare and unknown secrets, not only to disperse them publicly in this famous city, but in all the territories, that happily joy under the government of the most pious and magnificent states of Italy. But may some other gallant fellow say, 'O, there be divers that make professions to have as good, and as experimented receipts as yours:' indeed, very many have assayed, like apes, in imitation of that, which is really and essentially in me, to make of this oil; bestowed great cost in furnaces, stills, alembics, continual fires, and preparation of the ingredients, (as indeed there goes to it six hundred several simples, besides some quantity of human fat, for the conglutination, which we buy of the anatomists,) but, when these practitioners come to the last decoction, blow, blow, puff, puff, and all flies *in fumo:* ha, ha, ha! Poor wretches! I rather pity their folly and indescretion, than their loss of time and money; for these may be recovered by industry: but to be a fool born, is a disease incurable.

For myself, I always from my youth have endeavored to get the rarest secrets, and book them, either in exchange, or for money: I spared nor cost nor labor, where any thing was worthy to be learned. And, gentlemen, honorable gentlemen, I will undertake, by virtue of chemical art, out of the honorable hat that covers your head, to extract the four elements; that is to say, the fire, air, water, and earth, and return you your felt without burn or stain. For, whilst others have been at the balloo,[35]

PEREGRINE. All this, yet, will not do; eight crowns is high.

I have been at my book; and am now past the craggy paths of study, and come to the flowery plains of honor and reputation.

SIR POLITICK. I do assure you, sir, that is his aim.

VOLPONE. But to our price —

PEREGRINE And that withal, Sir Pol.

VOLPONE. You all know, honorable gentlemen, I never valued this *ampulla*, or vial, at less than eight crowns; but for this time, I am content to be deprived of it for six: six crowns is the price, and less in courtesy

[32] **Raymund Lully:** a Spanish philosopher of the 13th century.
[33] **Gonswart:** a Danish scholar of the 15th century.
[34] **Paracelsus:** a Swiss physician and alchemist of the 16th century.
[35] **Balloo:** a French or Italian game played with a large ball and a wooden bat.

I know you cannot offer me; take it or leave it, howsoever, both it and I am at your service. I ask you not as the value of the thing, for then I should demand of you a thousand crowns, so the cardinals Montalto, Fernese, the great Duke of Tuscany, my gossip,[36] with divers other princes, have given me; but I despise money. Only to show my affection to you, honorable gentlemen, and your illustrious State here, I have neglected the messages of these princes, mine own offices, framed my journey hither, only to present you with the fruits of my travels. — Tune your voices once more to the touch of your instruments, and give the honorable assembly some delightful recreation.

PEREGRINE. What monstrous and most painful circumstance
Is here, to get some three or four gazettes,[37]
Some three pence in the whole! for that 'twill come to.

NANO (*sings*). You that would last long, list to my song,
Make no more coil, but buy of this oil.
Would you be ever fair and young?
Stout of teeth, and strong of tongue?
Tart of palate? quick of ear?
Sharp of sight? of nostril clear?
Moist of hand? and light of foot?
Or, I will come nearer to't,
Would you live free from all diseases?
Do the act your mistress pleases,
Yet fright all aches from your bones?
Here's a medicine for the nones.[38]

VOLPONE. Well, I am in a humor at this time to make a present of the small quantity my coffer contains; to the rich in courtesy, and to the poor for God's sake. Wherefore now mark: I asked you six crowns; and six crowns, at other times, you have paid me; you shall not give me six crowns, nor five, nor four, nor three, nor two, nor one; nor half a ducat; no, nor a *moccinigo*.[39] Sixpence it will cost you, or six hundred pound — expect no lower price, for, by the banner of my front, I will not bate a bagatine,[40] — that I will have, only, a pledge of your loves, to carry something from amongst you, to show I am not condemned by you. Therefore, now, toss your handkerchiefs, cheerfully, cheerfully; and be advertised, that the first heroic spirit that deigns to grace me with a handkerchief, I will give it a little remembrance of something, beside, shall please it better, than if I had presented it with a double pistolet.[41]

[36] **My gossip**: close friends.
[37] **Gazettes**: small Venetian coins.
[38] **For the nones**: for the occasion, or nonce.
[39] ***Moccinigo:*** a small Venetian coin.
[40] **Bagatine**: a small Venetian coin.
[41] **Pistolet**: a gold coin.

PEREGRINE. Will you be that heroic spark, Sir Pol?

(CELIA *at a window above, throws down her handkerchief.*)

O, see! the window has prevented[42] you.

VOLPONE. Lady, I kiss your bounty; and for this timely grace you have done your poor Scoto of Mantua, I will return you, over and above my oil, a secret of that high and inestimable nature, shall make you for ever enamored on that minute, wherein your eye first descended on so mean, yet not altogether to be despised, an object. Here is a powder concealed in this paper, of which, if I should speak to the worth, nine thousand volumes were but as one page, that page as a line, that line as a word; so short is this pilgrimage of man (which some call life) to the expressing of it. Would I reflect on the price? why, the whole world is but as an empire, that empire as a province, that province as a bank, that bank as a private purse to the purchase of it. I will only tell you; it is the powder that made Venus a goddess (given her by Apollo), that kept her perpetually young, cleared her wrinkles, firmed her gums, filled her skin, colored her hair; from her derived to Helen, and at the sack of Troy unfortunately lost: till now, in this our age, it was as happily recovered, by a studious antiquary, out of some ruins of Asia, who sent a moiety of it to the court of France (but much sophisticated), wherewith the ladies there, now, color their hair. The rest, at this present, remains with me; extracted to a quintessence: so that, wherever it but touches, in youth it perpetually preserves, in age restores the complexion; seats your teeth, did they dance like virginal jacks,[43] firm as a wall; makes them white as ivory, that were black as —

(*Enter* CORVINO)

CORVINO. Spight o' the devil, and my shame! come down here;
Come down; — No house but mine to make your scene?
Signior Flaminio, will you down, sir? down?
What, is my wife your Franciscina, sir?
No windows on the whole Piazza, here,
To make your properties, but mine? but mine? (*Beats away* VOLPONE, NANO, *etc.*)
Heart! ere tomorrow I shall be new-christened,
And called the Pantalone di Besogniosi,[44]
About the town.

PEREGRINE. What should this mean, Sir Pol?

SIR POLITICK. Some trick of state, believe it; I will home.

[42] **Prevented:** preceded, anticipated, gotten ahead of.

[43] **Virginal jacks:** pieces of wood attached to the keys of the virginal.

[44] **Pantalone di Besogniosi:** Pantalone of the Beggars; Pantalone or Pantaloon was a stock character in the Italian comedy and pantomime, often an old dotard, the butt and accomplice of the clown.

PEREGRINE. It may be some design on you.
SIR POLITICK. I know not,
I'll stand upon my guard.
PEREGRINE. It is your best, sir.
SIR POLITICK. This three weeks, all my advices, all my letters,
They have been intercepted.
PEREGRINE. Indeed, sir!
Best have a care.
SIR POLITICK. Nay, so I will.
PEREGRINE. This knight,
I may not lose him, for my mirth, till night.

(*Exeunt.*)

Scene 2

(*A room in* VOLPONE'S *house. Enter* VOLPONE *and* MOSCA.)

VOLPONE. O, I am wounded!
MOSCA. Where, sir?
VOLPONE. Not without;
Those blows were nothing: I could bear them ever.
But angry Cupid, bolting from her eyes,
Hath shot himself into me like a flame;
Where, now, he flings about his burning heat,
As in a furnace an ambitious fire,
Whose vent is stopped. The fight is all within me.
I cannot live, except thou help me, Mosca;
My liver melts, and I, without the hope
Of some soft air, from her refreshing breath,
Am but a heap of cinders.
MOSCA. 'Las, good sir,
Would you had never seen her!
VOLPONE. Nay, would thou
Had'st never told me of her!
MOSCA. Sir, 'tis true;
I do confess I was unfortunate,
And you unhappy: but I'm bound in conscience,
No less than duty, to effect my best
To your release of torment, and I will, sir.
VOLPONE. Dear Mosca, shall I hope?
MOSCA. Sir, more than dear,
I will not bid you to despair of aught
Within a human compass.
VOLPONE. O, there spoke
My better angel. Mosca, take my keys,
Gold, plate, and jewels, all's at thy devotion;

Employ them how thou wilt; nay, coin me too:
So thou, in this, but crown my longings, Mosca.

MOSCA. Use but your patience.

VOLPONE. So I have.

MOSCA. I doubt not.
To bring success to your desires.

VOLPONE. Nay, then,
I not repent me of my late disguise.

MOSCA. If you can horn him, sir, you need not.

VOLPONE. True:
Besides, I never meant him for my heir. —
Is not the color of my beard and eyebrows
To make me known?

MOSCA. No jot.

VOLPONE. I did it well!

MOSCA. So well, would I could follow you in mine,
with half the happiness! — (*aside*) and yet I would
Escape your epilogue.[45]

VOLPONE. But were they gulled
With a belief that I was Scoto?

MOSCA. Sir,
Scoto himself could hardly have distinguished!
I have not time to flatter you now; we'll part;
And as I prosper, so applaud my art.

(*Exeunt.*)

Scene 3

(*A room in* CORVINO's *house. Enter* CORVINO, *with his sword in his hand, dragging in* CELIA.)

CORVINO. Death of mine honor, with the city's fool!
A juggling, tooth-drawing, prating mountebank!
And at a public window! where, whilst he,
With his strained action, and his dole of faces,
To his drug-lecture draws your itching ears,
A crew of old, unmarried, noted letchers,
Stood leering up like satyrs; and you smile
Most graciously, and fan your favors forth,
To give your hot spectators satisfaction!
What, was your mountebank their call? their whistle?
Or were you enamored on his copper rings,
His saffron jewel, with the toad-stone in't,
Or his embroidered suit, with the cope-stitch,

[45] **Escape your epilogue**: avoid your beating.

Made of a herse cloth? or his old tilt-feather?
Or his starched beard? Well, you shall have him, yes!
He shall come home, and minister unto you
The fricace for the mother. Or, let me see,
I think you'd rather mount; would you not mount?
Why, if you'll mount, you may; yes, truly, you may:
And so you may be seen, down to the foot.
Get you a cittern, Lady Vanity,
And be a dealer with the virtuous man;
Make one: I'll but protest myself a cuckold,
And save your dowry. I'm a Dutchman, I!
For, if you thought me an Italian,
You would be damned, ere you did this, you whore!
Thou'dst tremble, to imagine, that the murder
Of father, mother, brother, all thy race,
Should follow, as the subject of my justice.

CELIA. Good sir, have patience.

CORVINO. What couldst thou propose
Less to thyself, than in this heat of wrath.
And stung with my dishonor, I should strike
This steel into thee, with as many stabs,
As thou wert gazed upon with goatish eyes?

CELIA. Alas, sir, be appeased! I could not think
My being at the window should more now
Move your impatience, than at other times.

CORVINO. No! not to seek and entertain a parley
With a known knave, before a multitude!
You were an actor with your handkerchief,
Which he most sweetly kissed in the receipt,
And might, no doubt, return it with a letter,
And point the place where you might meet; your sister's,
Your mother's, or your aunt's might serve the turn.

CELIA. Why, dear sir, when do I make these excuses,
Or ever stir abroad, but to the church?
And that so seldom —

CORVINO. Well, it shall be less;
And thy restraint before was liberty,
To what I now decree: and therefore mark me.
First, I will have this bawdy light dammed up;
And till't be done, some two or three yards off,
I'll chalk a line: o'er which if thou but chance
To set thy desperate foot, more hell, more horror,
More wild remorseless rage shall seize on thee,
Than on a conjuror, that had heedless left
His circle's safety ere his devil was laid.
Then here's a lock which I will hang upon thee,
And, now I think on't, I will keep thee backwards;

Thy lodging shall be backwards; thy walks backwards;
Thy prospect, all be backwards; and no pleasure,
That thou shalt know but backwards: nay, since you force
My honest nature, know, it is your own,
Being too open, makes me use you thus.
Since you will not contain your subtle nostrils
In a sweet room, but they must snuff the air
Of rank and sweaty passengers.

(*Knocking within.*)

— One knocks.
Away, and be not seen, pain of thy life;
Nor look toward the window: if thou dost —
Nay, stay, here this — let me not prosper, whore,
But I will make thee an anatomy,
Dissect thee mine own self, and read a lecture
Upon thee to the city, and in public.
Away! —

(*Exit* CELIA. *Enter* SERVANT.)

Who's there?
SERVANT. 'Tis Signior Mosca, sir.

(*Enter* MOSCA.)

CORVINO. Let him come in.

(*Exit* SERVANT.)

His master's dead: there's yet
Some good to help the bad. — My Mosca, welcome!
I guess your news.
MOSCA. I fear you cannot, sir.
CORVINO. Is't not his death?
MOSCA. Rather the contrary.
CORVINO. Not his recovery?
MOSCA. Yes, sir.
CORVINO. I am cursed,
I am bewitched, my crosses meet to vex me.
How? how? how? how?
MOSCA. Why, sir, with Scoto's oil;
Corbaccio and Voltore brought of it,
Whilst I was busy in an inner room —
CORVINO. Death! that damned mountebank; but for the law
Now, I could kill the rascal; it cannot be,

His oil should have that virtue. Have not I
Known him a common rogue, come fiddling in
To the *osteria*,[46] with a tumbling whore,
And, when he has done all his forced tricks, been glad
Of a poor spoonful of dead wine, with flies in't?
It cannot be. All his ingredients
Are a sheep's gall, a roasted bitch's marrow,
Some few sod earwigs, pounded caterpillars,
A little capon's grease, and fasting spittle:
I know them to a dram.

MOSCA. I know not, sir;
But some on't, there, they poured into his ears,
Some in his nostrils, and recovered him;
Applying but the fricace.

CORVINO. Pox o' that fricace!

MOSCA. And since, to seem the more officious
And flatt'ring of his health, there, they have had,
At extreme fees, the College of Physicians
Consulting on him, how they might restore him;
Where one would have a cataplasm of spices,
Another a flayed ape clapped to his breast,
A third would have it a dog, a fourth an oil,
With wild cats' skins: at last, they all resolved
That, to preserve him, was no other means,
But some young woman must be straight sought out,
Lusty, and full of juice, to sleep by him;
And to this service, most unhappily,
And most unwillingly, am I now employed,
Which here I thought to pre-acquaint you with,
For your advice, since it concerns you most;
Because, I would not do that thing might cross
Your ends, on whom I have my whole dependence, sir:
Yet, if I do it not, they may delate
My slackness to my patron, work me out
Of his opinion; and there all your hopes,
Ventures, or whatsoever, are all frustrate!
I do but tell you, sir. Besides, they are all
Now striving, who shall first present him; therefore —
I could entreat you, briefly conclude somewhat;
Prevent them if you can.

CORVINO. Death to my hopes,
This is my villainous fortune! Best to hire
Some common courtesan.

MOSCA. Ay, I thought on that, sir;
But they are all so subtle, full of art —

[46] ***Osteria:*** hostelry, inn.

And age again doting and flexible,
So as — I cannot tell — we may, perchance,
Light on a quean may cheat us all.
CORVINO. 'Tis true.
MOSCA. No, no: it must be one that has no tricks, sir,
Some simple thing, a creature made unto it;
Some wench you may command. Have you no kinswoman?
Godso — Think, think, think, think, think, think, think, sir.
One o' the doctors offered there his daughter.
CORVINO. How!
MOSCA. Yes, Signior Lupo, the physician.
CORVINO. His daughter!
MOSCA. And a virgin, sir. Why, alas,
He knows the state of's body, what it is;
That nought can warm his blood, sir, but a fever;
Nor any incantation raise his spirit:
A long forgetfulness hath seized that part.
Besides sir, who shall know it? some one or two —
CORVINO. I pray thee give me leave. (*Walks aside.*) If any man
But I had had this luck — the thing in 'tself,
I know, is nothing — Wherefore should not I
As well command my blood and my affections,
As this dull doctor? In the point of honor,
The cases are all one of wife and daughter.
MOSCA (*aside*). I hear him coming.
CORVINO. She shall do't: 'tis done.
Slight! if this doctor, who is not engaged,
Unless 't be for his counsel, which is nothing,
Offer his daughter, what should I, that am
So deeply in? I will prevent him: Wretch!
Covetous wretch — Mosca, I have determined.
MOSCA. How, sir?
CORVINO. We'll make all sure. The party you wot of
Shall be mine own wife, Mosca.
MOSCA. Sir, the thing,
But that I would not seem to counsel you,
I should have motioned to you, at the first:
And make your count, you have cut all their throats.
Why, 'tis directly taking a possession!
And in his next fit, we may let him go.
'Tis but to pull the pillow from his head,
And he is throttled: it had been done before.
But for your scrupulous doubts.
CORVINO. Ay, a plague on't,
My conscience fools my wit! Well, I'll be brief,
And so be thou, lest they should be before us:
Go home, prepare him, tell him with what zeal

And willingness I do it; swear it was
On the first hearing, as thou may'st do, truly,
Mine own free motion.
MOSCA. Sir, I warrant you,
I'll so possess him with it, that the rest
Of his starved clients shall be banished all;
And only you received. But come not, sir,
Until I send, for I have something else
To ripen for your good, you must not know't.
CORVINO. But do not you forget to send now.
MOSCA. Fear not. (*Exit.*)
CORVINO. Where are you, wife? my Celia! wife!

(*Enter* CELIA.)

— What, blubbering?
Come, dry those tears. I think thou thought'st me in earnest;
Ha! by this light I talked so but to try thee:
Methinks the lightness of the occasion
Should have confirmed thee. Come, I am not jealous.
CELIA. No!
CORVINO. Faith I am not, I, nor never was;
It is a poor unprofitable humor.
Do not I know, if women have a will,
They'll do 'gainst all the watches of the world,
And that the fiercest spies are tamed with gold?
Tut, I am confident in thee, thou shalt see't;
And see I'll give thee cause too, to believe it.
Come kiss me. Go, and make thee ready, straight,
In all thy best attire, thy choicest jewels,
Put them all on, and, with them, thy best looks:
We are invited to a solemn feast,
At old Volpone's, where it shall appear
How far I am free from jealousy or fear.

(*Exeunt.*)

ACT THREE

Scene 1

(*A street. Enter* MOSCA.)

MOSCA. I fear, I shall begin to grow in love
With my dear self, and my most prosperous parts,
They do so spring and burgeon; I can feel

A whimsy in my blood: I know not how,
Success hath made me wanton. I could skip
Out of my skin, now, like a subtle snake,
I am so limber, O! your parasite
Is a most precious thing, dropped from above,
Not bred 'mongst clods and clodpoles, here on earth.
I muse, the mystery was not made a science,
It is so liberally professed! Almost
All the wise world is little else, in nature,
But parasites or sub-parasites. — And yet,
I mean not those that have your bare town-art,
To know who's fit to feed them; have no house,
No family, no care, and therefore mold
Tales for men's ears, to bait that sense; or get
Kitchen-invention, and some stale receipts
To please the belly, and the groin; nor those,
With their court dog-tricks, that can fawn and fleer,
Make their revenue out of legs and faces,
Echo my lord, and lick away a moth:
But your fine elegant rascal, that can rise,
And stoop, almost together, like an arrow;
Shoot through the air as nimbly as a star;
Turn short as doth a swallow; and be here,
And there, and here, and yonder, all at once;
Present to any humor, all occasion;
And change a visor, swifter than a thought!
This is the creature had the art born with him;
Toils not to learn it, but doth practise it
Out of most excellent nature: and such sparks
Are the true parasites, others but their zanies.

(*Enter* BONARIO.)

MOSCA. Who's this? Bonario, old Corbaccio's son?
The person I was bound to seek. — Fair sir,
You are happily met.
BONARIO. That cannot be by thee.
MOSCA. Why, sir?
BONARIO. Nay, pray thee, know thy way, and leave me:
I would be loth to interchange discourse
With such a mate as thou art.
MOSCA. Courteous sir,
Scorn not my poverty.
BONARIO. Not I, by heaven;
But thou shalt give me leave to hate thy baseness.
MOSCA. Baseness!
BONARIO. Ay; answer me, is not thy sloth

Sufficient argument? thy flattery?
Thy means of feeding?
MOSCA. Heaven be good to me!
These imputations are too common, sir,
And easily stuck on virtue when she's poor.
You are unequal[47] to me, and however
Your sentence may be righteous, yet you are not
That, ere you know me, thus proceed in censure:
St. Mark bear witness 'gainst you, 'tis inhuman. (*Weeps.*)
BONARIO (*aside*). What! does he weep? the sign is soft and good:
I do repent me that I was so harsh.
MOSCA. 'Tis true, that, swayed by strong necessity,
I am enforced to eat my careful bread
With too much obsequy: 'tis true, beside,
That I am fain to spin mine own poor raiment
Out of my mere observance, being not born
To a free fortune: but that I have done
Base offices, in rending friends asunder,
Dividing families, betraying counsels,
Whispering false lies, or mining men with praises,
Trained their credulity with perjuries,
Corrupted chastity, or am in love
With mine own tender ease, but would not rather
Prove the most rugged, and laborious course,
That might redeem my present estimation,
Let me here perish, in all hope of goodness.
BONARIO (*aside*). This cannot be a personated passion.—
I was to blame, so to mistake thy nature;
Prithee, forgive me: and speak out thy business.
MOSCA. Sir, it concerns you; and though I may seem,
At first to make a main offence in manners,
And in my gratitude unto my master;
Yet, for the pure love, which I bear all right,
And hatred of the wrong, I must reveal it.
This very hour your father is in purpose
To disinherit you —
BONARIO. How!
MOSCA. And thrust you forth,
As a mere stranger to his blood; 'tis true, sir,
The work no way engageth me, but, as
I claim an interest in the general state
Of goodness and true virtue, which I hear
To abound in you: and, for which mere respect,
Without a second aim, sir, I have done it.
BONARIO. This tale hath lost thee much of the late trust

[47] **Unequal:** unjust.

Thou hadst with me; it is impossible:
I know not how to lend it any thought,
My father should be so unnatural.
MOSCA. It is a confidence that well becomes
Your piety; and former, no doubt, it is
From your own simple innocence: which makes
Your wrong more monstrous and abhorred. But, sir,
I now will tell you more. This very minute,
It is, or will be doing; and, if you
Shall be but pleased to go with me, I'll bring you,
I dare not say where you shall see, but where
Your ear shall be a witness of the deed;
Hear yourself written bastard, and professed
The common issue of the earth.
BONARIO. I am amazed!
MOSCA. Sir, if I do it not, draw your just sword,
And score your vengeance on my front and face:
Mark me your villain: you have too much wrong,
And I do suffer for you, sir. My heart
Weeps blood in anguish —
BONARIO. Lead; I follow thee.

(*Exeunt.*)

Scene 2

(*A room in* VOLPONE'S *house. Enter* VOLPONE.)

VOLPONE. Mosca stays long, methinks. — Bring forth your sports,
And help to make the wretched time more sweet.

(*Enter* NANO, ANDROGYNO, *and* CASTRONE.)

NANO. Dwarf, fool, and eunuch, well met here we be.
A question it were now, whether of us three,
Being all the known delicates of a rich man,
In pleasing him, claim the precedency can?
CASTRONE. I claim for myself.
ANDROGYNO. And so doth the fool.
NANO. 'Tis foolish indeed: let me set you both to school.
First for your dwarf, he's little and witty,
And every thing, as it is little, is pretty;
Else why do men say to a creature of my shape,
So soon as they see him, "It's a pretty little ape"?
And why a pretty ape, but for pleasing imitation
Of greater men's actions, in a ridiculous fashion?

Beside, this feat[48] body of mine doth not crave
Half the meat, drink, and cloth, one of your bulks will have.
Admit your fool's face be the mother of laughter,
Yet, for his brain, it must always come after:
And though that do feed him, it's a pitiful case,
His body is beholding to such a bad face.

(*Knocking within.*)

VOLPONE. Who's there? my couch; away! look! Nano, see:

(*Exeunt* ANDROGYNO *and* CASTRONE.)

Give me my caps, first — go, enquire.

(*Exit* NANO.)

— Now, Cupid
Send it be Mosca, and with fair return!

NANO (*within*). It is the beauteous madam —

VOLPONE. Would-be — is it?

NANO. The same.

VOLPONE. Now torment on me! Squire her in;
For she will enter, or dwell here for ever:
Nay, quickly. (*Retires to his couch.*) — That my fit were past! I fear
A second hell too, that my loathing this
Will quite expel my appetite to the other:
Would she were taking now her tedious leave.
Lord, how it threats me what I am to suffer!

(*Enter* NANO, *with* LADY POLITICK WOULD-BE.)

LADY POLITICK. I thank you, good sir. 'Pray you signify
Unto your patron, I am here. — This band
Shows not my neck enough. — I trouble you, sir;
Let me request you bid one of my women
Come hither to me. — In good faith, I am dressed
Most favorably to-day! It is no matter:
'Tis well enough. —

(*Enter* FIRST WAITING-WOMAN.)

Look, see, these petulant things,
How they have done this!

[48] **Feat**: delicate.

VOLPONE (*aside*). I do feel the fever
Entering in at mine ears; O, for a charm,
To fright it hence!
LADY POLITICK. Come nearer: is this curl
In his right place, or thus? Why is this higher
Than all the rest? You have not washed your eyes yet!
Or do they not stand even in your head?
Where is your fellow? call her.

(*Exit* FIRST WAITING-WOMAN.)

NANO. Now, St. Mark
Deliver us, anon, she'll beat her women,
Because her nose is red.

(*Enter* FIRST *with* SECOND WAITING-WOMAN.)

LADY POLITICK. I pray you, view
This tire,[49] forsooth: are all things apt, or no?
FIRST WAITING-WOMAN. One hair a little, here, sticks out, forsooth.
LADY POLITICK. Does't so, forsooth! and where was your dear sight,
When it did so, forsooth! What now! bird-eyed?
And you, too? 'Pray you, both approach and mend it.
Now, by that light, I muse you are not ashamed!
I, that have preached these things so oft unto you,
Read you the principles, argued all the grounds,
Disputed every fitness, every grace,
Called you to counsel of so frequent dressings —
NANO (*aside*). More carefully than of your fame or honor.
LADY POLITICK. Made you acquainted, what an ample dowry
The knowledge of these things would be unto you,
Able alone, to get you noble husbands
At your return: and you thus to neglect it!
Besides you seeing what a curious nation
The Italians are, what will they say of me?
"The English lady cannot dress herself."
Here's a fine imputation to our country!
Well, go your ways, and stay in the next room.
This fucus[50] was too coarse too; it's no matter. —
Good sir, you'll give them entertainment?

(*Exeunt* NANO *and* WAITING-WOMEN.)

VOLPONE. The storm comes toward me.
LADY POLITICK (*goes to the couch*). How does my Volpone?

[49] **Tire**: hairdress, coiffure.
[50] **Fucus**: cosmetic preparation.

VOLPONE. Troubled with noise, I cannot sleep: I dreamt
That a strange fury entered, now, my house,
And, with the dreadful tempest of her breath,
Did cleave my roof asunder.

LADY POLITICK. Believe me, and I
Had the most fearful dream, could I remember't —

VOLPONE (*aside*). Out of my fate! I have given her the occasion
How to torment me: She will tell me hers.

LADY POLITICK. Methought, the golden mediocrity,
Polite and delicate —

VOLPONE. O, if you do love me,
No more: I sweat, and suffer, at the mention
Of any dream; feel how I tremble yet.

LADY POLITICK. Alas, good soul! the passion of the heart.
Seed-pearl were good now, boiled with syrup of apples,
Tincture of gold, and coral, citron-pills,
Your elicampane root, myrobalanes[51] —

VOLPONE (*aside*). Ah me, I have ta'en a grasshopper by the wing!

LADY POLITICK. Burnt silk, and amber: You have muscadel
Good in the house —

VOLPONE. You will not drink, and part?

LADY POLITICK. No, fear not that. I doubt, we shall not get
Some English saffron, half a dram would serve;
Your sixteen cloves, a little musk, dried mints,
Bugloss, and barley-meal —

VOLPONE (*aside*). She's in again!
Before I feigned diseases, now I have one.

LADY POLITICK. And these applied with a right scarlet cloth.

VOLPONE (*aside*). Another flood of words! a very torrent!

LADY POLITICK. Shall I, sir, make you a poultice?

VOLPONE. No, no, no,
I'm very well; you need prescribe no more.

LADY POLITICK. I have a little studied physic; but now,
I'm all for music, save, in the forenoons,
An hour or two for painting. I would have
A lady, indeed, to have all, letters and arts,
Be able to discourse, to write, to paint,
But principal, as Plato holds, your music,
And so does wise Pythagoras, I take it,
Is your true rapture: when there is consent
In fact, in voice, and clothes: and is, indeed,
Our sex's chiefest ornament.

VOLPONE. The poet
As old in time as Plato, and as knowing,
Says, that your highest female grace is silence.

[51] **Elicampane root, myrobalanes:** medicinal herbs.

LADY POLITICK. Which of your poets? Petrarch, or Tasso, or Dante?
Guarini? Ariosto? Aretine?
Cieco di Hadria? I have read them all.
VOLPONE (*aside*). Is every thing a cause to my destruction?
LADY POLITICK. I think I have two or three of them about me.
VOLPONE (*aside*). The sun, the sea, will sooner both stand still
Then her eternal tongue! nothing can 'scape it.
LADY POLITICK. Here's *Pastor Fido*[52] —
VOLPONE (*aside*). Profess obstinate silence;
That's now my safest.
LADY POLITICK. All our English writers,
I mean such as are happy in the Italian,
Will design to steal out of this author, mainly:
Almost as much as from Montagnié:
He has so modern and facile a vein,
Fitting the time, and catching the court-ear!
Your Petrarch is more passionate, yet he,
In days of sonnetting, trusted them with much:
Dante is hard, and few can understand him.
But, for a desperate wit, there's Aretine;
Only, his pictures are a little obscene —
You mark me not.
VOLPONE. Alas, my mind's perturbed.
LADY POLITICK. Why, in such cases, we must cure ourselves,
Make use of our philosophy —
VOLPONE. O me!
LADY POLITICK. And as we find our passions do rebel,
Encounter them with reason, or divert them,
By giving scope unto some other humor
Of lesser danger: as, in politic bodies,
There's nothing more doth overwhelm the judgment,
And cloud the understanding, than too much
Settling and fixing, and, as 'twere, subsiding
Upon one object. For the incorporating
Of these same outward things, into that part,
Which we call mental, leaves some certain *faeces*
That stop the organs, and as Plato says,
Assassinate our knowledge.
VOLPONE (*aside*). Now, the spirit
Of patience help me!
LADY POLITICK. Come, in faith, I must
Visit you more a days; and make you well:
Laugh and be lusty.
VOLPONE (*aside*). My good angel save me!
LADY POLITICK. There was but one sole man in all the world,

[52] *Pastor Fido:* the Faithful Shepherd.

With whom I e'er could sympathise; and he
Would lie you, often, three, four hours together
To hear me speak; and be sometimes so rapt,
As he would answer me quite from the purpose,
Like you, and you are like him, just. I'll discourse,
An't be but only, sir, to bring you asleep,
How we did spend our time and loves together,
For some six years.

VOLPONE. O, O, O, O, O, O!

LADY POLITICK. For we were *coætanei*[53] and brought up —

VOLPONE. Some power, some fate, some fortune rescue me!

(*Enter* MOSCA.)

MOSCA. God save you, madam!

LADY POLITICK. Good sir.

VOLPONE. Mosca! welcome,
Welcome to my redemption.

MOSCA. Why, sir?

VOLPONE. O,
Rid me of this my torture, quickly, there;
My madam, with the everlasting voice:
The bells, in time of pestilence, ne'er made
Like noise, or were in that perpetual motion!
The Cockpit comes not near it. All my house,
But now, steamed like a bath with her thick breath,
A lawyer could not have been heard; nor scarce
Another woman, such a hail of words
She has let fall. For hell's sake, rid her hence.

MOSCA. Has she presented?

VOLPONE. O, I do not care;
I'll take her absence, upon any price,
With any loss.

MOSCA. Madam —

LADY POLITICK. I have brought your patron
A toy, a cap here, of mine own work.

MOSCA. 'Tis well.
I had forgot to tell you, I saw your knight.
Where you would little think it. —

LADY POLITICK. Where?

MOSCA. Marry,
Where yet, if you make haste, you may apprehend
Rowing upon the water in a gondole
With the most cunning courtesan of Venice.

LADY POLITICK. Is't true?

[53] ***Coætanei:*** of the same age.

MOSCA. Pursue them, and believe your eyes:
Leave me, to make your gift:

(*Exit* LADY POLITICK *hastily*.)

— I knew 'twould take:
For, lightly, they that use themselves most license,
Are still most jealous.

VOLPONE. Mosca, hearty thanks,
For thy quick fiction, and delivery of me.
Now to my hopes, what say'st thou?

(*Enter* LADY POLITICK WOULD-BE.)

LADY POLITICK. But do you hear, sir? —

VOLPONE. Again! I fear a paroxysm.

LADY POLITICK. Which way
Rowed they together?

MOSCA. Toward the Rialto.

LADY POLITICK. I pray you lend me your dwarf.

MOSCA. I pray you take him. —

(*Exit* LADY POLITICK.)

Your hopes, sir, are like happy blossoms, fair,
And promise timely fruit, if you will stay
But the maturing; keep you at your couch,
Corbaccio will arrive straight, with the Will;
When he is gone, I'll tell you more. (*Exit*.)

VOLPONE. My blood,
My spirits are returned; I am alive:
And like your wanton gamester at primero,[54]
Whose thought had whispered to him, not go less,
Methinks I lie, and draw — for an encounter.[55]

(*The scene closes upon* VOLPONE.)

Scene 3

(*The passage leading to* VOLPONE'S *chamber. Enter* MOSCA *and* BONARIO.)

MOSCA. Sir, here concealed (*shows him a closet*), you may hear all.
But, pray you,
Have patience, sir;

[54] Primero: a card game.

[55] **Draw — for an encounter**: terms in primero, here used punningly by Volpone.

(*Knocking within.*)

— the same's your father knocks:
I am compelled to leave you. (*Exit.*)
BONARIO. Do so. — Yet
Cannot my thought imagine this a truth. (*Goes into the closet.*)

Scene 4

(*Another part of the same. Enter* MOSCA *and* CORVINO, CELIA *following.*)

MOSCA. Death on me! you are come too soon, what meant you?
Did not I say, I would send?
CORVINO. Yes, but I feared
You might forget it, and then they prevent us.
MOSCA (*aside*). Prevent! did e'er man haste so, for his horns?
A courtier would not ply it so, for a place.
(*To* CORVINO.) Well, now there is no helping it, stay here;
I'll presently return. (*Exit.*)
CORVINO. Where are you, Celia?
You know not wherefore I have brought you hither?
CELIA. Not well, except you told me.
CORVINO. Now, I will:
Hark hither.

(*Exeunt. Enter* MOSCA *and* BONARIO.)

MOSCA. Sir, your father hath sent word.
It will be half an hour ere he come;
And therefore, if you please to walk the while
Into that gallery — at the upper end,
There are some books to entertain the time:
And I'll take care no man shall come unto you, sir.
BONARIO. Yes, I will stay there. — (*Aside.*) I do doubt this fellow. (*Exit.*)
MOSCA (*looking after him*). There; he is far enough; he can hear nothing:
And, for his father, I can keep him off. (*Exit.*)

Scene 5

(VOLPONE'*s chamber.* — VOLPONE *on his couch.* MOSCA *sitting by him. Enter* CORVINO, *forcing in* CELIA.)

CORVINO. Nay, now, there is no starting back, and therefore,
Resolve upon it: I have so decreed.

It must be done. Nor would I move afore,
Because I would avoid all shifts and tricks,
That might deny me.

CELIA. Sir, let me beseech you,
Affect not these strange trials; if you doubt
My chastity, why, lock me up for ever;
Make me the heir of darkness. Let me live,
Where I may please your fears, if not your trust.

CORVINO. Believe it, I have no such humor, I.
All that I speak I mean; yet I'm not mad;
Nor horn-mad, see you? Go to, show yourself
Obedient, and a wife.

CELIA. O heaven!

CORVINO. I say it,
Do so.

CELIA. Was this the train?

CORVINO. I've told you reasons;
What the physicians have set down: how much
It may concern me; what my engagements are;
My means; and the necessity of those means,
For my recovery: wherefore, if you be
Loyal, and mine, be won, respect my venture.

CELIA. Before your honor?

CORVINO. Honor! tut, a breath:
There's no such thing in nature: a mere term
Invented to awe fools. What is my gold
The worse for touching, clothes for being looked on?
Why, this is no more. An old decrepit wretch,
That has no sense, no sinew; takes his meat
With others' fingers; only knows to gape,
When you do scald his gums; a voice, a shadow;
And, what can this man hurt you?

CELIA (*aside*). Lord! what spirit
Is this hath entered him?

CORVINO. And for your fame,
That's such a jig; as if I would go tell it,
Cry it on the Piazza! who shall know it,
But he that cannot speak it, and this fellow,
Whose lips are in my pocket? save yourself,
(If you'll proclaim't, you may), I know no other
Should come to know it.

CELIA. Are heaven and saints then nothing?
Will they be blind or stupid?

CORVINO. How!

CELIA. Good sir,
Be jealous still, emulate them; and think
What hate they burn with toward every sin.

CORVINO. I grant you: if I thought it were a sin,
I would not urge you. Should I offer this
To some young Frenchman, or hot Tuscan blood
That had read Aretine, conned all his prints,
Knew every quirk within lust's labyrinth,
And were professed critic in lechery;
And I would look upon him, and applaud him,
This were a sin: but here, 'tis contrary,
A pious work, mere charity for physic,
And honest polity, to assure mine own.
CELIA. O heaven! canst thou suffer such a change?
VOLPONE. Thou art mine honor, Mosca, and my pride,
My joy, my tickling, my delight! Go bring them.
MOSCA (*advancing*). Please you draw near, sir.
CORVINO. Come on, what —
You will not be rebellious? by that light —
MOSCA. Sir,
Signior Corvino, here, is come to see you.
VOLPONE. O!
MOSCA. And hearing of the consultation had,
So lately, for your health, is come to offer,
Or rather, sir, to prostitute —
CORVINO. Thanks, sweet Mosca.
MOSCA. Freely, unasked, or unintreated —
CORVINO. Well.
MOSCA. As the true fervent instance of his love.
His own most fair and proper wife; the beauty,
Only of price in Venice —
CORVINO. 'Tis well urged.
MOSCA. To be your comfortress, and to preserve you.
VOLPONE. Alas, I am past, already! Pray you, thank him
For his good care and promptness; but for that,
'Tis a vain labor e'en to fight 'gainst heaven;
Applying fire to stone — uh, uh, uh, uh (*coughing*)!
Making a dead leaf grow again. I take
His wishes gently, though; and you may tell him,
What I have done for him: marry, my state is hopeless.
Will him to pray for me; and to use his fortune
With reverence, when he comes to't.
MOSCA. Do you hear, sir?
Go to him with your wife.
CORVINO. Heart of my father!
Wilt thou persist thus? come, I pray thee, come.
Thou seest 'tis nothing, Celia. By this hand,
I shall grow violent. Come, do't, I say.
CELIA. Sir, kill me, rather: I will take down poison,
Eat burning coals, do any thing. —

CORVINO, Be damned!
Heart, I will drag thee hence, home, by the hair;
Cry thee a strumpet through the streets; rip up
Thy mouth unto thine ears; and slit thy nose,
Like a raw rochet![56] — Do not tempt me: come.
Yield, I am loth — Death! I will buy some slave
Whom I will kill, and bind thee to him, alive;
And at my window hang you forth, devising
Some monstrous crime, which I, in capital letters,
Will eat into thy flesh with aquafortis,
And burning corsives, on this stubborn breast.
Now, by the blood thou hast incensed, I'll do it!

CELIA. Sir, what you please, you may, I am your martyr.

CORVINO. Be not thus obstinate, I have not deserved it:
Think who it is intreats you. 'Prithee, sweet; —
Good faith, thou shalt have jewels, gowns, attires,
What thou wilt think, and ask. Do but go kiss him.
Or touch him, but. For my sake. — At my suit. —
This once. — No! not! I shall remember this.
Will you disgrace me thus? Do you thirst my undoing?

MOSCA. Nay, gentle lady, be advised.

CORVINO. No, no.
She has watched her time. God's precious, this is scurvy,
'Tis very scurvy; and you are —

MOSCA. Nay, good sir.

CORVINO. An arrant locust, by heaven, a locust!
Whore, crocodile, that hast thy tears prepared,
Expecting how thou'lt bid them flow —

MOSCA. Nay, 'pray you, sir!
She will consider.

CELIA. Would my life would serve
To satisfy —

CORVINO. S'death! if she would but speak to him,
And save my reputation, it were somewhat;
But spitefully to affect my utter ruin!

MOSCA. Ay, now you have put your fortune in her hands.
Why i' faith, it is her modesty, I must quit her.
If you were absent, she would be more coming;
I know it: and dare undertake for her.
What woman can before her husband? 'pray you,
Let us depart, and leave her here.

CORVINO. Sweet Celia,
Thou may'st redeem all, yet: I'll say no more:
If not, esteem yourself as lost. Nay, stay there.

[56] **Rochet**: a fish.

(CORVINO *shuts the door, and exits with* MOSCA.)

CELIA. O God, and his good angels! whither, whither,
Is shame fled human breasts? that with such ease,
Men dare put off your honors, and their own?
Is that, which ever was a cause of life,
Now placed beneath the basest circumstance,
And modesty an exile made, for money?

VOLPONE. Ay, in Corvino, and such earth-fed minds,
(*Leaping from his couch.*) That never tasted the true heaven of love.
Assure thee, Celia, he that would sell thee,
Only for hope of gain, and that uncertain,
He would have sold his part of Paradise
For ready money, had he met a cope-man.[57]
Why art thou mazed to see me thus revived?
Rather applaud thy beauty's miracle;
'Tis thy great work: that hath, not now alone,
But sundry times raised me, in several shapes,
And, but this morning, like a mountebank,
To see thee at thy window: ay, before
I would have left my practice, for thy love,
In varying figures, I would have contended
With the blue Proteus, or the horned flood.[58]
Now art thou welcome.

CELIA. Sir!

VOLPONE. Nay, fly me not.
Nor let thy false imagination
That I was bed-rid, make thee think I am so:
Thou shalt not find it. I am, now, as fresh,
As hot, as high, and in as jovial plight,
As when, in that so celebrated scene,
At recitation of our comedy,
For entertainment of the great Valois,[59]
I acted young Antinous; and attracted
The eyes and ears of all the ladies present
To admire each graceful gesture, note, and footing.

(*Sings.*) Come, my Celia, let us prove,
While we can, the sports of love,
Time will not be ours for ever,
He, at length, our goods will sever;
Spend not then his gifts in vain;

[57] **Cope-man:** chapman, dealer.

[58] **Proteus, or the horned flood:** Proteus was a Greek god capable of changing his shape at will. He frequently did so during the course of combat. The *horned flood* is the river god Achelous, who had the form of a bull with a human head.

[59] **Valois:** Henry III of France.

Suns, that set, may rise again;
But if once we lose this light,
'Tis with us perpetual night.
Why should we defer our joys?
Fame and rumor are but toys.
Cannot we delude the eyes
Of a few poor household spies?
Or his easier ears beguile,
Thus removed by our wile? —
'Tis no sin love's fruits to steal:
But the sweet thefts to reveal;
To be taken, to be seen,
These have crimes accounted been.

CELIA. Some serene[60] blast me, or dire lightning strike
This my offending face!
VOLPONE. Why droops my Celia?
Thou hast, in place of a base husband, found
A worthy lover: use thy fortune well,
With secrecy and pleasure. See, behold,
What thou art queen of; not in expectation,
As I feed others; but possessed and crowned.
See, here, a rope of pearl; and each, more orient
Than that the brave Egyptian queen caroused:
Dissolve and drink them. See, a carbuncle,
May put out both the eyes of our St. Mark;
A diamond, would have bought Lollia Paulina,[61]
When she came in like star-light, hid with jewels,
That were the spoils of provinces; take these,
And wear, and lose them: yet remains an ear-ring
To purchase them again, and this whole state.
A gem but worth a private patrimony,
Is nothing: we will eat such at a meal.
The heads of parrots, tongues of nightingales,
The brains of peacocks, and of ostriches,
Shall be our food: and, could we get the phoenix,
Though nature lost her kind, she were our dish.
CELIA. Good sir, these things might move a mind affected
With such delights; but I, whose innocence
Is all I can think wealthy, or worth th' enjoying,
And which, once lost, I have nought to lose beyond it,
Cannot be taken with these sensual baits:
If you have conscience —
VOLPONE. 'Tis the beggar's virtue;
If thou hast wisdom, hear me, Celia.

[60] **Serene**: serein; blight, unwholesome air, mildew.
[61] **Lollia Paulina**: A lady of Imperial Rome, famous for her jewels.

Thy baths shall be the juice of July-flowers,
Spirit of roses, and of violets,
The milk of unicorns, and panthers' breath
Gathered in bags, and mixed with Cretan wines.
Our drink shall be prepared gold and amber;
Which we will take, until my roof whirl round
With the vertigo: and my dwarf shall dance,
My eunuch sing, my fool make up the antic,
Whilst we, in changed shapes, act Ovid's tales,
Thou, like Europa now, and I like Jove,
Then I like Mars and thou like Erycine:
So, of the rest, till we have quite run through,
And wearied all the fables of the gods.
Then will I have thee in more modern forms,
Attired like some sprightly dame of France,
Brave Tuscan lady, or proud Spanish beauty;
Sometimes, unto the Persian sophy's wife;
Or the grand signior's mistress; and, for change,
To one of our most artful courtesans,
Or some quick Negro, or cold Russian;
And I will meet thee in as many shapes:
Where we may so transfuse our wandering souls
Out at our lips, and score up sums of pleasures,

(*Sings.*) That the curious shall not know
How to tell them as they flow;
And the envious, when they find
What their number is, be pined.

CELIA. If you have ears that will be pierced — or eyes
That can be opened — a heart that may be touched —
Or any part that yet sounds man about you —
If you have touch of holy saints — or heaven —
Do me the grace to let me 'scape — if not,
Be bountiful and kill me. You do know,
I am a creature, hither ill betrayed,
By one, whose shame I would forget it were:
If you will deign me neither of these graces,
Yet feed your wrath, sir, rather than your lust,
(It is a vice comes nearer manliness),
And punish that unhappy crime of nature,
Which you miscall my beauty: flay my face,
Or poison it with ointments, for seducing
Your blood to this rebellion. Rub these hands,
With what may cause an eating leprosy,
E'en to my bones and marrow: any thing,
That may disfavor me, save in my honor —
And I will kneel to you, pray for you, pay down

A thousand hourly vows, sir, for your health;
Report, and think you virtuous —
VOLPONE. Think me cold,
Frozen and impotent, and so report me?
That I had Nestor's hernia, thou wouldst think.
I do degenerate, and abuse my nation,
To play with opportunity thus long;
I should have done the act, and then have parleyed.
Yield, or I'll force thee. (*Seizes her.*)
CELIA. O! just God!
VOLPONE. In vain —
BONARIO (*rushing in*). Forbear, foul ravisher, libidinous swine!
Free the forced lady, or thou diest, impostor.
But that I'm loath to snatch thy punishment
Out of the hand of justice, thou shouldst, yet,
Be made the timely sacrifice of vengeance,
Before this altar, and this dross, thy idol. —
Lady, let's quit the place, it is the den
Of villainy; fear nought, you have a guard:
And he, ere long, shall meet his just reward.

(*Exeunt* BONARIO *and* CELIA.)

VOLPONE. Fall on me, roof, and bury me in ruin!
Become my grave, that wert my shelter! O!
I am unmasked, unspirited, undone,
Betrayed to beggary, to infamy —

(*Enter* MOSCA, *wounded and bleeding.*)

MOSCA. Where shall I run, most wretched shame of men,
To beat out my unlucky brains?
VOLPONE. Here, here.
What! dost thou bleed?
MOSCA. O that his well-driven sword
Had been so courteous to have cleft me down
Unto the navel, ere I lived to see
My life, my hopes, my spirits, my patron, all
Thus desperately engaged, by my error!
VOLPONE. Woe on thy fortune!
MOSCA. And my follies, sir.
VOLPONE. Thou hast made me miserable.
MOSCA. And myself, sir.
Who would have thought he would have hearkened so?
VOLPONE. What shall we do?
MOSCA. I know not; if my heart
Could expiate the mischance, I'd pluck it out.

Will you be pleased to hang me, or cut my throat?
And I'll requite you, sir. Let's die like Romans,
Since we have lived like Grecians.[62]

(*Knocking within.*)

VOLPONE. Hark! who's there?
I hear some footing; officers, the *saffi*,[63]
Come to apprehend us! I do feel the brand
Hissing already at my forehead; now,
Mine ears are boring.
MOSCA. To your couch, sir, you,
Make that place good, however.

(VOLPONE *lies down, as before.*)

Guilty men
Suspect what they deserve still.

(*Enter* CORBACCIO.)

Signior Corbaccio!
CORBACCIO. Why, how now, Mosca?
MOSCA. O, undone, amazed, sir.
Your son, I know not by what accident,
Acquainted with your purpose to my patron,
Touching your will, and making him your heir,
Entered our house with violence, his sword drawn
Sought for you, called you wretch, unnatural,
Vowed he would kill you.
CORBACCIO. Me!
MOSCA. Yes, and my patron.
CORBACCIO. This act shall disinherit him indeed;
Here is the will.
MOSCA. 'Tis well, sir.
CORBACCIO. Right and well:
Be you as careful now for me.

(*Enter* VOLTORE, *behind.*)

MOSCA. My life, sir,
Is not more tendered; I am only yours.
CORBACCIO. How does he? Will he die shortly, think'st thou?

[62] **Let's die like Romans, since we have lived like Grecians:** Let us die on each others' swords, since we have lived to the hilt.
[63] ***Saffi:*** policemen.

MOSCA. I fear
He'll outlast May.

CORBACCIO. Today?

MOSCA. No, last out May, sir.

CORBACCIO. Could'st thou not give him a dram?

MOSCA. O, by no means, sir.

CORBACCIO. Nay, I'll not bid you.

VOLTORE (*coming forward*). This is a knave, I see.

MOSCA (*seeing* VOLTORE, *aside*). How, Signior Voltore! did he hear me?

VOLTORE. Parasite!

MOSCA. Who's that? — O, sir, most timely welcome —

VOLTORE. Scarce
To the discovery of your tricks, I fear.
You are his, *only?* and mine also, are you not?

MOSCA. Who? I, sir?

VOLTORE. You, sir. What device is this
About a will?

MOSCA. A plot for you, sir.

VOLTORE. Come,
Put not your foists upon me; I shall scent them.

MOSCA. Did you not hear it?

VOLTORE. Yes, I hear Corbaccio
Hath made your patron there his heir.

MOSCA. 'Tis true,
By my device, drawn to it by my plot,
With hope —

VOLTORE. Your patron should reciprocate?
And you have promised?

MOSCA. For your good, I did, sir.
Nay, more, I told his son, brought, hid him here,
Where he might hear his father pass the deed;
Being persuaded to it by this thought, sir,
That the unnaturalness, first, of the act,
And then his father's oft disclaiming in him
(Which I did mean t'help on), would sure enrage him
To do some violence upon his parent,
On which the law should take sufficient hold,
And you be stated in a double hope:
Truth be my comfort, and my conscience,
My only aim was to dig you a fortune
Out of these two old rotten sepulchres —

VOLTORE. I cry thee mercy, Mosca.

MOSCA. Worth your patience,
And your great merit, sir. And see the change!

VOLTORE. Why, what success?

MOSCA. Most hapless! you must help, sir.

Whilst we expected the old raven, in comes
Corvino's wife, sent hither by her husband —
VOLTORE. What, with a present?
MOSCA. No, sir, on visitation
(I'll tell you how anon); and staying long,
The youth he grows impatient, rushes forth,
Seizeth the lady, wounds me, makes her swear
(Or he would murder her, that was his vow)
To affirm my patron to have done her rape:
Which how unlike it is, you see! and hence,
With that pretext he's gone, to accuse his father,
Defame my patron, defeat you —
VOLTORE. Where is her husband?
Let him be sent for straight.
MOSCA. Sir, I'll go fetch him.
VOLTORE. Bring him to the Scrutineo.[64]
MOSCA. Sir, I will.
VOLTORE. This must be stopped.
MOSCA. O you do nobly, sir.
Alas, 'twas labored all, sir, for your good;
Nor was there want of counsel in the plot:
But fortune can, at any time, o'erthrow
The projects of a hundred learned clerks, sir.
CORBACCIO (*listening*). What's that?
VOLTORE. Will't please you, sir, to go along?

(*Exit* CORBACCIO, *followed by* VOLTORE.)

MOSCA. Patron, go in, and pray for our success.
VOLPONE (*rising from his couch*). Need makes devotion: heaven your labor bless!

(*Exeunt.*)

ACT FOUR

Scene 1

(*A street. Enter* SIR POLITICK WOULD-BE *and* PEREGRINE.)

SIR POLITICK. I told you, sir, it was a plot; you see
What observation is! You mentioned me
For some instructions: I will tell you, sir,
(Since we are met here in this height of Venice),

[64] **Scrutineo:** Senate chambers.

Some few particulars I have set down,
Only for this meridian, fit to be known
Of your crude traveller; and they are these.
I will not touch, sir, at your phrase, or clothes,
For they are old.
PEREGRINE. Sir, I have better.
SIR POLITICK. Pardon,
I meant, as they are themes.
PEREGRINE. O, sir, proceed:
I'll slander you no more of wit, good sir.
SIR POLITICK. First for your garb, it must be grave and serious,
Very reserved and locked; not tell a secret
On any terms, not to your father; scarce
A fable, but with caution: made sure choice
Both of your company, and discourse; beware
You never speak a truth —
PEREGRINE. How!
SIR POLITICK. Not to strangers,
For those be they must converse with most;
Others I would not know, sir, but at distance,
So as I still might be a saver in them:
You shall have tricks else past upon you hourly.
And then, for your religion, profess none,
But wonder at the diversity, of all:
And, for your part, protest, were there no other
But simply the laws o' the land, you could content you.
Nic. Machiavel, and Monsieur Bodin,[65] both
Were of this mind. Then must you learn the use
And handling of your silver fork at meals,
The metal of your glass; (these are main matters
With your Italian;) and to know the hour
When you must eat your melons, and your figs.
PEREGRINE. Is that a point of state too?
SIR POLITICK. Here it is:
For your Venetian, if he see a man
Preposterous in the least, he has him straight;
He has; he strips him. I'll acquaint you, sir,
I now have lived here, 'tis some fourteen months
Within the first week of my landing here,
All took me for a citizen of Venice,
I know the forms so well —
PEREGRINE (*aside*). And nothing else.
SIR POLITICK. I had read Contarene,[66] took me a house,
Dealt with my Jews to furnish it with moveables —

[65] **Bodin**: an influential French political theorist of the 16th century.
[66] **Contarene**: author of a book about Venice.

Well, if I could but find one man, one man
To mine own heart, whom I durst trust, I would —
PEREGRINE. What, what, sir?
SIR POLITICK. Make him rich; make him a fortune:
He should not think again. I would command it.
PEREGRINE. As how?
SIR POLITICK. With certain projects that I have;
Which I may not discover.
PEREGRINE (*aside*). If I had
But one to wager with, I would lay odds now,
He tells me instantly.
SIR POLITICK. One is, and that
I care not greatly who knows, to serve the state
Of Venice with red herrings for three years,
And at a certain rate, from Rotterdam,
Where I have correspondence. There's a letter,
Sent me from one o' the states, and to that purpose:
He cannot write his name, but that's his mark.
PEREGRINE. He is a chandler?
SIR POLITICK. No, a cheesemonger.
There are some others too with whom I treat
About the same negotiation;
And I will undertake it: for, 'tis thus.
I'll do't with ease, I have cast it all: Your hoy
Carries but three men in her, and a boy;
And she shall make me three returns a year:
So, if there come but one of three, I save;
If two, I can defalk:[67] — but this is now,
If my main project fail.
PEREGRINE. Then you have others?
SIR POLITICK. I should be loath to draw the subtle air
Of such a place, without my thousand aims.
I'll not dissemble, sir: where'er I come,
I love to be considerative; and 'tis true,
I have at my free hours thought upon
Some certain goods unto the state of Venice,
Which I do call my Cautions; and, sir, which
I mean, in hope of pension, to propound
To the Great Council, then unto the Forty,
So to the Ten. My means are made already —
PEREGRINE. By whom?
SIR POLITICK. Sir, one that, though his place be obscure,
Yet he can sway, and they will hear him. He's
A *commandadore*.

[67] **Defalk:** cut off, deduct.

PEREGRINE. What! a common sergeant?
SIR POLITICK. Sir, such as they are, put it in their mouths,
What they should say, sometimes as well as greater:
I think I have my notes to show you —
PEREGRINE (*searching his pockets*). Good sir.
SIR POLITICK. But you shall swear unto me, on your gentry,
Not to anticipate —
PEREGRINE. I, sir!
SIR POLITICK. Nor reveal
A circumstance — My paper is not with me.
PEREGRINE. O, but you can remember, sir.
SIR POLITICK. My first is
Concerning tinder-boxes. You must know,
No family is here without its box.
Now, sir, it being so portable a thing,
Put case, that you or I were ill affected
Unto the state, sir; with it in our pockets,
Might not I go into the Arsenal,
Or you, come out again, and none the wiser?
PEREGRINE. Except yourself, sir.
SIR POLITICK. Go to, then. I therefore
Advertise to the state, how fit it were,
That none but such as were known patriots,
Sound lovers of their country, should be suffered
To enjoy them in their houses; and even those
Sealed at some office, and at such a bigness
As might not lurk in pockets.
PEREGRINE. Admirable!
SIR POLITICK. My next is, how to enquire, and be resolved,
By present demonstration, whether a ship,
Newly arrived from Soria, or from
Any suspected part of all the Levant,
Be guilty of the plague: and where they use
To lie out forty, fifty days, sometimes,
About the Lazaretto, for their trial;
I'll save that charge and loss unto the merchant,
And in an hour clear the doubt.
PEREGRINE. Indeed, sir!
SIR POLITICK. Or — I will lose my labor.
PEREGRINE. 'My faith, that's much.
SIR POLITICK. Nay, sir, conceive me. It will cost me in onions,
Some thirty livres —
PEREGRINE. Which is one pound sterling.
SIR POLITICK. Beside my waterworks: for this I do, sir.
First, I bring in your ship 'twixt two brick walls;
But those the state shall venture: On the one

I strain me a fair tarpauling, and in that
I stick my onions, cut in halves: the other
Is full of loopholes, out at which I thrust
The noses of my bellows; and those bellows
I keep, with waterworks, in perpetual motion,
Which is the easiest matter of a hundred.
Now, sir, your onion, which doth naturally
Attract the infection, and your bellows blowing
The air upon him, will show, instantly,
By his changed color, if there be contagion;
Or else remain as fair as at the first.
— Now it is known, 'tis nothing.

PEREGRINE. You are right, sir.

SIR POLITICK. I would I had my note.

PEREGRINE. 'Faith, so would I:
But you have done well for once, sir.

SIR POLITICK. Were I false,
Or would be made so, I could show you reasons
How I could sell this state now to the Turk,
Spite of their galleys or their — (*examining his papers*).

PEREGRINE. Pray you, Sir Pol.

SIR POLITICK. I have them not about me.

PEREGRINE. That I feared:
They are there, sir.

SIR POLITICK. No, this is my diary,
Wherein I note my actions of the day.

PEREGRINE. Pray you, let's see, sir. What is here? (*Reads.*) *Notandum*,
"A rat had gnawn my spur-leathers; notwithstanding,
I put on new, and did go forth: but first
I threw three beans over the threshold. Item,
I went and bought two toothpicks, whereof one
I burst immediately, in a discourse
With a Dutch merchant, 'bout *ragion del stato*.[68]
From him I went and paid a moccinigo
For piecing my silk stockings; by the way
I cheapened[69] sprats; and at St. Mark's I urined."
'Faith these are politic notes!

SIR POLITICK. Sir, I do slip
No action of my life, but thus I quote it.

PEREGRINE. Believe me, it is wise!

SIR POLITICK. Nay, sir, read forth.

(*Enter, at a distance,* LADY POLITICK WOULD-BE, NANO, *and two* WAITING-WOMEN.)

[68] ***Ragion del stato:*** politics.
[69] **Cheapened:** bargained for.

LADY POLITICK. Where should this loose knight be, trow? sure he's housed.

NANO. Why, then he's fast.

LADY POLITICK. Ay, he plays both with me.
I pray you stay. This heat will do more harm
To my complexion, than his heart is worth.
(I do not care to hinder, but to take him.)
How it comes off! (*Rubbing her cheeks.*)

FIRST WAITING-WOMAN. My master's yonder.

LADY POLITICK. Where?

SECOND WAITING-WOMAN. With a young gentleman.

LADY POLITICK. That same's the party;
In man's apparel! 'Pray you, sir, jog my knight:
I will be tender to his reputation,
However he demerit.

SIR POLITICK (*seeing her*). My lady!

PEREGRINE. Where?

SIR POLITICK. 'Tis she indeed, sir; you shall know her. She is,
Were she not mine, a lady of that merit,
For fashion and behavior; and for beauty
I durst compare —

PEREGRINE. It seems you are not jealous,
That dare commend her.

SIR POLITICK. Nay, and for discourse —

PEREGRINE. Being your wife, she cannot miss that.

SIR POLITICK (*introducing* PEREGRINE). Madam,
Here is a gentleman, pray you, use him fairly;
He seems a youth, but he is —

LADY POLITICK. None.

SIR POLITICK. Yes, one.
Has put his face as soon into the world —

LADY POLITICK. You mean, as early? but today?

SIR POLITICK. How's this?

LADY POLITICK. Why, in this habit, sir; you apprehend me: —
Well, Master Would-be, this doth not become you;
I had thought the odor, sir, of your good name
Had been more precious to you; that you would not
Have done this dire massacre on your honor;
One of your gravity and rank besides!
But knights, I see, care little for the oath
They make to ladies; chiefly, their own ladies.

SIR POLITICK. Now, by my spurs, the symbol of my knighthood, —

PEREGRINE (*aside*). Lord, how his brain is humbled for an oath!

SIR POLITICK. I reach you not.

LADY POLITICK. Right, sir, your policy
May bear it through thus. — Sir, a word with you.

(*To* PEREGRINE.) I would be loath to contest publicly
With any gentlewoman, or to seem
Forward, or violent, as the courtier says;
It comes too near rusticity in a lady,
Which I would shun by all means: and however
I may deserve from Master Would-be, yet
T'have one fair gentlewoman thus be made
The unkind instrument to wrong another,
And one she knows not, ay, and to persèver;
In my poor judgment, is not warranted
From being a solecism in our sex,
If not in manners.

PEREGRINE. How is this!

SIR POLITICK. Sweet madam,
Come nearer to your aim.

LADY POLITICK. Marry, and will, sir.
Since you provoke me with your impudence,
And laughter of your light land-siren here,
Your Sporus, your hermaphrodite —

PEREGRINE. What's here?
Poetic fury and historic storms!

SIR POLITICK. The gentleman, believe it, is of worth,
And of our nation.

LADY POLITICK. Ay, your Whitefriars[70] nation.
Come, I blush for you, Master Would-be, I;
And am ashamed you should have no more forehead,
Than thus to be the patron, or St. George,
To a lewd harlot, a base fricatrice,
A female devil, in a male outside.

SIR POLITICK. Nay,
An you be such a one, I must bid adieu
To your delights. The case appears too liquid. (*Exit.*)

LADY POLITICK. Ay, you may carry't clear, with your state-face! —
But for your carnival concupiscence,
Who here is fled for liberty of conscience,
From furious persecution of the marshal,
Her will I dis'ple.

PEREGRINE. This is fine, i' faith!
And do you use this often? Is this part
Of your wit's exercise, 'gainst you have occasion?
Madam —

LADY POLITICK. Go to, sir.

PEREGRINE. Do you hear me, lady?

70 **Whitefriars:** a disreputable section of London where underworld elements sought refuge.

Why, if your knight have set you to beg shirts,
Or to invite me home, you might have done it
A nearer way, by far.
LADY POLITICK. This cannot work you
Out of my snare.
PEREGRINE. Why, am I in it, then?
Indeed your husband told me you were fair.
And so you are; only your nose inclines,
That side that's next the sun, to the queenapple.
LADY POLITICK. This cannot be endured by any patience.

(*Enter* MOSCA.)

MOSCA. What is the matter, madam?
LADY POLITICK. If the senate
Right not my quest in this, I will protest them
To all the world, no aristocracy.
MOSCA. What is the injury, lady?
LADY POLITICK. Why, the callet
You told me of, here I have ta'en disguised.
MOSCA. Who? this! what means your ladyship? the creature
I mentioned to you is apprehended now,
Before the senate; you shall see her —
LADY POLITICK. Where?
MOSCA. I'll bring you to her. This young gentleman,
I saw him land this morning at the port.
LADY POLITICK. Is't possible! how has my judgment wandered?
Sir, I must, blushing, say to you, I have err'd;
And plead your pardon.
PEREGRINE. What, more changes yet!
LADY POLITICK. I hope you have not the malice to remember
A gentlewoman's passion. If you stay
In Venice here, please you to use me, sir —
MOSCA. Will you go, madam?
LADY POLITICK. 'Pray you, sir, use me; in faith,
The more you see me, the more I shall conceive
You have forgot our quarrel.

(*Exeunt* LADY WOULD-BE, MOSCA, NANO, WAITING-WOMEN.)

PEREGRINE. This is rare!
Sir Politick Would-be? no; Sir Politick Bawd,
To bring me thus acquainted with his wife!
Well, wise Sir Pol, since you have practiced thus
Upon my freshmanship, I'll try your salthead,
What proof it is against a counterplot. (*Exit.*)

Scene 2

(*The Scrutineo, or Senate House. Enter* VOLTORE, CORBACCIO, CORVINO, *and* MOSCA.)

VOLTORE. Well, now you know the carriage of the business,
Your constancy is all that is required
Unto the safety of it.
MOSCA. Is the lie
Safely conveyed amongst us? is that sure?
Knows every man his burden?
CORVINO. Yes.
MOSCA. Then shrink not.
CORVINO. But knows the advocate the truth?
MOSCA. O, sir,
By no means; I devised a formal tale,
That salved your reputation. But be valiant, sir.
CORVINO. I fear no one but him, that this his pleading
Should make him stand for a co-heir —
MOSCA. Co-halter!
Hang him; we will but use his tongue, his noise,
As we do croakers here.
CORVINO. Ay, what shall he do?
MOSCA. When we have done, you mean?
CORVINO. Yes.
MOSCA. Why, we'll think:
Sell him for mummia;[71] he's half dust already.
Do you not smile (*to* VOLTORE), to see this buffalo,
How he doth sport it with his head?[72] — I should,
If all were well and past (*aside*) — Sir (*to* CORBACCIO), only you
Are he that shall enjoy the crop of all,
And these not know for whom they toil.
CORBACCIO. Ay, peace.
MOSCA (*turning to* CORVINO). But you shall eat it. Much (*aside*)! — Worshipful sir,
(*To* VOLTORE). Mercury sit upon your thundering tongue,
Or the French Hercules, and make your language
As conquering as his club, to beat along,
As with a tempest, flat, our adversaries;
But much more yours, sir.
VOLTORE. Here they come, have done.
MOSCA. I have another witness, if you need, sir,
I can produce.

[71] **Mummia:** a preparation containing mummified flesh which supposedly has medicinal value.

[72] **Buffalo . . . doth sport it with his head:** an allusion to cuckoldry.

VOLTORE. Who is it?
MOSCA. Sir, I have her.

(*Enter* AVOCATORI *and take their seats,* BONARIO, CELIA, NOTARIO, COMMANDADORI, SAFFI, *and other* OFFICERS *of justice.*)

FIRST AVOCATORE. The like of this the senate never heard of.
SECOND AVOCATORE. 'Twill come most strange to them when we report it.
FOURTH AVOCATORE. The gentlewoman has been ever held
Of unreproved name.
THIRD AVOCATORE. So has the youth.
FOURTH AVOCATORE. The more unnatural part that of his father.
SECOND AVOCATORE. More of the husband.
FIRST AVOCATORE. I not know to give
His act a name, it is so monstrous!
FOURTH AVOCATORE. But the imposter, he's a thing created
To exceed example!
FIRST AVOCATORE. And all after-times!
SECOND AVOCATORE. I never heard a true voluptuary
Described, but him.
THIRD AVOCATORE. Appear yet those were cited?
NOTARIO. All but the old magnifico, Volpone.
FIRST AVOCATORE. Why is not he here?
MOSCA. Please your fatherhoods,
Here is his advocate: himself's so weak,
So feeble —
FOURTH AVOCATORE. What are you?
BONARIO. His parasite,
His knave, his pander: I beseech the court,
He may be forced to come, that your grave eyes
May bear strong witness of his strange impostures.
VOLTORE. Upon my faith and credit with your virtues,
He is not able to endure the air.
SECOND AVOCATORE. Bring him, however.
THIRD AVOCATORE. We will see him.
FOURTH AVOCATORE. Fetch him.
VOLTORE. Your fatherhoods' fit pleasures be obeyed;

(*Exeunt* OFFICERS.)

But sure, the sight will rather move your pities,
Than indignation. May it please the court,
In the mean time, he may be heard in me;
I know this place most void of prejudice,
And therefore crave it, since we have no reason
To fear our truth should hurt our cause.

THIRD AVOCATORE. Speak free.
VOLTORE. Then know, most honored fathers, I must now
Discover to your strangely abused ears,
The most prodigious and most frontless piece
Of solid impudence and treachery,
That ever vicious nature yet brought forth
To shame the state of Venice. This lewd woman,
That wants no artificial looks or tears
To help the vizor she has now put on,
Hath long been known a close adulteress
To that lascivious youth there; not suspected,
I say, but known, and taken in the act
With him; and by this man, the easy husband,
Pardoned; whose timeless bounty makes him now
Stand here, the most unhappy, innocent person,
That ever man's own goodness made accused.
For these not knowing how to owe a gift
Of that dear grace, but with their shame; being placed
So above all powers of their gratitude,
Began to hate the benefit; and, in place
Of thanks, devise to extirpe the memory
Of such an act: wherein I pray your fatherhoods
To observe the malice, yea, the rage of creatures
Discovered in their evils; and what heart
Such take, even from their crimes: — but that anon
Will make appear. — This gentleman, the father,
Hearing of this foul fact, with many others,
Which daily struck at his too tender ears,
And grieved in nothing more than that he could not
Preserve himself a parent (his son's ills
Growing to that strange flood), at last decreed
To disinherit him.
FIRST AVOCATORE. These be strange turns!
SECOND AVOCATORE. The young man's fame was ever fair and honest.
VOLTORE. So much more full of danger is his vice,
That can beguile so under shade of virtue.
But, as I said, my honored sires, his father
Having this settled purpose, by what means
To him betrayed, we know not, and this day
Appointed for the deed; that parricide,
I cannot style him better, by confederacy
Preparing this his paramour to be there,
Entered Volpone's house (who was the man,
Your fatherhoods must understand, designed
For the inheritance), there sought his father: —
But with what purpose sought he him, my lords?
I tremble to pronounce it, that a son

Unto a father, and to such a father,
Should have so foul, felonious intent!
It was to murder him: when being prevented
By his more happy absence, what then did he?
Not check his wicked thoughts; no, now new deeds
(Mischief doth never end where it begins),
An act of horror, fathers! he dragged forth
The aged gentleman that had there lain bedrid
Three years and more, out of his innocent couch,
Naked upon the floor, there left him; wounded
His servant in the face: and, with this strumpet
The stale[73] to his forged practice, who was glad
To be so active — (I shall here desire
Your fatherhoods to note but my collections,
As most remarkable —) thought at once to stop
His father's ends, discredit his free choice
In the old gentleman, redeem themselves,
By laying infamy upon this man,
To whom, with blushing, they should owe their lives.

FIRST AVOCATORE. What proofs have you of this?

BONARIO. Most honored fathers
I humbly crave there be no credit given
To this man's mercenary tongue.

SECOND AVOCATORE. Forbear.

BONARIO. His soul moves in his fee.

THIRD AVOCATORE. O sir.

BONARIO. This fellow,
For six sols more, would plead against his Maker.

FIRST AVOCATORE. You do forget yourself.

VOLTORE. Nay, nay, grave fathers,
Let him have scope: can any man imagine
That he will spare his accuser, that would not
Have spared his parent?

FIRST AVOCATORE. Well, produce your proofs.

CELIA. I would I could forget I were a creature.

VOLTORE. Signior Corbaccio!

(CORBACCIO *comes forward.*)

FOURTH AVOCATORE. What is he?

VOLTORE. The father.

SECOND AVOCATORE. Has he had an oath?

NOTARIO. Yes.

CORBACCIO. What must I do now?

[73] **Stale**: accomplice, shill, decoy.

NOTARIO. Your testimony's craved.
CORBACCIO. Speak to the knave?
I'll have my mouth first stopped with earth; my heart
Abhors his knowledge: I disclaim in him.
FIRST AVOCATORE. But for what cause?
CORBACCIO. The mere portent of nature!
He is an utter stranger to my loins.
BONARIO. Have they made you to this?
CORBACCIO. I will not hear thee,
Monster of men, swine, goat, wolf, parricide!
Speak not, thou viper.
BONARIO. Sir, I will sit down,
And rather wish my innocence should suffer,
Than I resist the authority of a father.
VOLTORE. Signior Corvino!

(CORVINO *comes forward.*)

SECOND AVOCATORE. This is strange.
FIRST AVOCATORE. Who's this?
NOTARIO. The husband.
FOURTH AVOCATORE. Is he sworn?
NOTARIO. He is.
THIRD AVOCATORE. Speak, then.
CORVINO. This woman, please your fatherhoods, is a whore,
Of most hot exercise, more than a partridge,
Upon record —
FIRST AVOCATORE. No more.
CORVINO. Neighs like a jennet.
NOTARIO. Preserve the honor of the court.
CORVINO. I shall,
And modesty of your most reverend ears.
And yet I hope that I may say, these eyes
Have seen her glued unto that piece of cedar,
That fine well-timbered gallant; and that here
The letters may be read thorough the horn,[74]
That makes the story perfect.
MOSCA. Excellent! sir.
CORVINO (*aside to* MOSCA). There is no shame in this now, is there?
MOSCA. None.
CORVINO. Or if I said, I hoped that she were onward
To her damnation, if there be a hell
Greater than whore and woman; a good Catholic
May make the doubt.

[74] **Horn:** an allusion to both cuckoldry and to the translucent horn covering of the children's primer called the hornbook.

THIRD AVOCATORE. His grief hath made him frantic.
FIRST AVOCATORE. Remove him hence.
SECOND AVOCATORE. Look to the woman.

(CELIA *swoons.*)

CORVINO. Rare!
Prettily feigned, again!
FOURTH AVOCATORE. Stand from about her.
FIRST AVOCATORE. Give her the air.
THIRD AVOCATORE (*to* MOSCA). What can you say?
MOSCA. My wound,
May it please your wisdoms, speaks for me, received
In aid of my good patron, when he missed
His sought-for father, when that well-taught dame
Had her cue given her to cry out, "A rape!"
BONARIO. O most laid impudence! Fathers —
THIRD AVOCATORE. Sir, be silent;
You had your hearing free, so must they theirs.
SECOND AVOCATORE. I do begin to doubt the imposture here.
FOURTH AVOCATORE. This woman has too many moods.
VOLTORE. Grave fathers,
She is a creature of a most professed
And prostituted lewdness.
CORVINO. Most impetuous,
Unsatisfied, grave fathers!
VOLTORE. May her feignings
Not take your wisdoms: but this day she baited
A stranger, a grave knight, with her loose eyes,
And more lascivious kisses. This man saw them
Together on the water, in a gondola.
MOSCA. Here is the lady herself, that saw them too;
Without; who then had in the open streets
Pursued them, but for saving her knight's honor.
FIRST AVOCATORE. Produce that lady.
SECOND AVOCATORE. Let her come.

(*Exit* MOSCA.)

FOURTH AVOCATORE. These things,
They strike with wonder.
THIRD AVOCATORE. I am turned a stone.

(*Enter* MOSCA *with* LADY WOULD-BE.)

MOSCA. Be resolute, madam.
LADY POLITICK. Ay, this same is she.

(*Pointing to* CELIA.) Out, thou camelion harlot! now thine eyes
Vie tears with the hyena. Dar'st thou look
Upon my wronged face? — I cry your pardons,
I fear I have forgettingly transgressed
Against the dignity of the court —
SECOND AVOCATORE. No, madam.
LADY POLITICK. And been exorbitant —
SECOND AVOCATORE. You have not, lady.
FOURTH AVOCATORE. These proofs are strong.
LADY POLITICK. Surely, I had no purpose
To scandalise your honors, or my sex's.
THIRD AVOCATORE. We do believe it.
LADY POLITICK. Surely, you may believe it.
SECOND AVOCATORE. Madam, we do.
LADY POLITICK. Indeed you may; my breeding
Is not so coarse —
FOURTH AVOCATORE. We know it.
LADY POLITICK. To offend
With pertinacy —
THIRD AVOCATORE. Lady —
LADY POLITICK. Such a presence!
No, surely.
FIRST AVOCATORE. We well think it.
LADY POLITICK. You may think it.
FIRST AVOCATORE. Let her o'ercome. What witnesses have you
To make good your report?
BONARIO. Our consciences.
CELIA. And heaven, that never fails the innocent.
FOURTH AVOCATORE. These are no testimonies.
BONARIO. Not in your courts,
Where multitude and clamor overcomes.
FIRST AVOCATORE. Nay, then, you do wax insolent.

(*Enter* OFFICERS, *bearing* VOLPONE *on a couch.*)

VOLTORE. Here, here.
The testimony comes, that will convince,
And put to utter dumbness their bold tongues:
See here, grave fathers, here's a ravisher,
The rider on men's wives, the great impostor,
The grand voluptuary! Do you not think
These limbs should affect venery? or these eyes
Covet a concubine? pray you mark these hands;
Are they not fit to stroke a lady's breasts? —
Perhaps he doth dissemble!
BONARIO. So he does.

VOLTORE. Would you have him tortured?
BONARIO. I would have him proved.
VOLTORE. Best try him then with goads, or burning irons;
Put him to the strappado: I have heard
The rack hath cured the gout; 'faith, give it him,
And help him of a malady; be courteous.
I'll undertake, before these honored fathers,
He shall have yet as many left diseases,
As she has known adulterers, or thou strumpets. —
O, my most equal hearers, if these deeds,
Acts of this bold and most exorbitant strain,
May pass with sufferance, what one citizen
But owes the forfeit of his life, yea, fame,
To him that dares traduce him? which of you
Are safe, my honored fathers? I would ask,
with leave of your grave fatherhoods, if their plot
Have any face or color like to truth?
Or if, unto the dullest nostril here.
It smell not rank, and most abhorred slander?
I crave your care of this good gentleman,
Whose life is much endangered by their fable;
And as for them, I will conclude with this,
That vicious persons, when they're hot and fleshed
In impious acts, their constancy abounds:
Damned deeds are done with greatest confidence.
FIRST AVOCATORE. Take them to custody, and sever them.
SECOND AVOCATORE. 'Tis pity two such prodigies should live.
FIRST AVOCATORE. Let the old gentleman be returned with care.

(*Exeunt* OFFICERS *with* VOLPONE.)

I'm sorry our credulity hath wronged him.
FOURTH AVOCATORE. These are two creatures.
THIRD AVOCATORE. I've an earthquake in me.
SECOND AVOCATORE. Their shame, even in their cradles, fled their faces.
FOURTH AVOCATORE (*to* VOLTORE). You have done a worthy service to the state, sir,
In their discovery.
FIRST AVOCATORE. You shall hear, ere night,
What punishment the court decrees upon them.

(*Exeunt* AVOCATORI, NOTARIO, *and* OFFICERS *with* BONARIO *and* CELIA.)

VOLTORE. We thank your fatherhoods. — How like you it?
MOSCA. Rare.
I'd have your tongue, sir, tipped with gold for this;
I'd have you be the heir to the whole city;

The earth I'd want men, ere you want living:
They're bound to erect your statue in St. Mark's.
Signior Corvino, I would have you go
And show yourself, that you have conquered.

CORVINO. Yes.

MOSCA. It was much better that you should profess
Yourself a cuckold thus, than that the other
Should have been proved.

CORVINO. Nay, I considered that:
Now it is her fault.

MOSCA. Then it had been yours.

CORVINO. True; I do doubt this advocate still.

MOSCA. I' faith
You need not, I dare ease you of that care.

CORVINO. I trust thee, Mosca. (*Exit.*)

MOSCA. As your own soul, sir.

CORBACCIO. Mosca!

MOSCA. Now for your business, sir.

CORBACCIO. How! have you business?

MOSCA. Yes, yours, sir.

CORBACCIO. O, none else?

MOSCA. None else, not I.

CORBACCIO. Be careful, then.

MOSCA. Rest you with both your eyes, sir.

CORBACCIO. Dispatch it.

MOSCA. Instantly.

CORBACCIO. And look that all,
Whatever, be put in, jewels, plate, moneys,
Household stuff, bedding, curtains.

MOSCA. Curtain rings, sir:
Only the advocate's fee must be deducted.

CORBACCIO. I'll pay him now; you'll be too prodigal.

MOSCA. Sir, I must tender it.

CORBACCIO. Two chequines is well.

MOSCA. No, six, sir.

CORBACCIO. 'Tis too much.

MOSCA. He talked a great while;
You must consider that, sir.

CORBACCIO. Well, there's three —

MOSCA. I'll give it him.

CORBACCIO. Do so, and there's for thee. (*Exit.*)

MOSCA (*aside*). Bountiful bones! What horrid strange offence
Did he commit 'gainst nature in his youth,
Worthy this age? (*Aside.*) — You see, sir (*to* VOLTORE), how I work
Unto your ends: take you no notice.

VOLTORE. No,
I'll leave you. (*Exit.*)

MOSCA. All is yours, the devil and all:
Good advocate! — Madam, I'll bring you home.
LADY POLITICK. No, I'll go see your patron.
MOSCA. That you shall not:
I'll tell you why. My purpose is to urge
My patron to reform his will; and for
The zeal you have shown today, whereas before
You were but third or fourth, you shall be now
Put in the first: which would appear as begged,
If you were present. Therefore —
LADY POLITICK. You shall sway me.

(*Exeunt.*)

ACT FIVE

Scene 1

(*A room in* VOLPONE's *house. Enter* VOLPONE.)

VOLPONE. Well, I am here, and all this brunt is past.
I ne'er was in dislike with my disguise
'Till this fled moment: here 'twas good, in private;
But in your public, — *cave*[75] whilst I breathe.
'Fore God, my left leg 'gan to have the cramp,
And I apprehended straight some power had struck me
With a dead palsy: Well! I must be merry,
And shake it off. A many of these fears
Would put me into some villainous disease,
Should they come thick upon me: I'll prevent 'em.
Give me a bowl of lusty wine, to fright
This humor from my heart. (*Drinks.*) — Hum, hum, hum!
'Tis almost gone already; I shall conquer.
Any device, now, of rare ingenious knavery,
That would possess me with a violent laughter,
Would make me up again. (*Drinks again.*) — So, so, so so!
This heat is life; 'tis blood by this time: — Mosca!

(*Enter* MOSCA.)

MOSCA. How now, sir? does the day look clear again?
Are we recovered, and wrought out of error,
Into our way, to see our path before us?
Is our trade free once more?

[75] *Cave:* beware!

VOLPONE. Exquisite Mosca!
MOSCA. Was it not carried learnedly?
VOLPONE. And stoutly:
Good wits are greatest in extremities.
MOSCA. It were a folly beyond thought, to trust
Any grand act unto a cowardly spirit:
You are not taken with it enough, methinks.
VOLPONE. O, more than if I had enjoyed the wench:
The pleasure of all womankind's not like it.
MOSCA. Why now you speak, sir. We must here be fixed;
Here we must rest; this is our masterpiece;
We cannot think to go beyond this.
VOLPONE. True,
Thou hast played thy prize, my precious Mosca.
MOSCA. Nay, sir,
To gull the court —
VOLPONE. And quite divert the torrent
Upon the innocent.
MOSCA. Yes, and to make
So rare a music out of discords —
VOLPONE. Right.
That yet to me's the strangest, how thou hast borne it!
That these, being so divided 'mongst themselves,
Should not scent somewhat, or in me or thee,
Or doubt their own side.
MOSCA. True, they will not see't.
Too much light blinds them, I think. Each of them
Is so possessed and stuffed with his own hopes,
That any thing unto the contrary,
Never so true, or never so apparent,
Never so palpable, they will resist it —
VOLPONE. Like a temptation of the devil.
MOSCA. Right, sir.
Merchants may talk of trade, and your great signiors
Of land that yields well; but if Italy
Have any glebe more fruitful than these fellows,
I am deceived. Did not your advocate rare?
VOLPONE. O — "My most honored fathers, my grave fathers,
Under correction of your fatherhoods,
What face of truth is here? If these strange deeds
May pass, most honored fathers" — I had much ado
To forbear laughing.
MOSCA. It seemed to me, you sweat, sir.
VOLPONE. In troth, I did a little.
MOSCA. But confess, sir,
Were you not daunted?
VOLPONE. In good faith, I was

A little in a mist, but not dejected;
Never, but still my self.
MOSCA. I think it, sir.
Now, so truth help me, I must needs say this, sir,
And out of conscience for your advocate,
He has taken pains, in faith, sir, and deserved,
In my poor judgment, I speak it under favor,
Not to contrary you, sir, very richly —
Well — to be cozened.
VOLPONE. Troth, and I think so too,
By that I heard him, in the latter end.
MOSCA. O, but before, sir: had you heard him first
Draw it to certain heads, then aggravate,
Then use his vehement figures — I looked still
When he would shift a shirt: and doing this
Out of pure love, no hope of gain —
VOLPONE. 'Tis right.
I cannot answer him, Mosca, as I would,
Not yet; but for thy sake, at thy entreaty,
I will begin, even now — to vex them all,
This very instant.
MOSCA. Good sir.
VOLPONE. Call the dwarf
And eunuch forth.
MOSCA. Castrone, Nano!

(*Enter* CASTRONE *and* NANO.)

NANO. Here.
VOLPONE. Shall we have a jig now?
MOSCA. What you please, sir.
VOLPONE. Go.
Straight give out about the streets, you two,
That I am dead; do it with constancy,
Sadly, do you hear? impute it to the grief
Of this late slander.

(*Exeunt* CASTRONE *and* NANO.)

MOSCA. What do you mean, sir?
VOLPONE. O,
I shall have instantly my Vulture, Crow,
Raven, come flying hither, on the news,
To peck for carrion, my she-wolf, and all,
Greedy, and full of expectation —
MOSCA. And then to have it ravished from their mouths!

VOLPONE. 'Tis true. I will have thee put on a gown,
And take upon thee, as thou wert mine heir:
Show them a will: Open that chest, and reach
Forth one of those that has the blanks: I'll straight
Put in thy name.

MOSCA. It will be rare, sir. (*Gives him a paper.*)

VOLPONE. Ay,
When they ev'n gape, and find themselves deluded —

MOSCA. Yes.

VOLPONE. And thou use them scurvily!
Dispatch, get on thy gown.

MOSCA (*putting on a gown*). But what, sir, if they ask
After the body?

VOLPONE. Say, it was corrupted.

MOSCA. I'll say, it stunk, sir; and was fain to have it
Coffined up instantly, and sent away.

VOLPONE. Any thing; what thou wilt. Hold, here's my will.
Get thee a cap, a count-book, pen and ink,
Papers afore thee; sit as thou wert taking
An inventory of parcels: I'll get up
Behind the curtain, on a stool, and hearken;
Sometime peep over, see how they do look,
With what degrees their blood doth leave their faces,
O, 'twill afford me a rare meal of laughter!

MOSCA (*putting on a cap, and setting out the table, etc.*). Your advocate will turn stark dull upon it.

VOLPONE. It will take off his oratory's edge.

MOSCA. But your clarissimo, old roundback, he
Will crump you like a hog-louse, with the touch.

VOLPONE. And what Corvino?

MOSCA. O, sir, look for him,
Tomorrow morning, with a rope and dagger,
To visit all the streets; he must run mad.
My lady too, that came into the court,
To bear false witness for your worship —

VOLPONE. Yes,
And kissed me 'fore the fathers, when my face
Flowed all with oils.

MOSCA. And sweat, sir. Why, your gold
Is such another med'cine, it dries up
All those offensive savors: it transforms
The most deformed, and restores them lovely,
As 'twere the strange poetical girdle.[76] Jove

[76] **Girdle:** Jonson's marginal note reads "Cestus," that is, Venus' girdle which had the power of exciting love.

Could not invent t' himself a shroud more subtle
To pass Acrisius'[77] guards. It is the thing
Makes all the world her grace, her youth, her beauty
VOLPONE. I think she loves me.
MOSCA. Who? the lady, sir?
She's jealous of you.
VOLPONE. Dost thou say so?

(*Knocking within.*)

MOSCA. Hark,
There's some already.
VOLPONE. Look.
MOSCA. It is the Vulture;
He has the quickest scent.
VOLPONE. I'll to my place,
Thou to thy posture. (*Goes behind the curtain.*)
MOSCA. I am set.
VOLPONE. But, Mosca,
Play the artificer now, torture them rarely.

(*Enter* VOLTORE.)

VOLTORE. How now, my Mosca?
MOSCA (*writing*). "Turkey carpets, nine —"
VOLTORE. Taking an inventory! that is well.
MOSCA. "Two suits of bedding, tissue —"
VOLTORE. Where's the will?
Let me read that the while.

(*Enter* SERVANTS, *with* CORBACCIO *in a chair.*)

CORBACCIO. So, set me down,
And get you home.

(*Exeunt* SERVANTS.)

VOLTORE. Is he come now, to trouble us!
MOSCA. "Of cloth of gold, two more —"
CORBACCIO. Is it done, Mosca?
MOSCA. "Of several velvets, eight —"
VOLTORE. I like his care.
CORBACCIO. Dost thou not hear?

(*Enter* CORVINO.)

[77] Acrisius: Danaë's father, who shut her in a bronze house open only at the top. Zeus obtained entrance in the form of a golden shower.

CORBACCIO. Ha! is the hour come, Mosca?

VOLPONE (*peeping over the curtain*). Ay, now they muster.

CORVINO. What does the advocate here,
Or this Corbaccio?

CORBACCIO. What do these here?

(*Enter* LADY POLITICK WOULD-BE.)

LADY POLITICK. Mosca!
Is his thread spun?

MOSCA. "Eight chests of linen — "

VOLPONE. O,
My fine dame Would-be, too!

CORVINO. Mosca, the will,
That I may show it these, and rid them hence.

MOSCA. "Six chests of diaper, four of damask." — There. (*Gives them the will carelessly, over his shoulder.*)

CORBACCIO. Is that the will?

MOSCA. "Downbeds and bolsters — "

VOLPONE. Rare!
Be busy still. Now they begin to flutter:
They never think of me. Look, see, see, see!
How their swift eyes run over the long deed,
Unto the name, and to the legacies,
What is bequeathed them there —

MOSCA. "Ten suits of hangings — "

VOLPONE. Ay, in their garters, Mosca. Now their hopes
Are at the gasp.

VOLTORE. Mosca the heir!

CORBACCIO. What's that?

VOLPONE. My advocate is dumb; look to my merchant,
He has heard of some strange storm, a ship is lost,
He faints; my lady will swoon. Old glazen eyes,
He hath not reached his despair yet.

CORBACCIO. All these
Are out of hope; I am, sure, the man. (*Takes the will.*)

CORVINO. But, Mosca —

MOSCA. "Two cabinets."

CORVINO. Is this in earnest?

MOSCA. "One
Of ebony — "

CORVINO. Or do you but delude me?

MOSCA. "The other, mother of pearl" — I am very busy.
Good faith, it is a fortune thrown upon me —
"Item, one salt of agate" — not my seeking.

LADY POLITICK. Do you hear, sir?

MOSCA. "A perfumed box — " Pray you forbear,
You see I'm troubled — "made of an onyx — "
LADY POLITICK. How!
MOSCA. Tomorrow or next day, I shall be at leisure
To talk with you all.
CORVINO. Is this my large hope's issue?
LADY POLITICK. Sir, I must have a fairer answer.
MOSCA. Madam!
Marry, and shall: 'pray you, fairly quit my house.
Nay, raise no tempest with your looks; but hark you,
Remember what your ladyship offered me
To put you in an heir; go to, think on it:
And what you said e'en your best madams did
For maintenance; and why not you? Enough.
Go home, and use the poor Sir Pol, your knight, well,
For fear I tell some riddle, go, be melancholy.

(*Exit* LADY WOULD-BE.)

VOLPONE. O, my fine devil!
CORVINO. Mosca, 'pray you a word.
MOSCA. Lord! will you not take your dispatch hence yet?
Methinks, of all, you should have been the example.
Why should you stay here? with what thought, what promise?
Hear you; do not you know, I know you an ass,
And that you would most fain have been a wittol,
If fortune would have let you? that you are
A declared cuckold, on good terms? This pearl,
You'll say, was yours? right: this diamond?
I'll not deny't, but thank you. Much here else?
It may be so. Why, think that these good works
May help to hide your bad. I'll not betray you;
Although you be but extraordinary,
And have it only in title, it sufficeth:
Go home, be melancholy too, or mad.

(*Exit* CORVINO.)

VOLPONE. Rare Mosca! how his villainy becomes him!
VOLTORE. Certain he doth delude all these for me.
CORBACCIO. Mosca the heir!
VOLPONE. O, his four eyes have found it.
CORBACCIO. I am cozened, cheated, by a parasite slave;
Harlot, thou hast gulled me.
MOSCA. Yes, sir. Stop your mouth,
Or I shall draw the only tooth is left.
Are not you he, that filthy covetous wretch,

With the three legs, that here, in hope of prey,
Have, any time this three years, snuffed about,
With your most grovelling nose, and would have hired
Me to the poisoning of my patron, sir?
Are not you he that have today in court
Professed the disinheriting of your son?
Perjured yourself? Go home, and die, and stink.
If you but croak a syllable, all comes out:
Away, and call your porters!

(*Exit* CORBACCIO.)

Go, go, stink.

VOLPONE. Excellent varlet!

VOLTORE. Now, my faithful Mosca,
I find thy constancy.

MOSCA. Sir!

VOLTORE. Sincere.

MOSCA (*writing*). "A table
Of porphyry —" I marle[78] you'll be thus troublesome.

VOLTORE. Nay, leave off now, they are gone.

MOSCA. Why, who are you?
What! who did send for you? O, cry you mercy,
Reverend sir! Good faith, I am grieved for you,
That any chance of mine should thus defeat
Your (I must needs says) most deserving travails:
But I protest, sir, it was cast upon me,
And I could almost wish to be without it,
But that the will o' the dead must be observed.
Marry, my joy is that you need it not;
You have a gift, sir, (thank your education,)
Will never let you want, while there are men,
And malice, to breed causes. Would I had
But half the like, for all my fortune, sir!
If I have any suits, as I do hope,
Things being so easy and direct, I shall not,
I will make bold with your obstreperous aid,
Conceive me, — for your fee, sir. In mean time,
You that have so much law, I know the conscience
Not to be covetous of what is mine.
Good sir, I thank you for my plate; 'twill help
To set up a young man. Good faith, you look
As you were costive; best go home and purge, sir.

(*Exit* VOLTORE.)

[78] **Marle**: marvel.

VOLPONE (*comes from behind the curtain*). Bid him eat lettuce[79] well. My witty mischief,
Let me embrace thee. O that I could now
Transform thee to a Venus! — Mosca, go,
Straight take my habit of clarissimo,
And walk the streets; be seen, torment them more:
We must pursue, as well as plot. Who would
Have lost this feast?

MOSCA. I doubt it will lose them.

VOLPONE. O, my recovery shall recover all.
That I could now but think on some disguise
To meet them in, and ask them questions:
How I would vex them still at every turn!

MOSCA. Sir, I can fit you.

VOLPONE. Canst thou?

MOSCA. Yes, I know
One o' the commandadori, sir, so like you;
Him will I straight make drunk, and bring you his habit.

VOLPONE. A rare disguise, and answering thy brain!
O, I will be a sharp disease unto them.

MOSCA. Sir, you must look for curses —

VOLPONE. Till they burst;
The Fox fares ever best when he is cursed.

(*Exeunt.*)

Scene 2

(*A hall in* SIR POLITICK'S *house. Enter* PEREGRINE *disguised, and three* MERCHANTS.)

PEREGRINE. Am I enough disguised?

FIRST MERCHANT. I warrant you.

PEREGRINE. All my ambition is to fright him only.

SECOND MERCHANT. If you could ship him away, 'twere excellent.

THIRD MERCHANT. To Zant, or to Aleppo?

PEREGRINE. Yes, and have his
Adventures put i' the *Book of Voyages*,
And his gulled story registered for truth.
Well, gentlemen, when I am in a while,
And that you think us warm in our discourse,
Know your approaches.

FIRST MERCHANT. Trust it to our care.

(*Exeunt* MERCHANTS. *Enter* WAITING-WOMAN.)

[79] **Lettuce:** regarded as a soporific.

PEREGRINE. Save you, fair lady! Is Sir Pol within?
WAITING-WOMAN. I do not know, sir.
PEREGRINE. Pray you say unto him,
Here is a merchant, upon earnest business,
Desires to speak with him.
WAITING-WOMAN. I will see, sir. (*Exit.*)
PEREGRINE. Pray you.—
I see the family is all female here.

(*Enter* WAITING-WOMAN.)

WAITING-WOMAN. He says, sir, he has weighty affairs of state,
That now require him whole; some other time
You may possess him.
PEREGRINE. Pray you say again,
If those require him whole, these will exact him,
Whereof I bring him tidings.

(*Exit* WAITING-WOMAN.)

—What might be
His grave affair of state now; how to make
Bolognian sausages here in Venice, sparing
One o' the ingredients?

(*Enter* WAITING-WOMAN.)

WAITING-WOMAN. Sir, he says, he knows
By your word *tidings*, that you are no statesman,
And therefore wills you stay.
PEREGRINE. Sweet, pray you return him;
I have read so many proclamations,
And studied them for words, as he has done—
But—here he deigns to come.

(*Exit* WAITING-WOMAN. *Enter* SIR POLITICK.)

SIR POLITICK. Sir, I must crave
Your courteous pardon. There hath chanced today,
Unkind disaster 'twixt my lady and me;
And I was penning my apology,
To give her satisfaction, as you came now.
PEREGRINE. Sir, I am grieved I bring you worse disaster:
The gentleman you met at the port today,
That told you, he was newly arrived—
SIR POLITICK. Ay, was
A fugitive punk?

PEREGRINE. No, sir, a spy set on you;
And he has made relation to the senate,
That you professed to him to have a plot
To sell the State of Venice to the Turk.

SIR POLITICK. O me!

PEREGRINE. For which, warrants are signed by this time,
To apprehend you, and to search your study
For papers —

SIR POLITICK. Alas, sir, I have none, but notes
Drawn out of playbooks —

PEREGRINE. All the better, sir.

SIR POLITICK. And some essays. What shall I do?

PEREGRINE. Sir, best
Convey yourself into a sugar chest;
Or, if you could lie round, a frail[80] were rare,
And I could send you aboard.

SIR POLITICK. Sir, I but talked so,
For discourse sake merely.

(*Knocking within.*)

PEREGRINE. Hark! they are there.

SIR POLITICK. I am a wretch, a wretch!

PEREGRINE. What will you do, sir?
Have you ne'er a currant-butt to leap into?
They'll put you to the rack; you must be sudden.

SIR POLITICK. Sir, I have an engine —

THIRD MERCHANT (*within*). Sir Politick Would-be!

SECOND MERCHANT (*within*). Where is he?

SIR POLITICK. That I have thought upon before time.

PEREGRINE. What is it?

SIR POLITICK. I shall ne'er endure the torture.
Marry, it is, sir of a tortoiseshell,
Fitted for these extremities: pray you, sir, help me.
Here I've a place, sir, to put back my legs,
Please you to lay it on, sir (*lies down while* PEREGRINE *places the shell upon him*) — with this cap,
And my black gloves. I'll lie, sir, like a tortoise,
'Til they are gone.

PEREGRINE. And call you this an engine?

SIR POLITICK. Mine own device — Good sir, bid my wife's women
To burn my papers.

(*Exit* PEREGRINE. *The three* MERCHANTS *rush in.*)

[80] **Frail:** a basket.

FIRST MERCHANT. Where is he hid?
THIRD MERCHANT. We must,
And will sure find him.
SECOND MERCHANT. Which is his study?

(*Enter* PEREGRINE.)

FIRST MERCHANT. What
Are you, sir?
PEREGRINE. I am a merchant, that came here
To look upon this tortoise.
THIRD MERCHANT. How!
FIRST MERCHANT. St. Mark!
What beast is this!
PEREGRINE. It is a fish.
SECOND MERCHANT. Come out here!
PEREGRINE. Nay, you may strike him, sir, and tread upon him;
He'll bear a cart.
FIRST MERCHANT. What, to run over him?
PEREGRINE. Yes, sir.
THIRD MERCHANT. Let's jump upon him.
SECOND MERCHANT. Can he not go?
PEREGRINE. He creeps, sir.
FIRST MERCHANT. Let him creep.
PEREGRINE. No, good sir, you will hurt him.
SECOND MERCHANT. Heart, I will see him creep, or prick his guts.
THIRD MERCHANT. Come out here!
PEREGRINE (*aside to* SIR POLITICK). Pray you, sir! — Creep a little.
FIRST MERCHANT. Forth.
SECOND MERCHANT. Yet farther.
PEREGRINE. Good sir! — Creep.
SECOND MERCHANT. We'll see his legs.

(*They pull off the shell and discover him.*)

THIRD MERCHANT. Ods so, he has garters!
FIRST MERCHANT. Ay, and gloves!
SECOND MERCHANT. Is this
Your fearful tortoise?
PEREGRINE (*discovering himself*). Now, Sir Pol, we are even:
For your next project I shall be prepared:
I am sorry for the funeral of your notes, sir.
FIRST MERCHANT. 'Twere a rare motion to be seen in Fleet Street.
SECOND MERCHANT. Ay, in the Term.
FIRST MERCHANT. Or Smithfield, in the fair.
THIRD MERCHANT. Methinks 'tis but a melancholy sight.

PEREGRINE. Farewell, most politic tortoise!

(*Exeunt* PEREGRINE *and* MERCHANTS. *Enter* WAITING-WOMAN.)

SIR POLITICK. Where's my lady?
Knows she of this?

WAITING-WOMAN. I know not, sir.

SIR POLITICK. Inquire —
O, I shall be the fable of all feasts,
The freight of the *gazetti*,[81] ship boy's tale;
And, which is worst, even talk for ordinaries.

WAITING-WOMAN. My lady's come most melancholic home,
And says, sir, she will straight to sea for physic.

SIR POLITICK. And I to shun this place and clime for ever,
Creeping with house on back, and think it well
To shrink my poor head in my politic shell.

(*Exeunt.*)

Scene 3

(*A room in* VOLPONE'S *house. Enter* MOSCA *in the habit of a clarissimo, and* VOLPONE *in that of a commandadore.*)

VOLPONE. Am I then like him?

MOSCA. O, sir, you are he:
No man can sever you.

VOLPONE. Good.

MOSCA. But what am I?

VOLPONE. 'Fore heaven, a brave clarissimo; thou becom'st it!
Pity thou wert not born one.

MOSCA (*aside*). If I hold
My made one, 'twill be well.

VOLPONE. I'll go and see
What news first at the court. (*Exit.*)

MOSCA. Do so. My Fox
Is out of his hole, and ere he shall re-enter,
I'll make him languish in his borrowed case,
Except he come to composition with me. —
Androgyno, Castrone, Nano!

(*Enter* ANDROGYNO, CASTRONE, *and* NANO.)

ALL. Here.

MOSCA. Go, recreate yourselves abroad; go sport. —

(*Exeunt.*)

[81] **Freight of the *gazetti*:** theme of the newspapers.

So, now I have the keys, and am possessed.
Since he will needs be dead afore his time,
I'll bury him, or gain by him: I am his heir,
And so will keep me, till he share at least.
To cozen him of all, were but a cheat
Well placed; no man would construe it a sin:
Let his sport pay for't. This is called the Fox-trap. (*Exit.*)

Scene 4

(*A street. Enter* CORBACCIO *and* CORVINO.)

CORBACCIO. They say, the court is set.
CORVINO. We must maintain
Our first tale good, for both our reputations.
CORBACCIO. Why, mine's no tale: my son would there have killed me.
CORVINO. That's true, I had forgot: — (*aside*) mine is, I'm sure.
But for your will, sir.
CORBACCIO. Ay, I'll come upon him
For that hereafter, now his patron's dead.

(*Enter* VOLPONE.)

VOLPONE. Signior Corvino! and Corbaccio! sir,
Much joy unto you.
CORVINO. Of what?
VOLPONE. The sudden good
Dropped down upon you —
CORBACCIO. Where?
VOLPONE. And none knows how,
From old Volpone, sir.
CORBACCIO. Out, arrant knave!
VOLPONE. Let not your too much wealth, sir, make you furious.
CORBACCIO. Away, thou varlet!
VOLPONE. Why, sir?
CORBACCIO. Dost thou mock me?
VOLPONE. You mock the world, sir; did you not change wills?
CORBACCIO. Out, harlot!
VOLPONE. O! belike you are the man,
Signior Corvino? 'faith, you carry it well;
You grow not mad withal; I love your spirit:
You are not overleavened with your fortune.
You should have some would swell now, like a wine-fat,
With such an autumn — Did he give you all, sir?
CORVINO. Avoid, you rascal!
VOLPONE. Troth, your wife has shown
Herself a very woman; but you are well,

You need not care, you have a good estate,
To bear it out, sir, better by this chance:
Except Corbaccio have a share.
CORBACCIO. Hence, varlet!
VOLPONE. You will not be acknown, sir; why, 'tis wise.
Thus do all gamesters, at all games, dissemble:
No man will seem to win.

(*Exeunt* CORVINO *and* CORBACCIO.)

— Here comes my Vulture,
Heaving his beak up in the air, and snuffing.

(*Enter* VOLTORE.)

VOLTORE. Outstripped thus, by a parasite! a slave,
Would run on errands, and make legs for crumbs!
Well, what I'll do —
VOLPONE. The court stays for your worship.
I e'en rejoice, sir, at your worship's happiness,
And that it fell into so learned hands,
That understand the fingering —
VOLTORE. What do you mean?
VOLPONE. I mean to be a suitor to your worship,
For the small tenement, out of reparations,[82]
That, at the end of your long row of houses,
By the Piscaria: it was, in Volpone's time,
Your predecessor, ere he grew diseased,
A handsome, pretty, customed[83] bawdy-house
As any was in Venice, none dispraised;
But fell with him: his body and that house
Decayed together.
VOLTORE. Come, sir, leave your prating.
VOLPONE. Why, if your worship give me but your hand,
That I may have the refusal, I have done.
Tis a mere toy to you, sir; candle-rents;
As your learned worship knows —
VOLTORE. What do I know?
VOLPONE. Marry, no end of your wealth, sir: God decrease it!
VOLTORE. Mistaking knave! what, mock'st thou my misfortune? (*Exit.*)
VOLPONE. His blessing on your heart, sir; would 'twere more! —
Now to my first again, at the next corner. (*Exit.*)

[82] **Out of reparations**: out of repair.
[83] **Customed**: frequented.

Scene 5

(*Another part of the street. Enter* CORBACCIO *and* CORVINO; MOSCA *passes over the stage, before them.*)

CORBACCIO. See, in our habit! see the impudent varlet!
CORVINO. That I could shoot mine eyes at him like gunstones!

(*Enter* VOLPONE.)

VOLPONE. But is this true, sir, of the parasite?
CORBACCIO. Again, to afflict us! monster!
VOLPONE. In good faith, sir,
I'm heartily grieved, a beard of your grave length
Should be so overreached. I never brooked
That parasite's hair; methought his nose should cozen:
There still was somewhat in his look, did promise
The bane of a clarissimo.
CORBACCIO. Knave —
VOLPONE. Methinks
Yet you, that are so traded in the world,
A witty merchant, the fine bird, Corvino,
That have such moral emblems on your name,
Should not have sung your shame, and dropped your cheese
To let the Fox laugh at your emptiness.
CORVINO. Sirrah, you think the privilege of the place,
And your red saucy cap, that seems to me
Nailed to your jolthead with those two chequines,
Can warrant your abuses; come you hither:
You shall perceive, sir, I dare beat you; approach.
VOLPONE. No haste, sir, I do know your valor well,
Since you durst publish what you are, sir.
CORVINO. Tarry,
I'd speak with you.
VOLPONE. Sir, sir, another time —
CORVINO. Nay, now.
VOLPONE. O lord, sir! I were a wise man,
Would stand the fury of a distracted cuckold.

(*As he is running off, enter* MOSCA.)

CORBACCIO. What, come again!
VOLPONE. Upon 'em, Mosca; save me.
CORBACCIO. The air's infected where he breathes.
CORVINO. Let's fly him.

(*Exeunt* CORVINO *and* CORBACCIO.)

VOLPONE. Excellent basilisk![84] turn upon the vulture.

(*Enter* VOLTORE.)

VOLTORE. Well, flesh-fly, it is summer with you now;
Your winter will come on.
MOSCA. Good advocate,
Prithee not rail, nor threaten out of place thus;
Thou'lt make a solecism, as madam says.
Get you a biggin[85] more, your brain breaks loose. (*Exit.*)
VOLTORE. Well, sir.
VOLPONE. Would you have me beat the insolent slave,
Throw dirt upon his first good clothes?
VOLTORE. This same
Is doubtless some familiar.
VOLPONE. Sir, the court,
In troth, stays for you. I am mad, a mule
That never read Justinian, should get up,
And ride an advocate. Had you no quirk
To avoid gullage, sir, by such a creature?
I hope you do but jest; he has not done it,
'Tis but confederacy, to blind the rest.
You are the heir.
VOLTORE. A strange, officious,
Troublesome knave! thou dost torment me.
VOLPONE. I know—
It cannot be, sir, that you should be cozened;
'Tis not within with the wit of man to do it;
You are so wise, so prudent; and 'tis fit
That wealth and wisdom still should go together.

(*Exeunt.*)

Scene 6

(*The Scrutineo, or Senate House. Enter* AVOCATORI, NOTARIO, BONARIO, CELIA, CORBACCIO, CORVINO, COMMANDADORI, SAFFI, *etc.*)

FIRST AVOCATORE. Are all the parties here?
NOTARIO. All but the advocate.
SECOND AVOCATORE. And here he comes.

(*Enter* VOLTORE *and* VOLPONE.)

[84] **Basilisk:** a fabulous serpent or dragon whose breath or look could kill.
[85] **Biggin:** an infant's cap worn until the sutures of the skull had closed; it seems also to have designated the cap worn by lawyers.

FIRST AVOCATORE. Then bring them forth to sentence.
VOLTORE. O, my most honored fathers, let your mercy
Once win upon your justice, to forgive —
I am distracted —
VOLPONE (*aside*). What will he do now?
VOLTORE. O,
I know not which to address myself to first;
Whether your fatherhoods, or these innocents —
CORVINO (*aside*). Will he betray himself?
VOLTORE. Whom equally
I have abused, out of most covetous ends —
CORVINO. The man is mad!
CORBACCIO. What's that?
CORVINO. He is possessed.
VOLTORE. For which, now struck in conscience, here, I prostrate
Myself at your offended feet, for pardon.
FIRST, SECOND AVOCATORI. Arise.
CELIA. O heaven, how just thou art!
VOLPONE (*aside*). I am caught
In mine own noose —
CORVINO (*to* CORBACCIO). Be constant, sir: nought now
Can help, but impudence.
FIRST AVOCATORE. Speak forward.
COMMANDADORE. Silence!
VOLTORE. It is not passion in me, reverend fathers,
But only conscience, conscience, my good sires,
That makes me now tell truth. That parasite,
That knave, hath been the instrument of all.
FIRST AVOCATORE. Where is that knave? fetch him.
VOLPONE. I go. (*Exit.*)
CORVINO. Grave fathers,
This man's distracted; he confessed it now:
For, hoping to be old Volpone's heir,
Who now is dead —
THIRD AVOCATORE. How!
SECOND AVOCATORE. Is Volpone dead?
CORVINO. Dead since, grave fathers.
BONARIO. O sure vengeance!
FIRST AVOCATORE. Stay,
Then he was no deceiver.
VOLTORE. O no, none:
The parasite, grave fathers.
CORVINO. He does speak
Out of mere envy, 'cause the servant's made
The thing he gaped for: please your fatherhoods,
This is the truth, though I'll not justify
The other, but he may be some deal faulty.

VOLTORE. Ay, to your hopes, as well as mine, Corvino:
But I'll use modesty. Pleaseth your wisdoms,
To view these certain notes, and but confer them;
As I hope favor, they shall speak clear truth.
CORVINO. The devil has entered him!
BONARIO. Or bides in you.
FOURTH AVOCATORE. We have done ill, by a public officer
To send for him, if he be heir.
SECOND AVOCATORE. For whom?
FOURTH AVOCATORE. Him that they call the parasite.
THIRD AVOCATORE. 'Tis true,
He is a man of great estate, now left.
FOURTH AVOCATORE. Go you, and learn his name, and say, the court
Entreats his presence here, but to the clearing
Of some few doubts.

(*Exit* NOTARIO.)

SECOND AVOCATORE. This same's a labyrinth!
FIRST AVOCATORE. Stand you unto your first report?
CORVINO. My state,
My life, my fame —
BONARIO. Where is it?
CORVINO. Are at the stake.
FIRST AVOCATORE. Is yours so too?
CORBACCIO. The advocate's a knave,
And has a forked tongue —
SECOND AVOCATORE. Speak to the point.
CORBACCIO. So is the parasite too.
FIRST AVOCATORE. This is confusion.
VOLTORE. I do beseech your fatherhoods, read but those — (*giving them papers*).
CORVINO. And credit nothing the false spirit hath writ:
It cannot be, but he's possessed, grave fathers.

(*The scene closes.*)

Scene 7

(*A street. Enter* VOLPONE.)

VOLPONE. To make a snare for mine own neck! and run
My head into it, wilfully! with laughter!
When I had newly 'scaped, was free, and clear,
Out of mere wantonness! O, the dull devil
Was in this brain of mine, when I devised it,
And Mosca gave it second; he must now

Help to sear up this vein, or we bleed dead.—

(*Enter* NANO, ANDROGYNO, *and* CASTRONE.)

How now! who let you loose? whither go you now?
What, to buy gingerbread, or to drown kitlings?
NANO. Sir, Master Mosca called us out of doors,
And bid us all go play, and took the keys.
ANDROGYNO. Yes.
VOLPONE. Did Master Mosca take the keys? why so!
I'm farther in. These are my fine conceits!
I must be merry, with a mischief to me!
What a vile wretch was I, that could not bear
My fortune soberly? I must have my crotchets,
And my conundrums! Well, go you, and seek him:
His meaning may be truer than my fear.
Bid him, he straight come to me to the court;
Thither will I, and, if't be possible,
Unscrew my advocate, upon new hopes:
When I provoked him, then I lost myself.

(*Exeunt.*)

Scene 8

(*The Scrutineo, or Senate House.* AVOCATORI, BONARIO, CELIA, CORBACCIO, CORVINO, COMMANDADORI, SAFFI, *etc., as before.*)

FIRST AVOCATORE. These things can ne'er be reconciled. He here (*showing the papers*)
Professeth, that the gentleman was wronged,
And that the gentlewoman was brought thither,
Forced by her husband, and there left.
VOLTORE. Most true.
CELIA. How ready is heaven to those that pray!
FIRST AVOCATORE. But that
Volpone would have ravished her, he holds
Utterly false, knowing his impotence.
CORVINO. Grave fathers, he's possessed; again, I say,
Possessed: nay, if there be possession, and
Obsession, he had both.
THIRD AVOCATORE. Here comes our officer.

(*Enter* VOLPONE.)

VOLPONE. The parasite will straight be here, grave fathers.
FOURTH AVOCATORE. You might invent some other name, sir varlet.

THIRD AVOCATORE. Did not the notary meet him?
VOLPONE. Not that I know.
FOURTH AVOCATORE. His coming will clear all.
SECOND AVOCATORE. Yet, it is misty.
VOLTORE. May't please your fatherhoods —
VOLPONE (*whispers* VOLTORE). Sir, the parasite
Willed me to tell you, that his master lives;
That you are still the man; your hopes the same;
And this was only a jest —
VOLTORE. How?
VOLPONE. Sir, to try
If you were firm, and how you stood affected.
VOLTORE. Art sure he lives?
VOLPONE. Do I live, sir?
VOLTORE. O me!
I was too violent.
VOLPONE. Sir, you may redeem it.
They said, you were possessed; fall down, and seem so;
I'll help to make it good.

(VOLTORE *falls*.)

— God bless the man! —
Stop your wind hard, and swell — See, see, see, see!
He vomits crooked pins! his eyes are set,
Like a dead hare's hung in a poulter's shop!
His mouth's running away! Do you see, signior?
Now it is in his belly.
CORVINO. Ay, the devil!
VOLPONE. Now in his throat.
CORVINO. Ay, I perceive it plain.
VOLPONE. 'Twill out, 'twill out! stand clear. See where it flies,
In shape of a blue toad, with a bat's wings!
Do you not see it, sir?
CORBACCIO. What? I think I do.
CORVINO. 'Tis too manifest.
VOLPONE. Look! he comes to himself!
VOLTORE. Where am I?
VOLPONE. Take good heart, the worst is past, sir.
You are dispossessed.
FIRST AVOCATORE. What accident is this!
SECOND AVOCATORE. Sudden, and full of wonder!
THIRD AVOCATORE. If he were
Possessed, as it appears, all this is nothing.
CORVINO. He has been often subject to these fits.
FIRST AVOCATORE. Show him that writing: — do you know it, sir?
VOLPONE (*whispers* VOLTORE). Deny it, sir, forswear it; know it not.

VOLTORE. Yes, I do know it well, it is my hand;
But all that it contains is false.

BONARIO. O practice!

SECOND AVOCATORE. What maze is this!

FIRST AVOCATORE. Is he not guilty then,
Whom you there name the parasite?

VOLTORE. Grave fathers,
No more than his good patron, old Volpone.

FOURTH AVOCATORE. Why, he is dead.

VOLTORE. O no, my honored fathers,
He lives —

FIRST AVOCATORE. How! lives?

VOLTORE. Lives.

SECOND AVOCATORE. This is subtler yet!

THIRD AVOCATORE. You said he was dead.

VOLTORE. Never.

THIRD AVOCATORE. You said so.

CORVINO. I heard so.

FOURTH AVOCATORE. Here comes the gentleman; make him way.

(*Enter* MOSCA.)

THIRD AVOCATORE. A stool.

FOURTH AVOCATORE (*aside*). A proper man; and, were Volpone dead
A fit match for my daughter.

THIRD AVOCATORE. Give him way.

VOLPONE (*aside to* MOSCA). Mosca, I was almost lost; the advocate
Had betrayed all; but now it is recovered;
All's on the hinge again —— Say, I am living.

MOSCA. What busy knave is this! — Most reverend fathers,
I sooner had attended your grave pleasures,
But that my order for the funeral
Of my dear patron, did require me —

VOLPONE (*aside*). Mosca!

MOSCA. Whom I intend to bury like a gentleman.

VOLPONE (*aside*). Ay, quick, and cozen me of all.

SECOND AVOCATORE. Still stranger.
More intricate!

FIRST AVOCATORE. And come about again!

FOURTH AVOCATORE (*aside*). It is a match, my daughter is bestowed.

MOSCA (*aside to* VOLPONE). Will you give me half?

VOLPONE. First, I'll be hanged.

MOSCA. I know
Your voice is good, cry not so loud.

FIRST AVOCATORE. Demand
The advocate — Sir, did you not affirm
Volpone was alive?

VOLPONE. Yes, and he is;
This gentleman told me so. — (*Aside to* MOSCA.) Thou shalt have half. —

MOSCA. Whose drunkard is this same? speak, some that know him:
I never saw his face. — (*Aside to* VOLPONE.) I cannot now
Afford it you so cheap.

VOLPONE. No!

FIRST AVOCATORE. What say you?

VOLTORE. The officer told me.

VOLPONE. I did, grave fathers,
And will maintain he lives, with mine own life,
And that this creature (*points to* MOSCA) told me. — (*Aside.*) I was born
With all good stars my enemies.

MOSCA. Most grave fathers,
If such an insolence as this must pass
Upon me, I am silent: 'twas not this
For which you sent, I hope.

SECOND AVOCATORE. Take him away.

VOLPONE. Mosca!

THIRD AVOCATORE. Let him be whipped.

VOLPONE. Wilt thou betray me?
Cozen me?

THIRD AVOCATORE. And taught to bear himself
Toward a person of his rank.

FOURTH AVOCATORE. Away.

(*The* OFFICERS *seize* VOLPONE.)

MOSCA. I humbly thank your fatherhoods.

VOLPONE (*aside*). Soft, soft: Whipped!
And lose all that I have! If I confess,
It cannot be much more.

FOURTH AVOCATORE. Sir, are you married?

VOLPONE. They'll be allied anon; I must be resolute:
The Fox shall here uncase. (*Throws off his disguise.*)

MOSCA. Patron!

VOLPONE. Nay, now
My ruins shall not come alone: your match
I'll hinder sure: my substance shall not glue you,
Nor screw you into a family.

MOSCA. Why, patron!

VOLPONE. I am Volpone, and this is my knave (*pointing to* MOSCA);
This (*to* VOLTORE), his own knave; this (*to* CORBACCIO), avarice's fool;
This (*to* CORVINO), a chimera of wittol, fool, and knave:
And, reverend fathers, since we all can hope
Nought but a sentence, let's not now despair it.
You hear me brief.

CORVINO. May it please your fatherhoods —

COMMANDADORE. Silence.

FIRST AVOCATORE. The knot is now undone by miracle.

SECOND AVOCATORE. Nothing can be more clear.

THIRD AVOCATORE. Or can more prove
These innocent.

FIRST AVOCATORE. Give them their liberty.

BONARIO. Heaven could not long let such gross crimes be hid.

SECOND AVOCATORE. If this be held the highway to get riches,
May I be poor!

THIRD AVOCATORE. This is not the gain, but torment.

FIRST AVOCATORE. These possess wealth, as sick men possess fevers,
Which trulier may be said to possess them.

SECOND AVOCATORE. Disrobe that parasite.

CORVINO. MOSCA. } Most honored fathers! —

FIRST AVOCATORE. Can you plead aught to stay the course of justice?
If you can, speak.

CORVINO. VOLTORE. } We beg favor.

CELIA. And mercy.

FIRST AVOCATORE. You hurt your innocence, suing for the guilty.
Stand forth; and first the parasite: You appear
T'have been the chiefest minister, if not plotter,
In all these lewd impostures; and now, lastly,
Have with your impudence abused the court,
And habit of a gentleman of Venice,
Being a fellow of no birth or blood:
For which our sentence is, first, thou be whipped;
Then live perpetual prisoner in our galleys.

VOLPONE. I thank you for him.

MOSCA. Bane to thy wolvish nature!

FIRST AVOCATORE. Deliver him to the *saffi*.

(MOSCA *is carried out.*)

— Thou, Volpone,
By blood and rank a gentleman, canst not fall
Under like censure; but our judgment on thee
Is, that thy substance all be straight confiscate
To the hospital of the Incurabili:
And, since the most was gotten by imposture,
By feigning lame, gout, palsy, and such diseases,
Thou art to lie in prison, cramped with irons,
Till thou be'st sick and lame indeed. — Remove him.

(VOLPONE *is taken from the bar.*)

VOLPONE. This is called mortifying of a Fox.

FIRST AVOCATORE. Thou, Voltore, to take away the scandal
Thou hast given all worthy men of thy profession,
Art banished from their fellowship, and our state.
Corbaccio! — bring him near — We here possess
Thy son of all thy state, and confine thee
To the monastery of San Spirito;
Where, since thou knewest not how to live well here,
Thou shalt be learned to die well.

CORBACCIO. Ah! what said he?

COMMANDADORE. You shall know anon, sir.

FIRST AVOCATORE. Thou, Corvino, shalt
Be straight embarked from thine own house, and rowed
Round about Venice, through the Grand Canal,
Wearing a cap, with fair long ass's ears,
Instead of horns; and so to mount, a paper
Pinned on thy breast, to the *Berlina*[86] —

CORVINO. Yes,
And have mine eyes beat out with stinking fish,
Bruised fruit, and rotten eggs — 'Tis well. I am glad
I shall not see my shame yet.

FIRST AVOCATORE. And to expiate
Thy wrongs done to thy wife, thou art to send her
Home to her father, with her dowry trebled:
And these are all your judgments.

ALL. Honored fathers. —

FIRST AVOCATORE. Which may not be revoked. Now you begin,
When crimes are done, and past, and to be punished,
To think what your crimes are: away from them.
Let all that see these vices thus rewarded,
Take heart and love to study 'em! Mischiefs feed
Like beasts, till they be fat, and then they bleed.

(*Exeunt.*)

VOLPONE (*comes forward*).

The seasoning of a play is the applause.
Now, though the Fox be punished by the laws,
He yet doth hope, there is no suffering due,
For any fact which he hath done 'gainst you;
If there be, censure him; here he doubtful stands:
If not, fare jovially, and clap your hands. (*Exit.*)

Curtain

[86] **Berlina**: a pillory.

Although the Christian Church has managed, through the ages, to sustain itself and its claims with Divine Revelation — which is, by definition, incapable of material demonstration — it has also leaned heavily on the elaborate structure of inductive and deductive logic. The Jesuits, for example, made themselves justly famous for their skills in explaining or defending religious mysteries and metaphysical speculations with logic.

The rule of reason, then, being a strong adjunct to faith and morality, it is surprising to moderns to learn how furiously Church authorities reacted to Molière (1622–1673) when he offered *Tartuffe, or The Hypocrite* (1664) for the enjoyment and edification of court and public audiences. First of all, Tartuffe is not, as he is occasionally played, a priest or a monk; the clergy, as such, are not being attacked in this drama. He is, rather, a lay member of a religious group which busies itself with the daily observance of Christian duties, their activities being directed not so much toward their own virtue and salvation as toward monitoring the lives of their neighbors. Although such groups may have had the support and encouragement of Churchmen, they were not in any sense ordained — and they obviously did much meddling and even some deliberate harm under the protective cloak of their piety.

Tartuffe is a universally recognizable character. Today he may be present in society as the kind of municipal meddler who no longer needs an ecclesiastical seal of approval to hide behind. Some men, it must be understood, censure others out of the questionable belief that they are themselves morally or intellectually superior. They may feel they are sharing their saintliness or their wisdom with their more corrupt or less thoughtful fellow citizens for the good of all. That, even with the best of intentions, is irritating to the objects of their attentions, but when it is pursued with fanaticism, it becomes dangerous. When it is pursued with fanaticism mixed generously with hypocrisy, it is volatile.

Molière offers examples of both for contrast and comedy. He attacks a serious problem with the tools of antic farce. Tartuffe seems a fanatic for goodness and piety, and he has certainly won the foolish, well-meaning Orgon over to a similar fanaticism — so much so that Orgon's own ordinarily sensible judgment has been affected by it. The fundamental difference is that Orgon really believes in the program of religion and decency which Tartuffe demands, while Tartuffe, the hypocrite, does not. He is merely using it. Both men are revealed by Molière with comic exaggeration. Orgon, reaching the limits of dedicated fanaticism, disinherits his son and tries to force his daughter to marry Tartuffe, in the madly mistaken belief that this man deserves the best Orgon can give him. This could be merely unpleasant — and it does come close — but Molière redeems it as farce. Tartuffe, an overreacher of another kind, pushes both his sham piety and his real hypocrisy too far. His essential dishonesty is discovered to Orgon in a most direct, painful way — though hilarious for theatre audiences — but only after Orgon's long-suffering wife sets a trap for Tartuffe. It is one of the funniest bits of visual farce in all Molière's works. Even then, when the tables should be turned on Tartuffe, they cannot be, since Orgon has given the villain everything and is now to be dispossessed.

The device Molière uses to punish the evil-doer and to reward the now chastened Orgon — as well as his spectators — with a happy ending is perhaps a bit too pat. Certainly it is fortuitous in the extreme. As things stand in the final moments of the comedy, Orgon has not only signed away his goods and lands to Tartuffe, but he has put into the scoundrel's hands certain papers which can implicate him in treason to the crown. It has been made clear earlier that Orgon has these papers only to protect a friend, the duties of true friendship sometimes taking precedence over duties to one's sovereign. Fortunately for Orgon and the tradition of the conventional comic close, the King well understands that, has not forgotten Orgon's virtues, and also knows Tartuffe for the villain he is.

Molière takes great pains not only to show Tartuffe as a nonordained phony, a faker who discredits the Church and who deserves to be exposed and punished, but also to stress that the worth of religion and the value of the Church are not to be damaged by the excesses of a common criminal like Tartuffe. What Molière is really attacking in the drama is the human failings of Tartuffe, Orgon, Mme. Pernelle, and others, not God or the Church. Today, perhaps, it may seem difficult to understand what the Church authorities could have found in *Tartuffe* to condemn. But certainly some members of the clergy did feel they were being attacked. They may well have known, in their secret hearts, that they were hypocritical and small of spirit. After all, this was an age dominated by an insecure religion which bolstered a shoddy system with ritual props. Any humorous satire involving an aspect of faith or its symbolic observation — even if the critique was both just and witty — was bound to be viewed as an intolerable assault on things sacred.

If the spirits of love, leniency, understanding, and mature judgment prevail in a society which is secure, balanced, and orderly, there is no reason to fear making a little fun of the excessively pious or the hypocritically virtuous. Where the folly of overzealous piety is taking root, a gentle comic nudge may be enough to restore a good man to his senses. That is what Molière is doing, in a general way, for his own society, his audiences, even for his modern readers. But when the folly is out of hand, as it is with Orgon, much stronger measures must be invoked.

G. L.

MOLIÈRE

Tartuffe

TRANSLATED BY JAMES L. ROSENBERG

Characters

MADAME PERNELLE, *mother of Orgon*
ORGON
ELMIRE, *Orgon's wife*
DAMIS, *son of Orgon, stepson of Elmire*
MARIANE, *daughter of Orgon and stepdaughter of Elmire*
VALÈRE
CLÉANTE, *brother-in-law of Orgon, brother of Elmire*
TARTUFFE
DORINE, *companion of Mariane*
MONSIEUR LOYAL, *bailiff*
A POLICE OFFICER
FLIPOTE, *Madame Pernelle's servant*

(*The setting throughout is the salon of* ORGON'S *house in Paris. The furnishings are those of a well-to-do-bourgeois.*)

ACT ONE

Scene 1

(MADAME PERNELLE, FLIPOTE, ELMIRE, MARIANE, DORINE, DAMIS, *and* CLÉANTE.)

MME. PERNELLE. Come on, Flipote, away from their mad chatter.
ELMIRE. Heavens, Madame! Now what can be the matter?
MME. PERNELLE. Enough, enough; spare me their smiling faces.
I can well dispense with certain airs and graces.
ELMIRE. Madame, no one has given you cause to grieve;
Why, I pray, are you so resolved to leave?
MME. PERNELLE. I cannot stand this place a minute more;
My every wish is trampled and spurned to the floor.
I leave your house no wiser, but much sadder,
And now — heigh ho! — you ask me what's the matter.
None honors age, all speak with impudence,
This house has become like a Court of Insolence.

DORINE. If . . .

MME. PERNELLE. You are, my girl, a humble maid, a minion,
And yet you talk and give us your free opinion
Like the veriest, blabbiest, gabbling hobbledehoy!

DAMIS. But . . .

MME. PERNELLE. In words of single syllables, my boy,
You are a fool. And that's all there is to that.
You've no more common sense than my old cat.
I've warned your father, not once, but a hundred times
That in the end you'd not be worth a dime.

MARIANE. I think . . .

MME. PERNELLE. And you, his sister, so demure and shy!
But I suspect that sparkle in your eye;
I note the adage about waters running deep
When I hear you sweetly sigh and softly weep.

ELMIRE. But, mother . . .

MME. PERNELLE. And you who should above all play the role
Of modesty and grace; upon the whole
I find your conduct shocking. Is it your place
To squander your husband's money, paint your face,
And boldly parade your charms before the world
Like a golden galleon with all her sails unfurled?
A woman who only seeks to attract her spouse
Does not so gaily decorate the house!

CLÉANTE. But, madame, after all . . .

MME. PERNELLE. And you, my lad,
I honor, love and respect you, need I add?
But if I were in my son her husband's place
I'd earnestly ask you not to show your face
Ever again in my house. It seems you preach
Tireless moral maxims, but what you teach
And what you live do not precisely agree.
Forgive my bluntness; my manner of speech is free.

DAMIS. I'm sure, madame, your Tartuffe is fortunate . . .

MME. PERNELLE. He is a man you might well imitate,
And it makes me furious through and through
To hear him maligned by a fool and a dolt like you.

DAMIS. What the devil? (Pardon the expression!)
Am I to live at the bigoted discretion
Of a puritanical tyrant and beg his consent
To live or breathe in my father's establishment?

DORINE. According to him and his maxims, we can't begin
To wiggle a toe without committing a sin.
He's got his nose in everything, sniffing out wrongs.

MME. PERNELLE. Wherever his nose is, there, I'm sure, it belongs.
He seeks to lead you with him on Heaven's path,
And you, like silly geese, just sit and laugh.

DAMIS. Neither the due respect I owe to my father
Nor anything else could make me go to the bother
Of trying to like that unctuous hypocrite,
And I cannot live at ease with myself and sit
At the table with him, smiling and wishing him well,
Or wishing, in short, he were anywhere else but in Hell!
DORINE. Indeed, I say it's a monstrous and scandalous thing
To see a stranger come and put a ring
In the master's nose and lead him around like a bull —
A penniless tramp whose belly was seldom full,
Whose shoes and coat were as holy as now he allows
His precious soul is — having the run of the house!
MME. PERNELLE. Ah! mercy on us! how happy we would be
If we all obeyed his wise and pious decrees.
DORINE. He's a shining saint in your imagination
But a hypocrite in our frank estimation.
MME. PERNELLE. Hold your tongue!
DORINE. I wouldn't trust him, by the book,
As far as I could throw a ten-ton rock.
MME. PERNELLE. All your malicious lies leave me unmoved.
In my opinion, Tartuffe stands approved
In every way. You hate him, you foolish things,
Because he tells you of your faults and brings
A message calling your souls away from sin.
Heaven's all he's interested in.
DORINE. Oh, yes, indeed! But tell me why, I pray,
He wants to drive all visitors away.
When someone calls, is Heaven so offended
That he must rave as though the world had ended?
Do you know what I think of the affair? (*Pointing to* ELMIRE.)
I think he's jealous of Madame — so there!
MME. PERNELLE. Hold your tongue and mind what you are saying.
He's not alone in finding your giddy playing
And all your social life a bit too much:
These carriages and servants, crowds and such,
Disturb the neighborhood with an uproar
The like of which has not been heard before
By decent folk. No doubt there's no harm done,
But gossip breeds like flies in the summer sun.
CLÉANTE. Ah, madame, would you cure the human race
Of gossiping or showing the double face?
And what a sorry world now this would be
If every little lie that touched on me
Forced me to lose a friend. The fact
Is, no one's ever legislated tact.
No one's safe against the tongue of slander
Or those malicious souls who long to pander

To the mob's desire for scandal. No, each man
Must merely live as wisely as he can.

DORINE. Isn't it old Daphne and that shrimp
Of a husband of hers — the little pimp! —
Who've been busy spreading their gossip and lies
About us? We're sinners in their eyes,
Or so they say. But why, pray, is it those
Whose own inane behavior, Heaven knows,
Is always most ridiculous or suspect
Who seem to feel it's their duty to inflict
Their stupid opinions upon the rest of us?
Can it be these peccadilloes they discuss
Are exactly the things they're up to on the sly
And they think the insinuating lie
Of who was seen ascending someone's stairs
Will leave them free to conduct their own affairs?

MME. PERNELLE. All this chitchat's quite beside the point.
You all, I'm sure, know my dear friend Orante,
A good and saintly woman, full of grace;
She's not pleased with what goes on in this place.

DORINE. A fine example, and a most chaste wife!
It's true indeed she lives an austere life,
But age has waked that cold reforming zeal;
The fire dies down when one runs out of fuel.
Many a prude's born when youth's beauty dies
And looks perforce on life with saintly eyes.
Orante now hides beneath discretion's veil
Those fading charms that from henceforth must fail
To win esteem. These veteran coquettes
Revenge themselves on a world that soon forgets
Their fast-decaying beauty and retire
To rectitude, renouncing all desire;
Cheated of love, they turn to criticism
And make Morality their catechism;
They censure all who taste the joy of life
And concentrate on stirring endless strife.
Not principle, but envy, activates
Their tireless tongues and bitterly creates
That twisted malice which insanely drives them
To hate those pleasures of which age deprives them.

MME. PERNELLE (*to* ELMIRE). These are the things that you delight to hear,
And it seems this gracious lady has your ear
And is allowed to go on talking all the day
While I must keep my peace and go my way.
Alas, the sins of this world! Yet I'll be heard
And give you, will-you nill-you, this last word:

The wisest decision my son has ever made
Was in taking this holy man to be his guide;
God has sent him here to redeem your sins
And show you where the road to Heaven begins.
All those balls and dances, conversations,
Those goings to and fro, those visitations
Are surely inspired by the Evil One's decrees;
One never hears a pious word or sees
A modest action; all come in for their share
In the tide of malicious gossip running there.
In short, all sensible people lose their sense
In that sea of shallow frippery and pretense.
A thousand silly stories spread in a day,
And I heard a certain noted doctor say
This house has become a virtual Tower of Babel
Where everyone talks as fast and loud as he's able.
And to explain how this comment came to be . . . (*pointing to* CLÉANTE)
But I see yon gentleman secretly smiling at me.
Eh bien, go find the fools who make you gay. (*To* ELMIRE.)
To you, my daughter, I've nothing more to say,
Except that I disapprove of your home and friends;
Good-bye. Farewell. Here our acquaintance ends. (*Giving* FLIPOTE *a box on the ear.*)
Come on, wake up, you silly gaping goose!
I'll fetch you a wallop will knock your senses loose!
Come on, away, away!

Scene 2

(CLÉANTE *and* DORINE.)

CLÉANTE. I'll not go rushing
After her, for fear of more tongue-lashing.
That old battle-axe . . .
DORINE. Ah, it's a pity
She can't hear you. What a lively ditty
She would sing you now — she'd shout and scold
To let you know she's not so awfully old!
CLÉANTE. How angry she was with us, and all for nothing!
Tartuffe has got her poor old brain a-buzzing.
DORINE. All this is a minor situation
Compared to the master's infatuation.
If you could only see him, you'd say he's turned
An utter fool. In recent years he'd earned
The reputation of a man of sense,
But since Tartuffe's bewitched him, all pretense
Of plain intelligence has left his head.

He calls him "brother" and has often said
He loves him more than daughter, son, or wife.
He makes him the director of his life
And his secret soul's true confidant;
A mistress or a sweetheart couldn't want
More tender demonstrations of his love;
At the dining table, Tartuffe sits above
In the place of honor, like a greedy glutton
Devouring vast slabs of beef and mutton;
The choicest cuts are his, let him but "hic"
The master cries "God bless you!" double quick.
In short, he dotes upon him like a fool;
Tartuffe's his hero, and he's the villain's tool.
He quotes him with the wildest admiration
And praises him on every least occasion.
Tartuffe, who knows a sucker when he sees him,
Employs a hundred little arts to please him;
He steals him blind, meanwhile, with pious maxims,
While criticizing all the family's actions.
Even that sneering jackanapes of a boy
Who serves him as a page seems to enjoy
The freedom of the house and has the power
To lecture and correct us hour by hour.
A handkerchief of mine drew his complaints
Because he found it pressed in a Book of Saints.

Scene 3

(ELMIRE, MARIANE, DAMIS, CLÉANTE, *and* DORINE.)

ELMIRE. You're lucky, brother, your ears were not made sore
By her haranguing all the way to the door.
But I saw my husband as I was passing the stair;
I'll be in my room, if he wishes to see me there.
CLÉANTE. Thanks. I'll wait, despite your friendly warning,
And try at least to wish him a "Good morning."

Scene 4

(CLÉANTE, DAMIS, *and* DORINE.)

DAMIS. Speak to him, if you will, about Mariane.
You know I'm interested in her plan
To marry Valère. I fear my father's delay
Is based on Tartuffe's dislike of the wedding day.
If Valère and my sister marry, it may be

My own joy with his sister I may see
Quite soon . . .
CLÉANTE. Here he comes.

Scene 5

(ORGON, CLÉANTE, *and* DORINE.)

ORGON. Ah, good morning, brother.
CLÉANTE. Dear Orgon, I am glad to have another
Chance to speak to you. The fields are drying . . .
ORGON. Forgive me, brother, but I'm dying
To hear the latest news about the household
From the greatest drawing-room to the smallest mousehole. (*To* DORINE.)
Has all gone happily since yesterday?
How's everybody's health? Tell me, I pray!
DORINE. Madame was feverish and had to take
A medicine to cure a vile headache.
ORGON. And Tartuffe?
DORINE. Tartuffe? Healthy, stout and merry,
Bright as paint and ruddy as a cherry.
ORGON. Poor man!
DORINE. Last night, her headache grew so bad
She scarce could stir out of her bed
And could not eat a bit of dinner.
ORGON. And Tartuffe?
DORINE. He ate — that well-fed sinner —
A brace of good plump partridges, done brown.
With a bottle of red wine to wash them down.
ORGON. Poor man!
DORINE. She passed a tortured, sleepless night
In endless pain; the morning's cold gray light
At last relieved her fever, but we sat
Beside her all night long; just think of that!
ORGON. And Tartuffe?
DORINE. Replete and sleepy, satisfied,
He drifted from the meal to his fireside,
Crept thence into his warm and cozy bed
And snored till dawn, the comfy sleepy-head.
ORGON. Poor man!
DORINE. Madame, agreeing to our fond persuasions,
Consented to the doctor's ministrations
And, bled and physicked, felt somewhat relieved.
ORGON. And Tartuffe?
DORINE. Not, I must confess, unduly grieved
By Madame's illness, but right valiantly

Took arms against foul trouble's surging sea
And drank some wine to replace the blood she'd lost.
ORGON. Poor man!
DORINE. I'm happy to report the danger's past,
And now I'll hasten to inform my mistress
How pleased you are she's cured of her distress.

Scene 6

(ORGON *and* CLÉANTE.)

CLÉANTE. Brother, she's laughing in your very face
And, though I'm far from wishing you disgrace,
I must say that she's right in her estimation.
Who ever saw such a mad infatuation?
Is it possible this man has charmed you so
That you can forget all else for him, and go
Running about to do his commands? I swear
I've never seen such nonsense . . .
ORGON. Stop right there;
For you don't know the man of whom you speak.
CLÉANTE. All right, then. I don't know him, if you like,
But I know various things that I have heard.
ORGON. To know him is to love him, take my word.
I model myself on him whenever I can;
He is a man who . . . well, in short, a man.
Whoever follows his precepts lives in peace
And sees the rest of the world as so much dross.
Yes, I have changed since he came into my life;
He's taught me not to waste my love on my wife
Or on any mortal thing; what's more,
I could see my children turned away from my door,
Thanks to him, without the least concern.
CLÉANTE. These are surely humane truths to learn!
ORGON. Ah, if you could have seen him when at first
We met, in the days when my life was still accursed!
Each day in church he came and, if you please,
Fell with a crash before me to his knees.
He drew the attention of everybody there
With the ardency and loudness of his prayer.
He sighed, stretched flatly forth on his abdomen,
And kissed the floor with every passing moment.
When I departed, he ran along before me
And lightly sprinkled holy water o'er me.
I made inquiries of his servant, and he
Told me of who he was, and his poverty
Described so movingly, I could not choose

But offer gifts to him, which he'd refuse,
Forever crying, "No, no, it's too much;
I am unworthy, no, I dare not touch
A penny of it!" And, if I persisted,
He'd give it to the poor. Oh, he assisted
Many a one that way. Chaste Heaven, at last,
Moved me to take him in here as my guest.
Since then, all prospers. Sternly he reproves
All sinful and suspect behavior, moves
Particularly to guard my sacred honor
Where my wife's concerned. He keeps upon her
A most strict watch, and is indeed more jealous
Of all those coxcombs and conceited fellows
Who hang around her than *I* am, I feel;
You'd scarce believe the extent of his pious zeal.
One day he killed a flea with too much pique,
Then scourged himself and fasted for a week.

CLÉANTE. Brother, I swear, there's something wrong with your head.
Are you laughing at me with all this that you've said?
What does it mean? This madness worries me . . .

ORGON. Your language, brother, savors of heresy.
Your thinking's somewhat tainted by that vice,
And, as I've had to warn you once or twice,
You're liable to a judgment on your head.

CLÉANTE. To think like you is worse than being dead.
You voluntary blind men always call
The rest of us "freethinkers," whereas all
We're guilty of is scorning empty shows
And faithlessness. And now do you suppose
Your veiled denunciations frighten me?
My heart is open for all men to see.
I am no dupe of formalistic panders;
Religion, like the throne, has false pretenders.
And as the truly brave aren't always those
Who trumpet loudest or with gaudy shows
Paint their performance, so the true devout
Don't always pray the loudest or go about
With piously exaggerated gestures;
True worth does not reside in outward vestures,
Hypocrisy too often masks religion,
And men like you confuse life's true condition
By judging that the mask must be the face;
But don't you see such judgment's a disgrace?
The shadow, not the substance, is your God;
The false coin's what you worship, not the good.
Man must be, indeed, a curious creature
Who can't obey the simple laws of nature.

Reason seems to hem him in too tightly,
And so he never plays his part quite rightly.
He ruins every act by exaggeration
In trying to advance in estimation.
And, brother, by the way, a word to the wise . . .

ORGON. Well, you must be a scholar in disguise,
For clearly all the wisdom of the ages
Has found its home in you; the greatest sages
Are nothing unto you — you are a Cato,
A Socrates, a Zeno, or a Plato!

CLÉANTE. I'm not a doctor of philosophy,
And all life's wisdom doesn't reside in me.
My science lies in being able to see
Distinctions between truth and falsity.
And as I know of nothing more commendable
Than the honest piety of dependable
And devoted holy men, so too I find
Nothing's worse than those whose double mind
Betrays true holiness, those hypocrites
Upon whose subtle faces triumph sits
In smiling sacrilegious impudence,
Whose lives are nothing but one long pretense
Of piousness, the while they make a mock
Of all that's good, and while they fleece the flock
Of silly sheep by various devices
Designed to line their pockets; all their vices
Masquerade as virtue; on their way
To Heaven they contrive to jest and play
In secrecy, maintaining the disguise
Of holiness by lifting up their eyes
In pious, zealous ardor; who, in short,
While living in the luxury of Court,
Dryly preach abstinence, plain living,
And retirement; who, without misgiving,
Can reconcile their vices and their zeal;
Passionate, revengeful, they conceal
Their petty jealousies beneath the cloak
Of piety and goodness and invoke
God's name to consecrate their evils,
So bold and fearless are these subtle devils.
They place themselves upon the side of Heaven
And assassinate their foes with a sacred weapon.
This modern age, I fear, too rankly teems
With such pretenders, but although it seems
Hard to detect them, still true piety
Is never really difficult to see:
Look at Ariston, look at Périandre,

Oronte, Alcidamas, Polydore, and Clitandre.
No one would dare deny to them the title
Of honesty in any true recital
Of virtue's servants; never do they show
This ostentatious righteousness or go
Meddling into other folk's affairs
And giving themselves these smug and holy airs.
Their goodness is direct and free and simple
And only by their own benign example
Do they ever even so much as venture
To subject others unto moral censure.
They do not trust the face that evil shows
But are the first to think the best of those
Whom lying slander villainously attacks.
We find no intrigues or no secret pacts
Among them; virtue's what they're interested in;
They love the sinner, though they hate the sin.
Above all, they're embarrassed to disclose
Toward Heaven greater zeal than Heaven shows
Toward them. Such people truly share my heart.

ORGON. And have you finally spoken all your part?

CLÉANTE. Yes.

ORGON. Your servant, sir. I bid you a good day.

CLÉANTE. A moment, brother. Please don't run away.
Do you recall your promise to Valère?

ORGON. Yes.

CLÉANTE. And that you'd blessed the happy, loving pair?

ORGON. That's true.

CLÉANTE. Why, then, is there this great delay?

ORGON. I don't know.

CLÉANTE. You're planning for another day?

ORGON. Perhaps.

CLÉANTE. You mean you'd break your word?

ORGON. I don't say that.

CLÉANTE. From what I've heard,
You have no reason to delay things thus.

ORGON. That depends.

CLÉANTE. There certainly should be no fuss.

ORGON. I suppose not.

CLÉANTE. What shall I tell Valère?

ORGON. Whatever you please.

CLÉANTE. But don't you care
To make your wishes clear?

ORGON. I care
Only to do what Heaven wills.

CLÉANTE. Come, now,
You gave the lad your sacred vow.

ORGON. Farewell. (*Exits.*)
CLÉANTE. I fear the worst in this affair.
I must speak further quickly with Valère.

ACT TWO

Scene 1

(ORGON *and* MARIANE.)

ORGON. Mariane.
MARIANE. Father?
ORGON. Come closer; let me speak
To you.
MARIANE (*to* ORGON, *who is peering off stage*). What is it there that you seek?
ORGON. I'm looking to see if anyone's eavesdropping.
This is a likely place for tricksy snooping.
There now. All's well. Now then, my dear,
There's something that I wish for you to hear;
You know I've always held you in my heart.
MARIANE. You've always played a loving father's part.
ORGON. Well said! And to deserve that love, my treasure,
You should think of nothing but your father's pleasure.
MARIANE. I hope I never merit your reproof.
ORGON. Splendid! Tell me, what do you think of Tartuffe?
MARIANE. Who, I?
ORGON. You. Take care with your answer, pray.
MARIANE. Alas! I'll say whatever you wish me to say.

(DORINE *enters quietly and stands behind* ORGON *without his seeing her.*)

Scene 2

(ORGON, MARIANE, *and* DORINE.)

ORGON. Ah, wisely spoken. Then say, my dearest dove,
He has inspired your heart with tender love
And that the crown of joy upon your life
Descends the day that you become his wife.
MARIANE. What?
ORGON. Eh?
MARIANE. What did you say?
ORGON. Me?
MARIANE. Heavens above!
Who is it that's inspired my heart with love?

Who'll place the crown of joy upon my life
The day that I agree to be his wife?
ORGON. Tartuffe.
MARIANE. But, father, I feel nothing of the sort.
Would you have me betray the truth of my true heart?
ORGON. But I *want* it to be true. It should suffice
That my wishes in this matter are precise.
MARIANE. What? You wish . . . ?
ORGON. I intend, you see,
To firmly unite Tartuffe to my family
By marrying him to you. With that in view,
I'm resolved this marriage must . . . (*sees* DORINE). Ha! You!
Your curiosity must be a powerful passion
To make you come and eavesdrop in this fashion.
DORINE. I must say, sir, I don't know whether I can
Tell whether the rumor arose by careful plan
Or accident, but when somebody spoke
Of such a marriage, I treated it all as a joke.
ORGON. And what is so incredible, I pray?
DORINE. I'm sorry. I can't believe a word that you say.
ORGON. I know how to make you believe it, I'll tell you that.
DORINE. Ha! What a tale! You're talking through your hat!
ORGON. I'm telling you what will very soon prove true.
DORINE. Nonsense!
ORGON. Now, daughter, I mean what I say, I'm warning you.
DORINE. Ha, ha! Don't believe him! He's only laughing!
ORGON. I tell you . . .
DORINE. What stuff! Get out! You must be chaffing!
ORGON. I warn you now, take care; my anger's rising!
DORINE. Well, I must say, it's surely most surprising.
Are we to believe a man as wise as you
With that splendid beard and eyes of baby blue
Would be so big a fool! . . .
ORGON. Now listen here!
You're taking certain liberties, my dear,
Which do not please me at all, I can't deny.
DORINE. Come, let's speak calmly, sir, if we can, and try
To understand each other. Of course, you're joking.
Your daughter to marry a bigot, whose manner of speaking
Would scarce melt butter? And explain, if you can,
What such an alliance would bring to you, a man
Of notable wealth — to corrupt your daughter's love
By marrying her off to a beggar . . .
ORGON. That's enough!
I tell you that's the reason I revere him.
His poverty is honest. If you could hear him
Spurning worldly wealth and vulgar rank

As gross deceptions, then, my girl, you'd thank
Your father for marrying you to a saint,
A man who never has a word of complaint,
Whatever his woes. But with my modest aid
He'll soon regain the splendid role he played
In happier days. He once owned property
And was a landed squire in his home county.

DORINE. Yes, so he says; I say his vanity
Does not sort well with all his piety.
When you set up in business as a saint,
You shouldn't boast and brag without restraint.
Humility and love and true devotion
Are strange bedmates, indeed, for gross ambition.
Why be so haughty? But I see that you
Don't care at all for this. Then let's turn to
His person, not his claims to noble rank;
Doesn't it make you sometimes shudder or shrink
To think of a hypocritical fool
Like that corrupting the innocent soul
Of a girl like this? Stop and consider
The consequences, if you commit her
To such a loathsome and revolting marriage.
You'd better save your breath to cool your porridge
Than try to lecture a young and ardent wife
Who's bound by marriage to a hateful life.
Those husbands who wear horns upon their heads
Have driven their wives away from their weary beds
By their stupidities; and woe to those fathers
Who make such marriages for their poor daughters!
Beware of driving her to be a wife.

ORGON. It's nice of you to tell me about life!

DORINE. You could do worse than follow my advice.

ORGON. I'm sure these learned strictures are very nice.
But, daughter, you will do what I command.
Obey your father: that's the law of the land.
At one time, true, I'd pledged you to Valère,
But now I'm much disturbed by what I hear
Of that young man: free-thinking, playing cards, and such.

DORINE. And next you'll say you don't see him in church
Like those who go for advertising's sake.

ORGON. May I remind you that I didn't make
A special request for *your* precise advice.
I don't intend to speak to you more than twice.
The other man of whom we speak, I say,
Has made his peace with Heaven. That's the way
To build a marriage rich in every blessing.
You'll love each other. There'll be no transgressing.

You'll coo and gurgle like two doting turtles
And grow to be the happiest of mortals.
You'll make of him whatever you wish to make.

DORINE. She'll furnish him with horns within a week.

ORGON. What? What's that?

DORINE. He's got the head for it,
And I fear the melancholy aspect of his planet,
Despite your daughter's virtue, will prove too strong.

ORGON. *I* say stop interrupting and hold your tongue!
Mind your business; stop this damnable meddling.

DORINE. I'm only trying to stop your foolish fiddling.

ORGON. That's very kind of you. Now please be silent.

DORINE. If I didn't love you, sir . . .

ORGON. I'm growing violent.

DORINE. I want to help you, sir, despite your ire.

ORGON. Ha!

DORINE. It's true. Believe me, I can't bear
All the mocking you'd be subject to.

ORGON. You won't shut up?

DORINE. Whatever else, I'm true,
True-blue, to my employer all the way.

ORGON. Serpent! Silence! The next word you say . . . !

DORINE. A holy man like you, in such a temper?

ORGON. You plague me so, I find I can't remember
What I started to say. Not one more squawk!

DORINE. All right, but I can think, if I can't talk.

ORGON. Think, if you like, but see that you don't dare
To utter a word. (*To* MARIANE.) I'll grant you that Valère
Is a handsome chap . . .

DORINE. It drives me simply crazy
Not to be able to speak.

ORGON. Though no fop or daisy,
Tartuffe has looks . . .

DORINE. Indeed! To stop a clock.

ORGON. And, too, he comes of very ancient stock.
His other gifts . . .

DORINE. Oh, you fortunate girl!
If I were forced to marry such a churl,
I'd have my sweet revenge already planned
And prove a woman always has at hand
Those weapons that will give her the last hit.

ORGON. You won't obey my orders? Is that it?

DORINE. What's your trouble? I'm not talking to you.

ORGON. To whom, pray tell?

DORINE. Why, to myself, that's who.

ORGON (*aside*). *Eh bien.* There's only one recourse in such a case
And that's to give her a slap across the face.

(*Raises his hand to give her a blow, but whenever he looks at her, she stands mute and motionless.*)

Daughter, you ought to think well of my scheme;
Tartuffe's the answer to a maiden's dream.
(*To* DORINE.) Why don't you speak?
DORINE. I've nothing more to say.
ORGON. Go on. One little word.
DORINE. Thanks, not today.
ORGON. I'm all ready for you.
DORINE. I'm not *that* dumb.
ORGON (*to* MARIANE). It's not that I want my daughter under my thumb,
But you must learn to accept a father's rule.
DORINE (*fleeing*). I'd die before I'd marry that fat fool!

(ORGON *tries to slap her but misses and falls down as she runs out.*)

ORGON. I can't live any longer with that pest
Or I'll suffer the sin of anger. I must rest.
I'm not in any state to go on with our talk.
Excuse me while I go and take a walk.

(*Exit* ORGON. DORINE *re-enters cautiously.*)

Scene 3

(MARIANE *and* DORINE.)

DORINE. Mariane — ye gods — have you nothing to say?
And must I play the part that you should play?
A proposition utterly absurd,
And yet you don't defend yourself with a word!
MARIANE. His power is absolute. What can I do?
DORINE. Anything, except what he wants you to.
MARIANE. What?
DORINE. Tell him that a girl can't love by proxy.
And when it comes to marrying a foxy
And bigoted old hypocrite — *mon Dieu!* —
Your wishes ought to count for something, too.
If he loves Tartuffe dearer than a brother,
Then — Devil take it! — Let them marry each other!
MARIANE. I know, but father is so overbearing,
I don't dare raise my voice within his hearing.
DORINE. Look here. Let's think this through. Valère, you know,
Has offered you his hand. Is that not so?

MARIANE. Stop it, Dorine! Of course I love Valère
More than words can tell, and I can't bear
To think of looking at another lover;
But I've repeated all this ten times over.

DORINE. I'm sometimes doubtful of such a coy admission
And wonder if you're merely feigning passion.

MARIANE. You do me wrong in doubting me, my dear.
I'd thought that you believed I was sincere.

DORINE. In short, you love the boy?

MARIANE. Oh, yes, with passion!

DORINE. And it would seem he loves you in like fashion?

MARIANE. I think so.

DORINE. And the way to happiness
For both of you is marriage?

MARIANE. Yes, oh yes!

DORINE. And what about Tartuffe, love's adversary?

MARIANE. I'll kill myself, if that seems necessary.

DORINE. Oh, fine! "I'll kill myself," the maid replied.
The answer to life's grief is suicide.
A sovereign cure! It makes me mad clear through
To hear that kind of crazy talk from you.

MARIANE. Good heavens, what a temper! There you go!
You don't much sympathize with others' woe.

DORINE. I don't much sympathize with those who drivel,
Like you; then, when the test comes, shrivel.

MARIANE. You know I've always been a timid sort.

DORINE. But love demands a strong, courageous heart.

MARIANE. Loyalty to Valère's my firm intent,
But he must ask, and gain, Papa's consent.

DORINE. But if your father is an utter goof
Who's so infatuated with Tartuffe
He'll break the promise that he's pledged you to,
What is there left for poor Valère to do?

MARIANE. If I confess my true scorn for Tartuffe,
Won't I reveal unconsciously the truth
Of my affections? Though I love Valère,
Should I abandon modesty and dare
To flaunt my love for all the world to see?

DORINE. Oh, never mind. At least it's clear to me
You really want to be Madame Tartuffe,
And I was wrong to offer my reproof.
Why should I argue with two loving hearts?
The match would be ideal on both your parts.
Monsieur Tartuffe! a pretty pouter pigeon!
Tartuffe the Great! A man of high position!
A lucky girl she is who is his wife!

She royally has fixed herself for life.
Every day, each hour, you hear his praises
Sung by choirs in half a dozen places;
His ears are red as is the richest rose,
Only surpassed in glory by his nose.

MARIANE. Oh, God!

DORINE. What ecstasy will fill your loving breast
When you go home to share his little nest.

MARIANE. Stop this agonizing talk! Not one more word!
I cannot stand it any more. I've heard
Enough. Tell me how I can escape his clutches.

DORINE. A daughter should obey her father's wishes,
Although he choose a monkey for her mate.
I'd like to help, but really, it's too late.
Just think, you'll have a splendid horse and carriage
To help you ease the boredom of your marriage.
You can go calling on aunts, uncles, cousins,
Whom you'll find round the city by the dozens.
You'll call upon the Lord High Mayoress
And on the tax-collector's wife, no less,
Who'll seat you on a stool, the place of honor,
And might invite you to stay on for dinner;
A round of balls — as much as once a year —
Two bagpipes for a band, some watery beer;
Perhaps a puppet show, complete with monkey.
However, if your husband . . .

MARIANE. Oh, that donkey!
Dorine, for heaven's sake, I need advice.

DORINE. You must excuse me.

MARIANE. Please, I've asked you twice.

DORINE. To punish you, this marriage must go through.

MARIANE. Dorine!

DORINE. No!

MARIANE. I'll speak to father, as you wish me to.

DORINE. You've made your choice. It's clear Tartuffe's your man.

MARIANE. No more, Dorine. I've done all that I can.
My tears and sighs don't even leave you ruffled.

DORINE. As far as I'm concerned, you'll be Tartuffled.

MARIANE. Since my unhappiness can't move your heart,
I must surrender to despair and start
To search out methods of escaping life:
A little vial of poison or a knife.

DORINE. Here, here, come back. I'll put aside my ire
And help you to attain your true desire.

MARIANE. Dorine, if they insist on martyring me,
I'll simply die. I'll end my life. You'll see.

DORINE. Don't worry. We can find a way to spare
Your life, I'm sure. But look, here comes Valère.

(*Enter* VALÈRE. *He speaks at first jestingly.*)

Scene 4

(VALÈRE, MARIANE, *and* DORINE.)

VALÈRE. Mademoiselle, a story's reached my ears
Confirming all my wildest doubts and fears.
MARIANE. What's that?
VALÈRE. You're marrying Tartuffe.
MARIANE. That's true.
My father wishes . . . What else can I do?
VALÈRE. Your father, mademoiselle . . .
MARIANE. Has changed his mind.
Tartuffe's the man for whom I am designed.
VALÈRE. Is he serious?
MARIANE. As serious as serious can be.
He just was urging this affair to me.
VALÈRE. What's your opinion of this serious prank,
Pray tell?
MARIANE. I just don't know.
VALÈRE. Well, at least, that's frank.
You don't know?
MARIANE. No.
VALÈRE. No?
MARIANE. What's your advice?
VALÈRE. Accept this splendid husband. Don't think twice.
MARIANE. That's your advice?
VALÈRE. Yes.
MARIANE. Really?
VALÈRE. Absolutely.
You must pursue this rare chance resolutely.
MARIANE. I'm much obliged to you for this sage counsel.
VALÈRE. No thanks are due. I scarcely strained a tonsil.
MARIANE. I'll ponder your advisements at my leisure.
VALÈRE. I gave the counsel but to give you pleasure.
DORINE (*aside*). I wonder how this all is going to end?
VALÈRE. I owe you thanks for frankness, at least, my friend.
When you . . .
MARIANE. I beg you not to talk like that.
You told me in so many words I should accept
The man my father chose to pledge me to;

I'm saying that's what I intend to do;
I'm simply following your own advice.

VALÈRE. Don't fob me off with that antique device.
Before I ever spoke, your mind was fixed
And now you're seizing on some frivolous pretext
To justify your falsehood to my face.

MARIANE. Well put! Quite true.

VALÈRE. The plain facts of the case
Are that you've never loved me for a minute.

MARIANE. Think what you will, if you take pleasure in it.

VALÈRE. Pleasure? Ha! The hurt you've dealt my heart
Is deep, but I'll learn to make a second start
And find more sympathy and warmth than I do here.

MARIANE. I don't doubt that. What girl would not admire
Your character?

VALÈRE. Forget my character.
It's not so hot. I'm crooked as a barrister,
Blind as a fool in love, yes, even blinder,
But there's a girl somewhere who may be kinder
Than you. She'll take me on the rebound, if she must.

MARIANE. The loss is not so great. Somehow, I trust,
I'll manage to sustain it stoically.

VALÈRE. I'm sure you will comport yourself heroically.
And, as for me, it's never very pleasant
To find oneself forgotten. For the present,
I'll do my best to sigh, smile and forget,
Or, if I can't forget, pretend. And yet
There's something weak and pitiful and wilted
About a man who weeps when he's been jilted.

MARIANE. A lofty sentiment, indeed, if true.

VALÈRE. More people should approve it, as you do.
What! Would you have me keep within my heart
My love for you unchanging from the start,
See you go happy to another's arms
And not seek solace in a lady's charms?

MARIANE. Why, not at all! That's what I most desire —
A new romance to set your heart afire!

VALÈRE. You'd like that?

MARIANE. Yes.

VALÈRE. Enough of this detraction!
I'll try to give you instant satisfaction. (*Starts to leave and returns through the next few speeches.*)

MARIANE. Good.

VALÈRE. Kindly remember that, for good or ill,
I follow your example.

MARIANE. As you will.

VALÈRE. Your wishes are quite clear. I will comply.
MARIANE. Fine!
VALÈRE. Enough. You get no more of me. Good-by.
MARIANE. Excellent!
VALÈRE. Eh?
MARIANE. What?
VALÈRE. I thought I heard my name.
MARIANE. You must be hearing things.
VALÈRE. This game
Begins to weary me. Farewell.
MARIANE. Adieu.
DORINE. May I
Speak up now as a humble stander-by
And say I think you both are addled
And ought to have your backsides paddled?
Monsieur Valère!

(*She takes him by the arm; he feigns resistance.*)

VALÈRE. What do you want, Dorine?
DORINE. Come here!
VALÈRE. No, no! I'm in a rage. You've seen
I'm doing what she wants. Don't interfere.
DORINE. Stop!
VALÈRE. The matter is all settled, that's quite clear.
DORINE. Ha!
MARIANE. My presence here clearly annoys someone.
It's wiser if I leave him quite alone.

(DORINE *leaves* VALÈRE *and runs to* MARIANE.)

DORINE. Where are you going?
MARIANE. Let me alone!
DORINE. Come back!
MARIANE. No use, Dorine. You try another tack.
VALÈRE. It's clear it tortures her to look at me.
I'll just remove myself and set her free.
DORINE (*leaving* MARIANE *and running to* VALÈRE). What the deuce? What's all this that I hear?
Now stop this nonsense! Both of you come here! (*She pulls at them, one with each hand.*)
VALÈRE. What are you up to?
MARIANE. What do you think you're doing?
DORINE. Trying to get you two to billing and cooing.
VALÈRE. You must be crazy, as far as I can see.
Didn't you hear the way she talked to me?

DORINE (*to* MARIANE). You act as if you're going off your head.
MARIANE. Didn't you hear the awful things he said?
DORINE. You're crazy, both of you. (*To* VALÈRE.) Now I am sure
The only thing she wants is to be yours.
(*To* MARIANE.) He loves you only; I'm prepared to swear
That marriage — and to you — is his desire.
MARIANE (*to* VALÈRE). Why did you give me, then, your vile advice?
VALÈRE (*to* MARIANE). Your asking for it wasn't exactly nice.
DORINE. I said you both were crazy. Give me your hand.
Yours, now.
VALÈRE. Why give you my hand?
DORINE. You'll understand.
MARIANE. What *is* all this?
DORINE. Just this. You're both in love
More than you're either of you conscious of.
VALÈRE. Well, there's no harm — at least once in a while —
In giving a man a little friendly smile.

(MARIANE *looks at* VALÈRE *and smiles feebly.*)

DORINE. The fact is, lovers are completely daft.
VALÈRE. *I've* reason to complain, you know. You laughed
At me and scorned me with reproof
Because I thought you'd said "Yes" to Tartuffe.
MARIANE. But you yourself . . . it really is a shame . . .
DORINE. Let's leave this issue for another time.
The thing we need now is a cunning plan.
MARIANE. Speak up, Dorine. We'll do all that we can.
DORINE. There are a lot of tricks that we can play.
Your father's bluffing, surely, but the way
For you to get around him is to feign
Complete compliance with his mad design,
So that, in case of crisis, you can manage
To keep postponing this unwelcome marriage.
Time has many virtues; it can heal
Many a wound that seems beyond repeal.
And there are many tricks. Say you fell ill;
No one can force you then against your will.
Or maybe some dire omen greets your eyes:
A funeral in the street (a grim surprise),
A broken mirror, auguring the worst,
A black cat, which suggests your life is cursed —
A dozen dodges. But I would much rather
You two would not be seen like this together.
(*To* VALÈRE.) Now go and use the help of all your friends
To win the girl that clearly Fate intends

For you. (*To* MARIANE.) I'm sure you'll get your brother
To help you, not to mention your stepmother.
Good-by!

VALÈRE (*to* MARIANE). We all will do whatever we can do,
But my best hope and love resides in you.

MARIANE. I don't know what my father may decide.
I only know I'll not be Tartuffe's bride.

VALÈRE. You make me very happy. And if ever . . .

DORINE. Lovers are never tired. They talk forever.
Come on, get going!

VALÈRE. Farewell . . .

DORINE. Oh, talk, talk, talk!
You that way, and you this. Come on, now! Walk!

ACT THREE

Scene 1

(DAMIS *and* DORINE.)

DAMIS. Let Heaven strike me with a lightning bolt,
Let all the world call me a rogue, a dolt;
No talk of filial respect, no father's power
Will hold me back; I'll act within the hour!

DORINE. For Heaven's sake, enough of this mad chatter;
Your father's merely talked about the matter.
Need I remind you that there's many a slip
Betwixt the smooth cup and the slippery lip?

DAMIS. I'll stop that fat conspirator's career;
I'll speak a word or two into his ear.

DORINE. Easy does it, boy; let your stepmother
Handle him, the way she does your father.
Tartuffe becomes like putty in her hands
And easily agrees to her demands.
I think he eyes her with a secret yen;
Lord knows, I hope that that's the case, for then
She'll come to interview him, for your sake,
Learn what his feelings are and make
Him understand what troubles will be brewing
If he continues as he has been doing.
His valet tells me that he's at his prayers;
No one can see him; he's alone upstairs.
But he'll be coming down in a minute or two.
So beat it, please; I'll see what I can do.

DAMIS. I must be present when he talks to her.

DORINE. Never! Beat it!
DAMIS. I won't speak or stir.
DORINE. Nonsense! I know how you fly off the handle,
And that's the surest way to snuff the candle.
Go on!
DAMIS. I promise I won't rage or shout.
DORINE. Oh, what a pest you are! Look, here he comes! Get out!

(DORINE *pushes him out.* TARTUFFE *enters and, seeing* DORINE, *calls off stage.*)

Scene 2

(TARTUFFE *and* DORINE.)

TARTUFFE (*calls off stage*). Put away my hair shirt and my scourge
And pray perpetually that Heaven may purge
Our souls of sin. If someone asks for me,
I've gone to bless the poor with charity.
DORINE (*aside*). What hogwash! What a stupid thing to say!
TARTUFFE. What do you want?
DORINE. I . . .
TARTUFFE (*drawing out a kerchief*). Wait! I pray,
Take this handkerchief before you speak.
DORINE. Why?
TARTUFFE. Cover that bosom which demurely peeks
Above your bodice. Such forbidden sights
May well give rise to slightly carnal thoughts.
DORINE. You must be quite concupiscently queasy
If a little flesh can make you so uneasy.
Of course, I don't know how you're stimulated
But I'm not quite so easily elated.
Why, I could see you nude without a qualm;
In fact, I think I'd stay supremely calm.
TARTUFFE. A bit more modesty in speech, my dear,
Or I'll withdraw and leave you standing here.
DORINE. No, I will go and leave you here alone,
But first, there's something that you should have known;
Madame Elmire will soon come into view.
She'd like to have a word or two with you.
TARTUFFE. Delighted!
DORINE (*aside*). He leaps and bleats just like a woolly lamb.
I'm right, he has a hankering for madame.
TARTUFFE. She's coming soon?
DORINE. Yes, here she comes this way;
I'll leave you two together, if I may. (*Exit.*)

Scene 3

(ELMIRE *and* TARTUFFE.)

TARTUFFE. May Heaven's grace, madame, preserve you whole
And sound in mind, in body, and in soul,
And bless your days according to the prayers
Of one who's much concerned with your affairs.
ELMIRE. I'm deeply grateful for your pieties.
Let us sit down and chat more at our ease.
TARTUFFE. I trust, madame, your fever's not persisted?
ELMIRE. I'm feeling well; the fever's quite arrested.
TARTUFFE. My poor and humble prayers here in this place
Seem all too small to have brought down such grace
Upon you from on high; yet I confess
My constant thoughts are of your happiness.
ELMIRE. Your pious zeal is rather overpowering.
TARTUFFE. Pray Heaven that the heavens keep on showering
Blessings on you; I'd give my life for yours.
ELMIRE. There's no need for such drastic overtures.
But I'm indebted to you for your prayers.
TARTUFFE. Dear lady, *any*thing to ease your cares . . .

(DAMIS *enters unseen behind them.*)

ELMIRE. I wanted to speak privately to you.
I'm glad we're here out of the public view.
TARTUFFE. And so am I! Dear Heaven, but it's sweet
To be beside you, madame, on this seat.
This is a chance for which I've often prayed;
It seems a stroke of luck that Fate has made.
ELMIRE. I know, my friend, exactly what you mean.
I've often longed for a chat like this, unseen.
TARTUFFE. Oh, how I've prayed that we could freely share
Our thoughts and words, that I could boldly bare
My soul unto you, that I might explain
My distaste for the friends you entertain
Springs not from my dislike of your devotion
To them, but rather from my own profound emotion
Which fairly chokes me . . .
ELMIRE. Well, your zeal
Is something, sir, that you need not conceal.
TARTUFFE (*taking her hand and squeezing her fingers*). How hard I pray for you, and even harder . . .
ELMIRE. Ouch! You're hurting me!
TARTUFFE. Forgive my ardor!

I had no idea of hurting you, I swear!
It's just . . . (*puts his hand on her knee*).

ELMIRE. Your hand. What is it doing there?

TARTUFFE. Just feeling the material; it's nice!

ELMIRE. I'm ticklish. Please, don't make me ask you twice.

(*She moves her chair away;* TARTUFFE *brings his closer. This continues throughout the scene.*)

TARTUFFE. I am a great admirer of fine lace.
The workmanship, the beauty, and the grace
Of the design. What lovely decoration!

ELMIRE. Perhaps. But now, sir, to our conversation.
I hear my husband wants to marry you
To Mariane. Pray tell me, is that true?

TARTUFFE. He's mentioned it. But, lady, need I say
That's not the joy I dream of night and day?
It's elsewhere that I see the lovely fire
Which blazes with the beauties I desire.

ELMIRE. You mean you don't love earthly things alone?

TARTUFFE. I mean, madame, my heart's not made of stone.

ELMIRE. I see. You mean your thoughts are turned to Heaven,
Toward which your yearning spirit long has striven.

TARTUFFE. The love which draws us toward eternal beauty
Does not release us from our earthly duty
To love each other. Heaven often forms
A vessel whose supernal beauty warms
Our earthly blood. And such a one are you;
My spirit soars when you come into view.
Heaven's glories shine within your face;
Your form and figure testify to Grace.
O perfect beauty, perfect in each feature!
In you I worship great creating Nature.
Fair goddess! wondrous woman; in your eyes
I see the will of Heaven and am wise.
At first I trembled, lest my sacred passion
For you prove false, a hindrance to salvation,
Perhaps — who knows? — a horrid stratagem
Of the Evil One, a trap to catch me in.
I even thought to flee in foolish fashion,
But then I came to see that such a passion,
Inspired by Heaven as it is, undoubtedly,
Need not be inconsistent with true modesty.
And so I gave my eager heart full rein.
I know I should not hope that you will deign
To smile with condescension on my suit;
But still, when Heaven calls, dare man be mute?

In you is all my hope, my good, my peace;
In you rests my damnation or release.
I may taste bliss or be tormented still;
It all will be according to your will.

ELMIRE. This is indeed a gallant declaration.
I must confess, though, to some consternation.
You should have steeled your feelings somewhat better;
Why, what would happen if my husband ever
Heard words like this from such a pious man? . . .

TARTUFFE. Though I am pious, I am still a man,
An erring, mortal man, and when your beauties
Flame on my sight, all my religious duties
Grow somewhat blurred. I know such an appraisal
May shock you somewhat. Still, I'm not an angel.
And if you view my conduct with alarm,
You must accuse your own bewitching charm.
Since I first viewed your beauty's flawless art,
You've been the sovereign of my secret heart.
My poor soul struggled, but alas! in vain
Against your distant beauty and disdain;
In vain, in vain my fasting, prayers and tears.
Each soft breeze blew your sweet name to my ears.
How long I've sought to say this with my eyes;
Now hear it in my words and in my sighs.
And if you look with pity and compassion
Upon this poor unworthy slave of passion,
If you consent to bring me consolation
And bring about my yearning soul's salvation,
I'll swear to you with most profound emotion
Unending service and a true devotion.
And in my hands be sure a lady's honor
Is safe, no danger that there'll come upon her
The smallest breath of scandal. These young sparks
That ladies dote on are unsafe. Their larks,
Their jokes, their boasts about the wars of love
Leave ladies' reputations not above
Reproach, and many ladies have been tarnished
By faithless gallants whose careers have furnished
Examples of betrayal and deceit.
But fear me not, dear lady; I'm discreet.
The care a man like me takes of his name
Is guarantee that you need fear no shame;
You buy, if you accept my heart, my dear,
Love without scandal, pleasure without fear.

ELMIRE. I'm fascinated; and your rhetoric
Effectively removes all the inveterate
Fears I might have felt; but don't *you* fear

That I might speak a word in Orgon's ear
About your strange behavior here today?
If I did, what do you think he'd say?

TARTUFFE. I know you are too merciful and good
And that my love is not misunderstood.
Pity for human frailty will excuse
My over-ardent voicing of such views.
Although I yearn toward the True and Good,
Still I am human, merely flesh and blood.

ELMIRE. Another woman might, indeed, repeat
This story; but I too can be discreet.
I'll not tell Orgon of your strange behavior;
In turn I'll beg of you a certain favor:
I want you to speak boldly and declare
That you support the marriage of Valère
And Mariane, that you renounce the claim
By which you would usurp another's name,
And . . .

Scene 4

(ELMIRE, DAMIS *and* TARTUFFE.)

DAMIS (*emerging*). No, madame, no! This news must come to light!
I've been this while concealed there, within sight
And hearing. Heaven's favor led me there
To trap this hypocrite in his own snare
And place within my hands at last the power
Of sweet revenge. Aha! Within the hour
I'll undeceive my father and he'll know
The gross sins of that fat Lothario!

ELMIRE. No, Damis, it's enough if he repents.
I'll count that a sufficient recompense.
I've promised it; don't make me break a vow.
No nasty scenes; I'm willing to allow
The whole affair to pass and not displease
My husband's ears with such absurdities.

DAMIS. You may have reason, madame, to be lenient,
But I do not consider it convenient
To lose this chance of pricking his fat bubble
And plunging him up to the ears in trouble.
His sanctimonious impudence too long
Has stirred up trouble in our home; too long
He's bilked my father, led him by the nose.
And now with vengeance sure, do you suppose
I'll overlook my opportunity?
It is a grace that Heaven's conferred on me.

Now and henceforth I am Heaven's debtor,
And Heaven knows when I will find a better
Chance to give this slippery fox a jolt.
If I passed up this chance, I'd be a dolt.

ELMIRE. Damis . . .

DAMIS. I must do what I think is justified.
I've never felt so richly satisfied.
Please don't deter me. Try to understand
My joy in holding vengeance in my hand.
I'll have full satisfaction, I vow,
And see, here comes my opportunity, right now.

Scene 5

(ORGON, ELMIRE, DAMIS, *and* TARTUFFE.)

DAMIS (*continuing, to* ORGON, *who enters*). Father, I've got a bit of a surprise
For you; some news to open up your eyes.
Your kindnesses have here been well repaid;
This gentleman, behind your back, has made
Proposals to madame which cast upon her
A curious light and work to your dishonor.
In short, I've just surprised this monstrous beast
In making love to her and, sir, he ceased
Only when I spoke. Madame implored
I spare you this recital, but I've stored
A thirst for vengeance in my hungry heart,
And I don't choose to play a forgiving part.

ELMIRE. I think a wife ought never to annoy
Her husband with such silly tales. My boy,
A woman likes to handle such affairs
In her own way, so that nobody shares
The knowledge of the circumstances. You'd be
Silent now if you were ruled by me. (*Exit.*)

Scene 6

(ORGON, DAMIS, *and* TARTUFFE.)

ORGON. Oh, gracious Heavens! Can I trust my ears?

TARTUFFE. Alas, the case is just as it appears:
I am a sinner lost in deep iniquity,
One who would let mere physical propinquity
Corrupt his holy purposes and stain
His spotless shield of honor; don't refrain
From heaping censure on me. I'm a beast.

My life's a mass of crime; there's not the least
Extenuation possible for me.
Heaven has contrived all this, I see,
As punishment for my most rank misdeeds
And Heaven has ordained that no one pleads
For me. Let no man speak. Let me be driven
Out of your house, out of the sight of Heaven.

ORGON (*to* DAMIS). Traitor! How do you dare, with nasty lies,
To bring the innocent tears into his eyes?

DAMIS. Don't tell me all this blubbering and bluster
Is going to make you think . . .

ORGON. Be silent, monster!

TARTUFFE. Ah, let him speak! How wrongly you accuse him!
Believe his words! It's wrong if you refuse him
Your trusting ears. Why put your faith in me?
How do you know what sort of man I might be?
Brother, how can you trust my outward seeming?
Perhaps when you look at me you're merely dreaming.
No, no, my outward semblance may deceive;
Within, I am far worse than you believe.
Although I commonly pass for a man of virtue,
You sadly let my outer surface cheat you. (*to* DAMIS)
Speak, dear boy, call me a vile traitor,
Perfidious, a liar, a betrayer
Of friendship's trust; call me the vilest term
You can imagine; I'm lower than a worm (*on his knees*).
Let me acknowledge here upon my knees
My horrid crimes. Condemn me, if you please.

ORGON. Brother, this is too much! (*To* DAMIS.) So — your heart
Remains unmoved?

DAMIS. He's merely playing a part!

ORGON. Silence, scoundrel! (*To* TARTUFFE.) My brother, I beg you, stand!
(*To* DAMIS.) Rascal!

DAMIS. He can . . .

ORGON. Silence!

DAMIS. Don't you understand?

ORGON. Just one more word, and I'll punch you in the nose!

TARTUFFE. Do not be angry, brother. Do you suppose
I would not rather suffer indignity
Than have him suffer the slightest scratch for me?

ORGON (*to* DAMIS). Ingrate!

TARTUFFE. Leave him in peace! See, I'm kneeling
To ask you for his pardon.

ORGON. Oh, what feeling! (*Falling on his knees and embracing* TARTUFFE.)
Observe his goodness!

DAMIS. But . . .
ORGON. Peace!
DAMIS. But, I . . .
ORGON. Quiet!
I understand why you're raising all this riot.
You hate him, all of you: my faithful wife,
My children, servants — why, upon my life!
It's a conspiracy to drive this saint
Out of my house. And this absurd complaint
Against him doesn't move me, not a whit.
I'll stand with him forever, you can sit
And spin your lies; I'll hasten with my plan
To marry this wronged saint to Mariane.

DAMIS. You think you'll force her into such a plight?

ORGON. Yes, and, to spite you all, this very night!
Oh, I defy you! Defy you, do you hear?
I'll show you, mark my words, who's master here!
Take back your wicked words, you monster, and entreat
His pardon. I command you, fall at his feet!

DAMIS. What? Fall at the feet of this repulsive liar?

ORGON. Ah, you resist my will? You've roused my ire!
Give me a stick, a stick! Don't hold me back!
Out of my sight! I'll deal you such a crack
Your ears will ring! Out! Out of my place!

DAMIS. All right, I'll go, but . . .

ORGON. Don't let me see your face!
Reptile, I'll remove you from my will!
Take my curse, and go — wherever you will.

(*Exit* DAMIS.)

Scene 7

(ORGON *and* TARTUFFE.)

ORGON (*continuing, to* TARTUFFE). Think of offering such insults to you!

TARTUFFE. May Heaven pardon him, as I would do.
Ah, could you know how bitterly I suffer
To hear such words spoken to my brother . . .

ORGON. Alas!

TARTUFFE. Merely to think of such ingratitude
Makes my heart ache. Words so rough and crude
Fill my soul with a horror that's so deep
I can do nothing but beat my breast and weep!

ORGON (*runs to the door where he has driven* DAMIS). Villain! I'm sorry I didn't knock you down
When I had the chance! Liar! Monster! Clown!

TARTUFFE. Brother, compose yourself. Don't be distressed.
Let's have no more of this. I think it best
That I should leave your home, dear friend, right now.
I'll never return to bother you, I vow.

ORGON. You're jesting!

TARTUFFE. No, no, they all hate me here.
They'd even question my sincerity, I fear.

ORGON. Do you think I listen to anything they say?

TARTUFFE. But they'll go on with their tales, day after day.
These stories that today have left you grieved
Tomorrow may be readily believed.

ORGON. Oh, never, brother, never!

TARTUFFE. Brother, a wife
May sway a husband's mind and rule his life.

ORGON. You shall not go! Never! I will not hear it!

TARTUFFE. Well, I'll remain, to mortify my spirit.
Still, if you desired it . . .

ORGON. Oh!

TARTUFFE. Well, no more.
I'll not behave as I have done before.
Honor is delicate, and, like Caesar's wife,
I must be past suspicion. On my life,
I'll flee the presence of madame and call . . .

ORGON. No, you'll attend her, to defy them all.
My one desire now is to fully spite them;
You must be with her constantly — we'll fight them,
Fire with fire, slander with suspicion,
To keep their tongues a-wagging. In addition,
I'm firm resolved that you must be my heir.
I'll change my will today, and I'll declare
That all my wealth is yours by legal right.
I tell you, brother, I take more delight
In you, my heir, than in all my family.

TARTUFFE. May Heaven's will be done eternally.

ORGON. Come, let's change the document; meanwhile,
Let the jealous choke on their own bile!

ACT FOUR

Scene 1

(CLÉANTE *and* TARTUFFE.)

CLÉANTE. Everywhere I go I hear this story;
It's one that doesn't add unto your glory;
And I am glad, sir, I've run into you
So I can tell you briefly what my view

Of the matter is. I won't weigh right and wrong;
In any case, the evidence is strong.
But let's assume the tale Damis propounded
Was false, and the whole thing was unfounded.
Should not a Christian pardon the mistake,
Turning the other cheek for charity's sake?
Should such a quarrel, by purpose or by chance
Be cause for Damis' disinheritance?
In perfect frankness, sir, let me repeat:
The story's spreading; everyone you meet
Is talking of it. Look at what you've done!
It's not too late for father and for son
To reconcile; if you promote this union,
You'll bring yourself back into good opinion.

TARTUFFE. Alas, how happy I would be, if this could be!
God knows, my heart of rancor is quite free.
I would not harm him, bless you, if I could;
I long with all my heart to do him good.
But Heaven's will doesn't always fit my heart;
If he returns to the house, I must depart.
No, no, I couldn't stay with him in this place,
Not without a sense of complete disgrace;
It would be an intolerable situation;
Why, people might accuse me of calculation.
They'd say I was pretending, as a ruse, sir,
False charity to silence my accuser.
They'd say I kept him here beneath surveillance
Merely to ensure his guilty silence.

CLÉANTE. Your statements have some plausibility,
But still it all sounds quite far-fetched to me.
Since when are you the self-appointed judge
Of who must cringe beneath great Heaven's scourge?
Let God decide on matters of election
And let him implement his own correction.
And he who's moved by Heaven, not his humors,
Should not be sensitive to idle rumors.
No need, I'm sure, for fearing idle tongues
When you act truly to correct great wrongs,
And he who would take justice in his hands
Should first be sure he's tuned to God's commands.

TARTUFFE. My one desire's to be obedient
To God, whenever it's expedient.
But, after Damis' recent rude behavior,
I'd not forgive him, no, were I the Savior.

CLÉANTE. And does God order you to punish him
By aiding and abetting Orgon's whim
To disinherit him? And does God know
How you will profit by his overthrow?

TARTUFFE. No one who's plumbed the true depths of my spirit
Could think a thing like that of me, or fear it.
The riches of this world are dross to me;
Their gleaming superficiality
Does not seduce me; and if I accept
Something of the wealth Orgon has kept
Hidden away, my motives are quite pure:
To keep it out of the hands of an evildoer,
Someone who might, alas! make evil use
Of it, or squander it without excuse;
How better, then, to give it to one who swore he
Would dedicate its use to Heaven's glory?
CLÉANTE. Your reasons are somewhat sophistical,
If not, indeed, a trifle egotistical.
Why not let Damis have his proper wealth,
As long as you have liberty and health?
Better, indeed, to let the lad misuse it
Than countenance the rumor you'd abuse it
For your own purposes. I'm amazed
You could have heard this plan and not have raised
Your voice in protest. As far as I'm aware,
God doesn't condone defrauding a son and heir.
And if God in truth your heart has steeled
Against Damis, then why not quit the field
As any honorable adversary should
And leave the house to him? I'm sure I would.
Believe me, sir, it does you no great credit
To have this story spread, and if you let it
Gain further credence, your basic piety
Will seem . . .
TARTUFFE. Excuse me, sir, it's half-past three;
I must retire to prayers and meditations;
I leave you with my best felicitations. (*Exit.*)

Scene 2

(ELMIRE, MARIANE, CLÉANTE, *and* DORINE.)

DORINE. Sir, can't you help her soul gain some relief,
For she is suffering a most cruel grief?
This hateful marriage pledge her father's made
Has sickened her poor heart, and it's betrayed
Her fondest hopes. He's coming now. Let's try
To undermine this project on the sly,
And unite this poor maid and Valère.

(*Enter* ORGON.)

Scene 3

(ORGON, ELMIRE, MARIANE, CLÉANTE, *and* DORINE.)

ORGON. I'm glad to find you all assembled here. (*To* MARIANE.)
There's something in this deed to make you smile,
And I'll reveal it in a little while.

MARIANE. Father, I call on Heaven, which knows my grief!
Look in your heart and offer me relief
From this oppressive sorrow; oh, relax
The rights of fatherhood, I pray. Don't tax
My frail forbearance, so that I must cry
In bitter protest unto God on high.
Don't make a senseless tragedy
Out of that life which you have given me.
Though you forbid my wedding the one I love,
At least, I beg, by all the powers above,
Don't bring me to this miserable estate
By forcing me to marry one I hate.
Don't drive me to an act of blind despair
By bringing all your legal powers to bear.

ORGON (*aside*). Be strong, my heart! Don't yield to human frailty!

MARIANE. I'm not distressed by your continued loyalty
To him. Give him your wealth, if that's what you want to do
And, if that's not enough, why, take mine too.
Give him all that I have; it cannot worsen
My grief. But don't consign to him my person!
Just spare me that. Then, when the deed is done,
Let me retire to spend my life as a nun.

ORGON. You think, by waxing weepy and despondent,
And talking crazily about a convent,
You'll frighten me? Get up! I say, the more
Your heart recoils, the more you'll answer for.
So mortify your senses by your yielding
Meekly to the power that I'm wielding.

DORINE. But what . . . ?

ORGON. Be silent! Speak when you're spoken to!
I don't want to hear a syllable out of you!

CLÉANTE. If you'll permit me to offer some advice . . .

ORGON. Your words, dear brother, always are quite nice,
And your advice is always full of merit,
So much so, I'd prefer just not to hear it.

ELMIRE (*to* ORGON). Seeing all this, I find myself struck dumb.
I can't believe how blind you have become.
You must be hypnotized, or else insane,
To doubt our word about this recent scene.

ORGON. I believe your words, dear, one by one,

And I know how fond you are of my rascal son.
Clearly you were afraid to disavow
The fraud he tried to perpetrate just now.
And you were, I must protest, a shade too calm;
A woman in your place should have showed alarm.

ELMIRE. Should a woman's honor be so stirred
If someone offers her a wicked word?
And does a mere suggestion then require
Denunciations and a tongue of fire?
Why, all I do is laugh at such advances;
To me, they're unimportant circumstances.
I try to wear my virtue modestly
And not like some protesting prudes I see
Whose virtue comes full-armed with teeth and claws
Ready to scratch and bite at the slightest cause.
Heaven preserve me from such purity!
True Virtue needs no arms and need not be
Masked by scowls. A firm and simple "No"
Will tell unwelcome lovers where to go.

ORGON. You needn't try to make a dupe of me.

ELMIRE. I can't believe your gullibility!
Could I shake your blind, unthinking faith
By making you witness to the truth?

ORGON. Witness?

ELMIRE. Yes.

ORGON. Nonsense!

ELMIRE. Suppose
I show you the fact before your very eyes?

ORGON. Balderdash!

ELMIRE. Oh, what a man! It's too absurd!
You obviously won't believe a word.
Suppose we could place you here concealed
Where you could see what would be revealed,
And you saw the truth? Then what would you do?

ORGON. I'd say in that case . . . well, I'd say "Pooh pooh!"
For it cannot be.

ELMIRE. You've been too long unwise,
And you've accused me for too long of telling lies.
Now, for my satisfaction and your proof,
I'll make you witness to the living truth.

ORGON. I'll take you up on that! Let's see your scheme.
The truth will be far stranger than you dream.

ELMIRE (*to* DORINE). Send him in here.

DORINE. He's clever as a fox
And he won't be easily trapped within a box.

ELMIRE. Some men are easily fooled by infatuation;
Such blindness must be cured by illumination.

Have him come down. (*To* CLÉANTE *and* MARIANE.) And, you two, please go.

(*Exeunt* DORINE, CLÉANTE, *and* MARIANE.)

Scene 4

(ELMIRE *and* ORGON.)

ELMIRE (*continuing, to* ORGON). See that table? There's your place — below.

ORGON. What?

ELMIRE. You'll have to hide yourself, that's clear.

ORGON. But why beneath the table?

ELMIRE. Get under here!
I have my plan; you'll see how it works out;
Under the table, quick, and when you're set,
Not a whisper. Don't make any comments.

ORGON. I must say, I'm most patient with your nonsense.
Well, let me see you wiggle out of this one.

ELMIRE. Remember, there are one or two conditions:
Since this is a rather ticklish situation,
I must behave according to the occasion;
Pray don't be scandalized if I seem to behave
Quite forwardly; I do it for you, to save
Your sanity; some questions I may ask
Are merely traps to tempt him to unmask,
And if I smile upon his lewd desires
It's merely to arouse his amorous fires.
Remember: for your sake and his confusion
I have consented here in this seclusion
To meet with him. The action will subside
As soon as you feel fully satisfied.
Your task will be, concealed there as you are,
To call a halt if things have gone too far.
A husband, after all, should shield his wife
From the unpleasant perils of this life;
You are the master in the house, and your will
Should be obeyed . . . Sh! Here he comes! Be still!

Scene 5

(TARTUFFE, ELMIRE, *and* ORGON. ORGON *is under the table.*)

TARTUFFE. They said, dear lady, you were waiting here.

ELMIRE. Yes. I've a secret for your private ear.

But close that door first, please, and peep
About the room. Let's not be caught asleep.

(TARTUFFE *shuts the door and looks about.*)

We certainly don't want again, you know,
The sort of scene we had a while ago.
That was most disagreeable, it's true,
And I was in a panic because of you.
You saw I did my best to keep him quiet,
But he was clearly determined to raise a riot.
Of course, I was so alarmed — I was nearly dead! —
I didn't think to deny the things he'd said.
But, Heaven be praised, it all worked out ideally
And everything is understood — yes, really!
Your reputation's so strong, it cannot fall,
And my husband does not suspect you, not at all.
In fact, to still the voice of slander, he
Wants us to be together continually.
So now we're able to be sequestered here
Behind locked doors and free of blame or fear,
And I can reveal what my true feelings are
About you, sir — but perhaps I go too far.

TARTUFFE. This talk is rather baffling, I'll admit;
You've changed, madame, since the last time we met.

ELMIRE. Why, if you're angry at my earlier rebuff,
You don't know women's hearts quite well enough.
You don't know what our hearts are trying to speak
When our defense seems languid, slow, and weak.
And ever our modesty must make a show
Of struggling valiantly to overthrow
Our feelings, which, the while we're yielding,
We blush to find our words have been revealing.
At first we fight against them, but our tender
Sighs betray our swift complete surrender.
For honor's sake, we put our hearts on trial
And promise everything with a denial.
I fear I'm speaking much too honestly
And overlooking proper modesty.
But, since I'm speaking frankly, don't you see
Why I didn't struggle to restrain Damis?
And would I, pray, so graciously, so long,
Have listened to your offer, and so long
Have let you pour your heart out in full measure
If the affair did not afford me pleasure?
And when I argued with such force and courage
To get you to renounce your coming marriage

Why would my claims have been so strongly pressed
Except for my own selfish interest?
In short, I feared this marriage might divide
A heart I wanted whole, and near my side.

TARTUFFE. Ah, madame, it gives me joy extreme
To hear such words from you. It's like a dream!
Their honey pours into my tortured brain;
Their liquid sweetness flows through every vein.
My aim's to please you, all things else above;
My heart's beatitude lies in your love.
And yet I hope you'll not think me suspicious
To dare to doubt my joys are so delicious.
I could almost suspect a sly arrangement
To get me to break off my late engagement.
And so, madame, to put the matter bluntly,
And much as I enjoy your lovely company,
I'll dare to doubt your tender words until
Some tangible favors indicate your will,
Implanting in my wavering soul a faith
That your dear bounty's not a vagrant wraith.

ELMIRE (*coughing to warn* ORGON). What do you mean? Don't tell me that you think
You can rush love to its climax in a wink!
I've forced myself to make a rash admission,
But now you'd add, I see, another condition,
And you won't be satisfied until you win
Love's final favors almost before you begin.

TARTUFFE. The less one merits, the less one dares to hope;
Where talk is cheap, each parish priest's a Pope.
One easily mistrusts a promised bliss
And can't believe it till it's really his.
Knowing how little I am worthy of you,
I doubt I'll ever be allowed to love you.
In short, madame, I'll not believe a word
Till facts confirm these promises I've heard.

ELMIRE. Dear me! Your love is really quite tyrannical.
I'd hate to think I'm being puritanical,
But, mercy me! love drives men quite insane,
So powerful and violent is its reign;
Can I not raise my hands in weak defense?
Is there no way to curb your violence?
Take pity on a lady, sir, and send her
Reprieve. Complete, abject surrender
Is frightening, you know, and it may cost
You a regard you'd rather not have lost.

TARTUFFE. If you receive my homage with compassion,
Then why withhold love's tangible expression?

ELMIRE. But, if I consent, won't Heaven be offended?
This is your constant theme, and I commend it.

TARTUFFE. Pooh! If Heaven's all that's worrying you,
I'll take care of that, and easily too;
I can remove such obstacles with ease.

ELMIRE. And yet they threaten us so with Heaven's decrees!

TARTUFFE. I can banish such superstitious fear.
There is an art, you know, in making clear
Heaven's will, and though Heaven may proscribe
Certain joys, a bit of a spiritual bribe
Can clear the path sometimes. There is a science
Of loosening the conscience so compliance
Is easy, and the evil of an action
Is rectified to Heaven's satisfaction.
I'll teach you all these secrets; you will see.
But you must put your confidence in me.
Content my longings, lady; do not fear.
The risk is mine; don't hesitate, my dear.

(ELMIRE *coughs.*)

You have a nasty cough . . .

ELMIRE. It's most distressing.

TARTUFFE. I have some cough drops. Try one, with my blessing.

ELMIRE. I've had this cough for weeks, would you believe it?
I fear that all your cough drops can't relieve it.

TARTUFFE. Very annoying.

ELMIRE. Yes, it's quite severe.

TARTUFFE. Well, at least I can dispel your fear.
Your secret is known to us alone,
And evil's not evil until it's known
To the world at large, and, as for sin,
To sin in silence is not to sin.

ELMIRE (*coughs*). In short, I see that I shall have to yield
And, fleeing, leave you master of the field
Of my poor honor, for I can't convince
A man who demands such tangible evidence.
I must admit I fear to go so far,
But who cares what my foolish scruples are?
And since I'm driven to it cruelly
By one who seems to find my pleas unduly
Quibbling and demands complete conviction
I must decide to render satisfaction
Unto his claims. If there is any crime
In such consent, it's clear the blame's not mine.
Surely I am not responsible.

TARTUFFE. Of course not, lady! Why, the thought's impossible!

ELMIRE. But first, please open the door — but not too wide —
And see if my husband's lurking there outside.
TARTUFFE. Pooh! Why worry about dolts like those?
He's the type you can lead around by the nose,
The type to abet our little intimacies;
Why, we can make him believe whatever we please.
ELMIRE. All the same, I'd feel much more secure
If you'd take a look around just to be sure.

(*Exit* TARTUFFE.)

Scene 6

(ORGON *and* ELMIRE.)

ORGON (*emerging from under the table*). Such wickedness is inconceivable!
I'm thunderstruck! It's unbelievable!
ELMIRE. What, crawling out so soon? Don't be absurd!
Creep in again and wait. You haven't heard
A fraction yet. Wait, and you'll correct your
Ideas further, and it won't be mere conjecture.
ORGON. Nothing more wicked has ever come out of hell!
ELMIRE. Don't be too quick to believe the tales they tell
About him. Perhaps you are mistaken
And you've let your faith be far too lightly shaken . . .

(*As* TARTUFFE *re-enters,* ELMIRE *quickly hides* ORGON *behind her.*)

Scene 7

(TARTUFFE, ELMIRE, *and* ORGON.)

TARTUFFE. Everything's working out, madame, for the best.
The coast is clear. It seems that Heaven has blessed
This moment. My senses are delighted . . .

(*As he advances to embrace* ELMIRE, *she steps aside, and he walks into the arms of* ORGON.)

ORGON. Hold on a minute! Don't get so excited!
Don't let your passions carry you away!
Aha! You pious soul, you thought to betray
Your benefactor by seducing his wife,
Wedding his daughter and fixing yourself for life!
I've long suspected that some day I would see
You're not all that you're cracked up to be.

But now I've seen enough, yes, and I've heard
More than enough. No, not another word.

ELMIRE (*to* TARTUFFE). It's not my manner to tease and betray,
But I've been forced to treat you in this way.

TARTUFFE (*to* ORGON). What, can you believe . . . ?

ORGON. Let no more be said.
Get out of here before I lose my head.

TARTUFFE. I only sought . . .

ORGON. To secretly seduce my spouse!
I know. This minute — get out of my house!

TARTUFFE. But, just a moment — *you* are the one to leave.
This house belongs to me, I do believe.
There's no use trying to pick a quarrel with me
On such a poor excuse. You wait! You'll see!
You're in a poor position to evict me,
When *you're* the one to pack and leave — and quickly!
I have the power to avenge offended Heaven;
Please be gone by quarter past eleven. (*Exit.*)

Scene 8

(ELMIRE *and* ORGON.)

ELMIRE. What's he talking about? It's all a bluff.

ORGON. I wish it were. I fear he's serious enough.

ELMIRE. What is it?

ORGON. This is a pretty mess, indeed.
I made a great mistake when I gave him that deed.

ELMIRE. A deed?

ORGON. Yes, and it's signed and sealed.
But there may be even more to be revealed.

ELMIRE. What's that?

ORGON. I'll tell you later; first, I want to see
If my strongbox still is where it used to be.

ACT FIVE

Scene 1

(ORGON *and* CLÉANTE.)

CLÉANTE. Where are you going?

ORGON. I don't know.

CLÉANTE. It's clear
We need to talk about this dreadful affair.

ORGON. The strongbox mainly weighs upon my mind,
More than all the other matters combined.
CLÉANTE. This strongbox is an important mystery?
ORGON. It has a most unusual history.
My good friend Argas gave it to me in trust,
Impressing on me, come what may, I must
Keep it a secret; his life, his property
Depended on that box he gave to me.
CLÉANTE. Then why, pray tell, did you give it to Tartuffe?
ORGON. I know, dear brother; I merit your reproof.
I hoped to keep my conscience easy, though,
And he persuaded me to let it go
By telling me that, in case of investigation,
I might deny then any imputation
Of guilty knowledge and could take an oath
That would not be contrary to the truth.
CLÉANTE. I must confess, I fear you're on the rocks.
The deed of gift, the transfer of the box —
I speak the truth, I cannot deal in lies —
To put the matter gently, were most unwise.
With these as evidence, it's clear he's got you
Exactly where he wants you. You forgot you
Were dealing with a man of many schemes;
You never should have pushed him to extremes.
ORGON. Oh! Under such an outward show of piety
To hide such wickedness and impropriety!
To think I rescued him from sheer disgrace!
From now on, I renounce the human race.
Henceforth I'll shun them utterly and call
Myself a fool if I don't hate them all!
CLÉANTE. Now there you go, flying off the handle!
Won't you ever learn to burn the candle
At just one end? You waver wildly, brother,
From one grotesque extreme back to the other.
You see your error now and recognize
That you were taken in by pious lies,
But why correct your error and confusion
By falling into greater disillusion
And lump all mankind in one category
As though that told the full facts of the story?
Because a rascal cuts truth on the bias,
Pretending to be holy, good, and pious,
You would conclude that Chaos is upon us
And that the human race has turned dishonest.
Let the freethinkers think that, if they choose,
But learn to separate the external views

From the inner truth. And then don't rush away
Too hastily, but keep to the middle way.
Try not to be the dupe of charlatans,
But don't brand truly pious men as harlequins
And if you must make one or the other choice,
Then let excessive leniency be your vice.

Scene 2

(ORGON, CLÉANTE, *and* DAMIS.)

DAMIS. Father, is it true this brazen rogue,
Forgetting all the favors you've bestowed,
Has grown presumptuous and threatens
To use your benefits against you as his weapons?
ORGON. My son, I'm sorry to say it's all too true.
DAMIS. Give me the word, and I'll run him through and through
With a carving-knife. One should never waver
Before the impudence of that soul-saver!
I'll fix him so he'll never bother us again!
CLÉANTE. Ah, that's the speech of youth. But now and then
It's necessary to be more composed.
We're men, not beasts; the course that you've proposed
Is surely no way to resolve the matter.

Scene 3

(MADAME PERNELLE, ORGON, ELMIRE, CLÉANTE, MARIANE, DAMIS, *and* DORINE.)

MME. PERNELLE. Good Heavens, what's the meaning of all this chatter?
ORGON. Strange things indeed I've seen with my own eyes,
And a strange and most unpleasant kind of surprise!
I rescue a man from abject poverty,
Give him my home, my daughter, my property,
Treat him, in short, better than my brother,
Crown every benefit I give him with another,
And what is my reward, upon my life?
He seeks beneath my nose to seduce my wife,
And, still not fully satisfied with this,
He dares to use against me my own gifts,
Trying to bring me down by using the hold
I've given him by my kindness, and he's bold
Enough to kick me from under this roof that's covered him
And leave me in the gutter where I discovered him!

DORINE. The poor man!
MME. PERNELLE. My son, I can't imagine
He could behave in such a fashion.
ORGON. What!
MME. PERNELLE. People always envy pious men.
ORGON. Do I have to tell you all of this again?
MME. PERNELLE. I know that people here don't love him;
I know they're all quite jealous of him.
ORGON. And what's that got to do with this affair?
MME. PERNELLE. When you were a boy, I warned you to take care,
For virtue's always slandered by a lie;
Though envy perishes, the envious won't die.
ORGON. I don't see how any of this is apropos.
MME. PERNELLE. Liars will tirelessly spread their lies, you know.
ORGON. I tell you I saw it all with my very own eyes!
MME. PERNELLE. Ah, alas! that this world is so full of lies!
ORGON. You'll make me sin through anger. For the last time,
I tell you I *saw* his shameless attempt at crime!
MME. PERNELLE. This world is ever full of slanderous tongues
Ready to make up tales of imagined wrongs.
ORGON. What you are saying is absolute nonsense!
I saw the man! He hasn't the slightest defense!
I saw him try to do it! Do I have to yell
The simple truth in your ear or ring a bell?
MME. PERNELLE. Mercy me! Appearances often deceive.
Don't be overly rash in what you believe.
ORGON. You're driving me crazy!
MME. PERNELLE. False suspicion
Is common to one in your condition.
ORGON. Then he piously sought to improve my life
By making infamous love to my wife?
MME. PERNELLE. You need *facts* to support an accusation
Which might destroy a good man's reputation.
ORGON. *Facts?* How in the hell can I be more factual
Than to catch the scoundrel in the actual
Act of . . . no, you almost made me say it.
MME. PERNELLE. If there's evil in him, he doesn't betray it,
Not by the slightest glance or sneer;
I just can't believe these stories I hear.
ORGON. Good Lord, I'm so mad I could jump on my hat!
If you weren't my mother, I'd do worse than that!
DORINE (*to* ORGON). You wouldn't believe a word we'd say;
Now turn about, I'm afraid, is fair play.
CLÉANTE. We're wasting time here babbling like silly sheep;
When the wolf is on the prowl, one shouldn't sleep.
How are we going to meet that scoundrel's scheme?
DAMIS. He wouldn't have the nerve! He wouldn't dream . . . !

ELMIRE. I really doubt if he'd take legal action
Merely to obtain his satisfaction.

CLÉANTE. Don't be too sure. He's got tricks up his sleeve,
And we know he's slyer than anyone dare believe.
For less than this, men have served a spell
With bread and water in a prison cell.
And I repeat, since we know what his weapons are,
You made a mistake in pushing him so far.

ORGON. All right, all right, but what else could I do?
His impudence simply angered me through and through.

CLÉANTE. I wish with all my heart we could arrange
Some kind of fair and equitable exchange.

ELMIRE. If I had known he held such trumps in hand,
I'd have thought twice about the trick I planned.

(M. LOYAL *appears at the door;* DORINE *goes to meet him.*)

Scene 4

(ORGON, MADAME PERNELLE, ELMIRE, MARIANE, CLÉANTE, DAMIS, DORINE, *and* MONSIEUR LOYAL.)

ORGON. Who's that fellow? Tell him to go away.
I'm in no state to deal with callers today.

M. LOYAL. Sister, good morning. Your master, pray, where is he?
I must speak to him at once.

DORINE. He's busy.
He can't see anyone, I fear.

M. LOYAL. I shouldn't like to intrude upon him here.
But I don't think my business will upset him;
He can hear my news, if you will let him.

DORINE. Your name?

M. LOYAL. Just say I've come to bring him proof
Of the warm regard of Monsieur Tartuffe.

DORINE (*to* ORGON). He is a messenger, and quite soft-spoken,
From our old friend. He says he brings a token
Of Tartuffe's regard.

CLÉANTE. You'd better see
Who he is and what his news can be.

ORGON. Maybe he's coming to offer apologies.
Should I greet him politely and put him at his ease?

CLÉANTE. Speak softly, but don't vouchsafe any admission.
If he offers peace, though — better listen.

M. LOYAL. Greetings, good sir! May Heaven confound your foes
And shower you with love and sweet repose!

ORGON (*to* CLÉANTE). A most polite beginning! An indication
He wants a reconciliation.

M. LOYAL. Your family's interests have long been mine.
I served your worthy father many a time.
ORGON. I beg your pardon, sir, but to my shame
I must confess I don't recall your name.
M. LOYAL. My name is Loyal. I too have a confession.
I am a process server by profession.
For forty years it's been my pride and joy
To hold that honorable office, man and boy.
You asked my business here, sir? This is it·
To serve upon you this judicial writ.
ORGON. What!
M. LOYAL. Now, please, let's talk without unseemly friction.
It's just a little notice of eviction.
You and your family must get out,
Remove your goods and furniture, and in about —
Let's say, an hour — sooner, if you could.
ORGON. What, leave my house!
M. LOYAL. If you would be so good.
This house belongs, as you are well aware,
To good Monsieur Tartuffe. A deed I bear
Attests unto the fact beyond dispute,
So please don't force him, good sir, to bring suit
And call upon the law in his defense.
DAMIS. I'm simply staggered by such insolence!
M. LOYAL. Young man, my business here is not with you,
But with your father, a good man and true,
Who knows his legal duties, you may trust us,
And wouldn't dream of contravening justice.
ORGON. But . . .
M. LOYAL. Yes, I know that not for a fortune
Would you protest or would you importune
The court to contradict its stern commands
And remove this writ from out of your hands.
DAMIS. You might get a wholesome beating on the end
Of your black and gloomy coat, my friend!
M. LOYAL. Sir, bid your son be silent and retire.
I'd hate to have to report his ire
And his threats of violence and fits of pique.
DORINE (*aside*). He says his name is Loyal? I'd say, Sneak.
M. LOYAL. I have a great respect for honesty,
And I agreed to serve this writ, you see,
Just to oblige you and to give you pleasure,
For others might not execute the seizure
Of your goods with such consideration
As I, who feel for you such admiration.
ORGON. What could be worse, or could be a greater crime
Than evicting a man?

M. LOYAL. But, you see, I'm giving you time.
I will suspend till tomorrow, if you need
Some extra time, the service of the deed.
I'll merely come, with a dozen of my men,
To quietly spend the night with you, and then
I'll ask you to deliver to me the keys
Of the house before you go to bed, if you please.
Please be assured, we'll not trouble your repose;
It's just a matter of form, you know how it goes.
Tomorrow morning early you'll move out
All your furniture. I've picked some stout
And husky fellows; you'll find they're quite discreet,
As well as skilled at moving things out on the street.
No one, I think, could possibly act more fairly,
Nor put the matter before you more sincerely,
And as I'm giving you all this kind assistance
I must beg you to offer no resistance.
ORGON (*aside*). How happy I would be to give my last
Hundred louis for the chance to blast
This monster of pure impudence and clout
Him violently and squarely on the snout!
CLÉANTE. Easy, don't lose your head.
DAMIS. Oh, I insist.
Just one punch. I've got an itching fist.
DORINE. That noble back, monsieur, seems to demand
A good sound beating from a lady's hand.
M. LOYAL. Beware, my dear; the law makes no distinction
Regarding sex when it comes to legal action.
CLÉANTE. No more of this, sir; whatever the law allows,
Just give us the writ, and then get out of the house.
M. LOYAL. Au revoir, gentlemen! May God content you! (*Exit.*)

Scene 5

(ORGON, MADAME PERNELLE, ELMIRE, CLÉANTE, MARIANE, DAMIS, *and* DORINE.)

ORGON. May He confound you and the man who sent you! (*To* MME. PERNELLE.)
Well, Mother, tell me, was I right
About this monster who is your delight?
MME. PERNELLE. I'm flabbergasted! I can't believe my ears!
DORINE. Well, maybe it's all better than it appears.
His goal is good; he's doing all he can
To demonstrate how he loves his fellow-man.
He knows the soul's corrupted by the love

Of money, so he'll lovingly remove
Temptation from his friends, for their salvation.
ORGON. Oh, shut up! Stop this bickering! Damnation!
CLÉANTE. Let's try to think of the proper course to take.
ELMIRE. Let's tell the world he's a hypocritical fake.
These despicable tricks he has employed
Would render any contract null and void.
Public opinion, once his deeds are known,
Will surely rise, and its power will be shown.

Scene 6

(VALÈRE, ORGON, MADAME PERNELLE, ELMIRE, CLÉANTE, MARIANE, DAMIS, *and* DORINE.)

VALÈRE. I'm sorry, sir, to cause you any distress,
But I feel obliged to by the present mess
You're in; a very old and trusted friend
Who knows my interest has dared to send
Me word of your affairs, in violation
Of that high secrecy belonging to his station.
The news he sends is bitter, curt, and tight:
Your only possible recourse is flight.
He who has swindled you of everything
Has made an accusation to the King,
And has supported his charges, sad to relate,
With the strongbox of an outlaw of the state,
The which he found, he says, in your possession.
Proof of your most traitorous transgression.
I don't know whether you're innocent or not,
But you're ordered to be arrested on the spot,
And Tartuffe himself has been commended
And charged to see that you are apprehended.
CLÉANTE. Thus armed might assists him in his schemes
And helps him realize his evil dreams.
ORGON. Oh, that man is wicked past man's thought!
VALÈRE. Any delay will be fatal, so I've brought
My carriage round to whisk you safely away
And a thousand louis to help you on your way.
So don't waste time; this is a fearful blow;
Escape is the only answer that I know.
I'll find you a hiding-place with another friend
And I'll stay by your side until the end.
ORGON. I owe so much to your kind consideration,
But that can wait for a happier occasion;
I only pray that Heaven gives me the power

To fitly remember your goodness in this hour.
Good-bye, my friends . . .
CLÉANTE. Hurry! No delays! Don't fear,
We'll take care of everything right here.

(*Enter* TARTUFFE *and a* POLICE OFFICER. *As* ORGON *starts to exit,* TARTUFFE *seizes him.*)

Scene 7

(TARTUFFE, *a* POLICE OFFICER, MADAME PERNELLE, ORGON, ELMIRE, CLÉANTE, MARIANE, VALÈRE, DAMIS, *and* DORINE.)

TARTUFFE. Here now, good sir! Don't run away so fast!
A lodging's ready for you. No need for haste.
I take you prisoner, in the name of the King.
ORGON. Villain, you are guilty of everything;
You duped me into listening to your counsel
So that you might bring about my utter downfall!
TARTUFFE. I will not flinch, although you rave quite wildly.
Heaven has taught me to suffer insults mildly.
CLÉANTE. So these are the lessons your religion has given!
DAMIS. How impudently he plays with the name of Heaven!
TARTUFFE. You cannot move me by your enmity;
To do my duty means everything to me.
MARIANE. Much glory you will draw from this affair,
And maybe more honor than even you can bear!
TARTUFFE. Glory only accrues unto an action
Blessed and commanded by the royal sanction.
ORGON. Have you forgotten it was my charity
That rescued you from the depths of poverty?
TARTUFFE. True, you helped me with an occasional loan,
But my highest duty is to the royal throne.
This sacred and compelling obligation
Extinguishes all small considerations
Of petty gratitude. Upon my life,
I place it ahead of children, family, or wife!
ELMIRE. Impostor!
DORINE. This treacherous, sly snake would
Twist and mock all values we hold sacred!
CLÉANTE. But if this noble and religious zeal
Is quite as perfect as you'd have us feel,
How is it that it waited to appear
Till you were caught embracing Madame here?
Why did you delay your denunciation
Till you were trapped in that curious situation?
I won't allege, though it might have played a part,

That deed of gift from the goodness of his heart,
But why accept the money, then and later,
Of a man whom you denounce now as a traitor?

TARTUFFE (*to the* POLICE OFFICER). Deliver me, monsieur, from attacks like these
And execute your orders, if you please.

OFFICER. Yes, I've delayed too long now, at the best;
And, aptly enough, you're the one who makes the request.
So here's the order: kindly follow me
To the prison cell that is your home-to-be.

TARTUFFE. Who, me?

OFFICER. Yes, you.

TARTUFFE. What do you mean? You must be insane!

OFFICER. You're not the one to whom I must explain. (*To* ORGON.)
You've had a nasty scare, but, praised be God,
Our present King is an enemy of fraud;
His eyes can penetrate his subjects' hearts
And he's not deluded by a trickster's arts.
His great spirit, mighty, calm, and wise,
Watches his kingdom with discerning eyes.
Charlatans and practicers of treason
Cannot delude or shake his sovereign reason.
To worthy men he gives due recompense,
Yet he's not blind to fraud and false pretense.
His love for truth, however, does not eclipse
The horror one should feel for hypocrites.
Tartuffe was not the type who could hoodwink him:
The King is more perceptive than men think him.
Immediately and subtly he divined
The vile conniving of an evil mind.
This man betrayed himself by his accusation
And by a process of due retribution
The King identified him as a thief
With a criminal record almost past belief,
A man of various names, whose numerous crimes
Have been recorded a good many times.
In short, His Majesty found so abhorrent
This man's career, that it was ample warrant
For his arrest. This additional crime
Only sealed his fate. That's why I'm
With him today. The King commanded me
To accompany him today and see
What impudence he would dare as a last evasion.
Now I shall force him to make you reparation,
Seizing the powers that he might have destroyed;
The King declares the contract null and void
Which might have made Tartuffe your legal heir

And he pardons that transgression where
You erred but to protect a friend.
Thus he rewards you, thus does he commend
Your past fidelity in the civil wars,
Proving his heart remembers and rewards
A loyal subject; like the King of paradise,
He's mindful more of virtue than of vice.

DORINE. May Heaven be praised!

MME. PERNELLE. Ah, I'm so relieved!

ELMIRE. All's well again!

MARIANE. This scarcely can be believed!

ORGON (*to* TARTUFFE). So now we've got you, villain . . .

(*The* OFFICER *drags* TARTUFFE *away.*)

Scene 8

(MADAME PERNELLE, ORGON, ELMIRE, MARIANE, CLÉANTE, VALÈRE, DAMIS, *and* DORINE.)

CLÉANTE. Please; moderation.
Don't yield to an unworthy exultation.
Leave the wretched man to his wretched fate;
He's already bowed beneath the heavy weight
Of his own remorse. Why not hope, rather,
That his heart may undergo a change, dear brother,
And by progressing to better from the worse, he
May move the King to temper justice with mercy.
The while you kneel before the royal throne
To beg that Tartuffe's fate might be like your own.

ORGON. Well said, indeed. So let us, at his feet,
Thank him for his kindness and entreat
Mercy for our enemies. This done,
There's one more crown of joy left to be won,
And that's for me to happily declare
Mariane shall be the bride of Valère.

Curtain

There is a curious tendency among those who love theatre but do not know its history or literature very well to refer to *The School for Scandal* (1777) as a Restoration play. Since the restoration of the monarchy in England took place in 1660, Sheridan's comedy arrived a bit late for the honors so often erroneously bestowed on it.

Such mistakes are partly understandable, however, when they are based on superficial similarities between plays like *The School for Scandal* and *The Country Wife* (1675) by William Wycherley. Both in Restoration and eighteenth-century plays, one finds the convention of giving characters names which are apt, even amusing descriptions of their qualities. This recalls the Jonsonian device of the Comedy of Humors. Also, though separated by a hundred years, Wycherley and Sheridan were both writing comedies of manners, though the codes of conduct had necessarily changed in a century.

"Social comedy" has since become more popular as a term for that drama which acts as a critique and a corrective of the way we behave toward one another, but the genre has become firmly established. In the very limited, very special world of the Restoration, an artificiality of behavior and expression prevailed which might suggest that a comedy of manners is in fact a comedy of the highly *mannered*. Actually, for those of the aristocracy and the *demi-monde* who frequented the Restoration theatre, what they saw and heard was the world in which they lived and moved, only slightly exaggerated. That was still at least partly true of the eighteenth-century Comedy of Manners, precious as the characters, dialogue, and events may seem today.

What is odd is that Sheridan's comedies remain generally more popular with modern audiences than do the works of wits like Wycherley, Congreve, and Farquhar. Scholars, paying due respect to Sheridan, often show more interest in and affection for his Restoration predecessors. A fundamental difference between the comedies of the two periods lies in their attitude toward life. Restoration playwrights cynically approached their world with an uncompromising honesty men like Sheridan cleverly avoided. Restoration plays are noted for their direct treatment of love affairs and less exalted lustful couplings, so much so that nineteenth-century prudes brought the plays into such disrepute that many who have not studied the texts closely think of them today merely as smutty theatre. That they were intended to titillate is obvious, but they were written for an almost unshockable audience. This also encouraged a slashingly frank attack on folly and pretension — often directed at the more outrageous sensualists in the play. Thus, immoral conduct might be displayed to make a moral point.

Richard Brinsley Sheridan (1751–1816) retained some superficial appearances of these Restoration techniques, but they have been ordered and subdued to fit the dictates of sentimentality. Outbursts of bawdy behavior were not infrequent in the eighteenth century, but the theatre audience had come to be dominated by the rising, respectable middle class who disapproved of the manners and morals of the earlier time.

Characters in *The School for Scandal* are named after their comic qualities: Lady Sneerwell, Sir Benjamin Backbite, Mrs. Candour. Even the play's title, which echoes such Molière comedies as *The School for Wives,* is as descriptive as Restoration titles were. This "school," it should be noted, refers to the impromptu training ground which society offers for the skill in question. Sheridan is interested in scandal, in malice, obviously, and the play has been widely and justly admired for the portraits it gives in conversational viciousness. In fact, that is still one of its greatest audience appeals. Spectators clearly enjoy the malicious chatter of Lady Sneerwell's circle, in the same way that theatre buffs may revel in cutting criticism while simultaneously sympathizing with the targets. What this means is that Sheridan has made it possible for readers and spectators to achieve a special kind of purgation. In this play, the unworthy, harmful impulse toward malice is indulged on stage, then mocked, punished, and purged. The audience has the experience vicariously.

Another quality which endears *The School for Scandal* to many viewers is precisely the sentimentality which provides thrills without danger and happiness and justice for all — or almost all. An excellent example of how this differs from the Restoration attitude is shown in comparing The Country Wife, Margery Pinchwife, with Lady Teazle. Margery, like Lady Teazle, has been married to a grumpy older man. Pinchwife thinks he can keep his wife faithful by hiding her away, even by disguising her as a boy. He also thinks only he should be gratified, caring nothing about her wishes and dreams. When seduction rears its head, Margery is only too eager to help it succeed. Pinchwife learns to his cost the folly of age marrying youth. Lady Teazle teases old and young, and when Joseph Surface makes direct overtures, she is repelled and frightened. What could have been a naughty infidelity threatens to become a startling rape. Virtue — and sentimentality — triumph. The audience has the illicit thrill, then is snatched back from the brink of something unthinkable in its code of manners to be rewarded with a neat settling of accounts.

The play's plot projects the moral that appearances are deceiving. Joseph Surface is just that: superficial and also treacherous. He maligns those who think him a friend, seeks to disinherit his brother, and debauches foolish ladies when and as he can. His good brother, Charles, on the other hand, appears profligate, careless. That also is deceiving. He gives his last money to help another. Selling the family portraits to raise cash, he refuses to part with his uncle's picture. This is certainly sentimental, especially when the disguised uncle takes it as a sign of Charles's essential virtue. It also seems to be an example of judging by appearances. Deeper than that, though, is the notion that the portrait is only a symbol of the affection Charles has for his uncle, a regard Joseph only simulates.

G. L.

RICHARD BRINSLEY SHERIDAN

The School for Scandal

Characters

Sir Peter Teazle
Sir Oliver Surface
Joseph Surface
Charles Surface
Careless
Snake
Sir Benjamin Backbite
Crabtree
Rowley
Moses
Trip
Sir Harry Bumper
Lady Teazle
Maria
Lady Sneerwell
Mrs. Candour
Gentlemen, Maid, *and* Servants

(*The scene is London in the 1770's.*)

Prologue

Written by Mr. Garrick

Spoken by Sir Peter Teazle

A School for Scandal! tell me, I beseech you,
Needs there a school this modish art to teach you?
No need of lessons now, the knowing think;
We might as well be taught to eat and drink.
Caused by a dearth of scandal, should the vapors
Distress our fair ones — let them read the papers;
Their powerful mixtures such disorders hit;
Crave what you will — there's *quantum sufficit.*
"Lord!" cries my Lady Wormwood (who loves tattle,
And puts much salt and pepper in her prattle),
Just risen at noon, all night at cards when threshing

Strong tea and scandal — "Bless me, how refreshing!
Give me the papers, Lisp — how bold and free! (*Sips.*)
Last night Lord L. (*sips*) *was caught with Lady D.*
For aching heads what charming sal volatile! (*Sips.*)
If Mrs. B. will still continue flirting,
We hope she'll DRAW, *or we'll* UNDRAW *the curtain.*
Fine satire, poz — in public all abuse it,
But, by ourselves (*sips*), our praise we can't refuse it.
Now, Lisp, read you — there at that dash and star."
"Yes, ma'am — *A certain Lord had best beware,*
Who lives not twenty miles from Grosvenor Square;
For should he Lady W. find willing,
Wormwood is bitter" — "Oh, that's me! the villain!
Throw it behind the fire, and never more
Let that vile paper come within my door."
Thus at our friends we laugh, who feel the dart;
To reach our feelings, we ourselves must smart.
Is our young bard so young, to think that he
Can stop the full spring-tide of calumny?
Knows he the world so little, and its trade?
Alas! the devil's sooner raised than laid.
So strong, so swift, the monster there's no gagging:
Cut Scandal's head off, still the tongue is wagging.
Proud of your smiles once lavishly bestowed,
Again our young Don Quixote takes the road;
To show his gratitude he draws his pen,
And seeks his hydra, Scandal, in his den.
For your applause all perils he would through —
He'll fight — that's *write* — a cavalliero true,
Till every drop of blood — that's *ink* — is spilt for you.

ACT ONE

Scene 1

(LADY SNEERWELL's *dressing-room.* LADY SNEERWELL *at her dressing-table;* SNAKE *drinking chocolate.*)

LADY SNEERWELL. The paragraphs, you say, Mr. Snake, were all inserted?

SNAKE. They were, madam; and, as I copied them myself in a feigned hand, there can be no suspicion whence they came.

LADY SNEERWELL. Did you circulate the report of Lady Brittle's intrigue with Captain Boastall?

SNAKE. That's in as fine a train as your ladyship could wish. In the common course of things, I think it must reach Mrs. Clackitt's ears within four-and-twenty hours; and then, you know, the business is as good as done.

LADY SNEERWELL. Why, truly, Mrs. Clackitt has a very pretty talent, and a great deal of industry.

SNAKE. True, madam, and has been tolerably successful in her day. To my knowledge, she has been the cause of six matches being broken off, and three sons being disinherited: of four forced elopements, and as many close confinements; nine separate maintenances, and two divorces. Nay, I have more than once traced her causing a *tête-à-tête* in the *Town and Country Magazine*, when the parties, perhaps, had never seen each other's face before in the course of their lives.

LADY SNEERWELL. She certainly has talents, but her manner is gross.

SNAKE. 'Tis very true. She generally designs well, has a free tongue and a bold invention; but her coloring is too dark, and her outlines often extravagant. She wants that delicacy of tint, and mellowness of sneer, which distinguish your ladyship's scandal.

LADY SNEERWELL. You are partial, Snake.

SNAKE. Not in the least; everybody allows that Lady Sneerwell can do more with a word or look than many can with the most labored detail, even when they happen to have a little truth on their side to support it.

LADY SNEERWELL. Yes, my dear Snake; and I am no hypocrite to deny the satisfaction I reap from the success of my efforts. Wounded myself in the early part of my life, by the envenomed tongue of slander, I confess I have since known no pleasure equal to the reducing others to the level of my own injured reputation.

SNAKE. Nothing can be more natural. But, Lady Sneerwell, there is one affair in which you have lately employed me, wherein, I confess, I am at a loss to guess your motives.

LADY SNEERWELL. I conceive you mean with respect to my neighbor, Sir Peter Teazle, and his family?

SNAKE. I do. Here are two young men, to whom Sir Peter has acted as a kind of guardian since their father's death; the eldest possessing the most amiable character, and universally well spoken of — the youngest, the most dissipated and extravagant young fellow in the kingdom, without friends or character: the former an avowed admirer of your ladyship, and apparently your favorite; the latter attached to Maria, Sir Peter's ward, and confessedly beloved by her. Now, on the face of these circumstances, it is utterly unaccountable to me why you, the widow of a city knight, with a good jointure, should not close with the passion of a man of such character and expectations as Mr. Surface; and more so, why you should be so uncommonly earnest to destroy the mutual attachment subsisting between his brother Charles and Maria.

LADY SNEERWELL. Then, at once to unravel this mystery, I must inform you that love has no share whatever in the intercourse between Mr. Surface and me.

SNAKE. No!

LADY SNEERWELL. His real attachment is to Maria or her fortune; but, finding in his brother a favorite rival, he has been obliged to mask his pretensions and profit by my assistance.

SNAKE. Yet still I am more puzzled why you should interest yourself in his success.

LADY SNEERWELL. Heavens! how dull you are! Cannot you surmise the weakness which I hitherto, through shame, have concealed even from you? Must I confess that Charles — that libertine, that extravagant, that bankrupt in fortune and reputation — that he it is for whom I am thus anxious and malicious, and to gain whom I would sacrifice everything?

SNAKE. Now, indeed, your conduct appears consistent; but how came you and Mr. Surface so confidential?

LADY SNEERWELL. For our mutual interest. I have found him out a long time since. I know him to be artful, selfish, and malicious — in short, a sentimental knave; while with Sir Peter, and indeed with all his acquaintance, he passes for a youthful miracle of prudence, good sense, and benevolence.

SNAKE. Yes! yet Sir Peter vows he has not his equal in England; and, above all, he praises him as a man of sentiment.

LADY SNEERWELL. True; and with the assistance of his sentiment and hypocrisy he has brought Sir Peter entirely into his interest with regard to Maria; while poor Charles has no friend in the house — though, I fear, he has a powerful one in Maria's heart, against whom we must direct our schemes.

(*Enter* SERVANT.)

SERVANT. Mr. Surface.

LADY SNEERWELL. Show him up.

(*Exit* SERVANT.)

He generally calls about this time. I don't wonder at people giving him to me for a lover.

(*Enter* JOSEPH SURFACE.)

JOSEPH SURFACE. My dear Lady Sneerwell, how do you do today? Mr. Snake, your most obedient.

LADY SNEERWELL. Snake has just been rallying me on our mutual attachment; but I have informed him of our real views. You know how useful he has been to us; and, believe me, the confidence is not ill placed.

JOSEPH SURFACE. Madam, it is impossible for me to suspect a man of Mr. Snake's sensibility and discernment.

LADY SNEERWELL. Well, well, no compliments now; but tell me when you saw your mistress, Maria — or, what is more material to me, your brother.

JOSEPH SURFACE. I have not seen either since I left you; but I can inform you that they never meet. Some of your stories have taken a good effect on Maria.

LADY SNEERWELL. Ah, my dear Snake! the merit of this belongs to you. But do your brother's distresses increase?

JOSEPH SURFACE. Every hour. I am told he has had another execution in the house yesterday. In short, his dissipation and extravagance exceed anything I have ever heard of.

LADY SNEERWELL. Poor Charles!

JOSEPH SURFACE. True, madam; notwithstanding his vices one can't help feeling for him. Poor Charles! I'm sure I wish it were in my power to be of any essential service to him; for the man who does not share in the distresses of a brother, even though merited by his own misconduct, deserves —

LADY SNEERWELL. O Lud! you are going to be moral and forget that you are among friends.

JOSEPH SURFACE. Egad, that's true! I'll keep that sentiment till I see Sir Peter. However, it is certainly a charity to rescue Maria from such a libertine, who, if he is to be reclaimed, can be so only by a person of your ladyship's superior accomplishments and understanding.

SNAKE. I believe, Lady Sneerwell, here's company coming. I'll go and copy the letter I mentioned to you. Mr. Surface, your most obedient.

JOSEPH SURFACE. Sir, your very devoted.

(*Exit* SNAKE.)

Lady Sneerwell, I am very sorry you have put any further confidence in that fellow.

LADY SNEERWELL. Why so?

JOSEPH SURFACE. I have lately detected him in frequent conference with old Rowley, who was formerly my father's steward and has never, you know, been a friend of mine.

LADY SNEERWELL. And do you think he would betray us?

JOSEPH SURFACE. Nothing more likely: take my word for't, Lady Sneerwell, that fellow hasn't virtue enough to be faithful even to his own villainy. Ah, Maria!

(*Enter* MARIA.)

LADY SNEERWELL. Maria, my dear, how do you do? What's the matter?

MARIA. Oh! there's that disagreeable lover of mine, Sir Benjamin Backbite, has just called at my guardian's with his odious uncle, Crabtree; so I slipped out and ran hither to avoid them.

LADY SNEERWELL. Is that all?

JOSEPH SURFACE. If my brother Charles had been of the party, madam, perhaps you would not have been so much alarmed.

LADY SNEERWELL. Nay, now you are severe; for I dare swear the truth of the matter is, Maria heard you were here. But, my dear, what has Sir Benjamin done that you should avoid him so?

MARIA. Oh, he has done nothing — but 'tis for what he has said. His conversation is a perpetual libel on all his acquaintance.

JOSEPH SURFACE. Ay, and the worst of it is, there is no advantage in not knowing him, for he'll abuse a stranger just as soon as his best friend; and his uncle's as bad.

LADY SNEERWELL. Nay, but we should make allowance; Sir Benjamin is a wit and a poet.

MARIA. For my part, I own, madam, wit loses its respect with me when I see it in company with malice. What do you think, Mr. Surface?

JOSEPH SURFACE. Certainly, madam. To smile at the jest which plants a thorn in another's breast is to become a principal in the mischief.

LADY SNEERWELL. Psha! there's no possibility of being witty without a little ill nature. The malice of a good thing is the barb that makes it stick. What's your opinion, Mr. Surface?

JOSEPH SURFACE. To be sure, madam; that conversation, where the spirit of raillery is suppressed, will ever appear tedious and insipid.

MARIA. Well, I'll not debate how far scandal may be allowable; but in a man, I am sure, it is always contemptible. We have pride, envy, rivalship, and a thousand motives to depreciate each other; but the male slanderer must have the cowardice of a woman before he can traduce one.

(*Enter* SERVANT.)

SERVANT. Madam, Mrs. Candour is below, and, if your ladyship's at leisure, will leave her carriage.

LADY SNEERWELL. Beg her to walk in.

(*Exit* SERVANT.)

Now, Maria, here is a character to your taste; for, though Mrs. Candour is a little talkative, everybody knows her to be the best natured and best sort of woman.

MARIA. Yes, with a very gross affection of good nature and benvolence, she does more mischief than the direct malice of old Crabtree.

JOSEPH SURFACE. I'faith that's true, Lady Sneerwell: whenever I hear the current running against the characters of my friends, I never think them in such danger as when Candour undertakes their defence.

LADY SNEERWELL. Hush! — here she is!

(*Enter* MRS. CANDOUR.)

MRS. CANDOUR. My dear Lady Sneerwell, how have you been this century? — Mr. Surface, what news do you hear? — though indeed it is no matter, for I think one hears nothing else but scandal.

JOSEPH SURFACE. Just so, indeed, ma'am.

MRS. CANDOUR. Oh, Maria! child — what, is the whole affair off between you and Charles? His extravagance, I presume — the town talks of nothing else.

MARIA. I am very sorry, ma'am, the town has so little to do.

MRS. CANDOUR. True, true, child: but there's no stopping people's tongues. I own I was hurt to hear it, as I indeed was to learn, from the same quarter, that your guardian, Sir Peter, and Lady Teazle have not agreed lately as well as could be wished.

MARIA. 'Tis strangely impertinent for people to busy themselves so.

MRS. CANDOUR. Very true, child; but what's to be done? People will talk — there's no preventing it. Why, it was but yesterday I was told that Miss Gadabout had eloped with Sir Filagree Flirt. But, Lord! there's no minding what one hears; though, to be sure, I had this from very good authority.

MARIA. Such reports are highly scandalous.

MRS. CANDOUR. So they are, child — shameful, shameful! But the world is so censorious, no character escapes. Lord, now who would have suspected your friend, Miss Prim, of an indiscretion? Yet such is the ill nature of people that they say her uncle stopped her last week just as she was stepping into the York diligence with her dancing-master.

MARIA. I'll answer for't there are no grounds for that report.

MRS. CANDOUR. Ah, no foundation in the world, I dare swear: no more, probably, than for the story circulated last month, of Mrs. Festino's affair with Colonel Cassino — though, to be sure, that matter was never rightly cleared up.

JOSEPH SURFACE. The license of invention some people take is monstrous indeed.

MARIA. 'Tis so; but, in my opinion, those who report such things are equally culpable.

MRS. CANDOUR. To be sure they are; tale bearers are as bad as the tale makers — 'tis an old observation and a very true one: but what's to be done, as I said before? how will you prevent people from talking? Today, Mrs. Clackitt assured me Mr. and Mrs. Honeymoon were at last become mere man and wife like the rest of their acquaintance. She likewise hinted that a certain widow in the next street had got rid of her dropsy and recovered her shape in a most surprising manner. And at the same time Miss Tattle, who was by, affirmed that Lord Buffalo had discovered his lady at a house of no extraordinary fame; and that Sir Harry Bouquet and Tom Saunter were to measure swords on a similar provocation. But, Lord, do you think I would report these things! No, no! tale bearers, as I said before, are just as bad as the tale makers.

JOSEPH SURFACE. Ah! Mrs. Candour, if everybody had your forbearance and good nature!

MRS. CANDOUR. I confess, Mr. Surface, I cannot bear to hear people attacked behind their backs; and when ugly circumstances come out against our acquaintance, I own I always love to think the best. By-the-bye, I hope 'tis not true that your brother is absolutely ruined?

JOSEPH SURFACE. I am afraid his circumstances are very bad indeed, ma'am.

MRS. CANDOUR. Ah! — I heard so — but you must tell him to keep up his spirits; everybody almost is in the same way: Lord Spindle, Sir Thomas Splint, Captain Quinze, and Mr. Nickit — all up, I hear, within this week; so, if Charles is undone, he'll find half his acquaintance ruined too; and that, you know, is a consolation.

JOSEPH SURFACE. Doubtless, ma'am — a very great one.

(*Enter* SERVANT.)

SERVANT. Mr. Crabtree and Sir Benjamin Backbite. (*Exit.*)

LADY SNEERWELL. So, Maria, you see your lover pursues you; positively you shan't escape.

(*Enter* CRABTREE *and* SIR BENJAMIN BACKBITE.)

CRABTREE. Lady Sneerwell, I kiss your hand. Mrs. Candour, I don't believe you are acquainted with my nephew, Sir Benjamin Backbite? Egad, ma'am, he has a pretty wit and is a pretty poet too. Isn't he, Lady Sneerwell?

SIR BENJAMIN. Oh, fie, uncle!

CRABTREE. Nay, egad it's true: I back him at a rebus or a charade against the best rhymer in the kingdom. Has your ladyship heard the epigram he wrote last week on Lady Frizzle's feather catching fire? — Do, Benjamin, repeat it, or the charade you made last night extempore at Mrs. Drowzie's *conversazione*. Come now; your first is the name of a fish, your second a great naval commander, and —

SIR BENJAMIN. Uncle, now — prithee —

CRABTREE. I'faith, ma'am, 'twould surprise you to hear how ready he is at all these sort of things.

LADY SNEERWELL. I wonder, Sir Benjamin, you never publish anything.

SIR BENJAMIN. To say truth, ma'am, 'tis very vulgar to print; and, as my little productions are mostly satires and lampoons on particular people, I find they circulate more by giving copies in confidence to the friends of the parties. However, I have some love elegies, which, when favored with this lady's smiles, I mean to give the public.

CRABTREE (*to* MARIA). 'Fore heaven, ma'am, they'll immortalize you — you will be handed down to posterity like Petrarch's Laura, or Waller's Sacharissa.

SIR BENJAMIN (*to* MARIA). Yes, madam, I think you will like them when you shall see them on a beautiful quarto page, where a neat rivulet of text shall meander through a meadow of margin. 'Fore gad, they will be the most elegant things of their kind!

CRABTREE. But, ladies, that's true — have you heard the news?

MRS. CANDOUR. What, sir, do you mean the report of —

CRABTREE. No, ma'am, that's not it. Miss Nicely is going to be married to her own footman.

MRS. CANDOUR. Impossible!

CRABTREE. Ask Sir Benjamin.

SIR BENJAMIN. 'Tis very true, ma'am: everything is fixed and the wedding liveries bespoke.

CRABTREE. Yes — and they do say there were pressing reasons for it.

LADY SNEERWELL. Why, I have heard something of this before.

MRS. CANDOUR. It can't be — and I wonder any one should believe such a story of so prudent a lady as Miss Nicely.

SIR BENJAMIN. O lud! ma'am, that's the very reason 'twas believed at once. She has always been so cautious and so reserved, that everybody was sure there was some reason for it at bottom.

MRS. CANDOUR. Why, to be sure, a tale of scandal is as fatal to the credit of a prudent lady of her stamp as a fever is generally to those of the strongest constitution. But there is a sort of puny, sickly reputation, that is always ailing, yet will outlive the robuster characters of a hundred prudes.

SIR BENJAMIN. True, madam, there are valetudinarians in reputation as well as constitution, who, being conscious of their weak part, avoid the least breath of air and supply their want of stamina by care and circumspection.

MRS. CANDOUR. Well, but this may be all a mistake. You know, Sir Benjamin, very trifling circumstances often give rise to the most injurious tales.

CRABTREE. That they do, I'll be sworn, ma'am. Did you ever hear how Miss Piper came to lose her lover and her character last summer at Tunbridge? Sir Benjamin, you remember it?

SIR BENJAMIN. Oh, to be sure! — the most whimsical circumstance.

LADY SNEERWELL. How was it, pray?

CRABTREE. Why, one evening at Mrs. Ponto's assembly, the conversation happened to turn on the breeding Nova Scotia sheep in this country. Says a young lady in company, "I have known instances of it; for Miss Letitia Piper, a first cousin of mine, had a Nova Scotia sheep that produced her twins." "What!" cries the Lady Dowager Dundizzy (who you know is as deaf as a post), "has Miss Piper had twins?" This mistake, as you may imagine, threw the whole company into a fit of laughter. However, 'twas the next morning everywhere reported, and in a few days believed by the whole town, that Miss Letitia Piper had actually been brought to bed of a fine boy and a girl: and in less than a week there were some people who could name the father, and the farm-house where the babies were put to nurse.

LADY SNEERWELL. Strange, indeed!

CRABTREE. Matter of fact, I assure you. O lud! Mr. Surface, pray is it true that your uncle, Sir Oliver, is coming home?

JOSEPH SURFACE. Not that I know of, indeed, sir.

CRABTREE. He has been in the East Indies a long time. You can scarcely remember him, I believe? Sad comfort, whenever he returns, to hear how your brother has gone on!

JOSEPH SURFACE. Charles has been imprudent, sir, to be sure; but I hope no busy people have already prejudiced Sir Oliver against him. He may reform.

SIR BENJAMIN. To be sure he may. For my part I never believed him to be so utterly void of principle as people say; and though he has lost all his friends, I am told nobody is better spoken of by the Jews.

CRABTREE. That's true, egad, nephew. If the old Jewry was a ward, I believe Charles would be an alderman: no man more popular there, 'fore gad! I hear he pays as many annuities as the Irish tontine; and that whenever he is sick they have prayers for the recovery of his health in all the synagogues.

SIR BENJAMIN. Yet no man lives in greater splendor. They tell me, when he entertains his friends he will sit down to dinner with a dozen of his own securities, have a score of tradesmen in the ante-chamber, and an officer behind every guest's chair.

JOSEPH SURFACE. This may be entertainment to you gentlemen, but you pay very little regard to the feelings of a brother.

MARIA (*aside*). Their malice is intolerable! — (*Aloud.*) Lady Sneerwell, I must wish you a good morning: I'm not very well. (*Exit.*)

MRS. CANDOUR. O dear! she changes color very much.

LADY SNEERWELL. Do, Mrs. Candour, follow her; she may want assistance.

MRS. CANDOUR. That I will, with all my soul, ma'am. Poor dear girl, who knows what her situation may be! (*Exit.*)

LADY SNEERWELL. 'Twas nothing but that she could not bear to hear Charles reflected on, notwithstanding their difference.

SIR BENJAMIN. The young lady's *penchant* is obvious.

CRABTREE. But, Benjamin, you must not give up the pursuit for that: follow her and put her into good humor. Repeat her some of your own verses. Come, I'll assist you.

SIR BENJAMIN. Mr. Surface, I did not mean to hurt you; but depend on't your brother is utterly undone.

CRABTREE. O lud, ay! undone as ever man was — can't raise a guinea!

SIR BENJAMIN. And everything sold, I'm told, that was movable.

CRABTREE. I have seen one that was at his house. Not a thing left but some empty bottles that were overlooked and the family pictures which I believe are framed in the wainscots.

SIR BENJAMIN (*going*). And I'm very sorry also to hear some bad stories against him.

CRABTREE. Oh, he has done many mean things, that's certain.

SIR BENJAMIN (*going*). But, however, as he's your brother —

CRABTREE. We'll tell you all another opportunity.

(*Exeunt* CRABTREE *and* SIR BENJAMIN.)

LADY SNEERWELL. Ha, ha! 'tis very hard for them to leave a subject they have not quite run down.

JOSEPH SURFACE. And I believe the abuse was no more acceptable to your ladyship than to Maria.

LADY SNEERWELL. I doubt her affections are further engaged than we imagine. But the family are to be here this evening, so you may as well dine where you are and we shall have an opportunity of observing further. In the meantime, I'll go and plot mischief and you shall study sentiment.

Scene 2

(SIR PETER TEAZLE'S *house.* SIR PETER.)

SIR PETER. When an old bachelor marries a young wife, what is he to expect? 'Tis now six months since Lady Teazle made me the happiest of men — and I have been the most miserable dog ever since! We tiffed a little going to church and fairly quarrelled before the bells had done ringing. I was more than once nearly choked with gall during the honeymoon, and had lost all comfort in life before my friends had done wishing me joy. Yet I chose with caution — a girl bred wholly in the country, who never knew luxury beyond one silk gown, nor dissipation above the annual gala of a race ball. Yet she now plays her part in all the extravagant fopperies of fashion and the town, with as ready a grace as if she never had seen a bush or a grass-plot out of Grosvenor Square! I am sneered at by all my acquaintance and paragraphed in the newspapers. She dissipates my fortune, and contradicts all my humors; yet the worst of it is, I doubt I love her, or I should never bear all this. However, I'll never be weak enough to own it.

(*Enter* ROWLEY.)

ROWLEY. Oh! Sir Peter, your servant: how is it with you, sir?

SIR PETER. Very bad, Master Rowley, very bad. I meet with nothing but crosses and vexations.

ROWLEY. What can have happened to trouble you since yesterday?

SIR PETER. A good question to a married man!

ROWLEY. Nay, I'm sure, Sir Peter, your lady can't be the cause of your uneasiness.

SIR PETER. Why, has anybody told you she was dead?

ROWLEY. Come, come, Sir Peter, you love her, notwithstanding your tempers don't exactly agree.

SIR PETER. But the fault is entirely hers, Master Rowley. I am myself the sweetest tempered man alive, and hate a teasing temper; and so I tell her a hundred times a day.

ROWLEY. Indeed!

SIR PETER. Ay; and what is very extraordinary, in all our disputes she is always in the wrong! But Lady Sneerwell and the set she meets at her house encourage the perverseness of her disposition. Then, to complete my vexation, Maria, my ward, whom I ought to have the power of a father over, is determined to turn rebel too and absolutely refuses the man whom I have long resolved on for her husband; meaning, I suppose, to bestow herself on his profligate brother.

ROWLEY. You know, Sir Peter, I have always taken the liberty to differ with you on the subject of these two young gentlemen. I only wish you may not be deceived in your opinion of the elder. For Charles, my life on't! he will retrieve his errors yet. Their worthy father, once my honored master, was, at his years, nearly as wild a spark; yet, when he died, he did not leave a more benevolent heart to lament his loss.

SIR PETER. You are wrong, Master Rowley. On their father's death, you know, I acted as a kind of guardian to them both till their uncle Sir Oliver's liberality gave them an early independence. Of course no person could have more opportunity of judging of their hearts, and I was never mistaken in my life. Joseph is indeed a model for the young men of the age. He is a man of sentiment and acts up to the sentiments he professes; but, for the other, take my word for't, if he had any grain of virtue by descent, he has dissipated it with the rest of his inheritance. Ah! my old friend Sir Oliver will be deeply mortified when he finds how part of his bounty has been misapplied.

ROWLEY. I am sorry to find you so violent against the young man, because this may be the most critical period of his fortune. I came hither with news that will surprise you.

SIR PETER. What! let me hear.

ROWLEY. Sir Oliver is arrived, and at this moment in town.

SIR PETER. How! you astonish me! I thought you did not expect him this month.

ROWLEY. I did not: but his passage has been remarkably quick.

SIR PETER. Egad, I shall rejoice to see my old friend. 'Tis sixteen years since we met. We have had many a day together: but does he still enjoin us not to inform his nephews of his arrival?

ROWLEY. Most strictly. He means, before it is known, to make some trial of their dispositions.

SIR PETER. Ah! There needs no art to discover their merits — however, he shall have his way; but, pray, does he know I am married?

ROWLEY. Yes, and will soon wish you joy.

SIR PETER. What, as we drink health to a friend in consumption! Ah, Oliver will laugh at me. We used to rail at matrimony together, but he has been steady to his text. Well, he must be soon at my house, though — I'll instantly give orders for his reception. But, Master Rowley, don't drop a word that Lady Teazle and I ever disagree.

ROWLEY. By no means.

SIR PETER. For I should never be able to stand Noll's jokes; so I'll have him think, Lord forgive me! that we are a very happy couple.

ROWLEY. I understand you: but then you must be very careful not to differ while he is in the house with you.

SIR PETER. Egad, and so we must — and that's impossible. Ah! Master Rowley, when an old bachelor marries a young wife, he deserves — no — the crime carries its punishment along with it.

ACT TWO

Scene 1

(SIR PETER TEAZLE'S *house.* SIR PETER *and* LADY TEAZLE.)

SIR PETER. Lady Teazle, Lady Teazle, I'll not bear it!

LADY TEAZLE. Sir Peter, Sir Peter, you may bear it or not as you please; but I ought to have my own way in everything, and what's more, I will too. What though I was educated in the country, I know very well that women of fashion in London are accountable to nobody after they are married.

SIR PETER. Very well, ma'am, very well; so a husband is to have no influence, no authority?

LADY TEAZLE. Authority! No, to be sure. If you wanted authority over me, you should have adopted me and not married me: I am sure you were old enough.

SIR PETER. Old enough! ay, there it is! Well, well, Lady Teazle, though my life may be made unhappy by your temper, I'll not be ruined by your extravagance!

LADY TEAZLE. My extravagance! I'm sure I'm not more extravagant than a woman of fashion ought to be.

SIR PETER. No, no, madam, you shall throw away no more sums on such unmeaning luxury. 'Slife! to spend as much to furnish your dressing-room with flowers in winter as would suffice to turn the Pantheon into a greenhouse, and give a *fête champêtre* at Christmas.

LADY TEAZLE. And am I to blame, Sir Peter, because flowers are dear in cold weather? You should find fault with the climate, and not with me. For my part, I'm sure I wish it was spring all the year round and that roses grew under our feet!

SIR PETER. Oons! madam — if you had been born to this, I shouldn't wonder at your talking thus; but you forget what your situation was when I married you.

LADY TEAZLE. No, no, I don't; 'twas a very disagreeable one, or I should never have married you.

SIR PETER. Yes, yes, madam, you were then in somewhat a humbler style — the daughter of a plain country squire. Recollect, Lady Teazle, when I saw you first sitting at your tambour in a pretty figured linen gown with a bunch of keys at your side, your hair combed smooth over a roll and your apartment hung round with fruits in worsted of your own working.

LADY TEAZLE. Oh, yes! I remember it very well, and a curious life I led. My daily occupation to inspect the dairy, superintend the poultry, make extracts from the family receipt-book, and comb my aunt Deborah's lapdog.

SIR PETER. Yes, yes, ma'am, 'twas so indeed.

LADY TEAZLE. And then, you know, my evening amusements! To draw patterns for ruffles, which I had not the materials to make up; to play Pope Joan with the Curate; to read a sermon to my aunt; or to be stuck down to an old spinet to strum my father to sleep after a fox-chase.

SIR PETER. I am glad you have so good a memory. Yes, madam, these were the recreations I took you from; but now you must have your coach — *vis-à-vis* — and three powdered footmen before your chair; and, in the summer, a pair of white cats to draw you to Kensington Gardens. No recollection, I suppose, when you were content to ride double, behind the butler, on a docked coach-horse?

LADY TEAZLE. No — I swear I never did that; I deny the butler and the coach-horse.

SIR PETER. This, madam, was your situation; and what have I done for you? I have made you a woman of fashion, of fortune, of rank — in short, I have made you my wife.

LADY TEAZLE. Well, then, and there is but one thing more you can make me to add to the obligation, that is —

SIR PETER. My widow, I suppose?

LADY TEAZLE. Hem! hem!

SIR PETER. I thank you, madam — but don't flatter yourself; for, though your ill-conduct may disturb my peace it shall never break my heart, I promise you. However, I am equally obliged to you for the hint.

LADY TEAZLE. Then why will you endeavor to make yourself so disagreeable to me and thwart me in every little elegant expense?

SIR PETER. 'Slife, madam, I say; had you any of these little elegant expenses when you married me?

LADY TEAZLE. Lud, Sir Peter! would you have me be out of the fashion?

SIR PETER. The fashion, indeed! what had you to do with the fashion before you married me?

LADY TEAZLE. For my part, I should think you would like to have your wife thought a woman of taste.

SIR PETER. Ay — there again — taste! Zounds! madam, you had no taste when you married me!

LADY TEAZLE. That's very true, indeed, Sir Peter! and after having married you, I should never pretend to taste again, I allow. But now, Sir Peter, since we have finished our daily jangle, I presume I may go to my engagement at Lady Sneerwell's?

SIR PETER. Ay, there's another precious circumstance — a charming set of acquaintance you have made there!

LADY TEAZLE. Nay, Sir Peter, they are all people of rank and fortune and remarkably tenacious of reputation.

SIR PETER. Yes, egad, they are tenacious of reputation with a vengeance; for they don't choose anybody should have a character but themselves! Such a crew! Ah! many a wretch has rid on a hurdle who has done less mischief than these utterers of forged tales, coiners of scandal, and clippers of reputation.

LADY TEAZLE. What, would you restrain the freedom of speech?

SIR PETER. Ah! they have made you just as bad as any one of the society.

LADY TEAZLE. Why, I believe I do bear a part with a tolerable grace. But I vow I bear no malice against the people I abuse: when I say an ill natured thing, 'tis out of pure good humor; and I take it for granted they deal exactly in the same manner with me. But, Sir Peter, you know you promised to come to Lady Sneerwell's too.

SIR PETER. Well, well, I'll call in just to look after my own character.

LADY TEAZLE. Then, indeed, you must make haste after me or you'll be too late. So goodbye to ye.

(*Exit* LADY TEAZLE.)

SIR PETER. So — I have gained much by my intended expostulation! Yet with what a charming air she contradicts everything I say, and how pleasantly she shows her contempt for my authority! Well, though I can't make her love me, there is great satisfaction in quarrelling with her; and I think she never appears to such advantage as when she is doing everything in her power to plague me.

Scene 2

(LADY SNEERWELL'S *house.* LADY SNEERWELL, MRS. CANDOUR, CRABTREE, SIR BENJAMIN BACKBITE *and* JOSEPH SURFACE.)

LADY SNEERWELL. Nay, positively, we will hear it.

JOSEPH SURFACE. Yes, yes, the epigram by all means.

SIR BENJAMIN. O plague on't, uncle! 'tis mere nonsense.

CRABTREE. No, no; 'fore gad, very clever for an extempore!

SIR BENJAMIN. But, ladies, you should be acquainted with the circumstance. You must know, that one day last week as Lady Betty Curricle was taking the dust in Hyde Park, in a sort of duodecimo phaeton, she desired me to write some verses on her ponies; upon which, I took out my pocket-book, and in one moment produced the following: —

Sure never were seen two such beautiful ponies;
Other horses are clowns, but these macaronies:
To give them this title I am sure can't be wrong.
Their legs are so slim, and their tails are so long.

CRABTREE. There, ladies, done in the smack of a whip, and on horseback too.

JOSEPH SURFACE. A very Phœbus mounted — indeed, Sir Benjamin!

SIR BENJAMIN. Oh dear, sir! — trifles — trifles.

(*Enter* LADY TEAZLE *and* MARIA.)

MRS. CANDOUR. I must have a copy.

LADY SNEERWELL. Lady Teazle, I hope we shall see Sir Peter?

LADY TEAZLE. I believe he'll wait on your ladyship presently.

LADY SNEERWELL. Maria, my love, you look grave. Come, you shall sit down to piquet with Mr. Surface.

MARIA. I take very little pleasure in cards — however, I'll do as your ladyship pleases.

LADY TEAZLE (*aside*). I am surprised Mr. Surface should sit down with her; I thought he would have embraced this opportunity of speaking to me before Sir Peter came.

MRS. CANDOUR. Now, I'll die; but you are so scandalous, I'll forswear your society.

LADY TEAZLE. What's the matter, Mrs. Candour?

MRS. CANDOUR. They'll not allow our friend Miss Vermillion to be handsome.

LADY SNEERWELL. Oh, surely she is a pretty woman.

CRABTREE. I am very glad you think so, ma'am.

MRS. CANDOUR. She has a charming fresh color.

LADY TEAZLE. Yes, when it is fresh put on.

MRS. CANDOUR. Oh, fie! I'll swear her color is natural: I have seen it come and go!

LADY TEAZLE. I dare swear you have, ma'am: it goes off at night and comes again in the morning.

SIR BENJAMIN. True, ma'am it not only comes and goes; but, what's more, egad, her maid can fetch and carry it!

MRS. CANDOUR. Ha! ha! ha! how I hate to hear you talk so! But surely, now, her sister is, or was, very handsome.

CRABTREE. Who? Mrs. Evergreen? O Lord! she's six-and-fifty if she's an hour!

MRS. CANDOUR. Now positively you wrong her; fifty-two or fifty-three is the utmost — and I don't think she looks more.

SIR BENJAMIN. Ah! there's no judging by her looks, unless one could see her face.

LADY SNEERWELL. Well, well, if Mrs. Evergreen does take some pains to repair the ravages of time, you must allow she effects it with great ingenuity; and surely that's better than the careless manner in which the widow Ochre caulks her wrinkles.

SIR BENJAMIN. Nay, now, Lady Sneerwell, you are severe upon the widow. Come, come, 'tis not that she paints so ill — but, when she has finished her face, she joins it on so badly to her neck, that she looks like a mended statue, in which the connoisseur may see at once that the head's modern, though the trunk's antique!

CRABTREE. Ha! ha! ha! Well said, nephew!

MRS. CANDOUR. Ha! ha! ha! Well, you make me laugh; but I vow I hate you for it. What do you think of Miss Simper?

SIR BENJAMIN. Why, she has very pretty teeth.

LADY TEAZLE. Yes; and on that account, when she is neither speaking nor laughing (which very seldom happens), she never absolutely shuts her mouth, but leaves it always on ajar, as it were — thus. (*Shows her teeth.*)

MRS. CANDOUR. How can you be so ill natured?

LADY TEAZLE. Nay, I allow even that's better than the pains Mrs. Prim takes to conceal her losses in front. She draws her mouth till it positively resembles the aperture of a poor's-box, and all her words appear to slide out edgewise, as it were — thus: *How do you do, madam? Yes, madam.*

LADY SNEERWELL. Very well, Lady Teazle; I see you can be a little severe.

LADY TEAZLE. In defence of a friend it is but justice. But here comes Sir Peter to spoil our pleasantry.

(*Enter* SIR PETER.)

SIR PETER. Ladies, your most obedient — (*Aside.*) Mercy on me, here is the whole set! a character dead at every word, I suppose.

MRS. CANDOUR. I am rejoiced you are come, Sir Peter. They have been so censorious — and Lady Teazle as bad as any one.

SIR PETER. That must be very distressing to you, Mrs. Candour, I dare swear.

MRS. CANDOUR. Oh, they will allow good qualities to nobody; not even good nature to our friend Mrs. Pursy.

LADY TEAZLE. What, the fat dowager who was at Mrs. Quadrille's last night?

MRS. CANDOUR. Nay, her bulk is her misfortune; and, when she takes so much pains to get rid of it, you ought not to reflect on her.

LADY SNEERWELL. That's very true, indeed.

LADY TEAZLE. Yes, I know she almost lives on acids and small whey; laces herself by pulleys; and often, in the hottest noon in summer, you may see her on a little squat pony, with her hair plaited up behind like a drummer's and puffing round the Ring on a full trot.

MRS. CANDOUR. I thank you, Lady Teazle, for defending her.

SIR PETER. Yes, a good defence, truly.

MRS. CANDOUR. Truly, Lady Teazle is as censorious as Miss Sallow.

CRABTREE. Yes, and she is a curious being to pretend to be censorious — an awkward gawky, without any one good point under heaven.

MRS. CANDOUR. Positively you shall not be so very severe. Miss Sallow is a near relation of mine by marriage, and, as for her person, great allowance is to be made; for, let me tell you, a woman labors under many disadvantages who tries to pass for a girl of six-and-thirty.

LADY SNEERWELL. Though, surely she is handsome still — and for the weakness in her eyes, considering how much she reads by candlelight, it is not to be wondered at.

MRS. CANDOUR. True; and then as to her manner, upon my word, I think it is particularly graceful, considering she never had the least education; for you know her mother was a Welsh milliner, and her father a sugar-baker at Bristol.

SIR BENJAMIN. Ah! you are both of you too good natured!

SIR PETER (*aside*). Yes, damned good natured! This their own relation! mercy on me!

MRS. CANDOUR. For my part, I own I cannot bear to hear a friend ill spoken of.

SIR PETER. No, to be sure.

SIR BENJAMIN. Oh! you are of a moral turn. Mrs. Candour and I can sit for an hour and hear Lady Stucco talk sentiment.

LADY TEAZLE. Nay, I vow Lady Stucco is very well with the dessert after dinner; for she's just like the French fruit one cracks for mottoes — made up of paint and proverb.

MRS. CANDOUR. Well, I will never join in ridiculing a friend; and so I constantly tell my cousin Ogle, and you all know what pretensions she has to be critical on beauty.

CRABTREE. Oh, to be sure! she has herself the oddest countenance that ever was seen; 'tis a collection of features from all the different countries of the globe.

SIR BENJAMIN. So she has, indeed — an Irish front —

CRABTREE. Caledonian locks —

SIR BENJAMIN. Dutch nose —

CRABTREE. Austrian lips —

SIR BENJAMIN. Complexion of a Spaniard —

CRABTREE. And teeth *à la Chinoise* —

SIR BENJAMIN. In short, her face resembles a *table d'hôte* at Spa — where no two guests are of a nation —

CRABTREE. Or a congress at the close of a general war — wherein all the members, even to her eyes, appear to have a different interest, and her nose and chin are the only parties likely to join issue.

MRS. CANDOUR. Ha! ha! ha!

SIR PETER (*aside*). Mercy on my life! — a person they dine with twice a week!

LADY SNEERWELL. Go — go — you are a couple of provoking toads.

MRS. CANDOUR. Nay, but I vow you shall not carry the laugh off so — for give me leave to say, that Mrs. Ogle —

SIR PETER. Madam, madam, I beg your pardon — there's no stopping these good gentlemen's tongues. But when I tell you, Mrs. Candour, that the lady they are abusing is a particular friend of mine, I hope you'll not take her part.

LADY SNEERWELL. Ha! ha! ha! well said, Sir Peter! but you are a cruel creature — too phlegmatic yourself for a jest, and too peevish to allow wit in others.

SIR PETER. Ah, madam, true wit is more nearly allied to good nature than your ladyship is aware of.

LADY TEAZLE. True, Sir Peter: I believe they are so near akin that they can never be united.

SIR BENJAMIN. Or rather, madam, I suppose them man and wife because one seldom sees them together.

LADY TEAZLE. But Sir Peter is such an enemy to scandal, I believe he would have it put down by Parliament.

SIR PETER. 'Fore heaven, madam, if they were to consider the sporting with reputation of as much importance as poaching on manors, and pass an act for the preservation of fame, I believe many would thank them for the bill.

LADY SNEERWELL. O Lud! Sir Peter; would you deprive us of our privileges?

SIR PETER. Ay, madam; and then no person should be permitted to kill characters and run down reputations, but qualified old maids and disappointed widows.

LADY SNEERWELL. Go, you monster!

MRS. CANDOUR. But, surely, you would not be quite so severe on those who only report what they hear?

SIR PETER. Yes, madam, I would have law merchant for them too; and in all cases of slander currency, whenever the drawer of the lie was not to be found, the injured parties should have a right to come on any of the indorsers.

CRABTREE. Well, for my part, I believe there never was a scandalous tale without some foundation.

LADY SNEERWELL. Come, ladies, shall we sit down to cards in the next room?

(*Enter* SERVANT, *who whispers* SIR PETER.)

SIR PETER. I'll be with them directly.

(*Exit* SERVANT.)

(*Aside.*) I'll get away unperceived.

LADY SNEERWELL. Sir Peter, you are not going to leave us?

SIR PETER. Your ladyships must excuse me: I'm called away by particular business. But I leave my character behind me. (*Exit.*)

SIR BENJAMIN. Well — certainly, Lady Teazle, that lord of yours is a strange being. I could tell you some stories of him would make you laugh heartily if he were not your husband.

LADY TEAZLE. Oh, pray don't mind that; come, do let's hear them.

(*Exeunt all but* JOSEPH SURFACE *and* MARIA.)

JOSEPH SURFACE. Maria, I see you have no satisfaction in this society.

MARIA. How is it possible I should? If to raise malicious smiles at the infirmities or misfortunes of those who have never injured us be the province of wit or humor, Heaven grant me a double portion of dullness!

JOSEPH SURFACE. Yet they appear more ill natured than they are; they have no malice at heart.

MARIA. Then is their conduct still more contemptible; for in my opinion, nothing could excuse the intemperance of their tongues but a natural and uncontrollable bitterness of mind.

JOSEPH SURFACE. Undoubtedly, madam; and it has always been a sentiment of mine that to propagate a malicious truth wantonly is more despicable than to falsify from revenge. But can you, Maria, feel thus for others, and be unkind to me alone? Is hope to be denied the tenderest passion?

MARIA. Why will you distress me by renewing this subject?

JOSEPH SURFACE. Ah, Maria! you would not treat me thus, and oppose your guardian, Sir Peter's will, but that I see that profligate Charles is still a favored rival.

MARIA. Ungenerously urged! But whatever my sentiments are for that unfortunate young man, be assured I shall not feel more bound to give him up, because his distresses have lost him the regard even of a brother.

JOSEPH SURFACE. Nay, but, Maria, do not leave me with a frown: by all that's honest, I swear —

(*He kneels. Enter* LADY TEAZLE.)

(*Aside.*) Gad's life, here's Lady Teazle. — (*Aloud to* MARIA.) You must not — no, you shall not — for, though I have the greatest regard for Lady Teazle —

MARIA. Lady Teazle!

JOSEPH SURFACE. Yet were Sir Peter to suspect —

LADY TEAZLE (*coming forward*). What is this, pray? Do you take her for me? — Child, you are wanted in the next room.—

(*Exit* MARIA.)

What is all this, pray?

JOSEPH SURFACE. Oh, the most unlucky circumstance in nature! Maria has somehow suspected the tender concern I have for your happiness, and threatened to acquaint Sir Peter with her suspicions, and I was just endeavoring to reason with her when you came in.

LADY TEAZLE. Indeed! but you seemed to adopt a very tender mode of reasoning — do you usually argue on your knees?

JOSEPH SURFACE. Oh, she's a child and I thought a little bombast — but, Lady Teazle, when are you to give me your judgment on my library, as you promised?

LADY TEAZLE. No, no; I begin to think it would be imprudent, and you know I admit you as a lover no farther than fashion requires.

JOSEPH SURFACE. True — a mere Platonic cicisbeo, what every wife is entitled to.

LADY TEAZLE. Certainly, one must not be out of the fashion. However, I have so many of my country prejudices left that, though Sir Peter's ill humor may vex me ever so, it never shall provoke me to —

JOSEPH SURFACE. The only revenge in your power. Well, I applaud your moderation.

LADY TEAZLE. Go — you are an insinuating wretch! But we shall be missed — let us join the company.

JOSEPH SURFACE. But we had best not return together.

LADY TEAZLE. Well, don't stay; for Maria shan't come to hear any more of your reasoning, I promise you. (*Exit.*)

JOSEPH SURFACE. A curious dilemma, truly, my politics have run me into! I wanted, at first, only to ingratiate myself with Lady Teazle, that she might not be my enemy with Maria; and I have, I don't know how, become her serious lover. Sincerely I begin to wish I had never made such a point of gaining so very good a character; for it has led me into so many cursed rogueries that I doubt I shall be exposed at last.

Scene 3

(SIR PETER TEAZLE'S *house.* SIR OLIVER SURFACE *and* ROWLEY.)

SIR OLIVER. Ha! ha! ha! so my old friend is married, hey? — a young wife out of the country. Ha! ha! ha! that he should have stood bluff to old bachelor so long and sink into a husband at last!

ROWLEY. But you must not rally him on the subject, Sir Oliver; 'tis a tender point, I assure you, though he has been married only seven months.

SIR OLIVER. Then he has been just half a year on the stool of repentance! — Poor Peter! But you say he has entirely given up Charles — never sees him, hey?

ROWLEY. His prejudice against him is astonishing, and I am sure greatly increased by a jealousy of him with Lady Teazle, which he has industriously been led into by a scandalous society in the neighborhood, who have contributed not a little to Charles's ill name. Whereas the truth is, I believe, if the lady is partial to either of them, his brother is the favorite.

SIR OLIVER. Ay, I know there are a set of malicious, prating, prudent gossips, both male and female, who murder characters to kill time, and will rob a young fellow of his good name before he has years to know the value of it. But I am not to be prejudiced against my nephew by such, I promise you! No, no; if Charles has done nothing false or mean, I shall compound for his extravagance.

ROWLEY. Then, my life on't, you will reclaim him. Ah, sir, it gives me new life to find that your heart is not turned against him, and that the son of my good old master has one friend, however, left.

SIR OLIVER. What! shall I forget, Master Rowley, when I was at his years myself? Egad, my brother and I were neither of us very prudent youths; and yet, I believe, you have not seen many better men than your old master was?

ROWLEY. Sir, 'tis this reflection gives me assurance that Charles may yet be a credit to his family. But here comes Sir Peter.

SIR OLIVER. Egad, so he does! Mercy on me, he's greatly altered, and seems to have a settled married look! One may read *husband* in his face at this distance!

(*Enter* SIR PETER.)

SIR PETER. Ha! Sir Oliver — my old friend! Welcome to England a thousand times!

SIR OLIVER. Thank you, thank you, Sir Peter! and i'faith I am glad to find you well, believe me!

SIR PETER. Oh! 'tis a long time since we met — fifteen years, I doubt, Sir Oliver, and many a cross accident in the time.

SIR OLIVER. Ay, I have had my share. But, what! I find you are married, hey, my old boy? Well, well, it can't be helped; and so — I wish you joy with all my heart!

SIR PETER. Thank you, thank you, Sir Oliver. — Yes, I have entered into — the happy state; but we'll not talk of that now.

SIR OLIVER. True, true, Sir Peter; old friends should not begin on grievances at first meeting. No, no, no.

ROWLEY (*aside to* SIR OLIVER). Take care, pray, sir.

SIR OLIVER. Well, so one of my nephews is a wild rogue, hey?

SIR PETER. Wild! Ah! my old friend, I grieve for your disappointment there; he's a lost young man, indeed. However, his brother will make you amends; Joseph is, indeed, what a youth should be — everyone in the world speaks well of him.

SIR OLIVER. I am sorry to hear it; he has too good a character to be an honest fellow. Everyone speaks well of him! Psha! then he has bowed as low to knaves and fools as to the honest dignity of genius and virtue.

SIR PETER. What, Sir Oliver! do you blame him for not making enemies?

SIR OLIVER. Yes, if he has merit enough to deserve them.

SIR PETER. Well, well — you'll be convinced when you know him. 'Tis edification to hear him converse; he professes the noblest sentiments.

SIR OLIVER. Oh, plague of his sentiments! If he salutes me with a scrap of morality in his mouth, I shall be sick directly. But, however, don't mistake me, Sir Peter; I don't mean to defend Charles's errors: but, before I form my judgment of either of them, I intend to make a trial of their hearts; and my friend Rowley and I have planned something for the purpose.

ROWLEY. And Sir Peter shall own for once he has been mistaken.

SIR PETER. Oh, my life on Joseph's honor!

SIR OLIVER. Well — come, give us a bottle of good wine, and we'll drink the lads' health and tell you our scheme.

SIR PETER. *Allons*, then!

SIR OLIVER. And don't, Sir Peter, be so severe against your old friend's son. Odds my life! I am not sorry that he has run out of the course a little. For my part, I hate to see prudence clinging to the green suckers of youth; 'tis like ivy round a sapling, and spoils the growth of the tree.

ACT THREE

Scene 1

(SIR PETER TEAZLE'S *house.* SIR PETER TEAZLE, SIR OLIVER SURFACE, *and* ROWLEY.)

SIR PETER. Well, then, we will see this fellow first and have our wine afterwards. But how is this, Master Rowley? I don't see the jet of your scheme.

ROWLEY. Why, sir, this Mr. Stanley, whom I was speaking of, is nearly related to them by their mother. He was once a merchant in Dublin, but has been ruined by a series of undeserved misfortunes. He has applied, by letter, since his confinement, both to Mr. Surface and Charles. From the former he has received nothing but evasive promises of future service, while Charles has done all that his extravagance has left him power to do; and he is, at this time, endeavoring to raise a sum of money, part of which, in the midst of his own distresses, I know he intends for the service of poor Stanley.

SIR OLIVER. Ah, he is my brother's son.

SIR PETER. Well, but how is Sir Oliver personally to —

ROWLEY. Why, sir, I will inform Charles and his brother that Stanley has obtained permission to apply personally to his friends; and, as they have neither of them ever seen him, let Sir Oliver assume his character, and he will have a fair opportunity of judging, at least, of the benevolence of their dispositions; and believe me, sir, you will find in the youngest brother one who, in the midst of folly and dissipation, has still, as our immortal bard expresses it, —

. . . a tear for pity, and a hand
Open as day, for melting charity.

SIR PETER. Psha! What signifies his having an open hand or purse either, when he has nothing left to give? Well, well, make the trial, if you please. But where is the fellow whom you brought for Sir Oliver to examine relative to Charles's affairs?

ROWLEY. Below, waiting his commands, and no one can give him better intelligence. — This, Sir Oliver, is a friendly Jew, who, to do him justice, has done everything in his power to bring your nephew to a proper sense of his extravagance.

SIR PETER. Pray let us have him in.

ROWLEY (*calls to* SERVANT). Desire Mr. Moses to walk upstairs.

SIR PETER. But, pray, why should you suppose he will speak the truth?

ROWLEY. Oh, I have convinced him that he has no chance of recovering certain sums advanced to Charles but through the bounty of Sir Oliver, who he knows is arrived; so that you may depend on his fidelity to his own interests. I have also another evidence in my power, one Snake, whom I have detected in a matter little short of forgery and shall shortly produce to remove some of your prejudices, Sir Peter, relative to Charles and Lady Teazle.

SIR PETER. I have heard too much on that subject.

ROWLEY. Here comes the honest Israelite.

(*Enter* MOSES.)

— This is Sir Oliver.

SIR OLIVER. Sir, I understand you have lately had great dealings with my nephew Charles.

MOSES. Yes, Sir Oliver, I have done all I could for him; but he was ruined before he came to me for assistance.

SIR OLIVER. That was unlucky, truly; for you have had no opportunity of showing your talents.

MOSES. None at all; I hadn't the pleasure of knowing his distress till he was some thousands worse than nothing.

SIR OLIVER. Unfortunate, indeed! But I suppose you have done all in your power for him, honest Moses?

MOSES. Yes, he knows that. This very evening I was to have brought him a gentleman from the city, who does not know him, and will, I believe, advance him some money.

SIR PETER. What, one Charles has never had money from before?

MOSES. Yes, Mr. Premium, of Crutched Friars, formerly a broker.

SIR PETER. Egad, Sir Oliver, a thought strikes me! — Charles, you say, does not know Mr. Premium?

MOSES. Not at all.

SIR PETER. Now then, Sir Oliver, you may have a better opportunity of satisfying yourself than by an old romancing tale of a poor relation. Go with my friend Moses and represent Premium, and then, I'll answer for it, you'll see your nephew in all his glory.

SIR OLIVER. Egad, I like this idea better than the other and I may visit Joseph afterwards as old Stanley.

SIR PETER. True — so you may.

ROWLEY. Well, this is taking Charles rather at a disadvantage, to be sure. However, Moses, you understand Sir Peter, and will be faithful!

MOSES. You may depend upon me. — This is near the time I was to have gone.

SIR OLIVER. I'll accompany you as soon as you please, Moses — But hold! I have forgot one thing — how the plague shall I be able to pass for a Jew?

MOSES. There's no need — the principal is Christian.

SIR OLIVER. Is he? I'm very sorry to hear it. But, then again, an't I rather too smartly dressed to look like a money-lender?

SIR PETER. Not at all; 'twould not be out of character, if you went in your carriage — would it, Moses?

MOSES. Not in the least.

SIR OLIVER. Well, but how must I talk? there's certainly some cant of usury and mode of treating that I ought to know.

SIR PETER. Oh, there's not much to learn. The great point, as I take it, is to be exorbitant enough in your demands. Hey, Moses?

MOSES. Yes, that's a very great point.

SIR OLIVER. I'll answer for't I'll not be wanting in that. I'll ask him eight or ten per cent on the loan, at least.

MOSES. If you ask him no more than that, you'll be discovered immediately.

SIR OLIVER. Hey! what, the plague! how much then?

MOSES. That depends upon the circumstances. If he appears not very anxious for the supply, you should require only forty or fifty per cent; but if you find him in great distress, and want the moneys very bad, you may ask double.

SIR PETER. A good honest trade you're learning, Sir Oliver!

SIR OLIVER. Truly I think so — and not unprofitable.

MOSES. Then, you know, you haven't the moneys yourself, but are forced to borrow them for him of a friend.

SIR OLIVER. Oh! I borrow it of a friend, do I?

MOSES. And your friend is an unconscionable dog: but you can't help that.

SIR OLIVER. My friend an unconscionable dog, is he?

MOSES. Yes, and he himself has not the moneys by him, but is forced to sell stocks at a great loss.

SIR OLIVER. He is forced to sell stocks at a great loss, is he? Well, that's very kind of him.

SIR PETER. I'faith, Sir Oliver — Mr. Premium, I mean — you'll soon be master of the trade. But, Moses! would not you have him run out a little against the Annuity Bill? That would be in character, I should think.

MOSES. Very much.

ROWLEY. And lament that a young man now must be at years of discretion before he is suffered to ruin himself?

MOSES. Ay, great pity!

SIR PETER. And abuse the public for allowing merit to an act whose only object is to snatch misfortune and imprudence from the rapacious grip of usury, and give the minor a chance of inheriting his estate without being undone by coming into possession.

SIR OLIVER. So, so — Moses shall give me further instructions as we go together.

SIR PETER. You will not have much time, for your nephew lives hard by.

SIR OLIVER. Oh, never fear! my tutor appears so able, that though Charles lived in the next street, it must be my own fault if I am not a complete rogue before I turn the corner.

(*Exit with* MOSES.)

SIR PETER. So, now, I think Sir Oliver will be convinced; you are partial, Rowley, and would have prepared Charles for the other plot.

ROWLEY. No, upon my word, Sir Peter.

SIR PETER. Well, go bring me this Snake, and I'll hear what he has to say presently. I see Maria and want to speak with her.

(*Exit* ROWLEY.)

I should be glad to be convinced my suspicions of Lady Teazle and Charles were unjust. I have never yet opened my mind on this subject to my friend Joseph — I am determined I will do it — he will give me his opinion sincerely.

(*Enter* MARIA.)

So, child, has Mr. Surface returned with you?

MARIA. No, sir; he was engaged.

SIR PETER. Well, Maria, do you not reflect, the more you converse with that amiable young man, what return his partiality for you deserves?

MARIA. Indeed, Sir Peter, your frequent importunity on this subject distresses me extremely — you compel me to declare, that I know no man who has ever paid me a particular attention whom I would not prefer to Mr. Surface.

SIR PETER. So — here's perverseness! No, no, Maria, 'tis Charles only whom you would prefer. 'Tis evident his vices and follies have won your heart.

MARIA. This is unkind sir. You know I have obeyed you in neither seeing nor corresponding with him: I have heard enough to convince me that he is unworthy my regard. Yet I cannot think it culpable, if, while my understanding severely condemns his vices, my heart suggests some pity for his distress.

SIR PETER. Well, well, pity him as much as you please; but give your heart and hand to a worthier object.

MARIA. Never to his brother!

SIR PETER. Go, perverse and obstinate! But take care, madam; you have never yet known what the authority of a guardian is. Don't compel me to inform you of it.

MARIA. I can only say, you shall not have just reason. 'Tis true, by my father's will I am for a short period bound to regard you as his substitute; but must cease to think you so, when you would compel me to be miserable. (*Exit.*)

SIR PETER. Was ever man so crossed as I am, everything conspiring to fret me! I had not been involved in matrimony a fortnight, before her father, a hale and hearty man, died, on purpose, I believe, for the pleasure of plaguing me with the care of his daughter.

(LADY TEAZLE *sings without.*)

But here comes my helpmate! She appears in great good humor. How happy I should be if I could tease her into loving me, though but a little!

(*Enter* LADY TEAZLE.)

LADY TEAZLE. Lud! Sir Peter, I hope you haven't been quarrelling with Maria? It is not using me well to be ill humored when I am not by.

SIR PETER. Ah, Lady Teazle, you might have the power to make me good humored at all times.

LADY TEAZLE. I am sure I wish I had; for I want you to be in a charming sweet temper at this moment. Do be good humored now, and let me have two hundred pounds, will you?

SIR PETER. Two hundred pounds; what, an't I to be in a good humor without paying for it! But speak to me thus, and i'faith there's nothing I could refuse you. You shall have it; but seal me a bond for the repayment.

LADY TEAZLE. Oh, no — there — my note of hand will do as well. (*Offering her hand.*)

SIR PETER. And you shall no longer reproach me with not giving you an independent settlement. I mean shortly to surprise you; but shall we always live thus, hey?

LADY TEAZLE. If you please; I'm sure I don't care how soon we leave off quarrelling, provided you'll own you were tired first.

SIR PETER. Well — then let our future contest be, who shall be most obliging.

LADY TEAZLE. I assure you, Sir Peter, good nature becomes you. You look now as you did before we were married, when you used to walk with me under the elms, and tell me stories of what a gallant you were in your youth, and chuck me under the chin, you would; and ask me if I thought I could love an old fellow who would deny me nothing — didn't you?

SIR PETER. Yes, yes, and you were as kind and attentive —

LADY TEAZLE. Ay, so I was, and would always take your part, when my acquaintance used to abuse you, and turn you into ridicule.

SIR PETER. Indeed!

LADY TEAZLE. Ay, and when my cousin Sophy has called you a stiff, peevish old bachelor, and laughed at me for thinking of marrying one who might be my father, I have always defended you, and said, I didn't think you so ugly by any means, and that I dared say you'd make a very good sort of a husband.

SIR PETER. And you prophesied right; and we shall now be the happiest couple —

LADY TEAZLE. And never differ again?

SIR PETER. No, never — though at the same time, indeed, my dear Lady Teazle, you must watch your temper very seriously; for in all our little quarrels, my dear, if you recollect, my love, you always began first.

LADY TEAZLE. I beg your pardon, my dear Sir Peter: indeed, you always gave the provocation.

SIR PETER. Now, see, my angel! take care — contradicting isn't the way to keep friends.

LADY TEAZLE. Then, don't you begin it, my love!

SIR PETER. There now! you — you are going on. You don't perceive, my life, that you are just doing the very thing which you know always makes me angry.

LADY TEAZLE. Nay, you know if you will be angry without any reason, my dear —

SIR PETER. There! now you want to quarrel again.

LADY TEAZLE. No, I'm sure I don't; but, if you will be so peevish —

SIR PETER. There now! who begins first?

LADY TEAZLE. Why, you to be sure. I said nothing — but there's no bearing your temper.

SIR PETER. No, no madam: the fault's in your own temper.

LADY TEAZLE. Ay, you are just what my cousin Sophy said you would be.

SIR PETER. Your cousin Sophy is a forward, impertinent gypsy.

LADY TEAZLE. You are a great bear, I am sure, to abuse my relations.

SIR PETER. Now may all the plagues of marriage be doubled on me if ever I try to be friends with you any more!

LADY TEAZLE. So much the better.

SIR PETER. No, no, madam. 'Tis evident you never cared a pin for me, and I was a madman to marry you — a pert, rural coquette, that had refused half the honest squires in the neighborhood!

LADY TEAZLE. And I am sure I was a fool to marry you — an old dangling bachelor, who was single at fifty, only because he never could meet with any one who would have him.

SIR PETER. Ay, ay, madam; but you were pleased enough to listen to me: you never had such an offer before.

LADY TEAZLE. No! didn't I refuse Sir Tivy Terrier, who everybody said would have been a better match? for his estate is just as good as yours, and he has broke his neck since we have been married.

SIR PETER. I have done with you, madam! You are an unfeeling, ungrateful — but there's an end of everything. I believe you capable of everything that is bad. Yes, madam, I now believe the reports relative to you and Charles, madam. Yes, madam, you and Charles are, not without grounds —

LADY TEAZLE. Take care, Sir Peter! you had better not insinuate any such thing! I'll not be suspected without cause, I promise you.

SIR PETER. Very well, madam! very well! a separate maintenance as soon as you please. Yes, madam, or a divorce! I'll make an example of myself for the benefit of all old bachelors. Let us separate, madam.

LADY TEAZLE. Agreed! agreed! And now, my dear Sir Peter, we are of a mind once more, we may be the happiest couple, and never differ again, you know: ha! ha! ha! Well, you are going to be in a passion, I see, and I shall only interrupt you — so, bye! bye! (*Exit.*)

SIR PETER. Plagues and tortures! can't I make her angry either! Oh, I am the most miserable fellow! But I'll not bear her presuming to keep her temper: no! she may break my heart, but she shan't keep her temper.

Scene 2

(CHARLES SURFACE'S *house.* TRIP, MOSES, *and* SIR OLIVER SURFACE.)

TRIP. Here, Master Moses! if you'll stay a moment; I'll try whether — what's the gentleman's name?

SIR OLIVER (*aside to* MOSES). Mr. Moses, what is my name?

MOSES. Mr. Premium.

TRIP. Premium — very well. (*Exit, taking snuff.*)

SIR OLIVER. To judge by the servants, one wouldn't believe the master was ruined. But what! — sure, this was my brother's house?

MOSES. Yes, sir; Mr. Charles bought it of Mr. Joseph, with the furniture, pictures, etc., just as the old gentleman left it. Sir Peter thought it a piece of extravagance in him.

SIR OLIVER. In my mind, the other's economy in selling it to him was more reprehensible by half.

(*Re-enter* TRIP.)

TRIP. My master says you must wait, gentlemen: he has company, and can't speak with you yet.

SIR OLIVER. If he knew who it was wanted to see him, perhaps he would not send such a message?

TRIP. Yes, yes, sir; he knows you are here — I did not forget little Premium: no, no, no.

SIR OLIVER. Very well; and I pray, sir, what may be your name?

TRIP. Trip, sir; my name is Trip, at your service.

SIR OLIVER. Well, then, Mr. Trip, you have a pleasant sort of place here, I guess?

TRIP. Why, yes — here are three or four of us to pass our time agreeably enough; but then our wages are sometimes a little in arrear — and not very great either — but fifty pounds a year, and find our own bags and bouquets.

SIR OLIVER (*aside*). Bags and bouquets! halters and bastinadoes!

TRIP. And *à propos*, Moses, have you been able to get me that little bill discounted?

SIR OLIVER (*aside*). Wants to raise money, too! — mercy on me! Has his distresses too, I warrant, like a lord, and affects creditors and duns.

MOSES. 'Twas not to be done, indeed, Mr. Trip.

TRIP. Good lack, you surprise me! My friend Brush has indorsed it, and I thought when he put his name at the back of a bill 'twas the same as cash.

MOSES. No, 'twouldn't do.

TRIP. A small sum — but twenty pounds. Hark'ee, Moses, do you think you couldn't get it me by way of annuity?

SIR OLIVER (*aside*). An annuity! ha! ha! a footman raise money by way of annuity. Well done, luxury, egad!

MOSES. Well, but you must insure your place.

TRIP. Oh, with all my heart! I'll insure my place and my life too, if you please.

SIR OLIVER (*aside*). It's more than I would your neck.

MOSES. But is there nothing you could deposit?

TRIP. Why, nothing capital of my master's wardrobe has dropped lately; but I could give you a mortgage on some of his winter clothes, with equity of redemption before November — or you shall have the reversion of the French velvet, or a post-obit on the blue and silver. These, I should think, Moses, with a few pair of point ruffles, as a collateral security — hey, my little fellow?

MOSES. Well, well.

(*Bell rings.*)

TRIP. Egad. I heard the bell! I believe, gentlemen, I can now introduce you. Don't forget the annuity, little Moses! This way gentlemen, I'll insure my place, you know.

SIR OLIVER (*aside*). If the man be a shadow of the master, this is the temple of dissipation indeed!

(*Exeunt.*)

Scene 3

(*Another room.* CHARLES SURFACE, CARELESS, SIR HARRY BUMPER, *and others, at a table with wine, etc.*)

CHARLES SURFACE. 'Fore heaven, 'tis true! there's the great degeneracy of the age. Many of our acquaintance have taste, spirit, and politeness; but plague on't they won't drink.

CARELESS. It is so, indeed, Charles! they give in to all the substantial luxuries of the table, and abstain from nothing but wine and wit. Oh, certainly society suffers by it intolerably! for now, instead of the social spirit of raillery that used to mantle over a glass of bright Burgundy, their conversation is become just like the Spa-water they drink, which has all the pertness and flatulency of champagne, without its spirit or flavor.

FIRST GENTLEMAN. But what are they to do who love play better than wine?

CARELESS. True! there's Sir Harry diets himself for gaming, and is now under a hazard regimen.

CHARLES SURFACE. Then he'll have the worst of it. What! you wouldn't train a horse for the course by keeping him from corn? For my part, egad, I'm never so successful as when I am a little merry. Let me throw on a bottle of champagne and I never lose — at least I never feel my losses, which is exactly the same thing.

SECOND GENTLEMAN. Ay, that I believe.

CHARLES SURFACE. And then, what man can pretend to be a believer in love who is an abjurer of wine? 'Tis the test by which the lover knows his own heart. Fill a dozen bumpers to a dozen beauties, and she that floats at the top is the maid that has bewitched you.

CARELESS. Now then, Charles, be honest, and give us your real favorite.

CHARLES SURFACE. Why, I have withheld her only in compassion to you. If I toast her, you must give her a round of her peers, which is impossible — on earth.

CARELESS. Oh, then we'll find some canonized vestals or heathen goddesses that will do, I warrant!

CHARLES SURFACE. Here then, bumpers, you rogues! bumpers! Maria! Maria —

SIR HARRY. Maria who?

CHARLES SURFACE. Oh, damn the surname — 'tis too formal to be registered in Love's calender — but now, Sir Harry, beware, we must have beauty superlative.

CARELESS. Nay, never study, Sir Harry: we'll stand to the toast, though your mistress should want an eye, and you know you have a song will excuse you.

SIR HARRY. Egad, so I have! and I'll give him the song instead of the lady. (*Sings.*)

Here's to the maiden of bashful fifteen;
  Here's to the widow of fifty;
Here's to the flaunting extravagant quean,
  And here's to the housewife that's thrifty.

Chorus Let the toast pass,
  Drink to the lass,
I'll warrant she'll prove an excuse for a glass!

Here's to the charmer whose dimples we prize;
Now to the maid who has none, sir;
Here's to the girl with a pair of blue eyes,
And here's to the nymph with but one, sir.

Chorus Let the toast pass,
Drink to the lass,
I'll warrant she'll prove an excuse for a glass.

Here's to the maid with a bosom of snow;
Now to her that's as brown as a berry;
Here's to the wife with a face full of woe,
And now to the damsel that's merry.

Chorus Let the toast pass,
Drink to the lass,
I'll warrant she'll prove an excuse for a glass.

For let 'em be clumsy, or let 'em be slim,
Young or ancient, I care not a feather;
So fill a pint bumper quite up to the brim,
And let us e'en toast them together.

Chorus Let the toast pass,
Drink to the lass,
I'll warrant she'll prove an excuse for a glass.

ALL. Bravo! Bravo!

(*Enter* TRIP, *and whispers to* CHARLES SURFACE.)

CHARLES SURFACE. Gentlemen, you must excuse me a little. Careless, take the chair, will you?

CARELESS. Nay, prithee, Charles, what now? This is one of your peerless beauties, I suppose, has dropped in by chance?

CHARLES SURFACE. No, faith! To tell you the truth, 'tis a Jew and a broker, who are come by appointment.

CARELESS. Oh, damn it! let's have the Jew in.

FIRST GENTLEMAN. Ay, and the broker too, by all means.

SECOND GENTLEMAN. Yes, yes, the Jew, and the broker!

CHARLES SURFACE. Egad, with all my heart! — Trip, bid the gentlemen walk in.

(*Exit* TRIP.)

Though there's one of them a stranger I can tell you.

CARELESS. Charles, let us give them some generous Burgundy and perhaps they'll grow conscientious.

CHARLES SURFACE. Oh, hang 'em, no! wine does but draw forth a man's natural qualities; and to make them drink would only be to whet their knavery.

(*Enter* TRIP, *with* SIR OLIVER SURFACE *and* MOSES.)

CHARLES SURFACE. So, honest Moses; walk in, pray, Mr. Premium — that's the gentleman's name, isn't it, Moses?

MOSES. Yes, sir.

CHARLES SURFACE. Set chairs, Trip. — Sit down, Mr. Premium. Glasses, Trip. — Sit down, Moses. — Come, Mr. Premuim, I'll give you a sentiment; here's *Success to usury!* — Moses, fill the gentleman a bumper.

MOSES. Success to usury! (*Drinks.*)

CARELESS. Right, Moses — usury is prudence and industry, and deserves to succeed.

SIR OLIVER. Then here's — all the success it deserves! (*Drinks.*)

CARELESS. No, no, that won't do! Mr. Premium, you have demurred at the toast, and must drink it in a pint bumper.

FIRST GENTLEMAN. A pint bumper, at least!

MOSES. Oh, pray, sir, consider — Mr. Premium's a gentleman.

CARELESS. And therefore loves good wine.

SECOND GENTLEMAN. Give Moses a quart glass — this is mutiny, and a high contempt for the chair.

CARELESS. Here now for't! I'll see justice done, to the last drop of my bottle.

SIR OLIVER. Nay, pray, gentlemen — I did not expect this usage.

CHARLES SURFACE. No, hang it, you shan't; Mr. Premium's a stranger.

SIR OLIVER (*aside*). Odd! I wish I was well out of their company.

CARELESS. Plague on 'em then! if they won't drink, we'll not sit down with them. Come, Harry, the dice are in the next room. — Charles, you'll join us when you have finished your business with the gentlemen?

CHARLES SURFACE. I will! I will!

(*Exeunt* GENTLEMEN.)

Careless!

CARELESS (*returning*). Well?

CHARLES SURFACE. Perhaps I may want you.

CARELESS. Oh, you know I am always ready: word, note, or bond, 'tis all the same to me. (*Exit.*)

MOSES. Sir, this is Mr. Premium, a gentleman of the strictest honor and secrecy; and always performs what he undertakes. Mr. Premium, this is —

CHARLES SURFACE. Psha! have done. Sir, my friend Moses is a very honest fellow, but a little slow at expression: he'll be an hour giving us our titles. Mr. Premium, the plain state of the matter is this: I am an extravagant young fellow who wants to borrow money; you I take to be a prudent old fellow, who has got money to lend. I am blockhead enough to give fifty per cent sooner than not have it! and you, I presume, are rogue enough to take a hundred if you can get it. Now, sir, you see we are acquainted at once, and may proceed to business without further ceremony.

SIR OLIVER. Exceeding frank, upon my word. I see, sir, you are not a man of many compliments.

CHARLES SURFACE. Oh, no, sir! plain dealing in business I always think best.

SIR OLIVER. Sir, I like you the better for it. However, you are mistaken in one thing. I have no money to lend, but I believe I could procure some of a friend; but then he's an unconscionable dog. Isn't he, Moses? And must sell stock to accommodate you. Mustn't he, Moses?

MOSES. Yes, indeed! You know I always speak the truth, and scorn to tell a lie!

CHARLES SURFACE. Right. People that speak truth generally do. But these are trifles, Mr. Premium. What! I know money isn't to be bought without paying for't!

SIR OLIVER. Well, but what security could you give? You have no land, I suppose?

CHARLES SURFACE. Not a mole-hill, nor a twig, but what's in the bough-pots out of the window!

SIR OLIVER. Nor any stock, I presume?

CHARLES SURFACE. Nothing but live stock — and that's only a few pointers and ponies. But pray, Mr. Premium, are you acquainted at all with any of my connections?

SIR OLIVER. Why, to say the truth, I am.

CHARLES SURFACE. Then you must know that I have a devilish rich uncle in the East Indies, Sir Oliver Surface, from whom I have the greatest expectations?

SIR OLIVER. That you have a wealthy uncle, I have heard; but how your expectations will turn out is more, I believe, than you can tell.

CHARLES SURFACE. Oh, no! — there can be no doubt. They tell me I'm a prodigious favorite, and that he talks of leaving me everything.

SIR OLIVER. Indeed! this is the first I've heard of it.

CHARLES SURFACE. Yes, yes, 'tis just so. Moses knows 'tis true; don't you, Moses?

MOSES. Oh, yes! I'll swear to't.

SIR OLIVER (*aside*). Egad, they'll persuade me presently I'm at Bengal.

CHARLES SURFACE. Now I propose, Mr. Premium, if it's agreeable to you, a post-obit on Sir Oliver's life: though at the same time the old fellow has been so liberal with me, that I give you my word, I should be very sorry to hear that anything had happened to him.

SIR OLIVER. Not more than I should, I assure you. But the bond you mention happens to be just the worst security you could offer me — for I might live to be a hundred and never see the principal.

CHARLES SURFACE. Oh, yes, you would! the moment Sir Oliver dies, you know, you would come on me for the money.

SIR OLIVER. Then I believe I should be the most unwelcome dun you ever had in your life.

CHARLES SURFACE. What! I suppose you're afraid that Sir Oliver is too good a life?

SIR OLIVER. No, indeed I am not; though I have heard he is as hale and healthy as any man of his years in Christendom.

CHARLES SURFACE. There again, now, you are misinformed. No, no, the climate has hurt him considerably, poor uncle Oliver. Yes, yes, he breaks apace, I'm told — and is so much altered lately that his nearest relations would not know him.

SIR OLIVER. No! Ha! ha! ha! so much altered lately that his nearest relations would not know him! Ha! ha! ha! egad — ha! ha! ha!

CHARLES SURFACE. Ha! ha! — you're glad to hear that, little Premium.

SIR OLIVER. No, no, I'm not.

CHARLES SURFACE. Yes, yes, you are — ha! ha! ha! — you know that mends your chance.

SIR OLIVER. But I'm told Sir Oliver is coming over; nay, some say he has actually arrived.

CHARLES SURFACE. Psha! sure I must know better than you whether he's come or not. No, no, rely on't he's at this moment at Calcutta. Isn't he, Moses?

MOSES. Oh, yes, certainly.

SIR OLIVER. Very true, as you say, you must know better than I, though I have it from a pretty good authority. Haven't I, Moses?

MOSES. Yes, most undoubted!

SIR OLIVER. But, sir, as I understand you want a few hundreds immediately, is there nothing you could dispose of?

CHARLES SURFACE. How do you mean?

SIR OLIVER. For instance, now, I have heard that your father left behind him a great quantity of massy old plate.

CHARLES SURFACE. O lud, that's gone long ago. Moses can tell you how better than I can.

SIR OLIVER (*aside*). Good lack! all the family race-cups and corporation-bowls! — (*Aloud.*) Then it was also supposed that his library was one of the most valuable and compact.

CHARLES SURFACE. Yes, yes, so it was — vastly too much for a private gentleman. For my part, I was always of a communicative disposition, so I thought it a shame to keep so much knowledge to myself.

SIR OLIVER (*aside*). Mercy upon me! learning that had run in the family like an heirloom! — (*Aloud.*) Pray, what has become of the books?

CHARLES SURFACE. You must inquire of the auctioneer, Master Premium, for I don't believe even Moses can direct you.

MOSES. I know nothing of books.

SIR OLIVER. So, so, nothing of the family property left, I suppose?

CHARLES SURFACE. Not much, indeed; unless you have a mind to the family pictures. I have got a room full of ancestors above; and if you have a taste for old paintings, egad, you shall have 'em a bargain!

SIR OLIVER. Hey! what the devil! sure, you wouldn't sell your forefathers, would you?

CHARLES SURFACE. Every man of them, to the best bidder.

SIR OLIVER. What! your great-uncles and aunts?

CHARLES SURFACE. Ay, and my great-grandfathers and grandmothers too.

SIR OLIVER (*aside*). Now I give him up! — (*Aloud.*) What the plague, have you no bowels for your own kindred? Odd's life! do you take me for Shylock in the play, that you would raise money of me on your own flesh and blood?

CHARLES SURFACE. Nay, my little broker, don't be angry. What need you care, if you have your money's worth?

SIR OLIVER. Well, I'll be the purchaser. I think I can dispose of the family canvas. — (*Aside.*) Oh, I'll never forgive him this! never!

(*Enter* CARELESS.)

CARELESS. Come, Charles, what keeps you?

CHARLES SURFACE. I can't come yet. I'faith, we are going to have a sale above stairs; here's little Premium will buy all my ancestors!

CARELESS. Oh, burn your ancestors!

CHARLES SURFACE. No, he may do that afterwards, if he pleases. Stay, Careless, we want you: egad, you shall be auctioneer — so come along with us.

CARELESS. Oh, have with you, if that's the case. I can handle a hammer as well as a dice box!

SIR OLIVER (*aside*). Oh, the profligates!

CHARLES SURFACE. Come, Moses, you shall be appraiser, if we want one. Gad's life, little Premium, you don't seem to like the business?

SIR OLIVER. Oh, yes, I do, vastly! Ha! ha! ha! yes, yes, I think it a rare joke to sell one's family by auction — ha! ha! — (*Aside.*) Oh, the prodigal!

CHARLES SURFACE. To be sure! when a man wants money, where the plague should he get assistance if he can't make free with his own relations?

(*Exeunt.*)

ACT FOUR

Scene 1

(*Picture room at* CHARLES'S. *Enter* CHARLES SURFACE, SIR OLIVER SURFACE, MOSES, *and* CARELESS.)

CHARLES SURFACE. Walk in, gentlemen, pray walk in — here they are, the family of the Surfaces up to the Conquest.

SIR OLIVER. And, in my opinion, a goodly collection.

CHARLES SURFACE. Ay, ay, these are done in the true spirit of portrait-painting; no *volontière grace* or expression. Not like the works of your modern Raphaels, who give you the strongest resemblance, yet contrive to make your portrait independent of you; so that you may sink the original and not hurt the picture. No, no; the merit of these is the inveterate likeness — all stiff and awkward as the originals, and like nothing in human nature besides.

SIR OLIVER. Ah! we shall never see such figures of men again.

CHARLES SURFACE. I hope not. Well, you see, Master Premium, what a domestic character I am; here I sit of an evening surrounded by my family. But come, get to your pulpit, Mr. Auctioneer; here's an old gouty chair of my grandfather's will answer the purpose.

CARELESS. Ay, ay, this will do. But, Charles, I haven't a hammer; and what's an auctioneer without his hammer?

CHARLES SURFACE. Egad, that's true. What parchment have we here? Oh, our genealogy in full. Here, Careless, you shall have no common bit of mahogany, here's the family tree for you, you rogue! This shall be your hammer, and now you may knock down my ancestors with their own pedigree.

SIR OLIVER (*aside*). What an unnatural rogue! — an ex *post facto* parricide!

CARELESS. Yes, yes, here's a list of your generation indeed; — faith, Charles, this is the most convenient thing you could have found for the business, for 'twill not only serve as a hammer, but a catalogue into the bargain. Come, begin — A-going, a-going, a-going!

CHARLES SURFACE. Bravo, Careless! Well, here's my great uncle, Sir Richard Raveline, a marvellous good general in his day, I assure you. He served in all the Duke of Marlborough's wars, and got that cut over his eye at the battle of Malplaquet. What say you, Mr. Premium? look at him — there's a hero! not cut out of his feathers, as your modern clipped captains are, but enveloped in wig and regimentals as a general should be. What do you bid?

MOSES. Mr. Premium would have you speak.

CHARLES SURFACE. Why, then, he shall have him for ten pounds, and I'm sure that's not dear for a staff-officer.

SIR OLIVER (*aside*). Heaven deliver me! his famous uncle Richard for ten pounds! — (*Aloud.*) Very well, sir. I take him at that.

CHARLES SURFACE. Careless, knock down my uncle Richard. — Here, now, is a maiden sister of his, my great-aunt Deborah, done by Kneller, in his best manner, and a very formidable likeness. There she is, you see, a shepherdess feeding her flock. You shall have her for five pounds ten — the sheep are worth the money.

SIR OLIVER (*aside*). Ah! poor Deborah! a woman who set such a value on herself! — (*Aloud.*) Five pounds ten — she's mine.

CHARLES SURFACE. Knock down my aunt Deborah! Here, now, are two that were a sort of cousins of theirs — You see, Moses, these pictures were done some time ago, when beaux wore wigs, and the ladies their own hair.

SIR OLIVER. Yes, truly, head-dresses appear to have been a little lower in those days.

CHARLES SURFACE. Well, take that couple for the same.

MOSES. 'Tis a good bargain.

CHARLES SURFACE. Careless — this, now, is a grandfather of my mother's, a learned judge, well known on the western circuit. — What do you rate him at, Moses?

MOSES. Four guineas.

CHARLES SURFACE. Four guineas! Gad's life, you don't bid me the price of his wig. — Mr. Premium, you have more respect for the woolsack, do let us knock his Lordship down at fifteen.

SIR OLIVER. By all means.

CARELESS. Gone!

CHARLES SURFACE. And there are two brothers of his, William and Walter Blunt, Esquires, both members of Parliament, and noted speakers; and, what's very extraordinary, I believe, this is the first time they were ever bought or sold.

SIR OLIVER. That is very extraordinary, indeed! I'll take them at your own price, for the honor of Parliament.

CARELESS. Well said, little Premium! I'll knock them down at forty.

CHARLES SURFACE. Here's a jolly fellow — I don't know what relation, but he was mayor of Manchester: take him at eight pounds.

SIR OLIVER. No, no, six will do for the mayor.

CHARLES SURFACE. Come, make it guineas, and I'll throw you the two aldermen there into the bargain.

SIR OLIVER. They're mine.

CHARLES SURFACE. Careless, knock down the mayor and aldermen. But, plague on't! we shall be all day retailing in this manner: do let us deal wholesale: what say you, little Premium? Give me three hundred pounds for the rest of the family in the lump.

CARELESS. Ay ay, that will be the best way.

SIR OLIVER. Well, well, anything to accommodate you; they are mine. But there is one portrait which you have always passed over.

CARELESS. What, that ill-looking little fellow over the settee?

SIR OLIVER. Yes, sir, I mean that; though I don't think him so ill-looking a little fellow, by any means.

CHARLES SURFACE. What, that? Oh; that's my uncle Oliver! 'Twas done before he went to India.

CARELESS. Your uncle Oliver! Gad, then you'll never be friends, Charles. That, now, to me, is as stern a looking rogue as ever I saw; an unforgiving eye, and a damned disinheriting countenance! an inveterate knave, depend on't. Don't you think so little Premium?

SIR OLIVER. Upon my soul, sir, I do not; I think it is as honest a looking face as any in the room, dead or alive. But I suppose uncle Oliver goes with the rest of the lumber?

CHARLES SURFACE. No, hang it! I'll not part with poor Noll. The old fellow has been very good to me, and, egad, I'll keep his picture while I've a room to put it in.

SIR OLIVER (*aside*). The rogue's my nephew after all! — (*Aloud.*) But, sir, I have somehow taken a fancy to that picture.

CHARLES SURFACE. I'm sorry for't, for you certainly will not have it. Oons, haven't you got enough of them?

SIR OLIVER (*aside*). I forgive him everything! — (*Aloud.*) But, sir, when I take a whim in my head, I don't value money. I'll give you as much for that as for all the rest.

CHARLES SURFACE. Don't tease me, master broker; I tell you I'll not part with it, and there's an end of it.

SIR OLIVER (*aside*). How like his father the dog is! — (*Aloud.*) Well, well, I have done. — (*Aside.*) I did not perceive it before, but I think I never saw such a striking resemblance. — (*Aloud.*) Here is a draught for your sum.

CHARLES SURFACE. Why, 'tis for eight hundred pounds!

SIR OLIVER. You will not let Sir Oliver go?

CHARLES SURFACE. Zounds! no! I tell you, once more.

SIR OLIVER. Then never mind the difference, we'll balance that another time. But give me your hand on the bargain; you are an honest fellow, Charles — I beg pardon, sir, for being so free. — Come, Moses.

CHARLES SURFACE. Egad, this is a whimsical old fellow! — But hark'ee, Premium, you'll prepare lodgings for these gentlemen.

SIR OLIVER. Yes, yes, I'll send for them in a day or two.

CHARLES SURFACE. But hold; do now send a genteel conveyance for them, for, I assure you, they were most of them used to ride in their own carriages.

SIR OLIVER. I will, I will — for all but Oliver.

CHARLES SURFACE. Ay, all but the little nabob.

SIR OLIVER. You're fixed on that?

CHARLES SURFACE. Peremptorily.

SIR OLIVER (*aside*). A dear extravagant rogue! — (*Aloud.*) Good day! — Come, Moses. — (*Aside.*) Let me hear now who dares call him profligate!

(*Exeunt* SIR OLIVER *and* MOSES.)

CARELESS. Why, this is the oddest genius of the sort I ever met with!

CHARLES SURFACE. Egad, he's the prince of brokers, I think. I wonder how the devil Moses got acquainted with so honest a fellow.— Ha! here's Rowley.—Do, Careless, say I'll join the company in a few moments.

CARELESS. I will—but don't let that old blockhead persuade you to squander any of that money on old musty debts, or any such nonsense; for tradesmen, Charles, are the most exorbitant fellows.

CHARLES SURFACE. Very true, and paying them is only encouraging them.

CARELESS. Nothing else.

CHARLES SURFACE. Ay, ay, never fear.—

(*Exit* CARELESS.)

So! this was an odd old fellow, indeed. Let me see, two-thirds of this is mine by right: five hundred and thirty odd pounds. 'Fore heaven! I find one's ancestors are more valuable relations than I took them for!— Ladies and gentlemen, your most obedient and very grateful servant.

(*Bows to the pictures. Enter* ROWLEY.)

Ha! old Rowley! egad, you are just come in time to take leave of your old acquaintance.

ROWLEY. Yes, I heard they were a-going. But I wonder you can have such spirits under so many distresses.

CHARLES SURFACE. Why, there's the point! my distresses are so many that I can't afford to part with my spirits; but I shall be rich and splenetic, all in good time. However, I suppose you are surprised that I am not more sorrowful at parting with so many near relations; to be sure, 'tis very affecting; but you see they never move a muscle, so why should I?

ROWLEY. There's no making you serious a moment.

CHARLES SURFACE. Yes, faith, I am so now. Here, my honest Rowley, here, get me this changed directly and take a hundred pounds of it immediately to old Stanley.

ROWLEY. A hundred pounds! Consider only—

CHARLES SURFACE. Gad's life, don't talk about it! poor Stanley's wants are pressing, and, if you don't make haste, we shall have some one call that has a better right to the money.

ROWLEY. Ah! there's the point! I never will cease dunning you with the old proverb—

CHARLES SURFACE. "Be just before you're generous."—Why, so I would if I could; but Justice is an old lame, hobbling beldame, and I can't get her to keep pace with Generosity, for the soul of me.

ROWLEY. Yet, Charles, believe me, one hour's reflection—

CHARLES SURFACE. Ay, ay, it's very true; but, hark'ee, Rowley, while I have, by Heaven I'll give; so, damn your economy! and now for hazard.

(*Exeunt.*)

Scene 2

(*The parlor. Enter* SIR OLIVER SURFACE *and* MOSES.)

MOSES. Well, sir, I think as Sir Peter said, you have seen Mr. Charles in high glory; 'tis great pity he's so extravagant.

SIR OLIVER. True, but he would not sell my picture.

MOSES. And loves wine and women so much.

SIR OLIVER. But he would not sell my picture.

MOSES. And games so deep.

SIR OLIVER. But he would not sell my picture. Oh, here's Rowley.

(*Enter* ROWLEY.)

ROWLEY. So, Sir Oliver, I find you have made a purchase —

SIR OLIVER. Yes, yes, our young rake has parted with his ancestors like old tapestry.

ROWLEY. And here has he commissioned me to re-deliver you part of the purchase-money — I mean, though, in your necessitous character of old Stanley.

MOSES. Ah! there is the pity of all: he is so damned charitable.

ROWLEY. And I left a hosier and two tailors in the hall, who I'm sure, won't be paid, and this hundred would satisfy them.

SIR OLIVER. Well, well, I'll pay his debts, and his benevolence too. But now I am no more a broker, and you shall introduce me to the elder brother as old Stanley.

ROWLEY. Not yet awhile; Sir Peter, I know, means to call there about this time.

(*Enter* TRIP.)

TRIP. Oh, gentlemen, I beg pardon for not showing you out; this way — Moses, a word.

(*Exit with* MOSES.)

SIR OLIVER. There's a fellow for you! Would you believe it, that puppy intercepted the Jew on our coming, and wanted to raise money before he got to his master!

ROWLEY. Indeed.

SIR OLIVER. Yes, they are now planning an annuity business. Ah, Master Rowley, in my days servants were content with the follies of their masters when they were worn a little threadbare; but now they have their vices, like their birthday clothes, with the gloss on.

(*Exeunt.*)

Scene 3

(*A library in* JOSEPH SURFACE's *house.* JOSEPH SURFACE *and* SERVANT.)

JOSEPH SURFACE. No letter from Lady Teazle?

SERVANT. No, sir.

JOSEPH SURFACE (*aside*). I am surprised she has not sent, if she is prevented from coming. Sir Peter certainly does not suspect me. Yet I wish I may not lose the heiress through the scrape I have drawn myself into with the wife. However, Charles's imprudence and bad character are great points in my favor.

(*Knocking.*)

SERVANT. Sir, I believe that must be Lady Teazle.

JOSEPH SURFACE. Hold! See whether it is or not before you go to the door. I have a particular message for you if it should be my brother.

SERVANT. 'Tis her ladyship, sir; she always leaves the chair at the milliner's in the next street.

JOSEPH SURFACE. Stay, stay! Draw that screen before the window — that will do. My opposite neighbor is a maiden lady of so curious a temper.

(SERVANT *draws the screen, and exits.*)

I have a difficult hand to play in this affair. Lady Teazle has lately suspected my views on Maria; but she must by no means be let into that secret — at least, till I have her more in my power.

(*Enter* LADY TEAZLE.)

LADY TEAZLE. What, sentiment in soliloquy now? Have you been very impatient? O lud! don't pretend to look grave. I vow I couldn't come before.

JOSEPH SURFACE. O madam, punctuality is a species of constancy very unfashionable in a lady of quality.

LADY TEAZLE. Upon my word, you ought to pity me. Do you know Sir Peter is grown so ill-natured to me of late, and so jealous of Charles too — that's the best of the story, isn't it?

JOSEPH SURFACE (*aside*). I am glad my scandalous friends keep that up.

LADY TEAZLE. I am sure I wish he would let Maria marry him, and then perhaps he would be convinced; don't you, Mr. Surface?

JOSEPH SURFACE (*aside*). Indeed I do not. — (*Aloud.*) Oh, certainly I do! for then my dear Lady Teazle would also be convinced how wrong her suspicions were of my having any design on the silly girl.

LADY TEAZLE. Well, well, I'm inclined to believe you. But isn't it provoking to have the most ill-natured things said at one? And there's my friend Lady Sneerwell has circulated I don't know how many scandalous tales of me, and all without any foundation, too; that's what vexes me.

JOSEPH SURFACE. Ay, madam, to be sure, that is the provoking circumstance — without foundation. Yes, yes, there's the mortification, indeed; for, when a scandalous story is believed against one, there certainly is no comfort like the consciousness of having deserved it.

LADY TEAZLE. No, to be sure, then I'd forgive their malice; but to attack me, who am really so innocent, and who never say an ill-natured thing of anybody — that is, of any friend; and then Sir Peter, too, to have him so peevish, and so suspicious, when I know the integrity of my own heart — indeed 'tis monstrous!

JOSEPH SURFACE. But, my dear Lady Teazle, 'tis your own fault if you suffer it. When a husband entertains a groundless suspicion of his wife, and withdraws his confidence from her, the original compact is broken, and she owes it to the honor of her sex to endeavor to outwit him.

LADY TEAZLE. Indeed! So that, if he suspects me without cause, it follows, that the best way of curing his jealousy is to give him reason for't?

JOSEPH SURFACE. Undoubtedly — for your husband should never be deceived in you: and in that case it becomes you to be frail in compliment to his discernment.

LADY TEAZLE. To be sure, what you say is very reasonable, and when the consciousness of my innocence —

JOSEPH SURFACE. Ah, my dear madam, there is the great mistake; 'tis this very conscious innocence that is of the greatest prejudice to you. What is it makes you negligent of forms, and careless of the world's opinion? why, the consciousness of your own innocence. What makes you thoughtless in your conduct and apt to run into a thousand little imprudences? why, the consciousness of your own innocence. What makes you impatient of Sir Peter's temper, and outrageous at his suspicions? why, the consciousness of your innocence.

LADY TEAZLE. 'Tis very true!

JOSEPH SURFACE. Now, my dear Lady Teazle, if you would but once make a trifling *faux pas*, you can't conceive how cautious you would grow, and how ready to humor and agree with your husband.

LADY TEAZLE. Do you think so?

JOSEPH SURFACE. Oh, I'm sure on't! and then you would find all scandal would cease at once, for — in short, your character at present is like a person in a plethora, absolutely dying from too much health.

LADY TEAZLE. So, so; then I perceive your prescription is that I must sin in my own defence, and part with my virtue to preserve my reputation?

JOSEPH SURFACE. Exactly so, upon my credit, ma'am.

LADY TEAZLE. Well, certainly this is the oddest doctrine, and the newest receipt for avoiding calumny.

JOSEPH SURFACE. An infallible one, believe me. Prudence, like experience, must be paid for.

LADY TEAZLE. Why, if my understanding were once convinced —

JOSEPH SURFACE. Oh, certainly, madam, your understanding should be convinced. Yes, yes — Heaven forbid I should persuade you to do anything you thought wrong. No, no, I have too much honor to desire it.

LADY TEAZLE. Don't you think we may as well leave honor out of the argument? (*Rises.*)

JOSEPH SURFACE. Ah, the ill effects of your country education, I see, still remain with you.

LADY TEAZLE. I doubt they do, indeed; and I will fairly own to you, that if I could be persuaded to do wrong, it would be by Sir Peter's ill usage sooner than your honorable logic, after all.

JOSEPH SURFACE. Then, by this hand, which he is unworthy of (*taking her hand*) —

(*Enter* SERVANT.)

'Sdeath, you blockhead — what do you want?

SERVANT. I beg your pardon, sir, but I thought you would not choose Sir Peter to come up without announcing him.

JOSEPH SURFACE. Sir Peter! — Oons — the devil!

LADY TEAZLE. Sir Peter! O lud! I'm ruined! I'm ruined!

SERVANT. Sir, 'twasn't I let him in.

LADY TEAZLE. Oh! I'm quite undone! What will become of me now, Mr. Logic? — Oh! mercy, he's on the stairs — I'll get behind here — and if ever I'm so imprudent again — (*Goes behind the screen.*)

JOSEPH SURFACE. Give me that book.

(*Sits down.* SERVANT *pretends to adjust his chair. Enter* SIR PETER TEAZLE.)

SIR PETER. Ay, ever improving himself. Mr. Surface, Mr. Surface —

JOSEPH SURFACE. Oh, my dear Sir Peter, I beg your pardon. (*Gaping, throws away the book.*) I have been dozing over a stupid book. Well, I am much obliged to you for this call. You haven't been here, I believe, since I fitted up this room. Books, you know, are the only things I am a coxcomb in.

SIR PETER. 'Tis very neat indeed. Well, well, that's proper; and you can make even your screen a source of knowledge — hung, I perceive, with maps.

JOSEPH SURFACE. Oh, yes, I find great use in that screen.

SIR PETER. I dare say you must, certainly, when you want to find anything in a hurry.

JOSEPH SURFACE (*aside*). Ay, or to hide anything in a hurry either.

SIR PETER. Well, I have a little private business —

JOSEPH SURFACE (*to* SERVANT). You need not stay.

SERVANT. No, sir. (*Exit.*)

JOSEPH SURFACE. Here's a chair, Sir Peter — I beg —

SIR PETER. Well, now we are alone, there is a subject, my dear friend, on which I wish to unburden my mind to you — a point of the greatest moment to my peace; in short, my good friend, Lady Teazle's conduct of late has made me very unhappy.

JOSEPH SURFACE. Indeed! I am very sorry to hear it.

SIR PETER. Yes, 'tis but too plain she has not the least regard for me; but, what's worse, I have pretty good authority to suppose she has formed an attachment to another.

JOSEPH SURFACE. Indeed! you astonish me!

SIR PETER. Yes! and, between ourselves, I think I've discovered the person.

JOSEPH SURFACE. How! you alarm me exceedingly.

SIR PETER. Ay, my dear friend, I knew you would sympathize with me!

JOSEPH SURFACE. Yes, believe me, Sir Peter, such a discovery would hurt me just as much as it would you.

SIR PETER. I am convinced of it. Ah! it is a happiness to have a friend whom we can trust even with one's family secrets. But have you no guess who I mean?

JOSEPH SURFACE. I haven't the most distant idea. It can't be Sir Benjamin Backbite!

SIR PETER. On, no! what say you to Charles?

JOSEPH SURFACE. My brother! impossible!

SIR PETER. Oh, my dear friend, the goodness of your own heart misleads you. You judge of others by yourself.

JOSEPH SURFACE. Certainly, Sir Peter, the heart that is conscious of its own integrity is ever slow to credit another's treachery.

SIR PETER. True; but your brother has no sentiment — you never hear him talk so.

JOSEPH SURFACE. Yet I can't think Lady Teazle herself has too much principle.

SIR PETER. Ay; but what is principle against the flattery of a handsome, lively young fellow?

JOSEPH SURFACE. That's very true.

SIR PETER. And then, you know, the difference of our ages makes it very improbable that she should have any great affection for me; and if she were to be frail, and I were to make it public, why the town would only laugh at me, the foolish old bachelor who had married a girl.

JOSEPH SURFACE. That's true, to be sure — they would laugh.

SIR PETER. Laugh! ay, and make ballads, and paragraphs, and the devil knows what of me.

JOSEPH SURFACE. No, you must never make it public.

SIR PETER. But then again — that the nephew of my old friend, Sir

Oliver, should be the person to attempt such a wrong, hurts me more nearly.

JOSEPH SURFACE. Ay, there's the point. When ingratitude barbs the dart of injury, the wound has double danger in it.

SIR PETER. Ay — I that was, in a manner, left his guardian, in whose house he had been so often entertained, who never in my life denied him — my advice!

JOSEPH SURFACE. Oh, 'tis not to be credited! There may be a man capable of such baseness, to be sure; but, for my part, till you can give me positive proofs, I cannot but doubt it. However, if it should be proved on him, he is no longer a brother of mine — I disclaim kindred with him: for the man who can break the laws of hospitality and tempt the wife of his friend, deserves to be branded as the pest of society.

SIR PETER. What a difference there is between you! What noble sentiments!

JOSEPH SURFACE. Yet I cannot suspect Lady Teazle's honor.

SIR PETER. I am sure I wish to think well of her, and to remove all ground of quarrel between us. She has lately reproached me more than once with having made no settlement on her; and, in our last quarrel, she almost hinted that she should not break her heart if I was dead. Now, as we seem to differ in our ideas of expense, I have resolved she shall have her own way and be her own mistress in that respect for the future; and, if I were to die, she will find I have not been inattentive to her interest while living. Here, my friend, are the drafts of two deeds, which I wish to have your opinion on. By one, she will enjoy eight hundred a year independent while I live; and by the other, the bulk of my fortune at my death.

JOSEPH SURFACE. This conduct, Sir Peter, is indeed truly generous. (*Aside.*) I wish it may not corrupt my pupil.

SIR PETER. Yes, I am determined she shall have no cause to complain, though I would not have her acquainted with the latter instance of my affection yet awhile.

JOSEPH SURFACE (*aside*). Nor I, if I could help it.

SIR PETER. And now, my dear friend, if you please, we will talk over the situation of your hopes with Maria.

JOSEPH SURFACE (*softly*). Oh, no, Sir Peter; another time, if you please.

SIR PETER. I am sensibly chagrined at the little progress you seem to make in her affections.

JOSEPH SURFACE (*softly*). I beg you will not mention it. What are my disappointments when your happiness is in debate! (*Aside.*) 'Sdeath, I shall be ruined every way!

SIR PETER. And though you are averse to my acquainting Lady Teazle with your passion, I'm sure she's not your enemy in the affair.

JOSEPH SURFACE. Pray, Sir Peter, now oblige me. I am really too much affected by the subject we have been speaking of to bestow a thought on my own concerns. The man who is entrusted with his friend's distress can never —

(*Enter* SERVANT.)

Well, sir?

SERVANT. Your brother, sir, is speaking to a gentleman in the street, and says he knows you are within.

JOSEPH SURFACE. 'Sdeath, blockhead, I'm not within — I'm out for the day.

SIR PETER. Stay — hold — a thought has struck me: you shall be at home.

JOSEPH SURFACE. Well, well, let him up.

(*Exit* SERVANT.)

(*Aside.*) He'll interrupt Sir Peter, however.

SIR PETER. Now, my good friend, oblige me, I entreat you. Before Charles comes, let me conceal myself somewhere, then do you tax him on the point we have been talking, and his answer may satisfy me at once.

JOSEPH SURFACE. Oh, fie, Sir Peter! would you have me join in so mean a trick? — to trepan my brother too?

SIR PETER. Nay, you tell me you are sure he is innocent; if so, you do him the greatest service by giving him an opportunity to clear himself, and you will set my heart at rest. Come, you shall not refuse me: here, behind the screen will be — Hey! what the devil! there seems to be one listener here already — I'll swear I saw a petticoat!

JOSEPH SURFACE. Ha! ha! ha! Well, this is ridiculous enough. I'll tell you, Sir Peter, though I hold a man of intrigue to be a most despicable character, yet you know, it does not follow that one is to be an absolute Joseph either! Hark'ee, 'tis a little French milliner, a silly rogue that plagues me; and having some character to lose, on your coming, sir, she ran behind the screen.

SIR PETER. Ah, you rogue — But, egad, she has overheard all I have been saying of my wife.

JOSEPH SURFACE. Oh, 'twill never go any farther, you may depend upon it!

SIR PETER. No! then, faith, let her hear it out. — Here's a closet will do as well.

JOSEPH SURFACE. Well, go in there.

SIR PETER. Sly rogue! sly rogue! (*Goes into the closet.*)

JOSEPH SURFACE. A narrow escape, indeed! and a curious situation I'm in, to part man and wife in this manner.

LADY TEAZLE (*peeping*). Couldn't I steal off?

JOSEPH SURFACE. Keep close, my angel.

SIR PETER (*peeping*). Joseph, tax me home!

JOSEPH SURFACE. Back, my dear friend!

LADY TEAZLE (*peeping*). Couldn't you lock Sir Peter in?

JOSEPH SURFACE. Be still, my life!

SIR PETER (*peeping*). You're sure the little milliner won't blab?

JOSEPH SURFACE. In, in, my dear Sir Peter! — 'Fore gad, I wish I had a key to the door!

(*Enter* CHARLES SURFACE.)

CHARLES SURFACE. Holla! brother, what has been the matter? Your fellow would not let me up at first. What! have you had a Jew or a wench with you?

JOSEPH SURFACE. Neither, brother, I assure you.

CHARLES SURFACE. But what has made Sir Peter steal off? I thought he had been with you.

JOSEPH SURFACE. He was, brother; but, hearing you were coming, he did not choose to stay.

CHARLES SURFACE. What! was the old gentleman afraid I wanted to borrow money of him!

JOSEPH SURFACE. No, sir: but I am sorry to find, Charles, you have lately given that worthy man grounds for great uneasiness.

CHARLES SURFACE. Yes, they tell me I do that to a great many worthy men. But how so, pray?

JOSEPH SURFACE. To be plain with you, brother, he thinks you are endeavoring to gain Lady Teazle's affections from him.

CHARLES SURFACE. Who, I? O lud! not I, upon my word. — Ha! ha! ha! ha! so the old fellow has found out that he has got a young wife, has he? — or, what's worse, Lady Teazle has found out she has an old husband?

JOSEPH SURFACE. This is no subject to jest on, brother. He who can laugh —

CHARLES SURFACE. True, true, as you were going to say — then, seriously, I never had the least idea of what you charge me with, upon my honor.

JOSEPH SURFACE (*in a loud voice*). Well, it will give Sir Peter great satisfaction to hear this.

CHARLES SURFACE. To be sure, I once thought the lady seemed to have taken a fancy to me; but, upon my soul, I never gave her the least encouragement. Besides, you know my attachment to Maria.

JOSEPH SURFACE. But sure, brother, even if Lady Teazle had betrayed the fondest partiality for you —

CHARLES SURFACE. Why, look'ee, Joseph, I hope I shall never deliberately do a dishonorable action; but if a pretty woman were purposely to throw herself in my way — and that pretty woman married to a man old enough to be her father —

JOSEPH SURFACE. Well!

CHARLES SURFACE. Why, I believe I should be obliged to borrow a little of your morality, that's all. But, brother, do you know now that you surprise me exceedingly by naming me with Lady Teazle; for i'faith, I always understood you were her favorite.

JOSEPH SURFACE. Oh, for shame, Charles! This retort is foolish.

CHARLES SURFACE. Nay, I swear I have seen you exchange such significant glances —

JOSEPH SURFACE. Nay, nay, sir, this is no jest.

CHARLES SURFACE. Egad, I'm serious! Don't you remember one day when I called here —

JOSEPH SURFACE. Nay, prithee, Charles —

CHARLES SURFACE. And found you together —

JOSEPH SURFACE. Zounds, sir, I insist —

CHARLES SURFACE. And another time, when your servant —

JOSEPH SURFACE. Brother, brother, a word with you! (*Aside.*) Gad, I must stop him.

CHARLES SURFACE. Informed, I say, that —

JOSEPH SURFACE. Hush! I beg your pardon, but Sir Peter has overheard all we have been saying. I knew you would clear yourself, or I should not have consented.

CHARLES SURFACE. How, Sir Peter! Where is he?

JOSEPH SURFACE. Softly, there! (*Points to the closet.*)

CHARLES SURFACE. Oh, 'fore Heaven, I'll have him out. Sir Peter, come forth!

JOSEPH SURFACE. No, no —

CHARLES SURFACE. I say, Sir Peter, come into court. (*Pulls in* SIR PETER.) What! my old guardian! — What! turn inquisitor and take evidence incog.?

SIR PETER. Give me your hand, Charles — I believe I have suspected you wrongfully; but you mustn't be angry with Joseph — 'twas my plan!

CHARLES SURFACE. Indeed!

SIR PETER. But I acquit you. I promise you I don't think near so ill of you as I did. What I have heard has given me great satisfaction.

CHARLES SURFACE. Egad, then, 'twas lucky you didn't hear any more. Wasn't it, Joseph?

SIR PETER. Ah! you would have retorted on him.

CHARLES SURFACE. Ah, ay, that was a joke.

SIR PETER. Yes, yes, I know his honor too well.

CHARLES SURFACE. But you might as well have suspected him as me in this matter, for all that. Mightn't he, Joseph?

SIR PETER. Well, well, I believe you.

JOSEPH SURFACE (*aside*). Would they were both out of the room!

SIR PETER. And in future, perhaps, we may not be such strangers.

(*Enter* SERVANT *and whispers* JOSEPH SURFACE.)

JOSEPH SURFACE. Gentlemen, I beg pardon — I must wait on you downstairs; here's a person come on particular business.

CHARLES SURFACE. Well, you can see him in another room. Sir Peter and I have not met a long time, and I have something to say to him.

JOSEPH SURFACE (*aside*). They must not be left together — (*Aloud.*) I'll send Lady Sneerwell away, and return directly. (*Aside to* SIR PETER.) Sir Peter, not a word of the French milliner.

SIR PETER (*aside to* JOSEPH SURFACE). I! not for the world! —

(*Exit* JOSEPH SURFACE.)

Ah, Charles, if you associated more with your brother, one might indeed hope for your reformation. He is a man of sentiment. Well, there is nothing in the world so noble as a man of sentiment.

CHARLES SURFACE. Psha! he is too moral by half; and so apprehensive of his good name, as he calls it, that I suppose he would as soon let a priest into his house as a wench.

SIR PETER. No, no — come, come, — you wrong him. No, no, Joseph is no rake, but he is no such saint either, in that respect. (*Aside.*) I have a great mind to tell him — we should have such a laugh at Joseph.

CHARLES SURFACE. Oh, hang him! he's a very anchorite, a young hermit!

SIR PETER. Hark'ee — you must not abuse him: he may chance to hear of it again I promise you.

CHARLES SURFACE. Why, you won't tell him?

SIR PETER. No — but — this way. (*Aside.*) Egad, I'll tell him. (*Aloud.*) Hark'ee, have you a mind to have a good laugh at Joseph?

CHARLES SURFACE. I should like it of all things.

SIR PETER. Then, i'faith, we will! I'll be quit with him for discovering me. He had a girl with him when I called.

CHARLES SURFACE. What! Joseph? you jest.

SIR PETER. Hush! — a little French milliner — and the best of the jest is — she's in the room now.

CHARLES SURFACE. The devil she is!

SIR PETER. Hush! I tell you. (*Points to the screen.*)

CHARLES SURFACE. Behind the screen! S'life, let's unveil her!

SIR PETER. No, no, he's coming. You shan't, indeed!

CHARLES SURFACE. Oh, egad, we'll have a peep at the little milliner!

SIR PETER. Not for the world! — Joseph will never forgive me.

CHARLES SURFACE. I'll stand by you —

SIR PETER. Odds, here he is!

(JOSEPH SURFACE *enters just as* CHARLES *throws down the screen.*)

CHARLES SURFACE. Lady Teazle, by all that's wonderful!

SIR PETER. Lady Teazle, by all that's damnable!

CHARLES SURFACE. Sir Peter, this is one of the smartest French milliners I ever saw. Egad, you seem all to have been diverting yourselves here at hide and seek, and I don't see who is out of the secret. Shall I beg your ladyship to inform me? Not a word! — Brother, will you be pleased to explain this matter? What! is Morality dumb too? — Sir Peter, though I found you in the dark, perhaps you are not so now! All mute! Well — though I can make nothing of the affair, I suppose you perfectly understand one another; so I'll leave you to yourselves. (*Going.*) Brother, I'm sorry to find you have given that worthy man grounds for so much uneasiness. — Sir Peter! there's nothing in the world so noble as a man of sentiment!

(*Exit* CHARLES SURFACE. *They stand for some time looking at each other.*)

JOSEPH SURFACE. Sir Peter — notwithstanding — I confess — that appearances are against me — if you will afford me your patience — I make no doubt — but I shall explain everything to your satisfaction.

SIR PETER. If you please, sir.

JOSEPH SURFACE. The fact is, sir, that Lady Teazle, knowing my pretensions to your ward Maria — I say, sir, Lady Teazle, being apprehensive of the jealousy of your temper — and knowing my friendship to the family — she, sir, I say — called here — in order that — I might explain these pretensions — but on your coming — being apprehensive — as I said — of your jealousy — she withdrew — and this, you may depend on it, is the whole truth of the matter.

SIR PETER. A very clear account, upon my word; and I dare swear the lady will vouch for every article of it.

LADY TEAZLE. For not one word of it, Sir Peter!

SIR PETER. How! don't you think it worth while to agree in the lie?

LADY TEAZLE. There is not one syllable of truth in what that gentleman has told you.

SIR PETER. I believe you, upon my soul, ma'am!

JOSEPH SURFACE (*aside to* LADY TEAZLE). 'Sdeath, madam, will you betray me?

LADY TEAZLE. Good Mr. Hypocrite, by your leave, I'll speak for myself.

SIR PETER. Ay, let her alone, sir; you'll find she'll make out a better story than you, without prompting.

LADY TEAZLE. Hear me, Sir Peter! I came here on no matter relating to your ward, and even ignorant of this gentleman's pretensions to her. But I came, seduced by his insidious arguments, at least to listen to his pretended passion, if not to sacrifice your honor to his baseness.

SIR PETER. Now, I believe, the truth is coming, indeed!

JOSEPH SURFACE. The woman's mad!

LADY TEAZLE. No, sir; she has recovered her senses, and your own arts have furnished her with the means. Sir Peter, I do not expect you to credit me — but the tenderness you expressed for me, when I am sure you could not think I was a witness to it, has penetrated so to my heart, that had I left the place without the shame of this discovery, my future life should have spoken the sincerity of my gratitude. As for that smooth-tongued hypocrite, who would have seduced the wife of his too credulous friend, while he affected honorable addresses to his ward — I behold him now in a light so truly despicable that I shall never again respect myself for having listened to him. (*Exit.*)

JOSEPH SURFACE. Notwithstanding all this, Sir Peter, Heaven knows —

SIR PETER. That you are a villain! and so I leave you to your conscience.

JOSEPH SURFACE. You are too rash, Sir Peter, you shall hear me. The man who shuts out conviction by refusing to —

(*Exeunt,* JOSEPH SURFACE *talking.*)

ACT FIVE

Scene 1

(*The library in* JOSEPH SURFACE'S *house.* JOSEPH SURFACE *and* SERVANT.)

JOSEPH SURFACE. Mr. Stanley! and why should you think I would see him? you must know he comes to ask something.

SERVANT. Sir, I should not have let him in, but that Mr. Rowley came to the door with him.

JOSEPH SURFACE. Psha! blockhead! to suppose that I should now be in a temper to receive visits from poor relations! — Well, why don't you show the fellow up?

SERVANT. I will, sir. — Why, sir, it was not my fault that Sir Peter discovered my lady —

JOSEPH SURFACE. Go, fool!

(*Exit* SERVANT.)

Sure fortune never played a man of my policy such a trick before! My character with Sir Peter, my hopes with Maria, destroyed in a moment! I'm in a rare humor to listen to other people's distresses! I shan't be able to bestow even a benevolent sentiment on Stanley. — So! here he comes, and Rowley with him. I must try to recover myself, and put a little charity in my face, however.

(*Exit. Enter* SIR OLIVER SURFACE *and* ROWLEY.)

SIR OLIVER. What! does he avoid us? That was he, was it not?

ROWLEY. It was, sir. But I doubt you are coming a little too abruptly.

His nerves are so weak that the sight of a poor relation may be too much for him. I should have gone first to break it to him.

SIR OLIVER. Oh, plague of his nerves! Yet this is he whom Sir Peter extols as a man of the most benevolent way of thinking!

ROWLEY. As to his way of thinking, I cannot pretend to decide; for, to do him justice, he appears to have as much speculative benevolence as any private gentleman in the kingdom, though he is seldom so sensual as to indulge himself in the exercise of it.

SIR OLIVER. Yet he has a string of charitable sentiments at his fingers' ends.

ROWLEY. Or, rather, at his tongue's end, Sir Oliver; for I believe there is no sentiment he has such faith in as that "Charity begins at home."

SIR OLIVER. And his, I presume, is of that domestic sort which never stirs abroad at all.

ROWLEY. I doubt you'll find it so; — but he's coming. I mustn't seem to interrupt you; and you know, immediately as you leave him, I come in to announce your arrival in your real character.

SIR OLIVER. True; and afterwards you'll meet me at Sir Peter's.

ROWLEY. Without losing a moment. (*Exit.*)

SIR OLIVER. I don't like the complaisance of his features.

(*Enter* JOSEPH SURFACE.)

JOSEPH SURFACE. Sir, I beg you ten thousand pardons for keeping you a moment waiting. — Mr. Stanley, I presume.

SIR OLIVER. At your service.

JOSEPH SURFACE. Sir, I beg you will do me the honor to sit down — I entreat you, sir.

SIR OLIVER. Dear sir — there's no occasion. (*Aside.*) Too civil by half!

JOSEPH SURFACE. I have not the pleasure of knowing you, Mr. Stanley; but I am extremely happy to see you look so well. You were nearly related to my mother, I think, Mr. Stanley?

SIR OLIVER. I was, sir; so nearly that my present poverty, I fear, may do discredit to her wealthy children, else I should not have presumed to trouble you.

JOSEPH SURFACE. Dear sir, there needs no apology: he that is in distress, though a stranger, has a right to claim kindred with the wealthy. I am sure I wish I was one of that class, and had it in my power to offer you even a small relief.

SIR OLIVER. If your uncle, Sir Oliver, were here, I should have a friend.

JOSEPH SURFACE. I wish he was, sir, with all my heart: you should not want an advocate with him, believe me, sir.

SIR OLIVER. I should not need one — my distresses would recommend me. But I imagined his bounty would enable you to become the agent of his charity.

JOSEPH SURFACE. My dear sir, you were strangely misinformed. Sir Oliver is a worthy man, a very worthy man, but avarice, Mr. Stanley, is the vice of age. I will tell you, my good sir, in confidence, what he has done for me has been a mere nothing; though, people, I know, have thought otherwise; and, for my part, I never choose to contradict the report.

SIR OLIVER. What! has he never transmitted you bullion — rupees — pagodas?

JOSEPH SURFACE. Oh, dear sir, nothing of the kind; no, no; a few presents now and then — china, shawls, congou tea, avadavats[1], and Indian crackers[2] — little more, believe me.

SIR OLIVER (*aside*). Here's gratitude for twelve thousand pounds! — Avadavats and Indian crackers!

JOSEPH SURFACE. Then, my dear sir, you have heard, I doubt not, of the extravagance of my brother; there are very few would credit what I have done for that unfortunate young man.

SIR OLIVER (*aside*). Not I, for one!

JOSEPH SURFACE. The sums I have lent him! Indeed I have been exceedingly to blame; it was an amiable weakness; however, I don't pretend to defend it — and now I feel it doubly culpable, since it has deprived me of the pleasure of serving you, Mr. Stanley, as my heart indicates.

SIR OLIVER (*aside*). Dissembler! (*Aloud.*) Then, sir, you can't assist me?

JOSEPH SURFACE. At present, it grieves me to say, I cannot; but, whenever I have the ability, you may depend upon hearing from me.

SIR OLIVER. I am extremely sorry —

JOSEPH SURFACE. Not more than I, believe me; to pity, without the power to relieve, is still more painful than to ask and be denied.

SIR OLIVER. Kind sir, your most obedient humble servant.

JOSEPH SURFACE. You leave me deeply affected, Mr. Stanley. — William, be ready to open the door.

SIR OLIVER. Oh, dear sir, no ceremony.

JOSEPH SURFACE. Your very obedient.

SIR OLIVER. Sir, your most obsequious.

JOSEPH SURFACE. You may depend upon hearing from me, whenever I can be of service.

SIR OLIVER. Sweet sir, you are too good.

JOSEPH SURFACE. In the meantime I wish you health and spirits.

SIR OLIVER. Your ever grateful and perpetual humble servant.

JOSEPH SURFACE. Sir, yours as sincerely.

SIR OLIVER (*aside*). Charles! — you are my heir. (*Exit.*)

JOSEPH SURFACE. This is one bad effect of a good character; it invites application from the unfortunate, and there needs no small degree of address to gain the reputation of benevolence without incurring the ex-

[1] **Avadavats:** Small songbirds from India. [2] **Indian crackers:** firecrackers.

pense. The silver ore of pure charity is an expensive article in the catalogue of a man's good qualities; whereas the sentimental French plate I use instead of it makes just as good a show, and pays no tax.

(*Enter* ROWLEY.)

ROWLEY. Mr. Surface, your servant: I was apprehensive of interrupting you, though my business demands immediate attention, as this note will inform you.

JOSEPH SURFACE. Always happy to see Mr. Rowley. — (*Reads.*) Sir Oliver Surface! My uncle arrived!

ROWLEY. He is, indeed: we have just parted — quite well, after a speedy voyage, and impatient to embrace his worthy nephew.

JOSEPH SURFACE. I am astonished! — William! stop Mr. Stanley, if he's not gone.

ROWLEY. Oh, he's out of reach, I believe.

JOSEPH SURFACE. Why did you not let me know this when you came in together?

ROWLEY. I thought you had particular business. But I must be gone to inform your brother and appoint him here to meet your uncle. He will be with you in a quarter of an hour.

JOSEPH SURFACE. So he says. Well, I am strangely overjoyed at his coming. — (*Aside.*) Never, to be sure, was anything so damned unlucky!

ROWLEY. You will be delighted to see how well he looks.

JOSEPH SURFACE. Oh! I'm overjoyed to hear it. — (*Aside.*) Just at this time!

ROWLEY. I'll tell him how impatiently you expect him.

JOSEPH SURFACE. Do, do; pray give my best duty and affection. Indeed, I cannot express the sensations I feel at the thought of seeing him.

(*Exit* ROWLEY.)

Certainly his coming just at this time is the cruellest piece of ill fortune. (*Exit.*)

Scene 2

(SIR PETER TEAZLE'S *house. Enter* MRS. CANDOUR *and* MAID.)

MAID. Indeed, ma'am, my lady will see nobody at present.

MRS. CANDOUR. Did you tell her it was her friend Mrs. Candour?

MAID. Yes, ma'am; but she begs you will excuse her.

MRS. CANDOUR. Do go again; I shall be glad to see her, if it be only for a moment, for I am sure she must be in great distress.

(*Exit* MAID.)

Dear heart, how provoking! I'm not mistress of half the circumstances! We shall have the whole affair in the newspapers, with the names of the parties at length, before I have dropped the story at a dozen houses.

(*Enter* SIR BENJAMIN BACKBITE.)

Oh, dear Sir Benjamin! you have heard, I suppose —

SIR BENJAMIN. Of Lady Teazle and Mr. Surface —

MRS. CANDOUR. And Sir Peter's discovery —

SIR BENJAMIN. Oh, the strangest piece of business, to be sure!

MRS. CANDOUR. Well, I never was so surprised in my life. I am so sorry for all parties, indeed.

SIR BENJAMIN. Now, I don't pity Sir Peter at all: he was so extravagantly partial to Mr. Surface.

MRS. CANDOUR. Mr. Surface! Why, 'twas with Charles Lady Teazle was detected.

SIR BENJAMIN. No, no, I tell you: Mr. Surface is the gallant.

MRS. CANDOUR. No such thing! Charles is the man. 'Twas Mr. Surface brought Sir Peter on purpose to discover them.

SIR BENJAMIN. I tell you I had it from one —

MRS. CANDOUR. And I have it from one —

SIR BENJAMIN. Who had it from one, who had it —

MRS. CANDOUR. From one immediately — But here comes Lady Sneerwell; perhaps she knows the whole affair.

(*Enter* LADY SNEERWELL.)

LADY SNEERWELL. So, my dear Mrs. Candour, here's a sad affair of our friend Lady Teazle!

MRS. CANDOUR. Ay, my dear friend, who would have thought —

LADY SNEERWELL. Well, there is no trusting to appearances; though indeed, she was always too lively for me.

MRS. CANDOUR. To be sure, her manners were a little too free; but then she was so young!

LADY SNEERWELL. And had, indeed, some good qualities.

MRS. CANDOUR. So she had, indeed. But have you heard the particulars?

LADY SNEERWELL. No; but everybody says that Mr. Surface —

SIR BENJAMIN. Ay, there; I told you Mr. Surface was the man.

MRS. CANDOUR. No, no: indeed the assignation was with Charles.

LADY SNEERWELL. With Charles! You alarm me, Mrs. Candour.

MRS. CANDOUR. Yes, yes: he was the lover. Mr. Surface, to do him justice, was only the informer.

SIR BENJAMIN. Well, I'll not dispute with you, Mrs. Candour; but, be it which it may, I hope that Sir Peter's wound will not —

MRS. CANDOUR. Sir Peter's wound! Oh, mercy! I didn't hear a word of their fighting.

LADY SNEERWELL. Nor I, a syllable.

SIR BENJAMIN. No! what, no mention of the duel?

MRS. CANDOUR. Not a word.

SIR BENJAMIN. Oh, yes: they fought before they left the room.

LADY SNEERWELL. Pray let us hear.

MRS. CANDOUR. Ay, do oblige us with the duel.

SIR BENJAMIN. "Sir," says Sir Peter, immediately after the discovery, "you are a most ungrateful fellow."

MRS. CANDOUR. Ay, to Charles —

SIR BENJAMIN. No, no — to Mr. Surface — "a most ungrateful fellow; and old as I am, sir," says he, "I insist on immediate satisfaction."

MRS. CANDOUR. Ay, that must have been to Charles; for 'tis very unlikely Mr. Surface should fight in his own house.

SIR BENJAMIN. 'Gad's life, ma'am, not at all — "giving me immediate satisfaction" — On this, ma'am, Lady Teazle, seeing Sir Peter in such danger, ran out of the room in strong hysterics, and Charles after her, calling out for hartshorn and water; then, madam, they began to fight with swords —

(*Enter* CRABTREE.)

CRABTREE. With pistols, nephew — pistols; I have it from undoubted authority.

MRS. CANDOUR. Oh, Mr. Crabtree, then it is all true!

CRABTREE. Too true, indeed, madam, and Sir Peter is dangerously wounded —

SIR BENJAMIN. By a thrust in *seconde* quite through his left side —

CRABTREE. By a bullet lodged in the thorax.

MRS. CANDOUR. Mercy on me! Poor Sir Peter!

CRABTREE. Yes, madam; though Charles would have avoided the matter, if he could.

MRS. CANDOUR. I knew Charles was the person.

SIR BENJAMIN. My uncle, I see, knows nothing of the matter.

CRABTREE. But Sir Peter taxed him with the basest ingratitude —

SIR BENJAMIN. That I told you, you know —

CRABTREE. Do, nephew, let me speak! — and insisted on immediate —

SIR BENJAMIN. Just as I said —

CRABTREE. Odds life, nephew, allow others to know something too! A pair of pistols lay on the bureau (for Mr. Surface, it seems, had come home the night before late from Salthill where he had been to see the Montem with a friend who has a son at Eton) so, unluckily, the pistols were left charged.

SIR BENJAMIN. I heard nothing of this.

CRABTREE. Sir Peter forced Charles to take one, and they fired, it seems, pretty nearly together. Charles's shot took effect, as I tell you, and Sir Peter's missed; but, what is very extraordinary, the ball struck against a little bronze Shakespeare that stood over the fireplace, grazed out of the window at a right angle, and wounded the postman who was just coming to the door with a double letter from Northamptonshire.

SIR BENJAMIN. My uncle's account is more circumstantial, I confess; but I believe mine is the true one for all that.

LADY SNEERWELL (*aside*). I am more interested in this affair than they imagine, and must have better information. (*Exit.*)

SIR BENJAMIN. Ah! Lady Sneerwell's alarm is very easily accounted for.

CRABTREE. Yes, yes, they certainly do say — but that's neither here nor there.

MRS. CANDOUR. But, pray, where is Sir Peter at present?

CRABTREE. Oh! they brought him home, and he is now in the house, though the servants are ordered to deny him.

MRS. CANDOUR. I believe so, and Lady Teazle, I suppose, attending him.

CRABTREE. Yes, yes; and I saw one of the faculty enter just before me.

SIR BENJAMIN. Hey! who comes here?

CRABTREE. Oh, this is he: the physician, depend on't.

MRS. CANDOUR. Oh, certainly; it must be the physician; and now we shall know.

(*Enter* SIR OLIVER SURFACE.)

CRABTREE. Well, doctor, what hopes?

MRS. CANDOUR. Ay, doctor, how's your patient?

SIR BENJAMIN. Now, doctor, isn't it a wound with a smallsword?

CRABTREE. A bullet lodged in the thorax, for a hundred!

SIR OLIVER. Doctor! a wound with a smallsword; and a bullet in the thorax? — Oons! are you mad, good people?

SIR BENJAMIN. Perhaps, sir, you are not a doctor?

SIR OLIVER. Truly, I am to thank you for my degree, if I am.

CRABTREE. Only a friend of Sir Peter's, then, I presume. But, sir, you must have heard of his accident?

SIR OLIVER. Not a word!

CRABTREE. Not of his being dangerously wounded?

SIR OLIVER. The devil he is!

SIR BENJAMIN. Run through the body —

CRABTREE. Shot in the breast —

SIR BENJAMIN. By one Mr. Surface —

CRABTREE. Ay, the younger.

SIR OLIVER. Hey! what the plague! you seem to differ strangely in your accounts: however, you agree that Sir Peter is dangerously wounded.

SIR BENJAMIN. Oh, yes, we agree there.

CRABTREE. Yes, yes, I believe there can be no doubt in that.

SIR OLIVER. Then, upon my word, for a person in that situation, he is the most imprudent man alive; for here he comes, walking as if nothing at all was the matter.

(*Enter* SIR PETER TEAZLE.)

Odds heart, Sir Peter! you are come in good time, I promise you; for we had just given you over!

SIR BENJAMIN (*aside to* CRABTREE). Egad, uncle, this is the most sudden recovery!

SIR OLIVER. Why, man! what do you do out of bed with a smallsword through your body and a bullet lodged in your thorax?

SIR PETER. A smallsword and a bullet?

SIR OLIVER. Ay; these gentlemen would have killed you without law or physic, and wanted to dub me a doctor, to make me an accomplice.

SIR PETER. Why, what is all this?

SIR BENJAMIN. We rejoice, Sir Peter, that the story of the duel is not true and are sincerely sorry for your other misfortune.

SIR PETER (*aside*). So, so; all over the town already.

CRABTREE. Though, Sir Peter, you were certainly vastly to blame to marry at your years.

SIR PETER. Sir, what business is that of yours?

MRS. CANDOUR. Though, indeed, as Sir Peter made so good a husband, he's very much to be pitied.

SIR PETER. Plague on your pity, ma'am! I desire none of it.

SIR BENJAMIN. However, Sir Peter, you must not mind the laughing and jests you will meet with on the occasion.

SIR PETER. Sir, sir! I desire to be master in my own house.

CRABTREE. 'Tis no uncommon case, that's one comfort.

SIR PETER. I insist on being left to myself. Without ceremony, I insist on your leaving my house directly!

MRS. CANDOUR. Well, well, we are going; and depend on't, we'll make the best report of it we can. (*Exit.*)

SIR PETER. Leave my house!

CRABTREE. And tell how hardly you've been treated. (*Exit.*)

SIR PETER. Leave my house!

SIR BENJAMIN. And how patiently you bear it. (*Exit.*)

SIR PETER. Fiends! vipers! furies! Oh! that their own venom would choke them!

SIR OLIVER. They are very provoking indeed, Sir Peter.

(*Enter* ROWLEY.)

ROWLEY. I heard high words: what has ruffled you, sir?

SIR PETER. Psha! what signifies asking? Do I ever pass a day without my vexations?

ROWLEY. Well, I'm not inquisitive.

SIR OLIVER. Well, Sir Peter, I have seen both my nephews in the manner we proposed.

SIR PETER. A precious couple they are!

ROWLEY. Yes, and Sir Oliver is convinced that your judgment was right, Sir Peter.

SIR OLIVER. Yes, I find Joseph is indeed the man, after all.

ROWLEY. Ay, as Sir Peter says, he is a man of sentiment.

SIR OLIVER. And acts up to the sentiments he professes.

ROWLEY. It certainly is edification to hear him talk.

SIR OLIVER. Oh, he's a model for the young men of the age! But how's this, Sir Peter? you don't join us in your friend Joseph's praise, as I expected.

SIR PETER. Sir Oliver, we live in a damned wicked world, and the fewer we praise the better.

ROWLEY. What! do you say so, Sir Peter, who were never mistaken in your life?

SIR PETER. Psha! plague on you both! I see by your sneering you have heard the whole affair. I shall go mad among you!

ROWLEY. Then, to fret you no longer, Sir Peter, we are indeed acquainted with it all. I met Lady Teazle coming from Mr. Surface's so humbled, that she deigned to request me to be her advocate with you.

SIR PETER. And does Sir Oliver know all this?

SIR OLIVER. Every circumstance.

SIR PETER. What, of the closet and the screen, hey?

SIR OLIVER. Yes, yes, and the little French milliner. Oh, I have been vastly diverted with the story! ha! ha! ha!

SIR PETER. 'Twas very pleasant.

SIR OLIVER. I never laughed more in my life, I assure you: ha! ha! ha!

SIR PETER. Oh, vastly diverting! ha! ha! ha!

ROWLEY. To be sure, Joseph with his sentiments! ha! ha! ha!

SIR PETER. Yes, yes, his sentiments! ha! ha! ha! Hypocritical villain!

SIR OLIVER. Ay, and the rogue Charles to pull Sir Peter out of the closet: ha! ha! ha!

SIR PETER. Ha! ha! 'twas devilish entertaining, to be sure!

SIR OLIVER. Ha! ha! ha! Egad, Sir Peter, I should like to have seen your face when the screen was thrown down: ha! ha.

SIR PETER. Yes, yes, my face when the screen was thrown down: ha! ha! ha! Oh, I must never show my head again!

SIR OLIVER. But come, come, it isn't fair to laugh at you neither, my old friend; though, upon my soul, I can't help it.

SIR PETER. Oh, pray, don't restrain your mirth on my account: it does not hurt me at all! I laugh at the whole affair myself. Yes, yes, I think being a standing jest for all one's acquaintance a very happy situation. Oh, yes, and then of a morning to read the paragraphs about Mr. S—, Lady T—, and Sir P—, will be so entertaining!

ROWLEY. Without affection, Sir Peter, you may despise the ridicule of fools. But I see Lady Teazle going towards the next room, I am sure you must desire a reconciliation as earnestly as she does.

SIR OLIVER. Perhaps my being here prevents her coming to you. Well, I'll leave honest Rowley to mediate between you; but he must bring you all presently to Mr. Surface's where I am now returning, if not to reclaim a libertine, at least to expose hypocrisy.

SIR PETER. Ah, I'll be present at your discovering yourself there with all my heart; though 'tis a vile unlucky place for discoveries.

ROWLEY. We'll follow.

(*Exit* SIR OLIVER.)

SIR PETER. She is not coming here, you see, Rowley.

ROWLEY. No, but she has left the door of the room open, you perceive. See, she is in tears.

SIR PETER. Certainly a little mortification appears very becoming in a wife. Don't you think it will do her good to let her pine a little?

ROWLEY. Oh, this is ungenerous in you!

SIR PETER. Well, I know not what to think. You remember the letter I found of hers evidently intended for Charles!

ROWLEY. A mere forgery, Sir Peter! laid in your way on purpose. This is one of the points which I intend Snake shall give you conviction of.

SIR PETER. I wish I were once satisfied of that. She looks this way. What a remarkably elegant turn of the head she has! Rowley, I'll go to her.

ROWLEY. Certainly.

SIR PETER. Though, when it is known that we are reconciled, people will laugh at me ten times more.

ROWLEY. Let them laugh, and retort their malice only by showing them you are happy in spite of it.

SIR PETER. I'faith, so I will! and, if I'm not mistaken, we may yet be the happiest couple in the country.

ROWLEY. Nay, Sir Peter, he is who once lays aside suspicion —

SIR PETER. Hold, Master Rowley! if you have any regard for me, never let me hear you utter anything like a sentiment. I have had enough of them to serve me the rest of my life.

Scene 3

(*The library in* JOSEPH SURFACE'S *house.* JOSEPH SURFACE *and* LADY SNEERWELL.)

LADY SNEERWELL. Impossible! Will not Sir Peter immediately be reconciled to Charles, and of course no longer oppose his union with Maria? The thought is distraction to me.

JOSEPH SURFACE. Can passion furnish a remedy?

LADY SNEERWELL. No, nor cunning either. Oh, I was a fool, an idiot, to league with such a blunderer!

JOSEPH SURFACE. Sure, Lady Sneerwell, I am the greatest sufferer; yet you see I bear the accident with calmness.

LADY SNEERWELL. Because the disappointment doesn't reach your heart; your interest only attached you to Maria. Had you felt for her what I have for that ungrateful libertine, neither your temper nor hypocrisy could prevent your showing the sharpness of your vexation.

JOSEPH SURFACE. But why should your reproaches fall on me for this disappointment?

LADY SNEERWELL. Are you not the cause of it? Had you not a sufficient field for your roguery in imposing upon Sir Peter, and supplanting your brother, but you must endeavor to seduce his wife? I hate such an avarice of crimes; 'tis an unfair monopoly, and never prospers.

JOSEPH SURFACE. Well, I admit I have been to blame. I confess I deviated from the direct road of wrong, but I don't think we're so totally defeated neither.

LADY SNEERWELL. No?

JOSEPH SURFACE. You tell me you have made a trial of Snake since we met, and that you still believe him faithful to us?

LADY SNEERWELL. I do believe so.

JOSEPH SURFACE. And that he has undertaken, should it be necessary, to swear and prove that Charles is at this time contracted by vows and honor to your ladyship, which some of his former letters to you will serve to support?

LADY SNEERWELL. This, indeed, might have assisted.

JOSEPH SURFACE. Come, come; it is not too late yet.

(*Knocking at the door.*)

But hark! this is probably my uncle, Sir Oliver: retire to that room; we'll consult further when he's gone.

LADY SNEERWELL. Well, but if he should find you out too.

JOSEPH SURFACE. Oh, I have no fear of that. Sir Peter will hold his tongue for his own credit's sake — and you may depend on it I shall soon discover Sir Oliver's weak side!

LADY SNEERWELL. I have no diffidence of your abilities! only be constant to one roguery at a time. (*Exit.*)

JOSEPH SURFACE. I will, I will! So! 'tis confounded hard, after such bad fortune, to be baited by one's confederate in evil. Well, at all events, my character is so much better than Charles's that I certainly — hey! — what — this is not Sir Oliver, but old Stanley again. Plague on't that he should return to tease me just now! I shall have Sir Oliver come and find him here — and —

(*Enter* SIR OLIVER SURFACE.)

Gad's life, Mr. Stanley, why have you come back to plague me at this time? You must not stay now, upon my word.

SIR OLIVER. Sir, I hear your uncle Oliver is expected here, and though he has been so penurious to you, I'll try what he'll do for me.

JOSEPH SURFACE. Sir, 'tis impossible for you to stay now, so I must beg — Come any other time, and I promise you, you shall be assisted.

SIR OLIVER. No: Sir Oliver and I must be acquainted.

JOSEPH SURFACE. Zounds, sir! then I insist on your quitting the room directly.

SIR OLIVER. Nay, sir —

JOSEPH SURFACE. Sir, I insist on't — Here, William! show this gentleman out. Since you compel me, sir, not one moment — this is such insolence!

(*Going to push him out. Enter* CHARLES SURFACE.)

CHARLES SURFACE. Heyday! what's the matter now? What the devil have you got hold of my little broker here? Zounds, brother, don't hurt little Premium. What's the matter, my little fellow?

JOSEPH SURFACE. So! he has been with you, too, has he?

CHARLES SURFACE. To be sure he has. Why, he's as honest a little — But sure, Joseph, you have not been borrowing money too, have you?

JOSEPH SURFACE. Borrowing! no! But, brother, you know we expect Sir Oliver here every —

CHARLES SURFACE. O gad, that's true! Noll mustn't find the little broker here, to be sure.

JOSEPH SURFACE. Yet, Mr. Stanley insists —

CHARLES SURFACE. Stanley! why his name's Premium.

JOSEPH SURFACE. No, sir, Stanley.

CHARLES SURFACE. No, no, Premium.

JOSEPH SURFACE. Well, no matter which — but —

CHARLES SURFACE. Ay, ay, Stanley or Premium, 'tis the same thing, as you say; for I suppose he goes by half a hundred names, besides A. B. at the coffee-house.

(*Knocking.*)

JOSEPH SURFACE. 'Sdeath! here's Sir Oliver at the door. Now I beg, Mr. Stanley —

CHARLES SURFACE. Ay, ay, and I beg, Mr. Premium —

SIR OLIVER. Gentlemen —

JOSEPH SURFACE. Sir, by heaven you shall go!

CHARLES SURFACE. Ay, out with him, certainly!

SIR OLIVER. This violence —

JOSEPH SURFACE. Sir, 'tis your own fault.

CHARLES SURFACE. Out with him, to be sure!

(*Both forcing* SIR OLIVER *out. Enter* SIR PETER *and* LADY TEAZLE, MARIA, *and* ROWLEY.)

SIR PETER. My old friend, Sir Oliver — hey! What in the name of wonder! — here are dutiful nephews — assault their uncle at first visit!

LADY TEAZLE. Indeed, Sir Oliver, 'twas well we came in to rescue you.

ROWLEY. Truly it was; for I perceive, Sir Oliver, the character of old Stanley was no protection to you.

SIR OLIVER. Nor of Premium either: the necessities of the former could not extort a shilling from that benevolent gentleman; and now, egad, I stood a chance of faring worse than my ancestors and being knocked down without being bid for.

JOSEPH SURFACE. Charles!

CHARLES SURFACE. Joseph!

JOSEPH SURFACE. 'Tis now complete!

CHARLES SURFACE. Very!

SIR OLIVER. Sir Peter, my friend, and Rowley too — look on that elder nephew of mine. You know what he has already received from my bounty; and you also know how gladly I would have regarded half my fortune as held in trust for him? judge, then, my disappointment in discovering him to be destitute of truth, charity, and gratitude!

SIR PETER. Sir Oliver, I should be more surprised at this declaration, if I had not myself found him to be mean, treacherous, and hypocritical.

LADY TEAZLE. And if the gentleman pleads not guilty to these, pray let him call me to his character.

SIR PETER. Then, I believe, we need add no more: if he knows himself, he will consider it as the most perfect punishment that he is known to the world.

CHARLES SURFACE (*aside*). If they talk this way to Honesty, what will they say to me, by-and-by?

SIR OLIVER. As for that prodigal, his brother, there —

CHARLES SURFACE (*aside*). Ay, now comes my turn: the damned family pictures will ruin me!

JOSEPH SURFACE. Sir Oliver — uncle, will you honor me with a hearing?

CHARLES SURFACE (*aside*). Now, if Joseph would make one of his long speeches, I might recollect myself a little.

SIR OLIVER (to JOSEPH). I suppose you would undertake to justify yourself entirely?

JOSEPH SURFACE. I trust I could.

SIR OLIVER (to CHARLES). Well, sir! — and you could justify yourself too, I suppose?

CHARLES SURFACE. Not that I know of, Sir Oliver.

SIR OLIVER. What! — Little Premium has been let too much into the secret, I suppose?

CHARLES SURFACE. True, sir; but they were family secrets, and should not be mentioned again, you know.

ROWLEY. Come, Sir Oliver, I know you cannot speak of Charles's follies with anger.

SIR OLIVER. Odd's heart, no more I can; nor with gravity either. Sir Peter, do you know the rogue bargained with me for all his ancestors; sold me judges and generals by the foot, and maiden aunts as cheap as broken china.

CHARLES SURFACE. To be sure, Sir Oliver, I did make a little free with the family canvas, that's the truth on't. My ancestors may rise in judgment against me, there's no denying it; but believe me sincere when I tell you — and upon my soul I would not say so if I was not — that if I do not appear mortified at the exposure of my follies, it is because I feel at this moment the warmest satisfaction at seeing you, my liberal benefactor.

SIR OLIVER. Charles, I believe you. Give me your hand again: the ill looking little fellow over the settee has made your peace.

CHARLES SURFACE. Then, sir, my gratitude to the original is still increased.

LADY TEAZLE. Yet, I believe, Sir Oliver, here is one whom Charles is still more anxious to be reconciled to. (*Pointing to* MARIA.)

SIR OLIVER. Oh, I have heard of his attachment there; and, with the young lady's pardon, if I construe right — that blush —

SIR PETER. Well, child, speak your sentiments.

MARIA. Sir, I have little to say, but I shall rejoice to hear that he is happy; for me, whatever claim I had to his attention, I willingly resign to one who has a better title.

CHARLES SURFACE. How, Maria!

SIR PETER. Heyday! what's the mystery now? While he appeared an incorrigible rake, you would give your hand to no one else; and now that he is likely to reform I'll warrant you won't have him.

MARIA. His own heart and Lady Sneerwell know the cause.

CHARLES SURFACE. Lady Sneerwell!

JOSEPH SURFACE. Brother, it is with great concern I am obliged to speak on this point, but my regard to justice compels me, and Lady Sneerwell's injuries can no longer be concealed.

(*Opens the door. Enter* LADY SNEERWELL.)

SIR PETER. So! another French milliner! Egad, he has one in every room in the house, I suppose!

LADY SNEERWELL. Ungrateful Charles! Well may you be surprised, and feel for the indelicate situation your perfidy has forced me into.

CHARLES SURFACE. Pray, uncle, is this another plot of yours? For, as I have life, I don't understand it.

JOSEPH SURFACE. I believe, sir, there is but the evidence of one person more necessary to make it extremely clear.

SIR PETER. And that person, I imagine, is Mr. Snake. Rowley, you were perfectly right to bring him with us, and pray let him appear.

ROWLEY. Walk in, Mr. Snake.

(*Enter* SNAKE.)

I thought his testimony might be wanted; however, it happens unluckily, that he comes to confront Lady Sneerwell, not to support her.

LADY SNEERWELL. A villain! Treacherous to me at last! Speak, fellow, have you too conspired against me?

SNAKE. I beg your ladyship ten thousand pardons: you paid me extremely liberally for the lie in question; but I unfortunately have been offered double to speak the truth.

SIR PETER. Plot and counterplot, egad!

LADY SNEERWELL. The torments of shame and disappointment on you all!

LADY TEAZLE. Hold, Lady Sneerwell — before you go, let me thank you for the trouble you and that gentleman have taken in writing letters from me to Charles, and answering them yourself; and let me also request you to make my respects to the scandalous college, of which you are president, and inform them that Lady Teazle, licentiate, begs leave to return the diploma they granted her, as she leaves off practice and kills characters no longer.

LADY SNEERWELL. You too, madam! — provoking — insolent! May your husband live these fifty years! (*Exit.*)

SIR PETER. Oons! what a fury!

LADY TEAZLE. A malicious creature, indeed!

SIR PETER. Hey! not for her last wish?

LADY TEAZLE. Oh, no!

SIR OLIVER. Well, sir, and what have you to say now?

JOSEPH SURFACE. Sir, I am so confounded, to find that Lady Sneerwell could be guilty of suborning Mr. Snake in this manner, to impose on us all, that I know not what to say: however, lest her revengeful spirit should prompt her to injure my brother, I had certainly better follow her directly. (*Exit.*)

SIR PETER. Moral to the last drop!

SIR OLIVER. Ay, and marry her, Joseph, if you can. Oil and vinegar — egad, you'll do very well together.

ROWLEY. I believe we have no more occasion for Mr. Snake at present?

SNAKE. Before I go, I beg pardon once for all, for whatever uneasiness I have been the humble instrument of causing to the parties present.

SIR PETER. Well, well, you have made atonement by a good deed at last.

SNAKE. But I must request of the company, that it shall never be known.

SIR PETER. Hey! what the plague! are you ashamed of having done a right thing once in your life?

SNAKE. Ah, sir, consider — I live by the badness of my character; I have nothing but my infamy to depend on; and, if it were once known that I had been betrayed into an honest action, I should lose every friend I have in the world.

SIR OLIVER. Well, well — we'll not traduce you by saying anything in your praise, never fear.

(*Exit* SNAKE.)

SIR PETER. There's a precious rogue!

LADY TEAZLE. See, Sir Oliver, there needs no persuasion now to reconcile your nephew and Maria.

SIR OLIVER. Ay, ay, that's as it should be; and, egad, we'll have the wedding tomorrow morning.

CHARLES SURFACE. Thank you, dear uncle.

SIR PETER. What, you rogue! don't you ask the girl's consent first?

CHARLES SURFACE. Oh, I have done that a long time — a minute ago — and she has looked yes.

MARIA. For shame, Charles! — I protest, Sir Peter, there has not been a word —

SIR OLIVER. Well, then, the fewer the better: may your love for each other never know abatement.

SIR PETER. And may you live as happily together as Lady Teazle and I intend to do!

CHARLES SURFACE. Rowley, my old friend, I am sure you congratulate me; and I suspect that I owe you much.

SIR OLIVER. You do, indeed, Charles.

ROWLEY. If my efforts to serve you had not succeeded, you would have been in my debt for the attempt — but deserve to be happy — and you overpay me.

SIR PETER. Ay, honest Rowley always said you would reform.

CHARLES SURFACE. Why as to reforming, Sir Peter, I'll make no promises, and that I take to be a proof that I intend to set about it. But here shall be my monitor — my gentle guide. — Ah! can I leave the virtuous path those eyes illumine?

> Though thou, dear maid, shouldst wave thy beauty's sway,
> Thou still must rule, because I will obey:
> An humble fugitive from Folly view,
> No sanctuary near but Love — and you (*to the audience*):
> You can, indeed, each anxious fear remove,
> For even Scandal dies, if you approve.

EPILOGUE

Written by MR. COLMAN

Spoken by LADY TEAZLE

I, who was late so volatile and gay,
Like a trade-wind must now blow all one way,
Bend all my cares, my studies, and my vows,
To one dull rusty weathercock — my spouse!
So wills our virtuous bard — the motley Bayes
Of crying epilogues and laughing plays!

Old bachelors, who marry smart young wives —
Learn from our play to regulate your lives:
Each bring his dear to town, all faults upon her —
London will prove the very source of honor.
Plunged fairly in, like a cold bath it serves,
When principles relax, to brace the nerves.
Such is my case; and yet I must deplore
That the gay dream of dissipation's o'er.
And say, ye fair! was ever lively wife,
Born with a genius for the highest life,
Like me untimely blasted in her bloom.
Like me condemned to such a dismal doom?
Save money — when I just knew how to waste it!
Leave London — just as I began to taste it!
Must I then watch the early-crowing cock,
The melancholy ticking of a clock;
In a lone rustic hall for ever pounded,
With dogs, cats, rats, and squalling brats surrounded?
With humble curate can I now retire,
(While good Sir Peter boozes with the squire,)
And at backgammon mortify my soul,
That pants for loo, or flutters at a vole.
Seven's the main! Dear sound that must expire,
Lost at hot cockles round a Christmas fire;
The transient hour of fashion too soon spent,
Farewell the tranquil mind, farewell content!
Farewell the pluméd head, the cushioned tête,
That takes the cushion from its proper seat!
That spirit-stirring drum — card drums I mean,
Spadille — odd trick — pam — basto — king and queen!
And you, ye knockers that with brazen throat
The welcome visitors' approach denote;
Farewell all quality of high renown,
Pride, pomp, and circumstance of glorious town!
Farewell! your revels I partake no more,
And Lady Teazle's occupation's o'er!
All this I told our bard; he smiled, and said 'twas clear,
I ought to play deep tragedy next year.
Meanwhile he drew wise morals from his play,
And in these solemn periods stalked away: —
"Blessed were the fair like you; her faults who stopped.
And closed her follies when the curtain dropped!
No more in vice or error to engage,
Or play the fool at large on life's great stage."

Curtain

The Importance of Being Earnest (1895) is not easy to classify. In that it depends on bizarre action, unexpected plot twists, puns, and similar nonsense, it is farce. But it is also social satire, with its polished verbal wit and its incisive jabs at nineteenth-century manners and behavior. In this dualism lies part of the fascination of the play: the contrast between crazy events and witty dialogue. Writing in the tradition of eighteenth-century Comedy of Manners, Oscar Wilde (1854–1900) was also clearly aware of the nineteenth-century melodrama. Without the knowing audience of the eighteenth century, the last one to recognize that manners are graces and wit an exercise of the mind on the things of the world, Wilde had to overlay his irony with farce to get his satire across. And at the same time, this whole process is exactly his point: the play in many ways is an attack on Victorian solemnity, hypocrisy, priggishness, and lack of true wit and manners.

The celebrated interview scene between Lady Bracknell and Jack Worthing is probably the best example in the play of the interplay between satire and farce. It is a festival of disjunctive humor and punning. Lady Bracknell's nonsensical reactions to Jack's honest and straightforward answers are howlingly funny. They take on a different kind of humor, though, when they are more closely considered in terms of the questions themselves. At first glance, the questions about money, family, career, prospects, friends, vices, and opinions seem the routine ones any Victorian mother might want to have answered. What Wilde has actually achieved, however, is a brilliant satire on the custom of conducting premarital inquisitions and on the superficial, materialistic standards which governed the making of marriages in his time. This is subtle but incisive social commentary.

That is the curious quality of the entire play. Both plot and characters operate on at least two levels constantly, one serious and one facetious. The double plot, based on the ancient device of the lost child and the romantic conceit of being in love with *names* instead of men, can be viewed simply as farcical nonsense, though the "importance of being Earnest" is a serious pun. But for those who are familiar with the gimmick of the orphan long separated from its true parents — Oedipus began it — or with the romantic notions which pervaded nineteenth-century dramas and novels, the plot, on a much higher level, is an artful parody of the style and content of much of the popular literary output of Wilde's time. Similarly, the dialogue can be appreciated quite simply for its disjunctive jokes and puns. But much of that is peripheral to the real social satire on standards and attitudes of the times. For example, Algernon's sweet slander of a recent widow — "I hear her hair has turned quite gold from grief" — is viciously funny in itself, but it also tells quite a lot about Algernon and the sentiments of the turn-of-the-century upper class.

Wilde's characters may be stereotypes, but then some of his models —

thanks to the hypocritical codes under which they lived or dissembled — behaved and talked like types rather than individuals. Algernon, Lady Bracknell, Cecily, and the others are based firmly on reality. Young men and women did indeed behave much as they do in *Earnest;* matriarchs did give such careful and superficial attention to the men their daughters married. But the wonderful twist that sharpens the duality of the characters as stereotypes and real people is the satirical theme of the whole play: that life should be treated with irony, not earnestness.

As a subheading to the title, Wilde describes *Earnest* as "A Trivial Comedy for Serious People." This very well combines the paradoxical duality of an almost nonsensical plot and seemingly inane dialogue with a deeper probing of the hypocrisy and sentimentality of Victorian society. In some of Gwendolen's conversational exchanges, deliberate superficiality is mingled with a naive directness which suggests simultaneously that training and manners have bred artificiality, though there is still a sensible mind behind the artifice.

That is all the more remarkable since Wilde is so often admired for his witticisms — usually in isolation from their dramatic functions. It should be clear to the reader that he is not just studding his farce with irrelevant jibes and quips. Even the most idiotic or dislocated dialogue manages to make a comment on character or society. A classic Wildean aphorism is Algernon's remark: "All women become like their mothers. That is their tragedy. No man does. That's his." It is neat, pat, slickly put, but it is not really true. As an aphorism, it sounds well, but as an analysis, it is valueless. So much so that it prompts the question from Jack: "Is that clever?" The retort does not quite answer that query: "It is perfectly phrased! and quite as true as any observation in civilized life should be." That, of course, is part of Wilde's satire — to echo fashionable comments, distorting them ever so slightly to expose the emptiness behind them.

In making "Earnest" a magic name for the two girls, Wilde shows also his contempt for people who are content to judge by such tags rather than by personal merit. Not only is the conversation trivial by design and custom, but the interractions of the characters are just as trivial, for much the same reasons.

The device of the lost child is central to resolving the problems Wilde has invented for his characters, but the equally venerable ploy of mistaken identity — in this case, an assumed identity — is also essential. That Wilde uses these tricks to advance and tie up his plot, while at the same time making fun of them as dramatic clichés, is a measure of his talent as a critic of theatre and of manners. He parodies postures, styles, and forms — human and literary.

G. L.

OSCAR WILDE

The Importance of Being Earnest

A Trivial Comedy for Serious People

Characters

JOHN WORTHING, J.P.
ALGERNON MONCRIEFF
REV. CANON CHASUBLE, D.D.
MERRIMAN, *butler*
LANE, *manservant*
LADY BRACKNELL
HON. GWENDOLEN FAIRFAX
CECILY CARDEW
MISS PRISM, *governess*
FOOTMAN

ACT ONE

(*Morning-room in* ALGERNON'S *flat in Half-Moon Street. The room is luxuriously and artistically furnished. The sound of a piano is heard in the adjoining room.*

LANE *is arranging afternoon tea on the table, and after the music has ceased,* ALGERNON *enters.*)

ALGERNON. Did you hear what I was playing, Lane?

LANE. I didn't think it polite to listen, sir.

ALGERNON. I'm sorry for that, for your sake. I don't play accurately — any one can play accurately — but I play with wonderful expression. As far as the piano is concerned, sentiment is my forte. I keep science for Life.

LANE. Yes, sir.

ALGERNON. And, speaking of the science of Life, have you got the cucumber sandwiches cut for Lady Bracknell?

LANE. Yes, sir. (*Hands them on a salver.*)

ALGERNON (*inspects them, takes two, and sits down on the sofa*). Oh! . . . by the way, Lane, I see from your book that on Thursday night, when Lord Shoreman and Mr. Worthing were dining with me, eight bottles of champagne are entered as having been consumed.

LANE. Yes, sir; eight bottles and a pint.

ALGERNON. Why is it that at a bachelor's establishment the servants invariably drink the champagne? I ask merely for information.

LANE. I attribute it to the superior quality of the wine, sir. I have often observed that in married households the champagne is rarely of a first-rate brand.

ALGERNON. Good heavens! Is marriage so demoralizing as that?

LANE. I believe it *is* a very pleasant state, sir. I have had very little experience of it myself up to the present. I have only been married once. That was in consequence of a misunderstanding between myself and a young person.

ALGERNON (*languidly*). I don't know that I am much interested in your family life, Lane.

LANE. No, sir; it is not a very interesting subject. I never think of it myself.

ALGERNON. Very natural, I am sure. That will do, Lane, thank you.

LANE. Thank you, sir. (*Goes out.*)

ALGERNON. Lane's views on marriage seem somewhat lax. Really, if the lower orders don't set us a good example, what on earth is the use of them? They seem, as a class, to have absolutely no sense of moral responsibility.

(*Enter* LANE.)

LANE. Mr. Ernest Worthing.

(*Enter* JACK. LANE *goes out.*)

ALGERNON. How are you, my dear Ernest? What brings you up to town?

JACK. Oh, pleasure, pleasure! What else should bring one anywhere? Eating as usual, I see, Algy!

ALGERNON (*stiffly*). I believe it is customary in good society to take some slight refreshment at five o'clock. Where have you been since last Thursday?

JACK (*sitting down on the sofa*). In the country.

ALGERNON. What on earth do you do there?

JACK (*pulling off his gloves*). When one is in town one amuses oneself. When one is in the country one amuses other people. It is excessively boring.

ALGERNON. And who are the people you amuse?

JACK (*airily*). Oh, neighbours, neighbours.

ALGERNON. Got nice neighbours in your part of Shropshire?

JACK. Perfectly horrid! Never speak to one of them.

ALGERNON. How immensely you must amuse them! (*Goes over and takes sandwich.*) By the way, Shropshire is your county, is it not?

JACK. Eh? Shropshire? Yes, of course. Hallo! Why all these cups? Why cucumber sandwiches? Why such reckless extravagance in one so young? Who is coming to tea?

ALGERNON. Oh! merely Aunt Augusta and Gwendolen.

JACK. How perfectly delightful!

ALGERNON. Yes, that is all very well; but I am afraid Aunt Augusta won't quite approve of your being here.

JACK. May I ask why?

ALGERNON. My dear fellow, the way you flirt with Gwendolen is perfectly disgraceful. It is almost as bad as the way Gwendolen flirts with you.

JACK. I am in love with Gwendolen. I have come up to town expressly to propose to her.

ALGERNON. I thought you had come up for pleasure? . . . I call that business.

JACK. How utterly unromantic you are!

ALGERNON. I really don't see anything romantic in proposing. It is very romantic to be in love. But there is nothing romantic about a definite proposal. Why, one may be accepted. One usually is, I believe. Then the excitement is all over. The very essence of romance is uncertainty. If ever I get married, I'll certainly try to forget the fact.

JACK. I have no doubt about that, dear Algy. The Divorce Court was specially invented for people whose memories are so curiously constituted.

ALGERNON. Oh! there is no use speculating on that subject. Divorces are made in Heaven —

(JACK *puts out his hand to take a sandwich.* ALGERNON *at once interferes.*)

Please don't touch the cucumber sandwiches. They are ordered specially for Aunt Augusta. (*Takes one and eats it.*)

JACK. Well, you have been eating them all the time.

ALGERNON. That is quite a different matter. She is my aunt. (*Takes plate from below.*) Have some bread and butter. The bread and butter is for Gwendolen. Gwendolen is devoted to bread and butter.

JACK (*advancing to table and helping himself*). And very good bread and butter it is too.

ALGERNON. Well, my dear fellow, you need not eat as if you were going to eat it all. You behave as if you were married to her already. You are not married to her already, and I don't think you ever will be.

JACK. Why on earth do you say that?

ALGERNON. Well, in the first place, girls never marry the men they flirt with. Girls don't think it right.

JACK. Oh, that is nonsense!

ALGERNON. It isn't. It is a great truth. It accounts for the extraordinary number of bachelors that one sees all over the place. In the second place, I don't give my consent.

JACK. Your consent!

ALGERNON. My dear fellow, Gwendolen is my first cousin. And before I allow you to marry her, you will have to clear up the whole question of Cecily. (*Rings bell.*)

JACK. Cecily! What on earth do you mean? What do you mean, Algy, by Cecily? I don't know any one of the name of Cecily.

(*Enter* LANE.)

ALGERNON. Bring me that cigarette case Mr. Worthing left in the smoking-room the last time he dined here.

LANE. Yes, sir. (*Goes out.*)

JACK. Do you mean to say you have had my cigarette case all this time? I wish to goodness you had let me know. I have been writing frantic letters to Scotland Yard about it. I was very nearly offering a large reward.

ALGERNON. Well, I wish you would offer one. I happen to be more than usually hard up.

JACK. There is no good offering a large reward now that the thing is found.

(*Enter* LANE *with the cigarette case on a salver.* ALGERNON *takes it at once.* LANE *goes out.*)

ALGERNON. I think that is rather mean of you, Ernest, I must say. (*Opens case and examines it.*) However, it makes no matter, for now that I look at the inscription inside, I find that the thing isn't yours after all.

JACK. Of course it's mine. (*Moving to him.*) You have seen me with it a hundred times, and you have no right whatsoever to read what is written inside. It is a very ungentlemanly thing to read a private cigarette case.

ALGERNON. Oh! it is absurd to have a hard and fast rule about what one should read and what one shouldn't. More than half of modern culture depends on what one shouldn't read.

JACK. I am quite aware of the fact, and I don't propose to discuss modern culture. It isn't the sort of thing one should talk of in private. I simply want my cigarette case back.

ALGERNON. Yes; but this isn't your cigarette case. This cigarette case is a present from someone of the name of Cecily, and you said you didn't know anyone of that name.

JACK. Well, if you want to know, Cecily happens to be my aunt.

ALGERNON. Your aunt!

JACK. Yes. Charming old lady she is, too. Lives at Tunbridge Wells. Just give it back to me, Algy.

ALGERNON (*retreating to back of sofa*). But why does she call herself little Cecily if she is your aunt and lives at Tunbridge Wells. (*Reading.*) "From little Cecily with her fondest love."

JACK (*moving to sofa and kneeling upon it*). My dear fellow, what on earth is there in that? Some aunts are tall, some aunts are not tall. That is a matter that surely an aunt may be allowed to decide for herself. You seem to think that every aunt should be exactly like your aunt! That is absurd. For Heaven's sake give me back my cigarette case. (*Follows* ALGERNON *round the room.*)

ALGERNON. Yes. But why does your aunt call you her uncle? "From little Cecily, with her fondest love to her dear Uncle Jack." There is no objection. I admit, to an aunt being a small aunt, but why an aunt, no matter what her size may be, should call her own nephew her uncle, I can't quite make out. Beside, your name isn't Jack at all; it is Ernest.

JACK. It isn't Ernest; it's Jack.

ALGERNON. You have always told me it was Ernest. I have introduced you to everyone as Ernest. You answer to the name of Ernest. You look as if your name was Ernest. You are the most earnest-looking person I ever saw in my life. It is perfectly absurd your saying that your name isn't Ernest. It's on your cards. Here is one of them (*taking it from case*). "Mr. Ernest Worthing, B.4, The Albany." I'll keep this as a proof that your name is Ernest if ever you attempt to deny it to me, or to Gwendolen, or to any one else. (*Puts the card in his pocket.*)

JACK. Well, my name is Ernest in town and Jack in the country, and the cigarette case was given to me in the country.

ALGERNON. Yes, but that does not account for the fact that your small Aunt Cecily, who lives at Tunbridge Wells, calls you her dear uncle. Come, old boy, you had much better have the thing out at once.

JACK. My dear Algy, you talk exactly as if you were a dentist. It is very vulgar to talk like a dentist when one isn't a dentist. It produces a false impression.

ALGERNON. Well, that is exactly what dentists always do. Now, go on! Tell me the whole thing. I may mention that I have always suspected you of being a confirmed and secret Bunburyist, and I am quite sure of it now.

JACK. Bunburyist? What on earth do you mean by a Bunburyist?

ALGERNON. I'll reveal to you the meaning of that incomparable expression as soon as you are kind enough to inform me why you are Ernest in town and Jack in the country.

JACK. Well, produce my cigarette case first.

ALGERNON. Here it is. (*Hands cigarette case.*) Now produce your explanation, and pray make it improbable. (*Sits on sofa.*)

JACK. My dear fellow, there is nothing improbable about my explanation at all. In fact it's perfectly ordinary. Old Mr. Thomas Cardew, who adopted me when I was a little boy, made me in his will guardian to his granddaughter, Miss Cecily Cardew. Cecily, who addresses me as her uncle from motives of respect that you could not possibly appreciate, lives at my place in the country under the charge of her admirable governess, Miss Prism.

ALGERNON. Where is that place in the country, by the way?

JACK. That is nothing to you, dear boy. You are not going to be invited.... I may tell you candidly that the place is not in Shropshire.

ALGERNON. I suspected that, my dear fellow! I have Bunburyed all over Shropshire on two separate occasions. Now, go on. Why are you Ernest in town and Jack in the country?

JACK. My dear Algy, I don't know whether you will be able to understand my real motives. You are hardly serious enough. When one is placed in the position of guardian, one has to adopt a very high moral tone on all subjects. It's one's duty to do so. And as a high moral tone can hardly be said to conduce very much to either one's health or one's happiness, in order to get up to town I have always pretended to have a younger brother of the name of Ernest, who lives in the Albany, and gets into the most dreadful scrapes. That, my dear Algy, is the whole truth pure and simple.

ALGERNON. The truth is rarely pure and never simple. Modern life would be very tedious if it were either, and modern literature a complete impossibility!

JACK. That wouldn't be at all a bad thing.

ALGERNON. Literary criticism is not your forte, my dear fellow. Don't try it. You should leave that to people who haven't been at a University. They do it so well in the daily papers. What you really are is a Bunburyist. I was quite right in saying you were a Bunburyist. You are one of the most advanced Bunburyists I know.

JACK. What on earth do you mean?

ALGERNON. You have invented a very useful young brother called Ernest, in order that you may be able to come up to town as often as you like. I have invented an invaluable permanent invalid called Bunbury, in order that I may be able to go down into the country whenever I choose. Bunbury is perfectly invaluable. If it wasn't for Bunbury's extraordinary bad health, for instance, I wouldn't be able to dine with you at Willis's tonight, for I have been really engaged to Aunt Augusta for more than a week.

JACK. I haven't asked you to dine with me anywhere tonight.

ALGERNON. I know. You are absurdly careless about sending out invitations. It is very foolish of you. Nothing annoys people so much as not receiving invitations.

JACK. You had much better dine with your Aunt Augusta.

ALGERNON. I haven't the smallest intention of doing anything of the kind. To begin with, I dined there on Monday, and once a week is quite enough to dine with one's own relations. In the second place, whenever I do dine there I am always treated as a member of the family, and sent down with either no woman at all, or two. In the third place, I know perfectly well whom she will place me next to, tonight. She will place me next to Mary Farquhar, who always flirts with her own husband across the dinner table. That is not very pleasant. Indeed, it is not even decent . . . and that sort of thing is enormously on the increase. The amount of women in London who flirt with their own husbands is perfectly scandalous. It looks so bad. It is simply washing one's clean linen in public.

Besides, now that I know you to be a confirmed Bunburyist I naturally want to talk to you about Bunburying. I want to tell you the rules.

JACK. I'm not a Bunburyist at all. If Gwendolen accepts me, I am going to kill my brother, indeed I think I'll kill him in any case. Cecily is a little too much interested in him. It is rather a bore. So I am going to get rid of Ernest. And I strongly advise you to do the same with Mr. . . . with your invalid friend who has the absurd name.

ALGERNON. Nothing will induce me to part with Bunbury, and if you ever get married, which seems to me extremely problematic, you will be very glad to know Bunbury. A man who marries without knowing Bunbury has a very tedious time of it.

JACK. That is nonsense. If I marry a charming girl like Gwendolen, and she is the only girl I ever saw in my life that I would marry, I certainly won't want to know Bunbury.

ALGERNON. Then your wife will. You don't seem to realize, that in married life three is company and two is none.

JACK (*sententiously*). That, my dear young friend, is the theory that the corrupt French Drama has been propounding for the last fifty years.

ALGERNON. Yes! and that the happy English home has proved in half the time.

JACK. For heaven's sake, don't try to be cynical. It's perfectly easy to be cynical.

ALGERNON. My dear fellow, it isn't easy to be anything nowadays. There's such a lot of beastly competition about.

(*The sound of an electric bell is heard.*)

Ah! that must be Aunt Augusta. Only relatives, or creditors, ever ring in that Wagnerian manner. Now, if I get her out of the way for ten minutes, so that you can have an opportunity for proposing to Gwendolen, may I dine with you tonight at Willis's?

JACK. I suppose so, if you want to.

ALGERNON. Yes, but you must be serious about it. I hate people who are not serious about meals. It is so shallow of them.

(*Enter* LANE.)

LANE. Lady Bracknell and Miss Fairfax.

(ALGERNON *goes forward to meet them. Enter* LADY BRACKNELL *and* GWENDOLEN.)

LADY BRACKNELL. Good afternoon, dear Algernon, I hope you are behaving very well.

ALGERNON. I'm feeling very well, Aunt Augusta.

LADY BRACKNELL. That's not quite the same thing. In fact the two things rarely go together. (*Sees* JACK *and bows to him with icy coldness.*)

ALGERNON (*to* GWENDOLEN). Dear me, you are smart!

GWENDOLEN. I am always smart! Am I not, Mr. Worthing?

JACK. You're quite perfect, Miss Fairfax.

GWENDOLEN. Oh! I hope I am not that. It would leave no room for developments, and I intend to develop in many directions.

(GWENDOLEN *and* JACK *sit down together in the corner.*)

LADY BRACKNELL. I'm sorry if we are a little late, Algernon, but I was obliged to call on dear Lady Harbury. I hadn't been there since her poor husband's death. I never saw a woman so altered; she looks quite twenty years younger. And now I'll have a cup of tea and one of those nice cucumber sandwiches you promised me.

ALGERNON. Certainly, Aunt Augusta. (*Goes over to tea-table.*)

LADY BRACKNELL. Won't you come and sit here, Gwendolen?

GWENDOLEN. Thanks, mamma, I'm quite comfortable where I am.

ALGERNON (*picking up empty plate in horror*). Good heavens! Lane! Why are there no cucumber sandwiches? I ordered them specially.

LANE (*gravely*). There were no cucumbers in the market this morning, sir. I went down twice.

ALGERNON. No cucumbers!

LANE. No, sir. Not even for ready money.

ALGERNON. That will do, Lane, thank you.

LANE. Thank you, sir. (*Goes out.*)

ALGERNON. I am greatly distressed, Aunt Augusta, about there being no cucumbers, not even for ready money.

LADY BRACKNELL. It really makes no matter, Algernon. I had some crumpets with Lady Harbury, who seems to me to be living entirely for pleasure now.

ALGERNON. I hear her hair has turned quite gold from grief.

LADY BRACKNELL. It certainly has changed its colour. From what cause I, of course, cannot say.

(ALGERNON *crosses and hands tea.*)

Thank you. I've quite a treat for you tonight, Algernon. I am going to send you down with Mary Farquhar. She is such a nice woman, and so attentive to her husband. It's delightful to watch them.

ALGERNON. I am afraid, Aunt Augusta, I shall have to give up the pleasure of dining with you tonight after all.

LADY BRACKNELL (*frowning*). I hope not, Algernon. It would put my table completely out. Your uncle would have to dine upstairs. Fortunately he is accustomed to that.

ALGERNON. It is a great bore, and, I need hardly say, a terrible disappointment to me, but the fact is I have just had a telegram to say that my poor friend Bunbury is very ill again. (*Exchanges glances with* JACK.) They seem to think I should be with him.

LADY BRACKNELL. It is very strange. This Mr. Bunbury seems to suffer from curiously bad health.

ALGERNON. Yes; poor Bunbury is a dreadful invalid.

LADY BRACKNELL. Well, I must say, Algernon, that I think it is high time that Mr. Bunbury made up his mind whether he was going to live or to die. This shilly-shallying with the question is absurd. Nor do I in any way approve of the modern sympathy with invalids. I consider it morbid. Illness of any kind is hardly a thing to be encouraged in others. Health is the primary duty of life. I am always telling that to your poor uncle, but he never seems to take much notice . . . as far as any improvement in his ailments goes. I should be much obliged if you would ask Mr. Bunbury, from me, to be kind enough not to have a relapse on Saturday, for I rely on you to arrange my music for me. It is my last reception, and one wants something that will encourage conversation, particularly at the end of the season when every one has practically said whatever they had to say, which, in most cases, was probably not much.

ALGERNON. I'll speak to Bunbury, Aunt Augusta, if he is still conscious, and I think I can promise you he'll be all right by Saturday. Of course the music is a great difficulty. You see, if one plays good music, people don't listen, and if one plays bad music, people don't talk. But I'll run over the programme I've drawn out, if you will kindly come into the next room for a moment.

LADY BRACKNELL. Thank you, Algernon. It is very thoughtful of you. (*Rising, and following* ALGERNON.) I'm sure the programme will be delightful, after a few expurgations. French songs I cannot possibly allow. People always seem to think that they are improper, and either look shocked, which is vulgar, or laugh, which is worse. But German sounds a thoroughly respectable language, and, indeed I believe is so. Gwendolen, you will accompany me.

GWENDOLEN. Certainly, mamma.

(LADY BRACKNELL *and* ALGERNON *go into the music-room;* GWENDOLEN *remains behind.*)

JACK. Charming day it has been, Miss Fairfax.

GWENDOLEN. Pray don't talk to me about the weather, Mr. Worthing. Whenever people talk to me about the weather, I always feel quite certain that they mean something else. And that makes me so nervous.

JACK. I do mean something else.

GWENDOLEN. I thought so. In fact, I am never wrong.

JACK. And I would like to be allowed to take advantage of Lady Bracknell's temporary absence . . .

GWENDOLEN. I would certainly advise you to do so. Mamma has a way of coming back suddenly into a room that I have often had to speak to her about.

JACK (*nervously*). Miss Fairfax, ever since I met you I have admired you more than any girl . . . I have ever met since . . . I met you.

GWENDOLEN. Yes, I am quite aware of the fact. And I often wish that in public, at any rate, you had been more demonstrative. For me you have always had an irresistible fascination. Even before I met you I was far from indifferent to you.

(JACK *looks at her in amazement.*)

We live, as I hope you know, Mr. Worthing, in an age of ideals. The fact is constantly mentioned in the more expensive monthly magazines, and has reached the provincial pulpits, I am told; and my ideal has always been to love some one of the name of Ernest. There is something in that name that inspires absolute confidence. The moment Algernon first mentioned to me that he had a friend called Ernest, I knew I was destined to love you.

JACK. You really love me, Gwendolen?

GWENDOLEN. Passionately!

JACK. Darling! You don't know how happy you've made me.

GWENDOLEN. My own Ernest!

JACK. But you don't really mean to say that you couldn't love me if my name wasn't Ernest?

GWENDOLEN. But your name is Ernest.

JACK. Yes, I know it is. But supposing it was something else? Do you mean to say you couldn't love me then?

GWENDOLEN (*glibly*). Ah! that is clearly a metaphysical speculation, and like most metaphysical speculations has very little reference at all to the actual facts of real life, as we know them.

JACK. Personally, darling, to speak quite candidly, I don't much care about the name of Ernest. . . . I don't think the name suits me at all.

GWENDOLEN. It suits you perfectly. It is a divine name. It has a music of its own. It produces vibrations.

JACK. Well, really, Gwendolen, I must say that I think there are lots of other much nicer names. I think Jack, for instance, a charming name.

GWENDOLEN. Jack? . . . No, there is very little music in the name Jack, if any at all, indeed. It does not thrill. It produces absolutely no vibrations. . . . I have known several Jacks, and they all, without exception, were more than usually plain. Besides, Jack is a notorious domesticity for John! And I pity any woman who is married to a man called John. She would probably never be allowed to know the entrancing pleasure of a single moment's solitude. The only really safe name is Ernest.

JACK. Gwendolen, I must get christened at once — I mean we must get married at once. There is no time to be lost.

GWENDOLEN. Married, Mr. Worthing?

JACK (*astounded*). Well . . . surely. You know that I love you, and you led me to believe, Miss Fairfax, that you were not absolutely indifferent to me.

GWENDOLEN. I adore you. But you haven't proposed to me yet. Nothing has been said at all about marriage. The subject has not even been touched on.

JACK. Well . . . may I propose to you now?

GWENDOLEN. I think it would be an admirable opportunity. And to spare you any possible disappointment, Mr. Worthing, I think it only fair to tell you quite frankly beforehand that I am fully determined to accept you.

JACK. Gwendolen!

GWENDOLEN. Yes, Mr. Worthing, what have you got to say to me?

JACK. You know what I have got to say to you.

GWENDOLEN. Yes, but you don't say it.

JACK. Gwendolen, will you marry me? (*Goes on his knees.*)

GWENDOLEN. Of course I will, darling. How long you have been about it! I am afraid you have had very little experience in how to propose.

JACK. My own one, I have never loved any one in the world but you.

GWENDOLEN. Yes, but men often propose for practice. I know my brother Gerald does. All my girl-friends tell me so. What wonderfully blue eyes you have, Ernest! They are quite, quite blue. I hope you will always look at me just like that, especially when there are other people present.

(*Enter* LADY BRACKNELL.)

LADY BRACKNELL. Mr. Worthing! Rise, sir, from this semi-recumbent posture. It is most indecorous.

GWENDOLEN. Mamma! (*He tries to rise; she restrains him.*) I must beg you to retire. This is no place for you. Besides, Mr. Worthing has not quite finished yet.

LADY BRACKNELL. Finished what, may I ask?

GWENDOLEN. I am engaged to Mr. Worthing, mamma.

(*They rise together.*)

LADY BRACKNELL. Pardon me, you are not engaged to anyone. When you do become engaged to some one, I, or your father, should his health permit him, will inform you of the fact. An engagement should come on a young girl as a surprise, pleasant or unpleasant, as the case may be. It is hardly a matter that she could be allowed to arrange for herself. . . . And now I have a few questions to put to you, Mr. Worthing. While I am making these inquiries, you, Gwendolen, will wait for me below in the carriage.

GWENDOLEN (*reproachfully*). Mamma!

LADY BRACKNELL. In the carriage, Gwendolen!

(GWENDOLEN *goes to the door. She and* JACK *blow kisses to each other behind* LADY BRACKNELL'*s back.* LADY BRACKNELL *looks vaguely about as if she could not understand what the noise was. Finally turns around.*)

Gwendolen, the carriage!

GWENDOLEN. Yes, mamma. (*Goes out, looking back at* JACK.)

LADY BRACKNELL (*sitting down*). You can take a seat, Mr. Worthing. (*Looks in her pocket for notebook and pencil.*)

JACK. Thank you, Lady Bracknell, I prefer standing.

LADY BRACKNELL (*pencil and notebook in hand*). I feel bound to tell you that you are not down on my list of eligible young men, although I have the same list as the dear Duchess of Bolton has. We work together, in fact. However, I am quite ready to enter your name, should your answers be what a really affectionate mother requires. Do you smoke?

JACK. Well, yes, I must admit I smoke.

LADY BRACKNELL. I am glad to hear it. A man should always have an occupation of some kind. There are far too many idle men in London as it is. How old are you?

JACK. Twenty-nine.

LADY BRACKNELL. A very good age to be married at. I have always been of the opinion that a man who desires to get married should know either everything or nothing. Which do you know?

JACK (*after some hesitation*). I know nothing, Lady Bracknell.

LADY BRACKNELL. I am pleased to hear it. I do not approve of anything that tampers with natural ignorance. Ignorance is like a delicate exotic fruit; touch it and the bloom is gone. The whole theory of modern education is radically unsound. Fortunately in England, at any rate, education produces no effect whatsoever. If it did, it would prove a serious danger to the upper classes, and probably lead to acts of violence in Grosvenor Square. What is your income?

JACK. Between seven and eight thousand a year.

LADY BRACKNELL (*makes a note in her book*). In land, or in investments?

JACK. In investments, chiefly.

LADY BRACKNELL. That is satisfactory. What between the duties expected of one during one's lifetime, and the duties exacted from one after one's death, land has ceased to be either a profit or a pleasure. It gives one position, and prevents one from keeping it up. That's all that can be said about land.

JACK. I have a country house with some land, of course, attached to it, about fifteen hundred acres, I believe; but I don't depend on that for my real income. In fact, as far as I can make out, the poachers are the only people who make anything out of it.

LADY BRACKNELL. A country house! How many bedrooms? Well, that point can be cleared up afterwards. You have a town house, I hope? A girl with a simple, unspoiled nature, like Gwendolen, could hardly be expected to reside in the country.

JACK. Well, I own a house in Belgrave Square, but it is let by the year to Lady Bloxham. Of course, I can get it back whenever I like, at six months' notice.

LADY BRACKNELL. Lady Bloxham? I don't know her.

JACK. Oh, she goes about very little. She is a lady considerably advanced in years.

LADY BRACKNELL. Ah, nowadays that is no guarantee of respectability of character. What number in Belgrave Square?

JACK. 149.

LADY BRACKNELL (*shaking her head*). The unfashionable side. I thought there was something. However, that could easily be altered.

JACK. Do you mean the fashion, or the side?

LADY BRACKNELL (*sternly*). Both, if necessary, I presume. What are your politics?

JACK. Well, I am afraid I really have none. I am a Liberal Unionist.

LADY BRACKNELL. Oh, they count as Tories. They dine with us. Or come in the evening, at any rate. Now to minor matters. Are your parents living?

JACK. I have lost both my parents.

LADY BRACKNELL. To lose one parent, Mr. Worthing, may be regarded as a misfortune; to lose both looks like carelessness. Who was your father? He was evidently a man of some wealth. Was he born in what the Radical papers call the purple of commerce, or did he rise from the ranks of the aristocracy?

JACK. I am afraid I really don't know. The fact is, Lady Bracknell, I said I had lost my parents. It would be nearer the truth to say that my parents seem to have lost me. . . . I don't actually know who I am by birth. I was . . . well, I was found.

LADY BRACKNELL. Found!

JACK. The late Mr. Thomas Cardew, an old gentleman of a very charitable and kindly disposition, found me, and gave me the name of Worthing, because he happened to have a first-class ticket for Worthing in his pocket at the time. Worthing is a place in Sussex. It is a seaside resort.

LADY BRACKNELL. Where did the charitable gentleman who had a first-class ticket for this seaside resort find you?

JACK (*gravely*). In a handbag.

LADY BRACKNELL. A handbag?

JACK (*very seriously*). Yes, Lady Bracknell. I was in a handbag — a somewhat large, black leather handbag, with handles to it — an ordinary handbag in fact.

LADY BRACKNELL. In what locality did this Mr. James, or Thomas, Cardew come across this ordinary handbag?

JACK. In the cloakroom at Victoria Station. It was given to him in mistake for his own.

LADY BRACKNELL. The cloakroom at Victoria Station?

JACK. Yes. The Brighton line.

LADY BRACKNELL. The line is immaterial. Mr. Worthing, I confess I feel somewhat bewildered by what you have just told me. To be born, or at any rate bred, in a handbag, whether it had handles or not, seems to me to display a contempt for the ordinary decencies of family life that reminds one of the worst excesses of the French Revolution. And I presume you know what that unfortunate movement led to? As for the particular locality in which the handbag was found, a cloakroom at a railway station might serve to conceal a social indiscretion — has probably, indeed, been used for that purpose before now — but it could hardly be regarded as an assured basis for a recognized position in good society.

JACK. May I ask you then what you would advise me to do? I need hardly say I would do anything in the world to ensure Gwendolen's happiness.

LADY BRACKNELL. I would strongly advise you, Mr. Worthing, to try and acquire some relations as soon as possible, and to make a definite effort to produce at any rate one parent, of either sex, before the season is quite over.

JACK. Well, I don't see how I could possibly manage to do that. I can produce the handbag at any moment. It is in my dressing-room at home. I really think that should satisfy you, Lady Bracknell.

LADY BRACKNELL. Me, sir! What has it to do with me? You can hardly imagine that I and Lord Bracknell would dream of allowing our only daughter — a girl brought up with the utmost care — to marry into a cloakroom, and form an alliance with a parcel. Good morning, Mr. Worthing!

(LADY BRACKNELL *sweeps out in majestic indignation.*)

JACK. Good morning!

(ALGERNON, *from the other room, strikes up the* Wedding March. JACK *looks perfectly furious, and goes to the door.*)

For goodness' sake don't play that ghastly tune, Algy! How idiotic you are!

(*The music stops and* ALGERNON *enters cheerily.*)

ALGERNON. Didn't it go off all right, old boy? You don't mean to say Gwendolen refused you? I know it is a way she has. She is always refusing people. I think it is most ill-natured of her.

JACK. Oh, Gwendolen is as right as a trivet. As far as she is concerned, we are engaged. Her mother is perfectly unbearable. Never met such a Gorgon. . . . I don't really know what a Gorgon is like, but I am quite sure that Lady Bracknell is one. In any case, she is a monster, without being a myth, which is rather unfair. . . . I beg your pardon, Algy, I suppose I shouldn't talk about your own aunt in that way before you.

ALGERNON. My dear boy, I love hearing my relations abused. It is the only thing that makes me put up with them at all. Relations are simply a tedious pack of people, who haven't got the remotest knowledge of how to live, nor the smallest instinct about when to die.

JACK. Oh, that is nonsense!

ALGERNON. It isn't!

JACK. Well, I won't argue about the matter. You always want to argue about things.

ALGERNON. That is exactly what things were originally made for.

JACK. Upon my word, if I thought that, I'd shoot myself. . . . (*A pause.*) You don't think there is any chance of Gwendolen becoming like her mother in about a hundred and fifty years, do you, Algy?

ALGERNON. All women become like their mothers. That is their tragedy. No man does. That's his.

JACK. Is that clever?

ALGERNON. It is perfectly phrased! and quite as true as any observation in civilized life should be.

JACK. I am sick to death of cleverness. Everybody is clever nowadays. You can't go anywhere without meeting clever people. The thing has become an absolute public nuisance. I wish to goodness we had a few fools left.

ALGERNON. We have.

JACK. I should extremely like to meet them. What do they talk about?

ALGERNON. The fools? Oh! about the clever people, of course.

JACK. What fools.

ALGERNON. By the way, did you tell Gwendolen the truth about your being Ernest in town, and Jack in the country?

JACK (*in a very patronizing manner*). My dear fellow, the truth isn't quite the sort of thing one tells to a nice, sweet, refined girl. What extraordinary ideas you have about the way to behave to a woman!

ALGERNON. The only way to behave to a woman is to make love to her, if she is pretty, and to someone else, if she is plain.

JACK. Oh, that is nonsense.

ALGERNON. What about your brother? What about the profligate Ernest?

JACK. Oh, before the end of the week I shall have got rid of him. I'll say he died in Paris of apoplexy. Lots of people die of apoplexy, quite suddenly, don't they?

ALGERNON. Yes, but it's hereditary, my dear fellow. It's a sort of thing that runs in families. You had much better say a severe chill.

JACK. You are sure a severe chill isn't hereditary, or anything of that kind?

ALGERNON. Of course it isn't!

JACK. Very well, then. My poor brother Ernest is carried off suddenly, in Paris, by a severe chill. That gets rid of him.

ALGERNON. But I thought you said that . . . Miss Cardew was a little too much interested in your poor brother Ernest? Won't she feel his loss a good deal?

JACK. Oh, that is all right. Cecily is not a silly romantic girl, I am glad to say. She has got a capital appetite, goes on long walks, and pays no attention at all to her lessons.

ALGERNON. I would rather like to see Cecily.

JACK. I will take very good care you never do. She is excessively pretty, and she is only just eighteen.

ALGERNON. Have you told Gwendolen yet that you have an excessively pretty ward who is only just eighteen?

JACK. Oh! one doesn't blurt these things out to people. Cecily and Gwendolen are perfectly certain to be extremely great friends. I'll bet you anything you like that half an hour after they have met, they will be calling each other sister.

ALGERNON. Women only do that when they have called each other a lot of other things first. Now, my dear boy, if we want to get a good table at Willis's, we really must go and dress. Do you know it is nearly seven?

JACK (*irritably*). Oh! it always is nearly seven.

ALGERNON. Well, I'm hungry.

JACK. I never knew you when you weren't. . . .

ALGERNON. What shall we do after dinner? Go to a theatre?

JACK. Oh no! I loathe listening.

ALGERNON. Well, let us go to the Club?

JACK. Oh, no! I hate talking.

ALGERNON. Well, we might trot round to the Empire at ten?

JACK. Oh, no! I can't bear looking at things. It is so silly.

ALGERNON. Well, what shall we do?

JACK. Nothing!

ALGERNON. It is awfully hard work doing nothing. However, I don't mind hard work where there is no definite object of any kind.

(*Enter* LANE.)

LANE. Miss Fairfax.

(*Enter* GWENDOLEN. LANE *goes out.*)

ALGERNON. Gwendolen, upon my word!

GWENDOLEN. Algy, kindly turn your back. I have something very particular to say to Mr. Worthing.

ALGERNON. Really, Gwendolen, I don't think I can allow this at all.

GWENDOLEN. Algy, you always adopt a strictly immoral attitude towards life. You are not quite old enough to do that.

(ALGERNON *retires to the fireplace.*)

JACK. My own darling!

GWENDOLEN. Ernest, we may never be married. From the expression on mamma's face I fear we never shall. Few parents nowadays pay any regard to what their children say to them. The old-fashioned respect for the young is fast dying out. Whatever influence I ever had over mamma,

I lost at the age of three. But although she may prevent us from becoming man and wife, and I may marry someone else, and marry often, nothing that she can possibly do can alter my eternal devotion to you.

JACK. Dear Gwendolen!

GWENDOLEN. The story of your romantic origin, as related to me by mamma, with unpleasing comments, has naturally stirred the deeper fibres of my nature. Your Christian name has an irresistible fascination. The simplicity of your character makes you exquisitely incomprehensible to me. Your town address at the Albany I have. What is your address in the country?

JACK. The Manor House, Woolton, Hertfordshire.

(ALGERNON, *who has been carefully listening, smiles to himself, and writes the address on his shirt-cuff. Then picks up the Railway Guide.*)

GWENDOLEN. There is a good postal service, I suppose? It may be necessary to do something desperate. That of course will require serious consideration. I will communicate with you daily.

JACK. My own one!

GWENDOLEN. How long do you remain in town?

JACK. Till Monday.

GWENDOLEN. Good! Algy, you may turn round now.

ALGERNON. Thanks, I've turned round already.

GWENDOLEN. You may also ring the bell.

JACK. You will let me see you to your carriage, my own darling?

GWENDOLEN. Certainly.

JACK (*to* LANE, *who now enters*). I will see Miss Fairfax out.

LANE. Yes, sir.

(JACK *and* GWENDOLEN *go off.* LANE *presents several letters on a salver to* ALGERNON. *It is to be surmised that they are bills, as* ALGERNON, *after looking at the envelopes, tears them up.*)

ALGERNON. A glass of sherry, Lane.

LANE. Yes, sir.

ALGERNON. Tomorrow, Lane, I'm going Bunburying.

LANE. Yes, sir.

ALGERNON. I shall probably not be back till Monday. You can put up my dress clothes, my smoking jacket, and all the Bunbury suits . . .

LANE. Yes, sir. (*Handing sherry.*)

ALGERNON. I hope tomorrow will be a fine day, Lane.

LANE. It never is, sir.

ALGERNON. Lane, you're a perfect pessimist.

LANE. I do my best to give satisfaction, sir.

(*Enter* JACK. LANE *goes off.*)

JACK. There's a sensible, intellectual girl; the only girl I ever cared for in my life.

(ALGERNON *is laughing immoderately.*)

What on earth are you so amused at?

ALGERNON. Oh, I'm a little anxious about poor Bunbury, that is all.

JACK. If you don't take care, your friend Bunbury will get you into a serious scrape some day.

ALGERNON. I love scrapes. They are the only things that are never serious.

JACK. Oh, that's nonsense, Algy. You never talk anything but nonsense.

ALGERNON. Nobody ever does.

(JACK *looks indignantly at him, and leaves the room.* ALGERNON *lights a cigarette, reads his shirt-cuff, and smiles.*)

ACT TWO

(*Garden at the Manor House. A flight of grey stone steps leads up to the house. The garden, an old-fashioned one, full of roses. Time of year, July. Basket chairs, and a table covered with books, are set under a large yew-tree.*

MISS PRISM *discovered seated at the table.* CECILY *is at the back, watering flowers.*)

MISS PRISM (*calling*). Cecily, Cecily! Surely such a utilitarian occupation as the watering of flowers is rather Moulton's duty than yours? Especially at a moment when intellectual pleasures await you. Your German grammar is on the table. Pray open it at page fifteen. We will repeat yesterday's lesson.

CECILY (*coming over very slowly*). But I don't like German. It isn't at all a becoming language. I know perfectly well that I look quite plain after my German lesson.

MISS PRISM. Child, you know how anxious your guardian is that you should improve yourself in every way. He laid particular stress on your German, as he was leaving for town yesterday. Indeed, he always lays stress on your German when he is leaving for town.

CECILY. Dear Uncle Jack is so very serious! Sometimes he is so serious that I think he cannot be quite well.

MISS PRISM (*drawing herself up*). Your guardian enjoys the best of health, and his gravity of demeanor is especially to be commended in one so comparatively young as he is. I know no one who has a higher sense of duty and responsibility.

CECILY. I suppose that is why he often looks a little bored when we three are together.

MISS PRISM. Cecily! I am surprised at you. Mr. Worthing has many troubles in his life. Idle merriment and triviality would be out of place in his conversation. You must remember his constant anxiety about that unfortunate young man, his brother.

CECILY. I wish Uncle Jack would allow that unfortunate young man, his brother, to come down here sometimes. We might have a good influence over him, Miss Prism. I am sure you certainly would. You know German, and geology, and things of that kind influence a man very much. (CECILY *begins to write in her diary.*)

MISS PRISM (*shaking her head*). I do not think that even I could produce any effect on a character that according to his own brother's admission is irretrievably weak and vacillating. Indeed I am not sure that I would desire to reclaim him. I am not in favor of this modern mania for turning bad people into good people at a moment's notice. As a man sows so let him reap. You must put away your diary, Cecily. I really don't see why you should keep a diary at all.

CECILY. I keep a diary in order to enter the wonderful secrets of my life. If I didn't write them down, I should probably forget all about them.

MISS PRISM. Memory, my dear Cecily, is the diary that we all carry about with us.

CECILY. Yes, but it usually chronicles the things that have never happened, and couldn't possibly have happened. I believe that Memory is responsible for nearly all the three-volume novels that Mudie sends us.

MISS PRISM. Do not speak slightingly of the three-volume novel, Cecily. I wrote one myself in earlier days.

CECILY. Did you really, Miss Prism? How wonderfully clever you are! I hope it did not end happily! I don't like novels that end happily. They depress me so much.

MISS PRISM. The good ended happily, and the bad unhappily. That is what Fiction means.

CECILY. I suppose so. But it seems very unfair. And was your novel ever published?

MISS PRISM. Alas! no. The manuscript unfortunately was abandoned.

(CECILY *starts.*)

I used the word in the sense of lost or mislaid. To your work, child, these speculations are profitless.

CECILY (*smiling*). But I see dear Dr. Chasuble coming up through the garden.

MISS PRISM (*rising and advancing*). Dr. Chasuble! This is indeed a pleasure.

(*Enter* CANON CHASUBLE.)

CHASUBLE. And how are we this morning? Miss Prism, you are, I trust, well?

CECILY. Miss Prism has just been complaining of a slight headache. I think it would do her so much good to have a short stroll with you in the Park, Dr. Chasuble.

MISS PRISM. Cecily, I have not mentioned anything about a headache.

CECILY. No, dear Miss Prism, I know that, but I felt instinctively that you had a headache. Indeed I was thinking about that, and not about my German lesson, when the Rector came in.

CHASUBLE. I hope, Cecily, you are not inattentive.

CECILY. Oh, I am afraid I am.

CHASUBLE. That is strange. Were I fortunate enough to be Miss Prism's pupil, I would hang upon her lips.

(MISS PRISM *glares.*)

I spoke metaphorically.—My metaphor was drawn from bees. Ahem! Mr. Worthing, I suppose, has not returned from town yet?

MISS PRISM. We do not expect him till Monday afternoon.

CHASUBLE. Ah yes, he usually likes to spend his Sunday in London. He is not one of those whose sole aim is enjoyment, as, by all accounts, that unfortunate young man his brother seems to be. But I must not disturb Egeria and her pupil any longer.

MISS PRISM. Egeria? My name is Laetitia, Doctor.

CHASUBLE (*bowing*). A classical allusion merely, drawn from the Pagan authors. I shall see you both no doubt at Evensong?

MISS PRISM. I think, dear Doctor, I will have a stroll with you. I find I have a headache after all, and a walk might do it good.

CHASUBLE. With pleasure, Miss Prism, with pleasure. We might go as far as the schools and back.

MISS PRISM. That would be delightful. Cecily, you will read your Political Economy in my absence. The chapter on the Fall of the Rupee you may omit. It is somewhat too sensational. Even these metallic problems have their melodramatic side. (*Goes down the garden with* DR. CHASUBLE.)

CECILY (*picks up books and throws them back on table*). Horrid Political Economy! Horrid Geography! Horrid, horrid German!

(*Enter* MERRIMAN *with a card on a salver.*)

MERRIMAN. Mr. Ernest Worthing has just driven over from the station. He has brought his luggage with him.

CECILY (*takes the card and reads it*). "Mr. Ernest Worthing, B.4, The Albany, W." Uncle Jack's brother! Did you tell him Mr. Worthing was in town?

MERRIMAN. Yes, Miss. He seemed very much disappointed. I mentioned that you and Miss Prism were in the garden. He said he was anxious to speak to you privately for a moment.

CECILY. Ask Mr. Ernest Worthing to come here. I suppose you had better talk to the housekeeper about a room for him.

MERRIMAN. Yes, Miss. (*Goes off.*)

CECILY. I have never met any really wicked person before. I feel rather frightened. I am so afraid he will look just like every one else.

(*Enter* ALGERNON, *very gay and debonnaire.*)

He does!

ALGERNON (*raising his hat*). You are my little cousin Cecily, I'm sure.

CECILY. You are under some strange mistake. I am not little. In fact, I believe I am more than usually tall for my age.

(ALGERNON *is rather taken aback.*)

But I am your cousin Cecily. You, I see from your card, are Uncle Jack's brother, my cousin Ernest, my wicked cousin Ernest.

ALGERNON. Oh! I am not really wicked at all, Cousin Cecily. You mustn't think that I am wicked.

CECILY. If you are not, then you have certainly been deceiving us all in a very inexcusable manner. I hope you have not been leading a double life, pretending to be wicked and being really good all the time. That would be hypocrisy.

ALGERNON (*looks at her in amazement*). Oh! Of course I have been rather reckless.

CECILY. I am glad to hear it.

ALGERNON. In fact, now you mention the subject, I have been very bad in my own small way.

CECILY. I don't think you should be so proud of that, though I am sure it must have been very pleasant.

ALGERNON. It is much pleasanter being here with you.

CECILY. I can't understand how you are here at all. Uncle Jack won't be back till Monday afternoon.

ALGERNON. That is a great disappointment. I am obliged to go up by the first train on Monday morning. I have a business appointment that I am anxious . . . to miss!

CECILY. Couldn't you miss it anywhere but in London?

ALGERNON. No: the appointment is in London.

CECILY. Well, I know, of course, how important it is not to keep a business engagement, if one wants to retain any sense of the beauty of life, but still I think you had better wait till Uncle Jack arrives. I know he wants to speak to you about your emigrating.

ALGERNON. About my what?

CECILY. Your emigrating. He has gone up to buy your outfit.

ALGERNON. I certainly wouldn't let Jack buy my outfit. He has no taste in neckties at all.

CECILY. I don't think you will require neckties. Uncle Jack is sending you to Australia.

ALGERNON. Australia! I'd sooner die.

CECILY. Well, he said at dinner on Wednesday night, that you would have to choose between this world, the next world, and Australia.

ALGERNON. Oh, well! The accounts I have received of Australia and the next world are not particularly encouraging. This world is good enough for me, Cousin Cecily.

CECILY. Yes, but are you good enough for it?

ALGERNON. I'm afraid I'm not that. That is why I want you to reform me. You might make that your mission, if you don't mind, Cousin Cecily.

CECILY. I'm afraid I've no time, this afternoon.

ALGERNON. Well, would you mind my reforming myself this afternoon?

CECILY. It is rather Quixotic of you. But I think you should try.

ALGERNON. I will. I feel better already.

CECILY. You are looking a little worse.

ALGERNON. That is because I am hungry.

CECILY. How thoughtless of me. I should have remembered that when one is going to lead an entirely new life, one requires regular and wholesome meals. Won't you come in?

ALGERNON. Thank you. Might I have a buttonhole first? I never have any appetite unless I have a buttonhole first.

CECILY. A Maréchal Niel? (*Picks up scissors.*)

ALGERNON. No, I'd sooner have a pink rose.

CECILY. Why? (*Cuts a flower.*)

ALGERNON. Because you are like a pink rose, Cousin Cecily.

CECILY. I don't think it can be right for you to talk to me like that. Miss Prism never says such things to me.

ALGERNON. Then Miss Prism is a shortsighted old lady.

(CECILY *puts the rose in his buttonhole.*)

You are the prettiest girl I ever saw.

CECILY. Miss Prism says that all good looks are a snare.

ALGERNON. They are a snare that every sensible man would like to be caught in.

CECILY. Oh, I don't think I would care to catch a sensible man. I shouldn't know what to talk to him about.

(*They pass into the house.* MISS PRISM *and* DR. CHASUBLE *return.*)

MISS PRISM. You are too much alone, dear Dr. Chasuble. You should get married. A misanthrope I can understand — a womanthrope, never!

CHASUBLE (*with a scholar's shudder*). Believe me, I do not deserve so neologistic a phrase. The precept as well as the practice of the Primitive Church was distinctly against matrimony.

MISS PRISM (*sententiously*). That is obviously the reason why the Primitive Church has not lasted up to the present day. And you do not seem to realize, dear Doctor, that by persistently remaining single, a man converts himself into a permanent public temptation. Men should be more careful; this very celibacy leads weaker vessels astray.

CHASUBLE. But is a man not equally attractive when married?

MISS PRISM. No married man is ever attractive except to his wife.

CHASUBLE. And often, I've been told, not even to her.

MISS PRISM. That depends on the intellectual sympathies of the woman. Maturity can always be depended on. Ripeness can be trusted. Young women are green.

(DR. CHASUBLE *starts.*)

I spoke horticulturally. My metaphor was drawn from fruits. But where is Cecily?

CHASUBLE. Perhaps she followed us to the schools.

(*Enter* JACK *slowly from the back of the garden. He is dressed in the deepest mourning, with crepe hatband and black gloves.*)

MISS PRISM. Mr. Worthing!

CHASUBLE. Mr. Worthing?

MISS PRISM. This is indeed a surprise. We did not look for you till Monday afternoon.

JACK (*shakes* MISS PRISM'S *hand in a tragic manner*). I have returned sooner than I expected. Dr. Chasuble, I hope you are well?

CHASUBLE. Dear Mr. Worthing, I trust this garb of woe does not betoken some terrible calamity?

JACK. My brother.

MISS PRISM. More shameful debts and extravagance?

CHASUBLE. Still leading his life of pleasure?

JACK (*shaking his head*). Dead!

CHASUBLE. Your brother Ernest dead?

JACK. Quite dead.

MISS PRISM. What a lesson for him! I trust he will profit by it.

CHASUBLE. Mr. Worthing, I offer you my sincere condolence. You have at least the consolation of knowing that you were always the most generous and forgiving of brothers.

JACK. Poor Ernest! He had many faults, but it is a sad, sad blow.

CHASUBLE. Very sad indeed. Were you with him at the end?

JACK. No. He died abroad; in Paris, in fact. I had a telegram last night from the manager of the Grand Hotel.

CHASUBLE. Was the cause of death mentioned?

JACK. A severe chill, it seems.

MISS PRISM. As a man sows, so shall he reap.

CHASUBLE (*raising his hand*). Charity, dear Miss Prism, charity! None of us is perfect. I myself am peculiarly susceptible to draughts. Will the interment take place here?

JACK. No. He seems to have expressed a desire to be buried in Paris.

CHASUBLE. In Paris! (*Shakes his head.*) I fear that hardly points to any very serious state of mind at the last. You would no doubt wish me to make some slight allusion to this tragic domestic affliction next Sunday.

(JACK *presses his hand convulsively.*)

My sermon on the meaning of the manna in the wilderness can be adapted to almost any occasion, joyful, or, as in the present case, distressing.

(*All sigh.*)

I have preached it at harvest celebrations, christenings, confirmations, on days of humiliation and festal days. The last time I delivered it was in the Cathedral, as a charity sermon on behalf of the Society for the Prevention of Discontent among the Upper Orders. The Bishop, who was present, was much struck by some of the analogies I drew.

JACK. Ah! that reminds me, you mentioned christenings, I think, Dr. Chasuble? I suppose you know how to christen all right?

(DR. CHASUBLE *looks astounded.*)

I mean, of course, you are continually christening aren't you?

MISS PRISM. It is, I regret to say, one of the Rector's most constant duties in this parish. I have often spoken to the poorer classes on the subject. But they don't seem to know what thrift is.

CHASUBLE. But is there any particular infant in whom you are interested, Mr. Worthing? Your brother was, I believe, unmarried, was he not?

JACK. Oh yes.

MISS PRISM (*bitterly*). People who live entirely for pleasure usually are.

JACK. But it is not for any child, dear Doctor. I am very fond of children. No! the fact is, I would like to be christened myself, this afternoon, if you have nothing better to do.

CHASUBLE. But surely, Mr. Worthing, you have been christened already?

JACK. I don't remember anything about it.

CHASUBLE. But have you any grave doubts on the subject?

JACK. I certainly intend to have. Of course I don't know if the thing would bother you in any way, or if you think I am a little too old now.

CHASUBLE. Not at all. The sprinkling, and, indeed, the immersion of adults is a perfectly canonical practice.

JACK. Immersion!

CHASUBLE. You need have no apprehensions. Sprinkling is all that is necessary, or indeed I think advisable. Our weather is so changeable. At what hour would you wish the ceremony performed?

JACK. Oh, I might trot round about five if that would suit you.

CHASUBLE. Perfectly, perfectly! In fact I have two similar ceremonies to perform at that time. A case of twins that occurred recently in one of the outlying cottages on your own estate. Poor Jenkins the carter, a most hard-working man.

JACK. Oh! I don't see much fun in being christened along with other babies. It would be childish. Would half-past five do?

CHASUBLE. Admirably! Admirably! (*Takes out watch.*) And now, dear Mr. Worthing, I will not intrude any longer into a house of sorrow. I would merely beg you not to be too much bowed down by grief. What seem to us bitter trials are often blessings in disguise.

MISS PRISM. This seems to me a blessing of an extremely obvious kind.

(*Enter* CECILY *from the house.*)

CECILY. Uncle Jack! Oh, I am pleased to see you back. But what horrid clothes you have got on. Do go and change them.

MISS PRISM. Cecily!

CHASUBLE. My child! My child!

(CECILY *goes towards* JACK; *he kisses her brow in a melancholy manner.*)

CECILY. What is the matter, Uncle Jack? Do look happy! You look as if you had toothache, and I have got such a surprise for you. Who do you think is in the dining-room? Your brother!

JACK. Who?

CECILY. Your brother Ernest. He arrived about half an hour ago.

JACK. What nonsense! I haven't got a brother.

CECILY. Oh, don't say that. However badly he may have behaved to you in the past he is still your brother. You couldn't be so heartless as to disown him. I'll tell him to come out. And you will shake hands with him, won't you, Uncle Jack? (*Runs back into the house.*)

CHASUBLE. These are very joyful tidings.

MISS PRISM. After we had all been resigned to his loss, his sudden return seems to me peculiarly distressing.

JACK. My brother is in the dining-room? I don't know what it all means. I think it is perfectly absurd.

(*Enter* ALGERNON *and* CECILY *hand in hand. They come slowly up to* JACK.)

JACK. Good heavens! (*Motions* ALGERNON *away.*)

ALGERNON. Brother John, I have come down from town to tell you that I am very sorry for all the trouble I have given you, and that I intend to lead a better life in the future.

(JACK *glares at him and does not take his hand.*)

CECILY. Uncle Jack, you are not going to refuse your own brother's hand?

JACK. Nothing will induce me to take his hand. I think his coming down here disgraceful. He knows perfectly well why.

CECILY. Uncle Jack, do be nice. There is some good in everyone. Ernest has just been telling me about his poor invalid friend Mr. Bunbury whom he goes to visit so often. And surely there must be much good in one who is kind to an invalid, and leaves the pleasures of London to sit by a bed of pain.

JACK. Oh! he has been talking about Bunbury, has he?

CECILY. Yes, he has told me all about poor Mr. Bunbury, and his terrible state of health.

JACK. Bunbury! Well, I won't have him talk to you about Bunbury or about anything else. It is enough to drive one perfectly frantic.

ALGERNON. Of course I admit that the faults were all on my side. But I must say that I think that Brother John's coldness to me is peculiarly painful. I expected a more enthusiastic welcome, especially considering it is the first time I have come here.

CECILY. Uncle Jack, if you don't shake hands with Ernest I will never forgive you.

JACK. Never forgive me?

CECILY. Never, never, never!

JACK. Well, this is the last time I shall ever do it. (*Shakes hands with* ALGERNON *and glares.*)

CHASUBLE. It's pleasant, is it not, to see so perfect a reconciliation? I think we might leave the two brothers together.

MISS PRISM. Cecily, you will come with us.

CECILY. Certainly, Miss Prism. My little task of reconcilation is over.

CHASUBLE. You have done a beautiful action today, dear child.

MISS PRISM. We must not be premature in our judgements.

CECILY. I feel very happy.

(*They all go off except* JACK *and* ALGERNON.)

JACK. You young scoundrel, Algy, you must get out of this place as soon as possible. I don't allow any Bunburying here.

(*Enter* MERRIMAN.)

MERRIMAN. I have put Mr. Ernest's things in the room next to yours, sir. I suppose that is all right?

JACK. What?

MERRIMAN. Mr. Ernest's luggage, sir. I have unpacked it and put it in the room next to your own.

JACK. His luggage?

MERRIMAN. Yes sir. Three portmanteaus, a dressing-case, two hat-boxes, and a large luncheon-basket.

ALGERNON. I am afraid I can't stay more than a week this time.

JACK. Merriman, order the dogcart at once. Mr. Ernest has been suddenly called back to town.

MERRIMAN. Yes, sir. (*Goes back into the house.*)

ALGERNON. What a fearful liar you are, Jack. I have not been called back to town at all.

JACK. Yes, you have.

ALGERNON. I haven't heard any one call me.

JACK. Your duty as a gentleman calls you back.

ALGERNON. My duty as a gentleman has never interfered with my pleasures in the smallest degree.

JACK. I can quite understand that.

ALGERNON. Well, Cecily is a darling.

JACK. You are not to talk of Miss Cardew like that. I don't like it.

ALGERNON. Well, I don't like your clothes. You look perfectly ridiculous in them. Why on earth don't you go up and change? It is perfectly childish to be in deep mourning for a man who is actually staying for a whole week with you in your house as a guest. I call it grotesque.

JACK. You are certainly not staying with me for a whole week as a guest or anything else. You have got to leave . . . by the four-five train.

ALGERNON. I certainly won't leave you so long as you are in mourning. It would be most unfriendly. If I were in mourning you would stay with me, I suppose. I should think it very unkind if you didn't.

JACK. Well, will you go if I change my clothes?

ALGERNON. Yes, if you are not too long. I never saw anybody take so long to dress, and with such little result.

JACK. Well, at any rate, that is better than being always overdressed as you are.

ALGERNON. If I am occasionally a little overdressed, I make up for it by being always immensely overeducated.

JACK. Your vanity is ridiculous, your conduct an outrage, and your presence in my garden utterly absurd. However, you have got to catch the four-five, and I hope you will have a pleasant journey back to town. This Bunburying, as you call it, has not been a great success for you. (*Goes into the house.*)

ALGERNON. I think it has been a great success. I'm in love with Cecily, and that is everything.

(*Enter* CECILY *at the back of the garden. She picks up the can and begins to water the flowers.*)

But I must see her before I go, and make arrangements for another Bunbury. Ah, there she is.

CECILY. Oh, I merely came back to water the roses. I thought you were with Uncle Jack.

ALGERNON. He's gone to order the dogcart for me.

CECILY. Oh, is he going to take you for a nice drive?

ALGERNON. He's going to send me away.

CECILY. Then have we got to part?

ALGERNON. I am afraid so. It's a very painful parting.

CECILY. It is always painful to part from people whom one has known for a very brief space of time. The absence of old friends one can endure with equanimity. But even a momentary separation from anyone to whom one has just been introduced is almost unbearable.

ALGERNON. Thank you.

(*Enter* MERRIMAN.)

MERRIMAN. The dogcart is at the door, sir.

(ALGERNON *looks appealingly at* CECILY.)

CECILY. It can wait, Merriman . . . for . . . five minutes.

MERRIMAN. Yes, miss. (*Exit.*)

ALGERNON. I hope, Cecily, I shall not offend you if I state quite frankly and openly that you seem to me to be in every way the visible personification of absolute perfection.

CECILY. I think your frankness does you great credit, Ernest. If you will allow me, I will copy your remarks into my diary. (*Goes over to table and begins writing in diary.*)

ALGERNON. Do you really keep a diary? I'd give anything to look at it. May I?

CECILY. Oh no. (*Puts her hand over it.*) You see, it is simply a very young girl's record of her own thoughts and impressions, and consequently meant for publication. When it appears in volume form I hope you will order a copy. But pray, Ernest, don't stop. I delight in taking down from dictation. I have reached "absolute perfection." You can go on. I am quite ready for more.

ALGERNON (*somewhat taken aback*). Ahem! Ahem!

CECILY. Oh, don't cough, Ernest. When one is dictating one should speak fluently and not cough. Besides, I don't know how to spell a cough. (*Writes as* ALGERNON *speaks.*)

ALGERNON (*speaking very rapidly*). Cecily, ever since I first looked upon your wonderful and incomparable beauty, I have dared to love you wildly, passionately, devotedly, hopelessly.

CECILY. I don't think that you should tell me that you love me wildly, passionately, devotedly, hopelessly. Hopelessly doesn't seem to make much sense, does it?

ALGERNON. Cecily.

(*Enter* MERRIMAN.)

MERRIMAN. The dogcart is waiting, sir.

ALGERNON. Tell it to come round next week, at the same hour.

MERRIMAN (*looks at* CECILY, *who makes no sign*). Yes, sir. (MERRIMAN *retires.*)

CECILY. Uncle Jack would be very much annoyed if he knew you were staying on till next week, at the same hour.

ALGERNON. Oh, I don't care about Jack. I don't care for anybody in the whole world but you. I love you, Cecily. You will marry me, won't you?

CECILY. You silly boy! Of course. Why, we have been engaged for the last three months.

ALGERNON. For the last three months?

CECILY. Yes, it will be exactly three months on Thursday.

ALGERNON. But how did we become engaged?

CECILY. Well, ever since dear Uncle Jack first confessed to us that he had a younger brother who was very wicked and bad, you of course have formed the chief topic of conversation between myself and Miss Prism. And of course a man who is much talked about is always very attractive. One feels there must be something in him, after all. I daresay it was foolish of me, but I fell in love with you, Ernest.

ALGERNON. Darling. And when was the engagement actually settled?

CECILY. On the 14th of February last. Worn out by your entire ignorance of my existence, I determined to end the matter one way or the other, and after a long struggle with myself I accepted you under this dear old tree here. The next day I bought this little ring in your name, and this is the little bangle with the true lovers' knot I promised you always to wear.

ALGERNON. Did I give you this? It's very pretty, isn't it?

CECILY. Yes, you've wonderfully good taste, Ernest. It's the excuse I've always given for your leading such a bad life. And this is the box in which I keep all your dear letters. (*Kneels at table, opens box, and produces letters tied up with blue ribbon.*)

ALGERNON. My letters! But, my own sweet Cecily, I have never written you any letters.

CECILY. You need hardly remind me of that, Ernest. I remember only too well that I was forced to write your letters for you. I wrote always three times a week, and sometimes oftener.

ALGERNON. Oh, do let me read them, Cecily?

CECILY. Oh, I couldn't possibly. They would make you far too conceited. (*Replaces box.*) The three you wrote me after I had broken off the engagement are so beautiful, and so badly spelled, that even now I can hardly read them without crying a little.

ALGERNON. But was our engagement ever broken off?

CECILY. Of course it was. On the 22nd of last March. You can see the entry if you like. (*Shows diary.*) "Today I broke off my engagement with Ernest. I feel it is better to do so. The weather still continues charming."

ALGERNON. But why on earth did you break it off? What had I done? I had done nothing at all. Cecily, I am very much hurt indeed to hear you broke it off. Particularly when the weather was so charming.

CECILY. It would hardly have been a really serious engagement if it hadn't been broken off at least once. But I forgave you before the week was out.

ALGERNON (*crossing to her, and kneeling*). What a perfect angel you are, Cecily.

CECILY. You dear romantic boy. (*He kisses her, she puts her fingers through his hair.*) I hope your hair curls naturally, does it?

ALGERNON. Yes darling, with a little help from others.

CECILY. I am so glad.

ALGERNON. You'll never break off our engagement again, Cecily?

CECILY. I don't think I could break it off now that I have actually met you. Besides, of course, there is the question of your name.

ALGERNON. Yes, of course. (*Nervously.*)

CECILY. You must not laugh at me, darling, but it had always been a girlish dream of mine to love some one whose name was Ernest.

(ALGERNON *rises*, CECILY *also.*)

There is something in that name that seems to inspire absolute confidence. I pity any poor married woman whose husband is not called Ernest.

ALGERNON. But, my dear child, do you mean to say you could not love me if I had some other name?

CECILY. But what name?

ALGERNON. Oh, any name you like — Algernon — for instance . . .

CECILY. But I don't like the name of Algernon.

ALGERNON. Well, my own dear sweet, loving little darling, I really can't see why you should object to the name of Algernon. It is not at all a bad name. In fact, it is rather an aristocratic name. Half of the chaps who get into the Bankruptcy Court are called Algernon. But seriously, Cecily . . . (*moving to her*) if my name was Algy, couldn't you love me?

CECILY (*rising*). I might respect you, Ernest, I might admire your character, but I fear that I should not be able to give you my undivided attention.

ALGERNON. Ahem! Cecily! (*Picking up hat.*) Your Rector here is, I suppose, thoroughly experienced in the practice of all the rites and ceremonials of the Church?

CECILY. Oh, yes. Dr. Chasuble is a most learned man. He has never written a single book, so you can imagine how much he knows.

ALGERNON. I must see him at once on a most important christening — I mean on most important business.

CECILY. Oh!

ALGERNON. I shan't be away more than half an hour.

CECILY. Considering that we have been engaged since February the 14th, and that I only met you today for the first time, I think it is rather hard that you should leave me for so long a period as half an hour. Couldn't you make it twenty minutes?

ALGERNON. I'll be back in no time. (*Kisses her and rushes down the garden.*)

CECILY. What an impetuous boy he is! I like his hair so much. I must enter his proposal in my diary.

(*Enter* MERRIMAN.)

MERRIMAN. A Miss Fairfax just called to see Mr. Worthing. On very important business, Miss Fairfax states.

CECILY. Isn't Mr. Worthing in his library?

MERRIMAN. Mr. Worthing went over in the direction of the Rectory some time ago.

CECILY. Pray ask the lady to come out here; Mr. Worthing is sure to be back soon. And you can bring tea.

MERRIMAN. Yes, Miss. (*Goes out.*)

CECILY. Miss Fairfax! I suppose one of the many good elderly women who are associated with Uncle Jack in some of his philanthropic work in London. I don't quite like women who are interested in philanthropic work. I think it is so forward of them.

(*Enter* MERRIMAN.)

MERRIMAN. Miss Fairfax.

(*Enter* GWENDOLEN. *Exit* MERRIMAN.)

CECILY (*advancing to meet her*). Pray let me introduce myself to you. My name is Cecily Cardew.

GWENDOLEN. Cecily Cardew? (*Moving to her and shaking hands.*) What a very sweet name! Something tells me that we are going to be great friends. I like you already more than I can say. My first impressions of people are never wrong.

CECILY. How nice of you to like me so much after we have known each other such a comparatively short time. Pray sit down.

GWENDOLEN (*still standing up*). I may call you Cecily, may I not?

CECILY. With pleasure!

GWENDOLEN. And you will always call me Gwendolen, won't you?

CECILY. If you wish.

GWENDOLEN. Then that is all quite settled, is it not?

CECILY. I hope so. (*A pause. They both sit down together.*)

GWENDOLEN. Perhaps this might be a favorable opportunity for my mentioning who I am. My father is Lord Bracknell. You have never heard of papa, I suppose?

CECILY. I don't think so.

GWENDOLEN. Outside the family circle, papa, I am glad to say, is entirely unknown. I think that is quite as it should be. The home seems to me to be the proper sphere for the man. And certainly once a man begins to neglect his domestic duties he becomes painfully effeminate, does he not? And I don't like that. It makes men so very attractive. Cecily, mamma, whose views on education are remarkably strict, has brought me up to be extremely shortsighted; it is part of her system; so do you mind my looking at you through my glasses?

CECILY. Oh! not at all, Gwendolen. I am very fond of being looked at.

GWENDOLEN (*after examining* CECILY *carefully through a lorgnette*). You are here on a short visit, I suppose.

CECILY. Oh no! I live here.

GWENDOLEN (*severely*). Really? Your mother, no doubt, or some female relative of advanced years, resides here also?

CECILY. Oh no! I have no mother, nor, in fact, any relations.

GWENDOLEN. Indeed?

CECILY. My dear guardian, with the assistance of Miss Prism, has the arduous task of looking after me.

GWENDOLEN. Your guardian?

CECILY. Yes, I am Mr. Worthing's ward.

GWENDOLEN. Oh! It is strange he never mentioned to me that he had a ward. How secretive of him! He grows more interesting hourly. I am not sure, however, that the news inspires me with feelings of unmixed delight. (*Rising and going to her.*) I am very fond of you, Cecily; I have liked you ever since I met you! But I am bound to state that now I know that you are Mr. Worthing's ward, I cannot help expressing a wish you were — well, just a little older than you seem to be — and not quite so very alluring in appearance. In fact, if I may speak candidly —

CECILY. Pray do! I think that whenever one has anything unpleasant to say, one should always be quite candid.

GWENDOLEN. Well, to speak with perfect candor, Cecily, I wish that you were fully forty-two, and more than usually plain for your age. Ernest has a strong upright nature. He is the very soul of truth and honor. Disloyalty would be as impossible to him as deception. But even men of the noblest possible moral character are extremely susceptible to the influence of the physical charms of others. Modern, no less than Ancient History, supplies us with many most painful examples of what I refer to. If it were not so, indeed, History would be quite unreadable.

CECILY. I beg your pardon, Gwendolen, did you say Ernest?

GWENDOLEN. Yes.

CECILY. Oh, but it is not Mr. Ernest Worthing who is my guardian. It is his brother — his elder brother.

GWENDOLEN (*sitting down again*). Ernest never mentioned to me that he had a brother.

CECILY. I am sorry to say they have not been on good terms for a long time.

GWENDOLEN. Ah! that accounts for it. And now that I think of it I have never heard any man mention his brother. The subject seems distasteful to most men. Cecily, you have lifted a load from my mind. I was growing almost anxious. It would have been terrible if any cloud had come across a friendship like ours, would it not? Of course you are quite, quite sure that it is not Mr. Worthing who is your guardian?

CECILY. Quite sure. (*A pause.*) In fact, I am going to be his.

GWENDOLEN (*inquiringly*). I beg your pardon?

CECILY (*rather shy and confidingly*). Dearest Gwendolen, there is no reason why I should make a secret of it to you. Our little country newspaper is sure to chronicle the fact next week. Mr. Ernest Worthing and I are engaged to be married.

GWENDOLEN (*quite politely, rising*). My darling Cecily, I think there must be some slight error. Mr. Ernest Worthing is engaged to me. The announcement will appear in the *Morning Post* on Saturday at the latest.

CECILY (*very politely, rising*). I am afraid you must be under some misconception. Ernest proposed to me exactly ten minutes ago. (*Shows diary.*)

GWENDOLEN (*examines diary through her lorgnette carefully*). It is very curious, for he asked me to be his wife yesterday afternoon at 5:30. If you would care to verify the incident, pray do so. (*Produces diary of her own.*) I never travel without my diary. One should always have something sensational to read in the train. I am so sorry, dear Cecily, if it is any disappointment to you, but I am afraid I have the prior claim.

CECILY. It would distress me more than I can tell you, dear Gwendolen, if it caused you any mental or physical anguish, but I feel bound to point out that since Ernest proposed to you he clearly has changed his mind.

GWENDOLEN (*meditatively*). If the poor fellow has been entrapped into any foolish promise I shall consider it my duty to rescue him at once, and with a firm hand.

CECILY (*thoughtfully and sadly*). Whatever unfortunate entanglement my dear boy may have got into, I will never reproach him with it after we are married.

GWENDOLEN. Do you allude to me, Miss Cardew, as an entanglement? You are presumptuous. On an occasion of this kind it becomes more than a moral duty to speak one's mind. It becomes a pleasure.

CECILY. Do you suggest, Miss Fairfax, that I entrapped Ernest into an engagement? How dare you? This is no time for wearing the shallow mask of manners. When I see a spade I call it a spade.

GWENDOLEN (*satirically*). I am glad to say that I have never seen a spade. It is obvious that our social spheres have been widely different.

(*Enter* MERRIMAN, *followed by the* FOOTMAN. *He carries a salver, table cloth, and plate stand.* CECILY *is about to retort. The presence of the servants exercises a restraining influence, under which both girls chafe.*)

MERRIMAN. Shall I lay tea here as usual, Miss?

CECILY (*sternly, in a calm voice*). Yes, as usual.

(MERRIMAN *begins to clear table and lay cloth. A long pause.* CECILY *and* GWENDOLEN *glare at each other.*)

GWENDOLEN. Are there many interesting walks in the vicinity, Miss Cardew?

CECILY. Oh! yes! a great many. From the top of one of the hills quite close one can see five counties.

GWENDOLEN. Five counties! I don't think I should like that; I hate crowds.

CECILY (*sweetly*). I suppose that is why you live in town?

(GWENDOLEN *bites her lip, and beats her foot nervously with her parasol.*)

GWENDOLEN (*looking round*). Quite a well-kept garden this is, Miss Cardew.

CECILY. So glad you like it, Miss Fairfax.

GWENDOLEN. I had no idea there were any flowers in the country.

CECILY. Oh, flowers are as common here, Miss Fairfax, as people are in London.

GWENDOLEN. Personally I cannot understand how anybody manages to exist in the country, if anybody who is anybody does. The country always bores me to death.

CECILY. Ah! This is what the newspapers call agricultural depression, is it not? I believe the aristocracy are suffering very much from it just at present. It is almost an epidemic amongst them, I have been told. May I offer you some tea, Miss Fairfax?

GWENDOLEN (*with elaborate politeness*). Thank you. (*Aside.*) Detestable girl! But I require tea!

CECILY (*sweetly*). Sugar?

GWENDOLEN (*superciliously*). No, thank you. Sugar is not fashionable any more.

(CECILY *looks angrily at her, takes up the tongs and puts four lumps of sugar into the cup.*)

CECILY (*severely*). Cake or bread and butter?

GWENDOLEN (*in a bored manner*). Bread and butter, please. Cake is rarely seen at the best houses nowadays.

CECILY (*cuts a very large slice of cake and puts it on the tray*). Hand that to Miss Fairfax.

(MERRIMAN *does so, and goes out with* FOOTMAN. GWENDOLEN *drinks the tea and makes a grimace. Puts down cup at once, reaches out her hand to the bread and butter, looks at it, and finds it is cake. Rises in indignation.*)

GWENDOLEN. You have filled my tea with lumps of sugar, and though I asked most distinctly for bread and butter, you have given me cake. I am known for the gentleness of my disposition, and the extraordinary sweetness of my nature, but I warn you, Miss Cardew, you may go too far.

CECILY (*rising*). To save my poor, innocent, trusting boy from the machinations of any other girl there are no lengths to which I would not go.

GWENDOLEN. From the moment I saw you I distrusted you. I felt that you were false and deceitful. I am never deceived in such matters. My first impressions of people are invariably right.

CECILY. It seems to me, Miss Fairfax, that I am trespassing on your valuable time. No doubt you have many other calls of a similar character to make in the neighbourhood.

(*Enter* JACK.)

GWENDOLEN (*catching sight of him*). Ernest! My own Ernest!

JACK. Gwendolen! Darling! (*Offers to kiss her.*)

GWENDOLEN (*drawing back*). A moment! May I ask if you are engaged to be married to this young lady? (*Points to* CECILY.)

JACK (*laughing*). To dear little Cecily! Of course not! What could have put such an idea into your pretty little head?

GWENDOLEN. Thank you. You may! (*Offers her cheek.*)

CECILY (*very sweetly*). I knew there must be some misunderstanding, Miss Fairfax. The gentleman whose arm is at present round your waist is my dear guardian, Mr. John Worthing.

GWENDOLEN. I beg your pardon?

CECILY. This is Uncle Jack.

GWENDOLEN (*receding*). Jack! Oh!

(*Enter* ALGERNON.)

CECILY. Here is Ernest.

ALGERNON (*goes straight over to* CECILY *without noticing anyone else*). My own love! (*Offers to kiss her.*)

CECILY (*drawing back*). A moment, Ernest! May I ask you — are you engaged to be married to this young lady?

ALGERNON (*looking round*). To what young lady? Good heavens! Gwendolen!

CECILY. Yes: to good heavens, Gwendolen, I mean to Gwendolen.

ALGERNON (*laughing*). Of course not! What could have put such an idea into your pretty little head?

CECILY. Thank you. (*Presenting her cheek to be kissed.*) You may.

(ALGERNON *kisses her.*)

GWENDOLEN. I felt there was some slight error, Miss Cardew. The gentleman who is now embracing you is my cousin, Mr. Algernon Moncrieff.

CECILY (*breaking away from* ALGERNON). Algernon Moncrieff! Oh!

(*The two girls move towards each other and put their arms round each other's waists as if for protection.*)

CECILY. Are you called Algernon?

ALGERNON. I cannot deny it.

CECILY. Oh!

GWENDOLEN. Is your name really John?

JACK (*standing rather proudly*). I could deny it if I liked. I could deny anything if I liked. But my name certainly is John. It has been John for years.

CECILY (*to* GWENDOLEN). A gross deception has been practiced on both of us.

GWENDOLEN. My poor wounded Cecily!

CECILY. My sweet wronged Gwendolen!

GWENDOLEN (*slowly and seriously*). You will call me sister, will you not?

(*They embrace.* JACK *and* ALGERNON *groan and walk up and down.*)

CECILY (*rather brightly*). There is just one question I would like to be allowed to ask my guardian.

GWENDOLEN. An admirable idea! Mr. Worthing, there is just one question I would like to be permitted to put to you. Where is your brother Ernest? We are both engaged to be married to your brother Ernest, so it is a matter of some importance to us to know where your brother Ernest is at present.

JACK (*slowly and hesitatingly*). Gwendolen — Cecily — it is very painful for me to be forced to speak the truth. It is the first time in my life that I have ever been reduced to such a painful position, and I am really quite inexperienced in doing anything of the kind. However, I will tell you quite frankly that I have no brother Ernest. I have no brother at all. I never had a brother in my life, and I certainly have not the smallest intention of ever having one in the future.

CECILY (*surprised*). No brother at all?

JACK (*cheerily*). None!

GWENDOLEN (*severely*). Had you never a brother of any kind?

JACK (*pleasantly*). Never. Not even of any kind.

GWENDOLEN. I am afraid it is quite clear, Cecily, that neither of us is engaged to be married to anyone.

CECILY. It is not a very pleasant position for a young girl suddenly to find herself in. Is it?

GWENDOLEN. Let us go into the house. They will hardly venture to come after us there.

CECILY. No, men are so cowardly, aren't they?

(*They retire into the house with scornful looks.*)

JACK. This ghastly state of things is what you call Bunburying, I suppose?

ALGERNON. Yes, and a perfectly wonderful Bunbury it is. The most wonderful Bunbury I have ever had in my life.

JACK. Well, you've no right whatsoever to Bunbury here.

ALGERNON. That is absurd. One has a right to Bunbury anywhere one chooses. Every serious Bunburyist knows that.

JACK. Serious Bunburyist? Good heavens!

ALGERNON. Well, one must be serious about something, if one wants to have any amusement in life. I happen to be serious about Bunburying. What on earth you are serious about I haven't got the remotest idea. About everything, I should fancy. You have such an absolutely trivial nature.

JACK. Well, the only small satisfaction I have in the whole of this wretched business is that your friend Bunbury is quite exploded. You won't be able to run down to the country quite so often as you used to do, dear Algy. And a very good thing too.

ALGERNON. Your brother is a little off color, isn't he, dear Jack? You won't be able to disappear to London quite so frequently as your wicked custom was. And not a bad thing either.

JACK. As for your conduct towards Miss Cardew, I must say that your taking in a sweet, simple, innocent girl like that is quite inexcusable. To say nothing of the fact that she is my ward.

ALGERNON. I can see no possible defence at all for your deceiving a brilliant, clever, thoroughly experienced young lady like Miss Fairfax. To say nothing of the fact that she is my cousin.

JACK. I wanted to be engaged to Gwendolen, that is all. I love her.

ALGERNON. Well, I simply wanted to be engaged to Cecily. I adore her.

JACK. There is certainly no chance of your marrying Miss Cardew.

ALGERNON. I don't think there is much likelihood, Jack, of you and Miss Fairfax being united.

JACK. Well, that is no business of yours.

ALGERNON. If it was my business, I wouldn't talk about it. (*Begins to eat muffins.*) It is very vulgar to talk about one's business. Only people like stockbrokers do that, and then merely at dinner parties.

JACK. How you can sit there, calmly eating muffins, when we are in this horrible trouble, I can't make out. You seem to me to be perfectly heartless.

ALGERNON. Well, I can't eat muffins in an agitated manner. The butter would probably get on my cuffs. One should always eat muffins quite calmly. It is the only way to eat them.

JACK. I say it's perfectly heartless your eating muffins at all, under the circumstances.

ALGERNON. When I am in trouble, eating is the only thing that consoles me. Indeed, when I am in really great trouble, as any one who knows me intimately will tell you, I refuse everything except food and drink. At the present moment I am eating muffins because I am unhappy. Besides, I am particularly fond of muffins. (*Rising.*)

JACK (*rising*). Well, there is no reason why you should eat them all in that greedy way. (*Takes muffins from* ALGERNON.)

ALGERNON (*offering tea-cake*). I wish you would have tea-cake instead. I don't like tea-cake.

JACK. Good heavens! I suppose a man may eat his own muffins in his own garden.

ALGERNON. But you have just said it was perfectly heartless to eat muffins.

JACK. I said it was perfectly heartless of you, under the circumstances. That is a very different thing.

ALGERNON. That may be. But the muffins are the same. (*He seizes the muffin-dish from* JACK.)

JACK. Algy, I wish to goodness you would go.

ALGERNON. You can't possibly ask me to go without having some dinner. It's absurd. I never go without my dinner. No one ever does, except vegetarians and people like that. Besides I have just made arrangements with Dr. Chasuble to be christened at a quarter to six under the name of Ernest.

JACK. My dear fellow, the sooner you give up that nonsense the better. I made arrangements this morning with Dr. Chasuble to be christened myself at 5:30, and I naturally will take the name of Ernest. Gwendolen would wish it. We can't both be christened Ernest. It's absurd. Besides, I have a perfect right to be christened if I like. There is no evidence at all that I have ever been christened by anybody. I should think it extremely probable I never was, and so does Dr. Chasuble. It is entirely different in your case. You have been christened already.

ALGERNON. Yes, but I have not been christened for years.

JACK. Yes, but you have been christened. That is the important thing.

ALGERNON. Quite so. So I know my constitution can stand it. If you are not quite sure about your ever having been christened, I must say I think it rather dangerous your venturing on it now. It might make you very unwell. You can hardly have forgotten that someone very closely connected with you was very nearly carried off this week in Paris by a severe chill.

JACK. Yes, but you said yourself that a severe chill was not hereditary.

ALGERNON. It usen't to be, I know — but I daresay it is now. Science is always making wonderful improvements in things.

JACK (*picking up the muffin-dish*). Oh, that is nonsense; you are always talking nonsense.

ALGERNON. Jack, you are at the muffins again! I wish you wouldn't. There are only two left. (*Takes them.*) I told you I was particularly fond of muffins.

JACK. But I hate tea-cake.

ALGERNON. Why on earth then do you allow tea-cake to be served up for your guests? What ideas you have of hospitality!

JACK. Algernon! I have already told you to go. I don't want you here. Why don't you go?

ALGERNON. I haven't quite finished my tea yet! and there is still one muffin left.

(JACK *groans, and sinks into a chair.* ALGERNON *still continues eating.*)

ACT THREE

(*Morning-room at the Manor House.* GWENDOLEN *and* CECILY *are at the window, looking out into the garden.*)

GWENDOLEN. The fact that they did not follow us at once into the house, as any one else would have done, seems to me to show that they have some sense of shame left.

CECILY. They have been eating muffins. That looks like repentance.

GWENDOLEN (*after a pause*). They don't seem to notice us at all. Couldn't you cough?

CECILY. But I haven't got a cough.

GWENDOLEN. They're looking at us. What effrontery!

CECILY. They're approaching. That's very forward of them.

GWENDOLEN. Let us preserve a dignified silence.

CECILY. Certainly. It's the only thing to do now.

(*Enter* JACK *followed by* ALGERNON. *They whistle some dreadful popular air from a British opera.*)

GWENDOLEN. This dignified silence seems to produce an unpleasant effect.

CECILY. A most distasteful one.

GWENDOLEN. But we will not be the first to speak.

CECILY. Certainly not.

GWENDOLEN. Mr. Worthing, I have something very particular to ask you. Much depends on your reply.

CECILY. Gwendolen, your common sense is invaluable. Mr. Moncrieff, kindly answer me the following question. Why did you pretend to be my guardian's brother?

ALGERNON. In order that I might have an opportunity of meeting you.

CECILY (*to* GWENDOLEN). That certainly seems a satisfactory explanation, does it not?

GWENDOLEN. Yes, dear, if you can believe him.

CECILY. I don't. But that does not affect the wonderful beauty of his answer.

GWENDOLEN. True. In matters of grave importance, style, not sincerity, is the vital thing. Mr. Worthing, what explanation can you offer to me for pretending to have a brother? Was it in order that you might have an opportunity of coming up to town to see me as often as possible?

JACK. Can you doubt it, Miss Fairfax?

GWENDOLEN. I have the gravest doubts upon the subject. But I intend to crush them. This is not the moment for German scepticism. (*Moving to* CECILY.) Their explanations appear to be quite satisfactory, especially Mr. Worthing's. That seems to me to have the stamp of truth upon it.

CECILY. I am more than content with what Mr. Moncrieff said. His voice alone inspires one with absolute credulity.

GWENDOLEN. Then you think we should forgive them?

CECILY. Yes. I mean no.

GWENDOLEN. True! I had forgotten. There are principles at stake that one cannot surrender. Which of us should tell them? The task is not a pleasant one.

CECILY. Could we not both speak at the same time?

GWENDOLEN. An excellent idea! I nearly always speak at the same time as other people. Will you take the time from me?

CECILY. Certainly.

(GWENDOLEN *beats time with uplifted finger.*)

GWENDOLEN *and* CECILY (*speaking together*). Your Christian names are still an insuperable barrier. That is all!

JACK *and* ALGERNON (*speaking together*). Our Christian names! Is that all? But we are going to be christened this afternoon.

GWENDOLEN (*to* JACK). For my sake you are prepared to do this terrible thing?

JACK. I am.

CECILY (*to* ALGERNON). To please me you are ready to face this fearful ordeal?

ALGERNON. I am!

GWENDOLEN. How absurd to talk of the equality of the sexes! Where questions of self-sacrifice are concerned, men are infinitely beyond us.

JACK. We are. (*Clasps hands with* ALGERNON.)

CECILY. They have moments of physical courage of which we women know absolutely nothing.

GWENDOLEN (*to* JACK). Darling!

ALGERNON (*to* CECILY). Darling!

(*They fall into each other's arms. Enter* MERRIMAN. *When he enters he coughs loudly, seeing the situation.*)

MERRIMAN. Ahem! Ahem! Lady Bracknell.

JACK. Good heavens!

(*Enter* LADY BRACKNELL. *The couples separate in alarm. Exit* MERRIMAN.)

LADY BRACKNELL. Gwendolen! What does this mean?

GWENDOLEN. Merely that I am engaged to be married to Mr. Worthing, mamma.

LADY BRACKNELL. Come here. Sit down. Sit down immediately. Hesitation of any kind is a sign of mental decay in the young, of physical weakness in the old. (*Turns to* JACK.) Apprised, sir, of my daughter's sudden flight by her trusty maid, whose confidence I purchased by means of a small coin, I followed her at once by a luggage train. Her unhappy father is, I am glad to say, under the impression that she is attending a more than usually lengthy lecture by the University Extension Scheme on the Influence of a Permanent Income on Thought. I do not propose to undeceive him. Indeed I have never undeceived him on any question. I would consider it wrong. But of course, you will clearly understand that all communication between yourself and my daughter must cease immediately from this moment. On this point, as indeed on all points, I am firm.

JACK. I am engaged to be married to Gwendolen, Lady Bracknell!

LADY BRACKNELL. You are nothing of the kind, sir. And now as regards Algernon! . . . Algernon!

ALGERNON. Yes, Aunt Augusta.

LADY BRACKNELL. May I ask if it is in this house that your invalid friend Mr. Bunbury resides?

ALGERNON (*stammering*). Oh! no! Bunbury doesn't live here. Bunbury is somewhere else at present. In fact, Bunbury is dead.

LADY BRACKNELL. Dead! When did Mr. Bunbury die? His death must have been extremely sudden.

ALGERNON (*airily*). Oh! I killed Bunbury this afternoon. I mean poor Bunbury died this afternoon.

LADY BRACKNELL. What did he die of?

ALGERNON. Bunbury? Oh, he was quite exploded.

LADY BRACKNELL. Exploded! Was he the victim of a revolutionary outrage? I was not aware that Mr. Bunbury was interested in social legislation. If so, he is well punished for his morbidity.

ALGERNON. My dear Aunt Augusta, I mean he was found out! The doctors found out that Bunbury could not live, that is what I mean — so Bunbury died.

LADY BRACKNELL. He seems to have had great confidence in the opinion of his physicians. I am glad, however, that he made up his mind at the last to some definite course of action, and acted under proper medical advice. And now that we have finally got rid of this Mr. Bunbury, may I ask, Mr. Worthing, who is that young person whose hand my nephew Algernon is now holding in what seems to me a peculiarly unnecessary manner?

JACK. That lady is Miss Cecily Cardew, my ward.

(LADY BRACKNELL *bows coldly to* CECILY.)

ALGERNON. I am engaged to be married to Cecily, Aunt Augusta.

LADY BRACKNELL. I beg your pardon?

CECILY. Mr. Moncrieff and I are engaged to be married, Lady Bracknell.

LADY BRACKNELL (*with a shiver, crossing to the sofa and sitting down*). I do not know whether there is anything peculiarly exciting in the air of this particular part of Hertfordshire, but the number of engagements that go on seems to me considerably above the proper average that statistics have laid down for our guidance. I think some preliminary inquiry on my part would not be out of place. Mr. Worthing, is Miss Cardew at all connected with any of the larger railway stations in London? I merely desire information. Until yesterday I had no idea that there were any families or persons whose origin was a Terminus.

(JACK *looks perfectly furious, but restrains himself.*)

JACK (*in a cold, clear voice*). Miss Cardew is the granddaughter of the late Mr. Thomas Cardew of 149 Belgrave Square, S.W.; Gervase Park, Dorking, Surrey; and the Sporran, Fifeshire, N.B.

LADY BRACKNELL. That sounds not unsatisfactory. Three addresses always inspire confidence, even in tradesmen. But what proof have I of their authenticity?

JACK. I have carefully preserved the Court Guides of the period. They are open to your inspection, Lady Bracknell.

LADY BRACKNELL (*grimly*). I have known strange errors in that publication.

JACK. Miss Cardew's family solicitors are Messrs. Markby, Markby, and Markby.

LADY BRACKNELL. Markby, Markby, and Markby? A firm of the very highest position in their profession. Indeed I am told that one of the Mr. Markbys is occasionally to be seen at dinner parties. So far I am satisfied.

JACK (*very irritably*). How extremely kind of you, Lady Bracknell! I have also in my possession, you will be pleased to hear, certificates of Miss Cardew's birth, baptism, whooping cough, registration, vaccination, confirmation, and the measles; both the German and the English variety.

LADY BRACKNELL. Ah! A life crowded with incident, I see; though perhaps somewhat too exciting for a young girl. I am not myself in favor of premature experiences. (*Rises, looks at her watch.*) Gwendolen! the time approaches for our departure. We have not a moment to lose. As a matter of form, Mr. Worthing, I had better ask you if Miss Cardew has any little fortune?

JACK. Oh! about a hundred and thirty thousand pounds in the Funds. That is all. Good-bye, Lady Bracknell. So pleased to have seen you.

LADY BRACKNELL (*sitting down again*). A moment, Mr. Worthing.

A hundred and thirty thousand pounds! And in the Funds! Miss Cardew seems to me a most attractive young lady, now that I look at her. Few girls of the present day have any really solid qualities, any of the qualities that last, and improve with time. We live, I regret to say, in an age of surfaces. (*To* CECILY.) Come over here, dear.

(CECILY *goes across.*)

Pretty child! your dress is sadly simple, and your hair seems almost as Nature might have left it. But we can soon alter all that. A thoroughly experienced French maid produces a really marvellous result in a very brief space of time. I remember recommending one to young Lady Lancing, and after three months her own husband did not know her.

JACK. And after six months nobody knew her.

LADY BRACKNELL (*glares at* JACK *for a few moments. Then bends, with a practiced smile, to* CECILY). Kindly turn round, sweet child.

(CECILY *turns completely round.*)

No, the side view is what I want.

(CECILY *presents her profile.*)

Yes, quite as I expected. There are distinct social possibilities in your profile. The two weak points in our age are its want of principle and its want of profile. The chin a little higher, dear. Style largely depends on the way the chin is worn. They are worn very high, just at present. Algernon!

ALGERNON. Yes, Aunt Augusta!

LADY BRACKNELL. There are distinct social possibilities in Miss Cardew's profile.

ALGERNON. Cecily is the sweetest, dearest, prettiest girl in the whole world. And I don't care twopence about social possibilities.

LADY BRACKNELL. Never speak disrespectfully of Society, Algernon. Only people who can't get into it do that. (*To* CECILY.) Dear child, of course you know that Algernon has nothing but his debts to depend upon. But I do not approve of mercenary marriages. When I married Lord Bracknell I had no fortune of any kind. But I never dreamed for a moment of allowing that to stand in my way. Well, I suppose I must give my consent.

ALGERNON. Thank you, Aunt Augusta.

LADY BRACKNELL. Cecily, you may kiss me!

CECILY (*kisses her*). Thank you, Lady Bracknell.

LADY BRACKNELL. You may also address me as Aunt Augusta for the future.

CECILY. Thank you, Aunt Augusta.

LADY BRACKNELL. The marriage, I think, had better take place quite soon.

ALGERNON. Thank you, Aunt Augusta.

CECILY. Thank you, Aunt Augusta.

LADY BRACKNELL. To speak frankly, I am not in favor of long engagements. They give people the opportunity of finding out each other's character before marriage, which I think is never advisable.

JACK. I beg your pardon for interrupting you, Lady Bracknell, but this engagement is out of the question. I am Miss Cardew's guardian, and she cannot marry without my consent until she comes of age. That consent I absolutely decline to give.

LADY BRACKNELL. Upon what grounds, may I ask? Algernon is an extremely, I may almost say an ostentatiously, eligible young man. He has nothing, but he looks everything. What more can one desire?

JACK. It pains me very much to have to speak frankly to you, Lady Bracknell, about your nephew, but the fact is that I do not approve at all of his moral character. I suspect him of being untruthful.

(ALGERNON *and* CECILY *look at him in indignant amazement.*)

LADY BRACKNELL. Untruthful! My nephew Algernon? Impossible! He is an Oxonian.

JACK. I fear there can be no possible doubt about the matter. This afternoon during my temporary absence in London on an important question of romance, he obtained admission to my house by means of the false pretence of being my brother. Under an assumed name he drank, I've just been informed by my butler, an entire pint bottle of my Perrier-Jouet, Brut, '89; wine I was specially reserving for myself. Continuing his disgraceful deception, he succeeded in the course of the afternoon in alienating the affections of my only ward. He subsequently stayed to tea, and devoured every single muffin. And what makes his conduct all the more heartless is, that he was perfectly well aware from the first that I have no brother, that I never had a brother, and that I don't intend to have a brother, not even of any kind. I distinctly told him so myself yesterday afternoon.

LADY BRACKNELL. Ahem! Mr. Worthing, after careful consideration I have decided entirely to overlook my nephew's conduct to you.

JACK. That is very generous of you, Lady Bracknell. My own decision, however, is unalterable. I decline to give my consent.

LADY BRACKNELL (*to* CECILY). Come here, sweet child.

(CECILY *goes over.*)

How old are you, dear?

CECILY. Well, I am really only eighteen, but I always admit to twenty when I go to evening parties.

LADY BRACKNELL. You are perfectly right in making some slight alteration. Indeed, no woman should ever be quite accurate about her age. It looks so calculating. . . . (*In a meditative manner.*) Eighteen, but admitting to twenty at evening parties. Well, it will not be very long before you are of age and free from the restraints of tutelage. So I don't think your guardian's consent is, after all, a matter of any importance.

JACK. Pray excuse me, Lady Bracknell, for interrupting you again, but it is only fair to tell you that according to the terms of her grandfather's will Miss Cardew does not come legally of age till she is thirty-five.

LADY BRACKNELL. That does not seem to me to be a grave objection. Thirty-five is a very attractive age. London society is full of women of the very highest birth who have, of their own free choice, remained thirty-five for years. Lady Dumbleton is an instance in point. To my own knowledge she has been thirty-five ever since she arrived at the age of forty, which was many years ago now. I see no reason why our dear Cecily should not be even still more attractive at the age you mention than she is at present. There will be a large accumulation of property.

CECILY. Algy, could you wait for me till I was thirty-five?

ALGERNON. Of course I could, Cecily. You know I could.

CECILY. Yes, I felt it instinctively, but I couldn't wait all that time. I hate waiting even five minutes for anybody. It always makes me rather cross. I am not punctual myself, I know, but I do like punctuality in others, and waiting, even to be married, is quite out of the question.

ALGERNON. Then what is to be done, Cecily?

CECILY. I don't know, Mr. Moncrieff.

LADY BRACKNELL. My dear Mr. Worthing, as Miss Cardew states positively that she cannot wait till she is thirty-five — a remark which I am bound to say seems to me to show a somewhat impatient nature — I would beg of you to reconsider your decision.

JACK. But my dear Lady Bracknell, the matter is entirely in your own hands. The moment you consent to my marriage with Gwendolen, I will most gladly allow your nephew to form an alliance with my ward.

LADY BRACKNELL (*rising and drawing herself up*). You must be quite aware that what you propose is out of the question.

JACK. Then a passionate celibacy is all that any of us can look forward to.

LADY BRACKNELL. That is not the destiny I propose for Gwendolen. Algernon, of course, can choose for himself. (*Pulls out her watch.*) Come, dear (GWENDOLEN *rises*), we have already missed five, if not six, trains. To miss any more might expose us to comment on the platform.

(*Enter* DR. CHASUBLE.)

CHASUBLE. Everything is quite ready for the christenings.

LADY BRACKNELL. The christenings, sir! Is not that somewhat premature?

CHASUBLE (*looking rather puzzled, and pointing to* JACK *and* ALGERNON). Both these gentlemen have expressed a desire for immediate baptism.

LADY BRACKNELL. At their age? The idea is grotesque and irreligious! Algernon, I forbid you to be baptized. I will not hear of such excesses. Lord Bracknell would be highly displeased if he learned that that was the way in which you wasted your time and money.

CHASUBLE. Am I to understand then that there are to be no christenings at all this afternoon?

JACK. I don't think that, as things are now, it would be of much practical value to either of us, Dr. Chasuble.

CHASUBLE. I am grieved to hear such sentiments from you, Mr. Worthing. They savour of the heretical views of the Anabaptists, views that I have completely refuted in four of my unpublished sermons. However, as your present mood seems to be one peculiarly secular, I will return to the church at once. Indeed, I have just been informed by the pew-opener that for the last hour and a half Miss Prism has been waiting for me in the vestry.

LADY BRACKNELL (*starting*). Miss Prism! Did I hear you mention a Miss Prism?

CHASUBLE. Yes, Lady Bracknell. I am on my way to join her.

LADY BRACKNELL. Pray allow me to detain you for a moment. This matter may prove to be one of vital importance to Lord Bracknell and myself. Is this Miss Prism a female of repellent aspect, remotely connected with education?

CHASUBLE (*somewhat indignantly*). She is the most cultivated of ladies, and the very picture of respectability.

LADY BRACKNELL. It is obviously the same person. May I ask what position she holds in your household?

CHASUBLE (*severely*). I am a celibate, madam.

JACK (*interposing*). Miss Prism, Lady Bracknell, has been for the last three years Miss Cardew's esteemed governess and valued companion.

LADY BRACKNELL. In spite of what I hear of her, I must see her at once. Let her be sent for.

CHASUBLE (*looking off*). She approaches; she is nigh.

(*Enter* MISS PRISM *hurriedly.*)

MISS PRISM. I was told you expected me in the vestry, dear Canon. I have been waiting for you there for an hour and three-quarters. (*Catches sight of* LADY BRACKNELL, *who has fixed her with a stony glare.* MISS PRISM *grows pale and quails. She looks anxiously round as if desirous to escape.*)

LADY BRACKNELL (*in a severe, judicial voice*). Prism!

(MISS PRISM *bows her head in shame.*)

Come here, Prism!

(MISS PRISM *approaches in a humble manner.*)

Prism! Where is that baby?

(*General consternation. The* CANON *starts back in horror.* ALGERNON *and* JACK *pretend to be anxious to shield* CECILY *and* GWENDOLEN *from hearing the details of a terrible public scandal.*)

Twenty-eight years ago, Prism, you left Lord Bracknell's house, Number 104, Upper Grosvenor Square, in charge of a perambulator that contained a baby of the male sex. You never returned. A few weeks later, through the elaborate investigations of the Metropolitan police, the perambulator was discovered at midnight standing by itself in a remote corner of Bayswater. It contained the manuscript of a three-volume novel of more than usually revolting sentimentality.

(MISS PRISM *starts in involuntary indignation.*)

But the baby was not there.

(*Everyone looks at* MISS PRISM.)

Prism! Where is that baby?

(*A pause.*)

MISS PRISM. Lady Bracknell, I admit with shame that I do not know. I only wish I did. The plain facts of the case are these. On the morning of the day you mention, a day that is for ever branded on my memory, I prepared as usual to take the baby out in its perambulator. I had also with me a somewhat old, but capacious handbag in which I had intended to place the manuscript of a work of fiction that I had written during my few unoccupied hours. In a moment of mental abstraction, for which I can never forgive myself, I deposited the manuscript in the bassinette and placed the baby in the handbag.

JACK (*who has been listening attentively*). But where did you deposit the handbag?

MISS PRISM. Do not ask me, Mr. Worthing.

JACK. Miss Prism, this is a matter of no small importance to me. I insist on knowing where you deposited the handbag that contained that infant.

MISS PRISM. I left it in the cloakroom of one of the larger railway stations in London.

JACK. What railway station?

MISS PRISM (*quite crushed*). Victoria. The Brighton line. (*Sinks into a chair.*)

JACK. I must retire to my room for a moment. Gwendolen, wait here for me.

GWENDOLEN. If you are not too long, I will wait here for you all my life.

(*Exit* JACK *in great excitement.*)

CHASUBLE. What do you think this means, Lady Bracknell?

LADY BRACKNELL. I dare not even suspect, Dr. Chasuble. I need hardly tell you that in families of high position strange coincidences are not supposed to occur. They are hardly considered the thing.

(*Noises heard overhead as if some one was throwing trunks about. Everyone looks up.*)

CECILY. Uncle Jack seems strangely agitated.

CHASUBLE. Your guardian has a very emotional nature.

LADY BRACKNELL. This noise is extremely unpleasant. It sounds as if he was having an argument. I dislike arguments of any kind. They are always vulgar, and often convincing.

CHASUBLE (*looking up*). It has stopped now.

(*The noise is redoubled.*)

LADY BRACKNELL. I wish he would arrive at some conclusion.

GWENDOLEN. This suspense is terrible. I hope it will last.

(*Enter* JACK *with a handbag of black leather in his hand.*)

JACK (*rushing over to* MISS PRISM). Is this the handbag, Miss Prism? Examine it carefully before you speak. The happiness of more than one life depends on your answer.

MISS PRISM (*calmly*). It seems to be mine. Yes, here is the injury it received through the upsetting of a Gower Street omnibus in younger and happier days. Here is the stain on the lining caused by the explosion of a temperance beverage, an incident that occurred at Leamington. And here, on the lock, are my initials. I had forgotten that in an extravagant mood I had had them placed there. The bag is undoubtedly mine. I am delighted to have it so unexpectedly restored to me. It has been a great inconvenience being without it all these years.

JACK (*in a pathetic voice*). Miss Prism, more is restored to you than this handbag. I was the baby you placed in it.

MISS PRISM (*amazed*). You?

JACK (*embracing her*). Yes . . . mother!

MISS PRISM (*recoiling in indignant astonishment*). Mr. Worthing, I am unmarried!

JACK. Unmarried! I do not deny that is a serious blow. But after all, who has the right to cast a stone against one who has suffered? Cannot repentance wipe out an act of folly? Why should there be one law for men, and another for women? Mother, I forgive you. (*Tries to embrace her again.*)

MISS PRISM (*still more indignant*). Mr. Worthing, there is some error. (*Pointing to* LADY BRACKNELL.) There is the lady who can tell you who you really are.

JACK (*after a pause*). Lady Bracknell, I hate to seem inquisitive, but would you kindly inform me who I am?

LADY BRACKNELL. I am afraid that the news I have to give you will not altogether please you. You are the son of my poor sister, Mrs. Moncrieff, and consequently Algernon's elder brother.

JACK. Algy's elder brother! Then I have a brother after all. I knew I had a brother! I always said I had a brother! Cecily — how could you have ever doubted that I had a brother? (*Seizes hold of* ALGERNON.) Dr. Chasuble, my unfortunate brother. Miss Prism, my unfortunate brother. Gwendolen, my unfortunate brother. Algy, you young scoundrel, you will have to treat me with more respect in the future. You have never behaved to me like a brother in all your life.

ALGERNON. Well, not till today, old boy, I admit. I did my best, however, though I was out of practice. (*Shakes hands.*)

GWENDOLEN (*to* JACK). My own! But what own are you? What is your Christian name, now that you have become someone else?

JACK. Good heavens! . . . I had quite forgotten that point. Your decision on the subject of my name is irrevocable, I suppose?

GWENDOLEN. I never change, except in my affections.

CECILY. What a noble nature you have, Gwendolen!

JACK. Then the question had better be cleared up at once. Aunt Augusta, a moment. At the time when Miss Prism left me in the handbag, had I been christened already?

LADY BRACKNELL. Every luxury that money could buy, including christening, had been lavished on you by your fond and doting parents.

JACK. Then I was christened! That is settled. Now, what name was I given? Let me know the worst.

LADY BRACKNELL. Being the eldest son you were naturally christened after your father.

JACK (*irritably*). Yes, but what was my father's Christian name?

LADY BRACKNELL (*meditatively*). I cannot at the present moment recall what the General's Christian name was. But I have no doubt he had one. He was eccentric, I admit. But only in later years. And that was the result of the Indian climate, and marriage, and indigestion, and other things of that kind.

JACK. Algy! Can't you recollect what our father's Christian name was?

ALGERNON. My dear boy, we were never even on speaking terms. He died before I was a year old.

JACK. His name would appear in the Army Lists of the period, I suppose, Aunt Augusta?

LADY BRACKNELL. The General was essentially a man of peace, except in his domestic life. But I have no doubt his name would appear in any military directory.

JACK. The Army Lists of the last forty years are here. These delightful records should have been my constant study. (*Rushes to bookcase and tears the books out.*) M. Generals . . . Mallam, Maxbohm, Magley —

what ghastly names they have — Markby, Migsby, Mobbs, Moncrieff! Lieutenant 1840, Captain, Lieutenant-Colonel, Colonel, General 1869, Christian names, Ernest John. (*Puts book very quietly down and speaks quite calmly.*) I always told you, Gwendolen, my name was Ernest, didn't I? Well, it is Ernest after all. I mean it naturally is Ernest.

LADY BRACKNELL. Yes, I remember now that the General was called Ernest. I knew I had some particular reason for disliking the name.

GWENDOLEN. Ernest! My own Ernest! I felt from the first that you could have no other name!

JACK. Gwendolen, it is a terrible thing for a man to find out suddenly that all his life he has been speaking nothing but the truth. Can you forgive me?

GWENDOLEN. I can. For I feel that you are sure to change.

JACK. My own one!

CHASUBLE (*to* MISS PRISM). Laetitia! (*Embraces her.*)

MISS PRISM (*enthusiastically*). Frederick! At last!

ALGERNON. Cecily! (*Embraces her.*) At last!

JACK. Gwendolen! (*Embraces her.*) At last!

LADY BRACKNELL. My nephew, you seem to be displaying signs of triviality.

JACK. On the contrary, Aunt Augusta, I've now realized for the first time in my life the vital Importance of Being Earnest.

Curtain

If *Uncle Vanya* (1899) can be viewed as a tragicomedy [see *The Forms of Drama* in this series], then it is no more difficult to accept *The Cherry Orchard* (1904) as a comedy. Or the other way around, if the truth be known. So much depends on the way the reader of the script or the director of a production chooses to approach either drama. Chekhov (1860–1904) himself called most of his plays comedies and is reported to have been annoyed when they were performed differently by Konstantin Stanislavsky and his company at the Moscow Art Theatre. The essence of Chekhov's comedies is his recognition of the disparity between the facts of our existence and the ideals and aspirations by which we attempt — usually unsuccessfully — to live. Life in a Chekhov play is both meaningful and painful, pathetic and ludicrous. But it is never melodramatic.

The Cherry Orchard, of course, deals with the breaking down of an older order: it reveals the condition of the life of the old landowners, personified by Mme. Ranevsky and Gaev, and the new guard, in the person of Lopahin. Chekhov satirizes the rural landowners he had met as a young man, their unbelievable incompetence not only in managing their estates but in carrying on the most ordinary responsibilities of daily life. Out of touch with reality, sentimental and romantic, they indulged themselves in dreams and idleness. Crises, when they appeared, were met with confusion and surprise. If devoted servants or sympathetic, hard-headed businessmen did not come to their rescue, they were lost.

Chekhov was amused and angered by these foolish people, both of which feelings are obvious in *The Cherry Orchard*. The play depicts a wryly ironical comic scene, a scene which is not without pathos and some tattered nostalgia. But it is also a scene which Chekhov implies is vanishing — disappearing thanks to the self-destructive impulses of stupid, deluded, and irresponsible landowners. In the picture he paints, the faint shadows of the coming Russian Revolution can be seen on the horizon. His human understanding of the characters and their dilemmas gives the play the dimension of sympathy that often encourages directors and performers to present it as a tragedy or tragicomedy. But the suppressed indignation apparent in his subtle satires gives the play the humorous balance it needs to keep it from becoming melodramatic or pathetic.

Mme. Ranevsky is perhaps the epitome of a Chekhovian heroine. She is *not* a beautiful, fragile lady of great taste and refinement who is being cruelly deprived of all she holds dear. She is a foolish, middle-aged woman, flighty, sentimental, irresponsible, with a lover who has been using her guilt, grief, and good nature to his advantage. She is not a bad woman; she is simply not very bright. Sentiment, rather than sense, animates her.

Mme. Ranevsky has lived and spent prodigally in Paris. Her return home is dictated partly by lack of funds, partly by the defection of her lover. Meanwhile, back at the estate her brother Gaev, a lazy, foolish, idle incompetent, has been letting everything go to pieces. Lopahin, rich and earnest, the grandson of a former serf on the estate, proposes cutting down the famous cherry orchard in order to develop summer homes. Not only will this pay off the estate's debts, but it will provide a handy profit — at least 25,000 rubles a year — enough to support the irresponsible Ranevskys indefinitely, leaving the rest of the estate untouched.

Cutting down the orchard is not great cruelty perpetrated on the Ranevskys. It is made quite clear that the orchard is dying anyway; a crop grows only every other year, and there is no market for it. Ignorant romanticism, *not* a tragic flaw, makes Gaev and Mme. Ranevsky recoil from Lopahin's intelligent suggestion. Indeed, the cherry orchard is often viewed as a Chekhovian symbol for the Ranevskys themselves: dying, used up, ineffectual, ready to be cut down and replaced with something new and functional. They manage to miss or mangle every opportunity to do something positive to save the estate. After Lopahin has purchased the estate, it could still remain in the family if either he or Varya could muster the courage to suggest marriage. They miss even that chance because they are unable to come to terms with reality.

The play is an intricately plotted web of such complications, almost all of them provoked by the various characters' ludicrously human lack of self-knowledge, not by their nobility. They have vague feelings, vague desires, but none emerges clearly enough for them to act forcefully, positively. Even when choices are obvious, they manage to sink into confusion. Oddly, only such lower-class people as Lopahin, Yasha, and Dunyasha have a clear idea of what they want and how to get it, and even *they* usually strive ineffectually.

The plot may be subtle, but it is *not* confused. The action of the play is fundamentally mental, rather than physical, though there are a number of important visible actions which reveal or demonstrate mental attitudes. Because this is a drama of Realism, a record of life as it was lived at this time on the Russian estates, no detail is meaningless. All are part of the whole and must be seen in that light. Even random remarks, conversations to which no one listens — all are threads of this life-fabric. Thus the characters are necessary, functional; they are not merely added for atmosphere. Without any one of them, certain moments of conflict or revelation would not be possible in this drama. That might not be immediately apparent in reading, but seeing the play professionally produced leaves no doubt of the brilliantly plotted interrelations. If the stagings do not stress this, it is because the directors have not understood Chekhov's meaning and method.

This is no pastoral idyll. That twang in the orchard tells us that the silver cord has snapped not only for the dying trees, but also for the doomed and dying aristocracy.

G. L.

ANTON CHEKHOV

The Cherry Orchard

TRANSLATED BY ROBERT W. CORRIGAN

Characters

LYUBOV ANDREYEVNA RANEVSKY, *owner of the cherry orchard*
ANYA, *her daughter, age 17*
VARYA, *her adopted daughter, age 24*
LEONID ANDREYEVICH GAEV, *Lyubov's brother*
YERMOLAY ALEXEYEVICH LOPAHIN, *a business man*
PYOTR SERGEYEVICH TROFIMOV, *a student*
BORIS BORISOVICH SEMYONOV-PISHCHIK, *a landowner*
CHARLOTTA IVANOVNA, *a governess*
SEMYON PANTALEYEVICH EPIHODOV, *a clerk on the Ranevsky estate*
DUNYASHA, *a maid*
FEERS, *an old servant, age 87*
YASHA, *a young servant*
A TRAMP
THE STATION MASTER
A POST-OFFICE CLERK
Guests and Servants

(*The action takes place on the estate of Madame Ranevsky.*)

ACT ONE

(*A room which used to be the children's room and is still called the nursery. Several doors, one leading into* ANYA's *room. It is early in the morning and the sun is rising. It is early in May, but there is a morning frost. The windows are closed but through them can be seen the blossoming cherry trees. Enter* DUNYASHA, *carrying a candle, and* LOPAHIN *with a book in his hand.*)

LOPAHIN. The train's arrived, thank God. What time is it?

DUNYASHA. It's nearly two. (*Blows out the candle.*) It's daylight already.

LOPAHIN. The train must have been at least two hours late. (*Yawns and stretches.*) And what a fool I am! I make a special trip out here to meet them at the station, and then I fall asleep. . . . Just sat down in the chair and dropped off. What a nuisance. Why didn't you wake me up?

DUNYASHA. I thought you'd gone. (*Listens.*) I think they're coming.

LOPAHIN (*also listens*). No . . . I should've been there to help them with their luggage and other things. . . . (*Pause.*) Lyubov Andreyevna has been abroad for five years. I wonder what she's like now. She used to be such a kind and good person. So easy to get along with and always considerate. Why, I remember when I was fifteen, my father — he had a store in town then — hit me in the face and it made my nose bleed. . . . We'd come out here for something or other, and he was drunk. Oh, I remember it as if it happened yesterday. . . . She was so young and beautiful . . . Lyubov Andreyevna brought me into this very room — the nursery — and she fixed my nose and she said to me, "Don't cry, little peasant, it'll be better by the time you get married." . . . (*Pause.*) "Little peasant" . . . She was right, my father was a peasant. And look at me now — going about in a white waistcoat and brown shoes, like a crow in peacock's feathers. Oh, I am rich all right, I've got lots of money, but when you think about it, I'm still just a peasant. (*Turning over pages of the book.*) Here, I've been reading this book, and couldn't understand a word of it. Fell asleep reading it. (*Pause.*)

DUNYASHA. The dogs have been awake all night: they know their mistress is coming.

LOPAHIN. Why, what's the matter with you, Dunyasha?

DUNYASHA. My hands are shaking. I think I'm going to faint.

LOPAHIN. You've become too delicate and refined, Dunyasha. You get yourself all dressed up like a lady, and you fix your hair like one, too. You shouldn't do that, you know. You must remember your place.

(*Enter* EPIHODOV *with a bouquet of flowers; he wears a jacket and brightly polished high boots which squeak loudly. As he enters he drops the flowers.*)

EPIHODOV (*picks up the flowers*). The gardener sent these. He says they're to go in the dining room. (*Hands the flowers to* DUNYASHA.)

LOPAHIN. And bring me some kvass.

DUNYASHA. All right.

EPIHODOV. It's chilly outside this morning, three degrees of frost, and here the cherry trees are all in bloom. I can't say much for this climate of ours, you know. (*Sighs.*) No, I really can't. It doesn't contribute to — well, you know — things. . . . And what do you think, Yermolay Alexeyevich, the day before yesterday I bought myself a pair of boots and they squeak so much . . . well, I mean to say, they're impossible. . . . What can I use to fix them?

LOPAHIN. Oh, be quiet! And don't bother me!

EPIHODOV. Every day something unpleasant happens to me. But I don't complain; I'm used to it, why, I even laugh.

(*Enter* DUNYASHA; *she serves* LOPAHIN *with kvass.*)

Well, I have to be going. (*Bumps into a chair which falls over.*) There, you see! (*Triumphantly.*) You can see for yourself what I mean, you see . . . so to speak . . . It's absolutely amazing! (*Goes out.*)

DUNYASHA. I must tell you a secret, Yermolay Alexeyevich. Epihodov proposed to me.

LOPAHIN. Really!

DUNYASHA. I don't know what to do. . . . He's a quiet man, but then sometimes he starts talking, and then you can't understand a word he says. It sounds nice, and he says it with so much feeling, but it doesn't make any sense. I think I like him a little, and he's madly in love with me. But the poor man, he's sort of unlucky! Do you know, something unpleasant seems to happen to him every day. That's why they tease him and call him "two-and-twenty misfortunes."

LOPAHIN (*listens*). I think I hear them coming. . . .

DUNYASHA. Coming! . . . Oh, what's the matter with me? . . . I feel cold all over.

LOPAHIN. Yes, they're really coming! Let's go and meet them at the door. I wonder if she'll recognize me? We haven't seen each other for five years.

DUNYASHA (*agitated*). I'm going to faint . . . Oh, I'm going to faint!

(*The sound of two carriages driving up to the house can be heard.* LOPAHIN *and* DUNYASHA *hurry out. The stage is empty. Then there are sounds of people arriving in the next room.* FEERS, *who has gone to meet the train, enters the room leaning on a cane. He crosses the stage as rapidly as he can. He is dressed in an old-fashioned livery coat and a top hat and is muttering to himself, though it is impossible to make out what he is saying. The noises off-stage become louder.*)

VOICE (*off-stage*). Let's go through here.

(*Enter* LYUBOV ANDREYEVNA, ANYA, *and* CHARLOTTA IVANOVNA, *leading a small dog, all in traveling clothes,* VARYA, *wearing an overcoat and a kerchief over her head,* GAEV, SEMYONOV-PISHCHIK, LOPAHIN, DUNYASHA, *carrying a bundle and parasol and other servants with luggage.*

ANYA. Let's go through here. Do you remember what room this is, Mamma?

LYUBOV (*joyfully, through her tears*). The nursery!

VARYA. How cold it is! My hands are numb. (*To* LYUBOV.) Your rooms are the same as always, Mamma dear, the white one, and the lavender one.

LYUBOV. The nursery, my dear, beautiful room! . . . I used to sleep here when I was little. (*Cries.*) And here I am again, like a little child . . . (*She kisses her brother, then* VARYA, *then her brother again.*) And Varya hasn't changed a bit, looking like a nun. And I recognized Dunyasha, *too.* (*Kisses* DUNYASHA.)

GAEV. The train was two hours late. Just think of it! Such efficiency!

CHARLOTTA (*to* PISHCHIK). And my dog eats nuts, too.

PISHCHIK (*astonished*). Think of that!

(*They all go out except* ANYA *and* DUNYASHA.)

DUNYASHA. We've waited and waited for you . . . (*Helps* ANYA *to take off her hat and coat.*)

ANYA. I haven't slept for four nights . . . I'm freezing.

DUNYASHA. It was Lent when you left, and it was snowing and freezing; but it's spring now. Darling! (*She laughs and kisses her.*) Oh, how I've missed you! I could hardly stand it. My pet, my precious . . . But I must tell you . . . I can't wait another minute . . .

ANYA (*without enthusiasm*). What time is it? . . .

DUNYASHA. Epihodov, the clerk, proposed to me right after Easter.

ANYA. You never talk about anything else . . . (*Tidies her hair.*) I've lost all my hairpins. . . . (*She's so tired she can hardly keep on her feet.*)

DUNYASHA. I really don't know what to think. He loves me . . . he loves me very much!

ANYA (*looking through the door into her room, tenderly*). My own room, my own windows, just as if I'd never left them! I'm home again! Tomorrow I'm going to get up and run right to the garden! Oh, if only I could fall asleep! I couldn't sleep all the way back, I've been so worried.

DUNYASHA. Pyotr Sergeyevich came the day before yesterday.

ANYA (*joyfully*). Petya!

DUNYASHA. We put him in the bathhouse, he's probably asleep now. He said he didn't want to inconvenience you. (*Looks at her watch.*) I should have gotten him up, but Varya told me not to. "Don't you dare get him up," she said.

(*Enter* VARYA *with a bunch of keys at her waist.*)

VARYA. Dunyasha, get some coffee, and hurry! Mamma wants some.

DUNYASHA. I'll get it right away. (*Goes out.*)

VARYA. Thank God, you're back! You're home again. (*Embracing her.*) My little darling's come home! How are you, my precious?

ANYA. If you only knew what I've had to put up with!

VARYA. I can just imagine . . .

ANYA. You remember, I left just before Easter and it was cold then. And Charlotta never stopped talking the whole time, talking and those silly tricks of hers. Why did you make me take Charlotta?

VARYA. But you couldn't go all alone, darling. At seventeen!

ANYA. When we got to Paris it was cold and snowing. My French was terrible. Mamma was living on the fifth floor, and the place was filled with people — some French ladies, and an old priest with a little book, and the room was full of cigarette smoke. It was so unpleasant. All of a sudden I felt so sorry for Mamma that I put my arms around her neck and hugged her and wouldn't let go, I was so upset. Later Mamma cried and was very kind.

VARYA (*tearfully*). I can't stand to hear it! . . .

ANYA. She had already sold her villa at Mentone, and she had nothing left, not a thing. And I didn't have any money left either, not a penny. In fact, I barely had enough to get to Paris. And Mamma didn't understand it at all. On the way, we'd eat at the best restaurants and she'd order the most expensive dishes and tip the waiters a rouble each. Charlotta's the same way. And Yasha expected a full-course dinner for himself; it was horrible. You know, Yasha is Mamma's valet, now, we brought him with us.

VARYA. Yes, I've seen the scoundrel.

ANYA. Well, how's everything here? Have you paid the interest on the mortgage?

VARYA. With what?

ANYA. Oh dear! Oh dear!

VARYA. The time runs out in August, and then it will be up for sale.

ANYA. Oh dear!

LOPAHIN (*puts his head through the door and moos like a cow*). Moo-o. . . . (*Disappears.*)

VARYA (*tearfully*). I'd like to hit him . . . (*Clenches her fist.*)

ANYA (*her arms round* VARYA, *dropping her voice*). Varya, has he proposed to you? (VARYA *shakes her head.*) But he loves you. . . . Why don't you talk to him, what are you waiting for?

VARYA. Nothing will come of it. He's too busy to have time to think of me . . . He doesn't notice me at all. It's easier when he isn't around, it makes me miserable just to see him. Everybody talks of our wedding and congratulates me, but in fact there's nothing to it, it's all a dream. (*In a different tone.*) You've got a new pin, it looks like a bee.

ANYA (*sadly*). Mamma bought it for me. (*She goes into her room and then with childlike gaiety.*) Did you know that in Paris I went up in a balloon?

VARYA. My darling's home again! My precious one's home.

(DUNYASHA *returns with a coffeepot and prepares coffee.*)

(*Standing by* ANYA's *door.*) You know, all day long, as I go about the house doing my work, I'm always dreaming. If only we could marry you to some rich man, I'd be more at peace. Then I could go away; first I'd go to the cloisters, and then I'd go on a pilgrimage to Kiev, and then Moscow . . . I'd spend my life just walking from one holy place to another. On and on. Oh, what a wonderful life that would be!

ANYA. The birds are singing in the garden. What time is it?

VARYA. It must be nearly three. Time you went to bed, darling. (*Goes into* ANYA'S *room.*) Oh, what a wonderful life!

(*Enter* YASHA, *with a blanket and a small bag.*)

YASHA (*crossing the stage, in an affectedly genteel voice*). May I go through here?

DUNYASHA. My, how you've changed since you've been abroad, Yasha. I hardly recognized you.

YASHA. Hm! And who are you?

DUNYASHA. When you went away, I was no bigger than this . . . (*shows her height from the floor*). I'm Dunyasha, Fyodor's daughter. You don't remember me!

YASHA. Hm! You're quite a little peach! (*Looks around and embraces her; she screams and drops a saucer.* YASHA *goes out quickly.*)

VARYA (*in the doorway, crossly*). What's happening in here?

DUNYASHA (*tearfully*). I've broken a saucer.

VARYA. That's good luck.

ANYA (*coming out of her room*). We ought to warn Mamma that Petya's here.

VARYA. I gave strict orders not to wake him up.

ANYA (*pensively*). Six years ago father died, and then a month later Grisha was drowned in the river. He was such a beautiful little boy — and only seven! Mamma couldn't stand it so she went away . . . and never looked back. (*Shivers.*) How well I understand her! If she only knew! (*Pause.*) And, Petya was Grisha's tutor, he might remind her . . .

(*Enter* FEERS, *wearing a jacket and a white waistcoat.*)

FEERS (*goes over and is busy with the samovar*). The mistress will have her coffee in here. (*Puts on white gloves.*) Is it ready? (*To* DUNYASHA, *severely.*) Where's the cream?

DUNYASHA. Oh, I forgot! (*Goes out quickly.*)

FEERS (*fussing around the coffeepot*). That girl's hopeless. . . . (*Mutters.*) They've come from Paris . . . Years ago the master used to go to Paris . . . used to go by carriage. . . . (*Laughs.*)

VARYA. Feers, what are you laughing at?

FEERS. What would you like? (*Happily.*) The mistress has come home! Home at last! I don't mind if I die now . . . (*Weeps with joy.*)

(*Enter* LYUBOV, LOPAHIN, GAEV *and* SEMYONOV-PISHCHIK, *the latter in a long peasant coat of fine cloth and full trousers tucked inside high boots.* GAEV, *as he comes in, moves his arms and body as if he were playing billiards.*)

LYUBOV. How does it go now? Let me think . . . The red off the side and into the middle pocket!

GAEV. That's right! Then I put the white into the corner pocket! . . . Years ago we used to sleep in this room, and now I'm fifty-one, strange as it may seem.

LOPAHIN. Yes, time flies.

GAEV. What?

LOPAHIN. Time flies, I say.

GAEV. This place smells of patchouli . . .

ANYA. I'm going to bed. Goodnight, Mamma. (*Kisses her.*)

LYUBOV. My precious child! (*Kisses her hands.*) Are you glad you're home? I still can't get used to it.

ANYA. Goodnight, Uncle.

GAEV (*kisses her face and hands*). God bless you. You're so much like your mother! (*To his sister.*) You looked exactly like her at her age, Lyuba.

(ANYA *shakes hands with* LOPAHIN *and* PISHCHIK, *goes out and shuts the door after her.*)

LYUBOV. She's very tired.

PISHCHIK. It's been a long trip for her.

VARYA (*to* LOPAHIN *and* PISHCHIK). Well, gentlemen? It's nearly three o'clock, time to say good-bye.

LYUBOV (*laughs*). You haven't changed a bit, Varya. (*Draws* VARYA *to her and kisses her.*) Let me have some coffee, then we'll all turn in.

(FEERS *places a cushion under her feet.*)

Thank you, my dear. I've got into the habit of drinking coffee. I drink it day and night. Thank you, my dear old friend. (*Kisses* FEERS.)

VARYA. I'd better see if they brought all the luggage in. (*Goes out.*)

LYUBOV. Is it really me sitting here? (*Laughing.*) I'd like to dance and wave my arms about. (*Covering her face with her hands.*) But am I just dreaming? God, how I love it here — my own country! Oh, I love it so much, I could hardly see anything from the train, I was crying so hard. (*Through tears.*) Here, but I must drink my coffee. Thank you, Feers, thank you, my dear old friend, I'm so glad you're still alive.

FEERS. The day before yesterday.

GAEV. He doesn't hear very well.

LOPAHIN. I've got to leave for Kharkov a little after four. What a nuisance! It's so good just to see you, and I want to talk with you . . . You look as lovely as ever.

PISHCHIK (*breathing heavily*). Prettier. In her fancy Parisian clothes . . . she's simply ravishing!

LOPAHIN. Your brother here — Leonid Andreyevich — says that I'm nothing but a hick from the country, a tight-fisted peasant, but it doesn't bother me. Let him say what he likes. All I want is that you trust me as you always have. Merciful God! My father was your father's serf, and your grandfather's, too, but you've done so much for me that I've forgotten all that. I love you as if you were my own sister . . . more than that even.

LYUBOV. I just can't sit still, I can't for the life of me! (*She jumps up and walks about in great excitement.*) I'm so happy, it's too much for me. It's all right, you can laugh at me. I know I'm being silly . . . My wonderful old bookcase! (*Kisses bookcase.*) And my little table!

GAEV. You know, the old Nurse died while you were away.

LYUBOV (*sits down and drinks coffee*). Yes, you wrote to me about it. May she rest in peace.

GAEV. Anastasy died, too. And Petrushka quit and is working in town for the chief of police. (*Takes a box of gumdrops out of his pocket and puts one in his mouth.*)

PISHCHIK. My daughter, Dashenka, sends you her greetings.

LOPAHIN. I feel like telling you some good news, something to cheer you up. (*Looks at his watch.*) I'll have to leave in a minute, so there's not much time to talk. But briefly it's this. As you know, the cherry orchard is going to be sold to pay your debts. They've set August 22nd as the date for the auction, but you can sleep in peace and not worry about it; there's a way out. Here's my plan, so please pay close attention. Your estate is only twenty miles from town, and the railroad is close by. Now, if the cherry orchard and the land along the river were subdivided and leased for the building of summer cottages, you'd have a yearly income of at least twenty-five thousand roubles.

GAEV. Such nonsense!

LYUBOV. I'm afraid I don't quite understand, Yermolay Alexeyevich.

LOPAHIN. You'd divide the land into one acre lots and rent them for at least twenty-five roubles a year. I'll bet you that if you advertise it now there won't be a lot left by the fall; they'll be snapped up almost at once. You see, you're saved! And really, I must congratulate you; it's a perfect setup. The location is marvelous and the river's deep enough for swimming. Of course, the land will have to be cleared and cleaned up a bit. For instance, all those old buildings will have to be torn down . . . and this house, too . . . but then it's not really good for anything any more. . . . And then, the old cherry orchard will have to be cut down . . .

LYUBOV. Cut down? My good man, forgive me, but you don't seem to understand. If there's one thing that's interesting and really valuable in this whole part of the country, it's our cherry orchard.

LOPAHIN. The only valuable thing about it is that it's very large. It only produces a crop every other year and then who wants to buy it?

GAEV. Why, this orchard is even mentioned in the Encyclopedia.

LOPAHIN (*looking at his watch*). If you don't decide now, and do something about it before August, the cherry orchard as well as the estate will be auctioned off. So make up your minds! There's no other way out, I promise you. There's no other way.

FEERS. In the old days, forty or fifty years ago, the cherries were dried, preserved, pickled, made into jam, and sometimes . . .

GAEV. Be quiet, Feers.

FEERS. And sometimes whole wagon-loads of dried cherries were shipped to Moscow and Kharkov. We used to make a lot of money on them then! And the dried cherries used to be soft, juicy, sweet, and very good . . . They knew how to do it then . . . they had a way of cooking them . . .

LYUBOV. And where is that recipe now?

FEERS. They've forgotten it. Nobody can remember it.

PISHCHIK (*to* LYUBOV). What's it like in Paris? Did you eat frogs?

LYUBOV. I ate crocodiles.

PISHCHIK. Well, will you imagine that!

LOPAHIN. Until recently only rich people and peasants lived in the country, but now lots of people come out for the summer. Almost every town, even the small ones, is surrounded with summer places. And probably within the next twenty years there'll be more and more of these people. Right now, all they do is sit on the porch and drink tea, but later on they might begin to grow a few things, and then your cherry orchard would be full of life again . . . rich and prosperous.

GAEV (*indignantly*). Such a lot of nonsense!

(*Enter* VARYA *and* YASHA.)

VARYA. There were two telegrams for you, Mamma dear. (*Takes out the keys and opens the old bookcase, making a great deal of noise.*) Here they are.

LYUBOV. They're from Paris. (*Tears them up without reading them.*) I'm through with Paris.

GAEV. Do you know, Lyuba, how old this bookcase is? Last week I pulled out the bottom drawer, and I found the date it was made burned in the wood. Just think, it's exactly a hundred years old. What do you think of that, eh? We ought to celebrate its anniversary. I know it's an inanimate object, but still — it's a bookcase!

PISHCHIK (*astonished*). A hundred years! Can you imagine that!

GAEV. Yes . . . that's quite something. (*Feeling round the bookcase with his hands.*) Dear, most honored bookcase! I salute you! For one hundred years you have served the highest ideals of goodness and justice. For one hundred years you have made us aware of the need for creative work; several generations of our family have had their courage sustained and their faith in a brighter future fortified by your silent call; you have fostered in us the ideals of public service and social consciousness. (*Pause.*)

LOPAHIN. Yes . . .

LYUBOV. You haven't changed a bit, Leonid.

GAEV (*slightly embarrassed*). I shoot it off the corner into the middle pocket! . . .

LOPAHIN (*looks at his watch*). Well, I've got to go.

YASHA (*brings medicine to* LYUBOV). Would you like to take your pills now; it's time.

PISHCHIK. You shouldn't take medicine, my dear . . . they don't do you any good . . . or harm either. Let me have them. (*Takes the box from her, pours the pills into the palm of his hand, blows on them, puts them all into his mouth and drinks them down with kvass*). There!

LYUBOV (*alarmed*). You're out of your mind!

PISHCHIK. I took all the pills.

LOPAHIN. What a stomach! (*All laugh.*)

FEERS. His honor was here during Holy Week, and he ate half a bucket of pickles. (*Mutters.*)

LYUBOV. What's he saying?

VARYA. He's been muttering like that for three years now. We're used to it.

YASHA. It's his age. . . .

(CHARLOTTA IVANOVNA, *very thin, and tightly laced in a white dress, with a lorgnette at her waist, passes across the stage.*)

LOPAHIN. Excuse me, Charlotta Ivanovna, for not greeting you. I didn't have a chance. (*Tries to kiss her hand.*)

CHARLOTTA (*withdrawing her hand*). If I let you kiss my hand, then you'd want to kiss my elbow next, and then my shoulder.

LOPAHIN. This just isn't my lucky day. (*All laugh.*) Charlotta Ivanovna, do a trick for us.

CHARLOTTA. Not now. I want to go to bed. (*Goes out.*)

LOPAHIN. I'll be back in three weeks. (*Kisses* LYUBOV'*s hand.*) It's time I'm going so I'll say good-bye. (*To* GAEV.) Au revoir. (*Embraces* PISHCHIK). Au revoir. (*Shakes hands with* VARYA, *then with* FEERS *and* YASHA.) I don't want to go, really. (*To* LYUBOV.) Think over the idea of the summer cottages and if you decide anything, let me know, and I'll get you a loan of at least fifty thousand. So think it over seriously.

VARYA (*crossly*). Won't you ever go?

LOPAHIN. I'm going, I'm going. (*Goes out.*)

GAEV. What a boor! I beg your pardon . . . Varya's going to marry him, he's Varya's fiancé.

VARYA. Please don't talk like that, Uncle.

LYUBOV. Well, Varya, I'd be delighted. He's a good man.

PISHCHIK. He's a man . . . you have to say that . . . a most worthy fellow . . . My Dashenka says so too . . . she says all sorts of things. . . . (*He drops asleep and snores, but wakes up again at once.*) By the way, my dear, will you lend me two hundred and forty roubles? I've got to pay the interest on the mortgage tomorrow . . .

VARYA (*in alarm*). We haven't got it, really we haven't!

LYUBOV. It's true, I haven't got a thing.

PISHCHIK. It'll turn up. (*Laughs.*) I never lose hope. There are times when I think everything's lost, I'm ruined, and then — suddenly! — a railroad is built across my land, and they pay me for it! Something's bound to happen, if not today, then tomorrow, or the next day. Perhaps Dashenka will win two hundred thousand — she's got a lottery ticket.

LYUBOV. Well, we've finished our coffee; now we can go to bed.

FEERS (*brushing* GAEV, *admonishing him*). You've got on those trousers again! What am I going to do with you?

VARYA (*in a low voice*). Anya's asleep. (*Quietly opens a window.*) The sun's rising and see how wonderful the trees are! And the air smells so fragrant! The birds are beginning to sing.

GAEV (*coming to the window*). The orchard is all white. You haven't forgotten, Lyuba? How straight that lane is . . . just like a ribbon. And how it shines on moonlight nights. Do you remember? You haven't forgotten, have you?

LYUBOV (*looks through the window at the orchard*). Oh, my childhood, my innocent childhood! I used to sleep here, and I'd look out at the orchard and every morning when I woke up I was so happy. The orchard was exactly the same, nothing's changed. (*Laughs happily.*) All, all white! Oh, my orchard! After the dark, gloomy autumn and the cold winter, you are young again and full of joy; the angels have not deserted you! If only this burden could be taken from me, if only I could forget my past!

GAEV. Yes, and now the orchard's going to be sold to pay our debts, how strange it all is.

LYUBOV. Look, there's Mother walking through the orchard . . . dressed all in white! (*Laughs happily.*) It is Mother!

GAEV. Where?

VARYA. Oh, please, Mamma dear!

LYUBOV. You're right, it's no one, I only imagined it. Over there, you see, on the right, by the path that goes to the arbor, there's a small white tree that's bending so it looks just like a woman.

(*Enter* TROFIMOV. *He is dressed in a shabby student's uniform and wears glasses.*)

What a wonderful orchard! Masses of white blossoms, the blue sky . . .

TROFIMOV. Lyubov Andreyevna! (*She turns to him.*) I'll just say hello and leave at once. (*Kisses her hand warmly.*) They told me to wait until morning, but I couldn't wait any longer. (LYUBOV *looks at him, puzzled.*)

VARYA (*through tears*). This is Petya Trofimov.

TROFIMOV. Petya Trofimov, I was Grisha's tutor. Have I changed that much?

(LYUBOV *puts her arms round him and weeps quietly.*)

GAEV (*embarrassed*). Now, now, Lyuba . . .

VARYA (*weeps*). Didn't I tell you to wait until tomorrow, Petya?

LYUBOV. My Grisha . . . my little boy . . . oh, Grisha . . . my son . . .

VARYA. Don't cry, Mamma darling. There's nothing we can do, it was God's will.

TROFIMOV (*gently, with emotion*). Don't, don't . . . please.

LYUBOV (*weeping quietly*). My little boy was lost . . . drowned . . . Why? Why, my friend? (*More quietly.*) Anya's asleep in there, and here I'm crying and making a scene. But tell me, Petya, what's happened to your good looks? You've aged so.

TROFIMOV. A peasant woman on the train called me "that moth-eaten man."

LYUBOV. You used to be such an attractive boy, a typical young student. But now your hair is thin and you wear glasses. Are you still a student? (*She walks to the door.*)

TROFIMOV. I expect I'll be a student as long as I live.

LYUBOV (*kisses her brother, then* VARYA). Well, go to bed now. You have aged, too, Leonid.

PISHCHIK (*following her*). Yes, I suppose it's time to get to bed. Oh, my gout! I'd better spend the night here, and in the morning, Lyubov Andreyevna, my dear, I'd like to borrow the two hundred and forty roubles.

GAEV. Don't you ever stop?

PISHCHIK. Just two hundred and forty roubles . . . To pay the interest on my mortgage.

LYUBOV. I haven't any money, my friend.

PISHCHIK. Oh, I'll pay you back, my dear. It's not much, after all.

LYUBOV. Oh, all right. Leonid will give it to you. You give him the money, Leonid.

GAEV. Why, of course; glad to. As much as he wants!

LYUBOV. What else can we do? He needs it. He'll pay it back.

(LYUBOV, TROFIMOV, PISHCHIK *and* FEERS *go out.* GAEV, VARYA *and* YASHA *remain.*)

GAEV. My sister hasn't lost her habit of throwing money away. (*To* YASHA.) Get out of the way, you smell like a barnyard.

YASHA (*with a sneer*). And you haven't changed either, have you, Leonid Andreyevich?

GAEV. What's that? (*To* VARYA.) What did he say?

VARYA (*to* YASHA). Your mother came out from town yesterday to see you, and she's been waiting out in the servants' quarters ever since.

YASHA. I wish she wouldn't bother me.

VARYA. Oh, you ought to be ashamed of yourself.

YASHA. What's she in such a hurry for? She could have come tomorrow. (YASHA *goes out.*)

VARYA. Mamma hasn't changed a bit. She'd give away everything we had, if she could.

GAEV. Yes . . . You know, when many things are prescribed to cure a disease, that means it's incurable. I've been wracking my brains to find an answer, and I've come up with several solutions, plenty of them — which means there aren't any. It would be wonderful if we could inherit some money, or if our Anya were to marry some very rich man, or if one of us went to Yaroslavl and tried our luck with our old aunt, the Countess. You know she's very rich.

VARYA (*weeping*). If only God would help us.

GAEV. Oh, stop blubbering! The Countess is very rich, but she doesn't like us . . . To begin with, my sister married a lawyer, and not a nobleman . . . (ANYA *appears in the doorway.*) She married a commoner . . . and since then no one can say she's behaved in the most virtuous way possible. She's good, kind, and lovable, and I love her very much, but no matter how much you may allow for extenuating circumstances, you've got to admit that her morals have not been beyond reproach. You can sense it in everything she does . . .

VARYA (*in a whisper*). Anya's standing in the doorway.

GAEV. What? (*A pause.*) Isn't that strange, something's gotten into my right eye . . . I'm having a terrible time seeing. And last Thursday, when I was in the District Court . . .

(ANYA *comes in.*)

VARYA. Anya, why aren't you asleep?

ANYA. I don't feel like sleeping. I just can't.

GAEV. My dear little girl! (*Kisses* ANYA'*s face and hands.*) My child! (*Tearfully.*) You're not just my niece, you're an angel, my whole world. Please believe me, believe . . .

ANYA. I believe you, Uncle. Everyone loves you, respects you . . . but, dear Uncle, you shouldn't talk so much, just try to keep quiet. What were you saying just now about mother, about your own sister? What made you say that?

GAEV. Yes, yes! (*He takes her hand and puts it over his face.*) You're quite right, it was a horrible thing to say! My God! My God! And that speech I made to the bookcase . . . so stupid! As soon as I finished it, I realized how stupid it was.

VARYA. It's true, Uncle dear, you oughtn't to talk so much. Just keep quiet, that's all.

ANYA. If you keep quiet, you'll find life is more peaceful.

GAEV. I'll be quiet. (*Kisses* ANYA'*s and* VARYA'*s hands.*) I'll be quiet. But I must tell you something about all this business, it's important. Last Thursday I went to the District Court, and I got talking with some friends, and from what they said it looks as if it might be possible to get a second mortgage so we can pay the interest to the bank.

VARYA. If only God would help us!

GAEV. I'm going again on Tuesday to talk with them some more. (*To* VARYA.) Oh, stop crying. (*To* ANYA.) Your mother's going to talk with Lopahin, and he certainly won't refuse her. And after you've had a little rest, you can go to Yaroslavl to see your great-aunt, the Countess. You see, we'll attack the problem from three sides, and — it's as good as solved! We'll pay the interest, I'm sure of it. (*He eats a gumdrop.*) On my honor, on anything you like, I swear the estate'll not be sold! (*Excited.*) I'll bet my happiness on it! Here's my hand, you can call me a worthless liar if I allow the auction to take place. I swear it with all my soul!

ANYA (*calmer, with an air of happiness*). How good you are, Uncle, and how sensible! (*Embracing him.*) I'm not afraid any more. I feel so happy and at peace.

(*Enter* FEERS.)

FEERS (*reproachfully*). Leonid Andreyevich, aren't you ashamed of yourself? When are you going to bed?

GAEV. In a minute. Now you go away, Feers. I can get ready for bed myself. Come along, children, time for bed. We'll talk about it some more tomorrow, you must go to bed now. (*Kisses* ANYA *and* VARYA.) You know, I'm a man of the 'eighties. People don't think much of that period these days, but still I can say that I've suffered a great deal in my lifetime because of my convictions. There's a reason why the peasants love me. You have to know the peasants! You have to know . . .

ANYA. You're beginning again, Uncle!

VARYA. Yes, you'd better keep quiet, Uncle dear.

FEERS (*sternly*). Leonid Andreyevich!

GAEV. I'm coming, I'm coming! Go to bed now! Bank the white into the side pocket. There's a shot for you . . . (*Goes out;* FEERS *hobbles after him.*)

ANYA. I feel better now, although I don't want to go to Yaroslavl, I don't like the Countess at all. But then, thanks to Uncle, we really don't have to worry at all. (*She sits down.*)

VARYA. I've got to get some sleep. I'm going. Oh, by the way, we had a terrible scene while you were gone. You know, there are only a few old servants left out in the servants' quarters: just Yefmushka, Polya, Yevstignay, and Karp. Well, they let some tramp sleep out there, and at first I didn't say anything about it. But then later, I heard people saying that I had given orders to feed them nothing but beans. Because I was stingy, you see . . . Yevstignay was the cause of it all. "Well," I think to myself, "if that's how things are, just you wait!" So I called Yevstignay in. (*Yawns.*) So he came. "What's all this, Yevstignay," I said to him, "you're such a fool." (*She walks up to* ANYA.) Anichka! (*A pause.*) She's asleep! . . . (*Takes her arm.*) Let's go to bed! Come! (*Leads her away.*) My darling's fallen asleep! Come . . .

(*They go towards the door. The sound of a shepherd's pipe is heard from far away, beyond the orchard.* TROFIMOV *crosses the stage, but, seeing* VARYA *and* ANYA, *stops.*)

Sh-sh! She's asleep . . . asleep . . . Come along, come along.

ANYA (*softly, half-asleep*). I'm so tired. . . . I can hear the bells ringing all the time. . . . Uncle . . . dear . . . Mamma and Uncle . . .

VARYA. Come, darling, come. . . . (*They go into* ANYA'*s room.*)

TROFIMOV (*deeply moved*). Oh, Anya . . . my sunshine! My spring!

ACT TWO

(*An old abandoned chapel in a field. Beside it are a well, an old bench, and some tombstones. A road leads to the Ranevsky estate. On one side a row of poplars casts a shadow; at that point the cherry orchard begins. In the distance, a line of telegraph poles can be seen, and beyond them on the horizon is the outline of a large town, visible only in very clear weather. It's nearly sunset.* CHARLOTTA, YASHA *and* DUNYASHA *are sitting on the bench;* EPIHODOV *is standing near by, playing a guitar; everyone is lost in thought.* CHARLOTTA *is wearing an old hunting cap; she has taken a shotgun off her shoulder and is adjusting the buckle on the strap.*)

CHARLOTTA (*thoughtfully*). I don't know how old I am. For you see, I haven't got a passport . . . but I keep pretending that I'm still very young. When I was a little girl, my father and mother traveled from fair to fair giving performances — oh, very good ones. And I used to do the "*salto-mortale*" and all sorts of other tricks, too. When Papa and Mamma died, a German lady took me to live with her and sent me to school. So when I grew up I became a governess. But where I come from and who I am, I don't know. Who my parents were — perhaps they weren't even married — I don't know. (*Taking a cucumber from her pocket and beginning to eat it.*) I don't know anything. (*Pause.*) I'm longing to talk to someone, but there isn't anybody. I haven't anybody . . .

EPIHODOV (*plays the guitar and sings*). "What care I for the noisy world? . . . What care I for friends and foes?" How pleasant it is to play the mandolin!

DUNYASHA. That's a guitar, not a mandolin. (*She looks at herself in a little mirror and powders her face.*)

EPIHODOV. To a man who's madly in love this is a mandolin. (*Sings quietly.*) "If only my heart were warmed by the fire of love requited." . . . (YASHA *joins in.*)

CHARLOTTA. How dreadfully these people sing! . . . Ach! Like a bunch of jackals.

DUNYASHA (*to* YASHA). You're so lucky to have been abroad!

YASHA. Of course I am. Naturally. (*Yawns, then lights a cigar.*)

EPIHODOV. Stands to reason. Abroad everything's reached its maturity . . . I mean to say, everything's been going on for such a long time.

YASHA. Obviously.

EPIHODOV. Now, I'm a cultured man, I read all kinds of extraordinary books, you know, but somehow I can't seem to figure out where I'm going, what it is I really want, I mean to say — whether to live or to shoot myself. Nevertheless, I always carry a revolver on me. Here it is. (*Shows the revolver.*)

CHARLOTTA. That's finished, so now I'm going. (*Slips the strap of the gun over her shoulder.*) Yes, Epihodov, you are a very clever man, and frightening, too; the women must be wild about you! Brr! (*Walks off.*) All these clever people are so stupid, I haven't anyone to talk to. I'm so lonely, always alone, I have nobody and . . . and who I am and what I'm here for, nobody knows . . . (*Wanders out.*)

EPIHODOV. Frankly, and I want to keep to the point, I have to admit that Fate, so to speak, treats me absolutely without mercy, like a small ship is buffeted by the storm, as it were. I mean to say, suppose I'm mistaken, then why for instance should I wake up this morning and suddenly see a gigantic spider sitting on my chest? Like this . . . (*showing the size with both hands*). Or if I pick up a jug to have a drink of kvass, there's sure to be something horrible, like a cockroach, inside it. (*Pause.*) Have you read Buckle? (*Pause.*) May I trouble you for a moment, Dunyasha? I'd like to speak with you.

DUNYASHA. Well, go ahead.

EPIHODOV. I'd very much like to speak with you alone. (*Sighs.*)

DUNYASHA (*embarrassed*). Oh, all right . . . But first bring me my little cape . . . it's hanging by the cupboard. It's getting terribly chilly . . .

EPIHODOV. Very well, I'll get it. . . . Now I know what to do with my revolver. (*Takes his guitar and goes off playing it.*)

YASHA. Two-and-twenty misfortunes! Just between you and me, he's a stupid fool. (*Yawns.*)

DUNYASHA. I hope to God he doesn't shoot himself. (*Pause.*) He makes me so nervous and I'm always worrying about him. I came to live here when I was still a little girl. Now I no longer know how to live a simple life, and my hands are as white . . . as white as a lady's. I've become such a delicate and sensitive creature. I'm afraid of everything . . . so frightened. If you deceive me, Yasha, I don't know what will happen to my nerves.

YASHA (*kisses her*). You sweet little peach! Just remember, a girl must always control herself. Personally I think nothing is worse than a girl who doesn't behave herself.

DUNYASHA. I love you so much, so passionately! You're so intelligent, you can talk about anything. (*Pause.*)

YASHA (*yawns*). Yes, I suppose so . . . In my opinion, it's like this: if a girl loves someone it means she's immoral. (*Pause.*) I enjoy smoking a cigar in the fresh air . . . (*Listens.*) Someone's coming. It's the ladies and gentlemen. . . . (DUNYASHA *impulsively embraces him.*) Go to the house now, as though you'd been swimming down at the river. No, this way or they'll see you. I wouldn't want them to think I was interested in you.

DUNYASHA (*coughing softly*). That cigar has given me such a headache . . . (*Goes out.*)

(YASHA *remains sitting by the shrine. Enter* LYUBOV, GAEV *and* LOPAHIN.)

LOPAHIN. You've got to make up your minds once and for all; there's no time to lose. After all, it's a simple matter. Will you lease your land for the cottages, or won't you? You can answer in one word: yes or no? Just one word!

LYUBOV. Who's been smoking such wretched cigars? (*Sits down.*)

GAEV. How very convenient everything is with the railroad nearby. (*Sits down.*) Well, here we are — we've been to town, had lunch and we're home already. I put the red into the middle pocket! I'd like to go in . . . just for one game. . . .

LYUBOV. You've got lots of time.

LOPAHIN. Just one word! (*Beseechingly.*) Please give me an answer!

GAEV (*yawns*). What did you say?

LYUBOV (*looking into her purse*). Yesterday I had lots of money, but today there's practically none left. My poor Varya feeds us all milk soups to economize; the old servants in the kitchen have nothing but dried peas, and here I am wasting money senselessly, I just don't understand it. . . . (*She drops her purse, scattering gold coins.*) Now I've dropped it again. . . . (*Annoyed.*)

YASHA. Allow me, madam, I'll pick them right up. (*Picks up the money.*)

LYUBOV. Thank you, Yasha . . . And why did we go out for lunch today? And that restaurant of yours . . . the food was vile, the music ghastly, and the tablecloths smelled of soap. And Leonid, why do you drink so much? And eat so much? And talk so much? Today at the restaurant you were at it again, and it was all so pointless. About the seventies, and the decadents. And to whom? Really, talking to the waiters about the decadents!

LOPAHIN. Yes, that's too much.

GAEV (*waving his hand*). I know I'm hopeless. (*To* YASHA, *irritably.*) Why are you always bustling about in front of me?

YASHA (*laughs*). The minute you open your mouth I start laughing.

GAEV (*to his sister*). Either he goes, or I do. . . .

LYUBOV. Get along, Yasha, you'd better leave us now.

YASHA (*hands the purse to* LYUBOV). I'm going. (*He can hardly restrain his laughter.*) Right this minute. . . . (*Goes out.*)

LOPAHIN. You know, that rich merchant Deriganov is thinking of buying your estate. They say he's coming to the auction himself.

LYUBOV. Where did you hear that?

LOPAHIN. That's what they say in town.

GAEV. Our aunt in Yaroslavl has promised to send us some money, but when and how much we don't know.

LOPAHIN. How much will she send? A hundred thousand? Two hundred?

LYUBOV. Well, hardly . . . Ten or fifteen thousand, perhaps. And we should be thankful for that.

LOPAHIN. Forgive me for saying it, but really, in my whole life I've never met such unrealistic, unbusinesslike, queer people as you. You're told in plain language that your estate's going to be sold, and you don't seem to understand it at all.

LYUBOV. But what are we to do? Please, tell us.

LOPAHIN. I keep on telling you. Every day I tell you the same thing. You must lease the cherry orchard and the rest of the land for summer cottages, and you must do it now, as quickly as possible. It's almost time for the auction. Please, try to understand! Once you definitely decide to lease it for the cottages, you'll be able to borrow as much money as you like, and you'll be saved.

LYUBOV. Summer cottages and vacationers! Forgive me, but it's so vulgar.

GAEV. I agree with you entirely.

LOPAHIN. Honestly, I'm going to burst into tears, or scream, or faint. I can't stand it any more! It's more than I can take! (*To* GAEV.) And you're an old woman!

GAEV. What did you say?

LOPAHIN. I said, you're an old woman!

LYUBOV (*alarmed*). No, don't go, please stay. I beg you! Perhaps we can think of something.

LOPAHIN. What's there to think of?

LYUBOV. Please don't go! I feel so much more cheerful when you're here. (*Pause.*) I keep expecting something horrible to happen . . . as though the house were going to collapse on top of us.

GAEV (*in deep thought*). I bank it off the cushions, and then into the middle pocket. . . .

LYUBOV. We've sinned too much. . . .

LOPAHIN. Sinned! What sins have you . . .

GAEV (*putting a gumdrop into his mouth*). They say I've eaten up my fortune in gumdrops. (*Laughs.*)

LYUBOV. Oh, my sins! Look at the way I've always wasted money. It's madness. And then I married a man who had nothing but debts. And he was a terrible drinker . . . champagne killed him! And then, as if I hadn't enough misery, I fell in love with someone else. We went off together, and just at that time — it was my first punishment, a blow that broke my heart — my little boy was drowned right here in this river . . . So I went abroad. I went away for good, never to return, never to see this river again . . . I just shut my eyes and ran away in a frenzy of grief, but *he* . . . he followed me. It was so cruel and brutal of him! I bought a villa near Mentone because he fell ill there, and for three years, day and night, I never had any rest. He was very sick, and he completely exhausted me; my soul dried up completely. Then, last year when the villa had to be sold to pay the debts, I went to Paris, and there he robbed me of everything I had and left me for another woman. . . . I tried to poison myself. . . . It was all so stupid, so shameful! And then suddenly I felt an urge to come back to Russia, to my own country, to my little girl . . . (*Dries her tears.*) Oh, Lord, Lord, be merciful, forgive my sins! Don't punish me any more! (*Takes a telegram out of her pocket.*) This came from Paris today. He's asking my forgiveness, he's begging me to return. (*Tears up the telegram.*) Sounds like music somewhere. (*Listens.*)

GAEV. That's our famous Jewish orchestra. Don't you remember, four violins, a flute, and a bass?

LYUBOV. Are they still playing? Sometime we should have a dance and they could play for us.

LOPAHIN (*listens*). I can't hear anything . . . (*Sings quietly.*) "And the Germans, if you pay, will turn Russians into Frenchmen, so they say" . . . (*Laughs.*) I saw a wonderful play last night. It was so funny.

LYUBOV. It probably wasn't funny at all. Instead of going to plays, you should take a good look at yourself. Just think how dull your life is, and how much nonsense you talk!

LOPAHIN. That's true, I admit it! Our lives are stupid . . . (*Pause.*) My father was a peasant, an idiot. He knew nothing and he taught me nothing. He only beat me when he was drunk, and always with a stick. And as a matter of fact, I'm just as much an idiot myself. I don't know anything and my handwriting's awful. I'm ashamed for people to see it — it's like a pig's.

LYUBOV. You ought to get married, my friend.

LOPAHIN. Yes . . . that's true.

LYUBOV. You ought to marry our Varya. She's a fine girl.

LOPAHIN. Yes.

LYUBOV. She comes from simple people, and she works hard all day long without stopping. But the main thing is she loves you, and you've liked her for a long time yourself.

LOPAHIN. Well . . . I think it's a fine idea . . . she's a nice girl. (*Pause.*)

GAEV. I've been offered a job at the bank. Six thousand a year. Did I tell you?

LYUBOV. Yes, you did. You'd better stay where you are.

(FEERS *enters, bringing an overcoat.*)

FEERS (*to* GAEV). Please put it on, sir, you might catch cold.

GAEV (*puts on the overcoat*). Oh, you are a nuisance.

FEERS. You must stop this! You went off this morning without letting me know. (*Looks him over.*)

LYUBOV. How you've aged, Feers!

FEERS. What can I do for you, Madam?

LOPAHIN. She says you've aged a lot.

FEERS. I've lived for a long time. They were planning to marry me before your father was born. (*Laughs.*) Why, I was already head butler at the time of the emancipation, but I wouldn't take my freedom, I stayed on with the master and mistress. . . . (*Pause.*) I remember everyone was happy at the time, but what they were happy about, they didn't know themselves.

LOPAHIN. That was the good life all right! All the peasants were flogged!

FEERS (*not having heard him*). That's right! The peasants belonged to their masters, and the masters belonged to the peasants; but now everything's all confused, and people don't know what to make of it.

GAEV. Be quiet, Feers. Tomorrow I've got to go to town. I've been promised an introduction to some general or other who might lend us some money for the mortgage.

LOPAHIN. Nothing will come of it. And how would you pay the interest, anyway?

LYUBOV. He's talking nonsense again. There aren't any generals.

(*Enter* TROFIMOV, ANYA *and* VARYA.)

GAEV. Here come the children.

ANYA. There's Mamma.

LYUBOV. Come here, my dears. Oh, my darling children. . . . (*Embraces* ANYA *and* VARYA.) If you only knew how much I love you! Here now, sit down beside me.

(*All sit down.*)

LOPAHIN. Our perennial student is always with the girls.

TROFIMOV. It's none of your business.

LOPAHIN. He'll soon be fifty, and he's still a student.

TROFIMOV. Oh, stop your stupid jokes.

LOPAHIN. What's bothering you? My, you *are* a strange fellow!

TROFIMOV. Why do you keep pestering me?

LOPAHIN (*laughs*). Just let me ask you one question: what's your opinion of me?

TROFIMOV. My opinion of you, Yermolay Alexeyevich, is this: you're a rich man, and soon you'll be a millionaire. For the same reason that wild beasts are necessary to maintain nature's economic laws, you are necessary, too — each of you devours everything that gets in his way.

(*Everybody laughs.*)

VARYA. You'd better talk about the planets, Petya.

LYUBOV. No, let's go on with the conversation we had yesterday.

TROFIMOV. What was that?

GAEV. About pride.

TROFIMOV. We talked for a long time yesterday, but we didn't agree on anything. The proud man, the way you use the word, has some mysterious quality about him. Perhaps you're right in a way, but if we look at it simply, without trying to be too subtle, you have to ask yourself why should we be proud at all? Why be proud when you realize that Man, as a species, is poorly constructed physiologically, and is usually coarse, stupid, and profoundly unhappy, too? We ought to put an end to such vanity and just go to work. That's right, we ought to work.

GAEV. You'll die just the same, no matter what you do.

TROFIMOV. Who knows? And anyway, what does it mean — to die? It could be that man has a hundred senses, and when he dies only the five that are known perish, while the other ninety-five go on living.

LYUBOV. How clever you are, Petya!

LOPAHIN (*ironically*). Oh, very clever!

TROFIMOV. Humanity is continually advancing, is continually seeking to perfect its powers. Some day all the things which we can't understand now will be made clear. But if this is to happen, we've got to work, work with all our might to help those who are searching for truth. Up until now, here in Russia only a few have begun to work. Nearly all of the intelligentsia that I know have no commitment, they don't do anything and are as yet incapable of work. They call themselves "the intelligentsia," but they still run roughshod over their servants, and they treat the peasants like animals, they study without achieving anything, they read only childish drivel, and they don't do a thing. As for their knowledge of science, it's only jargon, and they have no appreciation of art either. They are all so serious, and they go about important matters; and yet before our very eyes our workers are poorly fed, they live in the worst kind of squalor, sleeping not on beds but on the floor thirty to forty in a room — with roaches, odors, dampness, and depravity everywhere. It's perfectly clear that all our moralizing is intended to deceive not only ourselves but others as well. Tell me, where are the nursery schools we're always talking about, where are the libraries? We only write about them in novels, but in actuality there aren't any. There's nothing but dirt, vulgarity, and decadent Orientalism. . . . I'm afraid of those serious faces, I don't like them; I'm afraid of serious talk. It would be better if we'd just keep quiet.

LOPAHIN. Well, let me tell you that *I'm* up before five every morning, and I work from morning till night. I always have money, my own and other people's, and I have lots of opportunities to see what the people around me are like. You only have to start doing something to realize how few honest, decent people there are. Sometimes, when I can't sleep, I start thinking about it. God's given us immense forests and wide-open fields and unlimited horizons — living in such a world we ought to be giants!

LYUBOV. But why do you want giants? They're all right in fairy tales, anywhere else they're terrifying.

(EPIHODOV *crosses the stage in the background, playing his guitar.*)

LYUBOV (*pensively*). There goes Epihodov. . . .

ANYA (*pensively*). There goes Epihodov. . . .

GAEV. The sun's gone down, my friends.

TROFIMOV. Yes.

GAEV (*in a subdued voice, as if reciting a poem*). Oh, glorious Nature, shining with eternal light, so beautiful, yet so indifferent to our fate . . .

you, whom we call Mother, the wellspring of Life and Death, you live and you destroy. . . .

VARYA (*imploringly*). Uncle, please!

ANYA. You're doing it again, Uncle!

TROFIMOV. You'd better bank the red into the middle pocket.

GAEV. All right, I'll keep quiet.

(*They all sit deep in thought; the only thing that can be heard is the muttering of* FEERS. *Suddenly there is a sound in the distance, as if out of the sky, like the sound of a harp string breaking, gradually and sadly dying away.*)

LYUBOV. What was that?

LOPAHIN. I don't know. Sounded like a cable broke in one of the mines. But it must've been a long way off.

GAEV. Perhaps it was a bird . . . a heron, maybe.

TROFIMOV. Or an owl. . . .

LYUBOV (*shudders*). Whatever it was, it sounded unpleasant . . . (*A pause.*)

FEERS. It was the same way before the disaster: the owl hooted and the samovar was humming.

GAEV. What disaster?

FEERS. Before they freed us.

(*A pause.*)

LYUBOV. We'd better get started, my friends. It's getting dark and we should get home. (*To* ANYA.) You're crying, my darling! What's wrong? (*She embraces her.*)

ANYA. Nothing, Mamma. It's nothing.

TROFIMOV. Someone's coming.

(*Enter* A TRAMP *in a battered white hunting cap and an overcoat; he's slightly drunk.*)

TRAMP. Excuse me, but can I get to the station through here?

GAEV. Yes, just follow the road.

TRAMP. Much obliged to you, sir. (*Coughs.*) It's a beautiful day today. (*Declaiming.*) "Oh, my brother, my suffering brother! . . . Come to the Volga, whose groans . . ." (*To* VARYA.) Mademoiselle, could a poor starving Russian trouble you for just enough to . . .

(VARYA *cries out, frightened.*)

LOPAHIN (*angrily*). Really, this is too much!

LYUBOV (*at a loss what to do*). Here, take this . . . here you are. (*Looks in her purse.*) I haven't any silver . . . but that's all right, here's a gold one. . . .

TRAMP. Thank you very much! (*Goes off.*)

(*Laughter.*)

VARYA (*frightened*). I'm going . . . I'm going . . . Oh, Mamma, you know there's not even enough to eat in the house, and you gave him all that!

LYUBOV. Well, what can you do with a silly woman like me? I'll give you everything I've got as soon as we get home. Yermolay Alexeyevich, you'll lend me some more, won't you?

LOPAHIN. Why, of course I will.

LYUBOV. Come, it's time to go now. By the way, Varya, we've just about arranged your marriage. Congratulations!

VARYA (*through her tears*). Don't joke about things like that, Mother!

LOPAHIN. Go to a nunnery, Okhmelia! . . .

GAEV. Look at how my hands are trembling: I haven't had a game for so long.

LOPAHIN. Okhmelia, nymph, remember me in your prayers!

LYUBOV. Come along, everybody. It's almost supper time.

VARYA. That man frightened me so. My heart's still pounding.

LOPAHIN. My friends, just one thing, please, just a word: the cherry orchard's to be sold on the 22nd of August. Remember that! Think of that. . . .

(*All go out except* TROFIMOV *and* ANYA.)

ANYA (*laughs*). We can thank the tramp for a chance to be alone! He frightened Varya so.

TROFIMOV. Varya's afraid — she's afraid we might fall in love — so she follows us about all day long. She's so narrow-minded, she can't understand that we're above falling in love. To free ourselves of all that's petty and ephemeral, all that prevents us from being free and happy, that's the whole aim and meaning of our life. Forward! We march forward irresistibly towards that bright star shining there in the distance! Forward! Don't fall behind, friends!

ANYA (*raising her hands*). How beautifully you talk! (*A pause.*) It's wonderful here today.

TROFIMOV. Yes, the weather's marvelous.

ANYA. What have you done to me, Petya? Why don't I love the cherry orchard like I used to? I used to love it so very much I used to think that there wasn't a better place in all the world than our orchard.

TROFIMOV. The whole of Russia is our orchard. The earth is great and beautiful and there are many wonderful places in it. (*A pause.*) Just think, Anya: your grandfather and your great-grandfather and all your ancestors were serf owners — they owned living souls. Don't you see human beings staring at you from every tree in the orchard, from every leaf and every trunk? Don't you hear their voices? . . . They owned living souls — and it has made you all different persons, those who came before you, and you who are living now, so that your mother, your uncle and you yourself don't even notice that you're living on credit, at the expense of other people, people you don't admit any further than your kitchen. We're at least two hundred years behind the times; we have no real values, no sense of our past, we just philosophize and complain of how depressed we feel and drink vodka. Yet it's obvious that if we're ever to live in the present, we must first atone for our past and make a clean break with it, and we can only atone for it by suffering, by extraordinary, unceasing work. You've got to understand that, Anya.

ANYA. The house we live in hasn't really been ours for a long time. I'll leave it, I promise you.

TROFIMOV. Yes, leave it, and throw away the keys. Be free as the wind.

ANYA (*in rapture*). How beautifully you say things.

TROFIMOV. You must believe me, Anya, you must. I'm not thirty yet, I'm young, and I'm still a student, but I've suffered so much already. As soon as winter comes, I'll be hungry and sick and nervous, poor as a beggar. Fate has driven me everywhere! And yet, my soul is always — every moment of every day and every night — it's always full of such marvelous hopes and visions. I have a premonition of happiness, Anya, I can sense it's coming. . . .

ANYA (*pensively*). The moon's coming up.

(EPIHODOV *is heard playing the same melancholy tune on his guitar. The moon comes up. Somewhere near the poplars* VARYA *is looking for* ANYA *and calling.*)

VARYA (*off-stage*). Anya! Where are you?

TROFIMOV. Yes, the moon is rising. (*A pause.*) There it is — happiness — it's coming nearer and nearer. Already, I can hear its footsteps. And if we never see it, if we never know it, what does it matter? Others will see it!

VARYA'S *voice*. Anya! Where are you?

TROFIMOV. It's Varya again! (*Angrily.*) It's disgusting!

ANYA. Well? Let's go to the river. It's lovely there.

TROFIMOV. Yes, let's.

(TROFIMOV *and* ANYA *go out.*)

VARYA'S *voice*. Anya! Anya!

ACT THREE

(*The drawing room separated by an arch from the ballroom. The same Jewish orchestra that was mentioned in Act Two is playing off-stage. The chandelier is lighted. It is evening. In the ballroom they are dancing the*

Grand-rond. SEMYONOV-PISHCHIK *is heard calling: "Promenade à une paire!" Then they all enter the drawing room.* PISHCHIK *and* CHARLOTTA IVANOVNA *are the first couple, followed by* TROFIMOV *and* LYUBOV, ANYA *and a* POST-OFFICE CLERK, VARYA *and* THE STATION MASTER, *etc.* VARYA *is crying softly and wipes away her tears as she dances.* DUNYASHA *is in the last couple.* PISHCHIK *shouts: "Grand-rond balancez!" and "Les cavaliers à genoux et remerciez vos dames!"* FEERS, *wearing a dress coat, crosses the room with soda water on a tray.* PISHCHIK *and* TROFIMOV *come back into the drawing room.*)

PISHCHIK. I've got this high blood-pressure — I've had two strokes already, you know — and it makes dancing hard work for me; but, as they say, if you're one of a pack, you wag your tail, whether you bark or not. Actually I'm as strong as a horse. My dear father — may he rest in peace — had a little joke. He used to say that the ancient line of Semyonov-Pishchik was descended from the very same horse that Caligula made a member of the Senate. (*Sitting down.*) But my trouble is, I haven't any money. A starving dog can think of nothing but food . . . (*Starts to snore, but wakes up almost at once.*) That's just like me — I can't think of anything but money. . . .

TROFIMOV. You know, you're right, there *is* something horsy about you.

PISHCHIK. Well, a horse is a fine animal, you can sell a horse. . . .

(*The sound of someone playing billiards is heard in the next room.* VARYA *appears under the arch to the ballroom.*)

TROFIMOV (*teasing her*). Madame Lopahin! Madame Lopahin!

VARYA (*angrily*). The "moth-eaten man"!

TROFIMOV. Yes, I am a moth-eaten man, and I'm proud of it.

VARYA (*thinking bitterly*). Now we've hired an orchestra — but how are we going to pay for it? (*Goes out.*)

TROFIMOV (*to* PISHCHIK). If all the energy you've spent during your life looking for money to pay the interest on your debts had been used for something useful, you'd have probably turned the world upside down by now.

PISHCHIK. The philosopher Nietzsche, the greatest, the most famous — a man of the greatest intelligence, in fact — says it's quite all right to counterfeit.

TROFIMOV. Oh, you've read Nietzsche?

PISHCHIK. Of course not, Dashenka told me. But right now I'm in such an impossible position that I could forge a few notes. The day after tomorrow I've got to pay 310 roubles. I've borrowed 130 already. . . . (*Feels in his pockets, in alarm.*) The money's gone! I've lost the money. (*Tearfully.*) Where's the money? (*Joyfully.*) Oh, here it is, inside the lining! I'm so upset, I'm sweating all over! . . .

(*Enter* LYUBOV *and* CHARLOTTA.)

LYUBOV (*humming the "Lezginka"*). What's taking Leonid so long? What's he doing in town? (*To* DUNYASHA.) Dunyasha, offer the musicians some tea.

TROFIMOV. The auction was probably postponed.

LYUBOV. The orchestra came at the wrong time, and the party started at the wrong time . . . Oh, well . . . never mind . . . (*She sits down and hums quietly.*)

CHARLOTTA (*hands a deck of cards to* PISHCHIK). Here's a deck of cards — think of any card.

PISHCHIK. I've thought of one.

CHARLOTTA. Now shuffle the deck. That's right. Now give it to me, my dear Monsieur Pishchik. *Ein, zwei, drei!* Why look! There it is, in your coat pocket.

PISHCHIK (*takes the card out of his coat pocket*). The eight of spades, that's right! (*In astonishment.*) Isn't that amazing!

CHARLOTTA (*holding the deck of cards on the palm of her hand, to* TROFIMOV). Quickly, which card's on the top?

TROFIMOV. Well . . . ahh . . . the queen of spades.

CHARLOTTA. You're right, here it is! Now, which card?

PISHCHIK. The ace of hearts.

CHARLOTTA. Right again! (*She claps her hand over the pack of cards, which disappears.*) What beautiful weather we're having today! (*A woman's voice, as if coming from underneath the floor, answers her.*)

VOICE. Oh yes, indeed, the weather's perfectly marvelous!

CHARLOTTA (*addressing the voice*). How charming you are! I'm fond of you!

VOICE. And I like you very much, too.

STATION MASTER (*applauding*). Bravo, Madame ventriloquist! Bravo!

PISHCHIK (*astonished*). Isn't that amazing! Charlotta Ivanovna, you're absolutely wonderful! I'm completely in love with you!

CHARLOTTA (*shrugging her shoulders*). In love? What do you know about love? "*Guter Mensch, aber schlechter Musikant.*"

TROFIMOV (*slaps* PISHCHIK *on the shoulder*). He's just an old horse, he is!

CHARLOTTA. Your attention please! Here's one more trick. (*She takes a shawl from a chair.*) Now there's this very nice shawl . . . (*shakes it out*). Who'd like to buy it?

PISHCHIK (*amazed*). Imagine that!

CHARLOTTA. *Ein, zwei, drei!*

(*She lifts up the shawl and* ANYA *is standing behind it;* ANYA *curtsies, runs to her mother, gives her a hug, and runs back to the ballroom. Everybody's delighted.*)

LYUBOV (*clapping*). Bravo, bravo!

CHARLOTTA. Once more. *Ein, zwei, drei!*

(*Lifts the shawl again; behind it is* VARYA, *who bows.*)

PISHCHIK (*amazed*). Isn't that amazing!

CHARLOTTA. It's all over! (*She throws the shawl over* PISHCHIK, *curtsies, and runs into the ballroom.*)

PISHCHIK (*going after her*). You little rascal! . . . Have you ever seen anything like her? What a girl . . . (*Goes out.*)

LYUBOV. Leonid's still not here. I can't understand what's keeping him all this time in town. Anyway, by now everything's been settled; either the estate's been sold or the auction didn't take place. Why does he wait so long to let us know?

VARYA (*trying to comfort her*). Uncle's bought it, I'm sure he did.

TROFIMOV (*sarcastically*). Why, of course he did!

VARYA. Our great-aunt sent him power of attorney to buy it in her name, and transfer the mortgage to her. She's done it for Anya's sake . . . God will look after us, I'm sure of it — Uncle will buy the estate.

LYUBOV. Your great-aunt sent us fifteen thousand to buy the estate in her name — she doesn't trust us — but that's not enough to even pay the interest. (*She covers her face with her hands.*) My fate is being decided today, my fate. . . .

TROFIMOV (*to* VARYA, *teasingly*). Madame Lopahin!

VARYA (*crossly*). The perpetual student! Why, you've been thrown out of the university twice already!

LYUBOV. But why get so cross, Varya? He's only teasing you about Lopahin, there's no harm in that, is there? If you want to, why don't you marry him; he's a fine man, and he's interesting, too. Of course, if you don't want to, don't. No one's trying to force you, darling.

VARYA. I'm very serious about this, Mother . . . and I want to be frank with you . . . he's a good man and I like him.

LYUBOV. Then marry him. What are you waiting for? I don't understand you at all.

VARYA. But, Mother, I can't propose to him myself, can I? It's been two years now since everybody began talking to me about him, and everybody's talking, but he doesn't say a word, or when he does, he just jokes with me. I understand, of course. He's getting rich and his mind's busy with other things, and he hasn't any time for me. If only I had some money, even a little, just a hundred roubles, I'd leave everything and go away, the farther the better. I'd go into a convent.

TROFIMOV. How beautiful!

VARYA (*to* TROFIMOV). Of course, a student like you has to be so intelligent! (*Quietly and tearfully.*) How ugly you've become, Petya, how much older you look! (*To* LYUBOV, *her tearfulness gone.*) The only thing I can't stand, Mother, is not having any work to do. I've got to stay busy.

(*Enter* YASHA.)

YASHA (*with difficulty restraining his laughter*). Epihodov's broken a cue! . . . (*Goes out.*)

VARYA. But what's Epihodov doing here? Who let him play billiards? I don't understand these people. . . . (*Goes out.*)

LYUBOV. Please don't tease her, Petya. Don't you see she's upset already?

TROFIMOV. Oh, she's such a busy-body — always sticking her nose into other people's business. She hasn't left Anya and me alone all summer. She's afraid we might fall in love. What difference should it make to her? Besides, I didn't give her any reason to think so. I don't believe in such trivialities. We're above love!

LYUBOV. And I suppose I'm below love. (*Uneasily.*) Why isn't Leonid back? If only I knew whether the estate's been sold or not. It's such an incredible calamity that for some reason I don't know what to think, I feel so helpless. I think I'm going to scream this very minute . . . I'll do something silly. Help me, Petya. Talk to me, say something!

TROFIMOV. What difference does it make whether the estate's sold today or not? It was gone a long time ago. You can't turn back, the path's lost. You mustn't worry, and above all you mustn't deceive yourself. For once in your life you must look the truth straight in the face.

LYUBOV. What truth? *You* know what truth is and what it isn't, but I've lost such visionary powers. I don't see anything. You're able to solve all your problems so decisively — but, tell me, my dear boy, isn't that because you're young, because life is still hidden from your young eyes, because you can't believe anything horrible will ever happen to you and you don't expect it to? Oh, yes, you're more courageous and honest and serious than we are, but put yourself in our position, try to be generous — if only a little bit — and have pity on me. I was born here, you know, and my father and mother lived here, and my grandfather, too, and I love this house — I can't conceive of life without the cherry orchard, and if it really has to be sold, then sell me with it . . . (*Embraces* TROFIMOV, *kisses him on the forehead.*) You know, my little boy was drowned here. . . . (*Weeps.*) Have pity on me, my dear, kind friend.

TROFIMOV. You know that I sympathize with you from the bottom of my heart.

LYUBOV. But you should say it differently . . . differently. (*Takes out her handkerchief and a telegram falls on to the floor.*) There's so much on my mind today, you can't imagine. It's so noisy around here that my soul trembles with every sound, and I'm shaking all over — yet I can't go to my room because the silence of being alone frightens me. . . . Don't blame me, Petya. . . . I love you as if you were my own son. I'd gladly let Anya marry you, honestly I would, but, my dear boy, you must study, you've got to graduate. You don't do anything, Fate tosses you from one place to another — it's so strange. Well, it is, isn't it? Isn't it? And you should do something about your beard, make it grow somehow. . . . (*Laughs.*) You look so funny!

TROFIMOV (*picks up the telegram*). I don't care how I look. That's so superficial.

LYUBOV. This telegram's from Paris. I get one every day . . . yesterday, today. That beast is sick again, and everything's going wrong for him. . . . He wants me to forgive him, he begs me to return, and, really, I suppose I should go to Paris and stay with him for a while. You're looking very stern, Petya, but what am I to do, my dear boy, what am I to do? He's sick and lonely and unhappy, and who'll take care of him, who'll stop him from making a fool of himself and give him his medicine at the right time? And anyway, why should I hide it, or keep quiet about it? I love him; yes, I love him. I do, I do. . . . He's a stone around my neck, and I'm sinking to the bottom with him — but I love him and I can't live without him. (*She presses* TROFIMOV'*s hand.*) Don't think I'm evil, Petya, don't say anything, please don't. . . .

TROFIMOV (*with strong emotion*). Please — forgive my frankness, but that man's swindling you!

LYUBOV. No, no, no, you mustn't talk like that. . . . (*Puts her hands over her ears.*)

TROFIMOV. But he's a scoundrel, and you're the only one who doesn't know it! He's a despicable, worthless scoundrel. . . .

LYUBOV (*angry, but in control of herself*). You're twenty-six or twenty-seven years old, but you're talking like a schoolboy!

TROFIMOV. Say whatever you want!

LYUBOV. You should be a man at your age, you ought to understand what it means to be in love. And you should be in love. . . . Tell me, why haven't you fallen in love! (*Angrily.*) Yes, yes! Oh, you're not so "pure," your purity is a perversion, you're nothing but a ridiculous prude, a freak. . . .

TROFIMOV (*horrified*). What is she saying?

LYUBOV. "I'm above love!" You're not above love, you're useless, as Feers would say. Imagine not having a mistress at your age! . . .

TROFIMOV (*horrified*). This is terrible! What's she saying? (*Goes quickly towards the ballroom, clutching his head between his hands.*) This is dreadful. . . . I can't stand it, I'm going. . . . (*Goes out, but returns at once.*) Everything's over between us! (*Goes out through the door into the hall.*)

LYUBOV (*calls after him*). Petya, wait! You funny boy, I was only joking! Petya!

(*Someone can be heard running quickly downstairs and suddenly falling down with a crash.* ANYA *and* VARYA *scream, and then begin laughing.*)

What's happened?

(ANYA *runs in.*)

ANYA (*laughing*). Petya fell down the stairs. (*Runs out.*)

LYUBOV. What a strange boy he is!

(*The* STATION MASTER *stands in the middle of the ballroom and begins to recite "The Sinner" by Alexey Tolstoy. The others listen to him, but he's hardly had time to recite more than a little bit when a waltz is played, and he stops. Everyone dances.* TROFIMOV, ANYA, VARYA *come in from the hall.*)

Poor Petya . . . there, my dear boy . . . please forgive me . . . Come, let's dance . . .

(*She dances with* PETYA. ANYA *and* VARYA *dance. Enter* FEERS, *then* YASHA. FEERS *leans on his cane by the side door.* YASHA *looks at the dancers from the drawing room.*)

YASHA. How are you, old boy?

FEERS. Not too well . . . We used to have generals, barons, and admirals at our parties . . . long ago, but now we send for the post-office clerk and the station master, and even they don't want to come, it seems. I seem to be getting weaker somehow . . . My old master, the mistress' grandfather, used to make everyone take sealing wax no matter what was wrong with them. I've been taking it every day for the last twenty years, maybe even longer. Perhaps that's why I'm still alive.

YASHA. How you bore me, old man! (*Yawns.*) Why don't you just go away and die . . . it's about time.

FEERS. Eh, you! . . . You're useless . . . (*Mutters.*)

(TROFIMOV *and* LYUBOV *dancing, come into the drawing room.*)

LYUBOV. Thank you. I think I'll sit down for a bit. (*Sits down.*) I'm tired.

(*Enter* ANYA.)

ANYA (*agitated*). There's a man in the kitchen who's been saying that the cherry orchard was sold today.

LYUBOV. Sold? To whom?

ANYA. He didn't say. He's gone.

(*She and* TROFIMOV *dance into the ballroom.*)

YASHA. There was some old man gossiping there. A stranger.

FEERS. Leonid Andreyevich isn't back yet, he hasn't come yet. And he's only got his light overcoat on; he'll probably catch a cold. Oh, these youngsters!

LYUBOV. I've got to know, or I think I'll die. Yasha, go and find out who bought it.

YASHA. But the old guy went away a long time ago. (*Laughs.*)

LYUBOV (*with a touch of annoyance*). What are you laughing at? What's so humorous?

YASHA. Epihodov's so funny — he's so stupid. Two-and-twenty misfortunes!

LYUBOV. Feers, if the estate's sold, where will you go?

FEERS. I'll go wherever you tell me to go.

LYUBOV. Why are you looking like that? Aren't you well? You ought to be in bed.

FEERS. Yes . . . (*with a faint smile*). But if I went to bed, who'd take care of the guests and keep things going? There's no one in the house but me.

YASHA (*to* LYUBOV). Lyubov Andreyevna! I want to ask you something! If you go back to Paris, will you please take me with you? I couldn't stand staying here. (*Looking round and speaking in a low voice.*) I don't have to say it, you can see for yourself how uncivilized everything is here. The people are immoral, it's frightfully dull, and the food is terrible. And then there's that Feers walking about the place and muttering all sorts of stupid things. Take me with you, please!

(*Enter* PISHCHIK.)

PISHCHIK. May I have this dance, beautiful lady . . .

(LYUBOV *gets up to dance.*)

I'll have that 180 roubles from you yet, you enchantress . . . yes, I will . . . (*Dances.*) Just 180 roubles, that's all . . .

(*They go into the ballroom.*)

YASHA (*sings quietly*). "Don't you understand the passion in my soul? . . ."

(*In the ballroom a woman in a grey top hat and check trousers starts jumping and throwing her arms about; shouts of:* "Bravo, Charlotta Ivanovna!"

DUNYASHA (*stops to powder her face*). Anya told me to dance: there are so many men and not enough ladies; but I get so dizzy from dancing and it makes my heart beat so fast. Feers Nikolayevich, the post-office clerk said something to me just now that completely took my breath away. (*The music stops.*)

FEERS. What did he say?

DUNYASHA. You're like a flower, he said.

YASHA (*yawns*). What ignorance! . . . (*Goes out.*)

DUNYASHA. Like a flower . . . I'm so sensitive, I love it when people say beautiful things to me.

FEERS. You'll be having your head turned if you're not careful.

(*Enter* EPIHODOV.)

EPIHODOV. Avdotya Fyodorovna, you act as if you don't want to see me . . . as if I were some kind of insect. (*Sighs.*) Such is life!

DUNYASHA. What do you want?

EPIHODOV. But then, you may be right. (*Sighs.*) Of course, if one looks at it from a certain point of view — if I may so express myself, and please excuse my frankness, you've driven me into such a state . . . Oh, I know what my fate is; every day some misfortune's sure to happen to me, but I've long since been accustomed to that, so I look at life with a smile. You gave me your word, and though I . . .

DUNYASHA. Please, let's talk later, just let me alone now. I'm lost in a dream. (*Plays with her fan.*)

EPIHODOV. Some misfortune happens to me every day, but I — how should I put it — I just smile, I even laugh.

(VARYA *enters from the ballroom.*)

VARYA. Are you still here, Semyon? Your manners are abominable, really! (*To* DUNYASHA.) You'd better go now, Dunyasha.

(DUNYASHA *goes out.*)

(*To* EPIHODOV.) First you play billiards and break a cue, and now you're going about the drawing room like one of the guests.

EPIHODOV. Permit me to inform you, but you have no right to attack me like this.

VARYA. I'm not attacking, I'm telling you. You just wander from one place to another, instead of doing your work. We've hired a clerk, but why no one knows.

EPIHODOV (*offended*). Whether I work, wander, eat, or play billiards, the only people who are entitled to judge my actions are those who are older than me and have some idea of what they're talking about.

VARYA. How dare you say that to me? (*Beside herself with anger.*) You dare to say that? Are you suggesting that I don't know what I'm talking about? Get out of here! Right now!

EPIHODOV (*cowed*). I wish you'd express yourself more delicately.

VARYA (*beside herself*). Get out this minute! Get out!

(*He goes to the door, she follows him.*)

Two-and-twenty misfortunes! Get out of here! I don't want ever to see you again!

EPIHODOV (*goes out; his voice is heard from outside the door*). I'm going to complain.

VARYA. Oh, you're coming back, are you? (*She seizes the stick which* FEERS *left by the door.*) Well, come along, come in . . . I'll show you! So, you're coming back . . . are you? There, take that . . .

(*Swings the stick, and at that moment* LOPAHIN *comes in.*)

LOPAHIN (*whom the stick did not, in fact, touch*). Thank you very much!

VARYA (*angry and ironically*). I'm sorry!

LOPAHIN. Don't mention it. I'm much obliged to you for the kind reception.

VARYA. That's quite all right. (*Walks away and then looks around and asks gently.*) I haven't hurt you, have I?

LOPAHIN. No, not at all. . . . But there's going to be a huge bump, though.

VOICES (*in the ballroom*). Lopahin's here! Yermolay Alexeyevich!

PISHCHIK. There he is! You can see him, do you hear him? . . . (*Embraces* LOPAHIN.) You smell of cognac, my good fellow! . . . Well we're having a party here, too.

(*Enter* LYUBOV.)

LYUBOV. It's you, Yermolay Alexeyevich? What's taken you so long? Where's Leonid?

LOPAHIN. Leonid Andreyevich's here, he'll be along in a minute.

LYUBOV (*agitated*). Well, what happened? Was there an auction? Tell me!

LOPAHIN (*embarrassed, afraid of betraying his joy*). The auction was over by four o'clock . . . We missed our train and had to wait until nine-thirty. (*Sighs heavily.*) Ugh! I feel a little dizzy . . .

(*Enter* GAEV; *he carries packages in his right hand and wipes away his tears with his left.*)

LYUBOV. Leonid, what happened? Leonid? (*Impatiently, with tears.*) Tell me quickly, for God's sake! . . .

GAEV (*doesn't answer, but waves his hand. To* FEERS, *crying*). Here, take these . . . it's some anchovies and Kerch herrings . . . I haven't eaten all day . . . What I've been through!

(*Through the open door leading to the ballroom a game of billiards can be heard and* YASHA'*s voice is heard.*)

YASHA. Seven and eighteen.

GAEV (*his expression changes and he stops crying*). I'm very tired.

Come, Feers, I want to change my things. (*Goes out through the ballroom, followed by* FEERS.)

PISHCHIK. Well, what happened at the auction? Come on, tell us!

LYUBOV. Has the cherry orchard been sold?

LOPAHIN. It has.

LYUBOV. Who bought it?

LOPAHIN. I did.

(*A pause.* LYUBOV *is overcome; only the fact that she is standing beside a table and a chair keeps her from falling.* VARYA *takes the keys from her belt, throws them on the floor in the middle of the room and goes out.*)

I bought it. Wait a moment, ladies and gentlemen, please. I'm so mixed up, I don't quite know what to say . . . (*Laughs.*) When we got to the auction, Deriganov was already there. Leonid had only fifteen thousand roubles, and immediately Deriganov bid thirty thousand over and above the mortgage. I saw how things were, so I stepped in and raised it to forty. He bid forty-five, I went to fifty-five; he kept on raising five thousand and I raised it ten thousand. Well, finally it ended — I bid ninety thousand over and above the mortgage, and it went to me. The cherry orchard's mine now! All right, tell me I'm drunk, tell me I'm crazy and that I'm just imagining all this. . . . (*Stamps his feet.*) Don't laugh at me! If only my father and grandfather could rise from their graves and see all that's happened . . . how their Yermolay, their ignorant, beaten Yermolay, the little boy that ran around in his bare feet in the winter . . . if only they could see that he's bought this estate, the most beautiful place in the world! Yes, he's bought the very estate where his father and grandfather were slaves and where they weren't even admitted to the kitchen! I must be asleep, I'm dreaming, it only seems to be true . . . it's all just my imagination, my imagination must be confused . . . (*Picks up the keys, smiling gently.*) She threw these down because she wanted to show that she's not the mistress here any more. (*Jingles the keys.*) Well, never mind.

(*The orchestra is heard tuning up.*)

Hey there! you musicians, play something for us! I want some music! My friends, come along and soon you'll see Yermolay Lopahin take an axe to the cherry orchard, you'll see the trees come crashing to the ground! We're going to build hundreds of summer cottages, and our children and our grandchildren will see a whole new world growing up here . . . So play, let's have some music!

(*The band plays.* LYUBOV *has sunk into a chair and is crying bitterly.*)

(*Reproachfully.*) Why, why didn't you listen to me? My poor, dear lady, you'll never get it back now. (*With tears.*) Oh, if only all this could be over soon, if only we could change this unhappy and disjointed life of ours somehow!

PISHCHIK (*taking his arm, in a low voice*). She's crying. Come into the ballroom, let her be by herself. . . . Come on . . . (*takes his arm and leads him away to the ballroom*).

LOPAHIN. What's the matter! Where's the music? Come on, play! Play! Everything will be as *I* want it now. (*Ironically.*) Here comes the new owner, here comes the owner of the cherry orchard! (*He tips over a little table accidentally and nearly upsets the candelabra.*) Don't worry about it, I can pay for everything! (*Goes out with* PISHCHIK.)

(*There is no one left in the ballroom or drawing room but* LYUBOV, *who sits huddled up in a chair, crying bitterly. The orchestra continues to play quietly.* ANYA *and* TROFIMOV *enter quickly;* ANYA *goes up to her mother and kneels beside her,* TROFIMOV *remains at the entrance to the ballroom.*)

ANYA. Mamma! . . . Mamma, you're crying. Dear, kind, good Mamma, my precious one, I love you! God bless you, Mamma! The cherry orchard's sold, that's true, it's gone, but don't cry, Mamma, you still have your life ahead of you, you still have your good, innocent heart. You must come with me, Mamma, away from here! We'll plant a new orchard, even more wonderful than this one — and when you see it, you'll understand everything, and your heart will be filled with joy, like the sun in the evening; and then you'll smile again, Mamma! Come, dearest one, come with me! . . .

ACT FOUR

(*The same setting as for Act One. There are no pictures on the walls or curtains at the windows; most of the furniture is gone and the few remaining pieces are stacked in a corner, as if for sale. There is a sense of desolation. Beside the door, suitcases and other luggage have been piled together. The voices of* VARYA *and* ANYA *can be heard through the door on the left, which is open.* LOPAHIN *stands waiting;* YASHA *is holding a tray with glasses of champagne. In the hall* EPIHODOV *is tying up a large box. Off-stage there is a low hum of voices; the peasants have called to say good-bye.* GAEV'*s voice from off-stage.*)

GAEV. Thank you, friends, thank you.

YASHA. The peasants have come to say good-bye. In my opinion, Yermolay Alexeyevich, they're good people, but they don't know much.

(*The hum subsides.* LYUBOV *and* GAEV *enter from the hall;* LYUBOV *is not crying but her face is pale and it quivers. She is unable to speak.*)

GAEV. You gave them everything you had, Lyuba. You shouldn't have done that. You really shouldn't.

LYUBOV. I couldn't help it! I couldn't help it! (*Both go out.*)

LOPAHIN (*calls after them through the door*). Please, have some champagne, please do! Just a little glass before you go. I didn't think to bring some from town, and at the station I could find only this one bottle. Please have some. (*A pause.*) You don't want any, my friends? (*Walks away from the door.*) If I'd known that, I wouldn't have brought it. . . . Well, then, I won't have any either.

(YASHA *carefully puts the tray on a chair.*)

Have a drink, Yasha, nobody else wants any.

YASHA. To the travelers! And to those staying behind. (*Drinks.*) This champagne isn't the real thing, believe me.

LOPAHIN. What do you mean, eight roubles a bottle. (*A pause.*) God, it's cold in here.

YASHA. The stoves weren't lit today. What difference does it make since we're leaving? (*Laughs.*)

LOPAHIN. Why are you laughing?

YASHA. Because I feel good.

LOPAHIN. It's October already, but it's still sunny and clear, just like summer. Good building weather. (*Looks at his watch, then at the door.*) Ladies and gentlemen, the train leaves in forty-seven minutes. We've got to start in twenty minutes. So hurry up.

(TROFIMOV, *wearing an overcoat, comes in from outdoors.*)

TROFIMOV. It's time we got started. The horses are ready. God knows where my galoshes are, they've disappeared. (*Calls through the door.*) Anya, my galoshes aren't here; I can't find them.

LOPAHIN. I've got to go to Kharkov. I'm taking the same train. I'll be spending the winter in Kharkov. I've stayed around here too long, and it drives me crazy having nothing to do. I can't be without work: I just don't know what to do with my hands; they hang there, as if they didn't belong to me.

TROFIMOV. We'll be gone soon, then you can start making money again.

LOPAHIN. Have a drink.

TROFIMOV. No, thanks.

LOPAHIN. So, you're going to Moscow?

TROFIMOV. Yes, I'll go with them to town, and then tomorrow I'll leave for Moscow.

LOPAHIN. I suppose the professors are waiting for you to come before they begin classes.

TROFIMOV. That's none of your business.

LOPAHIN. How many years have you been studying at the university?

TROFIMOV. Can't you say something new for a change? That's getting pretty old. (*Looks for his galoshes.*) By the way, since we probably won't see each other again, let me give you a bit of advice, as we say good-bye: stop waving your arms! Try to get rid of that habit of making wide, sweeping gestures. And another thing, all this talk about building estates, these calculations about summer tourists that are going to buy property, all these predictions — they're all sweeping gestures, too. . . . You know, in spite of everything, I like you. You've got beautiful delicate fingers, like an artist's, you've a fine, sensitive soul. . . .

LOPAHIN (*embraces him*). Good-bye, my friend. Thanks for everything. I can give you some money for your trip, if you need it.

TROFIMOV. What for? I don't need it.

LOPAHIN. But you haven't got any!

TROFIMOV. Yes, I have, thank you. I got some money for a translation. Here it is, in my pocket. (*Anxiously.*) But I can't find my galoshes.

VARYA (*from the other room*). Here, take the nasty things! (*She throws a pair of rubber galoshes into the room.*)

TROFIMOV. What are you so angry about, Varya? Hm . . . but these aren't my galoshes!

LOPAHIN. I sowed three thousand acres of poppies last spring, and I've made forty thousand on it. And when they were in bloom, what a picture it was! What I mean to say is that I've made the forty thousand, so now I can lend you some money. Why be so stuck up? So I'm a peasant . . . I speak right out.

TROFIMOV. Your father was a peasant, mine was a druggist. What's that got to do with it?

(LOPAHIN *takes out his wallet.*)

Forget it, put it away . . . Even if you offered me two hundred thousand, I wouldn't take it. I'm a free man. And all that you rich men — and poor men too — all that you value so highly doesn't have the slightest power over me — it's all just so much fluff floating about in the air. I'm strong and I'm proud! I can get along without you, I can pass you by. Humanity is advancing towards the highest truth, the greatest happiness that it's possible to achieve on earth, and I'm one of the avant-garde!

LOPAHIN. Will you get there?

TROFIMOV. Yes. (*A pause.*) I'll get there myself, or show others the way to get there.

(*The sound of an axe hitting a tree is heard in the distance.*)

LOPAHIN. Well, my friend, it's time to go. Good-bye. We show off in front of one another, and all the time life is slipping by. When I work all day long, without resting, I'm happier and sometimes I even think I know why I exist. But how many people there are in Russia, my friend, who exist for no reason at all. But never mind, it doesn't matter. They say Leonid Andreyevich has a job at the bank at six thousand a year. That won't last long; he's too lazy. . . .

ANYA (*in the doorway*). Mamma begs you not to let them cut down the orchard until we've left.

TROFIMOV. Really, haven't you got any tact? (*Goes out through the hall.*)

LOPAHIN. All right, I'll take care of it. . . . These people! (*Follows* TROFIMOV.)

ANYA. Has Feers been taken to the hospital?

YASHA. I told them to take him this morning. He's gone, I think.

ANYA (*to* EPIHODOV, *who passes through the ballroom*). Semyon Pantaleyevich, will you please find out whether Feers has been taken to the hospital?

YASHA (*offended*). I told Yegor this morning. Why ask a dozen times?

EPIHODOV. That old Feers — frankly speaking, I mean — he's beyond repair, it's time he joined his ancestors. As for me, I can only envy him. (*He places a suitcase on top of a cardboard hatbox and squashes it.*) There you are, you see! . . . I might have known it! (*Goes out.*)

YASHA (*sardonically*). Two-and-twenty misfortunes!

VARYA (*from behind the door*). Has Feers been taken to the hospital?

ANYA. Yes.

VARYA. Why wasn't the letter to the doctor taken, then?

ANYA. I'll send someone after them with it . . . (*Goes out.*)

VARYA (*from the adjoining room*). Where's Yasha? Tell him his mother is here and wants to say good-bye to him.

YASHA (*waves his hand*). This is too much! I'll lose my patience.

(*While the foregoing action has been taking place,* DUNYASHA *has been busy with the luggage; now that* YASHA *is alone, she comes up to him.*)

DUNYASHA. If only you'd look at me just once, Yasha! You're going . . . you're leaving me! . . . (*She cries and throws her arms around his neck.*)

YASHA. What are you crying for? (*Drinks champagne.*) In a week I'll be in Paris again. Tomorrow we'll get on the train — and off we'll go — gone! I can't believe it. *Vive la France!* I can't stand it here and could never live here — nothing ever happens. I've seen enough of all this ignorance. I've had enough of it. (*Drinks.*) What are you crying for? Behave yourself properly, then you won't cry.

DUNYASHA (*looking into a handmirror and powdering her nose*). Please, write to me from Paris. You know how much I've loved you, Yasha. Oh, I've loved you so much! I'm very sensitive, Yasha!

YASHA. Sshh, someone's coming. (*Pretends to be busy with a suitcase, humming quietly.*)

(*Enter* LYUBOV ANDREYEVNA, GAEV, ANYA *and* CHARLOTTA IVANOVNA.)

GAEV. We've got to leave soon. There isn't much time left. (*Looks at* YASHA.) What a smell! Who's been eating herring?

LYUBOV. We'll have to leave in the carriage in ten minutes. (*Looks about the room.*) Good-bye, dear house, the home of our fathers. Winter will pass and spring will come again, and then you won't be here any more, you'll be torn down. How much these walls have seen! (*Kisses her daughter passionately.*) My little treasure, how radiant you look, your eyes are shining like diamonds. Are you glad? Very glad?

ANYA. Oh, yes, very glad, Mamma! Our new life is just beginning!

GAEV (*gaily*). Really, everything's all right now. Before the cherry orchard was sold we were all worried and upset, but as soon as things were settled once and for all, we all calmed down and even felt quite cheerful. I'm working in a bank now, a real financier. . . . The red into the side pocket . . . And say what you like, Lyuba, you're looking much better. No doubt about it.

LYUBOV. Yes, that's true, my nerves are better. (*Someone helps her on with her hat and coat.*) I'm sleeping better, too. Take out my things, Yasha, it's time. (*To* ANYA.) My little darling, we'll be seeing each other again soon. I'm going to Paris — I'll live on the money which your Grandmother sent us to buy the estate — God bless Grandmamma! — but that money won't last very long either.

ANYA. You'll come back soon, Mamma . . . won't you? I'll study and pass my exams and then I'll work and help you. We'll read together, Mamma . . . all sorts of things . . . won't we? (*She kisses her mother's hands.*) We'll read during the long autumn evenings. We'll read lots of books, and a new wonderful world will open up before us . . . (*Dreamily.*) Mamma, come back soon . . .

LYUBOV. I'll come back, my precious. (*Embraces her.*)

(*Enter* LOPAHIN. CHARLOTTA *quietly sings to herself.*)

GAEV. Happy Charlotta! She's singing.

CHARLOTTA (*picks up a bundle that looks like a baby in a blanket.*) Bye-bye, little baby. (*A sound like a baby crying is heard.*) Hush, be quiet, my darling, be a good little boy. (*The "crying" continues.*) Oh, my baby, you poor thing! (*Throws the bundle down.*) Are you going to find me another job? If you don't mind, I've got to have one.

LOPAHIN. We'll find you one, Charlotta Ivanovna, don't worry.

GAEV. Everybody's leaving us, Varya's going away . . . all of a sudden nobody wants us.

CHARLOTTA. There's no place for me to live in town. I'll have to go. (*Hums.*) Oh, well, what do I care.

(*Enter* PISHCHIK.)

LOPAHIN. Look what's here!

PISHCHIK (*gasping for breath*). Oohhh, let me get my breath . . . I'm worn out . . . My good friends . . . give me some water . . .

GAEV. I suppose you want to borrow some money? I'm going . . . Excuse me . . . (*Goes out.*)

PISHCHIK. I haven't seen you for a long time . . . my beautiful lady . . . (*To* LOPAHIN.) You're here, too . . . glad to see you . . . you're a man of great intelligence . . . here . . . take this . . . (*gives money to* LOPAHIN). Four hundred roubles . . . I still owe you eight hundred and forty. . . .

LOPAHIN (*shrugging his shoulders in amazement*). It's like a dream. . . . Where did you get it?

PISHCHIK. Wait a minute . . . I'm so hot . . . A most extraordinary thing happened. Some Englishmen came along and discovered some kind of white clay on my land. . . . (*To* LYUBOV.) Here's four hundred for you also, my dear . . . enchantress . . . (*gives her the money*). You'll get the rest later. (*Takes a drink of water.*) A young man on the train was just telling me that some great philosopher advises people to jump off roofs. You just jump off, he says, and that settles the whole problem. (*Amazed at what he has just said.*) Imagine that! More water, please.

LOPAHIN. What Englishmen?

PISHCHIK. I leased the land to them for twenty-four years. . . . And now you must excuse me, I'm in a hurry and have to get on. I'm going to Znoikov's, then to Kardamonov's . . . I owe them all money. (*Drinks.*) Your health. I'll come again on Thursday . . .

LYUBOV. We're just leaving for town, and tomorrow I'm going abroad.

PISHCHIK. What's that? (*In agitation.*) Why to town? Oh, I see . . . this furniture and the suitcases. . . . Well, never mind . . . (*Tearfully.*) What difference does it make? . . . These Englishmen, you know, they're very intelligent . . . Never mind. . . . I wish you all the best, God bless you. Never mind, everything comes to an end eventually. (*Kisses* LYUBOV'*s hand.*) And when you hear that my end has come, just think of a horse, and say: "There used to be a man like that once . . . his name was Semyonov-Pishchik — God bless him!" Wonderful weather we're having. Yes . . . (*Goes out embarrassed, but returns at once and stands in the doorway.*) Dashenka sends her greetings. (*Goes out.*)

LYUBOV. Well, we can get started now. I'm leaving with two worries on my mind. One is Feers — he's sick. (*Glances at her watch.*) We've still got five minutes. . . .

ANYA. Mamma, Feers has been taken to the hospital. Yasha sent him this morning.

LYUBOV. The other is Varya. She's used to getting up early and working, and now, with nothing to do, she's like a fish out of water. She's gotten so thin and pale, and she cries a lot, the poor dear. (*A pause.*) You know very well, Yermolay Alexeyevich, that I've been hoping you two would get married . . . and everything pointed to it. (*Whispers to* ANYA *and motions to* CHARLOTTA, *and they both go out.*) She loves you, and you're fond of her, too . . . I just don't know, I don't know why you seem to avoid each other. I don't understand it.

LOPAHIN. Neither do I, I admit it. The whole thing's so strange. . . .

If there's still time, I'm ready to. . . . Let's settle it at once — and get it over with! Without you here, I don't feel I'll ever propose to her.

LYUBOV. That's an excellent idea! You won't need more than a minute. I'll call her at once.

LOPAHIN. And there's champagne here, too, we'll celebrate. (*Looks at the glasses.*) They're empty, someone's drunk it all. (YASHA *coughs.*) They must have poured it down.

LYUBOV (*with animation*). Oh, I'm so glad. I'll call her, and we'll leave you alone. Yasha, *allez!* (*Through the door.*) Varya, come here for a minute, leave what you're doing and come here! Varya!

(*Goes out with* YASHA.)

LOPAHIN (*looking at his watch*). Yes. . . .

(*A pause. Whispering and suppressed laughter are heard behind the door, then* VARYA *comes in and starts fussing with the luggage.*)

VARYA. That's strange, I can't find it. . . .

LOPAHIN. What are you looking for?

VARYA. I packed it myself, and I can't remember . . .

(*A pause.*)

LOPAHIN. Where are you going to now, Varvara Mihailovna?

VARYA. I? To the Rogulins. I've taken a job as their housekeeper.

LOPAHIN. That's in Yashnevo, isn't it? Almost seventy miles from here.

(*A pause.*)

So this is the end of life in this house. . . .

VARYA (*still fussing with the luggage*). Where could it be? Perhaps I put it in the trunk? Yes, life in this house has come to an end . . . there won't be any more. . . .

LOPAHIN. And I'm going to Kharkov. . . . On the next train. I've got a lot of work to do there. I'm leaving Epihodov here. . . . I've hired him.

VARYA. Really! . . .

LOPAHIN. Remember, last year at this time it was snowing already, but now it's still so bright and sunny. Though it's cold . . . three degrees of frost.

VARYA. I haven't looked.

(*A pause.*)

Besides, our thermometer's broken. . . .

(*A pause. A voice is heard from outside the door.*)

VOICE. Yermolay Alexeyevich!

LOPAHIN (*as if he had been waiting for it*). I'm coming! Right away! (*Goes out quickly.*)

(VARYA *sits on the floor, with her head on a bundle of clothes, crying quietly. The door opens,* LYUBOV *enters hesitantly.*)

LYUBOV. Well? (*A pause.*) We must be going.

VARYA (*stops crying and wipes her eyes*). Yes, Mamma, it's time we got started. I'll just have time to get to the Rogulins today, if we don't miss the train.

LYUBOV (*calls through the door*). Anya, put your things on.

(*Enter* ANYA, *followed by* GAEV *and* CHARLOTTA. GAEV *wears a heavy overcoat with a hood. Servants and coachmen come into the room.* EPIHODOV *is picking up the luggage.*)

Now we can begin our journey!

ANYA (*joyfully*). Our journey!

GAEV. My friends, my dear, beloved friends! As I leave this house forever, how can I be silent, how can I refrain from expressing to you, as I say good-bye for the last time, the feelings which now overwhelm me. . . .

ANYA (*begging*). Uncle!

VARYA. Uncle, please don't!

GAEV (*downcast*). I put the red into the corner and then . . . I'll keep quiet.

(*Enter* TROFIMOV *and* LOPAHIN.)

TROFIMOV. Well, ladies and gentlemen, it's time we got started.

LOPAHIN. Epihodov, my coat!

LYUBOV. I'll just stay for one more minute. It seems as if I'd never seen the walls and ceilings of this house before, and now I look at them with such longing, such love. . . .

GAEV. I remember when I was six — it was Trinity Sunday . . . I was sitting here at this window watching father on his way to church. . . .

LYUBOV. Have they taken everything out?

LOPAHIN. It looks like it. (*To* EPIHODOV, *as he puts on his coat.*) Be sure to take care of everything, Epihodov.

EPIHODOV (*in a husky voice*). Don't worry, Yermolay Alexeyevich!

LOPAHIN. What is wrong with your voice?

EPIHODOV. I just had some water, and it went down the wrong throat.

YASHA (*with contempt*). What a fool!

LYUBOV. After we leave, there won't be a soul here. . . .

LOPAHIN. Not until spring.

(VARYA *pulls an umbrella from a bundle of clothes;* LOPAHIN *pretends to be afraid.*)

What are you doing that for? . . . I didn't mean to . . .

TROFIMOV. Ladies and gentlemen, hurry up, it's time. The train will be here soon.

VARYA. Petya, here are your galoshes beside the suitcase. (*Tearfully.*) How dirty and old they are! . . .

TROFIMOV (*puts them on*). Hurry up, ladies and gentlemen!

GAEV (*greatly embarrassed, afraid of breaking into tears*). The train, the station . . . The red off the white into the middle pocket. . . .

LYUBOV. Let us go!

LOPAHIN. Are we all here? No one left? (*Locks the door on the left.*) There are some things stored in there, best to keep it locked up. Come along!

ANYA. Good-bye, old house! Good-bye, old life!

TROFIMOV. Welcome to the new life! . . . (*Goes out with* ANYA.)

(VARYA *looks around the room and goes out slowly.* YASHA *and* CHARLOTTA, *with her little dog, follow.*)

LOPAHIN. And so, until the spring. Come, my friends. . . . Au revoir! (*Goes out.*)

(LYUBOV *and* GAEV *alone. They seem to have been waiting for this moment, and now they embrace each other and cry quietly, with restraint, so as not to be heard.*)

GAEV (*in despair*). Sister, my sister. . . .

LYUBOV. Oh, my orchard, my beloved, my beautiful orchard! My life, my youth, my happiness . . . good-bye! . . . Good-bye!

ANYA (*off-stage, calling gaily*). Mamma! . . .

TROFIMOV (*off-stage, gaily and excitedly*). Yoo-hoo! . . .

LYUBOV. Just one last time — to look at these walls, these windows. . . . Mother loved to walk in this room. . . .

GAEV. Sister, my sister . . .

ANYA (*off-stage*). Mamma!

TROFIMOV (*off-stage*). Yoo-hoo!

LYUBOV. We're coming . . . (*They go out.*)

(*The stage is empty. The sound of doors being locked and then of carriages driving off. Silence. In the stillness the dull sounds of an axe striking on a tree can be heard. They sound mournful and sad. Footsteps are heard and from the door on the right* FEERS *enters. He is dressed, as usual, in a coat and white waistcoat, and is wearing slippers. He is ill.*)

FEERS (*walks up to the middle door and tries the handle*). Locked. They've gone . . . (*Sits down on a sofa.*) They've forgotten me. Never mind. . . . I'll sit here for a bit. I don't suppose Leonid Andreyevich put on his fur coat, he probably wore his light one. (*Sighs, preoccupied.*) I didn't take care of it . . . These young people! . . . (*Mutters something unintelligible.*) My life's slipped by as if I'd never lived. . . . (*Lies down.*) I'll lie down a bit. You haven't got any strength left, nothing's left, nothing. . . . Oh, you . . . you old good-for-nothing! . . . (*Lies motionless.*)

(*A distant sound that seems to come out of the sky, like a breaking harp string, slowly and sadly dying away. Then all is silent, except for the sound of an axe striking a tree in the orchard far away.*)

Curtain

John Millington Synge (1871–1909), unlike some Irish dramatists who thought they could best serve the cause of nationalism by glorifying their countrymen and their myths beyond all recognition, moved in the opposite direction — with correspondingly more rewarding results. It is not that Synge portrays his fellow citizens as grotesques or that he holds their beliefs, customs, and attitudes up to ribald ridicule. He never goes quite that far. The effect, rather, is of verisimilitude pushed toward comic exaggeration. This truth-to-life, heightened by Synge's own genius for capturing the poetic quality of Irish peasant speech, gives his dramas a unique appeal for readers today.

Urged by William Butler Yeats, the champion of a distinctly Irish literature, poetry, and theatre, Synge spent several summers in the bleak Aran Islands, studying the speech of the people, analyzing the language usages and the patterns of rhythm. But it was not only the way they spoke that fascinated him; what they spoke about intrigued him as well. Their dreams and fears, simple but often supernatural, became the stuff of his plays.

The Playboy incorporates Synge's feelings about the peasants, their stories, and their language. It is a fantasy based on reality; just such an incident actually occurred. The theme is Oedipal — the symbolic murder of our parents before we can hope to find ourselves — placed in the context of a seeming fairy tale. Through the three "murders" of his father — the first by accidental violence, the second by purposeful violence, and the third by the symbolic violence of dominating his once proud father — Christy becomes the man the villagers all thought him to be when first he came with his boasting story of parricide. As with any fairy-tale hero, Christy's wish to be somebody is initially transformed into *seeming* reality by the will of others, Pegeen and the rest. When that magic of belief fails them — and him — Christy uses his own will to attain the reality of manhood. Being a playboy did not mean, however, that Christy Mahon had anything in common with devotees of *Playboy* magazine. To the inhabitants of Western Ireland — the Western World — it meant merely that he was a good athlete, a hoaxer, and a bit of a braggart.

A group which feels inferior often inflates its sagging ego with unrealistic fairy tales about itself and its ambitions. That does not necessarily mean that the group really is inferior. What it does mean is that lack of opportunity may have prevented the development and effective exploitation of talents and abilities to enable the people to compete with their more secure neighbors.

This was what was happening in Ireland at the time Synge was writing. After centuries of subjugation — physical, emotional, and intellectual — at the hands of the English, the emerging Irish nationalist movement quite naturally encouraged a vision of its country and its citizens which was glowingly patriotic, enthusiastically optimistic, and outrageously unreal. This is partly what Synge is satirizing in *The Playboy*. The lionizing of Christy, the presumed father-killer, is the action of a group of villagers starved for romance, excitement, and heroes to worship. But it is, in small, also the larger Irish community longing for the same things.

Synge's relentless honesty in depicting characters and attitudes is tinged with good-humored compassion for the all-too-human faults his creations display. But it was finally too direct, too honest to be endured complacently. The play, it was alleged, was obscene. It showed, some charged, that Irishmen admired murderers. It slandered the entire country. It suggested that Irish ladies and lasses were starved for male companionship. It implied that the Irish peasant was a treacherous, fickle, mean-spirited fellow. It tried to calumniate the flower of Irish manhood by throwing doubts upon its courage. In short, angry opponents to the play insisted, it presented the plain Irishman as a fool.

When *The Playboy* opened at the Abbey Theatre in Dublin, Synge's antagonists threw old potatoes — something the Irish had in abundance — and eggs at the stage. At the close, Yeats stepped forward, as Marc Connelly tells the story, glared at his countrymen, and said, "Well, once again you've managed to disgrace yourselves!" Some American Irishmen agreed with their Dublin brothers. Even before the Abbey Theatre group arrived for a tour of the United States in 1911–1912, emigrant sons of Erin started agitating against the play. On opening night in New York, they provoked a riot. Only the published admiration of President Theodore Roosevelt restored some measure of calm and helped win the play and production the attention and consideration they deserved.

If telling the truth dramatically is a crime, then perhaps Synge was guilty. But unless modern readers clearly see the truth that is in *The Playboy*, they may react as the first audience did and miss the point completely.

The play does not really glorify Christy's false bravado or his alleged act of murder. Not at all. It is, rather, about his eventual assimilation of the role of the playboy, a role he has longed for and which he first claims as his own by lying. In this act, and as a result of the disillusion that follows from it, he grows from boy to man, winning courage and independence. He is shocked to discover that the villagers prefer the tall tale to the reality. His report of killing his father engrosses them; the real thing — as it seems to them — is repellent. Christy learns to judge character better: his own, Pegeen's, the villagers'. They, however, are condemned to continue evading reality with tall tales and tall ales.

G. L.

JOHN MILLINGTON SYNGE

The Playboy of the Western World*

Characters

CHRISTOPHER MAHON
OLD MAHON, *his father — a squatter*
MICHAEL JAMES FLAHERTY, *called* MICHAEL JAMES, *a publican*
MARGARET FLAHERTY, *called* PEGEEN MIKE, *his daughter*
WIDOW QUIN, *a woman of about thirty*
SHAWN KEOGH, *her cousin, a young farmer*
PHILLY CULLEN *and* JIMMY FARRELL, *small farmers*
SARA TANSEY, SUSAN BRADY, *and* HONOR BLAKE, *village girls*
A BELLMAN
Some Peasants

(*The action takes place near a village, on a wild coast of Mayo. The first act passes on an evening of autumn, the other two acts on the following day.*)

ACT ONE

(SCENE: *Country public-house or shebeen, very rough and untidy. There is a sort of counter on the right with shelves, holding many bottles and jugs, just seen above it. Empty barrels stand near the counter. At back, a little to left of counter, there is a door into the open air, then, more to the left, there is a settle with shelves above it, with more jugs, and a table beneath a window. At the left there is a large open fire-place, with turf fire, and a small door into inner room.* PEGEEN, *a wild-looking but fine girl, of about twenty, is writing at table. She is dressed in the usual peasant dress.*)

PEGEEN (*slowly as she writes*). Six yards of stuff for to make a yellow gown. A pair of lace boots with lengthy heels on them and brassy eyes. A hat is suited for a wedding day. A fine tooth comb. To be sent with three barrels of porter in Jimmy Farrell's creel cart on the evening of the

*__Playboy:__ Irish slang for hoaxer, con-man, braggart. __Western World:__ Irish folk term for the West Coast of Ireland.

coming Fair to Mister Michael James Flaherty. With the best compliments of this season. Margaret Flaherty.

SHAWN KEOGH (*a fat and fair young man comes in as she signs, looks round awkwardly, when he sees she is alone*). Where's himself?

PEGEEN (*without looking at him*). He's coming. (*She directs the letter.*) To Mister Sheamus Mulroy, Wine and Spirit Dealer, Castlebar.

SHAWN (*uneasily*). I didn't see him on the road.

PEGEEN. How would you see him (*licks stamp and puts it on letter*) and it dark night this half hour gone by?

SHAWN (*turning towards the door again*). I stood a while outside wondering would I have a right to pass on or to walk in and see you, Pegeen Mike (*comes to fire*), and I could hear the cows breathing, and sighing in the stillness of the air, and not a step moving any place from this gate to the bridge.

PEGEEN (*putting letter in envelope*). It's above at the crossroads he is, meeting Philly Cullen; and a couple more are going along with him to Kate Cassidy's wake.

SHAWN (*looking at her blankly*). And he's going that length in the dark night?

PEGEEN (*impatiently*). He is surely, and leaving me lonesome on the scruff of the hill. (*She gets up and puts envelope on dresser, then winds clock.*) Isn't it long the nights are now, Shawn Keogh, to be leaving a poor girl with her own self counting the hours to the dawn of day?

SHAWN (*with awkward humour*). If it is, when we're wedded in a short while you'll have no call to complain, for I've little will to be walking off to wakes or weddings in the darkness of the night.

PEGEEN (*with rather scornful good humour*). You're making mighty certain, Shaneen,[1] that I'll wed you now.

SHAWN. Aren't we after making a good bargain, the way we're only waiting these days on Father Reilly's dispensation from the bishops, or the Court of Rome.

PEGEEN (*looking at him teasingly, washing up at dresser*). It's a wonder, Shaneen, the Holy Father'd be taking notice of the likes of you; for if I was him I wouldn't bother with this place where you'll meet none but Red Linahan, has a squint in his eye, and Patcheen is lame in his heel, or the mad Mulrannies were driven from California and they lost in their wits. We're a queer lot these times to go troubling the Holy Father on his sacred seat.

SHAWN (*scandalized*). If we are, we're as good this place as another, maybe, and as good these times as we were for ever.

PEGEEN (*with scorn*). As good, is it? Where now will you meet the like of Daneen Sullivan knocked the eye from a peeler,[2] or Marcus Quin,

Act One. [1] **Shaneen** = Shawn + een. Equivalent of "Johnnie" in English. The Irish suffix "-een," a diminutive, sometimes connotes endearment, as the English "-ie." Hence Peg*een*, priest*een*, sup*een*, etc.

[2] **peeler:** slang for policeman, derived from the name of the founder of the Metropolitan (London) Police, Sir Robert Peel.

God rest him, got six months for maiming ewes, and he a great warrant to tell stories of holy Ireland till he'd have the old women shedding down tears about their feet. Where will you find the like of them, I'm saying?

SHAWN (*timidly*). If you don't, it's a good job, maybe; for (*with peculiar emphasis on the words*) Father Reilly has small conceit[3] to have that kind walking around and talking to the girls.

PEGEEN (*impatiently, throwing water from basin out of the door*). Stop tormenting me with Father Reilly (*imitating his voice*) when I'm asking only what way I'll pass these twelve hours of dark, and not take my death with the fear. (*Looking out of door.*)

SHAWN (*timidly*). Would I fetch you the Widow Quin, maybe?

PEGEEN. Is it the like of that murderer? You'll not, surely.

SHAWN (*going to her, soothingly*). Then I'm thinking himself will stop along with you when he sees you taking on, for it'll be a long night-time with great darkness, and I'm after feeling a kind of fellow above in the furzy[4] ditch, groaning wicked like a maddening dog, the way it's good cause you have, maybe, to be fearing now.

PEGEEN (*turning on him sharply*). What's that? Is it a man you seen?

SHAWN (*retreating*). I couldn't see him at all; but I heard him groaning out, and breaking his heart. It should have been a young man from his words speaking.

PEGEEN (*going after him*). And you never went near to see was he hurted or what ailed him at all?

SHAWN. I did not, Pegeen Mike. It was a dark, lonesome place to be hearing the like of him.

PEGEEN. Well, you're a daring fellow, and if they find his corpse stretched above in the dews of dawn, what'll you say then to the peelers, or the Justice of the Peace?

SHAWN (*thunderstruck*). I wasn't thinking of that. For the love of God, Pegeen Mike, don't let on I was speaking of him. Don't tell your father and the men is coming above; for if they heard that story, they'd have great blabbing this night at the wake.

PEGEEN. I'll maybe tell them, and I'll maybe not.

SHAWN. They are coming at the door. Will you whisht,[5] I'm saying?

PEGEEN. Whisht yourself.

(*She goes behind counter.* MICHAEL JAMES, *fat jovial publican, comes in followed by* PHILLY CULLEN, *who is thin and mistrusting, and* JIMMY FARRELL, *who is fat and amorous, about forty-five.*)

MEN (*together*). God bless you. The blessing of God on this place.

PEGEEN. God bless you kindly.

MICHAEL (*to men who go to the counter*). Sit down now, and take

[3] **has small conceit:** doesn't like.

[4] **furzy:** an evergreen shrub; also called gorse.

[5] **whisht:** be quiet, "shush."

your rest. (*Crosses to* SHAWN *at the fire.*) And how is it you are, Shawn Keogh? Are you coming over the sands to Kate Cassidy's wake?

SHAWN. I am not, Michael James. I'm going home the short cut to my bed.

PEGEEN (*speaking across the counter*). He's right too, and have you no shame, Michael James, to be quitting off for the whole night, and leaving myself lonesome in the shop?

MICHAEL (*good-humouredly*). Isn't it the same whether I go for the whole night or a part only? and I'm thinking it's a queer daughter you are if you'd have me crossing backward through the Stooks of the Dead Women,[6] with a drop taken.

PEGEEN. If I am a queer daughter, it's a queer father'd be leaving me lonesome these twelve hours of dark, and I piling the turf with the dogs barking, and the calves mooing, and my own teeth rattling with the fear.

JIMMY (*flatteringly*). What is there to hurt you, and you a fine, hardy girl would knock the head of any two men in the place?

PEGEEN (*working herself up*). Isn't there the harvest boys with their tongues red for drink, and the ten tinkers is camped in the east glen, and the thousand militia — bad cess[7] to them! — walking idle through the land. There's lots surely to hurt me, and I won't stop alone in it, let himself do what he will.

MICHAEL. If you're that afeard, let Shawn Keogh stop along with you. It's the will of God, I'm thinking, himself should be seeing to you now.

(*They all turn on* SHAWN.)

SHAWN (*in horrified confusion*). I would and welcome, Michael James, but I'm afeard of Father Reilly; and what at all would the Holy Father and the Cardinals of Rome be saying if they heard I did the like of that?

MICHAEL (*with contempt*). God help you! Can't you sit in by the hearth with the light lit and herself beyond in the room? You'll do that surely, for I've heard tell there's a queer fellow above, going mad or getting his death, maybe, in the gripe[8] of the ditch, so she'd be safer this night with a person here.

SHAWN (*with plaintive despair*). I'm afeard of Father Reilly, I'm saying. Let you not be tempting me, and we near married itself.

PHILLY (*with cold contempt*). Lock him in the west room. He'll stay then and have no sin to be telling to the priest.

MICHAEL (*to* SHAWN, *getting between him and the door*). Go up now.

SHAWN (*at the top of his voice*). Don't stop me, Michael James. Let me out of the door, I'm saying, for the love of the Almighty God.

[6] **Stooks of the Dead Women**: a stretch of seashore with rocks piled high like *stooks*, sheaves of wheat or oats stacked to dry. According to legend (see *In West Kerry*), a boat with twelve dead women on board ran aground here.

[7] **cess**: luck.

[8] **gripe**: gutter, trough.

Let me out. (*Trying to dodge past him.*) Let me out of it, and may God grant you His indulgence in the hour of need.

MICHAEL (*loudly*). Stop your noising, and sit down by the hearth. (*Gives him a push and goes to counter laughing.*)

SHAWN (*turning back, wringing his hands*). Oh, Father Reilly and the saints of God, where will I hide myself to-day? Oh, St. Joseph and St. Patrick and St. Brigid, and St. James, have mercy on me now! (SHAWN *turns round, sees door clear, and makes a rush for it.*)

MICHAEL (*catching him by the coat tail*). You'd be going, is it?

SHAWN (*screaming*). Leave me go, Michael James, leave me go, you old Pagan, leave me go, or I'll get the curse of the priests on you, and of the scarlet-coated bishops of the courts of Rome. (*With a sudden movement he pulls himself out of his coat, and disappears out of the door, leaving his coat in* MICHAEL'*s hands.*)

MICHAEL (*turning round, and holding up coat*). Well, there's the coat of a Christian man. Oh, there's sainted glory this day in the lonesome west; and by the will of God I've got you a decent man, Pegeen, you'll have no call to be spying after if you've a score of young girls, maybe, weeding in your fields.

PEGEEN (*taking up the defence of her property*). What right have you to be making game of a poor fellow for minding the priest, when it's your own the fault is, not paying a penny pot-boy to stand along with me and give me courage in the doing of my work? (*She snaps the coat away from him, and goes behind counter with it.*)

MICHAEL (*taken aback*). Where would I get a pot-boy? Would you have me send the bellman screaming in the streets of Castlebar?

SHAWN (*opening the door a chink and putting in his head, in a small voice*). Michael James!

MICHAEL (*imitating him*). What ails you?

SHAWN. The queer dying fellow's beyond looking over the ditch. He's come up, I'm thinking, stealing your hens. (*Looks over his shoulder.*) God help me, he's following me now (*he runs into room*), and if he's heard what I said, he'll be having my life, and I going home lonesome in the darkness of the night.

(*For a perceptible moment they watch the door with curiosity. Some one coughs outside. Then* CHRISTY MAHON, *a slight young man, comes in very tired and frightened and dirty.*)

CHRISTY (*in a small voice*). God save all here!

MEN. God save you kindly.

CHRISTY (*going to the counter*). I'd trouble for a glass of porter,[9] woman of the house. (*He puts down coin.*)

PEGEEN (*serving him*). You're one of the tinkers, young fellow, is beyond camped in the glen?

CHRISTY. I am not; but I'm destroyed walking.

[9] **porter**: a weak, sweet beer, about 4 per cent alcohol.

MICHAEL (*patronizingly*). Let you come up then to the fire. You're looking famished with the cold.

CHRISTY. God reward you. (*He takes up his glass and goes a little way across to the left, then stops and looks about him.*) Is it often the police do be coming into this place, master of the house?

MICHAEL. If you'd come in better hours, you'd have seen "Licensed for the sale of Beer and Spirits, to be consumed on the premises," written in white letters above the door, and what would the polis want spying on me, and not a decent house within four miles, the way every living Christian is a bona fide,[10] saving one widow alone?

CHRISTY (*with relief*). It's a safe house, so. (*He goes over to the fire, sighing and moaning. Then he sits down, putting his glass beside him and begins gnawing a turnip, too miserable to feel the others staring at him with curiosity.*)

MICHAEL (*going after him*). Is it yourself is fearing the polis? You're wanting, maybe?

CHRISTY. There's many wanting.

MICHAEL. Many surely, with the broken harvest and the ended wars. (*He picks up some stockings, etc., that are near the fire, and carries them away furtively.*) It should be larceny, I'm thinking?

CHRISTY (*dolefully*). I had it in my mind it was a different word and a bigger.

PEGEEN. There's a queer lad. Were you never slapped in school, young fellow, that you don't know the name of your deed?

CHRISTY (*bashfully*). I'm slow at learning, a middling scholar only.

MICHAEL. If you're a dunce itself, you'd have a right to know that larceny's robbing and stealing. Is it for the like of that you're wanting?

CHRISTY (*with a flash of family pride*). And I the son of a strong farmer (*with a sudden qualm*), God rest his soul, could have bought up the whole of your old house a while since, from the butt[11] of his tailpocket, and not have missed the weight of it gone.

MICHAEL (*impressed*). If it's not stealing, it's maybe something big.

CHRISTY (*flattered*). Aye; it's maybe something big.

JIMMY. He's a wicked-looking young fellow. Maybe he followed after a young woman on a lonesome night.

CHRISTY (*shocked*). Oh, the saints forbid, mister; I was all times a decent lad.

PHILLY (*turning on* JIMMY). You're a silly man, Jimmy Farrell. He said his father was a farmer a while since, and there's himself now in a poor state. Maybe the land was grabbed from him, and he did what any decent man would do.

MICHAEL (*to* CHRISTY, *mysteriously*). Was it bailiffs?

CHRISTY. The divil a one.[12]

[10] **bona fide:** person who could be served drinks after tavern hours; had to have slept at least three miles away from the tavern the night before.

[11] **butt:** literally, end; in this case, bottom.

[12] **The divil a one:** not at all; "the devil it was."

MICHAEL. Agents?

CHRISTY. The divil a one.

MICHAEL. Landlords?

CHRISTY (*peevishly*). Ah, not at all, I'm saying. You'd see the like of them stories on any little paper of a Munster town. But I'm not calling to mind any person, gentle, simple, judge or jury, did the like of me.

(*They all draw nearer with delighted curiosity.*)

PHILLY. Well, that lad's a puzzle-the-world.

JIMMY. He'd beat Dan Davies' circus, or the holy missioners[13] making sermons on the villainy of man. Try him again, Philly.

PHILLY. Did you strike golden guineas out of solder, young fellow, or shilling coins itself?

CHRISTY. I did not, mister, not sixpence nor a farthing coin.

JIMMY. Did you marry three wives maybe? I'm told there's a sprinkling have done that among the holy Luthers of the preaching north.

CHRISTY (*shyly*). I never married with one, let alone with a couple or three.

PHILLY. Maybe he went fighting for the Boers, the like of the man beyond, was judged to be hanged, quartered and drawn. Were you off east, young fellow, fighting bloody wars for Kruger and the freedom of the Boers?

CHRISTY. I never left my own parish till Tuesday was a week.

PEGEEN (*coming from counter*). He's done nothing, so. (*To* CHRISTY.) If you didn't commit murder or a bad, nasty thing, or false coining, or robbery, or butchery, or the like of them, there isn't anything that would be worth your troubling for to run from now. You did nothing at all.

CHRISTY (*his feelings hurt*). That's an unkindly thing to be saying to a poor orphaned traveller, has a prison behind him, and hanging before, and hell's gap gaping below.

PEGEEN (*with a sign to the men to be quiet*). You're only saying it. You did nothing at all. A soft lad the like of you wouldn't slit the windpipe of a screeching sow.

CHRISTY (*offended*). You're not speaking the truth.

PEGEEN (*in mock rage*). Not speaking the truth, is it? Would you have me knock the head of you with the butt of the broom?

CHRISTY (*twisting round on her with a sharp cry of horror*). Don't strike me. I killed my poor father, Tuesday was a week, for doing the like of that.

PEGEEN (*with blank amazement*). Is it killed your father?

CHRISTY (*subsiding*). With the help of God I did surely, and that the Holy Immaculate Mother may intercede for his soul.

PHILLY (*retreating with* JIMMY). There's a daring fellow.

JIMMY. Oh, glory be to God!

[13] **missioners:** circuit priests.

MICHAEL (*with great respect*). That was a hanging crime, mister honey. You should have had good reason for doing the like of that.

CHRISTY (*in a very reasonable tone*). He was a dirty man, God forgive him, and he getting old and crusty, the way I couldn't put up with him at all.

PEGEEN. And you shot him dead?

CHRISTY (*shaking his head*). I never used weapons. I've no license, and I'm a law-fearing man.

MICHAEL. It was with a hilted knife maybe? I'm told, in the big world it's bloody knives they use.

CHRISTY (*loudly, scandalized*). Do you take me for a slaughter-boy?

PEGEEN. You never hanged him, the way Jimmy Farrell hanged his dog from the license,[14] and had it screeching and wriggling three hours at the butt of a string, and himself swearing it was a dead dog, and the peelers swearing it had life?

CHRISTY. I did not then. I just riz the loy[15] and let fall the edge of it on the ridge of his skull, and he went down at my feet like an empty sack, and never let a grunt or groan from him at all.

MICHAEL (*making a sign to* PEGEEN *to fill* CHRISTY'*s glass*). And what way weren't you hanged, mister? Did you bury him then?

CHRISTY (*considering*). Aye. I buried him then. Wasn't I digging spuds in the field?

MICHAEL. And the peelers never followed after you the eleven days that you're out?

CHRISTY (*shaking his head*). Never a one of them, and I walking forward facing hog, dog, or divil on the highway of the road.

PHILLY (*nodding wisely*). It's only with a common week-day kind of a murderer them lads would be trusting their carcase, and that man should be a great terror when his temper's roused.

MICHAEL. He should then. (*To* CHRISTY.) And where was it, mister honey, that you did the deed?

CHRISTY (*looking at him with suspicion*). Oh, a distant place, master of the house, a windy corner of high, distant hills.

PHILLY (*nodding with approval*). He's a close man, and he's right, surely.

PEGEEN. That'd be a lad with the sense of Solomon to have for a pot-boy, Michael James, if it's the truth you're seeking one at all.

PHILLY. The peelers is fearing him, and if you'd that lad in the house there isn't one of them would come smelling around if the dogs itself were lapping poteen[16] from the dung-pit of the yard.

JIMMY. Bravery's a treasure in a lonesome place, and a lad would kill his father, I'm thinking, would face a foxy divil with a pitch-pike[17] on the flags[18] of hell.

[14] **from the license**: because he had no license for it.
[15] **loy**: small spade for digging peat.
[16] **poteen**: illegally distilled whiskey.
[17] **pitch-pike**: pitchfork.
[18] **flags**: flagstones, therefore floor.

PEGEEN. It's the truth they're saying, and if I'd that lad in the house, I wouldn't be fearing the loosèd kharki cut-throats,[19] or the walking dead.

CHRISTY (*swelling with surprise and triumph*). Well, glory be to God!

MICHAEL (*with deference*). Would you think well to stop here and be pot-boy, mister honey, if we gave you good wages, and didn't destroy you with the weight of work?

SHAWN (*coming forward uneasily*). That'd be a queer kind to bring into a decent quiet household with the like of Pegeen Mike.

PEGEEN (*very sharply*). Will you whisht? Who's speaking to you?

SHAWN (*retreating*). A bloody-handed murderer the like of . . .

PEGEEN (*snapping at him*). Whisht I am saying; we'll take no fooling from your like at all. (*To* CHRISTY *with a honeyed voice.*) And you, young fellow, you'd have a right to stop, I'm thinking, for we'd do our all and utmost to content your needs.

CHRISTY (*overcome with wonder*). And I'd be safe in this place from the searching law?

MICHAEL. You would, surely. If they're not fearing you, itself, the peelers in this place is decent droughty[20] poor fellows, wouldn't touch a cur dog and not give warning in the dead of night.

PEGEEN (*very kindly and persuasively*). Let you stop a short while anyhow. Aren't you destroyed walking with your feet in bleeding blisters, and your whole skin needing washing like a Wicklow sheep.

CHRISTY (*looking round with satisfaction*). It's a nice room, and if it's not humbugging me you are, I'm thinking that I'll surely stay.

JIMMY (*jumps up*). Now, by the grace of God, herself will be safe this night, with a man killed his father holding danger from the door, and let you come on, Michael James, or they'll have the best stuff drunk at the wake.

MICHAEL (*going to the door with men*). And begging your pardon, mister, what name will we call you, for we'd like to know?

CHRISTY. Christopher Mahon.

MICHAEL. Well, God bless you, Christy, and a good rest till we meet again when the sun'll be rising to the noon of day.

CHRISTY. God bless you all.

MEN. God bless you.

(*They go out except* SHAWN, *who lingers at door.*)

SHAWN (*to* PEGEEN). Are you wanting me to stop along with you to keep you from harm?

PEGEEN (*gruffly*). Didn't you say you were fearing Father Reilly?

SHAWN. There'd be no harm staying now, I'm thinking, and himself in it too.

PEGEEN. You wouldn't stay when there was need for you, and let you step off nimble this time when there's none.

SHAWN. Didn't I say it was Father Reilly . . .

[19] **loosèd kharki cut-throats:** British soldiers.
[20] **droughty:** thirsty.

PEGEEN. Go on, then, to Father Reilly (*in a jeering tone*), and let him put you in the holy brotherhoods, and leave that lad to me.

SHAWN. If I meet the Widow Quin . . .

PEGEEN. Go on, I'm saying, and don't be waking this place with your noise. (*She hustles him out and bolts the door.*) That lad would wear the spirits from the saints of peace. (*Bustles about, then takes off her apron and pins it up in the window as a blind.* CHRISTY *watching her timidly. Then she comes to him and speaks with bland good humour.*) Let you stretch out now by the fire, young fellow. You should be destroyed travelling.

CHRISTY (*shyly again, drawing off his boots*). I'm tired, surely, walking wild eleven days, and waking fearful in the night. (*He holds up one of his feet, feeling his blisters, and looking at them with compassion.*)

PEGEEN (*standing beside him, watching him with delight*). You should have had great people in your family, I'm thinking, with the little, small feet you have, and you with a kind of a quality name, the like of what you'd find on the great powers and potentates of France and Spain.

CHRISTY (*with pride*). We were great surely, with wide and windy acres of rich Munster land.

PEGEEN. Wasn't I telling you, and you a fine, handsome young fellow with a noble brow?

CHRISTY (*with a flash of delighted surprise*). Is it me?

PEGEEN. Aye. Did you never hear that from the young girls where you come from in the west or south?

CHRISTY (*with venom*). I did not then. Oh, they're bloody liars in the naked parish where I grew a man.

PEGEEN. If they are itself, you've heard it these days, I'm thinking, and you walking the world telling out your story to young girls or old.

CHRISTY. I've told my story no place till this night, Pegeen Mike, and it's foolish I was here, maybe, to be talking free, but you're decent people, I'm thinking, and yourself a kindly woman, the way I wasn't fearing you at all.

PEGEEN (*filling a sack with straw*). You've said the like of that, maybe, in every cot and cabin where you've met a young girl on your way.

CHRISTY (*going over to her, gradually raising his voice*). I've said it nowhere till this night, I'm telling you, for I've seen none the like of you the eleven long days I am walking the world, looking over a low ditch or a high ditch on my north or my south, into stony scattered fields, or scribes[21] of bog, where you'd see young, limber girls, and fine prancing women making laughter with the men.

PEGEEN. If you weren't destroyed travelling, you'd have as much talk and streeleen,[22] I'm thinking, as Owen Roe O'Sullivan or the poets of the Dingle Bay, and I've heard all times it's the poets are your like, fine fiery fellows with great rages when their temper's roused.

[21] **scribes:** areas; patches.

[22] **streeleen:** blarney; charming nonsense.

CHRISTY (*drawing a little nearer to her*). You've a power of rings, God bless you, and would there be any offence if I was asking are you single now?

PEGEEN. What would I want wedding so young?

CHRISTY (*with relief*). We're alike, so.

PEGEEN (*she puts sack on settle and beats it up*). I never killed my father. I'd be afeard to do that, except I was the like of yourself with blind rages tearing me within, for I'm thinking you should have had great tussling when the end was come.

CHRISTY (*expanding with delight at the first confidential talk he has ever had with a woman*). We had not then. It was a hard woman was come over the hill, and if he was always a crusty kind when he'd a hard woman setting him on, not the divil himself or his four fathers[23] could put up with him at all.

PEGEEN (*with curiosity*). And isn't it a great wonder that one wasn't fearing you?

CHRISTY (*very confidentially*). Up to the day I killed my father, there wasn't a person in Ireland knew the kind I was, and I there drinking, waking, eating, sleeping, a quiet, simple poor fellow with no man giving me heed.

PEGEEN (*getting a quilt out of the cupboard and putting it on the sack*). It was the girls were giving you heed maybe, and I'm thinking it's most conceit[24] you'd have to be gaming with their like.

CHRISTY (*shaking his head, with simplicity*). Not the girls itself, and I won't tell you a lie. There wasn't anyone heeding me in that place saving only the dumb beasts of the field. (*He sits down at fire.*)

PEGEEN (*with disappointment*). And I thinking you should have been living the like of a king of Norway or the Eastern world.[25] (*She comes and sits beside him after placing bread and mug of milk on the table.*)

CHRISTY (*laughing piteously*). The like of a king, is it? And I after toiling, moiling,[26] digging, dodging from the dawn till dusk with never a sight of joy or sport saving only when I'd be abroad in the dark night poaching rabbits on hills, for I was a divil to poach, God forgive me, (*very naïvely*) and I near got six months for going with a dung fork and stabbing a fish.

PEGEEN. And it's that you'd call sport, is it, to be abroad in the darkness with yourself alone?

CHRISTY. I did, God help me, and there I'd be as happy as the sunshine of St. Martin's Day, watching the light passing the north or the patches of fog, till I'd hear a rabbit starting to screech and I'd go running in the furze. Then when I'd my full share I'd come walking down where you'd see the ducks and geese stretched sleeping on the highway of the road, and before I'd pass the dunghill, I'd hear himself snoring out, a

[23] **four fathers:** forefathers.

[24] **conceit:** opinion, idea, *i.e.*, the idea uppermost in his mind.

[25] **Eastern world:** Far East.

[26] **moiling:** drudging (usually in wet sand or dirt).

loud lonesome snore he'd be making all times, the while he was sleeping, and he a man'd be raging all times, the while he was waking, like a gaudy officer you'd hear cursing and damning and swearing oaths.

PEGEEN. Providence and Mercy, spare us all!

CHRISTY. It's that you'd say surely if you seen him and he after drinking for weeks, rising up in the red dawn, or before it maybe, and going out into the yard as naked as an ash tree in the moon of May, and shying clods against the visage of the stars till he'd put the fear of death into the banbhs[27] and the screeching sows.

PEGEEN. I'd be well-nigh afeard of that lad myself, I'm thinking. And there was no one in it but the two of you alone?

CHRISTY. The divil a one, though he'd sons and daughters walking all great states and territories of the world, and not a one of them, to this day, but would say their seven curses on him, and they rousing up to let a cough or sneeze, maybe, in the deadness of the night.

PEGEEN (*nodding her head*). Well, you should have been a queer lot. I never cursed my father the like of that, though I'm twenty and more years of age.

CHRISTY. Then you'd have cursed mine, I'm telling you, and he a man never gave peace to any, saving when he'd get two months or three, or be locked in the asylums for battering peelers or assaulting men (*with depression*) the way it was a bitter life he led me till I did up a Tuesday and halve his skull.

PEGEEN (*putting her hand on his shoulder*). Well, you'll have peace in this place, Christy Mahon, and none to trouble you, and it's near time a fine lad like you should have your good share of the earth.

CHRISTY. It's time surely, and I a seemly fellow with great strength in me and bravery of . . .

(*Someone knocks.*)

(*Clinging to* PEGEEN.) Oh, glory! it's late for knocking, and this last while I'm in terror of the peelers, and the walking dead.

(*Knocking again.*)

PEGEEN. Who's there?

VOICE (*outside*). Me.

PEGEEN. Who's me?

VOICE. The Widow Quin.

PEGEEN (*jumping up and giving him the bread and milk*). Go on now with your supper, and let on to be sleepy, for if she found you were such a warrant to talk, she'd be stringing gabble till the dawn of day.

(*He takes bread and sits shyly with his back to the door.*)

[27] **banbhs**: suckling pigs.

(*Opening door, with temper.*) What ails you, or what is it you're wanting at this hour of the night?

WIDOW QUIN (*coming in a step and peering at* CHRISTY). I'm after meeting Shawn Keogh and Father Reilly below, who told me of your curiosity man, and they fearing by this time he was maybe roaring, romping on your hands with drink.

PEGEEN (*pointing to* CHRISTY). Look now is he roaring, and he stretched away drowsy with his supper and his mug of milk. Walk down and tell that to Father Reilly and to Shaneen Keogh.

WIDOW QUIN (*coming forward*). I'll not see them again, for I've their word to lead that lad forward for to lodge with me.

PEGEEN (*in blank amazement*). This night, is it?

WIDOW QUIN (*going over*). This night. "It isn't fitting," says the priesteen, "to have his likeness lodging with an orphaned girl." (*To* CHRISTY.) God save you, mister!

CHRISTY (*shyly*). God save you kindly.

WIDOW QUIN (*looking at him with half-amazed curiosity*). Well, aren't you a little smiling fellow? It should have been great and bitter torments did arouse your spirits to a deed of blood.

CHRISTY (*doubtfully*). It should, maybe.

WIDOW QUIN. It's more than "maybe" I'm saying, and it'd soften my heart to see you sitting so simple with your cup and cake, and you fitter to be saying your catechism than slaying your da.

PEGEEN (*at counter, washing glasses*). There's talking when any'd see he's fit to be holding his head high with the wonders of the world. Walk on from this, for I'll not have him tormented and he destroyed travelling since Tuesday was a week.

WIDOW QUIN (*peaceably*). We'll be walking surely when his supper's done, and you'll find we're great company, young fellow, when it's of the like of you and me you'd hear the penny poets singing in an August Fair.

CHRISTY (*innocently*). Did you kill your father?

PEGEEN (*contemptuously*). She did not. She hit himself[28] with a worn pick, and the rusted poison did corrode his blood the way he never overed it, and died after. That was a sneaky kind of murder did win small glory with the boys itself. (*She crosses to* CHRISTY*'s left.*)

WIDOW QUIN (*with good humour*). If it didn't, maybe all knows a widow woman has buried her children and destroyed her man is a wiser comrade for a young lad than a girl, the like of you, who'd go helter-skeltering after any man would let you a wink upon the road.

PEGEEN (*breaking out into wild rage*). And you'll say that, Widow Quin, and you gasping with the rage you had racing the hill beyond to look on his face.

WIDOW QUIN (*laughing derisively*). Me, is it? Well, Father Reilly has cuteness to divide you now. (*She pulls* CHRISTY *up.*) There's great

[28] **himself**: her husband.

temptation in a man did slay his da, and we'd best be going, young fellow; so rise up and come with me.

PEGEEN (*seizing his arm*). He'll not stir. He's pot-boy in this place, and I'll not have him stolen off and kidnabbed while himself's abroad.

WIDOW QUIN. It'd be a crazy pot-boy'd lodge him in the shebeen where he works by day, so you'd have a right to come on, young fellow, till you see my little houseen, a perch[29] off on the rising hill.

PEGEEN. Wait till morning, Christy Mahon. Wait till you lay eyes on her leaky thatch is growing more pasture for her buck goat than her square of fields, and she without a tramp itself to keep in order her place at all.

WIDOW QUIN. When you see me contriving in my little gardens, Christy Mahon, you'll swear the Lord God formed me to be living lone, and that there isn't my match in Mayo for thatching, or mowing, or shearing a sheep.

PEGEEN (*with noisy scorn*). It's true the Lord God formed you to contrive indeed. Doesn't the world know you reared a black lamb at your own breast, so that the Lord Bishop of Connaught felt the elements of a Christian, and he eating it after in a kidney stew? Doesn't the world know you've been seen shaving the foxy skipper from France for a threepenny bit and a sop of grass tobacco would wring the liver from a mountain goat you'd meet leaping the hills?

WIDOW QUIN (*with amusement*). Do you hear her now young fellow? Do you hear the way she'll be rating at your own self when a week is by?

PEGEEN (*to* CHRISTY). Don't heed her. Tell her to go into her pigsty and not plague us here.

WIDOW QUIN. I'm going; but he'll come with me.

PEGEEN (*shaking him*). Are you dumb, young fellow?

CHRISTY (*timidly, to* WIDOW QUIN). God increase you; but I'm pot-boy in this place, and it's here I'd liefer stay.

PEGEEN (*triumphantly*). Now you have heard him, and go on from this.

WIDOW QUIN (*looking round the room*). It's lonesome this hour crossing the hill, and if he won't come along with me, I'd have a right maybe to stop this night with yourselves. Let me stretch out on the settle, Pegeen Mike; and himself can lie by the hearth.

PEGEEN (*short and fiercely*). Faith, I won't. Quit off or I will send you now.

WIDOW QUIN (*gathering her shawl up*). Well, it's a terror to be aged a score.[30] (*To* CHRISTY.) God bless you now, young fellow, and let you be wary, or there's right torment will await you here if you go romancing with her like, and she waiting only, as they bade me say, on a sheepskin parchment to be wed with Shawn Keogh of Killakeen. (*Goes out.*)

[29] **perch:** sixteen and a half feet; a rod.

[30] **it's a terror to be aged a score:** how earth-shaking it is to be twenty (sarcastic)!

CHRISTY (*going to* PEGEEN *as she bolts the door*). What's that she's after saying?

PEGEEN. Lies and blather, you've no call to mind. Well, isn't Shawn Keogh an impudent fellow to send up spying on me? Wait till I lay hands on him. Let him wait, I'm saying.

CHRISTY. And you're not wedding him at all?

PEGEEN. I wouldn't wed him if a bishop came walking for to join us here.

CHRISTY. That God in glory may be thanked for that.

PEGEEN. There's your bed now. I've put a quilt upon you I'm after quilting a while since with my own two hands, and you'd best stretch out now for your sleep, and may God give you a good rest till I call you in the morning when the cocks will crow.

CHRISTY (*as she goes to inner room*). May God and Mary and St. Patrick bless you and reward you, for your kindly talk.

(*She shuts the door behind her. He settles his bed slowly, feeling the quilt with immense satisfaction.*)

Well, it's a clean bed and soft with it, and it's great luck and company I've won me in the end of time — two fine women fighting for the likes of me — till I'm thinking this night wasn't I a foolish fellow not to kill my father in the years gone by.

ACT TWO

(SCENE: *As before. Brilliant morning light.* CHRISTY, *looking bright and cheerful, is cleaning a girl's boots.*)

CHRISTY (*to himself, counting jugs on dresser*). Half a hundred beyond. Ten there. A score that's above. Eighty jugs. Six cups and a broken one. Two plates. A power of glasses. Bottles, a school-master'd be hard set to count, and enough in them, I'm thinking, to drunken all the wealth and wisdom of the County Clare. (*He puts down the boot carefully.*) There's her boots now, nice and decent for her evening use, and isn't it grand brushes she has? (*He puts them down and goes by degrees to the looking-glass.*) Well, this'd be a fine place to be my whole life talking out with swearing Christians, in place of my old dogs and cat, and I stalking around, smoking my pipe and drinking my fill, and never a day's work but drawing a cork an odd time, or wiping a glass, or rinsing out a shiny tumbler for a decent man. (*He takes the looking-glass from the wall and puts it on the back of a chair; then sits down in front of it and begins washing his face.*) Didn't I know rightly I was handsome, though it was the divil's own mirror we had beyond, would twist a squint across an angel's brow; and I'll be growing fine from this day, the way I'll have a soft lovely skin on me and won't be the like of the clumsy young fellows do be ploughing all times in the earth and dung. (*He starts.*) Is she coming again? (*He looks out.*) Stranger girls. God help me, where'll I hide myself away and my long neck naked to the world? (*He looks out.*) I'd best go to the room maybe till I'm dressed again.

(*He gathers up his coat and the looking-glass, and runs into the inner room. The door is pushed open, and* SUSAN BRADY *looks in, and knocks on door.*)

SUSAN. There's nobody in it. (*Knocks again.*)

NELLY (*pushing her in and following her, with* HONOR BLAKE *and* SARA TANSEY). It'd be early for them both to be out walking the hill.

SUSAN. I'm thinking Shawn Keogh was making game of us and there's no such man in it at all.

HONOR (*pointing to straw and quilt*). Look at that. He's been sleeping there in the night. Well, it'll be a hard case[1] if he's gone off now, the way we'll never set our eyes on a man killed his father, and we after rising early and destroying ourselves running fast on the hill.

NELLY. Are you thinking them's his boots?

SARA (*taking them up*). If they are, there should be his father's track on them. Did you never read in the papers the way murdered men do bleed and drip?

SUSAN. Is that blood there, Sara Tansey?

SARA (*smelling it*). That's bog water, I'm thinking, but it's his own they are surely, for I never seen the like of them for whity mud, and red mud, and turf on them, and the fine sands of the sea. That man's been walking, I'm telling you. (*She goes down right, putting on one of his boots.*)

SUSAN (*going to window*). Maybe he's stolen off to Belmullet with the boots of Michael James, and you'd have a right so to follow after him, Sara Tansey, and you the one yoked the ass cart and drove ten miles to set your eyes on the man bit the yellow lady's[2] nostril on the northern shore. (*She looks out.*)

SARA (*running to window with one boot on*). Don't be talking, and we fooled today. (*Putting on other boot.*) There's a pair do fit me well, and I'll be keeping them for walking to the priest, when you'd be ashamed this place, going up winter and summer with nothing worth while to confess at all.

HONOR (*who has been listening at the door*). Whisht! there's someone inside the room. (*She pushes door a chink open.*) It's a man.

(SARA *kicks off boots and puts them where they were. They all stand in a line looking through chink.*)

Act Two. [1] **a hard case:** bad luck.

[2] **yellow lady:** "any notable blond. Mayo people are predominantly dark, and anyone with light hair and complexion would stand out and be remarked upon" (Boling).

SARA. I'll call him. Mister! Mister! (*He puts in his head.*) Is Pegeen within?

CHRISTY (*coming in as meek as a mouse, with the looking-glass held behind his back*). She's above on the cnuceen,[3] seeking the nanny goats, the way she'd have a sup of goat's milk for to color my tea.

SARA. And asking your pardon, is it you's the man killed his father?

CHRISTY (*sidling toward the nail where the glass was hanging*). I am, God help me!

SARA (*taking eggs she has brought*). Then my thousand welcomes to you, and I've run up with a brace of duck's eggs for your food today. Pegeen's ducks is no use, but these are the real rich sort. Hold out your hand and you'll see it's no lie I'm telling you.

CHRISTY (*coming forward shyly, and holding out his left hand*). They're a great and weighty size.

SUSAN. And I run up with a pat of butter, for it'd be a poor thing to have you eating your spuds dry, and you after running a great way since you did destroy your da.

CHRISTY. Thank you kindly.

HONOR. And I brought you a little cut of cake, for you should have a thin stomach on you, and you that length walking the world.

NELLY. And I brought you a little laying pullet — boiled and all she is — was crushed at the fall of night by the curate's car. Feel the fat of that breast, mister.

CHRISTY. It's bursting, surely. (*He feels it with the back of his hand, in which he holds the presents.*)

SARA. Will you pinch it? Is your right hand too sacred for to use at all? (*She slips round behind him.*) It's a glass he has. Well, I never seen to this day a man with a looking-glass held to his back. Them that kills their fathers is a vain lot surely.

(*Girls giggle.*)

CHRISTY (*smiling innocently and piling presents on glass*). I'm very thankful to you all today . . .

WIDOW QUIN (*coming in quickly, at door*). Sara Tansey, Susan Brady, Honor Blake! What in glory has you here at this hour of day?

GIRLS (*giggling*). That's the man killed his father.

WIDOW QUIN (*coming to them*). I know well it's the man; and I'm after putting him down in the sports below for racing, leaping, pitching, and the Lord knows what.

SARA (*exuberantly*). That's right, Widow Quin. I'll bet my dowry that he'll lick the world.

WIDOW QUIN. If you will, you'd have a right to have him fresh and nourished in place of nursing a feast.[4] (*Taking presents.*) Are you fasting or fed, young fellow?

[3] **cnuceen:** hill.

[4] **nursing a feast:** hungry. Double meaning here: Christy is holding the food the girls brought, literally nursing a feast.

CHRISTY. Fasting, if you please.

WIDOW QUIN (*loudly*). Well, you're the lot. Stir up now and give him his breakfast. (*To* CHRISTY.) Come here to me (*she puts him on bench beside her while the girls make tea and get his breakfast*) and let you tell us your story before Pegeen will come, in place of grinning your ears off like the moon of May.

CHRISTY (*beginning to be pleased*). It's a long story; you'd be destroyed listening.

WIDOW QUIN. Don't be letting on to be shy, a fine, gamey, treacherous lad the like of you. Was it in your house beyond you cracked his skull?

CHRISTY (*shy but flattered*). It was not. We were digging spuds in his cold, sloping, stony, divil's patch of a field.

WIDOW QUIN. And you went asking money of him, or making talk of getting a wife would drive him from his farm?

CHRISTY. I did not, then; but there I was, digging and digging, and "You squinting idiot," says he, "let you walk down now and tell the priest you'll wed the Widow Casey in a score of days."

WIDOW QUIN. And what kind was she?

CHRISTY (*with horror*). A walking terror from beyond the hills, and she two score and two hundredweights and five pounds in the weighing scales, with a limping leg on her, and a blinded eye, and she a woman of noted misbehavior with the old and young.

GIRLS (*clustering round him, serving him*). Glory be.

WIDOW QUIN. And what did he want driving you to wed with her? (*She takes a bit of the chicken.*)

CHRISTY (*eating with growing satisfaction*). He was letting on I was wanting a protector from the harshness of the world, and he without a thought the whole while but how he'd have her hut to live in and her gold to drink.[5]

WIDOW QUIN. There's maybe worse than a dry hearth and a widow woman and your glass at night. So you hit him then?

CHRISTY (*getting almost excited*). I did not. "I won't wed her," says I, "when all know she did suckle me for six weeks when I came into the world, and she a hag this day with a tongue on her has the crows and seabirds scattered, the way they wouldn't cast a shadow on her garden with the dread of her curse."

WIDOW QUIN (*teasingly*). That one should be right company.

SARA (*eagerly*). Don't mind her. Did you kill him then?

CHRISTY. "She's too good for the like of you," says he, "and go on now or I'll flatten you out like a crawling beast has passed under a dray." "You will not if I can help it," says I. "Go on," says he, "or I'll have the divil making garters of your limbs tonight." "You will not if I can help it," says I. (*He sits up, brandishing his mug.*)

[5] **gold to drink:** money with which to buy liquor.

SARA. You were right surely.

CHRISTY (*impressively*). With that the sun came out between the cloud and the hill, and it shining green in my face. "God have mercy on your soul," says he, lifting a scythe; "or on your own," says I, raising the loy.

SUSAN. That's a grand story.

HONOR. He tells it lovely.

CHRISTY (*flattered and confident, waving bone*). He gave a drive with the scythe, and I gave a lep to the east. Then I turned around with my back to the north, and I hit a blow on the ridge of his skull, laid him stretched out, and he split to the knob of his gullet. (*He raises the chicken bone to his Adam's apple.*)

GIRLS (*together*). Well, you're a marvel! Oh, God bless you! You're the lad surely!

SUSAN. I'm thinking the Lord God sent him this road to make a second husband to the Widow Quin, and she with a great yearning to be wedded, though all dread her here. Lift him on her knee, Sara Tansey.

WIDOW QUIN. Don't tease him.

SARA (*going over to dresser and counter very quickly, and getting two glasses and porter*). You're heroes surely, and let you drink a supeen with your arms linked like the outlandish lovers in the sailor's song. (*She links their arms and gives them the glasses.*) There now. Drink a health to the wonders of the western world, the pirates, preachers, poteen-makers, with the jobbing jockies,[6] parching peelers,[7] and the juries fill their stomachs selling judgments of the English law. (*Brandishing the bottle.*)

WIDOW QUIN. That's a right toast, Sara Tansey. Now, Christy.

(*They drink with their arms linked, he drinking with his left hand, she with her right. As they are drinking,* PEGEEN MIKE *comes in with a milk can and stands aghast. They all spring away from* CHRISTY. *He goes down left.* WIDOW QUIN *remains seated.*)

PEGEEN (*angrily, to* SARA). What is it you're wanting?

SARA (*twisting her apron*). A ounce of tobacco.

PEGEEN. Have you tuppence?

SARA. I've forgotten my purse.

PEGEEN. Then you'd best be getting it and not fooling us here. (*To the* WIDOW QUIN, *with more elaborate scorn.*) And what is it you're wanting, Widow Quin?

WIDOW QUIN (*insolently*). A penn'orth of starch.

PEGEEN (*breaking out*). And you without a white shift or a shirt in your whole family since the drying of the flood. I've no starch for the like of you, and let you walk on now to Killamuck.

[6] **jobbing jockies:** bootleggers.

[7] **parching peelers:** police who arrest illegal distillers, thereby drying up the countryside.

WIDOW QUIN (*turning to* CHRISTY, *as she goes out with the girls*). Well, you're mighty huffy this day, Pegeen Mike, and you, young fellow, let you not forget the sports and racing when the noon is by.

(*They go out.*)

PEGEEN (*imperiously*). Fling out that rubbish and put them cups away.

(CHRISTY *tidies away in great haste.*)

Shove in the bench by the wall.

(*He does so.*)

And hang that glass on the nail. What disturbed it at all?

CHRISTY (*very meekly*). I was making myself decent only, and this a fine country for young lovely girls.

PEGEEN (*sharply*). Whisht your talking of girls. (*Goes to counter — right.*)

CHRISTY. Wouldn't any wish to be decent in a place . . .

PEGEEN. Whisht I'm saying.

CHRISTY (*looks at her face for a moment with great misgivings, then as a last effort, takes up a loy, and goes towards her, with feigned assurance*). It was with a loy the like of that I killed my father.

PEGEEN (*still sharply*). You've told me that story six times since the dawn of day.

CHRISTY (*reproachfully*). It's a queer thing you wouldn't care to be hearing it and them girls after walking four miles to be listening to me now.

PEGEEN (*turning round astonished*). Four miles!

CHRISTY (*apologetically*). Didn't himself say there were only four bona fides living in this place?

PEGEEN. It's bona fides by the road they are, but that lot came over the river lepping the stones. It's not three perches when you go like that, and I was down this morning looking on the papers the post-boy does have in his bag. (*With meaning and emphasis.*) For there was great news this day, Christopher Mahon. (*She goes into room left.*)

CHRISTY (*suspiciously*). Is it news of my murder?

PEGEEN (*inside*). Murder, indeed.

CHRISTY (*loudly*). A murdered da?

PEGEEN (*coming in again and crossing right*). There was not, but a story filled half a page of the hanging of a man. Ah, that should be a fearful end, young fellow, and it worst of all for a man who destroyed his da, for the like of him would get small mercies, and when it's dead he is, they'd put him in a narrow grave, with cheap sacking wrapping him round, and pour down quicklime on his head, the way you'd see a woman pouring any frish-frash[8] from a cup.

CHRISTY (*very miserably*). Oh, God help me. Are you thinking I'm safe? You were saying at the fall of night, I was shut of jeopardy and I here with yourselves.

PEGEEN (*severely*). You'll be shut of jeopardy no place if you go talking with a pack of wild girls the like of them to be walking abroad with the peelers, talking whispers at the fall of night.

CHRISTY (*with terror*). And you're thinking they'd tell?

PEGEEN (*with mock sympathy*). Who knows, God help you.

CHRISTY (*loudly*). What joy would they have to bring hanging to the likes of me?

PEGEEN. It's queer joys they have, and who knows the thing they'd do, if it'd make the green stones cry itself to think of you swaying and swiggling[9] at the butt of a rope, and you with a fine, stout neck, God bless you! the way you'd be a half an hour, in great anguish, getting your death.

CHRISTY (*getting his boots and putting them on*). If there's that terror of them, it'd be best, maybe, I went on wandering like Esau or Cain and Abel on the sides of Neifin or the Erris plain.

PEGEEN (*beginning to play with him*). It would, maybe, for I've heard the Circuit Judges this place is a heartless crew.

CHRISTY (*bitterly*). It's more than Judges this place is a heartless crew. (*Looking up at her.*) And isn't it a poor thing to be starting again and I a lonesome fellow will be looking out on women and girls the way the needy fallen spirits do be looking on the Lord?

PEGEEN. What call have you to be that lonesome when there's poor girls walking Mayo in their thousands now?

CHRISTY (*grimly*). It's well you know what call I have. It's well you know it's a lonesome thing to be passing small towns with the lights shining sideways when the night is down, or going in strange places with a dog noising before you and a dog noising behind, or drawn to the cities where you'd hear a voice kissing and talking deep love in every shadow of the ditch, and you passing on with an empty, hungry stomach failing from your heart.

PEGEEN. I'm thinking you're an odd man, Christy Mahon. The oddest walking fellow I ever set my eyes on to this hour today.

CHRISTY. What would any be but odd men and they living lonesome in the world?

PEGEEN. I'm not odd, and I'm my whole life with my father only.

CHRISTY (*with infinite admiration*). How would a lovely handsome woman the like of you be lonesome when all men should be thronging around to hear the sweetness of your voice, and the little infant children should be pestering your steps I'm thinking, and you walking the roads.

[8] **frish-frash**: dregs.
[9] **swiggling**: swinging.

PEGEEN. I'm hard set to know what way a coaxing fellow the like of yourself should be lonesome either.

CHRISTY. Coaxing?

PEGEEN. Would you have me think a man never talked with the girls would have the words you've spoken today? It's only letting on you are to be lonesome, the way you'd get around me now.

CHRISTY. I wish to God I was letting on; but I was lonesome all times, and born lonesome, I'm thinking, as the moon of dawn. (*Going to door.*)

PEGEEN (*puzzled by his talk*). Well, it's a story I'm not understanding at all why you'd be worse than another, Christy Mahon, and you a fine lad with the great savagery to destroy your da.

CHRISTY. It's little I'm understanding myself, saving only that my heart's scalded this day, and I going off stretching out the earth between us, the way I'll not be waking near you another dawn of the year till the two of us do arise to hope or judgment with the saints of God, and now I'd best be going with my wattle[10] in my hand, for hanging is a poor thing (*turning to go*), and it's little welcome only is left me in this house today.

PEGEEN (*sharply*). Christy!

(*He turns round.*)

Come here to me.

(*He goes towards her.*)

Lay down that switch and throw some sods on the fire. You're pot-boy in this place, and I'll not have you mitch[11] off from us now.

CHRISTY. You were saying I'd be hanged if I stay.

PEGEEN (*quite kindly at last*). I'm after going down and reading the fearful crimes of Ireland for two weeks or three, and there wasn't a word of your murder. (*Getting up and going over to the counter.*) They've likely not found the body. You're safe so with ourselves.

CHRISTY (*astonished, slowly*). It's making game of me you were (*following her with fearful joy*), and I can stay so, working at your side, and I not lonesome from this mortal day.

PEGEEN. What's to hinder you from staying, except the widow woman or the young girls would inveigle you off?

CHRISTY (*with rapture*). And I'll have your words from this day filling my ears, and that look is come upon you meeting my two eyes, and I watching you loafing around in the warm sun, or rinsing your ankles when the night is come.

PEGEEN (*kindly, but a little embarrassed*). I'm thinking you'll be a loyal young lad to have working around, and if you vexed me a while

[10] **wattle:** switch.
[11] **mitch:** sneak.

since with your leaguing with the girls, I wouldn't give a thraneen[12] for a lad hadn't a mighty spirit in him and a gamey heart.

(SHAWN KEOGH *runs in carrying a cleeve*[13] *on his back, followed by the* WIDOW QUIN.)

SHAWN (*to* PEGEEN). I was passing below, and I seen your mountainy sheep eating cabbages in Jimmy's field. Run up or they'll be bursting surely.

PEGEEN. Oh, God mend them! (*She puts a shawl over her head and runs out.*)

CHRISTY (*looking from one to the other. Still in high spirits*). I'd best go to her aid maybe, I'm handy with ewes.

WIDOW QUIN (*closing the door*). She can do that much, and there is Shaneen has long speeches for to tell you now. (*She sits down with an amused smile.*)

SHAWN (*taking something from his pocket and offering it to* CHRISTY). Do you see that, mister?

CHRISTY (*looking at it*). The half of a ticket to the Western States![14]

SHAWN (*trembling with anxiety*). I'll give it to you and my new hat (*pulling it out of hamper*); and my breeches with the double seat (*pulling it off*); and my new coat is woven from the blackest shearings for three miles around (*giving him the coat*); I'll give you the whole of them, and my blessing, and the blessing of Father Reilly itself, maybe, if you'll quit from this and leave us in the peace we had till last night at the fall of dark.

CHRISTY (*with a new arrogance*). And for what is it you're wanting to get shut of me?

SHAWN (*looking to the* WIDOW *for help*). I'm a poor scholar with middling faculties to coin a lie, so I'll tell you the truth, Christy Mahon. I'm wedding with Pegeen beyond, and I don't think well of having a clever fearless man the like of you dwelling in her house.

CHRISTY (*almost pugnaciously*). And you'd be using bribery for to banish me?

SHAWN (*in an imploring voice*). Let you not take it badly, mister honey; isn't beyond the best place for you where you'll have golden chains and shiny coats and you riding upon hunters with the ladies of the land. (*He makes an eager sign to the* WIDOW QUIN *to come to help him.*)

WIDOW QUIN (*coming over*). It's true for him, and you'd best quit off and not have that poor girl setting her mind on you, for there's Shaneen thinks she wouldn't suit you though all is saying that she'll wed you now.

(CHRISTY *beams with delight.*)

[12] **thraneen:** straw, in the sense of "plugged nickel."
[13] **cleeve:** basket.
[14] **Western States:** United States.

SHAWN (*in terrified earnest*). She wouldn't suit you, and she with the divil's own temper the way you'd be strangling one another in a score of days. (*He makes the movement of strangling with his hands.*) It's the like of me only that she's fit for, a quiet simple fellow wouldn't raise a hand upon her if she scratched itself.

WIDOW QUIN (*putting* SHAWN'S *hat on* CHRISTY). Fit them clothes on you anyhow, young fellow, and he'd maybe loan them to you for the sports. (*Pushing him towards inner door.*) Fit them on and you can give your answer when you have them tried.

CHRISTY (*beaming, delighted with the clothes*). I will then. I'd like herself to see me in them tweeds and hat. (*He goes into room and shuts the door.*)

SHAWN (*in great anxiety*). He'd like herself to see them. He'll not leave us, Widow Quin. He's a score of divils in him the way it's well nigh certain he will wed Pegeen.

WIDOW QUIN (*jeeringly*). It's true all girls are fond of courage and do hate the like of you.

SHAWN (*walking about in desperation*). Oh, Widow Quin, what'll I be doing now? I'd inform again him, but he'd burst from Kilmainham[15] and he'd be sure and certain to destroy me. If I wasn't so God-fearing, I'd near have courage to come behind him and run a pike into his side. Oh, it's a hard case to be an orphan and not to have your father that you're used to, and you'd easy kill and make yourself a hero in the sight of all. (*Coming up to her.*) Oh, Widow Quin, will you find me some contrivance when I've promised you a ewe?

WIDOW QUIN. A ewe's a small thing, but what would you give me if I did wed him and did save you so?

SHAWN (*with astonishment*). You?

WIDOW QUIN. Aye. Would you give me the red cow you have and the mountainy ram, and the right of way across your rye path, and a load of dung at Michaelmas, and turbary[16] upon the western hill?

SHAWN (*radiant with hope*). I would surely, and I'd give you the wedding ring I have, and the loan of a new suit, the way you'd have him decent on the wedding day. I'd give you two kids for your dinner, and a gallon of poteen, and I'd call the piper on the long car[17] to your wedding from Crossmolina or from Ballina. I'd give you . . .

WIDOW QUIN. That'll do so, and let you whisht, for he's coming now again.

(CHRISTY *comes in very natty in the new clothes.* WIDOW QUIN *goes to him admiringly.*)

If you seen yourself now, I'm thinking you'd be too proud to speak to us at all, and it'd be a pity surely to have your like sailing from Mayo to the Western World.

[15] **Kilmainham:** prison near Dublin.
[16] **turbary:** right to cut turf on another's land.
[17] **on the long car:** "a kind of waggonette . . . used for postal services" (Henn).

CHRISTY (*as proud as a peacock*). I'm not going. If this is a poor place itself, I'll make myself contented to be lodging here.

(WIDOW QUIN *makes a sign to* SHAWN *to leave them.*)

SHAWN. Well, I'm going measuring the race-course while the tide is low, so I'll leave you the garments and my blessing for the sports today. God bless you! (*He wriggles out.*)

WIDOW QUIN (*admiring* CHRISTY). Well, you're mighty spruce, young fellow. Sit down now while you're quiet till you talk with me.

CHRISTY (*swaggering*). I'm going abroad on the hillside for to seek Pegeen.

WIDOW QUIN. You'll have time and plenty for to seek Pegeen, and you heard me saying at the fall of night the two of us should be great company.

CHRISTY. From this out I'll have no want of company when all sorts is bringing me their food and clothing (*he swaggers to the door, tightening his belt*), the way they'd set their eyes upon a gallant orphan cleft his father with one blow to the breeches belt. (*He opens door, then staggers back.*) Saints of glory! Holy angels from the throne of light!

WIDOW QUIN (*going over*). What ails you?

CHRISTY. It's the walking spirit of my murdered da.

WIDOW QUIN (*looking out*). Is it that tramper?

CHRISTY (*wildly*). Where'll I hide my poor body from that ghost of hell?

(*The door is pushed open, and old* MAHON *appears on threshold.* CHRISTY *darts in behind door.*)

WIDOW QUIN (*in great amusement*). God save you, my poor man.

MAHON (*gruffly*). Did you see a young lad passing this way in the early morning or the fall of night?

WIDOW QUIN. You're a queer kind to walk in not saluting at all.

MAHON. Did you see the young lad?

WIDOW QUIN (*stiffly*). What kind was he?

MAHON. An ugly young streeler[18] with a murderous gob[19] on him, and a little switch in his hand. I met a tramper seen him coming this way at the fall of night.

WIDOW QUIN. There's harvest hundreds do be passing these days for the Sligo boat. For what is it you're wanting him, my poor man?

MAHON. I want to destroy him for breaking the head on me with the clout of a loy. (*He takes off a big hat, and shows his head in a mass of bandages and plaster, with some pride.*) It was he did that, and amn't I a great wonder to think I've traced him ten days with that rent in my crown?

[18] **streeler:** stroller; tramp.
[19] **gob:** "mug."

WIDOW QUIN (*taking his head in both hands and examining it with extreme delight*). That was a great blow. And who hit you? A robber maybe?

MAHON. It was my own son hit me, and he the divil a robber, or anything else, but a dirty, stuttering lout.

WIDOW QUIN (*letting go his skull and wiping her hands in her apron*). You'd best be wary of a mortified[20] scalp, I think they call it, lepping around with that wound in the splendor of the sun. It was a bad blow surely, and you should have vexed him fearful to make him strike that gash in his da.

MAHON. Is it me?

WIDOW QUIN (*amusing herself*). Aye. And isn't it a great shame when the old and hardened do torment the young?

MAHON (*raging*). Torment him is it? And I after holding out with the patience of a martyred saint till there's nothing but destruction on, and I'm driven out in my old age with none to aid me.

WIDOW QUIN (*greatly amused*). It's a sacred wonder the way that wickedness will spoil a man.

MAHON. My wickedness, is it? Amn't I after saying it is himself has me destroyed, and he a liar on walls, a talker of folly, a man you'd see stretched the half of the day in the brown ferns with his belly to the sun.

WIDOW QUIN. Not working at all?

MAHON. The divil a work, or if he did itself, you'd see him raising up a haystack like the stalk of a rush, or driving our last cow till he broke her leg at the hip, and when he wasn't at that he'd be fooling over little birds he had — finches and felts[21] — or making mugs at his own self in the bit of a glass he had hung on the wall.

WIDOW QUIN (*looking at* CHRISTY). What way was he so foolish? It was running wild after the girls maybe?

MAHON (*with a shout of derision*). Running wild, is it? If he seen a red petticoat coming swinging over the hill, he'd be off to hide in the sticks, and you'd see him shooting out his sheep's eyes between the little twigs and the leaves, and his two ears rising like a hare looking out through a gap. Girls, indeed!

WIDOW QUIN. It was drink maybe?

MAHON. And he a poor fellow would get drunk on the smell of a pint. He'd a queer rotten stomach, I'm telling you, and when I gave him three pulls from my pipe a while since, he was taken with contortions till I had to send him in the ass cart to the females' nurse.

WIDOW QUIN (*clasping her hands*). Well, I never till this day heard tell of a man the like of that!

MAHON. I'd take a mighty oath you didn't surely, and wasn't he the laughing joke of every female woman where four baronies[22] meet, the way

[20] **mortified:** mortally infected.
[21] **felts:** thrushes.
[22] **baronies:** sections of land.

the girls would stop their weeding if they seen him coming the road to let a roar at him, and call him the looney of Mahon's.

WIDOW QUIN. I'd give the world and all to see the like of him. What kind was he?

MAHON. A small low fellow.

WIDOW QUIN. And dark?

MAHON. Dark and dirty.

WIDOW QUIN (*considering*). I'm thinking I seen him.

MAHON (*eagerly*). An ugly young blackguard.

WIDOW QUIN. A hideous, fearful villain, and the spit of you.

MAHON. What way is he fled?

WIDOW QUIN. Gone over the hills to catch a coasting steamer to the north or south.

MAHON. Could I pull up on him now?

WIDOW QUIN. If you'll cross the sands below where the tide is out, you'll be in it as soon as himself, for he had to go round ten miles by the top of the bay. (*She points to the door.*) Strike down by the head beyond and then follow on the roadway to the north and east.

(MAHON *goes abruptly.*)

(*Shouting after him.*) Let you give him a good vengeance when you come up with him, but don't put yourself in the power of the law, for it'd be a poor thing to see a judge in his black cap reading out his sentence on a civil warrior the like of you. (*She swings the door to and looks at* CHRISTY, *who is cowering in terror, for a moment, then she bursts into a laugh.*) Well, you're the walking Playboy of the Western World, and that's the poor man you had divided to his breeches belt.

CHRISTY (*looking out; then, to her*). What'll Pegeen say when she hears that story? What'll she be saying to me now?

WIDOW QUIN. She'll knock the head of you, I'm thinking, and drive you from the door. God help her to be taking you for a wonder, and you a little schemer making up the story you destroyed your da.

CHRISTY (*turning to the door, nearly speechless with rage, half to himself*). To be letting on he was dead, and coming back to his life, and following after me like an old weasel tracing a rat, and coming in here laying desolation between my own self and the fine women of Ireland, and he a kind of carcase that you'd fling upon the sea . . .

WIDOW QUIN (*more soberly*). There's talking for a man's one only son.

CHRISTY (*breaking out*). His one son, is it? May I meet him with one tooth and it aching, and one eye to be seeing seven and seventy divils in the twists of the road, and one old timber leg on him to limp into the scalding grave. (*Looking out.*) There he is now crossing the strands, and that the Lord God would send a high wave to wash him from the world.

WIDOW QUIN (*scandalized*). Have you no shame? (*Putting her hand on his shoulder and turning him round.*) What ails you? Near crying, is it?

CHRISTY (*in despair and grief*). Amn't I after seeing the love-light of the star of knowledge shining from her brow, and hearing words would put you thinking on the holy Brigid speaking to the infant saints, and now she'll be turning again, and speaking hard words to me, like an old woman with a spavindy[23] ass she'd have, urging on a hill.

WIDOW QUIN. There's poetry talk for a girl you'd see itching and scratching, and she with a stale stink of poteen on her from selling in the shop.

CHRISTY (*impatiently*). It's her like is fitted to be handling merchandise in the heavens above, and what'll I be doing now, I ask you, and I a kind of wonder was jilted by the heavens when a day was by.

(*There is a distant noise of girls' voices.* WIDOW QUIN *looks from window and comes to him, hurriedly.*)

WIDOW QUIN. You'll be doing like myself, I'm thinking, when I did destroy my man, for I'm above many's the day, odd times in great spirits, abroad in the sunshine, darning a stocking or stitching a shift; and odd times again looking out on the schooners, hookers, trawlers is sailing the sea, and I thinking on the gallant hairy fellows are drifting beyond, and myself long years living alone.

CHRISTY (*interested*). You're like me, so.

WIDOW QUIN. I am your like, and it's for that I'm taking a fancy to you, and I with my little houseen above where there'd be myself to tend you, and none to ask were you a murderer or what at all.

CHRISTY. And what would I be doing if I left Pegeen?

WIDOW QUIN. I've nice jobs you could be doing, gathering shells to make a whitewash for our hut within, building up a little goosehouse, or stretching a new skin on an old curragh[24] I have, and if my hut is far from all sides, it's there you'll meet the wisest old men, I tell you, at the corner of my wheel, and it's there yourself and me will have great times whispering and hugging. . . .

VOICES (*outside, calling far away*). Christy! Christy Mahon! Christy!

CHRISTY. Is it Pegeen Mike?

WIDOW QUIN. It's the young girls, I'm thinking, coming to bring you to the sports below, and what is it you'll have me to tell them now?

CHRISTY. Aid me for to win Pegeen. It's herself only that I'm seeking now.

(WIDOW QUIN *gets up and goes to window.*)

[23] **spavindy**: lame.
[24] **curragh**: small boat.

Aid me for to win her, and I'll be asking God to stretch a hand to you in the hour of death, and lead you short cuts through the Meadows of Ease, and up the floor of Heaven to the Footstool of the Virgin's Son.

WIDOW QUIN. There's praying.

VOICES (*nearer*). Christy! Christy Mahon!

CHRISTY (*with agitation*). They're coming. Will you swear to aid and save me for the love of Christ?

WIDOW QUIN (*looks at him for a moment*). If I aid you, will you swear to give me a right of way I want, and a mountainy ram, and a load of dung at Michaelmas, the time that you'll be master here?

CHRISTY. I will, by the elements and stars of night.

WIDOW QUIN. Then we'll not say a word of the old fellow, the way Pegeen won't know your story till the end of time.

CHRISTY. And if he chances to return again?

WIDOW QUIN. We'll swear he's a maniac and not your da. I could take an oath I seen him raving on the sands today.

(*Girls run in.*)

SUSAN. Come on to the sports below. Pegeen says you're to come.

SARA TANSEY. The lepping's beginning, and we've a jockey's suit to fit upon you for the mule race on the sands below.

HONOR. Come on, will you?

CHRISTY. I will then if Pegeen's beyond.

SARA TANSEY. She's in the boreen[25] making game of Shaneen Keogh.

CHRISTY. Then I'll be going to her now.

(*He runs out followed by the girls.*)

WIDOW QUIN. Well, if the worst comes in the end of all, it'll be great game to see there's none to pity him but a widow woman, the like of me, has buried her children and destroyed her man. (*She goes out.*)

ACT THREE

(SCENE: *As before. Later in the day.* JIMMY *comes in, slightly drunk.*)

JIMMY (*calls*). Pegeen! (*Crosses to inner door.*) Pegeen Mike! (*Comes back again into the room.*) Pegeen!

(PHILLY *comes in in the same state.*)

(*To* PHILLY.) Did you see herself?

PHILLY. I did not; but I sent Shawn Keogh with the ass cart for to bear him home. (*Trying cupboards which are locked.*) Well, isn't he a

[25] **boreen**: lane.

nasty man to get into such staggers at a morning wake? and isn't herself the divil's daughter for locking, and she so fussy after that young gaffer, you might take your death with drought and none to heed you?

JIMMY. It's little wonder she'd be fussy, and he after bringing bankrupt ruin on the roulette man, and the trick-o'-the-loop man, and breaking the nose of the cockshot-man, and winning all in the sports below, racing, lepping, dancing, and the Lord knows what! He's right luck, I'm telling you.

PHILLY. If he has, he'll be rightly hobbled yet, and he not able to say ten words without making a brag of the way he killed his father, and the great blow he hit with the loy.

JIMMY. A man can't hang by his own informing, and his father should be rotten by now.

(OLD MAHON *passes window slowly.*)

PHILLY. Supposing a man's digging spuds in that field with a long spade, and supposing he flings up the two halves of that skull, what'll be said then in the papers and the courts of law?

JIMMY. They'd say it was an old Dane, maybe, was drowned in the flood.

(OLD MAHON *comes in and sits down near door listening.*)

Did you never hear tell of the skulls they have in the city of Dublin, ranged out like blue jugs in a cabin of Connaught?

PHILLY. And you believe that?

JIMMY (*pugnaciously*). Didn't a lad see them and he after coming from harvesting in the Liverpool boat? "They have them there," says he, "making a show of the great people there was one time walking the world. White skulls and black skulls and yellow skulls, and some with full teeth, and some haven't only but one."

PHILLY. It was no lie, maybe, for when I was a young lad there was a graveyard beyond the house with the remnants of a man who had thighs as long as your arm. He was a horrid man, I'm telling you, and there was many a fine Sunday I'd put him together for fun, and he with shiny bones, you wouldn't meet the like of these days in the cities of the world.

MAHON (*getting up*). You wouldn't, is it? Lay your eyes on that skull, and tell me where and when there was another the like of it, is splintered only from the blow of a loy.

PHILLY. Glory be to God! And who hit you at all?

MAHON (*triumphantly*). It was my own son hit me. Would you believe that?

JIMMY. Well, there's wonders hidden in the heart of man!

PHILLY (*suspiciously*). And what way was it done?

MAHON (*wandering about the room*). I'm after walking hundreds and long scores of miles, winning clean beds and the fill of my belly four times in the day, and I doing nothing but telling stories of that naked truth. (*He comes to them a little aggressively.*) Give me a supeen and I'll tell you now.

(WIDOW QUIN *comes in and stands aghast behind him. He is facing* JIMMY *and* PHILLY, *who are on the left.*)

JIMMY. Ask herself beyond. She's the stuff hidden in her shawl.

WIDOW QUIN (*coming to* MAHON *quickly*). You here, is it? You didn't go far at all?

MAHON. I seen the coasting steamer passing, and I got a drought upon me and a cramping leg, so I said, "The divil go along with him," and turned again. (*Looking under her shawl.*) And let you give me a supeen, for I'm destroyed travelling since Tuesday was a week.

WIDOW QUIN (*getting a glass, in a cajoling tone*). Sit down then by the fire and take your ease for a space. You've a right to be destroyed indeed, with your walking, and fighting, and facing the sun. (*Giving him poteen from a stone jar she has brought in.*) There now is a drink for you, and may it be to your happiness and length of life.

MAHON (*taking glass greedily and sitting down by fire*). God increase you!

WIDOW QUIN (*taking men to the right stealthily*). Do you know what? That man's raving from his wound today, for I met him a while since telling a rambling tale of a tinker had him destroyed. Then he heard of Christy's deed, and he up and says it was his son had cracked his skull. O isn't madness a fright, for he'll go killing someone yet, and he thinking it's the man has struck him so?

JIMMY (*entirely convinced*). It's a fright, surely. I knew a party was kicked in the head by a red mare, and he went killing horses a great while, till he eat the insides of a clock and died after.

PHILLY (*with suspicion*). Did he see Christy?

WIDOW QUIN. He didn't. (*With a warning gesture.*) Let you not be putting him in mind of him, or you'll be likely summoned if there's murder done. (*Looking round at* MAHON.) Whisht! He's listening. Wait now till you hear me taking him easy and unravelling all. (*She goes to* MAHON.) And what way are you feeling, mister? Are you in contentment now?

MAHON (*slightly emotional from his drink*). I'm poorly only, for it's a hard story the way I'm left today, when it was I did tend him from his hour of birth, and he a dunce never reached his second book, the way he'd come from school, many's the day, with his legs lamed under him, and he blackened with his beatings like a tinker's ass. It's a hard story, I'm saying, the way some do have their next and nighest raising up a hand of murder on them, and some is lonesome getting their death with lamentation in the dead of night.

WIDOW QUIN (*not knowing what to say*). To hear you talking so quiet, who'd know you were the same fellow we seen pass today?

MAHON. I'm the same surely. The wrack and ruin of three score years; and it's a terror to live that length, I tell you, and to have your sons going to the dogs against you, and you wore out scolding them, and skelping[1] them, and God knows what.

PHILLY (*to* JIMMY). He's not raving. (*To* WIDOW QUIN.) Will you ask him what kind was his son?

WIDOW QUIN (*to* MAHON, *with a peculiar look*). Was your son that hit you a lad of one year and a score maybe, a great hand at racing and lepping and licking the world?

MAHON (*turning on her with a roar of rage*). Didn't you hear me say he was the fool of men, the way from this out he'll know the orphan's lot with old and young making game of him and they swearing, raging, kicking at him like a mangy cur.

(*A great burst of cheering outside, some way off.*)

(*Putting his hands to his ears.*) What in the name of God do they want roaring below?

WIDOW QUIN (*with the shade of a smile*). They're cheering a young lad, the champion Playboy of the Western World.

(*More cheering.*)

MAHON (*going to window*). It'd split my heart to hear them, and I with pulses in my brain-pan for a week gone by. Is it racing they are?

JIMMY (*looking from door*). It is then. They are mounting him for the mule race will be run upon the sands. That's the playboy on the winkered[2] mule.

MAHON (*puzzled*). That lad, is it? If you said it was a fool he was, I'd have laid a mighty oath he was the likeness of my wandering son. (*Uneasily, putting his hand to his head.*) Faith, I'm thinking I'll go walking for to view the race.

WIDOW QUIN (*stopping him, sharply*). You will not. You'd best take the road to Belmullet, and not be dilly-dallying in this place where there isn't a spot you could sleep.

PHILLY (*coming forward*). Don't mind her. Mount there on the bench and you'll have a view of the whole. They're hurrying before the tide will rise, and it'd be near over if you went down the pathway through the crags below.

MAHON (*mounts on bench,* WIDOW QUIN *beside him*). That's a right view again the edge of the sea. They're coming now from the point. He's leading. Who is he at all?

WIDOW QUIN. He's the champion of the world, I tell you, and there isn't a hop'orth[3] isn't falling lucky to his hands today.

Act Three. [1] **skelping:** beating.
[2] **winkered:** wearing blinders.
[3] **hop'orth:** Probably a corruption of *hap'orth,* a halfpenny's worth, although some critics read *hoopworth,* the amount of space between hoops on a quart pot.

PHILLY (*looking out, interested in the race*). Look at that. They're pressing him now.

JIMMY. He'll win it yet.

PHILLY. Take your time, Jimmy Farrell. It's too soon to say.

WIDOW QUIN (*shouting*). Watch him taking the gate. There's riding.

JIMMY (*cheering*). More power to the young lad!

MAHON. He's passing the third.

JIMMY. He'll lick them yet!

WIDOW QUIN. He'd lick them if he was running races with a score itself.

MAHON. Look at the mule he has, kicking the stars.

WIDOW QUIN. There was a lep! (*Catching hold of* MAHON *in her excitement.*) He's fallen! He's mounted again! Faith, he's passing them all!

JIMMY. Look at him skelping her!

PHILLY. And the mountain girls hooshing[4] him on!

JIMMY. It's the last turn! The post's cleared for them now!

MAHON. Look at the narrow place. He'll be into the bogs! (*With a yell.*) Good rider! He's through it again!

JIMMY. He's neck and neck!

MAHON. Good boy to him! Flames, but he's in!

(*Great cheering, in which all join.*)

(*With hesitation.*) What's that? They're raising him up. They're coming this way. (*With a roar of rage and astonishment.*) It's Christy! by the stars of God! I'd know his way of spitting and he astride the moon.

(*He jumps down and makes for the door, but* WIDOW QUIN *catches him and pulls him back.*)

WIDOW QUIN. Stay quiet, will you. That's not your son. (*To* JIMMY.) Stop him, or you'll get a month for the abetting of manslaughter and be fined as well.

JIMMY. I'll hold him.

MAHON (*struggling*). Let me out! Let me out, the lot of you! till I have my vengeance on his head today.

WIDOW QUIN (*shaking him, vehemently*). That's not your son. That's a man is going to make a marriage with the daughter of this house, a place with fine trade, with a license, and with poteen too.

MAHON (*amazed*). That man marrying a decent and a moneyed girl! Is it mad yous are? Is it in a crazy house for females that I'm landed now?

WIDOW QUIN. It's mad yourself is with the blow upon your head. That lad is the wonder of the Western World.

MAHON. I seen it's my son.

[4] **hooshing:** cheering.

WIDOW QUIN. You seen that you're mad. (*Cheering outside.*) Do you hear them cheering him in the zig-zags of the road? Aren't you after saying that your son's a fool, and how would they be cheering a true idiot born?

MAHON (*getting distressed*). It's maybe out of reason that the man's himself. (*Cheering again.*) There's none surely will go cheering him. Oh, I'm raving with a madness that would fright the world! (*He sits down with his hand to his head.*) There was one time I seen ten scarlet divils letting on they'd cork my spirit in a gallon can; and one time I seen rats as big as badgers sucking the life blood from the butt of my lug;[5] but I never till this day confused that dribbling idiot with a likely man. I'm destroyed surely.

WIDOW QUIN. And who'd wonder when it's your brain-pan that is gaping now?

MAHON. Then the blight of the sacred drought upon myself and him, for I never went mad to this day, and I not three weeks with the Limerick girls drinking myself silly, and parlatic[6] from the dusk to dawn. (*To* WIDOW QUIN, *suddenly.*) Is my visage[7] astray?

WIDOW QUIN. It is then. You're a sniggering maniac, a child could see.

MAHON (*getting up more cheerfully*). Then I'd best be going to the union[8] beyond, and there'll be a welcome before me, I tell you (*with great pride*), and I a terrible and fearful case, the way that there I was one time, screeching in a straitened waistcoat, with seven doctors writing out my sayings in a printed book. Would you believe that?

WIDOW QUIN. If you're a wonder itself, you'd best be hasty, for them lads caught a maniac one time and pelted the poor creature till he ran out, raving and foaming, and was drowned in the sea.

MAHON (*with philosophy*). It's true mankind is the divil when your head's astray. Let me out now and I'll slip down the boreen, and not see them so.

WIDOW QUIN (*showing him out*). That's it. Run to the right, and not a one will see.

(*He runs off.*)

PHILLY (*wisely*). You're at some gaming, Widow Quin; but I'll walk after him and give him his dinner and a time to rest, and I'll see then if he's raving or as sane as you.

WIDOW QUIN (*annoyed*). If you go near that lad, let you be wary of your head, I'm saying. Didn't you hear him telling he was crazed at times?

PHILLY. I heard him telling a power; and I'm thinking we'll have right sport, before night will fall. (*He goes out.*)

[5] **lug**: ear.
[6] **parlatic**: corruption of "paralytic"; paralyzed.
[7] **visage**: vision.
[8] **union**: workhouse and hospital for the poor.

JIMMY. Well, Philly's a conceited and foolish man. How could that madman have his senses and his brain-pan slit? I'll go after them and see him turn on Philly now.

(*He goes;* WIDOW QUIN *hides poteen behind counter. Then hubbub outside.*)

VOICES. There you are! Good jumper! Grand lepper! Darlint boy! He's the racer! Bear him on, will you!

(CHRISTY *comes in, in jockey's dress, with* PEGEEN MIKE, SARA, *and other girls, and men.*)

PEGEEN (*to crowd*). Go on now and don't destroy him and he drenching with sweat. Go along, I'm saying, and have your tug-of-warring till he's dried his skin.

CROWD. Here's his prizes! A bagpipes! A fiddle was played by a poet in the years gone by! A flat and three-thorned blackthorn[9] would lick the scholars[10] out of Dublin town!

CHRISTY (*taking prizes from the men*). Thank you kindly, the lot of you. But you'd say it was little only I did this day if you'd seen me a while since striking my one single blow.

TOWN CRIER (*outside, ringing a bell*). Take notice, last event of this day! Tug-of-warring on the green below! Come on, the lot of you! Great achievements for all Mayo men!

PEGEEN. Go on, and leave him for to rest and dry. Go on, I tell you, for he'll do no more.

(*She hustles crowd out;* WIDOW QUIN *following them.*)

MEN (*going*). Come on then. Good luck for the while!

PEGEEN (*radiantly, wiping his face with her shawl*). Well, you're the lad, and you'll have great times from this out when you could win that wealth of prizes, and you sweating in the heat of noon!

CHRISTY (*looking at her with delight*). I'll have great times if I win the crowning prize I'm seeking now, and that's your promise that you'll wed me in a fortnight, when our banns is called.

PEGEEN (*backing away from him*). You've right daring[11] to go ask me that, when all knows you'll be starting to some girl in your own townland, when your father's rotten in four months, or five.

CHRISTY (*indignantly*). Starting from you, is it? (*He follows her.*) I will not, then, and when the airs is warming in four months, or five, it's then yourself and me should be pacing Neifin in the dews of night, the

[9] **blackthorn:** heavy club made of blackthorn, a hard, gnarled, spiny tree.

[10] **scholars:** *English Protestant* scholars understood, *i.e.*, those at Trinity College, Dublin, which is affiliated with the Church of England.

[11] **You've right daring:** you've got a nerve.

times sweet smells do be rising, and you'd see a little shiny new moon, maybe, sinking on the hills.

PEGEEN (*looking at him playfully*). And it's that kind of a poacher's love you'd make, Christy Mahon, on the sides of Neifin, when the night is down?

CHRISTY. It's little you'll think if my love's a poacher's, or an earl's itself, when you'll feel my two hands stretched around you, and I squeezing kisses on your puckered lips, till I'd feel a kind of pity for the Lord God is all ages sitting lonesome in his golden chair.

PEGEEN. That'll be right fun, Christy Mahon, and any girl would walk her heart out before she'd meet a young man was your like for eloquence, or talk, at all.

CHRISTY (*encouraged*). Let you wait, to hear me talking, till we're astray in Erris, when Good Friday's by,[12] drinking a sup from a well, and making mighty kisses with our wetted mouths, or gaming in a gap or sunshine, with yourself stretched back onto your necklace, in the flowers of the earth.

PEGEEN (*in a lower voice, moved by his tone*). I'd be nice so, is it?

CHRISTY (*with rapture*). If the mitred bishops seen you that time, they'd be the like of the holy prophets, I'm thinking, do be straining the bars of Paradise to lay eyes on the Lady Helen of Troy, and she abroad, pacing back and forward, with a nosegay in her golden shawl.

PEGEEN (*with real tenderness*). And what is it I have, Christy Mahon, to make me fitting entertainment for the like of you, that has such poet's talking, and such bravery of heart?

CHRISTY (*in a low voice*). Isn't there the light of seven heavens in your heart alone, the way you'll be an angel's lamp to me from this out, and I abroad in the darkness, spearing salmons in the Owen, or the Carrowmore?

PEGEEN. If I was your wife, I'd be along with you those nights, Christy Mahon, the way you'd see I was a great hand at coaxing bailiffs, or coining funny nick-names for the stars of night.

CHRISTY. You, is it? Taking your death in the hailstones, or in the fogs of dawn.

PEGEEN. Yourself and me would shelter easy in a narrow bush (*with a qualm of dread*), but we're only talking, maybe, for this would be a poor, thatched place to hold a fine lad is the like of you.

CHRISTY (*putting his arm around her*). If I wasn't a good Christian, it's on my naked knees I'd be saying my prayers and paters to every jackstraw you have roofing your head, and every stony pebble is paving the laneway to your door.

PEGEEN (*radiantly*). If that's the truth, I'll be burning candles from this out to the miracles of God that have brought you from the south today, and I, with my gowns bought ready, the way that I can wed you, and not wait at all.

[12] **When Good Friday's by:** after good Friday. "A good Catholic does not make love in Lent" (Henn).

CHRISTY. It's miracles, and that's the truth. Me there toiling a long while, and walking a long while, not knowing at all I was drawing all times nearer to this holy day.

PEGEEN. And myself, a girl, was tempted often to go sailing the seas till I'd marry a Jew-man, with ten kegs of gold, and I not knowing at all there was the like of you drawing nearer, like the stars of God.

CHRISTY. And to think I'm long years hearing women talking that talk, to all bloody fools, and this the first time I've heard the like of your voice talking sweetly for my own delight.

PEGEEN. And to think it's me is talking sweetly, Christy Mahon, and I the fright of seven townlands for my biting tongue. Well, the heart's a wonder; and, I'm thinking, there won't be our like in Mayo, for gallant lovers, from this hour, today.

(*Drunken singing is heard outside.*)

There's my father coming from the wake, and when he's had his sleep we'll tell him, for he's peaceful then.

(*They separate.*)

MICHAEL (*singing outside.*)

The jailor and the turnkey
They quickly ran us down,
And brought us back as prisoners
Once more to Cavan town.

(*He comes in supported by* SHAWN.)

There we lay bewailing
All in a prison bound. . . .

(*He sees* CHRISTY. *Goes and shakes him drunkenly by the hand, while* PEGEEN *and* SHAWN *talk on the left.*)

(*To* CHRISTY.) The blessing of God and the holy angels on your head, young fellow. I hear tell you're after winning all in the sports below; and wasn't it a shame I didn't bear you along with me to Kate Cassidy's wake, a fine, stout lad, the like of you, for you'd never see the match of it for flows of drink, the way when we sunk her bones at noonday in her narrow grave, there were five men, aye, and six men, stretched out retching speechless on the holy stones.

CHRISTY (*uneasily, watching* PEGEEN). Is that the truth?

MICHAEL. It is then, and aren't you a louty schemer to go burying your poor father unbeknownst when you'd a right to throw him on the crupper of a Kerry mule and drive him westwards, like holy Joseph in the days gone by, the way we could have given him a decent burial, and not have him rotting beyond, and not a Christian drinking a smart drop to the glory of his soul?

CHRISTY (*gruffly*). It's well enough he's lying, for the likes of him.

MICHAEL (*slapping him on the back*). Well, aren't you a hardened slayer? It'll be a poor thing for the household man where you go sniffing for a female wife; and (*pointing to* SHAWN) look beyond at that shy and decent Christian I have chosen for my daughter's hand, and I after getting the gilded dispensation this day to wed them now.

CHRISTY. And you'll be wedding them this day, is it?

MICHAEL (*drawing himself up*). Aye. Are you thinking, if I'm drunk itself, I'd leave my daughter living single with a little frisky rascal is the like of you?

PEGEEN (*breaking away from* SHAWN). Is it the truth the dispensation's come?

MICHAEL (*triumphantly*). Father Reilly's after reading it in gallous[13] Latin, and "It's come in the nick of time," says he; "so I'll wed them in a hurry, dreading that young gaffer[14] who'd capsize the stars."

PEGEEN (*fiercely*). He's missed his nick of time, for it's that lad Christy Mahon, that I'm wedding now.

MICHAEL (*loudly with horror*). You'd be making him a son to me, and he wet and crusted with his father's blood?

PEGEEN. Aye. Wouldn't it be a bitter thing for a girl to go marrying the like of Shaneen, and he a middling kind of a scarecrow, with no savagery or fine words in him at all?

MICHAEL (*gasping and sinking on a chair*). Oh, aren't you a heathen daughter to go shaking the fat of my heart, and I swamped and drownded with the weight of drink? Would you have them turning on me the way that I'd be roaring to the dawn of day with the wind upon my heart? Have you not a word to aid me, Shaneen? Are you not jealous at all?

SHAWN (*in great misery*). I'd be afeard to be jealous of a man did slay his da.

PEGEEN. Well, it'd be a poor thing to go marrying your like. I'm seeing there's a world of peril for an orphan girl, and isn't it a great blessing I didn't wed you, before himself came walking from the west or south?

SHAWN. It's a queer story you'd go picking a dirty tramp up from the highways of the world.

PEGEEN (*playfully*). And you think you're a likely beau to go straying along with, the shiny Sundays of the opening year, when it's sooner on a bullock's liver[15] you'd put a poor girl thinking than on the lily or the rose?

SHAWN. And have you no mind of my weight of passion, and the holy dispensation, and the drift[16] of heifers I am giving, and the golden ring?

PEGEEN. I'm thinking you're too fine for the like of me, Shawn Keogh

[13] **gallous:** fine, magnificent, in the sense of fine-sounding.
[14] **gaffer:** trickster, hoaxer.
[15] **bullock's liver:** the coarse or earthy.
[16] **drift:** drove.

of Killakeen, and let you go off till you'd find a radiant lady with droves of bullocks on the plains of Meath,[17] and herself bedizened in the diamond jewelleries of Pharaoh's ma. That'd be your match, Shaneen. So God save you now! (*She retreats behind* CHRISTY.)

SHAWN. Won't you hear me telling you . . . ?

CHRISTY (*with ferocity*). Take yourself from this, young fellow, or I'll maybe add a murder to my deeds today.

MICHAEL (*springing up with a shriek*). Murder is it? Is it mad yous are? Would you go making murder in this place, and it piled with poteen for our drink tonight? Go on to the foreshore if it's fighting you want, where the rising tide will wash all traces from the memory of man. (*Pushing* SHAWN *towards* CHRISTY.)

SHAWN (*shaking himself free, and getting behind* MICHAEL). I'll not fight him, Michael James. I'd liefer live a bachelor, simmering in passions to the end of time, than face a lepping savage the like of him has descended from the Lord knows where. Strike him yourself, Michael James, or you'll lose my drift of heifers and my blue bull from Sneem.

MICHAEL. Is it me fight him, when it's father-slaying he's bred to now? (*Pushing* SHAWN.) Go on, you fool, and fight him now.

SHAWN (*coming forward a little*). Will I strike him with my hand?

MICHAEL. Take the loy is on your western side.

SHAWN. I'd be afeard of the gallows if I struck him with that.

CHRISTY (*taking up the loy*). Then I'll make you face the gallows or quit off from this.

(SHAWN *flies out of the door.*)

Well, fine weather be after him (*going to* MICHAEL, *coaxingly*), and I'm thinking you wouldn't wish to have that quaking blackguard in your house at all. Let you give us your blessing and hear her swear her faith to me, for I'm mounted on the springtide of the stars of luck, the way it'll be good for any to have me in the house.

PEGEEN (*at the other side of* MICHAEL). Bless us now, for I swear to God I'll wed him, and I'll not renege.

MICHAEL (*standing up in the center, holding on to both of them*). It's the will of God, I'm thinking, that all should win an easy or a cruel end, and it's the will of God that all should rear up lengthy families for the nurture of the earth. What's a single man, I ask you, eating a bit in one house and drinking a sup in another, and he with no place of his own, like an old braying jackass strayed upon the rocks? (*To* CHRISTY.) It's many would be in dread to bring your like into their house for to end them, maybe, with a sudden end; but I'm a decent man of Ireland, and I liefer face the grave untimely and I seeing a score of grandsons growing up little gallant swearers by the name of God, than go peopling my bedside with puny weeds the like of what you'd breed, I'm thinking, out of

[17] **plains of Meath**: fertile lands in the midlands.

Shaneen Keogh. (*He joins their hands.*) A daring fellow is the jewel of the world, and a man did split his father's middle with a single clout, should have the bravery of ten, so may God and Mary and St. Patrick bless you, and increase you from this mortal day.

CHRISTY *and* PEGEEN. Amen, O Lord!

(*Hubbub outside.* OLD MAHON *rushes in, followed by all the crowd, and* WIDOW QUIN. *He makes a rush at* CHRISTY, *knocks him down, and begins to beat him.*)

PEGEEN (*dragging back his arm*). Stop that, will you. Who are you at all?

MAHON. His father, God forgive me!

PEGEEN (*drawing back*). Is it rose from the dead?

MAHON. Do you think I look so easy quenched with the tap of a loy? (*Beats* CHRISTY *again.*)

PEGEEN (*glaring at* CHRISTY). And it's lies you told, letting on you had him slitted, and you nothing at all.

CHRISTY (*catching* MAHON'*s stick*). He's not my father. He's a raving maniac would scare the world. (*Pointing to* WIDOW QUIN.) Herself knows it is true.

CROWD. You're fooling Pegeen! The Widow Quin seen him this day, and you likely knew! You're a liar!

CHRISTY (*dumbfounded*). It's himself was a liar, lying stretched out with an open head on him, letting on he was dead.

MAHON. Weren't you off racing the hills before I got my breath with the start I had seeing you turn on me at all?

PEGEEN. And to think of the coaxing glory we had given him, and he after doing nothing but hitting a soft blow and chasing northward in a sweat of fear. Quit off from this.

CHRISTY (*piteously*). You've seen my doings this day, and let you save me from the old man; for why would you be in such a scorch of haste to spur me to destruction now?

PEGEEN. It's there your treachery is spurring me, till I'm hard set to think you're the one I'm after lacing in my heartstrings half-an-hour gone by. (*To* MAHON.) Take him on from this, for I think bad the world should see me raging for a Munster liar, and the fool of men.

MAHON. Rise up now to retribution, and come on with me.

CROWD (*jeeringly*). There's the playboy! There's the lad thought he'd rule the roost in Mayo. Slate him[18] now, mister.

CHRISTY (*getting up in shy terror*). What is it drives you to torment me here, when I'd asked the thunders of the might of God to blast me if I ever did hurt to any saving only that one single blow.

MAHON (*loudly*). If you didn't, you're a poor good-for-nothing, and isn't it by the like of you the sins of the whole world are committed?

CHRISTY (*raising his hands*). In the name of the Almighty God. . . .

[18] **Slate him**: let him have it; give it to him.

MAHON. Leave troubling the Lord God. Would you have him sending down droughts, and fevers, and the old hen and the cholera morbus?[19]

CHRISTY (*to* WIDOW QUIN). Will you come between us and protect me now?

WIDOW QUIN. I've tried a lot, God help me, and my share is done.

CHRISTY (*looking round in desperation*). And I must go back into my torment is it, or run off like a vagabond straying through the Unions with the dusts of August making mudstains in the gullet of my throat, or the winds of March blowing on me till I'd take an oath I felt them making whistles of my ribs within?

SARA. Ask Pegeen to aid you. Her like does often change.

CHRISTY. I will not then, for there's torment in the splendor of her like, and she a girl any moon of midnight would take pride to meet, facing southwards on the heaths of Keel. But what did I want crawling forward to scorch my understanding at her flaming brow?

PEGEEN (*to* MAHON, *vehemently, fearing she will break into tears*). Take him on from this or I'll set the young lads to destroy him here.

MAHON (*going to him, shaking his stick*). Come on now if you wouldn't have the company to see you skelped.

PEGEEN (*half laughing, through her tears*). That's it, now the world will see him pandied,[20] and he an ugly liar was playing off the hero, and the fright of men.

CHRISTY (*to* MAHON, *very sharply*). Leave me go!

CROWD. That's it. Now Christy. If them two set fighting, it will lick the world.

MAHON (*making a grab at* CHRISTY). Come here to me.

CHRISTY (*more threateningly*). Leave me go, I'm saying.

MAHON. I will maybe, when your legs is limping, and your back is blue.

CROWD. Keep it up, the two of you. I'll back the old one. Now the playboy.

CHRISTY (*in low and intense voice*). Shut your yelling, for if you're after making a mighty man of me this day by the power of a lie, you're setting me now to think if it's a poor thing to be lonesome, it's worse maybe to go mixing with the fools of earth.

(MAHON *makes a movement towards him.*)

(*Almost shouting.*) Keep off . . . lest I do show a blow unto the lot of you would set the guardian angels winking in the clouds above. (*He swings round with a sudden rapid movement and picks up a loy.*)

CROWD (*half frightened, half amused*). He's going mad! Mind yourselves! Run from the idiot!

CHRISTY. If I am an idiot, I'm after hearing my voice this day saying words would raise the topknot on a poet in a merchant's town.[21] I've won your racing, and your lepping, and . . .

[19] **the old hen . . . cholera morbus:** influenza and violent stomach pains.

[20] **pandied:** beaten, struck.

[21] **poet in a merchant's town:** "Christy has spoken so eloquently that even a refined city poet would be proud to have used his words" (Boling).

MAHON. Shut your gullet and come on with me.

CHRISTY. I'm going, but I'll stretch you first.

(*He runs at old* MAHON *with the loy, chases him out of the door, followed by* CROWD *and* WIDOW QUIN. *There is a great noise outside, then a yell, and dead silence for a moment.* CHRISTY *comes in, half dazed, and goes to fire.*)

WIDOW QUIN (*coming in, hurriedly, and going to him*). They're turning again you. Come on, or you'll be hanged, indeed.

CHRISTY. I'm thinking, from this out, Pegeen'll be giving me praises the same as in the hours gone by.

WIDOW QUIN (*impatiently*). Come by the back door. I'd think bad to have you stifled on the gallows tree.

CHRISTY (*indignantly*). I will not, then. What good'd be my lifetime, if I left Pegeen?

WIDOW QUIN. Come on, and you'll be no worse than you were last night; and you with a double murder this time to be telling to the girls.

CHRISTY. I'll not leave Pegeen Mike.

WIDOW QUIN (*impatiently*). Isn't there the match of her in every parish public,[22] from Binghamstown unto the plain of Meath? Come on, I tell you, and I'll find you finer sweethearts at each waning moon.

CHRISTY. It's Pegeen I'm seeking only, and what'd I care if you brought me a drift of chosen females, standing in their shifts itself, maybe, from this place to the Eastern World?

SARA (*runs in, pulling off one of her petticoats*). They're going to hang him. (*Holding out petticoat and shawl.*) Fit these upon him, and let him run off to the east.

WIDOW QUIN. He's raving now; but we'll fit them on him, and I'll take him, in the ferry, to the Achill boat.

CHRISTY (*struggling feebly*). Leave me go, will you? When I'm thinking of my luck today, for she will wed me surely, and I a proven hero in the end of all.

(*They try to fasten petticoat round him.*)

WIDOW QUIN. Take his left hand, and we'll pull him now. Come on, young fellow.

CHRISTY (*suddenly starting up*). You'll be taking me from her? You're jealous, is it, of her wedding me? Go on from this. (*He snatches up a stool, and threatens them with it.*)

WIDOW QUIN (*going*). It's in the mad-house they should put him, not in jail, at all. We'll go by the back door, to call the doctor, and we'll save him so.

(*She goes out, with* SARA, *through inner room. Men crowd in the doorway.* CHRISTY *sits down again by the fire.*)

[22] **public:** public house; tavern.

MICHAEL (*in a terrified whisper*). Is the old lad killed surely?

PHILLY. I'm after feeling the last gasps quitting his heart.

(*They peer in at* CHRISTY.)

MICHAEL (*with a rope*). Look at the way he is. Twist a hangman's knot on it, and slip it over his head, while he's not minding at all.

PHILLY. Let you take it, Shaneen. You're the soberest of all that's here.

SHAWN. Is it me to go near him, and he the wickedest and worst with me? Let you take it, Pegeen Mike.

PEGEEN. Come on, so.

(*She goes forward with the others, and they drop the double hitch over his head.*)

CHRISTY. What ails you?

SHAWN (*triumphantly, as they pull the rope tight on his arms*). Come on to the peelers, till they stretch you now.

CHRISTY. Me!

MICHAEL. If we took pity on you, the Lord God would, maybe, bring us ruin from the law today, so you'd best come easy, for hanging is an easy and a speedy end.

CHRISTY. I'll not stir. (*To* PEGEEN.) And what is it you'll say to me, and I after doing it this time in the face of all?

PEGEEN. I'll say, a strange man is a marvel, with his mighty talk; but what's a squabble in your back yard, and the blow of a loy, have taught me that there's a great gap between a gallous story and a dirty deed. (*To* MEN.) Take him on from this, or the lot of us will be likely put on trial for his deed today.

CHRISTY (*with horror in his voice*). And it's yourself will send me off, to have a horny-fingered hangman hitching his bloody slip-knots at the butt of my ear.

MEN (*pulling rope*). Come on, will you?

(*He is pulled down on the floor.*)

CHRISTY (*twisting his legs round the table*). Cut the rope, Pegeen, and I'll quit the lot of you, and live from this out, like the madmen of Keel,[23] eating muck and green weeds on the faces of the cliffs.

PEGEEN. And leave us to hang, is it, for a saucy liar, the like of you? (*To* MEN.) Take him on, out from this.

SHAWN. Pull a twist on his neck, and squeeze him so.

PHILLY. Twist yourself. Sure he cannot hurt you, if you keep your distance from his teeth alone.

[23] **madmen of Keel:** probably the local "naturals." "The standard activity of the Irish madman ever since the time of Sweeney the Mad has been to retire to the wilderness and live by eating watercress and other such green weeds" (Boling).

SHAWN. I'm afeard of him. (*To* PEGEEN.) Lift a lighted sod, will you, and scorch his leg.

PEGEEN (*blowing the fire, with a bellows*). Leave go now, young fellow, or I'll scorch your shins.

CHRISTY. You're blowing for to torture me. (*His voice rising and growing stronger.*) That's your kind, is it? Then let the lot of you be wary, for, if I've to face the gallows, I'll have a gay march down, I tell you, and shed the blood of some of you before I die.

SHAWN (*in terror*). Keep a good hold, Philly. Be wary, for the love of God. For I'm thinking he would liefest wreak his pains on me.

CHRISTY (*almost gaily*). If I do lay my hands on you, it's the way you'll be at the fall of night, hanging as a scarecrow for the fowls of hell. Ah, you'll have a gallous jaunt I'm saying, coaching out through Limbo with my father's ghost.

SHAWN (*to* PEGEEN). Make haste, will you? Oh, isn't he a holy terror, and isn't it true for Father Reilly, that all drink's a curse that has the lot of you so shaky and uncertain now?

CHRISTY. If I can wring a neck among you, I'll have a royal judgment looking on the trembling jury in the courts of law.[24] And won't there be crying out in Mayo the day I'm stretched upon the rope with ladies in their silks and satins snivelling in their lacy kerchiefs, and they rhyming songs and ballads on the terror of my fate? (*He squirms round on the floor and bites* SHAWN'S *leg.*)

SHAWN (*shrieking*). My leg's bit on me. He's the like of a mad dog, I'm thinking, the way that I will surely die.

CHRISTY (*delighted with himself*). You will then, the way you can shake out hell's flags of welcome for my coming in two weeks or three, for I'm thinking Satan hasn't many have killed their da in Kerry, and in Mayo too.

(OLD MAHON *comes in behind on all fours and looks on unnoticed.*)

MEN (*to* PEGEEN). Bring the sod, will you?

PEGEEN (*coming over*). God help him so. (*Burns his leg.*)

CHRISTY (*kicking and screaming*). O, glory be to God! (*He kicks loose from the table, and they all drag him towards the door.*)

JIMMY (*seeing old* MAHON). Will you look what's come in?

(*They all drop* CHRISTY *and run left.*)

CHRISTY (*scrambling on his knees face to face with old* MAHON). Are you coming to be killed a third time, or what ails you now?

MAHON. For what is it they have you tied?

CHRISTY. They're taking me to the peelers to have me hanged for slaying you.

[24] **I'll have a royal judgment . . . courts of law:** "At his imagined trial Christy will show formidable contempt towards the jury, just as he has to everyone he has met" (Boling).

MICHAEL (*apologetically*). It is the will of God that all should guard their little cabins from the treachery of law, and what would my daughter be doing if I was ruined or was hanged itself?

MAHON (*grimly, loosening* CHRISTY). It's little I care if you put a bag on her back, and went picking cockles till the hour of death; but my son and myself will be going our own way, and we'll have great times from this out telling stories of the villainy of Mayo, and the fools is here. (*To* CHRISTY, *who is freed.*) Come on now.

CHRISTY. Go with you, is it? I will then, like a gallant captain with his heathen slave. Go on now and I'll see you from this day stewing my oatmeal and washing my spuds, for I'm master of all fights from now. (*Pushing* MAHON.) Go on, I'm saying.

MAHON. Is it me?

CHRISTY. Not a word out of you. Go on from this.

MAHON (*walking out and looking back at* CHRISTY *over his shoulder*). Glory be to God! (*With a broad smile.*) I am crazy again! (*Goes.*)

CHRISTY. Ten thousand blessings upon all that's here, for you've turned me a likely gaffer in the end of all, the way I'll go romancing through a romping lifetime from this hour to the drawing of the judgment day. (*He goes out.*)

MICHAEL. By the will of God, we'll have peace now for our drinks. Will you draw the porter, Pegeen?

SHAWN (*going up to her*). It's a miracle Father Reilly can wed us in the end of all, and we'll have none to trouble us when his vicious bite is healed.

PEGEEN (*hitting him a box on the ear*). Quit my sight. (*Putting her shawl over her head and breaking out into wild lamentations.*) Oh my grief, I've lost him surely. I've lost the only Playboy of the Western World.

Curtain

Just when some thoughtful essayist has consigned George Bernard Shaw (1856–1950) and his comedies to a niche in the dramatic Hall of Fame, suggesting that they are splendid examples of a type and period which has passed over into history, a casual reader or an energetic director picks up a play like *Misalliance* (1919). One reading, seasoned with imagination and common sense, is enough to demonstrate that such works are as modern — if not as today — at least as yesterday.

It is true that a number of the battles Shaw was constantly joining in his dramatic dialogues have now been largely won. In some cases, they have been won and lost again, especially when they did not prove the panaceas Shaw and the Fabian Socialists thought they would be. Despite that, and despite the often outrageously willful manner in which Shaw molds his characters, orders their actions, and shapes their comments, there remains a basic truth to nature even in the most obviously manipulated personas, and a cynical romanticism in the most blatantly concocted situation.

Martin Meisel, in *Shaw and the Nineteenth Century Theatre,*[1] takes pains to explain the oddly comic mechanism of *Misalliance*, an unfairly neglected play whose humor goes far deeper than the easy laughter provoked by puns and literary jokes, or the sharply engineered contrasts of peculiar character types. What Shaw has done is to project a modern Discussion Play through the devices of the nineteenth-century Romantic Comedy. Characteristic story motifs of the Romantic Comedy are: 1) misalliance between the classes, 2) the Cinderella or Galatea syndrome, complete with testing to see if the transformation will succeed, and 3) the opposition of youth and age, often in competition for love. *Misalliance* has all of these, but Shaw was hardly copying conventional romantic dramas. He used the familiar devices instead to project some of his more paradoxical ideas.

The misalliance concept is used to compare differences among classes or conditions. The aristocracy, the wealthy middle class, the unfettered artist, and the slaving lower class are all forced into confrontations which are both painful and revealing. The results are not only amusing; they are almost farcical, revealing human attitudes recognizable even today.

Tests, of course, occur in several situations. Instead of bourgeois Hypatia's being tested by aristocratic Lord Summerhays to see whether she is fit to become his son's wife, Summerhays' son Bentley is himself being tested to discover whether he will be an asset to the Tarleton family industry and a suitable husband for Hypatia. The test for the Summerhays family is carried to an even greater extreme by Hypatia, who sets out to deceive Lord Summerhays into believing he is testing her. Awkardly enough, he misses the point that she and Bentley are considering marriage and proposes to her himself. Other members of the

[1] (Princeton, N.J.: Princeton University Press, 1963), pp. 307–314.

family circle, not to mention the visitors who "drop in," are also tested in various ways, unpleasant for them but amusing for readers and viewers.

Youth and age are in opposition in the wars of love. Both Lord Summerhays and John Tarleton declare their affection for younger women, and both are bested by their juniors. It is not only in affairs of the heart, however, that youth carries the day. In argument, in forthrightness, and in cruelty, the young people show themselves to be more adept than their elders. This may be one reason why this comedy seems so very modern, despite the now venerable quality of some of the questions of manners and morals, of capital and labor. It is really a confrontation of gracious, thoughtful, experienced Age with brash, impetuous, immature, unfeeling Youth. The vitality is all on the side of the young people, but it is impossible to empathize entirely with their energy or their victories because they exploit every advantage given them by youth, strength, or parental indulgence.

For once, it can be said that some sympathy is reserved for the pain, the inconvenience, and the defeat of the adults. What a good long gaze down into this Shavian Generation Gap reveals is that those who do the hurting and the demanding now will, in their turn, suffer the same at their children's hands.

Shaw called *Misalliance* "A Debate in One Sitting." It is useful to remember that description of the drama as a debate, for it stresses a fundamental fact about his comedies. He was not writing comedies of manners, amusing pieces which were content to mock or pillory conventional modes of behavior. Yet he does manage to include some biting comments and parodic exaggeration. The essence of his comedy is ideas. He is not going to reform society by merely making fun of popular poses and exposing inanity. What he offers are rather remarkable characters — men and women like Undershaft, Caesar, John Tanner, and St. Joan — who make meaningful social critique possible not by holding a mirror of mockery up to nature but by prescribing strong remedies for its improvement.

If Aristophanic comedy had a central "happy idea" to set its exposure of human frailties in motion, Shaw does something similar by creating characters and situations in which it is logical to effect a healthy change in the status quo — and at the same time to provoke laughter. However, the humor in Greek Old Comedy frequently comes from the ridiculous variations played on the basic theme or "happy idea." In Shaw's plays, the comedy often is generated by a briskly reasonable person applying common sense to aspects of a somewhat odd or unbalanced situation. It is also not uncommon for the characters, manufactured and manipulated by Shaw though they may be, to provide instructive amusement by discovering how wide the gap is between what they think they are and what they actually are. *Misalliance* exemplifies these comic qualities.

G. L.

BERNARD SHAW

Misalliance*

Characters

JOHNNY TARLETON
BENTLEY SUMMERHAYS
HYPATIA TARLETON
MRS TARLETON
LORD SUMMERHAYS
JOHN TARLETON
JOEY PERCIVAL
LINA SZCZEPANOWSKA
GUNNER

(JOHNNY TARLETON, *an ordinary young business man of thirty or less, is taking his weekly Friday to Tuesday in the house of his father,* JOHN TARLETON, *who has made a great deal of money out of Tarleton's Underwear. The house is in Surrey, on the slope of Hindhead; and* JOHNNY, *reclining, novel in hand, in a swinging chair with a little awning above it, is enshrined in a spacious half hemisphere of glass which forms a pavilion commanding the garden, and, beyond it, a barren but lovely landscape of hill profile with fir trees, commons of bracken and gorse, and wonderful cloud pictures.*

The glass pavilion springs from a bridgelike arch in the wall of the house, through which one comes into a big hall with tiled flooring, which suggests that the proprietor's notion of domestic luxury is founded on the lounges of week-end hotels. The arch is not quite in the centre of the wall. There is more wall to JOHNNY'S *right than to his left; and this space is occupied by a hat rack and umbrella stand in which tennis rackets, white parasols, caps, Panama hats, and other summery articles are bestowed. Just through the arch at this corner stands a new portable Turkish*

* This edition retains Shaw's idiosyncrasies in spelling — *shew* for *show*, *Shakespear* for *Shakespeare*, etc. — and punctuation: "The apostrophes in ain't, don't, haven't, etc., look so ugly that the most careful printing cannot make a page of colloquial dialogue as handsome as a page of classical dialogue. Besides, shan't should be sha"n't, if the wretched pedantry of indicating the elision is to be carried out. I have written aint, dont, havnt, shant, shouldnt and wont for twenty years with perfect impunity, using the apostrophe only where its omission would suggest another word: for example, hell for he'll. There is not the faintest reason for persisting in the ugly and silly trick of peppering pages with those uncouth bacilli. I also write thats, whats, lets, for the colloquial forms of that is, what is, let us; and I have not yet been prosecuted."

bath, recently unpacked, with its crate beside it, and on the crate the drawn nails and the hammer used in unpacking. Near the crate are open boxes of garden games: bowls and croquet. Nearly in the middle of the glass wall of the pavilion is a door giving on the garden, with a couple of steps to surmount the hot-water pipes which skirt the glass. At intervals round the pavilion are marble pillars with specimens of Viennese pottery on them, very flamboyant in colour and florid in design. Between them are folded garden chairs flung anyhow against the pipes. In the side walls are two doors: one near the hat stand, leading to the interior of the house, the other on the opposite side and at the other end, leading to the vestibule.

There is no solid furniture except a sideboard which stands against the wall between the vestibule door and the pavilion, a small writing table with blotter, rack for telegram forms and stationery, and a wastepaper basket, standing out in the hall near the sideboard, and a lady's worktable, with two chairs at it, towards the other side of the lounge. The writing table has also two chairs at it. On the sideboard there is a tantalus, liqueur bottles, a syphon, a glass jug of lemonade, tumblers, and every convenience for casual drinking. Also a plate of sponge cakes, and a highly ornate punchbowl in the same style as the keramic display in the pavilion. Wicker chairs and little bamboo tables with ash trays and boxes of matches on them are scattered in all directions. In the pavilion, which is flooded with sunshine, is the elaborate patent swing seat and awning in which JOHNNY *reclines with his novel. There are two wicker chairs right and left of him.*

BENTLEY SUMMERHAYS, *one of those smallish, thinskinned youths, who from 17 to 70 retain unaltered the mental airs of the later and the physical appearance of the earlier age, appears in the garden and comes through the glass door into the pavilion. He is unmistakably a grade above* JOHNNY *socially; and though he looks sensitive enough, his assurance and his high voice are a little exasperating.*)

JOHNNY. Hallo! Wheres your luggage?

BENTLEY. I left it at the station. Ive walked up from Haslemere. (*He goes to the hat stand and hangs up his hat.*)

JOHNNY (*shortly*). Oh! And whos to fetch it?

BENTLEY. Dont know. Dont care. Providence, probably. If not, your mother will have it fetched.

JOHNNY. Not her business, exactly, is it?

BENTLEY (*returning to the pavilion*). Of course not. That's why one loves her for doing it. Look here: chuck away your silly week-end novel, and talk to a chap. After a week at that filthy office my brain is simply blue-mouldy. Lets argue about something intellectual. (*He throws himself into the wicker chair on* JOHNNY*'s right.*)

JOHNNY (*straightening up in the swing with a yell of protest*). No. Now seriously, Bunny, Ive come down here to have a pleasant week-end;

and I'm not going to stand your confounded arguments. If you want to argue, get out of this and go over to the Congregationalist minister's. Hes a nailer at arguing. He likes it.

BENTLEY. You cant argue with a person when his livelihood depends on his not letting you convert him. And would you mind not calling me Bunny? My name is Bentley Summerhays, which you please.

JOHNNY. Whats the matter with Bunny?

BENTLEY. It puts me in a false position. Have you ever considered the fact that I was an afterthought?

JOHNNY. An afterthought? What do you mean by that?

BENTLEY. I —

JOHNNY. No, stop: I dont want to know. It's only a dodge to start an argument.

BENTLEY. Dont be afraid: it wont overtax your brain. My father was 44 when I was born. My mother was 41. There was twelve years between me and the next eldest. I was unexpected. I was probably unintentional. My brothers and sisters are not the least like me. Theyre the regular thing that you always get in the first batch from young parents: quite pleasant, ordinary, do-the-regular-thing sort: all body and no brains, like you.

JOHNNY. Thank you.

BENTLEY. Dont mention it, old chap. Now I'm different. By the time I was born, the old couple knew something. So I came out all brains and no more body than is absolutely necessary. I am really a good deal older than you, though you were born ten years sooner. Everybody feels that when they hear us talk; consequently, though it's quite natural to hear me calling you Johnny, it sounds ridiculous and unbecoming for you to call me Bunny. (*He rises.*)

JOHNNY. Does it, by George? You stop me doing it if you can: thats all.

BENTLEY. If you go on doing it after Ive asked you not, youll feel an awful swine. (*He strolls away carelessly to the sideboard with his eye on the sponge-cakes.*) At least I should; but I suppose youre not so particular.

JOHNNY (*rising vengefully and following* BENTLEY, *who is forced to turn and listen*). I'll tell you what it is, my boy: you want a good talking to; and I'm going to give it to you. If you think that because your father's a K.C.B., and you want to marry my sister, you can make yourself as nasty as you please and say what you like, youre mistaken. Let me tell you that except Hypatia, not one person in this house is in favor of her marrying you; and I dont believe shes happy about it herself. The match isnt settled yet: dont forget that. Youre on trial in the office because the Governor isnt giving his daughter money for an idle man to live on her. Youre on trial here because my mother thinks a girl should know what a man is like in the house before she marries him. Thats been going on for two months now; and whats the result? Youve got yourself thoroughly disliked in the office; and your getting yourself thoroughly disliked here, all through your bad manners and your conceit, and the damned impudence you think clever.

BENTLEY (*deeply wounded and trying hard to control himself*). Thats enough, thank you. You dont suppose, I hope, that I should have come down if I had known that that was how you all feel about me. (*He makes for the vestibule door.*)

JOHNNY (*collaring him*). No: you dont run away. I'm going to have this out with you. Sit down: d'y' hear?

(BENTLEY *attempts to go with dignity.* JOHNNY *slings him into a chair at the writing table, where he sits, bitterly humiliated, but afraid to speak lest he should burst into tears.*)

Thats the advantage of having more body than brains, you see: it enables me to teach you manners; and I'm going to do it too. Youre a spoilt young pup; and you need a jolly good licking. And if youre not careful youll get it: I'll see to that next time you call me a swine.

BENTLEY. I didnt call you a swine. But (*bursting into a fury of tears*) you *are* a swine: youre a beast: youre a brute: youre a cad: youre a liar: youre a bully: I should like to wring your damned neck for you.

JOHNNY (*with a derisive laugh*). Try it, my son.

(BENTLEY *gives an inarticulate sob of rage.*)

Fighting isnt in your line. Youre too small; and youre too childish. I always suspected that your cleverness wouldnt come to very much when it was brought up against something solid: some decent chap's fist, for instance.

BENTLEY. I hope your beastly fist may come up against a mad bull or a prizefighter's nose, or something solider than me. I don't care about your fist; but if everybody here dislikes me — (*he is checked by a sob*). Well, I dont care. (*Trying to recover himself.*) I'm sorry I intruded: I didnt know. (*Breaking down again.*) Oh you beast! you pig! Swine, swine, swine, swine, swine! Now!

JOHNNY. All right, my lad, all right. Sling your mud as hard as you please: it wont stick to me. What I want to know is this. How is it that your father, who I suppose is the strongest man England has produced in our time —

BENTLEY. You got that out of your halfpenny paper. A lot you know about him!

JOHNNY. I dont set up to be able to do anything but admire him and appreciate him and be proud of him as an Englishman. If it wasnt for my respect for him, I wouldnt have stood your cheek for two days, let alone two months. But what I cant understand is why he didnt lick it out of you when you were a kid. For twenty-five years he kept a place twice as big as England in order: a place full of seditious coffee-colored heathens and pestilential white agitators in the middle of a lot of savage tribes. And yet he couldnt keep you in order. I dont set up to be half the man your father undoubtedly is; but, by George, it's lucky for you you were not my son. I dont hold with my own father's views about corporal punishment being wrong. It's necessary for some people; and I'd have tried it on you until you first learnt to howl and then to behave yourself.

BENTLEY (*contemptuously*). Yes: behavior wouldnt come naturally to *your* son, would it?

JOHNNY (*stung into sudden violence*). Now you keep a civil tongue in your head. I'll stand none of your snobbery. I'm just as proud of Tarleton's Underwear as you are of your father's title and his K.C.B., and all the rest of it. My father began in a little hole of a shop in Leeds no bigger than our pantry down the passage there. He—

BENTLEY. Oh yes: I know. Ive read it. "The Romance of Business, or The Story of Tarleton's Underwear. Please Take One!" I took one the day after I first met Hypatia. I went and bought half a dozen unshrinkable vests for her sake.

JOHNNY. Well: did they shrink?

BENTLEY. Oh, dont be a fool.

JOHNNY. Never mind whether I'm a fool or not. Did they shrink? Thats the point. Were they worth the money?

BENTLEY. I couldnt wear them: do you think my skin's as thick as your customers' hides? I'd as soon have dressed myself in a nutmeg grater.

JOHNNY. Pity your father didnt give your thin skin a jolly good lacing with a cane!

BENTLEY. Pity you havnt got more than one idea! If you want to know, they did try that on me once, when I was a small kid. A silly governess did it. I yelled fit to bring down the house, and went into convulsions and brain fever and that sort of thing for three weeks. So the old girl got the sack; and serve her right! After that, I was let do what I liked. My father didnt want me to grow up a broken-spirited spaniel, which is your idea of a man, I suppose.

JOHNNY. Jolly good thing for you that my father made you come into the office and shew what you were made of. And it didnt come to much: let me tell you that. When the Governor asked me where I thought we ought to put you, I said "Make him the Office Boy." The Governor said you were too green. And so you were.

BENTLEY. I daresay. So would you be pretty green if you were shoved into my father's set. I picked up your silly business in a fortnight. Youve been at it ten years; and you havnt picked it up yet.

JOHNNY. Dont talk rot, child. You know you simply make me pity you.

BENTLEY. "Romance of Business" indeed! The real romance of Tarleton's business is the story that you understand anything about it. You never could explain any mortal thing about it to me when I asked you. "See what was done the last time": that was the beginning and the end of *your* wisdom. Youre nothing but a turnspit.

JOHNNY. A what!

BENTLEY. A turnspit. If your father hadnt made a roasting jack for you to turn, youd be earning twenty-four shillings a week behind a counter.

JOHNNY. If you dont take that back and apologize for your bad manners, I'll give you as good a hiding as ever —

BENTLEY. Help! Johnny's beating me! Oh! Murder! (*He throws himself on the ground, uttering piercing yells.*)

JOHNNY. Dont be a fool. Stop that noise, will you. I'm not going to touch you. Sh — sh —

(HYPATIA *rushes in through the inner door, followed by* MRS TARLETON, *and throws herself on her knees by* BENTLEY. MRS TARLETON, *whose knees are stiffer, bends over him and tries to lift him.* MRS TARLETON *is a shrewed and motherly old lady who has been pretty in her time, and is still very pleasant and likeable and unaffected.* HYPATIA *is a typical English girl of a sort never called typical: that is, she has an opaque white skin, black hair, large dark eyes with black brows and lashes, curved lips, swift glances and movements that flash out of a waiting stillness, boundless energy and audacity held in leash.*)

HYPATIA (*pouncing on* BENTLEY *with no very gentle hand*). Bentley: whats the matter? Dont cry like that: whats the use? Whats happened?

MRS TARLETON. Are you ill, child? (*They get him up.*) There, there, pet! It's all right: dont cry (*they put him into a chair*): there! there! there! Johnny will go for the doctor; and he'll give you something nice to make it well.

HYPATIA. What has happened, Johnny?

MRS TARLETON. Was it a wasp?

BENTLEY (*impatiently*). Wasp be dashed!

MRS TARLETON. Oh Bunny! that was a naughty word.

BENTLEY. Yes, I know: I beg your pardon. (*He rises, and extricates himself from them.*) Thats all right. Johnny frightened me. You know how easy it is to hurt me; and I'm too small to defend myself against Johnny.

MRS TARLETON. Johnny: how often have I told you that you must not bully the little ones. I thought youd outgrown all that.

HYPATIA (*angrily*). I do declare, mamma, that Johnny's brutality makes it impossible to live in the house with him.

JOHNNY (*deeply hurt*). It's fourteen years, mother, since you had that row with me for licking Robert and giving Hypatia a black eye because she bit me. I promised you then that I'd never raise my hand to one of them again; and Ive never broken my word. And now because this young whelp begins to cry out before he's hurt, you treat me as if I were a brute and a savage.

MRS TARLETON. No dear, not a savage; but you know you musnt call our visitor naughty names.

BENTLEY. Oh, let him alone —

JOHNNY (*fiercely*). Dont you interfere between my mother and me: d'y' hear?

HYPATIA. Johnny's lost his temper, mother. We'd better go. Come, Bentley.

MRS TARLETON. Yes: that will be best. (*To* BENTLEY.) Johnny doesnt mean any harm, dear: he'll be himself presently. Come.

(*The two ladies go out through the inner door with* BENTLEY, *who turns derisively at the door to cock a snook at* JOHNNY *as he goes out.*

JOHNNY, *left alone, clenches his fists and grinds his teeth, but can find no relief in that way for his rage. After choking and stamping for a moment, he makes for the vestibule door. It opens before he reaches it; and* LORD SUMMERHAYS *comes in.* JOHNNY *glares at him, speechless.* LORD SUMMERHAYS *takes in the situation, and quickly takes the punch-bowl from the sideboard and offers it to* JOHNNY.)

LORD SUMMERHAYS. Smash it. Dont hesitate: it's an ugly thing. Smash it: hard.

(JOHNNY, *with a stifled yell, dashes it in pieces, and then sits down and mops his brow.*)

Feel better now?

(JOHNNY *nods.*)

I know only one person alive who could drive me to the point of having either to break china or commit murder; and that person is my son Bentley. Was it he?

(JOHNNY *nods again, not yet able to speak.*)

As the car stopped I heard a yell which is only too familiar to me. It generally means that some infuriated person is trying to thrash Bentley. Nobody has ever succeeded, though almost everybody has tried.

(*He seats himself comfortably close to the writing table, and sets to work to collect the fragments of the punchbowl in the wastepaper basket whilst* JOHNNY, *with diminishing difficulty, collects himself.*)

Bentley is a problem which I confess I have never been able to solve. He was born to be a great success at the age of fifty. Most Englishmen of his class seem to be born to be great successes at the age of twenty-four at most. The domestic problem for me is how to endure Bentley until he is fifty. The problem for the nation is how to get itself governed by men whose growth is arrested when they are little more than college lads.

Bentley doesnt really mean to be offensive. You can always make him cry by telling him you dont like him. Only, he cries so loud that the experiment should be made in the open air: in the middle of Salisbury Plain if possible. He has a hard and penetrating intellect and a remarkable power of looking facts in the face; but unfortunately, being very young, he has no idea of how very little of that sort of thing most of us can stand. On the other hand, he is frightfully sensitive and even affectionate; so that he probably gets as much as he gives in the way of hurt feelings. Youll excuse me rambling on like this about my son.

JOHNNY (*who has pulled himself together*). You did it on purpose. I wasnt quite myself: I needed a moment to pull round. Thank you.

LORD SUMMERHAYS. Not at all. Is your father at home?

JOHNNY. No: hes opening one of his free libraries. Thats another nice little penny gone. He's mad on reading. He promised another free library last week. It's ruinous. Itll hit you as well as me when Bunny marries Hypatia. When all Hypatia's money is thrown away on libraries, where will Bunny come in? Cant you stop him?

LORD SUMMERHAYS. I'm afraid not. Hes a perfect whirlwind. Indefatigable at public work. Wonderful man, I think.

JOHNNY. Oh, public work! He does too much of it. It's really a sort of laziness, getting away from your own serious business to amuse yourself with other people's. Mind: I dont say there isnt another side to it. It has its value as an advertisement. It makes useful acquaintances and leads to valuable business connections. But it takes his mind off the main chance; and he overdoes it.

LORD SUMMERHAYS. The danger of public business is that it never ends. A man may kill himself at it.

JOHNNY. Or he can spend more on it than it brings him in: thats how I look at it. What I say is that everybody's business is nobody's business. I hope I'm not a hard man, nor a narrow man, nor unwilling to pay reasonable taxes, and subscribe in reason to deserving charities, and even serve on a jury in my turn; and no man can say I ever refused to help a friend out of a difficulty when he was worth helping. But when you ask me to go beyond that, I tell you frankly I dont see it. I never did see it, even when I was only a boy, and had to pretend to take in all the ideas the Governor fed me up with. I didnt see it; and I dont see it.

LORD SUMMERHAYS. There is certainly no business reason why you should take more than your share of the world's work.

JOHNNY. So I say. It's really a great encouragement to me to find you agree with me. For of course if nobody agrees with you, how are you to know that youre not a fool?

LORD SUMMERHAYS. Quite so.

JOHNNY. I wish youd talk to him about it. It's no use my saying anything: I'm a child to him still: I have no influence. Besides, you know how to handle men. See how you handled me when I was making a fool of myself about Bunny!

LORD SUMMERHAYS. Not at all.

JOHNNY. Oh yes I was: I know I was. Well, if my blessed father had come in he'd have told me to control myself. As if I was losing my temper on purpose!

(BENTLEY *returns, newly washed. He beams when he sees his father, and comes affectionately behind him and pats him on the shoulders.*)

BENTLEY. Hel-lo, commander! have you come? Ive been making a filthy silly ass of myself here. I'm awfully sorry, Johnny, old chap: I beg your pardon. Why dont you kick me when I go on like that?

LORD SUMMERHAYS. As we came through Godalming I thought I heard some yelling—

BENTLEY. I should think you did. Johnny was rather rough on me, though. He told me nobody here liked me; and I was silly enough to believe him.

LORD SUMMERHAYS. And all the women have been kissing you and pitying you ever since to stop your crying, I suppose. Baby!

BENTLEY. I did cry. But I always feel good after crying: it relieves my wretched nerves. I feel perfectly jolly now.

LORD SUMMERHAYS. Not at all ashamed of yourself, for instance?

BENTLEY. If I started being ashamed of myself I shouldnt have time for anything else all my life. I say: I feel very fit and spry. Lets all go down and meet the Grand Cham. (*He goes to the hatstand and takes down his hat.*)

LORD SUMMERHAYS. Does Mr Tarleton like to be called the Grand Cham, do you think, Bentley?

BENTLEY. Well, he thinks hes too modest for it. He calls himself Plain John. But you cant call him that in his own office: besides, it doesnt suit him: it's not flamboyant enough.

JOHNNY. Flam what?

BENTLEY. Flamboyant. Lets go and meet him. He's telephoned from Guildford to say hes on the road. The dear old son is always telephoning or telegraphing: he thinks hes hustling along like anything when hes only sending unnecessary messages.

LORD SUMMERHAYS. Thank you: I should prefer a quiet afternoon.

BENTLEY. Right o! I shant press Johnny: hes had enough of me for one week-end. (*He goes out through the pavilion into the grounds.*)

JOHNNY. Not a bad idea, that.

LORD SUMMERHAYS. What?

JOHNNY. Going to meet the Governor. You know you wouldnt think it; but the Governor likes Bunny rather. And Bunny is cultivating it. I shouldnt be surprised if he thought he could squeeze me out one of these days.

LORD SUMMERHAYS. You dont say so! Young rascal! I want to consult you about him, if you dont mind. Shall we stroll over to the Gibbet? Bentley is too fast for me as a walking companion; but I should like a short turn.

JOHNNY (*rising eagerly, highly flattered*). Right you are. Thatll suit me down to the ground. (*He takes a Panama and stick from the hat stand.*)

(MRS TARLETON *and* HYPATIA *come back just as the two men are going out.* HYPATIA *salutes* SUMMERHAYS *from a distance with an enigmatic lift of her eyelids in his direction and a demure nod before she sits down at the worktable and busies herself with her needle.* MRS TARLETON, *hospitably fussy, goes over to him.*)

MRS TARLETON. Oh, Lord Summerhays, I didnt know you were here. Wont you have some tea?

LORD SUMMERHAYS. No, thank you: I'm not allowed tea. And I'm ashamed to say Ive knocked over your beautiful punch-bowl. You must let me replace it.

MRS TARLETON. Oh, it doesnt matter: I'm only too glad to be rid of it. The shopman told me it was in the best taste; but when my poor old nurse Martha got cataract, Bunny said it was a merciful provision of Nature to prevent her seeing our china.

LORD SUMMERHAYS (*gravely*). That was exceedingly rude of Bentley, Mrs Tarleton. I hope you told him so.

MRS TARLETON. Oh, bless you! I dont care what he says; so long as he says it to me and not before visitors.

JOHNNY. We're going out for a stroll, mother.

MRS TARLETON. All right: dont let us keep you. Never mind about that crock: I'll get the girl to come and take the pieces away. (*Recollecting herself.*) There! Ive done it again!

JOHNNY. Done what?

MRS TARLETON. Called her the girl. You know, Lord Summerhays, it's a funny thing; but now I'm getting old, I'm dropping back into all the ways John and I had when we had barely a hundred a year. You should have known me when I was forty! I talked like a duchess; and if Johnny or Hypatia let slip a word that was like old times, I was down on them like anything. And now I'm beginning to do it myself at every turn.

LORD SUMMERHAYS. There comes a time when all that seems to matter so little. Even queens drop the mask when they reach our time of life.

MRS TARLETON. Let you alone for giving a thing a pretty turn! Youre a humbug, you know, Lord Summerhays. John doesnt know it; and Johnny doesnt know it; but you and I know it, dont we? Now thats something that even you cant answer; so be off with you for your walk without another word.

(LORD SUMMERHAYS *smiles; bows; and goes out through the vestibule door, followed by* JOHNNY. MRS TARLETON *sits down at the worktable and takes out her darning materials and one of her husband's socks.* HYPATIA *is at the other side of the table, on her mother's right. They chat as they work.*)

HYPATIA. I wonder whether they laugh at us when they are by themselves!

MRS TARLETON. Who?

HYPATIA. Bentley and his father and all the toffs in their set.

MRS TARLETON. Oh, thats only their way. I used to think that the aristocracy were a nasty sneering lot, and that they were laughing at me and John. Theyre always giggling and pretending not to care much about anything. But you get used to it: theyre the same to one another and to everybody. Besides, what does it matter what they think? It's far worse when theyre civil, because that always means that they want you to lend them money; and you must never do that, Hypatia, because they never pay. How can they? They dont make anything, you see. Of course, if you can make up your mind to regard it as a gift, thats different; but then they generally ask you again; and you may as well say no first as last. You neednt be afraid of the aristocracy, dear: theyre only human creatures like ourselves after all; and youll hold your own with them easy enough.

HYPATIA. Oh, I'm not a bit afraid of them, I assure you.

MRS TARLETON. Well, no, not afraid of them, exactly; but youve got to pick up their ways. You know, dear, I never quite agreed with your father's notion of keeping clear of them, and sending you to a school that was so expensive that they couldnt afford to send their daughters there; so that all the girls belonged to big business families like ourselves. It takes all sorts to make a world; and I wanted you to see a little of all sorts. When you marry Bunny, and go among the women of his father's set, theyll shock you at first.

HYPATIA (*incredulously*). How?

MRS TARLETON. Well, the things they talk about.

HYPATIA. Oh! scandalmongering?

MRS TARLETON. Oh no: we all do that: that's only human nature. But you know theyve no notion of decency. I shall never forget the first day I spent with a marchioness, two duchesses, and no end of Ladies This and That. Of course it was only a committee: theyd put me on to get a big subscription out of John. I'd never heard such talk in my life. The things they mentioned! And it was the marchioness that started it.

HYPATIA. What sort of things?

MRS TARLETON. Drainage!! She tried three systems in her castle; and she was going to do away with them all and try another. I didnt know which way to look when she began talking about it: I thought theyd all have got up and gone out of the room. But not a bit of it, if you please. They were all just as bad as she. They all had systems; and each of them swore by her own system. I sat there with my cheeks burning until one of the duchesses, thinking I looked out of it, I suppose, asked me what system I had. I said I was sure I knew nothing about such things, and hadnt we better change the subject. Then the fat was in the fire, I can tell you. There was a regular terror of a countess with an anaerobic system; and she told me, downright brutally, that I'd better learn something about them before my children died of diphtheria. That was just two months after I'd buried poor little Bobby; and that was the very thing he died of, poor little lamb! I burst out crying: I couldnt help it. It was as good as telling me I'd killed my own child. I had to go away; but before I was out of the door one of the duchesses — quite a young woman — began talking about what sour milk did in her inside and how she expected to live to be over a hundred if she took it regularly. And me listening to her, that had never dared to think that a duchess could have anything so common as an inside! I shouldnt have minded if it had been children's insides: we *have* to talk about them. But grown-up people! I *was* glad to get away that time.

HYPATIA. There was a physiology and hygiene class started at school; but of course none of our girls were let attend it.

MRS TARLETON. If it had been an aristocratic school plenty would have attended it. Thats what theyre like: theyve nasty minds. With really nice good women a thing is either decent or indecent; and if it's indecent, we just dont mention it or pretend to know about it; and theres an end of it. But all the aristocracy cares about is whether it can get any good out of the thing. Theyre what Johnny calls cynical-like. And of course nobody can say a word to them for it. Theyre so high up that they can do and say what they like.

HYPATIA. Well, I think they might leave the drains to their husbands, I shouldnt think much of a man that left such things to me.

MRS TARLETON. Oh, dont think that, dear, whatever you do. I never let on about it to you; but it's me that takes care of the drainage here. After what that countess said to me I wasnt going to lose another child nor trust John. And I dont want my grandchildren to die any more than my children.

HYPATIA. Do you think Bentley will ever be as big a man as his father? I dont mean clever: I mean big and strong.

MRS TARLETON. Not he. He's overbred, like one of those expensive little dogs. I like a bit of a mongrel myself, whether it's a man or a dog: theyre the best for everyday. But we all have our tastes: whats one woman's meat is another woman's poison. Bunny's a dear little fellow; but I never could have fancied him for a husband when I was your age.

HYPATIA. Yes; but he has some brains. He's not like all the rest. One cant have everything.

MRS TARLETON. Oh, youre quite right, dear: quite right. It's a great thing to have brains: look what it's done for your father! Thats the reason I never said a word when you jilted poor Jerry Mackintosh.

HYPATIA (*excusing herself*). I really couldnt stick it out with Jerry, mother. I know you liked him; and nobody can deny that hes a splendid animal —

MRS TARLETON (*shocked*). Hypatia! How can you! The things that girls say nowadays!

HYPATIA. Well, what else can you call him? If I'd been deaf or he'd been dumb, I could have married him. But living with father, Ive got accustomed to cleverness. Jerry would drive me mad: you know very well hes a fool: even Johnny thinks him a fool.

MRS TARLETON (*up in arms at once in defence of her boy*). Now dont begin about my Johnny. You know it annoys me. Johnny's as clever as anybody else in his own way. I dont say hes as clever as you in some ways; but hes a man, at all events, and not a little squit of a thing like your Bunny.

HYPATIA. Oh, I say nothing against your darling: we all know Johnny's perfection.

MRS TARLETON. Dont be cross, dearie. You let Johnny alone; and I'll let Bunny alone. I'm just as bad as you. There!

HYPATIA. Oh, I dont mind your saying that about Bentley. It's true. He *is* a little squit of a thing. I wish he wasnt. But who else is there? Think of all the other chances Ive had! Not one of them has as much brains in his whole body as Bentley has in his little finger. Besides, theyve no *distinction*. It's as much as I can do to tell one from the other. They wouldnt even have money if they werent the sons of their fathers, like Johnny. Whats a girl to do? I never met anybody like Bentley before. He may be small; but he's the best of the bunch: you cant deny that.

MRS TARLETON (*with a sigh*). Well, my pet, if you fancy him, theres no more to be said.

(*A pause follows this remark: the two women sewing silently.*)

HYPATIA. Mother: do you think marriage is as much a question of fancy as it used to be in your time and father's?

MRS TARLETON. Oh, it wasnt much fancy with me, dear: your father just wouldnt take no for an answer; and I was only too glad to be his wife instead of his shop-girl. Still, it's curious; but I had more choice than you in a way, because you see, I was poor; and there are so many more poor men than rich ones that I might have had more of a pick, as you might say, if John hadnt suited me.

HYPATIA. I can imagine all sorts of men I could fall in love with; but I never seem to meet them. The real ones are too small, like Bunny, or too silly, like Jerry. Of course one can get into a state about any man: fall in love with him if you like to call it that. But who would risk marrying a man for love? *I* shouldnt. I remember three girls at school who agreed that the one man you should never marry was the man you were in love with, because it would make a perfect slave of you. Theres a sort of instinct against it, I think, thats just as strong as the other instinct. One of them, to my certain knowledge, refused a man she was in love with, and married another who was in love with her; and it turned out very well.

MRS TARLETON. Does all that mean that youre not in love with Bunny?

HYPATIA. Oh, how could anybody be in love with Bunny? I like him to kiss me just as I like a baby to kiss me. I'm fond of him; and he never bores me; and I see that he's very clever; but I'm not what you call gone about him, if thats what you mean.

MRS TARLETON. Then why need you marry him?

HYPATIA. What better can I do? I must marry somebody, I suppose. Ive realized that since I was twenty-three. I always used to take it as a matter of course that I should be married before I was twenty.

BENTLEY'S VOICE (*in the garden*). Youve got to keep yourself fresh: to look at these things with an open mind.

JOHN TARLETON'S VOICE. Quite right, quite right: I always say so.

MRS TARLETON. Theres your father, and Bunny with him.

BENTLEY. Keep young. Keep your eye on me. Thats the tip for you.

(BENTLEY *and* MR TARLETON — *an immense and genial veteran of trade — come into view and enter the pavilion.*)

JOHN TARLETON. You think youre young, do you? You think I'm old? (*Energetically shaking off his motoring coat and hanging it up with his cap.*)

BENTLEY (*helping him with the coat*). Of course youre old. Look at your face and look at mine. What you call your youth is nothing but your levity. Why do we get on so well together? Because I'm a young cub and youre an old josser. (*He throws a cushion at* HYPATIA'*s feet and sits down on it with his back against her knees.*)

TARLETON. Old! Thats all you know about it, my lad. How do, Patsy! (HYPATIA *kisses him.*) How is my Chickabiddy? (*He kisses* MRS TARLETON'*s hand and poses expansively in the middle of the picture.*) Look at me! Look at these wrinkles, these grey hairs, this repulsive mask that you call old age! What is it? (*Vehemently.*) I ask you, what is it?

BENTLEY. Jolly nice and venerable, old man. Dont be discouraged.

TARLETON. Nice? Not a bit of it. Venerable? Venerable be blowed! Read your Darwin, my boy. Read your Weismann. (*He goes to the sideboard for a drink of lemonade.*)

MRS TARLETON. For shame, John! Tell him to read his Bible.

TARLETON (*manipulating the syphon*). Whats the use of telling children to read the Bible when you know they wont. I was kept away from the Bible for forty years by being told to read it when I was young. Then I picked it up one evening in a hotel in Sunderland when I had left all my papers in the train; and I found it wasnt half bad. (*He drinks, and puts down the glass with a smack of enjoyment.*) Better than most halfpenny papers, anyhow, if only you could make people believe it. (*He sits down by the writing-table, near his wife.*) But if you want to understand old age scientifically, read Darwin and Weismann. Of course if you want to understand it romantically, read about Solomon.

MRS TARLETON. Have you had tea, John?

TARLETON. Yes. Dont interrupt me when I'm improving the boy's mind. Where was I? This repulsive mask — Yes. (*Explosively.*) What is death?

MRS TARLETON. John!

HYPATIA. Death is a rather unpleasant subject, papa.

TARLETON. Not a bit. Not scientifically. Scientifically it's a delightful subject. You think death's natural. Well, it isnt. You read Weismann. There wasnt any death to start with. You go look in any ditch outside and youll find swimming about there as fresh as paint some of the identical little live cells that Adam christened in the Garden of Eden. But if big things like us didnt die, we'd crowd one another off the face of the globe. Nothing survived, sir, except the sort of people that had the sense and good manners to die and make room for the fresh supplies. And so death was introduced by Natural Selection. You get it out of your head, my lad, that I'm going to die because I'm wearing out or decaying. There's no such thing as decay to a vital man. I shall clear out; but I shant decay.

BENTLEY. And what about the wrinkles and the almond tree and the grasshopper that becomes a burden and the desire that fails?

TARLETON. Does it? by George! No, sir; it spiritualizes. As to your grasshopper, I can carry an elephant.

MRS TARLETON. You do say such things, Bunny! What does he mean by the almond tree?

TARLETON. He means my white hairs: the repulsive mask. That, my boy, is another invention of Natural Selection to disgust young women with me, and give the lads a turn.

MRS TARLETON. John: I wont have it. Thats a forbidden subject.

TARLETON. They talk of the wickedness and vanity of women painting their faces and wearing auburn wigs at fifty. But why shouldnt they? Why should a woman allow Nature to put a false mask of age on her when she knows that she's as young as ever? Why should she look in the glass and see a wrinkled lie when a touch of fine art will shew her a glorious truth? The wrinkles are a dodge to repel young men. Suppose she doesnt want to repel young men! Suppose she likes them!

MRS TARLETON. Bunny: take Hypatia out into the grounds for a walk: theres a good boy. John has got one of his naughty fits this evening.

HYPATIA. Oh, never mind me. I'm used to him.

BENTLEY. I'm not. I never heard such conversation: I cant believe my ears. And mind you, this is the man who objected to my marrying his daughter on the ground that a marriage between a member of the great and good middle class with one of the vicious and corrupt aristocracy would be a misalliance. A misalliance, if you please! This is the man Ive adopted as a father!

TARLETON. Eh? Whats that? Adopted me as a father, have you?

BENTLEY. Yes. Thats an idea of mine. I knew a chap named Joey Percival at Oxford (you know I was two months at Balliol before I was sent down for telling the old woman who was head of that silly college what I jolly well thought of him. He would have been glad to have me back, too, at the end of six months; but I wouldnt go: I just let him want: and serve him right!) Well, Joey was a most awfully clever fellow, and so nice! I asked him what made such a difference between him and all the other pups — they *were* pups, if you like. He told me it was very simple: they had only one father apiece; and he had three.

MRS TARLETON. Dont talk nonsense, child. How could that be?

BENTLEY. Oh, very simple. His father —

TARLETON. Which father?

BENTLEY. The first one: the regulation natural chap. He kept a tame philosopher in the house: a sort of Coleridge or Herbert Spencer kind of card, you know. That was the second father. Then his mother was an Italian princess; and she had an Italian priest always about. He was supposed to take charge of her conscience; but from what I could make out she jolly well took charge of his. The whole three of them took charge of Joey's conscience. He used to hear them arguing like mad about everything. You see, the philosopher was a freethinker, and always believed the latest thing. The priest didnt believe anything, because it was sure to get him into trouble with someone or another. And the natural father kept an open mind and believed whatever paid him best. Between the lot of them Joey got cultivated no end. He said if he could only have had three mothers as well, he'd have backed himself against Napoleon.

TARLETON (*impressed*). Thats an idea. Thats a most interesting idea: a most important idea.

MRS TARLETON. You always were one for ideas, John.

TARLETON. Youre right, Chickabiddy. What do I tell Johnny when he brags about Tarleton's Underwear? It's not the underwear. The underwear be hanged! Anybody can make underwear. Anybody can sell underwear. Tarleton's Ideas: thats whats done it. Ive often thought of putting that up over the shop.

BENTLEY. Take me into partnership when you do, old man. I'm wasted on the underwear; but I shall come in strong on the ideas.

TARLETON. You be a good boy; and perhaps I will.

MRS TARLETON (*scenting a plot against her beloved* JOHNNY). Now, John: you promised —

TARLETON. Yes, yes. All right, Chickabiddy: dont fuss. Your precious Johnny shant be interfered with. (*Bouncing up, too energetic to sit still.*) But I'm getting sick of that old shop. Thirty-five years Ive had of it: same blessed old stairs to go up and down every day: same old lot: same old game: sorry I ever started it now. I'll chuck it and try something else: something that will give a scope to all my faculties.

HYPATIA. Theres money in underwear: theres none in wild-cat ideas.

TARLETON. Theres money in *me*, madam, no matter what I go into.

MRS TARLETON. Dont boast, John. Dont tempt Providence.

TARLETON. Rats! You dont understand Providence. Providence likes to be tempted. Thats the secret of the successful man. Read Browning. Natural theology on an island, eh? Caliban was afraid to tempt Providence: that was why he was never able to get even with Prospero. What did Prospero do? Prospero didnt even tempt Providence: he was Providence. Thats one of Tarleton's ideas; and dont you forget it.

BENTLEY. You are full of beef today, old man.

TARLETON. Beef be blowed! Joy of life. Read Ibsen. (*He goes into the pavilion to relieve his restlessness, and stares out with his hands thrust deep in his pockets.*)

HYPATIA (*thoughtful*). Bentley: couldnt you invite your friend Mr Percival down here?

BENTLEY. Not if I know it. Youd throw me over the moment you set eyes on him.

MRS TARLETON. Oh, Bunny! For shame!

BENTLEY. Well, who'd marry me, dyou suppose, if they could get my brains with a full-sized body? No, thank you. I shall take jolly good care to keep Joey out of this until Hypatia is past praying for.

(JOHNNY *and* LORD SUMMERHAYS *return through the pavilion from their stroll.*)

TARLETON. Welcome! welcome! Why have you stayed away so long?

LORD SUMMERHAYS (*shaking hands*). Yes: I should have come sooner. But I'm still rather lost in England.

(JOHNNY *takes his hat and hangs it up beside his own.*)

Thank you.

(JOHNNY *returns to his swing and his novel.* LORD SUMMERHAYS *comes to the writing table.*)

The fact is that as Ive nothing to do, I never have time to go anywhere. (*He sits down next* MRS TARLETON.)

TARLETON (*following him and sitting down on his left*). Paradox, paradox. Good. Paradoxes are the only truths. Read Chesterton. But theres lots for you to do here. You have a genius for government. You learnt your job out there in Jinghiskahn. Well, we want to be governed here in England. Govern us.

LORD SUMMERHAYS. Ah yes, my friend; but in Jinghiskahn you have to govern the right way. If you dont, you go under and come home. Here everything has to be done the wrong way, to suit governors who understand nothing but partridge shooting (our English native princes, in fact) and voters who dont know what theyre voting about. I dont understand these democratic games; and I'm afraid I'm too old to learn. What can I do but sit in the window of my club, which consists mostly of retired Indian Civil servants? We look on at the muddle and the folly and amateurishness; and we ask each other where a single fortnight of it would have landed us.

TARLETON. Very true. Still, Democracy's all right, you know. Read Mill. Read Jefferson.

LORD SUMMERHAYS. Yes. Democracy reads well; but it doesnt act well, like some people's plays. No, no, my friend Tarleton: to make Democracy work, you need an aristocratic democracy. To make Aristocracy work, you need a democratic aristocracy. Youve got neither; and theres an end of it.

TARLETON. Still, you know, the superman may come. The superman's an idea. I believe in ideas. Read Whatshisname.

LORD SUMMERHAYS. Reading is a dangerous amusement, Tarleton. I wish I could persuade your free library people of that.

TARLETON. Why, man, it's the beginning of education.

LORD SUMMERHAYS. On the contrary, it's the end of it. How can you dare teach a man to read until youve taught him everything else first?

JOHNNY (*intercepting his father's reply by coming out of the swing and taking the floor*). Leave it at that. Thats good sense. Anybody on for a game of tennis?

BENTLEY. Oh, lets have some more improving conversation. Wouldnt you rather, Johnny?

JOHNNY. If you ask me, no.

TARLETON. Johnny: you dont cultivate your mind. You dont read.

JOHNNY (*coming between his mother and* LORD SUMMERHAYS, *book in hand*). Yes I do. I bet you what you like that, page for page, I read more than you, though I dont talk about it so much. Only, I dont read the same books. I like a book with a plot in it. You like a book with nothing in it but some idea that the chap that writes it keeps worrying, like a cat chasing its own tail. I can stand a little of it, just as I can stand watching the cat for two minutes, say, when Ive nothing better to do. But a man soon gets fed up with that sort of thing. The fact is, you look on an author as a sort of god. *I* look on him as a man that I pay to do a certain thing for me. I pay him to amuse me and to take me out of myself and make me forget.

TARLETON. No. Wrong principle. You want to remember. Read Kipling. "Lest we forget."

JOHNNY. If Kipling wants to remember, let him remember. If he had to run Tarleton's Underwear, he'd be jolly glad to forget. As he has a much softer job, and wants to keep himself before the public, his cry is, "Dont you forget the sort of things I'm rather clever at writing about." Well, I dont blame him: it's his business: I should do the same in his place. But what he wants and what I want are two different things. I want to forget; and I pay another man to make me forget. If I buy a book or go to the theatre, I want to forget the shop and forget myself from the moment I go in to the moment I come out. That what I pay my money for. And if I find that the author's simply getting at me the whole time, I consider that he's obtained my money under false pretences. I'm not a morbid crank: I'm a natural man; and, as such, I dont like being got at. If a man in my employment did it, I should sack him. If a member of my club did it, I should cut him. If he went too far with it, I should bring his conduct before the committee. I might even punch his head, if it came to that. Well, who and what is an author that he should be privileged to take liberties that are not allowed to other men?

MRS TARLETON. You see, John! What have I always told you? Johnny has as much to say for himself as anybody when he likes.

JOHNNY. I'm no fool, mother, whatever some people may fancy. I dont set up to have as many ideas as the Governor; but what ideas I have are consecutive, at all events. I can think as well as talk.

BENTLEY (*to* TARLETON, *chuckling*). Had you there, old man, hadnt he? You *are* rather all over the shop with your ideas, aint you?

JOHNNY (*handsomely*). I'm not saying anything against you, Governor. But I do say that the time has come for sane, healthy, unpretending men like me to make a stand against this conspiracy of the writing and talking and artistic lot to put us in the back row. It isnt a fact that we're inferior to them: it's a put-up job; and it's they that have put the job up. It's we that run the country for them; and all the thanks we get is to be told we're Philistines and vulgar tradesmen and sordid city men and so forth, and that theyre all angels of light and leading. The time has come to assert ourselves and put a stop to their stuck-up nonsense. Perhaps if we had nothing better to do than talking or writing, we could do it better than they. Anyhow, theyre the failures and refuse of business (hardly a man of them that didnt begin in an office) and we're the successes of it. Thank God I havnt failed yet at anything; and I dont believe I should fail at literature if it would pay me to turn my hand to it.

BENTLEY. Hear, hear!

MRS TARLETON. Fancy you writing a book, Johnny! Do you think he could, Lord Summerhays?

LORD SUMMERHAYS. Why not? As a matter of fact all the really prosperous authors I have met since my return to England have been very like him.

TARLETON (*again impressed*). Thats an idea. Thats a new idea. I believe I ought to have made Johnny an author. Ive never said so before for fear of hurting his feelings, because, after all, the lad cant help it; but Ive never thought Johnny worth tuppence as a man of business.

JOHNNY (*sarcastic*). Oh! You think youve always kept that to yourself, do you, Governor? I know your opinion of me as well as you know it yourself. It takes one man of business to appreciate another; and you arnt, and you never have been, a real man of business. I know where Tarleton's would have been three or four times if it hadnt been for me. (*With a snort and a nod to emphasize the implied warning, he retreats to the Turkish bath, and lolls against it with an air of good-humored indifference.*)

TARLETON. Well, who denies it? Youre quite right, my boy. I dont mind confessing to you all that the circumstances that condemned me to keep a shop are the biggest tragedy in modern life. I ought to have been a writer. I'm essentially a man of ideas. When I was a young man I sometimes used to pray that I might fail, so that I should be justified in giving up business and doing something: something first-class. But it was no good: I couldnt fail. I said to myself that if I could only once go to my Chickabiddy here and shew her a chartered accountant's statement proving that I'd made £20 less than last year, I could ask her to let me chance Johnny's and Hypatia's future by going into literature. But it was no good. First it was £250 more than last year. Then it was £700. Then it was £2000. Then I saw it was no use: Prometheus was chained to his rock: read Shelley: read Mrs Browning. Well, well, it was not to be. (*He rises solemnly.*) Lord Summerhays: I ask you to excuse me for a few moments. There are times when a man needs to meditate in solitude on his destiny. A chord is touched; and he sees the drama of his life as a spectator sees a play. Laugh if you feel inclined: no man sees the comic side of it more than I. In the theatre of life everyone may be amused except the actor. (*Brightening.*) Theres an idea in this: an idea for a picture. What a pity young Bentley is not a painter! Tarleton meditating on his destiny. Not in a toga. Not in the trappings of the tragedian or the philosopher. In plain coat and trousers: a man like any other man. And beneath that coat and trousers a human soul. Tarleton's Underwear! (*He goes out gravely into the vestibule.*)

MRS TARLETON (*fondly*). I suppose it's a wife's partiality, Lord Summerhays; but I do think John is really great. I'm sure he was meant to be a king. My father looked down on John, because he was a rate collector and John kept a shop. It hurt his pride to have to borrow money so often from John; and he used to console himself by saying, "After all, hes only a linendraper." But at last one day he said to me, "John is a king."

BENTLEY. How much did he borrow on that occasion?

LORD SUMMERHAYS (*sharply*). Bentley!

MRS TARLETON. Oh, dont scold the child: he'd have to say something like that if it was to be his last word on earth. Besides, hes quite right: my poor father had asked for his usual five pounds; and John gave him a hundred in his big way. Just like a king.

LORD SUMMERHAYS. Not at all. I had five kings to manage in Jinghiskahn; and I think you do your husband some injustice, Mrs Tarleton. They pretended to like me because I kept their brothers from murdering them; but I didnt like them. And I like Tarleton.

MRS TARLETON. Everybody does. I really must go and make the cook do him a Welsh rabbit. He expects one on special occasions. (*She goes to the inner door.*) Johnny: when he comes back ask him where we're to put that new Turkish bath. Turkish baths are his latest. (*She goes out.*)

JOHNNY (*coming forward again*). Now that the Governor has given himself away, and the old lady's gone, I'll tell you something, Lord

Summerhays. If you study men whove made an enormous pile in business without being keen on money, youll find that they all have a slate off. The Governor's a wonderful man; but he's not quite all there, you know. If you notice, he's different from me; and whatever my failings may be, I'm a sane man. Erratic: thats what he is. And the danger is that some day he'll give the whole show away.

LORD SUMMERHAYS. Giving the show away is a method like any other method. Keeping it to yourself is only another method. I should keep an open mind about it.

JOHNNY. Has it ever occurred to you that a man with an open mind must be a bit of a scoundrel? If you ask me, I like a man who makes up his mind once for all as to whats right and whats wrong and then sticks to it. At all events you know where to have him.

LORD SUMMERHAYS. That may not be his object.

BENTLEY. He may want to have *you*, old chap.

JOHNNY. Well, let him. If a member of my club wants to steal my umbrella, he knows where to find it. If a man put up for the club who had an open mind on the subject of property in umbrellas, I should blackball him. An open mind is all very well in clever talky-talky; but in conduct and in business give me solid ground.

LORD SUMMERHAYS. Yes: the quicksands make life difficult. Still, there they are. It's no use pretending theyre rocks.

JOHNNY. I dont know. You can draw a line and make other chaps toe it. Thats what I call morality.

LORD SUMMERHAYS. Very true. But you dont make any progress when youre toeing a line.

HYPATIA (*suddenly, as if she could bear no more of it*). Bentley: do go and play tennis with Johnny. You must take exercise.

LORD SUMMERHAYS. Do, my boy, do. (*To* JOHNNY.) Take him out and make him skip about.

BENTLEY (*rising reluctantly*). I promised you two inches more round my chest this summer. I tried exercises with an indiarubber expander; but I wasnt strong enough: instead of *my* expanding *it, it* crumpled *me* up. Come along, Johnny.

JOHNNY. Do you no end of good, young chap. (*He goes out with* BENTLEY *through the pavilion.*)

(HYPATIA *throws aside her work with an enormous sigh of relief.*)

LORD SUMMERHAYS. At last!

HYPATIA. At last. Oh, if I might only have a holiday in an asylum for the dumb. How I envy the animals! They cant talk. If Johnny could only put back his ears or wag his tail instead of laying down the law, how much better it would be! We should know when he was cross and when he was pleased; and thats all we know now, with all his talk. It never stops: talk, talk, talk, talk. Thats my life. All the day I listen to mamma talking; at dinner I listen to papa talking; and when papa stops for breath I listen to Johnny talking.

LORD SUMMERHAYS. You make me feel very guilty. I talk too, I'm afraid.

HYPATIA. Oh, I dont mind that, because your talk is a novelty. But it must have been dreadful for your daughters.

LORD SUMMERHAYS. I suppose so.

HYPATIA. If parents would only realize how they bore their children! Three or four times in the last half hour Ive been on the point of screaming.

LORD SUMMERHAYS. Were we very dull?

HYPATIA. Not at all: you were very clever. Thats whats so hard to bear, because it makes it so difficult to avoid listening. You see, I'm young; and I do so want something to happen. My mother tells me that when I'm her age, I shall be only too glad that nothing's happened; but I'm not her age; so what good is that to me? Theres my father in the garden, meditating on his destiny. All very well for him: he's had a destiny to meditate on; but I havnt had any destiny yet. Everything's happened to him: nothing's happened to me. Thats why this unending talk is so maddeningly uninteresting to me.

LORD SUMMERHAYS. It would be worse if we sat in silence.

HYPATIA. No it wouldnt. If you all sat in silence, as if you were waiting for something to happen, then there would be hope even if nothing did happen. But this eternal cackle, cackle, cackle about things in general is only fit for old, *old*, OLD people. I suppose it means something to them: theyve had their fling. All I listen for is some sign of it ending in something; but just when it seems to be coming to a point, Johnny or papa just starts another hare; and it all begins over again; and I realize that it's never going to lead anywhere and never going to stop. Thats when I want to scream. I wonder how you can stand it.

LORD SUMMERHAYS. Well, I'm old and garrulous myself, you see. Besides, I'm not here of my own free will, exactly. I came because you ordered me to come.

HYPATIA. Didnt you want to come?

LORD SUMMERHAYS. My dear: after thirty years of managing other people's business, men lose the habit of considering what they want or dont want.

HYPATIA. Oh, dont begin to talk about what men do, and about thirty years experience. If you cant get off that subject, youd better send for Johnny and papa and begin it all over again.

LORD SUMMERHAYS. I'm sorry. I beg your pardon.

HYPATIA. I asked you, didnt you want to come?

LORD SUMMERHAYS. I did not stop to consider whether I wanted or not, because when I read your letter I knew I had to come.

HYPATIA. Why?

LORD SUMMERHAYS. O come, Miss Tarleton! Really! really! Dont force me to call you a blackmailer to your face. You have me in your power; and I do what you tell me very obediently. Dont ask me to pretend I do it of my own free will.

HYPATIA. I dont know what a blackmailer is. I havnt even that much experience.

LORD SUMMERHAYS. A blackmailer, my dear young lady, is a person who knows a disgraceful secret in the life of another person, and extorts money from that other person by threatening to make his secret public unless the money is paid.

HYPATIA. I havnt asked you for money.

LORD SUMMERHAYS. No; but you asked me to come down here and talk to you; and you mentioned casually that if I didnt youd have nobody to talk about me to but Bentley. That was a threat, was it not?

HYPATIA. Well, I wanted you to come.

LORD SUMMERHAYS. In spite of my age and my unfortunate talkativeness?

HYPATIA. I like talking to you. I can let myself go with you. I can say things to you I cant say to other people.

LORD SUMMERHAYS. I wonder why?

HYPATIA. Well, you are the only really clever, grown-up, high-class, experienced man I know who has given himself away to me by making an utter fool of himself with me. You cant wrap yourself up in your toga after that. You cant give yourself airs with me.

LORD SUMMERHAYS. You mean you can tell Bentley about me if I do.

HYPATIA. Even if there wasnt any Bentley: even if you didnt care (and I really dont see why you should care so much) still, we never could be on conventional terms with one another again. Besides, Ive got a feeling for you: almost a ghastly sort of love for you.

LORD SUMMERHAYS (*shrinking*). I beg you — no, please.

HYPATIA. Oh, it's nothing at all flattering; and, of course, nothing wrong, as I suppose youd call it.

LORD SUMMERHAYS. Please believe that I know that. When men of my age —

HYPATIA (*impatiently*). Oh, do talk about yourself when you mean yourself, and not about men of your age.

LORD SUMMERHAYS. I'll put it as bluntly as I can. When, as you say, I made an utter fool of myself, believe me, I made a poetic fool of myself. I was seduced, not by appetites which, thank Heaven, Ive long outlived: not even by the desire of second childhood for a child companion, but by the innocent impulse to place the delicacy and wisdom and spirituality of my age at the affectionate service of your youth for a few years, at the end of which you would be a grown, strong, formed — widow. Alas, my dear, the delicacy of age reckoned, as usual, without the derision and cruelty of youth. You told me that you didnt want to be an old man's nurse, and that you didnt want to have undersized children like Bentley. It served me right: I dont reproach you: I was an old fool. But how you can imagine, after that, that I can suspect you of the smallest feeling for me except the inevitable feeling of early youth for late age, or imagine that I have any feeling for you except one of shrinking humiliation, I cant understand.

HYPATIA. I dont blame you for falling in love with me. I shall be grateful to you all my life for it, because that was the first time that anything really interesting happened to me.

LORD SUMMERHAYS. Do you mean to tell me that nothing of that kind had ever happened before? that no man had ever —

HYPATIA. Oh, lots. Thats part of the routine of life here: the very dullest part of it. The young man who comes a-courting is as familiar an incident in my life as coffee for breakfast. Of course, he's too much of a gentleman to misbehave himself; and I'm too much of a lady to let him; and he's shy and sheepish; and I'm correct and self-possessed; and at last, when I can bear it no longer, I either frighten him off or give him a chance of proposing, just to see how he'll do it, and refuse him because he does it in the same silly way as all the rest. You dont call that an event in one's life, do you? With you it was different. I should as soon have expected the North Pole to fall in love with me as you. You know I'm only a linendraper's daughter when all's said. I was afraid of you: you, a great man! a lord! and older than my father. And then, what a situation it was! Just think of it! I was engaged to your son; and you knew nothing about it. He was afraid to tell you: he brought you down here because he thought if he could throw us together I could get round you because I was such a ripping girl. We arranged it all: he and I. We got Papa and Mamma and Johnny out of the way splendidly; and then Bentley took himself off, and left us — you and me! — to take a walk through the heather and admire the scenery of Hindhead. You never dreamt that it was all a plan: that what made me so nice was the way I was playing up to my destiny as the sweet girl that was to make your boy happy. And then! and then! (*She rises to dance and clap her hands in her glee.*)

LORD SUMMERHAYS (*shuddering*). Stop, stop. Can no woman understand a man's delicacy?

HYPATIA (*revelling in the recollection*). And then — ha, ha! — you proposed. You! A father! For your son's girl!

LORD SUMMERHAYS. Stop, I tell you. Dont profane what you dont understand.

HYPATIA. That was something happening at last with a vengeance. It was splendid. It was my first peep behind the scenes. If I'd been seventeen I should have fallen in love with you. Even as it is, I feel quite differently towards you from what I do towards other old men. So (*offering her hand*) you may kiss my hand if that will be any fun for you.

LORD SUMMERHAYS (*rising and recoiling to the table, deeply revolted*). No, no, no. How dare you? (*She laughs mischievously.*) How callous youth is! How coarse! How cynical! How ruthlessly cruel!

HYPATIA. Stuff! It's only that youre tired of a great many things Ive never tried.

LORD SUMMERHAYS. It's not alone that. Ive not forgotten the brutality of my own boyhood. But do try to learn, glorious young beast that you are, that age is squeamish, sentimental, fastidious. If you cant understand my holier feelings, at least you know the bodily infirmities of the old. You know that I darent eat all the rich things you gobble up at every meal; that I cant bear the noise and racket and clatter that affect you no more than they affect a stone. Well, my soul is like that too. Spare it: be gentle with it. (*He involuntarily puts out his hands to plead: she takes them with a laugh.*) If you could possibly think of me as half an angel and half an invalid, we should get on much better together.

HYPATIA. We get on very well, I think. Nobody else ever called me a glorious young beast. I like that. Glorious young beast expresses exactly what I like to be.

LORD SUMMERHAYS (*extricating his hands and sitting down*). Where on earth did you get these morbid tastes? You seem to have been well brought up in a normal, healthy, respectable, middle-class family. Yet you go on like the most unwholesome product of the rankest Bohemianism.

HYPATIA. Thats just it. I'm fed up with—

LORD SUMMERHAYS. Horrible expression. Dont.

HYPATIA. Oh, I daresay it's vulgar; but theres no other word for it. I'm fed up with nice things: with respectability, with propriety! When a woman has nothing to do, money and respectability mean that nothing is ever allowed to happen to her. I dont want to be good; and I dont want to be bad: I just dont want to be bothered about either good or bad: I want to be an active verb.

LORD SUMMERHAYS. An active verb? Oh, I see. An active verb signifies to be, to do, or to suffer.

HYPATIA. Just so: how clever of you! I want to be; I want to do; and I'm game to suffer if it costs that. But stick here doing nothing but being good and nice and ladylike I simply *wont*. Stay down here with us for a week; and I'll shew you what it means: shew it to you going on day after day, year after year, lifetime after lifetime.

LORD SUMMERHAYS. Shew me what?

HYPATIA. Girls withering into ladies. Ladies withering into old maids. Nursing old women. Running errands for old men. Good for nothing else at last. Oh, you cant imagine the fiendish selfishness of the old people and the maudlin sacrifice of the young. It's more unbearable than any poverty: more horrible than any regular-right-down wickedness. Oh, home! home! parents! family! duty! how I loathe them! How I'd like to see them all blown to bits! The poor escape. The wicked escape. Well, I cant be poor: we're rolling in money: it's no use pretending we're not. But I can be wicked; and I'm quite prepared to be.

LORD SUMMERHAYS. You think that easy?

HYPATIA. Well, isnt it? Being a man, you ought to know.

LORD SUMMERHAYS. It requires some natural talent, which can no doubt be cultivated. It's not really easy to be anything out of the common.

HYPATIA. Anyhow, I mean to make a fight for living.

LORD SUMMERHAYS. Living your own life, I believe the Suffragist phrase is.

HYPATIA. Living *any* life. Living, instead of withering without even a gardener to snip you off when youre rotten.

LORD SUMMERHAYS. Ive lived an active life; but Ive withered all the same.

HYPATIA. No: youve worn out: thats quite different. And youve some life in you yet or you wouldnt have fallen in love with me. You can never imagine how delighted I was to find that instead of being the correct sort of big panjandrum you were supposed to be, you were really an old rip like papa.

LORD SUMMERHAYS. No, no: not about your father: I really cant bear it. And if you must say these terrible things: these heart-wounding shameful things, at least find something prettier to call me than an old rip.

HYPATIA. Well, what *would* you call a man proposing to a girl who might be —

LORD SUMMERHAYS. His daughter: yes, I know.

HYPATIA. I was going to say his granddaughter.

LORD SUMMERHAYS. You always have one more blow to get in.

HYPATIA. Youre too sensitive. Did you ever make mud pies when you were a kid — beg pardon: a child.

LORD SUMMERHAYS. I hope not.

HYPATIA. It's a dirty job; but Johnny and I were vulgar enough to like it. I like young people because theyre not too afraid of dirt to live. Ive grown out of the mud pies; but I like slang; and I like bustling you up by saying things that shock you; and I'd rather put up with swearing and smoking than with dull respectability; and there are lots of things that would just shrivel you up that I think rather jolly. Now!

LORD SUMMERHAYS. Ive not the slightest doubt of it. Dont insist.

HYPATIA. It's not your ideal, is it?

LORD SUMMERHAYS. No.

HYPATIA. Shall I tell you why? Your ideal is an old woman. I daresay she's got a young face; but she's an old woman. Old, old, old. Squeamish. Cant stand up to things. Cant enjoy things: not real things. Always on the shrink.

LORD SUMMERHAYS. On the shrink! Detestable expression.

HYPATIA. Bah! you cant stand even a little thing like that. What good are you? Oh, what good are you?

LORD SUMMERHAYS. Dont ask me. I dont know. I dont know.

(TARLETON *returns from the vestibule.* HYPATIA *sits down demurely.*)

HYPATIA. Well, papa: have you meditated on your destiny?

TARLETON (*puzzled*). What? Oh! my destiny. Gad, I forgot all about it: Jock started a rabbit and put it clean out of my head. Besides, why should I give way to morbid introspection? It's a sign of madness.

Read Lombroso. (*To* LORD SUMMERHAYS.) Well, Summerhays, has my little girl been entertaining you?

LORD SUMMERHAYS. Yes. She is a wonderful entertainer.

TARLETON. I think my idea of bringing up a young girl has been rather a success. Dont you listen to this, Patsy: it might make you conceited. She's never been treated like a child. I always said the same thing to her mother. Let her read what she likes. Let her do what she likes. Let her go where she likes. Eh, Patsy?

HYPATIA. Oh yes, if there had only been anything for me to do, any place for me to go, anything I wanted to read.

TARLETON. There, you see! She's not satisfied. Restless. Wants things to happen. Wants adventures to drop out of the sky.

HYPATIA (*gathering up her work*). If youre going to talk about me and my education, I'm off.

TARLETON. Well, well, off with you. (*To* LORD SUMMERHAYS.) She's active, like me. She actually wanted me to put her into the shop.

HYPATIA. Well, they tell me that the girls there have adventures sometimes. (*She goes out through the inner door.*)

TARLETON. She had me there, though she doesnt know it, poor innocent lamb! Public scandal exaggerates enormously, of course; but moralize as you will, superabundant vitality is a physical fact that cant be talked away. (*He sits down between the writing table and the sideboard.*) Difficult question this, of bringing up children. Between ourselves, it has beaten me. I never was so surprised in my life as when I came to know Johnny as a man of business and found out what he was really like. How did you manage with your sons?

LORD SUMMERHAYS. Well, I really hadnt time to be a father: thats the plain truth of the matter. Their poor dear mother did the usual thing while they were with us. Then of course Eton, Oxford, the usual routine of their class. I saw very little of them, and thought very little about them: how could I? with a whole province on my hands. They and I are — acquaintances. Not, perhaps, quite ordinary acquaintances: theres a sort of — er — I should almost call it a sort of remorse about the way we shake hands (when we do shake hands) which means, I suppose, that we're sorry we dont care more for one another; and I'm afraid we dont meet oftener than we can help. We put each other too much out of countenance. It's really a very difficult relation. To my mind not altogether a natural one.

TARLETON (*impressed, as usual*). Thats an idea, certainly. I dont think anybody has ever written about that.

LORD SUMMERHAYS. Bentley is the only one who was really my son in any serious sense. He was completely spoilt. When he was sent to a preparatory school he simply yelled until he was sent home. Eton was out of the question; but we managed to tutor him into Oxford. No use: he was sent down. By that time my work was over; and I saw a good deal of him. But I could do nothing with him — except look on. I should have thought your case was quite different. You keep up the middle-class tradition: the day school and the business training instead of the university. I believe in the day school part of it. At all events, you know your own children.

TARLETON. Do we? I'm not so sure of it. Fact is, my dear Summerhays, once childhood is over, once the little animal has got past the stage at which it acquires what you might call a sense of decency, it's all up with the relation between parent and child. You cant get over the fearful shyness of it.

LORD SUMMERHAYS. Shyness?

TARLETON. Yes, shyness. Read Dickens.

LORD SUMMERHAYS (*surprised*). Dickens!! Of all authors, Charles Dickens! Are you serious?

TARLETON. I dont mean his books. Read his letters to his family. Read any man's letters to his children. Theyre not human. Theyre not about himself or themselves. Theyre about hotels, scenery, about the weather, about getting wet and losing the train and what he saw on the road and all that. Not a word about himself. Forced. Shy. Duty letters. All fit to be published: that says everything. I tell you theres a wall ten feet thick and ten miles high between parent and child. I know what I'm talking about. Ive girls in my employment: girls and young men. I had ideas on the subject. I used to go to the parents and tell them not to let their children go out into the world without instruction in the dangers and temptations they were going to be thrown into. What did every one of the mothers say to me? "Oh, sir, how could I speak of such things to my own daughter?" The men said I was quite right; but they didnt do it, any more than I'd been able to do it myself to Johnny. I had to leave books in his way; and I felt just awful when I did it. Believe me, Summerhays, the relation between the young and the old should be an innocent relation. It should be something they could talk about. Well, the relation between parent and child may be an affectionate relation. But it can never be an innocent relation. Youd die rather than allude to it. Depend on it, in a thousand years itll be considered bad form to know who your father and mother are. Embarrassing. Better hand Bentley over to me. I can look him in the face and talk to him as man to man. You can have Johnny.

LORD SUMMERHAYS. Thank you. Ive lived so long in a country where a man may have fifty sons, who are no more to him than a regiment of soldiers, that I'm afraid Ive lost the English feeling about it.

TARLETON (*restless again*). You mean Jinghiskahn. Ah yes. Good thing the empire. Educates us. Opens our minds. Knocks the Bible out of us. And civilizes the other chaps.

LORD SUMMERHAYS. Yes: it civilizes *them*. And it uncivilizes us. Their gain. Our loss, Tarleton, believe me, our loss.

TARLETON. Well, why not? Averages out the human race. Makes the nigger half an Englishman. Makes the Englishman half a nigger.

LORD SUMMERHAYS. Speaking as the unfortunate Englishman in question, I dont like the process. If I had my life to live over again, I'd stay at home and supercivilize myself.

TARLETON. Nonsense! dont be selfish. Think how youve improved the other chaps. Look at the Spanish empire! Bad job for Spain, but splendid for South America. Look at what the Romans did for Britain! They burst up and had to clear out; but think of all they taught us! They were the making of us: I believe there was a Roman camp on Hindhead: I'll shew it to you tomorrow. Thats the good side of Imperialism: it's unselfish. I despise the Little Englanders: theyre always thinking about England. Smallminded. I'm for the Parliament of man, the federation of the world. Read Tennyson. (*He settles down again.*) Then theres the great food question.

LORD SUMMERHAYS (*apprehensively*). Need we go into that this afternoon?

TARLETON. No; but I wish youd tell the Chickabiddy that the Jinghiskahns eat no end of toasted cheese, and that it's the secret of their amazing health and long life!

LORD SUMMERHAYS. Unfortunately they are neither healthy nor long lived. And they dont eat toasted cheese.

TARLETON. There you are! They would be if they ate it. Anyhow, say what you like, provided the moral is a Welsh rabbit for my supper.

LORD SUMMERHAYS. British morality in a nutshell!

TARLETON. (*hugely amused*). Yes. Ha ha! Awful hypocrites, aint we? (*They are interrupted by excited cries from the grounds.*)

HYPATIA. Papa! Mamma! Come out as fast as you can. Quick. Quick.
BENTLEY. Hello, governor! Come out. An aeroplane. Look, look.

TARLETON (*starting up*). Aeroplane! Did he say an aeroplane?

LORD SUMMERHAYS. Aeroplane!

(*A shadow falls on the pavilion; and some of the glass at the top is shattered and falls on the floor.* TARLETON *and* LORD SUMMERHAYS *rush out through the pavilion into the garden.*)

HYPATIA. Take care. Take care of the chimney.
BENTLEY. Come this side: it's coming right where youre standing.
TARLETON. Hallo! where the devil are you coming? you'll have my roof off.
LORD SUMMERHAYS. He's lost control.

MRS TARLETON. Look, look, Hypatia. There are two people in it.

BENTLEY. Theyve cleared it. Well steered!

TARLETON. Yes; but theyre coming slam into the greenhouse.
LORD SUMMERHAYS. Look out for the glass.
MRS TARLETON. Theyll break all the glass. Theyll spoil all the grapes.
BENTLEY. Mind where youre coming. He'll save it. No: theyre down.

(*An appalling crash of breaking glass is heard. Everybody shrieks.*)

MRS TARLETON. Oh, are they killed? John: are they killed?
LORD SUMMERHAYS. Are you hurt? Is anything broken? Can you stand?
HYPATIA. Oh, you must be hurt. Are you sure? Shall I get you some water? Or some wine?
TARLETON. Are you all right? Sure you wont have some brandy just to take off the shock.

THE AVIATOR. No, thank you. Quite right. Not a scratch. I assure you I'm all right.

BENTLEY. What luck! And what a smash! You *are* a lucky chap, I can tell you.

(*The* AVIATOR *and* TARLETON *come in through the pavilion, followed by* LORD SUMMERHAYS *and* BENTLEY, *the* AVIATOR *on* TARLETON'*s right.* BENTLEY *passes the* AVIATOR *and turns to have an admiring look at him.* LORD SUMMERHAYS *overtakes* TARLETON *less pointedly on the opposite side with the same object.*)

THE AVIATOR. I'm really very sorry. I'm afraid Ive knocked your vinery into a cocked hat. (*Effusively.*) You dont mind, do you?

TARLETON. Not a bit. Come in and have some tea. Stay to dinner. Stay over the week-end. All my life Ive wanted to fly.

THE AVIATOR (*taking off his goggles*). Youre really more than kind.

BENTLEY. Why, it's Joey Percival.

PERCIVAL. Hallo, Ben! That you?

TARLETON. What! The man with three fathers!

PERCIVAL. Oh! has Ben been talking about me?

TARLETON. Consider yourself as one of the family — if you will do me the honor. And your friend too. Wheres your friend?

PERCIVAL. Oh, by the way! before he comes in: let me explain. I dont know him.

TARLETON. Eh?

PERCIVAL. Havnt even looked at him. I'm trying to make a club record with a passenger. The club supplied the passenger. He just got in; and Ive been too busy handling the aeroplane to look at him. I havnt said a word to him; and I cant answer for him socially; but he's an ideal passenger for a flyer. He saved me from a smash.

LORD SUMMERHAYS. I saw it. It was extraordinary. When you were thrown out he held on to the top bar with one hand. You came past him in the air, going straight for the glass. He caught you and turned you off into the flower bed, and then lighted beside you like a bird.

PERCIVAL. How he kept his head I cant imagine. Frankly, *I* didnt.

(*The* PASSENGER, *also begoggled, comes in through the pavilion with* JOHNNY *and the two ladies. The* PASSENGER *comes between* PERCIVAL *and* TARLETON, MRS TARLETON *between* LORD SUMMERHAYS *and her hus-*

band, HYPATIA *between* PERCIVAL *and* BENTLEY, *and* JOHNNY *to* BENTLEY'S *right.*)

TARLETON. Just discussing your prowess, my dear sir. Magnificent. Youll stay to dinner. Youll stay the night. Stay over the week. The Chickabiddy will be delighted.

MRS TARLETON. Wont you take off your goggles and have some tea?

(*The* PASSENGER *begins to remove the goggles.*)

TARLETON. Do. Have a wash. Johnny: take the gentleman to your room: I'll look after Mr Percival. They must —

(*By this time the* PASSENGER *has got the goggles off, and stands revealed as a remarkably good-looking woman.*)

MRS TARLETON.	Well I never ! ! !	(*All together.*)
BENTLEY.	(*in a whisper*) Oh, I say!	
JOHNNY.	By George!	
LORD SUMMERHAYS.	A lady!	
HYPATIA.	A woman!	
TARLETON.	(*to* PERCIVAL) You never told me —	
PERCIVAL.	I hadnt the least idea —	

(*An embarrassed pause.*)

PERCIVAL. I assure you if I'd had the faintest notion that my passenger was a lady I shouldnt have left you to shift for yourself in that selfish way.

LORD SUMMERHAYS. The lady seems to have shifted for both very effectually, sir.

PERCIVAL. Saved my life. I admit it most gratefully.

TARLETON. I must apologize, madam, for having offered you the civilities appropriate to the opposite sex. And yet, why opposite? We are all human: males and females of the same species. When the dress is the same the distinction vanishes. I'm proud to receive in my house a lady of evident refinement and distinction. Allow me to introduce myself: Tarleton: John Tarleton (*seeing conjecture in the* PASSENGER'S *eye*) — yes, yes: Tarleton's Underwear. My wife, Mrs Tarleton: youll excuse me for having in what I had taken to be a confidence between man and man alluded to her as the Chickabiddy. My daughter Hypatia, who has always wanted some adventure to drop out of the sky, and is now, I hope, satisfied at last. Lord Summerhays: a man known wherever the British flag waves. His son Bentley, engaged to Hypatia. Mr Joseph Percival, the promising son of three highly intellectual fathers.

HYPATIA (*startled*). Bentley's friend?

(BENTLEY *nods.*)

TARLETON (*continuing, to the* PASSENGER). May I now ask to be allowed the pleasure of knowing your name?

THE PASSENGER. My name is Lina Szczepanowska (*pronouncing it Sh-Chepanovska*).

PERCIVAL. Sh — I beg your pardon?

LINA. Szczepanowska.

PERCIVAL (*dubiously*). Thank you.

TARLETON (*very politely*). Would you mind saying it again?

LINA. Say fish.

TARLETON. Fish.

LINA. Say church.

TARLETON. Church.

LINA. Say fish church.

TARLETON (*remonstrating*). But it's not good sense.

LINA (*inexorable*). Say fish church.

TARLETON. Fish church.

LINA. Again.

TARLETON. No, but — (*resigning himself*) fish church.

LINA. Now say Szczepanowska.

TARLETON. Szczepanowska. Got it, by Gad.

(*A sibilant whispering becomes audible: they are all saying Sh-ch to themselves.*)

Szczepanowska! Not an English name, is it?

LINA. Polish. I'm a Pole.

TARLETON (*dithyrambically*). Ah yes. What other nation, madame, could have produced your magical personality? Your countrywomen have always appealed to our imagination. Women of Destiny! beautiful! musical! passionate! tragic! You will be at home here: my own temperament is pre-eminently Polish. Wont you sit down?

(*The group breaks up.* JOHNNY *and* BENTLEY *hurry to the pavilion and fetch the two wicker chairs.* JOHNNY *gives his to* LINA. HYPATIA *and* PERCIVAL *take the chairs at the worktable.* LORD SUMMERHAYS *gives the chair at the vestibule end of the writing table to* MRS TARLETON; *and* BENTLEY *replaces it with a wicker chair, which* LORD SUMMERHAYS *takes.* JOHNNY *remains standing behind the worktable,* BENTLEY *behind his father.*)

MRS TARLETON (*to* LINA). Have some tea now, wont you?

LINA. I never drink tea.

TARLETON (*sitting down at the end of the writing table nearest* LINA). Bad thing to aeroplane on, I should imagine. Too jumpy. Been up much?

LINA. Not in an aeroplane. Ive parachuted; but thats child's play.

MRS TARLETON. But arnt you very foolish to run such a dreadful risk?

LINA. You cant live without running risks.

MRS TARLETON. Oh, what a thing to say! Didnt you know you might have been killed?

LINA. That was why I went up.

HYPATIA. Of course. Cant you understand the fascination of the thing? the novelty! the daring! the sense of something happening!

LINA. Oh no. It's too tame a business for that. I went up for family reasons.

TARLETON. Eh? What? Family reasons?

MRS TARLETON. I hope it wasnt to spite your mother?

PERCIVAL (*quickly*). Or your husband?

LINA. I'm not married. And why should I want to spite my mother?

HYPATIA (*aside to* PERCIVAL). That was clever of you, Mr Percival.

PERCIVAL. What?

HYPATIA. To find out.

TARLETON. I'm in a difficulty. I cant understand a lady going up in an aeroplane for family reasons. It's rude to be curious and ask questions; but then it's inhuman to be indifferent, as if you didnt care.

LINA. I'll tell you with pleasure. For the last hundred and fifty years, not a single day has passed without some member of my family risking his life — or her life. It's a point of honor with us to keep up that tradition. Usually several of us do it; but it happens that just at this moment it is being kept up by one of my brothers only. Early this morning I got a telegram from him to say that there had been a fire, and that he could do nothing for the rest of the week. Fortunately I had an invitation from the Aerial League to see this gentleman try to break the passenger record. I appealed to the President of the League to let me save the honor of my family. He arranged it for me.

TARLETON. Oh, I must be dreaming. This is stark raving nonsense.

LINA (*quietly*). You are quite awake, sir.

JOHNNY. We cant all be dreaming the same thing, Governor.

TARLETON. Of course not, you duffer; but then I'm dreaming you as well as the lady.

MRS TARLETON. Dont be silly, John. The lady is only joking, I'm sure. (*To* LINA.) I suppose your luggage is in the aeroplane.

PERCIVAL. Luggage was out of the question. If I stay to dinner I'm afraid I cant change unless youll lend me some clothes.

MRS TARLETON. Do you mean *neither* of you?

PERCIVAL. I'm afraid so.

MRS TARLETON. Oh well, never mind: Hypatia will lend the lady a gown.

LINA. Thank you: I'm quite comfortable as I am. I am not accustomed to gowns: they hamper me and make me feel ridiculous; so if you dont mind I shall not change.

MRS TARLETON. Well, I'm beginning to think I'm doing a bit of dreaming myself.

HYPATIA (*impatiently*). Oh, it's all right, mamma. Johnny: look after Mr Percival. (*To* LINA, *rising.*) Come with me.

(LINA *follows her to the inner door. They all rise.*)

JOHNNY (*to* PERCIVAL). I'll shew you.
PERCIVAL. Thank you.

(LINA *goes out with* HYPATIA, *and* PERCIVAL *with* JOHNNY.)

MRS TARLETON. Well, this is a nice thing to happen! And look at the greenhouse! Itll cost thirty pounds to mend it. People have no right to do such things. And you invited them to dinner too! What sort of woman is that to have in our house when you know that all Hindhead will be calling on us to see that aeroplane? Bunny: come with me and help me to get all the people out of the grounds: I declare they came running as if theyd sprung up out of the earth. (*She makes for the inner door.*)

TARLETON. No: dont you trouble, Chickabiddy: I'll tackle em.

MRS TARLETON. Indeed youll do nothing of the kind: youll stay here quietly with Lord Summerhays. Youd invite them all to dinner. Come, Bunny.

(*She goes out, followed by* BENTLEY. LORD SUMMERHAYS *sits down again.*)

TARLETON. Singularly beautiful woman, Summerhays. What do you make of her? She must be a princess. Whats this family of warriors and statesmen that risk their lives every day?

LORD SUMMERHAYS. They are evidently not warriors and statesmen, or they wouldnt do that.

TARLETON. Well, then, what the devil are they?

LORD SUMMERHAYS. I think I know. The last time I saw that lady, she did something I should not have thought possible.

TARLETON. What was that?

LORD SUMMERHAYS. Well, she walked backwards along a taut wire without a balancing pole and turned a somersault in the middle. I remember that her name was Lina, and that the other name was foreign; though I dont recollect it.

TARLETON. Szcz! You couldnt have forgotten that if youd heard it.

LORD SUMMERHAYS. I didnt hear it: I only saw it on a program. But it's clear she's an acrobat. It explains how she saved Percival. And it accounts for her family pride.

TARLETON. An acrobat, eh? Good! good! good! Summerhays: that brings her within reach. Thats better than a princess. I steeled this evergreen heart of mine when I thought she was a princess. Now I shall let it be touched. She is accessible. Good.

LORD SUMMERHAYS. I hope you are not serious. Remember: you have a family. You have a position. You are not in your first youth.

TARLETON. No matter.

Theres magic in the night
When the heart is young.

My heart is young. Besides, I'm a married man, not a widower like you. A married man can do anything he likes if his wife dont mind. A widower cant be too careful. Not that I would have you think me an unprincipled man or a bad husband. I'm not. But Ive a superabundance of vitality. Read Pepys' Diary.

LORD SUMMERHAYS. The woman is your guest, Tarleton.

TARLETON. Well, is she? A woman I bring into my house is my guest. A woman you bring into my house is my guest. But a woman who drops bang down out of the sky into my greenhouse and smashes every blessed pane of glass in it must take her chance.

LORD SUMMERHAYS Still, you know that my name must not be associated with any scandal. Youll be careful, wont you?

TARLETON. Oh Lord, yes! Yes, yes, yes, yes, yes. I was only joking, of course.

(MRS TARLETON *comes back through the inner door.*)

MRS TARLETON. Well I never! John: I dont think that young woman's right in her head. Do you know what she's just asked for?

TARLETON. Champagne?

MRS TARLETON. No. She wants a Bible and six oranges.

TARLETON. What?

MRS TARLETON. A Bible and six oranges.

TARLETON. I understand the oranges: she's doing an orange cure of some sort. But what on earth does she want the Bible for?

MRS TARLETON. I'm sure I cant imagine. She cant be right in her head.

LORD SUMMERHAYS. Perhaps she wants to read it.

MRS TARLETON. But why should she? on a weekday at all events. What would you advise me to do, Lord Summerhays?

LORD SUMMERHAYS. Well, is there a Bible in the house?

TARLETON. Stacks of em. Theres the family Bible, and the Doré Bible, and the parallel revised version Bible, and the Doves Press Bible, and Johnny's Bible and Bobby's Bible and Patsy's Bible and the Chickabiddy's Bible and my Bible; and I daresay the servants could raise a few more between them. Let her have the lot.

MRS TARLETON. Dont talk like that before Lord Summerhays, John.

LORD SUMMERHAYS. It doesnt matter, Mrs Tarleton: in Jinghiskahn it was a punishable offense to expose a Bible for sale. The empire has no religion.

(LINA *comes in. She has left her cap in* HYPATIA'S *room, but has made no other change. She stops just inside the door, holding it open, evidently not intending to stay.*)

LINA. Oh, Mrs Tarleton, shall I be making myself very troublesome if I ask for a music-stand in my room as well?

TARLETON. Not at all. You can have the piano if you like. Or the gramophone. Have the gramophone?

LINA. No, thank you: no music.

MRS TARLETON (*going towards her*). Do you think it's good for you to eat so many oranges? Arnt you afraid of getting jaundice?

LINA. Not in the least. But billiard balls will do quite as well.

MRS TARLETON. But you cant eat billiard balls, child!

TARLETON. Get em, Chickabiddy. I understand. (*He imitates a juggler tossing up balls.*) Eh?

LINA (*going to him, past his wife*). Just so.

TARLETON. Billiard balls and cues? Plates, knives, and forks? Two paraffin lamps and a hatstand?

LINA. No: that is popular low-class business. In our family we touch nothing but classical work. Anybody can do lamps and hatstands. *I* can do silver bullets. That is really hard. (*She passes on to* LORD SUMMERHAYS, *and looks gravely down at him as he sits by the writing table.*)

MRS TARLETON. Well, I'm sure I dont know what youre talking about; and I only hope you know yourselves. However, you shall have what you want, of course. (*She goes out through the inner door.*)

LORD SUMMERHAYS. Will you forgive my curiosity? What is the Bible for?

LINA. To quiet my soul.

LORD SUMMERHAYS (*with a sigh*). Ah yes, yes. It no longer quiets mine, I am sorry to say.

LINA. That is because you do not know how to read it. Put it up before you on a stand; and open it at the Psalms. When you can read them and understand them, quite quietly and happily, and keep six balls in the air all the time, you are in perfect condition; and youll never make a mistake that evening. If you find you cant do that, then go and pray until you can. And be very careful *that* evening.

LORD SUMMERHAYS. Is that the usual form of test in your profession?

LINA. Nothing that we Szczepanowskis do is usual, my lord.

LORD SUMMERHAYS. Are you all so wonderful?

LINA. It is our profession to be wonderful.

LORD SUMMERHAYS. Do you never condescend to do as common people do? For instance, do you not pray as common people pray?

LINA. Common people do not pray, my lord: they only beg.

LORD SUMMERHAYS. You never ask for anything?

LINA. No.

LORD SUMMERHAYS. Then why do you pray?

LINA. To remind myself that I have a soul.

TARLETON (*walking about*). True. Fine. Good. Beautiful. All this damned materialism: what good is it to anybody? Ive got a soul, dont tell me I havnt. Cut me up and you cant find it. Cut up a steam engine and you cant find the steam. But, by George, it makes the engine go. Say what you will, Summerhays, the divine spark is a fact.

LORD SUMMERHAYS. Have I denied it?

TARLETON. Our whole civilization is a denial of it. Read Walt Whitman.

LORD SUMMERHAYS. I shall go to the billiard room and get the balls for you.

LINA. Thank you.

(LORD SUMMERHAYS *goes out through the vestibule door.*)

TARLETON (*going to her*). Listen to me. (*She turns quickly.*) What you said just now was beautiful. You touch chords. You appeal to the poetry in a man. You inspire him. Come now! Youre a woman of the world: youre independent: you must have driven lots of men crazy. You know the sort of man I am, dont you? See through me at a glance, eh?

LINA. Yes. (*She sits down quietly in the chair* LORD SUMMERHAYS *has just left.*)

TARLETON. Good. Well, do you like me? Dont misunderstand me: I'm perfectly aware that youre not going to fall in love at first sight with a ridiculous old shopkeeper. I cant help that ridiculous old shopkeeper. I have to carry him about with me whether I like it or not. I have to pay for his clothes, though I hate the cut of them: especially the waistcoat. I have to look at him in the glass while I'm shaving. I loathe him because he's a living lie. My soul's not like that: it's like yours. I want to make a fool of myself. About you. Will you let me?

LINA (*very calm*). How much will you pay?

TARLETON. Nothing. But I'll throw as many sovereigns as you like into the sea to shew you that I'm in earnest.

LINA. Are those your usual terms?

TARLETON. No. I never made that bid before.

LINA (*producing a dainty little book and preparing to write in it*). What did you say your name was?

TARLETON. John Tarleton. The great John Tarleton of Tarleton's Underwear.

LINA (*writing*). T-a-r-l-e-t-o-n. Er—? (*She looks up at him inquiringly.*)

TARLETON (*promptly*). Fifty-eight.

LINA. Thank you. I keep a list of all my offers. I like to know what I'm considered worth.

TARLETON. Let me look.

LINA (*offering the book to him*). It's in Polish.

TARLETON. Thats no good. Is mine the lowest offer?

LINA. No: the highest.

TARLETON. What do most of them come to? Diamonds? Motor cars? Furs? Villa at Monte Carlo?

LINA. Oh yes: all that. And sometimes the devotion of a lifetime.

TARLETON. Fancy that! A young man offering a woman his old age as a temptation!

LINA. By the way, you did not say how long.

TARLETON. Until you get tired of me.

LINA. Or until you get tired of me?

TARLETON. I never get tired. I never go on long enough for that. But when it becomes so grand, so inspiring that I feel that everything must be an anti-climax after that, then I run away.

LINA. Does she let you go without a struggle?

TARLETON. Yes. Glad to get rid of me. When love takes a man as it takes me — when it makes him great — it frightens a woman.

LINA. The lady here is your wife, isnt she? Dont you care for her?

TARLETON. Yes. And mind! she comes first always. I reserve her dignity even when I sacrifice my own. Youll respect that point of honor, wont you?

LINA. Only a point of honor?

TARLETON (*impulsively*). No, by God! a point of affection as well.

LINA (*smiling, pleased with him*). Shake hands, old pal. (*She rises and offers him her hand frankly.*)

TARLETON (*giving his hand rather dolefully*). Thanks. That means no, doesnt it?

LINA. It means something that will last longer than yes. I like you. I admit you to my friendship. What a pity you were not trained when you were young! Youd be young still.

TARLETON. I suppose, to an athlete like you, I'm pretty awful, eh?

LINA. Shocking.

TARLETON. Too much crumb. Wrinkles. Yellow patches that wont come off. Short wind. I know. I'm ashamed of myself. I could do nothing on the high rope.

LINA. Oh yes: I could put you in a wheelbarrow and run you along, two hundred feet up.

TARLETON (*shuddering*). Ugh! Well, I'd do even that for you. Read *The Master Builder.*

LINA. Have you learnt everything from books?

TARLETON. Well, have you learnt everything from the flying trapeze?

LINA. On the flying trapeze there is often another woman; and her life is in your hands every night and your life in hers.

TARLETON. Lina: I'm going to make a fool of myself. I'm going to cry. (*He crumples into the nearest chair.*)

LINA. Pray instead: dont cry. Why should you cry? Youre not the first Ive said no to.

TARLETON. If you had said yes, should I have been the first then?

LINA. What right have you to ask? Have I asked am *I* the first?

TARLETON. Youre right: a vulgar question. To a man like me, everybody is the first. Life renews itself.

LINA. The youngest child is the sweetest.

TARLETON. Dont probe too deep, Lina. It hurts.

LINA. You must get out of the habit of thinking that these things matter so much. It's linendraperish.

TARLETON. Youre quite right. Ive often said so. All the same, it *does* matter; for I want to cry. (*He buries his face in his arms on the work-table and sobs.*)

LINA (*going to him*). O la la! (*She slaps him vigorously, but not unkindly, on the shoulder.*) Courage, old pal, courage! Have you a gymnasium here?

TARLETON. Theres a trapeze and bars and things in the billiard room.

LINA. Come. You need a few exercises. I'll teach you how to stop crying. (*She takes his arm and leads him off into the vestibule.*)

(*A young man, cheaply dressed and strange in manner, appears in the garden; steals to the pavilion door; and looks in. Seeing that there is nobody, he enters cautiously until he has come far enough to see into the hatstand corner. He draws a revolver, and examines it, apparently to make sure that it is loaded. Then his attention is caught by the Turkish bath. He looks down the lunette, and opens the panels.*)

HYPATIA (*calling in the garden*). Mr Percival! Mr Percival! Where are you?

(*The young man makes for the door, but sees* PERCIVAL *coming. He turns and bolts into the Turkish bath, which he closes upon himself just in time to escape being caught by* PERCIVAL, *who runs in through the pavilion, bareheaded. He also, it appears, is in search of a hiding-place; for he stops and turns between the two tables to take a survey of the room; then runs into the corner between the end of the sideboard and the wall.* HYPATIA, *excited, mischievous, her eyes glowing, runs in, precisely on his trail; turns at the same spot; and discovers him just as he makes a dash for the pavilion door. She flies back and intercepts him.*)

HYPATIA. Aha! Arnt you glad Ive caught you?

PERCIVAL (*ill-humoredly turning away from her and coming towards the writing table*). No I'm not. Confound it, what sort of girl are you? What sort of house is this? Must I throw all good manners to the winds?

HYPATIA (*following him*). Do, do, do, do, do. This is the house of a respectable shopkeeper, enormously rich. This is the respectable shopkeeper's daughter, tired of good manners. (*Slipping her left hand into his right.*) Come, handsome young man, and play with the respectable shopkeeper's daughter.

PERCIVAL (*withdrawing quickly from her touch*). No, no: dont you know you mustnt go on like this with a perfect stranger?

HYPATIA. Dropped down from the sky. Dont you know that you must always go on like this when you get the chance? You must come to the top of the hill and chase me through the bracken. You may kiss me if you catch me.

PERCIVAL. I shall do nothing of the sort.

HYPATIA. Yes, you will: you cant help yourself. Come along. (*She seizes his sleeve.*) Fool, fool: come along. Dont you want to?

PERCIVAL. No: certainly not. I should never be forgiven if I did it.

HYPATIA. Youll never forgive yourself if you dont.

PERCIVAL. Nonsense. Youre engaged to Ben. Ben's my friend. What do you take me for?

HYPATIA. Ben's old. Ben was born old. Theyre all old here, except you and me and the man-woman or woman-man or whatever you call her that came with you. They never do anything: they only discuss whether what other people do is right. Come and give them something to discuss.

PERCIVAL. I will do nothing incorrect.

HYPATIA. Oh, dont be afraid, little boy: youll get nothing but a kiss; and I'll fight like the devil to keep you from getting that. But we must play on the hill and race through the heather.

PERCIVAL. Why?

HYPATIA. Because we want to, handsome young man.

PERCIVAL. But if everybody went on in this way —

HYPATIA. How happy! oh how happy the world would be!

PERCIVAL. But the consequences may be serious.

HYPATIA. Nothing is worth doing unless the consequences may be serious. My father says so; and I'm my father's daughter.

PERCIVAL. I'm the son of three fathers. I mistrust these wild impulses.

HYPATIA. Take care. Youre letting the moment slip. I feel the first chill of the wave of prudence. Save me.

PERCIVAL. Really, Miss Tarleton! (*She strikes him across the face.*) Damn you! (*Recovering himself, horrified at his lapse.*) I beg your pardon; but since weve both forgotten ourselves, youll please allow me to leave the house. (*He turns towards the inner door, having left his cap in the bedroom.*)

HYPATIA (*standing in his way*). Are you ashamed of having said "Damn you" to me?

PERCIVAL. I had no right to say it. I'm very much ashamed of it. I have already begged your pardon.

HYPATIA. And youre not ashamed of having said "Really, Miss Tarleton!"?

PERCIVAL. Why should I?

HYPATIA. O man, man! mean, stupid, cowardly, selfish, masculine male man! You ought to have been a governess. I was expelled from school for saying that the very next person that said "Really, Miss Tarleton!" to me, I would strike across the face. You were the next.

PERCIVAL. I had no intention of being offensive. Surely there is nothing that can wound any lady in — (*he hesitates, not quite convinced*). At least — er — I really didnt mean to be disagreeable.

HYPATIA. Liar.

PERCIVAL. Of course if youre going to insult me, I am quite helpless. Youre a woman: you can say what you like.

HYPATIA. And you can only say what you dare. Poor wretch: it isnt much. (*He bites his lip, and sits down, very much annoyed.*) Really, Mr Percival! You sit down in the presence of a lady and leave her standing.

(*He rises hastily.*) Ha, ha! Really, Mr Percival! Oh really, really, really really, really, Mr Percival! How do you like it? Wouldnt you rather I damned you?

PERCIVAL. Miss Tarleton —

HYPATIA (*caressingly*). Hypatia, Joey. Patsy, if you like.

PERCIVAL. Look here: this is no good. You want to do what you like.

HYPATIA. Dont you?

PERCIVAL. No. Ive been too well brought up. Ive argued all through this thing; and I tell you I'm not prepared to cast off the social bond. It's like a corset: it's a support to the figure even if it does squeeze and deform a bit. I want to be free.

HYPATIA. Well, I'm tempting you to be free.

PERCIVAL. Not at all. Freedom, my good girl, means being able to count on how other people will behave. If every man who dislikes me is to throw a handful of mud in my face, and every woman who likes me is to behave like Potiphar's wife, then I shall be a slave: the slave of uncertainty: the slave of fear: the worst of all slaveries. How would you like it if every laborer you met in the road were to make love to you? No. Give me the blessed protection of a good stiff conventionality among thoroughly well-brought up ladies and gentlemen.

HYPATIA. Another talker! Men like conventions because men made them. I didnt make them: I dont like them: I wont keep them. Now, what will you do?

PERCIVAL. Bolt. (*He runs out through the pavilion.*)

HYPATIA. I'll catch you. (*She dashes off in pursuit.*)

(*During this conversation the head of the scandalized man in the Turkish bath has repeatedly risen from the lunette, with a strong expression of moral shock. It vanishes abruptly as the two turn towards it in their flight. At the same moment* TARLETON *comes back through the vestibule door, exhausted by severe and unaccustomed exercise.*)

TARLETON (*looking after the flying figures with amazement*). Hallo, Patsy: whats up? Another aeroplane?

(*They are far too preoccupied to hear him; and he is left staring after them as they rush away through the garden. He goes to the pavilion door and looks up; but the heavens are empty. His exhaustion disables him from further inquiry. He dabs his brow with his handkerchief, and walks stiffly to the nearest convenient support, which happens to be the Turkish bath. He props himself upon it with his elbow, and covers his eyes with his hand for a moment. After a few sighing breaths, he feels a little better, and uncovers his eyes. The man's head rises from the lunette a few inches from his nose. He recoils from the bath with a violent start.*)

Oh Lord! My brain's gone. (*Calling piteously.*) Chickabiddy! (*He staggers down to the writing table.*)

THE MAN (*coming out of the bath, pistol in hand*). Another sound; and youre a dead man.

TARLETON (*braced*). Am I? Well, youre a live one: thats one comfort. I thought you were a ghost. (*He sits down, quite undisturbed by the pistol.*) Who are you; and what the devil were you doing in my new Turkish bath?

THE MAN (*with tragic intensity*). I am the son of Lucinda Titmus.

TARLETON (*the name conveying nothing to him*). Indeed? And how is she? Quite well, I hope, eh?

THE MAN. She is dead. Dead, my God! and you are alive.

TARLETON (*unimpressed by the tragedy, but sympathetic*). Oh! Lost your mother? Thats sad. I'm sorry. But we cant all have the luck to die before our mothers, and be nursed out of the world by the hands that nursed us into it.

THE MAN. Much you care, damn you!

TARLETON. Oh, dont cut up rough. Face it like a man. You see I didnt know your mother; but Ive no doubt she was an excellent woman.

THE MAN. Not know her! Do you dare to stand there by her open grave and deny that you knew her?

TARLETON (*trying to recollect*). What did you say her name was?

THE MAN. Lucinda Titmus.

TARLETON. Well, I ought to remember a rum name like that if I ever heard it. But I dont. Have you a photograph or anything?

THE MAN. Forgotten even the name of your victim!

TARLETON. Oh! she was my victim, was she?

THE MAN. She was. And you shall see her face again before you die, dead as she is. I *have* a photograph.

TARLETON. Good.

THE MAN. Ive two photographs.

TARLETON. Still better. Treasure the mother's pictures. Good boy!

THE MAN. One of them as you knew her. The other as she became when you flung her aside, and she withered into an old woman.

TARLETON. She'd have done that anyhow, my lad. We all grow old. Look at me! (*Seeing that the man is embarrassed by his pistol in fumbling for the photographs with his left hand in his breast pocket.*) Let me hold the gun for you.

THE MAN (*retreating to the worktable*). Stand back. Do you take me for a fool?

TARLETON. Well, youre a little upset, naturally. It does you credit.

THE MAN. Look here, upon this picture and on this. (*He holds out the two photographs like a hand at cards, and points to them with the pistol.*)

TARLETON. Good. Read Shakespear: he has a word for every occasion. (*He takes the photographs, one in each hand, and looks from one to the other, pleased and interested, but without any sign of recognition.*) What a pretty girl! Very pretty. I can imagine myself falling in love with her when I was your age. I wasnt a bad-looking young fellow myself in those days. (*Looking at the other.*) Curious that we should both have gone the same way.

THE MAN. You and she the same way! What do you mean?

TARLETON. Both got stout, I mean.

THE MAN. Would you have had her deny herself food?

TARLETON. No: it wouldnt have been any use. It is constitutional. No matter how little you eat you put on flesh if youre made that way. (*He resumes his study of the earlier photograph.*)

THE MAN. Is that all the feeling that rises in you at the sight of the face you once knew so well?

TARLETON (*too much absorbed in the portrait to heed him*). Funny that I cant remember! Let this be a lesson to you, young man. I could go into court tomorrow and swear I never saw that face before in my life if it wasnt for that brooch (*pointing to the photograph*). Have you got that brooch, by the way? (*The man again resorts to his breast pocket.*) You seem to carry the whole family property in that pocket.

THE MAN (*producing a brooch*). Here it is to prove my bona fides.

TARLETON (*pensively putting the photographs on the table and taking the brooch*). I bought that brooch in Cheapside from a man with a yellow wig and a cast in his left eye. Ive never set eyes on him from that day to this. And yet I remember that man; and I cant remember your mother.

THE MAN. Monster! Without conscience! without even memory! You left her to her shame—

TARLETON (*throwing the brooch on the table and rising pepperily*). Come, come, young man! none of that. Respect the romance of your mother's youth. Dont you start throwing stones at her. I dont recall her features just at this moment; but Ive no doubt she was kind to me and we were happy together. If you have a word to say against her, take yourself out of my house and say it elsewhere.

THE MAN. What sort of a joker are you? Are you trying to put me in the wrong, when you have to answer to me for a crime that would make every honest man spit at you as you passed in the street if I were to make it known?

TARLETON. You read a good deal, dont you?

THE MAN. What if I do? What has that to do with your infamy and my mother's doom?

TARLETON. There, you see! Doom! Thats not good sense; but it's literature. Now it happens that I'm a tremendous reader: always was. When I was your age I read books of that sort by the bushel: the Doom sort, you know. It's odd, isnt it, that you and I should be like one another in that respect? Can you account for it in any way?

THE MAN. No. What are you driving at?

TARLETON. Well, do you know who your father was?

THE MAN. I see what you mean now. You dare set up to be my father! Thank heaven Ive not a drop of your vile blood in my veins.

TARLETON (*sitting down again with a shrug*). Well, if you wont be civil, theres no pleasure in talking to you, is there? What do you want? Money?

THE MAN. How dare you insult me?

TARLETON. Well, what do you want?

THE MAN. Justice.

TARLETON. Youre quite sure thats all?

THE MAN. It's enough for me.

TARLETON. A modest sort of demand, isnt it? Nobody ever had it since the world began, fortunately for themselves; but you must have it, must you? Well, youve come to the wrong shop for it: youll get no justice here: we dont keep it. Human nature is what we stock.

THE MAN. Human nature! Debauchery! gluttony! selfishness! robbery of the poor! Is that what you call human nature?

TARLETON. No: thats what *you* call it. Come, my lad! Whats the matter with you? You dont look starved; and youve a decent suit of clothes.

THE MAN. Forty-two shillings.

TARLETON. They can do you a very decent suit for forty-two shillings. Have you paid for it?

THE MAN. Do you take me for a thief? And do you suppose I can get credit like you?

TARLETON. Then you were able to lay your hand on forty-two shillings. Judging from your conversational style, I should think you must spend at least a shilling a week on romantic literature.

THE MAN. Where would I get a shilling a week to spend on books when I can hardly keep myself decent? I get books at the Free Library.

TARLETON (*springing to his feet*). What!!!

THE MAN (*recoiling before his vehemence*). The Free Library. Theres no harm in that.

TARLETON. Ingrate! I supply you with free books; and the use you make of them is to persuade yourself that it's a fine thing to shoot me. (*He throws himself doggedly back into his chair.*) I'll never give another penny to a Free Library.

THE MAN. Youll never give another penny to anything. This is the end: for you and me.

TARLETON. Pooh! Come, come, man! talk business. Whats wrong? Are you out of employment?

THE MAN. No. This is my Saturday afternoon. Dont flatter yourself that I'm a loafer or a criminal. I'm a cashier; and I defy you to say that my cash has ever been a farthing wrong. Ive a right to call you to account because my hands are clean.

TARLETON. Well, call away. What have I to account for? Had you a hard time with your mother? Why didnt she ask me for money?

THE MAN. She'd have died first. Besides, who wanted your money? Do you suppose we lived in the gutter? My father maynt have been in as large a way as you; but he was better connected; and his shop was as respectable as yours.

TARLETON. I suppose your mother brought him a little capital.

THE MAN. I don't know. Whats that got to do with you?

TARLETON. Well, you say she and I knew one another and parted. She must have had something off me then, you know. One doesnt get out of these things for nothing. Hang it, young man: do you suppose Ive no heart? Of course she had her due; and she found a husband with it, and set him up in business with it, and brought you up respectably; so what the devil have you to complain of?

THE MAN. Are women to be ruined with impunity?

TARLETON. I havnt ruined any woman that I'm aware of. Ive been the making of you and your mother.

THE MAN. Oh, I'm a fool to listen to you and argue with you. I came here to kill you and then kill myself.

TARLETON. Begin with yourself, if you dont mind. Ive a good deal of business to do still before I die. Havnt you?

THE MAN. No. Thats just it: Ive no business to do. Do you know what my life is? I spend my days from nine to six — nine hours of daylight and fresh air — in a stuffy little den counting another man's money. Ive an intellect: a mind and a brain and a soul; and the use he makes of them is to fix them on his tuppences and his eighteenpences and his two pound seventeen and tenpences and see how much they come to at the end of the day and take care that no one steals them. I enter and enter, and add and add, and take money and give change, and fill cheques and stamp receipts; and not a penny of that money is my own: not one of those transactions has the smallest interest for me or anyone else in the world but him; and even he couldnt stand it if he had to do it all himself. And I'm envied: aye, envied for the variety and liveliness of my job, by the poor devil of a bookkeeper that has to copy all my entries over again. Fifty thousand entries a year that poor wretch makes; and not ten out of the fifty thousand ever has to be referred to again; and when all the figures are counted up and the balance sheet made out, the boss isnt a penny the richer than he'd be if bookkeeping had never been invented. Of all the damnable waste of human life that ever was invented, clerking is the very worst.

TARLETON. Why not join the territorials?

THE MAN. Because the boss wont let me. He hasnt the sense to see that it would pay him to get some cheap soldiering out of me. How can a man tied to a desk from nine to six be anything — be even a man, let alone a soldier? But I'll teach him and you a lesson. Ive had enough of living a dog's life and despising myself for it. Ive had enough of being talked down to by hogs like you, and wearing my life out for a salary that wouldnt keep you in cigars. Youll never believe that a clerk's a man until one of us makes an example of one of you.

TARLETON. Despotism tempered by assassination, eh?

THE MAN. Yes. Thats what they do in Russia. Well, a business office is Russia as far as the clerks are concerned. So dont you take it so coolly. You think I'm not going to do it; but I am.

TARLETON (*rising and facing him*). Come, now, as man to man! It's not my fault that youre poorer than I am; and it's not your fault that I'm richer than you. And if you could undo all that passed between me and your mother, you wouldnt undo it; and neither would she. But youre sick of your slavery; and you want to be the hero of a romance and to get into the papers. Eh? A son revenges his mother's shame. Villain weltering in his gore. Mother: look down from heaven and receive your unhappy son's last sigh.

THE MAN. Oh, rot! do you think I read novelettes? And do you suppose I believe such superstitions as heaven? I go to church because the boss told me I'd get the sack if I didnt. Free England! Ha!

(LINA *appears at the pavilion door, and comes swiftly and noiselessly forward on seeing the man with a pistol in his hand.*)

TARLETON. Youre afraid of getting the sack; but youre not afraid to shoot yourself.

THE MAN. Damn you! youre trying to keep me talking until somebody comes. (*He raises the pistol desperately, but not very resolutely.*)

LINA (*at his right elbow*). Somebody has come.

THE MAN (*turning on her*). Stand off. I'll shoot you if you lay a hand on me. I will, by God.

LINA. You cant cover me with that pistol. Try.

(*He tries, presenting the pistol at her face. She moves round him in the opposite direction to the hands of a clock with a light dancing step. He finds it impossible to cover her with the pistol: she is always too far to his left.* TARLETON, *behind him, grips his wrist and drags his arm straight up, so that the pistol points to the ceiling. As he tries to turn on his assailant,* LINA *grips his other wrist.*)

LINA. Please stop. I cant bear to twist anyone's wrist; but I must if you dont let the pistol go.

THE MAN (*letting* TARLETON *take it from him*). All right: I'm done. Couldnt even do that job decently. Thats a clerk all over. Very well: send for your damned police and make an end of it. I'm accustomed to prison from nine to six: I daresay I can stand from six to nine as well.

TARLETON. Dont swear. Thats a lady. (*He throws the pistol on the writing table.*)

THE MAN (*looking at* LINA *in amazement*). Beaten by a female! It needed only this. (*He collapses in the chair near the worktable, and hides his face. They cannot help pitying him.*)

LINA. Old pal: dont call the police. Lend him a bicycle and let him get away.

THE MAN. I cant ride a bicycle. I never could afford one. I'm not even that much good.

TARLETON. If I gave you a hundred pound note now to go and have a good spree with, I wonder would you know how to set about it. Do you ever take a holiday?

THE MAN. Take! I *got* four days last August.

TARLETON. What did you do?

THE MAN. I did a cheap trip to Folkestone. I spent sevenpence on dropping pennies into silly automatic machines and peepshows of rowdy girls having a jolly time. I spent a penny on the lift and fourpence on refreshments. That cleaned me out. The rest of the time I was so miserable that I was glad to get back to the office. Now you know.

LINA. Come to the gymnasium: I'll teach you how to make a man of yourself.

(*The man is about to rise irresolutely, from the mere habit of doing what he is told, when* TARLETON *stops him.*)

TARLETON. Young man: dont. Youve tried to shoot me; but I'm not vindictive. I draw the line at putting a man on the rack. If you want every joint in your body stretched until it's an agony to live — until you have an unnatural feeling that all your muscles are singing and laughing with pain — then go to the gymnasium with that lady. But youll be more comfortable in jail.

LINA (*greatly amused*). Was that why you went away, old pal? Was that the telegram you said you had forgotten to send?

(MRS TARLETON *comes in hastily through the inner door.*)

MRS TARLETON (*on the steps*). Is anything the matter, John? Nurse says she heard you calling me a quarter of an hour ago; and that your voice sounded as if you were ill. (*She comes between* TARLETON *and the man.*) Is anything the matter?

TARLETON. This is the son of an old friend of mine. Mr — er — Mr Gunner. (*To the man, who rises awkwardly.*) My wife.

MRS TARLETON. Good evening to you.

GUNNER. Er — (*He is too nervous to speak, and makes a shambling bow.*)

(BENTLEY *looks in at the pavilion door, very peevish, and too preoccupied with his own affairs to pay any attention to those of the company.*)

BENTLEY. I say: has anybody seen Hypatia? She promised to come out with me; and I cant find her anywhere. And wheres Joey?

GUNNER (*suddenly breaking out aggressively, being incapable of any middle way between submissiveness and violence*). *I* can tell you where Hypatia is. I can tell you where Joey is. And I say it's a scandal and an infamy. If people only knew what goes on in this so-called respectable house it would be put a stop to. These are the morals of our pious capitalist class! This is your rotten bourgeoisie! This —

MRS TARLETON. Dont you dare use such language in company. I wont allow it.

TARLETON. All right, Chickabiddy: it's not bad language: it's only Socialism.

MRS TARLETON. Well, I wont have any Socialism in my house.

TARLETON (*to* GUNNER). You hear what Mrs Tarleton says. Well, in this house everybody does what she says or out they go.

GUNNER. Do you suppose I want to stay? Do you think I would breathe this polluted atmosphere a moment longer than I could help?

BENTLEY (*running forward between* LINA *and* GUNNER). But what did you mean by what you said about Miss Tarleton and Mr Percival, you beastly rotter, you?

GUNNER (*to* TARLETON). Oh! is Hypatia your daughter? And Joey is *Mister* Percival, is he? One of your set, I suppose. One of the smart set! One of the bridge-playing, eighty-horse-power, week-ender set! One of the johnnies I slave for! Well, Joey has more decency than your daughter, anyhow. The women are the worst. I never believed it till I saw it with my own eyes. Well, it wont last for ever. The writing is on the wall. Rome fell. Babylon fell. Hindhead's turn will come.

MRS TARLETON (*naively looking at the wall for the writing*). Whatever are you talking about, young man?

GUNNER. I know what I'm talking about. I went into that Turkish bath a boy: I came out a man.

MRS TARLETON. Good gracious! he's mad. (*To* LINA.) Did John make him take a Turkish bath?

LINA. No. He doesnt need Turkish baths: he needs to put on a little flesh. I dont understand what it's all about. I found him trying to shoot Mr Tarleton.

MRS TARLETON (*with a scream*). Oh! and John encouraging him, I'll be bound! Bunny: you go for the police. (*To* GUNNER.) I'll teach you to come into my house and shoot my husband.

GUNNER. Teach away. I never asked to be let off. I'm ashamed to be free instead of taking my part with the rest. Women — beautiful women of noble birth — are going to prison for their opinions. Girl students in Russia go to the gallows; let themselves be cut in pieces with the knout, or driven through the frozen snows of Siberia, sooner than stand looking on tamely at the world being made a hell for the toiling millions. If you were not all skunks and cowards youd be suffering with them instead of battening here on the plunder of the poor.

MRS TARLETON (*much vexed*). Oh, did you ever hear such silly nonsense? Bunny: go and tell the gardener to send over one of his men to Grayshott for the police.

GUNNER. I'll go with him. I intend to give myself up. I'm going to expose what Ive seen here, no matter what the consequences may be to my miserable self.

TARLETON. Stop. You stay where you are, Ben. Chickabiddy: youve never had the police in. If you had, youd not be in a hurry to have them in again. Now, young man: cut the cackle; and tell us, as short as you can, what did you see?

GUNNER. I cant tell you in the presence of ladies.

MRS TARLETON. Oh, you *are* tiresome. As if it mattered to anyone what you saw. Me! A married woman that might be your mother. (*To* LINA.) And I'm sure *youre* not particular, if youll excuse my saying so.

TARLETON. Out with it. What did you see?

GUNNER. I saw your daughter with my own eyes — oh well, never mind what I saw.

BENTLEY (*almost crying with anxiety*). You beastly rotter. I'll get Joey to give you such a hiding —

TARLETON. You cant leave it at that, you know. What did you see my daughter doing?

GUNNER. After all, why shouldnt she do it? The Russian students do it. Women should be as free as men. I'm a fool. I'm so full of your bourgeois morality that I let myself be shocked by the application of my own revolutionary principles. If she likes the man why shouldnt she tell him so?

MRS TARLETON. I do wonder at you, John, letting him talk like this before everybody. (*Turning rather tartly to* LINA.) Would you mind going away to the drawing room just for a few minutes, Miss Chipenoska. This is a private family matter, if you dont mind.

LINA. I should have gone before, Mrs Tarleton, if there had been anyone to protect Mr Tarleton and the young gentleman. (*She goes out through the inner door.*)

GUNNER. There you are! It's all of a piece here. The men effeminate, the women unsexed —

TARLETON. Dont begin again, old chap. Keep it for Trafalgar Square.

HYPATIA'S VOICE OUTSIDE. No, no.

(*She breaks off in a stifled half laugh, half scream, and is seen darting across the garden with* PERCIVAL *in hot pursuit. Immediately afterwards she appears again, and runs into the pavilion. Finding it full of people, including a stranger, she stops; but* PERCIVAL, *flushed and reckless, rushes in and seizes her before he, too, realizes that they are not alone. He releases her in confusion. Dead silence. They are all afraid to look at one another except* MRS TARLETON, *who stares sternly at* HYPATIA. HYPATIA *is the first to recover her presence of mind.*)

HYPATIA. Excuse me rushing in like this. Mr Percival has been chasing me down the hill.

GUNNER. Who chased him up it? Dont be ashamed. Be fearless. Be truthful.

TARLETON. Gunner: will you go to Paris for a fortnight? I'll pay your expenses.

HYPATIA. What do you mean?

GUNNER. There was a silent witness in the Turkish bath.

TARLETON. I found him hiding there. Whatever went on here, he saw and heard. Thats what he means.

PERCIVAL (*sternly approaching* GUNNER, *and speaking with deep but contained indignation*). Am I to understand you as daring to put forward the monstrous and blackguardly lie that this lady behaved improperly in my presence?

GUNNER (*turning white*). You know what I saw and heard.

(HYPATIA, *with a gleam of triumph in her eyes, slips noiselessly into the swing chair, and watches* PERCIVAL *and* GUNNER, *swinging slightly, but otherwise motionless.*)

PERCIVAL. I hope it is not necessary for me to assure you all that there is not one word of truth — not one grain of substance — in this rascally calumny, which no man with a spark of decent feeling would have uttered even if he had been ignorant enough to believe it. Miss Tarleton's conduct, since I have had the honor of knowing her, has been, I need hardly say, in every respect beyond reproach. (*To* GUNNER.) As for you, sir, youll have the goodness to come out with me immediately. I have some business with you which cant be settled in Mrs Tarleton's presence or in her house.

GUNNER (*painfully frightened*). Why should I go out with you?

PERCIVAL. Because I intend that you shall.

GUNNER. I wont be bullied by you.

(PERCIVAL *makes a threatening step towards him.*)

Police!

(*He tries to bolt; but* PERCIVAL *seizes him.*)

Leave me go, will you? What right have you to lay hands on me?

TARLETON. Let him run for it, Mr Percival. He's very poor company. We shall be well rid of him. Let him go.

PERCIVAL. Not until he has taken back and made the fullest apology for the abominable lie he has told. He shall do that, or he shall defend himself as best he can against the most thorough thrashing I'm capable of giving him. (*Releasing* GUNNER, *but facing him ominously.*) Take your choice. Which is it to be?

GUNNER. Give me a fair chance. Go and stick at a desk from nine to six for a month, and let me have your grub and your sport and your lessons in boxing, and I'll fight you fast enough. You know I'm no good or you darent bully me like this.

PERCIVAL. You should have thought of that before you attacked a lady with a dastardly slander. I'm waiting for your decision. I'm rather in a hurry, please.

GUNNER. I never said anything against the lady.

MRS TARLETON. } Oh, listen to that!
BENTLEY. } What a liar!
HYPATIA. } Oh!
TARLETON. } Oh, come!

PERCIVAL. We'll have it in writing, if you dont mind. (*Pointing to the writing table.*) Sit down; and take that pen in your hand.

(GUNNER *looks irresolutely a little way round; then obeys.*)

Now write. "I," whatever your name is —

GUNNER (*after a vain attempt*). I cant. My hand's shaking too much. You see it's no use. I'm doing my best. I cant.

PERCIVAL. Mr Summerhays will write it: you can sign it.

BENTLEY (*insolently to* GUNNER). Get up.

(GUNNER *obeys; and* BENTLEY, *shouldering him aside towards* PERCIVAL, *takes his place and prepares to write.*)

PERCIVAL. Whats your name?

GUNNER. John Brown.

TARLETON. Oh come! Couldnt you make it Horace Smith? or Algernon Robinson?

GUNNER (*agitatedly*). But my name is John Brown. There are really John Browns. How can I help it if my name's a common one?

BENTLEY. Shew us a letter addressed to you.

GUNNER. How can I? I never get any letters: I'm only a clerk. I can shew you J. B. on my handkerchief. (*He takes out a not very clean one.*)

BENTLEY (*with disgust*). Oh, put it up again. Let it go at John Brown.

PERCIVAL. Where do you live?

GUNNER. 4 Chesterfield Parade, Kentish Town, N.W.

PERCIVAL (*dictating*). I, John Brown, of 4 Chesterfield Parade, Kentish Town, do hereby voluntarily confess that on the 31st May 1909 I — (*To* TARLETON.) What did he do exactly?

TARLETON (*dictating*). — I trespassed on the land of John Tarleton at Hindhead, and effected an unlawful entry into his house, where I secreted myself in a portable Turkish bath —

BENTLEY. Go slow, old man. Just a moment. "Turkish bath" — yes?

TARLETON (*continuing*). — with a pistol, with which I threatened to take the life of the said John Tarleton —

MRS TARLETON. Oh, John! You might have been killed.

TARLETON. — and was prevented from doing so only by the timely arrival of the celebrated Miss Lina Szczepanowska.

MRS TARLETON. Is she celebrated? (*Apologetically.*) I never dreamt —

BENTLEY. Look here: I'm awfully sorry; but I cant spell Szczepanowska.

PERCIVAL. I think it's S, z, c, z — Better say the Polish lady.

BENTLEY (*writing*). "the Polish lady"?

TARLETON (*to* PERCIVAL). Now it's your turn.

PERCIVAL (*dictating*). I further confess that I was guilty of uttering an abominable calumny concerning Miss Hypatia Tarleton, for which there was not a shred of foundation.

(*Impressive silence whilst* BENTLEY *writes.*)

BENTLEY. "foundation"?

PERCIVAL. I apologize most humbly to the lady and her family for my conduct — (*He waits for* BENTLEY *to write.*)

BENTLEY. "conduct"?

PERCIVAL. — and I promise Mr Tarleton not to repeat it, and to amend my life —

BENTLEY. "amend my life"?

PERCIVAL. — and to do what in me lies to prove worthy of his kindness in giving me another chance —

BENTLEY. "another chance"?

PERCIVAL. — and refraining from delivering me up to the punishment I so richly deserve.

BENTLEY. "richly deserve."

PERCIVAL (*to* HYPATIA). Does that satisfy you, Miss Tarleton?

HYPATIA. Yes: that will teach him to tell lies next time.

BENTLEY (*rising to make place for* GUNNER *and handing him the pen*). You mean it will teach him to tell the truth next time.

TARLETON. Ahem! Do you, Patsy?

PERCIVAL. Be good enough to sign.

(GUNNER *sits down helplessly and dips the pen in the ink.*)

I hope what you are signing is no mere form of words to you, and that you not only say you are sorry, but that you *are* sorry.

(LORD SUMMERHAYS *and* JOHNNY *come in through the pavilion door.*)

MRS TARLETON. Stop. Mr Percival: I think, on Hypatia's account, Lord Summerhays ought to be told about this.

(LORD SUMMERHAYS, *wondering what the matter is, comes forward between* PERCIVAL *and* LINA. JOHNNY *stops beside* HYPATIA.)

PERCIVAL. Certainly.

TARLETON (*uneasily*). Take my advice and cut it short. Get rid of him.

MRS TARLETON. Hypatia ought to have her character cleared.

TARLETON. You let well alone, Chickabiddy. Most of our characters will bear a little careful dusting; but they wont bear scouring. Patsy is jolly well out of it. What does it matter, anyhow?

PERCIVAL. Mr Tarleton: we have already said either too much or not enough. Lord Summerhays: will you be kind enough to witness the declaration this man has just signed?

GUNNER. I havnt yet. Am I to sign now?

PERCIVAL. Of course.

(GUNNER, *who is now incapable of doing anything on his own initiative, signs.*)

Now stand up and read your declaration to this gentleman.

(GUNNER *makes a vague movement and looks stupidly round.* PERCIVAL *adds peremptorily.*)

Now, please.

GUNNER (*rising apprehensively and reading without punctuation in a hardly audible voice, like a very sick man*). I John Brown of 4 Chesterfield Parade Kentish Town do hereby voluntarily confess that on the 31st May 1909 I trespassed on the land of John Tarleton at Hindhead and effected an unlawful entry into his house where I secreted myself in a portable Turkish bath with a pistol with which I threatened to take the life of the said John Tarleton and was prevented from doing so only by the timely arrival of the Polish lady. I further confess that I was guilty of uttering an abominable calumny concerning Miss Hypatia Tarleton for which there was not a shred of foundation I apologize most humbly to the lady and her family for my conduct and I promise Mr Tarleton not to repeat it and to amend my life and to do what in me lies to prove worthy of his kindness in giving me another chance and refraining from delivering me up to the punishment I so richly deserve.

(*A short and painful silence follows. Then* PERCIVAL *speaks.*)

PERCIVAL. Do you consider that sufficient, Lord Summerhays?

LORD SUMMERHAYS. Oh, quite, quite.

PERCIVAL (*to* HYPATIA). Lord Summerhays would probably like to hear you say that you are satisfied, Miss Tarleton.

HYPATIA (*coming out of the swing, and advancing between* PERCIVAL *and* LORD SUMMERHAYS). I must say that you have behaved like a perfect gentleman, Mr Percival.

PERCIVAL (*first bowing to* HYPATIA, *and then turning with cold contempt to* GUNNER, *who is standing helpless*). We need not trouble you any further.

(GUNNER *turns vaguely towards the pavilion.*)

JOHNNY (*with less refined offensiveness, pointing to the pavilion*). Thats your way. The gardener will shew you the shortest way into the road. Go the shortest way.

GUNNER (*oppressed and disconcerted, hardly knows how to get out of the room*). Yes, sir. I — (*He turns again, appealing to* TARLETON.) Maynt I have my mother's photographs back again?

(MRS TARLETON *pricks up her ears.*)

TARLETON. Eh? What? Oh, the photographs! Yes, yes, yes: take them.

(GUNNER *takes them from the table, and is creeping away, when* MRS TARLETON *puts out her hand and stops him.*)

MRS TARLETON. Whats this, John? What were you doing with his mother's photographs?

TARLETON. Nothing, nothing. Never mind, Chickabiddy: it's all right.

MRS TARLETON (*snatching the photographs from* GUNNER'S *irresolute fingers, and recognizing them at a glance*). Lucy Titmus! Oh John, John!

TARLETON (*grimly, to* GUNNER). Young man: youre a fool; but youve just put the lid on this job in a masterly manner. I knew you would. I told you all to let well alone. You wouldnt; and now you must take the consequences — or rather *I* must take them.

MRS TARLETON (*maternally*). Are you Lucy's son?

GUNNER. Yes!

MRS TARLETON. And why didnt you come to me? I didnt turn my back on your mother when she came to me in her trouble. Didnt you know that?

GUNNER. No. She never talked to me about anything.

TARLETON. How could she talk to her own son? Shy, Summerhays, shy. Parent and child. Shy. (*He sits down at the end of the writing table nearest the sideboard like a man resigned to anything that fate may have in store for him.*)

MRS TARLETON. Then how did you find out?

GUNNER. From her papers after she died.

MRS TARLETON (*shocked*). Is Lucy dead? And I never knew! (*With an effusion of tenderness.*) And you here being treated like that, poor orphan, with nobody to take your part! Tear up that foolish paper, child; and sit down and make friends with me.

JOHNNY. Hallo, mother: this is all very well, you know —
PERCIVAL. But may I point out, Mrs Tarleton, that —
BENTLEY. Do you mean that after what he said of —
HYPATIA. Oh, look here, mamma: this is really —

MRS TARLETON. Will you please speak one at a time?

(*Silence.*)

PERCIVAL (*in a very gentlemanly manner*). Will you allow me to remind you, Mrs Tarleton, that this man has uttered a most serious and disgraceful falsehood concerning Miss Tarleton and myself?

MRS TARLETON. I dont believe a word of it. If the poor lad was there in the Turkish bath, who has a better right to say what was going on here than he has? You ought to be ashamed of yourself, Patsy; and so ought you too, Mr Percival, for encouraging her.

(HYPATIA *retreats to the pavilion, and exchanges grimaces with* JOHNNY, *shamelessly enjoying* PERCIVAL'S *sudden reverse. They know their mother.*)

PERCIVAL (*gasping*). Mrs Tarleton: I give you my word of honor—

MRS TARLETON. Oh, go along with you and your word of honor. Do you think I'm a fool? I wonder you can look the lad in the face after bullying him and making him sign those wicked lies; and all the time you carrying on with my daughter before youd been half an hour in my house. Fie, for shame!

PERCIVAL. Lord Summerhays: I appeal to you. Have I done the correct thing or not?

LORD SUMMERHAYS. Youve done your best, Mr Percival. But the correct thing depends for its success on everybody playing the game very strictly. As a single-handed game, it's impossible.

BENTLEY (*suddenly breaking out lamentably*). Joey: have you taken Hypatia away from me?

LORD SUMMERHAYS (*severely*). Bentley! Bentley! Control yourself, sir.

TARLETON. Come, Mr Percival! the shutters are up on the gentlemanly business. Try the truth.

PERCIVAL. I am in a wretched position. If I tell the truth nobody will believe me.

TARLETON. Oh yes they will. The truth makes everybody believe it.

PERCIVAL. It also makes everybody pretend not to believe it. Mrs Tarleton: youre not playing the game.

MRS TARLETON. I dont think youve behaved at all nicely, Mr Percival.

BENTLEY. I wouldnt have played you such a dirty trick, Joey. (*Struggling with a sob.*) You beast.

LORD SUMMERHAYS. Bentley: you *must* control yourself. Let me say at the same time, Mr Percival, that my son seems to have been mistaken in regarding you either as his friend or as a gentleman.

PERCIVAL. Miss Tarleton: I'm suffering this for your sake. I ask you just to say that I am not to blame. Just that and nothing more.

HYPATIA (*gloating mischievously over his distress*). You chased me through the heather and kissed me. You shouldnt have done that if you were not in earnest.

PERCIVAL. Oh, this is really the limit. (*Turning desperately to* GUNNER.) Sir: I appeal to *you*. As a gentleman! as a man of honor! as a man bound to stand by another man! You were in that Turkish bath. You saw how it began. Could any man have behaved more correctly than I did? Is there a shadow of foundation for the accusations brought against me?

GUNNER (*sorely perplexed*). Well, what do you want me to say?

JOHNNY. He has said what he had to say already, hasnt he? Read that paper.

GUNNER. When I tell the truth, you make me go back on it. And now you want me to go back on myself! What is a man to do?

PERCIVAL (*patiently*). Please try to get your mind clear, Mr Brown. I pointed out to you that you could not, as a gentleman, disparage a lady's character. You agree with me, I hope.

GUNNER. Yes: that sounds all right.

PERCIVAL. But youre also bound to tell the truth. Surely youll not deny that.

GUNNER. Who's denying it? I say nothing against it.

PERCIVAL. Of course not. Well, I ask you to tell the truth simply and unaffectedly. Did you witness any improper conduct on my part when you were in the bath?

GUNNER. No, sir.

JOHNNY. Then what do you mean by saying that —
HYPATIA. Do you mean to say that I —
BENTLEY. Oh, you are a rotter. Youre afraid —

TARLETON (*rising*). Stop. (*Silence.*) Leave it at that. Enough said. You keep quiet, Johnny. Mr Percival: youre whitewashed. So are you, Patsy. Honors are easy. Lets drop the subject. The next thing to do is to open a subscription to start this young man on a ranch in some far country thats accustomed to be in a disturbed state. He —

MRS TARLETON. Now stop joking the poor lad, John: I wont have it. He's been worried to death between you all. (*To* GUNNER.) Have you had your tea?

GUNNER. Tea? No: it's too early. I'm all right; only I had no dinner: I didnt think I'd want it. I didnt think I'd be alive.

MRS TARLETON. Oh, what a thing to say! You mustnt talk like that.

JOHNNY. He's out of his mind. He thinks it's past dinnertime.

MRS TARLETON. Oh, youve no sense, Johnny. He calls his lunch his dinner, and has his tea at half-past six. Havnt you, dear?

GUNNER (*timidly*). Hasnt everybody?

JOHNNY (*laughing*). Well, by George, thats not bad.

MRS TARLETON. Now dont be rude, Johnny: you know I dont like it. (*To* GUNNER.) A cup of tea will pick you up.

GUNNER. I'd rather not. I'm all right.

TARLETON (*going to the sideboard*). Here! try a mouthful of sloe gin.

GUNNER. No, thanks. I'm a teetotaler. I cant touch alcohol in any form.

TARLETON. Nonsense! This isnt alcohol. Sloe gin. Vegetarian, you know.

GUNNER (*hesitating*). Is it a fruit beverage?

TARLETON. Of course it is. Fruit beverage. Here you are. (*He gives him a glass of sloe gin.*)

GUNNER (*going to the sideboard*). Thanks. (*He begins to drink it confidently; but the first mouthful startles and almost chokes him.*) It's rather hot.

TARLETON. Do you good. Dont be afraid of it.

MRS TARLETON (*going to him*). Sip it, dear. Dont be in a hurry.

(GUNNER *sips slowly, each sip making his eyes water.*)

JOHNNY (*coming forward into the place left vacant by* GUNNER'S *visit to the sideboard*). Well, now that the gentleman has been attended to, I should like to know where we are. It may be a vulgar business habit; but I confess I like to know where I am.

TARLETON. I dont. Wherever you are, youre there anyhow. I tell you again, leave it at that.

BENTLEY. I want to know too. Hypatia's engaged to me.

HYPATIA. Bentley: if you insult me again: if you say another word, I'll leave the house and not enter it until you leave it.

JOHNNY. Put that in your pipe and smoke it, my boy.

BENTLEY (*inarticulate with fury and suppressed tears*). Oh! Beasts! Brutes!

MRS TARLETON. Now dont hurt his feelings, poor little lamb!

LORD SUMMERHAYS (*very sternly*). Bentley: you are not behaving well. You had better leave us until you have recovered yourself.

(BENTLEY *goes out in disgrace, but gets no further than half way to the pavilion door, when, with a wild sob, he throws himself on the floor and begins to yell.*)

MRS TARLETON. (*running to him*) Oh, poor child, poor child! Dont cry, duckie: he didnt mean it: dont cry.
LORD SUMMERHAYS. Stop that infernal noise, sir: do you hear? Stop it instantly.
JOHNNY. Thats the game he tried on me. There you are! Now, mother! Now, Patsy! You see for yourselves.
HYPATIA. (*covering her ears*) Oh you little wretch! Stop him, Mr Percival. Kick him.
TARLETON. Steady on, steady on. Easy, Bunny, easy.

LINA (*appearing at the door*). Leave him to me, Mrs Tarleton. (*Clear and authoritative.*) Stand clear, please. (*She quickly lifts the upper half of* BENTLEY *from the ground; dives under him; rises with his body hanging across her shoulders; and runs out with him.*)

BENTLEY (*in scared, sobered, humble tones as he is borne off*). What are you doing? Let me down. Please, Miss Szczepanowska — (*They pass out of hearing.*)

(*An awestruck silence falls on the company as they speculate on* BENTLEY'S *fate.*)

JOHNNY. I wonder what she's going to do with him.

HYPATIA. Spank him, I hope. Spank him hard.

LORD SUMMERHAYS. I hope so. I hope so. Tarleton: I'm beyond measure humiliated and annoyed by my son's behavior in your house. I had better take him home.

TARLETON. Not at all: not at all. Now, Chickabiddy: as Miss Lina has taken away Ben, suppose you take away Mr Brown for a while.

GUNNER (*with unexpected aggressiveness*). My name isnt Brown.

(*They stare at him: he meets their stare defiantly, pugnacious with sloe gin; drains the last drop from his glass; throws it on the sideboard; and advances to the writing table.*)

My name's Baker: Julius Baker. *Mister* Baker. If any man doubts it, I'm ready for him.

MRS TARLETON. John: you shouldnt have given him that sloe gin. It's gone to his head.

GUNNER. Dont you think it. Fruit beverages dont go to the head; and what matter if they did? I say nothing to you, maam: I regard you with respect and affection. (*Lachrymosely.*) You were very good to my mother: my poor mother! (*Relapsing into his daring mood.*) But I say my name's Baker; and I'm not to be treated as a child or made a slave of by any man. Baker is my name. Did you think I was going to give you my real name? Not likely! Not me!

TARLETON. So you thought of John Brown. That *was* clever of you.

GUNNER. Clever! yes: we're not all such fools as you think: we clerks. It was the bookkeeper put me up to that. It's the only name that nobody gives as a false name, he said. Clever, eh? I should think so.

MRS TARLETON. Come now, Julius—

GUNNER (*reassuring her gravely*). Dont you be alarmed, maam. I know what is due to you as a lady and to myself as a gentleman. I regard you with respect and affection. If you had been my mother, as you ought to have been, I should have had more chance. But you shall have no cause to be ashamed of me. The strength of a chain is no greater than its weakest link; but the greatness of a poet is the greatness of his greatest moment. Shakespear used to get drunk. Frederick the Great ran away from a battle. But it was what they could rise to, not what they could sink to, that made them great. They werent good always; but they were good on their day. Well, on my day — on my day, mind you — I'm good for something too. I know that Ive made a silly exhibition of myself here. I know I didnt rise to the occasion. I know that if youd been my mother, youd have been ashamed of me. I lost my presence of mind: I was a contemptible coward. But (*slapping himself on the chest*) Im not the man I was then. This is my day. Ive seen the tenth possessor of a foolish face carried out kicking and screaming by a woman. (*To* PERCIVAL.) You crowed pretty big over me. You hypnotized me. But when you were put through the fire yourself, you were found wanting. I tell you straight I dont give a damn for you.

MRS TARLETON. No: thats naughty. You shouldnt say that before me.

GUNNER. I would cut my tongue out sooner than say anything vulgar in your presence; for I regard you with respect and affection. I was not swearing. I was affirming my manhood.

MRS TARLETON. What an idea! What puts all these things into your head?

GUNNER. Oh, dont think, because I'm only a clerk, that I'm not one of the intellectuals. I'm a reading man, a thinking man. I read in a book — a high class six shilling book — this precept: Affirm your manhood. It appealed to me. Ive always remembered it. I believe in it. I feel I must do it to recover your respect after my cowardly behavior. Therefore I affirm it in your presence. I tell that man who insulted me that I dont give a damn for him. And neither I do.

TARLETON. I say, Summerhays: did you have chaps of this sort in Jinghiskahn?

LORD SUMMERHAYS. Oh yes: they exist everywhere: they are a most serious modern problem.

GUNNER. Yes. Youre right. (*Conceitedly.*) I'm a problem. And I tell you that when we clerks realize that we're problems! well, look out: thats all.

LORD SUMMERHAYS (*suavely, to* GUNNER). You read a great deal, you say?

GUNNER. Ive read more than any man in this room, if the truth were known, I expect. Thats whats going to smash up your Capitalism. The problems are beginning to read. Ha! We're free to do that here in England. What would you do with me in Jinghiskahn if you had me there?

LORD SUMMERHAYS. Well, since you ask me so directly, I'll tell you. I should take advantage of the fact that you have neither sense enough nor strength enough to know how to behave yourself in a difficulty of any sort. I should warn an intelligent and ambitious policeman that you are a troublesome person. The intelligent and ambitious policeman would take an early opportunity of upsetting your temper by ordering you to move on, and treading on your heels until you were provoked into obstructing an officer in the discharge of his duty. Any trifle of that sort would be sufficient to make a man like you lose your self-possession and put yourself in the wrong. You would then be charged and imprisoned until things quieted down.

GUNNER. And you call that justice!

LORD SUMMERHAYS. No. Justice was not my business. I had to govern a province; and I took the necessary steps to maintain order in it. Men are not governed by justice, but by law or persuasion. When they refuse to be governed by law or persuasion, they have to be governed by force or fraud, or both. I used both when law and persuasion failed me. Every ruler of men since the world began has done so, even when he has hated both fraud and force as heartily as I do. It is as well that you should know this, my young friend; so that you may recognize in time that anarchism is a game at which the police can beat you. What have you to say to that?

GUNNER. What have I to say to it! Well, I call it scandalous: thats what I have to say to it.

LORD SUMMERHAYS. Precisely: thats all anybody has to say to it, except the British public, which pretends not to believe it. And now let me ask you a sympathetic personal question. Havnt you a headache?

GUNNER. Well, since you ask me, I have. Ive over-excited myself.

MRS TARLETON. Poor lad! No wonder, after all youve gone through! You want to eat a little and to lie down. You come with me. I want you to tell me about your poor dear mother and about yourself. Come along with me. (*She leads the way to the inner door.*)

GUNNER (*following her obediently*). Thank you kindly, madam.

(*She goes out. Before passing out after her, he partly closes the door and lingers for a moment to whisper.*)

Mind: I'm not knuckling down to any man here. I knuckle down to Mrs Tarleton because she's a woman in a thousand. I affirm my manhood all the same. Understand: I dont give a damn for the lot of you. (*He hurries out, rather afraid of the consequences of this defiance, which has provoked* JOHNNY *to an impatient movement towards him.*)

HYPATIA. Thank goodness he's gone! Oh, *what* a bore! WHAT a bore!!! Talk! talk! talk!

TARLETON. Patsy: it's no good. We're going to talk. And we're going to talk about you.

JOHNNY. It's no use shirking it, Pat. We'd better know where we are.

LORD SUMMERHAYS. Come, Miss Tarleton. Wont you sit down? I'm very tired of standing.

(HYPATIA *comes from the pavilion and takes a chair at the worktable.* LORD SUMMERHAYS *takes the opposite chair, on her right.* PERCIVAL *takes the chair* JOHNNY *placed for* LINA *on her arrival.* TARLETON *sits down at the end of the writing table.* JOHNNY *remains standing.* LORD SUMMERHAYS *continues, with a sigh of relief at being seated.*)

We shall now get the change of subject we are all pining for.

JOHNNY (*puzzled*). Whats that?

LORD SUMMERHAYS. The great question. The question that men and women will spend hours over without complaining. The question that occupies all the novel readers and all the playgoers. The question they never get tired of.

JOHNNY. But what question?

LORD SUMMERHAYS. The question which particular young man some young woman will mate with.

PERCIVAL. As if it mattered!

HYPATIA (*sharply*). Whats that you said?

PERCIVAL. I said: As if it mattered.

HYPATIA. I call that ungentlemanly.

PERCIVAL. Do you care about that? you who are so magnificently unladylike!

JOHNNY. Look here, Mr Percival: youre not supposed to insult my sister.

HYPATIA. Oh, shut up, Johnny. I can take care of myself. Dont you interfere.

JOHNNY. Oh, very well. If you choose to give yourself away like that — to allow a man to call you unladylike and then to be unladylike, Ive nothing more to say.

HYPATIA. I think Mr Percival is most ungentlemanly; but I wont be protected. I'll not have my affairs interfered with by men on pretence of protecting me. I'm not your baby. If I interfered between you and a woman, you would soon tell me to mind my own business.

TARLETON. Children: dont squabble. Read Dr Watts. Behave yourselves.

JOHNNY. Ive nothing more to say; and as I dont seem to be wanted here, I shall take myself off. (*He goes out with affected calm through the pavilion.*)

TARLETON. Summerhays: a family is an awful thing, an impossible thing. Cat and dog. Patsy: I'm ashamed of you.

HYPATIA. I'll make it up with Johnny afterwards; but I really cant have him here sticking his clumsy hoof into my affairs.

LORD SUMMERHAYS. The question is, Mr Percival, are you really a gentleman, or are you not?

PERCIVAL. Was Napoleon really a gentleman or was he not? He made the lady get out of the way of the porter and said, "Respect the burden, madam." That was behaving like a very fine gentleman; but he kicked Volney for saying that what France wanted was the Bourbons back again. That was behaving rather like a navvy. Now I, like Napoleon, am not all one piece. On occasion, as you have all seen, I can behave like a gentleman. On occasion, I can behave with a brutal simplicity which Miss Tarleton herself could hardly surpass.

TARLETON. Gentleman or no gentleman, Patsy: what are your intentions?

HYPATIA. My intentions! Surely it's the gentleman who should be asked his intentions.

TARLETON. Come now, Patsy! none of that nonsense. Has Mr Percival said anything to you that I ought to know or that Bentley ought to know? Have you said anything to Mr Percival?

HYPATIA. Mr Percival chased me through the heather and kissed me.

LORD SUMMERHAYS. As a gentleman, Mr Percival, what do you say to that?

PERCIVAL. As a gentleman, I do not kiss and tell. As a mere man: a cad, if you like, I say that I did so at Miss Tarleton's own suggestion.

HYPATIA. Beast!

PERCIVAL. I dont deny that I enjoyed it. But I did not initiate it. And I began by running away.

TARLETON. So Patsy can run faster than you, can she?

PERCIVAL. Yes, when she is in pursuit of me. She runs faster and faster. I run slower and slower. And these woods of yours are full of magic. There was a confounded fern owl. Did you ever hear the churr of a fern owl? Did you ever hear it create a sudden silence by ceasing? Did you ever hear it call its mate by striking its wings together twice and whistling that single note that no nightingale can imitate? That is what happened in the woods when I was running away. So I turned; and the pursuer became the pursued.

HYPATIA. I had to fight like a wild cat.

LORD SUMMERHAYS. Please dont tell us this. It's not fit for old people to hear.

TARLETON. Come: how did it end?

HYPATIA. It's not ended yet.

TARLETON. How is it going to end?

HYPATIA. Ask *him*.

TARLETON. How is it going to end, Mr Percival?

PERCIVAL. I cant afford to marry, Mr Tarleton. Ive only a thousand a year until my father dies. Two people cant possibly live on that.

TARLETON. Oh, cant they? When *I* married, I should have been jolly glad to have felt sure of the quarter of it.

PERCIVAL. No doubt; but I am not a cheap person, Mr Tarleton. I was brought up in a household which cost at least seven or eight times that; and I am in constant money difficulties because I simply dont know how to live on the thousand a year scale. As to asking a woman to share my degrading poverty, it's out of the question. Besides, I'm rather young to marry. I'm only 28.

HYPATIA. Papa: buy the brute for me.

LORD SUMMERHAYS (*shrinking*). My dear Miss Tarleton: dont be so naughty. I know how delightful it is to shock an old man; but there is a point at which it becomes barbarous. Dont. Please dont.

HYPATIA. Shall I tell Papa about *you*?

LORD SUMMERHAYS. Tarleton: I had better tell you that I once asked your daughter to become my widow.

TARLETON (*to* HYPATIA). Why didnt you accept him, you young idiot?

LORD SUMMERHAYS. I was too old.

TARLETON. All this has been going on under my nose, I suppose. You run after young men; and old men run after you. And I'm the last person in the world to hear of it.

HYPATIA. How could I tell you?

LORD SUMMERHAYS. Parents and children, Tarleton.

TARLETON. Oh, the gulf that lies between them! the impassable, eternal gulf! And so I'm to buy the brute for you, eh?

HYPATIA. If you please, papa.

TARLETON. Whats the price, Mr Percival?

PERCIVAL. We might do with another fifteen hundred if my father would contribute. But I should like more.

TARLETON. It's purely a question of money with you, is it?

PERCIVAL (*after a moment's consideration*). Practically yes: it turns on that.

TARLETON. I thought you might have some sort of preference for Patsy, you know.

PERCIVAL. Well, but does that matter, do you think? Patsy fascinates me, no doubt. I apparently fascinate Patsy. But, believe me, all that is not worth considering. One of my three fathers (the priest) has married hundreds of couples: couples selected by one another, couples selected by the parents, couples forced to marry one another by circumstances of one kind or another; and he assures me that if marriages were made by putting all the men's names into one sack and the women's names into another, and having them taken out by a blindfolded child like lottery numbers, there would be just as high a percentage of happy marriages as we have here in England. He said Cupid was nothing but the blindfolded child: pretty idea that, I think! I shall have as good a chance with Patsy as with anyone else. Mind: I'm not bigoted about it. I'm not a doctrinaire: not the slave of a theory. You and Lord Summerhays are experienced married men. If you can tell me of any trustworthy method of selecting a wife, I shall be happy to make use of it. I await your suggestions.

(*He looks with polite attention to* LORD SUMMERHAYS, *who, having nothing to say, avoids his eye. He looks to* TARLETON, *who purses his lips glumly and rattles his money in his pockets without a word.*)

Apparently neither of you has anything to suggest. Then Patsy will do as well as another, provided the money is forthcoming.

HYPATIA. Oh, you beauty! you beauty!

TARLETON. When I married Patsy's mother, I was in love with her.

PERCIVAL. For the first time?

TARLETON. Yes: for the first time.

PERCIVAL. For the last time?

LORD SUMMERHAYS (*revolted*). Sir: you are in the presence of his daughter.

HYPATIA. Oh, dont mind me. I dont care. I'm accustomed to Papa's adventures.

TARLETON (*blushing painfully*). Patsy, my child: that was not — not delicate.

HYPATIA. Well, papa, youve never shewn any delicacy in talking to me about my conduct; and I really dont see why I shouldnt talk to you about yours. It's such nonsense! Do you think young people dont know?

LORD SUMMERHAYS. I'm sure they dont feel. Tarleton: this is too horrible, too brutal. If neither of these young people have any — any — any —

PERCIVAL. Shall we say paternal sentimentality? I'm extremely sorry to shock you; but you must remember that Ive been educated to discuss human affairs with three fathers simultaneously. I'm an adult person. Patsy is an adult person. You do not inspire me with veneration. Apparently you do not inspire Patsy with veneration. That may surprise you. It may pain you. I'm sorry. It cant be helped. What about the money?

TARLETON. You dont inspire me with generosity, young man.

HYPATIA (*laughing with genuine amusement*). He had you there, Joey.

TARLETON. I havnt been a bad father to you, Patsy.

HYPATIA. I dont say you have, dear. If only I could persuade you Ive grown up, we should get along perfectly.

TARLETON. Do you remember Bill Burt?

HYPATIA. Why?

TARLETON (*to the others*). Bill Burt was a laborer here. I was going to sack him for kicking his father. He said his father had kicked him until he was big enough to kick back. Patsy begged him off. I asked that man what it felt like the first time he kicked his father, and found that it was just like kicking any other man. He laughed and said that it was the old man that knew what it felt like. Think of that, Summerhays! think of that!

HYPATIA. I havnt kicked you, papa.

TARLETON. Youve kicked me harder than Bill Burt ever kicked.

LORD SUMMERHAYS. It's no use, Tarleton. Spare yourself. Do you seriously expect these young people, at their age, to sympathize with what this gentleman calls your paternal sentimentality?

TARLETON (*wistfully*). Is it nothing to you but paternal sentimentality, Patsy?

HYPATIA. Well, I greatly prefer your superabundant vitality, papa.

TARLETON (*violently*). Hold your tongue, you young devil. The young are all alike: hard, coarse, shallow, cruel, selfish, dirty-minded. You can clear out of my house as soon as you can coax him to take you; and the sooner the better. (*To* PERCIVAL.) I think you said your price was fifteen hundred a year. Take it. And I wish you joy of your bargain.

PERCIVAL. If you wish to know who I am —

TARLETON. I dont care a tinker's curse who you are or what you are. Youre willing to take that girl off my hands for fifteen hundred a year: thats all that concerns me. Tell *her* who you are if you like: it's her affair, not mine.

HYPATIA. Dont answer him, Joey: it wont last. Lord Summerhays, I'm sorry about Bentley; but Joey's the only man for me.

LORD SUMMERHAYS. It may —

HYPATIA. Please dont say it may break your poor boy's heart. It's much more likely to break yours.

LORD SUMMERHAYS. Oh!

TARLETON (*springing to his feet*). Leave the room. Do you hear: leave the room.

PERCIVAL. Arnt we getting a little cross? Dont be angry, Mr Tarleton. Read Marcus Aurelius.

TARLETON. Dont you dare make fun of me. Take your aeroplane out of my vinery and yourself out of my house.

PERCIVAL (*rising, to* HYPATIA). I'm afraid I shall have to dine at the Beacon, Patsy.

HYPATIA (*rising*). Do. I dine with you.

TARLETON. Did you hear me tell you to leave the room?

HYPATIA. I did. (*To* PERCIVAL.) You see what living with one's parents means, Joey. It means living in a house where you can be ordered to leave the room. Ive got to obey: it's his house, not mine.

TARLETON. Who pays for it? Go and support yourself as I did if you want to be independent.

HYPATIA. I wanted to and you wouldnt let me. How can I support myself when I'm a prisoner?

TARLETON. Hold your tongue.

HYPATIA. Keep your temper.

PERCIVAL (*coming between them*). Lord Summerhays: youll join me, I'm sure, in pointing out to both father and daughter that they have now reached that very common stage in family life at which anything but a blow would be an anticlimax. Do you seriously want to beat Patsy, Mr Tarleton?

TARLETON. Yes. I want to thrash the life out of her. If she doesnt get out of my reach, I'll do it. (*He sits down and grasps the writing table to restrain himself.*)

HYPATIA (*coolly going to him and leaning with her breast on his writhing shoulders*). Oh, if you want to beat me just to relieve your feelings — just really and truly for the fun of it and the satisfaction of it, beat away. I dont grudge you that.

TARLETON (*almost in hysterics*). I used to think that this sort of thing went on in other families but that it never could happen in ours. And now — (*He is broken with emotion, and continues lamentably.*) I cant say the right thing. I cant do the right thing. I dont know what *is* the right thing. I'm beaten; and she knows it. Summerhays: tell me what to do.

LORD SUMMERHAYS. When my council in Jinghiskahn reached the point of coming to blows, I used to adjourn the sitting. Let us postpone the discussion. Wait until Monday: we shall have Sunday to quiet down in. Believe me, I'm not making fun of you; but I think theres something in this young gentleman's advice. Read something.

TARLETON. I'll read *King Lear.*

HYPATIA. Dont. I'm very sorry, dear.

TARLETON. Youre not. Youre laughing at me. Serve me right! Parents and children! No man should know his own child. No child should know its own father. Let the family be rooted out of civilization! Let the human race be brought up in institutions!

HYPATIA. Oh yes. How jolly! You and I might be friends then; and Joey could stay to dinner.

TARLETON. Let him stay to dinner. Let him stay to breakfast. Let him spend his life here. Dont you say I drove him out. Dont you say I drove *you* out.

PERCIVAL. I really have no right to inflict myself on you. Dropping in as I did—

TARLETON. Out of the sky. Ha! Dropping in. The new sport of aviation. You just see a nice house; drop in; scoop up the man's daughter; and off with you again.

(BENTLEY *comes back, with his shoulders hanging as if he too had been exercised to the last pitch of fatigue. He is very sad. They stare at him as he gropes to* PERCIVAL'*s chair.*)

BENTLEY. I'm sorry for making a fool of myself. I beg your pardon. Hypatia: I'm awfully sorry; but Ive made up my mind that I'll never marry. (*He sits down in deep depression.*)

HYPATIA (*running to him*). How nice of you, Bentley! Of course you guessed I wanted to marry Joey. What did the Polish lady do to you?

BENTLEY (*turning his head away*). I'd rather not speak of her, if you dont mind.

HYPATIA. Youve fallen in love with her. (*She laughs.*)

BENTLEY. It's beastly of you to laugh.

LORD SUMMERHAYS. You are not the first to fall today under the lash of that young lady's terrible derision, Bentley.

(LINA, *her cap on, and her goggles in her hand, comes impetuously through the inner door.*)

LINA (*on the steps*). Mr Percival: can we get that aeroplane started again? (*She comes down and runs to the pavilion door.*) I must get out of this into the air: right up into the blue.

PERCIVAL. Impossible. The frame's twisted. The petrol has given out: thats what brought us down. And how can we get a clear run to start with among these woods?

LINA (*swooping back through the middle of the pavilion*). We can straighten the frame. We can buy petrol at the Beacon. With a few laborers we can get her out on to the Portsmouth Road and start her along that.

TARLETON (*rising*). But why do you want to leave us, Miss Szcz?

LINA. Old pal: this is a stuffy house. You seem to think of nothing but making love. All the conversation here is about love-making. All the pictures are about love-making. The eyes of all of you are sheep's eyes. You are steeped in it, soaked in it: the very texts on the walls of your bedrooms are the ones about love. It is disgusting. It is not healthy. Your women are kept idle and dressed up for no other purpose than to be made love to. I have not been here an hour; and already everybody makes love to me as if because I am a woman it were my profession to be made love to. First you, old pal. I forgave you because you were nice about your wife.

HYPATIA. Oh! oh! oh! Oh, papa!

LINA. Then you, Lord Summerhays, come to me; and all you have to say is to ask me not to mention that you made love to me in Vienna two years ago. I forgave you because I thought you were an ambassador; and all ambassadors make love and are very nice and useful to people who travel. Then this young gentleman. He is engaged to this young lady; but no matter for that: he makes love to me because I carry him off in my arms when he cries. All these I bore in silence. But now comes your Johnny and tells me I'm a ripping fine woman, and asks me to marry him. I, Lina Szczepanowska, MARRY him!!!!! I do not mind this boy: he is a child: he loves me: I should have to give him money and take care of him: that would be foolish, but honorable. I do not mind you, old pal: you are what you call an old — ouf! but you do not offer to buy me: you say until we are tired — until you are so happy that you dare not ask for more. That is foolish too, at your age; but it is an adventure: it is not dishonorable. I do not mind Lord Summerhays: it was in Vienna: they had been toasting him at a great banquet: he was not sober. That is bad for the health; but it is not dishonorable. But your Johnny! Oh, your Johnny! with his marriage. He will do the straight thing by me. He will give me a home, a position. He tells me I must know that my present position is not one for a nice woman. This to me, Lina Szczepanowska! I am an honest woman: I earn my living. I am a free woman: I live in my own house. I am a woman of the world: I have thousands of friends: every night crowds of people applaud me, delight in me, buy my picture, pay hard-earned money to see me. I am strong: I am skillful: I am brave: I am independent: I am unbought: I am all that a woman ought to be; and in my family there has not been a single drunkard for four generations. And this Englishman! this linendraper! he dares to ask me to come and live with him in this rrrrrrabbit hutch, and take my bread from his hand, and ask him for pocket money, and wear soft clothes, and be his woman! his wife! Sooner than that, I would stoop to the lowest depths of my profession. I would stuff lions with food and pretend to tame them. I would deceive honest people's eyes with conjuring tricks instead of real feats of strength and skill. I would be a clown and set bad examples of conduct to little children. I would sink yet lower and be an actress or an opera singer, imperilling my soul by the wicked lie of pretending to be somebody else. All this I would do sooner than take my bread from the hand of a man and make him the master of my body and soul. And so you may tell your Johnny to buy an Englishwoman: he shall not buy Lina Szczepanowska; and I will not stay in the house where such dishonor is offered me. Adieu.

(*She turns precipitately to go, but is faced in the pavilion doorway by* JOHNNY, *who comes in slowly, his hands in his pockets, meditating deeply.*)

JOHNNY (*confidentially to* LINA). You wont mention our little conversation, Miss Shepanoska. It'll do no good; and I'd rather you didnt.

TARLETON. Weve just heard about it, Johnny.

JOHNNY (*shortly, but without ill-temper*). Oh: is that so?

HYPATIA. The cat's out of the bag, Johnny, about everybody. They were all beforehand with you: papa, Lord Summerhays, Bentley and all. Dont you let them laugh at you.

JOHNNY (*a grin slowly overspreading his countenance*). Well, theres no use my pretending to be surprised at *you*, Governor, is there? I hope you got it as hot as I did. Mind, Miss Shepanoska: it wasnt lost on me. I'm a thinking man. I kept my temper. Youll admit that.

LINA (*frankly*). Oh yes. I do not quarrel. You are what is called a chump; but you are not a bad sort of chump.

JOHNNY. Thank you. Well, if a chump may have an opinion, I should put it at this. You make, I suppose, ten pounds a night off your own bat, Miss Lina?

LINA (*scornfully*). Ten pounds a night! I have made ten pounds a minute.

JOHNNY (*with increased respect*). Have you indeed? I didnt know: youll excuse my mistake, I hope. But the principle is the same. Now I trust you wont be offended at what I'm going to say; but Ive thought about this and watched it in daily experience; and you may take it from me that the moment a woman becomes pecuniarily independent, she gets hold of the wrong end of the stick in moral questions.

LINA. Indeed! And what do you conclude from that, Mister Johnny?

JOHNNY. Well, obviously, that independence for women is wrong and shouldnt be allowed. For their own good, you know. And for the good of morality in general. You agree with me, Lord Summerhays, dont you?

LORD SUMMERHAYS. It's a very moral moral, if I may so express myself.

(MRS TARLETON *comes in softly through the inner door.*)

MRS TARLETON. Dont make too much noise. The lad's asleep.

TARLETON. Chickabiddy: we have some news for you.

JOHNNY (*apprehensively*). Now theres no need, you know, Governor, to worry mother with everything that passes.

MRS TARLETON (*coming to* TARLETON). Whats been going on? Dont you hold anything back from me, John. What have you been doing?

TARLETON. Patsy isnt going to marry Bentley.

MRS TARLETON. Of course not. Is that your great news? I never believed she'd marry him.

TARLETON. Theres something else. Mr Percival here —

MRS TARLETON (*to* PERCIVAL). Are you going to marry Patsy?

PERCIVAL (*diplomatically*). Patsy is going to marry me, with your permission.

MRS TARLETON. Oh, she has my permission: she ought to have been married long ago.

HYPATIA. Mother!

TARLETON. Miss Lina here, though she has been so short a time with us, has inspired a good deal of attachment in — I may say in almost all of us. Therefore I hope she'll stay to dinner, and not insist on flying away in that aeroplane.

PERCIVAL. You must stay, Miss Szczepanowska. I cant go up again this evening.

LINA. Ive seen you work it. Do you think I require any help? And Bentley shall come with me as a passenger.

BENTLEY (*terrified*). Go up in an aeroplane! I darent.

LINA. You must learn to dare.

BENTLEY (*pale but heroic*). All right. I'll come.

LORD SUMMERHAYS. } { No, no, Bentley, impossible. I shall not allow it.

MRS TARLETON. } { Do you want to kill the child? He shant go.

BENTLEY. I will. I'll lie down and yell until you let me go. I'm not a coward. I wont be a coward.

LORD SUMMERHAYS. Miss Szczepanowska: my son is very dear to me. I implore you to wait until tomorrow morning.

LINA. There may be a storm tomorrow. And I'll go: storm or no storm. I must risk my life tomorrow.

BENTLEY. I hope there will be a storm.

LINA (*grasping his arm*). You are trembling.

BENTLEY. Yes: it's terror, sheer terror. I can hardly see. I can hardly stand. But I'll go with you.

LINA (*slapping him on the back and knocking a ghastly white smile into his face*). You shall. I like you, my boy. We go tomorrow, together.

BENTLEY. Yes: together: tomorrow.

TARLETON. Well, sufficient unto the day is the evil thereof. Read the old book.

MRS TARLETON. Is there anything else?

TARLETON. Well, I — er (*he addresses* LINA, *and stops*). I — er (*he addresses* LORD SUMMERHAYS, *and stops*). I — er (*he gives it up*). Well, I suppose — er — I suppose theres nothing more to be said.

HYPATIA (*fervently*). Thank goodness!

Curtain

There is in madness occasionally a frightening sanity, especially in the madness of such characters as Countess Aurelia, Constance, Gabrielle, and Josephine. *The Madwoman of Chaillot* (1945) is a morality play which takes the world of the real, turns it upside down into fantasy, and populates it with madwomen who are remarkably sane about the things that matter; with simple, lovable, ordinary people who are almost too simple and lovable to be true; and with greedy, grasping monsters who are deliberately overdrawn to bring home the more rapacious aspects of the wielders of power and wealth.

Jean Giraudoux (1882–1944) was a playwright of incisive intelligence, yet that faculty does not manifest itself in his plays as tedious moralizing or ponderous lecturing. It is enhanced by a wit and charm so fundamental to his dramatic methods that the morals inherent in his stage parables are transmuted by the interesting nature of the action, the fascinating quality of the characters, and the delights of the dialogue into truths of human life which readers and viewers sense rather than know. That kind of learning experience is really the most effective anyway; it makes the play's moral part of one's emotional being, not just another memorized slogan or motto.

The Madwoman's Aristophanic comic elements have an undertone of bitterness, but the bitterness is more romantic than realistic, which explains why Giraudoux's attack on capitalism took this particular form. Among the realities of human life are such nagging concerns as earning a living, maintaining the fabric of a society by respecting its laws, and seeking some kind of meaningful advancement. All of these can take extreme forms; some people can push for more than they need or have a right to; some, beaten down in the struggle for bread, justice, and promotion, seem to end up with little or nothing, their hopes and energies destroyed.

Still, the highly articulated organization of most societies, whether they be fascist, democratic, or socialist, is such that an ideal distribution of goods, talents, positions, and leisure time — a distribution which would please everyone, hurt no one, and remove the evils of the passionate pursuit of power and wealth — is quite impossible. Giraudoux obviously was fascinated by the concept of such an ideal world, even if that world were limited to Paris. To make Paris the best place to live, however, Giraudoux had to remove the elements threatening life, love, beauty, and joy. And to do that, he had to retreat into fantasy. Otherwise, the brutal realities of social economics would have put a stop to the comedy of this drama before it got much farther than the plan to exploit the oil beneath the city of Paris.

Giraudoux's stereotypes of bankers, stock brokers, lawyers, and other members of the power elite are exaggerations, yet they have the ring of *comic* reality: the truth has been distorted, heightened, made ridiculous. The ordinary folk, however, are made into puppets by their leaders, who move money and men in patterns which only make themselves richer and more powerful — at least as Giraudoux sets up the social equation. These inoffensive little people are also oversimplified as characters. There is not so much simple virtue in ordinary men as the playwright wants his audience to believe, but then any fantasy requires a willing suspension of disbelief, and *The Madwoman* pleads for it in such a disarming, subtle way that only a reader or viewer with no feelings could really refuse. Plotting is not strong, but fantasy does not demand the hectic complications of a farce. *The Madwoman* is a comedy of moods and characters rather than of action, manners, or wit.

Sanity in the midst of insanity, in life as in fiction, brings one up short. The importance of illusion in giving people the strength to go on living is tenderly stressed. As Constance says: "Don't you suppose I know about Dickie? Don't you think I'd rather have him here alive and woolly and frisking around the way he used to? You have your Adolphe. Gabrielle has her birds. But I have only Dickie. Do you think I'd be so silly about him if it wasn't that it's only by pretending that he's here all the time that I get him to come sometimes, really? Next time I won't bring him!" After that revelation of a valiant attempt to escape from the prison of human loneliness, anyone who asks why Constance thinks she can leave a purely imaginary dog at home has partly missed the point of this touching, innocently charming play.

If Giraudoux's comic distortions of reality are zany and tender when he deals with the madwomen, his satiric attacks on the opportunism of unscrupulous businessmen do not seem very much more exaggerated than the reports of corporate mergers, financial miracles, and shrewd swindles to be found in any reliable newspaper. Here the playwright's fantasy is sustained and kept from lapsing into a realistic exposé of commercial corruption more appropriate to Ibsen or Odets by the staccato intercutting of dialogue, showing the rapidity and rapacity with which the speculators can make a deal. Its speed and cold calculation suggest that ordinary, honest people cannot counteract it — or even defend themselves against it.

That is why it remains for someone not at all ordinary, but *mad*, to protect them from the greedy destroyers of man and nature. The single-minded frenzy with which the Baron, the Broker, and the President pursue wealth, to the exclusion of the values which Giraudoux seems to say are really worthwhile in life, makes them also a bit mad, but in a different, frightening way. Countess Aurelia's madness threatens no one; it frightens no one. It even endears her to most people. But to put her mad mind to work on an equally insane scheme to disarm and remove the dangerous madness of the manipulators, she needs the facts and insights of the Ragpicker and the secrets of the Sewer Man. Thus, led by the logic of madness, even the sane can fight back, and this balances the play's whimsy with a kind of muscularity and vigor.

G. L.

JEAN GIRAUDOUX

The Madwoman of Chaillot

ADAPTED BY MAURICE VALENCY

Characters

THE WAITER
THE LITTLE MAN
THE PROSPECTOR
THE PRESIDENT
THE BARON
THERESE
THE STREET SINGER
THE PROFESSOR
THE FLOWER GIRL
THE RAGPICKER
PAULETTE
THE DEAF MUTE
IRMA
THE SHOELACE PEDDLER
THE BROKER
THE STREET JUGGLER
DR. JADIN
COUNTESS AURELIA, *The Madwoman of Chaillot*
THE DOORMAN
THE POLICEMAN
PIERRE
THE SERGEANT
THE SEWER MAN
CONSTANCE, *The Madwoman of Passy*
GABRIELLE, *The Madwoman of St. Sulpice*
JOSEPHINE, *The Madwoman of La Concorde*
THE PRESIDENTS
THE PROSPECTORS
THE PRESS AGENTS
THE LADIES
THE ADOLPHE BERTAUTS

ACT ONE

(SCENE: *The café terrace at Chez Francis, on the Place de l'Alma in Paris. The Alma is in the stately quarter of Paris known as Chaillot, be-*

tween the Champs Elysées and the Seine, across the river from the Eiffel Tower.

Chez Francis has several rows of tables set out under its awning, and, as it is lunch time, a good many of them are occupied. At a table, downstage, a somewhat obvious BLONDE *with ravishing legs is sipping a vermouth-cassis and trying hard to engage the attention of the* PROSPECTOR, *who sits at an adjacent table taking little sips of water and rolling them over his tongue with the air of a connoisseur. Downstage right, in front of the tables on the sidewalk, is the usual Paris bench, a stout and uncomfortable affair provided by the municipality for the benefit of those who prefer to sit without drinking. A* POLICEMAN *lounges about, keeping the peace without unnecessary exertion.*

TIME: *It is a little before noon in the spring of next year.*

AT RISE: *The* PRESIDENT *and the* BARON *enter with importance, and are ushered to a front table by the* WAITER.)

THE PRESIDENT. Baron, sit down. This is a historic occasion. It must be properly celebrated. The waiter is going to bring out my special port.

THE BARON. Splendid.

THE PRESIDENT (*offers his cigar case*). Cigar? My private brand.

THE BARON. Thank you. You know, this all gives me the feeling of one of those enchanted mornings in the *Arabian Nights* when thieves foregather in the market place. Thieves — pashas. . . . (*He sniffs the cigar judiciously, and begins lighting it.*)

THE PRESIDENT (*chuckles*). Tell me about yourself.

THE BARON. Well, where shall I begin?

(*The* STREET SINGER *enters. He takes off a battered black felt with a flourish and begins singing an ancient mazurka.*)

STREET SINGER (*sings*).

Do you hear, Mademoiselle,
Those musicians of hell?

THE PRESIDENT. Waiter! Get rid of that man.

WAITER. He is singing *La Belle Polonaise.*

THE PRESIDENT. I didn't ask for the program. I asked you to get rid of him.

(*The* WAITER *doesn't budge. The* SINGER *goes by himself.*)

As you were saying, Baron . . . ?

THE BARON. Well, until I was fifty . . .

(*The* FLOWER GIRL *enters through the café door, center.*)

. . . my life was relatively uncomplicated. It consisted of selling off one by one the various estates left me by my father. Three years ago, I parted with my last farm. Two years ago, I lost my last mistress. And now — all that is left me is . . .

THE FLOWER GIRL (*to the* BARON). Violets, sir?

THE PRESIDENT. Run along.

(*The* FLOWER GIRL *moves on.*)

THE BARON (*staring after her*). So that, in short, all I have left now is my name.

THE PRESIDENT. Your name is precisely the name we need on our board of directors.

THE BARON (*with an inclination of his head*). Very flattering.

THE PRESIDENT. You will understand when I tell you that mine has been a very different experience. I came up from the bottom. My mother spent most of her life bent over a washtub in order to send me to school. I'm eternally grateful to her, of course, but I must confess that I no longer remember her face. It was no doubt beautiful — but when I try to recall it, I see only the part she invariably showed me — her rear.

THE BARON. Very touching.

THE PRESIDENT. When I was thrown out of school for the fifth and last time, I decided to find out for myself what makes the world go round. I ran errands for an editor, a movie star, a financier. . . . I began to understand a little what life is. Then, one day, in the subway, I saw a face. . . . My rise in life dates from that day.

THE BARON. Really?

THE PRESIDENT. One look at that face, and I knew. One look at mine, and he knew. And so I made my first thousand — passing a boxful of counterfeit notes. A year later, I saw another such face. It got me a nice berth in the narcotics business. Since then, all I do is to look out for such faces. And now here I am — president of eleven corporations, director of fifty-two companies, and, beginning today, chairman of the board of the international combine in which you have been so good as to accept a post.

(*The* RAGPICKER *passes, sees something under the* PRESIDENT'S *table, and stoops to pick it up.*)

Looking for something?

THE RAGPICKER. Did you drop this?

THE PRESIDENT. I never drop anything.

THE RAGPICKER. Then this hundred-franc note isn't yours?

THE PRESIDENT. Give it here.

(*The* RAGPICKER *gives him the note, and goes out.*)

THE BARON. Are you sure it's yours?

THE PRESIDENT. All hundred-franc notes, Baron, are mine.

THE BARON. Mr. President, there's something I've been wanting to ask you. What exactly is the purpose of our new company? Or is that an indiscreet question . . . ?

THE PRESIDENT. Indiscreet? Not a bit. Merely unusual. As far as I know, you're the first member of a board of directors ever to ask such a question.

THE BARON. Do we plan to exploit a commodity? A utility?

THE PRESIDENT. My dear sir, I haven't the faintest idea.

THE BARON. But if you don't know — who does?

THE PRESIDENT. Nobody. And at the moment, it's becoming just a trifle embarrassing. Yes, my dear Baron, since we are now close business associates, I must confess that for the time being we're in a little trouble.

THE BARON. I was afraid of that. The stock issue isn't going well?

THE PRESIDENT. No, no — on the contrary. The stock issue is going beautifully. Yesterday morning at ten o'clock we offered 500,000 shares to the general public. By 10:05 they were all snapped up at par. By 10:20, when the police finally arrived, our offices were a shambles. . . . Windows smashed — doors torn off their hinges — you never saw anything so beautiful in your life! And this morning our stock is being quoted over the counter at 124 with no sellers, and the orders are still pouring in.

THE BARON. But in that case — what is the trouble?

THE PRESIDENT. The trouble is we have a tremendous capital, and not the slightest idea of what to do with it.

THE BARON. You mean all those people are fighting to buy stock in a company that has no object?

THE PRESIDENT. My dear Baron, do you imagine that when a subscriber buys a share of stock, he has any idea of getting behind a counter or digging a ditch? A stock certificate is not a tool, like a shovel or a commodity, like a pound of cheese. What we sell a customer is not a share in a business, but a view of the Elysian Fields. A financier is a creative artist. Our function is to stimulate the imagination. We are poets!

THE BARON. But in order to stimulate the imagination, don't you need some field of activity?

THE PRESIDENT. Not at all. What you need for that is a name. A name that will stir the pulse like a trumpet call, set the brain awhirl like a movie star, inspire reverence like a cathedral. *United General International Consolidated!* Of course that's been used. That's what a corporation needs.

THE BARON. And do we have such a name?

THE PRESIDENT. So far we have only a blank space. In that blank space a name must be printed. This name must be a masterpiece. And if I seem a little nervous today, it's because — somehow — I've racked my brains, but it hasn't come to me. Oho! Look at that! Just like the answer to a prayer . . . !

(*The* BARON *turns and stares in the direction of the* PROSPECTOR.)

You see? There's one. And what a beauty!

THE BARON. You mean that girl?

THE PRESIDENT. No, no, not the girl. That face. You see . . . ? The one that's drinking water.

THE BARON. You call that a face? That's a tombstone.

THE PRESIDENT. It's a milestone. It's a signpost. But is it pointing the way to steel, or wheat, or phosphates? That's what we have to find out. Ah! He sees me. He understands. He will be over.

THE BARON. And when he comes . . . ?

THE PRESIDENT. He will tell me what to do.

THE BARON. You mean business is done this way? You mean, you would trust a stranger with a matter of this importance?

THE PRESIDENT. Baron, I trust neither my wife, nor my daughter, nor my closest friend. My confidential secretary has no idea where I live. But a face like that I would trust with my inmost secrets. Though we have never laid eyes on each other before, that man and I know each other to the depths of our souls. He's no stranger — he's my brother, he's myself. You'll see. He'll be over in a minute.

(The DEAF MUTE *enters and passes slowly among the tables, placing a small envelope before each customer. He comes to the* PRESIDENT*'s table.)*

What is this anyway? A conspiracy? We don't want your envelopes. Take them away.

(The DEAF MUTE *makes a short but pointed speech in sign language.)*

Waiter, what the devil's he saying?

WAITER. Only Irma understands him.

THE PRESIDENT. Irma? Who's Irma?

WAITER *(calls)*. Irma! It's the waitress inside, sir. Irma!

*(*IRMA *comes out. She is twenty. She has the face and figure of an angel.)*

IRMA. Yes?

WAITER. These gentlemen would . . .

THE PRESIDENT. Tell this fellow to get out of here, for God's sake!

(The DEAF MUTE *makes another manual oration.)*

What's he trying to say, anyway?

IRMA. He say's it's an exceptionally beautiful morning, sir. . . .

THE PRESIDENT. Who asked him?

IRMA. But, he says, it was nicer before the gentleman stuck his face in it.

THE PRESIDENT. Call the manager!

(IRMA *shrugs. She goes back into the restaurant. The* DEAF MUTE *walks off, left. Meanwhile a* SHOELACE PEDDLER *has arrived.*)

PEDDLER. Shoelaces? Postcards?

THE BARON. I think I could use a shoelace.

THE PRESIDENT. No, no...

PEDDLER. Black? Tan?

THE BARON (*showing his shoes*). What would you recommend?

PEDDLER. Anybody's guess.

THE BARON. Well, give me one of each.

THE PRESIDENT (*putting a hand on the* BARON'S *arm*). Baron, although I am your chairman, I have no authority over your personal life — none, that is, except to fix the amount of your director's fees, and eventually to assign a motor car for your use. Therefore, I am asking you, as a personal favor to me, not to purchase anything from this fellow.

THE BARON. How can I resist so gracious a request?

(*The* PEDDLER *shrugs, and passes on.*)

But I really don't understand.... What difference would it make?

THE PRESIDENT. Look here, Baron. Now that you're with us, you must understand that between this irresponsible riff-raff and us there is an impenetrable barrier. We have no dealings whatever with *them.*

THE BARON. But without us, the poor devil will starve.

THE PRESIDENT. No, he won't. He expects nothing from us. He has a clientele of his own. He sells shoelaces exclusively to those who have no shoes. Just as the necktie peddler sells only to those who wear no shirts. And that's why these street hawkers can afford to be insolent, disrespectful, and independent. They don't need us. They have a world of their own. Ah! My broker. Splendid. He's beaming.

(*The* BROKER *walks up and grasps the* PRESIDENT'S *hand with enthusiasm.*)

BROKER. Mr. President! My heartiest congratulations! What a day! What a day!

(*The* STREET JUGGLER *appears, right. He removes his coat, folds it carefully, and puts it on the bench. Then he opens a suitcase, from which he extracts a number of colored clubs.*)

THE PRESIDENT (*presenting the* BROKER). Baron Tommard, of our Board of Directors. My broker.

(*The* BROKER *bows. So does the* JUGGLER. *The* BROKER *sits down and signals for a drink. The* JUGGLER *prepares to juggle.*)

What's happened?

BROKER. Listen to this. Ten o'clock this morning. The market opens.

(*As he speaks, the* JUGGLER *provides a visual counterpart to the* BROKER'S *lines, his clubs rising and falling in rhythm to the* BROKER'S *words.*)

Half million shares issued at par, par value a hundred, quoted on the curb at 124 and we start buying at 126, 127, 129 — and it's going up — up — up —

(*The* JUGGLER'S *clubs rise higher and higher.*)

— 132 — 133 — 138 — 141 — 141 — 141 — 141 . . .

THE BARON. May I ask . . .

THE PRESIDENT. No, no — any explanation would only confuse you.

BROKER. Ten forty-five we start selling short on rumors of a Communist plot, market bearish. . . . 141 — 138 — 133 — 132 — and it's down — down — down — 102 — and we start buying back at 93. Eleven o'clock, rumors denied — 95 — 98 — 101 — 106 — 124 — 141 — and by 11:30 we've got it all back — net profit three and a half million francs.

THE PRESIDENT. Classical. Pure.

(*The* JUGGLER *bows again.* A LITTLE MAN *leans over from a near-by table, listening intently, and trembling with excitement.*)

And how many shares do we reserve to each member of the board?

BROKER. Fifty, as agreed.

THE PRESIDENT. Bit stingy, don't you think?

BROKER. All right — three thousand.

THE PRESIDENT. That's a little better. (*To the* BARON.) You get the idea?

THE BARON. I'm beginning to get it.

BROKER. And now we come to the exciting part. . . .

(*The* JUGGLER *prepares to juggle with balls of fire.*)

Listen carefully: With 35 per cent of our funded capital under Section 32 I buy 50,000 United at 36 which I immediately reconvert into 32,000 National Amalgamated two's preferred which I set up as collateral on 150,000 General Consols which I deposit against a credit of fifteen billion to buy Eastern Hennequin which I immediately turn into Argentine wheat realizing 136 per cent of the original investment which naturally accrues as capital gain and not as corporate income thus saving twelve millions in taxes, and at once convert the 25 per cent cotton reserve into lignite, and as our people swing into action in London and New York, I beat up the price on greige goods from 26 to 92 — 114 — 203 — 306 —

(*The* JUGGLER *by now is juggling his fire-balls in the sky. The balls no longer return to his hands.*)

— 404 . . .

(*The* LITTLE MAN *can stand no more. He rushes over and dumps a sackful of money on the table.*)

LITTLE MAN. Here — take it — please, take it!

BROKER (*frigidly*). Who is this man? What is this money?

LITTLE MAN. It's my life's savings. Every cent. I put it all in your hands.

BROKER. Can't you see we're busy?

LITTLE MAN. But I beg you. . . . It's my only chance. . . . Please don't turn me away.

BROKER. Oh, all right. (*He sweeps the money into his pocket.*) Well?

LITTLE MAN. I thought — perhaps you'd give me a little receipt. . . .

THE PRESIDENT. My dear man, people like us don't give receipts for money. We take them.

LITTLE MAN. Oh, pardon. Of course. I was confused. Here it is. (*Scribbles a receipt.*) Thank you — thank you — thank you.

(*He rushes off joyfully. The* STREET SINGER *reappears.*)

STREET SINGER (*sings*).

Do you hear, Mademoiselle,
Those musicians of hell?

THE PRESIDENT. What, again? Why does he keep repeating those two lines like a parrot?

WAITER. What else can he do? He doesn't know any more and the song's been out of print for years.

THE BARON. Couldn't he sing a song he knows?

WAITER. He likes this one. He hopes if he keeps singing the beginning someone will turn up to teach him the end.

THE PRESIDENT. Tell him to move on. We don't know the song.

(*The* PROFESSOR *strolls by, swinging his cane. He overhears.*)

PROFESSOR (*stops and addresses the* PRESIDENT *politely*). Nor do I, my dear sir. Nor do I. And yet, I'm in exactly the same predicament. I remember just two lines of my favorite song, as a child. A mazurka also, in case you're interested. . . .

THE PRESIDENT. I'm not.

PROFESSOR. Why is it, I wonder, that one always forgets the words of a mazurka? I suppose they just get lost in that damnable rhythm. All I remember is (*he sings*):

From England to Spain
I have drunk, it was bliss . . . .

STREET SINGER (*walks over, and picks up the tune*).

Red wine and champagne
And many a kiss.

PROFESSOR. Oh, God! It all comes back to me . . . ! (*He sings.*)

Red lips and white hands I have known
Where the nightingales dwell. . . .

THE PRESIDENT (*holding his hands to his ears*). Please — please . . .

STREET SINGER (*sings*).

And to each one I've whispered, "My own,"
And to each one, I've murmured: "Farewell."

THE PRESIDENT. Farewell. Farewell.

STREET SINGER, PROFESSOR (*duo*).

But there's one I shall never forget. . . .

THE PRESIDENT. This isn't a café. It's a circus!

(*The two go off, still singing:* "There is one that's engraved in my heart." *The* PROSPECTOR *gets up slowly and walks toward the* PRESIDENT'S *table. He looks down without a word. There is a tense silence.*)

PROSPECTOR. Well?

THE PRESIDENT. I need a name.

PROSPECTOR (*nods, with complete comprehension*). I need fifty thousand.

THE PRESIDENT. For a corporation.

PROSPECTOR. For a woman.

THE PRESIDENT. Immediately.

PROSPECTOR. Before evening.

THE PRESIDENT. Something . . .

PROSPECTOR. Unusual?

THE PRESIDENT. Something . . .

PROSPECTOR. Provocative?

THE PRESIDENT. Something . . .

PROSPECTOR. Practical.

THE PRESIDENT. Yes.

PROSPECTOR. Fifty thousand. Cash.

THE PRESIDENT. I'm listening.

PROSPECTOR. *International Substrate of Paris, Inc.*

THE PRESIDENT (*snaps his fingers*). That's it! (*To the* BROKER.) Pay him off.

(*The* BROKER *pays with the* LITTLE MAN'S *money*.)

Now — what does it mean?

PROSPECTOR. It means what it says. I'm a prospector.

THE PRESIDENT (*rises*). A prospector! Allow me to shake your hand. Baron. You are in the presence of one of nature's noblemen. Shake his hand. This is Baron Tommard. (*They shake hands.*) It is this man, my dear Baron, who smells out in the bowels of the earth those deposits of metal or liquid on which can be founded the only social unit of which our age is capable — the corporation. Sit down, please. (*They all sit.*) And now that we have a name . . .

PROSPECTOR. You need a property.

THE PRESIDENT. Precisely.

PROSPECTOR. I have one.

THE PRESIDENT. A claim?

PROSPECTOR. Terrific.

THE PRESIDENT. Foreign?

PROSPECTOR. French.

THE BARON. In Indo-China?

BROKER. Morocco?

THE PRESIDENT. In France?

PROSPECTOR (*matter of fact*). In Paris.

THE PRESIDENT. In Paris? You've been prospecting in Paris?

THE BARON. For women, no doubt.

THE PRESIDENT. For art?

BROKER. For gold?

PROSPECTOR. Oil.

BROKER. He's crazy.

THE PRESIDENT. Sh! He's inspired.

PROSPECTOR. You think I'm crazy. Well, they thought Columbus was crazy.

THE BARON. Oil in Paris?

BROKER. But how is it possible?

PROSPECTOR. It's not only possible. It's certain.

THE PRESIDENT. Tell us.

PROSPECTOR. You don't know, my dear sir, what treasures Paris conceals. Paris is the least prospected place in the world. We've gone over the rest of the planet with a fine-tooth comb. But has anyone ever thought of looking for oil in Paris? Nobody. Before me, that is.

THE PRESIDENT. Genius!

PROSPECTOR. No. Just a practical man. I use my head.

THE BARON. But why has nobody ever thought of this before?

PROSPECTOR. The treasures of the earth, my dear sir, are not easy to find nor to get at. They are invariably guarded by dragons. Doubtless there is some reason for this. For once we've dug out and consumed the internal ballast of the planet, the chances are it will shoot off on some irresponsible tangent and smash itself up in the sky. Well, that's the risk we take. Anyway, that's not my business. A prospector has enough to worry about.

THE BARON. I know — snakes — tarantulas — fleas . . .

PROSPECTOR. Worse than that, sir. Civilization.

THE PRESIDENT. Does that annoy you?

PROSPECTOR. Civilization gets in our way all the time. In the first place, it covers the earth with cities and towns which are damned awkward to dig up when you want to see what's underneath. It's not only the real-estate people — you can always do business with them — it's human sentimentality. How do you do business with that?

THE PRESIDENT. I see what you mean.

PROSPECTOR. They say that where we pass, nothing ever grows again. What of it? Is a park any better than a coal mine? What's a mountain got that a slag pile hasn't? What would you rather have in your garden — an almond tree or an oil well?

THE PRESIDENT. Well . . .

PROSPECTOR. Exactly. But what's the use of arguing with these fools? Imagine the choicest place you ever saw for an excavation, and what do they put there? A playground for children! Civilization!

THE PRESIDENT. Just show us the point where you want to start digging. We'll do the rest. Even if it's in the middle of the Louvre. Where's the oil?

PROSPECTOR. Perhaps you think it's easy to make an accurate fix in an area like Paris where everything conspires to put you off the scent? Women — perfume — flowers — history. You can talk all you like about geology, but an oil deposit, gentlemen, has to be smelled out. I have a good nose. I go further. I have a phenomenal nose. But the minute I get the right whiff — the minute I'm on the scent — a fragrance rises from what I take to be the spiritual deposits of the past — and I'm completely at sea. Now take this very point, for example, this very spot.

THE BARON. You mean — right here in Chaillot?

PROSPECTOR. Right under here.

THE PRESIDENT. Good heavens! (*He looks under his chair.*)

PROSPECTOR. It's taken me months to locate this spot.

THE BARON. But what in the world makes you think . . . ?

PROSPECTOR. Do you know this place, Baron?

THE BARON. Well, I've been sitting here for thirty years.

PROSPECTOR. Did you ever taste the water?

THE BARON. The water? Good God, no!

PROSPECTOR. It's plain to see that you are no prospector! A prospector, Baron, is as addicted to water as a drunkard to wine. Water, gentlemen, is the one substance from which the earth can conceal nothing. It sucks out its innermost secrets and brings them to our very lips. Well — beginning at Notre Dame, where I first caught the scent of oil three months ago, I worked my way across Paris, glassful by glassful, sampling the water, until at last I came to this café. And here — just two days ago — I took a sip. My heart began to thump. Was it possible that I was deceived? I took another, a third, a fourth, a fifth. I was trembling like a leaf. But there was no mistake. Each time that I drank, my taste-buds thrilled to the most exquisite flavor known to a prospector — the flavor of — (*with utmost lyricism*) petroleum!

THE PRESIDENT. Waiter! Some water and four glasses. Hurry. This round, gentlemen, is on me. And as a toast — I shall propose International Substrate of Paris, Incorporated.

(*The* WAITER *brings a decanter and the glasses. The* PRESIDENT *pours out the water amid profound silence. They taste it with the air of connoisseurs savoring something that has never before passed human lips. Then they look at each other doubtfully. The* PROSPECTOR *pours himself a second glass and drinks it off.*)

Well . . .

BROKER. Ye-es . . .

THE BARON. Mm . . .

PROSPECTOR. Get it?

THE BARON. Tastes queer.

PROSPECTOR. That's it. To the unpracticed palate it tastes queer. But to the taste-buds of the expert — ah!

THE BARON. Still, there's one thing I don't quite understand . . .

PROSPECTOR. Yes?

THE BARON. This café doesn't have its own well, does it?

PROSPECTOR. Of course not. This is Paris water.

BROKER. Then why should it taste different here than anywhere else?

PROSPECTOR. Because, my dear sir, the pipes that carry this water pass deep through the earth, and the earth just here is soaked with oil, and this oil permeates the pores of the iron and flavors the water it carries. Ever so little, yes — but quite enough to betray its presence to the sensitive tongue of the specialist.

THE BARON. I see.

PROSPECTOR. I don't say everyone is capable of tasting it. No. But I — I can detect the presence of oil in water that has passed within fifteen miles of a deposit. Under special circumstances, twenty.

THE PRESIDENT. Phenomenal!

PROSPECTOR. And so here I am with the greatest discovery of the age on my hands — but the blasted authorities won't let me drill a single well unless I show them the oil! Now how can I show them the oil unless they let me dig? Completely stymied! Eh?

THE PRESIDENT. What? A man like you?

PROSPECTOR. That's what they think. That's what they want. Have you noticed the strange glamor of the women this morning? And the quality of the sunshine? And this extraordinary convocation of vagabonds buzzing about protectively like bees around a hive? Do you know why it is? Because they know. It's a plot to distract us, to turn us from our purpose. Well, let them try. I know there's oil here. And I'm going to dig it up, even if I . . . (*he smiles*). Shall I tell you my little plan?

THE PRESIDENT. By all means.

PROSPECTOR. Well . . . For heaven's sake, what's that?

(*At this point, the* MADWOMAN *enters. She is dressed in the grand fashion of 1885, a taffeta skirt with an immense train — which she has gathered up by means of a clothespin — ancient button shoes, and a hat in the style of Marie Antoinette. She wears a lorgnette on a chain, and an enormous cameo pin at her throat. In her hand she carries a small basket. She walks in with great dignity, extracts a dinner bell from the bosom of her dress, and rings it sharply.* IRMA *appears.*)

COUNTESS. Are my bones ready, Irma?

IRMA. There won't be much today, Countess. We had broilers. Can you wait? While the gentleman inside finishes eating?

COUNTESS. And my gizzard?

IRMA. I'll try to get it away from him.

COUNTESS. If he eats my gizzard, save me the giblets. They will do for the tomcat that lives under the bridge. He likes a few giblets now and again.

IRMA. Yes, Countess.

(IRMA *goes back into the café. The* COUNTESS *takes a few steps and stops in front of the* PRESIDENT'S *table. She examines him with undisguised disapproval.*)

THE PRESIDENT. Waiter. Ask that woman to move on.

WAITER. Sorry, sir. This is her café.

THE PRESIDENT. Is she the manager of the café?

WAITER. She's the Madwoman of Chaillot.

THE PRESIDENT. A Madwoman? She's mad?

WAITER. Who says she's mad?

THE PRESIDENT. You just said so yourself.

WAITER. Look, sir. You asked me who she was. And I told you. What's mad about her? She's the Madwoman of Chaillot.

THE PRESIDENT. Call a policeman.

(*The* COUNTESS *whistles through her fingers. At once, the* DOORMAN *runs out of the café. He has three scarves in his hands.*)

COUNTESS. Have you found it? My feather boa?

DOORMAN. Not yet, Countess. Three scarves. But no boa.

COUNTESS. It's five years since I lost it. Surely you've had time to find it.

DOORMAN. Take one of these, Countess. Nobody's claimed them.

COUNTESS. A boa like that doesn't vanish, you know. A feather boa nine feet long!

DOORMAN. How about this blue one?

COUNTESS. With my pink ruffle and my green veil? You're joking! Let me see the yellow. (*She tries it on.*) How does it look?

DOORMAN. Terrific.

(*With a magnificent gesture, she flings the scarf about her, upsetting the* PRESIDENT's *glass and drenching his trousers with water. She stalks off without a glance at him.*)

THE PRESIDENT. Waiter! I'm making a complaint.

WAITER. Against whom?

THE PRESIDENT. Against her! Against you! The whole gang of you! That singer! That shoelace peddler! That female lunatic! Or whatever you call her!

THE BARON. Calm yourself, Mr. President. . . .

THE PRESIDENT. I'll do nothing of the sort! Baron, the first thing we have to do is get rid of these people! Good heavens, look at them! Every size, shape, color and period of history imaginable. It's utter anarchy! I tell you, sir, the only safeguard of order and discipline in the modern world is a standardized worker with interchangeable parts. That would solve the entire problem of management. Here, the manager. . . . And there — one composite drudge grunting and sweating all over the world. Just we two. Ah, how beautiful! How easy on the eyes! How restful for the conscience!

THE BARON. Yes, yes — of course.

THE PRESIDENT. Order. Symmetry. Balance. But instead of that, what? Here in Chaillot, the very citadel of management, these insolent phantoms of the past come to beard us with their raffish individualism — with the right of the voiceless to sing, of the dumb to make speeches, of trousers to have no seats and bosoms to have dinner bells!

THE BARON. But, after all, do these people matter?

THE PRESIDENT. My dear sir, wherever the poor are happy, and the servants are proud, and the mad are respected, our power is at an end. Look at that! That waiter! That madwoman! That flower girl! Do I get that sort of service? And suppose that I — president of twelve corporations and ten times a millionaire — were to stick a gladiolus in my buttonhole and start yelling — (*he tinkles his spoon in a glass violently, yelling*) "Are my bones ready, Irma?"

THE BARON (*reprovingly*). Mr. President . . .

(*People at the adjoining tables turn and stare with raised eyebrows. The* WAITER *starts to come over.*)

THE PRESIDENT. You see? Now.

PROSPECTOR. We were discussing my plan.

THE PRESIDENT. Ah, yes, your plan. (*He glances in the direction of the* MADWOMAN'S *table.*) Careful — she's looking at us.

PROSPECTOR. Do you know what a bomb is?

THE PRESIDENT. I'm told they explode.

PROSPECTOR. Exactly. You see that white building across the river. Do you happen to know what that is?

THE PRESIDENT. I do not.

PROSPECTOR. That's the office of the City Architect. That man has stubbornly refused to give me a permit to drill for oil anywhere within the limits of the city of Paris. I've tried everything with him — influence, bribes, threats. He says I'm crazy. And now . . .

THE PRESIDENT. Oh, my God! What is this one trying to sell us?

(DR. JADIN, *a little old man, enters left, and doffs his hat politely. He is somewhat ostentatiously respectable — gloved, pomaded, and carefully dressed, with a white handkerchief peeping out of his breast pocket.*)

DR. JADIN. Nothing but health, sir. Or rather the health of the feet. But remember — as the foot goes, so goes the man. May I present myself . . . ? Dr. Gaspard Jadin, French Navy, retired. Former specialist in the extraction of ticks and chiggers. At present specializing in the extraction of bunions and corns. In case of sudden emergency, Martial the waiter will furnish my home address. My office is here, second row, third table, week days, twelve to five. Thank you very much. (*He sits at his table.*)

WAITER. Your vermouth, Doctor?

DR. JADIN. My vermouth. My vermouths. How are your gallstones today, Martial?

WAITER. Fine. Fine. They rattle like anything.

DR. JADIN. Splendid. (*He spies the* COUNTESS.) Good morning, Countess. How's the floating kidney? Still afloat? (*She nods graciously.*) Splendid. Splendid. So long as it floats, it can't sink.

THE PRESIDENT. This is impossible! Let's go somewhere else.

PROSPECTOR. No. It's nearly noon.

THE PRESIDENT. Yes. It is. Five to twelve.

PROSPECTOR. In five minutes' time you're going to see that City Architect blown up, building and all — boom!

BROKER. Are you serious?

PROSPECTOR. That imbecile has no one to blame but himself. Yesterday noon, he got my ultimatum — he's had twenty-four hours to think it over. No permit? All right. Within two minutes my agent is going to drop a little package in his coal bin. And three minutes after that, precisely at noon . . .

THE BARON. You prospectors certainly use modern methods.

PROSPECTOR. The method may be modern. But the idea is old. To get at the treasure, it has always been necessary to slay the dragon. I guarantee that after this, the City Architect will be more reasonable. The new one, I mean.

THE PRESIDENT. Don't you think we're sitting a little close for comfort?

PROSPECTOR. Oh no, no. Don't worry. And above all, don't stare. We may be watched.

(*A clock strikes.*)

Why, that's noon. Something's wrong! Good God! What's this?

(*A* POLICEMAN *staggers in bearing a lifeless body on his shoulders in the manner prescribed as "The Fireman's Lift."*)

It's Pierre! My agent! (*He walks over with affected nonchalance.*) I say, Officer, what's that you've got?

POLICEMAN. Drowned man. (*He puts him down on the bench.*)

WAITER. He's not drowned. His clothes are dry. He's been slugged.

POLICEMAN. Slugged is also correct. He was just jumping off the bridge when I came along and pulled him back. I slugged him, naturally, so he wouldn't drag me under. Life Saving Manual, Rule 5: "In cases where there is danger of being dragged under, it is necessary to render the subject unconscious by means of a sharp blow." He's had that. (*He loosens the clothes and begins applying artificial respiration.*)

PROSPECTOR. The stupid idiot! What the devil did he do with the bomb? That's what comes of employing amateurs!

THE PRESIDENT. You don't think he'll give you away?

PROSPECTOR. Don't worry. (*He walks over to the policeman.*) Say, what do you think you're doing?

POLICEMAN. Lifesaving. Artificial respiration. First aid to the drowning.

PROSPECTOR. But he's not drowning.

POLICEMAN. But he thinks he is.

PROSPECTOR. You'll never bring him round that way, my friend. That's meant for people who drown in water. It's no good at all for those who drown without water.

POLICEMAN. What am I supposed to do? I've just been sworn in. It's my first day on the beat. I can't afford to get in trouble. I've got to go by the book.

PROSPECTOR. Perfectly simple. Take him back to the bridge where you found him and throw him in. Then you can save his life and you'll get a medal. This way, you'll only get fined for slugging an innocent man.

POLICEMAN. What do you mean, innocent? He was just going to jump when I grabbed him.

PROSPECTOR. Have you any proof of that?

POLICEMAN. Well, I saw him.

PROSPECTOR. Written proof? Witnesses?

POLICEMAN. No, but . . .

PROSPECTOR. Then don't waste time arguing. You're in trouble. Quick — before anybody notices — throw him in and dive after him. It's the only way out.

POLICEMAN. But I don't swim.

THE PRESIDENT. You'll learn how on the way down. Before you were born, did you know how to breathe?

POLICEMAN (*convinced*). All right. Here we go. (*He starts lifting the body.*)

DR. JADIN. One moment, please. I don't like to interfere, but it's my professional duty to point out that medical science has definitely established the fact of intra-uterine respiration. Consequently, this policeman, even before he was born, knew not only how to breathe but also how to cough, hiccup, and belch.

THE PRESIDENT. Suppose he did — how does it concern you?

DR. JADIN. On the other hand, medical science has never established the fact of intra-uterine swimming or diving. Under the circumstances, we are forced to the opinion, Officer, that if you dive in you will probably drown.

POLICEMAN. You think so?

PROSPECTOR. Who asked you for an opinion?

THE PRESIDENT. Pay no attention to that quack, Officer.

DR. JADIN. Quack, sir?

PROSPECTOR. This is not a medical matter. It's a legal problem. The officer has made a grave error. He's new. We're trying to help him.

BROKER. He's probably afraid of the water.

POLICEMAN. Nothing of the sort. Officially, I'm afraid of nothing. But I always follow doctor's orders.

DR. JADIN. You see, Officer, when a child is born . . .

PROSPECTOR. Now, what does he care about when a child is born? He's got a dying man on his hands. . . . Officer, if you want my advice . . .

POLICEMAN. It so happens, I care a lot about when a child is born. It's part of my duty to aid and assist any woman in childbirth or labor.

THE PRESIDENT. Can you imagine!

POLICEMAN. Is it true, Doctor, what they say, that when you have twins, the first born is considered to be the youngest?

DR. JADIN. Quite correct. And what's more, if the twins happen to be born at midnight on December 31st, the older is a whole year younger. He does his military service a year later. That's why you have to keep your eyes open. And that's the reason why a queen always gives birth before witnesses. . . .

POLICEMAN. God! The things a policeman is supposed to know! Doctor, what does it mean if, when I get up in the morning sometimes . . .

PROSPECTOR (*nudging the* PRESIDENT *meaningfully*). The old woman.

BROKER. Come on, Baron.

THE PRESIDENT. I think we'd better all run along.

PROSPECTOR. Leave him to me.

THE PRESIDENT. I'll see you later.

(*The* PRESIDENT *steals off with the* BROKER *and the* BARON.)

POLICEMAN (*still in conference with* DR. JADIN). But what's really worrying me, Doctor, is this — don't you think it's a bit risky for a man to marry after forty-five?

(*The* BROKER *runs in breathlessly.*)

BROKER. Officer! Officer!
POLICEMAN. What's the trouble?
BROKER. Quick! Two women are calling for help — on the sidewalk — Avenue Wilson!
POLICEMAN. Two women at once? Standing up or lying down?
BROKER. You'd better go and see. Quick!
PROSPECTOR. You'd better take the Doctor with you.
POLICEMAN. Come along, Doctor, come along. . . . (*Pointing to* PIERRE.) Tell him to wait till I get back. Come along, Doctor.

(*He runs out, the* DOCTOR *following. The* PROSPECTOR *moves over toward* PIERRE, *but* IRMA *crosses in front of him and takes the boy's hand.*)

IRMA. How beautiful he is! Is he dead, Martial?
WAITER (*handing her a pocket mirror*). Hold this mirror to his mouth. If it clouds over . . .
IRMA. It clouds over.
WAITER. He's alive. (*He holds out his hand for the mirror.*)
IRMA. Just a sec—

(*She rubs it clean and looks at herself intently. Before handing it back, she fixes her hair and applies her lipstick. Meanwhile the* PROSPECTOR *tries to get around the other side, but the* COUNTESS' *eagle eye drives him off. He shrugs his shoulders and exits with the* BARON.)

Oh, look — he's opened his eyes!

(PIERRE *opens his eyes, stares intently at* IRMA *and closes them again with the expression of a man who is among the angels.*)

PIERRE (*murmurs*). Oh! How beautiful!
VOICE (*from within the café*). Irma!
IRMA. Coming. Coming.

(*She goes in, not without a certain reluctance. The* COUNTESS *at once takes her place on the bench, and also the young man's hand.* PIERRE *sits up suddenly, and finds himself staring, not at* IRMA, *but into the very peculiar face of the* COUNTESS. *His expression changes.*)

COUNTESS. You're looking at my iris? Isn't it beautiful?

PIERRE. Very. (*He drops back, exhausted.*)

COUNTESS. The Sergeant was good enough to say it becomes me. But I no longer trust his taste. Yesterday, the flower girl gave me a lily, and he said it didn't suit me.

PIERRE (*weakly*). It's beautiful.

COUNTESS. He'll be very happy to know that you agree with him. He's really quite sensitive. (*She calls.*) Sergeant!

PIERRE. No, please — don't call the police.

COUNTESS. But I must. I think I hurt his feelings.

PIERRE. Let me go, Madame.

COUNTESS. No, no. Stay where you are. Sergeant!

(PIERRE *struggles weakly to get up.*)

PIERRE. Please let me go.

COUNTESS. I'll do nothing of the sort. When you let someone go, you never see him again. I let Charlotte Mazumet go. I never saw her again.

PIERRE. Oh, my head.

COUNTESS. I let Adolphe Bertaut go. And I was holding him. And I never saw him again.

PIERRE. Oh, God!

COUNTESS. Except once. Thirty years later. In the market. He had changed a great deal — he didn't know me. He sneaked a melon from right under my nose, the only good one of the year. Ah, here we are. Sergeant!

(*The* POLICE SERGEANT *comes in with importance.*)

SERGEANT. I'm in a hurry, Countess.

COUNTESS. With regard to the iris. This young man agrees with you. He says it suits me.

SERGEANT (*going*). There's a man drowning in the Seine.

COUNTESS. He's not drowning in the Seine. He's drowning here. Because I'm holding him tight — as I should have held Adolphe Bertaut. But if I let him go, I'm sure he will go and drown in the Seine. He's a lot better looking than Adolphe Bertaut, wouldn't you say?

(PIERRE *sighs deeply.*)

SERGEANT. How would I know?

COUNTESS. I've shown you his photograph. The one with the bicycle.

SERGEANT. Oh, yes. The one with the harelip.

COUNTESS. I've told you a hundred times! Adolphe Bertaut had no harelip. That was a scratch in the negative.

(*The* SERGEANT *takes out his notebook and pencil.*)

What are you doing?

SERGEANT. I am taking down the drowned man's name, given name, and date of birth.

COUNTESS. You think that's going to stop him from jumping in the river? Don't be silly, Sergeant. Put that book away and try to console him.

SERGEANT. I should try and console him?

COUNTESS. When people want to die, it is your job as a guardian of the state to speak out in praise of life. Not mine.

SERGEANT. I should speak out in praise of life?

COUNTESS. I assume you have some motive for interfering with people's attempts to kill each other, and rob each other, and run each other over? If you believe that life has some value, tell him what it is. Go on.

SERGEANT. Well, all right. Now look, young man . . .

COUNTESS. His name is Roderick.

PIERRE. My name is not Roderick.

COUNTESS. Yes, it is. It's noon. At noon all men become Roderick.

SERGEANT. Except Adolphe Bertaut.

COUNTESS. In the days of Adolphe Bertaut, we were forced to change the men when we got tired of their names. Nowadays, we're more practical — each hour on the hour all names are automatically changed. The men remain the same. But you're not here to discuss Adolphe Bertaut, Sergeant. You're here to convince the young man that life is worth living.

PIERRE. It isn't.

SERGEANT. Quiet. Now then — what was the idea of jumping off the bridge, anyway?

COUNTESS. The idea was to land in the river. Roderick doesn't seem to be at all confused about that.

SERGEANT. Now how can I convince anybody that life is worth living if you keep interrupting all the time?

COUNTESS. I'll be quiet.

SERGEANT. First of all, Mr. Roderick, you have to realize that suicide is a crime against the state. And why is it a crime against the state? Because every time anybody commits suicide, that means one soldier less for the army, one taxpayer less for the . . .

COUNTESS. Sergeant, isn't there something about life that you really enjoy?

SERGEANT. That I enjoy?

COUNTESS. Well, surely, in all these years, you must have found something worth living for. Some secret pleasure, or passion. Don't blush. Tell him about it.

SERGEANT. Who's blushing? Well, naturally, yes — I have my passions — like everybody else. The fact is, since you ask me — I love — to play — casino. And if the gentleman would like to join me, by and by when I go off duty, we can sit down to a nice little game in the back room with a nice cold glass of beer. If he wants to kill an hour, that is.

COUNTESS. He doesn't want to kill an hour. He wants to kill himself. Well? Is that all the police force has to offer by way of earthly bliss?

SERGEANT. Huh? You mean — (*he jerks a thumb in the direction of the pretty* BLONDE, *who has just been joined by a* BRUNETTE *of the same stamp*) Paulette?

(PIERRE *groans.*)

COUNTESS. You're not earning your salary, Sergeant. I defy anybody to stop dying on your account.

SERGEANT. Go ahead, if you can do any better. But you won't find it easy.

COUNTESS. Oh, this is not a desperate case at all. A young man who has just fallen in love with someone who has fallen in love with him!

PIERRE. She hasn't. How could she?

COUNTESS. Oh, yes, she has. She was holding your hand, just as I'm holding it, when all of a sudden . . . Did you ever know Marshal Canrobert's[1] niece?

SERGEANT. How could he know Marshal Canrobert's niece?

COUNTESS. Lots of people knew her — when she was alive.

(PIERRE *begins to struggle energetically.*)

No, no, Roderick — stop — stop!

SERGEANT. You see? You won't do any better than I did.

COUNTESS. No? Let's bet. I'll bet my iris against one of your gold buttons. Right? — Roderick, I know very well why you tried to drown yourself in the river.

PIERRE. You don't at all.

COUNTESS. It's because that Prospector wanted you to commit a horrible crime.

PIERRE. How did you know that?

COUNTESS. He stole my boa, and now he wants you to kill me.

PIERRE. Not exactly.

COUNTESS. It wouldn't be the first time they've tried it. But I'm not so easy to get rid of, my boy, oh, no. . . . Because . . .

(*The* DOORMAN *rides in on his bicycle. He winks at the* SERGEANT, *who has now seated himself while the* WAITER *serves him a beer.*)

[1] Commander of French forces in the Crimean war, 1854–1855.

DOORMAN. Take it easy, Sergeant.

SERGEANT. I'm busy saving a drowning man.

COUNTESS. They can't kill me because — I have no desire to die.

PIERRE. You're fortunate.

COUNTESS. To be alive is to be fortunate, Roderick. Of course, in the morning, when you first awake, it does not always seem so very gay. When you take your hair out of the drawer, and your teeth out of the glass, you are apt to feel a little out of place in this world. Especially if you've just been dreaming that you're a little girl on a pony looking for strawberries in the woods. But all you need to feel the call of life once more is a letter in your mail giving you your schedule for the day — your mending, your shopping, that letter to your grandmother that you never seem to get around to. And so, when you've washed your face in rosewater, and powdered it — not with this awful rice-powder they sell nowadays, which does nothing for the skin, but with a cake of pure white starch — and put on your pins, your rings, your brooches, bracelets, earrings, and pearls — in short, when you are dressed for your morning coffee — and have had a good look at yourself — not in the glass, naturally — it lies — but in the side of the brass gong that once belonged to Admiral Courbet[2] — then, Roderick, then you're armed, you're strong, you're ready — you can begin again.

(PIERRE *is listening now intently. There are tears in his eyes.*)

PIERRE. Oh, Madame . . . ! Oh, Madame . . . !

COUNTESS. After that, everything is pure delight. First the morning paper. Not, of course, these current sheets full of lies and vulgarity. I always read the *Gaulois*, the issue of March 22, 1903. It's by far the best. It has some delightful scandal, some excellent fashion notes, and, of course, the last-minute bulletin on the death of Leonide Leblanc. She used to live next door, poor woman, and when I learn of her death every morning, it gives me quite a shock. I'd gladly lend you my copy, but it's in tatters.

SERGEANT. Couldn't we find him a copy in some library?

COUNTESS. I doubt it. And so, when you've taken your fruit salts — not in water, naturally — no matter what they say, it's water that gives you gas — but with a bit of spiced cake — then in sunlight or rain, Chaillot calls. It is time to dress for your morning walk. This takes much longer, of course — without a maid, impossible to do it in under an hour, what with your corset, corset-cover, and drawers all of which lace or button in the back. I asked Madame Lanvin, a while ago, to fit the drawers with zippers. She was quite charming, but she declined. She thought it would spoil the style.

(*The* DEAF MUTE *comes in.*)

[2] Admiral Courbet commanded the French fleet in the Far East, 1883–1884.

WAITER. I know a place where they put zippers on anything.

(*The* RAGPICKER *enters.*)

COUNTESS. I think Lanvin knows best. But I really manage very well, Martial. What I do now is, I lace them up in front, then twist them around to the back. It's quite simple, really. Then you choose a lorgnette, and then the usual fruitless search for the feather boa that the prospector stole — I know it was he: he didn't dare look me in the eye — and then all you need is a rubber band to slip around your parasol — I lost the catch the day I struck the cat that was stalking the pigeon — it was worth it — ah, that day I earned my wages!

THE RAGPICKER. Countess, if you can use it, I found a nice umbrella catch the other day with a cat's eye in it.

COUNTESS. Thank you, Ragpicker. They say these eyes sometimes come to life and fill with tears. I'd be afraid . . .

PIERRE. Go on, Madame, go on . . .

COUNTESS. Ah! So life is beginning to interest you, is it? You see how beautiful it is?

PIERRE. What a fool I've been!

COUNTESS. Then, Roderick, I begin my rounds. I have my cats to feed, my dogs to pet, my plants to water. I have to see what the evil ones are up to in the district — those who hate people, those who hate plants, those who hate animals. I watch them sneaking off in the morning to put on their disguises — to the baths, to the beauty parlors, to the barbers. But they can't deceive me. And when they come out again with blonde hair and false whiskers, to pull up my flowers and poison my dogs, I'm there, and I'm ready. All you have to do to break their power is to cut across their path from the left. That isn't always easy. Vice moves swiftly. But I have a good long stride and I generally manage. . . . Right, my friends?

(*The* WAITER *and the* RAGPICKER *nod their heads with evident approval.*)

Yes, the flowers have been marvelous this year. And the butcher's dog on the Rue Bizet, in spite of that wretch that tried to poison him, is friskier than ever. . . .

SERGEANT. That dog had better look out. He has no license.

COUNTESS. He doesn't seem to feel the need for one.

THE RAGPICKER. The Duchess de la Rochefoucauld's whippet is getting awfully thin. . . .

COUNTESS. What can I do? She bought that dog full grown from a kennel where they didn't know his right name. A dog without his right name is bound to get thin.

THE RAGPICKER. I've got a friend who knows a lot about dogs — an Arab . . .

COUNTESS. Ask him to call on the Duchess. She receives Thursdays, five to seven. You see, then, Roderick. That's life. Does it appeal to you now?

PIERRE. It seems marvelous.

COUNTESS. Ah! Sergeant. My button.

(*The* SERGEANT *gives her his button and goes off. At this point the* PROSPECTOR *enters.*)

That's only the morning. Wait till I tell you about the afternoon!

PROSPECTOR. All right, Pierre. Come along now.

PIERRE. I'm perfectly all right here.

PROSPECTOR. I said, come along now.

PIERRE (*to the* COUNTESS). I'd better go, Madame.

COUNTESS. No.

PIERRE. It's no use. Please let go my hand.

PROSPECTOR. Madame, will you oblige me by letting my friend go?

COUNTESS. I will not oblige you in any way.

PROSPECTOR. All right. Then I'll oblige you . . . !

(*He tries to push her away. She catches up a soda water siphon and squirts it in his face.*)

PIERRE. Countess . . .

COUNTESS. Stay where you are. This man isn't going to take you away. In the first place, I shall need you in a few minutes to take me home. I'm all alone here and I'm very easily frightened.

(*The* PROSPECTOR *makes a second attempt to drag* PIERRE *away. The* COUNTESS *cracks him over the skull with the siphon. They join battle. The* COUNTESS *whistles. The* DOORMAN *comes, then the other* VAGABONDS, *and lastly the* POLICE SERGEANT.)

PROSPECTOR. Officer! Arrest this woman!

SERGEANT. What's the trouble here?

PROSPECTOR. She refuses to let this man go.

SERGEANT. Why should she?

PROSPECTOR. It's against the law for a woman to detain a man on the street.

IRMA. Suppose it's her son whom she's found again after twenty years?

THE RAGPICKER (*gallantly*). Or her long-lost brother? The Countess is not so old.

PROSPECTOR. Officer, this is a clear case of disorderly conduct.

(*The* DEAF MUTE *interrupts with frantic signals.*)

COUNTESS. Irma, what is the Deaf Mute saying?

IRMA (*interpreting*). The young man is in danger of his life. He mustn't go with him.

PROSPECTOR. What does he know?

IRMA. He knows everything.

PROSPECTOR. Officer, I'll have to take your number.

COUNTESS. Take his number. It's 2133. It adds up to nine. It will bring you luck.

SERGEANT. Countess, between ourselves, what are you holding him for, anyway?

COUNTESS. I'm holding him because it's very pleasant to hold him. I've never really held anybody before, and I'm making the most of it. And because so long as *I* hold him, he's free.

PROSPECTOR. Pierre, I'm giving you fair warning . . .

COUNTESS. And I'm holding him because Irma wants me to hold him. Because if I let him go, it will break her heart.

IRMA. Oh, Countess!

SERGEANT (*to the* PROSPECTOR). All right, you — move on. Nobody's holding you. You're blocking traffic. Move on.

PROSPECTOR (*menacingly*). I have your number. (*And murderously, to* PIERRE.) You'll regret this, Pierre. (*Exit* PROSPECTOR.)

PIERRE. Thank you, Countess.

COUNTESS. They're blackmailing you, are they?

(PIERRE *nods.*)

What have you done? Murdered somebody?

PIERRE. No.

COUNTESS. Stolen something?

PIERRE. No.

COUNTESS. What then?

PIERRE. I forged a signature.

COUNTESS. Whose signature?

PIERRE. My father's. To a note.

COUNTESS. And this man has the paper, I suppose?

PIERRE. He promised to tear it up, if I did what he wanted. But I couldn't do it.

COUNTESS. But the man is mad! Does he really want to destroy the whole neighborhood?

PIERRE. He wants to destroy the whole city.

COUNTESS (*laughs*). Fantastic.

PIERRE. It's not funny, Countess. He can do it. He's mad, but he's powerful, and he has friends. Their machines are already drawn up and waiting. In three months' time you may see the city covered by a forest of derricks and drills.

COUNTESS. But what are they looking for? Have they lost something?

PIERRE. They're looking for oil. They're convinced that Paris is sitting on a lake of oil.

COUNTESS. Suppose it is. What harm does it do?

PIERRE. They want to bring the oil to the surface, Countess.

COUNTESS (*laughs*). How silly! Is that a reason to destroy a city? What do they want with this oil?

PIERRE. They want to make war, Countess.

COUNTESS. Oh, dear, let's forget about these horrible men. The world is beautiful. It's happy. That's how God made it. No man can change it.

WAITER. Ah, Countess, if you only knew . . .

COUNTESS. If I only knew what?

WAITER. Shall we tell her now? Shall we tell her?

COUNTESS. What is it you are hiding from me?

THE RAGPICKER. Nothing, Countess. It's you who are hiding.

WAITER. You tell her. You've been a pitchman. You can talk.

ALL. Tell her. Tell her. Tell her.

COUNTESS. You're frightening me, my friends. Go on. I'm listening.

THE RAGPICKER. Countess, there was a time when old clothes were as good as new — in fact, they were better. Because when people wore clothes, they gave something to them. You may not believe it, but right this minute, the highest-priced shops in Paris are selling clothes that were thrown away thirty years ago. They're selling them for new. That's how good they were.

COUNTESS. Well?

THE RAGPICKER. Countess, there was a time when garbage was a pleasure. A garbage can was not what it is now. If it smelled a little strange, it was because it was a little confused — there was everything there — sardines, cologne, iodine, roses. An amateur might jump to a wrong conclusion. But to a professional — it was the smell of God's plenty.

COUNTESS. Well?

THE RAGPICKER. Countess, the world has changed.

COUNTESS. Nonsense. How could it change? People are the same, I hope.

THE RAGPICKER. No, Countess. The people are not the same. The people are different. There's been an invasion. An infiltration. From another planet. The world is not beautiful any more. It's not happy.

COUNTESS. Not happy? Is that true? Why didn't you tell me this before?

THE RAGPICKER. Because you live in a dream, Countess. And we don't like to disturb you.

COUNTESS. But how could it have happened?

THE RAGPICKER. Countess, there was a time when you could walk around Paris, and all the people you met were just like yourself. A little cleaner, maybe, or dirtier, perhaps, or angry, or smiling — but you knew them. They were you. Well, Countess, twenty years ago, one day, on the street, I saw a face in the crowd. A face, you might say, without a face. The eyes — empty. The expression — not human. Not a human face. It saw me staring, and when it looked back at me with its gelatine eyes, I shuddered. Because I knew that to make room for this one, one of us must have left the earth. A while after, I saw another. And another. And since then, I've seen hundreds come in — yes — thousands.

COUNTESS. Describe them to me.

THE RAGPICKER. You've seen them yourself, Countess. Their clothes don't wrinkle. Their hats don't come off. When they talk, they don't look at you. They don't perspire.

COUNTESS. Have they wives? Have they children?

THE RAGPICKER. They buy the models out of shop windows, furs and all. They animate them by a secret process. Then they marry them. Naturally, they don't have children.

COUNTESS. What work do they do?

THE RAGPICKER. They don't do any work. Whenever they meet, they whisper, and then they pass each other thousand-franc notes. You see them standing on the corner by the Stock Exchange. You see them at auctions — in the back. They never raise a finger — they just stand there. In theater lobbies, by the box office — they never go inside. They don't do anything, but wherever you see them, things are not the same. I remember well the time when a cabbage could sell itself just by being a cabbage. Nowadays it's no good being a cabbage — unless you have an agent and pay him a commission. Nothing is free any more to sell itself or give itself away. These days, Countess, every cabbage has its pimp.

COUNTESS. I can't believe that.

THE RAGPICKER. Countess, little by little, the pimps have taken over the world. They don't do anything, they don't make anything — they just stand there and take their cut. It makes a difference. Look at the shopkeepers. Do you ever see one smiling at a customer any more? Certainly not. Their smiles are strictly for the pimps. The butcher has to smile at the meat-pimp, the florist at the rose-pimp, the grocer at the fresh-fruit-and-vegetable pimp. It's all organized down to the slightest detail. A pimp for birdseed. A pimp for fishfood. That's why the cost of living keeps going up all the time. You buy a glass of beer — it costs twice as much as it used to. Why? 10 per cent for the glass-pimp, 10 per cent for the beer-pimp, 20 per cent for the glass-of-beer pimp — that's where our money goes. Personally, I prefer the old-fashioned type. Some of those men at least were loved by the women they sold. But what feelings can a pimp arouse in a leg of lamb? Pardon my language, Irma.

COUNTESS. It's all right. She doesn't understand it.

THE RAGPICKER. So now you know, Countess, why the world is no longer happy. We are the last of the free people of the earth. You saw them looking us over today. Tomorrow, the street singer will start paying the song-pimp, and the garbage-pimp will be after me. I tell you, Countess, we're finished. It's the end of free enterprise in this world!

COUNTESS. Is this true, Roderick?

PIERRE. I'm afraid it's true.

COUNTESS. Did you know about this, Irma?

IRMA. All I know is the doorman says that faith is dead.

DOORMAN. I've stopped taking bets over the phone.

JUGGLER. The very air is different, Countess. You can't trust it any more. If I throw my torches up too high, they go out.

THE RAGPICKER. The sky-pimp puts them out.

FLOWER GIRL. My flowers don't last over night now. They wilt.

JUGGLER. Have you noticed, the pigeons don't fly any more?

THE RAGPICKER. They can't afford to. They walk.

COUNTESS. They're a lot of fools and so are you! You should have told me at once! How can you bear to live in a world where there is unhappiness? Where a man is not his own master? Are you cowards? All we have to do is to get rid of these men.

PIERRE. How can we get rid of them? They're too strong.

(*The* SERGEANT *walks up again.*)

COUNTESS (*smiling*). The Sergeant will help us.

SERGEANT. Who? Me?

IRMA. There are a great many of them, Countess. The Deaf Mute knows them all. They employed him once, years ago, because he was deaf.

(*The* DEAF MUTE *wigwags a short speech.*)

They fired him because he wasn't blind.

(*Another flash of sign language.*)

They're all connected like the parts of a machine.

COUNTESS. So much the better. We shall drive the whole machine into a ditch.

SERGEANT. It's not that easy, Countess. You never catch these birds napping. They change before your very eyes. I remember when I was in the detectives. . . . You catch a president, pfft! He turns into a trustee. You catch him as trustee, and pfft! he's not a trustee — he's an honorary vice-chairman. You catch a Senator dead to rights: he becomes Minister of Justice. You get after the Minister of Justice — he is Chief of Police. And there you are — no longer in the detectives.

PIERRE. He's right, Countess. They have all the power. And all the money. And they're greedy for more.

COUNTESS. They're greedy? Ah, then, my friends, they're lost. If they're greedy, they're stupid. If they're greedy — don't worry, I know exactly what to do. Roderick, by tonight you will be an honest man. And, Juggler, your torches will stay lit. And your beer will flow freely again, Martial. And the world will be saved. Let's get to work.

THE RAGPICKER. What are you going to do?

COUNTESS. Have you any kerosene in the house, Irma?

IRMA. Yes. Would you like some?

COUNTESS. I want just a little. In a dirty bottle. With a little mud. And some mange-cure, if you have it. (*To the* DEAF MUTE.) Deaf Mute! Take a letter.

(IRMA *interprets in sign language.*)

(*To the* SINGER.) Singer, go and find Madame Constance.

(IRMA *and the* WAITER *go into the café.*)

SINGER. Yes, Countess.
COUNTESS. Ask her to be at my house by two o'clock. I'll be waiting for her in the cellar. You may tell her we have to discuss the future of humanity. That's sure to bring her.
SINGER. Yes, Countess.
COUNTESS. And ask her to bring Mademoiselle Gabrielle and Madame Josephine with her. Do you know how to get in to speak to Madame Constance? You ring twice, and then meow three times like a cat. Do you know how to meow?
SINGER. I'm better at barking.
COUNTESS. Better practice meowing on the way. Incidentally, I think Madame Constance knows all the verses of your mazurka. Remind me to ask her.
SINGER. Yes, Countess. (*Exit.*)

(IRMA *comes in. She is shaking the oily concoction in a little perfume vial, which she now hands the* COUNTESS.)

IRMA. Here you are, Countess.
COUNTESS. Thanks, Irma. (*She assumes a presidential manner.*) Deaf Mute! Ready?

(IRMA *interprets in sign language. The* WAITER *has brought out a portfolio of letter paper and placed it on a table. The* DEAF MUTE *sits down before it, and prepares to write.*)

IRMA (*speaking for the* DEAF MUTE.) I'm ready.
COUNTESS. My dear Mr. — What's his name?

(IRMA *wigwags the question to the* DEAF MUTE, *who answers in the same manner. It is all done so deftly that it is as if the* DEAF MUTE *were actually speaking.*)

IRMA. They are all called Mr. President.
COUNTESS. My dear Mr. President: I have personally verified the existence of a spontaneous outcrop of oil in the cellar of number 21, rue de

Chaillot, which is at present occupied by a dignified person of unstable mentality. (*The* COUNTESS *grins knowingly.*) This explains why, fortunately for us, the discovery has so long been kept secret. If you should wish to verify the existence of this outcrop for yourself, you may call at the above address at 3:00 P.M. today. I am herewith enclosing a sample so that you may judge the quality and consistency of the crude. Yours very truly. Roderick, can you sign the prospector's name?

PIERRE. You wish me to?

COUNTESS. One forgery wipes out the other.

(PIERRE *signs the letter. The* DEAF MUTE *types the address on an envelope.*)

IRMA. Who is to deliver this?

COUNTESS. The Doorman, of course. On his bicycle. And as soon as you have delivered it, run over to the prospector's office. Leave word that the President expects to see him at my house at three.

DOORMAN. Yes, Countess.

COUNTESS. I shall leave you now. I have many pressing things to do. Among others, I must press my red gown.

RAGPICKER. But this only takes care of two of them, Countess.

COUNTESS. Didn't the Deaf Mute say they are all connected like the works of a machine?

IRMA. Yes.

COUNTESS. Then, if one comes, the rest will follow. And we shall have them all. My boa, please.

DOORMAN. The one that's stolen, Countess?

COUNTESS. Naturally. The one the prospector stole.

DOORMAN. It hasn't turned up yet, Countess. But someone has left an ermine collar.

COUNTESS. Real ermine?

DOORMAN. Looks like it.

COUNTESS. Ermine and iris were made for each other. Let me see it.

DOORMAN. Yes, Countess. (*Exit* DOORMAN.)

COUNTESS. Roderick, you shall escort me. You still look pale. I have some old Chartreuse at home. I always take a glass each year. Last year I forgot. You shall have it.

PIERRE. If there is anything I can do, Countess . . . ?

COUNTESS. There is a great deal you can do. There are all the things that need to be done in a room that no man has been in for twenty years. You can untwist the cord on the blind and let in a little sunshine for a change. You can take the mirror off the wardrobe door, and deliver me once and for all from the old harpy that lives in the mirror. You can let the mouse out of the trap. I'm tired of feeding it. (*To her friends.*) Each man to his post. See you later, my friends.

(*The* DOORMAN *puts the ermine collar around her shoulders.*)

Thank you, my boy. It's rabbit.

(*One o'clock strikes.*)

Your arm, Valentine.

PIERRE. Valentine?

COUNTESS. It's just struck one. At one, all men become Valentine.

PIERRE (*he offers his arm*). Permit me.

COUNTESS. Or Valentino. It's obviously far from the same, isn't it, Irma? But they have that much choice.

(*She sweeps out majestically with* PIERRE. *The others disperse. All but* IRMA.)

IRMA (*clearing off the table*). I hate ugliness. I love beauty. I hate meanness. I adore kindness. It may not seem so grand to some to be a waitress in Paris. I love it. A waitress meets all sorts of people. She observes life. I hate to be alone. I love people. But I have never said I love you to a man. Men try to make me say it. They put their arms around me — I pretend I don't see it. They pinch me — I pretend I don't feel it. They kiss me — I pretend I don't know it. They take me out in the evening and make me drink — but I'm careful, I never say it. If they don't like it, they can leave me alone. Because when I say I love you to Him, He will know just by looking in my eyes that many have held me and pinched me and kissed me, but I have never said I love you to anyone in the world before. Never. No. (*Looking off in the direction in which* PIERRE *has gone, she whispers softly.*) I love you.

VOICE (*from within the café*). Irma!

IRMA. Coming. (*Exits.*)

ACT TWO

(SCENE: *The cellar of the* COUNTESS' *house. An ancient vault set deep in the ground, with walls of solid masonry, part brick and part great ashlars, mossy and sweating. A staircase of medieval pattern is built into the thickness of the wall, and leads up to the street level from a landing halfway down. In the corners of the cellar are piled casks, packing cases, birdcages, and other odds and ends — the accumulation of centuries — the whole effect utterly fantastic.*

In the center of the vast underground room, some furniture has been arranged to give an impression of a sitting-room of the 1890's. There is a venerable chaise-longue piled with cushions that once were gay, three armchairs, a table with an oil lamp and a bowl of flowers, a shaggy rug. It is 2:00 P.M., *the same day.*

AT RISE: *The* COUNTESS *is sitting over a bit of mending, in one of the armchairs.* IRMA *appears on the landing and calls down.*)

IRMA. Countess! The Sewer Man is here.

COUNTESS. Thank goodness, Irma. Send him down.

(*The* SEWER MAN *enters. He carries his hip-boots in his hand.*)

How do you do, Mr. Sewer Man?

(*The* SEWER MAN *bows.*)

But why do you have your boots in your hand instead of on your feet?

SEWER MAN. Etiquette, Countess. Etiquette.

COUNTESS. How very American! I'm told that Americans nowadays apologize for their gloves if they happen to take one's hand. As if the skin of a human were nicer to touch than the skin of a sheep! And particularly if they have sweaty hands . . . !

SEWER MAN. My feet never sweat, Countess.

COUNTESS. How very nice! But please don't stand on ceremony here. Put your boots on. Put them on.

SEWER MAN (*complying*). Thanks very much, Countess.

COUNTESS (*while he draws on his boots*). I'm sure you must have a very poor opinion of the upper world, from what you see of it. The way people throw their filth into your territory is absolutely scandalous! I burn all my refuse, and I scatter the ashes. All I ever throw in the drain is flowers. Did you happen to see a lily float by this morning? Mine. But perhaps you didn't notice?

SEWER MAN. We notice a lot more down there, Countess, than you might think. You'd be surprised the things we notice. There's lots of things come along that were obviously intended for us — little gifts, you might call them — sometimes a brand-new shaving brush — sometimes *The Brothers Karamazov*. . . . Thanks for the lily, Countess. A very sweet thought.

COUNTESS. Tomorrow you shall have this iris. But now, let's come to the point. I have two questions to ask you.

SEWER MAN. Yes, Countess?

COUNTESS. First — and this has nothing to do with our problem — it's just something that has been troubling me. . . . Tell me, is it true that the sewer men of Paris have a king?

SEWER MAN. Oh, now, Countess, that's another of those fairy tales out of the Sunday supplements. It just seems those writers can't keep their minds off the sewers! It fascinates them. They keep thinking of us moving around in our underground canals like gondoliers in Venice, and it sends them into a fever of romance! The things they say about us! They say we have a race of girls down there who never see the light of day! It's completely fantastic! The girls naturally come out — every Christmas and Easter. And orgies by torchlight with gondolas and guitars! With troops of rats that dance as they follow the piper! What nonsense! The rats are not allowed to dance. No, no, no. Of course we have no king. Down in the sewers, you'll find nothing but good Republicans.

COUNTESS. And no queen?

SEWER MAN. No. We may run a beauty contest down there once in a while. Or crown a mermaid Queen of the May. But no queen what you'd call a queen. And, as for these swimming races they talk so much about . . . possibly once in a while — in the summer — in the dog days. . . .

COUNTESS. I believe you. I believe you. And now tell me. Do you remember that night I found you here in my cellar — looking very pale and strange — you were half-dead as a matter of fact — and I gave you some brandy . . .

SEWER MAN. Yes, Countess.

COUNTESS. That night you promised if ever I should need it — you would tell me the secret of this room.

SEWER MAN. The secret of the moving stone?

COUNTESS. I need it now.

SEWER MAN. Only the King of the Sewer Men knows this secret.

COUNTESS. I'm sure of it. I know most secrets, of course. As a matter of fact, I have three magic words that will open any door that words can open. I have tried them all — in various tones of voice. They don't seem to work. And this is a matter of life and death.

SEWER MAN. Look, Countess. (*He locates a brick in the masonry, and pushes it. A huge block of stone slowly pivots and uncovers a trap from which a circular staircase winds into the bowels of the earth.*)

COUNTESS. Good heavens! Where do those stairs lead?

SEWER MAN. Nowhere.

COUNTESS. But they must go somewhere.

SEWER MAN. They just go down.

COUNTESS. Let's go and see.

SEWER MAN. No, Countess. Never again. That time you found me, I had a pretty close shave. I kept going down and around, and down and around for an hour, a year — I don't know. There's no end to it, Countess. Once you start you can't stop. . . . Your head begins to turn — you're lost. No — once you start down, there's no coming up.

COUNTESS. You came up.

SEWER MAN. I — I am a special case. Besides, I had my tools, my ropes. And I stopped in time.

COUNTESS. You could have screamed — shouted.

SEWER MAN. You could fire off a cannon.

COUNTESS. Who could have built a thing like this?

SEWER MAN. Paris is old, you know. Paris is very old.

COUNTESS. You don't suppose, by any chance, there is oil down there?

SEWER MAN. There's only death down there.

COUNTESS. I should have preferred a little oil too — or a vein of gold — or emeralds. You're quite sure there is nothing?

SEWER MAN. Not even rats.

COUNTESS. How does one lower this stone?

SEWER MAN. Simple. To open, you press here. And to close it, you push there. (*He presses the brick. The stone descends.*) Now there's two of us in the world that knows it.

COUNTESS. I won't remember long. Is it all right if I repeat my magic words while I press it?

SEWER MAN. It's bound to help.

(IRMA *enters.*)

IRMA. Countess, Madame Constance and Mademoiselle Gabrielle are here.

COUNTESS. Show them down, Irma. Thank you very much, Mr. Sewer Man.

SEWER MAN. Like that story about the steam laundry that's supposed to be running day and night in my sewer . . . I can assure you . . .

COUNTESS (*edging him toward the door.*) Thank you very much.

SEWER MAN. Pure imagination! They never work nights. (*He goes off, bowing graciously.*)

(CONSTANCE, *the Madwoman of Passy, and* GABRIELLE, *the Madwoman of St. Sulpice,*[1] *come down daintily.* CONSTANCE *is all in white. She wears an enormous hat graced with ostrich plumes, and a lavender veil.* GABRIELLE *is costumed with the affected simplicity of the 1880's. She is atrociously made up in a remorseless parody of blushing innocence, and she minces down the stairs with macabre coyness.*)

CONSTANCE. Aurelia! Don't tell us they've found your feather boa?

GABRIELLE. You don't mean Adolphe Bertaut has proposed at last! I knew he would.

COUNTESS. How are you, Constance? (*She shouts.*) How are you, Gabrielle?

GABRIELLE. You needn't shout today, my dear. It's Wednesday. Wednesdays, I hear perfectly.

CONSTANCE. It's Thursday.

GABRIELLE. Oh, dear. Well, never mind. I'm going to make an exception just this once.

CONSTANCE (*to an imaginary dog who has stopped on the landing*). Come along, Dickie. Come along. And stop barking. What a racket you're making! Come on, darling — we've come to see the longest boa and the handsomest man in Paris. Come on.

COUNTESS. Constance, it's not a question of my boa today. Nor of poor Adolphe. It's a question of the future of the human race.

CONSTANCE. You think it has a future?

[1] Passy and St. Sulpice, like Chaillot, are fashionable sections of Paris.

COUNTESS. Please don't make silly jokes. Sit down and listen to me. Today we must make a decision which may alter the fate of the world.

CONSTANCE. Couldn't we do it tomorrow? I want to wash my slippers. Now, Dickie — please!

COUNTESS. We haven't a moment to waste. Where is Josephine? Well, we'd best have our tea, and the moment Josephine comes . . .

GABRIELLE. Josephine is sitting on her bench in front of the palace waiting for President Wilson to come out. She says she's sorry, but she positively must see him today.

CONSTANCE. Dickie!

COUNTESS. What a pity! (*She gets the tea things from the side table, pours tea and serves cake and honey.*) I wish she were here to help us. She has a first-class brain.

CONSTANCE. Go ahead, dear. We're listening. (*To* DICKIE.) What is it, Dickie? You want to sit in Aunt Aurelia's lap. All right, darling. Go on. Jump, Dickie.

COUNTESS. Constance, we love you, as you know. And we love Dickie. But this is a serious matter. So let's stop being childish for once.

CONSTANCE. And what does that mean, if you please?

COUNTESS. It means Dickie. You know perfectly well that we love him and fuss over him just as if he were still alive. He's a sacred memory and we wouldn't hurt his feelings for the world. But please don't plump him in my lap when I'm settling the future of mankind. His basket is in the corner — he knows where it is, and he can just go and sit in it.

CONSTANCE. So you're against Dickie too! You too!

COUNTESS. Constance! I'm not in the least against Dickie! I adore Dickie. But you know as well as I that Dickie is only a convention with us. It's a beautiful convention — but it doesn't have to bark all the time. Besides, it's you that spoil him. The time you went to visit your niece and left him with me, we got on marvelously together. He didn't bark, he didn't tear things, he didn't even eat. But when you're with him, one can pay attention to nothing else. I'm not going to take Dickie in my lap at a solemn moment like this, no, not for anything in the world. And that's that!

GABRIELLE (*very sweetly*). Constance, dear, I don't mind taking him in my lap. He loves to sit in my lap, don't you, darling?

CONSTANCE. Kindly stop putting on angelic airs, Gabrielle. I know you very well. You're much too sweet to be sincere. There's plenty of times that I make believe that Dickie is here, when really I've left him at home, and you cuddle and pet him just the same.

GABRIELLE. I adore animals.

CONSTANCE. If you adore animals, you shouldn't pet them when they're not there. It's a form of hypocrisy.

COUNTESS. Now, Constance, Gabrielle has as much right as you . . .

CONSTANCE. Gabrielle has no right to do what she does. Do you know what she does? She invites *people* to come to tea with us. *People* whom we know nothing about. *People* who exist only in her imagination.

COUNTESS. You think that's not an existence?

GABRIELLE. I don't invite them at all. They come by themselves. What can I do?

CONSTANCE. You might introduce us.

COUNTESS. If you think they're only imaginary, there's no point in your meeting them, is there?

CONSTANCE. Of course they're imaginary. But who likes to have imaginary people staring at one? Especially strangers.

GABRIELLE. Oh, they're really very nice. . . .

CONSTANCE. Tell me just one thing, Gabrielle — are they here now?

COUNTESS. Am I to be allowed to speak? Or is this going to be the same as the argument about inoculating Josephine's cat, when we didn't get to the subject at all?

CONSTANCE. Never! Never! Never! I'll never give my consent to that. (*To* DICKIE.) I'd never do a thing like that to you, Dickie sweet. . . . Oh, no! Oh, no! (*She begins to weep softly.*)

COUNTESS. Good heavens! Now we have her in tears. What an impossible creature! With the fate of humanity hanging in the balance! All right, all right, stop crying. I'll take him in my lap. Come, Dickie, Dickie.

CONSTANCE. No. He won't go now. Oh, how can you be so cruel? Don't you suppose I know about Dickie? Don't you think I'd rather have him here alive and woolly and frisking around the way he used to? You have your Adolphe. Gabrielle has her birds. But I have only Dickie. Do you think I'd be so silly about him if it wasn't that it's only by pretending that he's here all the time that I get him to come sometimes, really? Next time I won't bring him!

COUNTESS. Now let's not get ourselves worked up over nothing. Come here, Dickie. . . . Irma is going to take you for a nice walk. (*She rings her bell.*) Irma!

(IRMA *appears on the landing.*)

CONSTANCE. No. He doesn't want to go. Besides, I didn't bring him today. So there!

COUNTESS. Very well, then. Irma, make sure the door is locked.

IRMA. Yes, Countess. (IRMA *exits.*)

CONSTANCE. What do you mean? Why locked? Who's coming?

COUNTESS. If you'd let me get a word in, you'd know by now. A terrible thing has happened. This morning, this very morning, exactly at noon . . .

CONSTANCE (*thrilled*). Oh, how exciting!

COUNTESS. Be quiet. This morning, exactly at noon, thanks to a young man who drowned himself in the Seine . . . Oh, yes, while I think of it — do you know a mazurka called *La Belle Polonaise?*

CONSTANCE. Yes, Aurelia.

COUNTESS. Could you sing it now? This very minute?

CONSTANCE. Yes, Aurelia.

COUNTESS. All of it?

CONSTANCE. Yes, Aurelia. But who's interrupting now, Aurelia?

COUNTESS. You're right. Well, this morning, exactly at noon, I discovered a horrible plot. There is a group of men who intend to tear down the whole city!

CONSTANCE. Is that all?

GABRIELLE. But I don't understand, Aurelia. Why should men want to tear down the city? It was they themselves who put it up.

COUNTESS. You are so innocent, my poor Gabrielle. There are people in the world who want to destroy everything. They have the fever of destruction. Even when they pretend that they're building, it is only in order to destroy. When they put up a new building, they quietly knock down two old ones. They build cities so that they can destroy the countryside. They destroy space with telephones and time with airplanes. Humanity is now dedicated to the task of universal destruction. I am speaking, of course, primarily of the male sex.

GABRIELLE (*shocked*). Oh . . . !

CONSTANCE. Aurelia! Must you talk sex in front of Gabrielle?

COUNTESS. There *are* two sexes.

CONSTANCE. Gabrielle is a virgin, Aurelia!

COUNTESS. Oh, she can't be as innocent as all that. She keeps canaries.

GABRIELLE. I think you're being very cruel about men, Aurelia. Men are big and beautiful, and as loyal as dogs. I preferred not to marry, it's true. But I hear excellent reports from friends who have had an opportunity to observe them closely.

COUNTESS. My poor darling! You are still living in a dream. But one day, you will wake up as I have, and then you will see what is happening in the world. The tide has turned, my dear. Men are changing back into beasts. They know it. They no longer try to hide it. There was once such a thing as manners. I remember a time when the hungriest was the one who took the longest to pick up his fork. The one with the broadest grin was the one who needed most to go to the . . . It was such fun to keep them grinning like that for hours. But now they no longer pretend. Just look at them — snuffling their soup like pigs, tearing their meat like tigers, crunching their lettuce like crocodiles! A man doesn't take your hand nowadays. He gives you his paw.

CONSTANCE. Would that trouble you so much if they turned into animals? Personally, I think it's a good idea.

GABRIELLE. Oh, I'd love to see them like that. They'd be sweet.

CONSTANCE. It might be the salvation of the human race.

COUNTESS (*to* CONSTANCE). You'd make a fine rabbit, wouldn't you?

CONSTANCE. I?

COUNTESS. Naturally. You don't think it's only the men who are changing? You'd change along with them. Husbands and wives together. We're all one race, you know.

CONSTANCE. You think so? And why would my poor husband have to be a rabbit if he were alive?

COUNTESS. Remember his front teeth? When he nibbled his celery?

CONSTANCE. I'm happy to say, I remember absolutely nothing about him. All I remember on that subject is the time that Father Lacordaire tried to kiss me in the park.

COUNTESS. Yes, yes, of course.

CONSTANCE. And what does that mean, if you please, "Yes, yes, of course"?

COUNTESS. Constance, just this once, look us in the eye and tell us truly — did that really happen or did you read about it in a book?

CONSTANCE. Now I'm being insulted!

COUNTESS. We promise you faithfully that we'll believe it all over again afterwards, won't we, Gabrielle? But tell us the truth this once.

CONSTANCE. How dare you question my memories? Suppose I said your pearls were false!

COUNTESS. They were.

CONSTANCE. I'm not asking what they were. I'm asking what they are. Are they false or are they real?

COUNTESS. Everyone knows that little by little, as one wears pearls, they become real.

CONSTANCE. And isn't it exactly the same with memories?

COUNTESS. Now do not let us waste time. I must go on.

CONSTANCE. I think Gabrielle is perfectly right about men. There are still plenty who haven't changed a bit. There's an old Senator who bows to Gabrielle every day when he passes her in front of the palace. And he takes off his hat each time.

GABRIELLE. That's perfectly true, Aurelia. He's always pushing an empty baby carriage, and he always stops and bows.

COUNTESS. Don't be taken in, Gabrielle. It's all make-believe. And all we can expect from these make-believe men is itself make-believe. They give us facepowder made of stones, sausages made of sawdust, shirts made of glass, stockings made of milk. It's all a vulgar pretence. And if that is the case, imagine what passes, these days, for virtue, sincerity, generosity, and love! I warn you, Gabrielle, don't let this Senator with the empty baby carriage pull the wool over your eyes.

GABRIELLE. He's really the soul of courtesy. He seems very correct.

COUNTESS. Those are the worst. Gabrielle, beware! He'll make you put on black riding boots, while he dances the can-can around you, singing God knows what filth at the top of his voice. The very thought makes one's blood run cold!

GABRIELLE. You think that's what he has in mind?

COUNTESS. Of course. Men have lost all sense of decency. They are all equally disgusting. Just look at them in the evening, sitting at their tables in the café, working away in unison with their toothpicks, hour after hour, digging up roast beef, veal, onion . . .

CONSTANCE. They don't harm anyone that way.

COUNTESS. Then why do you barricade your door, and make your friends meow before you let them come up? Incidentally, we must make an interesting sight, Gabrielle and I, yowling together on your doorstep like a couple of tomcats!

CONSTANCE. There's no need at all for you to yowl together. One would be quite enough. And you know perfectly well why I have to do it. It's because there are murderers.

COUNTESS. I don't quite see what prevents murderers from meowing like anybody else. But why are there murderers?

CONSTANCE. Why? Because there are thieves.

COUNTESS. And why are there thieves? Why is there almost nothing but thieves?

CONSTANCE. Because they worship money. Because money is king.

COUNTESS. Ah — now we've come to it. Because we live in the reign of the Golden Calf. Did you realize that, Gabrielle? Men now publicly worship the Golden Calf!

GABRIELLE. How awful! Have the authorities been notified?

COUNTESS. The authorities do it themselves, Gabrielle.

GABRIELLE. Oh! Has anyone talked to the bishop?

COUNTESS. Nowadays only money talks to the bishop. And so you see why I asked you to come here today. The world has gone out of its mind. Unless we do something, humanity is doomed! Constance, have you any suggestions?

CONSTANCE. I know what I always do in a case like this. . . .

COUNTESS. You write to the Prime Minister.

CONSTANCE. He always does what I tell him.

COUNTESS. Does he ever answer your letters?

CONSTANCE. He knows I prefer him not to. It might excite gossip. Besides, I don't always write. Sometimes I wire. The time I told him about the Archbishop's frigidaire, it was by wire. And they sent a new one the very next day.

COUNTESS. There was probably a commission in it for someone. And what do you suggest, Gabrielle?

CONSTANCE. Now, how can she tell you until she's consulted her voices?

GABRIELLE. I could go right home and consult them, and we could meet again after dinner.

COUNTESS. There's no time for that. Besides, your voices are not real voices.

GABRIELLE (*furious*). How dare you say a thing like that?

COUNTESS. Where do your voices come from? Still from your sewing-machine?

GABRIELLE. Not at all. They've passed into my hot-water bottle. And it's much nicer that way. They don't chatter any more. They gurgle. But they haven't been a bit nice to me lately. Last night they kept telling me to let my canaries out. "Let them out. Let them out. Let them out."

CONSTANCE. Did you?

GABRIELLE. I opened the cage. They wouldn't go.

COUNTESS. I don't call that *voices*. Objects talk — everyone knows that. It's the principle of the phonograph. But to ask a hot-water bottle for advice is silly. What does a hot-water bottle know? No, all we have to consult here is our own judgment.

CONSTANCE. Very well then, tell us what you have decided. Since you're asking our opinion, you've doubtless made up your mind.

COUNTESS. Yes, I've thought the whole thing out. All I really needed to discover was the source of the infection. Today I found it.

CONSTANCE. Where?

COUNTESS. You'll see soon enough. I've baited a trap. In just a few minutes, the rats will be here.

GABRIELLE (*in alarm*). Rats!

COUNTESS. Don't be alarmed. They're still in human form.

GABRIELLE. Heavens! What are you going to do with them?

COUNTESS. That's just the question. Suppose I get these wicked men all here at once — in my cellar — have I the right to exterminate them?

GABRIELLE. To kill them?

(COUNTESS *nods.*)

CONSTANCE. That's not a question for us. You'll have to ask Father Bridet.

COUNTESS. I have asked him. Yes. One day, in confession, I told him frankly that I had a secret desire to destroy all wicked people. He said: "By all means, my child. And when you're ready to go into action, I'll lend you the jawbone of an ass."

CONSTANCE. That's just talk. You get him to put that in writing.

GABRIELLE. What's your scheme, Aurelia?

COUNTESS. That's a secret.

CONSTANCE. It's not so easy to kill them. Let's say you had a tank of vitriol all ready for them. You could never get them to walk into it. There's nothing so stubborn as a man when you want him to do something.

COUNTESS. Leave that to me.

CONSTANCE. But if they're killed, they're bound to be missed, and then we'll be fined. They fine you for every little thing these days.

COUNTESS. They won't be missed.

GABRIELLE. I wish Josephine were here. Her sister's husband was a lawyer. She knows all about these things.

COUNTESS. Do you miss a cold when it's gone? Or the germs that caused it? When the world feels well again, do you think it will regret its illness? No, it will stretch itself joyfully, and it will smile — that's all.

CONSTANCE. Just a moment! Gabrielle, are they here now? Yes or no?

COUNTESS. What's the matter with you now?

CONSTANCE. I'm simply asking Gabrielle if her friends are in the room or not. I have a right to know.

GABRIELLE. I'm not allowed to say.

CONSTANCE. I know very well they are. I'm sure of it. Otherwise you wouldn't be making faces.

COUNTESS. May I ask what difference it makes to you if her friends are in the room?

CONSTANCE. Just this: If they're here, I'm not going to say another word! I'm certainly not going to commit myself in a matter involving the death sentence in the presence of third parties, whether they exist or not.

GABRIELLE. That's not being very nice to my guests, is it?

COUNTESS. Constance, you must be mad! Or are you so stupid as to think that just because we're alone, there's nobody with us? Do you consider us so boring or repulsive that of all the millions of beings, imaginary or otherwise, who are prowling about in space, there's not one who might possibly enjoy spending a little time with us? On the contrary, my dear — my house is full of guests always. They know that here they have a place in the universe where they can come when they're lonely and be sure of a welcome. For my part, I'm delighted to have them.

GABRIELLE. Thank you, Aurelia.

CONSTANCE. You know perfectly well, Aurelia . . .

COUNTESS. I know perfectly well that at this moment the whole universe is listening to us — and that every word we say echoes to the remotest star. To pretend otherwise is the sheerest hypocrisy.

CONSTANCE. Then why do you insult me in front of everybody? I'm not mean. I'm shy. I feel timid about giving an opinion in front of such a crowd. Furthermore, if you think I'm so bad and so stupid, why did you invite me, in the first place?

COUNTESS. I'll tell you. And I'll tell you why, disagreeable as you are, I always give you the biggest piece of cake and my best honey. It's because when you come there's always someone with you — and I don't mean Dickie — I mean someone who resembles you like a sister, only she's young and lovely, and she sits modestly to one side and smiles at me tenderly all the time you're bickering and quarreling, and never says a word. That's the Constance to whom I give the cake that you gobble, and it's because of her that you're here today, and it's her vote that I'm asking you to cast in this crucial moment. And not yours, which is of no importance whatever.

CONSTANCE. I'm leaving.

COUNTESS. Be so good as to sit down. I can't let her go yet.

CONSTANCE (*crossing toward the stairs*). No. This is too much. I'm taking her with me.

(IRMA *enters.*)

IRMA. Madame Josephine.

COUNTESS. Thank heaven!

GABRIELLE. We're saved.

(JOSEPHINE, *the Madwoman of La Concorde,*[2] *sweeps in majestically in a get-up somewhere between the regal and the priestly.*)

JOSEPHINE. My dear friends, today once again, I waited for President Wilson — but he didn't come out.

COUNTESS. You'll have to wait quite a while longer before he does. He's been dead since 1924.

JOSEPHINE. I have plenty of time.

COUNTESS. In anyone else, Josephine, these extravagances might seem a little childish. But a person of your judgment doubtless has her reasons for wanting to talk to a man to whom no one would listen when he was alive. We have a legal problem for you. Suppose you had all the world's criminals here in this room. And suppose you had a way of getting rid of them forever. Would you have the right to do it?

JOSEPHINE. Why not?

COUNTESS. Exactly my point.

GABRIELLE. But, Josephine, so many people!

JOSEPHINE. *De minimis non curat lex.*[3] The more there are, the more legal it is. It's impersonal. It's even military. It's the cardinal principle of battle — you get all your enemies in one place, and you kill them all together at one time. Because if you had to track them down one by one in their houses and offices, you'd get tired, and sooner or later you'd stop. I believe your idea is very practical, Aurelia. I can't imagine why we never thought of it before.

GABRIELLE. Well, if you think it's all right to do it . . .

JOSEPHINE. By all means. Your criminals have had a fair trial, I suppose?

COUNTESS. Trial?

JOSEPHINE. Certainly. You can't kill anybody without a trial. That's elementary. "No man shall be deprived of his life, liberty, and property without due process of law."

COUNTESS. They deprive us of ours.

JOSEPHINE. That's not the point. You're not accused of anything. Every accused — man, woman, or child — has the right to defend himself at the bar of justice. Even animals. Before the Deluge, you will recall, the Lord permitted Noah to speak in defense of his fellow mortals. He evidently stuttered. You know the result. On the other hand, Captain Dreyfus was not only innocent — he was defended by a marvelous orator.

[2] The central square of Paris.

[3] The law does not concern itself with trifles.

The result was precisely the same. So you see, in having a trial, you run no risk whatever.

COUNTESS. But if I give them the slightest cause for suspicion — I'll lose them.

JOSEPHINE. There's a simple procedure prescribed in such cases. You can summon the defendants by calling them three times — mentally, if you like. If they don't appear, the court may designate an attorney who will represent them. This attorney can then argue their case to the court, *in absentia*, and a judgment can then be rendered, *in contumacio*.[4]

COUNTESS. But I don't know any attorneys. And we have only ten minutes.

GABRIELLE. Hurry, Josephine, hurry!

JOSEPHINE. In case of emergency, it is permissible for the court to order the first passer-by to act as attorney for the defense. A defense is like a baptism. Absolutely indispensable, but you don't have to know anything to do it. Ask Irma to get you somebody. Anybody.

COUNTESS. The Deaf Mute?

JOSEPHINE. Well — that's getting it down a bit fine. That might be questionable on appeal.

COUNTESS (*calls*). Irma! What about the Police Sergeant?

JOSEPHINE. He won't do. He's under oath to the state.

(IRMA *appears.*)

IRMA. Yes, Countess?

COUNTESS. Who's out there, Irma?

IRMA. All our friends, Countess. There's the Ragpicker and . . .

COUNTESS. Send down the Ragpicker.

CONSTANCE. Do you think it's wise to have all those millionaires represented by a ragpicker?

JOSEPHINE. It's a first-rate choice. Criminals are always represented by their opposites. Murderers, by someone who obviously wouldn't hurt a fly. Rapists, by a member of the League for Decency. Experience shows it's the only way to get an acquittal.

COUNTESS. But we must not have an acquittal. That would mean the end of the world!

JOSEPHINE. Justice is justice, my dear.

(*The* RAGPICKER *comes down, with a stately air. Behind him, on the landing, appear the other* VAGABONDS.)

THE RAGPICKER. Greetings, Countess. Greetings, ladies. My most sincere compliments.

COUNTESS. Has Irma told you . . . ?

[4] In contempt of court.

THE RAGPICKER. She said something about a trial.

COUNTESS. You have been appointed attorney for the defense.

THE RAGPICKER. Terribly flattered, I'm sure.

COUNTESS. You realize, don't you, how much depends on the outcome of this trial?

JOSEPHINE. Do you know the defendants well enough to undertake the case?

THE RAGPICKER. I know them to the bottom of their souls. I go through their garbage every day.

CONSTANCE. And what do you find there?

THE RAGPICKER. Mostly flowers.

GABRIELLE. It's true, you know, the rich are always surrounded with flowers.

CONSTANCE. How beautiful!

COUNTESS. Are you trying to prejudice the court?

THE RAGPICKER. Oh no, Countess, no.

COUNTESS. We want a completely impartial defense.

THE RAGPICKER. Of course, Countess, of course. Permit me to make a suggestion.

COUNTESS. Will you preside, Josephine?

THE RAGPICKER. Instead of speaking as attorney, suppose you let me speak directly as defendant. It will be more convincing, and I can get into it more.

JOSEPHINE. Excellent idea. Motion granted.

COUNTESS. We don't want you to be too convincing, remember.

THE RAGPICKER. Impartial, Countess, impartial.

JOSEPHINE. Well? Have you prepared your case?

THE RAGPICKER. How rich am I?

JOSEPHINE. Millions. Billions.

THE RAGPICKER. How did I get them? Theft? Murder? Embezzlement?

COUNTESS. Most likely.

THE RAGPICKER. Do I have a wife? A mistress?

COUNTESS. Everything.

THE RAGPICKER. All right. I'm ready.

GABRIELLE. Will you have some tea?

THE RAGPICKER. Is that good?

CONSTANCE. Very good for the voice. The Russians drink nothing but tea. And they talk like anything.

THE RAGPICKER. All right. Tea.

JOSEPHINE (*to the* VAGABONDS). Come in. Come in. All of you. You may take places. The trial is public.

(*The* VAGABONDS *dispose themselves on the steps and elsewhere.*)

Your bell, if you please, Aurelia.

COUNTESS. But what if I should need to ring for Irma?

JOSEPHINE. Irma will sit here, next to me. If you need her, she can ring for herself. (*To the* POLICE SERGEANT *and the* POLICEMAN.) Conduct the accused to the bar.

(*The officers conduct the* RAGPICKER *to a bar improvised with a rocking chair and a packing case marked FRAGILE. The* RAGPICKER *mounts the box. She rings the bell.*)

The court is now in session. (*All sit.*) Counsel for the defense, you may take the oath.

THE RAGPICKER. I swear to tell the truth, the whole truth, and nothing but the truth, so help me God.

JOSEPHINE. Nonsense! You're not a witness. You're an attorney. It's your duty to lie, conceal, and distort everything, and slander everybody.

THE RAGPICKER. All right. I swear to lie, conceal, and distort everything, and slander everybody.

JOSEPHINE (*rings stridently*). Quiet! Begin.

THE RAGPICKER. May it please the honorable, august and elegant Court . . .

JOSEPHINE. Flattery will get you nowhere. That will do. The defense has been heard. Cross-examination.

COUNTESS. Mr. President . . .

THE RAGPICKER (*bowing with dignity*). Madame.

COUNTESS. Do you know what you are charged with?

THE RAGPICKER. I can't for the life of me imagine. My life is an open book. My ways are known to all. I am a pillar of the church and the sole support of the Opera. My hands are spotless.

COUNTESS. What an atrocious lie! Just look at them!

CONSTANCE. You don't have to insult the man. He's only lying to please you.

COUNTESS. Be quiet, Constance! You don't get the idea at all. (*To the* RAGPICKER.) You are charged with the crime of worshipping money.

THE RAGPICKER. Worshipping money? Me?

JOSEPHINE. Do you plead guilty or not guilty? Which is it?

THE RAGPICKER. Why, Your Honor . . .

JOSEPHINE. Yes or no?

THE RAGPICKER. Yes or no? No! I don't worship money, Countess. Heavens, no! Money worships me. It adores me. It won't let me alone. It's damned embarrassing, I can tell you.

JOSEPHINE. Kindly watch your language.

COUNTESS. Defendant, tell the Court how you came by your money.

THE RAGPICKER. The first time money came to me, I was a mere boy, a little golden-haired child in the bosom of my dear family. It came to me suddenly in the guise of a gold brick which, in my innocence, I picked out of a garbage can one day while playing. I was horrified, as you can imagine. I immediately tried to get rid of it by swapping it for a little run-down one-track railroad which, to my consternation, at once sold itself for a hundred times its value. In a desperate effort to get rid of this money, I began to buy things. I bought the Northern Refineries, the Galeries Lafayette,[5] and the Schneider-Creusot Munition Works. And now I'm stuck with them. It's a horrible fate — but I'm resigned to it. I don't ask for your sympathy, I don't ask for your pity — all I ask for is a little common human understanding. . . . (*He begins to cry.*)

COUNTESS. I object. This wretch is trying to play on the emotions of the Court.

JOSEPHINE. The Court has no emotions.

THE RAGPICKER. Everyone knows that the poor have no one but themselves to blame for their poverty. It's only just that they should suffer the consequences. But how is it the fault of the rich if they're rich?

COUNTESS. Dry your tears. You're deceiving nobody. If, as you say, you're ashamed of your money, why is it you hold onto it with such a death-grip?

THE RAGPICKER. Me?

STREET PEDDLER. You never part with a franc!

JUGGLER. You wouldn't even give the poor Deaf Mute a sou!

THE RAGPICKER. Me, hold onto money? What slander! What injustice! What a thing to say to me in the presence of this honorable, august, and elegant Court! I spend all my time trying to spend my money. If I have tan shoes, I buy black ones. If I have a bicycle, I buy a motor car. If I have a wife, I buy . . .

JOSEPHINE (*rings*). Order!

THE RAGPICKER. I dispatch a plane to Java for a bouquet of flowers. I send a steamer to Egypt for a basket of figs. I send a special representative to New York to fetch me an ice-cream cone. And if it's not just exactly right, back it goes. But no matter what I do, I can't get rid of my money! If I play a hundred-to-one shot, the horse come in by twenty lengths. If I throw a diamond in the Seine, it turns up in the trout they serve me for lunch. Ten diamonds — ten trout. Well, now, do you suppose I can get rid of forty millions by giving a sou to a deaf-mute? Is it even worth the effort?

CONSTANCE. He's right.

THE RAGPICKER. Ah! You see, my dear? At last, there is somebody who understands me! Somebody who is not only beautiful, but extraordinarily sensitive and intelligent.

COUNTESS. I object!

JOSEPHINE. Overruled!

THE RAGPICKER. I should be delighted to send you some flowers, Miss — directly I'm acquitted. What flowers do you prefer?

CONSTANCE. Roses.

THE RAGPICKER. You shall have a bale every morning for the next five years. Money means nothing to me.

[5] One of the largest department stores in Paris.

CONSTANCE. And amaryllis.

THE RAGPICKER. I'll make a note of the name. (*In his best lyrical style.*) The lady understands, ladies and gentlemen. The lady is no fool. She's been around and she knows what's what. If I gave the Deaf Mute a franc, twenty francs, twenty million francs — I still wouldn't make a dent in the forty times a thousand million francs that I'm afflicted with! Right, little lady?

CONSTANCE. Right.

JOSEPHINE. Proceed.

THE RAGPICKER. Like on the Stock Exchange. If *you* buy a stock, it sinks at once like a plummet. But if *I* buy a stock, it turns around and soars like an eagle. If I buy it at 33 . . .

PEDDLER. It goes up to a thousand.

THE RAGPICKER. It goes to twenty thousand! That's how I bought my twelve chateaux, my twenty villas, my 234 farms. That's how I endow the Opera and keep my twelve ballerinas.

FLOWER GIRL. I hope every one of them deceives you every moment of the day!

THE RAGPICKER. How can they deceive me? Suppose they try to deceive me with the male chorus, the general director, the assistant electrician, or the English horn — I own them all, body and soul. It would be like deceiving me with my big toe.

CONSTANCE. Don't listen, Gabrielle.

GABRIELLE. Listen to what?

THE RAGPICKER. No. I am incapable of jealousy. I have all the women — or I can have them, which is the same thing. I get the thin ones with caviar — the fat ones with pearls. . . .

COUNTESS. So you think there are no women with morals?

THE RAGPICKER. I mix morals with mink — delicious combination. I drip pearls into protests. I adorn resistance with rubies. My touch is jeweled; my smile, a motor car. What woman can withstand me? I lift my little finger — and do they fall? — Like leaves in autumn — like tin cans from a second-story window.

CONSTANCE. That's going a little too far!

COUNTESS. You see where your money leads.

THE RAGPICKER. Of course. When you have no money, nobody trusts you, nobody believes you, nobody likes you. Because to have money is to be virtuous, honest, beautiful, and witty. And to be without is to be ugly and boring and stupid and useless.

COUNTESS. One last question. Suppose you find this oil you're looking for. What do you propose to do with it?

THE RAGPICKER. I propose to make war! I propose to conquer the world!

COUNTESS. You have heard the defense, such as it is. I demand a verdict of guilty.

THE RAGPICKER. What are you talking about? Guilty? I? I am never guilty!

JOSEPHINE. I order you to keep quiet.

THE RAGPICKER. I am never quiet!

JOSEPHINE. Quiet, in the name of the law!

THE RAGPICKER. I am the law. When I speak, that is the law. When I present my backside, it is etiquette to smile and to apply the lips respectfully. It is more than etiquette — it is a cherished national privilege, guaranteed by the Constitution.

JOSEPHINE. That's contempt of court. The trial is over.

COUNTESS. And the verdict?

ALL. Guilty!

JOSEPHINE. Guilty as charged.

COUNTESS. Then I have full authority to carry out the sentence?

ALL. Yes!

COUNTESS. I can do what I like with them?

ALL. Yes!

COUNTESS. I have the right to exterminate them?

ALL. Yes!

JOSEPHINE. Court adjourned!

COUNTESS (*to the* RAGPICKER). Congratulations, Ragpicker. A marvelous defense. Absolutely impartial.

THE RAGPICKER. Had I known a little before, I could have done better. I could have prepared a little speech, like the time I used to sell the Miracle Spot Remover. . . .

JOSEPHINE. No need for that. You did very well, extempore. The likeness was striking and the style reminiscent of Clemenceau. I predict a brilliant future for you. Good-bye, Aurelia. I'll take our little Gabrielle home.

CONSTANCE. I'm going to walk along the river. (*To* DICKIE.) Oh! So here you are. And your ear all bloody! Dickie! Have you been fighting again? Oh, dear . . . !

COUNTESS (*to the* RAGPICKER). See that she gets home all right, won't you? She loses everything on the way. And in the queerest places. Her prayer book in the butcher shop. And her corset in church.

THE RAGPICKER (*bowing and offering his arm*). Permit me, Madame.

STREET SINGER. Oh, Countess — my mazurka. Remember?

COUNTESS. Oh, yes. Constance, wait a moment. (*To the* SINGER.) Well? Begin.

SINGER (*sings*).

> Do you hear, Mademoiselle,
> Those musicians of hell?

CONSTANCE. Why, of course, it's *La Belle Polonaise*. . . . (*She sings.*)

> From Poland to France
> Comes this marvelous dance,
>   So gracious,
>   Audacious,
> Will you foot it, perchance?

SINGER. I'm saved!

JOSEPHINE (*reappearing at the head of the stairs*).

> Now my arm I entwine
> Round these contours divine,
> So pure, so impassioned,
> Which Cupid has fashioned. . . .

GABRIELLE (*reappearing also, she sings a quartet with the others*).

> Come, let's dance the mazurka,
> That devilish measure,
> 'Tis a joy that's reserved
> To the gods for their pleasure —
> Let's gallop, let's hop,
> With never a stop,
> My blond Polish miss,
> Let our heads spin and turn
> As the dance-floor we spurn —
> There was never such pleasure as this!

(*They all exit, dancing.*)

IRMA. It's time for your afternoon nap.

COUNTESS. But suppose they come, Irma!

IRMA. I'll watch out for them.

COUNTESS. Thank you, Irma. I *am* tired. (*She smiles.*) Did you ever see a trial end more happily in your life?

IRMA. Lie down and close your eyes a moment.

(*The* COUNTESS *stretches out on the chaise-longue and shuts her eyes.* IRMA *tiptoes out. In a moment,* PIERRE *comes down softly, the feather boa in his hands. He stands over the chaise-longue, looking tenderly down at the sleeping woman, then kneels beside her and takes her hand.*)

COUNTESS (*without opening her eyes*). Is it you, Adolphe Bertaut?

PIERRE. It's only Pierre.

COUNTESS. Don't lie to me, Adolphe Bertaut. These are your hands. Why do you complicate things always? Say that it's you.

PIERRE. Yes. It is I.

COUNTESS. Would it cost you so much to call me Aurelia?

PIERRE. It's I, Aurelia.

COUNTESS. Why did you leave me, Adolphe Bertaut? Was she so very lovely, this Georgette of yours?

PIERRE. No. You are a thousand times lovelier.

COUNTESS. But she was clever.

PIERRE. She was stupid.

COUNTESS. It was her soul, then, that drew you? When you looked into her eyes, you saw a vision of heaven, perhaps?

PIERRE. I saw nothing.

COUNTESS. That's how it is with men. They love you because you are beautiful and clever and soulful — and at the first opportunity they leave you for someone who is plain and dull and soulless. But why does it have to be like that, Adolphe Bertaut? Why?

PIERRE. Why, Aurelia?

COUNTESS. I know very well she wasn't rich. Because when I saw you that time at the grocer's, and you snatched the only good melon from right under my nose, your cuffs, my poor friend, were badly frayed. . . .

PIERRE. Yes. She was poor.

COUNTESS. "Was" poor? Is she dead then? If it's because she's dead that you've come back to me — then no. Go away. I will not take their leavings from the dead. I refuse to inherit you. . . .

PIERRE. She's quite well.

COUNTESS. Your hands are still the same, Adolphe Bertaut. Your touch is young and firm. Because it's the only part of you that has stayed with me. The rest of you is pretty far gone, I'm afraid. I can see why you'd rather not come near me when my eyes are open. It's thoughtful of you.

PIERRE. Yes. I've aged.

COUNTESS. Not I. I am young because I haven't had to live down my youth, like you. I have it with me still, as fresh and beautiful as ever. But when you walk now in the park at Colombes with Georgette, I'm sure . . .

PIERRE. There is no longer a park at Colombes.

COUNTESS. Is there a park still at St. Cloud? Is there a park at Versailles? I've never gone back to see. But I think, if they could move, those trees would have walked away in disgust the day you went there with Georgette. . . .

PIERRE. They did. Not many are left.

COUNTESS. You take her also, I suppose, to hear *Denise*?

PIERRE. No one hears *Denise* any more.

COUNTESS. It was on the way home from *Denise*, Adolphe Bertaut, that I first took your arm. Because it was windy and it was late. I have never set foot in that street again. I go the other way round. It's not easy, in the winter, when there's ice. One is quite apt to fall. I often do.

PIERRE. Oh, my darling — forgive me.

COUNTESS. No, never. I will never forgive you. It was very bad taste to take her to the very places where we'd been together.

PIERRE. All the same, I swear, Aurelia . . .

COUNTESS. Don't swear. I know what you did. You gave her the same flowers. You bought her the same chocolates. But has she any left? No. I have all your flowers still. I have twelve chocolates. No, I will never forgive you as long as I live.

PIERRE. I always loved you, Aurelia.

COUNTESS. You "loved" me? Then you too are dead, Adolphe Bertaut?

PIERRE. No. I love you. I shall always love you, Aurelia.

COUNTESS. Yes. I know. That much I've always known. I knew it the moment you went away, Adolphe, and I knew that nothing could ever change it. Georgette is in his arms now — yes. But he loves me. Tonight he's taken Georgette to hear *Denise* — yes. But he loves me. . . . I know it. You never loved her. Do you think I believed for one moment that absurd story about her running off with the osteopath? Of course not. Since you didn't love her, obviously she stayed with you. And, after that, when she came back, and I heard about her going off with the surveyor — I knew that couldn't be true, either. You'll never get rid of her, Adolphe Bertaut — never. Because you don't love her.

PIERRE. I need your pity, Aurelia. I need your love. Don't forget me. . . .

COUNTESS. Farewell, Adolphe Bertaut. Farewell. Let go my hand, and give it to little Pierre.

(PIERRE *lets go her hand, and after a moment takes it again. The* COUNTESS *opens her eyes.*)

Pierre? Ah, it's you. Has he gone?

PIERRE. Yes, Countess.

COUNTESS. I didn't hear him go. Oh, he knows how to make a quick exit, that one. (*She sees the boa.*) Good heavens! Wherever did you find it?

PIERRE. In the wardrobe, Countess. When I took off the mirror.

COUNTESS. Was there a purple felt shopping bag with it?

PIERRE. Yes, Countess.

COUNTESS. And a little child's sewing box?

PIERRE. No, Countess.

COUNTESS. Oh, they're frightened now. They're trembling for their lives. You see what they're up to? They're putting back all the things they have stolen. I never open that wardrobe, of course, on account of the old woman in the mirror. But I have sharp eyes. I don't need to open it to see what's in it. Up to this morning, that wardrobe was empty. And now — you see? But, dear me, how stupid they are! The one thing I really miss is my little sewing box. It's something they stole from me when I was a child. They haven't put it back? You're quite sure?

PIERRE. What was it like?

COUNTESS. Green cardboard with paper lace and gold stamping. I got it for Christmas when I was seven. They stole it the very next day. I cried my eyes out every time I thought of it — until I was eight.

PIERRE. It's not there, Countess.

COUNTESS. The thimble was gilt. I swore I'd never use any other. Look at my poor fingers. . . .

PIERRE. They've kept the thimble too.

COUNTESS. Splendid! Then I'm under no obligation to be merciful. Put the boa around my neck, Pierre. I want them to see me wearing it. They'll think it's a real boa.

(IRMA *runs in excitedly.*)

IRMA. Here they come, Countess! You were right — it's a procession. The street is full of limousines and taxis!

COUNTESS. I will receive them. (*As* PIERRE *hesitates to leave her.*) Don't worry. There's nothing to be frightened of.

(PIERRE *goes out.*)

Irma, did you remember to stir the kerosene into the water?

IRMA. Yes, Countess. Here it is.

COUNTESS (*looking critically at the bottle*). You might as well pour in what's left of the tea.

(IRMA *shakes up the liquid.*)

Don't forget, I'm supposed to be deaf. I want to hear what they're thinking.

IRMA. Yes, Countess.

COUNTESS (*putting the finishing touches to her make-up*). I don't have to be merciful — but, after all, I do want to be just. . . .

(IRMA *goes up to the landing and exits. As soon as she is alone, the* COUNTESS *presses the brick, and the trap door opens. There is a confused sound of auto horns in the street above, and the noise of an approaching crowd.*)

IRMA (*offstage*). Yes, Mr. President. Come in, Mr. President. You're expected, Mr. President. This way, Mr. President.

(*The* PRESIDENTS *come down, led by the* PRESIDENT. *They all look alike, are dressed alike, and all have long cigars.*)

The Countess is quite deaf, gentlemen. You'll have to shout. (*She announces.*) The presidents of the boards of directors!

THE PRESIDENT. I had a premonition, Madame, when I saw you this morning, that we should meet again. (*The* COUNTESS *smiles vaguely. He continues, a tone louder.*) I want to thank you for your trust. You may place yourself in our hands with complete confidence.

SECOND PRESIDENT. Louder. The old trot can't hear you.

THE PRESIDENT. I have a letter here, Madame, in which . . .

SECOND PRESIDENT. Louder. Louder.

THIRD PRESIDENT (*shouting*). Is it true that you've located . . . ? (*The* COUNTESS *stares at him blankly. He shouts at the top of his voice.*) Oil? (*The* COUNTESS *nods with a smile, and points down. The* PRESIDENT *produces a legal paper and a fountain pen.*) Sign here.

COUNTESS. What is it? I haven't my glasses.

THE PRESIDENT. Your contract. (*He offers the pen.*)

COUNTESS. Thank you.

SECOND PRESIDENT (*normal voice*). What is it?

THIRD PRESIDENT. Waiver of all rights. (*He takes it back signed.*) Thank you. (*He hands it to the* SECOND PRESIDENT.) Witness. (*The* SECOND PRESIDENT *witnesses it. The* PRESIDENT *passes it on to the* THIRD PRESIDENT.) Notarize. (*The paper is notarized. The* PRESIDENT *turns to the* COUNTESS *and shouts.*) My congratulations. And now, Madame— (*he produces a gold brick wrapped in tissue paper*). If you'll show us the well, this package is yours.

COUNTESS. What is it?

THE PRESIDENT. Pure gold. Twenty-four karat. For you.

COUNTESS. Thank you very much. (*She takes it.*) It's heavy.

SECOND PRESIDENT. Don't worry. We'll pick it up again on the way out. (*He shouts at the* COUNTESS, *pointing at the trap door.*) Is this the way?

COUNTESS. That's the way.

(*The* SECOND PRESIDENT *tries to slip in first. The* PRESIDENT *pulls him back.*)

THE PRESIDENT. Just a minute, Mr. President. After me, if you don't mind. And watch those cigars. It's oil, you know.

(*But as he is about to descend, the* COUNTESS *steps forward.*)

COUNTESS. Just one moment . . .

THE PRESIDENT. Yes?

COUNTESS. Did any of you happen to bring along a little sewing box?

THE PRESIDENT. Sewing box? (*He pulls back another impatient* PRESIDENT.) Take it easy.

COUNTESS. Or a little gold thimble?

THE PRESIDENT. Not me.

THE PRESIDENTS. Not us.

COUNTESS. What a pity!

THE PRESIDENT. Can we go down now? Watch your step!

(*They hurry down eagerly. When they have quite disappeared,* IRMA *appears on the landing and announces the next echelon.*)

IRMA. Countess, the Prospectors.

COUNTESS. Heavens! Are there more than one?

IRMA. There's a whole delegation.

COUNTESS. Send them down.

(*The* PROSPECTOR *comes in, following his nose.*)

IRMA. Come in, please.

THE PROSPECTOR (*sniffing the air like a bloodhound*). I smell something. . . . Who's that?

IRMA. The Countess. She is very deaf.

THE PROSPECTOR. Good.

(*The* PROSPECTORS *also look alike. Sharp clothes, Western hats, and long noses. They crowd down the stairs after the* PROSPECTOR, *sniffing in unison. The* PROSPECTOR *is especially talented. He casts about on the scent until it leads him to the decanter on the table. He pours himself a glass, drinks it off, and belches with much satisfaction. The others join him at once, and follow his example. They all belch in unison.*)

THE PROSPECTORS. Oil?

THE PROSPECTOR. Oil!

COUNTESS. Oil.

THE PROSPECTOR. Traces? Puddles?

COUNTESS. Pools. Gushers.

SECOND PROSPECTOR. Characteristic odor? (*He sniffs.*)

THE PROSPECTOR. Chanel Number 5. Nectar! Undoubtedly — the finest — rarest! (*He drinks.*) Sixty gravity crude: straight gasoline! (*To the* COUNTESS.) How found? By blast? Drill?

COUNTESS. By finger.

THE PROSPECTOR (*whipping out a document*). Sign here, please.

COUNTESS. What is it?

THE PROSPECTOR. Agreement for dividing the profits. . . .

(*The* COUNTESS *signs.*)

SECOND PROSPECTOR (*to* FIRST PROSPECTOR). What is it?

THE PROSPECTOR (*pocketing the paper*). Application to enter a lunatic asylum. Down there?

COUNTESS. Down there.

(*The* PROSPECTORS *go down, sniffing.* IRMA *enters.*)

IRMA. The gentlemen of the press are here.

COUNTESS. The rest of the machine! Show them in.

IRMA. The Public Relations Counselors!

(*They enter, all shapes and sizes, all in blue pin-striped suits and black homburg hats.*)

The Countess is very deaf, gentlemen. You'll have to shout!

FIRST PRESS AGENT. You don't say — Delighted to make the acquaintance of so charming and beautiful a lady. . . .

SECOND PRESS AGENT. Louder. She can't hear you.

FIRST PRESS AGENT. What a face! (*Shouts.*) Madame, we are the press. You know our power. We fix all values. We set all standards. Your entire future depends on us.

COUNTESS. How do you do?

FIRST PRESS AGENT. What will we charge the old trull? The usual thirty?

SECOND PRESS AGENT. Forty.

THIRD PRESS AGENT. Sixty.

FIRST PRESS AGENT. All right — seventy-five. (*He fills in a form and offers it to the* COUNTESS.) Sign here, Countess. This contract really gives you a break.

COUNTESS. That is the entrance.

FIRST PRESS AGENT. Entrance to what?

COUNTESS. The oil well.

FIRST PRESS AGENT. Oh, we don't need to see that, Madame.

COUNTESS. Don't need to see it?

FIRST PRESS AGENT. No, no — we don't have to see it to write about it. We can imagine it. An oil well is an oil well. "That's oil we know on earth, and oil we need to know." (*He bows.*)

COUNTESS. But if you don't see it, how can you be sure the oil is there?

FIRST PRESS AGENT. If it's there, well and good. If it's not, by the time we get through, it will be. You underestimate the creative aspect of our profession, Madame.

(*The* COUNTESS *shakes her head, handing back the papers.*)

I warn you, if you insist on rubbing our noses in this oil, it will cost you 10 per cent extra.

COUNTESS. It's worth it.

(*She signs. They cross toward the trapdoor.*)

SECOND PRESS AGENT (*descending*). You see, Madame, we of the press can refuse a lady nothing.

THIRD PRESS AGENT. Especially such a lady. (THIRD PRESS AGENT *starts going down.*)

SECOND PRESS AGENT (*going down; gallantly*). It's plain to see, Madame, that even fountains of oil have their nymphs. . . . I can use that somewhere. That's copy!

(*The* PRESS AGENTS *go down. As he disappears, the* FIRST PRESS AGENT *steals the gold brick and blows a kiss gallantly to the* COUNTESS, *who blows one back.*

There is a high-pitched chatter offstage, and IRMA *comes in, trying hard to hold back* THREE WOMEN *who pay no attention to her whatever. These* WOMEN *are tall, slender, and as soulless as if they were molded of wax.*

They march down the steps, erect and abstracted like animated window models, but chattering incessantly.)

IRMA. But, ladies, please — you have no business here — you are not expected. (*To the* COUNTESS.) There are some strange ladies coming. . . .

COUNTESS. Show them in, Irma.

(*The* WOMEN *come down, without taking the slightest interest in their surroundings.*)

Who are you?

FIRST WOMAN. Madame, we are the most powerful pressure group in the world.

SECOND WOMAN. We are the ultimate dynamic.

THIRD WOMAN. The mainspring of all combinations.

FIRST WOMAN. Nothing succeeds without our assistance. Is that the well, Madame?

COUNTESS. That is the well.

FIRST WOMAN. Put out your cigarettes, girls. We don't want any explosions. Not with my brand-new eyelashes.

(*They go down, still chattering. The* COUNTESS *crosses to the wall to close the trap. As she does so, there is a commotion on the landing.*)

IRMA. Countess . . .

(*The* LITTLE MAN *rushes in breathlessly.*)

MAN. Just a minute! Just a minute! (*He rushes for the trap door.*)

COUNTESS. Wait! Who are you?

MAN. I'm in a hurry. Excuse me. It's my only chance! (*He rushes down.*)

COUNTESS. But . . . (*But he is gone. She shrugs her shoulders, and presses the brick. The trap closes. She rings the bell for* IRMA.) My gold brick! Why, they've stolen my gold brick! (*She moves toward the trap. It is now closed.*) Well, let them take their god with them.

(IRMA *enters and sees with astonishment that the stage is empty of all but the* COUNTESS. *Little by little, the scene is suffused with light, faint at first, but increasing as if the very walls were glowing with the quiet radiance of universal joy. Only around the closed trap a shadow lingers.*)

IRMA. But what's happened? They've gone! They've vanished!

COUNTESS. They've evaporated, Irma. They were wicked. Wickedness evaporates.

(PIERRE *enters. He is followed by the* VAGABONDS, *all of them. The new radiance of the world is now very perceptible. It glows from their faces.*)

PIERRE. Oh, Countess . . . !

WAITER. Countess, everything's changed. Now you can breathe again. Now you can see.

PIERRE. The air is pure! The sky is clear!

IRMA. Life is beautiful again.

THE RAGPICKER (*rushes in*). Countess — the pigeons! The pigeons are flying!

FLOWER GIRL. They don't have to walk any more.

THE RAGPICKER. They're flying. . . . The air is like crystal. And young grass is sprouting on the pavements.

COUNTESS. Is it possible?

IRMA (*interpreting for the* DEAF MUTE). Now, Juggler, you can throw your fireballs up as high as you please — they won't go out.

SERGEANT. On the street, utter strangers are shaking hands, they don't know why, and offering each other almond bars!

COUNTESS. Oh, my friends . . .

WAITER. Countess, we thank you. . . .

(*They go on talking with happy and animated gestures, but we no longer hear them, for their words blend into a strain of unearthly music which seems to thrill from the uttermost confines of the universe. And out of this music comes a voice.*)

FIRST VOICE. Countess . . .

(*Only the* COUNTESS *hears it. She turns from the group of* VAGABONDS *in wonder.*)

SECOND VOICE. Countess . . .

THIRD VOICE. Countess . . .

(*As she looks up in rapture, the* FIRST VOICE *speaks again.*)

FIRST VOICE. Countess, we thank you. We are the friends of animals.

SECOND VOICE. We are the friends of people.

THIRD VOICE. We are the friends of friendship.

FIRST VOICE. You have freed us!

SECOND VOICE. From now on, there will be no hungry cats. . . .

THIRD VOICE. And we shall tell the Duchess her dog's right name!

(*The* VOICES *fade off. And now another group of voices is heard.*)

FIRST VOICE. Countess, we thank you. We are the friends of flowers.

SECOND VOICE. From now on, every plant in Paris will be watered. . . .

THIRD VOICE. And the sewers will be fragrant with jasmine!

(*These voices, too, are silent. For an instant, the stage is vibrant with music. Then the* DEAF MUTE *speaks, and his voice is the most beautiful of all.*)

DEAF MUTE. Sadness flies on the wings of the morning, and out of the heart of darkness comes the light.

(*Suddenly a group of figures detaches itself from the shadows. These are exactly similar in face and figure and in dress. They are shabby in the fashion of 1900 and their cuffs are badly frayed. Each bears in his hand a ripe melon.*)

FIRST ADOLPHE BERTAUT. Countess, we thank you. We, too, are freed at last. We are the Adolphe Bertauts of the world.

SECOND ADOLPHE BERTAUT. We are no longer timid.

THIRD ADOLPHE BERTAUT. We are no longer weak.

FIRST ADOLPHE BERTAUT. From this day on, we shall hold fast to what we love. For your sake, henceforth, we shall be handsome, and our cuffs forever immaculate and new. Countess, we bring you this melon and with it our hearts . . . ! (*They all kneel.*) Will you do us the honor to be our wife?

COUNTESS (*sadly*). Too late! Too late!

(*She waves them aside. They take up their melons sadly and vanish. The voices of the* VAGABONDS *are heard again, and the music dies.*)

Too late! Too late!

PIERRE. Too late, Countess?

IRMA. Too late for what?

COUNTESS. I say that it's too late for them. On the twenty-fourth of May, 1881, the most beautiful Easter in the memory of man, it was not too late. And on the fifth of September, 1887, the day they caught the trout and broiled it on the open fire by the brook at Villeneuve, it was not too late. And it was even not too late for them on the twenty-first of August, 1897, the day the Czar visited Paris with his guard. But they did nothing and they said nothing, and now — kiss each other, you two, this very instant!

IRMA. You mean . . . ?

PIERRE. You mean . . . ?

IRMA. But, Countess . . .

COUNTESS. It's three hours since you've met and known and loved each other. Kiss each other quickly.

(PIERRE *hesitates.*)

Look at him. He hesitates. He trembles. Happiness frightens him. . . . How like a man! Oh, Irma, kiss him, kiss him! If two people who love each other let a single instant wedge itself between them, it grows — it becomes a month, a year, a century; it becomes too late. Kiss him, Irma, kiss him while there is time, or in a moment his hair will be white and there will be another madwoman in Paris! Oh, make her kiss him, all of you!

(*They kiss.*)

Bravo! Oh, if only you'd had the courage to do that thirty years ago, how different I would be today! Dear Deaf Mute, be still — your words dazzle our eyes! And Irma is too busy to translate for you.

(*They kiss once more.*)

Well, there we are. The world is saved. And you see how simple it all was? Nothing is ever so wrong in this world that a sensible woman can't set it right in the course of an afternoon. Only, the next time, don't wait until things begin to look black. The minute you notice anything, tell me at once.

THE RAGPICKER. We will, Countess. We will.

COUNTESS (*puts on her hat; her tone becomes businesslike*). Irma. My bones. My gizzard.

IRMA. I have them ready, Countess.

COUNTESS. Good. (*She puts the bones into her basket and starts for the stairs.*) Well, let's get on to more important things. Four o'clock. My poor cats must be starved. What a bore for them if humanity had to be saved every afternoon. They don't think much of it, as it is.

Curtain

Bertolt Brecht (1898–1956) wrote *Puntila* (1940) in Finland, where he had taken shelter — in his flight from the Nazis — with the Finnish novelist Hella Wuolijoki. As with so many Brecht dramas, *Puntila* was not an original; he and Mrs. Wuolijoki adapted it from one of her novels during the first three weeks of September, 1940. If it was swiftly drafted, it was no less important to Brecht as an example of a genre he felt had been much neglected, one which could be valuable as both teaching and entertainment for the proletarian audience.

In an essay on the folk play, also written during his stay in Finland, Brecht said:

> The 'Volksstück' or folk play is normally a crude and humble kind of theatre which academic critics pass over in silence or treat with condescension. In the second case, they prefer it to be what it is, just as some regimes prefer their 'Volk' to be crude and humble. It is a mixture of earthy humor and sentimentality, homespun morality and cheap sex. The wicked get punished and the good get married off; the industrious get left legacies and the idle get left in the lurch. The technique of the people who write these plays is more or less international; it hardly ever varies. . . . It may seem unsuitable that a single small folk play, *Puntila,* should be the occasion for such a far-reaching commentary, for the conjuring up of such vast phantoms and finally for a demand for an entirely new art of theatrical representation. Yet, like it or not, this demand has got to be made; our whole repertoire calls for a new kind of art which is quite indispensable for the performance of the great masterpieces of the past. . . . The folk play is a type of work that has long been treated with contempt and left to amateurs and hacks. It is time it was infected with the high ideals to which its very name commits it.[1]

Puntila, then, was hardly a potboiler to Brecht, even though it was written with such dispatch. It was an exemplary experiment, and it succeeded in combining the admirable folk qualities, already so firmly entrenched with and beloved of unsophisticated audiences, with Brecht's own vision of the human condition, turning the fundamental morality play into an exercise in political indoctrination.

A problem of morality dramas has always been their oversimplification of characters, motives, and actions. The danger, all too often, is that elemental truth, instead of being made more obvious, will in fact be sentimentalized or distorted into falsehood. Puntila, a prosperous Finnish landowner, represents the power elite in a very small way indeed. His

[1] Quoted from John Willett, trans., *Brecht on Theatre* (New York: Hill and Wang, 1964), pp. 153, 156.

servant Matti is, of course, a heroic, long-suffering proletarian. To a Central European, this visualization of capital and labor in a materialist, nonsocialist system is perfectly understandable and often amusing. They recognize the types only too well.

But other lands, other customs. For readers and audiences in the more prosperous parts of America, Puntila is apt to seem more of a vulgar proletarian than Matti. Matti, in fact, is sketched like Nature's nobleman. In modern America, few masters can afford the services of such a paragon. Servants — as well as a class system based on the wealthy and the workers — are really no longer part of the American experience. American workers, especially the heavily unionized ones, are far too affluent to regard a herring a day as a good diet. The truly dispossessed, the real victims of poverty, are far worse off than Matti and lack his talents for changing matters. So we as Americans must use a great deal of imagination in understanding the European reality Brecht is trying to mock.

A sense of the Old World is necessary to comprehend this folk play. In many parts of Europe, the old class system still survives, battered perhaps, shaken by World War II certainly, but there. Puntila-types now go to colleges of engineering or agriculture or business. They acquire a surface sophistication which hides the fact that they may actually be cruel, overbearing, or gross.

Puntila, at least, hides nothing, drunk or sober. What is especially interesting about his alternation of states is that when he is drunk, he is his best, kindest, most sensible — or most playful — self. He knows the right, the natural, the enjoyable thing to do. He becomes the wooer of the neglected village maidens, and, so he thinks, the affectionate equal of his all-enduring servant Matti. In Puntila's wildest adventures, Matti is his tolerant assistant, waiting patiently for the return of sobriety — and arrogance — in his master.

This play, either in the reading or performance of an English translation, usually presents problems of interpretation and appreciation. The fundamental differences between the American and the European social situations have already been indicated, but the contrasts really have to be seen, to be experienced, to make *Puntila* thoroughly intelligible. Puntila may seem, to affluent Americans, like only a prosperous peasant, but in his proper Finnish milieu, he is the local capitalist.

Brecht's widow, Helene Weigel, has also stressed that available translations, though competent and useful for reading, usually miss the simple lyric quality and the rich, elemental humor of his works in German. And because *Puntila* is designed to be a folk play, the fun and the delight in language are bent to serve Brecht's purposes as a teacher, a polemicist, a reformer. He attempts to entertain at the same time that he moralizes. Perhaps if that formula were reversed, the translated version would be more immediately enjoyable to its readers.

G. L.

BERTOLT BRECHT

Puntila and His Hired Man

TRANSLATED BY GERHARD NELLHAUS

Characters

PUNTILA, *landowner*[1]
EVA, *his daughter*
MATTI, *his chauffeur*
THE WAITER
THE JUDGE
THE ATTACHÉ
THE HORSE DOCTOR
HOME-BREW EMMA
THE APOTHECARY MISS
THE MILKMAID
THE TELEPHONE OPERATOR
A FAT MAN
A STRONG WORKER
A RED-HEADED WORKER
A SCRAWNY WORKER
SURKKALA
SURKKALA'S CHILDREN
LAINA, *the cook*
FINA, *the kitchenmaid*
THE LAWYER
THE REVEREND
THE REVEREND'S WIFE
Other Workers

PROLOGUE

Spoken by Lisu, the MILKMAID

Ladies and gentlemen: It's a disgrace
This world's not yet a better place,
But nothing's gained without a laugh or two
And so we bring this comic play to you.

[1] Proper names of three syllables are accented on the first syllable, *e.g.*, Púntila, Kúrgela, etc.

We'll show all sides of man, shady and sunny,
And talk of human things like sex and money.
Just this we ask: don't weigh our tale
Like pills with a precision scale
But like potatoes in big sacks.
Sometimes, you'll see, we grind an ax
In showing you just how the human lot
Is hard when some men have and some have not.

You'll see the owner of a large estate,
Whose kind has long been out of date.
But here where feudal lords still have the upper hand,
With drunken pride he plagues the lovely land.
Now to it — and what our sets don't show,
We hope our words will let you know:
Nightless, a Finnish summer arches
Over villages, where 'neath a dome of birches
Milk cans make music and smoke rises gray
From shingled roofs, while cocks crow in the day.
All this and more we hope, you'll say you saw
In Bert Brecht's play of *Puntila*.

I. Puntila finds a human being

(*A side room in the Park Hotel in Tavastehus, Finland.* PUNTILA, JUDGE, *and* WAITER. *As the scene opens, the* JUDGE *falls off his chair, dead drunk.*)

PUNTILA. Waiter, how long have we been here?

WAITER. Two days, Mr. Puntila.

PUNTILA (*to the* JUDGE, *reproachfully*). Two short days. You hear that? And you're giving up already and pretending to be tired. But that's the way you all are: the least exertion and you're ready to collapse. The spirit is willing, but the flesh is weak. Just think what a bad example it is for the people of Tavastland to see a man like you, a Tavastland judge, unable to keep on your feet when you are in a tavern. If one of my hands were as lazy at plowing as you are at drinking, I'd fire him on the spot. Dog, I'd say to him, I'll teach you to take your duties lightly! Think of what people expect of you, Frederick — you, a man of culture, someone people look up to as a good example: to show them how much a man can bear, a man with a sense of responsibility. Why can't you pull yourself together and sit up and talk to me, you weakling? (*To* WAITER.) What day is today?

WAITER. Saturday, Mr. Puntila.

PUNTILA. That's a surprise. It ought to be Friday.

WAITER. Sorry, but it's Saturday.

PUNTILA. You're contradicting me! You're a fine waiter, you are. You try to make your customers angry so they'll leave. Listen, Waiter, I'm ordering another aquavit. And one Friday. Is that clear?

WAITER. Yes Mr. Puntila. (*He shuffles off.*)

PUNTILA (*to the* JUDGE, *still sleeping on the floor*). Wake up, weakling! . . . To surrender to a couple of bottles of aquavit! You've hardly had a good smell. You've cowered in the bottom of the boat while I rowed you across the aquavit. You didn't even dare look over the side. . . . Look, I'm even stepping out on the seas of aquavit and walking upon the waters. (*He climbs up on the table and walks about majestically.*) And do I go down?

(*He notices* MATTI, *his chauffeur, who has come in some time ago and has been standing by the door.*)

Who are you?

MATTI. I'm your chauffeur, Mr. Puntila.

PUNTILA (*suspicious*). You're what?

MATTI. I'm your chauffeur.

PUNTILA. Anybody can say that. I don't know you.

MATTI. Maybe you've never looked at me very closely. I've only been with you five weeks.

PUNTILA. And where did you just come from?

MATTI. From outside. I've been waiting for you two days in the car.

PUNTILA. In whose car?

MATTI. In yours. In the Studebaker —

PUNTILA. That sounds peculiar to me. Can you prove it?

MATTI. — and I'm not going to wait any longer, just so you'll know. I've had enough. You can't treat a man like that.

PUNTILA. What do you mean, "a man"? Are you a man? A minute ago you said you were a chauffeur! See, you're contradicting yourself already! Admit it!

MATTI. You'll soon find out that I'm a man, Mr. Puntila. You think you can treat me like a dog and keep me waiting out in the street for you 'till you're good and ready to come out? Pay me what you owe me, 175 marks, and I'll get my letter of reference later.

PUNTILA. Your voice sounds familiar. (*He climbs down from the table and walks around* MATTI, *looking him over like a strange kind of animal.*) It really sounds quite human. Sit down and have an aquavit. We should get to know each other.

WAITER (*coming in with a bottle*). Your aquavit, Mr. Puntila. And today is Friday.

PUNTILA (*pointing to* MATTI). This is a friend of mine.

WAITER. Yes, Mr. Puntila. Your chauffeur, Mr. Puntila.

PUNTILA. What? (*To* MATTI.) Are you a chauffeur? . . . I've always said, you meet the nicest people when you travel. Pour yourself a drink.

MATTI. I wonder what you're up to this time. I don't know if I'll drink your aquavit.

PUNTILA. You're a suspicious fellow, I see. . . . I can understand why, though. You shouldn't sit down at a table with strangers. But I'm Puntila! The biggest landowner around Lammi. I'm an honest man — I've got ninety cows. It's all right to drink with me, brother.

MATTI. Fine. I'm Matti Altonen. Glad to make your acquaintance. (*Pours himself a glass and drinks to* PUNTILA.)

PUNTILA. Matti, did I really keep you waiting out there all that time? That wasn't right. If I ever do it again, just take a monkey-wrench and hit me over the head. . . . Matti — are you my friend?

MATTI. No.

PUNTILA. Thank you. I knew you were . . . (*Beseechingly.*) Matti, look at me! Don't you see anything?

MATTI. I see a big piece of blubber, stinking drunk.

PUNTILA. That just shows how deceptive appearances can be. That's not the real me you're seeing, Matti; I'm altogether different. I'm really just a sick man.

MATTI. Very sick.

PUNTILA. I'm glad you noticed. Not everybody can tell. You'd never suspect it to look at me. . . . (*Gravely, looking sharply at* MATTI.) I get attacks.

MATTI. You don't say.

PUNTILA. No joking. They hit me at least once every three months. . . . I wake up and suddenly I'm absolutely, completely, stone-cold sober. What do you say to that?

MATTI. Do you get these attacks regularly?

PUNTILA. Regularly. It's like this: All the rest of the time I'm perfectly normal, just as you see me now. I'm in full possession of my mental powers, master of my five senses. . . . Then the attack strikes! First, something goes wrong with my eyes. (*He holds up a single fork.*) Instead of two forks, I see only one.

MATTI (*horrified*). Then you're half-blind!

PUNTILA. All I see then is half the world. But it gets even more dreadful. You see, while I'm sober — totally and senselessly sober — I lose all my inhibitions. What I do when I'm in that condition, you just can't hold against me. Not if you have a heart, and keep telling yourself that I'm a sick man. (*With terror in his voice.*) Why at times like that I'm even responsible. (*Eagerly.*) Do you know what that means, to be "responsible"? A responsible man is a man who might do most anything. No longer, for example, does he think of his child's welfare; friends count for nothing. He is ready to step over his own dead body. . . . And all just because he's "responsible," as they say in court.

MATTI. Can't you do anything about these attacks?

PUNTILA. Brother, I do whatever's possible. Whatever's humanly possible! (*He raises his glass.*) This is my only medicine. I swallow it down by the bucket, believe me! I fight these attacks of soberness like a man. . . . But what good does it do? They get me down again and again. Just take my total lack of consideration for you, such a splendid example of a human being. (*Offers him a plate of food that had been standing, covered, on the table.*) Here. Help yourself. Here's some meat. . . . Go ahead, eat it. Take all the time you want.

(MATTI *starts to eat.*)

Tell me, by what luck did you find me?

MATTI. By losing my last job — when it wasn't my fault.

PUNTILA. How did that happen?

MATTI. I saw ghosts.

PUNTILA. Real ones?

MATTI (*shrugs his shoulders*). At Mr. Pappmann's place. Nobody knew why there should have been ghosts. Before I came there never were any. If you ask me, I think it was because the food was bad. Mush lies heavy in people's stomachs, and they have bad dreams. I started talking gloomily in the kitchen, and before you knew it the kitchen-maid began to see children's heads sticking on fence-posts at night. And the dairy maid saw a big grey ball that looked like a skull come rolling along the floor of the cowbarn. The chambermaid left, because I saw a swarthy man walking around with his head under his arm near the bathhut about eleven at night — and he asked me for a match to light his pipe. When they all left, Mr. Pappmann hollered at me. Said it was all my fault, that there were no ghosts in the house. But he couldn't say anything when I told him that while Mrs. Pappmann was in the hospital having her baby, I saw a white ghost climb out of the window of one of the dairy-maids' rooms and go right into Mr. Pappmann's own window. . . . So he fired me. When I left I told him that if he saw to it that they fed the help better on his place, then maybe the ghosts would leave him in peace — they can't stand the smell of good meat.

PUNTILA. I see. Your liking to eat doesn't lower you any in my eyes — just so long as you handle my tractor well and behave yourself, and give to Puntila what is Puntila's due. We'll get along together; why, everybody gets along with Puntila. (*He sings.*)

"Why haul me into court, baby, tell me why?
When in bed together we see eye to eye!"

How Puntila would like to go out and chop down birch trees with you, and dig stones out of the fields, and drive the tractor. But does anybody let him do good, honest work like that? When I married into a sawmill and a papermill, I could throw a bull on his back. But before I knew it, they put a stiff collar around my neck — I've rubbed two chins bloody already. She said, "From now on it won't do for you to go out plowing. It won't do for you to drink coffee with laborers." And even before she died, my daughter started in on the same thing — that's one thing she learned. But I'm not going to stand for it anymore! I'm going to Kurgela to marry my daughter off to the Attaché and then there'll be nobody to keep after me. I'll be able to sit and eat in my shirtsleeves and as for that Klinckmann female, she'll take things lying down. I'll raise everyone's pay because the world is big, and I have woods — and there's enough for all of you, and for Puntila, too.

MATTI (*laughs*). That's right, Mr. Puntila.

PUNTILA. I just want to be sure there isn't any gulf between us anymore. Tell me there isn't any gulf! . . . Matti, I need your advice. It's about money.

MATTI. Any time you want, Mr. Puntila.

PUNTILA. But it's vulgar to talk about money!

MATTI. Well, all right, let's not talk about it then.

PUNTILA. Wrong. After all, why shouldn't we be vulgar. Aren't we free human beings?

MATTI. No.

PUNTILA. There, you see? And as free human beings we can do what we want; and now we want to be vulgar. . . . We have to scrape a dowry together for my only child; that's what we have to look in the eye now, cold, sharp, and drunk. . . . I see just two possibilities. I could sell one of my woods, or I could sell myself. What do you think?

MATTI. I wouldn't sell myself if I could sell a wood.

PUNTILA. What? Sell a wood? You disappoint me. Do you know what a wood is? Is a wood just ten thousand cords to burn? Do you want to sell a beautiful green joy? Shame on you!

MATTI. All right, then, sell yourself.

PUNTILA. "Et tu, Brute?" You really want me to sell myself?

MATTI. Well, how are you going to go about selling yourself anyway?

PUNTILA. Mrs. Klinckmann.

MATTI. The Attaché's aunt in Kurgela? Where we're going now?

PUNTILA. She's got a weakness for me.

MATTI. And you're going to sell your body to her? That's terrible.

PUNTILA. Absolutely not. But what will happen to our freedom, brother? Oh, well, I'll sacrifice myself; after all, what am I?

MATTI. You're right.

(The JUDGE *wakes up, and gropes about on the floor for an imaginary bell. He seems to find it, and shakes it vigorously.)*

JUDGE. Quiet in the courtroom!

PUNTILA. He thinks he's in court, sleeping so well. . . . Matti, you've decided the question of which is worth more: a wood like my wood, or a man like me. You're a wonderful fellow. . . . Here, take my wallet and pay the bill. Hold on to it; I'd only lose it. (*Pointing to the* JUDGE.) Now up with him! Out with him! . . . You know, the way I lose things, I wish I didn't own anything. Money's bad for you; remember that. My dream is to have nothing at all: the two of us going through our beautiful

Finland on foot, or maybe in a little car. The little gas it'd take they'd let us borrow someplace; and when we got tired we'd go into a little tavern like this one, and they'd give us a drink for chopping their wood. The chopping wouldn't be any trouble for you at all.

(*They go off,* MATTI *carrying the* JUDGE.)

I. (COOK *sweeps.*)

Mr. Puntila drank all night and day
In Tavastland's Park Hotel.
When he left, the waiter wouldn't say
Thank you or Fare-thee-well.
"Now, waiter, why behave that way?
Life is fun, don't you agree?"
The waiter said: "I couldn't say,
My feet are killing me.
  My feet are —
    My feet are —
My feet are killing me."

II. *Puntila is treated badly*

(*A large entrance hall in the manor house on the Klinckmann Estate in Kurgela.* EVA PUNTILA *is sitting, eating chocolates, waiting for her father. Eino Silakka, a diplomatic corps* ATTACHÉ, *appears at the top of the stairs. He seems very sleepy.*)

EVA. I can well imagine that Lady Klinckmann is annoyed.

ATTACHÉ. *Chère* Eva, my aunt never stays annoyed very long. But this time when I telephoned to see where they were, I was told that a car just drove past Kirchendorf with two roaring men in it.

EVA. That's them, for sure. There's no mistaking my father. I've always known right away when they were talking about him. When a man chases after a peasant with a horsewhip, or gives some poor cottager's widow a car for a present, that's my father.

ATTACHÉ. But this . . . *enfin* . . . is not the Puntila Estate! I say, it would be terribly embarrassing if there were a scandal. Quite possibly I haven't much sense for figures, or for how many gallons of milk we can send to Tavastehus — I never drink any, indeed, milk doesn't agree with me — but I am very sensitive to anything that might constitute a scandal. When the Attaché of the French Embassy in London after eight cognacs called across the table to the Duchess of Catrumple that she was a whore, I immediately predicted that there'd be a scandal. And I turned out to be absolutely right. I believe they're here. My dear, I'm a trifle weary. Forgive me if I retire!

(*He leaves in haste. A tremendous crash is heard outside as the gate is knocked down.*)

PUNTILA. Here we are at last. But don't go to any trouble, don't wake anybody, we'll drink just one more bottle to celebrate, and then we'll go to bed. Well, are you happy?

EVA. We expected you three days ago.

PUNTILA. We were detained on the road. But we brought everything. Matti, get that suitcase. I hope you held it in your lap carefully, so nothing broke. Or we'd die of thirst here. We hurried because we knew you'd be waiting, Eva.

JUDGE. Are congratulations in order, Eva?

EVA. You always upset things, Papa! For a week now I've had to sit here in a strange house with an old novel, the Attaché, and his aunt, dying of boredom.

PUNTILA. Didn't I just tell you how we rushed along, and I kept hurrying and saying we mustn't waste time, that the Attaché and I had still a couple of things to discuss about the engagement, and I was glad to know you were with the Attaché so you had someone to keep you company while we were detained? Be careful with that suitcase, Matti, we don't want any accidents.

(*With infinite care, he helps* MATTI *take the suitcase out of the car.*)

JUDGE. Did you have a falling out with the Attaché — complaining about being left alone with him?

EVA. Oh, it's not that. You can't really quarrel with him.

JUDGE. Puntila, your Eva doesn't sound the least bit enthusiastic. She says that you can't really quarrel with the Attaché. I had to rule in a divorce case once, where the woman complained that her husband never hit her back, even when she threw a lamp at him. She felt neglected.

PUNTILA. There, now, lucky once again. What Puntila touches, turns out lucky. What, you didn't have a good time? If you ask me, keep away from that Attaché. He's no man.

EVA (*seeing* MATTI *grin*). I only meant that I doubt if I could amuse myself alone with the Attaché.

PUNTILA. That's what I meant, too. . . . Take Matti here! Any woman could amuse herself with him.

EVA. You're impossible, Papa. I only said, "I doubt." (*To* MATTI.) Take that suitcase upstairs!

PUNTILA. Wait! First we'll have to have a drink while we talk over whether or not the Attaché suits me. Did you at least get engaged to him?

EVA. No. We didn't get engaged. We didn't even talk about such things. (*To* MATTI.) Don't you dare open that suitcase.

PUNTILA. What, three whole days and you didn't get engaged? Just what did you do? . . . (*To* MATTI.) I don't like that in a man. I get myself engaged in three minutes. Get him down here; I'll call in the kitchen-maids and I'll show him how to get engaged, quick as lightning. . . . Give me a bottle. The burgundy. No, some brandy.

EVA. No! You're not going to do any more drinking. (*To* MATTI.) Take that suitcase up to my room this minute. . . . Second door on the right.

PUNTILA (*in alarm, seeing* MATTI *lift up the suitcase*). Is that nice of you, Eva? You can't deny your own father a drink when he's thirsty. I promise to empty just one more bottle, very quietly, with the cook or the chambermaid, and Frederick here. He's still thirsty, too. Have a heart.

EVA. I stayed up just to keep you from disturbing the maids.

PUNTILA. I'm convinced that old lady Klinckmann — where is she, anyway? — would like to sit and talk with me a bit. We've always had a weakness for each other.

EVA. I wish you'd behave yourself. Lady Klinckmann was furious about your being three days late; I doubt if she'll even see you tomorrow.

PUNTILA. I'll go knock at her door and set everything straight. I know how to handle her. . . . You don't know anything about that sort of thing, Eva.

EVA. I only know that no woman would sit with you in your condition! (*To* MATTI.) I told you to take that suitcase upstairs! Waiting three days is enough!

PUNTILA. Eva, be reasonable. If you don't want me to go upstairs, you go get me the little roly-poly one — I think it's the housekeeper — and I'll talk things over with her.

EVA. Don't go too far, Papa, if you don't want me to carry the suitcase upstairs myself and let it come crashing down by accident.

(PUNTILA *is horrified.* MATTI *carries the suitcase upstairs,* EVA *follows him slowly.*)

PUNTILA (*with the pathos of King Lear*). That is how a child treats her father. Come on, Frederick.

JUDGE. What is your plan now, basically?

PUNTILA. I'm getting away from this place; I don't like it. Why, I hurried and got here late at night, and am I received with loving arms? . . . Think of the prodigal son, Frederick. What if they had not slaughtered the fatted calf, but offered him cold abuse? . . . I'm going.

JUDGE. Where?

PUNTILA. Why even ask? Didn't you see how my own daughter wouldn't let me have a drop? . . . So that now I have to go out into the night and look for someone to give me a bottle or two?

JUDGE. Be sensible, Puntila. You can't get any liquor at two-thirty in the morning. The serving or sale of alcoholic beverages during the night is strictly illegal without a doctor's prescription.

PUNTILA. So you're deserting me, too. . . . Me, not get any legal alcohol? I'll show you how I'll get legal alcohol — day or night!

EVA (*appears again at the top of the stairs*). Take your coat off this minute, Papa.

PUNTILA. Quiet, Eva! And honor your father and your mother, that your days may be long upon the earth. It's a fine house where the guts of the guests are hung up to dry on the clothesline! And not letting me get a woman! I'll show you. You tell that Klinckmann female I can do without her company! I consider her a foolish virgin with no oil in her lamp. And now I'm going to drive off, and the earth will groan and all the curves in the road straighten out from fright. (*He backs out with a roar.*)

EVA (*running downstairs, to* MATTI). You, stop him!

MATTI (*coming down the stairs behind her*). Too late! He's too fast.

JUDGE. I don't think I'll wait up for him. I'm not as young as I used to be, Eva. Where's my room? (*He starts upstairs.*)

EVA. Third on the right. (*To* MATTI.) Now we'll have to stay up and see to it that he doesn't drink with the servants and get familiar with them when he comes back.

MATTI. You never know what familiarity might breed.

EVA. People are forever taking advantage of Father because of his weakness. He's too good.

MATTI. It's lucky that he gets good and drunk at times.

EVA. I won't have you talking that way about the man you work for. And I don't like your taking everything so literally, like what my father said about the Attaché.

MATTI. That the Attaché isn't a man? . . . There are all sorts of opinions about what a man is.

EVA (*after a pause*). The Attaché is really greatly respected in the diplomatic service. He has a splendid career ahead of him; everyone should realize that. They all say he's one of the brightest of the younger men.

MATTI. I see.

EVA. What I meant a while ago was that I didn't have as good a time with him as my father meant. Of course, whether or not a man is amusing doesn't matter in the least.

MATTI. I knew a man who wasn't amusing at all and still made a fortune in margarine and fats.

EVA. . . . Our engagement has been planned for a long time. We've known each other since childhood. . . . Perhaps I'm just a very lively person and get bored easily.

MATTI. You mean you have your doubts?

EVA. I didn't say that. I only wanted to emphasize that the Attaché is a kind and intelligent man, and that you can't judge him by his look or by what he says and does. He would never do anything vulgar or parade his virility. He stands very high in my opinion. . . . But perhaps you are tired.

MATTI. Keep on talking. I'm only shutting my eyes so I can concentrate.

II. (COOK *dusts.*)

The owner's daughter had received
A higher education.
Her place, she'd been taught to believe,
Was special in creation.
One night she talked to the chauffeur
And saw him in a new light.
"Come, amuse me, Chauffeur, I hear,
You're a man in your own right.
  You're a man —
    You're a man —
You're a man in your own right."

III. Puntila gets engaged to four early risers

(*Early morning in the village. Small wooden houses, three of which are marked "Post Office," "Veterinary," and "Apothecary." In the middle of the square is a bright red telephone pole.* PUNTILA *has run his Studebaker into the telephone pole, and is cursing it as the curtain opens.*)

PUNTILA. Clear the roads in Tavastland! Out of Puntila's way! Who do you think you are? Do you have any cows? Any woods? . . . Back up! If I call the police and have you hauled away for being a Red, you'll be sorry! (*He climbs out of the car.*) About time you got out of my way!

(*He goes up to one of the houses and knocks on the window.* HOME-BREW EMMA *looks out.*)

Good morning, gracious lady. Did you sleep well? I have a slight request to make. I'm the owner of the Puntila Estate in Lammi, and I'm terribly distressed because I have to get some alcohol for my cows, poor beasts, who are sick and dying with scarlet fever. Where does the Horse Doctor live? I'll knock down your dirty little house if you don't show me where the Horse Doctor lives!

HOME-BREW EMMA. Keep your pants on, don't get so excited. The Horse Doctor lives right next door. . . . But what did I hear you say? You need alcohol? I've got some alcohol: nice, strong stuff. Made it myself.

PUNTILA. Get thee behind me, woman! How dare you tempt me with your illegal liquor? I only drink it when it's legal, otherwise I couldn't even get it down my throat. I'd rather be dead than not obey the Laws of Finland. Why, everything I do is according to the law. When I want to kill a man, I do it legally or not at all.

HOME-BREW EMMA. Your legality gives me a pain in the —.

(*She disappears into her house.* PUNTILA *runs to the* HORSE DOCTOR'S *house and rings the bell. The* HORSE DOCTOR *looks out of an upstairs window.*)

PUNTILA. Horse Doctor, Horse Doctor, there you are at last! I'm the owner of Puntila Estate at Lammi. I have ninety cows and all ninety of them have scarlet fever. That's why I've got to have some alcohol right away.

HORSE DOCTOR. I think you've come to the wrong place. . . . You'd better go along without any trouble.

PUNTILA. Horse Doctor, don't you disappoint me! Or maybe you're no horse doctor at all, or you'd know what everybody in Tavastland gives to Puntila when his cows have scarlet fever. Because I'm not lying! If I told you they had snot in their nose, then I'd be lying. But when I tell you it's scarlet fever, then it's a subtle hint between gentlemen.

HORSE DOCTOR. And what if I don't understand the hint?

PUNTILA. Then I think you ought to know that Puntila is the biggest roughneck in all of Tavastland. Why, there's a folksong about it. He's got three horse doctors on his conscience already. You understand me now, Doctor?

HORSE DOCTOR (*laughing*). Yes, now I understand. But how can I be sure that it's scarlet fever?

PUNTILA. Listen, when my cows have red spots, and two of the cows already have black spots, isn't that the disease in its most dreaded stage? And the headaches they have, tossing around, unable to sleep, and rolling back and forth the whole night through, thinking of nothing but their sins.

HORSE DOCTOR. In that case, of course, it's my duty to ease their pains. (*He throws the prescription down to* PUNTILA.)

PUNTILA. Send the bill to the Puntila Estate in Lammi.

(PUNTILA *runs to the Apothecary's and pulls the bell violently. As he stands waiting,* HOME-BREW EMMA *comes out of her house.*)

HOME-BREW EMMA. It was autumn in our village
Ripe the plums hung on the tree
When there drove up in his carriage
A young man, so handsome he.

(*She goes back into her house. The* APOTHECARY MISS *looks out of her window.*)

APOTHECARY MISS. Don't pull down the bell!

PUNTILA. Better pull the bell down than wait forever! I need liquor for ninety cows, my sweet. . . . You soft little thing.

APOTHECARY MISS. What you need most is for me to call a policeman.

PUNTILA. Why, baby! One policeman for a man like Puntila from Lammi? What good would one policeman do? There'd have to be at least two. But why policemen? I love policemen. They have bigger feet than anyone else, and five toes on each foot, because they stand for law and order; and I love law and order! (*He hands her the prescription.*) Here, my little dove, there's law and order.

(*The* APOTHECARY MISS *goes inside to get the liquor. While* PUNTILA *is waiting,* HOME-BREW EMMA *again steps out of her house.*)

HOME-BREW EMMA. In the grass he lay to watch us
As we picked plums from the trees,
And he laughed when he could catch us
With our skirts above our knees.

(*She goes back into her house. The* APOTHECARY MISS *comes out with a jug of liquor.*)

APOTHECARY MISS (*laughing*). It's an awfully big jug. (*She hands him the jug.*)

PUNTILA (*holding the jug to his ear*). Glug, glug, glugglug. Oh, you Finnish music, the most beautiful music in the world. . . . Oh my God, I almost forgot something! Now I've got liquor, but I haven't got a woman. You don't have any liquor, and you don't have a man either! . . . Beautiful Apothecary Miss, I'd like to get engaged to you.

APOTHECARY MISS. Thank you very much, Mr. Puntila from Lammi, but I only get engaged according to the law, with a ring and a drink of wine.

PUNTILA. That's fine; let's get engaged. It's high time you got engaged anyway. . . . Tell me about yourself. I've got to know those things if I'm going to get engaged to you.

APOTHECARY MISS. Me? This is the kind of life I lead: I had to study for four years and now the apothecary pays me less than he does his cook. I send half my pay home to my mother in Tavastehus. Every second night I'm on duty. The apothecary's wife is jealous because her husband is after me. The doctor's handwriting is bad; once I even got the prescription mixed up. I keep burning my clothes with the chemicals, and new ones are terribly expensive. I can't find a boy friend; the police lieutenant, the director of the cooperative, and the book dealer are all married already. . . . I think my life is rather sad.

PUNTILA. There, you see? Well, then — just stick to Puntila! Here, have a drink.

APOTHECARY MISS. But where's my ring? The law says: a ring and a drink of wine.

PUNTILA. . . . Haven't you any curtain-rings?

APOTHECARY MISS (*smiling*). How many do you need? Just one, or a lot?

PUNTILA. A lot, my girl, not just one. Puntila always needs lots of everything. He might not even notice just one girl.

(*While the* APOTHECARY MISS *goes to get the curtain-rings,* HOME-BREW EMMA *again comes out of her house.*)

HOME-BREW EMMA. Let me see what you are cooking,
He asked us as he came by.
But instead of simply looking,
Stuck his finger in each pie.

(*The* APOTHECARY MISS *has returned, and sliding the rings off the curtain-rod, hands them all to* PUNTILA.)

PUNTILA (*putting a ring on her finger*). Come to the Puntila Estate a week from next Sunday. There's going to be a big engagement party.

(PUNTILA *starts to walk away as the* MILKMAID *comes along, carrying her pail.*)

Wait a minute, my little dove. I can't do without you. Where are you off to so early in the morning?

MILKMAID. Milking.

PUNTILA. What? With nothing but a pail between your legs? Tell me what kind of life you lead; you fascinate me.

MILKMAID. This is the kind of life I lead. At half past three in the morning I have to get up, clean the manure out of the barn, and brush the cows. Then I have to do the milking, wash the pail with stuff that burns my hand, and clean the manure out again. Then I drink my coffee, eat a piece of bread and butter, and then I can sleep a little. For lunch I cook up some potatoes and gravy — I never see meat. . . . Then it starts all over again: I clean the manure out of the barn, brush the cows, do the milking, and wash the pail. Every fifth Sunday I have off, but sometimes I go dancing at night, and when things don't go right I get a baby. I have two dresses and a bicycle, too.

PUNTILA. I have an estate, a steammill, and a sawmill, but I don't have a woman. How about you, my little dove? Here's a ring. Take a drink from the jug and everything'll be legal and in order. Come out to the Puntila Estate a week from next Sunday. All right?

MILKMAID. All right.

PUNTILA (*walking on*). On and on, right down the village street. I'm curious to see who's up this early. You just can't resist them right after they crawl out of their feather-beds, when their eyes are so bright and sinful and the world's still young. (*He comes to the Post Office where the* TELEPHONE OPERATOR *is standing.*)

PUNTILA. Good morning, my wide-awake little dove. You're the girl who knows everything from listening in on the telephone. Good morning to you.

TELEPHONE OPERATOR. Good morning, Mr. Puntila. What's going on so early?

PUNTILA. I'm going a-courtin'!

TELEPHONE OPERATOR. You're the one I had to keep telephoning half the night for.

PUNTILA. I see, you know everything. . . . Did you have to stay up half the night? And all alone? What kind of life is that?

TELEPHONE OPERATOR. I can tell you what kind of life it is: I get fifty marks a month — but for that I haven't been able to leave my switchboard for eleven years. Whatever goes on in the village — and for miles around — I know about. You'd be surprised at a cobbler. Telephones, potato pancakes and herring, and knowing everything: that's my life.

PUNTILA. Then it's time for a change. And right away, too. Send a telegram this minute to the main post office, to tell them you're marrying Puntila from Lammi. There's the ring and here's a drink, everything legal, and eight days from Sunday come out to the Puntila Estate!

TELEPHONE OPERATOR (*laughing*). I'll be there. I know you'll be giving an engagement party for your daughter.

PUNTILA (*to* HOME-BREW EMMA). And you, gracious lady, you've seen how I've been getting myself engaged to everybody. You'll be there, too, I trust.

THE FOUR WOMEN. When the plums were gone, he left us
For another village then.
But we can't forget, believe us,
Our young and handsome man.

PUNTILA. And on and on I go, around the pond, and through the pines; and on to the market place to hire some workers for the season! On and on and on! Oh, you beautiful girls of Tavastland, all you who year after year rose early for nothing — till Puntila came by and made it all worth while. Come, all of you! Come, all of you who light the fires so early in the morning. Come in your bare feet; the fresh grass knows your steps and Puntila will hear!

III. (COOK *beats batter.*)

When Mr. Puntila went for a ride
He met an early riser.
"O Milkmaid with your breasts so white,
Why aren't you a little wiser?
You're off to milk my cows, I see,
While cocks crow cockadoo.
Why only rise to work for me,
Why not sleep with me, too?
Why not sleep —
Why not sleep —
Why not sleep with me, too?"

IV. Scandal on the Puntila Estate

(*The Puntila Estate. Before noon. In the courtyard there is a bathhut [sauna] of which the interior is visible.* LAINA, *the cook, and* FINA, *the kitchenmaid, are nailing a sign saying* "Welcome to the Engagement Party" *above the door of the manor house.* PUNTILA *and* MATTI *come through the gate, followed by several laborers.*)

COOK. Welcome home. Miss Eva and the Attaché and the District Judge all got here some time ago and are having their breakfast.

PUNTILA. What I want to know right now is: why is Surkkala packing?

COOK. But you promised the Reverend you'd send him away for being too political.

PUNTILA. What? Surkkala? The only intelligent man among my tenants? And him with four children? Tell Surkkala to come immediately, tell the children to come, too, all four of them. I want to express to them personally my regrets for the fear and insecurity I must have caused them.

COOK. You needn't do that, Mr. Puntila.

PUNTILA (*seriously*). Yes, I do. These gentlemen are staying (*pointing to the laborers*). Go, get them an aquavit, Fina, I want to hire some of them to work in the woods. And bring me some coffee.

COOK. I thought you were going to sell the woods to raise Miss Eva's dowry.

PUNTILA. Me? I'm not selling any woods. My daughter has her dowry between her legs, am I right? I can't stand hiring men in the market place, so I brought them along. When I go buying horses or cows I go to the market and think nothing of it, but you are human beings, and it's not right that you should be bargained for in the marketplace. Isn't that so?

A SCRAWNY WORKER. That's so, all right.

MATTI. Excuse me, Mr. Puntila, but that's not so. They need work, and you have work, and that means bargaining — whether it's at the market place, or in church, or here, it's a market all the same.

PUNTILA. What are you giving me the onceover for? Am I a lame horse?

MATTI. I take you on good faith, Mr. Puntila.

PUNTILA (*noting the* SCRAWNY WORKER). That one isn't bad. I like his eyes.

MATTI. Mr. Puntila, I don't want to interfere with what's your business, but that man won't do for you. He couldn't stand the work.

SCRAWNY WORKER. You ever hear the like? How do you know I won't be able to stand the work?

MATTI. Eleven and a half hours a day in the summer heat? I wouldn't want you to be disappointed, Mr. Puntila. Afterwards you'd have to get rid of him, when he couldn't take it.

PUNTILA. I'm going to take a steam bath. I'll have my coffee there.

(FINA *comes with glasses, a bottle of aquavit, and a pot of coffee.*)

MATTI (*to* FINA). He wants his coffee in there.

RED-HEADED WORKER. What's it like here?

MATTI. So-so. Four liters of milk; that's pretty good. You get potatoes. The room's small.

RED-HEADED WORKER. How far's the school? I've got a little girl.

MATTI. A good hour's walk.

RED-HEADED WORKER. In good weather, that's nothing. How about him?

MATTI. Him? Gets too familiar. You don't have to care, you're out in the woods. But me, he's got right in the car, and next thing you know, he talks to me man to man.

(SURKKALA *enters with his* CHILDREN.)

Surkkala! For God's sake, get away from here. By the time he's had his bath and swallows his coffee, he'll be cold sober. And heaven help you if he sees you around then! You'd better stay out of his way for the next few days.

(SURKKALA *nods and starts to leave quickly with his* CHILDREN.)

PUNTILA (*has been listening, but has not understood what has been said. Now, half-dressed, he looks out of the bathhut, and sees* SURKKALA *and his* CHILDREN). Surkkala! I'll be right with you. (*To* MATTI.) Matti, give him ten marks bonus.

MATTI. And how about these men? Couldn't you hire them now? Soon it'll be too late to get back to the market-place in time to find work for the season.

PUNTILA. Don't rush me. I don't buy people in cold blood. I want to give them a home here.

RED-HEADED WORKER. Then I'd better go. I need work. (*Off.*)

PUNTILA. Hey, wait! Now he's gone. I could have used him. (*To the* SCRAWNY WORKER.) Don't let him scare you away; you'll stand the work all right. (*To* MATTI.) Come in here. I need you to pour water over me. (*To the* SCRAWNY WORKER.) Why don't you come, too.

(PUNTILA, MATTI *and the* SCRAWNY WORKER *go into the bathhut.* MATTI *starts pouring water over* PUNTILA. SURKKALA *and his* CHILDREN *leave quickly.*)

One bucket's enough. I hate water.

MATTI. You'll have to take a couple more buckets and some more coffee, and you'll be ready to greet your guests.

PUNTILA. I'm ready right now. You're just trying to bully me.

SCRAWNY WORKER. I think one bucket's enough too. The water doesn't agree with Mr. Puntila, I can see that.

PUNTILA. See, Matti, that's the way a man talks who has some feelings for me. I wish you'd tell him how I fixed that fat fellow at the market. Fina can listen too.

(*She enters, and pours him another coffee.* PUNTILA *is in a story-telling mood.*)

Such a fat repulsive fellow he was, with pimples. He tried to get one of the workers to desert me. Go on, tell the rest, Matti; I've got to drink my coffee.

MATTI. Well, when we got back to the car, the fat man's buggy was standing right next to it. He got so mad when he saw Mr. Puntila coming, he took his whip and started beating his horse so hard, his horse reared up and clawed the air with his hoofs.

PUNTILA. I can't stand people who are cruel to animals.

MATTI. Mr. Puntila got hold of the reins and calmed the horse down. And he told the fat man what he thought of him. I thought Mr. Puntila was going to get a lashing too, but the fat fellow didn't dare, there were too many of us. So he just mumbled something about people without breeding, thinking maybe we wouldn't hear it. But Mr. Puntila's got a sharp ear when there's someone he can't stand, and right away Mr. Puntila asked him if he didn't know, since he was so smart, that few people died easily from apoplexy.

PUNTILA. Go on, tell how he got red as a turkey, and how he was so mad he couldn't think of a smart answer in front of all those people.

MATTI. He got red in the face like a turkey, and Mr. Puntila told him getting red in the face like that showed how the blood was rushing to his head.

PUNTILA. And then I told him how all physical exercise — like hitting horses with a whip — was like poison for him.

MATTI. I gave Mr. Puntila a lot of credit for talking to the fat man like that. Why, Mr. Puntila could have said to himself: It's none of my business. Why make enemies for myself in the neighborhood?

PUNTILA (*who has been drinking coffee steadily and is growing sober*). I'm not afraid of enemies.

MATTI. Now you'll have to send your mares someplace else, though.

FINA. What do you mean?

MATTI. Afterwards I learned that the fat man bought out Summala, and they have the only stud in 800 kilometers we can send our mares to.

FINA. That was the new owner? And you only found out afterwards?

(PUNTILA *stands up out of the tub and goes to pour another bucket of water over his head.*)

MATTI. Oh, Mr. Puntila really knew about it all along. He called after the fat man that his stallion was too played out for our mares anyway. How was it you said that?

PUNTILA (*coldly*). Some way.

FINA. But what a job to send our mares so far away to get covered!

PUNTILA (*ill-tempered*). More coffee.

FINA. Is it strong enough?

PUNTILA. Don't ask stupid questions. I drank it. (*To* MATTI.) Don't just stand around, do something! Don't contradict! And if I catch you loafing again, I'll put it in your letter of reference. Remember that! (PUNTILA *wraps his bathrobe around himself and walks off into the house angrily.*) Fina!

(*She follows him in.*)

MEN. Now what? Will he hire us now!

MATTI. You'd better leave!

PUNTILA. Fina!

(*She follows from behind, carrying his clothes.*)

Listen to what I've decided, so they don't twist my words around afterwards again. I might have taken that one, but his pants are too fine to suit me. I can take one look at a man and tell what's in him. As far as I'm concerned, the main thing is the man himself. I don't care if they're smart. The smart ones only try to figure out all day how many hours they're working. I don't like that. I want my workers and me to be friends. (*To a strong worker.*) Come with me; I'll give you the earnest money in the house. That reminds me. (*Calls* MATTI, *who is coming out of the bathhut.*) Give me your jacket, you. Your jacket, understand?

(MATTI *hands him the jacket.*)

I've got you now, you thief. (*Shows him the wallet.*) So that's what I find in your pocket. The first time I saw you, I knew you were a jailbird. Is that my wallet or not?

MATTI. Yes, Mr. Puntila.

PUNTILA. Now you're in for it. Ten years' prison.

MATTI. Yes, Mr. Puntila.

(EVA *has stepped out and stands listening.*)

PUNTILA. But that would be doing you too much of a favor. Letting you sit around in a cell, loafing and eating the taxpayer's bread! Especially right now, at harvest time! So you wouldn't have to drive the tractor! But I'll put it in your letter of reference, understand?

MATTI. Yes, Mr. Puntila.

(PUNTILA, *fuming, starts toward the house.*)

SCRAWNY WORKER. Should I come, too, Mr. Puntila?

PUNTILA. I couldn't use you. You couldn't stand the work.

SCRAWNY WORKER. But it's too late for the market now. The hiring's over.

PUNTILA. Why didn't you think of that sooner, instead of trying to take advantage of my friendly mood. Thinking it all over, I'm not going to take anybody. I'll probably sell a wood, and you can blame him (*pointing to* MATTI) there. He kept me in the dark about something I needed to know. I'll get even with him. (*Off into the house.*)

A WORKER. That's the way they are. First they bring you along in their car and then you can walk back — the whole nine kilometers. And no work.

SCRAWNY WORKER. I'll make a complaint.

MATTI. To whom?

(*The* WORKERS *walk off, grumbling bitterly.*)

EVA. Why didn't you defend yourself? We all know that when he's drunk he gives his wallet to other people to pay his bills.

MATTI. What for? I learned a long time ago that the people you work for don't like it when you defend yourself.

EVA. Don't act so humble and sanctimonious. I'm not in a joking mood today.

MATTI. I know. You're getting engaged to the Attaché.

EVA. Don't be so crude. The Attaché is a very fine man — just not for marrying.

MATTI. That's often the case.

EVA. My father's leaving it entirely up to me; you heard him say so himself. That's why he told me I could marry even you. Only he'd already promised my hand to the Attaché, and he doesn't want people to say he doesn't keep his word — which is the only reason I'm being so considerate and thinking of accepting him after all.

MATTI. Looks to me as if you're up the creek.

EVA. I am not up the creek, as you put it in your unrefined way. I don't know why I talk such intimate things over with you at all.

MATTI. That's quite a habit with humans, talking things over. It's the big advantage we're supposed to have over the animals. If cows could talk things over, for instance, there'd soon be no slaughterhouses.

EVA. What does that have to do with my saying that I probably won't be happy with the Attaché? And that he ought to withdraw his proposal? . . . Only how are we going to suggest it to him?

MATTI. Hitting him over the head with a fence post won't do it; it would take at least a telephone pole.

EVA. Just what do you mean by that?

MATTI. I mean I'd have to handle it myself. I'm crude.

EVA. Just how do you imagine you're going to be able to help me in such a delicate affair?

MATTI. Let's suppose I felt encouraged by Mr. Puntila's friendly suggestion that you marry me, which he let slip when he was drunk; and that you felt attracted by my brute strength; and that the Attaché caught us and said to himself: "She's not worthy of me — carrying on with a chauffeur."

EVA. I couldn't ask that much of you.

MATTI. It would be part of my job, just like fixing a tire. It'd hardly take fifteen minutes. All we have to do is show him we're intimate.

EVA. And how do you propose to do that?

MATTI. Sometime when he's around I could call you by your first name.

EVA. What would you say, for instance?

MATTI. "Your blouse is open at the neck, Eva."

EVA (*raises her hand to her throat*). But it's not — oh, you're acting your part already. . . . Well, that wouldn't bother him anyway. He's not as easily offended as all that. He's too deeply in debt.

MATTI. Well, then sort of by accident, I could pull a stocking of yours out of my pocket with my handkerchief — right in front of him, so he'd be sure to notice.

EVA. That's better. But still he'd only say that you'd snatched it when I wasn't around because you adored me secretly. (*Pause.*) Your imagination in things of this sort isn't bad, it seems.

MATTI. I do my best, Miss Eva. I'm imagining every possible sort of compromising situation for us two — trying to find something that'll do.

EVA. Don't be so conscientious.

MATTI. All right, then, I won't.

EVA. . . . Why, what did you have in mind?

MATTI. If his debts are really big, then he's got to see us coming out of the bathhut together. Anything less than that won't do. He'd always find some excuse to make it look harmless. For instance, if I only kissed you, he'd say I was forward because your beauty made me lose control of myself. And so on.

EVA. I never know when you're joking, or laughing at me behind my back. With you I'm never sure.

MATTI. What do you want to be sure for? Nobody is asking you to invest your money. To be unsure is much more human, as your father would say. . . . I like women unsure.

EVA. I can well imagine.

MATTI. You see? You don't have such a bad imagination yourself.

EVA. When you talk like that I can see that your idea of the bathhut wouldn't work out. You'd be sure to take advantage of the situation.

MATTI. Now there's something you're sure of again. . . . If you keep hemming and hawing much longer, Miss Eva, I'll lose interest in compromising you.

EVA. I'd just as soon your interest weren't so intense. . . . All right, I'll tell you something: I agree to the bathhut idea! I trust you. . . . They ought to be finished with their breakfast pretty soon, and they'll be sure to take a walk on the porch to talk over the engagement. We'll go into the bathhut at once.

MATTI. Go on ahead. . . . I'll get some cards first.

EVA. Why cards?

MATTI. How else are we going to pass the time?

(MATTI *goes behind the house, and* EVA *walks slowly toward the bathhut. The* COOK *appears, carrying her basket.*)

COOK. Good morning, Miss Eva, I'm going to get some cucumbers. Would you like to come?

EVA. No, I've got a little headache and want to take a steambath.

(EVA *goes into the sauna. The* COOK *stands looking after her shaking her head.* PUNTILA *and the* ATTACHÉ *come out of the house, both smoking cigars.*)

ATTACHÉ. You know, Puntila, I think I'm going to take Eva to the Riviera for our honeymoon and ask Baron Vaurien for his Rolls. It will be a splendid advertisement for Finland and its foreign policy.

PUNTILA (*to the* COOK). Where's Eva?

COOK. She's in the sauna, Mr. Puntila. She had such a bad headache she wanted to take a bath. (*She goes off.*)

PUNTILA. She's always getting notions like that. I've never heard of anyone taking a steambath for a headache.

ATTACHÉ. It's quite an original idea. But you know, Puntila, we make much too little of our Finnish sauna. That's what I told the First Privy Councilor at the time when the new loan was being discussed. Our Finnish Culture must be publicized from entirely new angles. Why, indeed, are there no saunas in Picadilly Circus?

PUNTILA. Tell me, is the foreign minister really coming to the engagement party?

ATTACHÉ. He gave me his word. He is under obligation to me, you know, because I introduced him to the Lehtinens of the Lehtinen National Trust. He is extremely fond of me. He told me once, "You can be sent anywhere and everywhere. You are soft-spoken and commit no indiscretions; you are not interested in politics." He means I am a representative par excellence.

PUNTILA. You're full of —, Eino. But no joking about the minister's coming. That will prove what they really think of you.

ATTACHÉ. Puntila, I'm absolutely sure he will come. I am always lucky. It's common knowledge around the ministry that when I lose something I always get it back.

(MATTI *appears with a towel thrown over his shoulder, and walks across the courtyard toward the sauna.*)

PUNTILA (*to* MATTI). What are you lolling around for, you? . . . If I loafed the way you do, I'd ask myself how I was earning my pay. I won't even give you a letter of reference.

MATTI. Yes, Mr. Puntila.

(PUNTILA *turns back to the* ATTACHÉ, *and* MATTI, *undisturbed, goes into the sauna.* PUNTILA *seems to think nothing of this at first, then suddenly, recollecting, he turns in astonishment toward the bathhut that* MATTI *has just closed behind him.*)

PUNTILA. By the way . . . (*He turns back to the* ATTACHÉ *and continues somewhat uneasily.*) How are you and Eva getting along?

ATTACHÉ. Excellently, why excellently. She is somewhat cool toward me to be sure, but that is her nature. The situation might be compared with our position regarding Russia. In diplomatic language, our relations are *comme il faut*. . . . Would you care to join me while I pick a bouquet of white roses for Eva?

PUNTILA (*looking back at the bathhut as he goes off with the* ATTACHÉ). Hmm, perhaps not a bad idea.

MATTI (*in the sauna*). They saw me come in. Everything's going fine.

EVA. I'm surprised my father didn't stop you. The cook told him I was in here.

MATTI. He thought of it too late, I suppose. He must have a terrible hangover today. . . . If he'd thought of it as I came in, though, it would have spoiled things. The timing would have been bad. The intention to compromise isn't enough. Something has to happen.

EVA. I doubt if they'll think anything bad about this at all. Nothing can happen in the middle of the morning.

MATTI. Why not? Pinochle? (*Shuffles cards.*) In love there are some people who never get enough. Your turn. You think the help in the cowbarn always wait till it's night? . . . Now that it's summertime everybody's in the mood. After all, people are people. So they go quickly off into the bathhut. . . . It's hot in here. (*He takes off his jacket and opens the front of his shirt.*) You can make yourself comfortable, too; my looking won't hurt. . . . We're playing a pfennig a point, all right?

EVA. Your talk is rather vulgar. Remember, I'm not a milkmaid.

MATTI. I've got nothing against milkmaids.

EVA. You don't show me the proper respect.

MATTI. I've been told that many times before. Chauffeurs generally lose their respect for the better sort of people. That's because we have the better sort of people behind us in the car. — That's one game for me. Want to play another?

EVA. In Switzerland where I went to school, conversation was always very proper.

MATTI. Who said anything about "proper" or "improper"? I'm talking about what's so and not so. . . . Your deal. Be sure to cut so there won't be any cheating.

(PUNTILA *and the* ATTACHÉ *come back into the courtyard. The* ATTACHÉ *is carrying a large bouquet of white roses.*)

ATTACHÉ. She is very witty, you know. I once said to her, "You would be perfect, if only you were not so rich." Said she without hesitation, "I find it rather pleasant being rich!" Hahaha! And do you know, Puntila, Mademoiselle de Rothschild gave me exactly the same answer when I was introduced to her at the villa of Baroness Vaurien? She is very witty, too.

MATTI. You'll have to giggle as if I were tickling you, or they won't even pay attention. They'll just walk by shamelessly.

(EVA *giggles a little while continuing to play cards.*)

That doesn't sound as if you're enjoying it enough.

ATTACHÉ (*stops and listens*). Isn't that Eva?

PUNTILA. Of course not! How could it be? It must be someone else.

MATTI (*loudly, still playing cards*). My, you're ticklish.

ATTACHÉ. Listen!

MATTI (*whispers*). Fight me off!

PUNTILA. I think perhaps you'd better take your bouquet inside the house.

EVA (*playing her role, cries out*). No! Don't!

MATTI. Oh, come on.

ATTACHÉ. You know, Puntila, that really sounds like Eva.

PUNTILA. Don't be insulting.

MATTI (*whispers*). Now little by little, start giving in and getting more familiar.

EVA (*in decreasing volume*). No! No! No! (*Whispers.*) What else should I say?

MATTI (*whispers*). Say, "We mustn't do this!" Put yourself into the situation! Be passionate!

EVA. We mustn't do this!

PUNTILA (*roars*). Eva!

MATTI (*whispers*). Go on! With passion! (*He puts the cards away as they continue the scene.*) If he comes in we'll just have to give him the real thing. We won't have any choice.

EVA. We can't do that!

MATTI (*he knocks a bench over with his foot*). Then get out — but better look like a wet hen!

PUNTILA. Eva!

(MATTI *runs his hand through* EVA's *hair to make it look disheveled.* EVA *unbuttons her blouse at the neck and steps out of the bathhut.*)

EVA. Did you call me, Papa? I was just changing my clothes to go swimming.

PUNTILA. What do you think you were doing in the bathhut? Don't you think we can hear?

ATTACHÉ. Now don't lose your temper, Puntila. Why shouldn't Eva go into the sauna if she wants to.

(MATTI *steps out of the bathhut and stands behind* EVA *who doesn't notice him.*)

EVA (*a little set back*). But there wasn't anything to hear, Papa. Really. It was nothing.

PUNTILA. You call that nothing! Maybe you'd better look behind you.

MATTI (*acting as if he were embarrassed*). Mr. Puntila, Miss Eva and I were only playing pinochle. Here are the cards, if you don't believe us. You mustn't misunderstand.

PUNTILA. Keep your mouth shut! You're fired! (*To* EVA.) What is Eino to think?

ATTACHÉ. You know, Puntila, if they were playing pinochle, then you really did misunderstand. Princess Bibesco once got so excited playing whist that she broke her pearl necklace. . . . I've brought you some white roses, Eva. (*He hands her the bouquet.*) Come, Puntila, let us go and play a round of billiards! (*He pulls* PUNTILA *by the sleeve.*)

PUNTILA (*fuming*). I'll have this out with you later, Eva! (*To* MATTI.) But you! If ever you so much as look crooked at my daughter — shut up! — you can go pack your dirty socks! You ought to look up to my daughter as to a higher sort of being who has come down to earth. . . . Don't stop me, Eino. Do you think I'm going to let something like this go on? (*To* MATTI.) Now tell me! What are you going to do?

MATTI. I shall look up to her as to a higher being who has come down to earth, Mr. Puntila.

PUNTILA. You open your eyes wide, in unbelieving amazement that such beings exist!

MATTI. I open my eyes wide in unbelieving amazement, Mr. Puntila.

PUNTILA. When you see a thing of such innocence you ought to fall to the ground. Understand?

MATTI. I understand.

(*The* ATTACHÉ *pulls* PUNTILA *into the house.*)

EVA (*to* MATTI). Damn.

MATTI. His debts are even bigger than we thought.

IV. (cook *beats eggs.*)

A sauna stands on Puntila's place
To keep a body clean and strong
When the owner's daughter goes to bathe
Why can't the chauffeur go along?
Mr. Puntila says: "My daughter's fiancé
As a diplomat never frets;
If a scandal's brewing, he looks away;
For I pay all his debts
  For I pay —
    For I pay —
For I pay all his debts."

V. *A conversation about crayfish*

(*The kitchen in the manor house on the Puntila Estate. It is evening. A slaughtered pig is hanging on a hook.* matti, *in his slippers, is sitting, reading the newspaper.* fina, *the kitchenmaid, comes in with some laundry and puts it in a large kettle which she takes from the stove. Dance music can be heard from time to time.*)

fina. Miss Eva wants to talk to you.

matti. I'm finishing my coffee.

fina. You don't have to finish it on account of me — just to make it look as if you weren't in a hurry. . . . I suppose you're getting big ideas because Miss Eva pays attention to you now and then — just because she doesn't have any other company here on the estate, and has to talk to somebody.

matti. On a night like this I have all sorts of ideas. For example, if you'd like to go look at the river with me, Fina, then I won't have heard of Miss Eva's needing me.

fina. I don't think I want to.

matti (*taking up his newspaper again*). Thinking of the school teacher?

fina. There was nothing between me and the teacher. He was a friendly sort and wanted to help educate me, so he lent me a book.

matti. Too bad he's so poorly paid, with all his education. I get two hundred marks and a teacher gets a hundred and fifty, but then I've got to know more. Why, if a teacher doesn't know anything, the worst that can happen is that the people in the village won't learn how to read the newspapers. Once, that would have been a step backwards, but what good is it reading the papers nowadays? What with censorship, there's nothing in them! I'd go as far as to say that if they'd get rid of school teachers altogether, they wouldn't *need* any censors and could save the state all the money they spend for their salaries. But, when the car gets stuck on the highway, then the gentlemen have to walk on foot through the filth, and they fall into the ditch because they're drunk.

(MATTI *beckons to* FINA; *she comes and sits on his knee. The* JUDGE *and the* LAWYER *enter, towels thrown over their shoulders, returning from the steambath.*)

JUDGE (*to* MATTI). You have anything to drink around? Maybe some of that wonderful buttermilk you used to have?

MATTI. You want the maid to bring you some?

JUDGE. No, just show us where it is.

(MATTI *gets up and ladles out two glasses for them as* FINA *goes off.*)

LAWYER. Excellent.

JUDGE. I always drink it after my steambath when I'm at Puntila's.

LAWYER. Ah, these Finnish summer nights . . .

JUDGE. They cause me a lot of work. Those suits for alimony are a Song of Songs about Finland's summer nights. In the courtroom you realize how beautiful a Finnish birchwood is. They can't even go down to the river without temptation. Around every bush along the side of the road there ought to be barbed wire. You just can't hold them back in the summertime. They climb off their bicycles; they crawl up into haylofts. It happens in the kitchen because it's too warm, and outdoors because such a fine breeze is blowing. Sometimes children do it because the summer's too short, and sometimes because the winter's too long.

LAWYER. How splendid it is that old folks, too, can share in it; they make such fine witnesses afterwards. They see the young couple disappear into the wood and they see the wooden shoes outside the hayloft. And they not only see; they also hear. Yes, with their eyes and ears the old folks share it — and enjoy the summer, too.

(*The servants' bell rings, but* MATTI *doesn't move.*)

JUDGE (*to* MATTI). Perhaps you'd better go in and see what they want . . . (*Starting to walk in himself.*) Well, we'll go tell them that there's an eight-hour day around here.

(*He goes off with the* LAWYER. MATTI *is still reading his paper.*)

EVA (*enters, swinging her hips and smoking a cigarette with an inordinately long cigarette-holder*). I rang for you. Are you still busy here?

MATTI. Me? No, I don't start work again till six.

EVA. I thought perhaps you'd row out with me to the little island to catch a few crayfish for my engagement party tomorrow.

MATTI. Isn't it time to go to bed?

EVA. I'm not the least tired. I always sleep badly in the summer; I don't know what comes over me. . . . Could you fall asleep now, if you went to bed?

MATTI. Yes.

EVA. I envy you. Well, get my fishing tackle ready anyway. My father wants some crayfish for the dinner. (*She turns on her heel and starts to go off, again swinging her hips in the manner of a movie siren.*)

MATTI (*changing his mind*). I think I will go along. I'll row you.

EVA. But aren't you too tired?

MATTI. No, I'm not as sleepy as I was and feel pretty good. You'd better go change your clothes, so you can wade better.

EVA. The tackle is in the harness shed.

(EVA *goes off.* MATTI *puts on his jacket.* EVA *returns, wearing a brief pair of shorts.*)

But you didn't get the tackle.

MATTI. We'll catch them with our hands. That's much nicer. I'll teach you.

EVA (*hesitating*). I'd rather take the tackle. We'll catch more.

MATTI. Do we need so many?

EVA. My father never eats anything if there isn't a lot of it.

MATTI. That sounds serious. I was thinking to myself, just a few, and then we'll amuse ourselves. It's such a nice night.

EVA. I wish you wouldn't say "nice" about everything. You better go get the tackle.

MATTI. Don't take your crayfish so seriously! A couple of pockets full will be enough. I know a place where there are plenty. In five minutes we'll have enough to show for the whole trip.

EVA. Just what do you mean by that? Perhaps you don't want to catch crayfish at all!

MATTI (*after a moment*). I suppose it is a little late. I've got to get up at six and pick up some of the guests at the station. If we wade around the little island until three, four o'clock, there won't be much time left for sleeping. . . . But I can row you over there, if you insist.

(EVA *turns around fuming, and walks off without a word.* MATTI *takes off his jacket, sits down, and again starts to read his newspaper. The* COOK *comes in from the steambath.*)

COOK. Fina and the head dairymaid asked if you'd like to come down to the water.

MATTI. I'm too tired.

COOK. Me, too, I'm just dead from all this baking — that's all engagement parties mean to me anyway. I hated to tear myself away to go to bed; it's so bright outside, it's a sin to go to sleep. (*As she goes off she looks out of the window.*) Maybe I will go down by the water for a while. The ostler will be playing on his harmonica again; I like to hear him play. (*She goes off tiredly but determinedly.*)

EVA (*comes in dressed for a trip, just as* MATTI *is about to leave by another door*). I want you to drive me to the station right away.

MATTI. It'll take a minute for me to turn the car around. I'll be waiting out front.

EVA. Good. . . . I notice you don't even ask what I'm going to do at the station.

MATTI. I suppose you're going to take the eleven-ten to Helsinki.

EVA. At any rate, I can see you're not surprised.

MATTI. Why should I be surprised? When chauffeurs are surprised it doesn't change a thing.

EVA. I'm going to Switzerland to a school friend's for a couple of weeks. Since I'd rather not bother my father about it right now, you'll have to lend me two hundred marks for the ticket. My father will pay you back, of course, as soon as I write him.

MATTI (*mimics*). Of course.

EVA. I hope you're not worried about your money. Even if my father doesn't care who I get engaged to, he wouldn't want to be in debt to you on my account.

MATTI (*doubtfully*). I'm not sure he'd feel he owed me anything if I lent the money to you.

EVA (*after a moment*). I'm sorry I even asked you for it.

MATTI. Your father has your best interests at heart, Miss Eva. He told me so himself. When he's had a drink too many, he doesn't always know what your best interests are; then he's ruled by his feelings. But when he is sober, then he knows what he's doing and buys you an Attaché and gets his money's worth, too.

EVA. So now you're advising me to accept the Attaché!

MATTI. Miss Eva, all I know is that in your financial position, you can't afford to cause your father any worry.

EVA. I see you've changed your opinion. You're a weathervane.

MATTI. That's right. But people just don't think when they talk about weathervanes. Weathervanes are made of iron, and that's pretty solid. They just don't have a solid base. Sorry, but I don't have a solid base either. (*He rubs thumb and forefinger together.*)

EVA. Then I'd better be careful about taking your advice, because you don't have the basis to give sound advice. Your fine words about my father only mean you don't want to risk lending me money.

MATTI. — Or losing my job either. It's not a bad one.

EVA. You're pretty much of a materialist, it seems, Mr. Altonen; or — as they'd say in your circles — you know which side your bread is buttered on. Anyhow, I've never seen anybody worry as much as you do about their money — or about their welfare generally. I can see, not only those who have money think about it all day.

MATTI. I'm sorry if I disappoint you. Money always leads to misunderstandings.

EVA (*sitting down*). I won't marry the Attaché.

MATTI. Thinking it over now, I don't see what you have against him in particular. To me, one of them seems pretty much like another. I ought to know, I've worked for them. They got culture and won't throw their shoes at you, not even when they're drunk — and they don't even watch what you're spending, especially when it's not their money. And they know how to appreciate you just like they know one wine from another, because that's something they've learned.

EVA. I won't have the Attaché. I think I'll take you.

MATTI. What does that mean?

EVA. My father could give us a sawmill. Us — when we're married.

MATTI. I had a job once on a place in Karelia, and the owner there had been a hired man. The mistress used to send him out fishing when the Reverend came to visit. Even their grown-up children called him by his first name. "Victor, go get our galoshes. And don't be so slow about it." . . . That's not for me, Miss Eva.

EVA. No, you'd want to be the master. I can well imagine how you'd treat a woman.

MATTI. Have you been thinking much about it?

EVA. Of course not. I suppose you think I do nothing else all day long but think about you! I don't know what ever gave you that idea. (*Stands.*) At any rate, I'm sick and tired of hearing you always talk about yourself, what you want, and what you like, and what you heard. I see right through your innocent stories and your insolence. I don't like selfish people — and I want you to know that I can't stand you!

V. (COOK *butters cake pan.*)

The owner's daughter one night late
Asked the chauffeur to come and fish.
He said: "You won't need any bait
To get you what you wish."
When she wasn't sure if it would do
To fish without tackle or net,
He said: "Why, Miss, it's up to you,
I haven't read my paper yet.
  I haven't read —
    I haven't read —
I haven't read my paper yet."

VI. *The League of Puntila's Brides*

(*The courtyard of the Puntila Estate. It is Sunday morning. On the balcony of the manor house,* PUNTILA *is seen shaving. He is arguing with*

EVA *who is holding the mirror for him. Church bells are heard in the distance.*)

PUNTILA. You'll marry the Attaché and that's that — or you'll not get a pfennig out of me. I'm responsible for your future.

EVA. Just the other day you said that I shouldn't marry him.

PUNTILA. I say lots of things when I've taken a drink to quench my thirst, and I don't like it when you put all sorts of meanings into what I say. If I catch you with that chauffeur once more you'll be in trouble. What if there had been some strangers around to see you coming out of the bathhut with the chauffeur? There would have been a scandal! (*Suddenly he looks away into the distance and shouts.*) What are the horses doing out in the clover?

VOICE. The ostler said to put them out!

PUNTILA. Get them in right away. (*To* EVA.) If I'm gone just one afternoon everything on the estate goes wrong. Why, I ask you, are the horses out in the clover? — Because the ostler's carrying on with the gardener's daughter. And why is that young cow, only a year and two months old, already with calf so she won't grow any more? — Because the chief dairymaid is carrying on with the young doctor. And of course she doesn't have time to see that the bull doesn't jump on my young cows. She just lets him jump on whichever ones he likes! And if that gardener's daughter — I'm going to have to talk to her — wouldn't lie around with the ostler, I wouldn't be selling only two hundred pounds of tomatoes this year. How can she expect to have any real affection left for my tomatoes? They were always a little mine. . . . I'm going to stop all this love-making on my estate; it's costing me too much, you hear? Just let me tell you and that chauffeur that I'm not going to have my estate ruined. There's a limit to everything!

EVA. Who's ruining the estate?

PUNTILA. I'm warning you, I won't stand for a scandal. I'm giving you a wedding that's costing six thousand marks, and I'm doing everything to get you married into the best circles; all of which is costing me a whole wood — do you know what a wood is? And you carry on with any Kretti and Pletti — and even my chauffeur!

(MATTI *steps out of the door below and listens to the conversation as he finishes dressing himself up.*)

PUNTILA. I didn't pay for your fine education in Brussels so you could throw yourself around the neck of a chauffeur. You should have learned to keep your distance with servants. If you don't, they get out of hand and try to rub bellies with you. Ten steps distance and no familiarities, or you'll have chaos. In this kind of thing I'm as hard as steel.

(PUNTILA *goes inside. The four "brides" from Kurgela appear at the gate. They take off their head-scarves and put wreaths of flowers on their heads. Then they send one girl off as a delegate: Sandra, the* TELEPHONE OPERATOR, *enters the courtyard.*)

TELEPHONE OPERATOR. Good morning. I'd like to speak to Mr. Puntila.

MATTI. I don't think he'll see anybody today. He isn't feeling too well.

TELEPHONE OPERATOR. I should think he'd want to see his fiancée.

MATTI. Are you his fiancée?

TELEPHONE OPERATOR. I should say I am.

PUNTILA'S VOICE. And I forbid you to talk of "love" — love, hah. I know what kind of filth you're talking about and I won't stand for such goings-on on my estate. And anyway, I've made my plans, and I want peace and quiet!

(MATTI *takes up a long broom and starts to sweep the yard.*)

TELEPHONE OPERATOR. That voice sounds familiar.

MATTI. No wonder; it's the voice of your fiancé.

TELEPHONE OPERATOR. It is and it isn't. The voice in Kurgela was different.

MATTI. Oh, so it was in Kurgela! Was it when we went there to get liquor?

TELEPHONE OERATOR. Maybe I don't recognize it because things were different. I could see the face and it was friendly. He was sitting in the car and the dawn was in his face.

MATTI. I know that face and I know that dawn. You'd better go home. Nobody wants you right now.

(HOME-BREW EMMA *comes into the courtyard. She acts as if she doesn't know the* TELEPHONE OPERATOR.)

HOME-BREW EMMA. Is Mr. Puntila here? I'd like to talk to him right away.

MATTI. Sorry, he isn't here. But there's his fiancée; you can talk to her.

TELEPHONE OPERATOR. Isn't that Emma Takinainen who makes illegal alcohol? (*Putting on an act.*)

HOME-BREW EMMA. What do I do? Make illegal alcohol? Just because I need a little alcohol when I massage the legs of the policeman's wife. So you can see it must be legal. . . . And whose fiancée did he say you were? Does the Telephone Operator from Kurgela claim to be engaged to my fiancé, Mr. Puntila? — who lives here, I've been told. — That's too much, you magpie!

TELEPHONE OPERATOR (*extending her ring finger and beaming*). What do you see there, you bathtub-brewer? What do you see on my ring finger?

HOME-BREW EMMA. A wart. What do you see on mine? I'm engaged, not you! As legal as can be, with a drink and a ring.

MATTI. Are both of you ladies from Kurgela? Seems we have fiancées here like fleas on a dog.

(*The* MILKMAID *and the* APOTHECARY MISS *come into the courtyard.*)

MILKMAID *and* APOTHECARY MISS (*in unison*). Does Mr. Puntila live here?

MATTI. Are you from Kurgela, too? Then he doesn't live here. I ought to know, I'm his chauffeur.

MILKMAID. But my name is Lisu Jackara. Mr. Puntila and I are really engaged! I can prove it. . . . (*Pointing to the* TELEPHONE OPERATOR.) And she can prove the same thing. She's engaged to him, too.

TELEPHONE OPERATOR *and* HOME-BREW EMMA (*in unison*). Yes, we can all prove it. We are all his legitimate fiancées.

(*The four laugh.*)

MATTI. I'm glad you can all prove it. I'll tell you honestly if there was only one legitimate bride, I couldn't be particularly interested, but I know the voice of the masses when I hear it. I hereby propose a League of Puntila's Brides. And with that I now raise an historical question: What is to be done?

HOME-BREW EMMA. That doesn't sound as if we're very welcome.

MATTI. I didn't say you weren't welcome. It's just that — from one point of view — you came a little too soon. I'll have to watch for the right time to take you in so you'll be acknowledged as the fiancées that you rightly are.

APOTHECARY MISS. We only want to have a little fun and kick up our heels a bit at the dance.

MATTI. If we pick the right time, it might work. As soon as they're drunk and things get going, they'll want something a little grotesque. Then four brides could make their appearance. The Reverend will be surprised, and the Judge will be a different and happier man to see the Reverend surprised. But it must be done in an orderly way — or Mr. Puntila won't know what's going on when the League of Brides marches into the big dining room singing the Tavastland Hymn and carrying a petticoat for a flag.

(*They all laugh.*)

HOME-BREW EMMA. You think we might get some coffee, and afterwards maybe a dance or two?

MATTI. That's a demand which the League should be able to push through.

APOTHECARY MISS. You, whatever your name is, maybe you could get us a glass of milk?

MATTI. Some milk? Not before lunch, you'd ruin your appetite.

MILKMAID. Don't worry.

MATTI. You'd have a nicer visit if I gave the groom a glass of something — and not milk.

TELEPHONE OPERATOR. His voice sounded a little dry, I must say.

MATTI. You see, Sandra, the Telephone Operator, understands why I can't go and get a glass of milk for you right now; she knows I'm trying to figure out how I'm going to get him to drink a glass of aquavit.

MILKMAID. I heard they have ninety cows on the Puntila Estate.

TELEPHONE OPERATOR. You heard that, all right, Lisu, but you didn't hear his voice.

(*The* COOK *and the* OSTLER *carry a slaughtered pig into the house.*)

THE FOUR WOMEN (*applauding loudly*). { That'll feed a lot of us!
Make it good and crisp!
Put some marjoram on it!

HOME-BREW EMMA. Do you think I could open the hooks of my skirt a little at dinner if nobody's looking? It's tight enough as it is.

APOTHECARY MISS. Mr Puntila might look.

TELEPHONE OPERATOR. Not at dinner.

MATTI. Do you know what kind of dinner it's going to be? You'll be sitting side by side with the Judge of the Supreme Court in Vyborg. (*The broom with which* MATTI *has been sweeping has a nail at the top of the handle. He plants the broom brush-end up on the ground. Assuming the manner of a lawyer, he addresses the broom as if it were the Chief Justice of Vyborg.*) I'll address him as follows: "Your honor. You see here before you four penniless women who are in great fear that their just claims might be cast aside. They have wandered great distances along dusty roads to join their bridegroom. Early one morning, exactly ten days ago, a fine fat gentleman came driving into their village in his Studebaker, and became legally engaged to them all with a ring and a drink. Now he is trying to deny everything. . . . I call upon you, your honor, to fulfill your duty, and pronounce sentence. And let me warn you that if you do not provide these four women with protection perhaps one day there will no longer be a Supreme Court in Vyborg."

TELEPHONE OPERATOR. Bravo!

MATTI. The lawyer will be drinking with you at the table, too. What will you tell him, Emma Takinainen?

HOME-BREW EMMA. I'll tell him I'm very pleased to make his acquaintance, and wouldn't he make out my tax form and be real tough with the tax collector. And couldn't he talk them into keeping my husband in the army a little longer. . . . And I'll tell him the storekeeper tries to cheat me right and left.

MATTI. That's using your opportunity wisely. But let's have no saving money on taxes if you marry Mr. Puntila. The one who gets him can afford to pay.

(*A* WORKER *rolls a beer barrel into the house.*)

HOME-BREW EMMA. Look! Real lager beer!

MATTI. And you'll be rubbing elbows with the Reverend, too. What will you tell him?

MILKMAID. I'll say to him: from now on I'll have lots and lots of time to come to church on Sunday if I take a notion.

MATTI. That's much too short for a dinner conversation. I'll add for you: Reverend, more than anything you should be pleased that today, Lisu, the Milkmaid, is eating off real china, too. Isn't it written that in God's eyes all men are the same, so why not in the eyes of Mr. Puntila?

(*While* MATTI *has been holding forth,* PUNTILA *has stepped out on the balcony and has been listening glumly.*)

PUNTILA. When you finish talking, let me know. . . . Who are they?

TELEPHONE OPERATOR (*laughing*). Your fiancées, Mr. Puntila. You recognize me, don't you?

PUNTILA. Me? I don't know any of you.

HOME-BREW EMMA. Of course, you know us — at least by our rings.

APOTHECARY MISS. The ones from the curtain rod in the Kurgela pharmacy.

PUNTILA. What are you all doing here? Raising a stink?

MATTI. Mr. Puntila, we were just talking about how they'd add to the amusement at the engagement party, and we founded a League of Puntila's Brides.

PUNTILA. Why not a labor union? You loafer! Your idleness is the root of all evil. I know you, Matti, I know what paper you read.

HOME-BREW EMMA. Excuse me, Mr. Puntila, it's only for fun and maybe a cup of coffee.

PUNTILA. I know your fun! You've come to blackmail me.

HOME-BREW EMMA. My, my!

PUNTILA. I'll teach you all to take advantage of my friendly moods. I advise you to get off my place before I chase you off and call the police! You there, you're the telephone operator from Kurgela; I recognize you. And the others — I'll find out who they are, too.

HOME-BREW EMMA. We understand. . . . You know, Mr. Puntila, just to have something to remember in our old age, I think I'll sit myself right down in your yard so I can say, "I once sat on Mr. Puntila's place. I was invited." (*She sits on the ground.*) Now, you see nobody can argue about it and deny it; I'm already sitting. I won't need to tell anyone that it wasn't on a chair but on the naked Tavastland earth — about which all the schoolbooks say, "It needs much toil, but the rewards are great." Of course, they didn't say who gets the toil and who gets the rewards.

PUNTILA. Get off my land, all of you.

(*He goes inside. The four women angrily throw down their wreaths of straw, and walk off dejectedly.* MATTI *sweeps the straw away.*)

VII. *Finnish tales*

(*A highway. It is evening. The four women are plodding homeward.*)

APOTHECARY MISS. How can anybody know what mood they'll be in?

HOME-BREW EMMA (*falling behind*). I must have a nail in my shoe. (*She hobbles to a low fence, sits down, and takes off her shoe. The others join her.*)

TELEPHONE OPERATOR. The sole's worn through too.

MILKMAID. Those shoes weren't made for walking five hours on the paved highway.

HOME-BREW EMMA. This walk has ruined them, all right. They should have lasted me another year. . . . Would somebody get me a stone?

(*The* TELEPHONE OPERATOR *brings her a stone which* HOME-BREW EMMA *uses to hammer her shoe. The* TELEPHONE OPERATOR *and the* MILKMAID *sit down beside her.*)

You can never tell what these gentlemen will do. One minute they're this way; the next minute they're that. They have short memories.

APOTHECARY MISS (*standing in front of the others*). Sometimes, though, their memories are awfully long. Like that Pekka man who went off to America and made a fortune, and came back twenty years later to visit his relatives. They were so poor that they had to beg potato peelings from my mother, but when he came to visit them they served him roast veal to put him in a good humor. Anyway, while he was eating, he reminded them that he'd lent them twenty marks once — and shook his head about their being so badly off that they couldn't even pay their debts.

(*They all laugh and the* APOTHECARY MISS *sits down.*)

TELEPHONE OPERATOR (*taking* HOME-BREW EMMA's *shoe and examining it*). They know how to take care of themselves, all right. (*Hands shoe back to* HOME-BREW EMMA.) A cottager near us took a rich landowner across the lake one night when it was frozen over that awful winter of 1908. They both knew that there was a break in the ice some place but they didn't know where, and the cottager had to go in front the whole twelve kilometers. The landowner got frightened and promised him a horse if they got across safely. When they were in the middle, he said: "If you find the way over and don't fall in, I'll give you a calf." A little later, they saw a light shining from the village, and the gentleman said: "Do a good job and you'll earn yourself a watch." Fifty yards from the shore he said something about a sack of potatoes; and when they were across, he gave him a mark and said: "What took you so long?"

HOME-BREW EMMA. They can drown for all I care.

TELEPHONE OPERATOR. . . . We're not smart enough for their jokes, and their tricks catch us every time. They look the same as we do, and that fools us. If they only looked like crocodiles or rattlesnakes, we'd be on guard.

APOTHECARY MISS (*to the* TELEPHONE OPERATOR). Don't joke with them, and don't accept anything from them.

TELEPHONE OPERATOR. "Don't accept anything from them!" That's good — when they have everything and we have nothing.

HOME-BREW EMMA (*ironically*). Take nothing from the river when you're dying of thirst!

APOTHECARY MISS. I'm awfully thirsty.

MILKMAID. Me too.

TELEPHONE OPERATOR. . . . Our kind always loses out.

MILKMAID. A dairymaid I know in Kausala was carrying on with the son of the owner of the place where she worked. She had a baby, but at the court in Helsinki the owner's son denied everything so he wouldn't have to pay for its support. Her mother got her a lawyer. He showed the court the love letters the son had written from the army. The letters left no doubt as to what the situation was. He ought to have gotten five years at least for perjury; but when the judge read the first letter — he read it very slowly — the girl stepped in front of him and asked to have the letters back. . . . So she didn't get any money for support. They said the tears ran out of her eyes like a river as she left the courthouse — with her mother furious at her. That scoundrel had a good laugh. That's what her love was like.

TELEPHONE OPERATOR. That's how stupid she was.

HOME-BREW EMMA (*puts on her shoe*). But sometimes people like her can be smart, too; it all depends. There was a young man from around Viborg. *He* wouldn't take anything from them. He was in the uprising in 1918, and they put him in the Tammersfors camp on account of it. He had to eat grass, he was so hungry. They didn't give them anything to eat. His mother went to visit him and brought him something. She had to go eighty kilometers. She was a cottager's widow, and the owner's wife had given her a fish and a pound of butter. The old woman went all the way on foot, except when a wagon came along, then maybe she'd get a short ride. She'd tell the man who gave her a ride, "I'm on my way to Tammersfors to visit my son, Athi, who is in the prison camp for the Reds. The landlord's wife gave me a fish for him, and a pound of butter, the kind soul." If the man who was giving her a ride was a kulak, he'd make her get off when he heard about her son. When she went by the washerwomen on the river bank, she said again, "I'm on my way to Tammersfors to visit my son, Athi, who is in the prison camp for the Reds. The landlord's wife gave me a fish for him, and a pound of butter, the kind soul." And when she came to Tammersfors, she even made her little speech to the Camp Commander; and he laughed and let her in, when everybody else was forbidden. . . . In front of the camp, grass still grew; but behind the barbed wire there wasn't a single blade, not even a leaf on a tree. They'd eaten everything. That's true, believe me. She hadn't seen Athi in two years, and what with the war and his being in prison he was very thin. "There you are, Athi. Look, here's a fish and some butter. The landlord's wife gave them to me, the kind soul." Athi asked her how she was, and how the neighbors were, and if her rheumatism had been bothering her — but the fish and the butter he wouldn't take for anything in the world. He got angry and said, "Did you go to the landlord's wife to beg for them? Then you might as well take it all back, I want nothing from them!" As hungry as Athi was she had to wrap her presents up again. She said goodbye and went all the way home on foot. Now she said to the women by the river, "My Athi in the prison camp wouldn't take the fish and butter because I'd begged them from the landlord's wife. He won't take anything from them." She said this to everyone she met along the way — the whole eighty kilometers — and the story impressed a lot of people.

MILKMAID. There are some men like Athi.

HOME-BREW EMMA. Too few.

(*The four women get up and continue their walk in silence.*)

VII. (COOK *polishes wine glass.*)

The Brides of Puntila, people say,
Then raised a song of scorn.
Their Sunday was a wasted day
And their shoes were badly torn.
If ever you put your faith into
The rich man's promised land ahead,
Look not to the hole that's in your shoe
But to the hole in your head.
  But to the —
    But to the —
But to the hole in your head.

(*The four women repeat the song.*)

VIII. *Puntila gives his daughter's hand to a human being*

(*The Puntila Estate. A large dining room, small tables and a large buffet table. The* REVEREND, *the* JUDGE, *and the* LAWYER *are standing smoking and drinking coffee.* PUNTILA *sits in a corner drinking silently. From the next room can be heard French dance music of the 1920's.*)

REVEREND. True faith is rarely found today. Instead, there is enough doubt and indifference to make one despair of our people. I drum it into them again and again that without Him not one gooseberry would grow.

Yet they take the fruits of Nature as something quite natural, and gobble them down as if that were the only way. Then, too, man is evil by nature. How else can I explain something like this: last week I was talking to a peasant on his death-bed about what awaits man in the Great Beyond; and he asked me, "Do you think the potatoes will stand the rain?" A thing like that makes me wonder if everything we do is just waste down the drain.

JUDGE. I know what you mean. Trying to instill culture in these louts is no picnic.

LAWYER. We lawyers don't have too easy a life either. We've always made our living from the peasants. In the old days, their iron character made them prefer to be beggars rather than give up their rights. Now — they'd still like to insult each other, and stick knives in each other's ribs, and sell each other lame horses — but as soon as they realize that it's going to cost them money to go to court, they quickly lose their enthusiasm. All for the love of Mammon.

JUDGE. That's this commercial age for you. Nowadays there's a certain shallowness about everything; the old values are disappearing. It's terribly difficult not to give up the common people in despair.

LAWYER. Puntila's fields keep growing year after year, but a lawsuit, on the other hand, is a terribly delicate plant. You have to be particularly careful in handling a suit when it's still in its infancy; that's when the mortality rate is highest. Once you've nursed it along into young adulthood, then it can get on quite nicely by itself. And ah, a suit that's more than four, five years old, can be fully expected to reach a ripe old age. But what a job to carry it that far! It's a dog's life!

(ATTACHÉ *enters with* REVEREND'S WIFE.)

REVEREND'S WIFE. Mr. Puntila, you really should pay some attention to your guests. His Excellency, the Foreign Minister, is dancing now with Miss Eva, but he's been asking for you.

(PUNTILA *doesn't answer.*)

ATTACHÉ. The Reverend's Wife just gave a delightfully witty answer to His Excellency, the Minister. He asked her if she cared for jazz. *Mon Dieu,* in my whole life I've never been in such suspense as to see how she'd solve the situation. She thought a moment and then answered as one couldn't dance to the church organ, it made little difference to her which instruments were used! His Excellency, the Minister, almost died from laughter. . . . What do you say to that, eh, Puntila?

PUNTILA. Nothing. . . . I don't go around criticizing my guests. (*Beckons to the* JUDGE.) What do you think of that face, Frederick?

JUDGE. Which face?

PUNTILA. The Attaché's. Seriously now, what do you think?

JUDGE. Be careful, Johannes, the drinks are pretty strong.

ATTACHÉ (*humming the melody being played in the next room, and keeping time with his foot*). It goes to one's feet, *n'est-ce pas?*

PUNTILA (*again beckoning to the* JUDGE, *who has been trying not to notice* PUNTILA). Frederick! . . . Look at that face, Frederick, and tell me how you like it. It's costing me a wood.

(*All the gentlemen hum* "Je cherche après Titine.")

ATTACHÉ (*not suspecting anything*). I could never remember verses, not even back in school, but I've got rhythm in my blood.

LAWYER (*seeing* PUNTILA *waving about wildly*). Hmmm, don't you think it's a little warm in here? Let's go into the billiard room. (*He wants to pull the* ATTACHÉ *away.*)

ATTACHÉ. The other day I did manage to remember a verse: "Yes, We Have No Bananas." I'm more optimistic now about my memory.

PUNTILA. Frederick, look at that face and render your verdict. Go on, Frederick.

JUDGE (*not answering* PUNTILA). Have any of you heard the joke about the Jew who went walking down the street with his duck? . . . It was during the war, and a policeman stopped him and said, "Jew! What do you feed the duck?" The Jew said, "I give him wheat." The policeman kicked him and said, "Jew! Don't you know that wheat is for the Army?" . . . A few streets farther on, another policeman stopped him and said, "Jew! What do you feed that duck?" The Jew answered softly, "I give him corn." The policeman kicked him and said, "Jew! Don't you know that corn is for the Army?" A little later still another policeman stopped him. "Jew!" said the policeman, "What do you feed that duck?" . . . "Oh," said the Jew in a small voice, "I give him a little money and let him buy what he wants."

(*Everybody laughs but the* ATTACHÉ.)

ATTACHÉ. . . . Was the duck trained?

(*There is an uncomfortable silence.*)

JUDGE. I don't think you quite get the point.

ATTACHÉ. Perhaps you'll have to explain it to me. If the duck wasn't specially trained, how could he take money to a shop and get the food?

PUNTILA (*in disgust*). Frederick!

JUDGE. . . . You don't understand. My dear Eino, the whole point is that the Jew didn't really give the duck any money at all.

ATTACHÉ. Oh, I see. He didn't really give the duck any money. You forgot to mention that. . . . (*Gives a polite bray.*) Hahahaha! What a magnificent joke. The most ingenious joke I've ever heard.

PUNTILA (*gets to his feet gloomily*). I've got to do something about this. I don't have to put up with such an insect. . . . A man without a sense of humor is no man at all. (*To the* ATTACHÉ *with dignity.*) Leave my house! Yes, you. Don't turn around as if I could possibly mean someone else.

JUDGE. Puntila, you've gone too far.

ATTACHÉ. Gentlemen, I beg of you, please forget the incident. You have no idea how precarious is the position of a member of the diplomatic corps. The slightest shadow on his moral reputation may well cause the failure of an entire mission of state. In Paris, at Montmartre, the mother-in-law of the First Secretary of the Roumanian Legation thrashed her lover with an umbrella, and instantly there was a scandal.

PUNTILA. A grasshopper in tails! A grasshopper who'd eat my woods!

ATTACHÉ (*eagerly*). Please understand! It's not that she had a lover — that's in perfectly good form. And it's not that she thrashed him — that's understandable enough. But to have done so with an umbrella! That was vulgar. Everything depends on the nuance!

LAWYER. He's right, Puntila. His honor is very delicate. He's in the diplomatic corps.

ATTACHÉ. Princess Bibesco herself a while ago made some flattering remarks about my sense of humor when she mentioned to Lady Oxford that I would laugh about a *bon mot* before it was even out, that is to say, I comprehend extremely quickly.

PUNTILA. Frederick! Listen! His sense of humor!

ATTACHÉ. As long as no names are mentioned, the situation is still amendable. It's only when insults and names are linked together that matters are beyond repair.

PUNTILA (*with heavy sarcasm*). Frederick, what am I going to do? I've forgotten his name — and according to what he says I'll never be able to get rid of him. . . . Now I remember! Thank God! I saw his name on a promissory note he once asked me to buy. It's Eino Silakka. Maybe he'll go now. What do you think?

ATTACHÉ. Gentlemen, a name has now been mentioned. From this moment on every word must be weighed like gold.

PUNTILA. What can a man do? (*Roaring out suddenly.*) Get out of here! Never show your face on my estate again. I'm not going to give my daughter to a grasshopper in tails!

ATTACHÉ (*turning to* PUNTILA). Puntila, you're beginning to be offensive. If you throw me out of your house, you will be starting to cross that delicate line where a scandal begins.

PUNTILA. That's too much. My patience is at an end. I had intended to let you know, between ourselves, that your presence was too much for my nerves, and that you had better leave; but now you force me to be very plain. . . . Get the hell out, you shit-head!

ATTACHÉ. Puntila, I am taking this amiss. . . . If you'll excuse me, *madame — messieurs?* (*Off.*)

PUNTILA. Don't be so slow! I want to see you run. I'll teach you to give me smart answers!

(PUNTILA *runs after the* ATTACHÉ *with everyone but the* REVEREND'S WIFE *and the* JUDGE *following, too.*)

REVEREND'S WIFE. There'll be a scandal.

(EVA *comes in.*)

EVA. What's going on? What's all the noise about in the courtyard?

REVEREND'S WIFE (*running toward* EVA). My dear child, something frightful has happened. You must fortify yourself with all the strength of your soul.

JUDGE (*bringing her a glass of sherry*). Drink this, Eva. . . . Your father drank a lot of punch and then he took a sudden dislike to Eino's face and chased him out of the house.

EVA (*drinking*). Hm, I can taste the cork. What did he tell him?

REVEREND'S WIFE. Aren't you dreadfully upset, Eva?

EVA. Why, of course.

(*The* REVEREND *returns.*)

REVEREND. It's dreadful. Simply dreadful.

REVEREND'S WIFE. What? What's happened?

REVEREND. There was a terrible scene in the yard. He threw stones at him.

EVA. Did he hit him?

REVEREND. I don't know. The lawyer came between them. — With the Minister right in the house!

EVA. Now I'm pretty certain he'll stay away, Uncle Frederick. It's a good thing we got the Minister to come. Without him the scandal wouldn't have been half so big.

REVEREND'S WIFE. Eva!

(PUNTILA *comes back in, followed by* MATTI, *the* COOK, *and the* KITCHENMAID.)

PUNTILA. Matti! Fina! Laina! I have just looked deep into the depravity of this world. I went into that room (*pointing*) with the best of intentions. I went to announce that a mistake had been made, that I'd almost given my only daughter's hand to a grasshopper, and that I was hastening to give her to a human being. Because a long time ago I decided to marry my daughter to a real man, to Matti Altonen, a capable chauffeur and my friend. I wanted all of them to drink to the happy, young pair. What do you think they did? The Minister, who is supposed to be a cultivated man, looked at me as if I were a toadstool and called for his car. And the others followed suit like monkeys. . . . It was sad. I felt like a Christian martyr before the lions. I couldn't keep it to myself; I had to tell the Minister what I thought. He was leaving fast, but luckily

I caught him in front of his car and told him that he was a shit-head, too! I trust I spoke for all of you.

MATTI. Mr. Puntila, I think we ought to go into the kitchen and discuss the whole thing over a bottle of aquavit.

PUNTILA. Why in the kitchen? We haven't even celebrated your engagement! We've only celebrated the wrong engagement, a mistake. . . . Put the tables together! Set up a banquet. Let's celebrate! Fina, here next to me.

(PUNTILA *sits down in the middle of the room while the others put the small tables together to build one long banquet table.* EVA *and* MATTI *bring the chairs.*)

Reverend next to the kitchenmaid. And you, Madam (*to the* REVEREND'S WIFE), next to the cook. Frederick, sit down to a decent table for once.

(*All sit down reluctantly. There is silence.*)

REVEREND'S WIFE (*to the* COOK). Have you put up your mushrooms this year?

COOK. I don't put them up. I dry them.

REVEREND'S WIFE. How do you do that?

COOK. I cut them into big pieces, string them up, and hang them in the sun.

PUNTILA. I'd like to say a word about my daughter's fiancé. . . . Matti, I've studied you secretly and gained insight into your character. I'm not talking about how the machines have all been in order since you've been here. No, it's the man in you I'm honoring now. . . . I haven't forgotten what happened this morning. I noticed the way you looked as I stood on the balcony like Nero and, in my blindness and error, chased those four dear guests out onto the dusty road. I've told you before about my attacks. I wouldn't be surprised if they lost faith in Puntila. But . . . I'm asking you now; can you forget that, Matti? (*Sits down.*)

MATTI. Mr. Puntila, consider everything forgotten. But you'd better tell your daughter, with all the weight of your authority, that she's not to marry a chauffeur.

REVEREND. Absolutely right.

EVA. Papa. Matti and I had a little argument. He won't believe that you'll give us a sawmill, and he thinks I couldn't stand living with him as just the wife of a chauffeur.

PUNTILA. What do you say to that, Frederick?

JUDGE. Don't ask me, Johannes. And don't look at me like a dying deer; ask Laina.

PUNTILA. Laina, I'm asking you if you think I'd be tightfisted with my daughter, and if you think a sawmill and a steammill — and a wood as well — are too little for her.

COOK (*interrupted in the whispered conversation she has been holding with the* REVEREND'S WIFE). I'd be glad to fix you some coffee, Mr. Puntila.

PUNTILA (*to* MATTI). Are you good at making love?

MATTI. Pretty decent.

PUNTILA. That's nothing. How about indecently, that's what counts. But you don't have to answer. I know you don't go around bragging about yourself.

MATTI. Never mind, Mr. Puntila.

(EVA, *a little drunk, stands up to make a speech.*)

EVA. Dear Matti, please make me your wife so I can have a man like other women. I really don't think as much of myself as you think I do, and I could live with you even if we were a little short of money.

PUNTILA. Bravo!

EVA. But if you think I'm not taking things seriously enough, I'll pack a little bag and go with you to see your mother. My father won't object.

PUNTILA. On the contrary, I'll be glad.

MATTI (*rises in his turn and rapidly drinks down two glasses*). Miss Eva, I can be talked into doing all sorts of foolish things, but I can't take you to my mother's. The old woman might have a heart attack. Why, at best there'd only be a couch for you. (*Turns.*) Reverend, tell Miss Eva what a poor cottager's kitchen with a bed in it looks like.

REVEREND (*gravely*). Most depressing.

EVA. Why describe it? I'll see for myself.

MATTI. — And you'll be asking my old mother for a bath!

EVA. I'll go to the public steambath.

MATTI. With the pay I get from Mr. Puntila? You've still got the owner of a sawmill in your head. . . . That'll all come to nothing because Mr. Puntila is a sensible man when he's himself — and he'll be himself again tomorrow morning.

PUNTILA. Don't go on! Don't talk about the Puntila who is our common enemy! That Puntila was drowned tonight in a bottle of aquavit, that terrible man; and here I stand, converted into a human being. All of you drink and become human like me! Never give up!

MATTI. I'm telling you I can't take you to my mother's. She'd beat my ears with her slippers if I dared to bring home such a wife, if you want to know the truth.

EVA. Matti, you shouldn't have said that.

PUNTILA. I think you're going too far myself, Matti. Eva has her faults, and maybe someday she'll get a little fat like her mother — though not before she's thirty or thirty-five — but now she can show herself wherever she likes.

MATTI. I'm not talking about her getting fat; I'm talking about her not being practical — and how she'd never make a wife for a chauffeur.

REVEREND. Precisely what I think.

MATTI. Don't laugh, Miss Eva, you'd soon stop laughing if my mother put you to the test. She'd take you down a peg or two.

EVA. Let's try, Matti. I'm a chauffeur's wife. Tell me what I have to do.

PUNTILA. Good idea! Bring in the sandwiches, Fina. We'll have a nice little snack, and Matti will test Eva till she's blue in the face!

MATTI. Stay where you are, Fina. We don't have servants around when guests drop in on us. And we don't have anything to eat but what we usually have. Bring in the herring, Eva.

EVA (*running off gaily*). No sooner said than done!

PUNTILA (*calling after her*). Don't forget the butter! (*To* MATTI.) I'm glad you decided to make yourself independent, and not to accept anything from me. Not everyone would show such character.

REVEREND'S WIFE (*to* COOK). But I don't put the mushrooms in salt water; I cook them with lemon and butter. They should be as small as buttons. I put up morels, too.

COOK. Those aren't really very delicate. The only really delicate mushrooms are the champignon and the yellow boletus.

EVA (*bringing back a herring on a silver platter*). In our kitchen, we don't have any butter. Am I right?

MATTI (*taking the platter*). Ah, there he is. How well I know him. I saw his brother only yesterday, and his cousin the day before, and back through many other members of his family since I've been old enough to reach for a plate. (*To* EVA.) How many times a week will you want to eat herring?

EVA. Three times, Matti, if I have to.

COOK. You'll have to eat it more often than that, whether you want to or not.

MATTI. You have a lot to learn. My mother, who's a cook, too, serves herring to the help five times a week; and Laina serves it eight times. (*Rising, he lifts up the herring by the tail.*) Welcome, O Herring, feeder of the poor! You, the appeaser of our hunger at any time of the day, the salty pain in our intestines. You are the fuel that drives the machines called working-men and working-women. O Herring, you dog! If it weren't for you, we might start asking for ham — and what would happen to Finland then? (*Puts the herring back on the platter and cuts it up, then passes it around the table, offering everyone a piece.*)

PUNTILA. To me it tasted like a delicacy, because I rarely eat it. . . . Such distinctions shouldn't exist. When you come right down to it, I'm really a radical — if I were a hired-man, I'd make Puntila's life a hell. . . . Go on with the examination.

MATTI. When I think of what a woman has to know before I'd take her to my mother, right away I think of my socks. (*He takes off one of his socks and gives it to* EVA.) Could you mend this?

JUDGE. That's asking a great deal. I didn't say anything about the herring, but Juliet's love for Romeo might not have stood the test of darning his socks. A love capable of such self-sacrifice is hard to bear, its nature too intense, and hence, the kind likely to end in court.

MATTI. With working people, socks aren't darned for the sake of love, but to save money.

REVEREND. I don't think that the *mesdemoiselles* who raised her in Switzerland ever considered this eventuality.

(EVA *returns with needle and thread and begins to darn the sock.*)

MATTI. What they neglected in her education, she's got to catch up on now. (*To* EVA.) I picked the sock on purpose, so I could really find out what was in you.

FINA. I could show Miss Eva how.

PUNTILA. Pay attention there, Eva. You've got a good head on you.

(EVA *finishes and, with hesitation, gives* MATTI *the sock. He lifts it up, then smiles wryly as he tries to insert his hand. The sock has been hopelessly sewn together.*)

FINA. Without a darning-egg, I couldn't have done any better.

PUNTILA. Then why didn't you get a darning egg?

MATTI. Ignorance. (*To the* JUDGE, *who is laughing.*) Don't laugh. My sock's ruined. (*To* EVA.) If you married a chauffeur, this would be a tragedy, because you'd have to stretch things hard to make both ends meet. But I'll give you another chance. (*He drags one of the parts of the banquet table some distance to one side.*) Chair!

EVA (*bringing over a chair, apologetically*). I admit I didn't do so well with the sock.

MATTI. Now let's say I'm a chauffeur. You help out around the estate — with the washing and in the winter with keeping the stoves going. . . . I come home at night. What do you do?

EVA. I'll do better this time, Matti. Come home!

(MATTI *walks away a few steps, then turns around and acts as if he is entering the door as he comes home.*)

Matti! (*She runs to him and gives him a kiss.*)

MATTI. First mistake. Intimacies and dilly-dallying when I come home tired. (MATTI *acts out going to the water faucet and washing his hands and face, then he stretches out his hand for a towel.*)

EVA (*not understanding, starts to chat*). Poor Matti, are you tired? I've been thinking the whole day about how hard you have to work.

FINA (*whispers*). Towel! (*Hands* EVA *a napkin.*)

EVA (*sadly, realizing her mistake*). Excuse me, I didn't understand what you wanted.

(MATTI, *having dried himself, sits down by the table he has dragged to one side. He sticks out his boots to* EVA.)

PUNTILA (*gets up and watches intently*). Pull!

(EVA *pulls hard at one boot. Suddenly it comes off and she falls on the floor.*)

REVEREND. I consider this a very sound lesson. All this is most unnatural.

MATTI. I don't always have you do this, but today I had to drive the tractor and I'm half dead. . . . What did you do today?

EVA. Wash, Matti.

MATTI. Did you get the water from a hose? Or did you have to carry it in a bucket because the hose leaks? — like on that Puntila place.

PUNTILA. Give it to me good and hard, Matti. I'm a terrible man.

EVA. I had to use a bucket.

MATTI (*lifts up her hand*). You broke your nails again. You'd better make a habit of putting some fat on your hands. My mother's have swollen up like this (*he demonstrates*) and gotten all red. . . . You're probably tired, but my work clothes still have to be washed. I need them clean for tomorrow.

EVA. Yes, Matti.

(MATTI *gropes for something on the table next to him.*)

(*Alarmed.*) What is it?

FINA (*whispers*). The paper.

(EVA *jumps up and pretends to hold a newspaper out to* MATTI. *He doesn't take it, but continues to grope gloomily on the table.*)

On the table!

(EVA *finally puts the imaginary newspaper down on the table.* MATTI *still has one boot on and stomps impatiently with it on the floor.* EVA *finally sits down to pull it off; then stands up, relieved, sighs and fixes her hair.*)

EVA. I fixed up my apron and put a little color in it. See? You can always have a little color without it costing too much; you only have to know how. How do you like it, Matti?

(MATTI, *disturbed in his reading, lowers his newspaper and gives* EVA *a long-suffering look. She looks back, intimidated.*)

FINA (*whispers*). Don't talk when he's reading the paper.

MATTI (*rising*). There. You see?

PUNTILA. I'm disappointed in you, Eva.

MATTI (*almost pityingly*). Everything's wrong. Not wanting to eat herring more than three times a week. No darning-egg for the sock. And when I come home at night, not enough sense to keep her mouth shut. . . . (*To* EVA.) Then they call me in the middle of the night to haul the old man home. What then?

EVA. I'll show you. (*She pretends to open a window and shouts excitedly.*) What? In the middle of the night? When my husband just got home and needs his sleep? That's the end! Let that souse sleep off his drunk in the gutter. Before I let my man go out tonight, I'll hide his pants.

PUNTILA. That's good, you'll have to admit that.

EVA. Getting people out of bed when it's time to sleep! As if they weren't worked to the bone all day long! I'm giving notice! . . . (*To* MATTI.) Is that better?

MATTI (*laughing*). That's pretty good, Eva. — I mean, they'll give me notice — but if my mother saw it, she'd be convinced. (*Jokingly, he slaps* EVA *on the behind.*)

EVA (*speechless at first; then furious*). Stop that!

MATTI. What's the matter?

EVA. How dare you hit me there?

JUDGE (*stands up and pats* EVA *on the shoulder*). I'm afraid, Eva, that despite everything, you've failed the examination.

PUNTILA. What's wrong with you?

MATTI. I shouldn't have slapped you there, is that it?

EVA (*now laughing again*). Papa, I don't think it will work out.

REVEREND. Truer words were never spoken.

PUNTILA. What do you mean, you "don't think it will work out"?

EVA. I realize now that I received the wrong education. I think I'll go upstairs.

PUNTILA. I'll have to do something about this. Eva, sit down. (*Pointing to her place at the table.*)

EVA. Papa, I think I'd better go. I'm sorry you can't have your engagement. Goodnight. (*Walks out.*)

PUNTILA. Eva!

(*The* REVEREND *and the* JUDGE *start to leave. The* COOK *and the* REVEREND'S WIFE, *however, are still talking about mushrooms.*)

REVEREND'S WIFE. You've almost convinced me, but I still feel safer putting them up. Though I peel them first.

COOK. Why do that? All you have to do is brush the dirt off.

REVEREND. Come along, Anna, it's getting late.

PUNTILA. Matti, I'm through with her. Here I got her a man, a splendid example of a human being — someone to make her happy, so she could get up every morning singing like a lark. But she's too fine for all that! . . . I cast her off. (*He runs to the door.*) I disown you! Do you think I didn't notice how you almost took the Attaché just because I ordered you to? You don't have any character. You dishrag, you! You aren't my daughter anymore.

REVEREND. Mr. Puntila, you've lost control of yourself.

PUNTILA. Leave me alone. Go do your preaching in church where there's nobody to hear!

REVEREND. If you'll excuse me, Mr. Puntila. . . . Anna!

PUNTILA. Yes, go away — leaving behind you a father bowed with grief! . . . How did I ever come to have the kind of a daughter who'd commit sodomy with a diplomatic grasshopper? Any milkmaid could tell her why the good Lord created her hind end in the sweat of His brow! (*To the* JUDGE.) And you didn't open your mouth once to try to drive all those unnatural things out of her! Get out of here!

JUDGE. That's enough now, Puntila. I wash my hands in innocence. (*Walks out with a smile.*)

PUNTILA. After doing that for thirty years, Frederick, they must be all washed away! You used to have the hands of a peasant before you became a judge — and started washing your hands in innocence!

REVEREND (*trying to draw his wife away from her conversation with the the* COOK). It's time to go, Anna.

REVEREND'S WIFE. No, I don't put them in cold water. And I don't cook the stems. How long do you let them cook?

COOK. I just let them boil up once.

REVEREND. I'm waiting, Anna.

REVEREND'S WIFE. I'm coming. . . . I let them cook ten minutes, myself.

(*The* REVEREND *goes out shrugging his shoulders.*)

PUNTILA (*back at the table*). Those aren't human beings. I don't consider them human.

MATTI. Strictly speaking they're human all right. I once knew a doctor who used to say when he'd see one of the peasants beating up his horses: Look, he's treating them real human again. You see, to say "real beastly" wouldn't have been proper.

PUNTILA. Now there's a deep truth. I'd like to have taken a drink or two with your doctor. Here, have a half a glass more. I liked that when you were testing her out, Matti.

MATTI. Forgive me for patting your daughter on the behind, Mr. Puntila. That wasn't part of the examination. I only meant it to encourage her, but it showed the gulf between us.

PUNTILA. There's nothing to forgive, Matti. I have no daughter anymore.

MATTI. . . . Don't be hardhearted, Mr. Puntila. (*To the* REVEREND'S WIFE *and the* COOK, *who are getting up.*) Did you two at least come to an agreement about the mushrooms?

REVEREND'S WIFE. And you put in the salt right at the beginning?

COOK. Right at the beginning.

(*Both off.*)

PUNTILA. . . . Listen, the help's still dancing down by the pond.
A VOICE (*singing in the distance. Tune of "Henry Martin"*).

There once was a countess in Sweden's great land.
She was so lovely and white.
"Oh, huntsman, oh huntsman, my garter came off —
It is off, it is off.
Huntsman, kneel down and tie it on right."

"O Countess, my Countess, don't look at me so.
Already your huntsman am I.
Your breasts are snow-white but your headman's ax cold —
It is cold, it is cold.
Sweet 'tis to love — but bitter to die."

(MATTI *rises and walks around the table to* FINA. *He takes her in his arms and, as the song continues, they slowly dance out of the room.*)

The huntsman, he fled her that very same night.
In haste he rode down to the sea.
"O boatman, O boatman, take me in your boat —
In your boat, in your boat —
I must flee to the end of the sea."

Now this was the love twixt a vixen and cock.
"Golden Cockerel, do you love me?"
Oh, the evening was fine, but then in the morn —
In the morn, in the morn —
His feathers lay scattered all under a tree.

PUNTILA. That song was meant for me. Songs like that touch me deeply.

VIII. (COOK *dries dishes.*)

Mr. Puntila on the engagement day
Against the Attaché rails.
He says: "Can I give my child away
To a grasshopper in tails?
Chauffeur, take my daughter — her figure is quite neat!
To be happy you don't have to be so rich."
The chauffeur said: "How can she make ends meet
When she doesn't know which end is which?
    When she doesn't —
        When she doesn't —
When she doesn't know which end is which?"

IX. Puntila and Matti climb Mt. Hatelma

(The billiard room on the Puntila estate. PUNTILA, *with a wet cloth around his head, groans as he is going over bills;* LAINA, *the Cook, stands beside him with a pan of water and another cloth.)*

PUNTILA. If the Attaché telephones Helsinki from here once more for a whole half hour, I'll break the engagement. I don't say anything when it's costing me a wood, but petty thefts like that make my blood boil.

FINA *(coming in)*. The Reverend and the lawyer for the Dairy Association are here to see you.

PUNTILA. I don't want to see anybody. My head's splitting. I think I'm getting pneumonia. Bring them in.

*(*FINA *escorts in the* REVEREND *and* LAWYER *and then leaves quickly.)*

REVEREND. Good morning, Mr. Puntila. I hope you slept well. We just happened to meet in the street, and thought we'd drop by to see you.

LAWYER. It was a night of misunderstandings, so to speak, wasn't it?

PUNTILA. I've already telephoned Eino, if that's what you mean. He made me a full apology and I accepted.

REVEREND. There is one point, dear Mr. Puntila, that remains to be considered, however. Insofar as any misunderstandings on the estate involve only your own family and your dealings with members of the government, they're completely your own affair. But, unfortunately, there are matters which are not.

PUNTILA. Don't keep beating around the bush. If any damage has been done, I'll pay for it.

REVEREND. Most regrettably, my dear Mr. Puntila, there are damages which cannot be rectified with money. In short, we have come as friends to speak to you about the Surkkala affair.

PUNTILA. What about Surkkala?

REVEREND. At one time, we heard you express your intention to discharge this man because he exercises a most pernicious influence upon the community.

PUNTILA. I said I'd kick him out.

REVEREND. Yesterday, Mr. Puntila, was the terminal date for giving notice. But you didn't give Surkkala notice, otherwise, I wouldn't have seen his eldest daughter yesterday at service.

PUNTILA. What? He didn't get his notice. Laina! Didn't Surkkala get his notice?

COOK. No.

PUNTILA. Why?

COOK. Instead of giving him notice, you gave him ten marks.

PUNTILA. What nerve of him to take ten marks from me — after I'd told him a dozen times that he'd have to leave the first of the month. . . . Fina!

(FINA *runs in.*)

Call Surkkala right away. . . . I've got a terrible headache.

(FINA *runs off.*)

LAWYER. It's the coffee!

PUNTILA. Right you are, Pekka, I must have been drunk. . . . I'm always doing things like that when I've had one too many. I could kick myself. That Surkkala belongs in prison. He took advantage of me.

REVEREND. I'm convinced of it, Mr. Puntila. All of us know you as a man whose heart is in the right place. This could only have happened under the influence of drink.

PUNTILA. This is terrible. (*In despair.*) What am I going to tell the Knights of Finland? I'll be boycotted. Nobody will buy my milk anymore. It's all my chauffeur's fault. He knows very well that I can't stand Surkkala, and still he let me give him ten marks.

REVEREND. There's no need for you to take the affair too tragically, Mr. Puntila. Things like this can happen, you know.

PUNTILA. What good's there in saying "things like that can happen," I'm ruined! — Don't just sit around, Pekka! Do something immediately; you're the lawyer for the Dairy Association. . . . I'll make a donation to the Knights of Finland. (*To the* COOK.) It's liquor that causes all this. It's ruining me!

LAWYER. All right. Then you'll pay Surkkala off. He's got to go; he's poisoning the atmosphere.

REVEREND. I think we'll say goodbye now, Mr. Puntila. No damage is irreparable where there is goodwill. Goodwill is everything, Mr. Puntila.

PUNTILA (*shaking his hand sadly*). Thank you.

REVEREND. You needn't thank us; we're only doing our duty. And let us all be prompt and effective in its performance.

LAWYER. And may I suggest you make a few inquiries about your chauffeur. He seems somewhat subversive, too.

(*The* REVEREND *and the* LAWYER *leave.*)

PUNTILA. Laina, I'll never touch another drop again, never. (*Grandly.*) Bring me all the liquor you can find. I'm going to smash every single bottle to pieces. — And don't tell me how expensive they are! Think of the good of the Estate.

COOK. Yes, Mr. Puntila, but are you sure you want to?

PUNTILA. This business with Surkkala — is enough of a lesson to me. . . . Have that chauffeur come here. He's my evil spirit.

COOK. Poor Surkkala. His family has just finished unpacking, and now they'll have to pack all over again.

(*The* COOK *runs off.* SURKKALA *and his* CHILDREN *come in.*)

PUNTILA. I didn't say anything about bringing your brats. I have to square my accounts with you.

SURKKALA. That's what I thought, Mr, Puntila; that's why I brought them along. They can listen and learn a thing or two.

(*There is a pause.* MATTI *enters.*)

MATTI. Good morning, Mr. Puntila. How's your headache?

PUNTILA. There you are, you son-of-a-bitch. What have you done behind my back now? Didn't I warn you only yesterday that I'd throw you out and not give you a letter of reference? . . . Shut up. I've had enough of your insolence and backtalk. My friends opened my eyes to you. How much did Surkkala pay you?

MATTI. I don't know what you're talking about, Mr. Puntila.

PUNTILA. I suppose now you're going to deny that you and Surkkala are hand in glove with each other. You kept me from getting rid of him in time!

MATTI. I'm sorry to differ with you, Mr. Puntila, but I only carried out your orders.

PUNTILA. You should have seen for yourself those orders made no sense!

MATTI. Beg your pardon, but you can't always tell about your orders. If I only carried out the orders that made sense, you'd fire me for being lazy.

PUNTILA. Don't be so smart, you thief! . . . When I do something like not giving Surkkala notice, it's because of liquor — now I'll have to give him three months' pay to get rid of him — but you had it all plotted!

(*All this time* FINA *and the* COOK *have been bringing in bottle after bottle.*)

But this time I'm in dead earnest. I'm actually going to destroy every last bottle! It's the root of all evil. I once read, "The first step to sobriety is: Don't buy any liquor." That's much too little known. — But if you already have some, then at least destroy it. (*To* MATTI.) I'm purposely having you, especially, watch. That will really put the fear of God into you.

MATTI. Yes, Mr. Puntila. Do you want me to smash the bottles out in the yard for you?

PUNTILA. No, I'll do it myself, you swindler. You'd really like that, wouldn't you? — getting rid of this beautiful schnapps (*lifting a bottle to examine it*) by swilling it down yourself.

COOK. Don't look at the bottle too long, Mr. Puntila.

PUNTILA. Absolutely right. (*He threatens* MATTI *with the bottle.*) You'll never get me to drink schnapps again, you bastard. You're only happy when you have everybody wallowing around you like pigs. You're a case for the police. And I caught you agitating with those women from

Kurgela, you Bolshevik! (*Absent-mindedly,* PUNTILA *begins to fill the glass, which* MATTI *had eagerly fetched.*) You're full of hate for me, and you'd like nothing better than for me to be fooled by your "Yes, Mr. Puntila; yes, Mr. Puntila."

COOK. Mr. Puntila!

PUNTILA. Oh, don't worry. I'm only trying it out to make sure the shopkeeper didn't cheat me again, and because I'm celebrating my irrevocable resolution. (*To* MATTI.) But I saw right through you from the start — and kept waiting for you to betray yourself. (*He continues drinking.*) You thought you could get me to lead a life of wine, women, and song and take advantage of me. But my friends opened my eyes to you; I'll drink this glass to their health. . . . I shudder when I think back on that life; three days in the Park Hotel, and then the search for legal alcohol and those women from Kurgela. What a life, without rhyme or reason. — I think of the milkmaid that morning! She tried to take advantage of the fact that I'd been drinking — and that she had a big bosom. I think her name was Lisu. You'll have to admit those were good times. But I'm not going to give you my daughter, you pig-head! You're not a shit-head, though, I'll have to admit that.

COOK. But you're drinking again, Mr. Puntila!

PUNTILA. Me drinking? You call this drinking — a bottle or two? (*He takes a new bottle, and gives the empty one to the* COOK.) Destroy this one; smash it. I never want to see it again, didn't I tell you that? And don't look at me the way our Lord looked at Peter when the cock crowed. I can't stand petty insistence on every little word a man says. (*Pointing to* MATTI.) That one drags me down, but you others want me to grow stale, and chew the nails on my feet from boredom. What kind of a life do I have here anyway? Nothing but driving people all day long, and figuring out what the fodder costs for the cows. Get out of here, you Lilliputians. (*He chases out* FINA *and the* COOK.) . . . Petty minds. . . . No imagination. (*To* SURKKALA'S CHILDREN.) Steal, rob, be Reds — but never be Lilliputians. That's Puntila's advice. (*To* SURKKALA.) Excuse me for interfering with the education of your children. (*To* MATTI.) Open this bottle. (*Drinks.*) For God's sake, Matti, take a bottle for yourself; I intend to celebrate my decisions, because they're irrevocable — which is always a calamity. . . . Your health, Surkkala.

MATTI. That means they can stay, Mr. Puntila?

PUNTILA. Do we have to talk about things like that? — Matti, I'm disappointed in you. Staying on here isn't enough for Surkkala. What is the Puntila Estate to him? I'd put him down in a salt mine so he could learn what it means to work — that leech! Am I right, Surkkala, don't be polite!

SURKKALA'S ELDEST CHILD. But we want to stay, Mr. Puntila.

PUNTILA. No, no. Your father is going and a hundred horses couldn't hold him back. (*He goes to the table and takes some money out of the drawer; then gives it to* SURKKALA, *keeping back ten marks.*) Less the ten marks. (*To the* CHILDREN.) Always be proud that your father is willing to stand up for his convictions. And you, Hella, as his eldest, should be his support. . . . And now the time has come to say goodbye.

(*He offers his hand to* SURKKALA. SURKKALA *ignores it.*)

SURKKALA. Come, Hella, we'll go home and pack. You've heard everything that's to be heard from Mr. Puntila. Come along. (*He leaves with his* CHILDREN.)

PUNTILA (*deeply hurt*). My hand wasn't good enough for him. What a bitter experience. (*He drinks.*) You and I, we're different, Matti. You're a friend and guide along my steep path. I get thirsty just looking at you. (*Drinks. Dreamily.*) Sometime, Matti, I'd like to climb Mt. Hatelma with you, so I could show you the wonderful country we live in. . . . Do you want to climb Mt. Hatelma now, Matti? We could do it in spirit, so to speak. With a couple of chairs it would be easy.

MATTI. Anything you say, Mr. Puntila, during working hours.

PUNTILA. I'm not sure you have enough imagination.

(MATTI *remains silent.*)

(*Explosively.*) Build me a mountain, Matti! Don't spare yourself. Leave nothing untried. Take the biggest pieces of rock, or it will never be Mt. Hatelma — and we won't get our view!

MATTI. It'll all be done exactly the way you wish, Mr. Puntila.

(MATTI *breaks up an old grandfather's clock and a gun cabinet, and with the doors and slides and a few chairs furiously builds a mountain on top of the billiard table.*)

PUNTILA. Take that chair there! You'll do best building Mt. Hatelma if you follow my orders. I know what has to be done and what doesn't. I have a sense of responsibility. Remember, you only care about having work, but I'm the one who has to make it pay off. . . . Now I've got to have a path up to my mountain, so I can carry up my 200 pounds comfortably. Without a path, your mountain isn't worth a good crap. — You see? You don't think enough. . . . I know how to handle people. I'd like to know how you'd get along without me.

MATTI. There you are. The mountain's ready. You can start climbing. It's a mountain with a path — in more usable condition than the ones God created in such a hurry, when He had only six days. . . . Afterwards, He had to create laborers, so you could get some good out of the mountains, Mr. Puntila.

PUNTILA (*beginning to climb*). I'll break my neck!

MATTI (*supporting* PUNTILA). You'd do the same on level ground if it weren't for me.

PUNTILA. That's why I'm taking you along, Matti; otherwise you'd never have a chance to see the beautiful land that gave you birth, and without which you'd be so much dirt. First we see the fields and meadows, then the woods. The woods with their pines that can live in the rock on nothing at all. A man marvels at how they can live on so little.

MATTI. They'd make ideal servants.

PUNTILA. We're climbing, Matti, we're going up! The buildings and structures built by man remain behind; we push forward now into pure nature, already it's taking on a more severe aspect. Leave behind all your petty worries, Matti; dedicate yourself to the grandeur of this experience.

MATTI. I'm doing my best, Mr. Puntila.

PUNTILA. Ah, thou blessed Tavastland! . . . Let's have another drink out of the bottle, so we can appreciate all the beauty.

MATTI. Just a minute! I'll scramble down the mountain and get it for you. (*He climbs down, and then back up again.*)

PUNTILA. I wonder if you can really see the beauty of this land. Are you from Tavastland?

MATTI. Yes.

PUNTILA. Then let me ask you: Where have you ever seen anything like the Tavastland sky? I hear that in some other places the sky's bluer, but the clouds are finer spun here. The Finnish winds are more gentle, and I wouldn't want any other blue even if I could have it. And when the wild swans fly out of the marshes, and the air hums with their wings — is that nothing to you? Don't listen to big stories about other places, Matti. They're just a pack of lies. Stick to Tavastland. I'm giving you good advice.

MATTI. Yes, Mr. Puntila.

PUNTILA. The lakes alone! Forget about the woods — those over there are mine! the one on the point I'm having cut down — but think of the lakes! Just think of one or two of them — and don't even count the fish they're filled with! Just think of the way they look in the morning! And we have eighty thousand lakes like that in Finland!

MATTI. All right, I'll just think about the way they look, Mr. Puntila.

PUNTILA. You see that little tugboat with the bulldog-chest towing logs in the light of the dawn? How they float through the clear water, beautifully tied and stripped of bark, a small fortune. I can smell freshly felled lumber ten kilometers away; can you? What smells we have here in Tavastland! They're a story in themselves; the berries, for instance. After the rain. And the leaves of the birch twigs you're beaten with after the steambath. . . . Where else in the world can you find a view like this?

MATTI. No place, Mr. Puntila.

PUNTILA. Look, there are some cows there, swimming across the lake.

MATTI. I see them. There must be about fifty.

PUNTILA. Sixty, at least. . . . And there goes the train. When I listen sharply, I can hear the milk sloshing in the cans.

MATTI. Very sharply.

PUNTILA. Now, what do you see to the left?

MATTI. . . . Well, what do I see?

PUNTILA. Fields! Fields are what you see as far as your eye can reach.

And Puntila's fields are among them, especially the turfland. The soil there is so rich that the cows I let into the clover can be milked three times a day, and the rye grows up to your chin twice a year. . . . Let's sing!

"And the waves of the beautiful Ruona
Are kissing the milk-white sand."

(FINA *and the* COOK *come in.*)

FINA. Heavens!
COOK. They've ruined everything!
MATTI. We're on top of Mt. Hatelma, enjoying the view.
PUNTILA. Everybody sing! Where's your patriotism?
ALL (*except* MATTI).

"And the waves of the beautiful Ruona
Are kissing the milk-white sand."

PUNTILA. O Tavastland, blessed above all! With your sky — your lakes — your people — and your woods! (*To* MATTI.) Go on, say your heart opens wide when you see all that.

MATTI. My heart opens wide when I see your woods, Mr. Puntila.

X. *Epilogue. Matti turns his back on Puntila*

(*Courtyard on the Puntila Estate. Early morning.* MATTI *appears carrying a small bag. The* COOK *follows him with a package.*)

COOK. There, go on, take the food, Matti. I don't understand why you're going away. Why don't you at least wait until Mr. Puntila is awake?

MATTI. I'd rather not take a chance on what might happen. Last night he got so drunk that toward morning he promised to turn over half his woods to me — and before witnesses, too. If he hears about that he'll send for the police for sure.

COOK. But if you go off without getting a letter of reference, you won't find a job.

MATTI. What good would a letter of reference do me if he writes in it that I'm an agitator — or a real human being? Neither would help me much in getting a job.

COOK. But he won't know what to do without you any more; he's so used to you.

MATTI. Well, he'll have to do the best he can. I've had enough. After all that's happened, I've learned my lesson. . . . His kind and mine can't get along together. . . . Thanks for the food, Laina . . . and goodbye.

COOK. Good luck.

(*She goes quickly indoors.* MATTI *starts to walk away, but after having gone a few steps, stops and addresses the audience reflectively.*)

MATTI. Our history's done, the curtain drawn.
Now, Mr. Puntila, I must be gone.
I've worked for worse men than for you —
When drunk, you're almost human, too.
But friends your kind and mine can't be.
"Who bosses who?" the workdays still decree.
And oil and water don't mix, that we know.
No use to cry about it though:
A fact's a fact, a spade a spade,
Most of men's troubles are self-made.
The time for change is long past due,
High time your servants turned their backs on you.
Masters and servants will be of one mind,
When men and masters are all of one kind.

Curtain

The mysteries of psychology and psychiatry are almost an obsession with many Americans. It is not at all unusual that a novelist of the caliber and inventiveness of Saul Bellow (1915–) should use the findings of psychoanalytic research as the comic stuff of a most unusual drama. The play's title not only accurately describes the events of the plot on several levels, but it also provides an obvious pun no less welcome for its obviousness.

When Bellow's play bowed on Broadway, it baffled many who saw it, including the critics. Its life there was very brief: a mere nineteen performances. Unfortunately, Bellow writes for readers, not for viewers. It is one thing to write a novel in dramatic form, complete with dialogue and stage directions. It is quite another to write a playable play. Bellow does have a good visual sense of the ridiculous, and there are a number of very funny moments for spectators in *The Last Analysis*. Nevertheless, much of what he has created has to be appreciated intellectually. It must be pondered, chewed over, disputed. The flow of ideas, the variety of images, the fund of satire is all so rich that only reading — and rereading — can give the potential audience effective access to it.

Despite its shortcomings as a play, though, *The Last Analysis* has much of the kind of bold, slashing satire that can be dramatically telling. Its frenetic assault on various aspects of modern materialism and human aggression gives it an almost lethal comic power. A little imagination and four years' residence in New York City, Miami, or Los Angeles can equip the reader for fleshing out Bellow's script indications for sight gags with solidly, satirically amusing visions. Bummidge is not surrounded, for instance, with sweet, sedate Middle-Western Methodist ladies. His world seethes with shrill *yentas* and grasping, opportunist males. It is bad enough that Bummidge's competitors and colleagues are willing to defraud him or exploit him when and as they can, but they also practice the popular New York custom of conducting social conversation in a series of insults — insults delivered with a smile. The insult has become the common currency of verbal intercourse. Though one might expect his own family to treat him with some affection and respect, Bellow shows that they are generally just as eager to get a share of anything that can be banked or spent as an outsider. What is doubly ironic about these family portraits is that they are more the New York reality than they are a Molière-like exaggeration.

The essence of Bummidge's character is not conventional common sense and the pursuit of material goals, but that purging passion for self-knowledge that modern psychology teaches us we all possess in some degree. And in Bummidge's brain, of course, psychiatric theory is reduced to the meaningless banality of cocktail-party cant — exactly what most of us know about psychology or psychiatry. Now, if people who have been or who are undergoing analysis are monumental bores, what can be said of those who assume as much authority with only Psych 1-A (three credits) to back them up, or a cursory reading of *The Basic Writings of Sigmund Freud*? To paraphrase an old saying, "A little psychiatry is a dangerous thing."

Bummidge is an enthusiastic amateur whose acquaintance with psychiatric lore has passed from familiarity to virtual incest. Schizoid incest at that, since he is his own analyst, playing doctor and patient by turns. On one level, this can be viewed as a wonderful parody of the national involvement with analysis as the magic solution to all one's personal and public difficulties. On another, however, it is a genuine exploration because Bummidge's sincere, don't-give-a-damn attitude encourages him to go to the roots, hiding nothing, sparing no one.

By creating his own self-analysis — *i.e.*, playing all the roles he has ever played — Bummidge is struggling for self-mastery and self-definition. By acting the roles of both doctor and patient in all the psychic crises of his past, he is producing a kind of Freudian "This is Your Life" show, built on the age-old pattern of life-death-rebirth. The pattern culminates in the reenactment of his own birth, which gives him a new awareness of himself and the world. He will not accept the world-on-a-string offered him by everyone who has seen and praised his television program; he does not need it, and he goes off to the Trilby Theatre where he first started as a vaudeville comic to found the Bummidge Institute of Nonsense. At the end of the play he says, "With my new self, which is really an understanding and acceptance of my old self, I won't return to the old patterns. I'm going to start a new pattern, which, given the world we live in, *must* be the Institute of Nonsense."

Bummidge is the prototype of the absurd man trying to come to terms with existence. He is a blend of the two archetypal characters of human absurdity, Hamlet and Don Quixote. To paraphrase Turgenev, the life strategies of these two figures — self-determination and escapism — are the only ones we have to cope with existence, and Bummidge uses both.

The dialogue in *The Last Analysis* often achieves added satiric sharpness by being so near to the actualities of cocktail chatter in the Manhattan Bummidge knows. At the same time, the quality and organization of many physical events are the stuff of farce. The reenactment of Bummidge's birth is a gem of parody: it spoofs the substance and form of Greek tragedy as well as modern productions of it, at the same time mocking the images and catchwords of Freudian psychiatry.

G. L.

SAUL BELLOW

The Last Analysis

Characters

BUMMIDGE: *A former star whose popularity has declined, now his own psychiatrist. I think of Bummidge as a large man, or at least a stout one. Nearing sixty, he is still eagerly mapping programs and hatching new projects. Half ravaged, half dignified, earnest when he is clowning and clowning when he means to be earnest, he represents the artist who is forced to be his own theoretician. The role requires great subtlety and charm, and extraordinary mimetic powers.*

WINKLEMAN: *Bummidge's cousin. A lawyer, authoritative and realistic, he has a deep voice, and a slightly oracular style. He has adopted, as Mott points out, the Harvard Club manner.*

BELLA: *Bummidge's estranged wife. Not as estranged as he would like her to be. Bella is proud of her businesslike ways, her air of command. She is an aggressive, hammering woman, large and masculine, elaborately made up, and wearing a bottle-green suit trimmed in fox fur, and spike-heeled shoes. She carries a whopping patent-leather purse.*

MADGE: *Bummidge's sister. The businesswoman, thinly disguised as a Westchester matron.*

MAX: *Bummidge's son is in his mid-thirties. Impeccably tailored, manicured, barbered, he is nevertheless the Angry Young Man.*

AUNT VELMA: *Bummidge's ancient aunt and midwife. At the edge of the grave, and tottering, she is still aggressive. Wears horn-rimmed glasses and smokes cigars.*

IMOGEN: *Bummidge's secretary. A little darling, the utterly credulous ingénue. Bummidge's relation to her is entirely fatherly.*

PAMELA: *Bummidge's paramour. The relationship has obviously faded. She does not expect to get much more from him and is tired of humoring him. Her face is masklike, with raised brows and prim, bland lips. She has a thin figure and is dressed in a modest suit.*

LOUIE MOTT: *Bummidge's old pal, the television technician, is desperately trying to keep youthful. He wears College Shop clothing — a turtle-necked shirt and white buckskin shoes.*

BERTRAM: *Bummidge's scientific collaborator, formerly a ratcatcher. A slender, elderly, terribly smiling man with high color and false teeth.*

GALLUPPO: *A private detective. Stocky, shifty, corrupt-looking, he chews a toothpick, at which he occasionally sniffs furtively.*

AUFSCHNITT: *The little Viennese tailor. The part was played to perfection by Mr. Will Lee at the Belasco Theatre.*

FIDDLEMAN: *An impresario. He wears a colored vest, has ducal grand manners in the Hollywood style, and speaks very impatiently.*

A TECHNICIAN.

A MESSENGER.

ACT ONE

(A two-story loft in a warehouse on the West Side of New York, brightly lighted by a studio window. Upstage left, a door to the fire escape. There are also exits to the library, stage right, and through an old-fashioned fire door, stage left. At the back of stage right is a little iron staircase leading to a small balcony. The bathroom door is at stage left. Characters arriving from the street enter through an elevator door, stage right.

The stage is not cluttered. It is hung with bright fabrics, though they are by no means new. The inhabitant of this loft is obviously eccentric. He keeps an old barber chair, downstage right, and an elegant old sofa such as an analyst of the Vienna school might have used, downstage left. The posters on the wall go back to the twenties and thirties — BUMMY, THE OLD TRILBY THEATRE. ZANY BUMMIDGE OF THE FOLLIES. KING OF THE CLOWNS. BUMMY WE LOVE YOU. *Television equipment has been coming in. Obviously, a broadcast is being prepared. There is a floodlamp on the wall, downstage right, in position to cover the barber chair. Near the sofa is a bust of Sigmund Freud. Behind it, bookcases with learned-looking tomes and journals. In center stage is a movable platform.*

At curtain, we discover BUMMIDGE *lying in the barber chair, completely covered by a sheet.* IMOGEN *sits by her desk on a swivel chair, legs crossed, eagerly transcribing notes from a stenographic pad to large file cards. Enter* WINKLEMAN.)

WINKLEMAN. Imogen, where's my cousin? Oh, there. Now, Bummy —

IMOGEN. Please, Lawyer Winkleman. I just got him to rest. The strain of today's broadcast is twisting his nerves.

WINKLEMAN (*looking about*). Ah, television equipment. But not the real thing. Only closed-circuit. There was a time when my cousin Bummidge was king of the networks — the greatest comedian of his time. Now look at him, almost destroyed by his ideas, mental experiments — home-brewed psychoanalysis. Poor has-been.

(BUMMIDGE *quivers under the sheet.*)

He spends his days in an old loft with his colleagues — (*a gesture at* IMOGEN) — acting out his neuroses. His traumas. The psychological crises of his life. It's very painful.

IMOGEN. It's almost deliberate, Mr. Winkleman, the way you refuse to understand.

WINKLEMAN. What's to understand?

BUMMIDGE (*tears off the sheet*). Don't waste your time, Imogen. He pretends to be a genuine lowbrow, a plebeian. *You* know, Winkie, why I act out my past life.

WINKLEMAN (*with heavy irony*). Yeah, self-knowledge.

BUMMIDGE. If a man like me needs insight, why should he go to some punk? I have my own method — *Existenz*-Action-Self-analysis.

WINKLEMAN. Once you were in a class with Bert Lahr, Groucho Marx. Now I foresee you waiting in an alley for a handout of dried eggs from Federal Surplus.

IMOGEN (*to* BUMMIDGE). Finish your rest. You have to have it.

WINKLEMAN. Lowbrow! For you no brow could ever be high enough. Some people are social climbers. You are a mental climber. I'm not against thought, but you're a comic, not a scientist. Is this a time to plunge into theory? Originality? Delirium! And now, with a secretary who used to be a bunny in the Playboy Club, and a collaborator who used to be a ratcatcher . . . now you spend your last dough on a closed circuit TV broadcast to a bunch of specialists at the American Psychiatric Association. How was it arranged? Whom did you bribe on the Program Committee?

BUMMIDGE (*nettled*). Bribe? They jumped at the chance to see my work.

IMOGEN. Rest . . . I don't know how his organism stands the strain. (*She draws the sheet over him.*)

WINKLEMAN. And whose equipment is this? (*Reads label.*) Diamond Electronics. I thought so. Louie Mott, your old Hungarian sidekick and errand boy. That swindler. Bummy, listen to me. We have ties. Why, my mother brought you into the world.

BUMMIDGE (*sits up*). Oh, Aunt Velma! That ancient thing, she still exists. She delivered me. She could clue me into the Unconscious in a dozen places. Where is she?

WINKLEMAN. Very busy, in her old age. She said you telephoned her.

IMOGEN. You haven't rested, haven't eaten in two weeks. You must relax a while before you face the cameras.

BUMMIDGE (*as she begins to cover him again*). Today my powers must be at their peak. I must convince everyone.

(*Enter* MOTT.)

MOTT. Well, my assistant is here. We can hook up the equipment. But first there's one matter to be took up — money, the balance.

(BUMMIDGE *pulls the sheet over his head.*)

WINKLEMAN. I knew you'd be mixed up in this, you devious Hungarian. Whenever he's on the brink of disaster, you're always right behind him.

MOTT. Go blow it out, Winkleman. I stood by him for years.

WINKLEMAN. Only because there were broads around.

MOTT. Wink the Fink!

WINKLEMAN. And now this TV racket. I bet you can't transmit to the Waldorf.

MOTT. I could transmit all the way to China, if I wanted. Look at this citation from the College of Surgeons. I filmed the heart operations at Rochester, you ambulance-chaser!

WINKLEMAN. Sex maniac! Deviant!

MOTT. Maybe you fool your pals at the Harvard Club, but not me. I know about your old-peoples'-home racket.

(WINKLEMAN *flinches.*)

IMOGEN. Nursing home?

MOTT. You bet. Cousin Winkie bought an old luxury hotel and filled it with ancient, senile old-folks.

WINKLEMAN. Perfectly legitimate. The old Ravenna Towers. Gorgeous! A work of art. The space, the gilt cornices. The doorknobs themselves are priceless.

MOTT. Three bunks to a single room. And your old lady is like the camp commandant.

(WINKLEMAN *is glaring.*)

BUMMIDGE. Imogen — tell them to wrangle outside.

MOTT. Bummy, the office insists on the final payment. Five grand.

IMOGEN. What about the thirty-five thousand he already paid you?

MOTT. I can't help it. And no funny stuff, Bummy.

BUMMIDGE (*sits up, the sheet clutched at his throat*). I thought you were pulling with me, Louie. I've invited all those distinguished people. They want to see the results of my research.

MOTT. Okay, fine. But the office . . .

BUMMIDGE (*earnest*). Don't sell out to the bookkeepers. This is of universal significance.

IMOGEN. I'll look for the checkbook.

(BUMMIDGE *detains her.*)

BUMMIDGE. Wink. (*Beckons him near, speaks sotto voce.*) Let me have the dough for a few days.

WINKLEMAN. Cousin, you're joking.

BUMMIDGE. Why joking? I need it. You made millions on me.

WINKLEMAN. Ancient history! That was when you let me do the thinking. I'd like to help. But I have my principles, too, just like you.

BUMMIDGE. O money! O, Plutus! O, Mammon!

WINKLEMAN. Is anything more horrible than a solemn buffoon. Where are your savings?

BUMMIDGE. In the separation Bella cleaned me out. Two millions.

WINKLEMAN. You made her furious. Your mistresses used her charge accounts.

BUMMIDGE. Don't you know what Freud says about gold? What does the color remind you of?

WINKLEMAN. Try giving Louie here (*gestures*) the other substance. See if he'll take it.

BUMMIDGE. For thirty years you sold me to the lousy public like dry cereal.

WINKLEMAN. Lousy? You lost your touch. They stopped laughing.

BUMMIDGE. I can make those apes laugh any time. At will. (*Pause.*) It's just that I can't stand the sound they make. And I feel hit by the blast of sickness from their lungs. It makes me shrink.

WINKLEMAN. And you're going to cure the ravaged psyche of the mass. Poor cousin!

BUMMIDGE. You exploited me. Dragged me down into affluence.

MOTT. Let's not forget that check.

IMOGEN (*crossing to desk*). You see me looking for it, don't you?

BUMMIDGE. You made me change my name. Lead a false life. Maybe an actor must — I'll give you that much. But (*with fervor*) now I want insight. Value. I'll die without value. And finally I've succeeded in getting off the mere surface of life. Wink, back me today.

WINKLEMAN (*wraps himself in his coat and sits on couch*). You're not the only one in trouble.

IMOGEN. I came to Mr. Bummidge's door with a questionnaire. Instead of answering my questions, he took me by the hand and said, "My dear, what do you consider funny?"

MOTT. What did you say?

IMOGEN. I just said, "Me, coming to your door to ask if you eat soup." And he laughed, and hired me. I believe in him. (*Her hand is on her breast.*) Mr. Winkleman, leading scientists have agreed to watch. Doctor Gumplovitch, Doctor Ratzenhofer, the giants of American psychiatry.

And people from Princeton and Johns Hopkins, the Ford Foundation. They know they're dealing with a great artist.

MOTT. I'm waiting!

BUMMIDGE. Calm! (*Throws himself back in the chair.*)

MOTT. Here's a check. Fill it in. Five zero zero zero and no one hundred cents.

(IMOGEN *writes.*)

WINKLEMAN. Between Bella, and his son Max, and his broads, especially the present one, Pamela, the ex-chorus girl, I figure he's been taken for ten million. Your sister Madge and I are worried. Your real friends.

MOTT. Let's have the signature, now.

BUMMIDGE (*as he signs*). Imogen, we must check out a few things. Where's Bertram? And Kalbfuss! Make sure Kalbfuss will be watching me. Phone his shop.

WINKLEMAN. Kalbfuss? Shop?

(*Enter a* TECHNICIAN, *pushing a television camera.*)

TECHNICIAN (*to* MOTT). Louie, is this the joint? The floor doesn't look solid enough. These boards waggle like loose teeth. (*Seeing* IMOGEN.) Well — hello, Miss.

IMOGEN. Bertram went to the Waldorf to see about the canapés and champagne.

WINKLEMAN. Champagne? And who is this Kalbfuss — the lord high egghead? (*Speaking to the* TECHNICIAN *and then to* IMOGEN.) Earnestness has been the ruin of my cousin. Highmindedness. The suckers had their mouths open for yucks — he fed them Aristotle, Kierkegaard, Freud. Who needs another homemade intellectual? One more self-nominated boring intellectual, sick with abstractions? An American intellectual?

TECHNICIAN (*pushing equipment before him*). Look out, friend.

WINKLEMAN. Reading! This man hid books in his dressing room. Huge volumes, thick journals. Booksellers were like dope-pushers to him. He was like a junkie — on thought.

IMOGEN. All I can say is that he's done great things for my mental development. He saw more than these externals. No other man has ever been willing to look past them.

(*The* TECHNICIAN *whistles at her.*)

MOTT (*sniffing her*). She's like a mound of nectarines. — Business first. I'll run down to the bank. (*Exit.*)

BUMMIDGE. Oh! (*Sits up.*) The time is short. I've got so much mental preparation to make, and I'm hampered, hindered, held back, obstructed, impeded, impaired. (*To* WINKLEMAN.) Where is your mother? I need those sagging bones. I want her here today. (*Crossing stage.*) And Bertram — Kalbfuss. He's crucial. Come, Imogen. (*Exit stage right.*)

(*As* IMOGEN *follows, the* TECHNICIAN *pinches her.*)

IMOGEN. Yes, Mr. Bummidge. (*To* TECHNICIAN.) Please! (*Exit.*)

WINKLEMAN. No matter what Bummy masterminded, no matter what he brewed, I could make use of it. It brought me a buck, and a tax-clean buck, too. With phantasmagoria like his there's only one thing to do: sell them! When he wanted to weave rugs, I put him into a Fifth Avenue window. If he wanted to paint action pictures, play the organ like Albert Schweitzer, I'd make a deal. But now he's lost his image with the public, he's confused the Plain Man, and that's the sonofabitch that pays for the whole show. . . . I admit I also have a bad character. It's true, I no longer care who lives and who dies. Still, I have to pursue my own way. It's a job, and jobs have to be done. And I'm in trouble myself. He's not the only one. (*Moves upstage and right.*) He doesn't know it yet, but he's going to save the day for me, as he's done before. Keep sharp, look sharp, Winkie. Lurk offshore. Rush in at the right moment and grab Bummy again. Hide, wait, listen, haunt the fringes, you'll get benefits. And now, a little oxygen for the system (*inhales*) and submerge. (*Exit, holding his nose like a swimmer.*)

(*Enter* BUMMIDGE *with a timer.*)

BUMMIDGE. Hours and minutes! No time. Curse that interfering Winkleman. I know he wants to exploit me. He and my sister Madge, they always work together. There's some intrigue. (*He wipes them away with a gesture.*) Now I am alone. (*Puts the timer on the platform, center.*) Ultimate reality — that's what we want. Deep, deep and final. The truth which daily life only distorts. Okay, Bummy. (*Sits on platform.*) What's on your mind? Come, boy, let's have it. Begin with the dreams you dreamt last night. Sleep is dotted with madness. Each dream is a tiny psychosis. The sleeper is a tranquil criminal. All right — the dreams. . . . What I dreamt! A huge white animal climbed into my bed. I thought, "A polar bear." I looked again and saw pig's feet. A white sow. But wait — I didn't do anything to her. A nursing pig. What's the symbolism of it? (*Ponders, then shrugs.*) I thought, "Live and let live. Let her lie there." I moved over on the diagonal. Part of my basic submissiveness. At least I didn't have to make love to her. But the dream, the dream! The pig squirmed and writhed like a phantom knockwurst, and turned into a fat, enormous man in a baggy sweater with little candy milk bottles sewn in rows. Like Hermann Goering with his medals. But was this fat man a man? In the unconscious, to be obese is female. Oh, that unconscious! Is it ever cunning! Repression! The power of the

Id! This was a male with breasts. (*Rises.*) I want notes on this, for the record. (*Calls.*) Imogen! Is that girl slipping, libido-wise? Wait, there's more. (*Crosses over and sits on his analytic sofa.*) Then he/she lay in bed with me, shaking, and all the little bottles clinked and jingled. He/she was laughing. (*Laughs in several keys, assuming various characters.*) He-he-he! Ha! Hoo-hoo-hoo! That laughter! (*Now he is grave.*) A nightmare. The creature mocked me. I'm afraid I may not be taken seriously in the field of science. And I no longer know what laughter is. I've lost my bearings and it all sounds wrong to me. In the dream I threw a fit. I puffed up with rage like a squid. My psyche let out angry ink. I almost levitated from the bed. And I cried out in many tongues — "*Nefesh, Ish. Ecce homo. Ho thanatos,*" in Hebrew, Latin, Greek, and bared my chest in the dead eye of the floating moon. Seen through the skylight. And . . . (*He staggers a bit.*)

(*Enter* IMOGEN, *with the* TECHNICIAN *close behind her.*)

IMOGEN. Please! You must let me alone!

BUMMIDGE. Imogen, is this one of your sexual lapses?

IMOGEN. Of course not, Mr. Bummidge.

BUMMIDGE (*to the* TECHNICIAN). I'm going to request that you leave this broad alone.

TECHNICIAN. *I*, let *her* alone? (*Laughs.*) Do I wear lipstick, use perfume, waggle my behind? *She* does it.

BUMMIDGE. Such random eroticism is a bad sign. Is your home life so inadequate that you become inflamed before dinner?

(*The* TECHNICIAN *laughs.* BUMMIDGE *is enraged.*)

Listen to that laugh. Is that neurotic, or is that neurotic? Boy, what decadence! Malignancy in the marrow of society. (*Sits in barber chair.*)

TECHNICIAN (*to* IMOGEN). Is he serious? (*Laughs.*) Is that Bummidge the comedian? He's lost his marbles. (*Exit.*)

BUMMIDGE. You'd better adjust yourself a bit.

(IMOGEN *turns her back to* BUMMIDGE. *He buttons her dress.*)

IMOGEN. It makes me so unhappy. I try to communicate with people, but they only pay attention to my body.

BUMMIDGE (*sympathetic*). Ah, yes.

IMOGEN (*sits on his knee, filially*). That's why I understand when you try to speak seriously, and they insist on treating you like a hambone comedian. They don't know how profound you are.

BUMMIDGE (*he has picked up a hand mirror and is grimacing into it*). I look frightful. Can people accept my message of sanity and health if I look like death or madness?

IMOGEN. But you're making faces before you look.

BUMMIDGE (*to the mirror*). Come on, you! I know your lousy tricks! Humankind must tear itself away from its nonsense.

IMOGEN. I just know you'll win today. It's bound to be a triumph. I feel it.

BUMMIDGE (*eager*). You think so? Thank you, Imogen. You help me bear my burden. What time is it?

IMOGEN. Two-oh-nine.

(*Both rise quickly.*)

BUMMIDGE. Even time is my enemy today. (*Crosses stage.*) I haven't decided on an opening for my TV appearance. What music shall we begin with?

IMOGEN (*looking through records*). Well, we have Wagner, Grieg, and here's "Les Sylphides."

BUMMIDGE (*stands beside bust of Freud*). Where shall I stand? Here? Maybe with this bust of Freud. Just the two of us. I'll wear a special coat I designed. Aufschnitt is bringing it. He'll want money too.

IMOGEN. Here's classical guitar music.

BUMMIDGE. No, something wilder. Music to denote that I've roused the sleeping Titans of the instincts. Wham! Crash! Thunder! Remember who'll be watching at the Waldorf. I've invited not only psychologists and analysts, but artists, too, and comedians. I want the comedians to see how the analysts laugh. I want the analysts to see how seriously the comedians take me. I must reach everyone. Everything. Heart, reason, comic spirit. I have something tremendous to say. I want to persuade them. Move them. Stun them . . . Oh, Imogen, I'm frightened. My fingers are freezing.

IMOGEN (*chafing his hands*). You'll do it. (*She begins to drape the barber chair with tapestries.*)

BUMMIDGE. The enterprise is bigger than me, but there's nobody else to do it. What are these fabrics?

IMOGEN. For a papal-throne effect.

BUMMIDGE. I've also invited the clergy. Where is Bertram? Louie — at the bank with my bad check. I must raise the money. Meantime, my schedule. My inner self. Oh-oh — my sordid sister.

(*Exit* IMOGEN, *as* MADGE *enters.* MADGE *is conservatively dressed; the matron from New Rochelle is what she tries to be.*)

MADGE. Well, Bummy, what's all the excitement?

BUMMIDGE (*at first trying to charm her*). Madge, dear, what a surprise! But I knew you'd come.

MADGE. Naturally. You were weeping on the phone. I thought you were dying. How nice to see TV equipment again. A reminder of your former greatness.

BUMMIDGE (*more charm*). Madge, I've missed you. You have Mama's sense of humor.

MADGE. The good old days! The big time, the celebrities, the beautiful trips. I'm often sorry for you, Philip.

BUMMIDGE. You think I goofed.

MADGE. Are you as prosperous in psychoanalysis as you were in show business?

BUMMIDGE. How's Harold?

MADGE (*indifferently*). The same.

(*They kiss.*)

BUMMIDGE. Madge, I need five thousand dollars.

MADGE (*laughs*). Oh, Bummy!

BUMMIDGE (*behaves oddly when she laughs; puts his ear to her chest like a physician*). That makes you laugh? Laugh again.

MADGE (*pushing him off*). First you read these books, then you turn into a mad scientist. You have to broadcast your message on closed-circuit.

BUMMIDGE. Any minute, Louie Mott will be back from the bank with a bad check.

MADGE. You're putting me on. It's just your idiosyncrasy to live in this warehouse and play psychologist with a dumb doll and a ratcatcher. You didn't let Max and Bella and Pamela take everything!

BUMMIDGE. Why leave yourself off the list? Madge, we're siblings. Sib-lings! From the same womb. It's not like being registered in the same hotel, different nights.

MADGE. I'm grateful to you for what little I have. But don't forget my problems. Why, Harold alone — first his prostate, then his coronary, then his eyes!

BUMMIDGE. I wish I were a modest failure like Harold — no broad perspectives, no ideas, adrift with bifocals. All I'm asking is five —

MADGE (*laughs*). Peanuts, to a former millionaire.

BUMMIDGE. Your laughter fascinates me. Mama had a throaty laugh. Yours has little screams and cries in it. (*Imitates.*) But don't make a poor mouth. (*Seizes her wrist.*) You took your diamonds off in the street. I can see the marks.

MADGE (*jerks away her arm*). Your sister will show you how broke she is. My very slip is torn. (*She shows the lace of her slip; it hangs loose.*)

BUMMIDGE (*voice rising*). Oh, my Lord! Your underwear. (*Fingers it.*) Your underwear!

MADGE. Now even you can understand how it is.

BUMMIDGE. Wait! What's happening. My unconscious is trying to tell me something. What, you primitive devil — guilt? Lust? Crime? Tell me! (*Prods his head.*)

MADGE. I hope you're satisfied.

BUMMIDGE. I hear the groaning past — like a bass fiddle. (*He makes deep sounds in his throat.*) Madge, you've mobilized ancient emotions.

MADGE. I can't stay.

BUMMIDGE (*clinging to the lace*). Wait!

(*They both tug.*)

MADGE. Let go my slip.

BUMMIDGE. Answer some questions about Williamsburg, where we lived behind the store.

MADGE. Hideous place. I was ashamed to bring a boy to the house.

BUMMIDGE. The scene of my infancy.

MADGE. So, put up a plaque — you're tearing my clothing, Bummy.

BUMMIDGE (*now on his knees*). I'm on an expedition to recover the forgotten truth. Madge, you have no idea what human beings really are; the stages of the psyche — polymorphous, oral, anal, narcissistic. It's fantastic, intricate, complicated, hidden. How can you live without knowing? Madge, look deep! Infinite and deep!

MADGE. You want me to be as confused as yourself? Get out from under my skirt. Freud is passé. Even I know it. (*Rises in haste.*)

BUMMIDGE (*tearing the lace from her slip*). I need that. (*Puts it to his nose.*)

MADGE. You're stripping me!

BUMMIDGE (*rises*). It's coming back to me. Ah! A sealed door has burst open. Dusty light is pouring out. Madge — Madge!

MADGE. I'm leaving.

BUMMIDGE (*stops her*). No. You have to share this with me — this trauma you gave me at eleven. You caught me fooling with the things in your dresser. We'll re-enact it. Eleven and thirteen. You catch me. Scream for Mama.

MADGE. No, I won't.

BUMMIDGE (*stamps his foot*). You will. You owe it to me. You damaged me. (*Changing tone.*) It'll do you good, too.

MADGE. It's crazy. Twenty-four hours a day, I have to defend myself from insanity.

BUMMIDGE (*leading her to his desk*). This is the dresser. You surprise me as I fondle your step-ins. Clutch my arm and shout *Mama, Mama!*

(*During the following action,* MAX, IMOGEN, BERTRAM, *and* WINKLEMAN *enter and watch.* BUMMIDGE *in pantomime opens a drawer and feels silks with adolescent lasciviousness.* MADGE *falls on him from behind with a sudden cry.*)

MADGE. Mama! Mama!

BUMMIDGE. That's not right. Give it more. Again, and use your nails, too.

MADGE. Mama!

BUMMIDGE. You're beginning to have that bitchy tone I remember. But more.

MADGE (*piercing*). Ma!

BUMMIDGE. More yet. (*Pinches her.*)

MADGE (*fiercely*). You nasty, sneaking little bastard.

BUMMIDGE (*triumphant*). The old Madge. You can hear it yourself.

MADGE (*inspired*). Look what I caught him doing, Mama. I'm the daughter, the only daughter, and I have no privacy in this filthy, foul, horrible hole. Look what I caught him doing. He'll end up with the whores yet. Dirty, snotty, cockeyed little poolroom bum!

BUMMIDGE (*squatting*). Right — right! And I crouch there, trapped, quivering, delight turning to horror. I'm the human Thing — the peculiar beast that feels shame. And now Mama's swinging at me.

(*He ducks.* MADGE *swipes at him with a broom.*)

Don't hit me.

MADGE (*shaken*). Who *am* I, anyway?

WINKLEMAN. If this isn't spooky. Playing with dead relatives.

MAX (*angry*). Hey, what about a minute for a living relative? It's me, your son, your only child. Remember? You damn well will. I'll see to that.

BUMMIDGE. One generation at a time. Bertram, did you see this?

BERTRAM. I sure did. You're all shook up.

BUMMIDGE. A petticoat. Lace. Hem. I was hemmed in. A boy's awakening sex cruelly suppressed. A drawer. Drawer — coffin — death. Poor things that we are. Binding with briars the joys and desires. Madge, you see how I work?

MADGE (*matronly composure beginning to return*). Ridiculous!

MAX. That's what I say. A crude joke.

BUMMIDGE (*turns to him*). Can you tell me what a joke is? (*He starts to leave.*)

MAX. Stay here. Once and for all, we're going to have it out.

BUMMIDGE. Come, Bert — Imogen. Help . . . upstairs. Consultation . . .

MAX. Pop, I warn you. . . .

IMOGEN. An artist like your father is entitled to respect.

MAX. Artist? Feet of clay, all the way up to the ears.

BUMMIDGE. Wink. Your mother. Tante Velma. Bring her.

(*Exit with* IMOGEN *and* BERTRAM, *smelling* MADGE's *lace.*)

WINKLEMAN. Would anyone pay to see him carry on like this?

MAX. An obsolete comedian? His generation is dead. Good riddance to that square old stuff. . . . What are you doing here, Winkie — you want to con something out of him?

WINKLEMAN. How delightful to hear a youthful point of view.

MAX (*to* MADGE). And what's your angle? You didn't come to give him a glass of Yiddisher tea.

MADGE. I'm his agent still. And Wink's his lawyer.

MAX. Parasites, germs and viruses. You two, and Pamela, the famous Southern choreographer . . .

MADGE. You went through quite a chunk of money yourself. Well, your mother took Bummy's millions; what do you want with him?

MAX. Yesterday my old man raised thirty-five thousand on the property in Staten Island. It's mine in trust. He's spending it on this TV production. . . . Pathetic show-off slob. But I'm going to stop him. (*Exit angry and determined.*)

WINKLEMAN. What's he up to? He probably owes his bookie. He's forever in a booth having long phone conversations with crooks. Dimes are like goof pills to him. I'm glad I never had a son, never married.

MADGE. Why didn't you?

WINKLEMAN. I know my married friends lead *lovely* lives. But me? (*An elaborate sigh, mocking himself and* MADGE.) There's an old poem —

> To hold a horse, you need a rein,
> To hold an elephant, a chain,
> To hold a woman, you need a heart. . . .

MADGE. Everyone has a heart.

WINKLEMAN. Every restaurant serves potatoes. (*Pause.*) We served too many potatoes to the old people. Now we're in trouble.

MADGE. Does Bummy suspect anything?

WINKLEMAN. So far I've kept it out of the news. Eight cases of malnutrition. If the inspector breaks it to the papers we're ruined. I socked a quarter of a million into this. I told you we couldn't feed 'em on a buck a day.

MADGE. We could, but your mother took kickbacks on meat, eggs, bread, milk. Face it, she starved them.

WINKLEMAN (*opens a newspaper*). You gave her a hopeless budget. Look at these prices. Pot roast sixty-eight cents. Ground meat forty-three cents. And what about special diets? Some of these people have diabetes, anemia.

MADGE. Why waste time here? I know, we need a lump of money to bribe our way out of a scandal. (*Pause.*) Only think, we used to get half a million a year out of Bummy. But that was before he shot his bolt.

WINKLEMAN. Still, he's never lost his audience sense.

MADGE. He did. He turned solemn, boring, a Dutch uncle, a scold.

WINKLEMAN. Scolding is a career too. Some of our biggest idealists make a fortune, scolding.

MADGE. He should have stuck to his nonsense.

WINKLEMAN. But that's just it. The great public is tired of the old nonsense-type nonsense. It's ready for serious-type nonsense. This psychological set-up is just the thing for a comeback. I would have given him the five thousand.

MADGE. Are you out of your head? Today? When we need every penny?

WINKLEMAN. I still say cooperate. I don't know what those highbrows at the Waldorf will think of his shenanigans, but what would Madison Ave. think?

MADGE (*pondering*). You always were a thoughtful, imaginative angler.

WINKLEMAN (*bows, acknowledging the compliment*). I've been in touch with Fiddleman.

MADGE (*thunderstruck*). Fiddleman! But he wrote Bummy off years ago.

WINKLEMAN. At this moment, Fiddleman, kingpin impresario, bigger than Hurok, is in his limousine en route to the Waldorf to watch the telecast at my invitation. Don't forget, those people are up against it for novelty. A billion-dollar industry, desperate for innovation. It fears death. It has to come up with something big, original, every month.

MADGE. Maybe. But would Bummy go commercial again? He's half nuts over Freud. Just as Freud becomes old hat.

WINKLEMAN. But on the lower levels the social order is just catching up with psychoanalysis. The masses want their share of insight. Anyway, put a five-million-dollar contract under Bummy's nose, and see what happens.

MADGE. Five! My commission is ten per cent. . . . Winkie, I'm sure he still has money stashed away. In this joint, too.

WINKLEMAN. Crafty he's always been.

MADGE. He'd never hide it. He always loved "The Purloined Letter." He'd put his dough in an obvious place. For instance, what's this old valise?

WINKLEMAN. Open it.

MADGE. It's locked. Chained to this barber chair.

WINKLEMAN. He's his own bag man. This is his loot.

MADGE. Tip the chair, and I'll slip the chain out.

WINKLEMAN. Theft? Me? I'm a lawyer. I may be disbarred as it is.

MADGE. Calling me poor-mouth.

WINKLEMAN. Reading me sermons on anality. Ha-ha! That nut. He has charm. You must admit it.

(*Shouting is heard above.*)

My ridiculous cousin. What's he yelling about?

MADGE. Let's have a talk.

(*They go. Enter* BERTRAM *and* IMOGEN, *supporting* BUMMIDGE.)

BERTRAM. Lucky I heard you. You almost fell out of the window.

IMOGEN. Why did you lean out so far?

BUMMIDGE. I saw Louie coming from the bank. Bertram, stall him. Keep the equipment coming.

BERTRAM. I'll do what I can. (*Exit.*)

BUMMIDGE (*calling after* BERTRAM). Bring me a sandwich. Imogen, where's the schedule? (*Reads schedule.*) Dreams. Madge. Aunt Velma. Couch work. I haven't done the couch work. Before the broadcast, I must. There's still a big block. (*Brings out a screen and places it at the head of the couch.*)

IMOGEN. You haven't eaten, haven't shaved.

BUMMIDGE. I can't stop. Must barrel through. This may be one of those central occasions in the history of civilization. I claim nothing personally. I'm the instrument of a purpose beyond ordinary purpose. I may be the only man on the Eastern Seaboard with a definitely higher purpose. What a thing to get stuck with!

IMOGEN. Ready for the session. (*Sits with stenographic pad.*) Number eight-one-oh-eight.

BUMMIDGE (*lying down*). Eight-one-oh-eight. (*Mutters*). One-oh-eight. (*Rises.*) Imogen, I can't do this alone. I must call in the analyst.

IMOGEN. I understand. The tension must be frightful.

BUMMIDGE (*goes behind the screen and emerges as the analyst, in horn-rimmed smoked glasses*). Well, Mr. Bummidge, how is the psyche today? Lie down, stretch out. How do you intend to proceed? I leave you complete freedom of choice, as an analyst should.

(*Throughout this scene, he wears glasses as the analyst. Removing them, he is the patient.*)

BUMMIDGE (PATIENT). Doctor, things are not good. Last night I dreamed of a male with breasts. After this I found myself in a swimming pool, not swimming, not wet. An old gentleman with a long beard floats by. Such a long white beard, and rosy cheeks.

BUMMIDGE (ANALYST). The material is quite mixed. Water stands for the amniotic bag-of-waters. A beard refers to the father-figure.

BUMMIDGE (PATIENT). I have to tell you, Doctor, I'm fed up with these boring figures in my unconscious. It's always Father, Mother. Or again, breast, castration, anxiety, fixation to the past. I am desperately bored with these things, sick of them!

BUMMIDGE (ANALYST). You're sick *from* them. Of course. We are all sick. That is our condition. Man is the sick animal. Repression is the root of his madness, and also of his achievements.

BUMMIDGE (PATIENT). Oh, Doctor, why can't I live without hope, like everybody else?

BUMMIDGE (ANALYST). Mr. Bummidge, you are timid but obstinate. Exceptional but commonplace. Amusing but sad. A coward but brave. You are stuck. The Id will not release you to the Ego, and the Ego cannot let you go to the Id.

BUMMIDGE (PATIENT). No resolution?

BUMMIDGE (ANALYST). Perhaps. If you can laugh. But face the void of death. Why do you dream of your father?

BUMMIDGE (PATIENT). But was it Papa? Papa had no beard. In his last illness, he shaved his mustache. (*Sits.*) I was shocked by this. Pa . . . oh, Pa, your lip is so white. Age and weakness have suddenly come over you. Too feeble to count out the *Daily Mirrors*. Mustache gone, face changed, your eyes are so flat, they show death. Death, what are you doing to Papa? You can't . . . Is this the mighty hero I feared? Him with the white lip? Papa, don't go from us.

BUMMIDGE (ANALYST). Don't be deceived by surface feelings, Mr. Bummidge. Remember — ambivalence. You may not really feel compassion. An old enemy and rival is going down. In your heart you also exulted. Maybe you wanted him to live only to see your success.

BUMMIDGE (PATIENT). I don't believe it.

IMOGEN (*applauding*). Good!

BUMMIDGE (PATIENT). You're a hard-nosed man. Why do you prefer the ugliest interpretations? Why do you pollute all my good impulses?

(*Enter* BERTRAM *with a sandwich.*)

I loved my old father. . . . I want to weep.

IMOGEN. He's giving it to himself today.

BUMMIDGE (ANALYST). Did I invent the human species? It can't be helped. I want to cry, too.

BUMMIDGE (PATIENT). My father couldn't bear the sight of me. I had adenoids, my mouth hung open — was that a thing to beat me for? I liked to hum to myself while eating — was that a thing to beat me for? I loved to read the funnies — is that any reason to whip a child? (*Looks into sandwich and mutters to* BERTRAM.) More mustard. (*His voice rises.*) Killjoy! A human life was in my breast, you old killjoy. You attacked all my pleasure sources. But I fought. I hid in the cellar. I forged your signature on my report card. I ate pork. I was a headliner at the good old Trilby. The good-for-nothing became a star and earned millions, making people laugh — all but Papa. He never laughed. What a peevish face. Laugh, you old Turk. Never! Censure. Always censure. Well, you grim old bastard, I made it. You're dead, and I'm still jumping. What do I care for your grave? Let Madge look after it. Down goes the coffin. Down. The hole fills with clay. But Bummidge is still spilling gravy at life's banquet, and out front they're laughing fit to bust. (*He laughs, close to tears.*) Yes, I am that crass man, Bummidge. Oh, how foul my soul is! I have the Pagliacci gangrene. Ha, ha, ha — weep, weep, weep! (*Buries his face in his hands.*)

BUMMIDGE (ANALYST). Do you see the Oedipal strain in this situation? What of your mother?

BUMMIDGE (PATIENT). I saw I'd have Mama to myself. *She* laughed. Oh what a fat throaty laugh she had. Her apron shook.

BUMMIDGE (ANALYST). But what did you want with your mother?

BUMMIDGE (PATIENT). You mean the mother who bathed me in the little tin tub by the kitchen stove? Oh, Doctor, what are you suggesting?

BUMMIDGE (ANALYST). Don't repress the poisonous truth. Go deeper.

BUMMIDGE (PATIENT). How deep?

BUMMIDGE (ANALYST). As deep as you can.

BUMMIDGE (PATIENT). Will there ever be a bottom?

BUMMIDGE (ANALYST). Does the universe have a bottom?

BUMMIDGE (PATIENT). How can I bear it? I, too, am blind. Like Oedipus, far gone in corrupt habits. Oh, hubris! I put a rose bush on Mama's grave. But Papa's grave is sinking, sinking. Weeds cover the tombstone. Oh, shame, Jocasta! (*Collapses on the sofa.*)

IMOGEN. Oh, Mr. Bummidge, marvelous!

BERTRAM. Quite extraordinary. If you perform like this on television, the analysts will give you an ovation.

IMOGEN. He ought to have the Nobel Prize. I think psychology is worth every sacrifice. I love it more and more.

BUMMIDGE. My whole brain is like a sea of light. (*He unlocks the valise. Now* BUMMIDGE THE PATIENT *puts twenty dollars on the chair.*) This is one point on which I can't break with orthodox Freudianism. You must pay the analyst.

(*Enter* MADGE.)

MADGE. What is this?

BUMMIDGE (ANALYST) (*picks up the money*). Thank you.

BERTRAM. Better lock up the doctor's money.

IMOGEN. Bank it for him.

BUMMIDGE. He prefers it this way.

(*Exit* BUMMIDGE, *with* BERTRAM *and* IMOGEN.)

MADGE (*going rapidly to the bag*). Money. Loaded.

(*Enter* MOTT.)

MOTT (*angry, shaken*). Boy, is he dishonest! Bummy! Where is he, your brother? He wrote a bad check.

MADGE. Oh, the poor kid. Stalling for a little time.

MOTT. I wouldn't believe the teller. No funds! "What?" I said — Bummy complains there are no more real underlings. Just bureaucrats, full of aggression.

MADGE (*soothing*). You won't pull out because of a few dollars. This broadcast is too important, Louie.

MOTT. No sweet talk, please. It's too late. Thirty years ago you turned me down flat.

MADGE (*shades of youthful allure*). I was a foolish girl. I thought you were attacking me. I'd be smarter now, maybe. You're still so youthful.

MOTT. Excuse me. . . . I didn't mean . . . I think you're lovely. Don't get me wrong. . . . I used to get such a flash when I saw you — in the old days.

MADGE (*with, alas, antiquated wiles*). You're a dear, Louie. Louie, we mustn't let my brother down. He's been a true friend. He saved you from those Boston hoodlums during Prohibition.

MOTT. True. I was in the dehydrated-wine business. Dry, purple bricks. Add water, make wine. Boston Blackie tried to muscle me out.

MADGE. Bummy saved you.

MOTT. Yes, true. I don't deny it. I tell everybody. But . . .

MADGE. He's always helped you. Staked you six different times. Covered for you with women. Even got you this little electronics racket.

MOTT. I admit that. He paid for the course. Enrolled me personally.

MADGE. Don't cry. I know how emotion tears your Hungarian heart.

MOTT (*moved*). Bummy says I suffer from moral dizziness. No roots. Only loose wires. It's all true. But when he gives bad checks . . .

MADGE. Louie, I myself will make it good.

MOTT. You? (*All business again.*) Sorry . . . but not in trade. I have to have cash.

MADGE (*stung*). Don't be nasty! (*Recovers.*) Old friend, I'll let you in on a good thing. We have people watching at the Waldorf. Fiddleman . . .

MOTT (*impressed*). Leslie — the impresario?

MADGE. You know my brother still has greatness in him. He's due for a revival. He'll be bigger than ever. I want you to pipe the performance not only to the scientists but also to an adjoining suite. NBC, CBS, MCA will be watching. With sponsors. The biggest.

MOTT. Is that so? That's clever. Can do. But the money . . .

MADGE. You'll be cut in. There's money for all. I guarantee it. (*She lightly kicks* BUMMIDGE'*s bag.*) You want it in black and white?

(*Enter* TECHNICIAN.)

TECHNICIAN. Well, what gives?

MOTT (*wavers, then decides*). We work. Start hooking up.

(MADGE *and* MOTT *shake hands. Exit* MADGE, *right. Enter* BUMMIDGE, *now wearing trousers and a T shirt.* MAX *follows him.*)

BUMMIDGE. Max, don't be destructive.

MAX. Take this crap out.

BUMMIDGE. Oh, Louie. Don't let me down over a few bucks. I know the check was rubber, but —

MOTT. It was a lousy thing to do. But I've thought it over and decided to do the big thing. You have another hour to raise the dough.

BUMMIDGE (*sincerely grateful*). Oh, you generous heart.

MAX (*seizing a cable*). You won't squander my inheritance.

(*He and* BUMMIDGE *and* MOTT *tug at cable.*)

TECHNICIAN. That line is hot. Watch it.

(*The fuses blow. The stage is plunged into darkness. Green and red sparks fly.* BUMMIDGE *screams.*)

BUMMIDGE. My son wants to electrocute me!
MOTT. He blew everything.
BUMMIDGE. Ruined! Lights, lights! Imogen! Bertram!
MOTT. My flashlight! We have to find the fusebox.

(BUMMIDGE *lights a candle,* MOTT *holding a flashlight.* MOTT *and* TECHNICIAN *run out.*)

BUMMIDGE. What the Christ do you think you're doing?

MAX. You're not throwing my dough out the window. I need it today. And the hell with your originality.

BUMMIDGE. Every moment is precious. Guests are waiting at the Waldorf — eminent people.

MAX. Sure, you're the center of everything. Everybody has to wait. You breathe all the air, eat all the food, and lay all the women.

BUMMIDGE (*alters his tone*). Poor child, master this Oedipal hate and love. You're no kid. You mustn't waste fifty years distorting simple facts. Your father is only flesh and blood. Reason is your only help. Think, Max, think for dear life.

MAX. You think. Why wouldn't you be Bella's husband, the public's favorite?

BUMMIDGE. You mean a nice, square, chuckling Santa Claus to entertain the expense-account aristocracy with gags.

MAX. What else are you good for?

BUMMIDGE. I'm all for the emancipation of youth. Even at your age. Fight with authority, yes. But what good is that doggish look, that cool, heavy, sullen expression? My boy, this war of fathers and sons is a racket. Humankind has a horrible instinct for complaint. It's one whole section of the death instinct.

MAX. If we're going to have one of these high-level theoretical talks, you might start by zipping your fly.

BUMMIDGE. Is it open? It isn't worth a glance.

MAX. Showoff! You want to be the great stud. And I'm just a sample of your marvelous work.

BUMMIDGE. Not true. You're still just one of these child fanatics.

MAX. You made me drive you and that choreographer to Boston on *business*. Well, she was giving me the high sign.

BUMMIDGE. Pamela? Why, you crumb. You — you ex-sperm, you.

MAX. Old egomaniac!

BUMMIDGE. Quick, before you provoke me to terrible violence, what do you want?

MAX. You grabbed my property on Staten Island. That's theft. You owe me a good start in life.

BUMMIDGE. You've had six, seven starts.

MAX (*in earnest*). Come clean with me. What's the reason for this analysis? You latch on to everybody who knocks at the door — delivery boys, ratcatchers, bill collectors. You make them act out psychological situations. Are you kidding your way to God? What makes a comic think he can cure human perversity? It'll only take different forms. If you change your vices, is that progress?

BUMMIDGE. *Only* a comic. Bummidge — he doesn't know Greek or calculus. But he knows what he knows. Have you ever watched audiences laughing? You should see how monstrous it looks; you should listen from my side of the footlights. Oh, the despair, my son! The stale hearts! The snarling and gasping! (*He imitates various kinds of laughter — snarling, savage, frightening, howling, quavering.*) "Ha, ha — I am a cow, a sheep, a wolf, a rat. I am a victim, a killer. Ha, ha — my soul is corked up forever. Let me out. My spirit is famished. I twist, and rub. Ha, ha, ha, I'm an impostor. Can't you see? Catch me, please. No, it's too late. Life has no meaning. Ha, ha, ha, ha, ha!"

MAX. Why take it on yourself? Do your work, draw your dough, and to hell with it.

BUMMIDGE. My work? It's being stolen from me. Sophistication is putting me out of business. Everybody is kidding, smiling. Every lie looks like a pleasantry. Destruction appears like horseplay. Chaos is turned into farce, because evil is clever. It knows you can get away with murder if you laugh. Sadism makes fun. Extermination is a riot. And this is what drives clowns to thought. (*Gravely.*) To thought.

MAX. Why, you have a lump in your throat, Dad.

BUMMIDGE. Max! You called me Dad. Max!

MAX. Pa! (*They are about to embrace. He turns.*) It's just an expression — don't get all shook up.

BUMMIDGE. But you said it. My son!

MAX. Oh . . . everybody's "Dad."

BUMMIDGE. Except your father.

MAX. Don't confuse everything. I'm here to talk business. Listen, Bummy, there's a shipment of toasters from Czechoslovakia, refused by the importer because the cords are faulty. I know where to put my hands on the right Japanese-made cords, and there's an importer from Honduras, waiting.

BUMMIDGE. What have I begotten?

MAX. Another father would be proud. I beat those Czechs down to nothing. Ten grand today gets me thirty tomorrow. For twenty I can buy into a frozen-lasagne operation. All I want from you is three grand. Deduct it from the thirty-five you stole from me.

BUMMIDGE. In other words, you have seven and need three. Max (*shifting his chair closer confidentially*) why don't you lend me five and take my note for thirty?

MAX (*recoiling*). What, invest in your fantasies?

BUMMIDGE. Me you accuse of fantasy? You with the toasters and the guys from Honduras and Japan who'll make you a fortune in lasagne?

MAX. Is that worse than this giant insanity about psychoanalysis and comedy — this Tower of Babel you're building singlehanded? You think you're a new Moses?

BUMMIDGE. In the sandbox I watched over you. In the incubator I read to you.

MAX. Lucky I couldn't understand. You would have addled my brains, too.

BUMMIDGE. I wanted to lead you out of the realm of projections into the light of sanity. But you prefer the institutionalized psychosis of business.

MAX. Old lunatic!

BUMMIDGE. You may not be my child. Men have been tricked before.

MAX. Profound old fart!

BUMMIDGE. Spirochete! Filterable virus! Go bug your mother!

(*Lights go on.*)

MAX. You wait. I'll show you what things are really like. I'll open your eyes about that Pamela broad; I'll plow you. You hocked my building. (*Jumps up and down in a tantrum.*) You could go to jail.

BUMMIDGE. From a winged boy into a tailored vulture.

MAX. I may have you committed. . . . You wait, I'll be back with a warrant. An injunction. There'll be no telecast. (*In running out he bumps into* MOTT, TECHNICIAN, *and* BERTRAM.) Get out of my way! (*Exit.*)

TECHNICIAN. What's eating him?

BUMMIDGE. My son has wounded me. Wounded me. (*Exit.*)

MOTT. Tough!

(*He and* TECHNICIAN *go about their work.* BERTRAM *is curious, watching.*)

BERTRAM. It all connects, eh? And you'll beam the lecture to the Waldorf?

MOTT. I could transmit it to Iceland, if I wanted. . . . I wonder how Bummy'll be.

BERTRAM. Brilliant.

MOTT. Didn't you first come here as the exterminator?

BERTRAM. As soon as I saw the place I realized there were rats. You ask me how? I feel the molding, the baseboards. Rats have greasy fur, and they always run along the wall. Also, a rat drops many pellets.

MOTT. Ugh!

BERTRAM. The expert can date these pellets accurately. By a gentle squeeze of thumb and forefinger. Infallible. He also puts an ear to the wall. Rats must gnaw to survive. Otherwise the fangs'd get too long to chew with, their mouths would lock, and they'd starve. Bummy and I have scientific interests in common. What now?

TECHNICIAN. We hook the A line to this camera.

BERTRAM. Bummy and I hit it off right away. I got involved in psychotherapy. He showed me that to go around killing rats meant I must be compulsive, obsessional. The rat often symbolizes the child, as in the "Pied Piper." The rat also stands for a primordial mystery. Earth mystery. Chthonic. But most of all, my sense of humor fascinated Bummy. I don't laugh at jokes.

MOTT (*curious*). Never?

BERTRAM. I can't. I'm too neurotic. (*He stands between* MOTT *and the* TECHNICIAN.) I have no sense of humor. I only have occasion to laugh.

TECHNICIAN. When does that happen?

BERTRAM. Mainly when I'm tickled.

(*They tickle him. He laughs horribly. They are aghast.*)

MOTT. Stop! Stop it!

BERTRAM. I know. It's pathological. Tickling shouldn't make a normal person laugh.

TECHNICIAN. Let's see.

(*He and* MOTT *solemnly tickle each other.*)

MOTT. I'm knocking myself out trying to understand about the broadcast. Bummy loves big gestures. Does he want to be a college professor?

(*Enter* IMOGEN.)

IMOGEN. Mr. Bummidge doesn't realize how fast time is passing.

(*Enter* BUMMIDGE.)

BUMMIDGE. To understand Max, I must revisit *my* father.

MOTT (*a bit shocked*). But he's dead. . . .

BUMMIDGE. In the unconscious, Louie, there is no time, no logic, and no death.

TECHNICIAN. We need a sound level.

MOTT. I'll set up these lights.

BUMMIDGE. Bertram, you'll play Father. We live behind the candy store in Williamsburg. . . . It was so dark there. Dark. And poverty.

MOTT (*as he works with lights*). Here goes the poor-childhood routine, again. How he fetched wood and coal. Was beaten. Peddled papers.

Froze his ears. How there was never real toilet paper in the house, only orange wrappers.

BUMMIDGE. Papa wouldn't allow me to have candy. I stole. I'd wolf down the stale chocolates, choking. Now Bert, as Papa, you discover a Mary Jane wrapper floating in the toilet. You clutch my ear and cry out, "Thief! Goniff!"

BERTRAM (*taking* BUMMIDGE *by the ear*). Thief — goniff.

IMOGEN. I wouldn't want Bertram to pinch my ear.

BUMMIDGE. Harder, Bert. Don't just squeeze — twist. It's essential to feel the pain.

BERTRAM (*warningly*). It's not a good idea to encourage my cruelty.

MOTT. Go on, Bert, turn it on.

(BERTRAM, *face transformed, twists.* BUMMIDGE *screams.*)

BUMMIDGE. That's it! Unbearable! (*Sinks to his knees.*) I haven't felt such agony in forty years. (*Supplicating.*) Papa, Papa! Don't! I'm only a child. I have an innocent craving for sweets. It's human nature. I inherit it from you. Papa, it's the pleasure principle. Jung and Freud would agree.

IMOGEN. He's read simply everything.

BERTRAM. Mine son stealing?

BUMMIDGE (*rises*). No, Bert, Papa had a ballsy voice. (*Imitates his father.*) "By thirteen I was already in the sweat shop, brought home pay. God helped, I got this lousy business. All day buried behind a dark counter with broken feet; with gall bladder; blood pressure. I sell egg-cream, mushmellows, cheap cigars, gumballs — all kinds of *dreck*. But you, your head lays in idleness? Play? Fun? Candy? You'll be a *mensch* or I'll kill you." (*Himself again.*) Desire pierced my glands and my mouth watered. I heard a subversive voice that whispered, "Joy, joy!" It made a criminal of me. (*Reflecting.*) A humorless savage, he was. But I loved him. Why won't my son love me? My father whipped me. (*Bending, he canes himself.*)

MOTT. Now he's a flagellant?

BUMMIDGE (*kneeling, head to the floor*). Flogged.

IMOGEN. Oh, dear, he'll have an attack of Humanitis.

TECHNICIAN. What's Humanitis?

BERTRAM. It's when the human condition is suddenly too much for you.

BUMMIDGE (*sitting on floor*). When he punished me, I took myself away and left an empty substitute in his hands. (*Crawls toward exit, sits again.*) I let myself be punished in effigy. I split up into fragments. There were two, four, an army, and the real Bummidge gets lost. I couldn't keep track. My self got lost. But where is the *me* that is me? What happened to it? (*Rises slowly.*) That was the beginning of my comic method.

(*Explaining the matter to himself, he goes.* BERTRAM *helps him off.*)

IMOGEN. We'll never be ready, at this rate.

MOTT (*to* TECHNICIAN). Run down to the truck and get the rest of those cables.

(*Exit* TECHNICIAN.)

I talked the office into giving Bummy a little more time.

IMOGEN. That's kind of you.

MOTT. That's the kind of friend I am. . . . Imogen. (*Takes her hand.*) As soon as I saw you, I had like a tremendous flash!

IMOGEN (*trying to free her hand*). Mr. Mott!

MOTT. You're my erotic type.

IMOGEN. Don't, Mr. Mott. I can't bear to be a sexy joke. I really am a serious person.

MOTT. This *is* serious. I'm a mature man, mature and single. Most important, I'm youthful. Most mature men in New York are married. The rest are queer, crazy, infected, dangerous. But I —

IMOGEN. No, no. Someone's coming. (*Flees.*)

MOTT. Wait!

(*Exit in pursuit. Enter* PAMELA. *She is, like* MADGE, *highly respectable in appearance, wears a knit suit, a modest hat; she has a slight Southern accent.*)

PAMELA. Bummy? Where are you, dear? (*Looks for him.*) I've come to be with you on this important day. (*Seeing she is alone.*) It's sure to be a bomb. Then what? Then we can stop pretending. I can't wait. Love, science. "Oh, value, value. I'll die without value." What a drag it's turned into. (*Listens.*) Footsteps? I'll surprise him.

(*She steps behind the screen.* MADGE *and* WINKLEMAN *enter.*)

WINKLEMAN. It's set, at the Waldorf. The networks, the agencies — Fiddleman. Phew. It took plenty of doing. Fiddleman will phone, the instant the broadcast is over.

MADGE. Bummy's got to get us off the hook. And listen, I saw Bella at Columbus Circle, waiting for a bus. With all her money, she won't take a taxi.

WINKLEMAN. Was she coming here?

MADGE. Where else? What a tough old broad she's become, loud, brassy, suspicious. She'll throw a monkey wrench in the works if she can.

WINKLEMAN. My contact, the inspector, said he'd wait one day. Tomorrow, at the latest, we have to bribe him. Does Bella know we're in a tight spot?

MADGE. She has everyone followed, investigated. She must suspect. How much is that guy holding us up for? . . . I still wonder about this valise of Bummy's. Could I work my hand in? Is it money? Winkie, it is — it is money!

(PAMELA *now steps out.* MADGE'*s wrist is caught in the valise.*)

WINKLEMAN (*trying to cover*). Why, it's Pamela.

PAMELA. Shall we play peek-a-boo? I love to catch people red-handed. Such a luxurious feeling.

MADGE. Help me.

(*With* PAMELA *and* WINKLEMAN *tugging,* MADGE *frees her hand, and falls backward.*)

PAMELA. You'll have to cut me in. Let's not waste time lying. I understand what you're up to. If Bummy gets offers, you'll need my help, my persuasive powers.

MADGE (*as she and* WINKLEMAN *exchange glances, shrug, accept the inevitable*). Okay.

PAMELA. Life isn't easy for a person like me. If we can put Bummy back in the big time I can lead the respectable life I've always longed for. I'll find out what he's got in this bag. He must carry the keys. Come, let's work out the details.

(*She and* MADGE *go off.*)

WINKLEMAN. Why didn't I retire two years ago, when I was ahead? Lead a quiet life? Write the Comedy Humane of New York? Maybe I was afraid to be left alone with my distorted heart. Oh, here comes my cousin. (*Exit.*)

(BUMMIDGE *and* BERTRAM *enter.* BUMMIDGE *is holding a child's potty.*)

BUMMIDGE. Bert, this was a real piece of luck. This is just like the one Mama sat me on. It will help me to re-enter my infancy.

BERTRAM. You won't sit on that during the broadcast, will you?

BUMMIDGE. I'm not sure. But the Ego has hung a veil, the veil of infantile amnesia, over the earliest facts of life. I have to tear it down. See the bare truth . . .

BERTRAM. Can it be done?

BUMMIDGE. Shush! (*Finger to lips.*) A quiet corner. A bit of reverie. We were all *body* once. Then we split.

BERTRAM. The trauma . . .

(PAMELA *comes in.*)

BUMMIDGE. O Trauma. O Regression — Sublimation! I think this is a good spot. (*He squats behind the sofa, so that only his head is visible.*)

BERTRAM (*catching sight of* PAMELA). Don't get settled yet.

BUMMIDGE. The mighty of the earth have put us in this position, and it's from here we must make our stand. This is a very small pot.

(BERTRAM *whispers to him.*)

Why didn't you say so?

BERTRAM. Get a grip on yourself.

PAMELA. Lover?

BUMMIDGE (*leaps up*). Just as I was beginning to feel something. Bert, go clear everything with Mott. There's still that headache about the money. Where's Aufschnitt with the coat? If these people trip me up before the broadcast, I'll murder them, cut my throat, and set fire to the building.

(*Exit* BERTRAM.)

PAMELA. What are you doing?

BUMMIDGE. Therapy, dear. Therapy. I didn't expect to see you.

PAMELA. On a day like this? I came to help.

BUMMIDGE. Help? You? That's a new one. Where have you been?

PAMELA. Thinking of you. Of your ideas. Our future. (*Sits on sofa.*)

BUMMIDGE (*pulling up a chair beside her*). Where were you last night? I phoned and phoned.

PAMELA. Why, darling, I was visiting Mother. You forgot.

BUMMIDGE. That madam? The hell you were.

PAMELA. We went out to U.S. One for a pizza pie. I told her how mad I am for you, and how happy we'd be if you became a professor of dramatic psychology. I'm sure Johns Hopkins will offer you the chair.

BUMMIDGE. There are times when I wish you didn't have that vapid look. I do love you, in my peculiar way.

PAMELA. A quiet, decent life. Straight. A real home.

BUMMIDGE. I've figured out the main forms of love. A man can love a woman on the tenderness system. That's very good. Or on the lust system. That's better than nothing. Or on the pride system. That's worse than nothing.

PAMELA. My lover! (*Embracing him.*) Your stomach is rumbling.

BUMMIDGE. It isn't rumbling. It's doing free association.

PAMELA. You're brain all over. Sheer brain.

(*They rise and move toward barber chair.*)

BUMMIDGE. Sweetheart — that diamond anklet (*points*). Bought when I was flush. I paid Tiffany twelve grand.

PAMELA. Kiss me, Bummy, hold me close. (*Goes through his pockets; gets the key to the valise.*)

BUMMIDGE. I could pawn it for five. Louie Mott would take it.

(*They are now back to back.* BUMMIDGE *holds* PAMELA*'s ankle and removes her shoe. She, meanwhile, is opening the valise.*)

PAMELA. All my life I've looked for nothing but peace, security, quiet, but I always wind up in some absurd mixup.

BUMMIDGE. You have big feet.

PAMELA. You swept me off them like a force of nature.

BUMMIDGE (*removing the anklet*). I've got it! (*They begin to part.*)

PAMELA. It's opening. Thousands! (*Turning to face him.*) You've got thousands here.

BUMMIDGE. But earmarked for a higher purpose. I can't use them.

PAMELA. My anklet! Give it back!

BUMMIDGE. Where did you get the keys? Shut my valise.

PAMELA. You thief!

BUMMIDGE. Calling *me* a thief?

(*He shuts and locks the valise while* PAMELA *tries to recover the anklet.* LOUIE MOTT *runs in.*)

MOTT. Your wife is below — Bella.

BUMMIDGE. Keep her away. . . . I don't want to see her.

MOTT. Can't you hear her hollering?

(*Enter* BERTRAM.)

BERTRAM. Bummy, your estranged Missis!

BUMMIDGE (*to* PAMELA). You'd better go.

PAMELA. Without my jewels? Like hell I will. (*In a temper.*) I came to help you.

BUMMIDGE. The screaming, the scratching, the hairpulling — you'll kill my broadcast. My scientific demonstration — the biggest thing in my life.

PAMELA. I won't go. Get rid of her. I'll wait.

BERTRAM. Where'll we put you? In the toilet? The broom closet?

PAMELA. I'd see you dead first, you creep.

MOTT. What about the fire escape?

PAMELA. I'll wait on the fire escape a few minutes. No longer. It's going to drizzle. And give me the anklet. My diamonds!

BUMMIDGE. Later, dear, later.

(BERTRAM *and* MOTT *hurry* PAMELA *to the fire escape.*)

Lock that door. Lock her out. Oh, my character has created another typical crisis. What crazy things we are! The repetition compulsion. (*To statue of Freud.*) O, Master, how deep you were! . . . Imogen! Where is she? Astray again? That poor sexual waif. Louie, pull the shade.

(*We now see nothing of* PAMELA *but an occasional silhouette through the shade.*)

How am I going to get rid of Bella?

(*Exit with* BERTRAM. *Enter* IMOGEN.)

IMOGEN. Did Mr. Bummidge call me?
MOTT. Imogen, as soon as I see you my pulses double and triple. Don't ask a man to waste such feelings.
IMOGEN (*fights him off*). Mr. Mott, don't. It's almost broadcast time.
MOTT. A flash! A red haze. And from below I get this gentle, gentle heat. Here. Feel . . . Where's your hand?

(*Pounding at the door, right.*)

IMOGEN (*struggling*). Someone's coming.
MOTT (*all over her*). I'm oblivious!
IMOGEN. You look so . . . icky.
MOTT. It's virility. You'll be astonished. Ecstatic. Wait till you see.

(*Someone is battering the door.* MOTT, *blowing a kiss, takes off.* IMOGEN'*s stockings are falling. Her dress has been pulled off the shoulders.*)

IMOGEN. How did he get to my garter belt? . . . Who is it? (*Trying to fasten her stockings.*) Coming . . .

(*She opens the door. Enter* AUFSCHNITT, *carrying a coat on a hanger wrapped in brown paper.*)

AUFSCHNITT (*crossing*). Is Mr. Bummidge here? I am his tailor.
IMOGEN. I thought you were his wife.
AUFSCHNITT. I came with the coat for his broadcast. But, please, I need C.O.D.

(*Enter* BELLA, *large and aggressive, pushing past them into the room, outlandishly dressed. One can see that* PAMELA *has made a study of* BUMMIDGE'*s wife in order to give him — or pretend to give him — all that* BELLA *could never conceivably offer.*)

BELLA. Where is he, that miserable man? And where is that cheap lay of his? I'll clobber them both. Then let them go on television with bloody faces.

AUFSCHNITT. Mrs. Bummidge, I have your husband's coat. But this time he must pay.

BELLA. I don't blame you. He wanted squalor, did he? Ugh! No self-respecting dog would throw up here. Imogen, tell him I've come. (*Sits.*)

IMOGEN. I'll try and find him. (*Exit.*)

BELLA. He's somewhere near, listening.

(*She looks for him. We see* PAMELA'*s silhouette. We hear the rumble of thunder. Enter* BERTRAM, *instructed to get rid of* BELLA.)

BERTRAM. Mrs. Bummidge, are you looking for your husband?

BELLA. So, where is the great mental wizard? Ah, it's the ratcatcher. How can he bear to have you around? You must get your suits in the morgue. They smell like it. Where is he?

BERTRAM. They're building that dam in the Nile. Abu Simbel. He wanted to have a look at those Pharaohs before the water covers them.

(*Enter* BUMMIDGE *as a little boy, playing hopscotch.*)

BELLA. So. With his psychology he's gone back to childhood. Here's our kiddy. Some people fade or subside, but not him. He'll go through every agony. How old are you, little man?

BUMMIDGE. Six and a half.

BELLA (*to* BERT). I wish he had gone to Ethiopia, you stooge. (*To* BUMMIDGE). And are you a good little boy?

BUMMIDGE. Oh, yes, otherwise my parents hit me with rulers. They slash me with straps. So I am.

BELLA. And what are you going to be when you grow up?

BUMMIDGE. With wings, but on foot like a goose.

AUFSCHNITT. Mr. Bummidge, are you ready for the coat?

BUMMIDGE (*looks at coat, pleased*). Ah!

AUFSCHNITT. So pay me.

BUMMIDGE (*face changing, he examines the coat*). What kind of a garment do you call this? Is that a buttonhole? Aufschnitt, have you lost all pride in your work?

AUFSCHNITT. Pride I can't eat. Pride doesn't pay the rent.

(BUMMIDGE *stands on the platform as* AUFSCHNITT *fits the coat, a garment resembling the one worn by the late Mr. Nehru.*)

BUMMIDGE. Affluence is finished. People are poor again. I've paid you thousands.

AUFSCHNITT. Not a cent in two years. In two years! What do I know from affluence!

BELLA (*laughing at* BUMMIDGE *in his coat*). Look at that! What a freak he is! Now you'll pay what — sixty G's? — to play the psychiatrist to that howling gang at the Waldorf.

BUMMIDGE. Who's howling? Have you been there?

BELLA. Certainly, and a rummier bunch I never saw. Gobbling up the caviar and lushing champagne. Who are those scientists? (*She puts her purse on chair near him and strides about.*)

BUMMIDGE (*when her back is turned examines her purse*). You saw the gate-crashers. You have to expect some of that at every affair. Now Bella, sweetheart . . .

BELLA (*snatches away her purse, shouting*). Don't you pull that sweetheart stuff on me, after my years of misery! I'll never let you snow me again.

BUMMIDGE (*angrily, pursuing her about stage as* AUFSCHNITT *tries to fit the coat*). Then what do you want? These fights with me are your bread and meat.

BELLA. I've come. I have my reasons, never mind. Legally I'm still your wife.

BUMMIDGE. You took everything. Two million dollars' worth of property. I have to squabble with ingrate buttonhole makers.

AUFSCHNITT (*running after him*). Don't move your arms too much. It's a rush job. The seams are weak.

BELLA. I had to stop you from squandering every last cent on broads. Especially this last one — the choreographer. A fancy word for whore.

BUMMIDGE (*again on the platform*). Don't talk like that. She loves me.

BELLA. Love? Don't talk to me about love. I've seen the bills.

(*The* TECHNICIAN *enters with a kit and begins to apply make-up to* BUMMIDGE*'s face.*)

TECHNICIAN. Let's see you under the lights. Your skin is peculiar.

BELLA. You took her to Europe on that disastrous tour of old opera houses. Me you left behind. You think Pamela loves you for your personality? For your brilliant mind? For your bad bridgework? And your belching, and getting up ten times a night to pee, so a person can't sleep? Is that what she loves you for? (*Her eye is caught by an open newspaper.*) Oh, General Electric, down three-eighths.

BUMMIDGE (*smoothing the front of his coat*). Bella, you're distracting me from my great purpose. Keep the two millions, but stop bothering me.

TECHNICIAN. Let me see what I can do with this complexion of yours. (*He drags a complaining* BUMMIDGE *to the barber chair.*)

BELLA. You sent me on phony errands to clear the decks for your orgies. I was a prisoner for six months on that milk farm in Wisconsin.

BUMMIDGE. Overweight. We had to think of your blood pressure.

BELLA. You put a pistol in my night table to suggest suicide.

BUMMIDGE. Maybe I wanted you to shoot me. (*To* TECHNICIAN.) I want you to emphasize the serenity of my brow and my eyes. Let's eliminate this clownish slant.

BELLA (*as she comes over to the barber chair we hear a rumble of thunder*). Bummy, tell me the truth. What's going to happen? I can't understand. I'm just an old-fashioned, goodhearted broad, an ordinary, practical, loyal woman.

BUMMIDGE (*to* TECHNICIAN). Recognize the party line?

(*The* TECHNICIAN *makes a broad grimace of agreement, but continues working.*)

BELLA. At one time, to me, you were everything. Why don't you explain it to me? . . . I think we're going to have a thundershower.

BUMMIDGE (*with an anxious glance toward the fire escape*). Listen, Bella, in eighteen fifty-nine Darwin published *The Origin of Species;* nineteen hundred, Freud came out with *The Interpretation of Dreams.*

BELLA. For God's sake, Bummy, have a little pride. Don't go tell those intellectuals what they already know. Elementary. They'll laugh at you.

BUMMIDGE. They know *nothing* about laughing. That's my field. . . . Bella, there's something I can't forgive you. Never. (*Leaves the chair.*)

BELLA (*follows him*). What, now? What?

BUMMIDGE. You want to be a business power, a tycoon. Well, you took the old building where I played in youth, the Trilby Theatre, and rented it for a meat market. Where names like "Bummidge," like "Jimmy Savo," used to be on the marquee, we now have "The Kalbfuss Palace of Meats. Pork Butts Today."

BELLA (*giving no ground*). So what?

BUMMIDGE. I'm going to restore it, rededicate it to comedy.

BELLA. Bring back vaudeville?

BUMMIDGE. No. I want to open it to the public. I want to make it a theatre of the soul. Let people come off the street to practice my *Existenz*-Action-Self-Analysis. Tickets at modest prices. Let the public step up and work with me — my method.

BELLA. You want to bring psychoanalysis to the vaudeville stage?

BUMMIDGE. You can't get the whole public on the couch. Theories have to be socially active, broad. The couch is for higher-income brackets. Bella, people make a career of their problems, a racket of their characters, an occupation of their personality traits. Take yourself, for instance. (*Parodies her.*) "An old-fashioned, goodhearted broad. To me you were everything." . . . How you belt it out! The throbbing heart! And love! Jesus, what a production you make of love! Warfare, that's what you really love. You spend your whole life playing the dramatic values of your Devotion, your Fate, your Sacrifice and Struggles. What corn! Aren't you ashamed of yourself? Bella, only laughter can save you from this. Such elaboration of personality is a joke.

BELLA (*stunned by this*). Reopen the Trilby. That's Utopian. Crazy. . . . Oh, one man's jokes are another man's theories. I don't get it.

BUMMIDGE. In this valise I have almost enough to buy the lease from Kalbfuss. Oh, Lord, and I have to scrape up the balance for Louie. (*Runs to desk.*) Somewhere in this mess is the receipt from Tiffany's. (*Pulls out drawers.*) Ah, here. More than I thought. Fourteen thousand.

AUFSCHNITT. I don't dare leave this coat without you pay me. My wife warned me.

BUMMIDGE. Bella, maybe you've got a few bucks.

BELLA. A headache from your theories, that's what I've got.

(*Enter* BERTRAM.)

Do you have aspirins in the medicine chest? I'm sure you have rats in that bathroom. Where's the light? (*Exit.*)

BERTRAM. I'll show you. . . . Rats?

AUFSCHNITT. Mr. Bummidge, you say plain, ordinary people could understand your psychology? I have plenty of trouble in my family. A sad daughter who won't even get out of bed.

BUMMIDGE. Single?

AUFSCHNITT. The bed or the daughter? . . . Both single.

(*Enter* IMOGEN.)

BUMMIDGE. Perhaps you and I could work together. Free of charge, of course.

AUFSCHNITT. For nothing?

IMOGEN. Mr. Bummidge, you have very little time.

BUMMIDGE. For instance.

IMOGEN. He's never too busy to hold out a hand to misery.

BUMMIDGE. Now Aufschnitt, listen to me.

IMOGEN. It's started to rain.

BUMMIDGE. Bertram, find an umbrella for you-know-who. Aufschnitt, I am six years old. My parents have bought me my first pair of galoshes for school. Gleaming black rubber, and such a delicious smell. They make beautiful tracks in the snow. But my mother warns me — the usual: We are poor people. You lose everything. Don't you come home without those galoshes. Papa will kill you stone dead!

(BERTRAM *frantically looks for an umbrella.* PAMELA *tries to make herself heard through the glass door.* BERTRAM *can find nothing but a little girl's pink parasol. When he opens the door a crack,* PAMELA *tries to fight her way in. He succeeds in locking the door.*)

BERTRAM. It's raining out there. A regular monsoon.

BUMMIDGE. Listen, Aufschnitt, my first-grade teacher, Miss Farnum, was a youthful rhubarb blonde. You be Miss Farnum, and I'll be six.

AUFSCHNITT. What should I do?

BUMMIDGE. Act and feel like my teacher.

(*Enter* MAX *and a private detective,* MR. GALLUPPO.)

MAX. Pop, Mr. Galluppo, here, is my lawyer, a private investigator.

BUMMIDGE. He looks like a blackmailer. I have no time for this.

MAX. Listen to his report.

GALLUPPO (*gazing about*). So this is what happens to stars in retirement. Substandard housing.

AUFSCHNITT. I'm not sure I can imitate a young teacher in a long dress.

BUMMIDGE. Of course you can. Do it for your daughter. This can help her. Like this. (*Enacts Miss Farnum.*)

AUFSCHNITT. Like this? (*He tries.*)

BUMMIDGE. Quite good for a first effort.

AUFSCHNITT. How could it help my poor daughter Joy?

BUMMIDGE. Concentrate with me, Aufschnitt. The other kids with their sheepskins and boots have gone home. But where are my galoshes?

(*He and* AUFSCHNITT *hunt under chairs for the galoshes.*)

MAX (*to* GALLUPPO). Give your report on his friend Pamela. Where was she last night?

GALLUPPO. In premises at Six-Y Jones Street. She had relations with a gentleman of the other sex. Every night a different person.

BUMMIDGE (*with some hauteur*). You must have the wrong party. Miss Sillerby is an artist from a distinguished Southern family. (*To* AUFSCHNITT.) Now Miss Farnum, I'm in a terrible spot. First you scold me. Then you make fun of me. You stick out your tongue. I start to bawl. . . . Max, why do you do this?

AUFSCHNITT. Now little boy, you'd better not cry.

(*Enter* MOTT. *The* TECHNICIAN *appears above.*)

MOTT. We've got to have a sound level, Bummy. Swing out the boom, John.

GALLUPPO. Is this a photo of the party in question?

MAX. You bet. Show it to my father.

IMOGEN (*trying to interpose herself*). Oh, don't do that. You'll upset everything.

BUMMIDGE. That's what he wants to do.

(GALLUPPO *shows photo to* AUFSCHNITT, *who can't bear to look.*)

AUFSCHNITT. Why me? I don't recognize these people. They have no clothes on.

GALLUPPO. Monday with a Wall Street broker. Tuesday with a bartender. Wednesday the super of her building.

BUMMIDGE. I'm crying over my galoshes. I'm not a day over six.

AUFSCHNITT. What a little crybaby! (*Puts out his tongue.*)

BUMMIDGE. She tried to make me laugh at my dread. I hated her for it. But she was right. She tried to teach me to reject ridiculous pain. (*He pounds at door of the fire escape, where we see* PAMELA'*s anguished figure in silhouette.*)

TECHNICIAN. What's he doing? What goes on?

IMOGEN. It's a cloudburst. They always affect him.

MOTT. Let's try those lights. Bert, give a hand here. Bummy, you've got only twenty minutes.

BUMMIDGE. What? (*Shakes his fist at door, then turns from it.*) Louie, take these rocks. Tiffany's. Here's the receipt. Worth eight grand at least. Oh Bummidge, you sucker, you patsy, you mark! Max, take this snooper away. It's nearly time for my broadcast. Louie, let's go.

AUFSCHNITT. Crybaby! Crybaby!

BUMMIDGE. I should have laughed, not wept. (*Tries laughter.*)

MAX. There'll be no broadcast.

(*Enter* BELLA.)

Mother, what are you doing here?

BELLA (*pointing to* GALLUPPO). Where did he come from? Does he do work for you too? I pay him fat fees. He takes from us both for the same information, I bet.

GALLUPPO. I didn't know you was related.

AUFSCHNITT. Crybaby! Crybaby!

BELLA. Shut up! My head is splitting.

(*Enter* WINKLEMAN *and* MADGE.)

I knew they'd show up!

TECHNICIAN (*holding up microphone*). Let's hear you speak a word or two.

BUMMIDGE. Help! Help!

(GALLUPPO *forces him to look at the photo.*)

Oh, the bitch!

(*There is a sharp rapping at the door. Lights are tested. Cables are draped over furniture. Enter a* MESSENGER.)

What do you want?

MESSENGER. Western Union.

IMOGEN. I'll take the wire.

(*Enter* AUNT VELMA *in a wheelchair. She carries a cane.*)

WINKLEMAN. Here's Mother.
BUMMIDGE. Tante Velma! She's come!
VELMA. Why is it so crowded and noisy?
BUMMIDGE. You were midwife at my birth. From the sightless universe into your hands!

(*Telephone rings.*)

Bertram, answer.
BERTRAM. Shouldn't I open that door?
BELLA. Is that a woman screaming somewhere?
BUMMIDGE. The wind! Wind and rain!
MADGE (*persuasive, cooperative*). Now listen to me, Bummy.
BUMMIDGE (*mistaking her tone*). You and Winkie are plotting against me. A conspiracy.
MADGE. But that's just paranoid.
AUFSCHNITT. You must pay me or I can't let you have the coat. (*Tries to remove it.*)
BUMMIDGE. Bella, won't you get this needle-pusher off my back?
BELLA. How much?
AUFSCHNITT. One twenty-five.
MAX (*tries to stop her*). Mother, don't.
BELLA (*fishing money out of her bosom*). You've ruined my life, but thank God I'm comfortably ruined.
BERTRAM. It's Doctor Ratzenhofer on the phone. He says how long will the broadcast be? He has appointments.
BUMMIDGE. Oh, Doctor Ratzenhofer?
WINKLEMAN. How can you start in all this chaos?
MOTT. How do I know these diamonds aren't paste?
IMOGEN. The wire is from Kalbfuss. He's standing by.
BUMMIDGE. Kalbfuss! (*Throws his arms upward.*) Thank heaven for his loyalty.
AUFSCHNITT. The seams! The seams are opening!
BELLA. These are the fruits of my husband's originality. Confusion!
VELMA (*rapping with her cane*). I think this floor is sagging.
BUMMIDGE. A mere symbol, Tante.
WINKLEMAN. Look here, Cousin, you've got Madge and me all wrong.
BELLA (*pushing forward*). We know about you. Starving old people. Conditions worse than Andersonville. Investigations. The whole story about to break. A hell of a note.
BUMMIDGE. You've all come to prevent my broadcast.
MAX. That's right.
GALLUPPO (*pulling out a paper*). I have a restraining order.
BELLA (*to* MAX). Don't try to shaft your father. He's got it coming from me.

BUMMIDGE. You want to make a farce of my serious intentions. But someone has to do something. Even if that someone is only me.

(MOTT *is about to hit the diamonds with a hammer to see if they are real.*)

Hold it!

(BUMMIDGE *restrains* MOTT. *There is silence. Then* BUMMIDGE *laughs strangely.*)

Ladies and gentlemen, I invite you to witness a typical moment of human existence, showing mankind as it makes the most of its universal opportunities, amid all the miracles of light and motion. . . .

(*The next group of speeches is spoken together, jumbled.*)

MAX. Now he's Cassandra.
MADGE. I never know what he's talking about. Let's start.
VELMA. Why did I even come? Family feeling? Big deal!
GALLUPPO. Fifty bucks an hour, I charge.
WINKLEMAN. We can't let this go on!

(*They fall silent.*)

BUMMIDGE (*violently*). Stop! Why are you here? I am your food, your prey. You have filled my life with stench and noise; dogged me night and day; lived on me like green fungus on pumpernickel. But you won't be happy till I'm crucified? You, a Roman crowd? I, an Asiatic slave?

MAX. Man, now he's on the Jesus kick.

BUMMIDGE (*holds up both hands, fingers widely spread*). Shall I submit?

WINKLEMAN (*trying vainly to soothe him*). Please come off it, Bummy. Don't be carried away.

MADGE. You'll forget your purpose.

VELMA. This is New York. Nineteen sixty-five A.D.

BUMMIDGE. All right, where is that staple gun? Imogen. (*He stands on a desk.*)

(IMOGEN *approaches with the stapler.*)

Staple Bummidge to the wall.

(IMOGEN *hesitates.* BERTRAM *staples* BUMMIDGE's *cuffs. His arms are outstretched.*)

MAX. The martyrdom bit!

WINKLEMAN. Wasted! He's using up his energy before the broadcast. Wait, Bummy.

MADGE. Save it for the cameras.

TECHNICIAN. I'm impressed.

GALLUPPO. Maybe I am a lousy crook, a double-dealing fink, but this is blasphemy.

IMOGEN. Not with Mr. Bummidge. It's real! Can't you see he's in pain? He's having an attack of Humanitis. Catch him.

BELLA. No, Bummy, no! I take it all back.

(PAMELA, *drenched, with the parasol, has forced her way in. She is gasping.*)

MOTT. We got just a little time before the broadcast. (*To* TECHNICIAN.) Let's take a five-minute break.

(*They kneel and shoot dice.*)

BELLA (*as* PAMELA *collapses at* BUMMIDGE'*s feet*). There's the whore in the picture. Now we got the full cast.

MOTT. Okay. Roll 'em.

BUMMIDGE. Forgive them, Father, for, for . . . What comes next?

ACT TWO

(*Minutes later:* BUMMIDGE *has been extricated from his coat, which hangs empty on the wall. Onstage are* PAMELA, *who has wrapped herself, shivering, in the tapestry on the barber chair;* AUFSCHNITT, *who is taking down the coat in order to mend it;* MADGE, *explaining the situation to* MAX *and* GALLUPPO. BELLA *appears skeptical but is really* [as always] *passionately in pursuit of her life's project: involvement with her husband's magical peculiarities.* TANTE VELMA, *legs boldly crossed, sits in her wheelchair smoking a cigar and studying business documents. Her kindly old eyeglasses have been pushed up on her forehead; without them she looks tough and severe.* MOTT *is looking at his wristwatch.*)

MOTT. We may have to call it all off.

MADGE. Nonsense! Too much is riding on Bummy for us all. Max understands now.

MAX. I see what you mean. I get it. He's going to do this anyway. We can't overcome his peculiar ideas, so we exploit them instead. Smart.

BELLA. You *think* you can outsmart him. Wait. You'll see how shifty and shrewd he is.

MADGE. Winkie is in the library with him, explaining that we offer full cooperation. All of us.

GALLUPPO. But what will CBS, NBC, MCA, Fiddleman, and the rest see in his shenanigans?

MAX. Madge and Winkie are right. There's nothing so extreme or kookie that the mass media won't try to use it. We talk of atomic explosion and population explosion, but in the twentieth century there's also an explosion of consciousness. Society needs the imagination of its most alienated members. They want to defy it? It doesn't care. It pays them millions. Money reconciles all tendencies.

VELMA. You're your father's son. You sound like him.

PAMELA. I'm soaked to the skin.

BELLA (*acid*). Undress. By now everybody knows how you look in the nude.

PAMELA. Without your corsets, you must be like a sea cow.

BELLA. The government should label people the way it does meat — prime, choice, and dog food.

PAMELA. You have a plain label — the ball-breaking wife.

(BELLA *is about to strike* PAMELA *with her purse;* PAMELA *prepares to defend herself with her high-heeled shoe;* MAX *restrains his mother.*)

MOTT. Minutes ticking away!

VELMA (*to* AUFSCHNITT *as he passes with the coat*). And what's he doing?

AUFSCHNITT. Mending the raiment. (*Exit.*)

MAX. The thing is, what will I get out of it?

MADGE. You? You're the heir.

VELMA. With Papa in the big money again? And doting on his sonny boy? Ha, *ha!*

PAMELA. So far, I've lost my anklet.

(MOTT *covertly lifts it from his pocket and looks at it.*)

MADGE (*suspicious*). Louie . . .

(*Enter* IMOGEN *and* BERTRAM. BERTRAM *carries an infant in his arms.*)

BERTRAM. Bummy wanted to see a little child. Where is he?

(*Enter* BUMMIDGE *with* WINKLEMAN.)

IMOGEN. Mr. Bummidge — an infant!

BUMMIDGE (*excited*). Undress it. I must see the original human material. The essential thing.

BELLA (*taking charge*). This child could use a clean diaper.

BERTRAM. Her mother is an alcoholic. I had to give her a twenty-dollar deposit.

IMOGEN. In the bar, across the street.

BUMMIDGE (*enraptured*). Look at this freedom! How the little belly rises and falls. The state of Nature! Life drifts into the infant. . . . (*Laves himself with air.*) Drifts, drifts. Precious, blessed infancy. Everything loathsome about the human species is forgiven time after time, and with every child we begin again.

GALLUPO. I don't dig it.

IMOGEN (*explaining*). Heaven lies about us in our infancy. Then comes repression. We lose Eternity. We get shut up in Time.

VELMA (*gestures with her cigar, looks upward*). Big deal. I delivered thousands of them, poor things.

MOTT. Bummy, it's practically zero hour.

(AUFSCHNITT *enters with the coat.*)

BUMMIDGE. Take the baby, Bertram. Wait, I must have one last look. (*He looks tenderly at infant, as if to memorize it.*)

AUFSCHNITT. I fixed the seams.

BERTRAM. I'm out of pocket twenty bucks.

BUMMIDGE (*as he is getting into the coat, looks at* BELLA). Bella . . .

BELLA. On twenty bucks the mother'll go on a two-day binge. Oh, well . . . (*digs again into her bosom*).

(BERTRAM *takes money and goes, with the infant under one arm.*)

PAMELA (*comes forward*). Bummy, I have to have dry clothes. And where's my anklet?

BUMMIDGE (*hurries to large wicker clothes hamper, opens it*). Here's something for you. (*Struck by an idea.*) There's something here for each of you. . . . Ah, yes. For each and every one. Marvelous! You'll all participate with me in the broadcast. Louie, throw away the old format.

WINKLEMAN. Ad lib? Now? But Bummy — think!

BUMMIDGE. I've never been so lucid. That little infant shows me the way. All impulse. Impulse is the soul of freedom. My deeper self is telling me what to do. (*Clutches his head, but smilingly.*)

PAMELA (*unfolding the garment*). Why, this is nothing but a burlesque stripper's outfit!

BUMMIDGE (*to* WINKLEMAN). You said everyone would stand behind me.

MADGE. To a man! I remember Doctor Ehrlich and the magic bullet.

WINKLEMAN. And Semmelweiss, and Pasteur!

MOTT. Don't forget Richard Nixon. How against him they all were until he went on television with that little dog.

BUMMIDGE. And Pamela? You, too?

PAMELA (*somewhat reluctant*). Yes, Bummy. You'll give back my diamonds, won't you? (*Exit.*)

BUMMIDGE (*as he watches her go*). The forms — the many forms that suffering takes. The compulsion to suffer. But for each and every one of these there is a method to evade suffering. Delusion. Intoxication. Ecstasy. And comedy. I must remember that for the broadcast. Now listen, all of you. I'm going back to my sources and you'll all wear costumes and step forward as I call on you. Imogen, hand them out. Louie, the hoodlum you were during Prohibition.

(MOTT *goes to change.*)

Madge, this flapper's dress with fringes.

(MADGE *goes.*)

Max, you'll represent my father. You resemble him.

(MAX *puts on a shopkeeper's apron and a broad-brimmed hat.*)

Bella, a bridal gown.

(BELLA *goes.*)

Winkie. These rompers.

WINKLEMAN. Must I?

BUMMIDGE. Your cooperation is essential.

(WINKLEMAN *goes.*)

There's a reason why they're all so obliging. Woe unto you when all men shall speak well of you.

(*Enter* BERTRAM.)

But it's woe anyway, wherever you look. Imogen, dear, will you assist?

IMOGEN. Of course, Mr. Bummidge.

VELMA. Where do I come in?

BUMMIDGE. Give the old bat this hat with fruit. Bertram, in my unconscious it turns out you have female characteristics. Wear this dress.

BERTRAM (*accepting*). Female? Curious!

BUMMIDGE. Isn't it? (*He marvels briefly.*)

IMOGEN. Mr. Bummidge, are you sure you know what you're doing?

BUMMIDGE. It is the right thing, my child — whatever *that* is. I feel inward confidence. Aufschnitt . . .

AUFSCHNITT. Am I in the broadcast too? I've never been on television.

BUMMIDGE. Man! That's who you'll be. Repressed, civilized Man. Poor humankind in bondage. Thread in your fingers and chains on your feet.

GALLUPPO. And me?

BUMMIDGE. Sly, smiling, menacing . . . I have it! Bella's father. Grinning, then violent. Yes!

(*Enter* TECHNICIAN.)

TECHNICIAN. Where's the opening setup?

(*Enter* MOTT *dressed as a neighborhood tough.*)

MOTT. Places! Let's have lights.

BUMMIDGE. Louie, iris in on me here, by this statue of Freud.

IMOGEN. I'm dying of excitement!

MOTT. Time! Five, four, three, two, one — you're on.

BUMMIDGE (*begins an attempt at smiling refinement*). Ladies and gentlemen of the psychiatric world. Honored guests. You know me, of course, as a comedian. But today I invite you to put away that old image. Look at this person, one of yourselves, a human being. See this hair, these eyes, these wattles, stubby hands, a heart that beats: Philip Bummidge, sixty years old. Sixty-one years ago I was literally nothing. I was merely possible. Then I was conceived, and became inevitable. When I die, I shall be *im*possible. Meanwhile, between two voids, past and future, I exist. Medically, I seem quite sound, though not in my first youth. Strong as a horse. (*Feels his muscles.*) Twenty-twenty vision. (*Pulls down his underlids.*) Powerful lungs. (*Shouts.*) Hoy! (*Pauses.*) Nothing wrong with the organism, hey? But up here. (*Suddenly gloomy.*) My mind! Inside my skull. My feelings, my emotions. (*Quite tragically.*) My personality, my mind! My mind has a will of its own. This psyche of mine is an outlaw. Can this be the normal human state? Is this what we are meant to be? Oh, my character! How did I ever get stuck with these monstrous peculiarities? Why so vivid within, so dead outside? I feel like a museum of all the perversity, sickness, and ugliness of mankind. Oh, Death, take me or leave me, but don't haunt me any more. But you see, ladies and gentlemen, brothers and sisters, it's because of death that we are individuals. Organisms without death have no true identity. But we are what we are owing to our morbidity. (*In earnest.*) I bless the day when I discovered how abnormal I was. I read all the books and, never forgetting that I was an actor, a comedian, I formed my own method. I learned to obtain self-knowledge by doing what I best knew how to do, acting out the main events of my life, dragging repressed material into the open by sheer force of drama. I'm not solely a man but also a man who is an artist, and an artist whose sphere is comedy. Though the conditions may be impossible, laughter in decay, there is nothing else for me to do but face those real conditions. (*The lecturer.*) A general increase of consciousness in civilized people accompanied by a decrease in the value they attach to themselves and one another is a prime condition. (*Dissatisfied with his own pomposity.*) But rather than lecture, I prefer to illustrate. Let me introduce, briefly, certain friends and relatives.

(*In the following scene, people come forward as called, in their costumes.*)

This is Aunt Velma, who delivered me. This, my tender bride. This is my son, who will represent my father. This proper lady is my sister. This is my colleague, Bertram, a mother figure.

(*Enter* WINKLEMAN *in a Lord Fauntleroy costume.*)

Oh, yes, this is my cousin Winkie, whose mother always dressed him absurdly.

WINKLEMAN. Excuse these knickers — one must humor a client, a man of genius with brilliant ideas.

(*Enter* PAMELA, *wearing her strip-tease costume.*)

BUMMIDGE. This little lady has offered to represent the grandeur and misery of the erotic life. She's something of an expert on this subject. These unfortunates are part of me, and I of them. Now, my method, on the most elementary level, opens a channel to the past. Like that old song (*sings*) "I'm just a kid again, doin' what I did again."

(*All sing in chorus. He leads them forward. The group stands about him.*)

I am convinced that lies are bad art. I reclaim my freedom by acting. I tear down the Bastille of censorship and distortion. No more isolation. Break out of jail! We must leap beyond repression. But look at these miserable creatures. I shall start with one of them, my old aunt. (*Wheels her forward.*) Tante, you bridge many generations, and you have a long memory.

VELMA. Like an old filing case, I am.

BUMMIDGE. Was mine a difficult birth?

VELMA. On your father's scales you weighed fourteen pounds. You gave lots of pain. It was tough, but I pulled you through.

BUMMIDGE (*to camera*). She thinks she's being funny. (*To her.*) — Now, when was I weaned?

VELMA. Late. On the way to Prospect Park, on your mama's lap, your feet were dragging on the floor of the streetcar. You didn't want the breast and your mama said, "All right, I'll give it to the conductor."

BUMMIDGE (*to camera*). An old gag. She's full of them. They're really sadistic threats in comic form. — Now, when was I toilet-trained?

VELMA. My sister and I kept clean houses. As soon as you could sit up.

BUMMIDGE (*somberly*). This is very bad!

MADGE. Was it so serious?

BUMMIDGE. Ah, Madge — my sister, my poor companion in abuse. Terrible! They ruined us. This is horrible information.

BELLA. Don't take it so hard.

BUMMIDGE. I never had a chance. How can I hold my head up?

VELMA. But nobody could keep you clean. You made in your pants. You were a wild, disobedient boy, like your Uncle Mitchell.

BUMMIDGE. Yes, tell everyone about him. (*To television audience.*) She thinks she's irresistible.

VELMA. He played baseball. Shortstop. The bus with his team fell in the Passaic River. It damaged his brains. On the Sea Beach Express, he exposed himself to some girls from the shirtwaist factory.

BUMMIDGE (*to camera*). This is her lifelong patter. Old lobster shells of wit. The meat is gone. — Tell the people more. . . .

VELMA. Then there was Uncle Harold. He was a saxophone performer. On the Weehawken Ferry. During the War, he passed the hat for the boys Over There.

MAX. But he put the money in his own pocket.

VELMA. He needed a start in business. That branch of the family did all right. Furthermore . . .

BUMMIDGE. Enough. She comes on like a charming old thing. From her jokes, you'd never guess what viciousness there was in her.

(VELMA *spreads her mouth with her fingers and makes a horrid face at him.*)

WINKLEMAN (*sternly*). Mother! On the air!

VELMA. Should I say more? Should I tell about Aunt Rose? (*Parodying her own family sentiments.*) All Perth Amboy listened in the street when she sang. Such a woice!

BUMMIDGE. No, enough. Take her away, Winkie.

VELMA. Give me a light, my child. (*Cigar, again.*)

BUMMIDGE. Infinite sadness salted with jokes. But . . . (*Lecturing.*) My method — as follows: I have trained myself to re-enter any phase of my life, at will. By bouncing a ball, rolling a hoop, sucking my thumb, I become a child. When I want to visit the remote parts of my mind, I take to the couch. (*Lies down.*) Doctor, I had a dream. (*As analyst.*) Tell me all about it. (*As patient.*) I dreamt I was at sea in an old shoebox. (*Rising.*) Thus, ladies and gentleman, I was able to isolate a hard core of problems, by adapting the methods of Freud — that Genius! (*Turns emotionally to bust.*) The disease I discovered in myself, I call Humanitis. An emotional disorder of our relation to the human condition. Suddenly, being human is too much for me. I faint, and stagger. (*He enacts the sick man. Holds dialogue with himself.*) "What's the matter, Bummidge? Don't you like other human beings?" "Like them! I adore them! Only I can't bear them." "I love 'em like a dog. So ardent, so smoochy. Wagging my tail. This sick, corrupt emotion leaks out of me." I don't have the strength to bear my feelings. (*Lecturing.*) This is the weakness of my comedy. When the laughing stops, there's still a big surplus of pain.

BERTRAM. He's going to explain about the Pagliacci gangrene.

BUMMIDGE. The Pagliacci gangrene! Caused as all gangrene is by a failure of circulation. Cut off by self-pity. Passivity. Fear. Masochistic rage. Now (*smiling and bowing*), I shall ask you to follow me into the library, where I have prepared an exhibit of charts and diagrams.

(*Exit, followed by the* TECHNICIAN *with camera and by* MOTT.)

GALLUPPO. You think you sell this? I'd walk out. Worst show I ever saw.

MAX. It's like a lecture at the New School, but crazier.

IMOGEN. Every word of it is clear to me.

BERTRAM. Plain as day.

WINKLEMAN. Take it from me, the industry is hard up for novelty. There is something here for the great public. (*Desperate.*) It's got to work.

MAX. If it doesn't, I've lost out on one of the biggest deals that ever came my way. My mother turned it down.

BELLA. Damn right I did.

PAMELA. I want my jewels back, at least. In this getup I deserve some consideration.

BELLA. It's a miracle you can keep them on those skinny wrists and ankles.

PAMELA. Better to be petite than built like a lady wrestler.

BELLA. Petite! Dry bones. You could do a fan dance with fly swatters.

(*They begin to fight.*)

GALLUPPO. Here, break it up. (*Takes a police grip on* PAMELA.)

MADGE. A cat fight is all we need. For heaven's sake, you've got to keep in line. If this fails, Winkie and I stand to lose a fortune.

BERTRAM. Bummy won't fail.

WINKLEMAN (*sweating, he tries to persuade them*). Freud has filtered down to the broad masses. He used to belong to the intellectuals and the upper middle class, but now the proles demand their share of this. As the standard of living rises, people claim the privilege of sickness, formerly one of the aristocratic prerogatives.

VELMA. Listen to my son! I had only one, but with the brains of five.

WINKLEMAN. Look! There's all this machinery of entertainment, publicity. A billion-dollar industry with administration, bureaucracy. It needs fresh material every week. And out there are millions of Americans, asking for nourishment. Bread. The industry gives 'em every substitute it can invent. Faith. I ask you to have a little faith. Haven't I always marketed whatever Bummy dreamed up?

IMOGEN. Mr. Bummidge isn't interested in being marketed.

MADGE. Isn't he? We'll see about that.

VELMA. Wheel me back. Here he comes.

(TECHNICIAN, *led by* MOTT, *comes in with camera.*)

MOTT. One side. Clear it. Get Bummidge as he enters the doorway. Go, camera.

BUMMIDGE. Such, my friends, is the Pagliacci gangrene, crying as you laugh, but making a fortune meanwhile. Now let us have a brief look at my career. At twenty I sing and dance at the Old Trilby. (*Sings and shuffles.*)

"Oh I went to school with Maggie Moiphy
And Maggie Moiphy went to school with me-e-e.
I tried to get the best of Maggie Moiphy,
But the sonofagun, she got the best of me."

(*Another routine.*)

"Lady, lady, put out your can
I think I hear the garbage man."

(*As lady, answering.*)

"But Mister, I don't want any garbage."

(*Lecturing again.*) By 1927 we're at the top of our fields, Coolidge and me. I tap-dance in the White House portico. (*Hoofing.*)

BELLA. I almost burst with pride.

BUMMIDGE (*strutting*). Three agents, two bodyguards, a fleet of Dusenbergs. Five paternity suits in one year. My own cigar vault at Dunhill's next to the Prince of Wales. I charter the Twentieth Century to take me to Saratoga for the races. People laugh at everything I say. "Nice day." (*To group.*) Laugh!

(*They laugh uproariously.*)

You see how it worked. "Nice day."

(*They laugh again. He sneezes.*)

AUFSCHNITT. *Gesundheit.*

BUMMIDGE. Now a dark subject. I should like to re-enact the circumstances of my marriage. I shall represent myself. Bella — Bella . . .

BELLA (*pushed forward*). Yes.

BUMMIDGE. You be Bella. The other characters will emerge as they are needed. Now, Bella, what were the first words that kicked us off into matrimony?

BELLA. The first words? It was on the telephone. I need a telephone.

(IMOGEN, *stooping, out of the way of camera, brings two phones. They ring.* BUMMIDGE *and* BELLA, *back to back, converse.*)

BUMMIDGE. Yes? Hello?

BELLA (*breathless*). Philip?

BUMMIDGE. Yes?

BELLA. I have bad news. I'm six weeks late.

BUMMIDGE. What? What was that?

BELLA. Late! You know what I'm talking about. Do I have to draw a picture?

BUMMIDGE (*to camera*). I wouldn't have understood the picture, either. (*To telephone.*) From that? We were just fooling. We didn't even undress.

BELLA. I admit there wasn't much to it.

MAX. They won't spare me a single detail!

BUMMIDGE. I'll come right over. (*Hangs up and speaks to camera.*) Passion on a grand scale is always safe. It's that miserable, neurotic poking around that causes trouble.

PAMELA. How can he be sure she didn't do it on purpose?

BUMMIDGE. The time is now a beautiful afternoon in May. The Trifflers are having a little party in the garden.

GALLUPPO. We Trifflers are rising in the world.

MADGE. Rising into the upper lower middle class of Brooklyn.

VELMA. Lovely house. Mission-style apricot stucco.

BUMMIDGE. I am sniffing lilacs, unaware that Bella has told her parents she's knocked up. Suddenly old Triffler swoops down and says, "What did you do to my child?"

GALLUPPO (*as old* TRIFFLER). What did you do to my child!

BUMMIDGE (*coaching*). "This you do to a father?"

GALLUPPO. This you do to a father?

BELLA. I stood under the weeping willow, when my mother ran up. (*Tapping* BERTRAM.) She hissed, "Arnold, a houseful of guests! Not now!"

BERTRAM. Arnold, a houseful of guests. Not now.

MADGE. My opinion was that they were framing him. Bella was an aggressive girl.

BELLA (*hotly*). A lot you know! But I recall the moment. My mother shouted —

VELMA. I was there. Your mother shouted, "He's so coarse! Couldn't it be a nice refined boy, you tramp? His habits are filthy. He cleans his ears in public and looks at the wax."

BELLA. She didn't call me tramp!

BUMMIDGE. She did. And she said, "Look how bad his skin is. He must have syphilis."

BELLA. She warned me you'd be a selfish husband. A hypochondriac. A tyrant. And you were. I told Mama, "He's everything you say."

MADGE. But you weren't getting any younger.

BELLA (*fiercely*). I was just a kid. My heart told me to marry him.

MADGE. Her heart! She was out to here, already. (*Indicates a swollen belly.*)

BUMMIDGE. Bella, you love melodrama, and you're happy when the materials of your personality turn into soap opera. You do have a sense of humor, of a grim sort, but you've neglected it.

BELLA. This proves my suffering never touched your heart. You didn't care.

BUMMIDGE. I said to Mama Triffler, "Don't you think I'm too immature to marry? I'm not ready yet."

BELLA. And you started to blubber.

BUMMIDGE. And then you hit me.

BELLA. I said, "Coward! I'll give you something to cry about!" (*She strikes him.*)

BUMMIDGE. (*reels*). Ow! (*Angry.*) This was harder than the first time. (*Holding his cheek.*) This is very rich material.

BELLA. You tried to escape out the gate. "You people are railroading me." We were a respectable family, till we met you. You twisted our behavior into comedy.

MAX. That sounds like the truth.

BUMMIDGE. Your so-called respectability was comical without twisting. Your father tried to throttle me, is that respectable? (*To* GALLUPPO.) Choke me.

GALLUPPO. Wait a minute. What's my responsibility if there's an injury? There's a legal point, here.

BUMMIDGE (*commanding*). My method requires reliving. Choke me.

BELLA. You were just slapped.

(*A* MESSENGER *has just entered the scene.*)

BUMMIDGE (*frantic*). I must have closure. We're on the air. You have to obey me.

GALLUPPO. No!

BUMMIDGE. Somebody — (*To* MESSENGER.) *You* choke me.

MADGE (*pushing the* MESSENGER *forward*). Choke him, and get it over with.

BELLA. Bummy, with all those intellectuals watching, don't be a goddam jerk!

BUMMIDGE (*on his toes, rigid*). Choke me!

MESSENGER (*to* VELMA). Hold this!

(*He brutally chokes* BUMMIDGE, *who falls to his knees.* BELLA, BERTRAM, *and* MOTT *try to drag him away from his victim.*)

WINKLEMAN. His face is getting purple.

IMOGEN. Enough! Stop!

MOTT (*he and* BERT *with difficulty pry the* MESSENGER'*s fingers loose*). This fellow's a killer.

BERTRAM. Who taught you to take life like that?

MESSENGER. He asked for it. I have to grab all opportunities.

MAX. Pop, are you all right?
BUMMIDGE (*feebly*). Tip the boy. . . .
IMOGEN. It's a telegram from Mr. Fiddleman.
MADGE (*grabbing wire*). For Winkleman.
MESSENGER. What's this, a TV show? Is that Bummy? The comic?
WINKLEMAN (*reading*). Great interest, so far.
MADGE. Oh, Winkie!

(MOTT *and* BERTRAM *throw the* MESSENGER *out.*)

BUMMIDGE (*to cameras*). This choking was an orgastic experience, almost. Suffering and agony can be repressive forms of gratification. Under conditions of general repression, that is how it works out. Under these conditions, man conceives the project of changing the external world, and the project of changing himself. There is no other creature that aims to change itself, or discover another kind of life. From top to bottom, each man rejects himself, denies what he is, and doesn't even know it. (*He laughs. He pushes the others and forces them to laugh with him.*) Isn't that funny?

(*General laughter.*)

You, too, Bert.
BERTRAM (*tries to laugh*). Heh, heh!
BUMMIDGE. Bertram is far too sick to laugh. . . . But now, my father has learned of my transgression with Bella, and waits for me on the stoop.
MAX (*as Father*). Outcast! Now you'll marry? On what?
BUMMIDGE. His favorite punishment was to strike me under the nose with his forefinger. Exceedingly castrating. My mother and sister weep in the background, and I am struck.

(MAX *flicks him under the nose.*)

Ow! That hurt. How did you learn to do it? (*He has a nosebleed.*) You see the technique? My father struck me, and now my son. . . . My nose! Oh, I'm bleeding! Give me something! Someone! A rag! Ice! Let me smell vinegar! Bella . . . I'm bleeding. I'm undone!

(BELLA *gives him a handkerchief. He collapses in barber chair.*)

MADGE. Just as things were going good. Take the camera off him.
MOTT. Somebody — do something.
AUFSCHNITT (*in the center of the stage, stunned, frightened as the camera turns on him*). Ladies and gentlemen, my name is Gerald Aufschnitt. I was born in Vienna, also the home of Mr. Freud. I am now Mr. Bummidge's tailor for thirty years. What a wonderful person. He helps me with my troubles. My daughter's troubles, too. I make his

costumes in my little shop on Columbus Avenue. He asked me to play in his show. I was just man, in the grip of relentless suppressions. I was never in a show before. How do I look?

MADGE. It's a fiasco. Wink, get on camera.

WINKLEMAN. Good evening. Yes, we are relatives. Were playmates. My cousin is a man of genius. Without him, my life would have been very empty. It is becoming rare for any person to need any other specific person. I mean, usually, if death removes the one before you, you can always get another. And if you die, it might be much the same to the rest. The parts are interchangeable. But Bummidge is *needed*. . . .

MADGE. Get off with that stuff.

MAX. Pamela! Dance — bumps, grinds — anything!

(BERTRAM *is now before the camera.*)

BERTRAM. By profession I was a zoologist, but got into the exterminating business. For every one of us, there is a rat. One to one. We seldom realize that rats are part of civilization. Rats came from Europe. They couldn't cross the continent until there was enough garbage from the covered wagons. They were pioneers, too. Mr. Bummidge understands. He has taken me on for training and study. He feels I tried to overcome my Oedipal problem by becoming father to myself. That is why I am so stern, why the rats are like children to me, and why I do not laugh. Unless tickled.

(MOTT *tickles him and* BERTRAM *laughs horribly. They push him from the spotlight.*)

MADGE. Pamela, take over.

(PAMELA *performs, something between modern dance and burlesque.*)

BELLA. It's a disaster! This broad will ruin him. I always said it.

BUMMIDGE (*rising from chair*). The bleeding has stopped. Where's the camera? Ladies and gentlemen, a violent father often has terrible effects on a son, if the son idolizes strength. (*He goes toward* MAX *but finds himself entangled in the arms and legs of* PAMELA.) Age twelve. I lose my virginity, as they say. Seduced on the counter of a dairy restaurant by a certain Mrs. Friedmacher. . . . (*Extricates himself.*) Locked in my bosom, a child, a little child who weeps. But now I am ten. The perils of reality surround the boy. He flirts with death on the fire escape, on the back of the trolley. Disease is trying to infect me. Time waits to consume me. The Id wants to detain me in infancy till I become like an ancient Mongolian idiot, old, wrinkled, yellow. I run and hide, steal, lie, cheat, hate, lust. Thus . . . my pursuit of happiness!

MADGE. Winkie, if he rambles on like this, we're sunk.

BUMMIDGE. And now I ask you to witness a pair of solemn events. At this moment I am yet unborn. We are behind the candy store in Williamsburg. A January night. (*Counts on his fingers.*) It must have been January. I don't exist. (*Covers his eyes.*) Oh, blackness, blackness, and frost. The stove is burning. A brass bedstead. And here they are. (*Points.*) My parents, male and female. Two apparitions. Oh! (*He turns away.*)

MADGE. When? Papa and Mama! What's he talking! Bummy, there are limits!

VELMA. Of such things the law should prohibit viewing. Even on closed-circuit.

BUMMIDGE (*pushes* MADGE *aside*). My little sister is sleeping. Unaware. And then (*pointing a trembling hand*) my father takes . . . And my mother . . . Oh, no, Mama, no! Pa! Ma! Wait! Hold it! Consider! Oh, don't do this to me. (*To the audience.*) It's the Primal Scene. Nobody can come between them. The action of Fate. I am being conceived. No, no, no, no, no! Pray, little Philip Bomovitch. Oh, pray! (*On his knees.*) But it's too late. My number is up! Bang! (*Claps hands to head.*) I'm doomed now to be born. May God have mercy on my soul — on all our souls.

WINKLEMAN. Brother! Even the old name, Bomovitch.

BUMMIDGE (*rising, before camera*). And now, ladies and gentlemen all . . . I will ask you to observe the projection of another most significant event. I shall try to penetrate the mystery of birth. I do this in the hope of renewal, or rebirth. This is the climax of my method. I invite you to watch a playlet which attempts to bring together the ancient and the avant-garde. (*To group.*) I have parts for all of you.

WINKLEMAN. Oh, God, now he's a playwright. Meantime, disaster waits for me.

MADGE. I've staked everything on this!

GALLUPPO (*to* MAX). You'll get a bill from me, buddy-boy.

IMOGEN. Here are the parts, Mr. Bummidge.

BUMMIDGE. Hand them out.

PAMELA. I thought it was all impulse.

(*A black cloth has been prepared on the sofa, midstage. There are holes in this cloth for the heads of the chorus. The company dons the cloth,* IMOGEN *assisting,* BUMMIDGE *supervising.*)

MAX. What is this?

BELLA. A Greek chorus?

GALLUPPO. Why am I the Second Voice?

VELMA. I'm no Greek.

(*Final adjustments of the black cloth are made.*)

BUMMIDGE. The title of this presentation is "The Upper Depths," or "The Birth of Philip Bomovitch." Ready . . . get set . . . Go. (*Lies on the sofa.*)

BELLA (*reading*). The babe is in the womb now.

WOMEN. What far-off force presides over this curious particle of matter?

VELMA. O Kronos!

MOTT (*to* TECHNICIAN). Who the hell is this Kronos?

VELMA. Speak, Tiresias. Speak, holy hermaphrodite. Blind, you know the darkness best. (*Continues to smoke her cigar.*)

MEN. The cells of the babe divide.

WINKLEMAN. Seeming chaos. A terrible order.

GALLUPPO. Iron. Proteins.

MAX. The swift enzymes. Transistors of flesh.

PAMELA. Matter torn away from other forms of being.

ALL. Will this be nothing but finite, mortal man?

BELLA. His eyes.

MADGE. Tongue.

PAMELA. Genitalia.

VELMA. His liver.

WINKLEMAN. And his nerves.

MAX. And within the soft skull, a soft mass of white cells which will judge the world.

BELLA. O Transfiguration!

ALL. He is being created.

GALLUPPO. Merely to jest? So that other animals may grin?

MAX. But there is no unmetaphysical calling.

PAMELA. And what is the mother doing? Does she go stately through the slums? Is her mind upon the gods? Does she understand what she is carrying?

MADGE. Not she. No thought, no prayer, no wine, no sacrifices. Only herring, potatoes, tea, cards, gossip, newspaper serials. How far is this Daughter of Man from authentic Being.

WINKLEMAN. The unborn Bummidge, afloat in Stygian darkness.

(BUMMIDGE *floats like an embryo.*)

ALL. He's folding, unfolding, refolding. Now he's a fish.

(BUMMIDGE *enacts the fish.*)

MAX. Dimly he beholds the geologic periods.

GALLUPPO *and* MADGE. The vacant lifeless seas.

BELLA *and* MAX. Things that crawl.

VELMA *and* WINKLEMAN. The ferns, the lumbering beasts.

MAX. From stone, from brine, sucking the seething power of the sun.

PAMELA. Now appears the backbone.

GALLUPPO. The gills.
WINKLEMAN. He's a reptile.
MADGE. A mammal. Higher. Up the vertebrate tree.
ALL. Up! Up! This thing is evolving into a man.

(BUMMIDGE *stands.*)

VELMA. Reason.
WINKLEMAN. Self-regard. Tragic apprehension. Comic knowledge.
BUMMIDGE (*getting back on sofa*). It's great in here. I like it.
BELLA. Blind and dumb, the babe. Sheer happiness — Nirvana!
GALLUPPO. But it can't last. The pains are starting.
ALL. Contractions.

(BUMMIDGE *sits up on sofa. The chorus makes the cloth billow behind him, by degrees more violently.*)

WINKLEMAN. Fifteen.
ALL. Ba-ba-ba-baboom!
WINKLEMAN. Ten.
ALL. Ba-ba-ba-baboom!
WINKLEMAN. Eight!
ALL. Ba-ba-ba-baboom!
WINKLEMAN. Four.
ALL. Ba-ba-ba-baboom!
WINKLEMAN. Two.
ALL. Ba-ba-ba-baboom!

(*The violent swelling of the cloth has put* BUMMIDGE *on his feet.*)

BUMMIDGE. Oh, Mother! Our time has come. (*Knocks as if on a door.*) Mother! (*Stamps his foot.*) Mother! The bag is broken. (*Sharp cry.*) Help! I'm grounded in here. Oh, terror, rage, suffocation! This is expulsion. I hear screams. I'd scream, too, if I could breathe. Tante Velma has me by the head dragging me, dragging me. Take it easy, Tante — I'm choking. Choking. Air, air, give me air. Agony to my lungs! Oxygen! The light is scalding my eyes. (*Newborn, with wrinkled blind face and clenched poor hand, he slaps himself on the behind and gives the feeble infant cry.*) Eh . . . Ehh! (*He squalls like a newborn infant.*)
BELLA. It tears your heart to hear that cry.
MAX. A tyrant. Utterly helpless. Absolute from weakness.
PAMELA. They cut the cord.

(BUMMIDGE *looks about.*)

WOMEN. So this is the world?

MEN. It is the Kingdom of Necessity.
ALL. *Sein! Dasein! Bewusstsein!*

(IMOGEN *presses an inflated balloon to his mouth.*)

BELLA. The breast. She holds him in her arms.
ALL. Bliss.
BELLA. He breathes. He suckles.
ALL. Bliss.
BUMMIDGE. Where do I end, and where does the world begin? I must be the world myself. I'm it. It's me.
MAX. A little moment of omnipotence.

(IMOGEN *pulls away the balloon, which is attached to a long string.*)

BUMMIDGE. So *that's* the way it is!
WINKLEMAN. Only the first lesson of reality.
BUMMIDGE (*raging*). Give it back!

(*The chorus now reads him a lesson.*)

MADGE. Strife.
PAMELA. Disappointment.
BELLA. Loss.
GALLUPPO. Law.
VELMA. Thou shalt not.
MADGE. Thou shalt not covet.
PAMELA. Stifle those horrible needs.
MAX. Bow your head as all mankind must, and submit to your burden.
WINKLEMAN. The war has begun between the instincts of life and the instincts of death.
ALL. *Ave atque vale* . . .

(*With this incantation they go off.*)

BUMMIDGE. Oh, my friends. Men, women, brothers, sisters, all . . . (*He crawls forward.*) You see me now in swaddling clothes. I thought I was born to life, to joy. Not so. I am a sad, vain, tangled thing. I cannot rest in any state. Would it have been better never to be summoned into this world? Should I pray to cease being? I was born once. Can I be born again from my own empty heart? I am one of certain voices entering the world, and have not spoken as I should. I chose to serve laughter, but the weight of suffering overcame me time and again. As I rose to my unsteady feet (*rises*) I heard the sins of history shouted in the street.
BERTRAM. The *Titanic*, sinking.
AUFSCHNITT. Clemenceau goes to the front.

MOTT. Lenin reaches Finland.

(*Sound of bells.*)

BUMMIDGE. Armistice Day, nineteen eighteen. From the abyss of blood, the sirens of peace. I have a vision of bandaged lepers screaming, "Joy, joy!" Twenty million mummy bundles of the dead grin as the child, Philip Bummidge, intuits the condition of man and succumbs for the first time to Humanitis, that dread plague. Being human is too much for flesh and blood. . . .

IMOGEN. He's having one of his attacks.

MAX. Jesus, Pop.

(BUMMIDGE *sinks into his barber chair, covers himself with the sheet.*)

What is he doing?

IMOGEN (*before the camera*). Mr. Bummidge foresaw he might be overcome during this broadcast, being a highly emotional man. As his colleagues, Bertram and I are prepared to spell out essential parts of his program.

BERTRAM (*reading*). "The spirit of Gargantua was captured by totalitarianism. When lampshades are made of human skin, we see that fun is very big in hell."

IMOGEN (*reading*). "Farce follows horror into darkness. Deeper, deeper."

BERTRAM (*reading*). "Sores and harsh pains, despair and death — those raise loud, brutal laughter."

IMOGEN (*reading*). "And what minor follies are there for the comedian to work with? If he tries to be an extremist, he finds the world is far more extreme than he can ever be."

BERTRAM (*reading*). "As the social order extends its monopoly of power, it takes over the fields of fantasy and comedy. It makes all the best jokes."

IMOGEN (*reading*). "Illuminated by Freudian and other studies, Bummidge tries to understand the situation." (*With a soft and graceful gesture of her arm, indicates the figure of* BUMMIDGE *covered by the cloth.*)

BERTRAM (*reading*). "For the spirit of man must preserve itself."

IMOGEN (*reading*). "And can preserve itself only upon a higher level than any yet attained."

BERTRAM (*reading*). "Investigators of sleep know that if you keep people from having dreams at night they begin to be crazy."

IMOGEN (*reading*). "And what is true of dreams is true of laughter, too. They come from the same source in the unconscious."

BERTRAM (*reading*). "So wit and comedy have to be recovered. So the social order does not keep the monopoly."

IMOGEN (*reading*). "Therefore Philip Bummidge, with this bag of money, his last savings, intends to buy, from Franklin Kalbfuss, the Trilby Theatre, which he has made into a butcher shop, and establish there a center, an academy or conservatory of comic art based on the latest psychological principles."

BERTRAM (*reading*). "The characters we are so proud of having, the personalities we show off, the conflicts about which we are so serious (little monsters of vanity that we are, fascinated by the dead matter produced by Ego and Superego), these are the materials of the new comedy. To disown the individual altogether is nihilism, which isn't funny at all. But suppose all we fumblers and bumblers, we cranks and creeps and cripples, we proud, sniffing, ragged-assed paupers of heart and soul, sick with every personal vice, rattled, proud, spoiled, and distracted — suppose we look again for the manhood we are born to inherit."

MAX. The Trilby! He's out of his head, completely. I may have to commit him.

BUMMIDGE (*rising*). I shall now die to the old corn. (*He begins to parody old routines.*) "Do you file your fingernails?" "No, I throw them away."

MAX. He thinks he's back in burlesque.

BUMMIDGE. "Why did the chicken cross the road?" "That was no chicken, Jack, that was my life."

PAMELA (*who has been in the wings, and now enters*). He's flipped.

MADGE (*also coming forward*). His mind was never strong.

BUMMIDGE. "What did the monkey say when he peed on the cash register?" "This is going to run into money. . . ." Farewell, old jokes. (*Waving his arms.*) Fly away, flap-flap, like clumsy old chickens. I am sinking . . . sinking . . .

(BELLA *comes forward, curious, from the wings.* WINKLEMAN *follows.*)

BELLA. What's happening to him?

WINKLEMAN. He looks as if he's dying. . . . Is he?

PAMELA. I never could be sure of anything, with him.

BUMMIDGE (*crawls into the wardrobe basket*). The dark night of my soul has begun. Oh, Lazarus, we are brothers. I die of banality. Lay me in this mirthless tomb, and cover me with corn. Let me hear the laughter of evil for the last time. Oh, demons who murder while guffawing, I have succumbed. (*Reaches for the lid of the basket.*) Consummatum est. It is ended. (*Shuts the top of the basket. He emerges seconds later from the back of the wicker wardrobe trunk.*) But I am Lazarus. I was sick unto death, died, and was buried. Now I await resurrection . . . the word, "Come forth, Lazarus." . . . (*He waits.*) Will no one speak? (*Waits.*) No one? (*Faintly, appealing.*) Someone has got to speak!

IMOGEN (*timidly raising her hand like a schoolgirl*). Come forth, Lazarus.

(BUMMIDGE *rises slowly.*)

BERTRAM. He's being reborn.

BELLA (*bossy, but stirred as well*). Come forth . . . okay already, come forth!

(*They break into Handel's "Hallelujah Chorus" and modulate into the anthem "America the Beautiful."* WINKLEMAN *brings in an American flag.* BUMMIDGE *is raised to the top of the wardrobe trunk.*)

MOTT. Cut . . . time. Time. Cut.

IMOGEN. He kept talking about the Last Analysis. Now I know what he meant. Mr. Bummidge! He's white, fainting. Help!

WINKLEMAN. I'll change and be back immediately. (*Exit.*)

MOTT. What sense of timing! Better than a clock. The broadcast is over.

PAMELA. I have to get out of this costume. Bert, lend me that dress. And I want my diamonds back. Who has them?

MAX (*bending over him*). What's the matter, Dad, is it for real?

BELLA. He's out cold. Emotion really overcame him. Loosen his collar.

TECHNICIAN. Well, that's it. Save the lights. Wrap it up.

BERTRAM. Louie and I will put Bummidge to bed.

(*They carry him out.* PAMELA *follows, unbuttoning* BERTRAM'*s dress from back.*)

MAX (*hurries to telephone*). I've got to see if my deal is still on.

MADGE. No. We're waiting for Fiddleman to call.

(*She and* MAX *pull at the phone. The wire is torn loose.*)

See what you've done! It's disconnected.

MAX. I? You did it!

MADGE. All these preparations. All these shenanigans, and you have to eff it all up. How will Fiddleman reach us?

IMOGEN. And Doctor Ratzenhofer, Doctor Gumplovitch. Mr. Bummidge will be very upset.

MAX. I'll run down, make my call, and phone a repairman. (*Exit.*)

BELLA. It was a fiasco anyway. Pathetic Bummy's always been. It's his charm — boorish and touching, also. But who could take this seriously?

IMOGEN. I have to tell him what's happening, as soon as he comes out of it. (*Exit.*)

MADGE. Bella, I'm bound to agree. And it's a sad, dismal day for me, too. I don't know what we'll do.

BELLA. I know, you hoped to hush up the scandal. That would take dough. But why did you starve those old people?

MADGE. It was Aunt Velma, chiseling. Malnutrition! I didn't know it was that bad. Handling the aged is a hell of a problem.

BELLA. I'd throw you and Winkie to them. Let them prod you to death with crutches and canes.

MADGE. Bella, help. We'll cut you in. You're a business woman. Handled right, this is a really profitable racket.

BELLA. I wouldn't have the heart for it, it's too sordid. . . . Make me a proposition.

MADGE. We have to move fast. There's an inspector who threatens to leak the story to the papers.

BELLA. Throw Aunt Velma to the wolves. Let her take the rap. A year in jail is just what she needs.

MADGE. No, Winkie is sentimental about his mother. . . . Anyway, I agree Bummy washed out. Fiddleman could *never* go for this stuff.

(*Police sirens are heard.*)

What is that?

BELLA. Sounds to me like the cops.

MADGE. Bella, whom do you suppose they want? Us?

BELLA. Get a grip on yourself. . . . What a chunk of money he blew on this today.

(*Enter* WINKLEMAN *in his own clothing.*)

WINKLEMAN. The police are making a terrible racket in the street. Has anyone telephoned?

MADGE. Max tore the wires out. I thought he was going to strike me. Today I wouldn't have minded so much.

BELLA. Winkleman, you know as well as I do Bummy's performance was a bomb.

WINKLEMAN. Ripped out the phone, you say! Fiddleman did send a wire, but that was early. I agree — that broadcast must have emptied the Waldorf. A man of genius turned into a crank is a painful sight. So foolish. And what is his big idea? The Trilby Theatre! So figmentary, improbable, Utopian. I really can't stand these Utopians. I could be sorry for him if I wasn't in such a mess myself.

(*Enter* FIDDLEMAN, *the great impresario.*)

MADGE. Fiddleman!

FIDDLEMAN. I'm here with a police escort.

WINKLEMAN. Now don't be sore, Mr. Fiddleman, we meant it for the best.

BELLA. What are you doing here, Leslie?

FIDDLEMAN. What are you asking? Didn't Winkleman get my wire? I'm here because of Bummy.

WINKLEMAN. Accept my apologies. We had no idea he was so twisted in his mind.

MADGE. Those insane theories.

FIDDLEMAN. What are you talking! I couldn't get you on the phone. He was a sensation!

MADGE. Please, Mr. Fiddleman, don't put us on.

WINKLEMAN. We admit it was a mistake. We're crushed already. Then why punish us with bitter jokes?

FIDDLEMAN. Would I waste time on jokes? This is no joke. He wowed everybody!

BELLA. I can't believe it. From here it looked like a monstrosity. But that's because we're not artists. Bummy is one, so the thing had form.

MADGE. So that's what happened. (*Incredulous, then brightening.*) Winkie.

WINKLEMAN. It worked. I'm vindicated. We're still with it. He'll pull us out of the ditch. (*Lays about with an imaginary whip.*) Pull, dammit, pull!

MADGE. We are saved!

WINKLEMAN. I'll go and fetch him.

MADGE. No, wait.

WINKLEMAN. Yes! Bide our time until we figure out the best way to handle this.

MADGE. How?

WINKLEMAN. I'm thinking. My heart is kicking like a child in the womb. Just because you're corrupt is no reason to quit. I know that now.

FIDDLEMAN. You know I was skeptical. Bummy? A has-been, a waste of time. But everybody was floored by him. The scientists? Don't even ask. And the show-business people, their mouths dropped open. Personally, the fellow just stormed my heart — right here. But what's with your phone? I got a squad-car escort from the police department.

BELLA. Tell us how it came over.

FIDDLEMAN. Beautiful. And the whole Waldorf was in those rooms. Everybody in New York, from caveman to egghead. What excitement! Since Valentino's funeral, I haven't seen such a spontaneous mob. Women kissed the television screens. And strangers were hugging and dancing. They wept with laughter, or else they grinned as they were sobbing — sometimes it's hard to tell. The place was like the deck of the *Titanic*.

BELLA. How could we doubt him? But it's like being in the orchestra. You play oompa-oompa-oompa, but out front it's Beethoven.

MADGE. Winkleman, are you thinking?

WINKLEMAN. I am. With all my might I am!

FIDDLEMAN. And when he was born, people were like fish in a net. Stripers, flounders, lobsters — gasping.

MADGE. What kind of money is there in it?

BELLA. Let Leslie finish.

FIDDLEMAN. Some of the toughest crooks in the industry broke up when he said that being born from an empty heart. They started gushing tears. In a way it was repulsive.

WINKLEMAN. From excess to excess.

FIDDLEMAN. Anyway, the networks, the public, the nation, the American people — they're all his. Where is Bummy?

BELLA. Resting.

(*Enter* MESSENGER.)

MESSENGER. I'm back.

BELLA. I'll take that wire.

WINKLEMAN. I'm his lawyer.

MADGE. His agent. Give it here. (*Opens.*) It's signed Kalbfuss.

(WINKLEMAN *drops a coin in the* MESSENGER'S *hat. Exit* MESSENGER.)

BELLA. Kalbfuss. The butcher who rents the old Trilby property.

FIDDLEMAN. What was that they said about the Trilby, that sagging old joint? It goes back to the Civil War. They used to have boxes with fruits and fiddles on their bellies, like marzipan.

WINKLEMAN. Forget it. . . . Madge, what does the butcher say? Maybe he'll kill the deal.

MADGE (*reading*). "Master, I did not know you were a great genius. Will give lease to property on your terms. A shrine. Should be preserved."

BELLA. He doesn't want it preserved but reopened as a theatre of the soul.

FIDDLEMAN (*loudly*). For Christ sakes! (*Softening his tone.*) What kind of *shtuss* is this from a woman like you, Bella?

BELLA. I'm just repeating what he said. You heard him. A theatre of the soul. People will come up from the audience and Bummy will work with them. They will act out pieces of life. Bummy thinks a man's character is a lot of old junk — rusty bedsprings, busted axles. We should stop carrying all this ridiculous scrap metal around, we —

FIDDLEMAN. Don't get all wound up. What's he going to run at the Trilby, a sanatorium?

MADGE. I pictured a mental spa.

WINKLEMAN. Is that the whole wire?

MADGE. There's more. (*Reads.*) "May I be allowed to work with you? My only wish. A man of blood. Living from dead beasts. Who wishes to be redeemed." Signed "Franklin Kalbfuss."

FIDDLEMAN. You see how he moves the people? A butcher! A lousy butcher!

BELLA. Everybody waiting, waiting, waiting for emotional truth. For even a little sign.

WINKLEMAN. And can recognize it only in absurd form. Now, Fiddleman, we have to move fast. You must have some ideas.

FIDDLEMAN. A hundred million dollars' worth.

(*Enter* BERTRAM, *carrying covered dishes.*)

BELLA. How's Bummy?

BERTRAM. Reviving. Breathing hard, but coming around.

FIDDLEMAN. Who's this?

BERTRAM. I prepared a little spread for after the broadcast. Chopped liver. With my own hands. Try some.

BELLA. Never!

FIDDLEMAN. I already got proposals, option checks. Sponsors were there. Here's one from King Cigarettes — two hundred and fifty grand. Chicken feed. Here's from Imperial Deodorants, half a million.

MADGE. Against what? Give it here.

WINKLEMAN. Let me see this.

BELLA. You must have something in mind, Leslie.

FIDDLEMAN. Of course, I saw it like a flash. Have him do his psychotherapy on TV with famous people — Casey Stengel, Marlon Brando, Artie Shaw.

WINKLEMAN. We'll be smart this time. Incorporate. Put everybody on the payroll. The company will buy real estate to take advantage of depreciation. . . .

BELLA. You'll sell him your lousy old-people's home and get out of the hole yourself. That's an inspiration straight from the sewer. How can you do it to him?

MADGE. Bella, be serious. This is a business discussion.

(*Enter* BUMMIDGE, *led by* IMOGEN; MOTT, PAMELA, *and* MAX *drift in soon after.*)

BUMMIDGE. Imogen, I feel very vague . . . awfully peculiar.

FIDDLEMAN (*confronting him*). Bummy, look. Who is this? *I* am here in your house. Do you know what it means?

BUMMIDGE (*shaking his head*). No. I don't understand.

WINKLEMAN. Come off it! Leslie Fiddleman!

BELLA. Bummy, you were right, and you only.

WINKLEMAN. Not he only. I said he'd make this comeback.

MAX. Comeback? I thought it was a bomb.

MADGE. No. It worked. See for yourself. Here's Fiddleman.

MOTT. So that's why the limousine is downstairs, and the cops, and the big crowd. Bummy, do you hear? We won the sweepstakes! (*To* FIDDLEMAN.) How was the reception? I must have sent a terrific picture.

PAMELA. Oh, lover, I'm so happy for you.

BELLA. We could have been the greatest family in America, on the cover of *Time*, if only the whores let him alone.

MAX. Pop doesn't seem to get it.

PAMELA. The broadcast was a smash.

IMOGEN. What about the scientific reaction?

FIDDLEMAN. There are about fifty of those longhaired guys trying to get in. I asked the cops to hold 'em back awhile.

IMOGEN. That isn't fair! It was all meant for them.

MAX. We've got business. Keep 'em out. Let the family settle first.

BERTRAM. Bummy, you do look strange.

BUMMIDGE. The grave . . .

MOTT. What does he mean?

BERTRAM. He's referring to Lazarus.

BUMMIDGE. I still feel deathy. I feel both old and new.

MADGE. You stunned everybody.

PAMELA. No more living in filth. What a future lies before us!

(BUMMIDGE *eyes her strangely; he seems far removed from them all.*)

FIDDLEMAN. Bummy, what's with the fish eye? Am I a stranger? We've known each other forty years.

BUMMIDGE. Is that so? (*Curiously distant.*) If you say so.

FIDDLEMAN. Of course I say. Since Boys High, on the gymnastic team. You got amnesia?

BUMMIDGE. All that was familiar is strange, and the strange is familiar. Life and death are two slopes under me. I can look down one side or the other. What was I before?

MADGE. Before, during, and after — a buffoon! Bummy dear, please don't fool around. There's so much at stake.

BUMMIDGE. A buffoon! Oh, how unfortunate. Forcing laughs, you mean? Sucking up to the paying public? Oh, my!

MAX. Now, Father! Are you serious?

BELLA. Yes, what is this, Bummy? Are you pulling something?

FIDDLEMAN. What's with him?

IMOGEN. He's gone through rebirth. He may not be the same person now.

BUMMIDGE (*mysteriously remote*). That . . . is the truth.

MADGE. Let's see if he'll deny his own sister.

MAX. Or me.

WINKLEMAN. Let me handle it.

(*All close in about* BUMMIDGE.)

BUMMIDGE. Please — please don't crowd. Oh, don't touch! It makes me cold in the bowels. I feel you breathing on me. See how my skin is wincing. (*He shrinks, draws up his shoulders, warms hands between his thighs.*)

BERTRAM. Step back, step back here. Give him air.

PAMELA (*to* BERTRAM). Hands off! (*To* BUMMIDGE.) You always liked me to touch you.

FIDDLEMAN. What is he? Putting us on?

MAX. He's trying to get away with something.

IMOGEN. Oh, what an unfair accusation.

BUMMIDGE. I'm not the person I was. Something has happened.

MOTT. Like what?

BUMMIDGE. I am drenched with new meaning. Wrapped in new mystery.

MAX. Oh, can it, Pop!

BUMMIDGE. Pop? (*He is mildly curious.*)

MADGE. Well, who are you?

BUMMIDGE. I'm waiting to find out. Chaos swallowed me up, now I am just coming out again.

MOTT. That sounds just great. You can use it in a show. Say, Mr. Fiddleman — anything specific?

WINKLEMAN (*showing him the checks*). A little option money.

MAX. Real dough? Let's see.

PAMELA. Show me those.

BELLA. Come on, Bummy — you know what's happening. The networks want you back.

IMOGEN (*she has found the butcher's wire*). A telegram came from Mr. Kalbfuss. He offers you the Trilby.

BUMMIDGE (*we can't be sure how much he understands*). The Trilby?

FIDDLEMAN. The old vaudeville dump where you used to perform. You said you wanted it back as a theatre of the soul, or something.

BUMMIDGE. Of the soul . . . I don't know what you're doing here. I wish you'd all go. I feel life drifting into me. Drift, drift. (*Laves his bosom with air.*)

MAX. He wants to drive us nuts!

IMOGEN. Don't you understand? He's been transfigured.

MADGE. As a school kid he'd pretend to be blind. He'd stare right through you and he'd stagger around. A whole week he made me feed him with a spoon.

BUMMIDGE. I have attained rebirth. I am in a pure condition which cannot be exploited. Noli me tangere. Noli, noli, noli . . .

FIDDLEMAN (*to others*). Can you guess how much my time is worth? Come on. A figure. Five hundred an hour? Ha! Guess again. I can't stick around here.

BUMMIDGE. I am not certain who I am. . . .

BELLA. We'll tell you. We'll straighten you out. Don't you worry, kid.

BUMMIDGE. Oh, fallen man, as you lie suffering in the profane, longing for what is absolutely real . . .

WINKLEMAN. Now he's a sage. I think I get it. You don't know who you are?

BUMMIDGE. But I do know who I am *not*. How many of you can say that?

PAMELA. Bummy, I am Pamela who loves you heart and soul.

BUMMIDGE (*viewing her*). Souls? Hearts? You?

PAMELA. How can you pretend not to know me?

BUMMIDGE. Pretend? (*To* IMOGEN.) Imogen, take a note. Write, "Weeping is the mother of music."

IMOGEN (*writing*). Yes, Mr. Bummidge.

MOTT. For God's sake!

FIDDLEMAN. He thinks he'll bring me to my knees. Not these knees. Never.

PAMELA. Maybe I deserve to be treated like this. All I know is I love you.

BUMMIDGE. A note, Imogen, a note: "Is pleasure the true object of desire? This may be the great modern error. We will revise Freud some more — respectfully."

PAMELA. Please look at me, dearest Bummy.

BUMMIDGE. I can't see clearly. It's like I have drops of argyrol in my eyes.

PAMELA. Look.

BUMMIDGE. I'll try.

PAMELA. What do you see?

BUMMIDGE. I'm not sure.

PAMELA. I want you to see me, dearest.

BUMMIDGE. Ah, yes.

PAMELA (*trying to control her vexation*). Yes what?

BUMMIDGE. Yes, of course.

PAMELA. What do you see?

BUMMIDGE. A bed. A king-sized bed. And a photograph on the wall. Is it a graduation picture? Is it an ikon?

PAMELA. Darling, a picture of *you!*

BUMMIDGE. Oh, I know who you are. You are the desire I tried very hard to have. How do you do?

PAMELA. Our love!

BUMMIDGE. "Love," but not right. Love, sweet but grimy. Like — I have it. Like eating ice cream from a coal scuttle.

PAMELA. You break my heart, Bummy!

BUMMIDGE. Imogen, a note: "Wouldn't it be better to have a rutting season? Once a year, but the real thing? When the willows turn yellow in March? But only animals are innocent." (*To* PAMELA.) O phantom of erections past, farewell! Bertram, show this lady out. (*He takes the bracelet from* MOTT'*s pocket and puts it in* PAMELA'*s hand.*)

PAMELA. I won't go. (*She resists* BERTRAM *and remains.*)

BELLA. I don't blame you, Bummy. It's high time, too. You don't know her, that's right. But you damn well know me.

BUMMIDGE. I faintly recall . . .

BELLA. The devotion of a wife.

BUMMIDGE. Something unpleasant. Like noisy supervision. Like suffocation for my own good. No, like West Point with a marriage license.

BELLA. What do you mean, West Point!

BUMMIDGE. "A-tten-shun! Inspec-shun! Let's see your nails. Your necktie. Your cuffs. Your heels. Your handkerchief. Lipstick? Where have you been? What did you do? Open your fly — hup-two-three-four. The greatest in America!" Bertram, will you escort this lady to the street?

BELLA. Put a rat-catching hand on me and I'll kick you in the head. (*She remains.*)

MAX. And what about me?

BUMMIDGE. You? I am newborn. . . .

MAX. Aren't you a little infantile for a father?

BUMMIDGE. Aren't you a little old to be still a son? (*To* WINKLEMAN.) I seem to remember you.

WINKLEMAN. You should. I made you great. And I'll make you greater than ever. I'll put you back to work. Because you've made a new discovery. And you have no time to think of the administration, Bummy. You're too creative. Leave it all to me. Please! Be sensible, I beg you.

BUMMIDGE. I definitely remember you. You make linoleum out of roses. You walk over my soul with gritty shoes. Yes, and you have a strange tic. You tell false falsehoods.

BELLA. Some rose!

BUMMIDGE. I may not be the bud of a flower, but neither am I an old rubber plant. (*To* MADGE.) And you, Madam . . . I believe we once played cards together. You got into the habit of cheating, and you cheated and you cheated and you cheated. . . . A note, Imogen.

IMOGEN. Ready, Mr. Bummidge.

BUMMIDGE. "How does the lonely cactus thrive in deserts dry."

MOTT. Bummy, have you flipped?

BUMMIDGE. "It has a mystery to guard. Otherwise, why stand in the sun — why buck the drought, why live with vultures and tarantulas?"

FIDDLEMAN. And me, Fiddleman?

BUMMIDGE (*hand to brow*). Pardon?

FIDDLEMAN. Where are those damn checks — give 'em here. (*Snatches them from* PAMELA *and* MOTT *and thrusts them on* BUMMIDGE.)

BUMMIDGE (*examining them*). Are these yours? I don't want them. Imogen, what I want to know is, where are my colleagues? Where are Doctors Gumplovitch and Ratzenhofer and the others?

IMOGEN. Trying to get up to see you. The police are holding them back.

BUMMIDGE. Police? . . . A note: "They say that tragedy makes us look better and comedy worse than we are. But that is puzzling. In the first place, what are we? And in the second place, what is worse?"

WINKLEMAN. Bummy wants to dump his friends, to try to make it as an intellectual. Yes, he's aiming very high. He wants power. Oh, cousin, look out. You'll shoot yourself in the foot. You shouldn't turn your back on us. In spite of everything, we love you.

BERTRAM. Isn't anybody going to taste my liver?

FIDDLEMAN. All right, Bummy. You've had your fun with me. I am shivering with insults. But okay. Now talk turkey. Those checks are nothing. We'll make millions. You'll be the biggest thing that ever hit the channels. A giant, a healer, a prophet. The man who went down into the hell of modern life and took comedy by the hand and brought it back again to every living room and bar in America. You want the old Trilby? I'll fix it for you. Sumptuous. New everything. Gold urinals, if you like. With the most advanced television equipment, and every night capacity houses.

BUMMIDGE. You make me recall the life I once agreed to live. All that I used to do, when only wind and fury could make flimsy things succeed. With forced breath and tired nerves. And an audience smelling like a swamp of martinis and half-digested steak. Well, of course it earned millions. (*Looks at checks again.*) The world *is* hard up for original inventions.

BERTRAM. Emerson, or was it Elbert Hubbard, said if you invented a better rat trap the world would beat a path to your door.

BUMMIDGE. Or you will be sucked out of your doorway, deep into the boundless universe, as by a vacuum cleaner. So (*to* FIDDLEMAN) as Aristotle said . . .

WINKLEMAN. My God — Madge, I think it's hopeless!

BUMMIDGE. As Aristotle said . . .

WINKLEMAN. Wait, you're overexcited. Sit down. I'll handle it. (*Helplessly.*) Aristotle . . .

BUMMIDGE. As *he* said, get out of here! (*Tears up checks.*) Beat it, the whole gang of you.

MOTT. What?

MAX. No, Father. . . .

MADGE. Are you crazy?

WINKLEMAN. I can't desert you. Abuse me all you like, but I'm too loyal.

BUMMIDGE. Without me you are ruined.

MADGE. Yes, and me. Your sister, I'm losing everything.

BUMMIDGE. Bertram, Bertram, throw them all out.

ALL. No. Keep your hands off. I've got old files. I'll sue.

BUMMIDGE. You compel me to take measures? You refuse to let me be? Bertram, the net.

BELLA. What's happening — what is this?

(*A device appears above.* BELLA, PAMELA, WINKLEMAN, MOTT, MADGE, FIDDLEMAN, *and* MAX *stare up.*)

WINKLEMAN. A net! Duck! Look out!

(*All are caught in the net.* BERTRAM *runs up like the ratcatcher he is to see what he has trapped.*)

BUMMIDGE (*dancing about in excitement*). Out, out! Drag 'em out!

BELLA. You lunatic!

MADGE. He's going to kill us!

IMOGEN. Don't hurt them, Mr. Bummidge, don't hurt them.

WINKLEMAN. Don't destroy a lifelong relationship.

BUMMIDGE. You came between me and my soul. Drag 'em away, Bertram. (*Jubilant.*) Oh, I can't bear to see them suffering. Ha, ha! They break my heart, throw them out.

FIDDLEMAN. I'll bring an action.

PAMELA. Oh, help me!

(BERTRAM *and* BUMMIDGE *drag all in the net through the doorway.* BUMMIDGE *slams the door, and then does a dance with* IMOGEN.)

BUMMIDGE. A new life. A new man. I really am reborn. (*Sprinkles water on his head from water jug.*) I baptize myself.

(BERTRAM *enters from other side.*)

BERTRAM. It worked. Technically perfect.

BUMMIDGE. Just perfect. I could vault over clouds.

BERTRAM (*looking down at scraps of paper*). You tore up nearly a million bucks.

IMOGEN. It had to be done. Bertram, you know it.

BUMMIDGE. No, no, Imogen. I wanted to do it. I did it of my own free will. (*Thinking.*) Or did those people force freedom on me? Now, where is the butcher's telegram? We have things to do. Work, work! Onwards, to the Trilby. We have to tear up the floors and purge the smell of blood. Go, Imogen, and let in my scientific colleagues. They've been waiting. I will put on my toga. The Trilby will be run like Plato's academy. (*Puts on toga, arranges folds.*) The Bummidge Institute of Nonsense. We deserve a modern skyscraper like the United Nations, but the poor, the sad, the bored and tedious of the earth will trust us better for beginning so humbly. And we will train people in the Method and send them as missionaries to England, to Germany, to all those bleak and sadistic countries. I am so moved! What a struggle I've had. It took me so long to get through the brutal stage of life. And when I was through with it, the mediocre stage was waiting for me. And now that's done with, and I am ready for the sublime. (*He raises his arms in a great gesture.*)

Curtain

PART TWO

DRAMATIC CRITICISM

GEORGE MEREDITH

from AN ESSAY ON COMEDY

There are plain reasons why the comic poet is not a frequent apparition, and why the great comic poet remains without a fellow. A society of cultivated men and women is required, wherein ideas are current, and the perceptions quick, that he may be supplied with matter and an audience. The semi-barbarism of merely giddy communities, and feverish emotional periods, repel him; and also a state of marked social inequality of the sexes; nor can he whose business is to address the mind be understood where there is not a moderate degree of intellectual activity.

Moreover, to touch and kindle the mind through laughter demands, more than sprightliness, a most subtle delicacy. That must be a natal gift in the comic poet. The substance he deals with will show him a startling exhibition of the dyer's hand, if he is without it. People are ready to surrender themselves to witty thumps on the back, breast, and sides; all except the head — and it is there that he aims. He must be subtle to penetrate. A corresponding acuteness must exist to welcome him. The necessity for the two conditions will explain how it is that we count him during centuries in the singular number. . . . Life, we know too well, is not a comedy, but something strangely mixed; nor is comedy a vile mask. The corrupted importation from France was noxious, a noble entertainment spoilt to suit the wretched taste of a villainous age; and the later imitations of it, partly drained of its poison and made decorous, became tiresome, notwithstanding their fun, in the perpetual recurring of the same situations, owing to the absence of original study and vigor of conception. Scene 5, Act 2, of the *Misanthrope,* owing, no doubt, to the fact of our not producing matter for original study, is repeated in succession by Wycherley, Congreve, and Sheridan, and, as it is at second hand, we have it done cynically — or such is the tone — in the manner of "below stairs." Comedy thus treated may be accepted as a version of the ordinary worldly understanding of our social life; at least, in accord with the current dicta concerning it. The epigrams can be made; but it is uninstructive, rather tending to do disservice. Comedy justly treated, as you find it in Molière, whom we so clownishly mishandled — the comedy of Molière throws no infamous reflection upon life. It is deeply conceived, in the first place, and therefore it cannot be impure. Meditate on that statement. Never

From "An Essay on Comedy" [1877] by George Meredith, in *Collected Works* (London: Chapman & Hall, 1885–1895).

did man wield so shrieking a scourge upon vice; but his consummate self-mastery is not shaken while administering it. Tartuffe and Harpagon, in fact, are made each to whip himself and his class — the false pietists, and the insanely covetous. Molière has only set them in motion. He strips Folly to the skin, displays the imposture of the creature and is content to offer her better clothing, with the lesson Chrysale reads to Philaminte and Bélise. He conceives purely, and he writes purely, in the simplest language, the simplest of French verse. The source of his wit is clear reason; it is a fountain of that soil, and springs to vindicate reason, common sense, rightness, and justice — for no vain purpose ever. The wit is of such pervading spirit that it inspires a pun with meaning and interest. His moral does not hang like a tail, or preach from one character incessantly cocking an eye at the audience, as in recent realistic French plays, but is in the heart of his work, throbbing with every pulsation of an organic structure. If life is likened to the comedy of Molière, there is no scandal in the comparison.

Congreve's *Way of the World* is an exception to our other comedies, his own among them, by virtue of the remarkable brilliancy of the writing, and the figure of Millamant. The comedy has no idea in it, beyond the stale one that so the world goes; and it concludes with the jaded discovery of a document at a convenient season for the descent of the curtain. A plot was an afterthought with Congreve. By the help of a wooden villain (Maskwell), marked gallows to the flattest eye, he gets a sort of plot in *The Double-Dealer*. His *Way of the World* might be called "The Conquest of a Town Coquette"; and Millamant is a perfect portrait of a coquette, both in her resistance to Mirabell and the manner of her surrender, and also in her tongue. The wit here is not so salient as in certain passages of *Love for Love*, where Valentine feigns madness, or retorts on his father, or Mrs. Frail rejoices in the harmlessness of wounds to a woman's virtue, if she keeps them "from air." In *The Way of the World*, it appears less prepared in the smartness, and is more diffused in the more characteristic style of the speakers. Here, however, as elsewhere, his famous wit is like a bullyfencer, not ashamed to lay traps for its exhibition, transparently petulant for the train between certain ordinary words and the powder-magazine of the improprieties to be fired. Contrast the wit of Congreve with Molière's. That of the first is a Toledo blade, sharp, and wonderfully supple for steel; cast for dueling, restless in the scabbard, being so pretty when out of it. To shine, it must have an adversary. Molière's wit is like a running brook, with innumerable fresh lights on it at every turn of the wood through which its business is to find a way. It does not run in search of obstructions, to be noisy over them; but when dead leaves and viler substances are heaped along the course, its natural song is heightened. Without effort, and with no dazzling flashes of achievement, it is full of healing, the wit of good breeding, the wit of wisdom.

"Genuine humor and true wit," says Landor, "require a sound and capacious mind, which is always a grave one." . . . The life of the comedy is in the idea. As with the singing of the skylark out of sight, you must love the bird to be attentive to the song, so in this highest flight of the comic Muse, you must love pure comedy warmly to understand the *Misanthrope;* you must be receptive of the idea of comedy. And to love comedy you must know the real world, and know men and women well enough not to expect too much of them, though you may still hope for good. . . .

Now, to look about us in the present time, I think it will be acknowledged that, in neglecting the cultivation of the comic idea, we are losing the aid of a powerful auxiliary. You see Folly perpetually sliding into new shapes in a society possessed of wealth and leisure, with many whims, many strange ailments and strange doctors. Plenty of common sense is in the world to thrust her back when she pretends to empire. But the first-born of common sense, the vigilant Comic, which is the genius of thoughtful laughter, which would readily extinguish her at the outset, is not serving as a public advocate.

You will have noticed the disposition of common sense, under pressure of some pertinacious piece of light-headedness, to grow impatient and angry. That is a sign of the absence, or at least of the dormancy, of the comic idea. For Folly is the natural prey of the Comic, known to it in all her transformations, in every disguise; and it is with the springing delight of hawk over heron, hound after fox, that it gives her chase, never fretting, never tiring, sure of having her, allowing her no rest.

Contempt is a sentiment that cannot be entertained by comic intelligence. What is it but an excuse to be idly-minded, or personally lofty, or comfortably narrow, not perfectly humane? If we do not feign when we say that we despise Folly, we shut the brain. There is a disdainful attitude in the presence of Folly, partaking of the foolishness to comic perception; and anger is not much less foolish than disdain. The struggle we have to conduct is essence against essence. Let no one doubt of the sequel when this emanation of what is firmest in us is launched to strike down the daughter of Unreason and Sentimentalism — such being Folly's parentage, when it is respectable.

Our modern system of combating her is too long defensive, and carried on too ploddingly with concrete engines of war in the attack. She has time to get behind entrenchments. She is ready to stand a siege, before the heavily-armed man of science and the writer of the leading article or elaborate essay have primed their big guns. It should be remembered that she has charms for the multitude; and an English multitude, seeing her make a gallant fight of it, will be half in love with her, certainly willing to lend her a cheer. Benevolent subscriptions assist her to hire her own man of science, her own organ in the press. If ultimately she is cast out and overthrown, she can stretch a finger at gaps in our ranks. She can say that she commanded an army, and seduced men, whom we thought sober men and safe, to act as her lieutenants. We learn rather gloomily, after she has flashed her lantern, that we have in our midst able men, and men with minds, for whom there is no pole-star in intellectual navigation. Comedy, or the comic element, is the specific for the poison of delusion while Folly is passing from the state of vapor to substantial form. . . .

The comic poet is in the narrow field, or enclosed square, of the society he depicts; and he addresses the still narrower enclosure of men's intellects, with reference to the operation of the social world upon their characters. He is not concerned with beginnings or endings or surroundings, but with what you are now weaving. To understand his work and value it, you must have a sober liking of your kind, and a sober estimate of our civilized qualities. The aim and business of the comic poet are misunderstood, his meaning is not seized nor his point of view taken, when he is accused of dishonoring our nature and being hostile to sentiment, tending to spitefulness and making an unfair use of laughter. Those who detect irony in comedy do so because they choose to see it in life. Poverty, says the satirist, 'has nothing harder in itself than that it makes men ridiculous.' But poverty is never ridiculous to comic perception until it attempts to make its rags conceal its bareness in a forlorn attempt at decency, or foolishly to rival ostentation. Caleb Balderstone, in his endeavor to keep up the honor of a noble household in a state of beggary, is an exquisitely comic character. In the case of "poor relatives," on the other hand, it is the rich, whom they perplex, that are really comic; and to laugh at the former, not seeing the comedy of the latter, is to betray dulness of vision. Humorist and satirist frequently hunt together as ironists in pursuit of the grotesque, to the exclusion of the comic. That was an affecting moment in the history of the Prince Regent, when the First Gentleman of Europe burst into tears at a sarcastic remark of Beau Brummell's on the cut of his coat. Humor, satire, irony, pounce on it altogether as their common prey. The Comic Spirit eyes, but does not touch, it. Put into action, it would be farcical. It is too gross for comedy.

Incidents of a kind casting ridicule on our unfortunate nature, instead of our conventional life, provoke derisive laughter, which thwarts the comic idea. But derision is foiled by the play of the intellect. Most of doubtful causes in contest are open to comic interpretation, and any intellectual pleading of a doubtful cause contains germs of an idea of comedy.

The laughter of satire is a blow in the back or the face. The laughter of comedy is impersonal and of unrivaled politeness, nearer a smile — often no more than a smile. It laughs through the mind, for the mind directs it; and it might be called the humor of the mind.

One excellent test of the civilization of a country, as I have said, I take to be the flourishing of the comic idea and comedy; and the test of true comedy is that it shall awaken thoughtful laughter.

HENRI BERGSON

from LAUGHTER

What does laughter mean? What is the basal element in the laughable? What common ground can we find between the grimace of a merry-andrew, a play upon words, an equivocal situation in a burlesque and a scene of high comedy? What method of distillation will yield us invariably the same essence from which so many different products borrow either their obtrusive odour or their delicate perfume? The greatest of thinkers, from Aristotle downwards, have tackled this little problem, which has a knack of baffling every effort, of slipping away and escaping only to bob up again, a pert challenge flung at philosophic speculation.

Our excuse for attacking the problem in our turn must lie in the fact that we shall not aim at imprisoning the comic spirit within a definition. We regard it, above all, as a living thing. However trivial it may be, we shall treat it with the respect due to life. We shall confine ourselves to watching it grow and expand. Passing by imperceptible gradations from one form to another, it will be seen to achieve the strangest metamorphoses. We shall disdain nothing we have seen. Maybe we may gain from this prolonged contact, for the matter of that, something more flexible than an abstract definition, — a practical, intimate acquaintance, such as springs from a long companionship. And maybe we may also find that, unintentionally, we have made an acquaintance that is useful. For the comic spirit has a logic of its own, even in its wildest eccentricities. It has a method in its madness. It dreams, I admit, but it conjures up in its dreams visions that are at once accepted and understood by the whole of a social group. Can it then fail to throw light for us on the way that human imagination works, and more particularly social, collective, and popular imagination? Begotten of real life and akin to art, should it not also have something of its own to tell us about art and life?

At the outset we shall put forward three observations which we look upon as fundamental. They have less bearing on the actually comic than on the field within which it must be sought.

The first point to which attention should be called is that the comic does not exist outside the pale of what is strictly *human*. A landscape may be beautiful, charming and sublime, or insignificant and ugly; it will never be laughable. You may laugh at an animal, but only because you have detected in it some human attitude or expression. You may laugh at a hat, but what you are making fun of, in this case, is not the piece of felt or straw, but the shape that men have given it, — the human caprice whose mould it has assumed. It is strange that so important a fact, and such a simple one too, has not attracted to a greater degree the attention of philosophers. Several have defined man as "an animal which laughs." They might equally well have defined him as an animal which is laughed at; for if any other animal, or some lifeless object, produces the same effect, it is always because of some resemblance to man, of the stamp he gives it or the use he puts it to.

Here I would point out, as a symptom equally worthy of notice, the *absence of feeling* which usually accompanies laughter. It seems as though the comic could not produce its disturbing effect unless it fell, so to say, on the surface of a soul that is thoroughly calm and unruffled. Indifference is its natural environment, for laughter has no greater foe than emotion. I do not mean that we could not laugh at a person who inspires us with pity, for instance, or even with affection, but in such a case we must, for the moment, put our affection out of court and impose silence upon our pity. In a society composed of pure intelligences there would probably be no more tears, though perhaps there would still be laughter; whereas highly emotional souls, in tune and unison with life, in whom every event would be sentimentally prolonged and re-echoed, would neither know nor understand laughter. Try, for a moment, to become interested in everything that is being said and done; act, in imagination, with those who act, and feel with those who feel; in a word, give your sympathy its widest expansion: as though at the touch of a fairy wand you will see the flimsiest of objects assume importance, and a gloomy hue spread over everything. Now step aside, look upon life as a disinterested spectator: many a drama will turn into a comedy. It is enough for us to stop our ears to the sound of music in a room, where dancing is going on, for the dancers at once to appear ridiculous. How many human actions would stand a similar test? Should we not see many of them suddenly pass from grave to gay, on isolating them from the accompanying music of sentiment? To produce the whole of its effect, then, the comic demands something like a momentary anesthesia of the heart. Its appeal is to intelligence, pure and simple.

This intelligence, however, must always remain in touch with other intelligences. And here is the third fact to which attention should be drawn. You would hardly appreciate the comic if you felt yourself isolated from others. Laughter appears to stand in need of an echo. Listen to it carefully: it is not an articulate, clear, well-defined sound; it is something which would fain be prolonged by reverberating from one to another, something beginning with a crash, to continue in successive rumblings, like thunder in a mountain. Still, this reverberation cannot go on for ever. It can travel within as wide a circle as you please: the circle remains, none the less, a closed one. Our laughter is always the laughter of a group. It may, perchance, have happened to you, when seated in a railway carriage or at *table d'hôte*, to hear travellers relating to one another stories which must have been comic to them, for they laughed heartily. Had you been one of their company, you would have laughed like them, but, as you were not, you had no desire whatever to do so. A man who was once asked why he did not weep at a sermon when everybody else was shedding tears replied: "I don't belong to the parish!" What that man thought of tears would be still more true of laughter. However spontaneous it seems, laughter always implies a kind of secret freemasonry, or even complicity, with other laughers, real or imaginary. How often has it been said that the fuller the theatre, the more uncontrolled the laughter of the audience! On the other hand, how often has the remark been made that many comic effects are incapable of translation from one language to another, because they refer to the customs and ideas of a particular social group! It is through not understanding the importance of this double fact that the comic has been looked upon as a mere curiosity in which the mind finds amusement, and laughter itself as a strange, isolated phenomenon, without any bearing on the rest of human activity. Hence those definitions which tend to make the comic into an abstract relation between ideas: "an intellectual contrast," "a patent absurdity," etc., definitions which, even were they really suitable to every form of the comic, would not in the least explain why the comic makes us laugh. How, indeed, should it come about that this particular logical relation, as soon as it is perceived, contracts, expands and shakes our limbs, whilst all other relations leave the body unaffected? It is not from this point of view that we shall approach the problem. To understand laughter, we must put it back into its natural environment, which is society, and above all must we determine the utility of its function, which is a social one. Such, let us say at once, will be the leading idea of all our investigations. Laughter must answer to certain requirements of life in common. It must have a *social* signification.

Let us clearly mark the point towards which our three preliminary observations are converging. The comic will come into being, it appears, whenever a group of men concentrate their attention on one of their number, imposing silence on their emotions and calling into play nothing but their intelligence. . . .

. . . .

Before going further, let us halt a moment and glance around. As we hinted at the outset of this study, it would be idle to attempt to derive every comic effect from one simple formula. The formula exists well enough in a certain sense, but its development does not follow a straightforward course. What I mean is that the process of deduction ought from time to time to stop and study certain culminating effects, and that these effects each appear as models round which new effects resembling them take their places in a circle. These latter are not deductions from the formula, but are comic through their relationship with those that are. To quote Pascal again, I see no objection, at this stage, to defining the process by the curve which that geometrician studied under the name of *roulette* or cycloid — the curve traced by a point in the circumference of a wheel when the carriage is advancing in a straight line: this point turns like the wheel, though it advances like the carriage. Or else we might think of an immense avenue such as are to be seen in the forest of Fontainebleau, with crosses at intervals to indicate the crossways: at each of these we shall walk round the cross, explore for a while the paths that open out before us, and then return to our original course. Now, we have just reached one of these mental crossways. *Something mechanical encrusted on the living* will represent a cross at which we must halt, a central image from which the imagination branches off in different directions. What are these directions? There appear to be three main ones. We will follow them one after the other, and then continue our onward course.

1. In the first place, this view of the mechanical and the living dovetailed into each other makes us incline towards the vaguer image of *some rigidity or other* applied to the mobility of life, in an awkward attempt to follow its lines and counterfeit its suppleness. Here we perceive how easy it is for a garment to become ridiculous. It might almost be said that every fashion is laughable in some respect. Only, when we are dealing with the fashion of the day, we are so accustomed to it that the garment seems, in our mind, to form one with the individual wearing it. We do not separate them in imagination. The idea no longer occurs to us to contrast the inert rigidity of the covering with the living suppleness of the object covered: consequently, the comic here remains in a latent condition. It will only succeed in emerging when the natural incompatibility is so deep-seated between the covering and the covered that even an immemorial association fails to cement this union: a case in point is our head and top hat. Suppose, however, some eccentric individual dresses himself in the fashion of former times our attention is immediately drawn to the clothes themselves; we absolutely distinguish them from the individual, we say that the latter *is disguising himself,* — as though every article of clothing were not a disguise! — and the laughable aspect of fashion comes out of the shadow into the light.

Here we are beginning to catch a faint glimpse of the highly intricate difficulties raised by this problem of the comic. One of the reasons that must have given rise to many erroneous or unsatisfactory theories of laughter is that many things are comic *de jure* without being comic *de facto,* the continuity of custom having deadened within them the comic quality. A sudden dissolution of continuity is needed, a break with fashion, for this quality to revive. Hence the impression that this dissolution of continuity is the parent of the comic, whereas all it does is to bring it to our notice. Hence, again, the explanation of laughter by *surprise, contrast,* etc., definition which would equally apply to a host of cases in which we have no inclination whatever to laugh. The truth of the matter is far from being so simple.

. . . .

2. Our starting-point is again "something mechanical encrusted upon the living." Where did the comic come from in this case? It came from the fact that the living body became rigid, like a machine. Accordingly, it seemed to us that the living body ought to be the perfection of suppleness, the ever-alert activity of a principle always at work. But this activity would really belong to the soul rather than to the body. It would be the very flame of life, kindled within us by a higher principle and perceived through the body, as though through a glass. When we see only gracefulness and suppleness in the living body, it is because we disregard in it the elements of weight, of resistance, and, in a word, of matter; we forget its materiality and think only of its vitality, a vitality which we regard as derived from the very principle of intellectual and moral life. Let us suppose, however, that our attention is drawn to this material side of the body; that, so far from sharing in the lightness and subtlety of the principle with which it is animated, the body is no more in our eyes than a heavy and cumbersome vesture, a kind of irksome ballast which holds down to earth a soul eager to rise aloft. Then the body will become to the soul what, as we have just seen, the garment was to the body itself — inert matter dumped down upon living energy. The impression of the comic will be produced as soon as we have a clear apprehension of this putting the one on the other. And we shall experience it most strongly when we are shown the soul *tantalised* by the needs of the body: on the one hand, the moral personality with its intelligently varied energy, and, on the other, the stupidly monotonous body, perpetually obstructing everything with its machine-like obstinacy. The more paltry and uniformly repeated these claims of the body, the more striking will be the result. But that is only a matter of degree, and the general law of these phenomena may be formulated as follows: *Any incident is comic that calls our attention to the physical in a person, when it is the moral side that is concerned.*

. . . .

3. Let us then return, for the last time, to our central image — something mechanical encrusted on something living. Here, the living being under discussion was a human being, a person. A mechanical arrangement, on the other hand, is a thing. What, therefore, incited laughter, was the momentary transformation of a person into a thing, if one considers the image from this standpoint. Let us then pass from the exact idea of a machine to the vaguer one of a thing in general. We shall have a fresh series of laughable images which will be obtained by taking a

blurred impression, so to speak, of the outlines of the former and will bring us to this new law: *We laugh every time a person gives us the impression of being a thing.*

. . . .

The comic is that side of a person which reveals his likeness to a thing, that aspect of human events which, through its peculiar inelasticity, conveys the impression of pure mechanism, of automatism, of movement without life. Consequently it expresses an individual or collective imperfection which calls for an immediate corrective. This corrective is laughter, a social gesture that singles out and represses a special kind of absentmindedness in men and in events.

. . . .

Hence the equivocal nature of the comic. It belongs neither altogether to art nor altogether to life. On the one hand, characters in real life would never make us laugh were we not capable of watching their vagaries in the same way as we look down at a play from our seat in a box; they are only comic in our eyes because they perform a kind of comedy before us. But, on the other hand, the pleasure caused by laughter, even on the stage, is not an unadulterated enjoyment; it is not a pleasure that is exclusively esthetic or altogether disinterested. It always implies a secret or unconscious intent, if not of each one of us, at all events of society as a whole. In laughter we always find an unavowed intention to humiliate, and consequently to correct our neighbour, if not in his will, at least in his deed. This is the reason a comedy is far more like real life than a drama is. The more sublime the drama, the more profound the analysis to which the poet has had to subject the raw materials of daily life in order to obtain the tragic element in its unadulterated form. On the contrary, it is only in its lower aspects, in light comedy and farce, that comedy is in striking contrast to reality: the higher it rises, the more it approximates to life; in fact, there are scenes in real life so closely bordering on high-class comedy that the stage might adopt them without changing a single word.

. . . .

SIGMUND FREUD

from JOKES AND THE COMIC

It is only with misgivings that I venture to approach the problem of the comic itself. It would be presumptuous to expect that my efforts would be able to make any decisive contribution to its solution when the works of a great number of eminent thinkers have failed to produce a wholly satisfactory explanation. My intention is in fact no more than to pursue the lines of thought that have proved valuable with jokes a short distance further into the sphere of the comic.

The comic arises in the first instance as an unintended discovery derived from human social relations. It is found in people — in their movements, forms, actions and traits of character, originally in all probability only in their physical characteristics but later in their mental ones as well or, as the case may be, in the expression of those characteristics. By means of a very common sort of personification, animals become comic too, and inanimate objects. At the same time, the comic is capable of being detached from people, in so far as we recognize the conditions under which a person seems comic. In this way the comic of situation comes about, and this recognition affords the possibility of making a person comic at one's will by putting him in situations in which his actions are subject to these comic conditions. The discovery that one has it in one's power to make someone else comic opens the way to an undreamt-of yield of comic pleasure and is the origin of a highly developed technique. One can make *oneself* comic, too, as easily as other people. The methods that serve to make people comic are: putting them in a comic situation, mimicry, disguise, unmasking, caricature, parody, travesty, and so on. It is obvious that these techniques can be used to serve hostile and aggressive purposes. One can make a person comic in order to make him become contemptible, to deprive him of his claim to dignity and authority. But even if such an intention habitually underlies making people comic, this need not be the meaning of what is comic spontaneously.

This irregular survey of the occurrences of the comic will already show us that a very extensive field of origin is to be ascribed to it and that such specialized conditions as we found, for instance, in the naïve are not to be expected in it. In order to get on the track of the determining condition that is valid for the comic, the most important thing is the choice of an introductory case. We shall choose the comic of movement, because we recollect that the most primitive kind of stage performance — the pantomime — uses that method for making us laugh. The answer to the question of why we laugh at the clown's movements is that they seem to us extravagant and inexpedient. We are laughing at an expenditure that is too large. Let us look now for the determining condition outside the comic that is artificially constructed — where it can be found unintended. A child's movements do not seem to us comic, although he kicks and jumps about. On the other hand, it is comic when a child who is learning to write follows the movements of his pen with his tongue stuck out; in these associated motions we see an unnecessary expenditure of movement which we should spare ourselves if we were carrying out the same activity. Similarly, other such associated motions, or merely exaggerated expressive movements, seem to us comic in adults too. Pure examples of this species of the comic are to be seen, for instance, in the movements of someone playing skittles who, after he has released the ball, follows its course as though he could still continue to direct it. Thus, too, all grimaces are comic which exaggerate the normal expression of the emotions, even if they are produced involuntarily as in sufferers from St. Vitus's dance (chorea). And in the same way, the passionate movements of a modern conductor seem comic to any unmusical person who cannot understand their necessity. Indeed, it is from this comic of movement that the comic of bodily shapes and facial features branches off; for these are regarded as though they were the outcome of an exaggerated or pointless movement. Staring eyes, a hooked nose hanging down to the mouth, ears sticking out, a hump-back — all such things probably only produce a comic effect in so far as movements are imagined which would be necessary to bring about these features; and here the nose, the ears and other parts of the body are imagined as more movable than they are in reality. There is no doubt that it is comic if someone can "waggle his ears", and it would certainly be still more comic if he could move his nose up and down. A good deal of the comic effect produced on us by animals comes from our perceiving in them movements such as these which we cannot imitate ourselves.

But how is it that we laugh when we have recognized that some other person's movements are exaggerated and inexpedient? By making a comparison, I believe, between the movement I observe in the other person and the one that I should have carried out myself in his place. The two things compared must of course be judged by the same standard, and this standard is my expenditure of innervation, which is linked to my idea of the movement in both of the two cases. . . .

Thus a uniform explanation is provided of the fact that a person appears comic to us if, in comparison with ourselves, he makes too great an expenditure on his bodily functions and too little on his mental ones; and it cannot be denied that in both these cases our laughter expresses a pleasurable sense of the superiority which we feel in relation to him. If the relation in the two cases is reversed — if the other person's physical expenditure is found to be less than ours or his mental expenditure greater — then we no longer laugh, we are filled with astonishment and admiration.[1] . . .

Mankind have not been content to enjoy the comic where they have come upon it in their experience; they have also sought to bring it about intentionally, and we can learn more about the nature of the comic if we study the means which serve to *make* things comic. First and foremost, it is possible to produce the comic in relation to oneself in order to amuse other people — for instance, by making oneself out clumsy or stupid. In that way one produces a comic effect exactly as though one really were these things, by fulfilling the condition of the comparison which leads to the difference in expenditure. But one does not in this way make oneself ridiculous or contemptible, but may in some circumstances even achieve admiration. The feeling of superiority does not arise in the other person if he knows that one has only been pretending; and this affords fresh evidence of the fundamental independence of the comic from the feeling of superiority.

As regards making *other people* comic, the principal means is to put them in situations in which a person becomes comic as a result of human dependence on external events, particularly on social factors, without regard to the personal characteristics of the individual concerned — that is to say, by employing the comic of situation. This putting of someone in a comic situation may be a *real* one (a practical joke) — by sticking out a leg so that someone trips over it as though he were clumsy, by making him seem stupid by exploiting his credulity, or trying to convince him of something nonsensical, and so on — or it may be simulated by speech or play. The aggressiveness, to which making a person comic usually ministers, is much assisted by the fact that the comic pleasure is independent of the reality of the comic situation, so that everyone is in fact exposed, without any defence, to being made comic.

. . . .

Every theory of the comic is objected to by its critics on the score that its definition overlooks what is essential to the comic: 'The comic is based on a contrast between ideas.' 'Yes, in so far as the contrast has a comic and not some other effect.' 'The feeling of the comic arises from the disappointment of an expectation.' 'Yes, unless the disappointment is in fact a distressing one.' No doubt the objections are justified; but we shall be over-estimating them if we conclude from them that the essential feature of the comic has hitherto escaped detection. What impairs the universal validity of these definitions are conditions which are indis-

[1] The contradictoriness with which the determining conditions of the comic are pervaded — the fact that sometimes an excess and sometimes an insufficiency seems to be the source of comic pleasure — has contributed no little to the confusion of the problem. Cf. Lipps (1898, 47).

pensable for the generating of comic pleasure; but we do not need to look for the essence of the comic in them. In any case, it will only become easy for us to dismiss the objections and throw light on the contradictions to the definitions of the comic if we suppose that the origin of comic pleasure lies in a comparison of the difference between two expenditures. Comic pleasure and the effect by which it is known — laughter — can only come about if this difference is unutilizable and capable of discharge. We obtain no pleasurable effect but at most a transient sense of pleasure in which the characteristic of being comic does not emerge, if the difference is put to another use as soon as it is recognized. Just as special contrivances have to be adopted in the case of jokes in order to prevent the use elsewhere of the expenditure that is recognized as superfluous, so, too, comic pleasure can only appear in circumstances that guarantee this same condition. For this reason occasions on which these differences in expenditure occur in our ideational life are uncommonly numerous, but the occasions on which the comic emerges from those differences are relatively quite rare.

. . . .

CHRISTOPHER FRY

COMEDY

A friend once told me that when he was under the influence of ether he dreamed he was turning over the pages of a great book, in which he knew he would find, on the last page, the meaning of life. The pages of the book were alternately tragic and comic, and he turned page after page, his excitement growing, not only because he was approaching the answer but because he couldn't know, until he arrived, on which side of the book the final page would be. At last it came: the universe opened up to him in a hundred words: and they were uproariously funny. He came back to consciousness crying with laughter, remembering everything. He opened his lips to speak. It was then that the great and comic answer plunged back out of his reach.

If I had to draw a picture of the person of Comedy it is so I should like to draw it: the tears of laughter running down the face, one hand still lying on the tragic page which so nearly contained the answer, the lips about to frame the great revelation, only to find it had gone as disconcertingly as a chair twitched away when we went to sit down. Comedy is an escape, not from truth but from despair: a narrow escape into faith. It believes in a universal cause for delight, even though knowledge of the cause is always twitched away from under us, which leaves us to rest on our own buoyancy. In tragedy every moment is eternity; in comedy eternity is a moment. In tragedy we suffer pain; in comedy pain is a fool, suffered gladly.

Charles Williams once said to me — indeed it was the last thing he said to me: he died not long after: and it was shouted from the tailboard of a moving bus, over the heads of pedestrians and bicyclists outside the Midland Station, Oxford — "When we're dead we shall have the sensation of having enjoyed life altogether, whatever has happened to us." The distance between us widened, and he leaned out into the space so that his voice should reach me: "Even if we've been murdered, what a pleasure to have been capable of it!"; and, having spoken the words for comedy, away he went like the revelation which almost came out of the ether.

He was not at all saying that everything is for the best in the best of all possible worlds. He was saying — or so it seems to me — that there is an angle of experience where the dark is distilled into light: either here or hereafter, in or out of time: where our tragic fate finds itself with perfect pitch, and goes straight to the key which creation was composed in. And comedy senses and reaches out to this experience. It says, in effect, that groaning as we may be, we move in the figure of a dance, and, so moving, we trace the outline of the mystery.

Laughter did not come by chance, but how or why it came is beyond comprehension, unless we think of it as a kind of perception. The human animal, beginning to feel his spiritual inches, broke in onto an unfamiliar tension of life, where laughter became inevitable. But how? Could he, in his first unlaughing condition, have contrived a comic view of life and then developed the strange rib-shaking response? Or is it not more likely that when he was able to grasp the tragic nature of time he was of a stature to sense its comic nature also; and, by the experience of tragedy and the intuition of comedy, to make his difficult way? The difference between tragedy and comedy is the difference between experience and intuition. In the experience we strive against every condition of our animal life: against death, against the frustration of ambition, against the instability of human love. In the intuition we trust the arduous eccentricities we're born to, and see the oddness of a creature who has never got acclimatized to being created. Laughter inclines me to know that man is essential spirit; his body, with its functions and accidents and frustrations, is endlessly quaint and remarkable to him; and though comedy accepts our position in time, it barely accepts our posture in space.

The bridge by which we cross from tragedy to comedy and back again is precarious and narrow. We find ourselves in one or the other by the turn of a thought; a turn such as we make when we turn from speaking to listening. I know that when I set about writing a comedy the idea presents itself to me first of all as tragedy. The characters press on to the theme with all their divisions and perplexities heavy about them; they are already entered for the race to doom, and good and evil are an infernal tangle skinning the fingers that try to unravel them. If the characters were not qualified for tragedy there would be no comedy, and to some extent I have to cross the one before I can light on the other. In a century less flayed and quivering we might reach it more directly; but not now, unless every word we write is going to mock us. A bridge has to be crossed, a thought has to be turned. Somehow the characters have to unmortify themselves: to affirm life and assimilate death and preserve in joy. Their hearts must be as determined as the phoenix; what burns must also light and renew: not by a vulnerable optimism but by a hard-won maturity of delight, by the intuition of comedy, an active patience declaring the solvency of good. The Book of Job is the great reservoir of comedy. "But there is a spirit in man . . . Fair weather cometh out of the north . . . The blessing of him that was ready to perish came upon me: And I caused the widow's heart to sing for joy."

I have come, you may think, to the verge of saying that comedy is greater than tragedy. On the verge I stand and go no further. Tragedy's experience hammers against the mystery to make a breach which would admit the whole triumphant answer. Intuition has no such potential. But there are times in the state of man when comedy has a special worth, and the present is one of them: a time when the loudest faith has been faith in a trampling materialism, when literature has been thought unrealistic which did not mark and remark our poverty and doom. Joy (of a kind) has been all on the devil's side, and one of the necessities of our time is to redeem it. If not, we are in poor sort to meet the circumstances, the circumstances being the contention of death with life, which is to say evil with good, which is to say desolation with delight. Laughter may seem to be only like an exhalation of air, but out of that air we came; in the beginning we inhaled it; it is a truth, not a fantasy, a truth voluble of good which comedy stoutly maintains.

WYLIE SYPHER

from THE MEANINGS OF COMEDY

I. Our New Sense of the Comic

Doubtless Meredith and Bergson were alike wearied by the "heavy moralizings" of the nineteenth century, with its "terrific tonnage," and thus sought relief in comedy of manners. For both really confine their idea of comedy within the range of comedy of manners; and they have given us our finest, most sensitive theory of that form. Comedy, says Bergson, is a game — a game that imitates life. And in writing the introduction to *The Egoist*, Meredith thinks of this game as dealing with human nature in the drawing room "where we have no dust of the struggling outer world, no mire, no violent crashes." The aftertaste of laughter may be bitter, Bergson grants, but comedy is itself only "a slight revolt on the surface of social life." Its gaiety happens like froth along a beach, for comedy looks at man from the outside: "It will go no farther."

For us, today, comedy goes a great deal farther — as it did for the ancients with their cruel sense of the comic. Indeed, to appreciate Bergson and Meredith we must see them both in a new perspective, now that we have lived amid the "dust and crashes" of the twentieth century and have learned how the direst calamities that befall man seem to prove that human life at its depths is inherently absurd. The comic and the tragic views of life no longer exclude each other. Perhaps the most important discovery in modern criticism is the perception that comedy and tragedy are somehow akin, or that comedy can tell us many things about our situation even tragedy cannot. At the heart of the nineteenth century Dostoevsky discovered this, and Søren Kierkegaard spoke as a modern man when he wrote that the comic and the tragic touch one another at the absolute point of infinity — at the extremes of human experience, that is. Certainly they touch one another in the naïve art of Paul Klee, whose "little scrawls" tell the ridiculous suffering of modern man. Klee adopts the child's drawing because there is a painful wisdom in the hobgoblin laughter of children: "The more helpless they are, the more instructive are the examples they offer us." The features of modern man, whose soul is torn with alarm, are to be seen in Klee's daemonic etchings, Perseus, The Triumph of Wit Over Suffering, of which the artist himself said: "A laugh is mingled with the deep lines of pain and finally gains the upper hand. It reduces to absurdity the unmixed suffering of the Gorgon's head, added at the side. The face is without nobility — the skull shorn of its serpentine adornment except for one ludicrous remnant." In our sculpture, too, the image of modern man is reduced to absurdity — in, for example, Giacometti's figures, worn thin to naked nerve patterns and racked by loneliness.

Our comedy of manners is a sign of desperation. Kafka's novels are a ghastly comedy of manners showing how the awkward and hopelessly maladroit hero, K, is inexorably an "outsider" struggling vainly somehow to "belong" to an order that is impregnably closed by some inscrutable authority. Kafka transforms comedy of manners to pathos by looking, or feeling, from the angle of the alien soul. He treats comedy of manners from the point of view of Dostoevsky's "underground man," and his heroes are absurd because their efforts are all seen from below, and from within. In his notebooks, Kafka described the anxiety with which his characters try to bear up under a perpetual judgment life passes upon them: "Watching, fearing, hoping, the answer steals round the question, peers despairingly in her enigmatic face, follows her through the maddest paths, that is, the paths leading farthest away from the answer." Kafka is a modern Jeremiah laughing in feverish merriment, prophetically writing the incredible — the depraved — comedy of our concentration camps, which are courts where the soul of contemporary man undergoes an absurd Trial by Ordeal. His comedy reaches the stage of the inarticulate, as tragedy does when Lear frets about the button.

Our new appreciation of the comic grows from the confusion in modern consciousness, which has been sadly wounded by the politics of power, bringing with it the ravage of explosion, the atrocious pain of inquisitions, the squalor of labor camps, and the efficiency of big lies. Wherever man has been able to think about his present plight he has felt "the suction of the absurd." He has been forced to see himself in unheroic positions. In his sanest moments the modern hero is aware that he is J. Alfred Prufrock, or Osric, an attendant lord — "Almost, at times, the Fool." Or else Sweeney, the apeneck, seeking low pleasures while death and the raven drift above.

We have, in short, been forced to admit that the absurd is more than ever inherent in human existence: that is, the irrational, the inexplicable, the surprising, the nonsensical — in other words, the comic. One of the evidences of the absurd is our "dissociation of sensibility," with the ironic lack of relation between one feeling and another; and the artist now must, as Eliot once said, accept the chaos which serves for our life, span the unstable consciousness of the ordinary man: "The latter falls in love or reads Spinoza, and these two experiences have nothing to do with each other, or with the noise of the typewriter or the smell of cooking." The fragmentary lives we live are an existential comedy, like the intense schizoid lives of Dostoevsky's characters. In *The Brothers Karamazov*, Ivan says, "Let me tell you that the absurd is only too necessary on earth.

The world stands on absurdities, and perhaps nothing would have come to pass without them." In our modern experiences the ethical "golden mean" seems to have broken down, and man is left face to face with the preposterous, the trivial, the monstrous, the inconceivable. The modern hero lives amid irreconcilables which, as Dostoevsky suggests, can be encompassed only by religious faith — or comedy.

The sense of the absurd is at the root of our characteristic philosophy — existentialism. The existential religious hero is Kierkegaard, who wrote "In truth, no age has so fallen victim to the comic as this." Kierkegaard, like Kafka, finds that "the comical is present in every stage of life, for wherever there is life there is contradiction, and wherever there is contradiction the comical is present." Kierkegaard's highest comedy is the comedy of faith; since the religious man is the one who knows by his very existence that there is an endless, yawning difference between God and man, and yet he has the infinite, obsessive passion to devote himself to God, who is all, whereas man is nothing. Without God man does not exist; thus "the more thoroughly and substantially a human being exists, the more he will discover the comical." Finite man must take the full risk of encountering an infinite God: "Existence itself, the act of existing, is a striving, and is both pathetic and comic in the same degree." Faith begins with a sense of "the discrepancy, the contradiction, between the infinite and the finite, the eternal and that which becomes." So the highest form of comedy is that "the infinite may move within a man, and no one, no one be able to discover it through anything appearing outwardly." The earnestness of one's faith is tested by one's "sensitiveness to the comical," for God is all and man is nothing, and man must come to terms with God. If one exists as a human being, he must be hypersensitive to the absurd; and the most absurd contradiction of all is that man must risk everything without insurance against losing everything. This is precisely what ordinary "Christians" refuse to do, Kierkegaard finds; they wish to find a "safe" way to salvation, to find God without being tormented, and to base their faith on what is probable, reasonable, assured. This is itself ludicrous — the despicable comedy of "Christendom," which requires religion to be comforting and "tranquilizing." Even in his religious life man is always being confronted with the extreme hazard in the guise of the absurd.

This sense of having to live amid the irrational, the ludicrous, the disgusting, or the perilous has been dramatized by the existentialists; and it has also been boldly exploited by propagandists and those who seize power by using "the big lie," that most cynical form of modern political comedy. For all our science, we have been living through an age of Un-reason, and have learned to submit to the Improbable, if not to the Absurd. And comedy is, in Gautier's words, a logic of the absurd.

. . . .

SUSANNE K. LANGER

from THE COMIC RHYTHM

. . . .

It is commonly assumed that comedy and tragedy have the same fundamental form, but differ in point of view — in the attitude the poet and his interpreters take, and the spectators are invited to take, toward the action.[1] But the difference really goes deeper than surface treatment (*i.e.*, relative levity or pathos). It is structural and radical. Drama abstracts from reality the fundamental forms of consciousness: the first reflection of natural activity in sensation, awareness, and expectation, which belongs to all higher creatures and might be called, therefore, the pure sense of life; and beyond that, the reflection of an activity which is at once more elaborate, and more integrated, having a beginning, efflorescence, and end — the personal sense of life, or self-realization. The latter probably belongs only to human beings, and to them in varying measure.

The pure sense of life is the underlying feeling of comedy, developed in countless different ways. To give a general phenomenon one name is not to make all its manifestations one thing, but only to bring them conceptually under one head. Art does not generalize and classify; art sets forth the individuality of forms which discourse, being essentially general, has to suppress. The sense of life is always new, infinitely complex, therefore infinitely variable in its possible expressions. This sense, or "enjoyment" as Alexander would call it,[2] is the realization in direct feeling of what sets organic nature apart from inorganic: self-preservation, self-restoration, functional tendency, purpose. Life is teleological, the rest of nature is, apparently, mechanical; to maintain the pattern of vitality in a non-living universe is the most elementary instinctual purpose. An orga-

Reprinted with the permission of Charles Scribner's Sons from *Feeling and Form*, pages 327–329, 330–331, and 349–350, by Susanne Langer. Copyright 1953 Charles Scribner's Sons. [Footnotes have been renumbered.]

[1] Cf., for instance, the letters of Athene Seyler and Stephen Haggard, published under the title: *The Craft of Comedy.* Miss Seyler writes: ". . . comedy is simply a point of view. It is a comment on life from outside, an observation on human nature. . . . Comedy seems to be the standing outside a character or situation and pointing out one's delight in certain aspects of it. For this reason it demands the cooperation of . . . the audience and is in essence the same as recounting a good story over the dining-table." (p. 9.)

[2] S. Alexander, *Space, Time and Deity.* See Vol. I, p. 12.

nism tends to keeps its equilibrium amid the bombardment of aimless forces that beset it, to regain equilibrium when it has been disturbed, and to pursue a sequence of actions dictated by the need of keeping all its interdependent parts constantly renewed, their structure intact. Only organisms have needs; lifeless objects whirl or slide or tumble about, are shattered, struck together, piled up, without showing any impulse to return to some pre-eminent condition and function. But living things strive to persist in a particular chemical balance, to maintain a particular temperature, to repeat particular functions, and to develop along particular lines, achieving a growth that seems to be preformed in their earliest, rudimentary, protoplasmic structure.

That is the basic biological pattern which all living things share: the round of conditioned and conditioning organic processes that produces the life rhythm. When this rhythm is disturbed, all activities in the total complex are modified by the break; the organism as a whole is out of balance. But, within a wide range of conditions, it struggles to retrieve its original dynamic form by overcoming and removing the obstacle, or if this proves impossible, it develops a slight variation of its typical form and activity and carries on life with a new balance of functions — in other words, it adapts itself to the situation. A tree, for instance, that is bereft of the sunshine it needs by the encroachment of other trees, tends to grow tall and thin until it can spread its own branches in the light. A fish that has most of its tail bitten off partly overcomes the disturbance of its locomotion patterns by growing new tissue, replacing some of the tail, and partly adapts to its new condition by modifying the normal uses of its fins, swimming effectively without trying to correct the list of its whole body in the water, as it did at first.

But the impulse to survive is not spent only in defense and accommodation; it appears also in the varying power of organisms to seize on opportunities. Consider how chimney swifts, which used to nest in crevasses among rocks, have exploited the products of human architecture, and how unfailingly mice find the warmth and other delights of our kitchens. All creatures live by opportunities, in a world fraught with disasters. That is the biological pattern in most general terms.

. . . .

Mankind has its rhythm of animal existence, too — the strain of maintaining a vital balance amid the alien and impartial chances of the world, complicated and heightened by passional desires The pure sense of life springs from that basic rhythm, and varies from the composed well-being of sleep to the intensity of spasm, rage, or ecstasy. But the process of living is incomparably more complex for human beings than for even the highest animals; man's world is, above all, intricate and puzzling. The powers of language and imagination have set it utterly apart from that of other creatures. In human society an individual is not, like a member of a herd or a hive, exposed only to others that visibly or tangibly surround him, but is consciously bound to people who are absent, perhaps far away, at the moment. Even the dead may still play into his life. His awareness of events is far greater than the scope of his physical perceptions. Symbolic construction has made this vastly involved and extended world: and mental adroitness is his chief asset for exploiting it. The pattern of his vital feeling, therefore, reflects his deep emotional relation to those symbolic structures that are his realities, and his instinctual life modified in almost every way by thought — a brainy opportunism in face of an essentially dreadful universe.

This human life-feeling is the essence of comedy. It is at once religious and ribald, knowing and defiant, social and freakishly individual. The illusion of life which the comic poet creates is the oncoming future fraught with dangers and opportunities, that is, with physical or social events occurring by chance and building up the coincidences with which individuals cope according to their lights. This ineluctable future — ineluctable because its countless factors are beyond human knowledge and control — is Fortune. Destiny in the guise of Fortune is the fabric of comedy; it is developed by comic action, which is the upset and recovery of the protagonist's equilibrium, his contest with the world and his triumph by wit, luck, personal power, or even humorous, or ironical, or philosophical acceptance of mischance. Whatever the theme — serious and lyrical as in *The Tempest*, coarse slapstick as in the *Schwänke* of Hans Sachs, or clever and polite social satire — the immediate sense of life is the underlying feeling of comedy, and dictates its rhythmically structured unity, that is to say its organic form.

Comedy is an art form that arises naturally wherever people are gathered to celebrate life, in spring festivals, triumphs, birthdays, weddings, or initiations. For it expresses the elementary strains and resolutions of animate nature, the animal drives that persist even in human nature, the delight man takes in his special mental gifts that make him the lord of creation; it is an image of human vitality holding its own in the world amid the surprises of unplanned coincidence. The most obvious occasions for the performance of comedies are thanks or challenges to fortune. What justifies the term "Comedy" is not that the ancient ritual procession, the Comus, honoring the god of that name, was the source of this great art form — for comedy has arisen in many parts of the world, where the Greek god with his particular worship was unknown — but that the Comus was a fertility rite, and the god it celebrated a fertility god, a symbol of perpetual rebirth, eternal life.

. . . .

The same impulse that drove people, even in prehistoric times, to enact fertility rites and celebrate all phases of their biological existence, sustains their eternal interest in comedy. It is in the nature of comedy to be erotic, risqué, and sensuous if not sensual, impious, and even wicked. This assures it a spontaneous emotional interest, yet a dangerous one: for it is easy and tempting to command an audience by direct stimulation of feeling and fantasy, not by artistic power. But where the formulation of feeling is really achieved, it probably reflects the whole development of mankind and man's world, for feeling is the intaglio image of reality. The sense of precariousness that is the typical tension of light comedy was undoubtedly developed in the eternal struggle with chance that every farmer knows only too well — with weather, blights, beasts, birds, and beetles. The embarrassments, perplexities and mounting panic which characterize that favorite genre, comedy of manners, may still reflect the toils of ritual and taboo that complicated the caveman's existence. Even the element of aggressiveness in comic action serves to develop a fundamental trait of the comic rhythm — the deep cruelty of it, as all life feeds on life. There is no biological truth that feeling does not reflect, and that good comedy, therefore, will not be prone to reveal.

But the fact that the rhythm of comedy is the basic rhythm of life does not mean that biological existence is the "deeper meaning" of all its themes, and that to understand the play is to interpret all the characters as symbols and the story as a parable, a disguised rite of spring or fertility magic, performed four hundred and fifty times on Broadway. The stock characters are probably symbolic both in origin and in appeal. There are such independently symbolic factors, or residues of them, in all the arts,[3] but their value for art lies in the degree to which their significance can be "swallowed" by the single symbol, the art work. Not the derivation of personages and situations, but of the rhythm of "felt life" that the poet puts upon them, seems to me to be of artistic importance: the essential comic feeling, which is the sentient aspect of organic unity, growth, and self-preservation.

[3] *E.g.*, the symbolization of the zodiac in some sacred architecture, of our bodily orientation in the picture plane, or of walking measure, a primitive measure of actual time, in music. But a study of such non-artistic symbolic functions would require a monograph.

ERIC BENTLEY

from THE LIFE OF THE DRAMA

. . . .

Tragedy and Comedy: Some Generalizations

We conventionally consider comedy a gay and lighthearted form of art, and we regard any contrasting element as secondary, an undertone, an interruption, an exception. I am proposing, instead, to regard misery as the basis of comedy and gaiety as an ever-recurring transcendence. Seen in this way, comedy, like tragedy, is a way of trying to cope with despair, mental suffering, guilt, and anxiety. But not the same way. The tragic injunction, in the words of Stein in *Lord Jim,* is: "In the destructive element, immerse!" It is: Walk, like Rilke, with death inside you! Take terror by the hand! More prosaically put: accept the obstacles life places in your way, and confront them! Now, of course, the comic stance is comparatively opportunistic. Its strategy is to evade and elude the enemy, rather than to tackle him. Inevitably the moralists will say that where tragedy is heroic and sublime, comedy is cowardly and frivolous — like Falstaff, its banner carrier. Serving survival better than morals, and traditionally hostile to the professional moralists, it will get better marks in biology than in religion. But since the goods it advertises are definitely pleasures, though it may lack champions, it can never lack customers.

The pleasures it peddles are, in the first instance, those of farce; for the higher forms include the lower. But, just as the satisfactions of tragedy transcend those of melodrama, so those of comedy transcend those of farce. I described in the last chapter how, in tragedy, fear turns to awe. And awe, whatever its intellectual content, if any, is an affirmative feeling, an inspired and numinous feeling, bordering upon ecstasy. The intensity and beauty of awe are in direct ratio to the quantity of horror overcome. Now it is much the same with that higher pleasure of comedy which we call joy. We can receive it only from an author in whom we sense joy's opposite. The comic dramatist's starting point is misery; the joy at his destination is a superb and thrilling transcendence. Given the misery of the human condition in general, what could be more welcome?

Tragedy is one long lament. Not restrained or elegiac but plangent and full-throated, it speaks all the pity of life and the terror. The comic poet does not speak his feelings directly but veils them, contradicts them with pranks or elegancies. It is not necessarily the feelings themselves that differ from those of tragedy, it can rather be the way they are veiled. Comedy is indirect, ironical. It says fun when it means misery. And when it lets the misery show, it is able to transcend it in joy.

All kinds of things have been said about the ending of *The Misanthrope*, but no one that I heard of ever suggested that Alceste will kill himself. He might be a more consistent character if he did. But it is tragic characters who are consistent in that way. "We are people," says Jean Anouilh's Antigone, "who ask questions right up to the end." That is just what Sophocles's Oedipus does despite Jocasta's warnings. In tragedy, but by no means in comedy, the self-preservation instinct is overruled.

At the core of any good tragedy is a profound disturbance of the human equilibrium. This is transcended, at least aesthetically, in the tragic poem itself; and such aesthetic transcendence argues a kind of courage. It is not so clear that each comedy reflects a particular experience of this kind. One cannot tell, because even if the experience were there, comedy would shield it from sight. What one can tell is that the comic writer knows about such things in his bones.

The tragic poet writes from a sense of crisis. It would never be hard to believe of any tragedy that it sprang from a particular crisis in the life of its author. The comic poet is less apt to write out of a particular crisis than from that steady ache of misery which in human life is even more common than crisis and so a more insistent problem. When we get up tomorrow morning, we may well be able to do without our tragic awareness for an hour or two but we shall desperately need our sense of the comic.

Tragedy says, with the Book of Common Prayer: "In the midst of life we are in death." The paradox of this sentiment is that, as it sinks in, the sense of life, of living, is renewed. And the man who truly feels that "the readiness is all" attains a rare serenity, not only in dying but in living. Comedy says, "In the midst of death we are in life." Whatever the hazards of air travel, we continue to plan for the morrow. We are not often in the mood of the tragic hero just before his end, when he has attained to a complete stillness of the will. "The readiness is all" is a noble sentiment but the exact reverse of it also has its human point.

I warmed both hands before the fire of life,

(so William Lyon Phelps parodied Landor):

It fades and I'm not ready to depart.

The desire to live is not merely love of living. It is also greed. Comedy deals with the itch to own the material world. Hence its interest in gluttons who imbibe part of this world, and misers who hoard another part. And from *devouring* and *clutching*, human nature makes a swift leap to *stealing*. In how many comic plots there is theft or the intention of theft! If men did not wish to break the tenth commandment, comic plotting, as we know it, could never have come into being.

It is possible that in my discussion of "Death in Everyday Life" I gave tragedy too benign an image. This would be the time to add that very often the subject of tragedy is not dying but killing. Tragic stories from *Agamemnon* to *Macbeth*, and from *The Duchess of Malfi* to *Penthesilea*, embody the impulse to kill. People who express surprise at the piles of corpses on the tragic stage are asking tragedy to reflect their actions, and they have not committed murder; but tragedy reflects their souls, and in their souls they *have* committed murder. Modern psychology, with its intensive study of daily living, daily imagining, has had no trouble demonstrating the ubiquity of murderous wishes. A human being, in sober fact, needs very little provocation to wish his neighbor dead. The joke behind the joke in the colloquial use of "Drop dead!" is that the phrase means exactly what it says. Children of three are also taken to be joking when they tell a parent they wish he or she were dead. The joke is on the parent, and it is gallows-humor at that.

Comedy is very often about theft, exactly as tragedy is very often about murder. Just as the tragic poets present few scenes of dying or being dead but many (on stage or off) of killing, so comedy has fewer scenes of possession than of expropriation (or the plan to expropriate). There is a technical reason in both cases: it is of the nature of dramatic art to show, not states of being, but what people do to people. Death is a state, possession is a state, murder and theft are what people do to people. But there is a nontechnical reason for the technical reason — as in art there always is. Drama, the art of the extreme, seeks out the ultimate act that corresponds to ultimate fact. In the tragic world, if death is the ultimate fact, the infliction of death is the ultimate act. In the comic world, if possession is the ultimate fact, dispossession is the ultimate act. The motor forces are hatred and greed respectively.

To steal is to falsify, for it is to forge, as it were, a title to ownership. The greed we find in comedy is an offshoot of the spirit of falsehood and mendacity. St. John's gospel speaks of Satan as both "the father of lies" and "a murderer from the beginning," and this is to say that the mischief in both comedy and tragedy is the very Devil and, conversely, that Satan has a great traditional genre to report each of his two favorite pastimes. "And of these two diabolical manifestations," a recent theological commentator adds, "it is arguable that falsity is the more essentially Satanic." It is arguable, as we have seen, that comedy is a blacker art than tragedy.

The other face of the greed in comedy is tenacity, by which men survive. It is hard to survive. The tragic hero, at the last, can attain to the readiness and ripeness that are all. The rest of us, first and last, cling to existence and on our deathbeds will regret only, as Fontenelle did on his in 1757, that it is so "difficult to be." "*Je sens une difficulté d'être*," he said, "I am finding it difficult to be." It is a difficulty, like death itself, that permeates all of life.

> In the last analysis [as Jean Cocteau put it], everything can be taken care of except the difficulty of being: the difficulty of being cannot be taken care of.

In the last analysis, it cannot. This comedy knows, and acknowledges in sadness or cynicism. And yet we do not live only in the last analysis, but serially, in analyses first, second, and third. Though in the last analysis, no priest and no physician can stop us from dying, it may be a comfort to have both of them on call until finally we are dead. The comic sense tries to cope with the daily, hourly, inescapable difficulty of being. For if everyday life has an undercurrent or cross-current of the tragic, the main current is material for comedy.

Yet, if comedy begins in the kitchen and the bedroom, it can walk out under the stars. It can attain to grandeur. If this is not generally admitted, it is only because any comedy that has grandeur is immediately stamped as Not a Comedy. (Someone should make an anthology of the various great works that have been called Not a Comedy, Not a Tragedy, and Not a Play. It would be one of the Hundred Great Books.) A comedy that achieves grandeur is also said to be veering toward tragedy. There is seldom any plausibility to the attribution. If any of these comedies were subtitled A Tragedy it would be said to be toppling toward Comedy.

Molière's *Don Juan* is an example. There is something marvelously lofty and mysterious about it. One would be at a loss to name any tragedy with an atmosphere of this type. The weighty world of tragedy is created the direct way: with weighty words to which in the theatre is added weighty acting. The world of Molière's *Don Juan* is created by the traditional dialectic of farce and comedy, that is, indirectly, with the weight only suggested, what is actually said and acted kept studiously flippant.

To think of Molière's *Don Juan* is to think of Mozart's *Don Giovanni*. Mozart also used the comic dialectic: it exactly corresponded to his own mentality, as it had to Molière's. Mozart early attached himself to the tradition of great comic theatre: he had completed a setting of a Goldoni play at the age of twelve. *La finta semplice* is musical farce. His development from there to *Cosí fan tutte* and *Don Giovanni* is not a progress toward tragedy. It is a progress from farce to comedy. What grows is his power to suggest the immensity of what lies underneath. But the comic surface is resolutely and scintillatingly maintained. To call *Don Giovanni* tragic makes no sense. We are in no way encouraged to identify ourselves with the Don's guilt. So far is such an attitude from Mozart that he can show the death of the Don (as Jonson shows us Volpone punished) without winning sympathy for him. The work is called tragic only by those who refuse to consider the possibility that such immensity and terror might be within the scope of comedy.

Though there are so many differences between tragedy and comedy, it is news as old as Plato that the two have something in common. Scholars are not agreed as to how to take the passage in the *Symposium* in which this point is made but, thinking for ourselves, and with so much drama to think about which Plato did not know, we can see that the two genres stand together in very many ways. For example, they stand in contrast to an art such as music which glories in the direct expression of affirmative sentiments like the feeling of triumph. Tragedy and comedy are alike negative arts in that they characteristically reach positive statement by inference from negative situations. "In stories like this," says the Gardener in Giraudoux's *Electra*, "the people won't stop killing and biting each other to tell you the one aim of life is to love."

Surprising though it may be, the ego takes as much punishment in comedy as in tragedy, even if it is the pretensions of knaves and fools that are cut down, and not the rashness of a hero. Both tragedy and comedy demonstrate, with plots and characters that provide horribly conclusive evidence, that life is not worth living; and yet they finally convey such a sense of the majesty of our sufferings or the poignancy of our follies that, lo and behold! the enterprise seems worth having been a part of. Both tragedy and comedy are about human weakness, but both, in the end, testify to human strength. In tragedy one is glad to be identified with a hero, whatever his flaw or his fate. In comedy, even if one cannot identify oneself with anybody on stage, one has a hero to identify with, nonetheless: the author. One is proud to be lent the spectacles of Jonson or Molière.

Like tragedy, comedy can achieve a transcendence over misery, an aesthetic transcendence (of art over life), and a transcending emotion (awe in tragedy, joy in comedy). Both tragedy and comedy amount to an affirmation made irrationally — that is, in defiance of the stated facts — like religious affirmation. Unlike the church, however, the theatre claims no metaphysical status for such affirmations.

Finally, tragedy and comedy have the same heuristic intent: self-knowledge. What tragedy achieves in this line by its incredibly direct rendering of sympathies and antipathies, comedy achieves by indirection, duality, irony. As Northrop Frye says, comedy is "designed, not to condemn evil, but to ridicule a lack of self-knowledge." To condemn evil would be direct, single, unironic, and therefore uncomic. To spend one's life condemning evil has all too often been to lack self-knowledge and to fail to see this. The classic condemners of evil are the Pharisees. And the Pharisees, then and now, cannot make use of comedy; they can only be made use of by it.

Molière, says Fernandez, "teaches us the unspeakably difficult art of seeing ourselves in spite of ourselves." We are mistaken about our own identities: comedy makes of mistaken identity a classic subject. And if "to be mistaken about" is a passive phenomenon, it has its active counterpart. We are not only mistaken in ourselves but the cause that mistakes are in other men. Deceiving ourselves, we deceive our fellows. Now the art of comedy is an undeceiving, an emancipation from error, an unmasking, an art, if you will, of denouement or "untying." But a knot cannot be untied without first having been tied. A denouement comes at the end: through most of the play we have in fact been fooled. Thus, by a truly comic paradox, the playwright who exposes our trickery does so by outtricking us. In that respect, he is his own chief knave, and has made of us, his audience, his principal fool. The bag of tricks of this prince of knaves is — the art of comedy.

ABCDEFGHIJ-CO-7654321